Street by Street

CHESHIRE

PLUS ALTRINCHAM, BRAMHALL, HAZEL GROVE, STOCKPORT, WHITCHURCH

Enlarged Areas Chester, Crewe, Ellesmere Port, Macclesfield, Nantwich, Northwich, Runcorn, Warrington, Widnes

Ist edition May 2001

© Automobile Association Developments Limited 2001

This product includes map data licensed from Ordnance Survey® with the permission of the Controller of Her Majesty's Stationery Office. © Crown copyright 2000. All rights reserved. Licence No: 399221.

Published by AA Publishing (a trading name of Automobile Association Developments Limited, whose registered office is Norfolk House, Priestley Road, Basingstoke, Hampshire, RG24 9NY. Registered number 1878835).

Mapping produced by the Cartographic Department of The Automobile Association.

A CIP Catalogue record for this book is available from the British Library.

Printed by G. Canale & C. S.P.A., Torino, Italy

The contents of this atlas are believed to be correct at the time of the latest revision. However, the publishers cannot be held responsible for loss occasioned to any person acting or refraining from action as a result of any material in this atlas, nor for any errors, omissions or changes in such material. The publishers would welcome information to correct any errors or omissions and to keep this atlas up to date. Please write to Publishing, The Automobile Association, Fanum House, Basing View, Basingstoke, Hampshire, RG21 4EA.

Ref: MX082

Key to map pages ii-iii

Key to map symbols iv-1

Enlarged scale pages 2-21

Street by Street 22-275

Index – towns & villages 276-277

Index – streets 278-316

Index – featured places 316-322

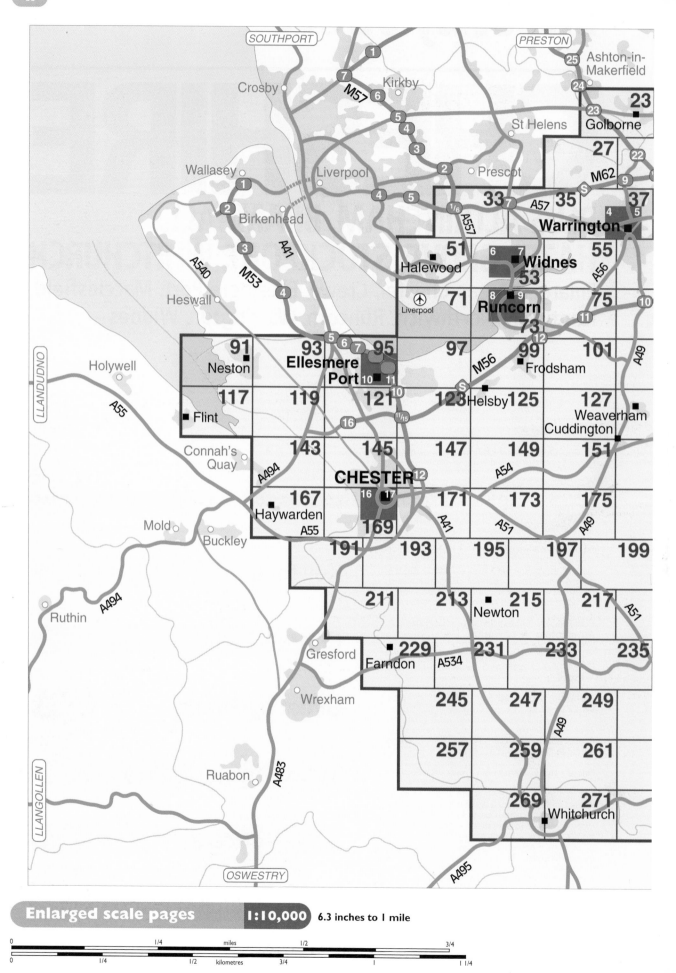

Enlarged scale pages 1:10,000 6.3 inches to 1 mile

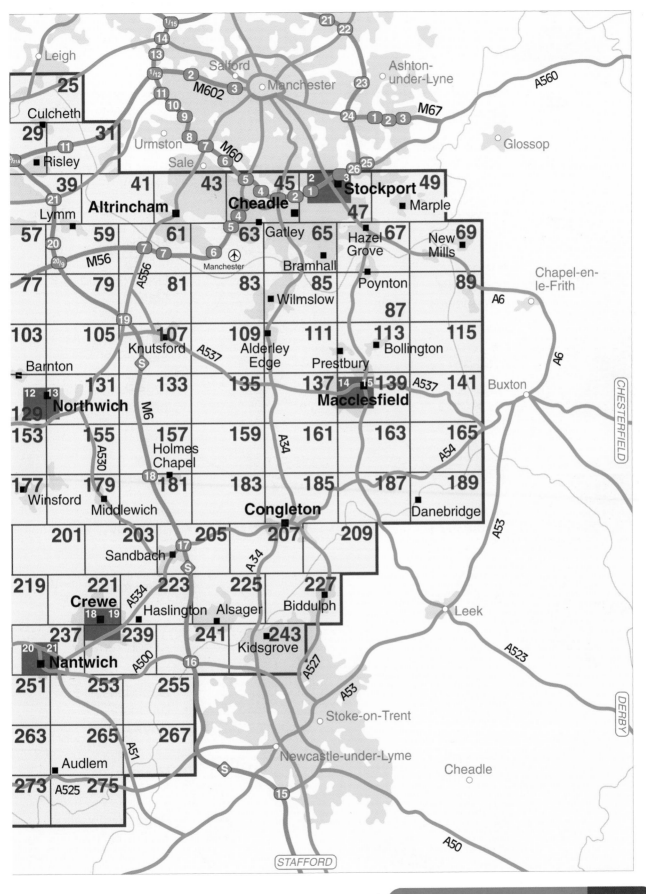

Junction 9	Motorway & junction
Services	Motorway service area
	Primary road single/dual carriageway
Services	Primary road service area
	A road single/dual carriageway
	B road single/dual carriageway
	Other road single/dual carriageway
	Restricted road
	Private road
← ←	One way street
	Pedestrian street
	Track/ footpath
	Road under construction
	Road tunnel
P	Parking

P+	Park & Ride
	Bus/coach station
	Railway & main railway station
	Railway & minor railway station
⊖	Underground station
⊖	Light railway & station
+++++++++	Preserved private railway
LC	Level crossing
• • • •	Tramway
----------	Ferry route
....	Airport runway
-·-·-·-·-	Boundaries- borough/ district
▼▼▼▼▼▼▼	Mounds
93	Page continuation 1:17,500
7	Page continuation to enlarged scale 1:10,000

	River/canal lake, pier		Toilet with disabled facilities
	Aqueduct lock, weir		Petrol station
465 ▲ Winter Hill	Peak (with height in metres)	PH	Public house
	Beach	PO	Post Office
	Coniferous woodland		Public library
	Broadleaved woodland	*i*	Tourist Information Centre
	Mixed woodland		Castle
	Park		Historic house/ building
	Cemetery	Wakehurst Place NT	National Trust property
	Built-up area	M	Museum/ art gallery
	Featured building	†	Church/chapel
	City wall		Country park
A&E	Accident & Emergency hospital		Theatre/ performing arts
	Toilet		Cinema

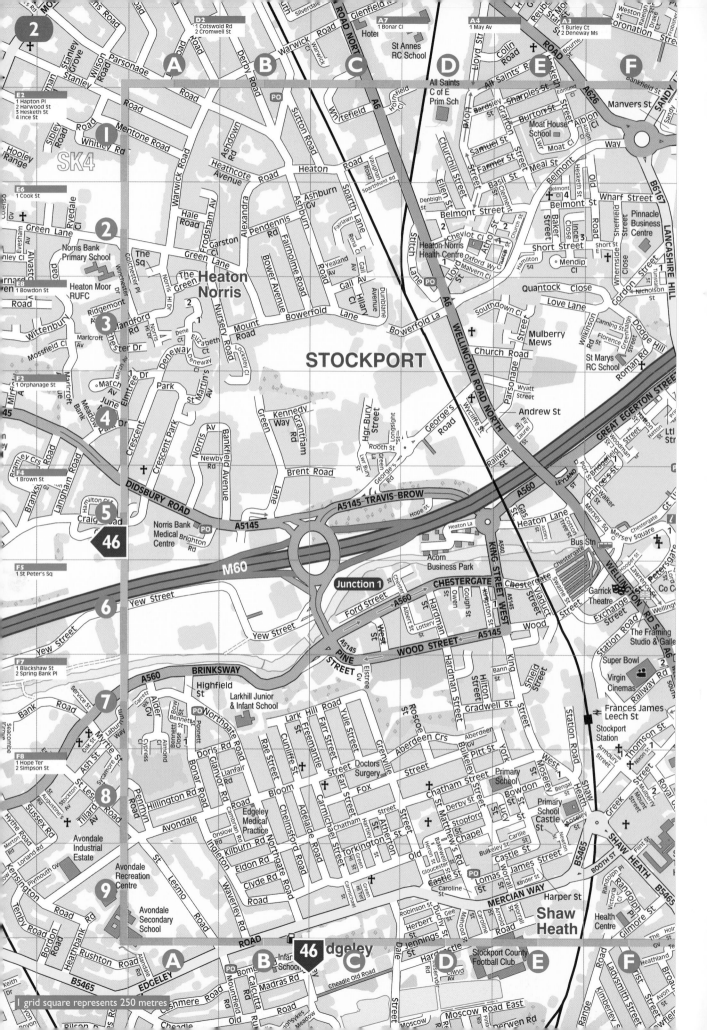

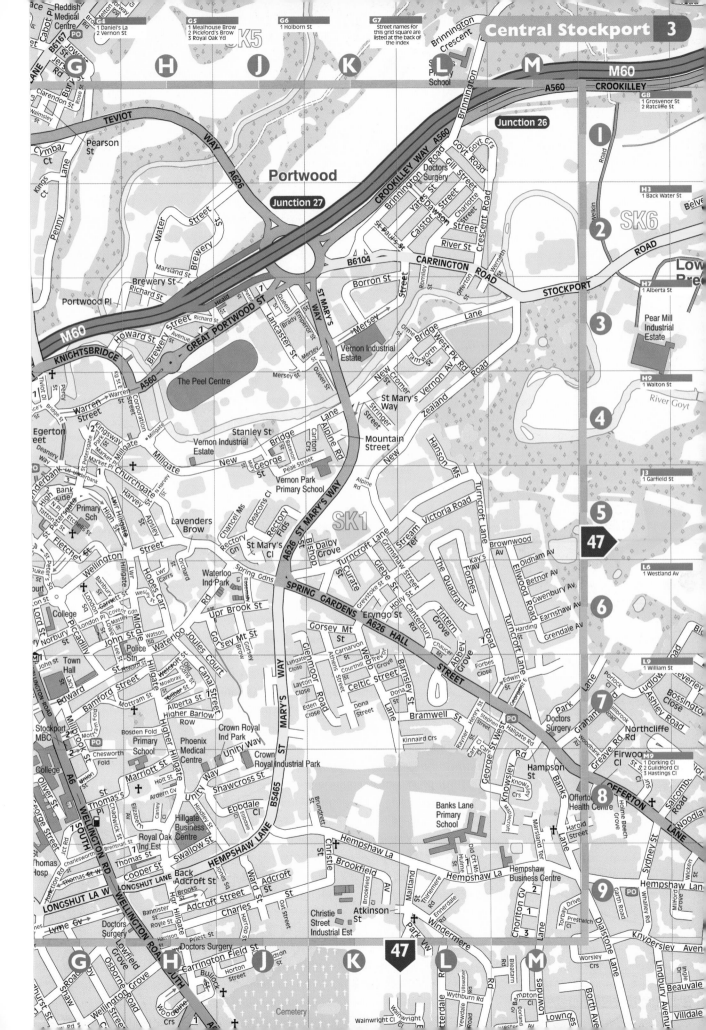

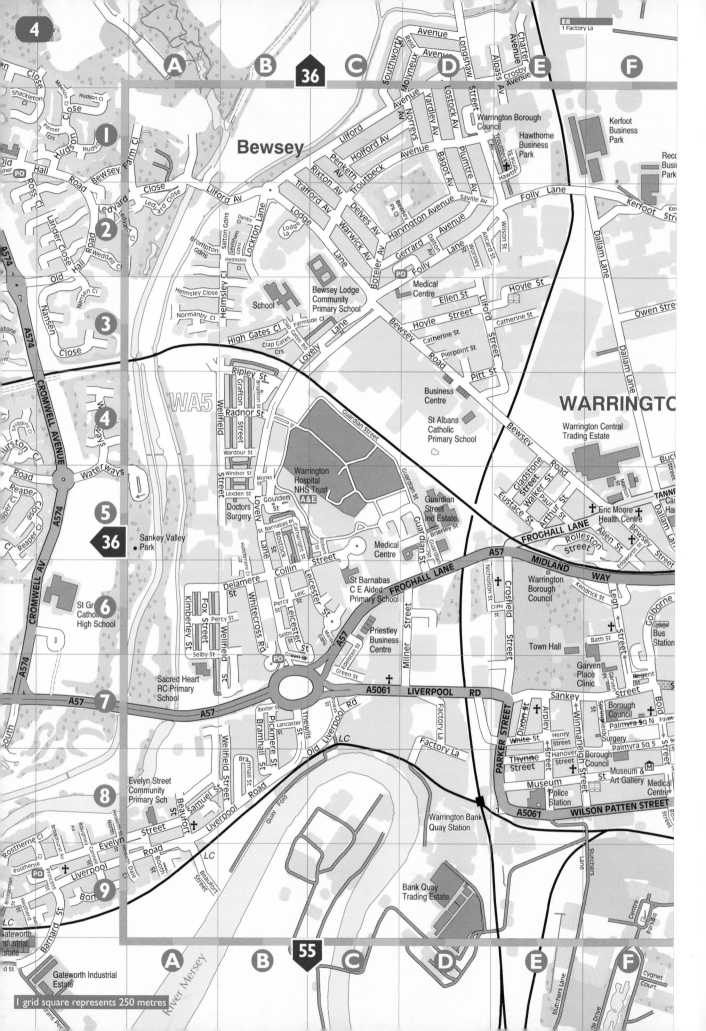

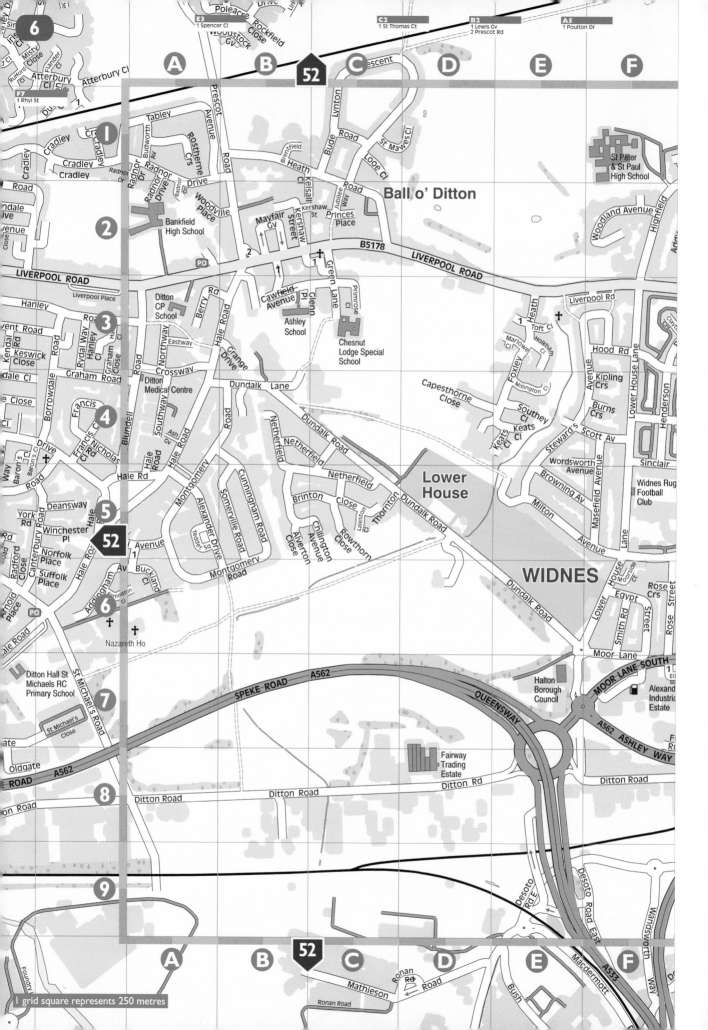

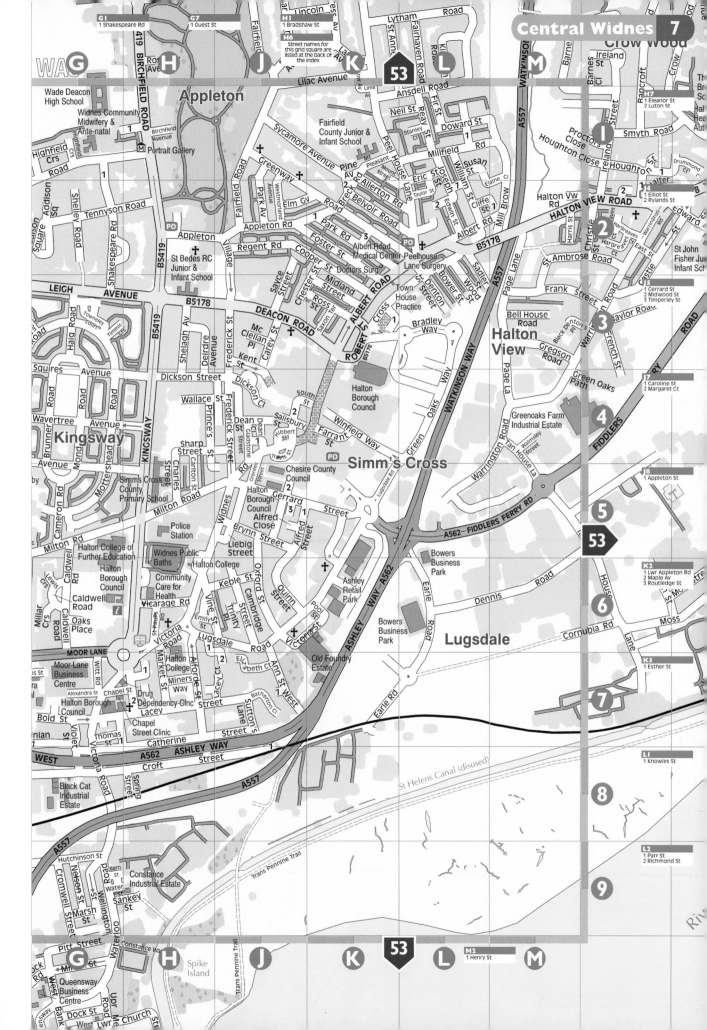

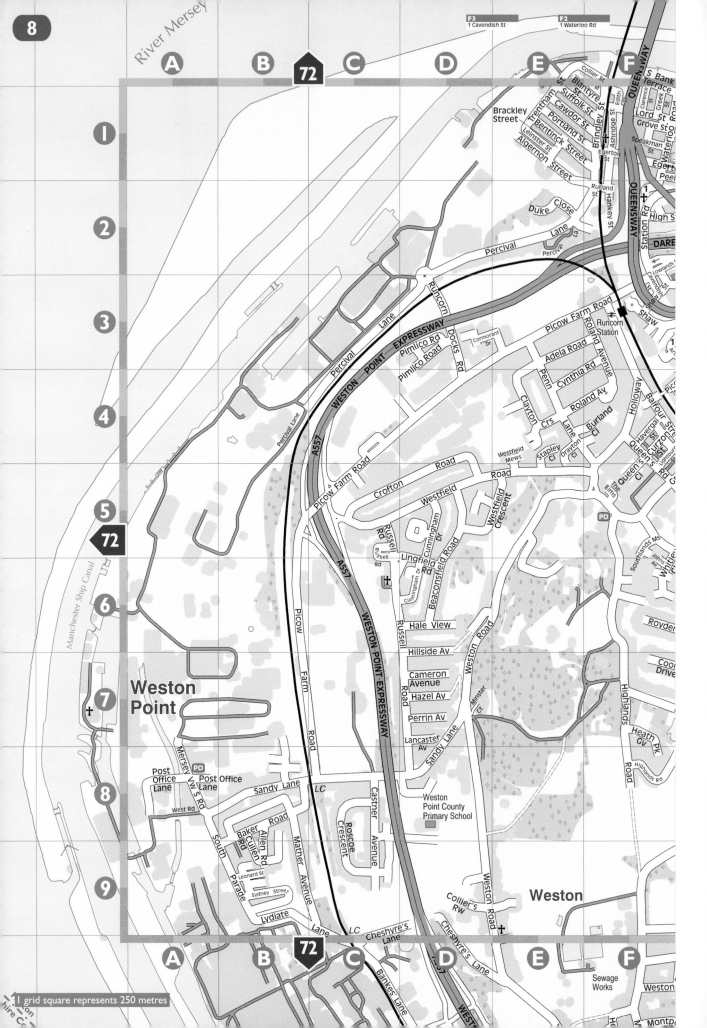

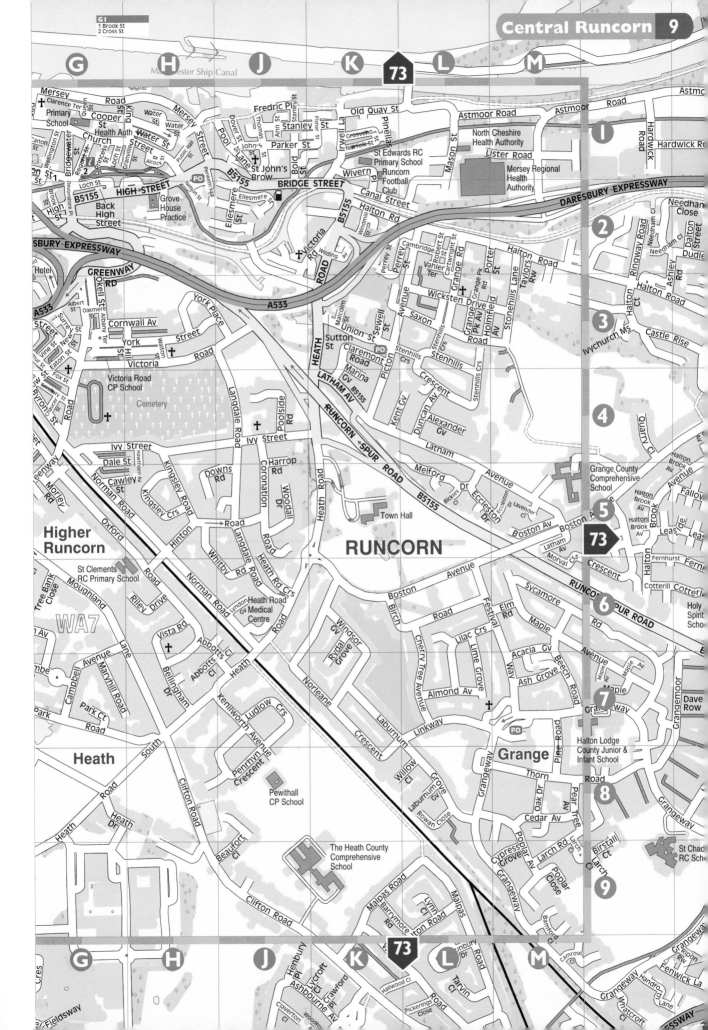

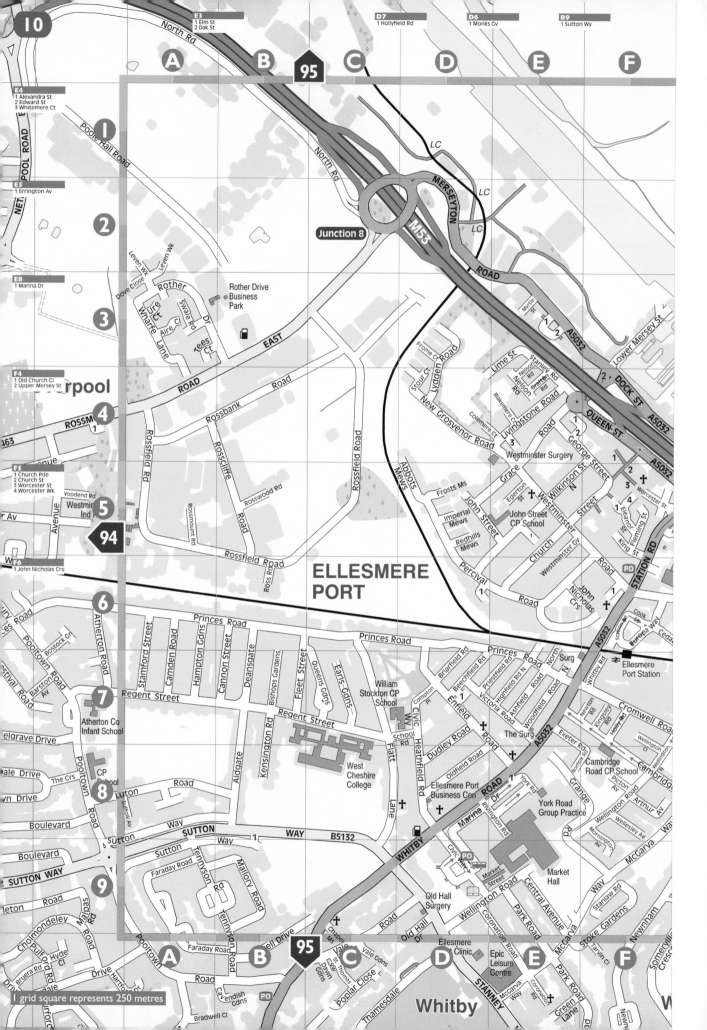

G5
1 John Nicholas Crs

G H J K 95 L River Mersey M

1
2
3
4
5
96
6
7
8
9

Boat Museum

South Pier Road

Canalside Industrial Estate

Canalside

Oil Sites Road

Manchester Ship Canal

CH65

Junction 9

M53

Westminster Retail Park

Crescent Road

Meadow Lane

Meadow Lane

Dock Yard Road

Oil Sites Road

Oil Sites Road

Bridges Road

Cromwell Road

Bridges Road

Bridges Road

Lees Lane

South Road

New Bridge Road

Cambridge Road

Marchwiel Rd

M53

Girton Cl

Girton Road

Girton Road

Lancing Road

Milton Road

Harrow Rd

Drive

Eton Road

Lees Lane

Repton Road

Oxford Road

Burnell Rd

Winchester AV

Thornton

G H J K 95 L M

Wolverham

PO

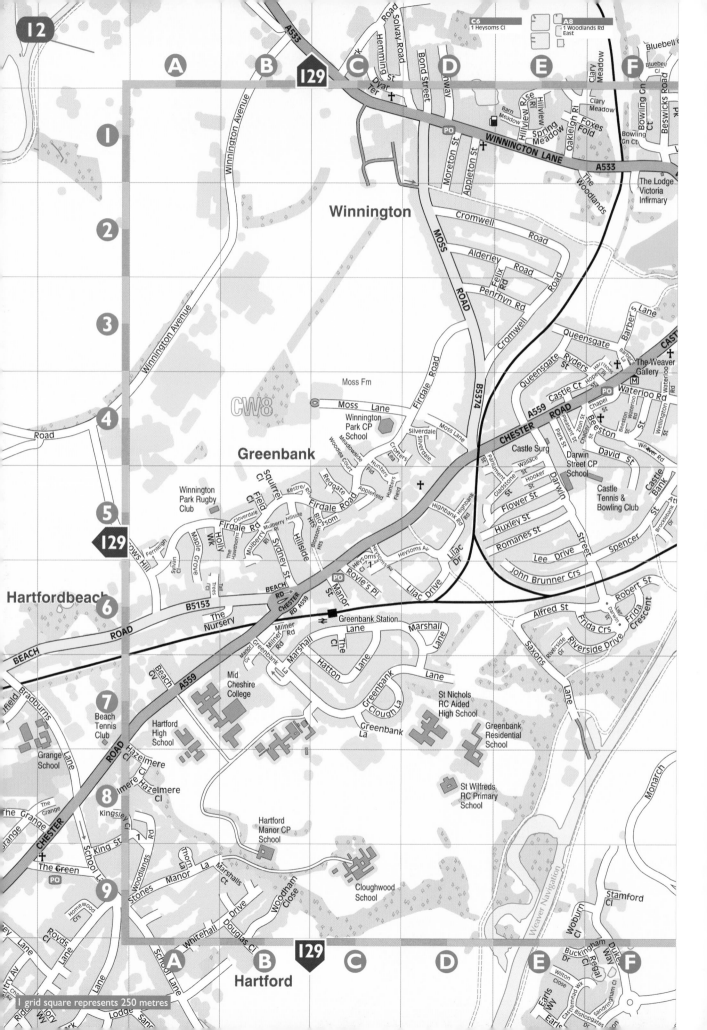

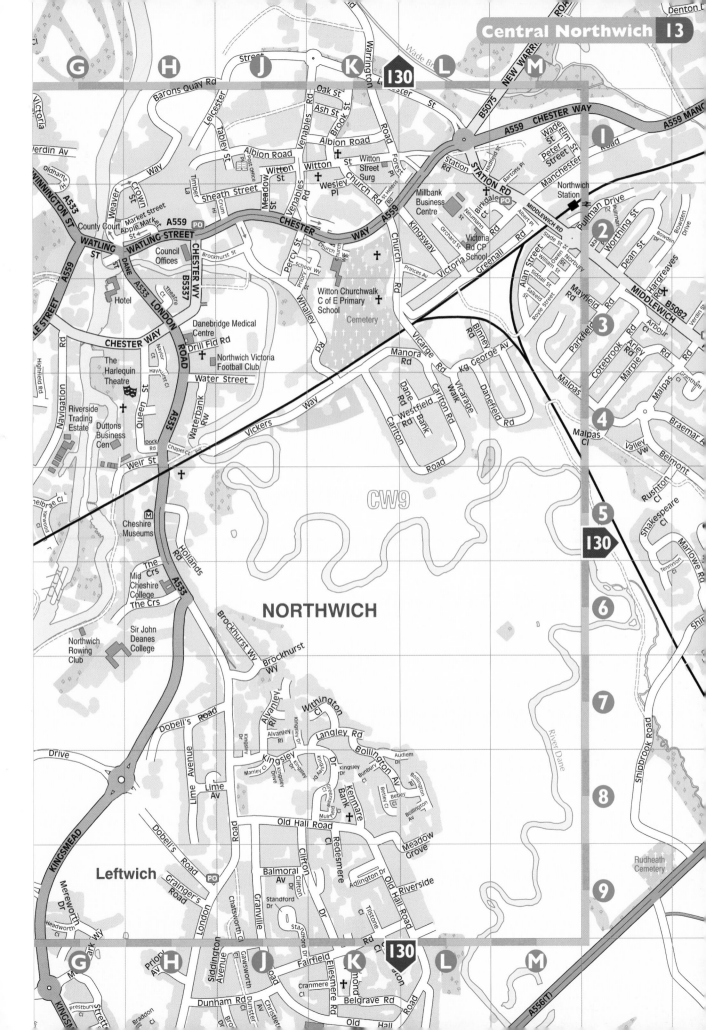

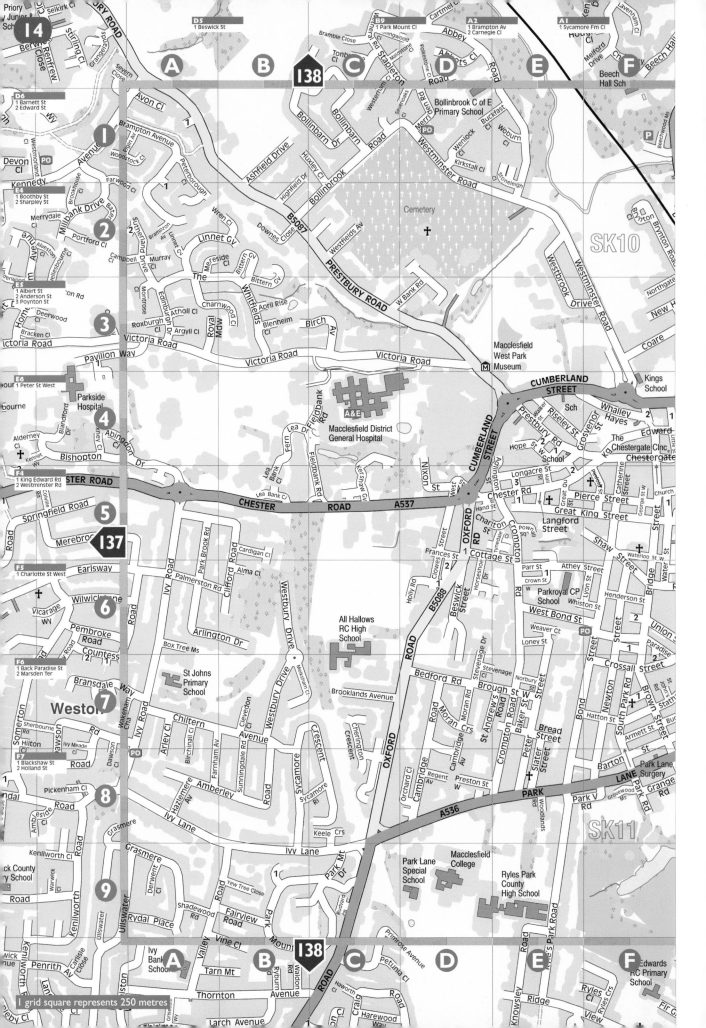

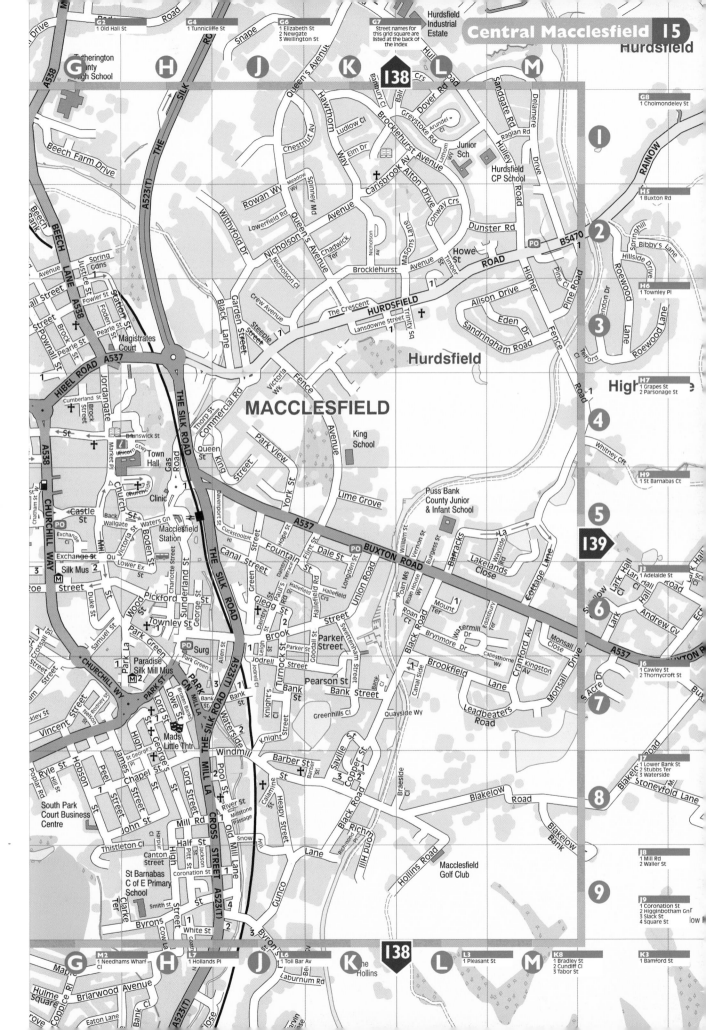

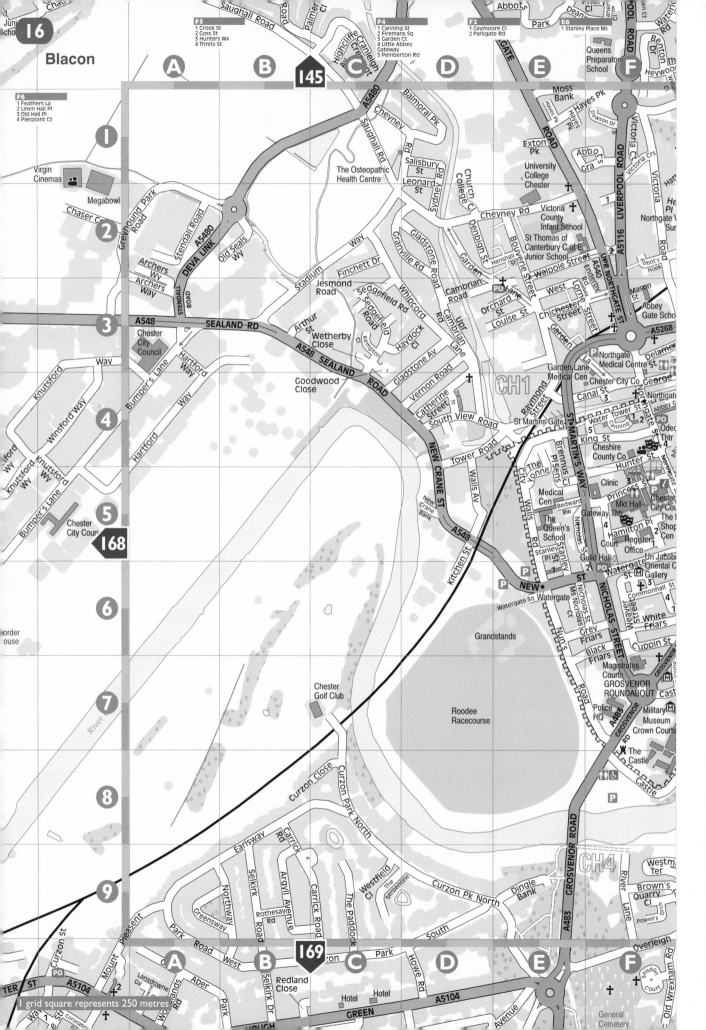

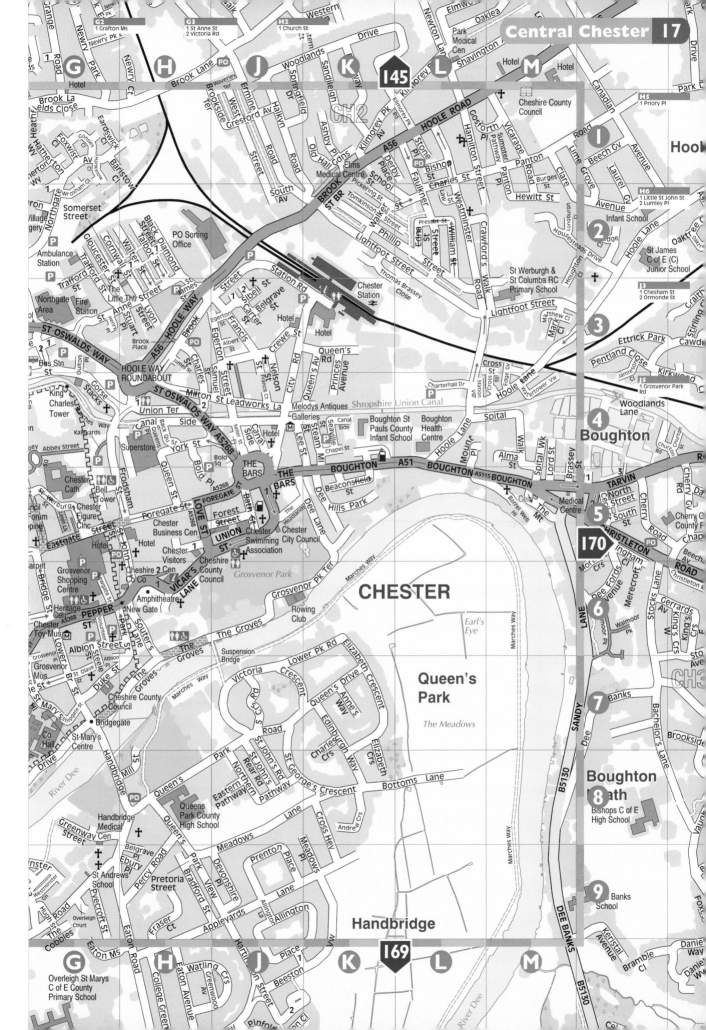

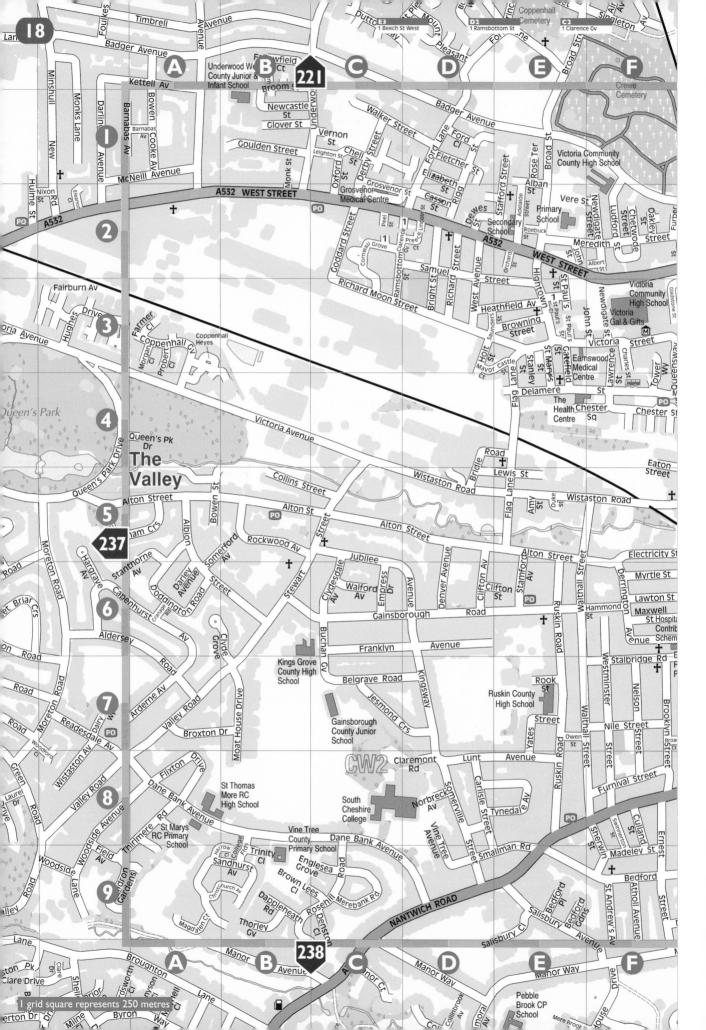

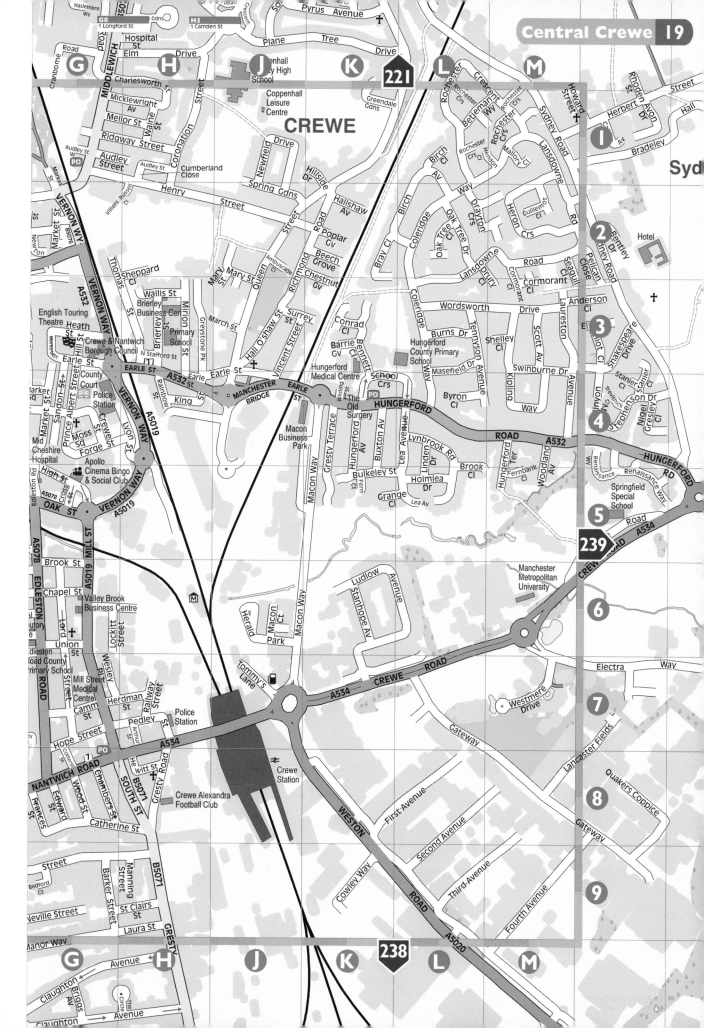

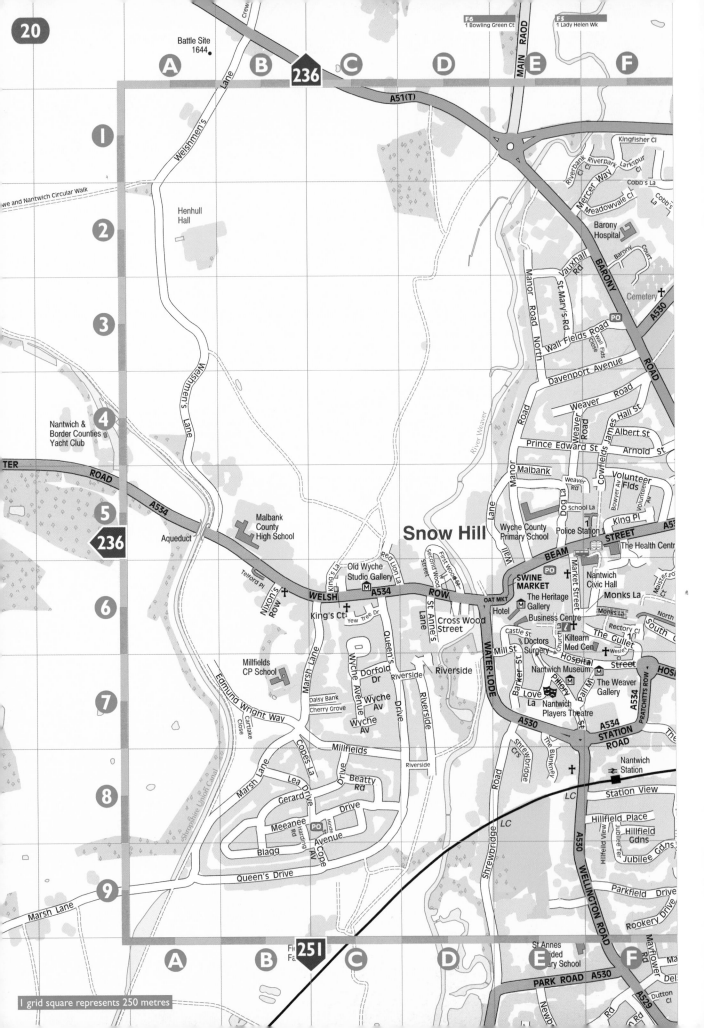

G H J K **237** L M

Red Hall

1
2
3
4
5
6
7
8
9

Alvaston Business Park

A500(T)

MIDDLEWICH ROAD

A530

MIDDLEWICH RD

Sycamore Cl

Nantwich Cricket & Rugby Union Football Club

Cemetery

Brook Farm

Ray Avenue

Sandford Road

Brereton Drive

Whitehouse Lane

Willow Ct

Willow Farm

Highfield County Primary School

The Barony

CW5

Baronia Pl

Park View

Heathfield Cl

Cumberland Avenue

Willow Bank

Birchwood Cl

Birchin Lane

Constant Ct

Highfield Dr

Birchin Close

Heathside

Penlington Ct

Penlington Ct

Princess Dr

A51

Baronia Pl

The Crs

Heathside

Mount Cl

Mount Drive

Princess Dr

Harvey Av

Hornby Dr

Hornby Dr

Birchin Lane

CREWE

237 Park Road

St Lawrence Rd

St Ct

St Lawrence Ct

NANTWICH

The Broadway

The Broadway

A534

CREWE ROAD

A500(T)

Willas

Scaife Road

Alvaston Rd

Monks Orchard

Croft

Crofts

Rookery

MILLSTONE LANE

A51

Turner St

PO

Brick Bank

Whitewell Close

Woodland Av

Nantwich Town Football Club

Jackson Av

CREWE ROAD A534

Cedar Gv

Gingerbread La

237

Colleys Lane

PITAL ST

Spring Gdns

Nuthurst Gardens

Beeches

Church's Mansion

Nantwich Town Football Club

College

Gingerbread Lane

Lewis Cl

St Josephs Way

Worthington Close

St Josephs Way

Brunner Gv

Brunner Gv

Brunner Gv

A51

St Josephs

Regents Ga

Stapeley Ter

LONDON ROAD

LC

LC

NEWCASTLE

ROAD

Cheerbrook Fm

Whitlow Av

Cronkinson Avenue

Cronkinson Oak

Cronkinson Oak

Pine Walk

Jan Palach Av

Brown Avenue

Ash Cv

rlowe Dr

amere

Windsor Rd

St Albans Dr

G H J K **252** L M

Stapely Water Gardens

LONDON

Wybunbu

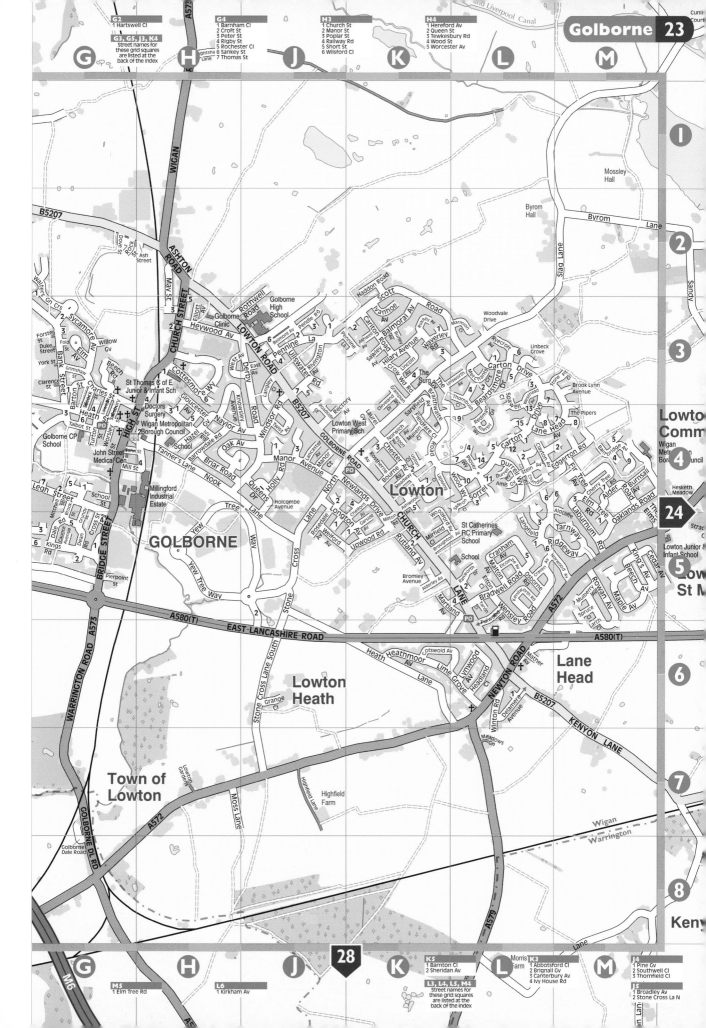

Mossley Hall

Byrom Hall

Byrom Lane

Woodvale Drive

Linbeck Grove

Brook Lynn Avenue

The Pipers

Lowto Comm

Wigan Metro Bor Council

Hesketh Meadow

24

Lowton Junior & Infant School

Low St M

Lowton

Golborne High School

Rothwell Road

Golborne Clinic

GOLBORNE

Golborne CP School

John Street Medical Cen

Millingford Industrial Estate

Lowton West Primary Sch

St Catherines RC Primary Sch

Lane Head

East Lancashire Road A580(T)

Lowton Heath

Town of Lowton

Highfield Farm

Golborne Dale Road

Wigan Warrington

Kenyon Lane B5207

Keny

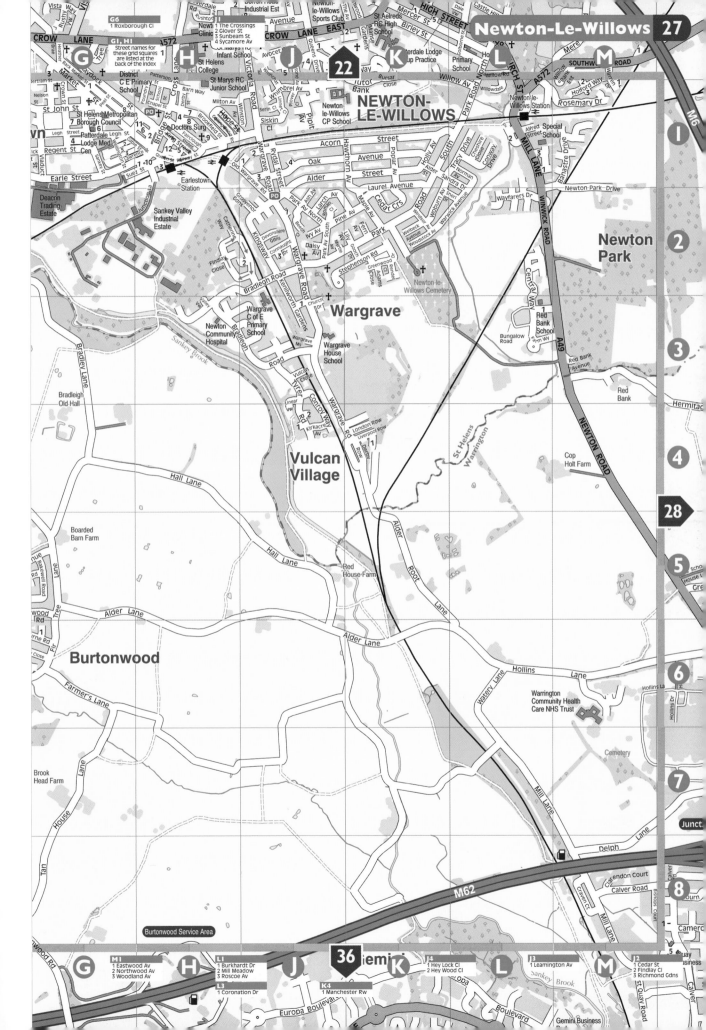

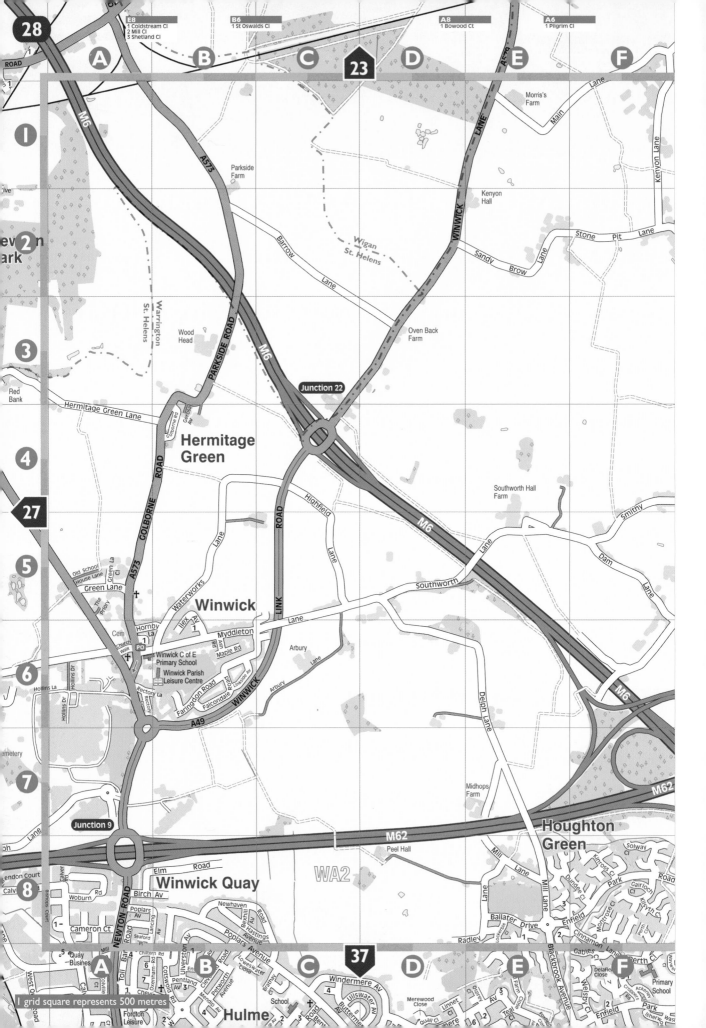

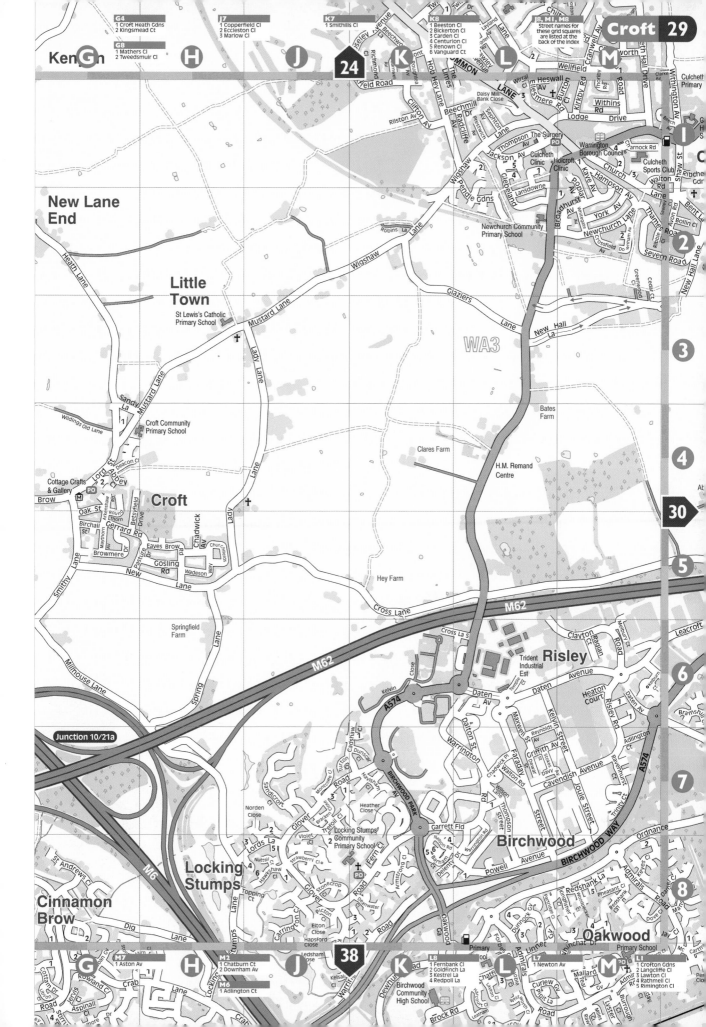

G   H   J   26   K   L   36   M

I

2

3

4

5

6

7

8

Home
Farm

Joy Lane

Limekiln Lane

Wright's Lane

Burtonwood Rd

M62

Whittle Avenue

Tunbridge Rd

Leamington Cl

**Lingley
Mere**

Lingley Green Av

Wensleydale

Lingley Green Avenue

Great Sankey
Community
High School

Sankey Medical
Centre

Barrow Hall
Community
Primary School

Whittle Brook

Thorntondale Drive
Farndale Cl
Kingsdale Road
Airedale
Bransdale Cl
Gorsedale
Barbondale Cl
Coverdale Cl
Widdale
Bishopdale Cl
Kingsdale Rd
Littledale Rd
Moscale Dr

Whittle Brook

Bembridge Cl

God's Hill

Whitwell Cl

Park Road

Woodale Cl

Swaledale

Deep
Dale

Alderfield
Road

A57

Dawson
House

Lingley Green

Foreland Cl

Shanklin Cl

Shorwell Cl

Tomta Cl

Mayfair Cl

Cronulla Drive

Warwick
Stanley
York
Princess

Barrow

North Vw

Mill Av

Chestnut Av

North Vw

Vine Crescent

Conifer

Rowan

Halton Rd

Wilmot Av

Whittle Hall Lane

A57

Muriel
Andore Cl
Piecroft Rd
Fraser
Road

Hilary
Paul St
Lingley
Kintore Dr
Keith Av

Lingley Green Av
Piecroft Cl

Kirkcaldy
Av

Cromdale Way
Community Hall
& Health Centre

Wroxham

Park Road
Community
Primary School

Cromdale
Way

Phillips
Drive

Park Road

Charles St

Wesbury Dr

Rd

Norfolk Drive

Lingwood
Rd

Campbell Crs

Belmont Crs

Hawthorne Av

Brook
Drive

Liverpool Road

Henderson Cl
Edward Road
Friends Lane

Thetford Road

Yarmouth Rd

LIVERPOOL ROAD

Sankey for
Penketh
Station

Forge Rd

PO

Station Road

Elmset Cl

Friars Avenue

Hadleigh Cl

Whitethorn Av

Highfield
Road

Penketh
Community
High School

Sandy Lane
Farm

St Helens

Warrington

Penketh

Susan
Dr
Groake
Dr

Stocks

Meeting
Lane

Kenyon Av
Walton Av
Denise
Norton Av

St Josephs
Catholic
Primary Sch

Windmill Lane

St Alban Rd
Holly

Walsingham

South Dale

St Stephen Rd

St Mary's Road

Dale
The

Burnham Cl
Upton Drive

Coronation Dr

Sandy

SOUTH

LANE

Coniston Avenue

Primary
School

Lynton Rd

Babbacombe Rd

Witnyclombe

Paignton

Sidmouth

Bideford Road

Honiton Way

Porlock

Penketh
Swimming
Baths

Barnstaple Way

Broad Oak Rd

Penketh
Health
Clinic

Avon

Greystone Road

Cherry
Tree Av

Formby
Ainsdale

Hillside

Birkdale Rd

Hesketh

The CV

Smythian

Sandy

A5080

Farnworth Rd

Rose
Cottage
Surg

Arlington

PO

WARRINGTON ROAD

A562

Ash Road

Lyons Rd

Maple

Neville
Rd

Grange Rd

Clifford Road

A5062

WIDNES ROAD

Padstow

Fenham Dr

Oak Rd

**Doe
Gr**   54   **ORTH
D**

Cuerdley Rd

Chapel Rd

Penryn

Newlyn Gdns

Mowcroft Lane

Tannery

Penrose Gdns

Rothay

Radlett
Close

St Vincents
Catholic

Falmouth Dr

Penketh South
Community
Primary School

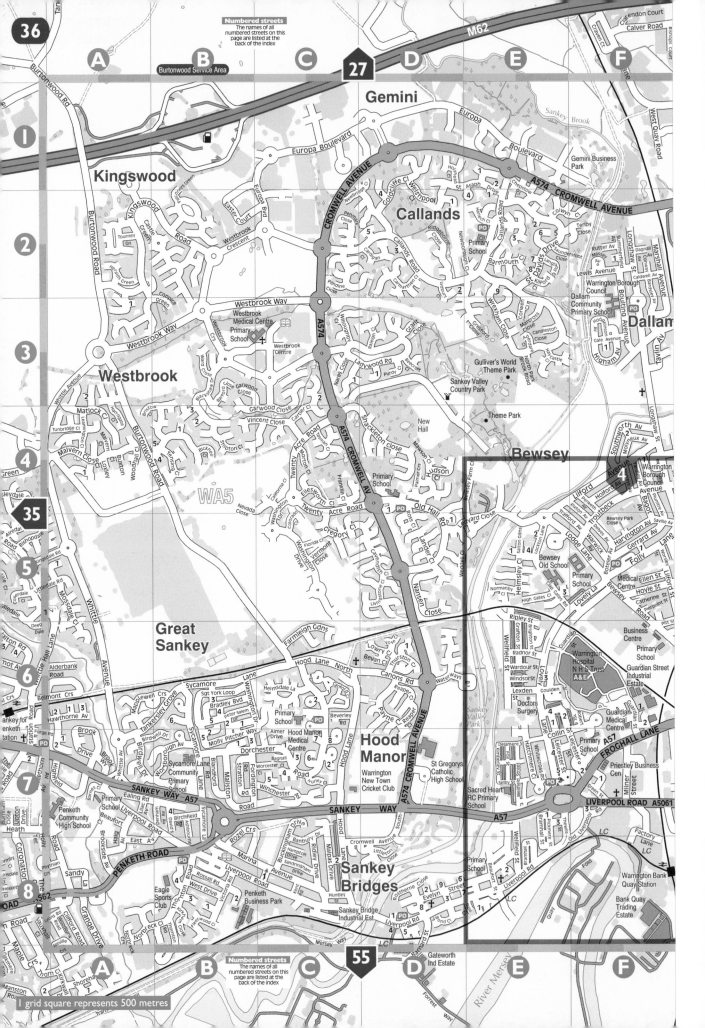

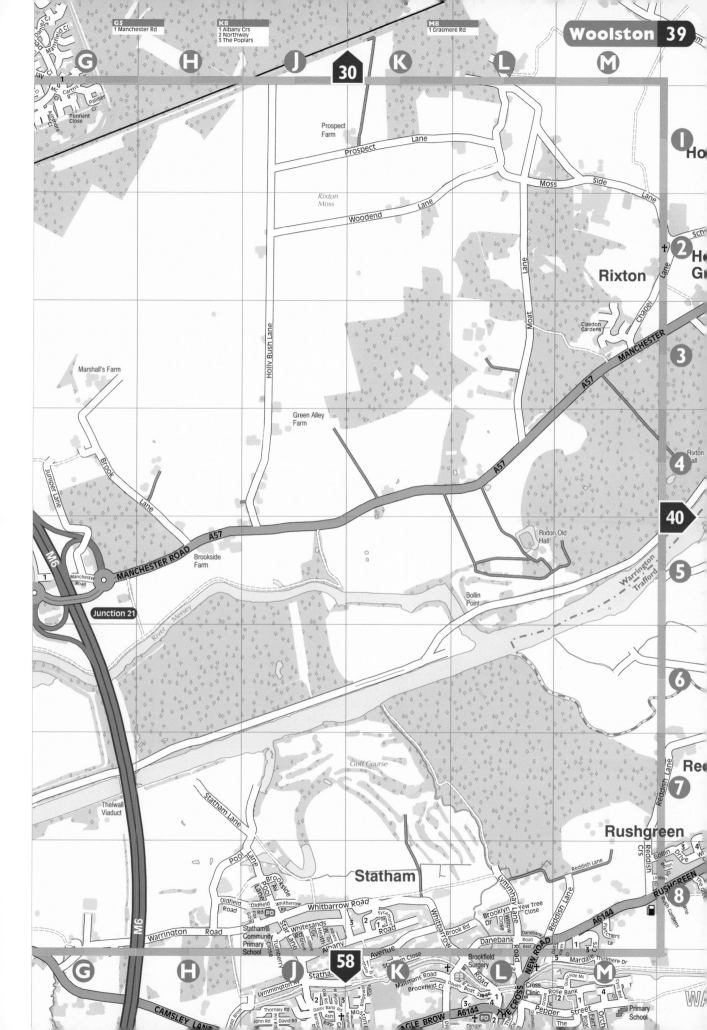

G5
1 Manchester Rd

K8
1 Albany Crs
2 Northway
3 The Poplars

M8
1 Grasmere Rd

G   H   J   30   K   L   M

I
Ho

Prospect Farm

Prospect Lane

Moss   Side Lane

2   He Gr

Rixton Moss

Rixton

Woodend Lane

Moat Lane

Chapel Lane

Claydon Gardens

MANCHESTER

A57

3

Marshall's Farm

Green Alley Farm

A57

Rixton Hall

4

40

Brook Lane

Juniper Lane

Rixton Old Hall

5

Warrington Trafford

M6

1

Manchester Road

MANCHESTER ROAD   A57

Brookside Farm

Bollin Point

Junction 21

River Mersey

6

Golf Course

Re

7

Statham Lane

Rushgreen

Thelwall Viaduct

Reddish Lane

Reddish Crs

Bollin Drive

3   4

Linden

RUSHGREEN

8

Pool Lane

Brookside Tw

Pool Lane

Statham

Reddish Lane

Danebank

Lymmhay Lane

Whitbarrow Road

Brook Rd

Brooklyn Dr

Yew Tree Close

Willow

Danebank Road East

Oldfield Road

Oldfield Rd

Whitbarrow Close

PO

Sycamore Road

Whitesands Rd

W Heath

Jubilee Gr

A6144

Fletchers

M6

Warrington   Road

Statham Community Primary School

Star Lane

Turnberry Close

Albany

Avenue

Statham Close

Maltmans Road

Brookfield Cl

Brookfield Surgery

NEW ROAD

THE CROSS

Mardale Rd   Thirlmere Dr

G   H   J   58   K   L   M

Lymmington Av

Thornley Rd

John Rd   David Rd

Daisy Bank Rd

Ash

Moss

Davies Wy   Boat La

Cross Clinic

Rose Bank

Grove

Pepper   Street

Orch   Fart

Primary School

CAMSLEY LANE

EAGLE BROW

A6144

PO

Dingle

The

Wa

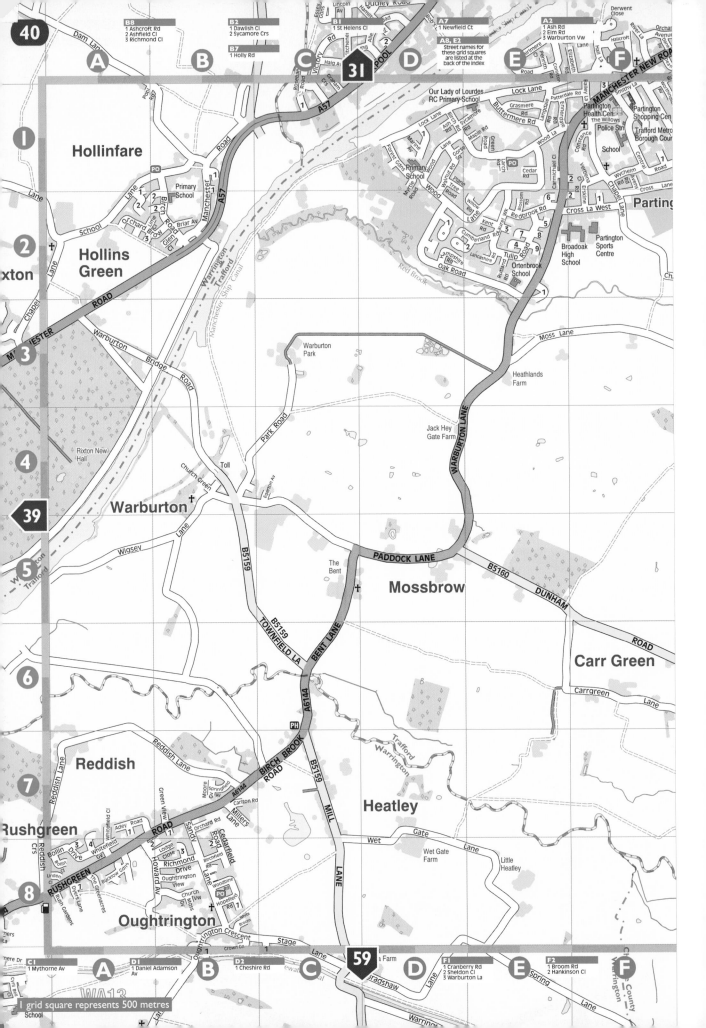

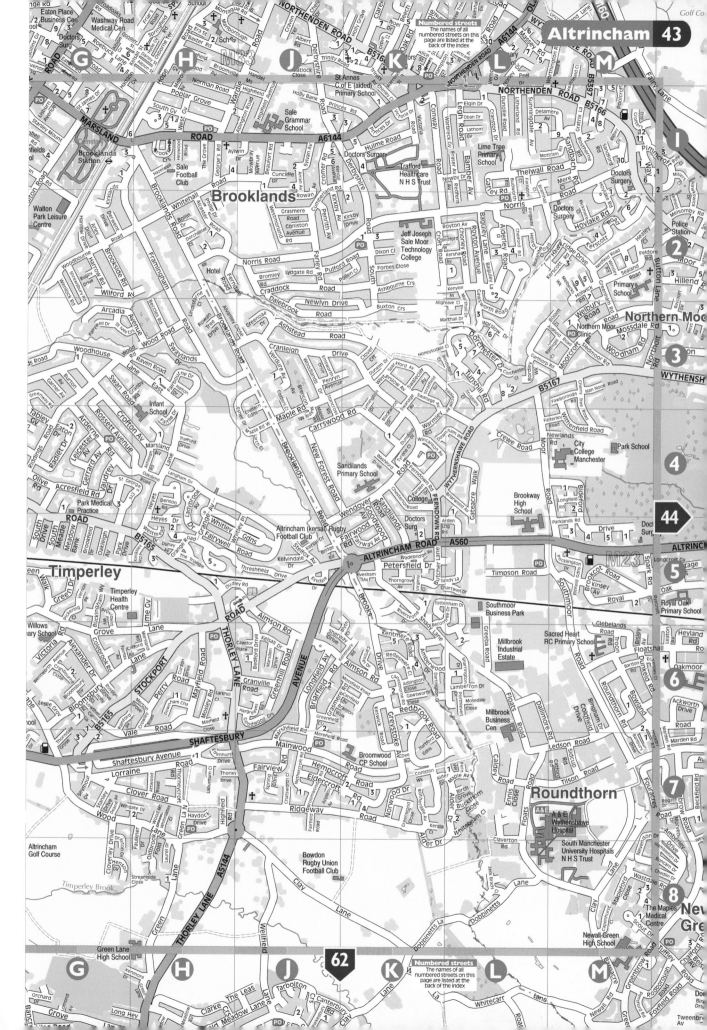

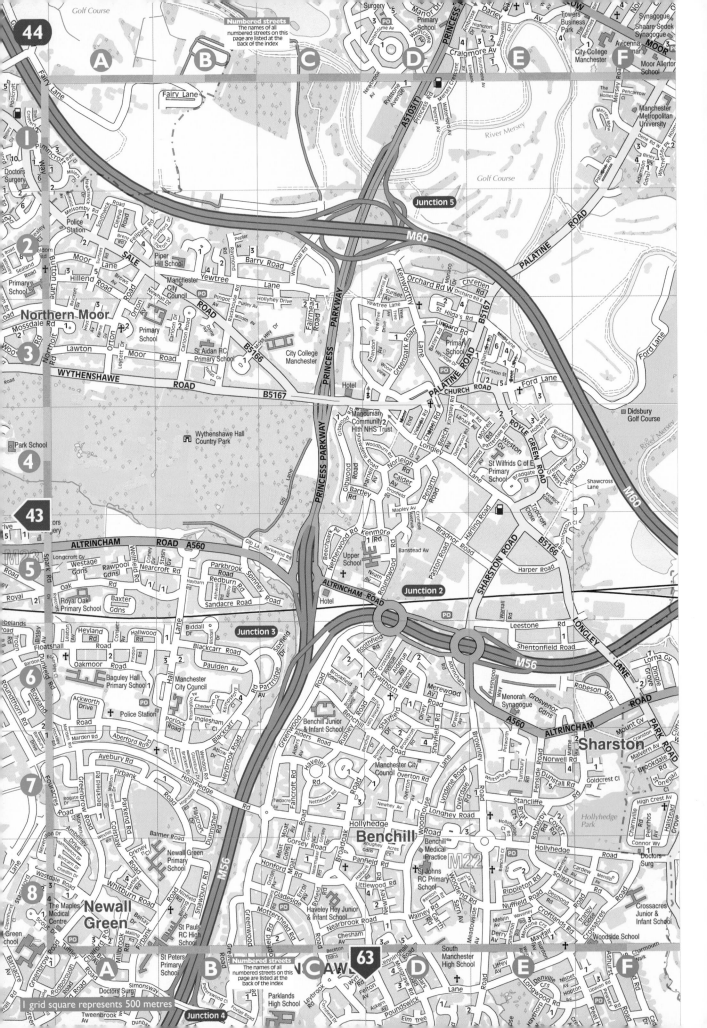

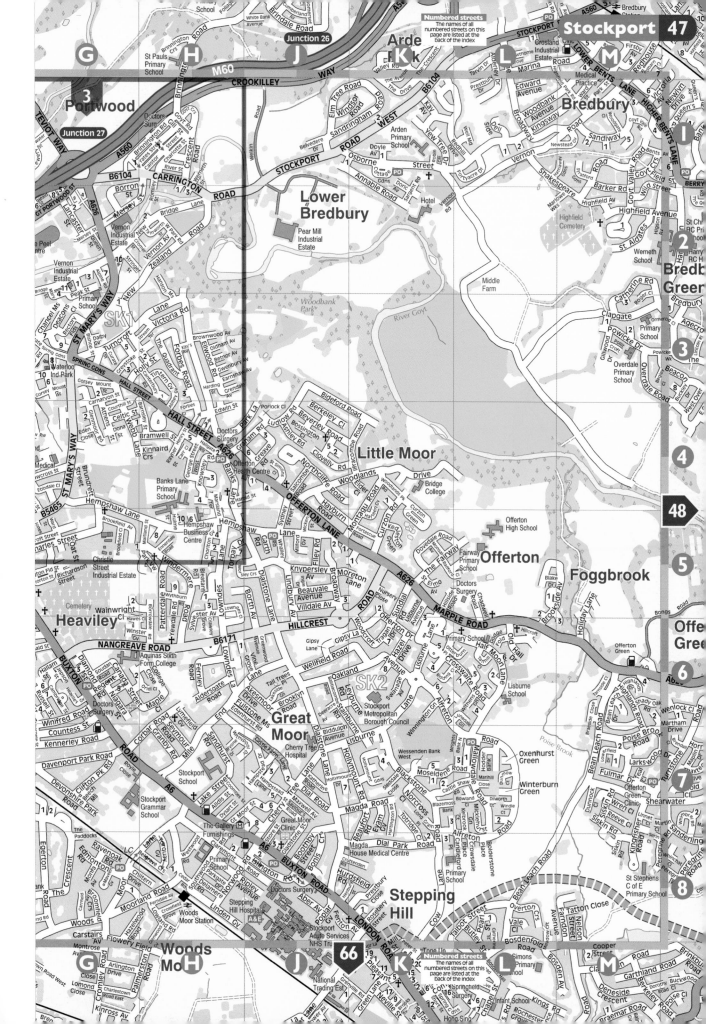

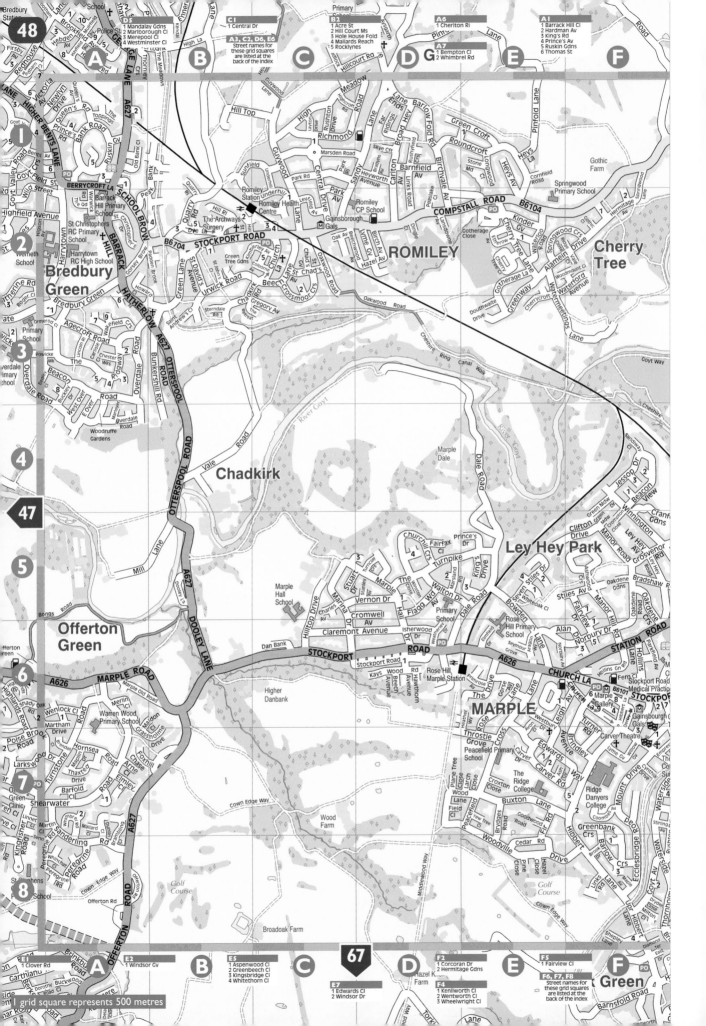

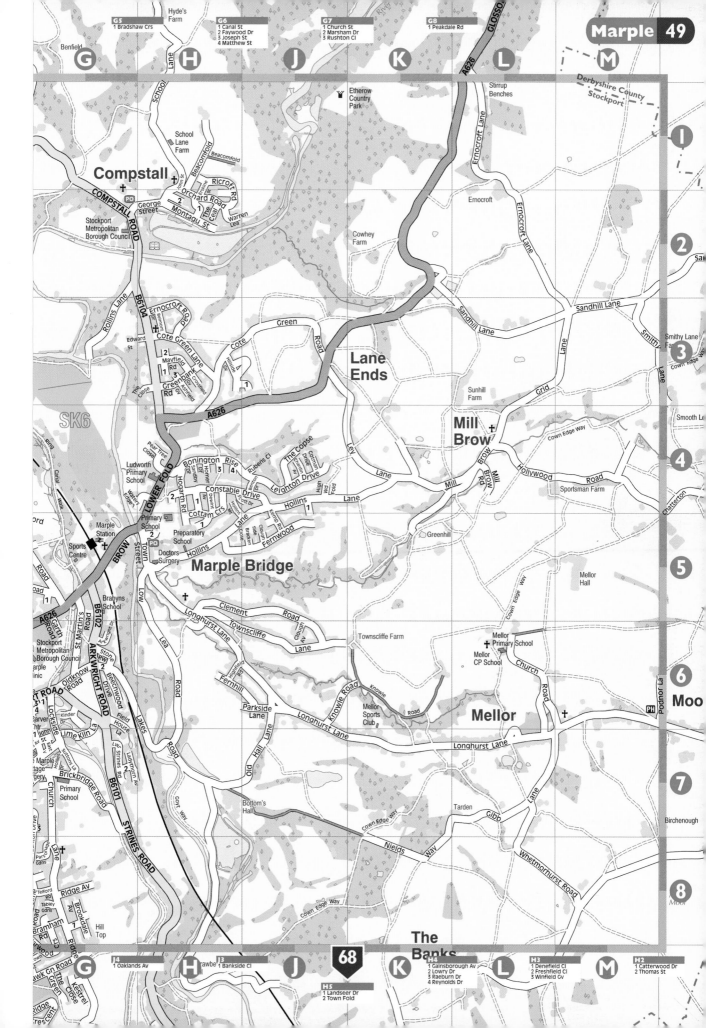

Tarbock Green

G1
1 Mardale Cl

G3
1 Abingdon Gv
2 Ambassador Dr
3 Wellbank Dr

G4
1 Graham Dr
2 Luscombe Cl

G   **H**   **J**   **32**   **K**   **L**   **M**

Stockswell

I

2

Lanc Avenue

3
Ditton Primar
tney Avenue

Ash

Dale
Clinctorts

4
Our Lady of Perp
Succour Junior School

52

5
SPEKE ROAD

Cross Hillocks Lane

B5178

Cross Hillocks Farm

Garnetts

A5500

Springfield Farm

Foxhill Farm

Lane

Wellingham Drive
Hever
Ashndown
Claydon Court

Court Av

Greensbridge Lane

Green's Bridge Farm

Greensbridge Lane

Halewood Church of England Primary School

L26

PO

Lower Cl

Lower Road

Ditton Brook

Knowsley Halton

ord Drive

Avenue

drive

Ronaldsway

wyn

Fir Cl
Fir Avenue

St Marks R C Primary School

Bailey's Lane

Birchen Rd

Highfield School

Hornbeam Road
Sharcombe Close

Penmann

Barn

Halewood Sports Centre

Kempsell Wy.

seheath Drive

Road

ere

Acre Gn

Winterley Dr
Willaston

Finch Lane

Finch Farm

Lower Road

Brook House Farm

A562

6

Old Hutte Lane

Sandhurst Rd
Aldersgate Dr

Higher Road   A562

Higher Road

Manor Farm

Higher Rd
Old

Higher Rd

Hale Bank Road

7

North Road

East Road

Higher Road

Carr Lane

Burnt Mill

Potters La

8

South Road

EKE BOULEVARD

The Margaret Thompson Medical Cen

Millwood

Ransfield

East

Maintree Crs
Cassley Rd
West Mains
Elloway Rd
Crovde Dr
Leveret Dr
Miners Wy
Oak Vw
Sandham Rd

G   **H**   **J**   **71**   **K**   **L**   **M**

H4
1 Rawlinson Crs

G8
1 Huttfield Rd
2 Millway Rd

G6
1 Haslington Gv
2 Rusholme Cl
3 Stapeley Gdns

G5
1 Merstone Cl

Ramsbro

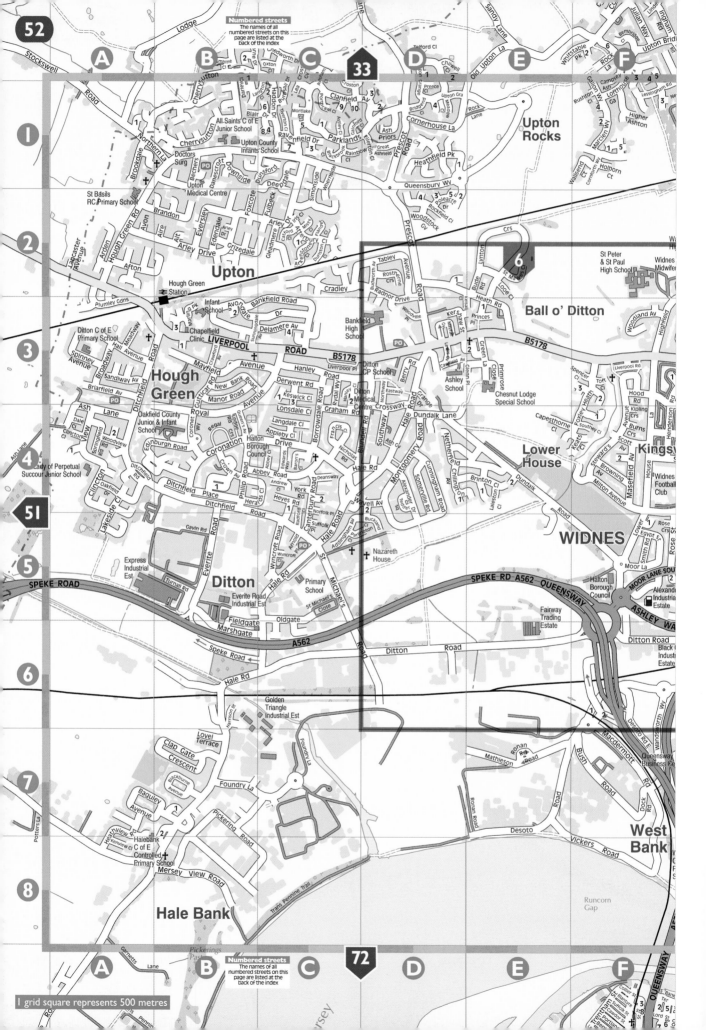

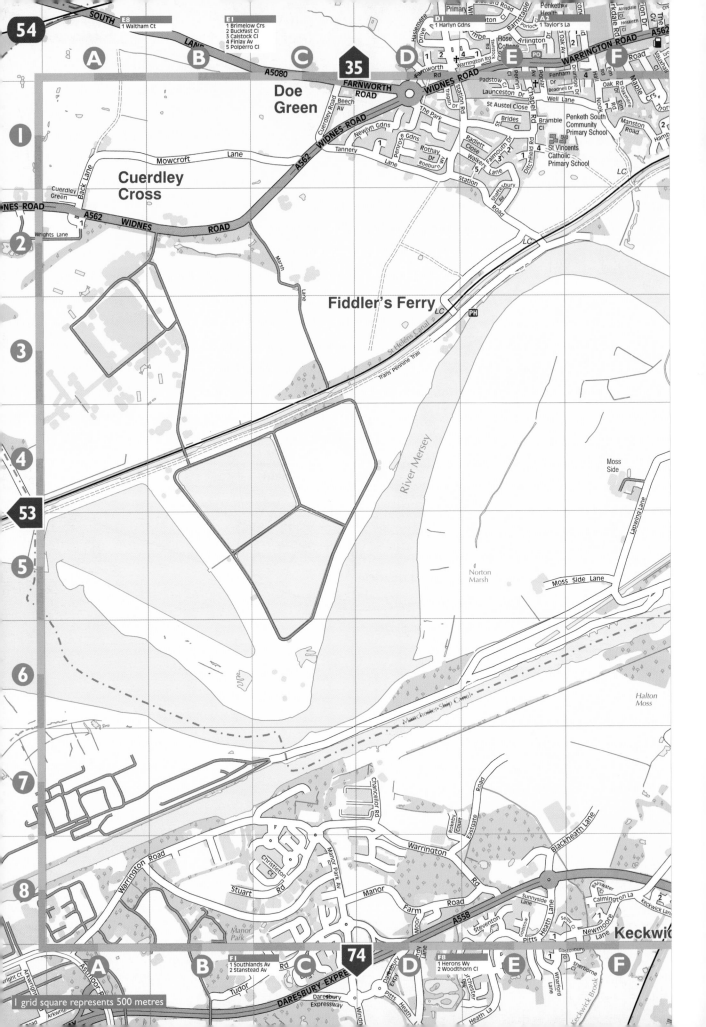

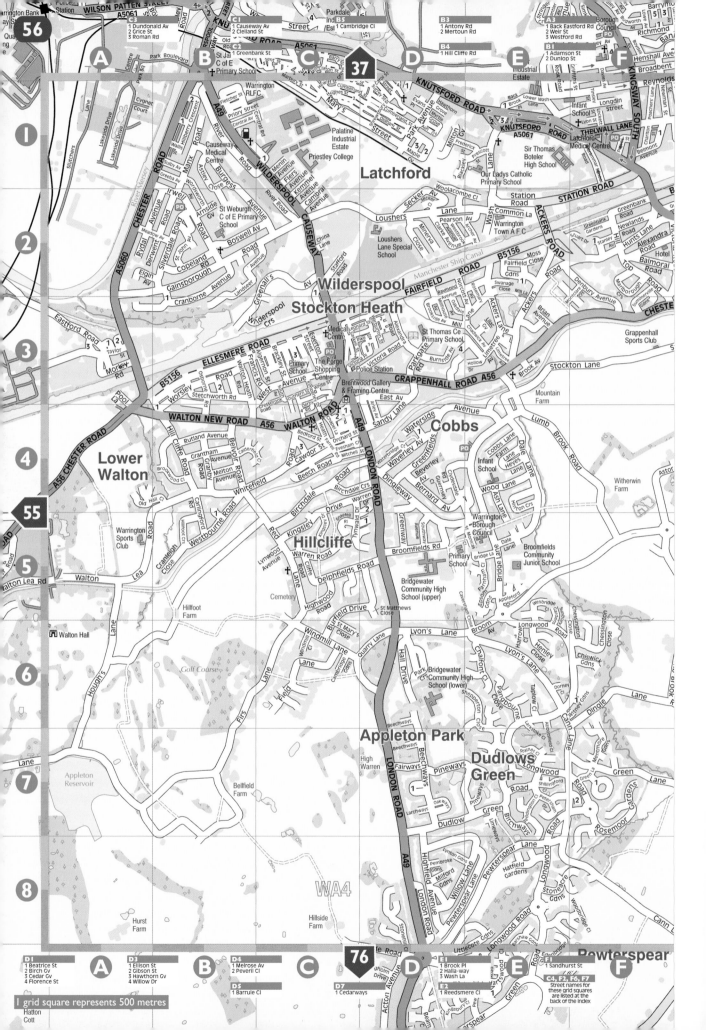

G1
1 Bruntleigh Av
2 Denver Rd
3 Selkirk Av

G2
1 Brookfield Pk

H2
1 Adamson Ct
2 Boydell Av
3 Meredith Av

38

Thelwall

Grappenhall

Grappenhall

STOCKPORT ROAD

KNUTSFORD ROAD

A50

KNUTSFORD ROAD

A50 CLIFF LANE

58

Junction 20

Wright's Green

GRAPPENHALL LANE

B5356

Appleton Thorn

77

G
Pepper Street
ROAD

H
Barley Castle Close

J
Arley

K
1 Brakenwood Ms
2 Hazelwood Ms

L
1 Coronation Av
2 Kensington Av

M
1 Buntingford Rd

I

2
Weaste

3

4
M6

5

6

7

8

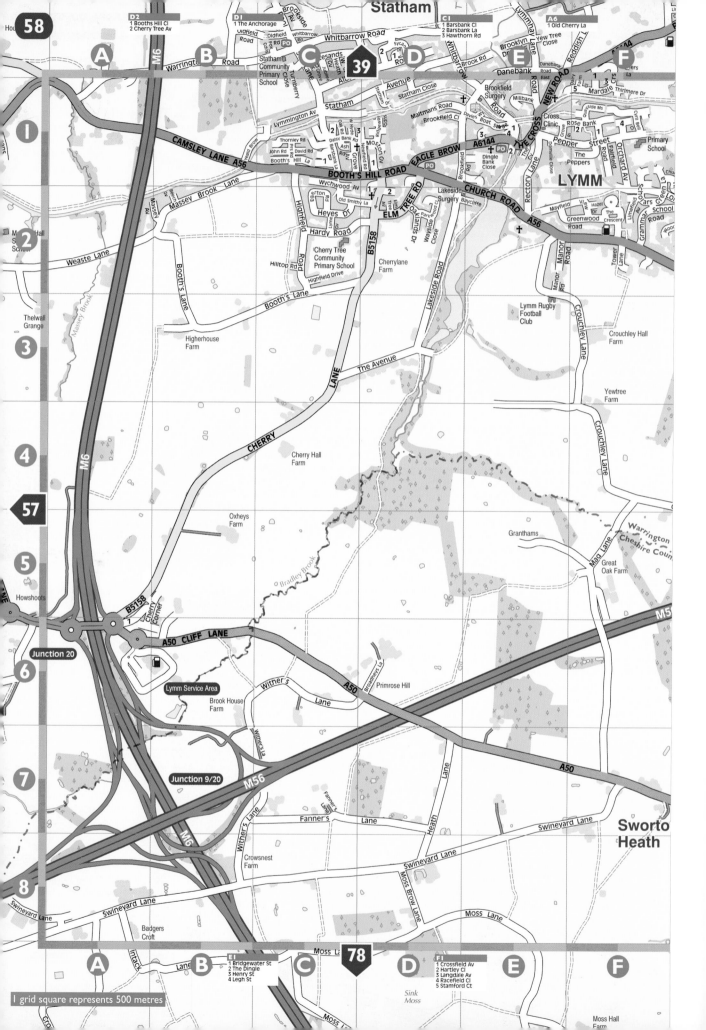

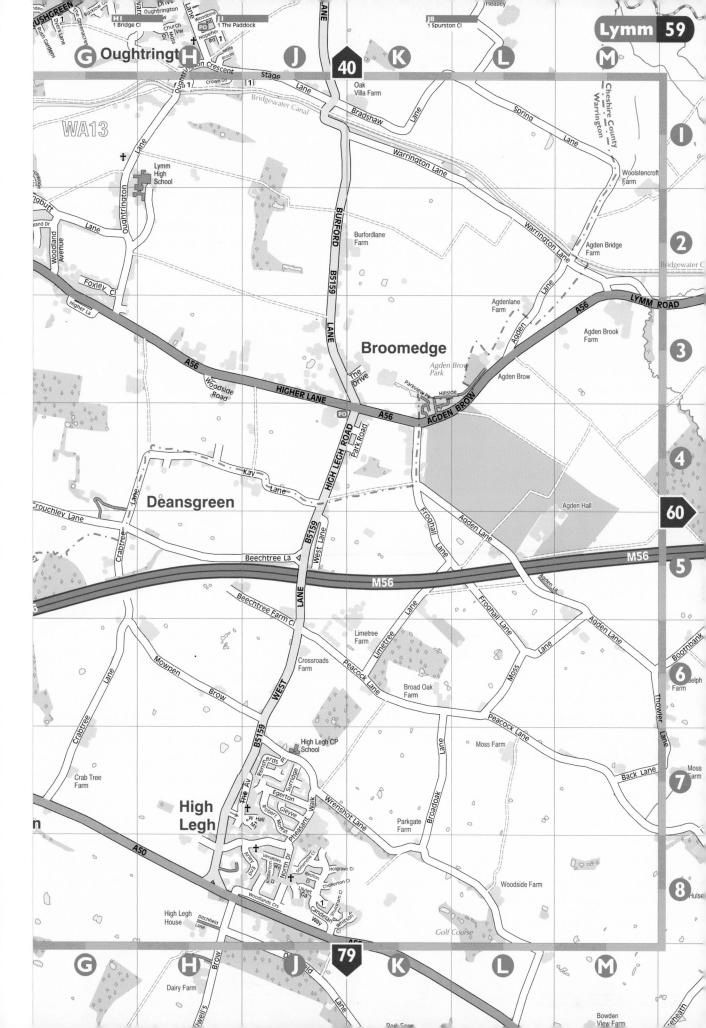

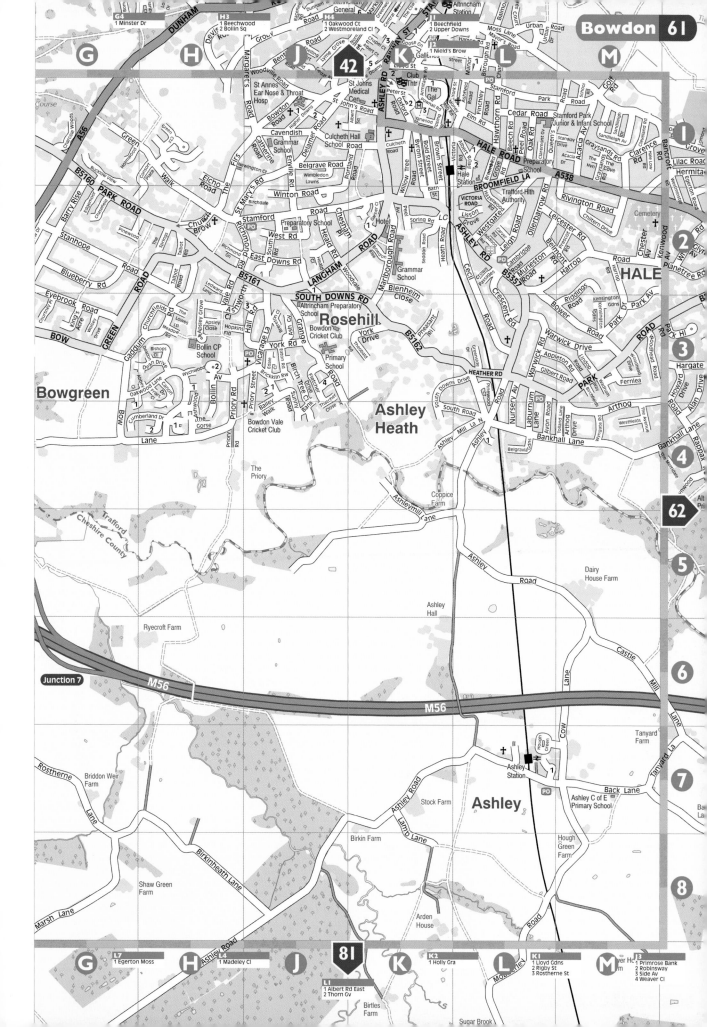

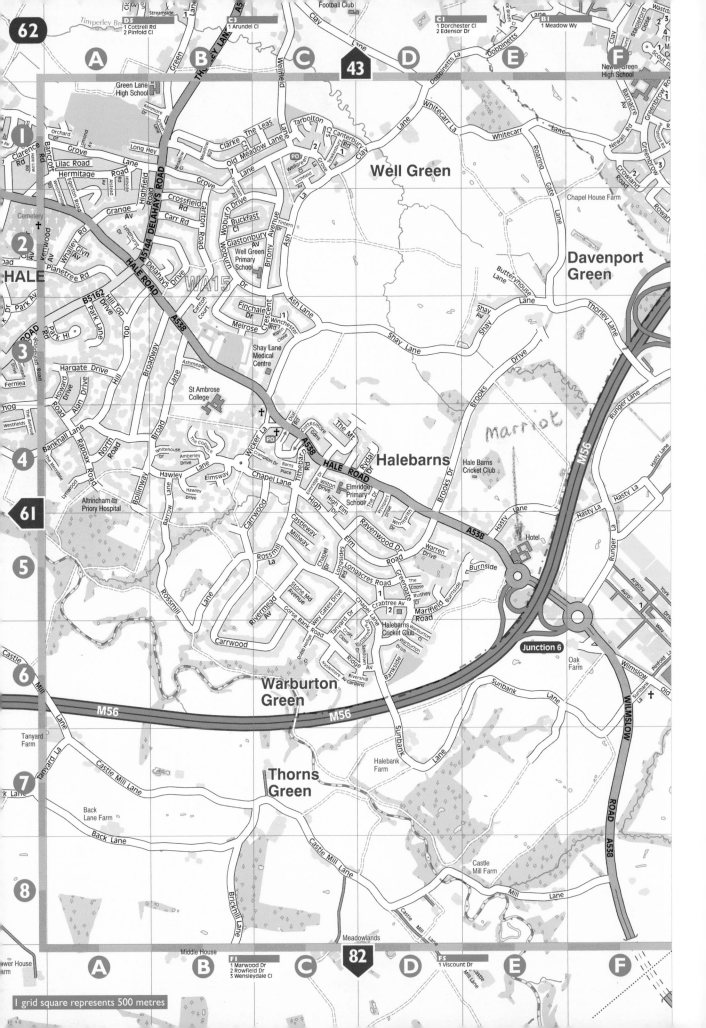

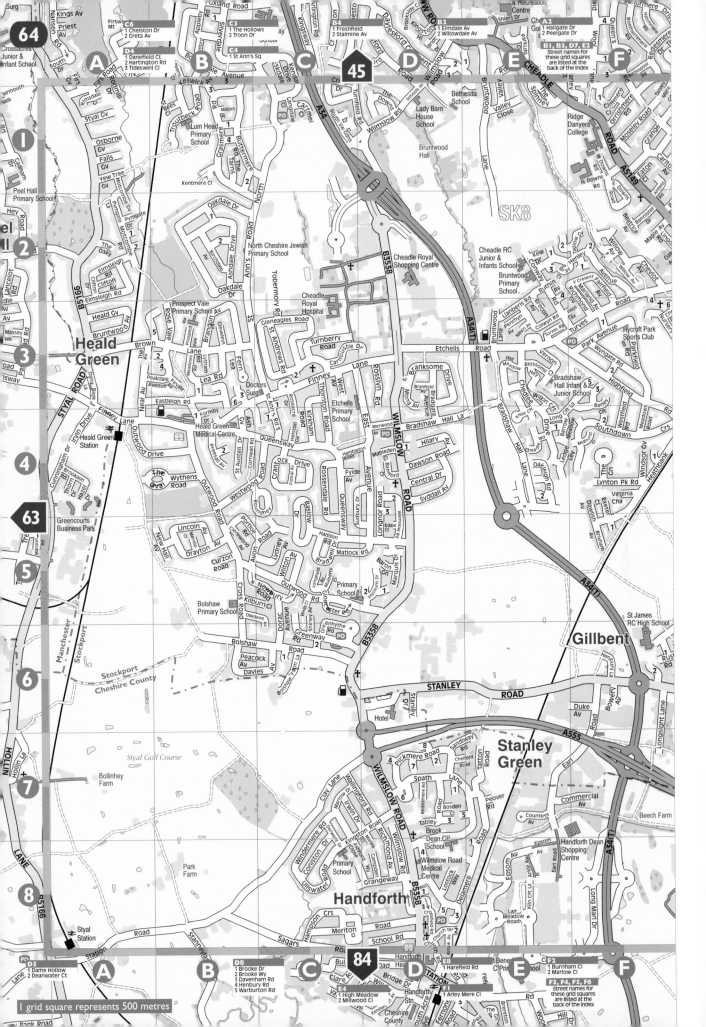

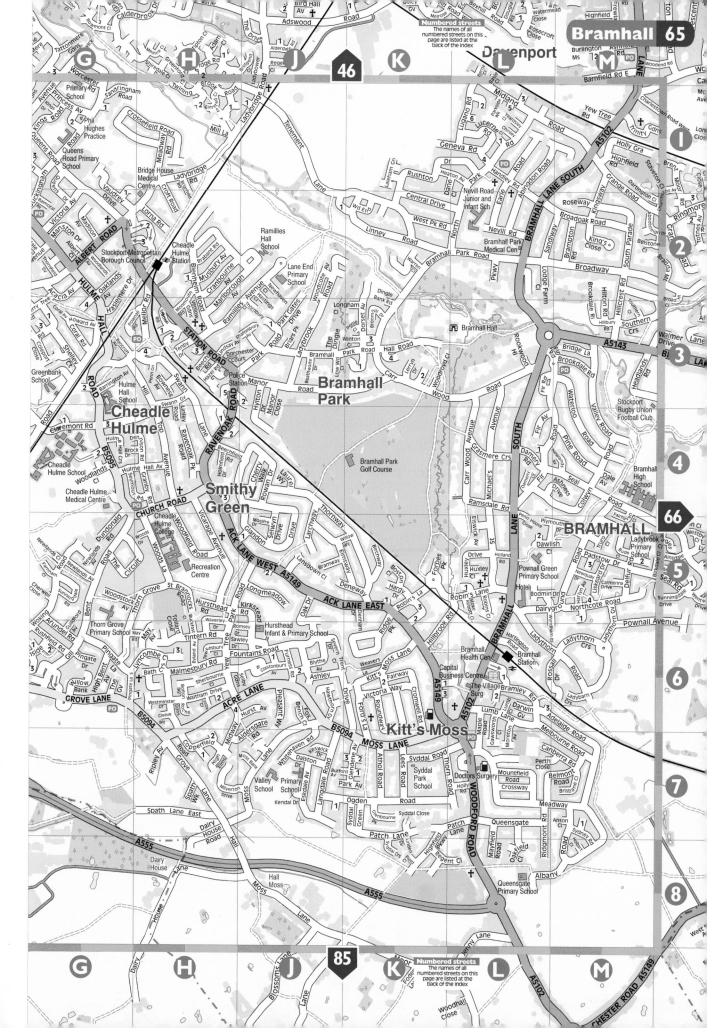

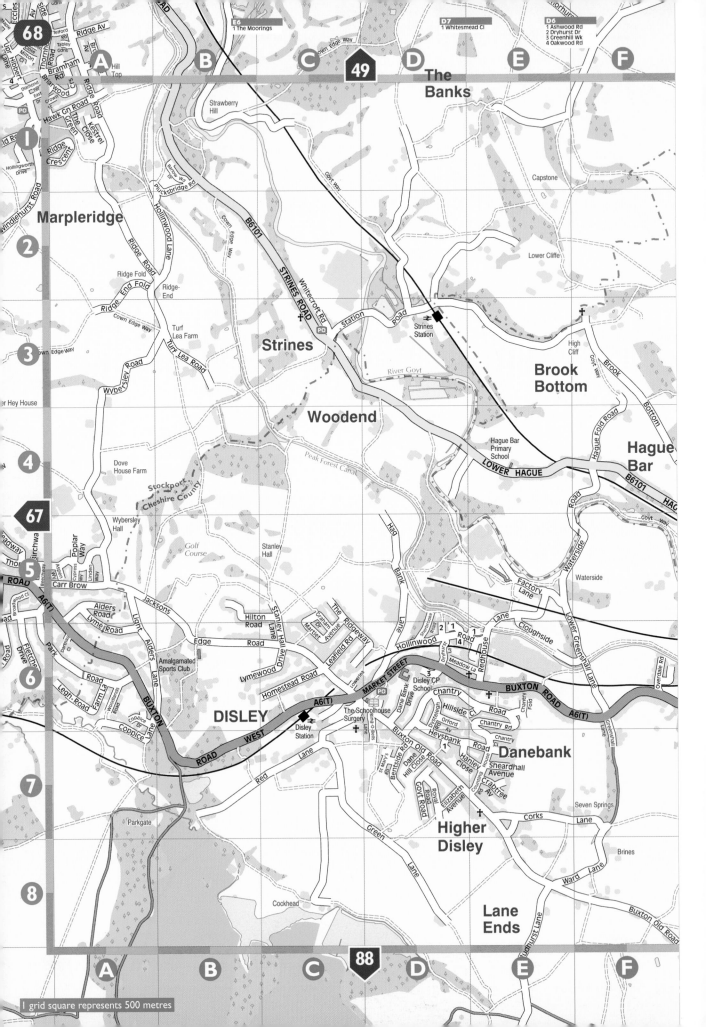

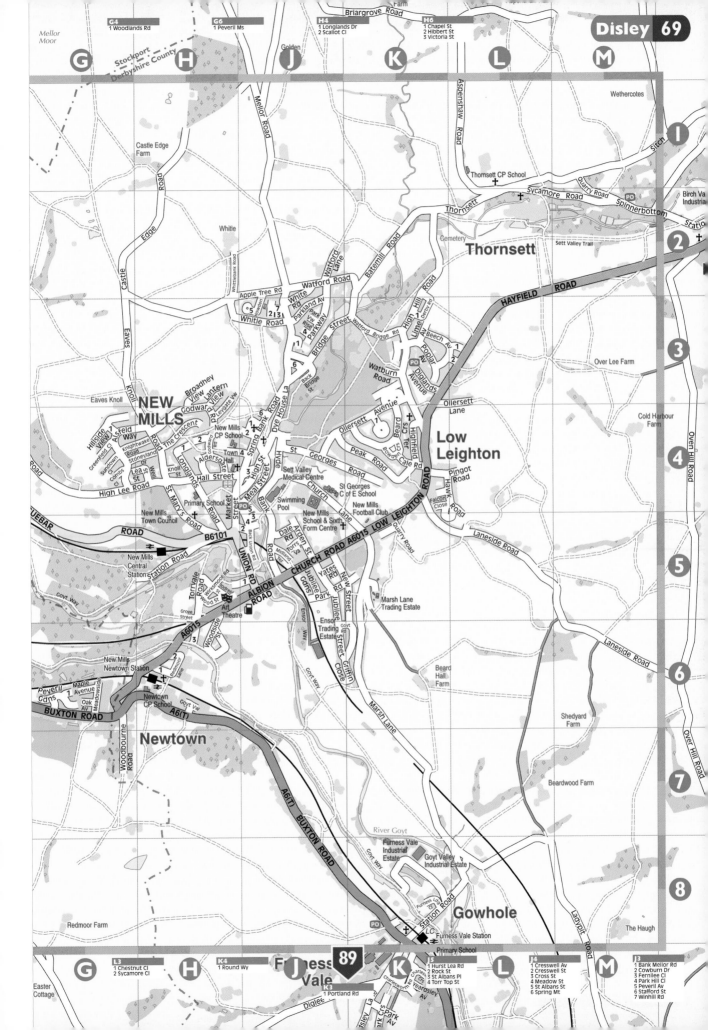

E2
1 Bramhall Cl
2 Ganworth Cl
3 Southern Rd

E1
1 Prenton Gn
2 Upton Cl
3 Upton Gn

D2
1 Fenton Gn
2 Marton Cl
3 Marton Gn

D1
1 Fenton Cl
2 Harefield Gn
3 Wellbrook Gn
4 Welton Cl
5 Welton Gn

A B C D E F

I

2

3

4

5

6

7

8

Speke

Oglet

River Mersey

Liverpool
Halton

Liverpool
Cheshire County

Speke Hall (NT)

Liverpool Airport

St Christophers Junior School
St Christophers Infant School
Speke Comprehensive School
Speke Community Comprehensive School
Stockton Wood JMI School
Alderwood CP School
Austin Rawlinson Sports Cen
Police Station
North Parade
Hlth Authority
South Parade
Speke Family Health Clinic
Wood Road Doctors Surgery

L24

Hale Road
Dam Wood Road
Hale Drive

Spindus Road
Dunlop Road
Central Avenue
Mersey Way
Oglet Lane
Dungeon Lane

1 grid square represents 500 metres

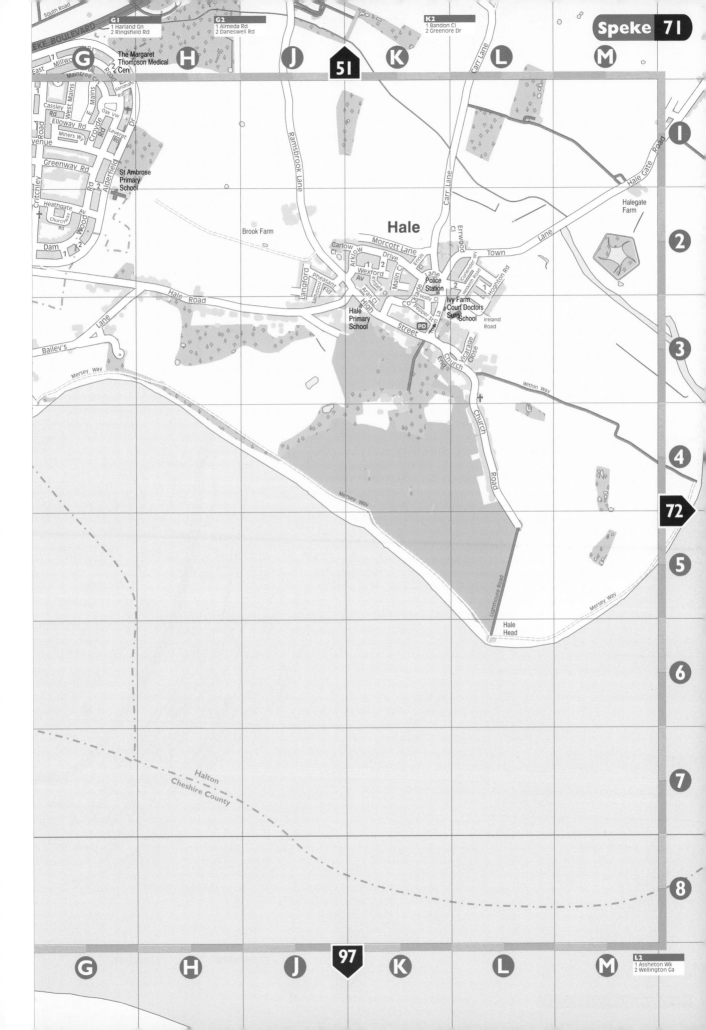

South Road

G1
1 Harland Gn
2 Ringsfield Rd

G2
1 Almeda Rd
2 Daneswell Rd

K2
1 Bandon Cl
2 Greenore Dr

SPEKE·BOULEVARD

G H J **51** K L M I

East Millwo 7

Maintree Cres

The Margaret
Thompson Medical
Cen

Carr Lane

Hale Gate Road

Cassley
Rd West Mains
Elloway Rd E Mains Oak VW
Croyle Rd Leveret
Road Miners Wy
Critchley Rd Alderfield
Avenue Greenway Rd

St Ambrose
Primary
School

Halegate
Farm

2

Heathgate
Av Wood
Church Rd
Dam 1 2

Brook Farm

Hale Road

Hale
Lane

Morcott Lane

Hale

Carr Lane

Errwood

Town Lane

Ivy Farm

3

Bailey's

Mersey Way

Ramsbrook Lane

Langford
Lanyford
Pheasant Fld

Carlow
Cl
Arklow Cl
Wexford
Av 1 2
Aran Cl
High
Street

Drive
Kildare Cl
Malin Cl
Ennis
Cockade
Holly Cl
Pepper St
Town La PO
Church

Police
Station

Carpenter W
Western Road
Hoghton Rd

2
Court Doctors
Surg School
Ireland
Road

Vicarage
Close

Within Way

Church

Road

72

4

Hale
Primary
School

5

Lighthouse Road

Mersey Way

Hale
Head

Mersey Way

6

Halton
Cheshire County

7

8

52
8
71
98

F2
1 Cavendish St
2 Hankey St
3 High St
4 Lowlands Rd
5 Rutland St
6 Shaw St
7 Waterloo Rd

E4
1 Lancaster Av
2 Lingfield Rd

E2
1 Runcorn Docks Rd

D5
1 Cullen Rd

A B C D E F

I

2

3

4

5

6

7

8

Mersey View Road
Trans Pennine Trail
e Park
Runcorn Gap

Garnetts Lane
Pickerings Pasture

Hale Gate Road
Trans Pennine Trail

Halegate Farm

River Mersey

Collier St
Surrey St
Brindley St
Trenwdor St
Portland St
35 Ashbury
Trent St
Bentinck St
Leinster St
Lord St
Waterloo

Algernon Street
Duke Cl
A533
Peel

Percival
Percival Lane
WESTON POINT EXPRESSWAY - A557
Cormorant Dr
Runcorn Station
Shaw

Pimlico Rd
Picow Farm
Adela Rd
Cynthia Rd
Roland Av
Penn Lane
Clayton Crs
Roland av
Queen's Rd

Picow
Crofton Road
Westfield
Westfield Crs
Weston Road
10
3
4

Cunningham
Beaconsfield Rd
Russell
PO
Higher Runcorn
8
2

Weston Point
Hale Vw
Hillside Av
Cameron Av
Hazel Av
Perrin Av
1
Royden Av
Coombe Dr
Park

A557

Highlands Road
Heath Park

Post Office
PO
Mersey Vw. 5 Rd
West Road
Sandy Lane
South Parade
Baker Road
Leonard St
Sydney
LC
Roscoe Crescent
Castner Av
Weston Point County Primary School
Weston Road

Weston

Highlands Road

Halton
Cheshire County

Lydiate
Cheshyre's La
Bankes's La
Cheshyre's La
Collier's Row
WESTON POINT EXPRESSWAY
Weston Road
Sewage Works
Heath Westo
Marion Rd
Montpa
Tilds
Lambs
4
Bankes's La
PO
South
Cavendi
A557

D4
1 Johns Av
2 Whitley Cl

F6
1 Ashton Cl
2 Company's Cl
3 Cresta Dr
4 Lambsickle Cl

A B C D E F

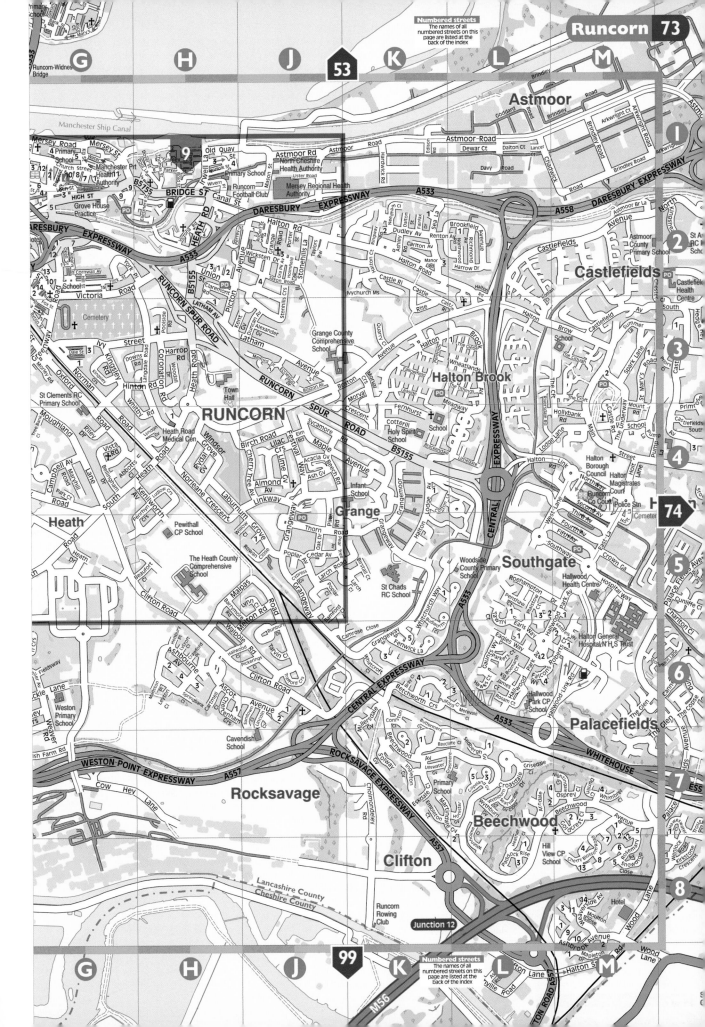

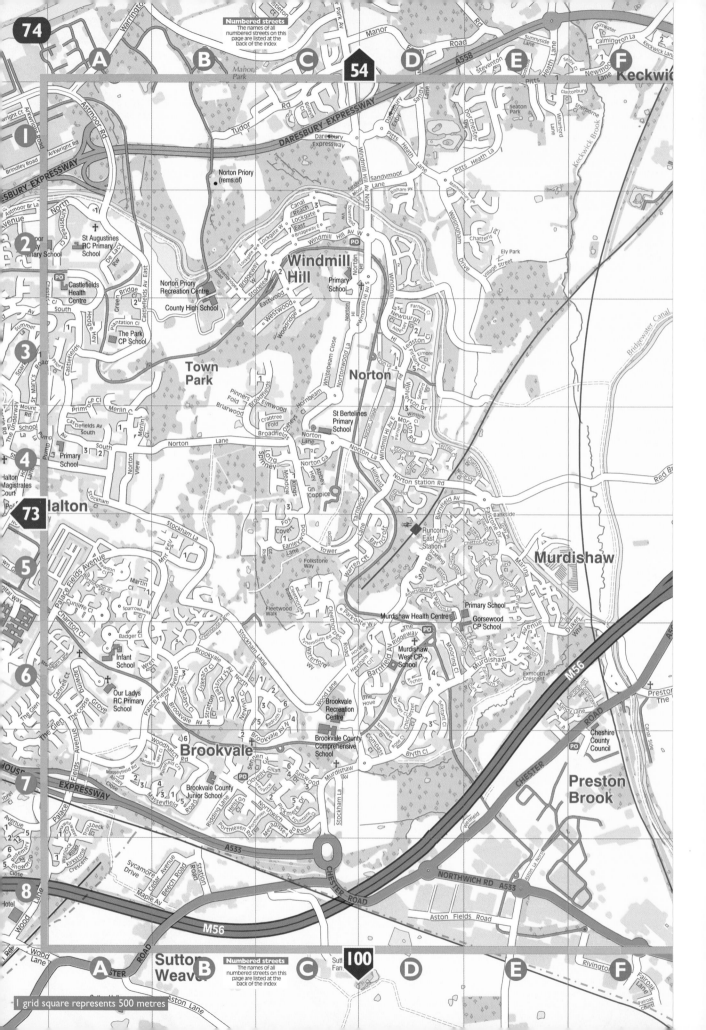

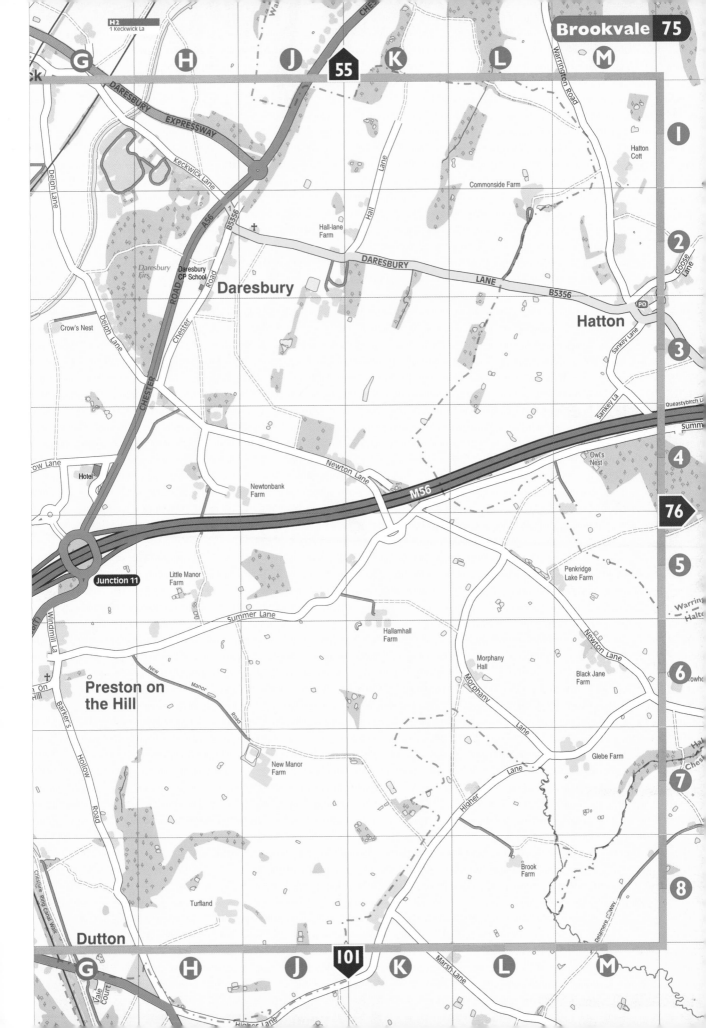

G H J K L M

H2
1 Keckwick La

55

I

DARESBURY EXPRESSWAY

Keckwick Lane

Warrington Road

Hatton Cott

Commonside Farm

2

Hall-lane Farm

DARESBURY LANE B5356

Goose Lane

Hall Lane

Chester Road

A56

B5356

Delph Lane

Daresbury Firs

Daresbury CP School

Daresbury

Crow's Nest

PO

Hatton

3

Sankey Lane

Chester Road

Sankey La

Queastybirch L

summ

4

Newton Lane

Owl's Nest

ow Lane

Hotel

Newtonbank Farm

M56

76

5

Junction 11

Little Manor Farm

Penkridge Lake Farm

Warring

Halto

Windmill La

Summer Lane

Hallamhall Farm

Morphany Hall

Newton Lane

Black Jane Farm

6

rowho

New Manor Road

Preston on the Hill

Morphany Lane

Glebe Farm

Hal

Chest

7

Barker's

Hollow Road

New Manor Farm

Higher Lane

Brook Farm

8

Turfland

Delamere way

Chesire Ring Canal Walk

Dutton

Vale Court

101

G H J K L M

Marsh Lane

Higher Lane

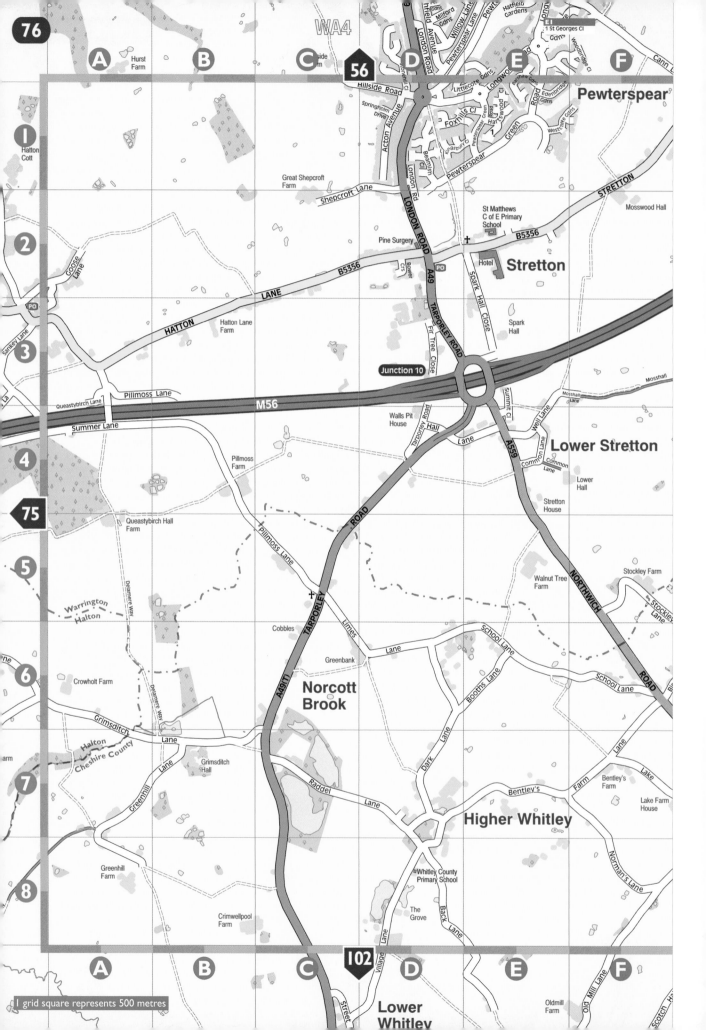

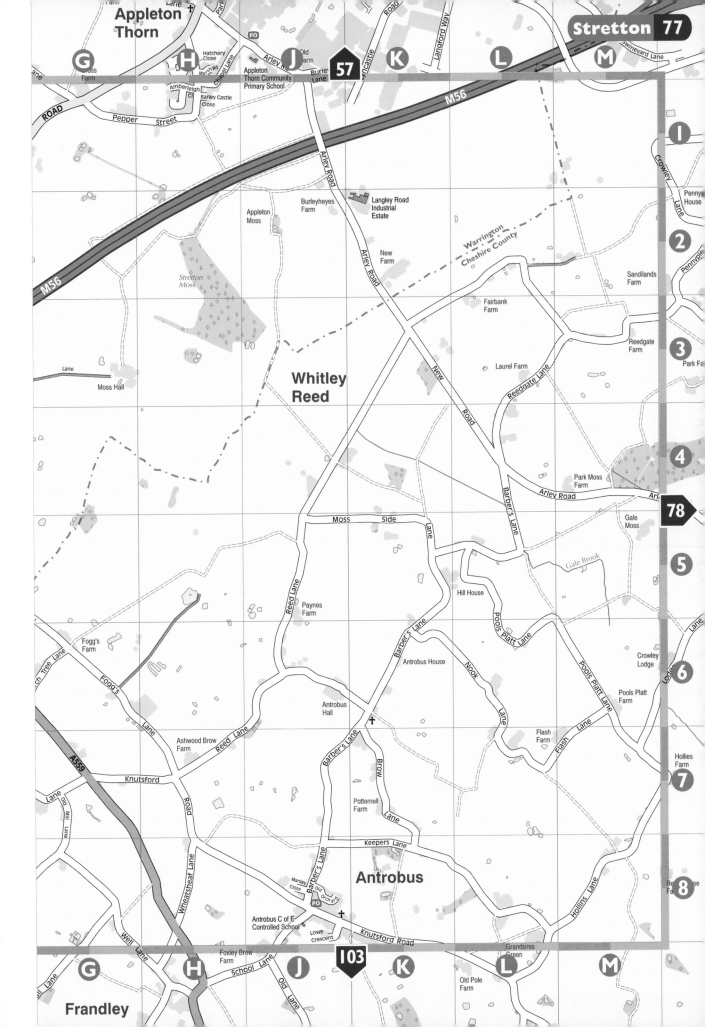

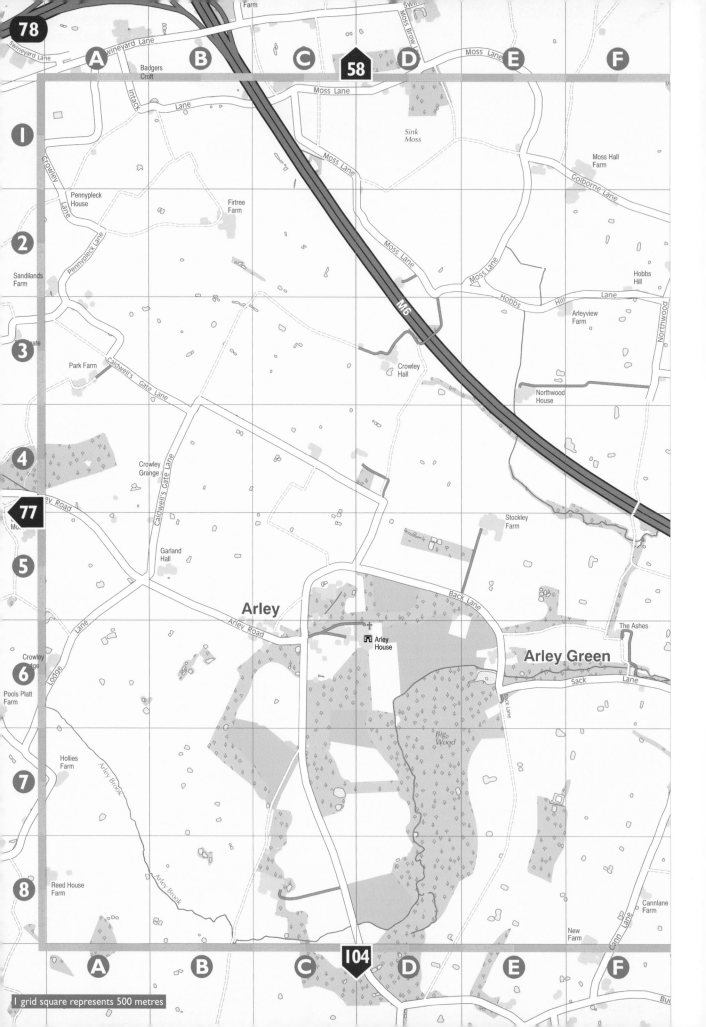

Woodside Farm

G   H   J   59   K   L   M

I

Woodlands Crs

Ditchfield
Lane

Ditchfield

Dairy Farm

Bowden
View Farm

Park Farm

Hoo Green

2   Hulme
Farm

PO

Golborne Lane

Bowden View Lane

A50

Lane

Rowley Bank Lane

Hoogreen Lane

Hoogreen Lane

3

Yew Tree
Hall Farm

Rowley   Rowleybank
Farm

Northwood

Goodiersgreen
Farm

4

Lane

Whitley Lane

Daisybank
Farm

Whitley
Brook Farm

80

Northwood
Hall Farm

Mere
Heyes

Winterbottom Lane

5

Whitley Lane

M6

6

Cann Lane

Litley
Farm

Winterbottom

Bentleyhurst
Farm

M6

7
**Ove
Tab**

Cann Lane

Hollowood
Farm

Gore Farm

Old Hall La

8   Ho

Feldy

Heyrose
Farm

Holehouses

dworth Road

Tableybrook
Farm

B5391

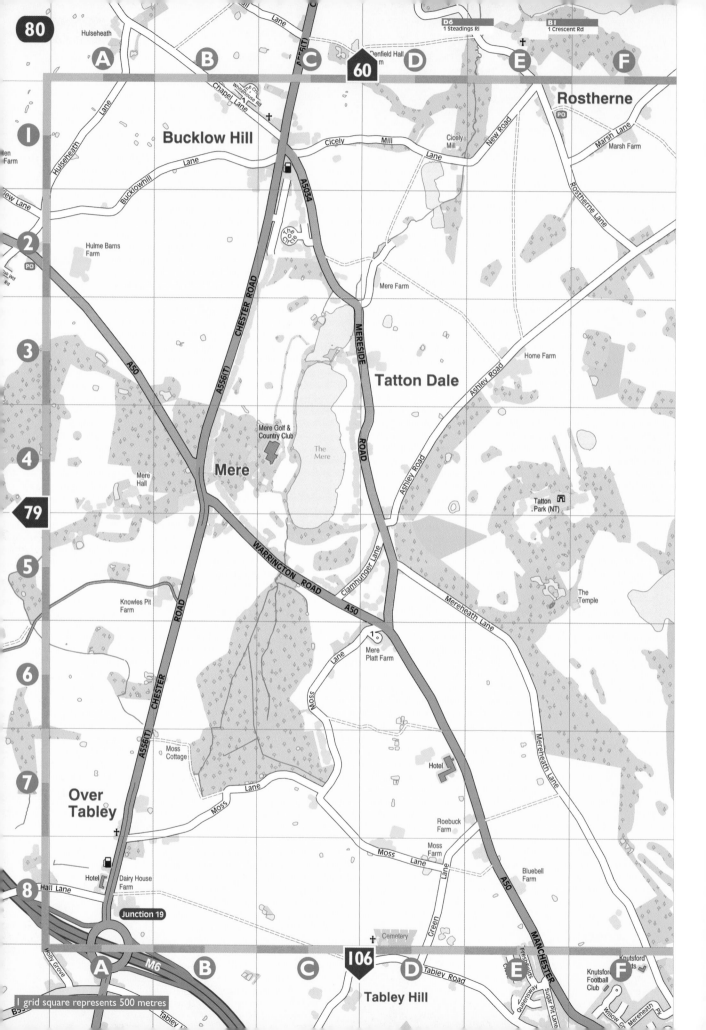

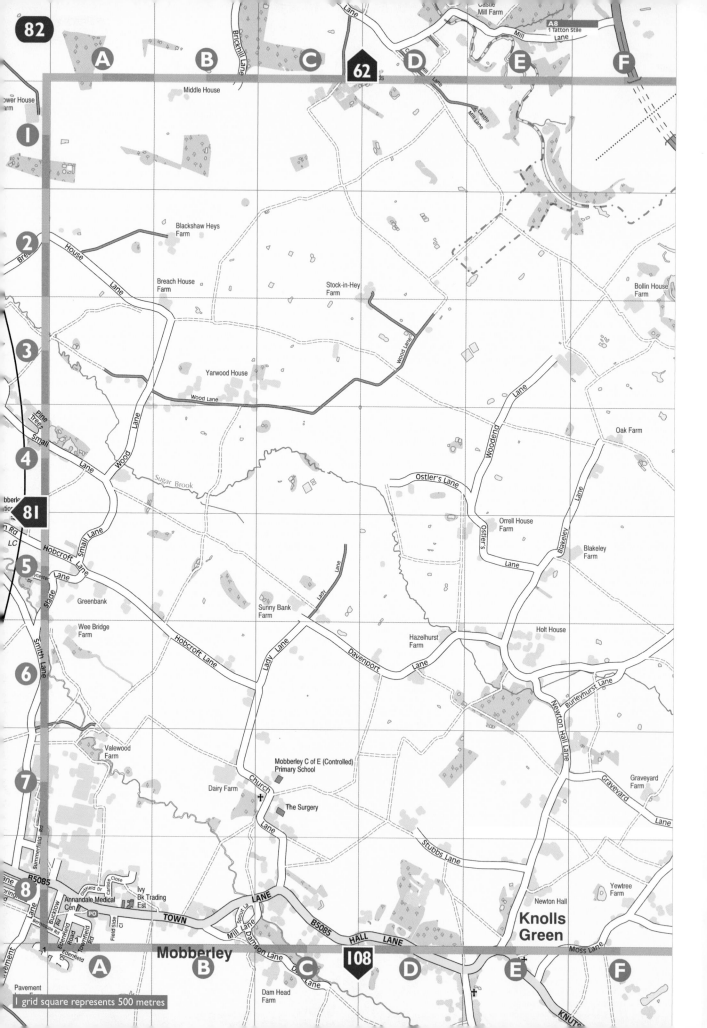

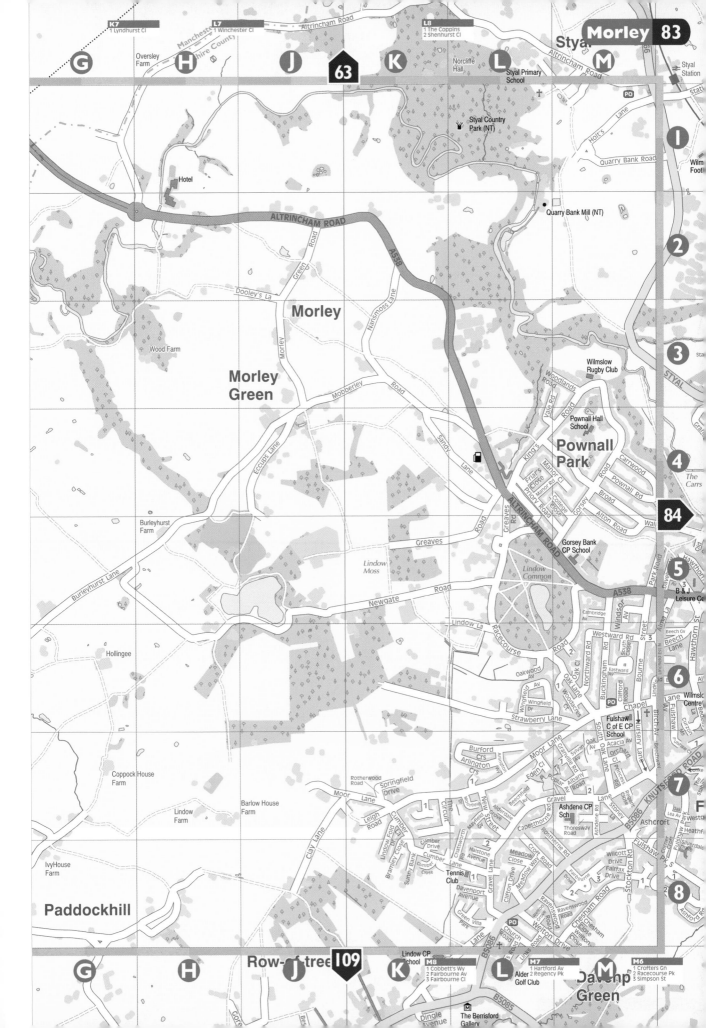

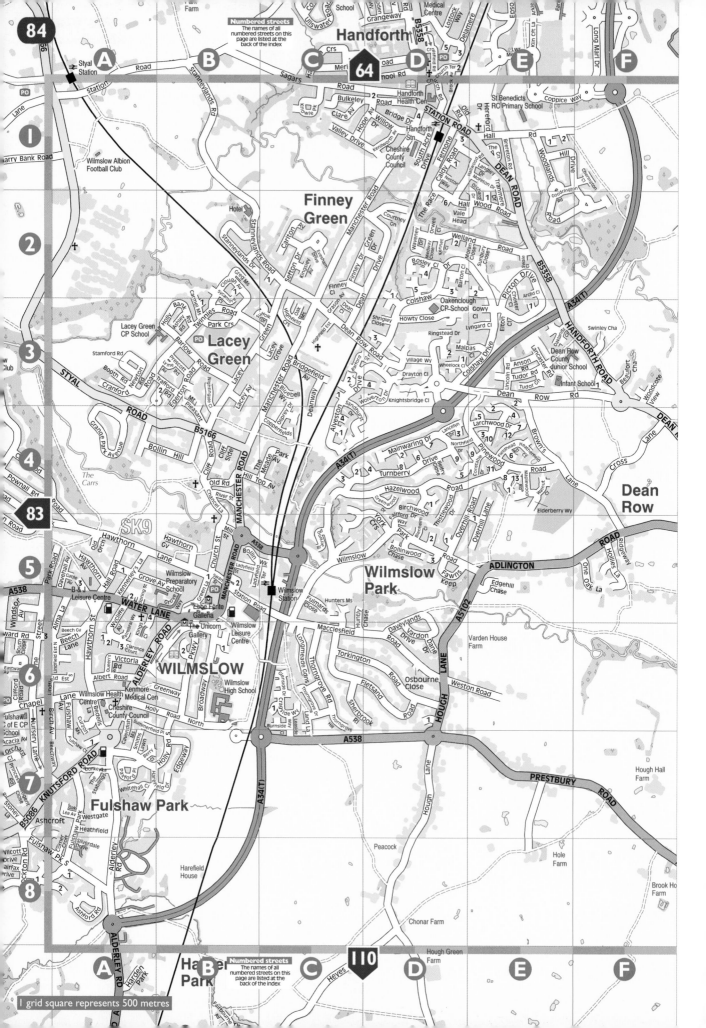

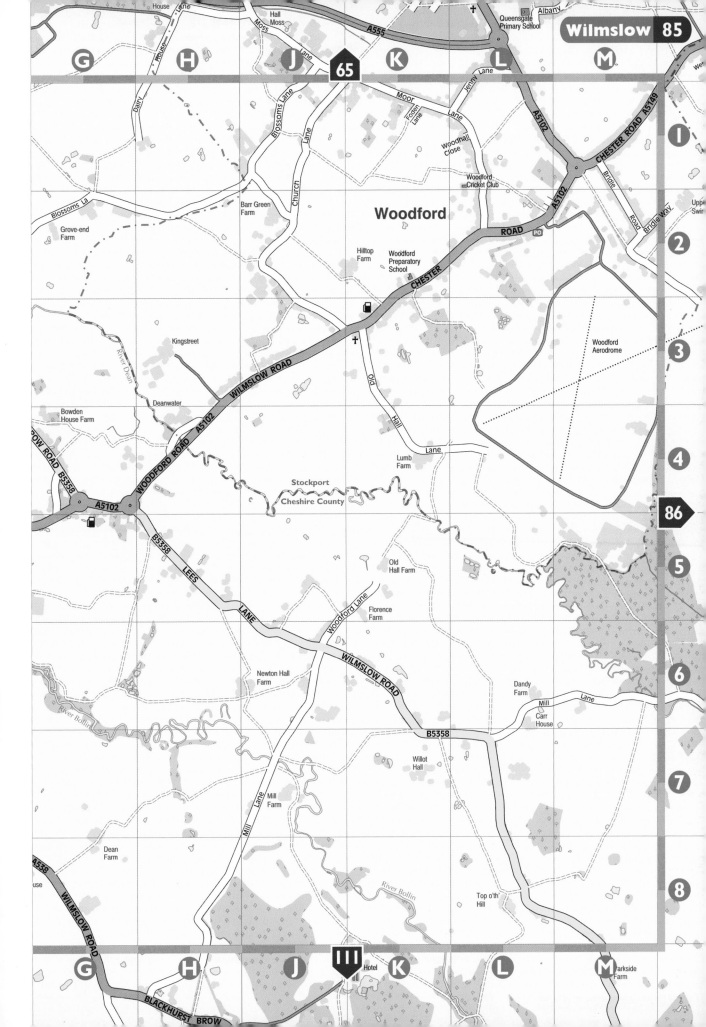

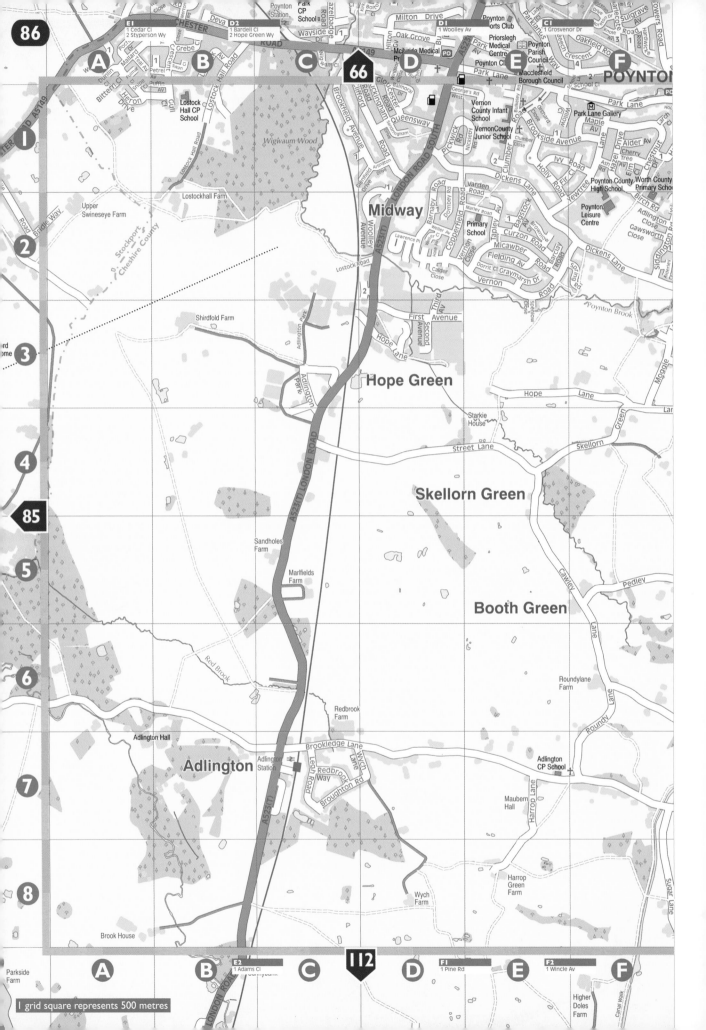

G1
1 Bosley Dr
2 Collingwood Cl
3 Nelson Cl
4 Trafalgar Cl

G2
1 Warford Av

H4
1 Meadowside

G **H** **J** **K** **L** **M**

67

Anson Road

SK12

Hockley

Hepley Rd

Coppice Road

PO

Higher Poynton

Green Lane

Lyme Rd

Hilltop Farm

Platt Wood Farm

Elm Beds Road

Sheldon Road

Middlewood Way

Shrigley Road

Haresteads Farm

Hagg Farm

Green Farm

Wardsend

Narrow Lane

Wood Lane End Farm

Yew Tree Road

Wood Lane North

Cheshire Ring Canal Walk

Mitchell Fold

Shrigley Road

Wood Lanes

Wood Lane West

Middlewood Way

Wood Lane South

Redacre Hall Farm

West Parkgate

Shrigley Road

88

Hill

Wood Lane East

Simpson Lane

5

Woodend Farm

Higher House Farm

Shrigley Road

6

Middlewood Way

Cheshire Ring Canal Walk

Springbank Farm

Harrop Brow

Birchencliff

Macclesfield Canal

Shrigley Road

7

Norman's Hall Farm

Shrigley Park Farm

Brookledge Lane

8

Styperson Park

Shrigley Park

Shrigley Hall Hotel Golf & Country Club

Moorside Lane

Bakestonedale Moor

Bakestonedale Road

113

Pott Shrigley

Pott Shrigley C of E Primary School

Andrew's Knob

Ellis Bar

G **H** **J** **K** **L** **M**

Clark Green

Long Lane

Shrigley Road

Sugar

A B C **68** D Lane End E F

I

2

3

87

4

5

6

7

8

A B **114** C D E F

Cockhead

Ward Lane

Buxton Old Road

Mudhurst Lane

Rocks Farm

Bolder Hall

Lyme Park Country Park

Lyme Park (NT)

Gritstone Trail

Cock-knoll

Higher Lane

Handleybarn

Cliff

Gritstone Bowstonegate Trail

Bailey's Farm

Park Moor

Gritstone Trail

Handley Fold Farm

411 Sponds Hill

Cliff Farms

Dunge Valley (gardens)

Kettleshulme

Paddock Lane

Flatts Lane

Side End Farm

Bakestonedale Road

Bakestonedale

Gritstone Trail

Farm

Brink

Bakestonedale Rd

MACCLESFIELD ROAD

Higher Lane

B5470

Close

I grid square represents 500 metres

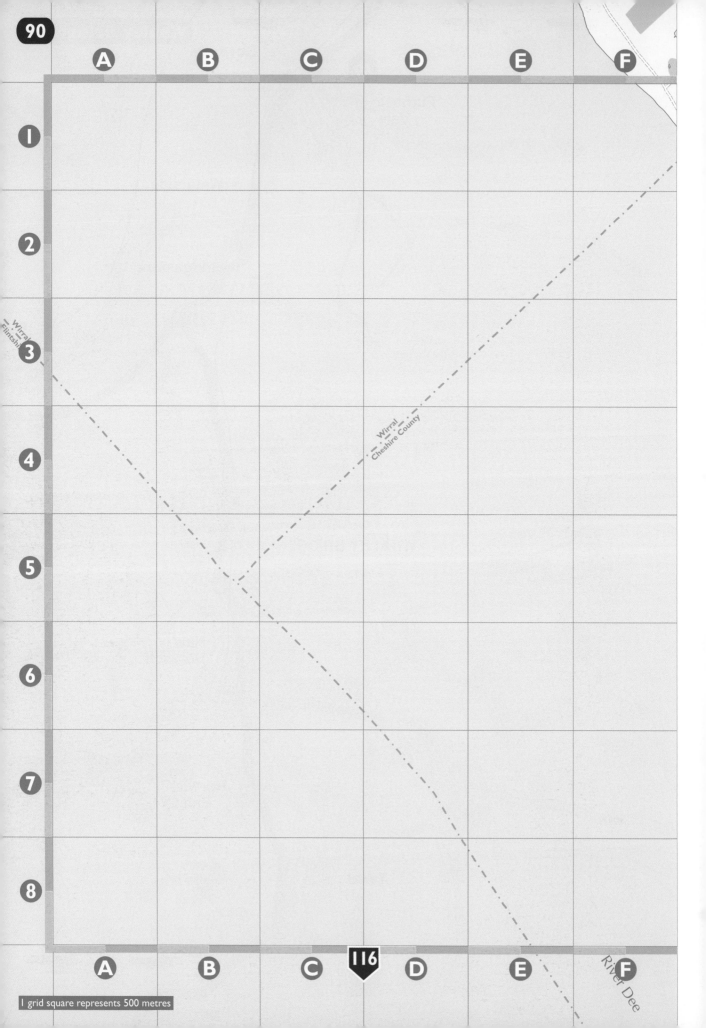

J3
1 Sandheys
H4
1 The Ropewalk
K3
1 Fairholme Av
L3
1 Spenser Rd

Leighton
Hall Farm

K5
1 Gladstone Rd
2 Marlowe Rd

H5
1 Old Quay Cl

The Grange
Country

CHESTER HIGH ROAD A540

LIVERPOOL ROAD B

Ashfield
Hall

Leighton
Road
LANE
B5135

BOATHOUSE

North Parade

Wirral Way

THE PARADE
B5135

The
Looms
Brook Hey
Tithebarn
Hamilton
Looms
Barnacre
Dr
Moorfield
Drive
Carlton
Drive
Brook La

Wood

Paddock Dr

Pinehey

Bevyl
Road
Hawthorn Road
Bowling
Green
Drive

Moorings
Cl

School

Brooklands
Road
Brooklands
Gardens

Parkgate CP
School

Wirral Way

Springcroft

Crenfell Pk

The
Square
Holtwell
Close
Little
La

PO

Mostyn
House
School

STATION RD

Neston
Cricket
Club

The
Parade

Memorial Road

Hunters Way

Memorial Road South

The
Anchorage

Emilie
Court

Heron'a
Ct

Moorside
Avenue

Moorside
Court

PARKGATE RD

Albert
Drive

The
Spinney

Earle

Earle
Crs

Woodlands Rd

Woodlands

Leighton
Pk

The
Leightons

Leighton Road

Buggen
Lane

Lane

B5135

Park St
The
Green

Mill
Street

Church
Street

Beechways Dr

Old
Quay
Lane

Moorside
Lane

Manor

Wesley
Pk

Boundary

Pinehey

Parkgate

Leighton
Drive

Abbots
Way

The
Priory

Leighton
Chase

Leighton
Cross

Syrch Croft
Neston
Station

Neston
Medical
Centre

Raby
Gdns

Raby
Rd

Tannery La

Brook
St

HIGH
ST

CHESTER
RD

News Gallery

Steeple
Ct

Bridge Street

Station   Road

Romney Way

Raeburn

Flint

Cottage Cl

Morland
Av

Allans Meadow

Allans
Cl

Crasmere

Meadow
Close

Meadow
Dr

Ardern
Dr

Sutton Av

Henley Rd

He ley
Rd

West
Dr

West

The Di
Stratford
Rd

Kenilworth

West

Leamington
Cross

Warwick Rd

Riverside
Walk

Hampton
Crs

Sandpiper
Dr

Marshlands

Orchard Cl

New St

Colliery
Green Dr

Snab
Gates
Cl

Quayside

Winstanley
Wy

Sunningdale Wy

Darby Rd

Sea Vw

Top Rd

Colliery Green Cl

Clifton
Rd

Snabwood

Greenfields Drive

Brook

Turrocks
Cl

Well

Wirral Crs

Furrocks La

Furrocks
Wy

Bankfield

Road

Hampton
Road

Somerville

Cliffe Rd

Riverview
Rd

Conation Rd

The
Maw

Girvin Dr

Burton

Road

Badger Bait

The
Bull

Cliffe

School Lane

Woodfall Lane

Furrocks La

Dawn Clse

Cumbers Dr

Neston Road

Well Lane

Talbot
Av

Talbot

Mellock
Lane

Neston
Surgery

Neston
Primary
School

Yewtree

Bushell Road

The
Quillet

Bendee Road

Ashtree Drive

Waterford Drive

Rockree
Edge

Stoneban k

Woodfall

San

VIC

LIVERPOOL ROAD

Ringway

Westlands

Westwood
Court

Water Tower

Long Acres
Road

Buildwas
Road

Coalbrookdale Rd

Clayhill

Art
Gallery

St Marys C of E
Primary School

Neston
County
High School

Recreation
Centre

Cemetery

Park
Road

Raby

Breezehill
Rd

Breezehill
Pk

Gunn
Grove

B5136

Drake
Road

Hawkins Road

Sidney
Road

Raleigh
Rd

Shakespeare
Rd

Frobisher Road

Jonson
Rd

Bunn
Rd

Blakeys Lane

Highfield
Close

Orchfield Rd

Olive Dr

Moorside

NESTON

Little
Neston

Nessholt

Parkgate

G
M7
1 Greenfields Cl
2 Woodham Gv

H
M4
1 Stanton Ct

M5
1 Station Cl
2 Windermere Cl

J

117

M3
1 Greenville Rd

K

L7
1 Bathwood Dr
2 Colliery Green Ct
3 Grampian Wy
4 Peerswood Ct
5 Turrocks Cl

L
L6
1 Hampton Cl

M
L5
1 Bridge Ct
2 Eldon Ter

G5
1 Tees Ct
2 Ure Ct

H6
1 Imperial Ms

H7
1 Hollyfield Rd

H8
1 Chapel Ms

G H J K L M

I

2

3

10

11

ELLESMERE PORT

4

96

5

6

7

8

River Mersey

Canal

M53

Junction 8

MERSEYTON RD

B5463

Rother Drive
Business Park

EAST ROAD

Rossbank Road

Rosscliffe Rd

Rosswood Rd

Rossmount Rd

Rossfield Road

Ross Rd

Rossfield Road

Westminster
Industrial Park

Stamford Street

Camden Rd

Hampton Gdns

Cannon St

Bishops Gdns

Deansgate

Queens Gdns

Earls Gdns

Fleet Gdns

Flatt Lane

Princes Road

Compton Place

Blairfield Rd

Beechfield Rd

Priestfield Rd

Highfield Rd

Woodford Rd

Enfield Rd

Dudley Rd

Oldfield Rd

Heathfield Rd

WHITBY ROAD

Regent Street

Kensington Drive

Aldgate

College

William Stockton
CP School

Ellesmere Port
Business Cen

Civic Lane

School Lane

York Rd
Clinic

York Road
Group Practice

Victoria Rd

Whitby Rd

Ellesmere
Port Station

Station Rd

STATION ROAD

King St

Crescent Rd

Meadow Lane

Cook St

Cedab
Road

The
Surg

Percival Road

Monks Gv

Church

Westminster Road

Percival Road

Wilkinson Street

John St

Grace Rd

Redhills

Frosts Ms

Westminster
Surgery

New Grosvenor Rd

Livingstone Rd

Lime St

Stanley Rd

Netson Rd

Coleman St

Stour Cl

Frome Rd

Abbots Ms

Abbots Road

QUEEN ST

George Street

Worcester

Egerton St

Exmouth St

QUEEN ST

Boat
Museum

Lower Mersey Street

Myrtle St

A5032

South Road

South Pier

Canalside

Oil Sites Road

Dock Yard Road

Canalside
Industrial
Estate

Manchester Ship Canal

Junction 9

M53

Oil Sites Road

Bridges Road

Cromwell Road

York Rd

Victoria Rd

Arthur St

Wellington Rd

Cambridge Road

Girton Cl

Cirton Rd

Lancing Rd

Milton Rd

Marchwiel
Road

Lees Lane

South Road

New Bridge Road

Telford Road

Thornton Road

Repton Rd

Winchester Rd

Newnham Drive

Somerville Crescent

Harrow Road

Eton Rd

McGarva Way

Grange Road

Market
Hall

Wellington Road

Central Drive

Park Road

Coronation Rd

Stove Gdns

Green Lane

Newnham

Sutton Way

SUTTON WAY B5132

Whitby Road

Faraday Rd

Mallory Rd

Tennyson

Cavell Drive

Faraday Rd

Thornton Cl

Poplar Cl

Vale Rd

Old Hall
Surg

Dr Ellesmere
Port Clinic

Old Hall Road

Thamesdale

A5032

Civic Way

Epic
Leisure
Centre

Wolverham

Whitby

G
Arthur Av

Tynesdale

Stanney Lane

STANNEY LANE

H
1 Coronation Rd
2 Mcgarva Wy
3 Stanlaw Rd
4 Tarvin Cl

121

Oval

Wolver

J

Marlborough Rd

Kilnbourne Rd

Rugby Rd

Hartech Way

K
1 Kingsley Rd
2 Mornington Av
3 Newton Rd
4 Picton Av
5 Wellington Cl

Rochester

L
1 Church St
2 Eleanor St
3 Errington Av
4 Fleming St
5 John Nicholas Crs
6 Westminster Gv
7 Worcester Wk

Ellesmere
Port
Stadium

Deans Road

Mill Lane
Industrial
Estate

Shropshire
Road

M
1 Blakemere Ct
2 Upper Mersey St
3 Whitemere Ct

Our Ladys RC
Infant School

Capenhurst Lane

High
School

Our Ladys RC
Infant School

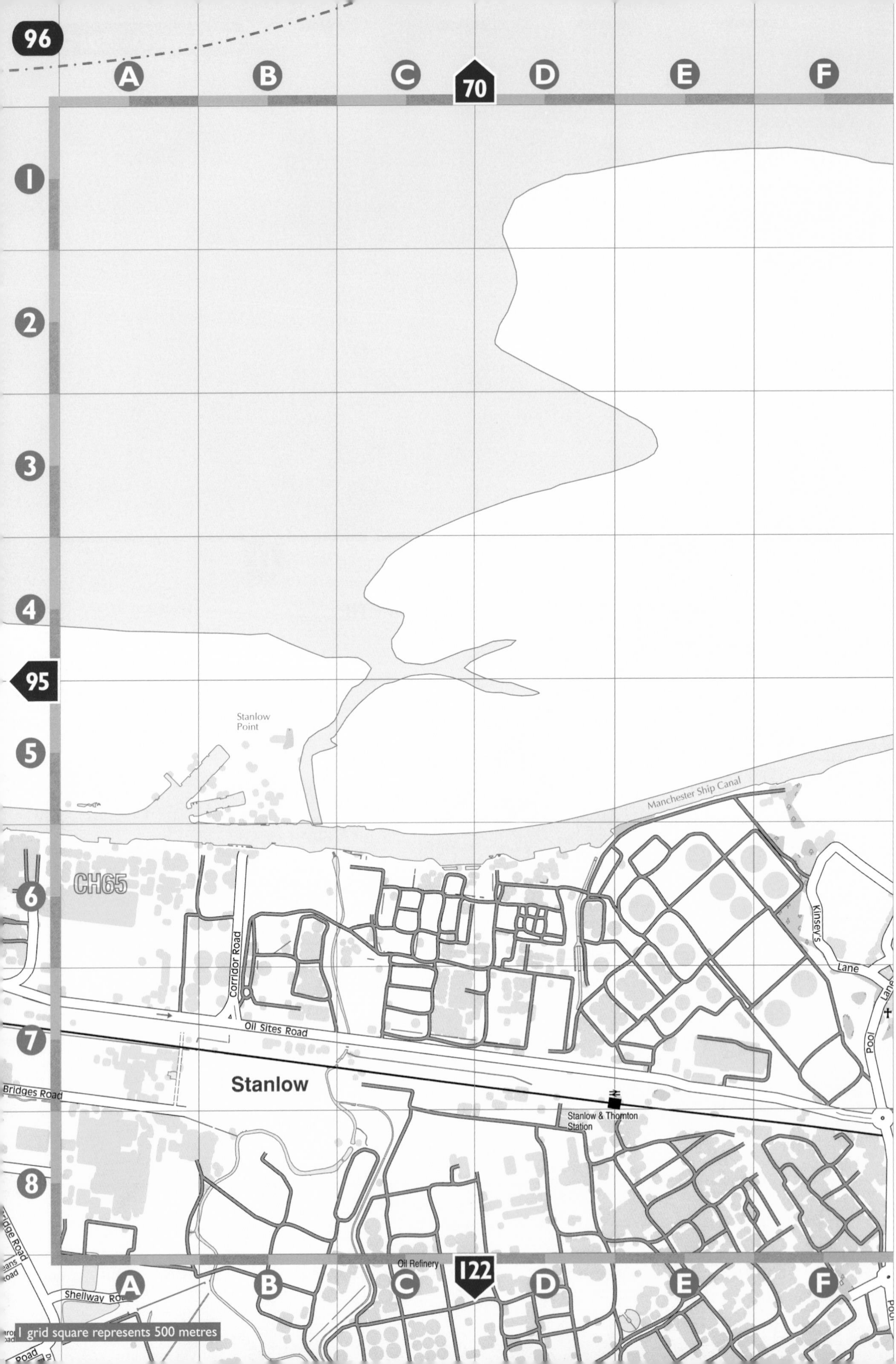

A B C **70** D E F

I

2

3

4

5

Stanlow
Point

Manchester Ship Canal

CH65

6

Corridor Road

Kinsey's

Lane

Oil Sites Road

Pool Lane

7

Stanlow

Bridges Road

Stanlow & Thornton
Station

8

Shellway Road

A B C **122** D E F

Oil Refinery

G   H   J   **71**   K   L   M

1
2
3
4
98
5
6
7
8

Ince
Banks

Manchester Ship Canal

Holme
Farm

Ince Marshes

Ince

Marsh Lane

Lordship Lane

Rake Lane

Hornsmill Brook

Station Road

Marsh Lane

Perimeter Road

Hoolpool Lane

Elton Lane

Ince Orchards

Ince & Elton Stn

Orchard Park Lane

Hapsford Lane

PO

Mt Pleasant

Highfield

Ince Lane

Coppice Green

Dove Cl

Redwood Dr

Greenfield

Elton

Elton County
Primary School

The Park

Ryecr

Whitefields

Marsh Lane

Holm Drive

Firbank

Mulberry Cl

Ash Road

M56

Farmdale Dr
Ferndale
Way
Deansfield
Ferndale Av
Brackendale

Meadow view

Hallfield Dr
Lawnswood
Grove
Ivanley View
School

Parkland

Pinewood Cl

G   H   **123**   J   K   L   M

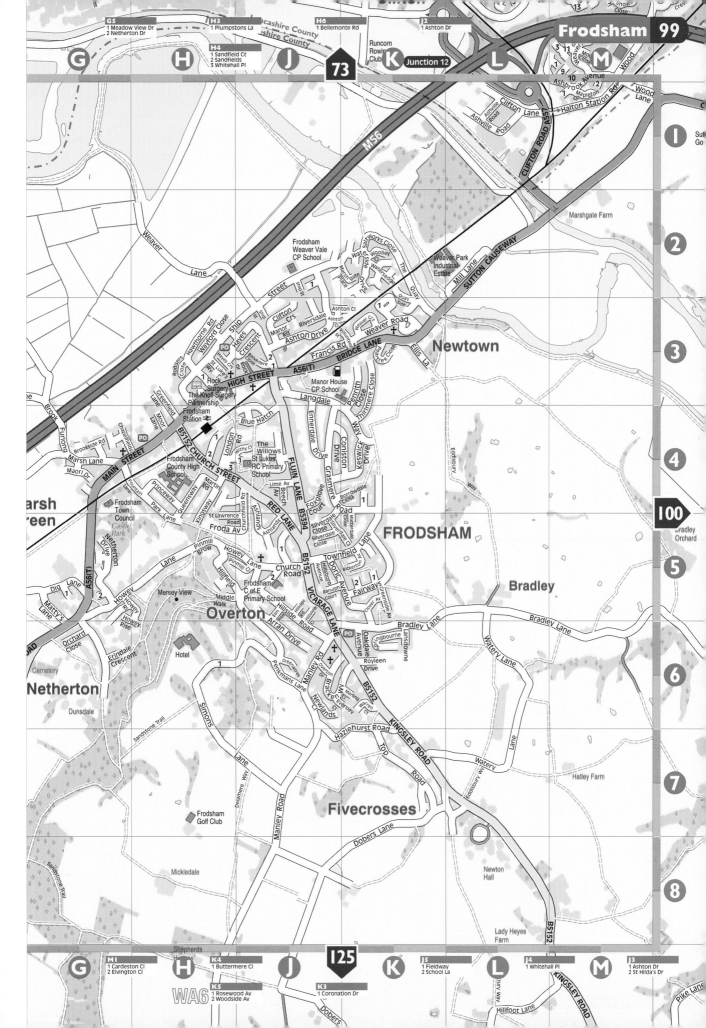

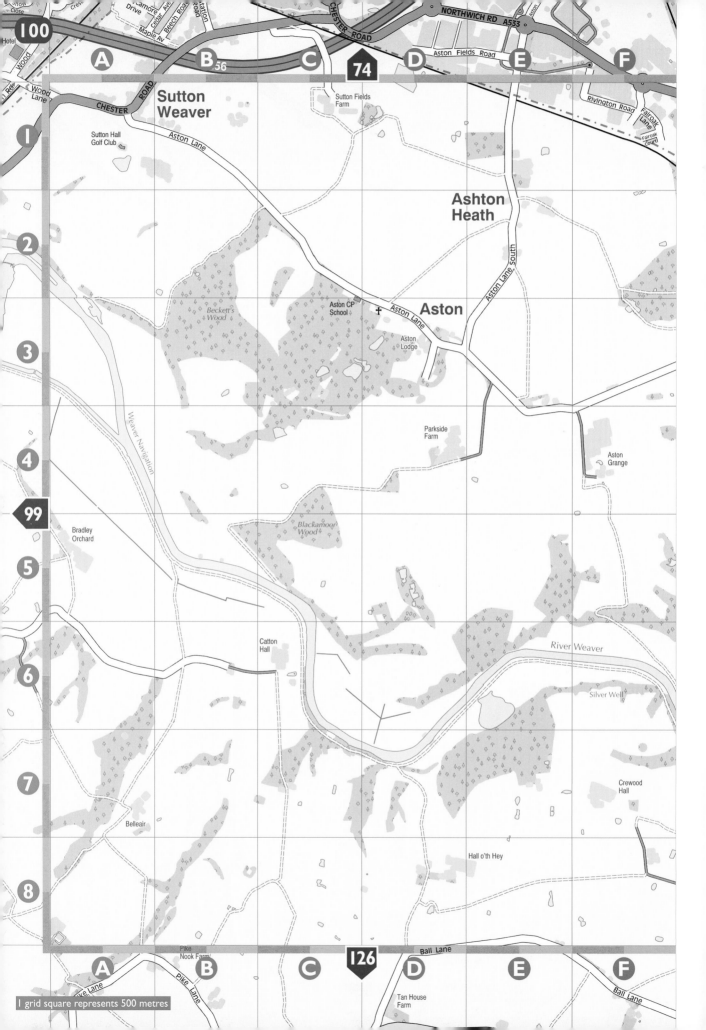

A B 56 C 74 D E F

NORTHWICH RD A533

CHESTER ROAD

Aston Fields Road

Rivington Road

Fairoak Lane

Fairoak Court

Wood Lane

CHESTER ROAD

Sutton
Weaver

Sutton Hall
Golf Club

Aston Lane

Sutton Fields
Farm

Ashton
Heath

1

2

Beckett's
Wood

Aston CP
School

Aston Lane

Aston

Aston Lane South

Weaver Navigation

Aston
Lodge

3

4

Parkside
Farm

Aston
Grange

Bradley
Orchard

Blackamoor
Wood

5

Catton
Hall

River Weaver

Silver Well

6

7

Belleair

Crewood
Hall

Hall o'th Hey

8

Pike
Nook Farm

Pike Lane

Ball Lane

126

Tan House
Farm

Ball Lane

A B C D E F

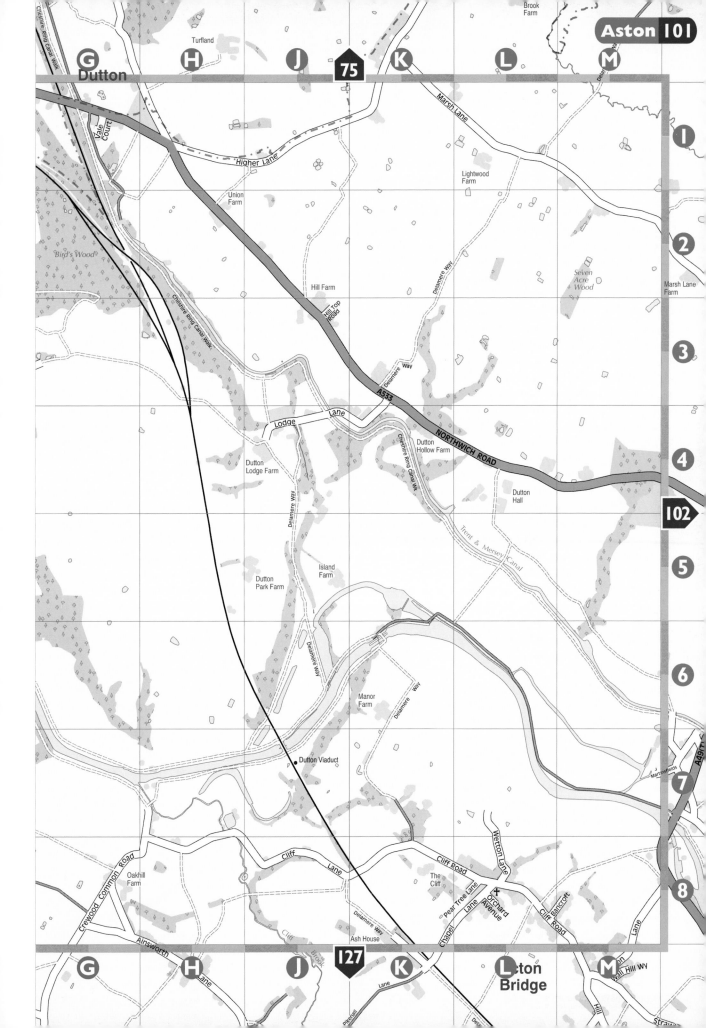

G **Dutton**

H

J **75**

K

L

M

1

2

3

4

102

5

6

7

8

Turfland

Brook Farm

Marsh Lane

Higher Lane

Vale Court

Union Farm

Lightwood Farm

Bird's Wood

Hill Farm

Seven Acre Wood

Marsh Lane Farm

Cheshire Ring Canal Walk

Hill Top Road

Delamere Way

Delamere Way

A533

Lodge Lane

NORTHWICH ROAD

Dutton Hollow Farm

Dutton Lodge Farm

Cheshire Ring Canal Wk.

Dutton Hall

Trent & Mersey Canal

Delamere Way

Island Farm

Dutton Park Farm

Delamere Way

Manor Farm

Delamere Way

Dutton Viaduct

Martinsfields

A49(T)

Oakhill Farm

Crewood Common Road

Cliff Lane

Cliff Road

Wetton Lane

The Cliff

Bancroft

Cliff Road

Pear Tree Lane

Chapel Lane

Orchard Avenue

Ainsworth

Cliff

Ash House

Delamere Way

Brook

G

H Lane

J

K **127**

L **eton Bridge**

M Wall Hill Wy

Hill

Strawb

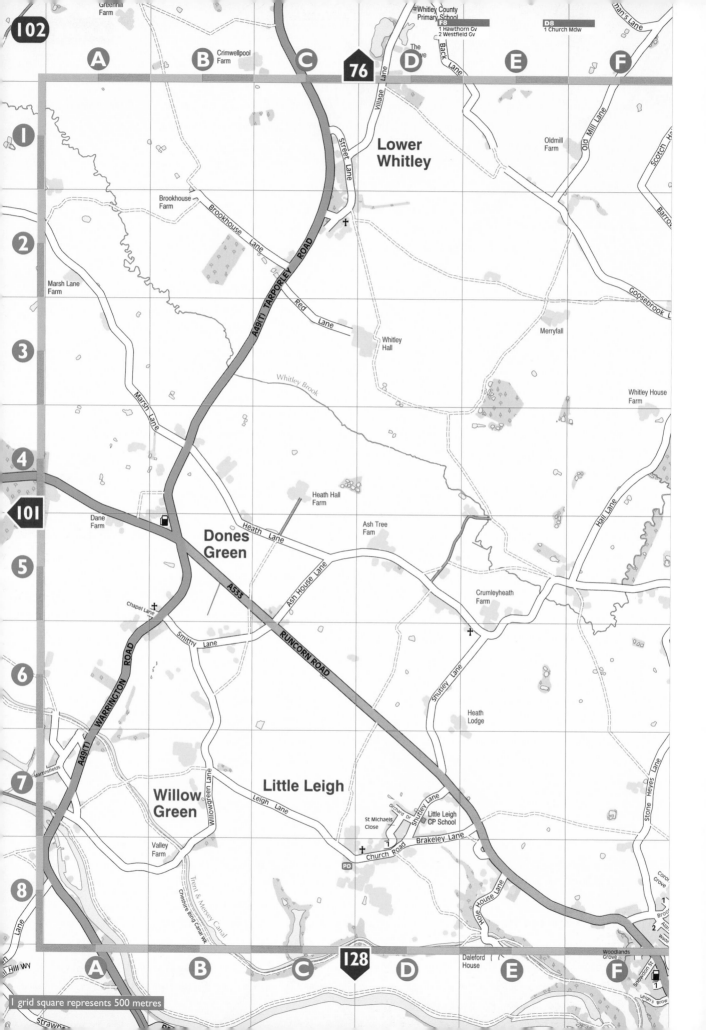

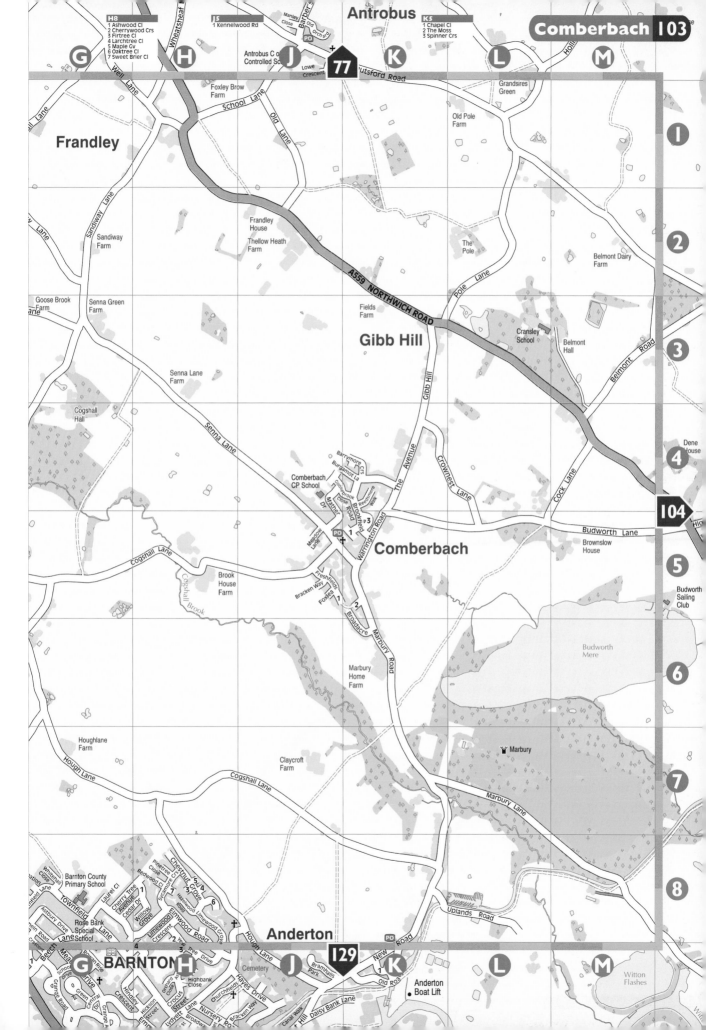

H8
1 Ashwood Cl
2 Cherrywood Crs
3 Firtree Cl
4 Larchtree Cl
5 Maple Gv
6 Oaktree Cl
7 Sweet Brier Cl

J5
1 Kennelwood Rd

K5
1 Chapel Cl
2 The Moss
3 Spinner Crs

Antrobus

G H J K L M

I

Frandley

Well Lane
Wheatsheaf
School Lane
Old Lane
Manley Close
Barber's
PO
Antrobus C of
Controlled Sc
Lowe Crescent
77
Knutsford Road
Grandsires Green
Hollins

2

Sandiway Lane
Sandiway Farm
Foxley Brow Farm
Frandley House
Thellow Heath Farm
A559 NORTHWICH ROAD
Old Pole Farm
The Pole
Belmont Dairy Farm

3

Goose Brook Farm
Senna Green Farm
Fields Farm
Gibb Hill
Pole Lane
Cransley School
Belmont Hall
Belmont Road

4

Senna Lane Farm
Cogshall Hall
Senna Lane
Gibb Hill
The Avenue
Crownest Lane
Cock Lane
Dene House

I04

Comberbach CP School
Barrymore Crs
Burgamot La
Cogbrook Close
Brookfield
Ravensmere Walk
Mather Dr
Brook Road
Meadow Lane
PO
1
3
Comberbach
Warrington Road
Budworth Lane
Brownslow House

5

Cogshall Lane
Cogshall Brook
Brook House Farm
Bracken Way
Freshfields
Foxlea
1
2
Broadacre
Marbury Road
Budworth Sailing Club

6

Marbury Home Farm
Budworth Mere

7

Houghlane Farm
Hough Lane
Cogshall Lane
Claycroft Farm
Marbury
Marbury Lane

8

Barnton County Primary School
Townfield
Whitenall
Rose Bank Special School
Astbury Drive
Laurel Cl
Cherry Tree Avenue
Cedar Dr
Redwood Cl
Pinetree Cl
Willow Grove
Chestnut Grove
Sycamore Rd
Hazelwood Cl
Limewood Grove
Limewood Crescent
Elmwood Road
Yew Tree Drive
Hough Lane
Uplands Road

Anderton
PO
Anderton Boat Lift

G BARNTON H
129
J
Cemetery
Bramhalls Park
Churchfields
Highbank Close
Hayes Drive
K
New Road
Old Road
L
M
Witton Flashes

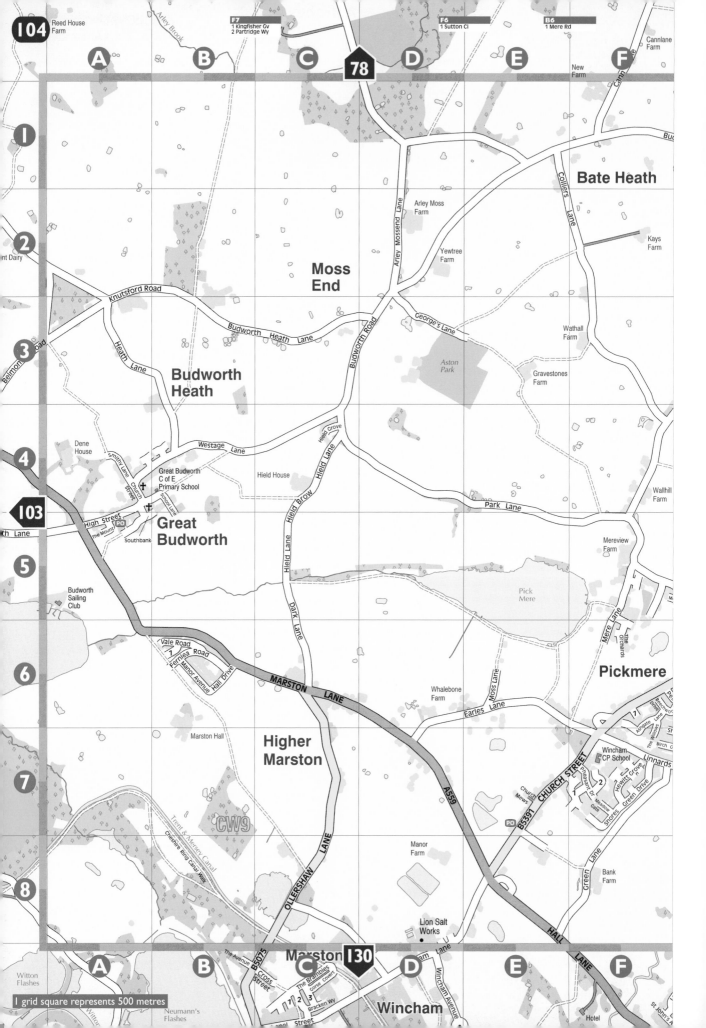

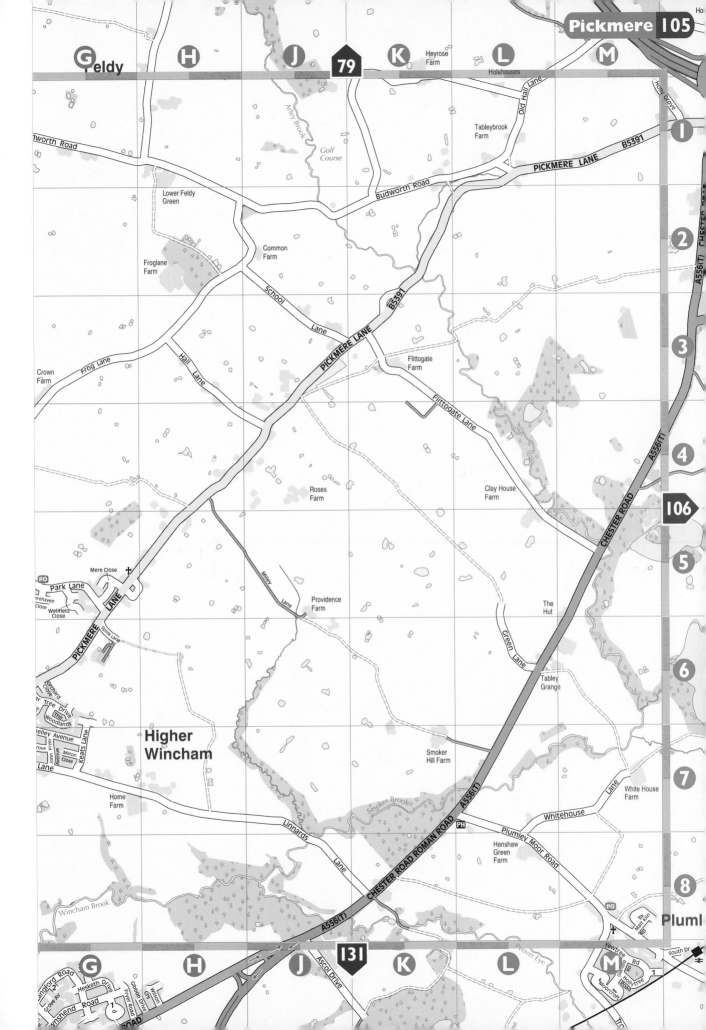

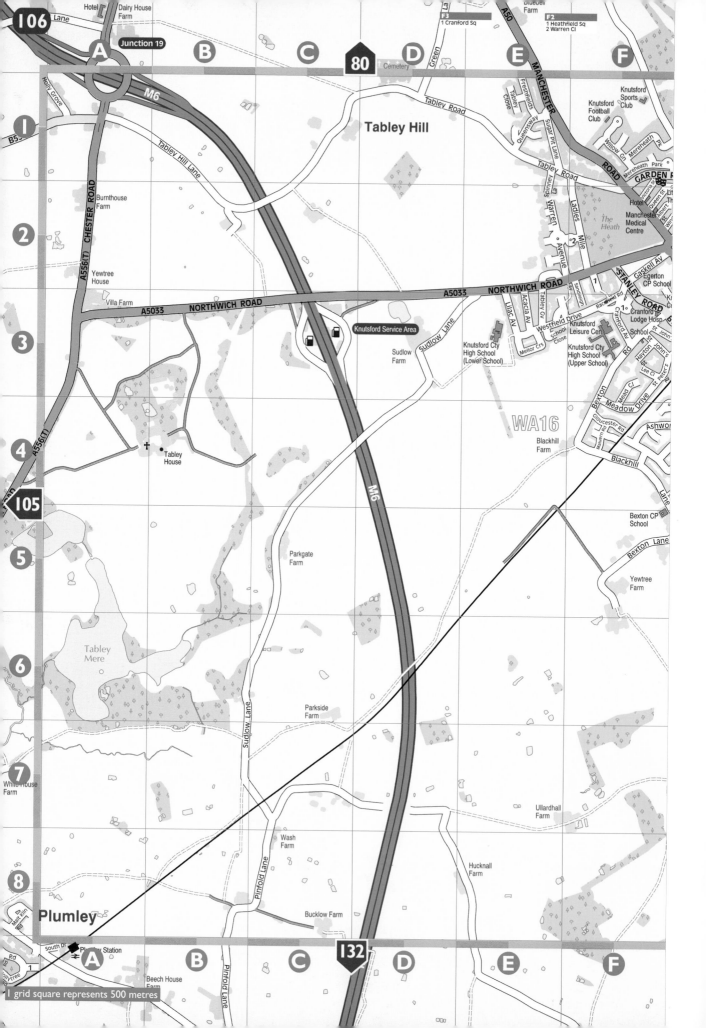

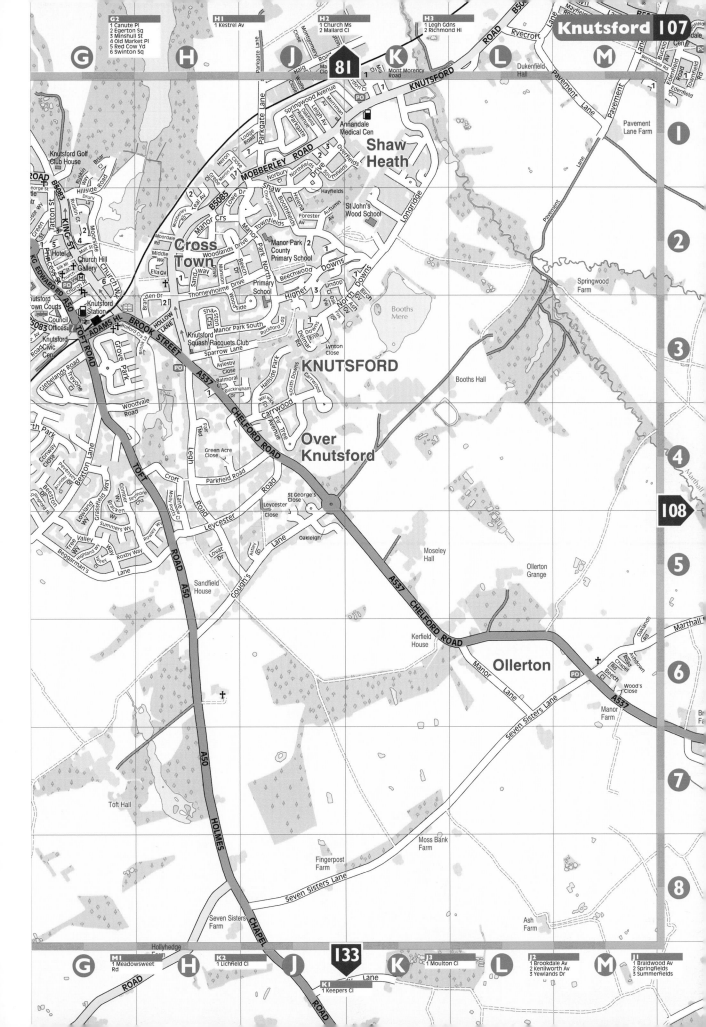

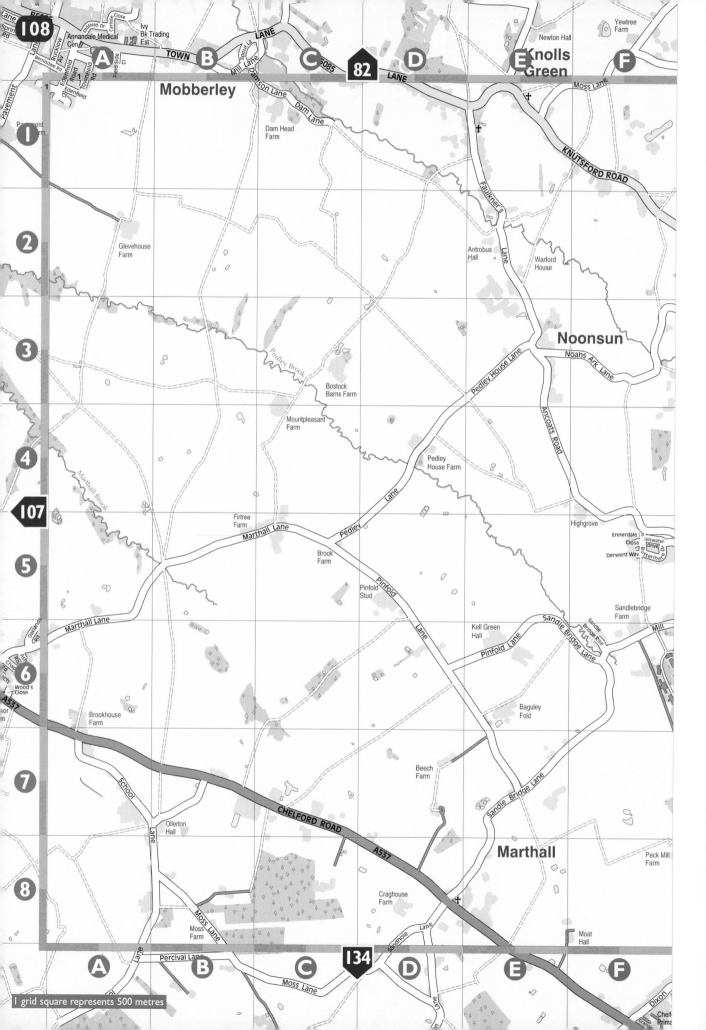

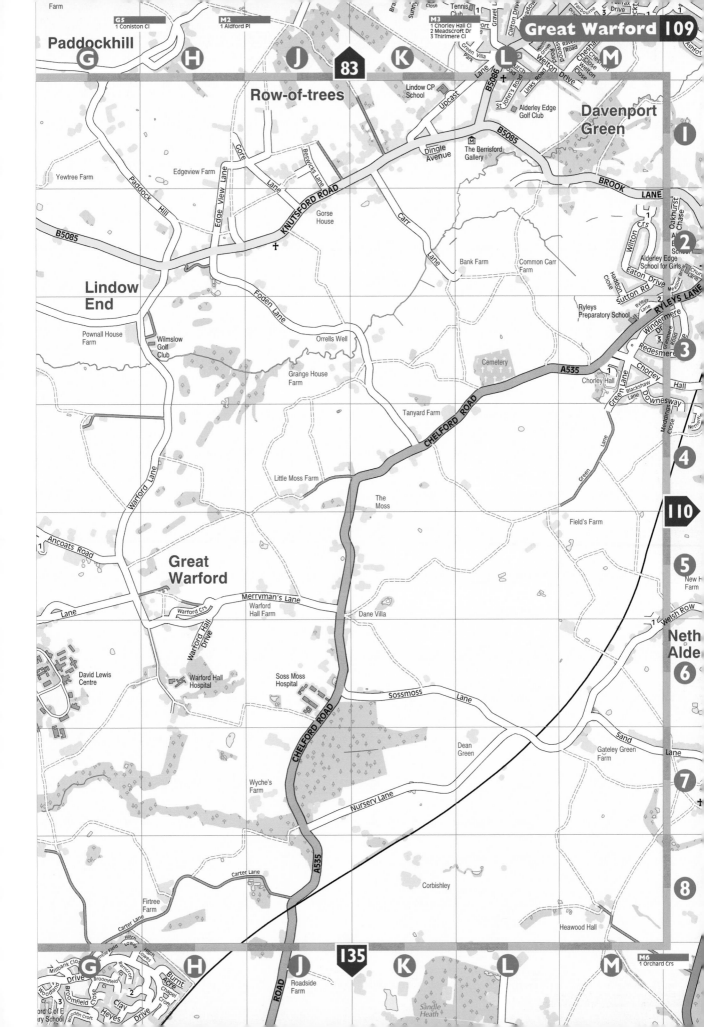

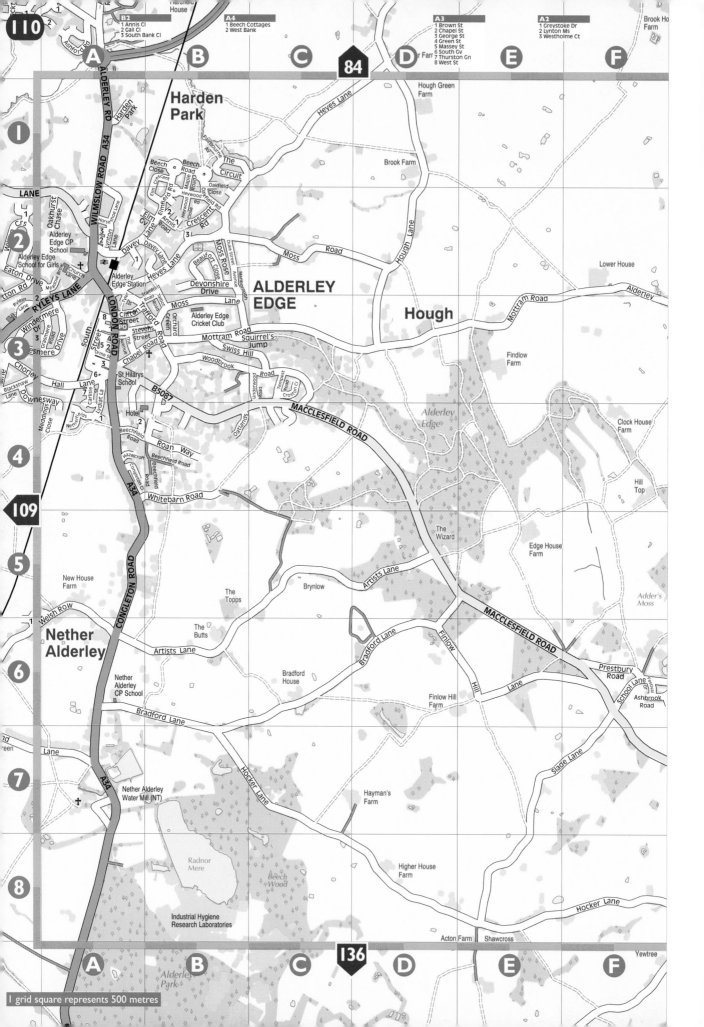

84
109
136

Index / Street references

Grid labels

A B C D E F

I 2 3 4 5 6 7 8

Place and road names

Harden Park

Brook Ho Farm

Hough Green Farm

Heyes Lane

Brook Farm

The Circuit

Beech Close

Beech Road

Oakfield Close

Heywood Field Rd

Crescent Rd

Moss Road

Hough Lane

Lower House

Alderley

Alderley Edge School for Girls

Alderley Edge CP School

Oakhurst Chase

Wilmslow Road A34

Harden Park

Elm Gv

Annis Road

Elm Gv

Moss Rose Avenue

Marlborough Avenue

Mottram Road

ALDERLEY EDGE

Hough

Eaton Drive

Church Lane

Meadow Bank

Ryleys Lane

Windermere Dr

Grasmere Road

Ullesmere Drive

Davey Lane

Davey Lane

Heyes Lane

Beaufort Close

Devonshire Drive

Lane

Stamford

Alderley Edge Cricket Club

Squirrel's Jump

Findlow Farm

Chorley Hall Lane

Blackshaw Lane

Downesway

Meddings Close

London Road

South Street

Trafford Road

Clifton Street PO

Stevens Street

Chapel Road

Orchard Green

Moss

Orchard Green

Mottram Road

Swiss Hill

Woodbrook

Underwood Road

Tennyson Road

Crofton Cl

Alderley Edge

St Hilarys School

Carlisle

Lydiat La

B5087

Hotel

Beechfield Road

Roan Way

Beechfield Road

Hazelcroft

Congleton Road

Whitebarn Road

Clock House Farm

Hill Top

A34

New House Farm

The Wizard

Edge House Farm

Adder's Moss

Welsh Row

Nether Alderley

Congleton Road

Artists Lane

The Topps

Brynlow

Artists Lane

Macclesfield Road

The Butts

Bradford Lane

Finlow Lane

Prestbury Road

School Lane

Ashbrook Road

Nether Alderley CP School

Bradford House

Bradford Lane

Finlow Hill Farm

Hill

Lane

Slade Lane

Lane

Hocker Lane

Nether Alderley Water Mill (NT)

Hayman's Farm

Radnor Mere

Beech Wood

Higher House Farm

Hocker Lane

Industrial Hygiene Research Laboratories

Acton Farm

Shawcross

Yewtree

Alderley Park

A34

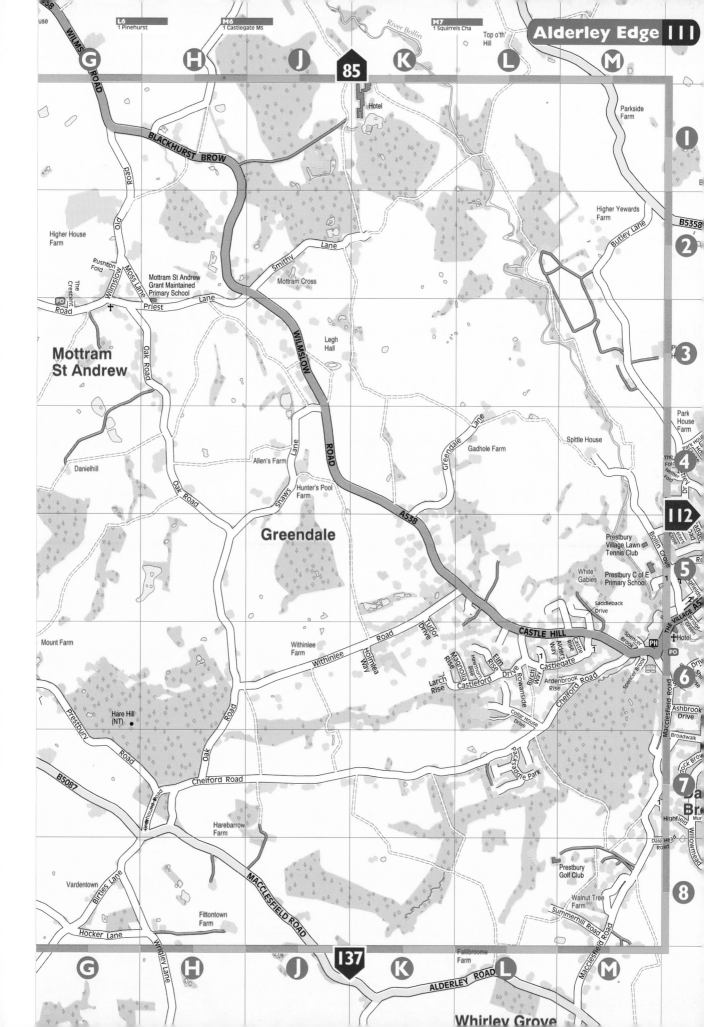

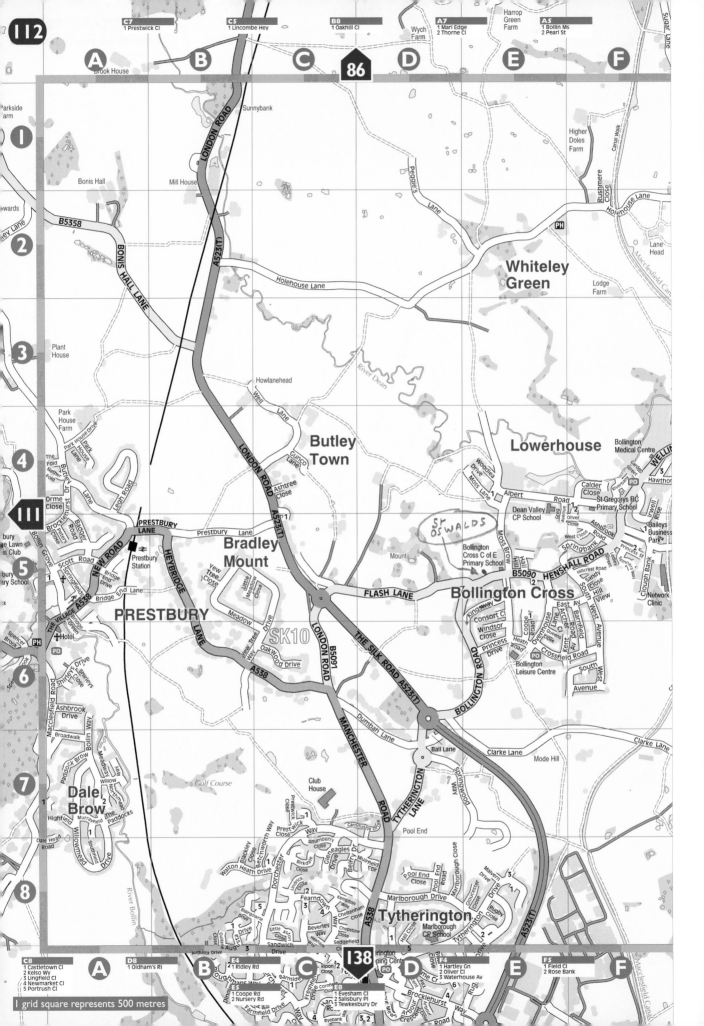

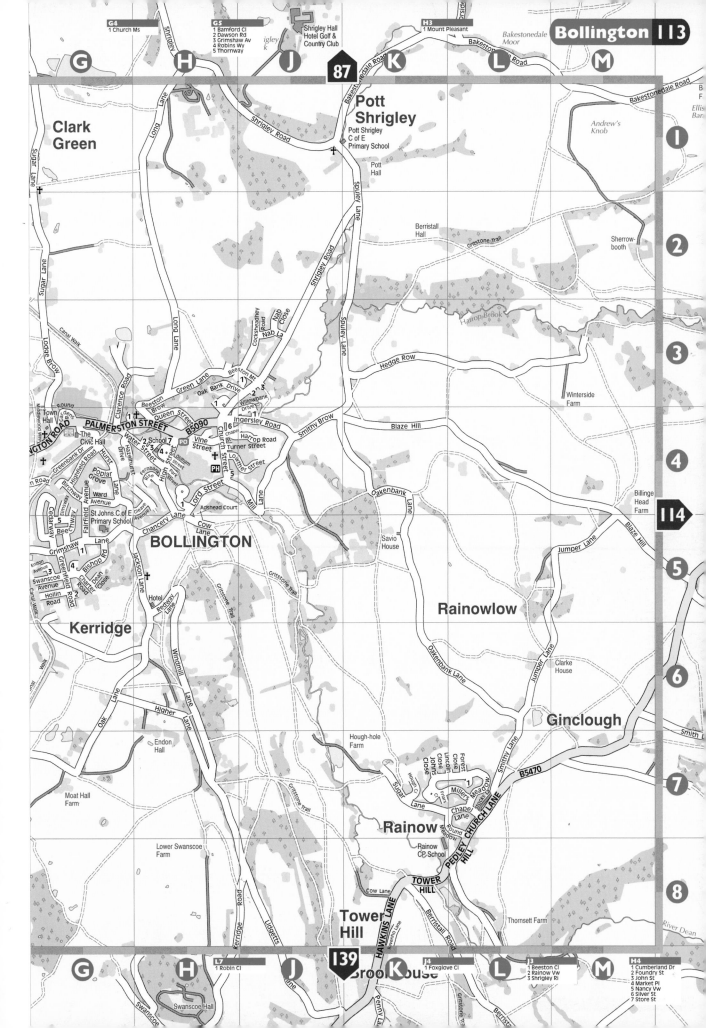

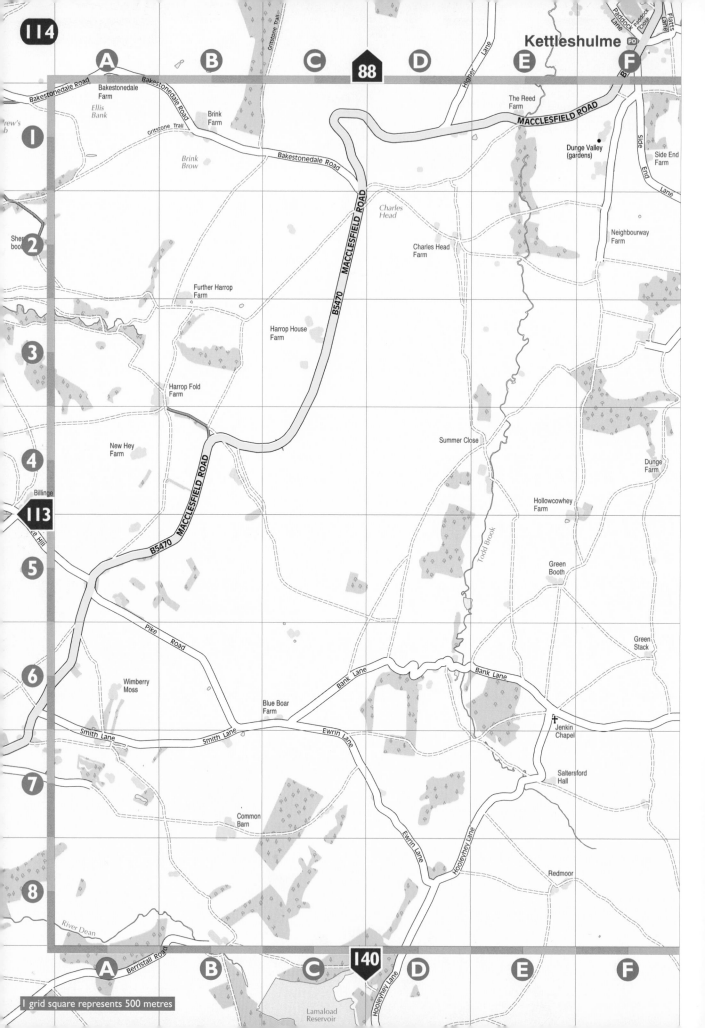

Taxal

Clayton Fold Farm

Shallcross Road

Shallcross Hall Farm

Old Hall Av

Shallcross Avenue

G **H** **J** **89** **K** **L** **M** or Lane Farm

Wright's Farm

Taxal Edge

Sitch House

River Goyt

Folds La

Elnor Lane

Old Road

I

2

Fivelane-ends

Taxal Moor Road

Crowhill

Whiteleas Road

Overton Hall Farm

Fernilee

A5004

Norman Wood

verhill

3

Windgather Rocks

Oldfield

4

Goyt Forest

Fernilee Reservoir

Long Hill

5

Hoo Moor

6

The Street

Goyt Valley

Embridge Causeway

7

The Street

8

Bunsal Cob

G **H** **J** **141** **K** **L** **M**

Derbyshire Co
Cheshire Co

90

River Dee

Cheshire County
Flintshire

B5
1 Lloyd St
2 Lower Mumforth St
3 Lower Sydney St
4 Salusbury St
5 Thomas St

A7
1 Mount Pleasant Av

A6
1 Chapel Street (Lon Y Capel)
2 Lon Odyn (Kiln Close)
3 St Catherine's Cl
4 Swinchiard La

A5
1 Chester Street (Heol Caer)
2 Feathers St
3 Sydney Wk
4 Trelawny Sq

Flint Marsh

Ashmount Industrial Centre

Ashmount Industrial Centre

HOLLYWELL ROAD

Rugby Union Football Club

Flintshire Retail Park

Flint Leisure Centre

Happy Feet Health Centre

Town Hall & Mayors Parlour

Flint Stn

Corporation St

Evans St
Castle St
Castle Dyke

New Russell St

Rugby Union Football Club

Flint Football Club

Marsh Lane

FLINT

Flint Community Hospital

HEOL-YR-EGLWYS

CHURCH ST

Flintshire County Council

Eyton Place Practice

Swinchiard Walk

Halkyn

Prince Drive

Gwynedd Drive

Duke St

Park Avenue

Borough Gv

CHESTER STREET

Henry Taylor St

County Primary School

Cornist Rd

Coed y Felin

Maes Afon

H6

Cemetery

Rectory Cl

Gwynedd CP Junior School

Flint Child Health Clinic

Trelawny Av

Maes-y-Dre Av

Woodfield Avenue

Queens Avenue

Kings Av

Maes Gwyn

Avenue

LC

Bryn Road

Coed Onn

Second Av

PO

First Av

Charles Dr

Florda Glynow

Florda Llewelyn

St Marys School

Cae Hir

Derw

Maes Alaw

Albert Av

Sirlol

Julius Close

Englefield Drive

Caesar Av

Deva Cl

Mill Croft

Artis Crt

Croes Atti La

PO

Mount Pleasant

A5119 ROAD

Third Avenue

Fourth Av

Sixth Avenue

Princes Drive

Edward Dr

Edwin Dr

Glan

Davids Cl

County Secondary School

Fifth Avenue

Tudor Av

Maes Teg

Min Awel

Marian

Bryn Gwyn

Coed Onn Road

St Richard Gwyn High School

Leadbrook

CHESTER ROAD A548

Paper Lane

Oakenholt

B6
1 Princes St
2 Queen St

B8
1 Bodiondeb
2 Bryn Derw
3 Bryn Heilig
4 Heol-y-bryn
5 Rhoswen
6 Swn-y-gwynt

1 grid square represents 500 metres

91

Denhall House
Farm

118

White
Sands

Kelsterton

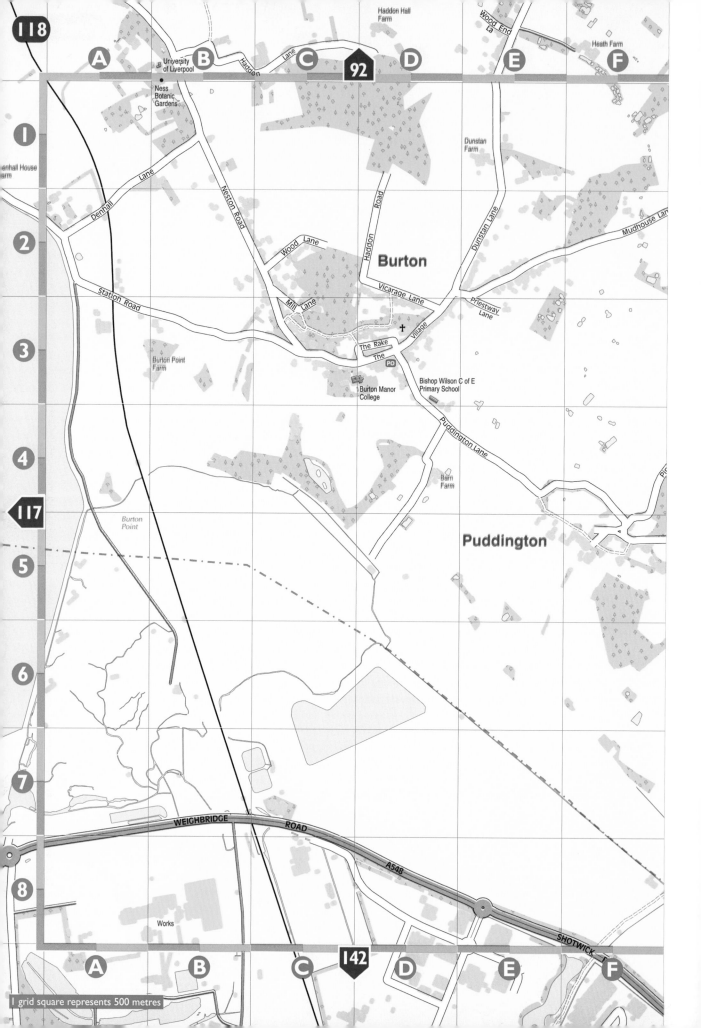

Ⓐ Ⓑ Ⓒ **92** Ⓓ Ⓔ Ⓕ

Haddon Hall Farm

Wood End La

Heath Farm

University of Liverpool

Haddon Lane

Ness Botanic Gardens

Ⓘ

enhall House arm

Dunstan Farm

Denhall Lane

Neston Road

Mudhouse Lan

Ⓒ **2**

Wood Lane

Haddon Road

Burton

Dunstan Lane

Station Road

Vicarage Lane

Priestway Lane

Mill Lane

Ⓒ **3**

Burton Point Farm

The Rake

The

PO

Village

✝

Bishop Wilson C of E Primary School

Burton Manor College

Puddington Lane

Barn Farm

Ⓒ **4**

Burton Point

Puddington

Ⓒ **5**

Ⓒ **6**

Ⓒ **7**

WEIGHBRIDGE ROAD

A548

Ⓒ **8**

Works

SHOTWICK

Ⓐ Ⓑ Ⓒ **142** Ⓓ Ⓔ Ⓕ

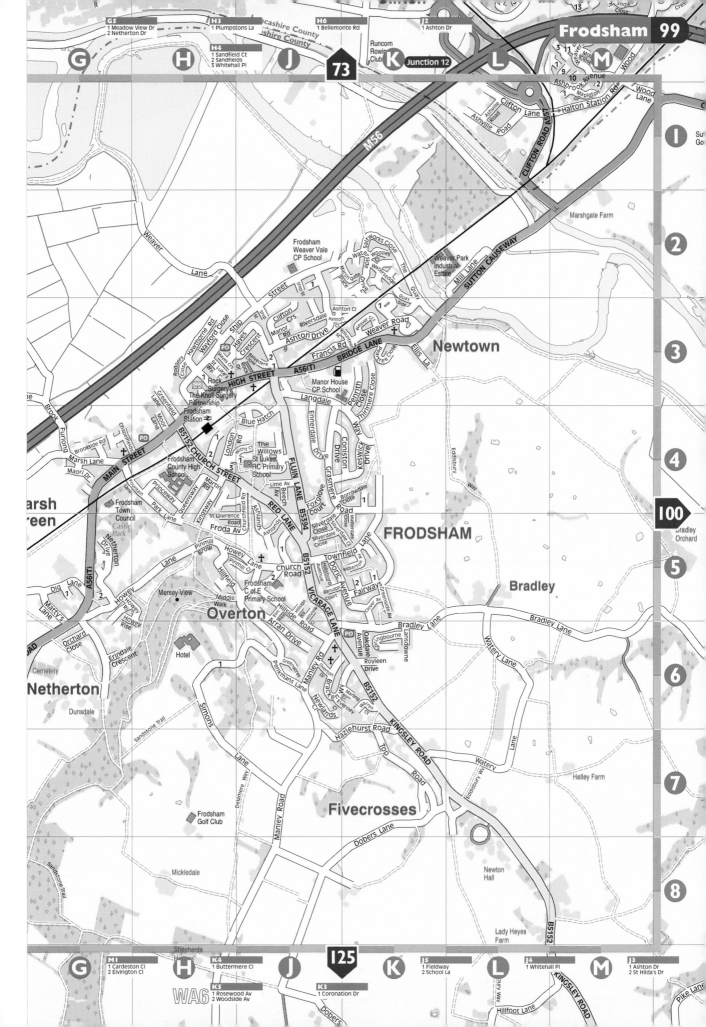

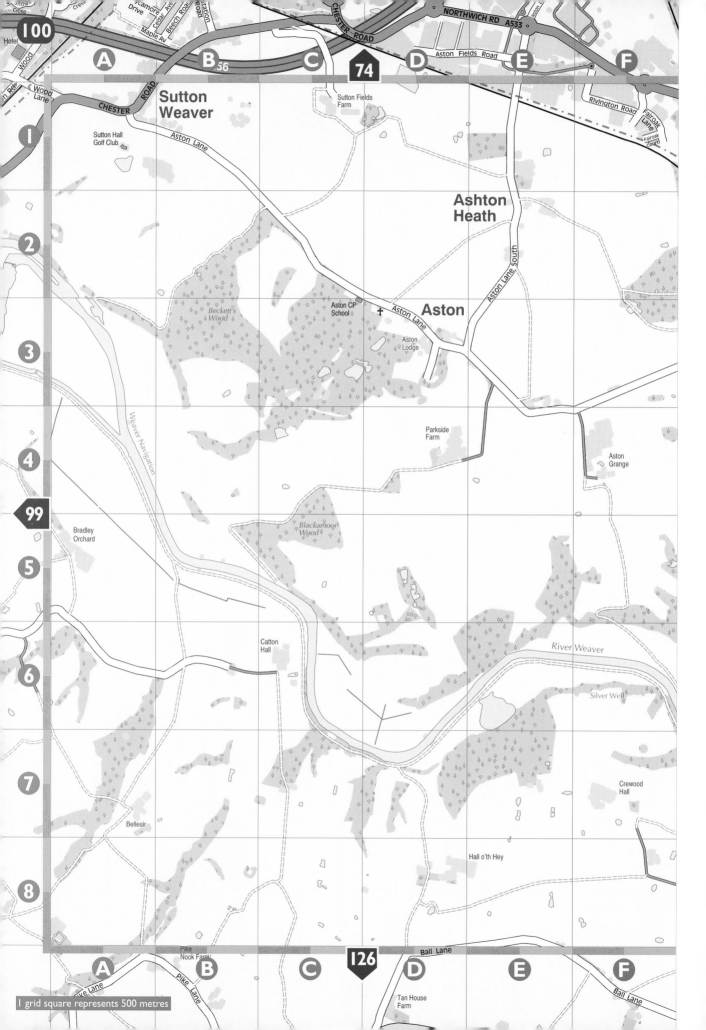

NORTHWICH RD A533

CHESTER ROAD

Aston Fields Road

A

B 56

C

D

E

F

Rivington Road

Fairoak Lane

Fairoak Court

CHESTER ROAD

Sutton Weaver

Sutton Fields Farm

1

Sutton Hall Golf Club

Aston Lane

Wood Lane

Wood Lane

Snow... Close

...more Ave

Cedar Ave

Beech Road

Maple Av

...tation Road

Ashton Heath

2

Beckett's Wood

Aston CP School

Aston

Aston Lane

Aston Lane South

3

Aston Lodge

Weaver Navigation

4

Parkside Farm

Aston Grange

Bradley Orchard

Blackamoor Wood

5

Catton Hall

River Weaver

6

Silver Well

7

Crewood Hall

Belleair

8

Hall o'th Hey

Pike Nook Farm

Pike Lane

...ve Lane

A

B

Ball Lane

C

D

E

F

Tan House Farm

Ball Lane

1 grid square represents 500 metres

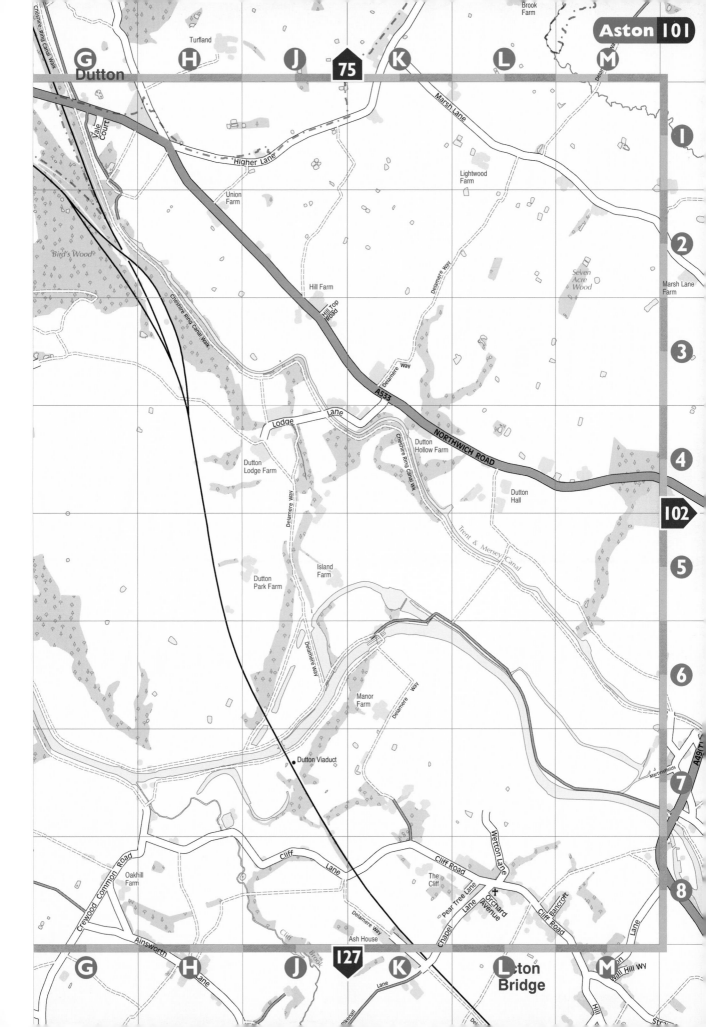

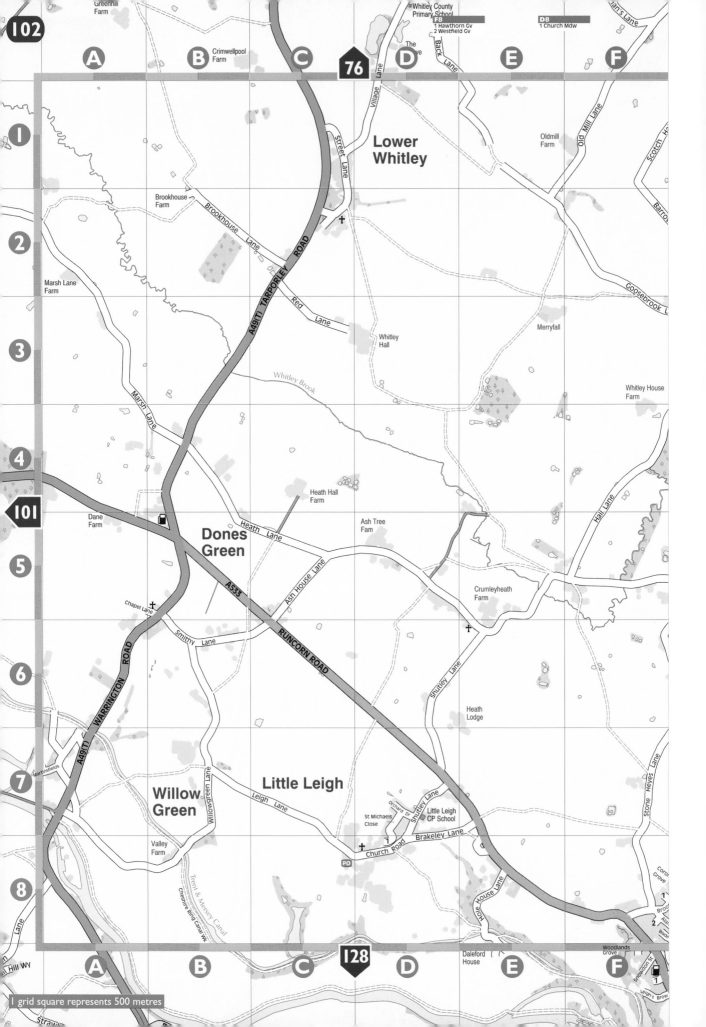

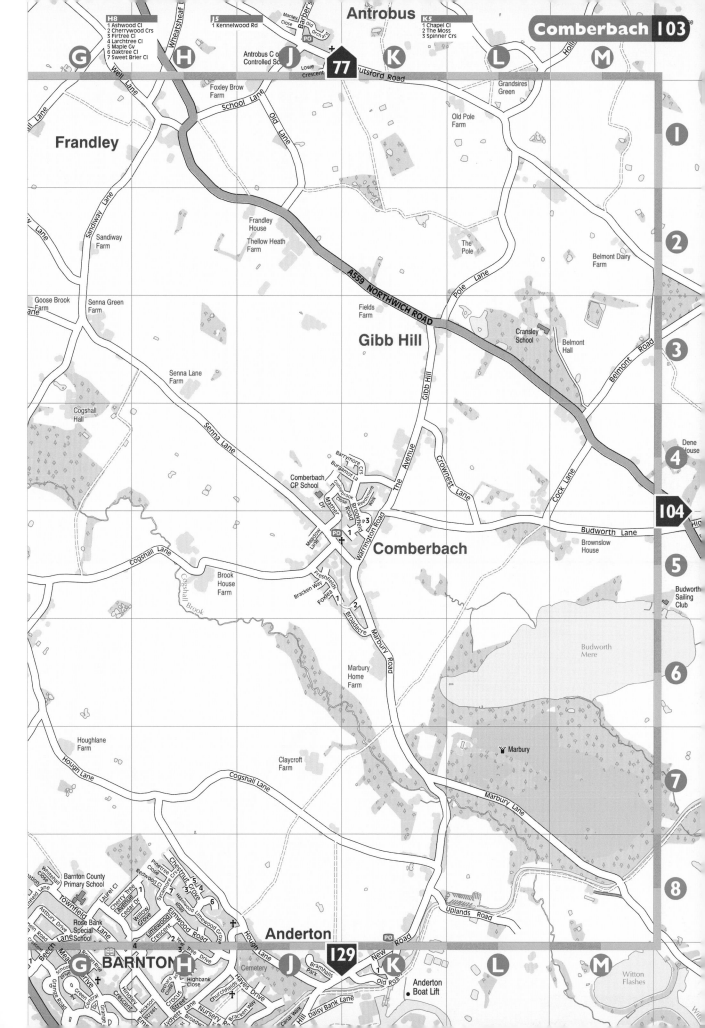

G   H   J   K   L   M

Antrobus

H8
1 Ashwood Cl
2 Cherrywood Crs
3 Firtree Cl
4 Larchtree Cl
5 Maple Gv
6 Oaktree Cl
7 Sweet Brier Cl

J5
1 Kennelwood Rd

K5
1 Chapel Cl
2 The Moss
3 Spinner Crs

Frandley

Well Lane
Wheatsheaf
School Lane
Old Lane
Manley Close
Lowe Crescent

77

Knutsford Road

Antrobus C of E
Controlled Sch

Foxley Brow Farm

Grandsires Green

Old Pole Farm

I

Sandiway Lane
Sandiway Farm

Frandley House
Thellow Heath Farm

The Pole

Belmont Dairy Farm

2

Goose Brook Farm
Senna Green Farm

A559 NORTHWICH ROAD

Fields Farm

Pole Lane

Belmont Road

3

Senna Lane Farm

Gibb Hill

Cransley School
Belmont Hall

Cogshall Hall

Senna Lane

Gibb Hill

The Avenue

Crownest Lane

Dene House

4

Barrymore Crs
Burgamot La
Comberbach CP School

Cock Lane

104

Mather Dr
Goldbrook Close
Brookfield
Revomere Walk

Warmington Road

Budworth Lane

Brownslow House

Meadow Lane
PO

3

Comberbach

5

Cogshall Lane
Cogshall Brook

Brook House Farm

Freshfield
Bracken Way
Foxlea
1

Broadacre

Marbury Road

Budworth Sailing Club

Budworth Mere

6

Houghlane Farm

Hough Lane

Cogshall Lane

Claycroft Farm

Marbury Home Farm

Marbury

7

Whitehill
Barnton County Primary School
Townfield

Cogshall Lane

Marbury Lane

8

Laurel Cl
Cherry Tree Avenue
Cedar Dr
Redwood Close
Pinetree Close
Chestnut Grove
Sycamore Close
Hazelwood Close
Limewood Grove

Willow Grove
Limewood Crescent
Elmwood Road
Yew Tree Drive

Rose Bank Special School

Uplands Road

Anderton Boat Lift

Beech Mead Drive
Hindley Crescent
Hickson Street
Lydyett Lane
Nursery Lane
Highbank Close
Churchfields
Hayes Drive
Hough Lane
Cemetery
Bramhalls Park
New Road

129

PO

Anderton

BARNTON

G   H   J   K   L   M

Witton Flashes

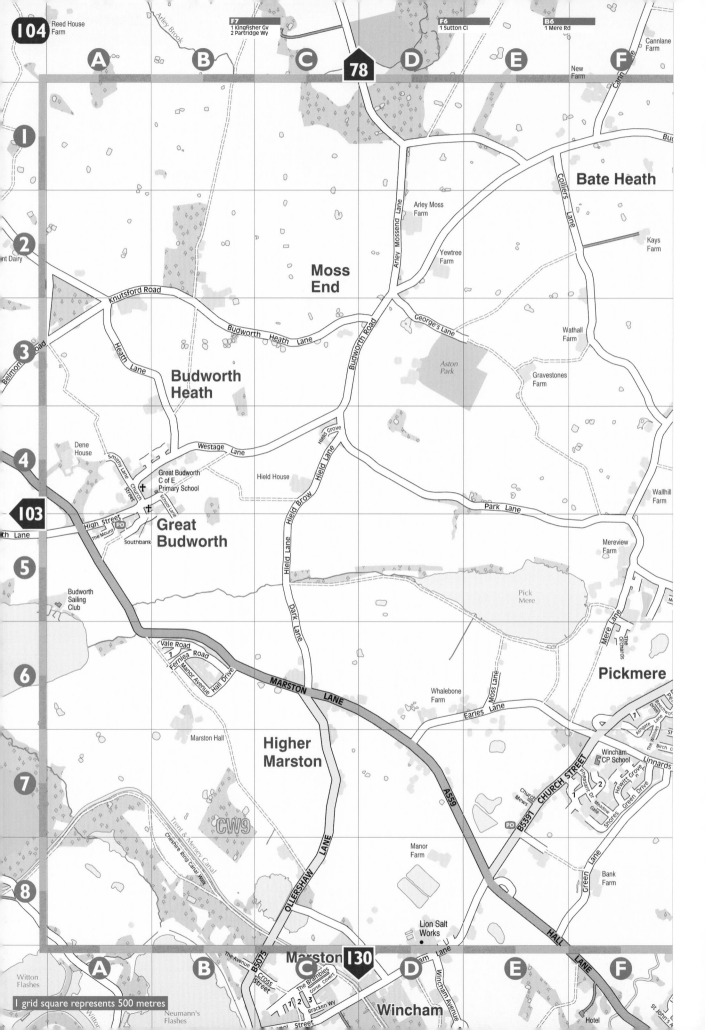

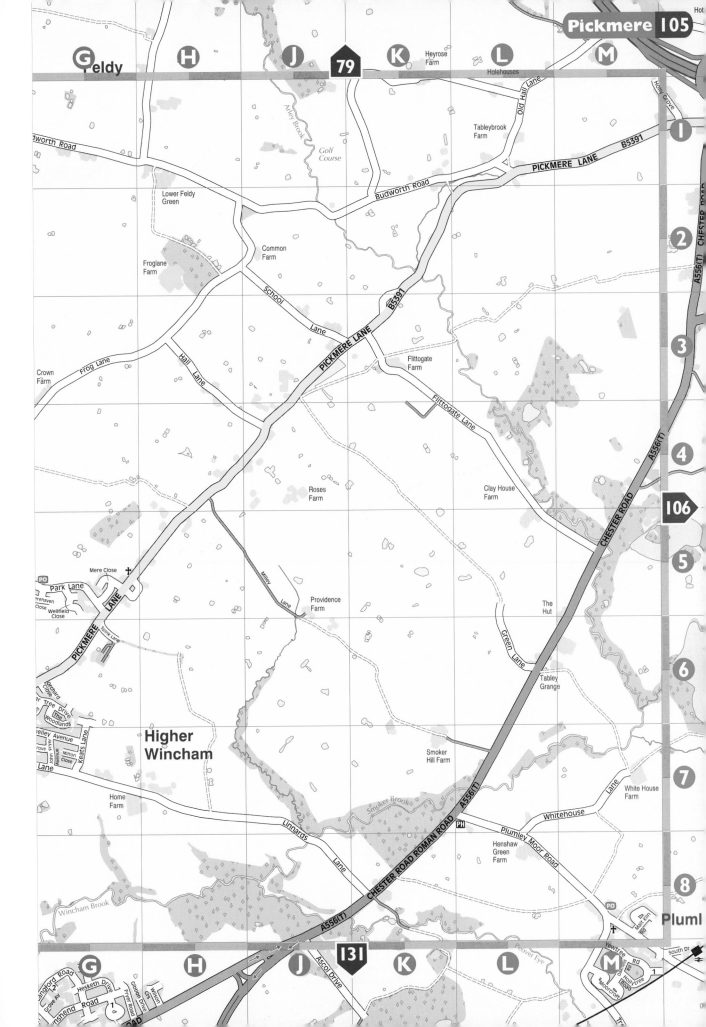

G Feldy
H
J
79
K
L
M

Higher Wincham

Heyrose Farm

Holehouses

Tableybrook Farm

Old Hall Lane

Holly Grove

PICKMERE LANE B5391

CHESTER ROAD

A556(T)

Budworth Road

udworth Road

Lower Feldy Green

Common Farm

Froglane Farm

School Lane

B5391

PICKMERE LANE

Flittogate Farm

Flittogate Lane

Crown Farm

Frog Lane

Hall Lane

Roses Farm

Clay House Farm

Green Lane

The Hut

Mere Close

PO

Park Lane

erenaven Close

Wellfield Close

PICKMERE LANE

Sink Lane

Milley Lane

Brook

Providence Farm

Orchard Close

Tree Drive

The Woodlands

helley Avenue

Grove

John Fryer Avenue

Milton Close

Keats Lane

Lane

Home Farm

Linnards Lane

Smoker Hill Farm

Smoker Brook

Tabley Grange

Whitehouse

Lane

White House Farm

Plumley Moor Road

PH

Henshaw Green Farm

A556(T)

CHESTER ROAD ROMAN ROAD

A556(T)

Wincham Brook

Peover Eye

PO

Pluml

South Dr

angford Road

Hesketh Drive

Grove Av

Gibbon Drive

Fryer Road

Wilson Cfs

ownshend Road

G
H
J
131
Ascol Drive
K
L
M

Malt Kiln

Yewtree

Garden Rd

MoorCroft

Holly Tree Road

1
2
3
4
5
6
7
8

Golf Course

Arley Brook

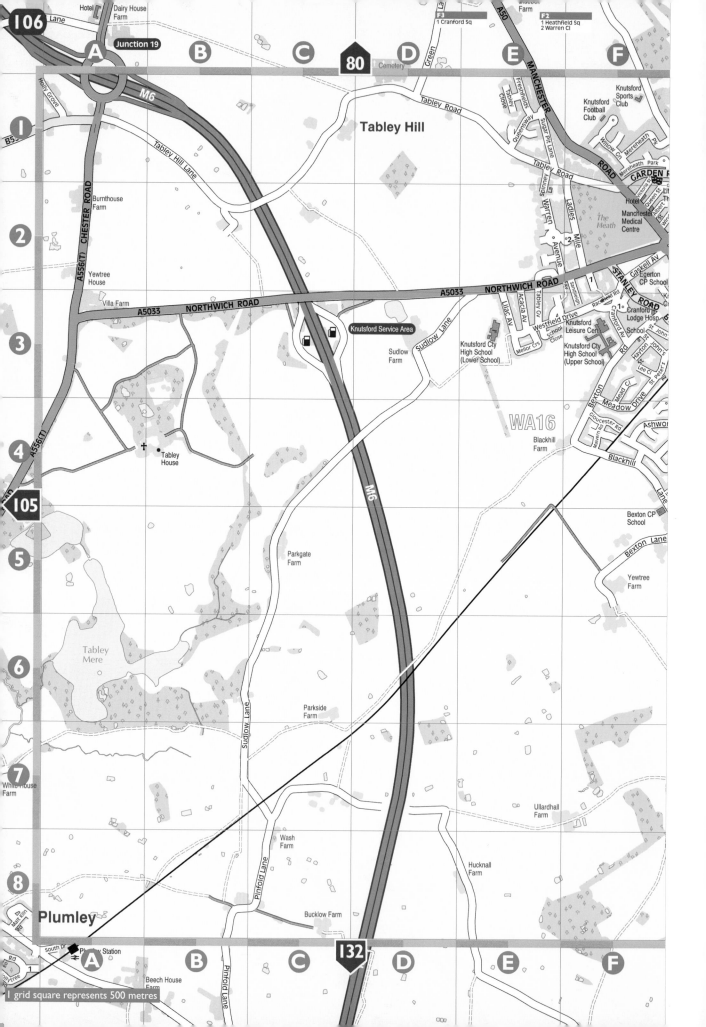

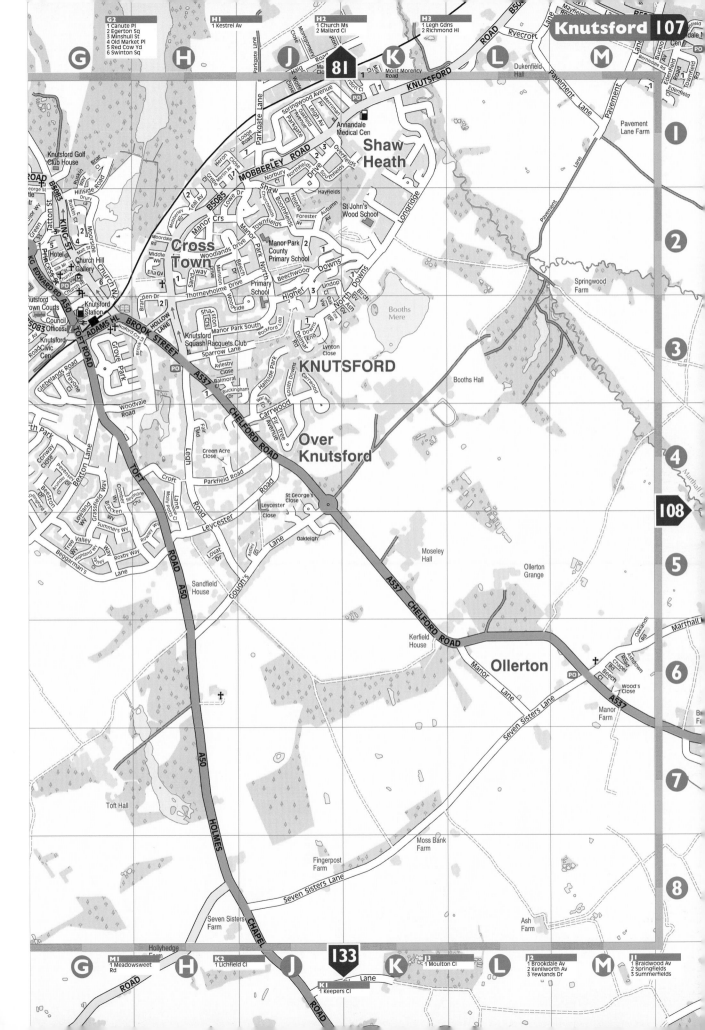

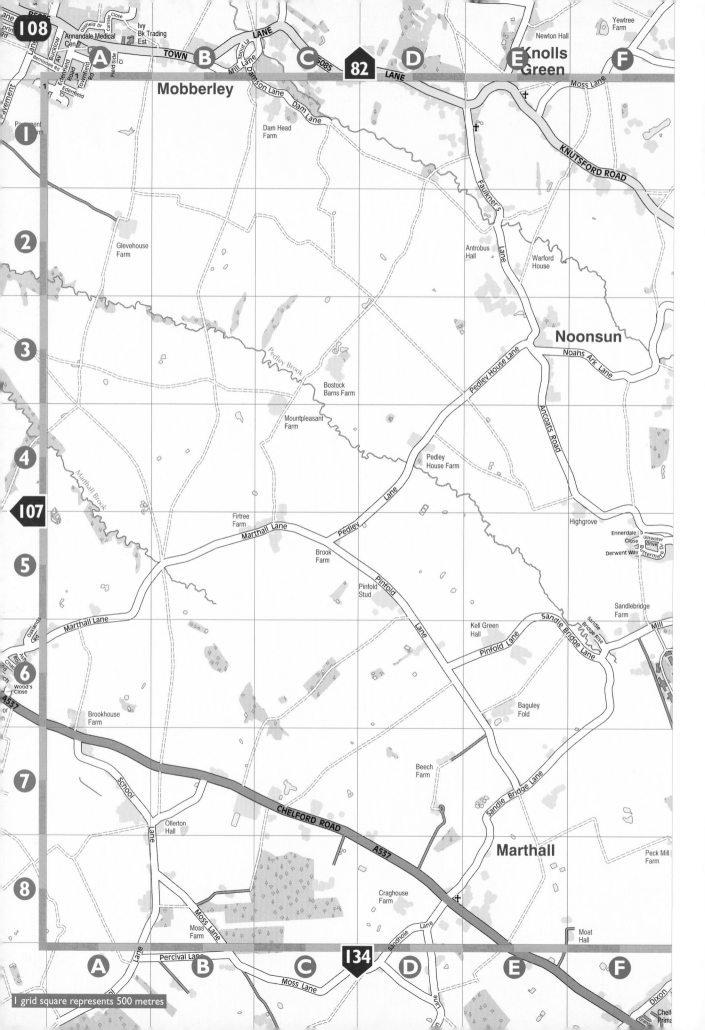

Mobberley

Annandale Medical Cen
Ivy Bk Trading Est
Oakfield Dr
Carlisle Close
Buckley
Edenfield Road
Edenfield
Bernisdale Rd
Field Side Cl
Townfield Rd
Pavement La
Lane

TOWN LANE
Mill Lane
Spout La
Damson Lane
Dam Lane
6085
LANE
Knolls Green
Newton Hall
Yewtree Farm
Moss Lane

A **B** **C** **D** **E** **F**

1
Pavement Farm

2
Glevehouse Farm
Dam Head Farm
Antrobus Hall
Warford House

3
Pedley Brook
Bostock Barns Farm
Noonsun
Noahs Ark Lane

4
Marthall Brook
Mountpleasant Farm
Pedley House Farm
Pedley House Lane
Ancoats Road

Firtree Farm
Marthall Lane
Pedley Lane
Highgrove
Ennerdale Close
Ullswater Drive
Derwent Way
Wastermere

5
Brook Farm
Pinfold Stud
Pinfold Lane
Sandlebridge Farm
Sandle Bridge Lane
Sandle Bridge Rise
Mill

Marthall Lane
Oaklands
Chat
ranch
Wood's Close

6
Kell Green Hall
Pinfold Lane
Baguley Fold

A537

7
Brookhouse Farm
School Lane
Ollerton Hall
Beech Farm
Sandle Bridge Lane

CHELFORD ROAD
A537
Marthall
Peck Mill Farm

8
Moss Lane
Moss Farm
Percival Lane
Craghouse Farm
Sandhole Lane
Moat Hall

A **B** **C** **D** **E** **F**

Moss Lane
Dixon
Chelf Prima

I grid square represents 500 metres

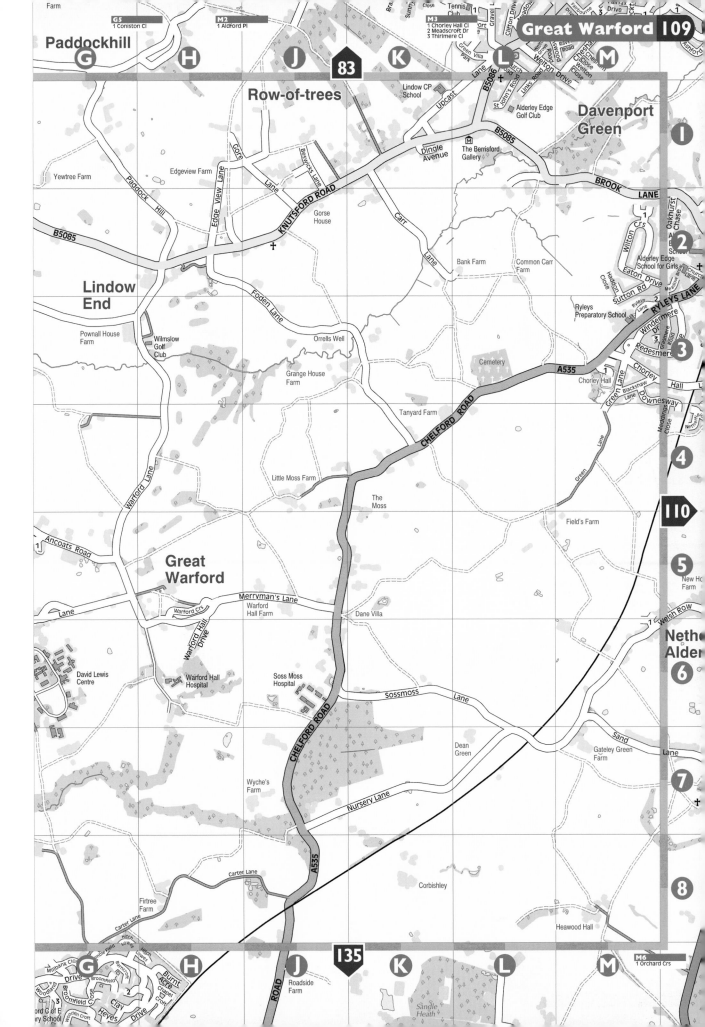

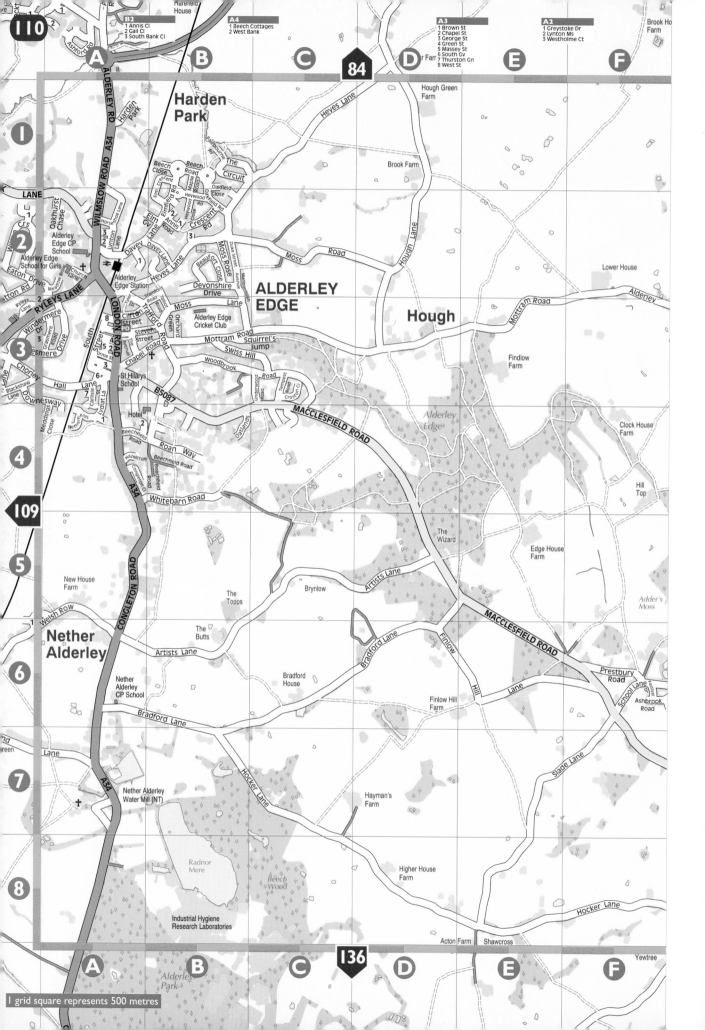

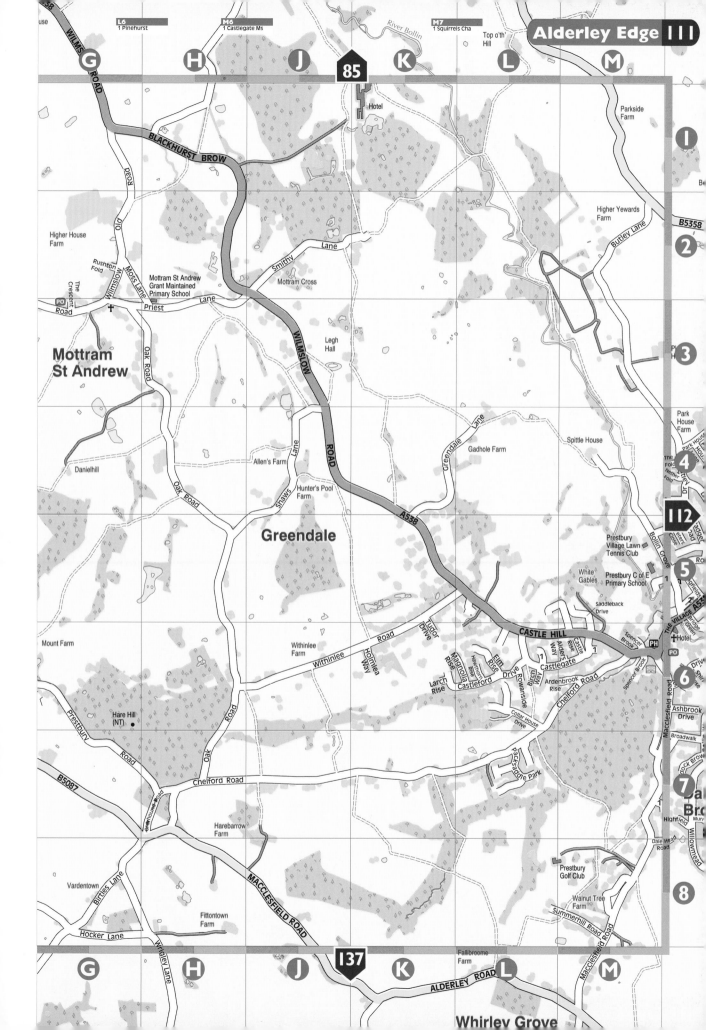

River Bollin

M7
1 Squirrels Cha

Top o'th'
Hill

Parkside
Farm

I

L6
1 Pinehurst

M6
1 Castlegate Ms

G **H** **J** **85** **K** **L** **M**

Hotel

B5358

2

Higher Yewards
Farm

WILMSLOW ROAD

BLACKHURST BROW

Butley Lane

Higher House
Farm

Old

Moss Lane

Rushton
Fold

Mottram St Andrew
Grant Maintained
Primary School

Smithy

Lane

Mottram Cross

Park
House
H

3

The
Crescent

Wilmslow

PO

Road

Priest

Lane

Legh
Hall

Park
House
Farm

Park House Road

**Mottram
St Andrew**

Oak Road

WILMSLOW

Greendale

Lane

Gadhole Farm

Spittle House

The
Fold

Nether
Fold

Jr.

4

Allen's Farm

ROAD

Danielhill

Shaws Lane

Hunter's Pool
Farm

A538

Prestbury
Village Lawn
Tennis Club

Bollin Grove

Waters Close

112

Greendale

White
Gables

Prestbury C of E
Primary School

THE VILLAGE A538

5

Mount Farm

Withinlee
Farm

Withinlee

Holmlea

Road

Way

Tudor

Drive

Road

Saddleback
Drive

CASTLE HILL

Magnolia
Rise

Hawthorn Rise

Elm
Rise

Drive

Rowanside

Castle
Rise

Alders
Way

Way

Castlegate

Spencer Brook

Spencer Brook

PH

Hotel

6

Drive

Prestbury

Road

Oak

Road

B5087

Hare Hill
(NT)

Larch
Rise

Castleford

Ardenbrook
Rise

Chelford
Road

Macclesfield road

PO

Ashbrook
Drive

Packsaddle Park

Broadwalk

Chelford Road

Collar House
Drive

7

Da
Bro

Highfield

Mur

Willowmead

Harebarrow
Farm

Dale Head
Road

8

Prestbury
Golf Club

Vardentown

Birties Lane

Greenhouse Road

Wrigley Lane

MACCLESFIELD ROAD

Walnut Tree
Farm

Summerhill Road

Macclesfield Road

Fittontown
Farm

Hocker Lane

G **H** **J** **137** **K** ALDERLEY ROAD **L** **M**

Fallibroome
Farm

Whirley Grove

A B C **86** D E F

C7
1 Prestwick Cl

C5
1 Lincombe Hey

B8
1 Oakhill Cl

A7
1 Marl Edge
2 Thorne Cl

A5
1 Bollin Ms
2 Pearl St

Wych Farm

Harrop Green Farm

I
2
3
4
III
5
6
7
8

Brook House

Parkside Farm

Sunnybank

Bonis Hall

Mill House

B5358

BONIS HALL LANE

LONDON ROAD

A523(T)

Holehouse Lane

Higher Doles Farm

Canal Walk

Rushmere Close

Holehouse Lane

Lane Head

Whiteley Green

Lodge Farm

Peggie's Lane

PH

Plant House

Park House Farm

Howlanehead

River Dean

Well Lane

Gunco Lane

Ashtree Close

Butley Town

Lowerhouse

Bollington Medical Centre

Woodlea Drive

Moss Lane

Albert Road

Dean Valley CP School

Calder Close

St Gregorys RC Primary School

Hawthorn

Baileys Business Park

The Fold Nether Fold

Orme Close

Brocklehurst

Badger Peter's

Leigh Road

PRESTBURY LANE

Prestbury Lane

Prestbury Lane

Bradley Mount

Mount

ST OSWALDS

Bollington Cross C of E Primary School

Moss Brow

Hall Hill

Springbank

West Close

Oliver Close

Ashbrook

Network Clinic

Bollin Grove

Scott Road

Springfields

New Road

Bridge End Drive

Prestbury Station

Heybridge Lane

Little Meadow Close

Yew Tree Close

Meadow Drive

Yew Tree Drive

Oakwood Drive

A538

SK10

LONDON ROAD

B5091

FLASH LANE

THE SILK ROAD A523(T)

Bollington Cross

B5090

HENSHALL ROAD

Kingsway

Consort Close

Windsor Close

Princess Drive

Heath Road

Cooke Road

Overhouse

Queens

Barnfield

Archer

Crossfield Road

East Av

Bollington Leisure Centre

PO

South West Avenue

Hillcrest Road

Sandy Close

Sonner's Way

South Hill View

Clough Bank

PRESTBURY

The Village A538

Hotel

PO

PH

Spencer Brook

Shirley's Drive

Shirers Close

Macclesfield Road

Ashbrook Drive

Broadwalk

Paddock Brow

Bollin Way

Meadway

Willow Bank

Northmead

Dale Brow

Highfield

Murrayfield

The Paddocks

Willowmead Drive

Southmead Drive

Dale Head Road

River Bollin

MANCHESTER ROAD

Golf Course

Club House

Prestwick Close

Dumbah Lane

Ball Lane

Clarke Lane

TYTHERINGTON LANE

Pool End

Springboom Way

BOLLINGTON ROAD

Mode Hill

Clarke Lane

A523(T)

Prestwick Way

Turnberry Close

Gleneagles Way

Belfry Dr

Carnoustie Dr

Pool End Close

Pool End Road

Marlborough Close

Malvern Drive

Gloucester Close

Rugby Drive

Walton Heath Drive

Blackley Close

Batchworth Way

Dorchester Close

Birkdale Close

Fearndown Way

Kempton Way

Chepstow Close

Cheltenham Close

Beverley Way

Sedgefield

Maryborough Drive

Marlborough CP School

Tytherington

Hall Close

Brairdowrie Drive

Little Aston Close

Sandwich Drive

Quillane Close

Augusta Drive

Augusta Drive

Beverley Way

Hexham Way

Sandwich Drive

A538

Brocklehurst Way

C8
1 Castletown Cl
2 Kelso Wy
3 Lingfield Cl
4 Newmarket Cl
5 Portrush Cl

D8
1 Oldham's Rl

E4
1 Ridley Rd

C1
1 Coope Rd
2 Nursery Rd

B1
1 Evesham Cl
2 Salisbury Pl
3 Tewkesbury Dr

D4
1 Hartley Gn
2 Oliver Cl
3 Waterhouse Av

F5
1 Field Cl
2 Rose Bank

Ripon Close

Freshfield Close

Cornium

Dina Close

Farmfield Drive

Ryebank

1 grid square represents 500 metres

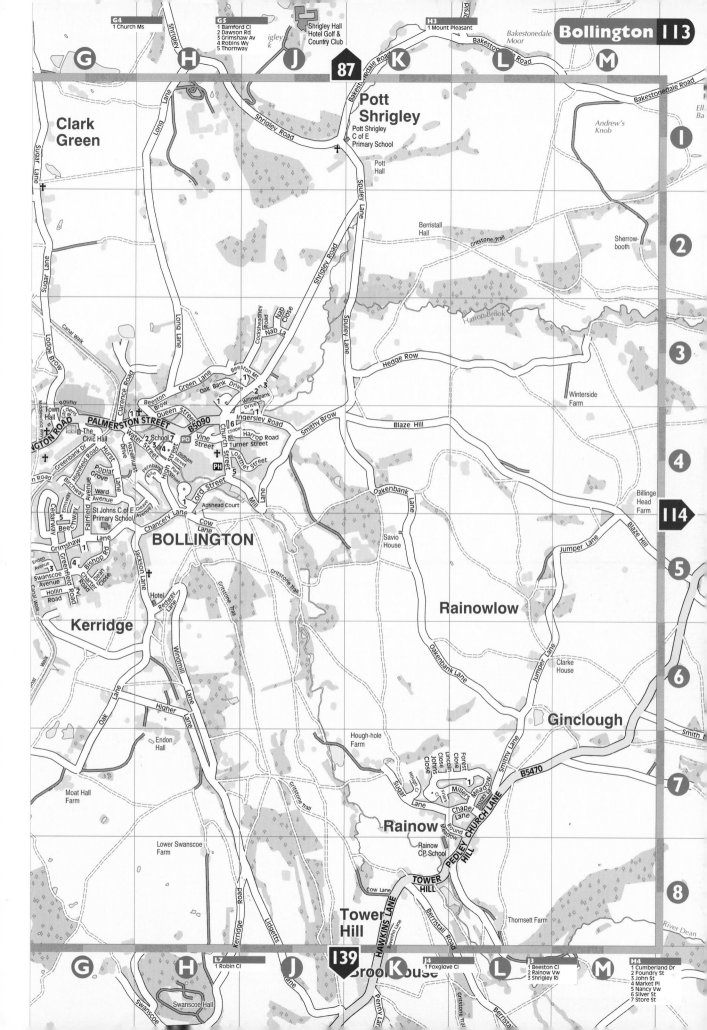

G4
1 Church Ms

G5
1 Bamford Cl
2 Dawson Rd
3 Grimshaw Av
4 Robins Wy
5 Thornway

H3
1 Mount Pleasant

G H J 87 K L M

I
2
3
4
114
5
6
7
8

Clark Green

Pott Shrigley

Pott Shrigley C of E Primary School

Shrigley Hall Hotel Golf & Country Club

Bakestonedale Moor

Bakestonedale Road

Andrew's Knob

Sherrow-booth

Pott Hall

Berristall Hall

Gritstone Trail

Harrop Brook

Hedge Row

Winterside Farm

Blaze Hill

Sugar Lane

Long Lane

Canal Walk

Lodge Brow

Middlewood Road

Town Hall

Clarence Road

Shrigley Road

Shrigley Lane

Spuley Lane

Cocksheadhey Road

Nab La

Nab Close

Beeston Ml

Green Lane

Oak Bank

Beeston Brow

Queen Street

Willowbank Drive

Ingersley Road

Smithy Brow

PALMERSTON STREET

B5090

Vine Street

School

Church Street

Harrop Road

Turner Street

Lowther Street

Oldham Street

Park Street

High Street

chapel

PO

The Civic Hall

Greenbank Dr

Hazelhurst

Hurst Drive

Fernbank Rise

Cleave Avenue

PH

Mill Lane

Oakbank Lane

Blaze Hill

Billinge Head Farm

Lord Street

Adshead Court

Cow Lane

Savio House

Rainowlow

Jumper Lane

Clarke House

Oakenbank Lane

Jumper Lane

Ginclough

Smith

Highfield Road

Birchway

Poplar Grove

Ward Avenue

Fairfield Avenue

Elmsway

Cedarway

Bee Chway

St Johns C of E Primary School

Grimshaw Lane

Bishop Rd

Charter Road

Greenfield Road

Dean Close

Jackson Lane

Chancery Lane

Gritstone Trail

BOLLINGTON

Endon Avenue

Swanscoe Avenue

Hollin Road

Canal Walk

Kerridge

Hotel

Redway Lane

Windmill Lane

Oak Lane

Higher Lane

Endon Hall

Moat Hall Farm

Gritstone Trail

Kerridge Road

Liggetts

Lower Swanscoe Farm

Hough-hole Farm

Sugar Lane

Forest Close

Lincoln Close

Johns Close

Friars

Miller's Meadow

Chapel Lane

Round Meadow

Smithy Lane

B5470

Rainow

Rainow CP School

PEDLEY CHURCH LANE HILL

TOWER HILL

Tower Hill

HAWKINS LANE

Ravensnan Lane

Berristall Road

Thornsett Farm

River Dean

Cow Lane

Gritstone Trail

Swanscoe Hall

L7
1 Robin Cl

J4
1 Foxglove Cl

L
1 Beeston Cl
2 Rainow Vw
3 Shrigley Ri

H4
1 Cumberland Dr
2 Foundry St
3 John St
4 Market Pl
5 Nancy Vw
6 Silver St
7 Store St

Brook House

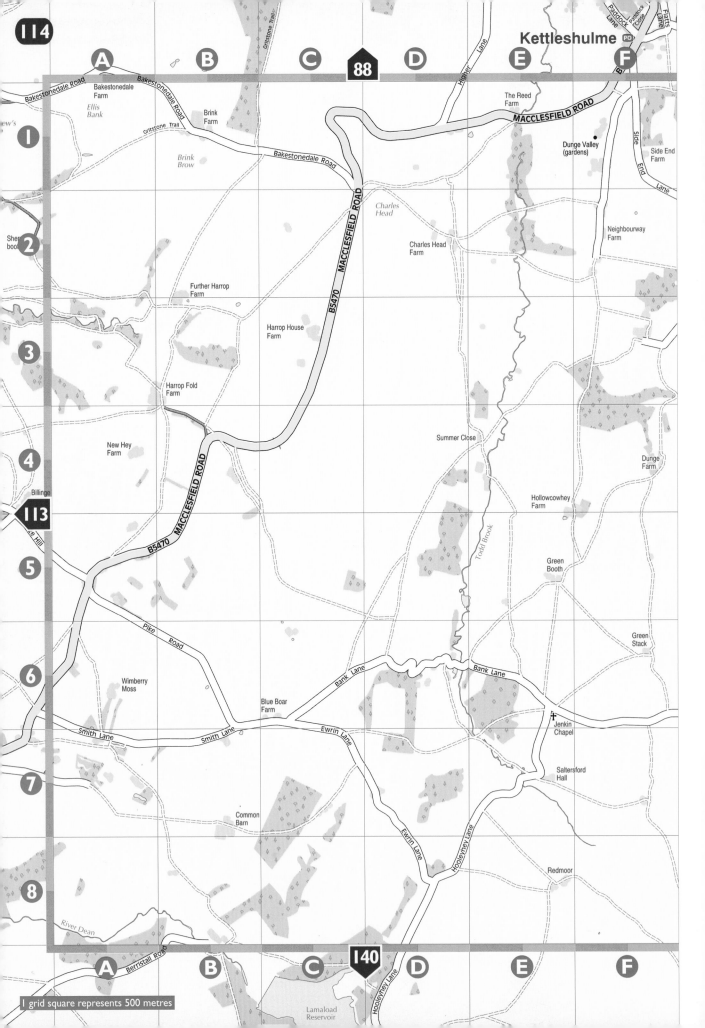

88

113

140

A B C D E F

I
2
3
4
5
6
7
8

Bakestonedale Road
Bakestonedale Farm
Ellis Bank
Bakestonedale Road
Brink Farm
Gritstone Trail
Brink Brow
Sher book
Further Harrop Farm
Harrop House Farm
Harrop Fold Farm
New Hey Farm
Billinge
e Hill
B5470 MACCLESFIELD ROAD
Charles Head
Charles Head Farm
The Reed Farm
MACCLESFIELD ROAD
Dunge Valley (gardens)
Side End Farm
Side End Lane
Neighbourway Farm
Summer Close
Dunge Farm
Hollowcowhey Farm
Todd Brook
Green Booth
Green Stack
Pike Road
Wimberry Moss
Bank Lane
Bank Lane
Blue Boar Farm
Smith Lane
Smith Lane
Ewrin Lane
Jenkin Chapel
Saltersford Hall
Common Barn
Ewrin Lane
Hooleyhey Lane
Redmoor
River Dean
Berristall Road
Lamaload Reservoir
Higher Lane
Paddock Lane
Paddock Close
Flatts Lane

PO

1 grid square represents 500 metres

Taxal

Clayton Fold
Farm

Wright's
Farm

Taxal
Edge

Sitch House

Shallcross Road

Shallcross Hall
Farm

Shallcross
Avenue

Moor Lane
Farm

Folds
La.

Einor Lane

Old Road

1

2

Fivelane-
ends

Taxal Moor Road

Crowhill

Whiteleas Road

Overton
Hall Farm

A5004

Fernilee

verhill

3

Windgather
Rocks

Norman
Wood

Oldfield

4

Goyt
Forest

Fernilee
Reservoir

Long Hill

5

Hoo
Moor

Goyt
Valley

6

The Street

Embridge Causeway

The Street

7

Bunsal
Cob

8

Derbyshire Co
Cheshire Co

116

90

B5
1 Lloyd St
2 Lower Mumforth St
3 Lower Sydney St
4 Salusbury St
5 Thomas St

A7
1 Mount Pleasant Av

A6
1 Chapel Street (Lon Y Capel)
2 Lon Odyn (Kiln Close)
3 St Catherine's Cl
4 Swinchiard La

A5
1 Chester Street (Heol Caer)
2 Feathers St
3 Sydney Wk
4 Trelawny Sq

B6
1 Princes St
2 Queen St

B8
1 Bodlondeb
2 Bryn Derw
3 Bryn Hellg
4 Heol-y-bryn
5 Rhoswen
6 Swn-y-gwynt

River Dee

Cheshire County
Flintshire

A B C D E F

1 grid square represents 500 metres

FLINT

Mount Pleasant

Oakenholt

91

118

Denhall House Farm

White Sands

Kelsterton

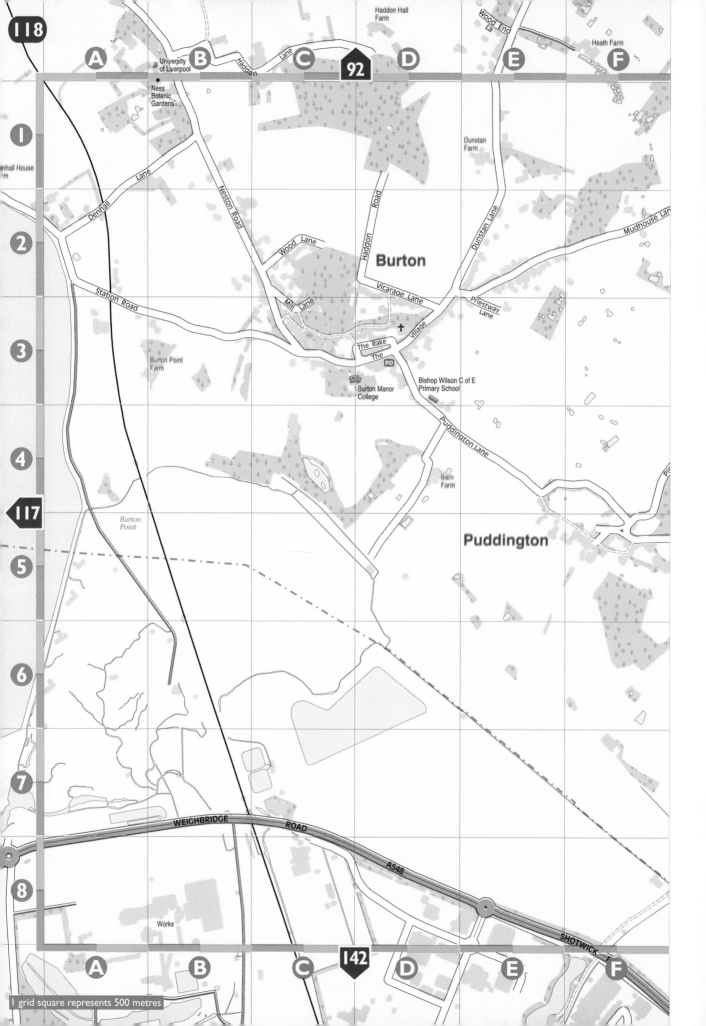

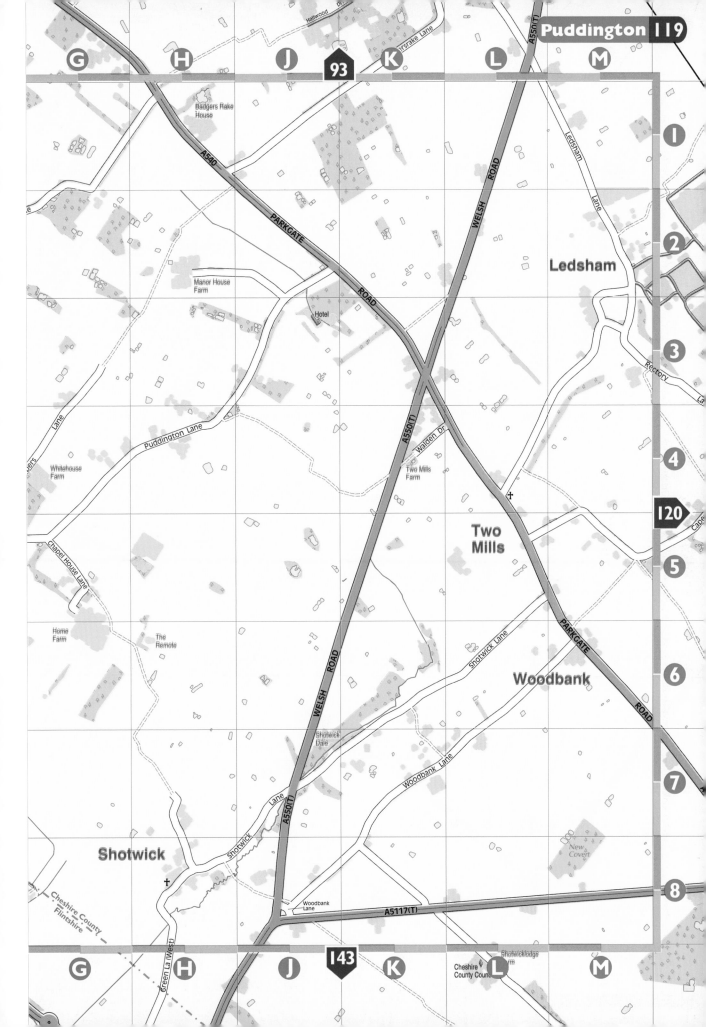

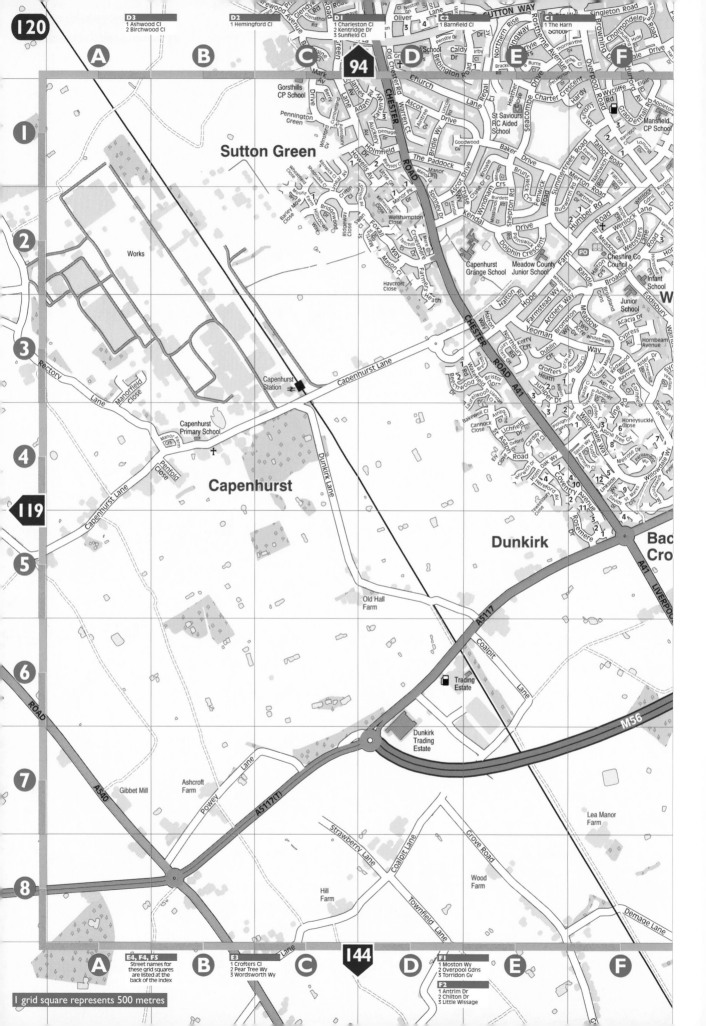

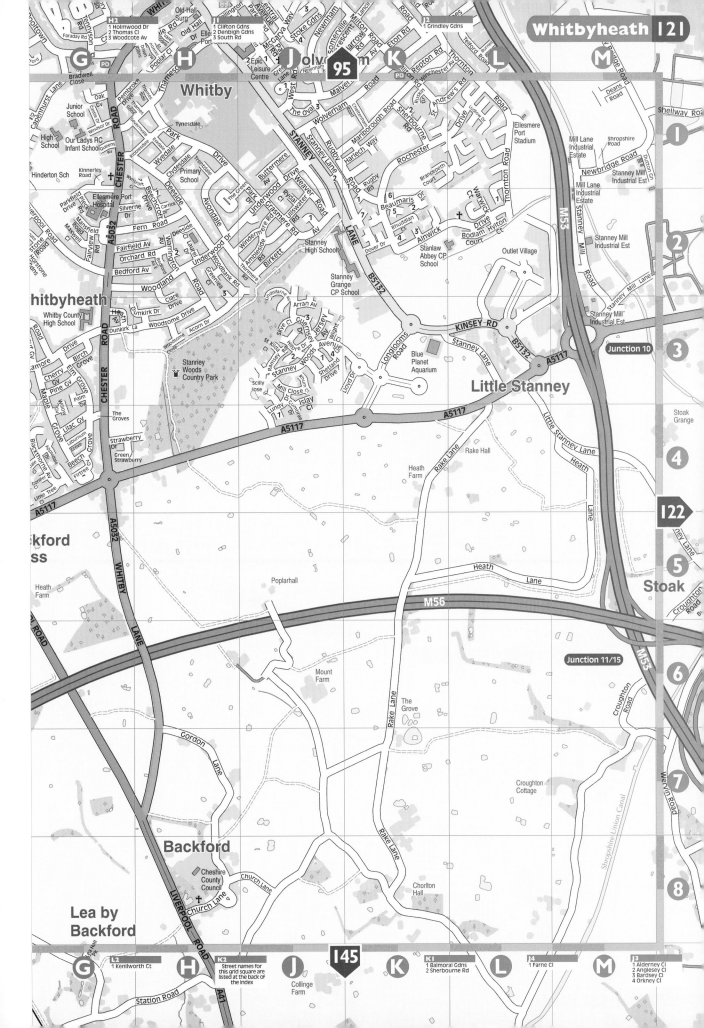

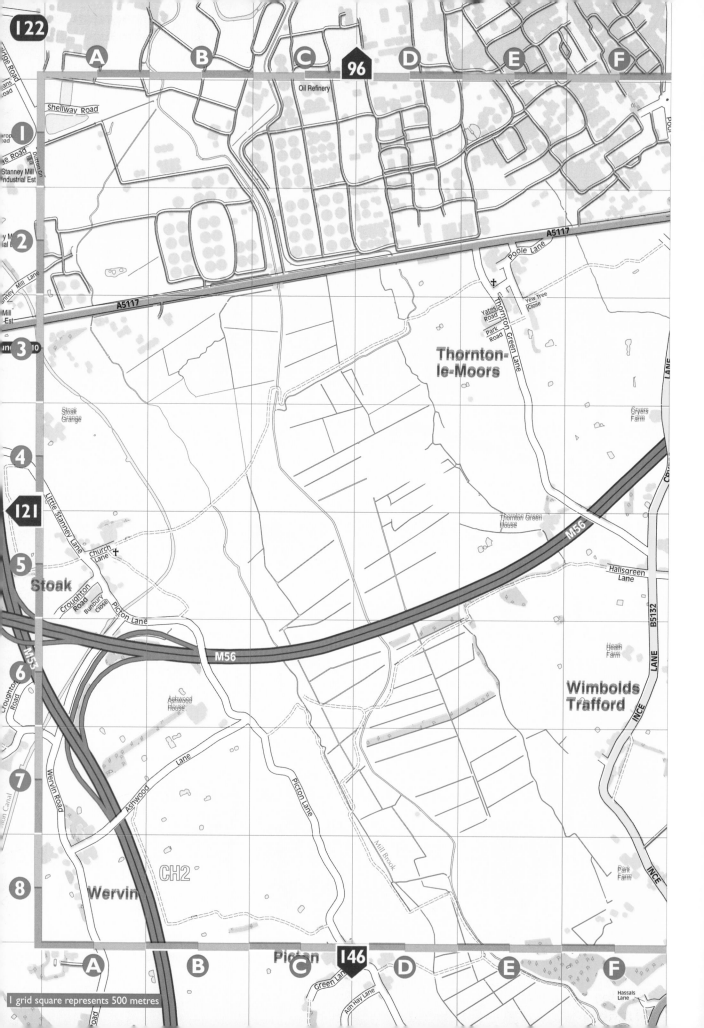

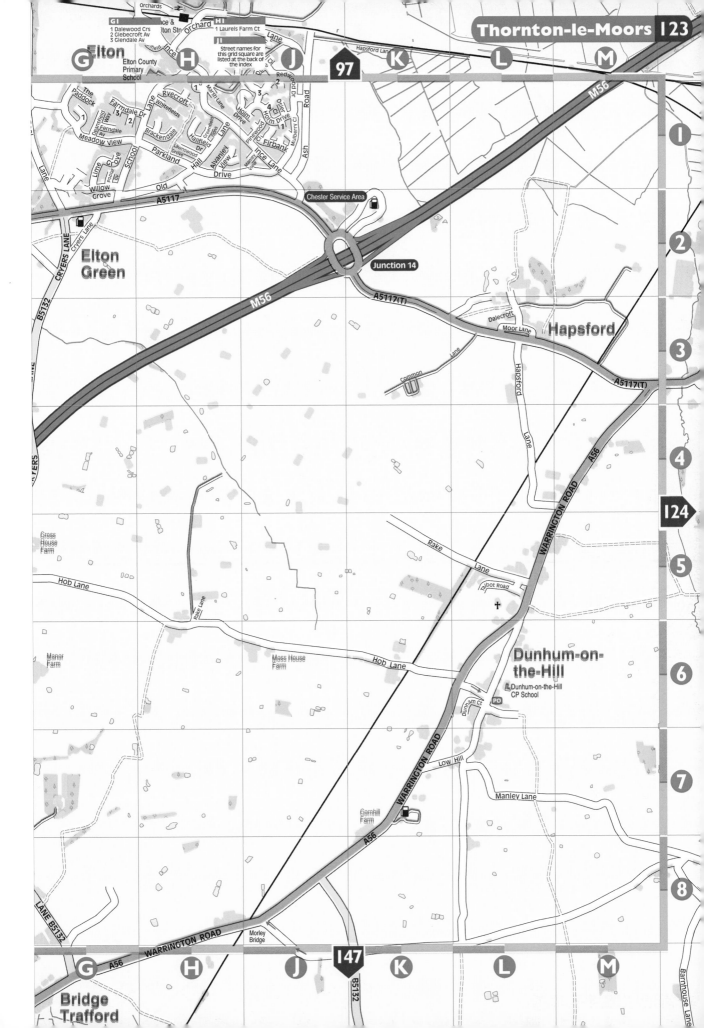

G H J 97 K L M

I

2

124

5

6

7

8

G H 147 K L M

Elton

Elton County
Primary
School

G1 1 Dalewood Crs
2 Glebecroft Av
3 Glendale Av

H1 1 Laurels Farm Ct

I1 Street names for
this grid square are
listed at the back of
the index

The
Paddock

Farndale Dr

Deansfield
Way

Ferndale
Av

Meadow View

Ferndale
Av

Parkland

Lime
Grove

Willow
Grove

School
Lane

Rycecroft

whitefields

Brackendale

Hallfield
Dr

Greenfield
Close

Lawnswood
Grove

Hall

Alvanley
View

Drive

Marsh
Lane

Holm
Drive

Pinewood
Dr

Manley
View

Firbank

Osier
Drive

Mulberry Cl

Ince Lane

Redwood Dr

Ash
Road

Orchard
Lane

Hapsford Lane

Ince

Elton Stn

Orchards

A5117

**Elton
Green**

CRYERS LANE

Cryers Lane

B5132

LTERS

Chester Service Area

Junction 14

M56

A5117(T)

Dalecroft

Moor Lane

Hapsford

A5117(T)

Common
Lane

Hapsford
Lane

A56

WARRINGTON ROAD

Cross
House
Farm

Hob Lane

Manor
Farm

Rake Lane

Moss House
Farm

Hob Lane

Rake
Lane

Talbot Road

✝

**Dunhum-on-
the-Hill**

Dunhum-on-the-Hill
CP School

PO

Dunham Ct

Low Hill

Manley Lane

Cornhill
Farm

A56

LANE B5132

WARRINGTON ROAD

A56

Morley
Bridge

B5132

**Bridge
Trafford**

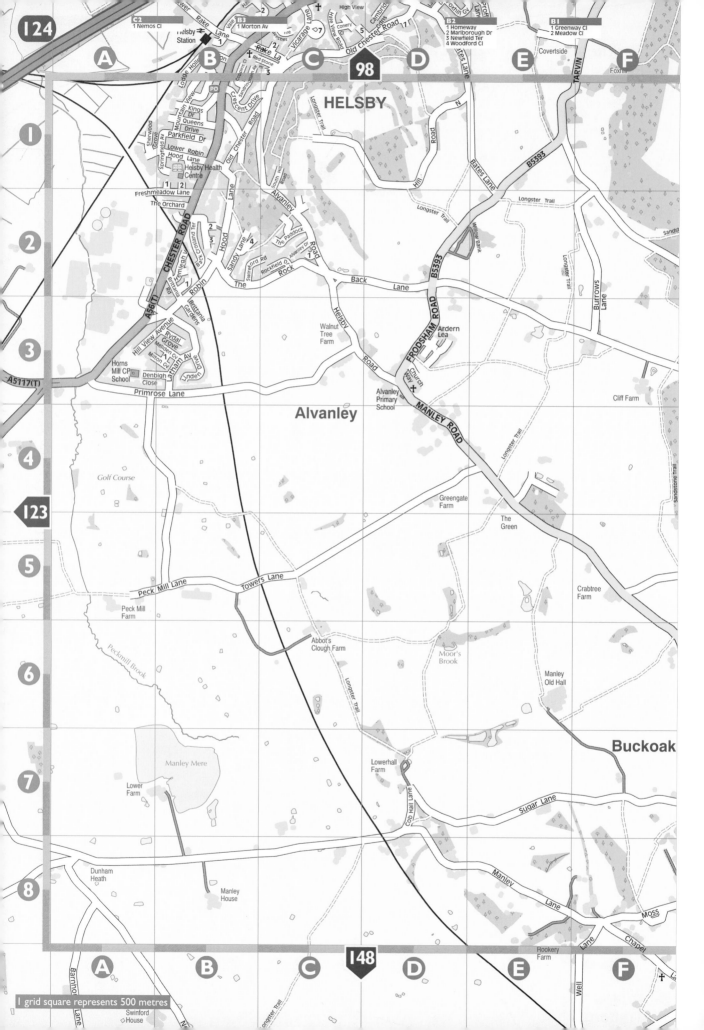

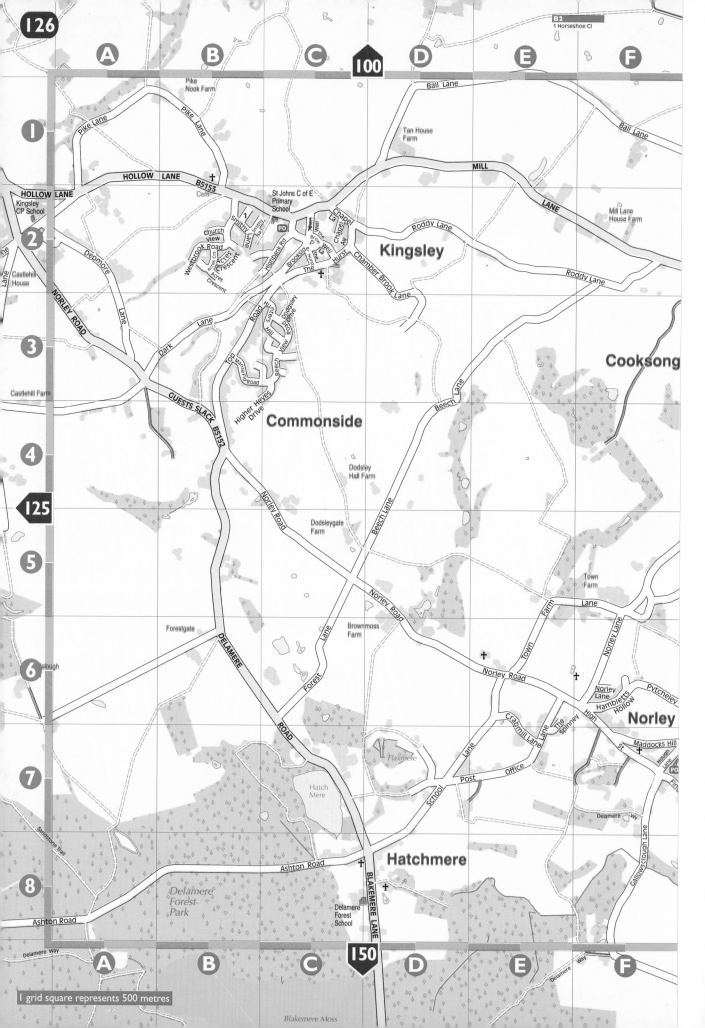

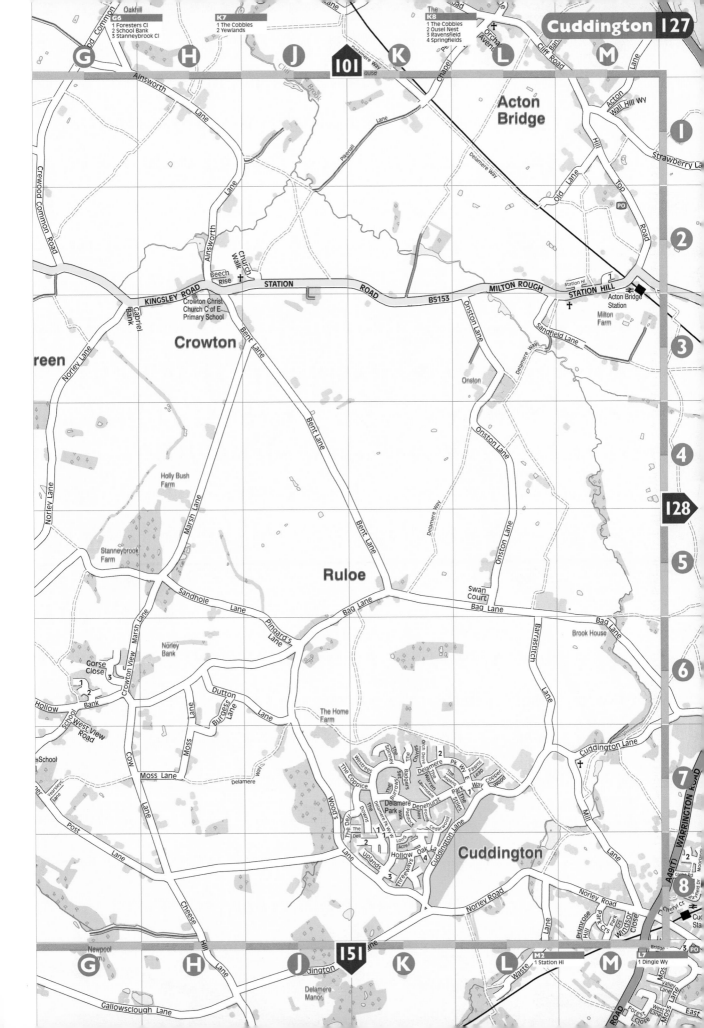

G7
Oakhill
1 Foresters Cl
2 School Bank
3 Stanneybrook Cl

K7
1 The Cobbles
2 Yewlands

K8
1 The Cobbles
2 Ousel Nest
3 Ravensfield
4 Springfields

G H J 101 K L M

I

2

3

128

4

5

6

7

8

3

Acton Bridge

Ainsworth Lane

Cliff Brook

Delamere Way

Chapel Lane

Pikenall Lane

Orcha Avenu

Cliff Road

Acton Lane

Top Road

Wall Hill Wy

Strawberry La

Crewood Common Road

Ainsworth Lane

Church Walk

Beech Rise

KINGSLEY ROAD

Gabriel Bank

Crowton Christ Church C of E Primary School

STATION ROAD

B5153

MILTON ROUGH

STATION HILL

Old Lane

Delamere Way

PO

Station Hl

Acton Bridge Station

Milton Farm

Crowton

reen

Norley Lane

Bent Lane

Marsh Lane

Onston Lane

Onston

Delamere Way

Sandfield Lane

Holly Bush Farm

Stanneybrook Farm

Norley Lane

Bent Lane

Ruloe

Delamere Way

Swan Court

Bag Lane

Sandhole Lane

Pingard's Lane

Bag Lane

Bag Lane

Barrastitch Lane

Brook House

Norley Bank

Gorse Close
1
2
3

Crowton View

Marsh Lane

Dutton Lane

Burgess's Lane

The Home Farm

Cuddington Lane

Hollow Bank

School

West View Road

Cow Lane

Moss Lane

Moss Lane

Delamere Way

Wood's Lane

Yearsleys Lane

Delamere Park

The Spinney
The Birches
The Warren
The Aspens
Orch Dene
Delamere Walk
Fawns Leap
Copper Wood
Park Way
PK Wy
The Stiles
Foxes
Cedarwood
Denehurst
The Coppice
Westrees
The Burrows
The Dell
The Downs
Long Acre
Hollow Oak
Threeway
Uplands
1
2
3
4

Cuddington Lane

Cuddington

Mill Lane

Norley Road

WARRINGTON ROAD

A49 (T)

Cud Sta

PO

Post Lane

Cheese Hill Lane

Newpool

Norley Road

Primrose Hill

Windsor Close

Park Cl's

Cts Park

Cheryl Ct

Moorgate

Gilfield Dr

Dingle Wy

Bridge

G H J 151 K L M2 M L7

M2
1 Station Hl

Waste

L7

Delamere Manor

Gallowsclough Lane

Gallowsclough Lane

BARNTON

G **H** **J** Anderton **103** **K** **L** **M**

I
2
3
I3
4
I30
5
6
7
8

I2

Winnington

Greenbank

Hartfordbeach

Leftwich

B5153

153

G **H** **J** **K** Hartford L **L** **M**

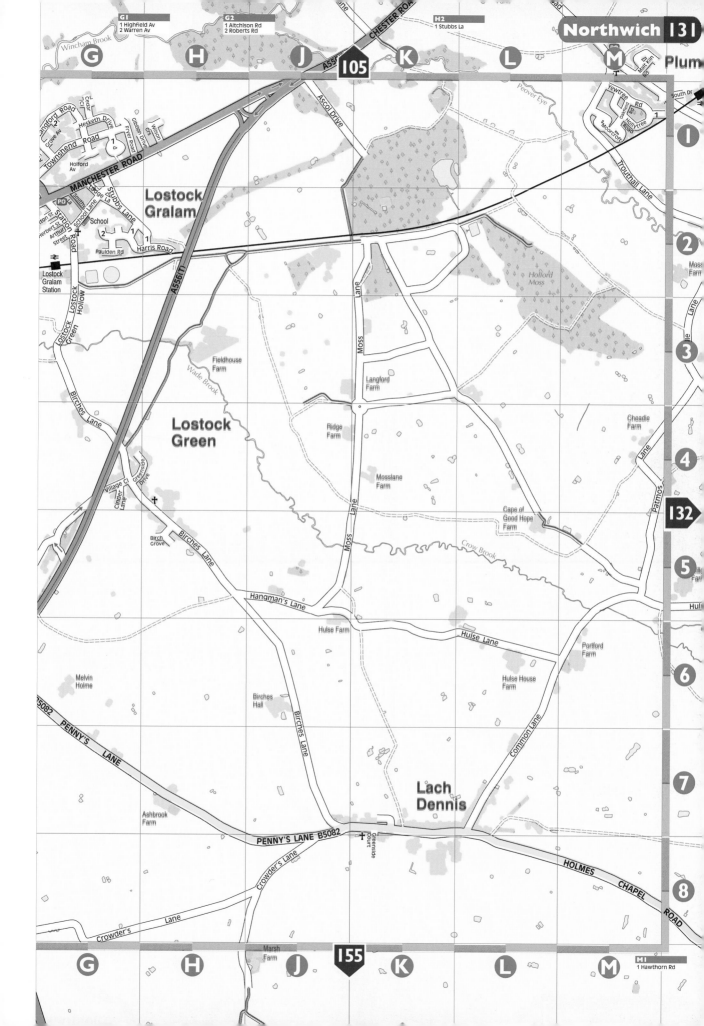

G1
1 Highfield Av
2 Warren Av

G2
1 Aitchison Rd
2 Roberts Rd

H2
1 Stubbs La

G **H** **J** A55 CHESTER ROAD **105** **K** **L** **M** Marl Run Rd Plum

Wincham Brook

South Dr

Peover Eye

Yewtree Rd
Garfield Rd
Holly Tree Rd
Moorcroft

I

Langford Road
Cedar Grove Av
Hesketh Drive
Wilson Cres
Gibbon Drive
Frier Road
Townshend Road
Holford Av
MANCHESTER ROAD

Trouthall Lane

Lostock Gralam

Stubbs Lane
School Lane
Lodge La

Moss Farm

2

PO
Station St
Herbert St
Arthur Street
Station Road
School

Paulden Rd Harris Road

2 1 1

A556(T)

Holford Moss

Lostock Gralam Station

Lane

3

Lostock Hollow
Lostock Green

Birches Lane

Fieldhouse Farm

Moss Lane

Langford Farm

Cheadle Farm

Wade Brook

Lostock Green

Ridge Farm

Patmos Lane

4

Greenside Drive
Village Cl
Cinder Lane

Mosslane Farm

Cape of Good Hope Farm

132

Birch Grove

Birches Lane

Moss Lane

Crow Brook

5 Fari
Hul

Hangman's Lane

Hulse Farm

Hulse Lane

Portford Farm

6

Melvin Holme

Birches Hall

Hulse House Farm

Common Lane

B5082 PENNY'S LANE

Birches Lane

7

Ashbrook Farm

Lach Dennis

PENNY'S LANE B5082

Greenside Court

HOLMES CHAPEL ROAD

8

Crowder's Lane

Crowder's Lane

Marsh Farm

M1
1 Hawthorn Rd

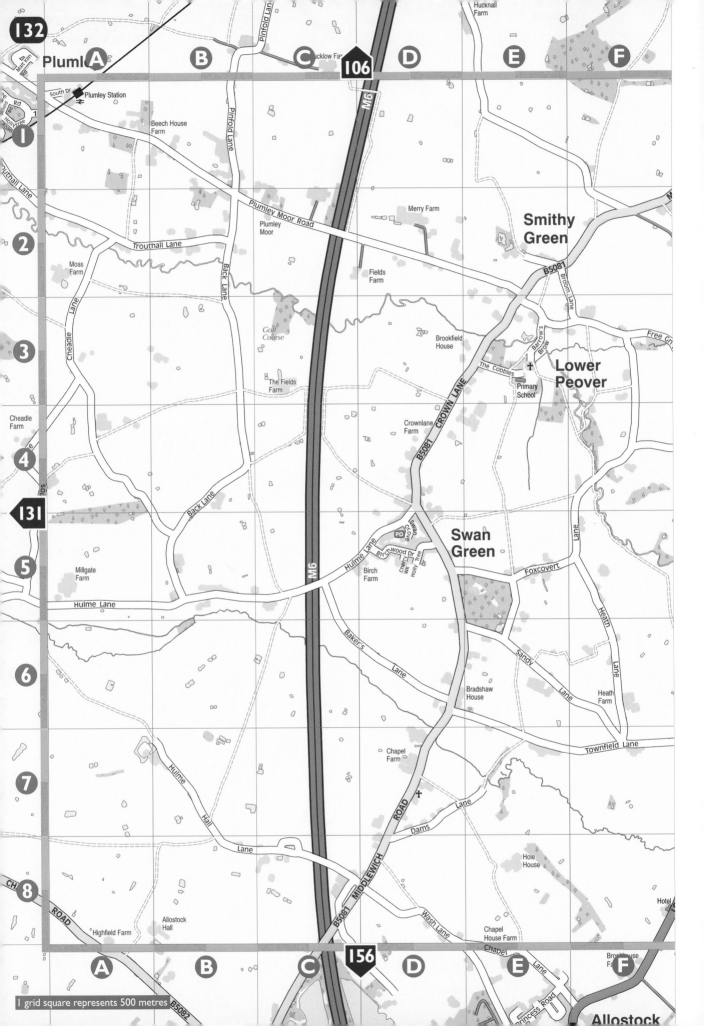

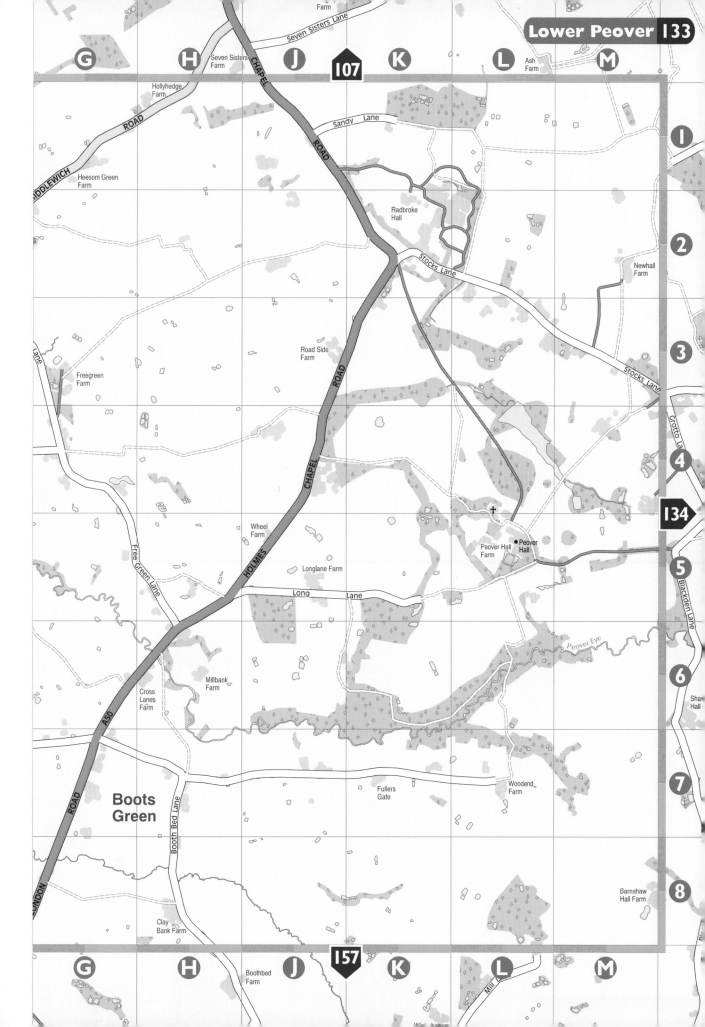

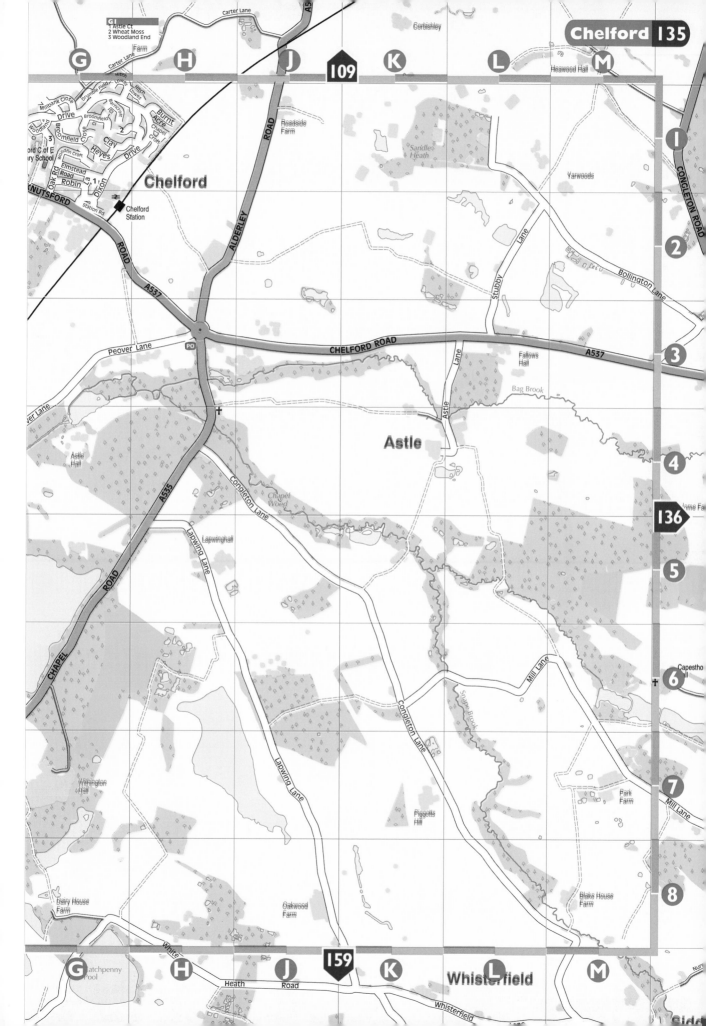

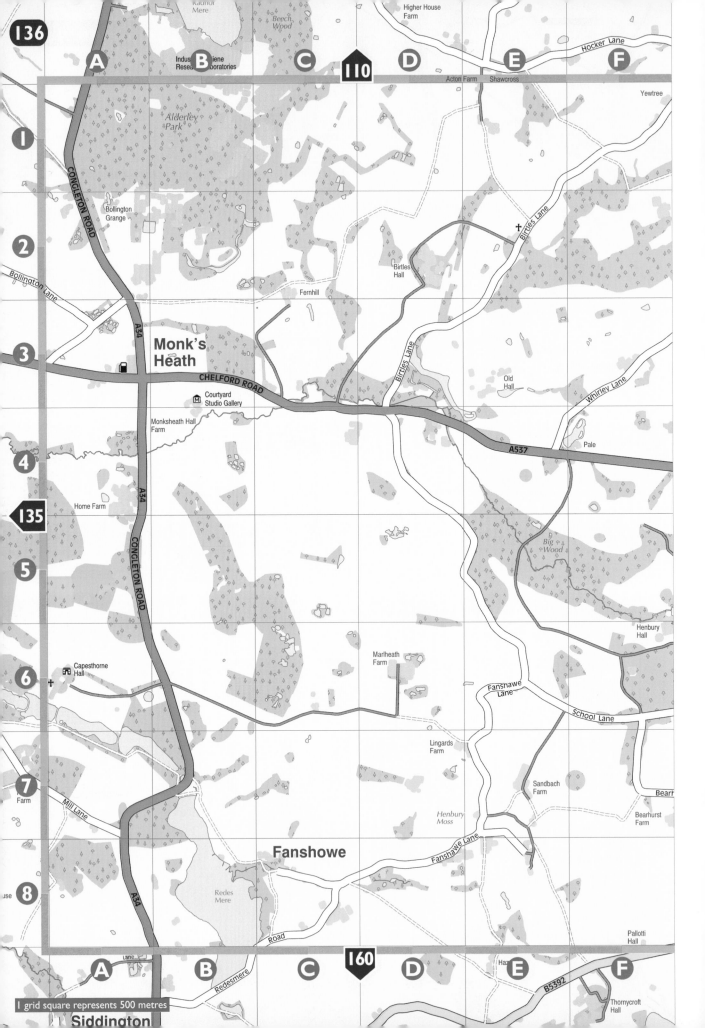

A B C **110** D E F

Hocker Lane

Acton Farm   Shawcross

Higher House
Farm

Yewtree

Industrial
Research
Laboratories

Biene
Laboratories

Beech
Wood

Radnor
Mere

Alderley
Park

1

Bollington
Grange

Birtles Lane

Birtles
Hall

2

Bollington Lane

Fernhill

3

CONGLETON ROAD

A34

**Monk's
Heath**

CHELFORD ROAD

Courtyard
Studio Gallery

Birtles Lane

Old
Hall

Whirley Lane

A537

Pale

4

Monksheath Hall
Farm

135

Home Farm

Big
Wood

5

Henbury
Hall

Marlheath
Farm

Fanshawe
Lane

School Lane

6

Capesthorne
Hall

CONGLETON ROAD

Lingards
Farm

Sandbach
Farm

Bear

Bearhurst
Farm

7

Farm

Mill Lane

Fanshowe

Henbury
Moss

Fanshawe Lane

8

use

A34

Redes
Mere

Road

Pallotti
Hall

A B **160** C D E F

Lane

Redesmere

B5392

Haz

Thornycroft
Hall

Siddington

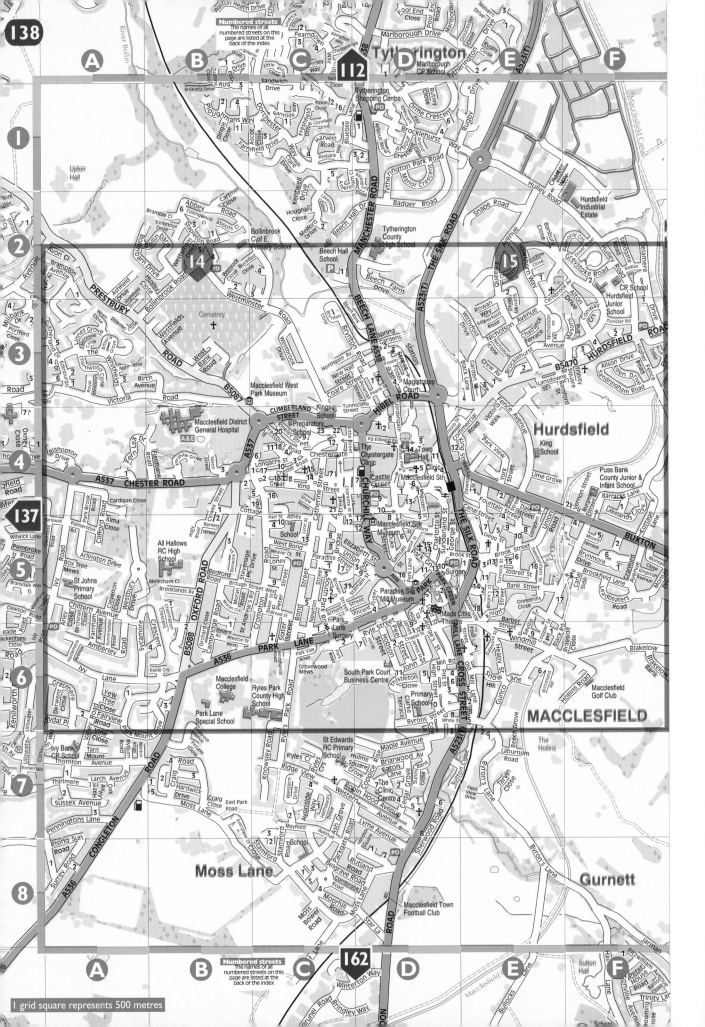

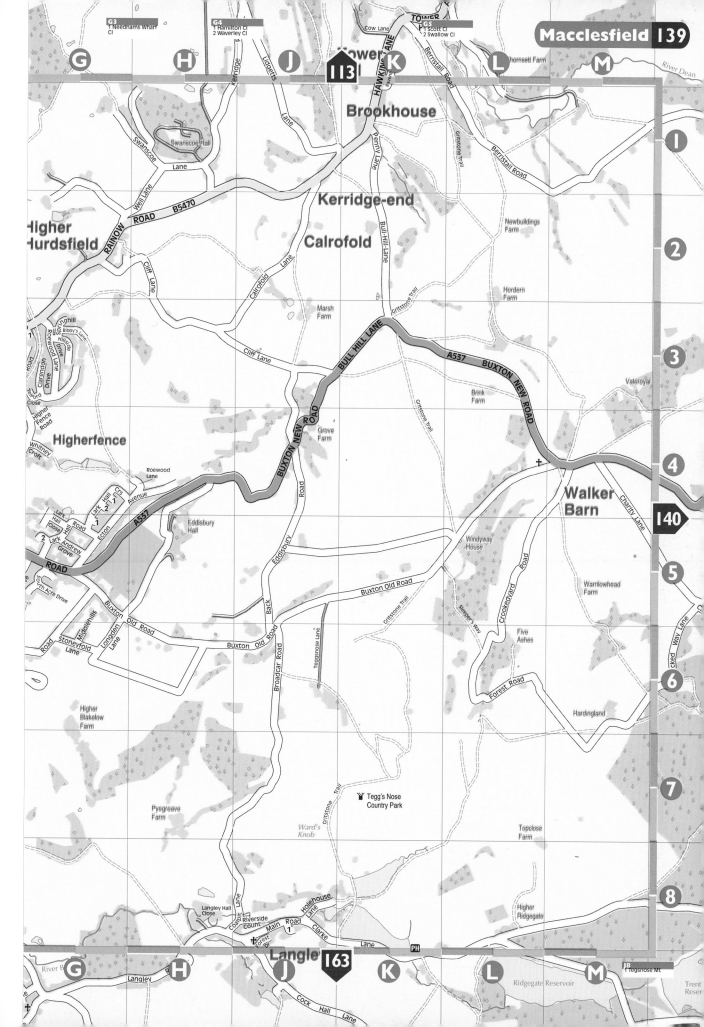

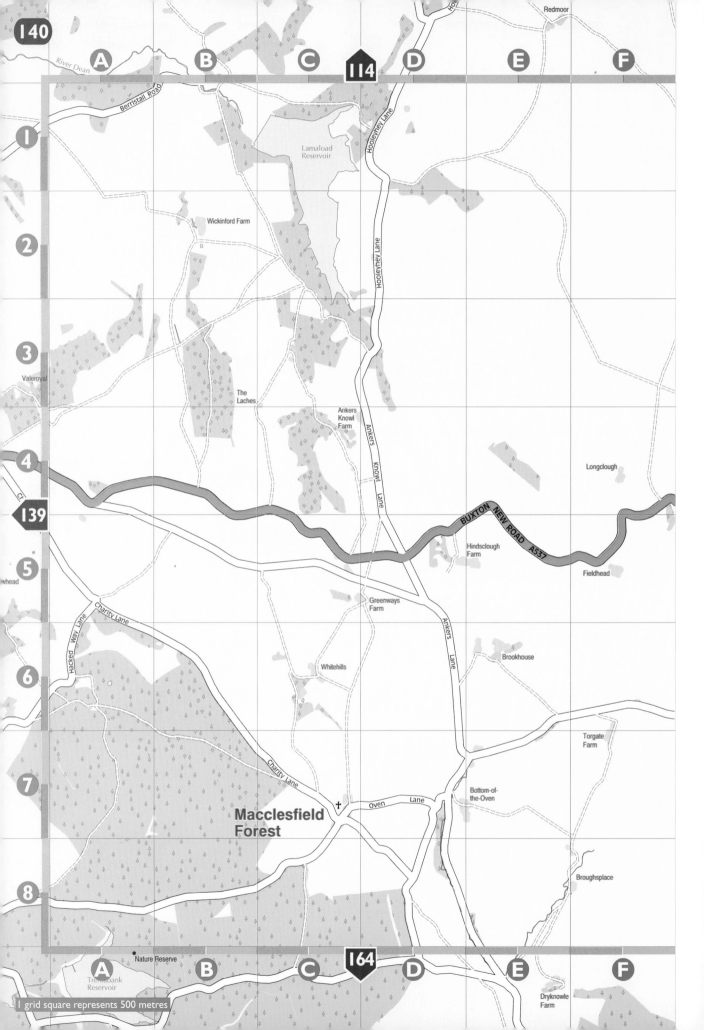

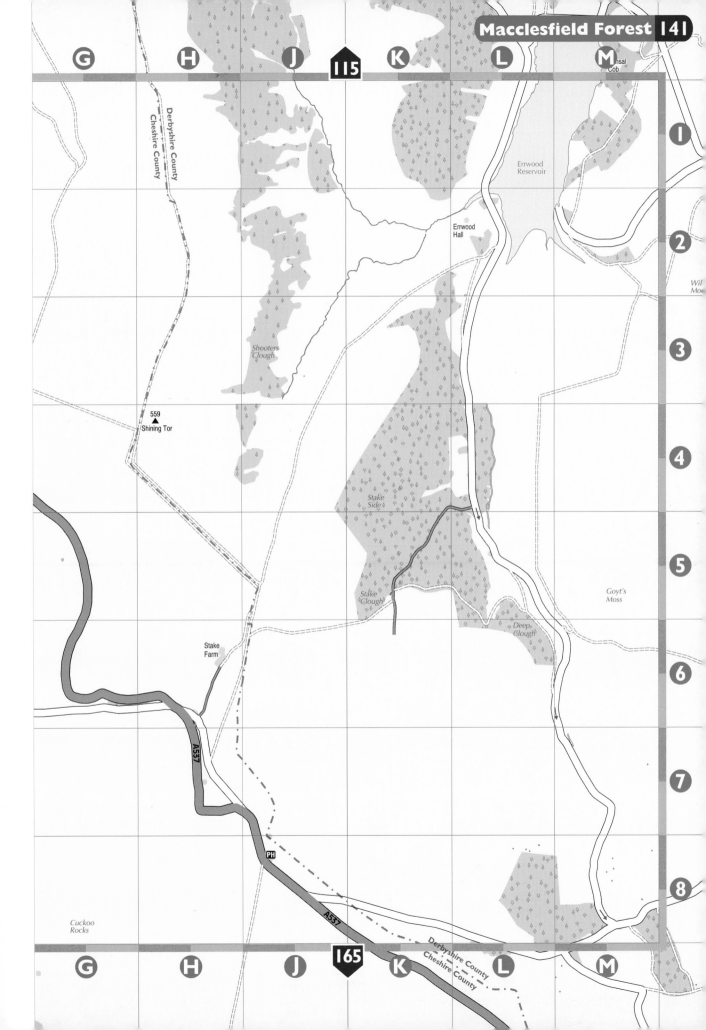

G   H   J   115   K   L   M   Monsal
                                     Cob

I

2
                                                     Wil
                                                     Moe

Errwood
Reservoir

Errwood
Hall

3

Shooters
Clough

559
Shining Tor

4

Stake
Side

5
                                                     Goyt's
                                                     Moss

Stake
Clough

Deep
Clough

Stake
Farm   6

A537

7

PH

8

A537

Cuckoo
Rocks

Derbyshire County
Cheshire County

G   H   J   165   K   Derbyshire County   L   M
                    Cheshire County

Derbyshire County
Cheshire County

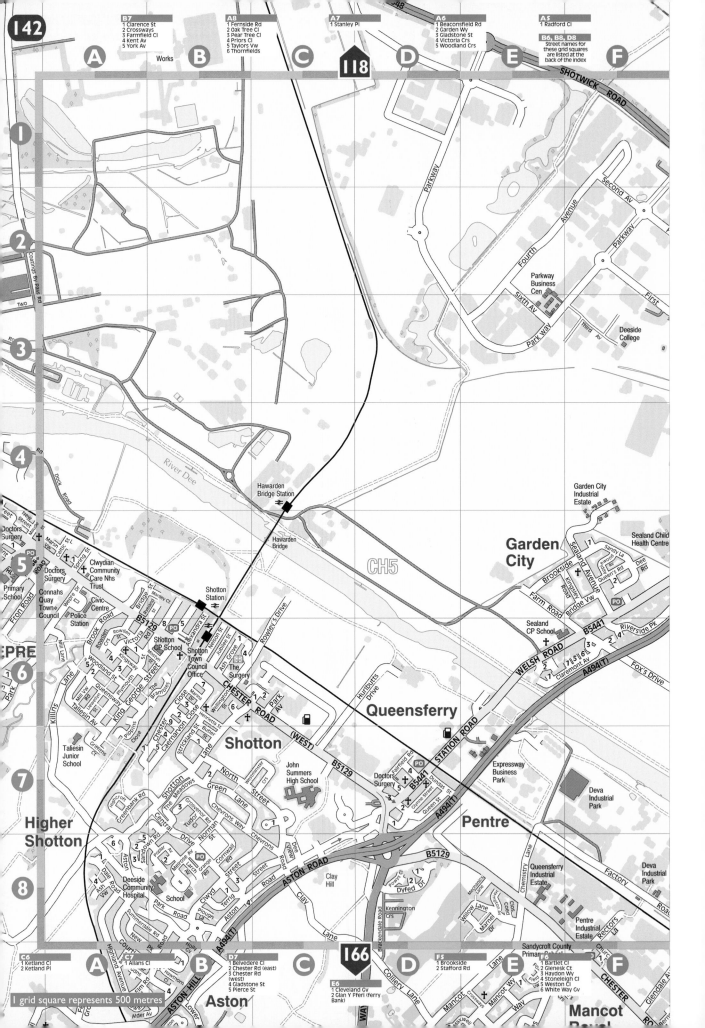

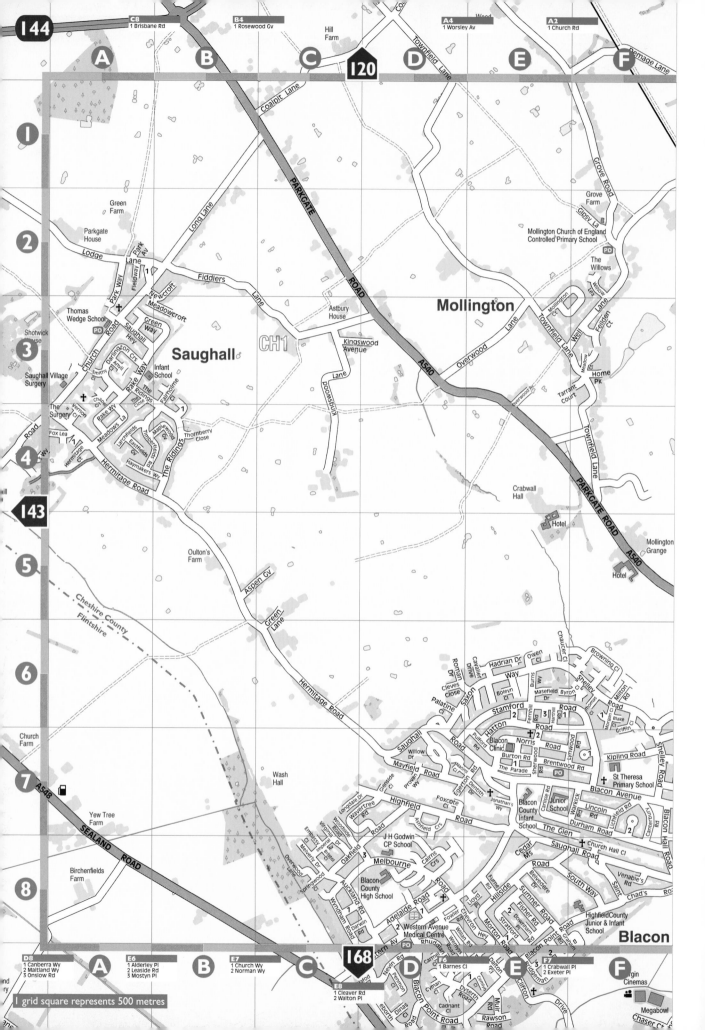

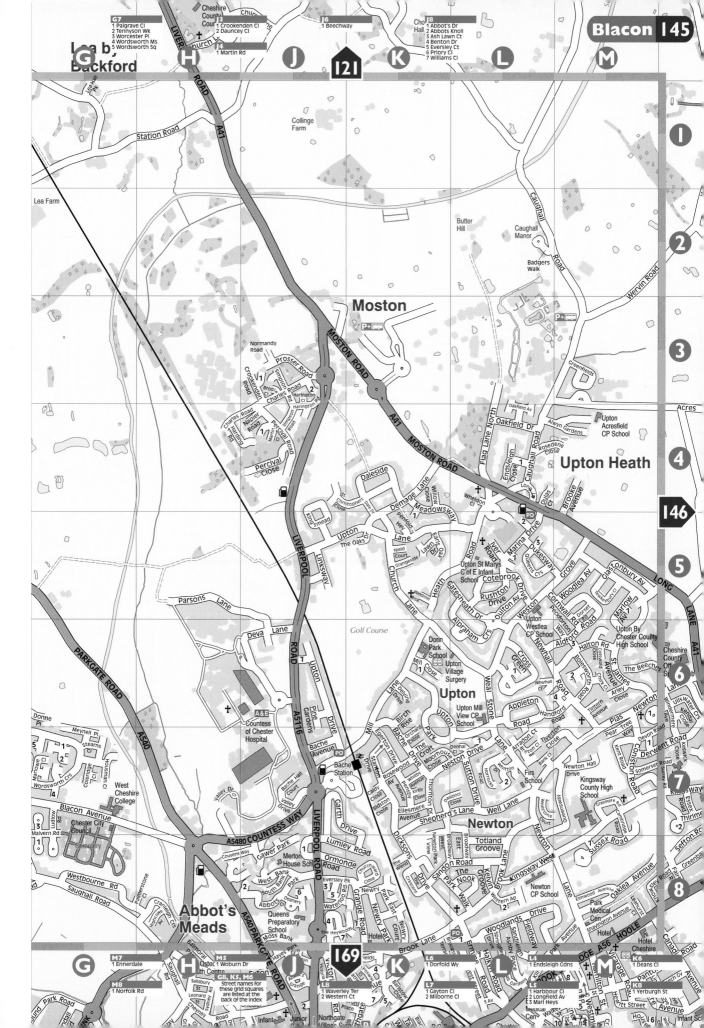

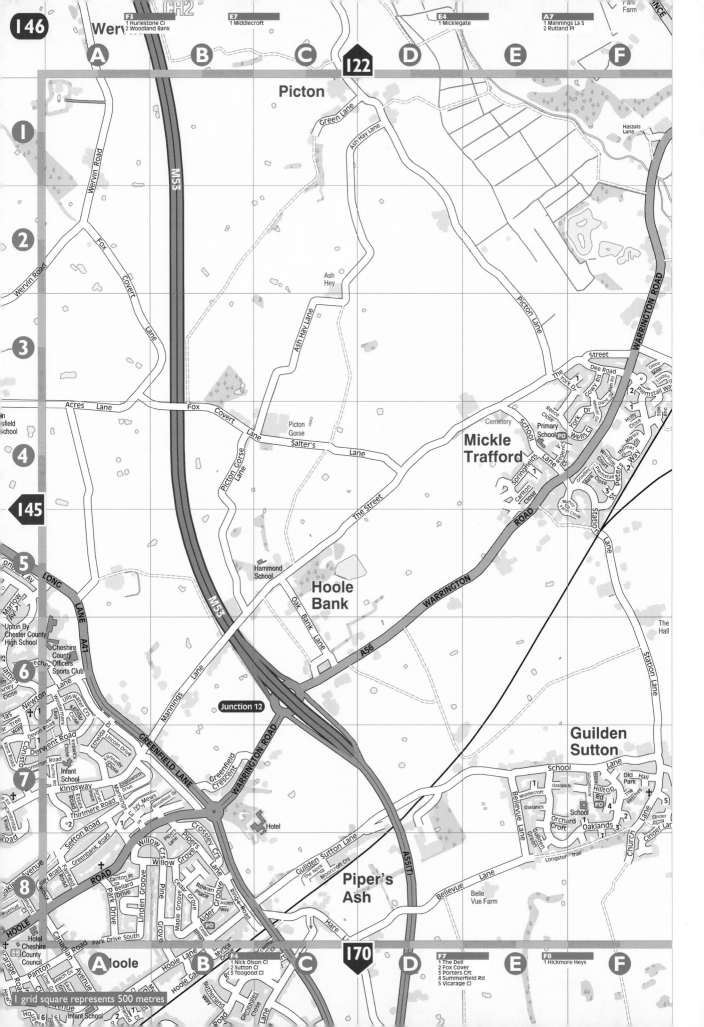

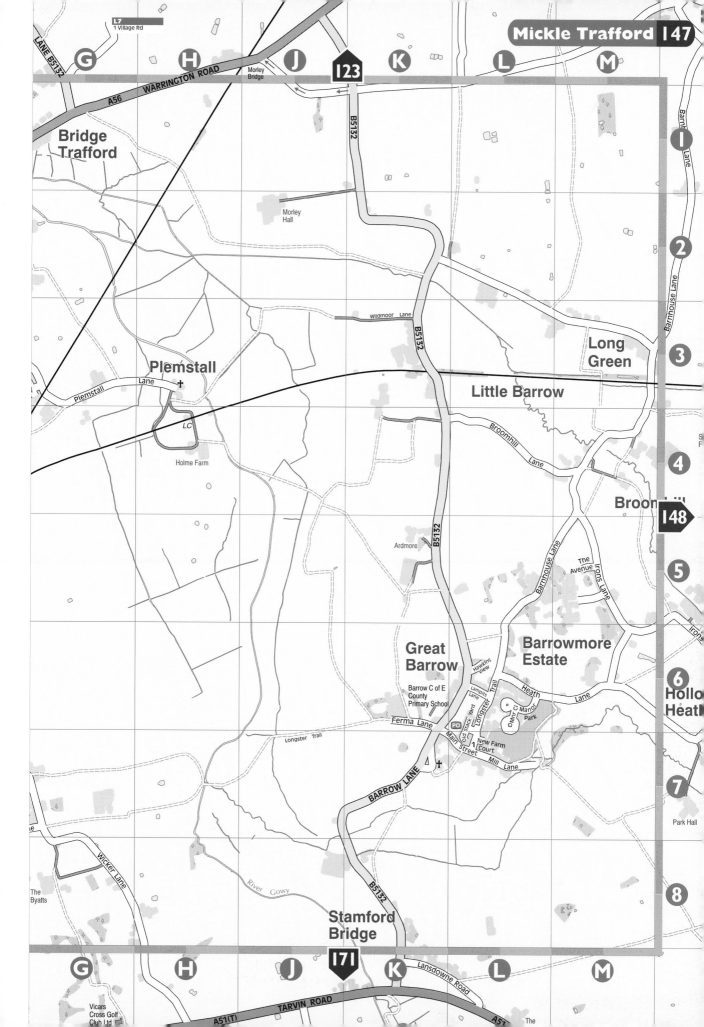

L7
1 Village Rd

G   H   J   123   K   L   M

LANE B5132
A56   **WARRINGTON ROAD**   Morley Bridge   B5132

Bridge Trafford

Morley Hall

Wildmoor Lane

Long Green

Plemstall
Plemstall   Lane
LC
Holme Farm

Little Barrow

Broomhill Lane

Broom Hill   148

Ardmore

B5132

The Avenue
Irons Lane

5

Great Barrow   **Barrowmore Estate**

Hawkins View
Barrow C of E County Primary School
Lampits Lane
Longster Trail
Heath   Lane
Barnhouse Lane
Manor Park
Mnr Cl

6   **Hollo Heath**

Ferma Lane
PO
Old Stack Yard
New Farm Court
Main Street
Mill Lane

Longster Trail

7

Park Hall

BARROW LANE

Wicker Lane

The Byatts

River   Gowy

B5132

Stamford Bridge   171

G   H   J   171   K   Lansdowne Road   L   M

TARVIN ROAD
A51(T)   A51

Vicars Cross Golf Club Ltd

Barnhouse Lane

I
2
3
4
5
6
7
8

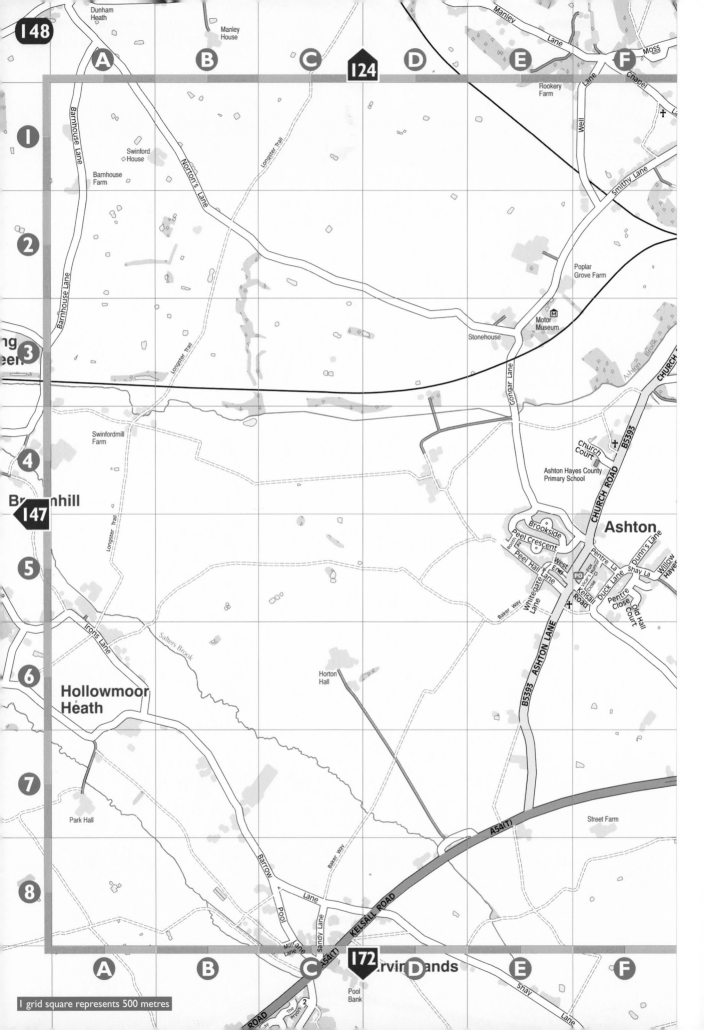

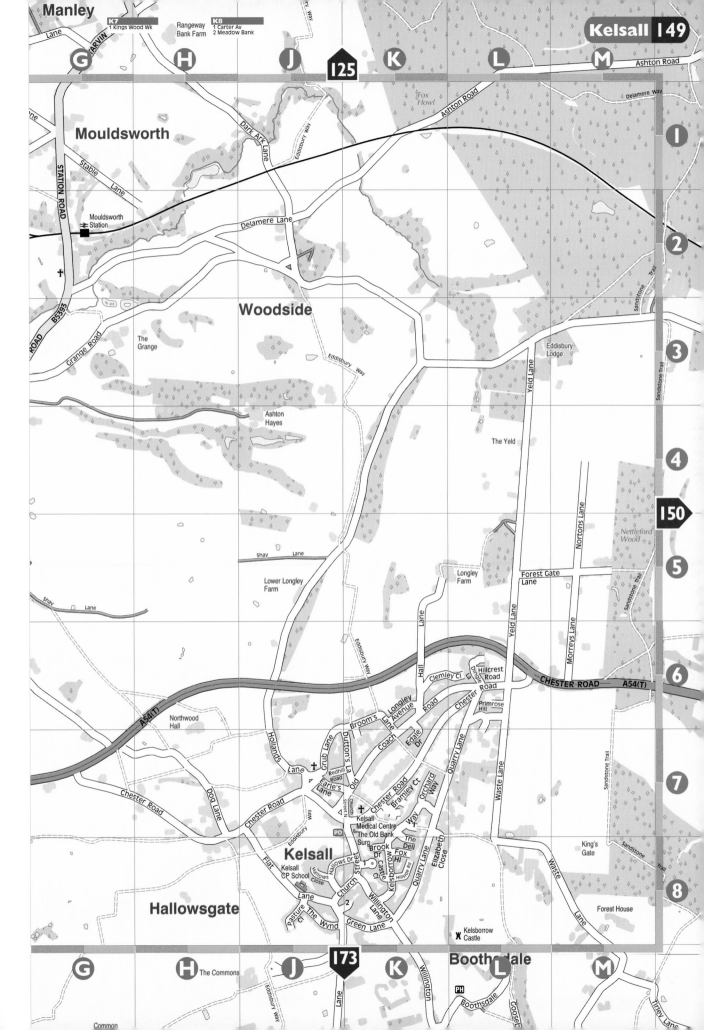

150

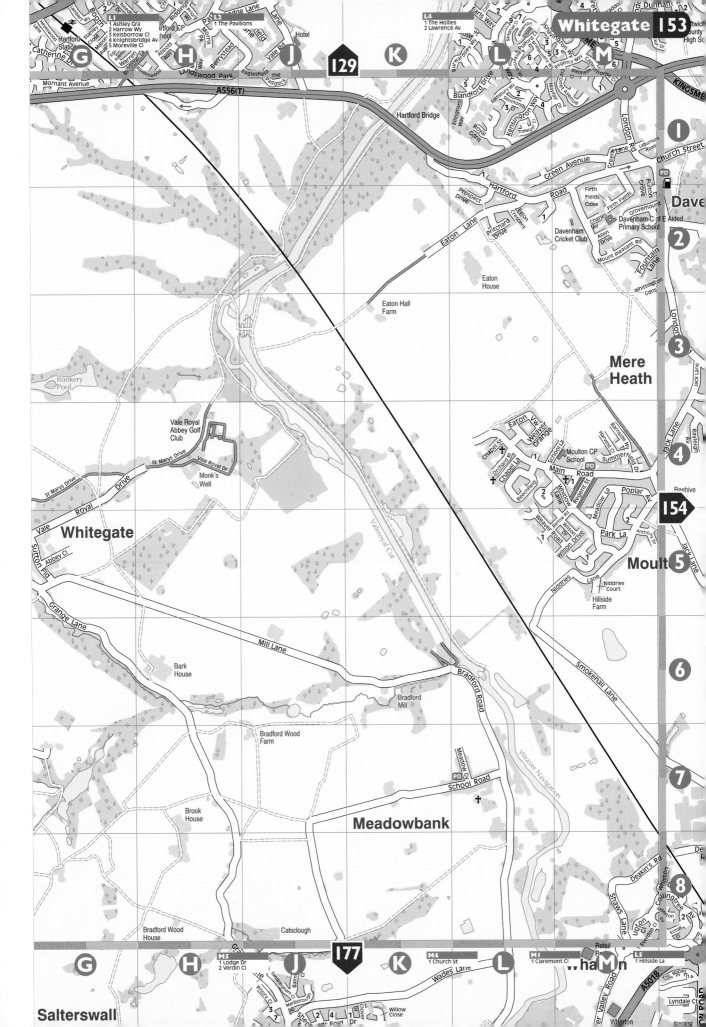

Map labels

Top row (grid letters): G H J 129 K L M

Right side (grid numbers): I 2 3 4 154 5 6 7 8

Bottom row (grid letters): G H J 177 K M5 M4 L M1 M

Place names and features

Hartford Station
Hartford CP School
Hotel
Landswood Park
Eaglesfield
The Paddock
A556(T)
Hartford Bridge
Blandford Drive
Kensington Way
Green Lane
Green Avenue
Church Street
Dave...
Firth Fields Close
Firth Fields
Fulton Grove
Grovemount
Davenham C of E Aided Primary School
Davenham Cricket Club
Mount Pleasant Rd
Fountain Lane
Prospect Drive
Hartford Road
Eaton Lane
Pritchard Drive
Eaton Crescent
Eaton House
Whittington Gdns
London Rd
Mere Heath
Rookery Pool
Vale Royal Abbey Golf Club
St Marys Drive
Vale Royal Dr
Monk's Well
Eaton Vw
Weaver Grange
Chapel St
Orchard Cl
Chapel La
School La
Moulton CP School
Summerfield Dr
Barnside Wy
Harvest Cl
Main Road
Beechfield
Willow Lane
Regent St
Wilson Rd
Poplar Av
Park La
Beehive
154
Moult
Valeroyal Cut
Weaver Road
Wilson Drive
Meadow La
Nidderies Lane
Niddries Court
Hillside Farm
Vale Royal Drive
Whitegate
Sutton Fld
Abbey Cl
Grange Lane
Mill Lane
Smokehall Lane
Bark House
Bradford Mill
Bradford Road
Weaver Navigation
Bradford Wood Farm
Meadow Cl
School Road
Brook House
Meadowbank
Bradford Wood House
Catsclough
Salterswall
Wades Lane
Willow Close
Shaws Lane
Collingtree
Upton
Retail...
Wharton
Lyndale Cl
A5018
The Maples

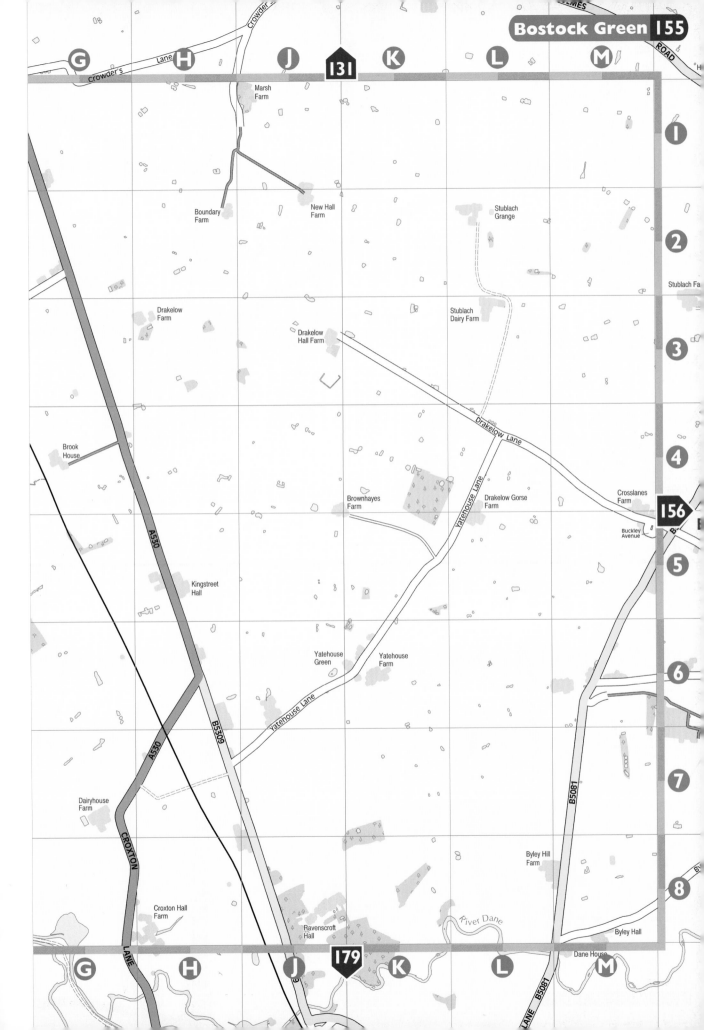

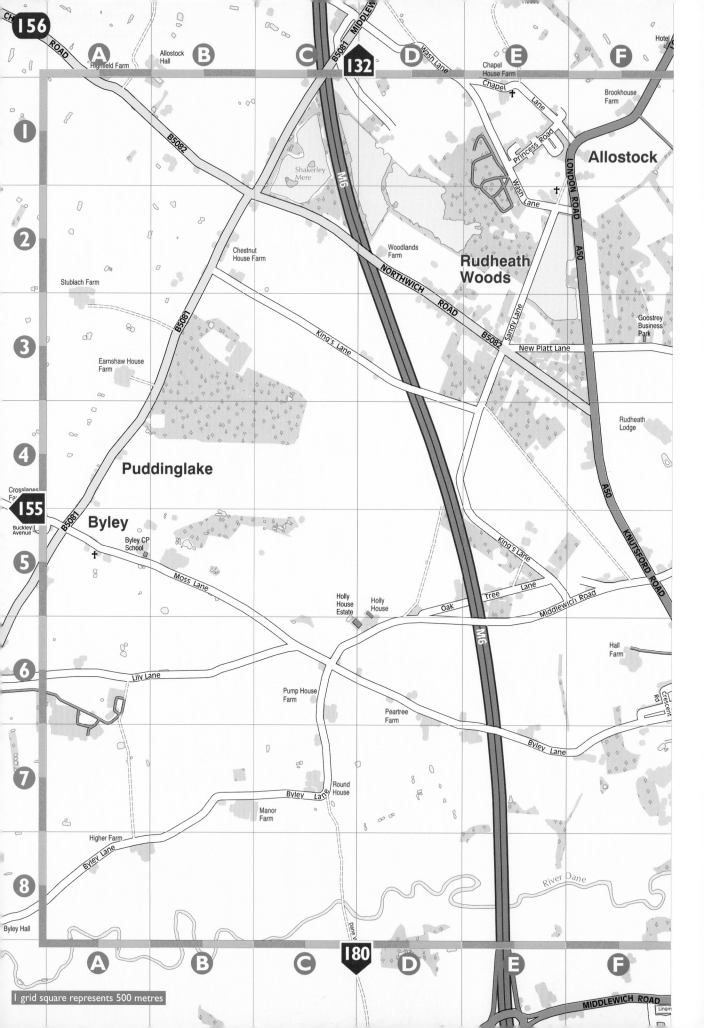

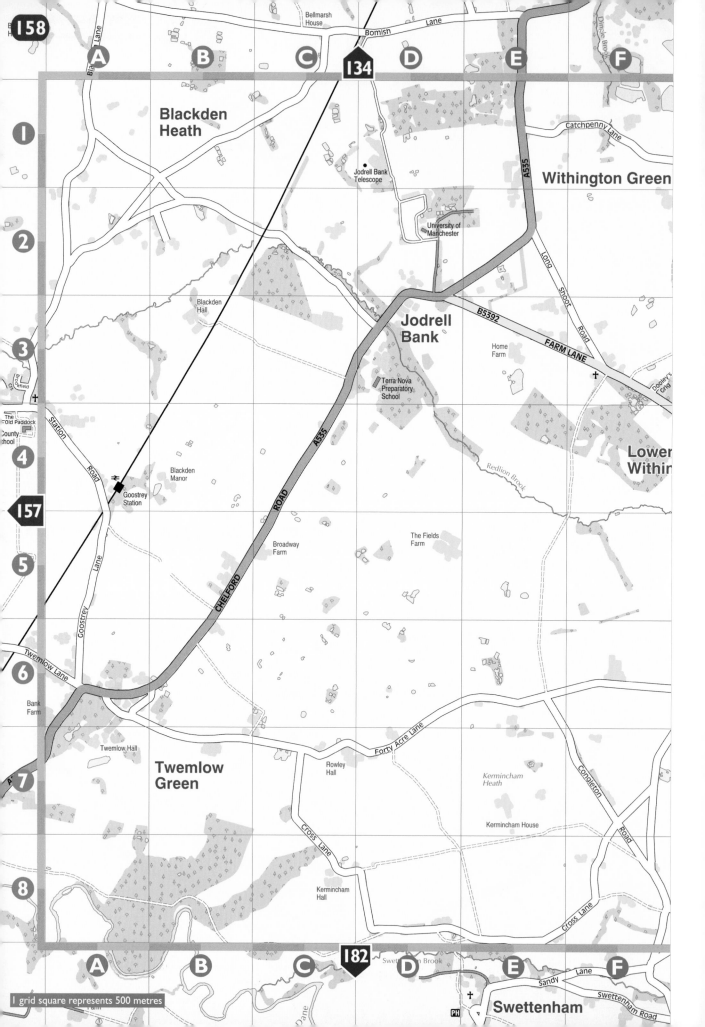

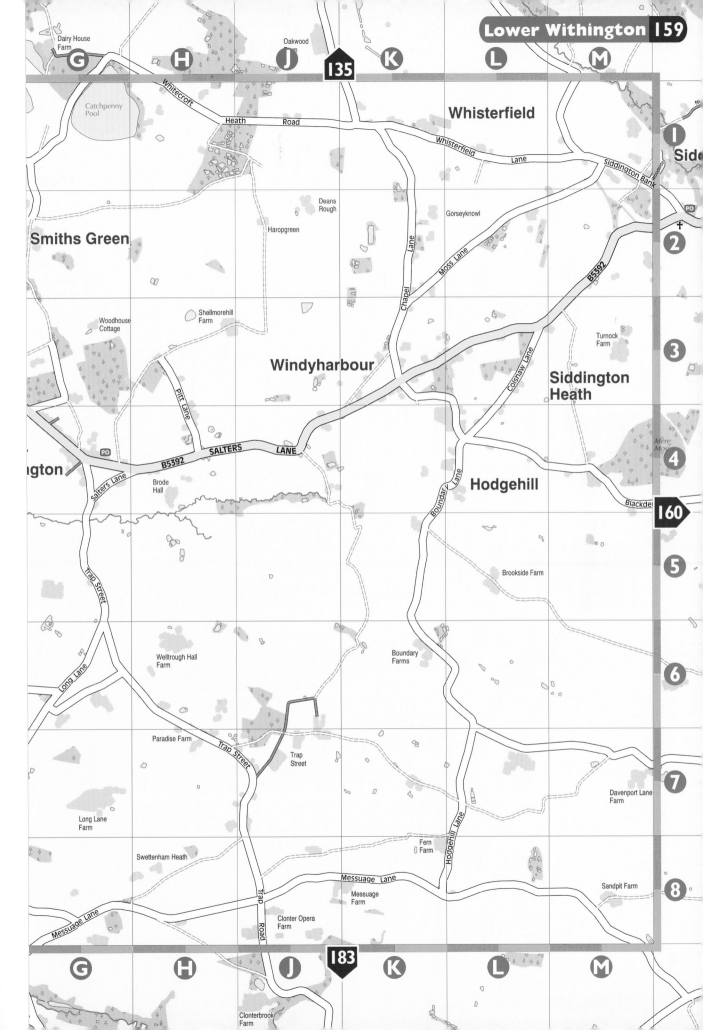

G H J 135 K L M

Dairy House Farm

Catchpenny Pool

Whitecroft

Heath Road

Oakwood

Whisterfield

Whisterfield Lane

Siddington Bank

I

Sid

PO

†

2

Deans Rough

Gorseyknowl

Haropgreen

Smiths Green

Chapel Lane

Moss Lane

B5392

Woodhouse Cottage

Shellmorehill Farm

Turnock Farm

3

Windyharbour

Colshaw Lane

Siddington Heath

Mere Mos

Pitt Lane

4

Brode Hall

B5392

SALTERS LANE

PO

ngton

Salters Lane

Boundary Lane

Hodgehill

Blackde

160

Trap Street

Brookside Farm

5

Long Lane

Welltrough Hall Farm

Boundary Farms

6

Paradise Farm

Trap Street

Trap Street

Davenport Lane Farm

7

Long Lane Farm

Hodgehill Lane

Fern Farm

Sandpit Farm

8

Swettenham Heath

Messuage Lane

Messuage Farm

Trap Road

Messuage Lane

Clonter Opera Farm

G H J 183 K L M

Clonterbrook Farm

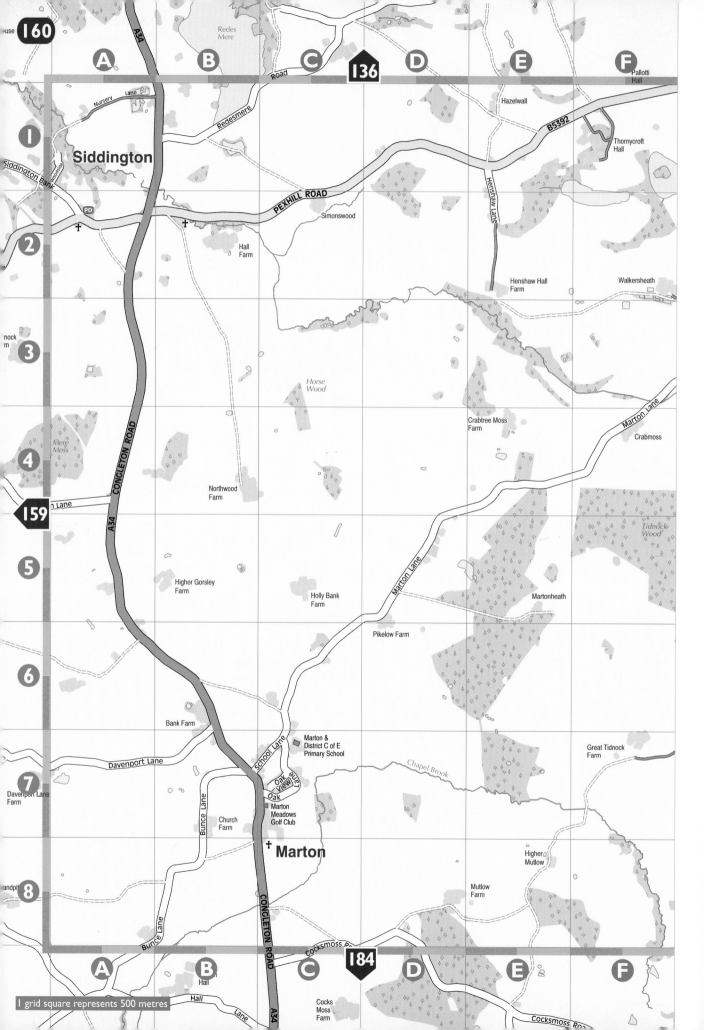

A B C **136** D E F

1

Redes
Mere

Road

Pallotti
Hall

Nursery   Lane

Hazelwall

B5392

Siddington

Thornycroft
Hall

Siddington Bank

Redesmere

PO

PEXHILL ROAD

2

Simonswood

Hall
Farm

Henshaw Lane

Henshaw Hall
Farm

Walkersheath

nock
m

3

Horse
Wood

Crabtree Moss
Farm

Marton Lane

Crabmoss

Mere
Moss

4

CONGLETON ROAD

Northwood
Farm

Tidnock
Wood

159

n Lane

A34

5

Higher Gorsley
Farm

Holly Bank
Farm

Marton Lane

Martonheath

Pikelow Farm

6

Bank Farm

School Lane

Great Tidnock
Farm

Davenport Lane

Marton &
District C of E
Primary School

Chapel Brook

7

Davenport Lane
Farm

Bunce Lane

Oak View Lane

Oak

Church
Farm

Marton
Meadows
Golf Club

Higher
Mutlow

† Marton

Mutlow
Farm

andpit

8

CONGLETON ROAD

Bunce Lane

Hall

Cocksmoss Ro

A34

A B C **184** D E F

Hall

Lane

Cocks
Moss
Farm

Cocksmoss Roa

1 grid square represents 500 metres

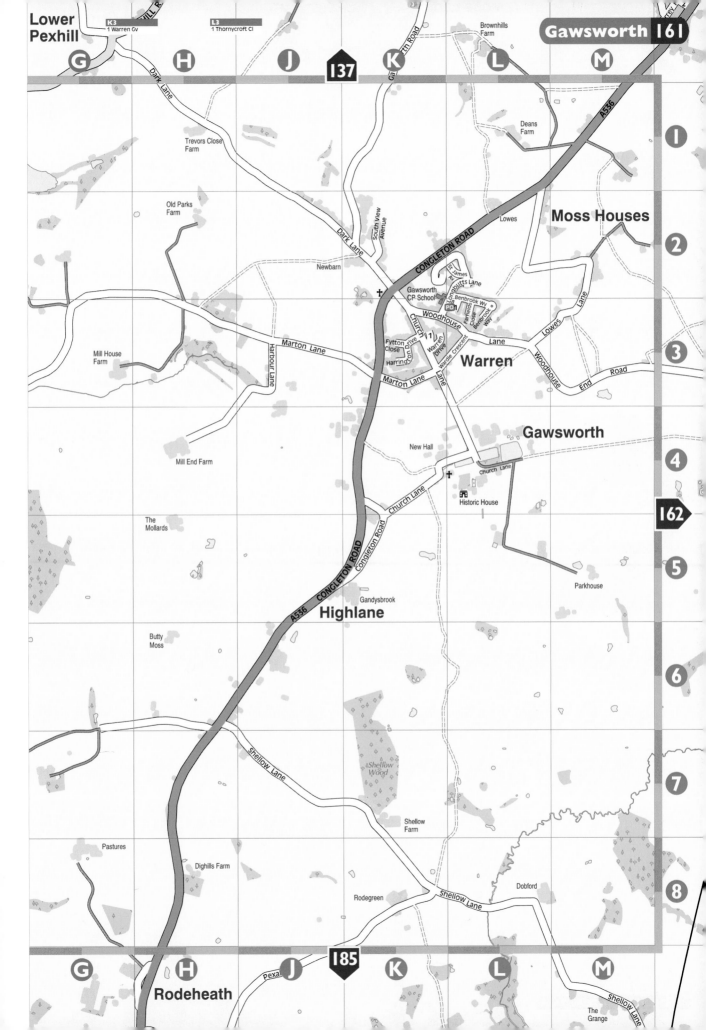

Lower
Pexhill

K3
1 Warren Gv

L3
1 Thornycroft Cl

Trevors Close
Farm

Old Parks
Farm

Newbarn

Dark Lane

Dark Lane

South View Avenue

Mill House
Farm

Harbour Lane

Marton Lane

Mill End Farm

The
Mollards

CONGLETON ROAD

A536

Butty
Moss

Gandysbrook

Highlane

Shellow Lane

Shellow
Wood

Shellow
Farm

Pastures

Dighills Farm

Rodegreen

Shellow Lane

Dobford

Brownhills
Farm

Deans
Farm

A536

CONGLETON ROAD

Lowes

St James Lane

Longbutts Lane

Gawsworth
CP School

Woodhouse Lane

Benbrook Wy

Fairfields
Close

Benbrook
Way

Fytton
Close

Church Drive

Harrington

Warren
Drive

Wardle Crescent

Warren

Church Lane

Marton Lane

Woodhouse

Lane

Lowes
Lane

Woodhouse End Road

Moss Houses

Gawsworth

New Hall

Church Lane

Church Lane

Historic House

Parkhouse

Pexall

Rodeheath

Shellow Lane

The
Grange

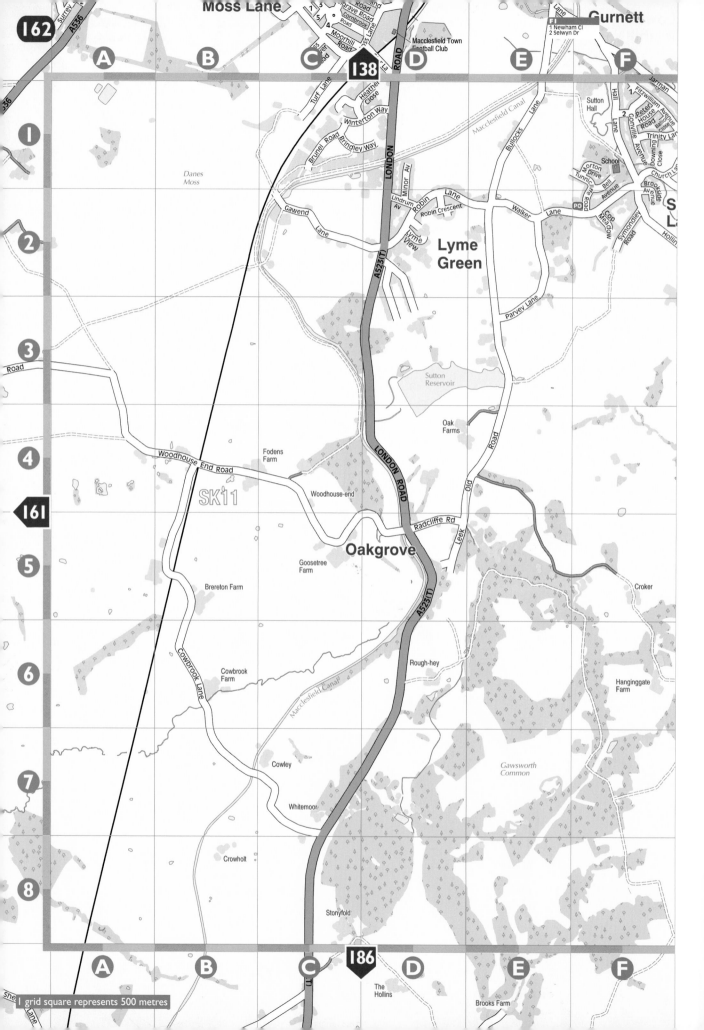

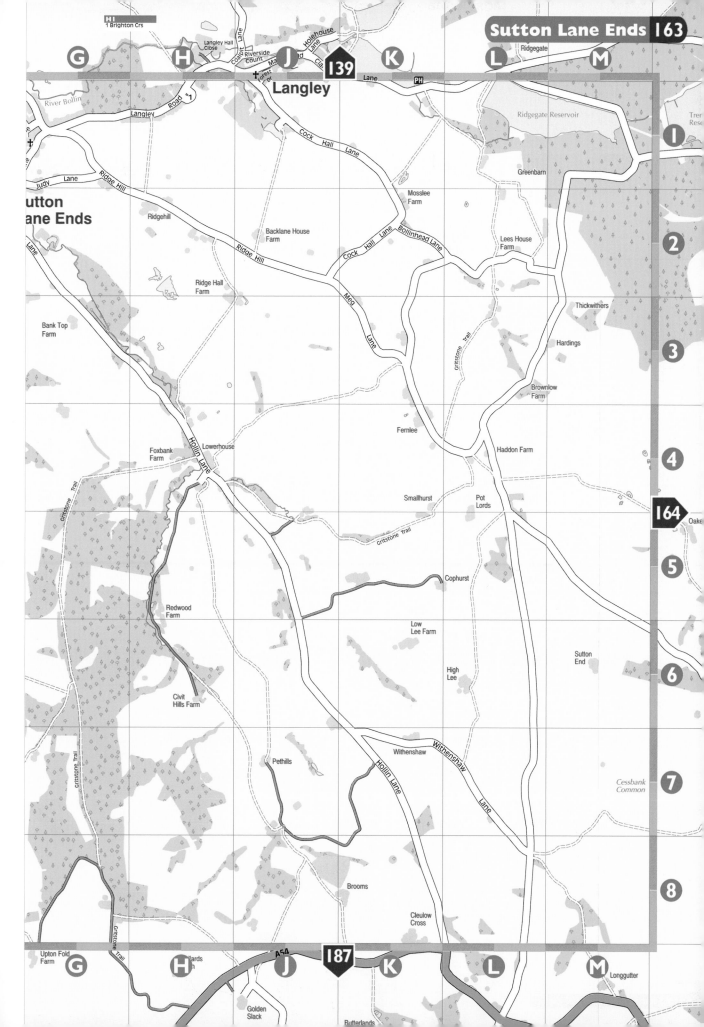

G **H** **J** **K** **L** **M**

HI
1 Brighton Crs

Langley Hall
Close

Coalpit Lane

Riverside
Count

Holehouse
Lane

Forest Dr

Ma

Cla

139

Langley

†

PH

Ridgegate

I

River Bollin

Langley Road

Langley Hall
Close

Cock Hall Lane

Ridgate
Reservoir

Greenbarn

Judy Lane

Ridge Hill

Mosslee
Farm

Ridgehill

Backlane House
Farm

Cock Hall Lane

Bollinhead Lane

Lees House
Farm

2

Sutton
Lane Ends

Ridge Hill

Ridge Hall
Farm

Meg Lane

Gritstone Trail

Thickwithers

Hardings

3

Bank Top
Farm

Brownlow
Farm

Fernlee

Haddon Farm

4

Foxbank
Farm

Lowerhouse

Hollin Lane

Gritstone Trail

Smallhurst

Pot
Lords

164

Oake

Gritstone Trail

Cophurst

5

Redwood
Farm

Low
Lee Farm

Sutton
End

High
Lee

6

Civit
Hills Farm

Gritstone Trail

Pethills

Withenshaw

Withenshaw Lane

Hollin Lane

Cessbank
Common

7

Brooms

Cleulow
Cross

8

Upton Fold
Farm

Gritstone Trail

ards

A54

187

Longgutter

G **H** **J** **K** **L** **M**

Golden
Slack

Butterlands

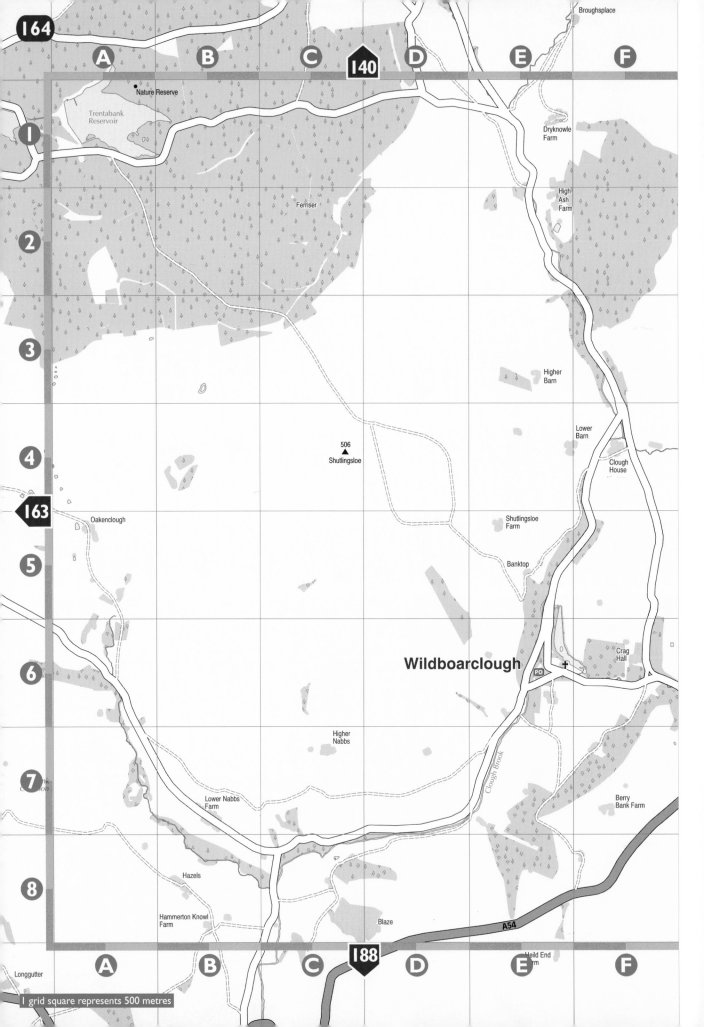

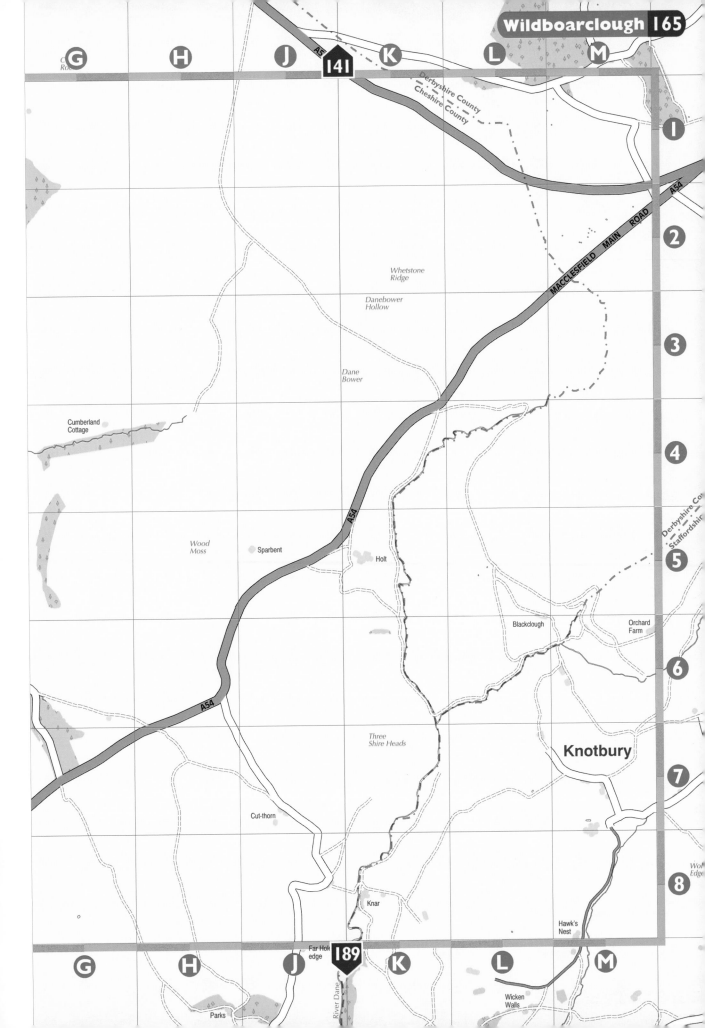

G H J **141** K L M

I

A54

A5

Derbyshire County
Cheshire County

MACCLESFIELD MAIN ROAD

A54

2

3

4

Derbyshire Co...
Staffordshir...

5

*Whetstone
Ridge*

*Danebower
Hollow*

*Dane
Bower*

Cumberland
Cottage

*Wood
Moss*

Sparbent

A54

Holt

Blackclough

Orchard
Farm

6

Three
Shire Heads

Knotbury

7

A54

Cut-thorn

Wo...
Edge...

8

Knar

Hawk's
Nest

G H J **189** K L M

Far Hol...
edge

River Dane

Parks

Wicken
Walls

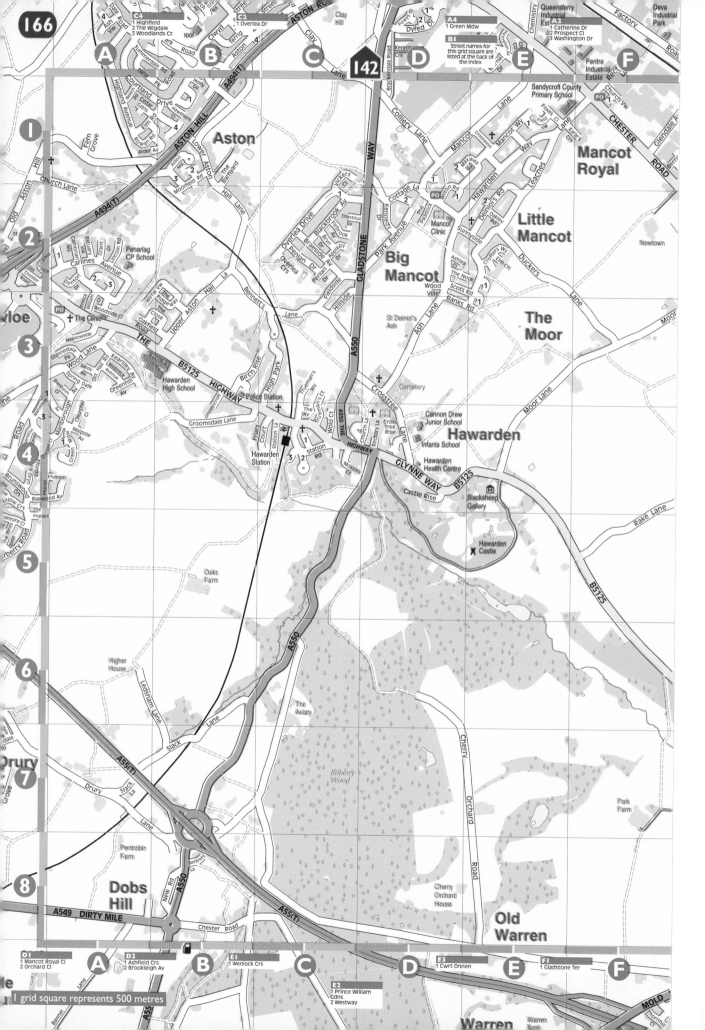

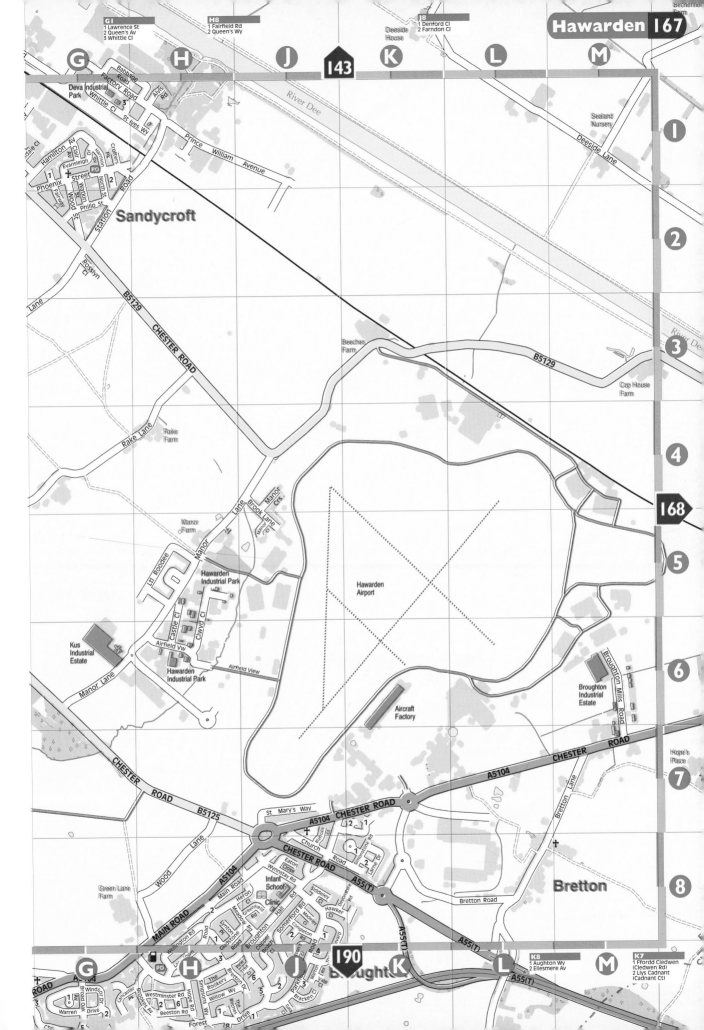

G1
1 Lawrence St
2 Queen's Av
3 Whittle Cl

H8
1 Fairfield Rd
2 Queen's Wy

J8
1 Denford Cl
2 Farndon Cl

Deeside House

G   H   J   143   K   L   M

River Dee

I   2

Deeside Lane

Sealand Nursery

Deva Industrial Park

Babbage Road

Factory Road

Avis Rd

Whittle Cl   St Ives Wy   3

Prince   William   Avenue

River Dee   3

B5129

Hamilton Av   Clair Av   JO St   Harrison   Crofters Pk   PO   North St   2

Phoenix   Evansleigh   Street   Watkin   Wood St   Philip St   Fairway

Sandycroft

Station Road

Cop House Farm

Rosslyn Ct

Lane

B5129   CHESTER ROAD

Beeches Farm

4

Rake Lane   Rake Farm

168

Manor Crks

Brook Lane

Manor Lane

5

Manor Farm

Manor   Ltd   Rogdee

Hawarden Industrial Park

Castle Cl   Clwyd Cl

Hawarden Airport

Broughton Mills Road

6

Kus Industrial Estate

Airfield Vw

Airfield View

Broughton Industrial Estate

Hawarden Industrial Park

Manor Lane

Hope's Place

7

Aircraft Factory

CHESTER   ROAD   A5104

ROAD   B5125   CHESTER   A5104

St Mary's Way   CHESTER ROAD

2   1

Wood   Lane

Church   Road   Simonstone Rd   Lane Dr

Bretton Lane

Green Lane Farm

A5104   Main Road   Eaton Close   Wynnstay Rd

Infant School

Clinic

Siddeley

Broughton

Bretton Road

Bretton

8

MAIN ROAD   Wellington Rd   Heron   Meadow Greenfield Rd   Hall   Somerford Rd   Hawker Cl

A55(T)

Lynton Gladstone   Hope Rd   Copper Beech   Congleton

A55(T)

G   Broad Oak   Windsor Dr   H   The Rookery   J   190   K   L   A55(T)   M

ROAD   A5104   Lancaster   Brookena   Westminster Rd   Bretton Cl   Parkfield   Willow Wy   Broughton   Vale

Warren   Beeston Rd   Hope Rd   The Birches   The Drive   Bracken

Forest

K8
1 Aughton Wy
2 Ellesmere Av

K7
1 Ffordd Cledwen
(Cledwen Rd)
2 Llys Cadnant
(Cadnant Ct)

A B C **144** D E F **Blacon**

Blacon
County
High School

Highfield
Junior &
School

Virgin
Cinemas

Megabowl

Chaser Ct

1

Birchenfields
Farm

Bank
Farm

Point House
Farm

SEALAND ROAD A548

Chester City
Council
Way

2

Thornleigh
Park

Ferry Lane
Farm

Chantry
Court

Knutsford Way

Winsford Way

3

River Dee

Cop House
Farm

Ferry Lane

Fir Tree
Farm

Chester City
Football Club

Chester
City
Council

Border
House

River Dee

4

Higher Ferry
House

Mill
Farm

Bumper's Lane

Cheshire County
Flintshire

167

North
St

Ewart Street

Brymau One
Trading Estate

5

Brymau Five
Trading Estate

Chesterbank
Business
Park

River Lane

Brymau Three
Trading Estate

Brymau
Two Trading
Estate

CHESTER STREET

Brymau
Four Trading Estate

St Davids
Trading Estate

Marley Wy

Wood
Memorial CP
School

6

Well House
Farm

St Davids
High School

Saltney Clinic

CHESTER ROAD A5104

HIGH STREET

School

Lache

7

Hope's
Place

Saltney

8

Bretton
Hall

Flintshire
shire County

A B C **191** D E F

The Laene
Eyes

1 grid square represents 500 metres

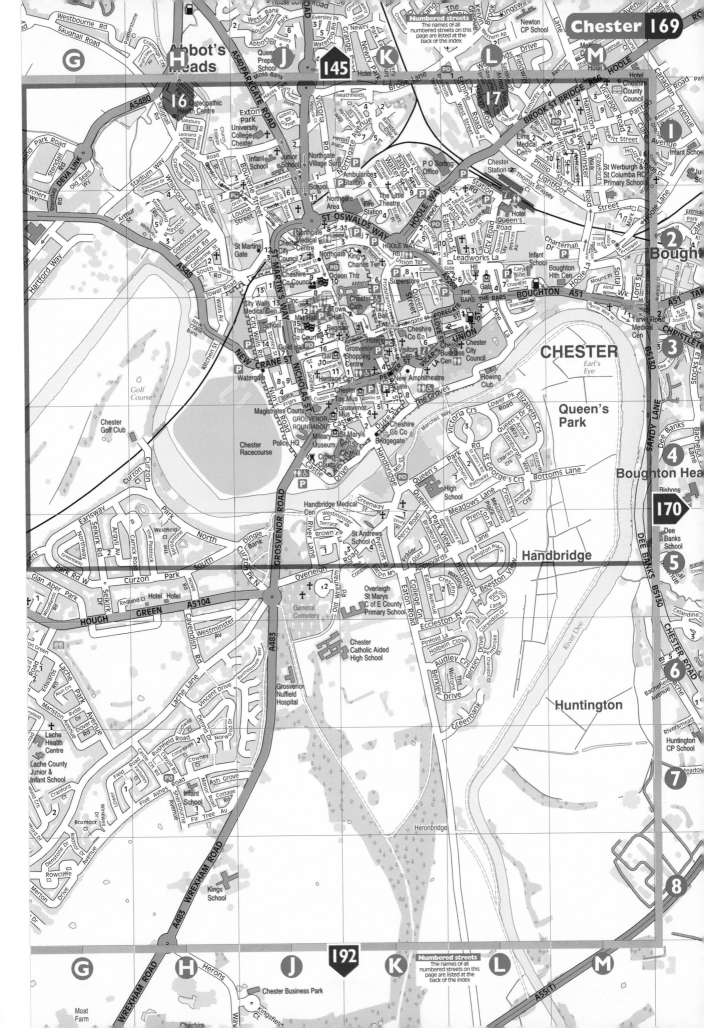

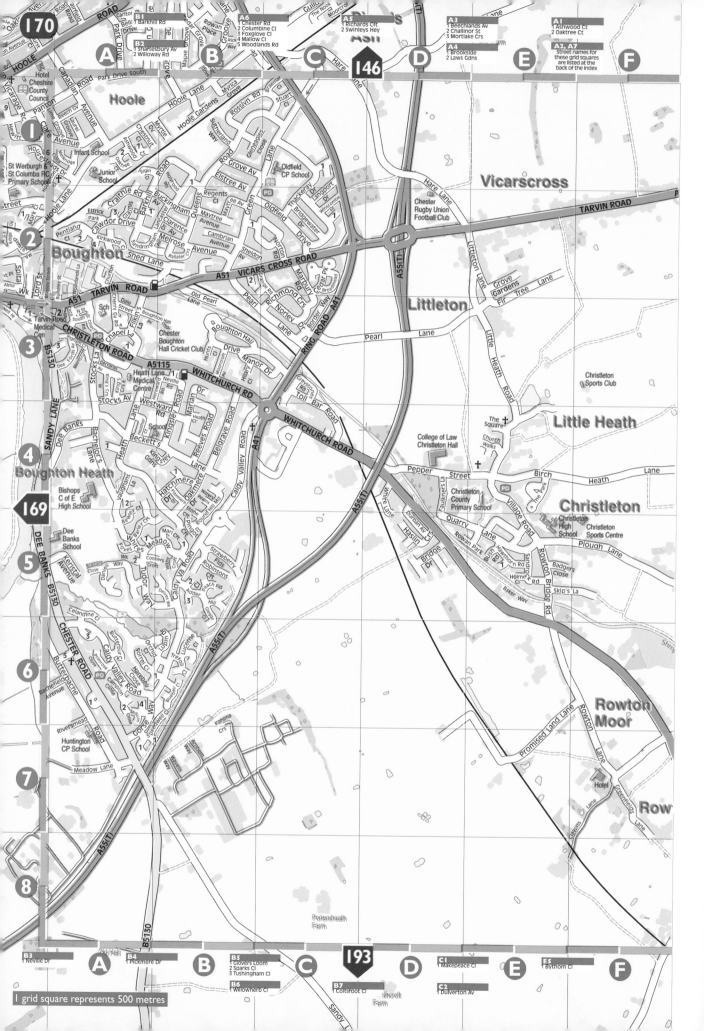

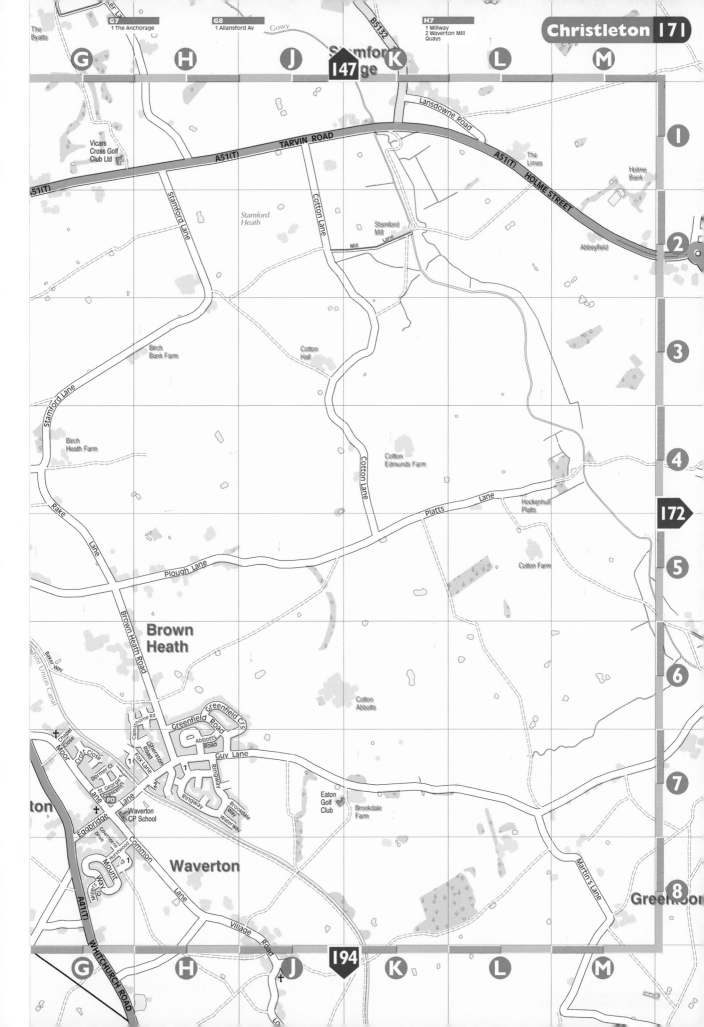

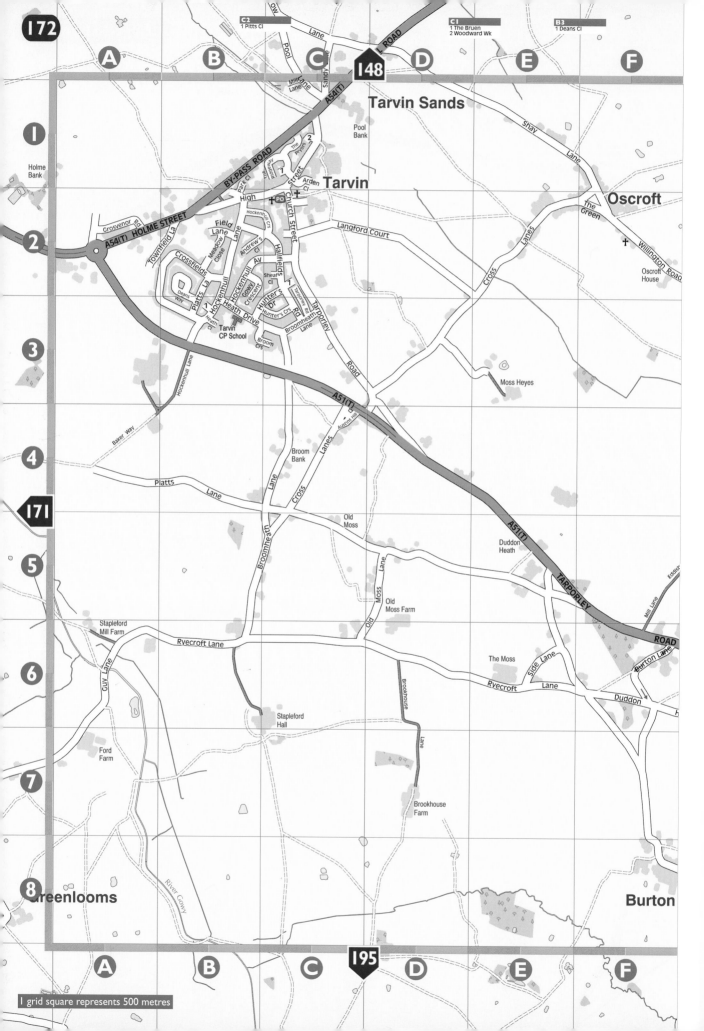

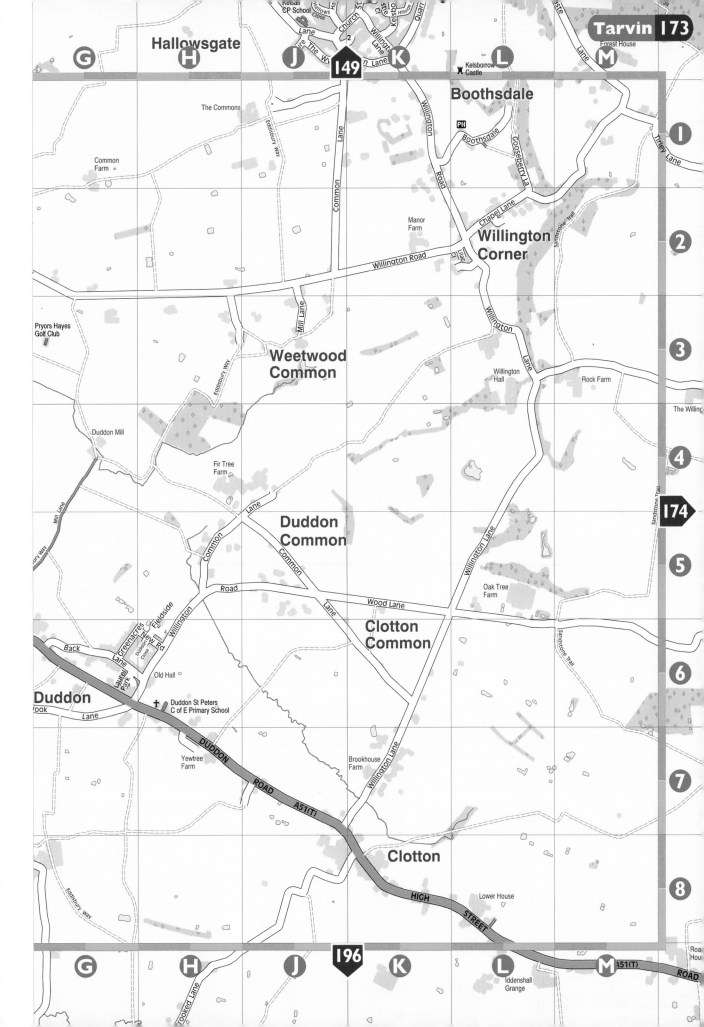

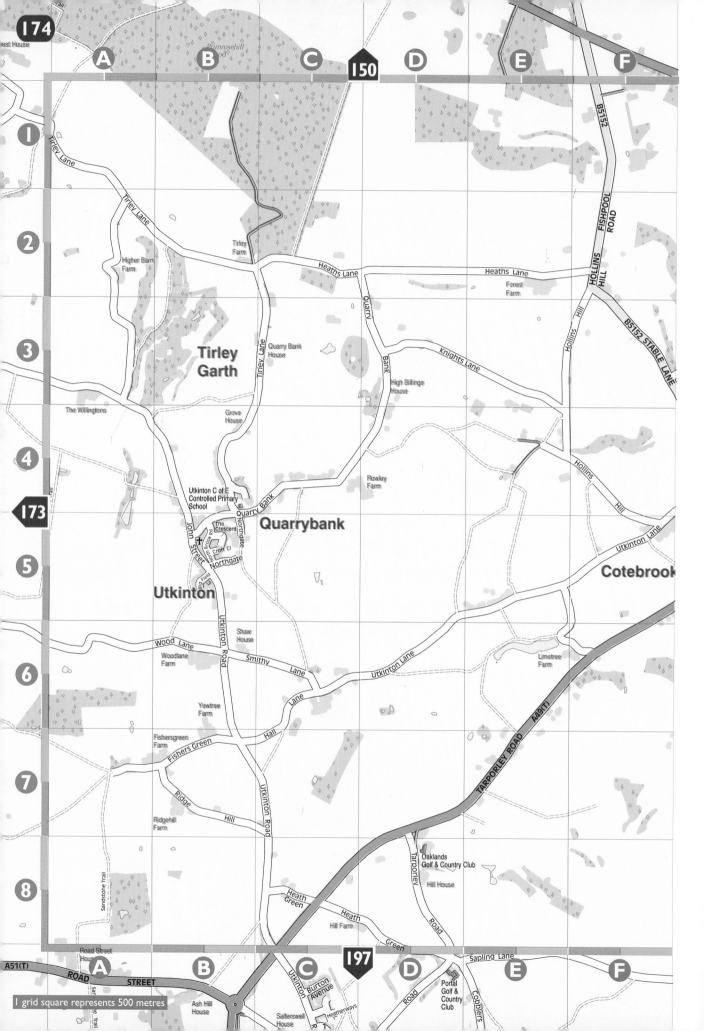

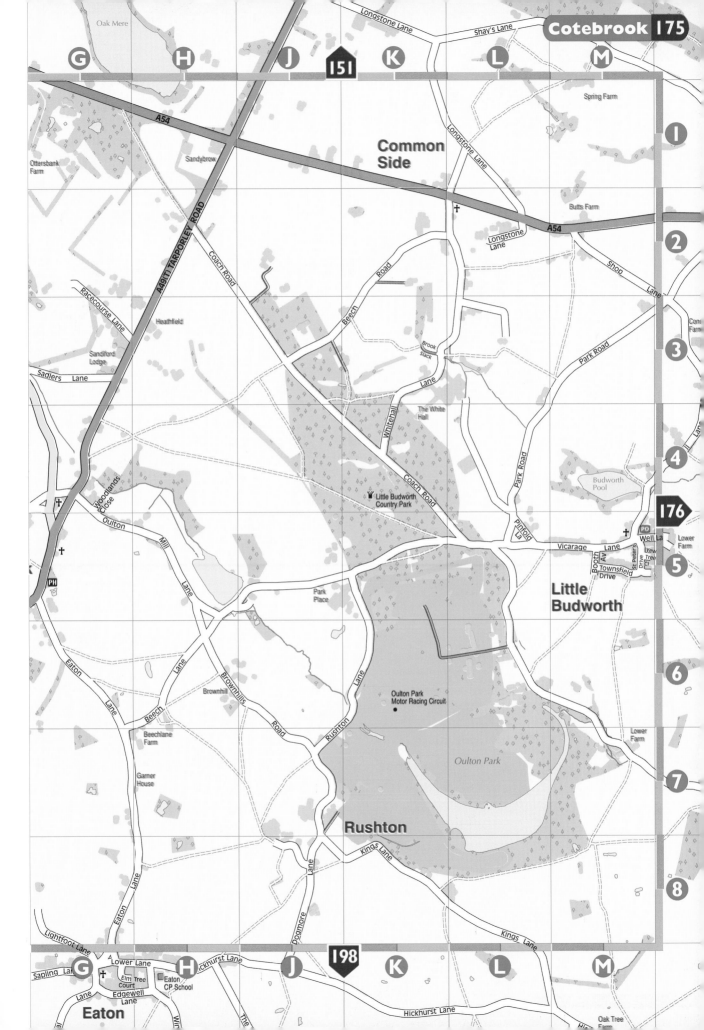

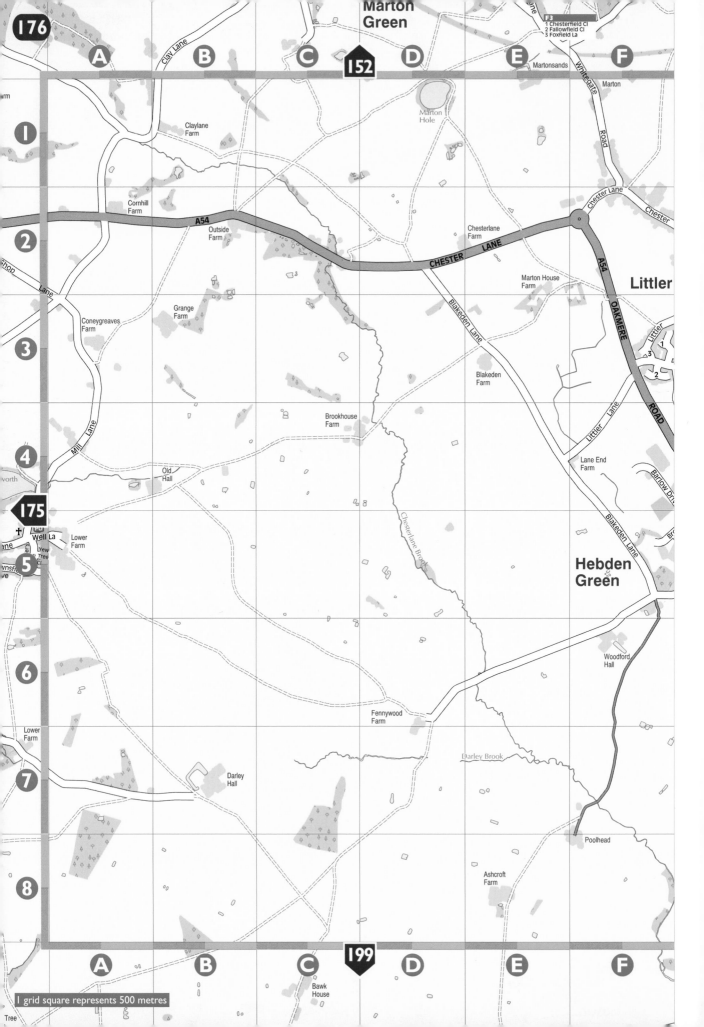

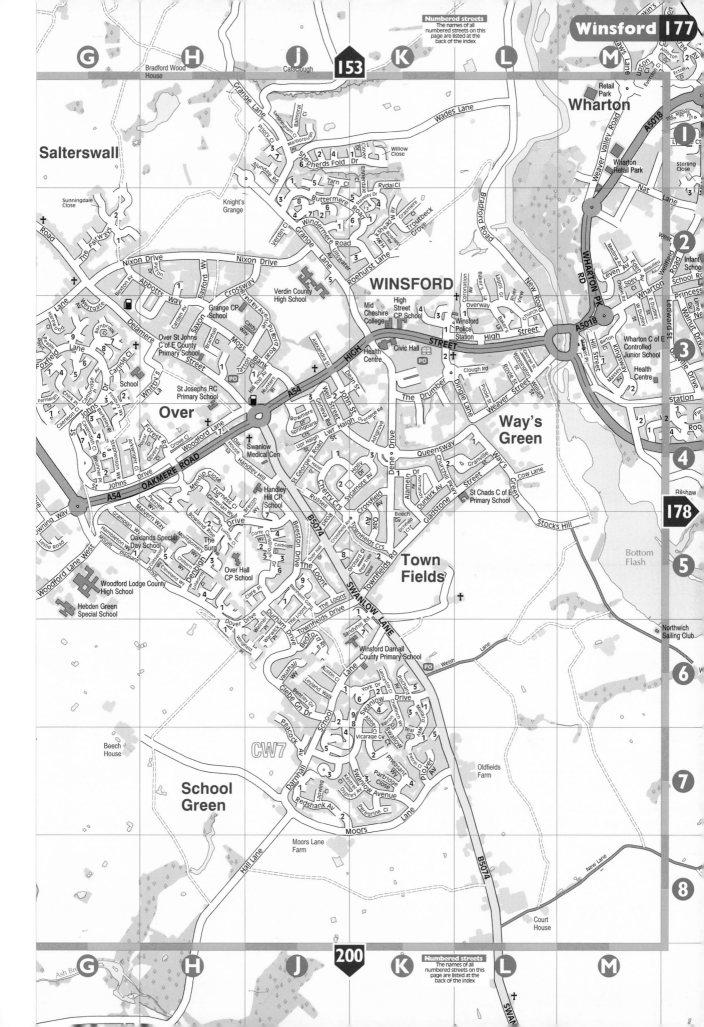

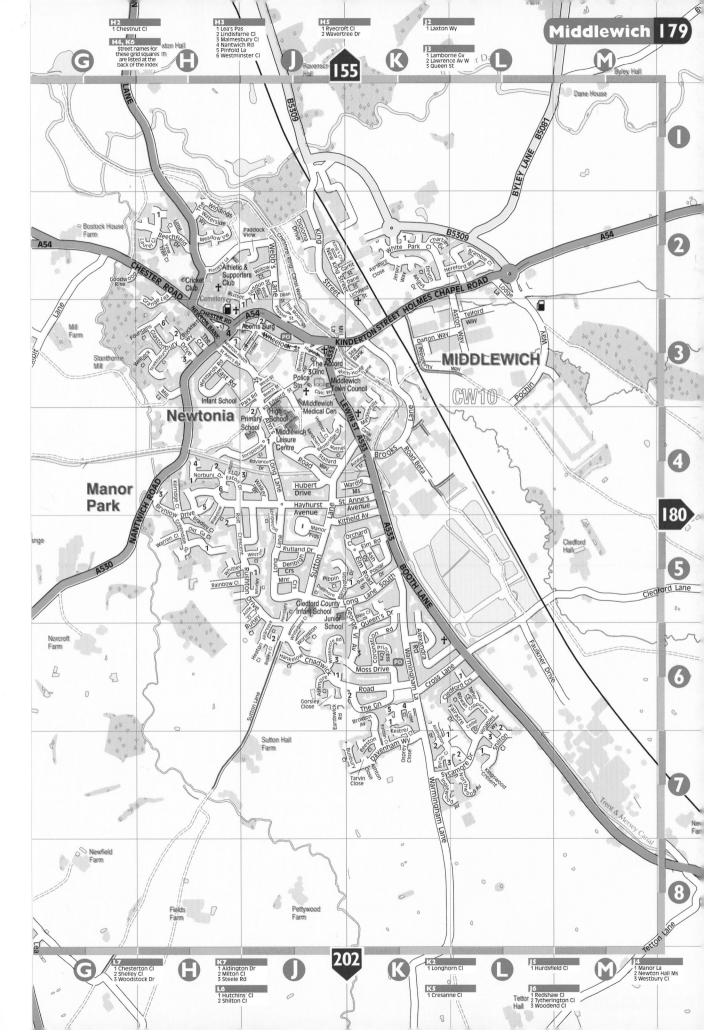

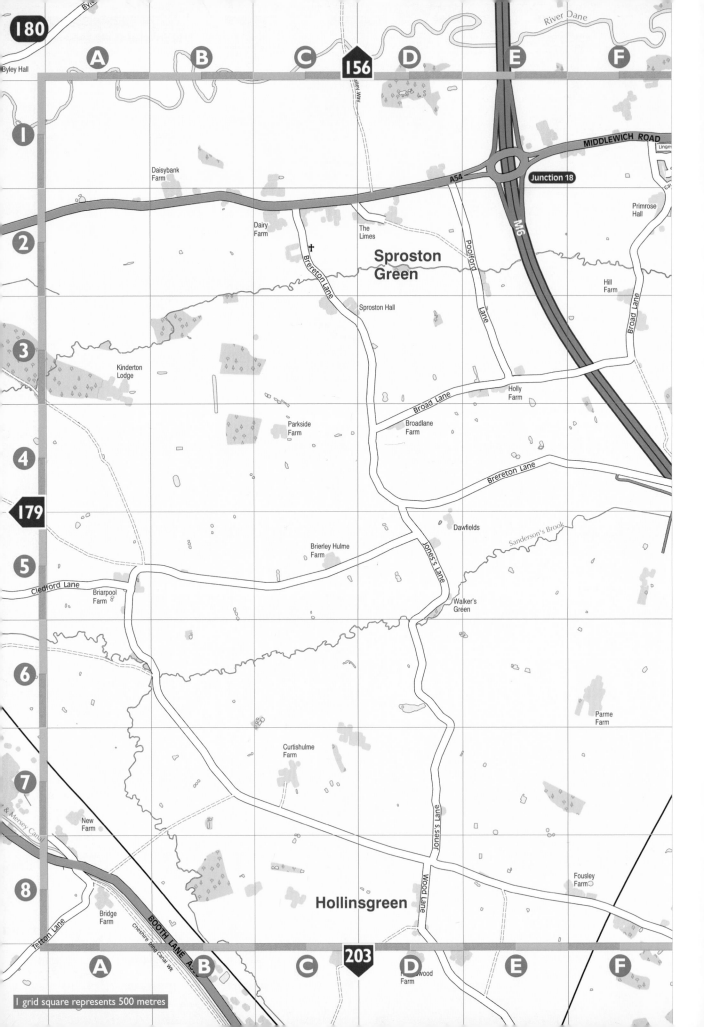

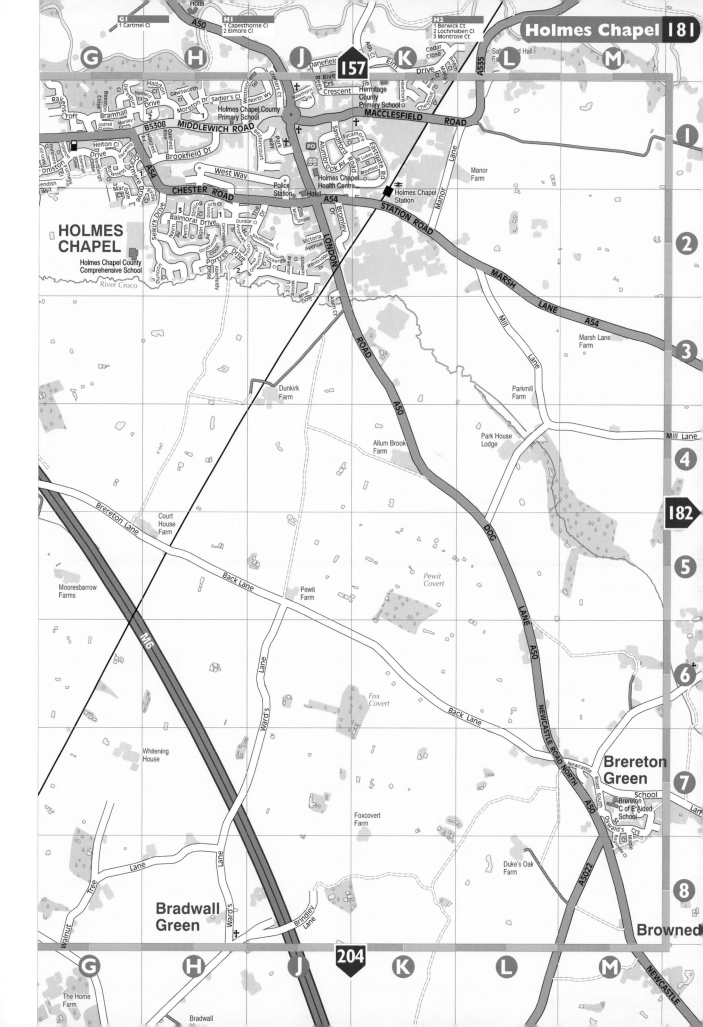

G1
1 Cartmel Cl

H1
1 Capesthorne Cl
2 Elmore Cl

H2
1 Berwick Ct
2 Lochmaben Cl
3 Montrose Ct

G H J 157 K L M

A50

Danefield

Crofters Ct
Rive Rees
Hawthorn
Crescent

Hermitage
County
Primary School

Ash Cl
Elm Cl
Cedar Close
Beech
Maple

A535
Sa... Hall

MACCLESFIELD   ROAD

I

MIDDLEWICH ROAD
B5308

Ravenscroft
Bramhall
Hadron
Drive
Gawsworth Cl
Sadler's Cl
Moreton Dr
Manley
Jodrell
Hatfield
Dene
Oakfield Rise

Holmes Chapel County
Primary School

North Wy
Westmorland
Park Way
Beswicourt

Chestnut

Manor
Farm

Holmes Chapel

Coniston
Furness
Drive
Helton Cl
Hillcrest
Brookfield Dr
Ellesmere Drive
A54
Brookfield Dr

West Way

CHESTER ROAD

Police
Station

Holmes Chapel
Health Centre

PO

Sandiford
Road
Alumbrook Av
Sycamore
Eastgate Rd
Mayfield
St Lukes

Lane
Manor

Station Drive

2

HOLMES
CHAPEL

Holmes Chapel County
Comprehensive School

Selkirk Drive
Nairn
Perth
Elgin Av
Stirling
Loch Ct
Dunbar Cl
Andrews
Southlands
Balmoral Drive
Strathmore
Glenashlee
Lockerbie
Braemar
Glendon
Dunoon
Aberfeldy
Arran Close
Portree Drive
Victoria
Avenue
Galloway
Ironbridge Dr
Bromley
Dr
LONDON

A54
Holmes Chapel
Station

STATION ROAD

A54

Mill Lane
MARSH   LANE   A54

Manor
Farm

I

River Croco

ROAD

A50

Dunkirk
Farm

Allum Brook
Farm

Park House
Lodge

Parkmill
Farm

Marsh Lane
Farm

Mill Lane

3

4

182

Brereton Lane

Court
House
Farm

Back Lane

Mooresbarrow
Farms

M6

Pewit
Farm

Ward's

Lane

Pewit
Covert

DOG

LANE

A50

5

6

Whitening
House

Fox
Covert

Back Lane

NEWCASTLE ROAD NORTH

Newcastle
Road
South

Brereton
Green

School
Brereton
C of E Aided
School

7

Foxcovert
Farm

Duke's Oak
Farm

St Oswald's
Maple Crs

A5022

Tree
Lane
Walnut
Lane

Bradwall
Green

Ward's
Lane

Brindley
Lane

A50

Browned

8

The Home
Farm

Bradwall

G H J 204 K L M

NEWCASTLE

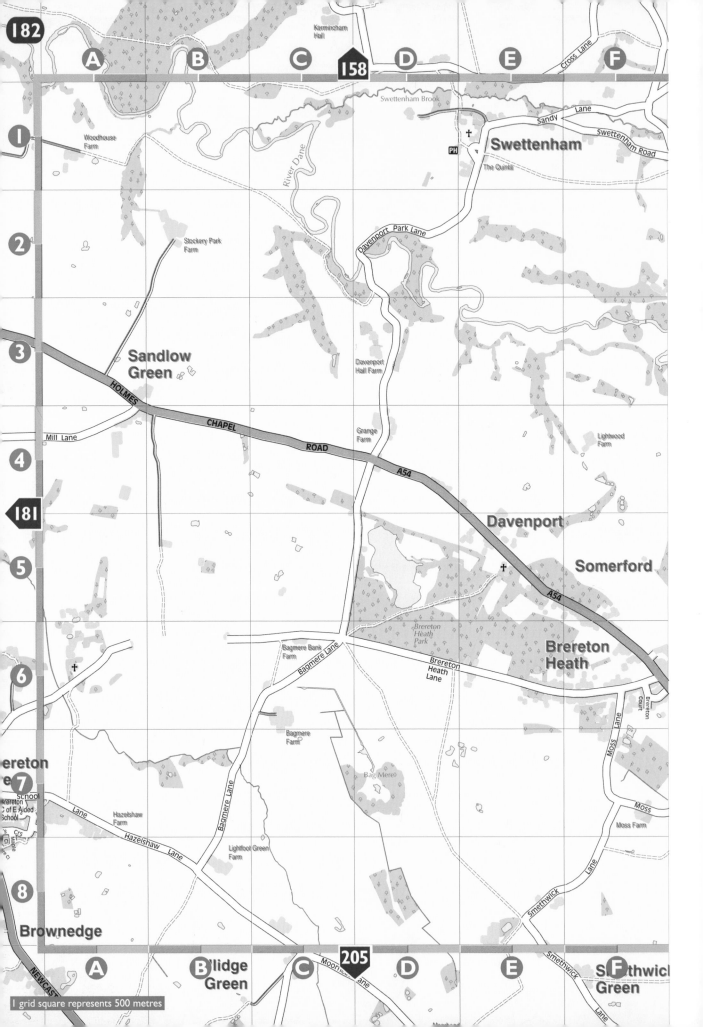

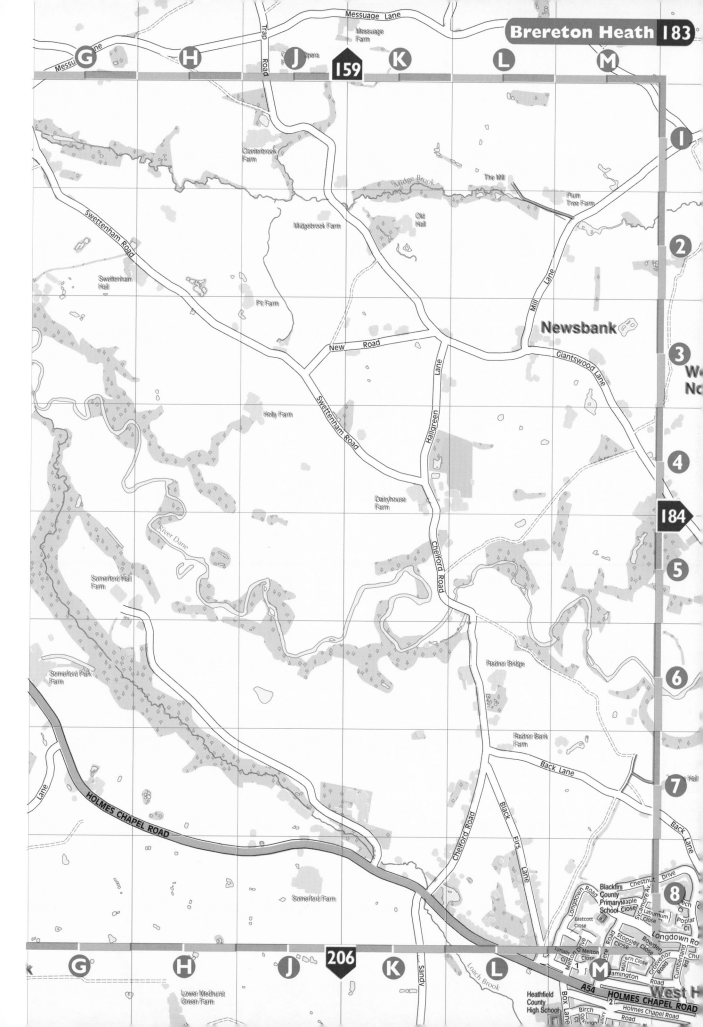

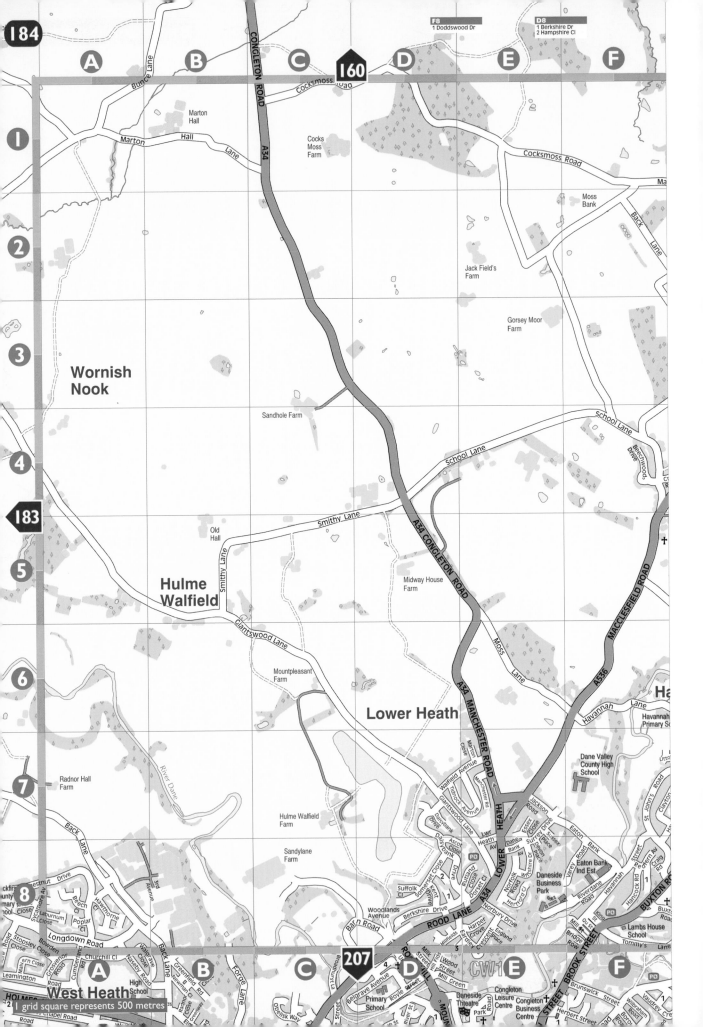

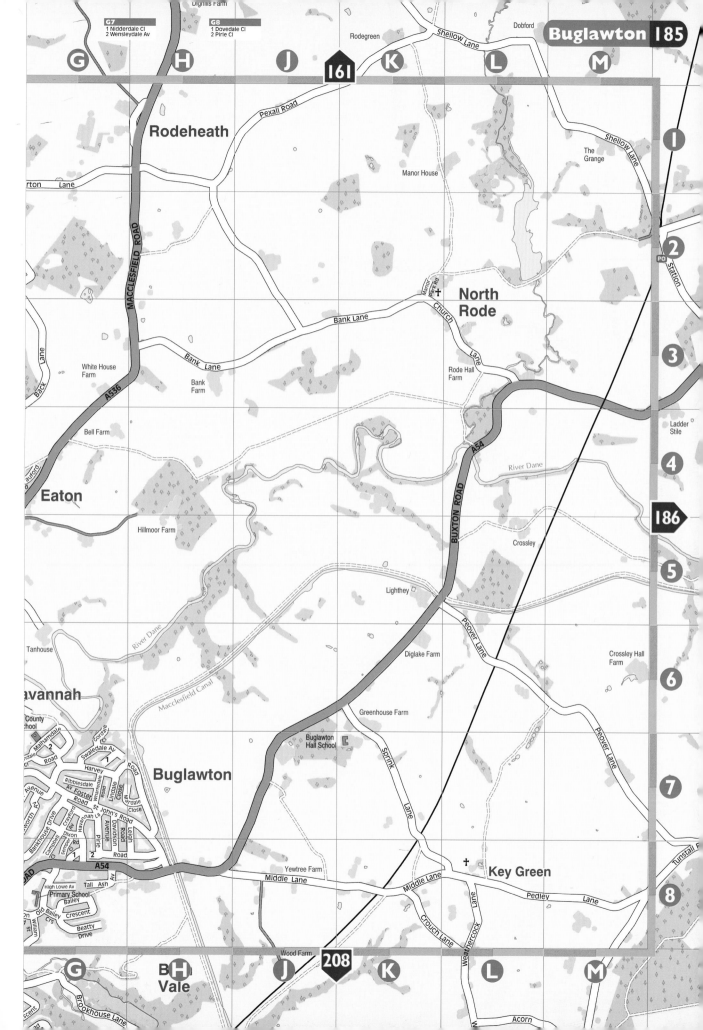

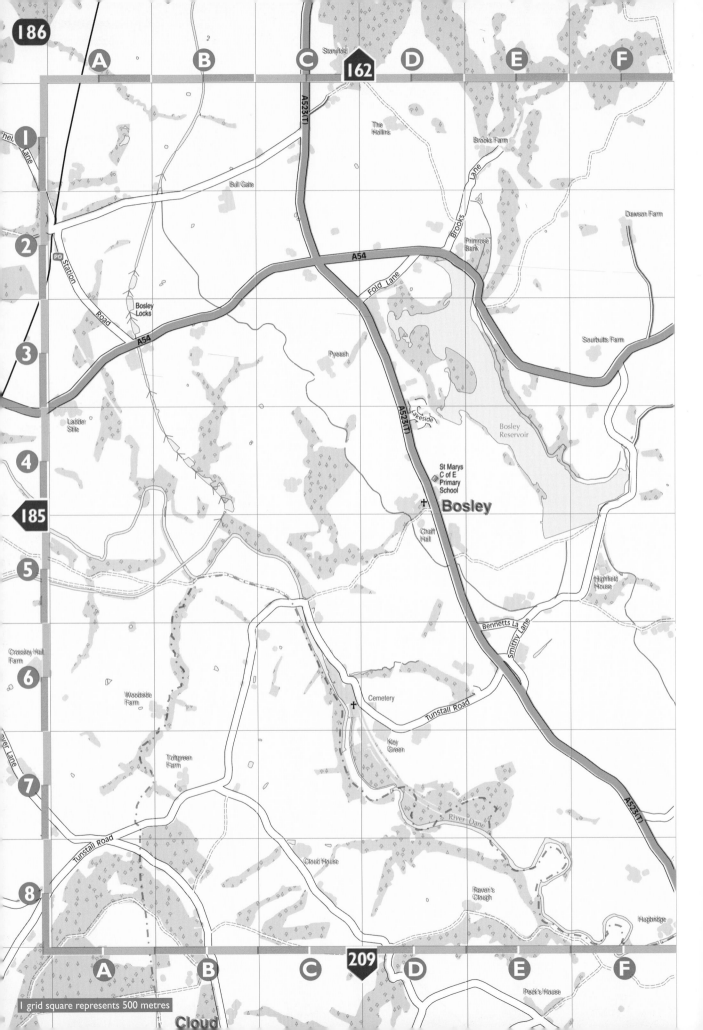

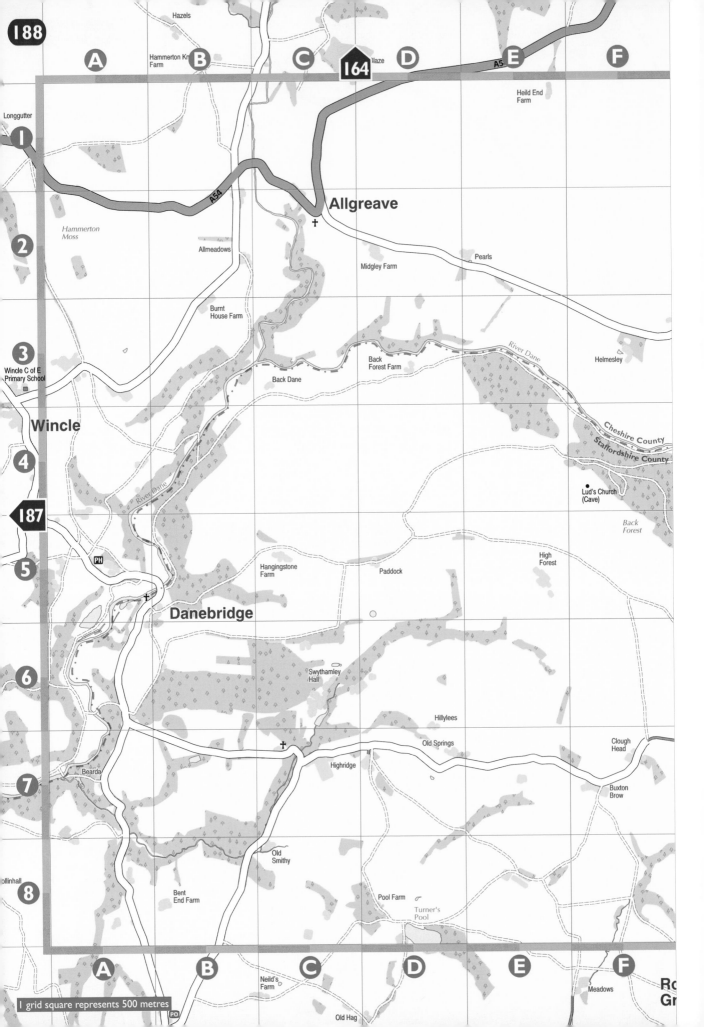

G H J K L M

165

I
2
3
4
5
6
7
8

Knar
Far Hole-edge
River Dane
Parks

Hawk's Nest
Wicken Walls

Spring Head

Greens
Wildstone Rock

Burntcliff Top
Wildstone Rock

Flash Bottom

Gradbach
Green Gutter Head

Middle Edge
Little Hillend

Black Brook

Goldsitch Moss

Roach End
Goldsitch House
Blackbank
Black Brook

Brownsett
Newstone Farm
Shaw Bottom

Hazel Barrow

G H J K L M

The Roaches

oche ange

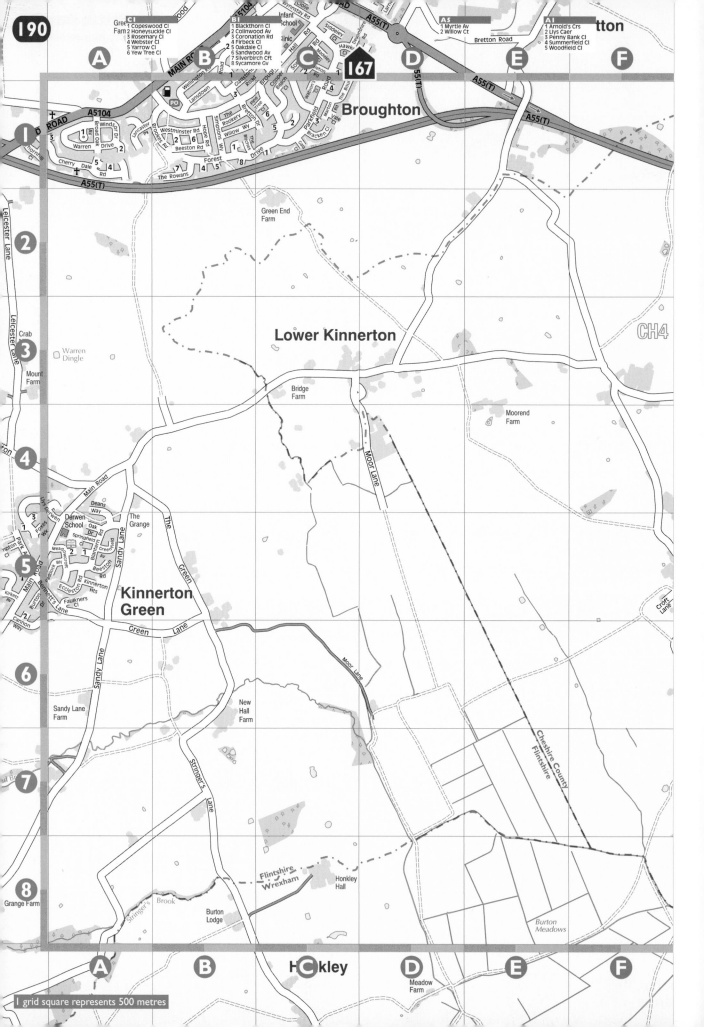

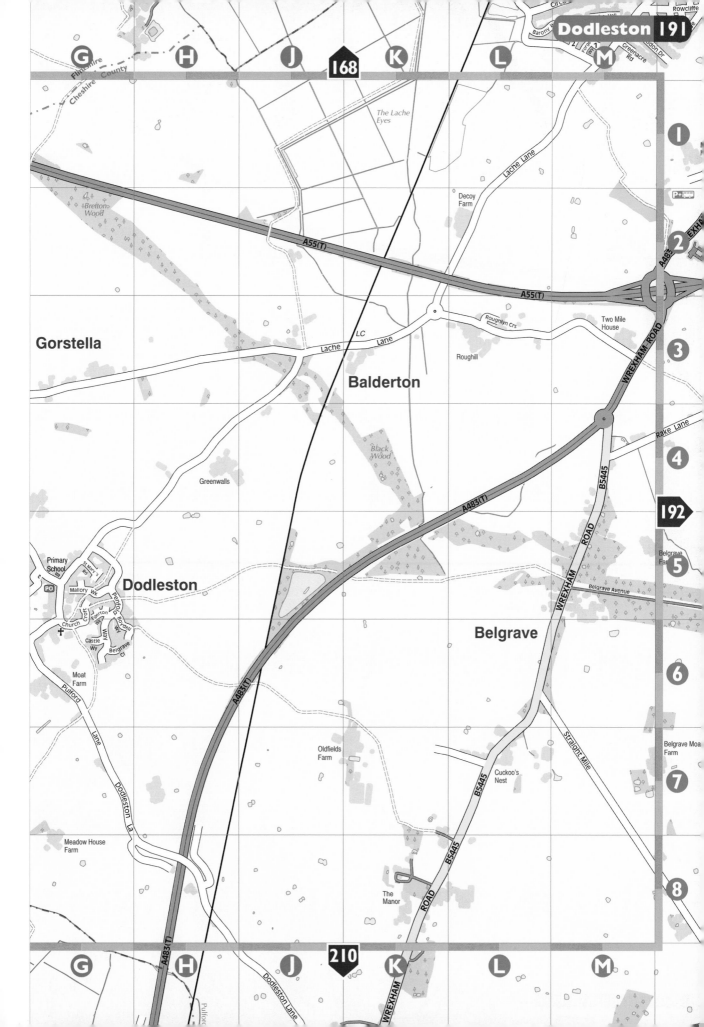

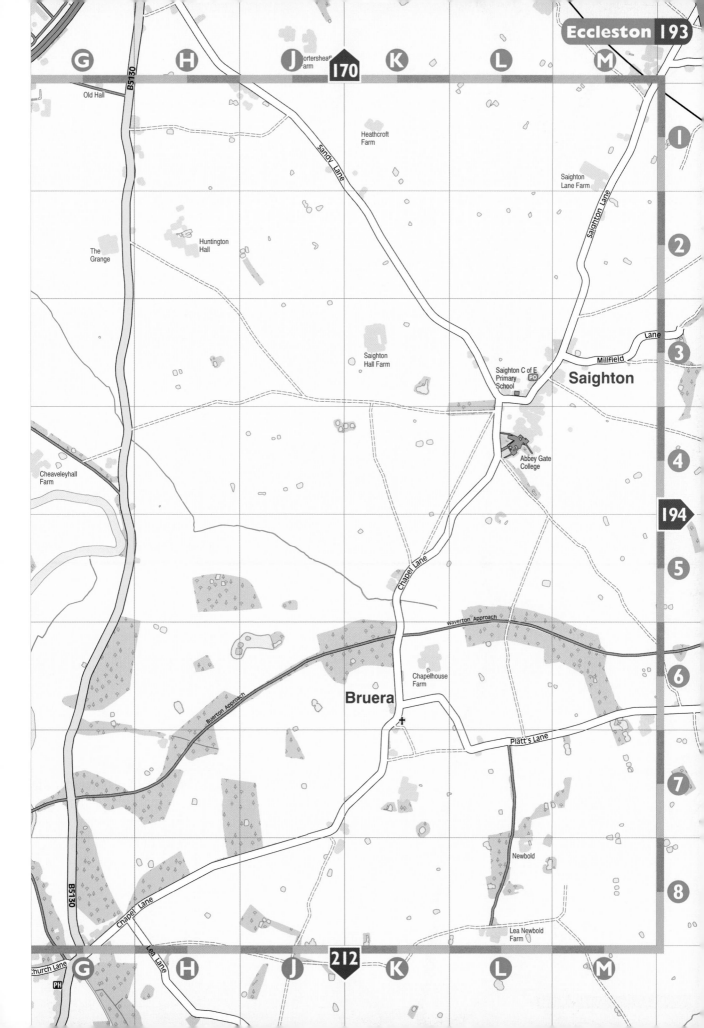

G H J 170 K L M

I
2
3
4
194
5
6
7
8

Old Hall

B5130

Sandy Lane

Heathcroft Farm

ortersheath Farm

Saighton Lane Farm

Saighton Lane

The Grange

Huntington Hall

Saighton Hall Farm

Saighton C of E Primary School PO

Millfield

Lane

Saighton

Abbey Gate College

Cheaveleyhall Farm

Chapel Lane

Waverton Approach

Chapelhouse Farm

Bruera

Buerton Approach

Platt's Lane

Newbold

B5130

Chapel Lane

Lea Lane

Lea Newbold Farm

Church Lane

PH

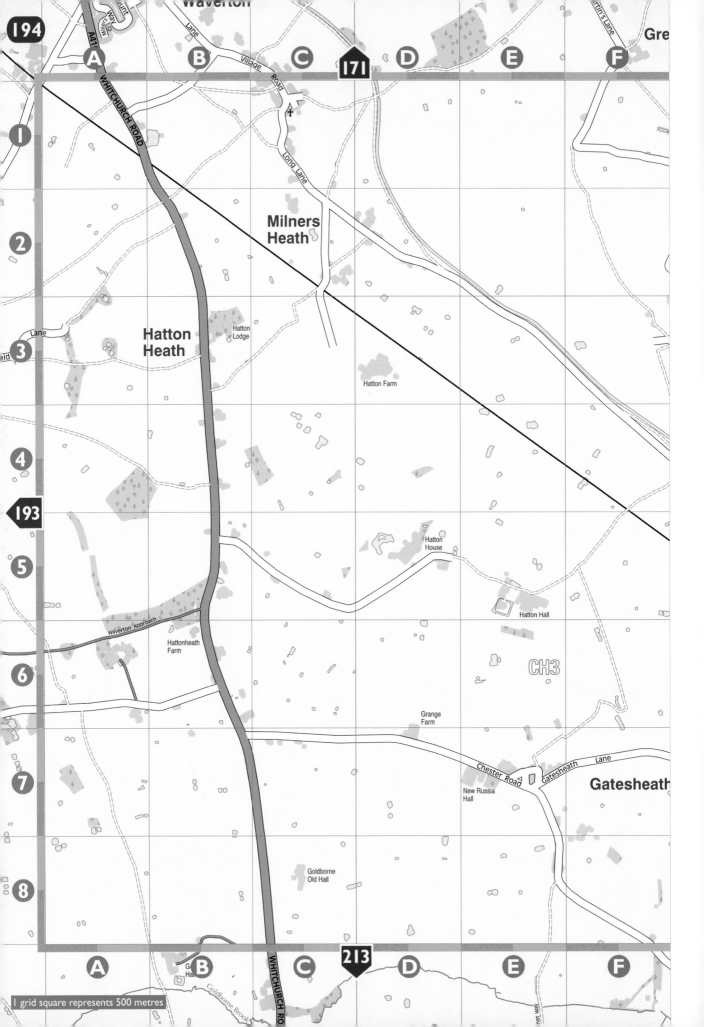

Gre

A **B** **C** 171 **D** **E** **F**

Waverton

Village Road

Long Lane

I

**Milners
Heath**

2

Lane

**Hatton
Heath**
Hatton
Lodge

3

Hatton Farm

4

193

Hatton
House

5

Hatton Hall

Waverton Approach

6
Hattonheath
Farm

CH3

Grange
Farm

Chester Road
Gatesheath Lane

7
New Russia
Hall

Gatesheath

Goldborne
Old Hall

8

WHITCHURCH ROAD

A41 WHITCHURCH ROAD

A **B** **C** 213 **D** **E** **F**

Goldborne Brook

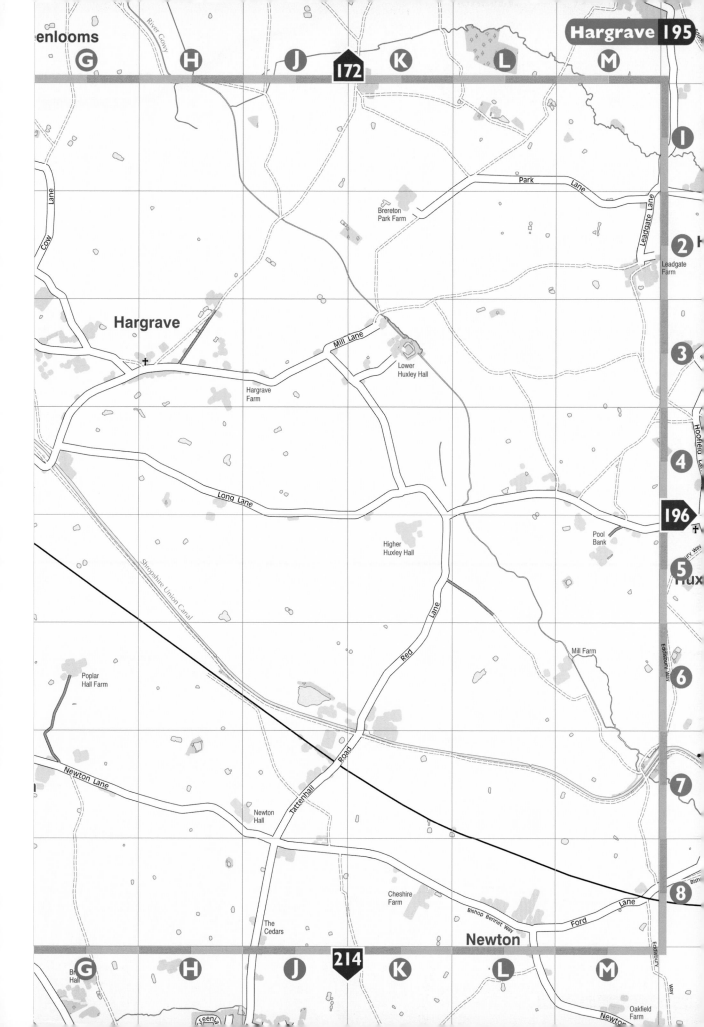

enlooms

Greenlooms

G

River Cowy

H

J

172

K

L

M

I

2

Park Lane

Brereton
Park Farm

Leadgate
Farm

Leadgate Lane

Hargrave

†

Mill Lane

Lower
Huxley Hall

Hargrave
Farm

3

Hoofield Lane

4

196 †

Long Lane

Shropshire Union Canal

Higher
Huxley Hall

Pool
Bank

Hux

5

Cow Lane

Poplar
Hall Farm

Red Lane

Mill Farm

Edgbury Way

6

Newton Lane

Tattenhall Road

7

Newton
Hall

8

Cheshire
Farm

Ford Lane

Bishop Bennet Way

Eddisbury Way

The
Cedars

Newton

G

Br
Hall

H

J

214

K

L

M

Oakfield
Farm

Newton

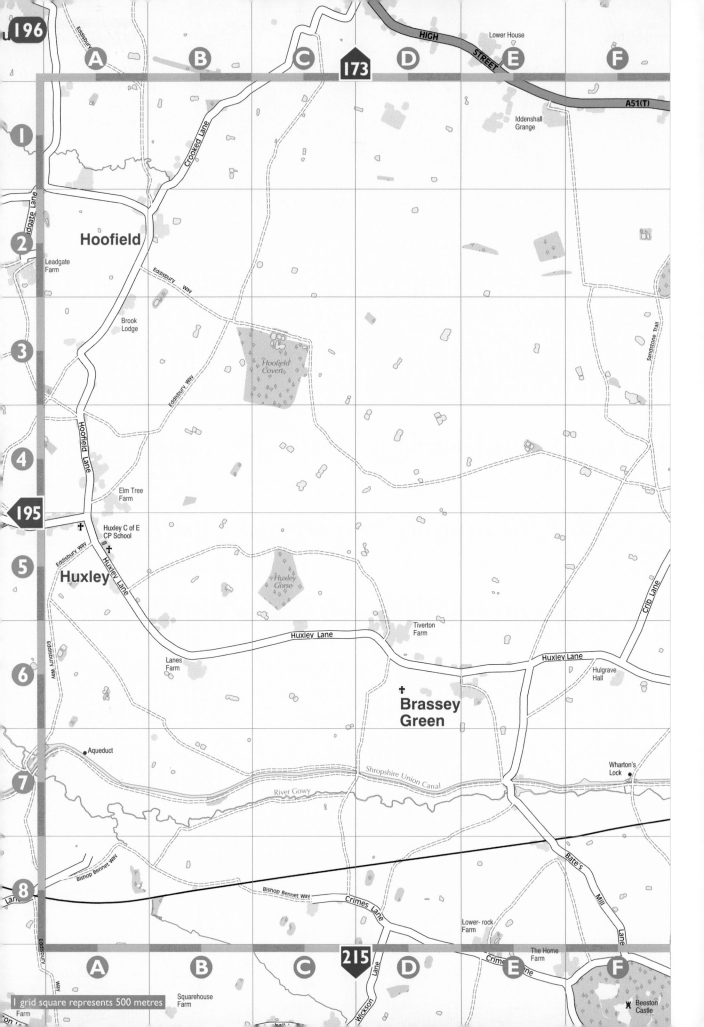

G   H   J   K   L   M

J1 1 The Blythings
J2 1 Henry St
J3 1 Bridgedown

174

Road Street House
Ash Hill House
ROAD STREET
Sandstone Trail
Back Lane
A49(T)
Moss Lane
Utkinton Road
Heath Green
Hill F

Burton Avenue
Salterswell House
Heatherways
Cedarwood Court

Forest Road
Woodlands Way
Lime Cl
Fir Cl
High Street
Mill Field
South
Elm Cl
Ash Cl
Chestnut Cl
Oaktree

Sapling Lane
Portal Golf & Country Club
Cobblers Cross Lane
Portal
Arderne Hall
Eaton Lane
Royal
Sapling La
Lightfo

Tarporley

PO
Bell Meadow Court
Market Court
Park Road
Tarporley War Memorial Hospital
Doctors Surgery
Police Station
Tarporley C of E (Controlled) Primary School
Copperfields
Torrise
Greenland
Peakwood
Close
Foxhill Ct
Rhuddall Heath
Flaxyard Farm

The Avenue
Oathills Cl
Oathills Drive
Churchill Dr
Eaton Road
Walkers Lane
CW6

Meadowfield
Honey Flds
Tarporley Business Centre
Eaton
Bowmere Road
The Paddock
Warren
Bowmere Wy
Oakdene Wy

Arden's Meadow
Nantwich Road
Spring Hill
Tarporley County High School
Brook Way
Bohars
Brookfield Close
Brook Road
Eaton Lane

Birch Heath Road
Birch Heath

Crib Lane

198

A49(T)
NANTWICH ROAD

Heath Way
Brook Farm Residential Special School

Ferney Lees
Pudding Lane
Sandstone Trail

Town Fields
Townfield Lane

Tiresford
Four Lane Ends

Tilstone Lodge

Tilstone Fearnall

Tiverton Hall
The Dale

Hand Green

Huxley Lane
A49(T)

Tiverton

Sandstone Trail

Beeston Hall Farm

Tilstone Bank

216

Dean Bank

Castlegate Farm

Hotel

G   H   J   K   L   M

K3 1 The Hawthorns 2 Windsor Av
K2 Rathbone Pk
1 Rathbone Pk
J4 1 The Mews

1
2
3
4
5
6
7
8

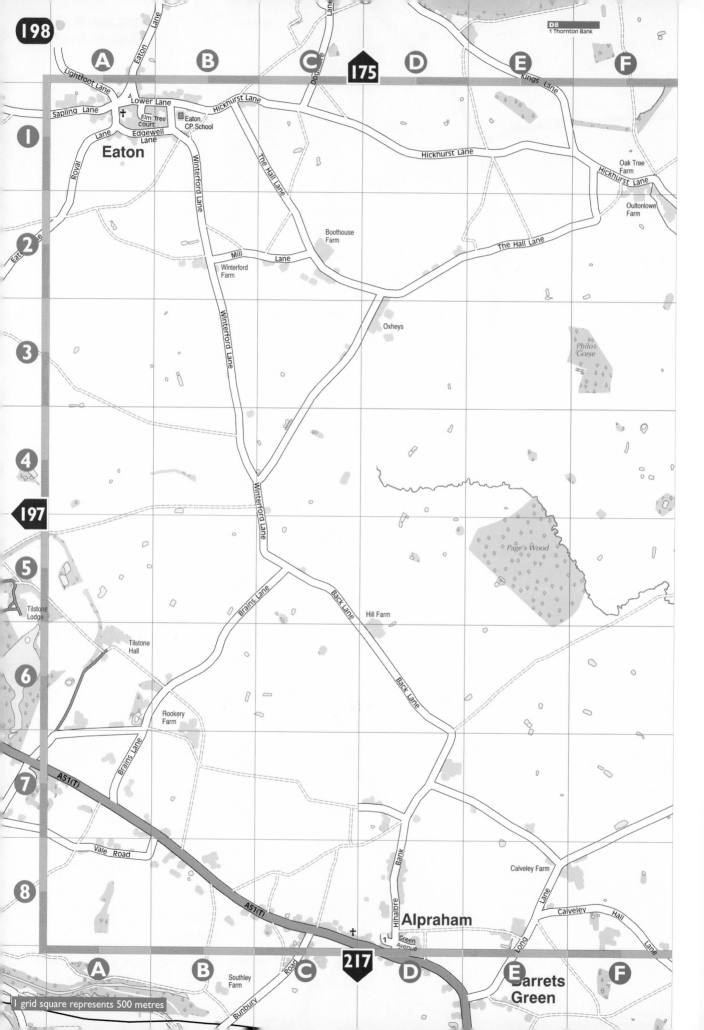

198

A   B   C   175   D   E   D8
1 Thornton Bank

Lightfoot Lane
Eaton Lane
Dog Lane
Rings Lane
F

1
Sapling Lane
Lower Lane
Hickhurst Lane
Hickhurst Lane
Oak Tree Farm
Hickhurst Lane
Edgewell Lane
Elm Tree Court
Eaton CP School
Eaton
Royal Lane
Eaton Lane
Winterford Lane
The Hall Lane
Oultonlowe Farm

2
Mill   Lane
Winterford Farm
Boothouse Farm
The Hall Lane

3
Oxheys
Philo Gorse
Winterford Lane

4
197

Page's Wood

5
Tilstone Lodge
Brains Lane
Back Lane
Hill Farm

6
Tilstone Hall
Back Lane

Rookery Farm
Brains Lane

7
A51(T)

Vale   Road
Calveley Farm

8
A51(T)
Bank
Hihalbre
Calveley   Hall
Long   Lane
Alpraham
Green Avenue

A   B   C   217   D   E   F
Southley Farm
Bunbury   Road
Barrets Green

I grid square represents 500 metres

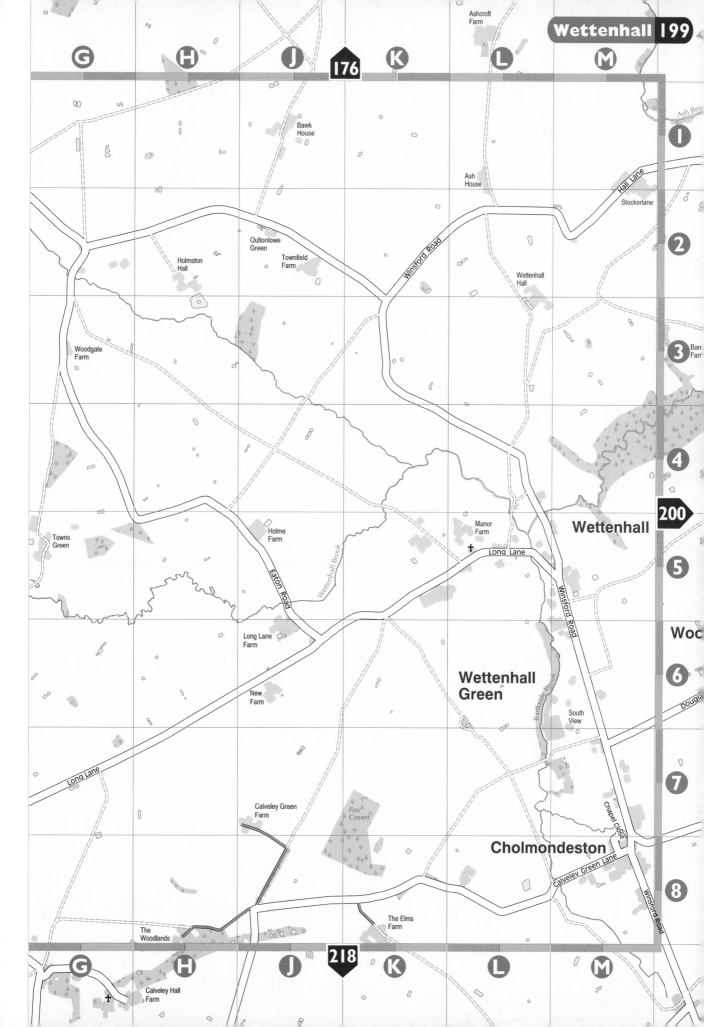

G H J **176** K L M

1

2

3

4

200

5

6

7

8

Ashcroft
Farm

Ash Bro

Hall Lane

Stockerlane

Bawk
House

Ash
House

Winsford Road

Wettenhall
Hall

Ban
Farr

Oultonlowe
Green

Townfield
Farm

Holmston
Hall

Woodgate
Farm

Manor
Farm

Wettenhall

Long Lane

Woc

Towns
Green

Holme
Farm

Wettenhall Brook

Eaton Road

Winsford Road

Long Lane
Farm

**Wettenhall
Green**

Bankside Brook

South
View

Doug

New
Farm

Long Lane

Calveley Green
Farm

Fox
Covert

Chapel Close

Cholmondeston

Calveley Green Lane

Winsford Road

The Woodlands

The Elms
Farm

G H J **218** K L M

Calveley Hall
Farm

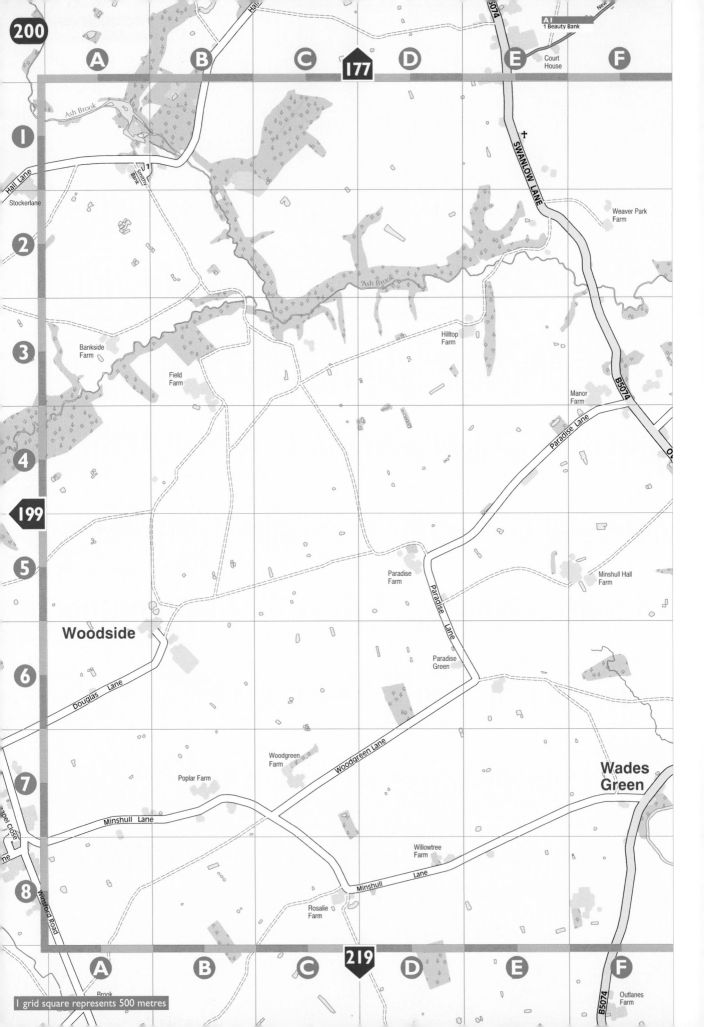

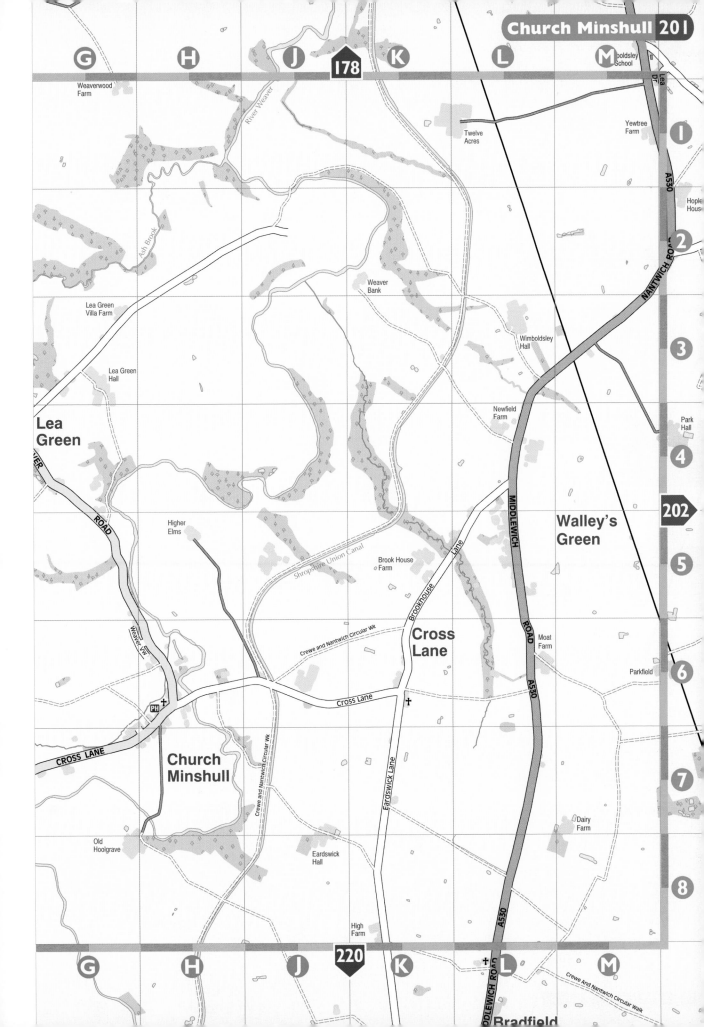

G   H   J   **178**   K   L   M   oldsley School

Weaverwood Farm

River Weaver

Twelve Acres

Yewtree Farm

Lea DF

A530

1

Hople Hous

2

NANTWICH ROAD

Ash Brook

Lea Green Villa Farm

Weaver Bank

Wimboldsley Hall

3

Lea Green Hall

Newfield Farm

Park Hall

4

Lea Green

202

MIDDLEWICH

Higher Elms

Shropshire Union Canal

Brook House Farm

Brookhouse Lane

Walley's Green

5

ROAD

Moat Farm

A530

Parkfield

6

Weaver Vw

Crewe and Nantwich Circular Wk

Cross Lane

RIVER

ROAD

PH ✝

CROSS LANE

Cross Lane

✝

7

Eardswick Lane

Crewe and Nantwich Circular Wk

Church Minshull

Dairy Farm

Old Hoolgrave

Eardswick Hall

8

High Farm

DDLEWICH ROAD

A530

✝

Crewe And Nantwich Circular Walk

Bradfield

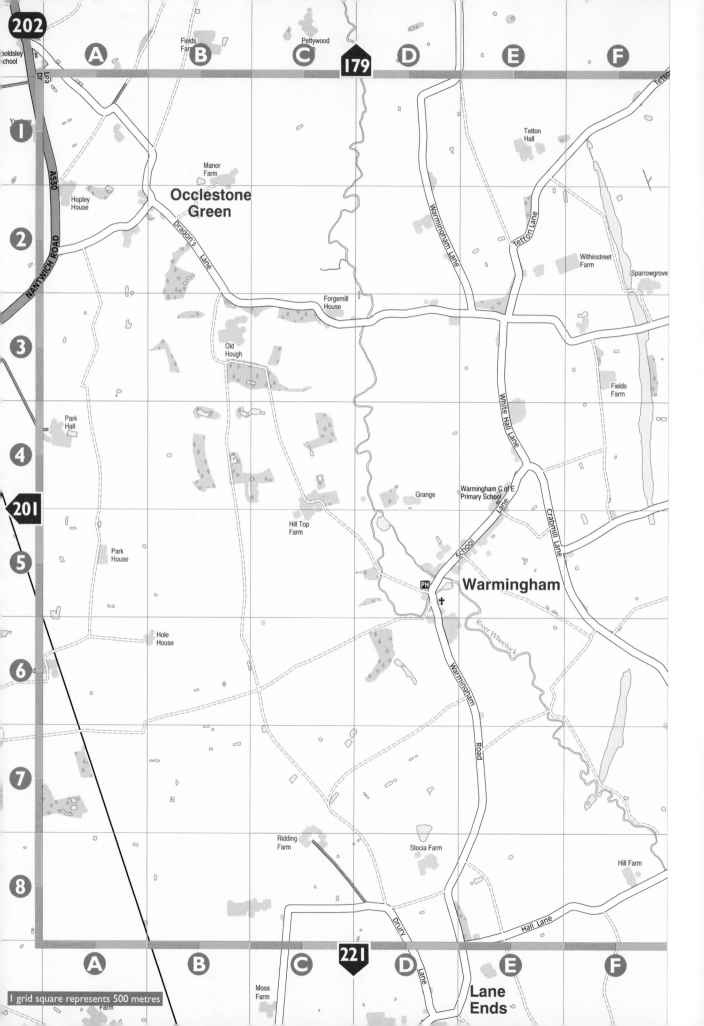

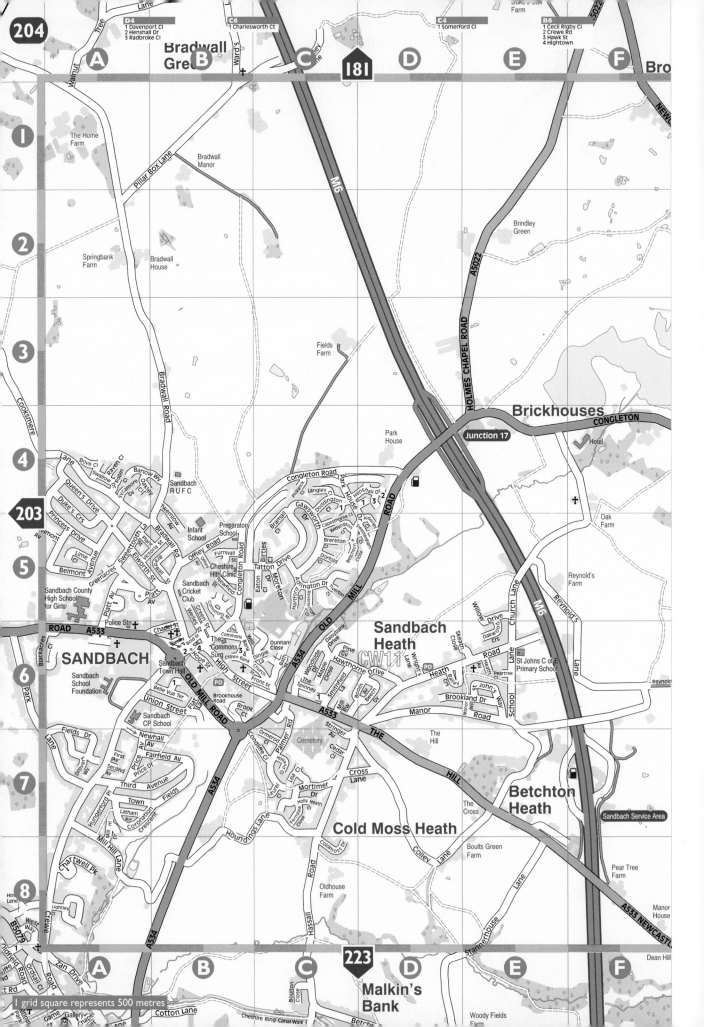

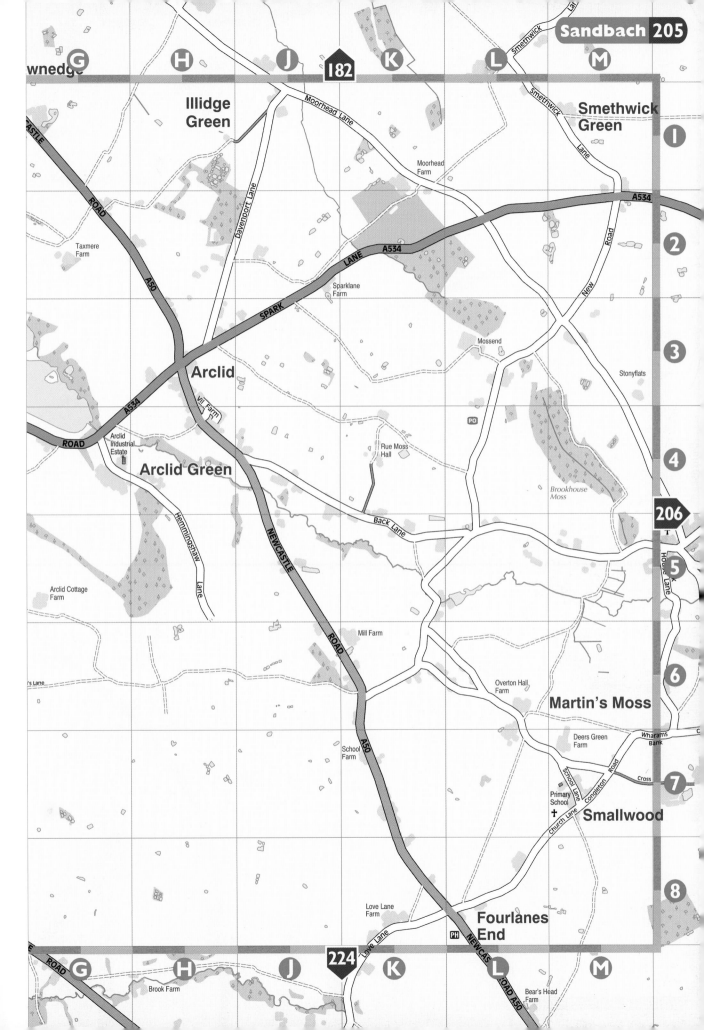

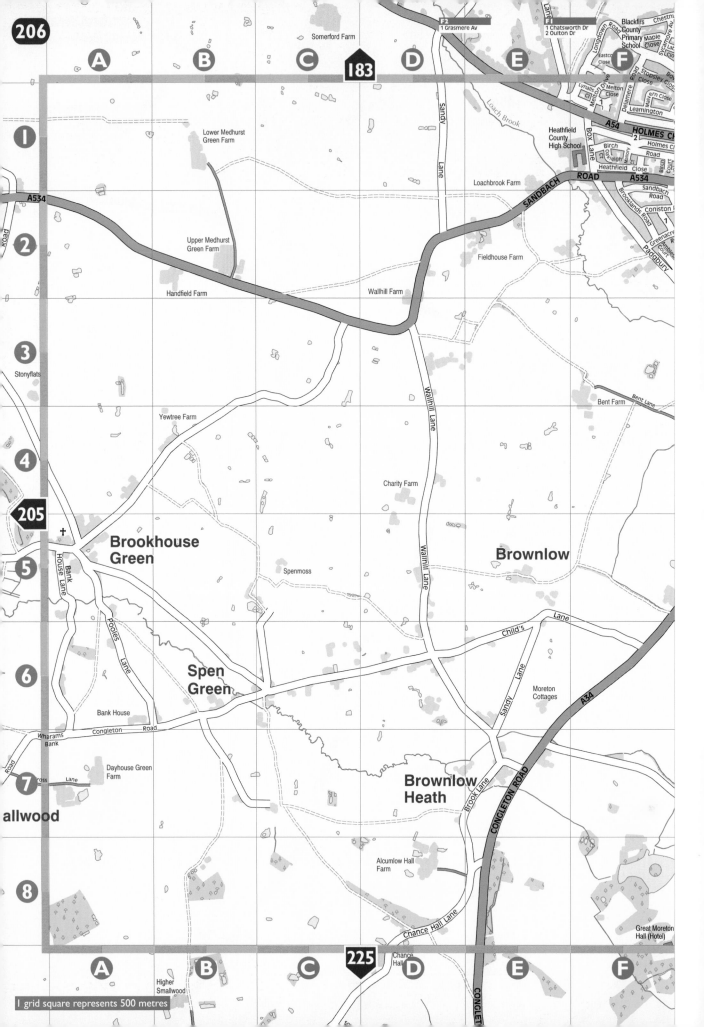

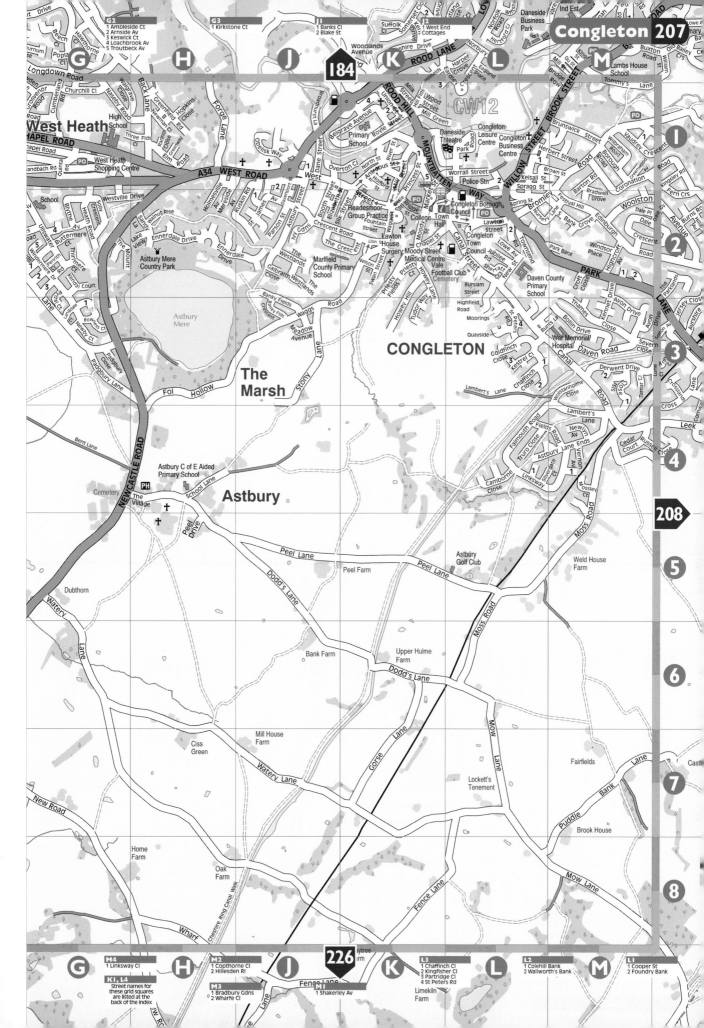

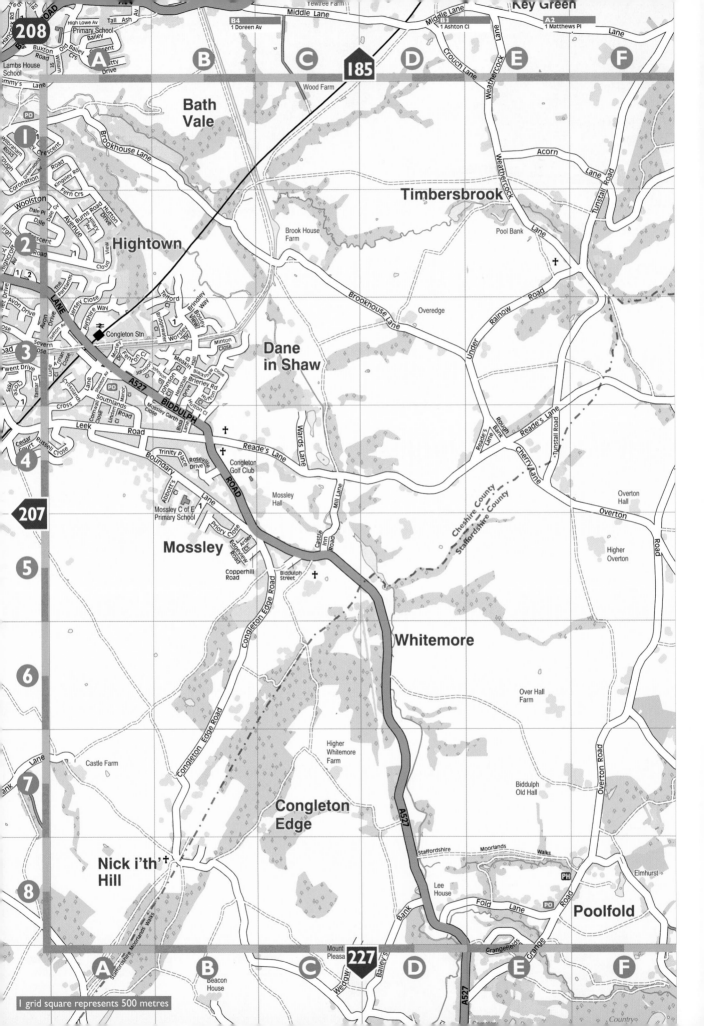

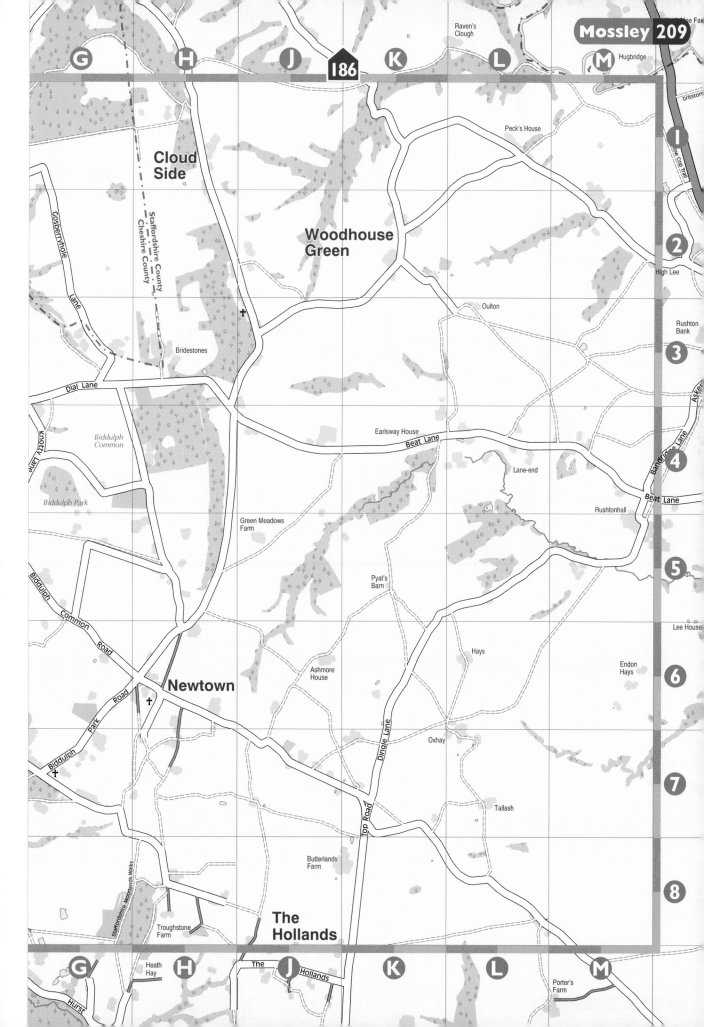

186

Cloud
Side

Woodhouse
Green

Raven's
Clough

Peck's House

Hugbridge

Gritston

High Lee

Oulton

Rushton
Bank

Gosberryhole Lane

Staffordshire County
Cheshire County

Bridestones

Dial Lane

Earlsway House

Beat Lane

Lane-end

Bandridge Lane

Asker

Beat Lane

Knotty Lane

Biddulph
Common

Biddulph Park

Rushtonhall

Green Meadows
Farm

Pyat's
Barn

Lee House

Biddulph Common Road

Hays

Endon
Hays

Newtown

Ashmore
House

Park Road

Biddulph

Dingle Lane

Oxhay

Top Road

Tallash

Butterlands
Farm

Staffordshire Moorlands Walks

Troughstone
Farm

The
Hollands

Heath
Hay

Hurst

The
Hollands

Porter's
Farm

G H J K L M

G H J K L M

I

2

3

4

5

6

7

8

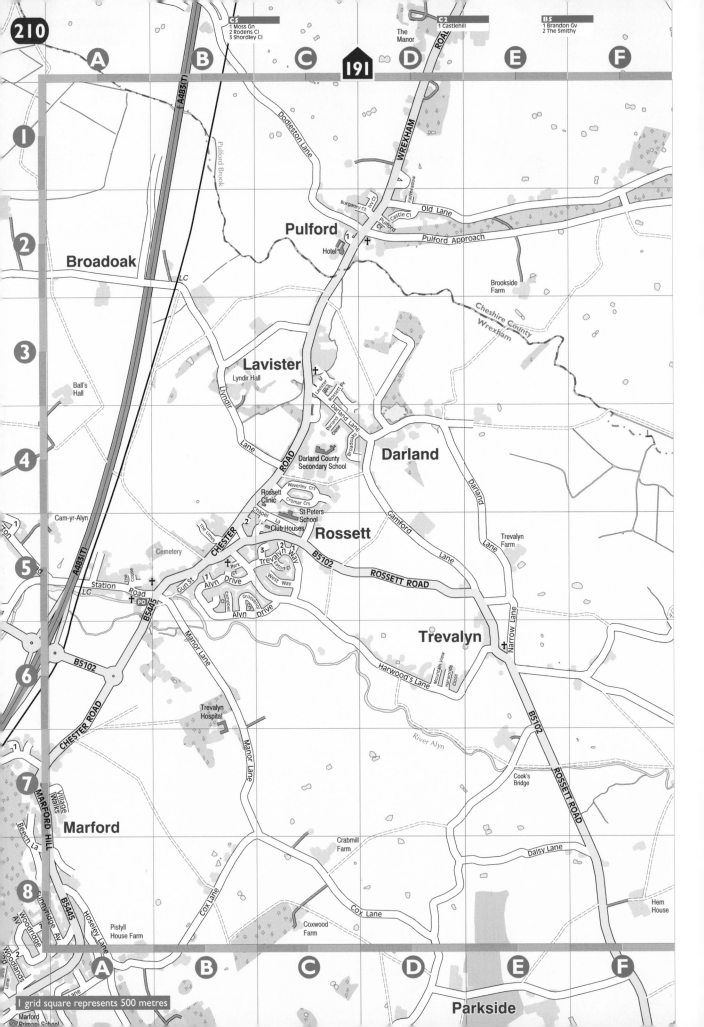

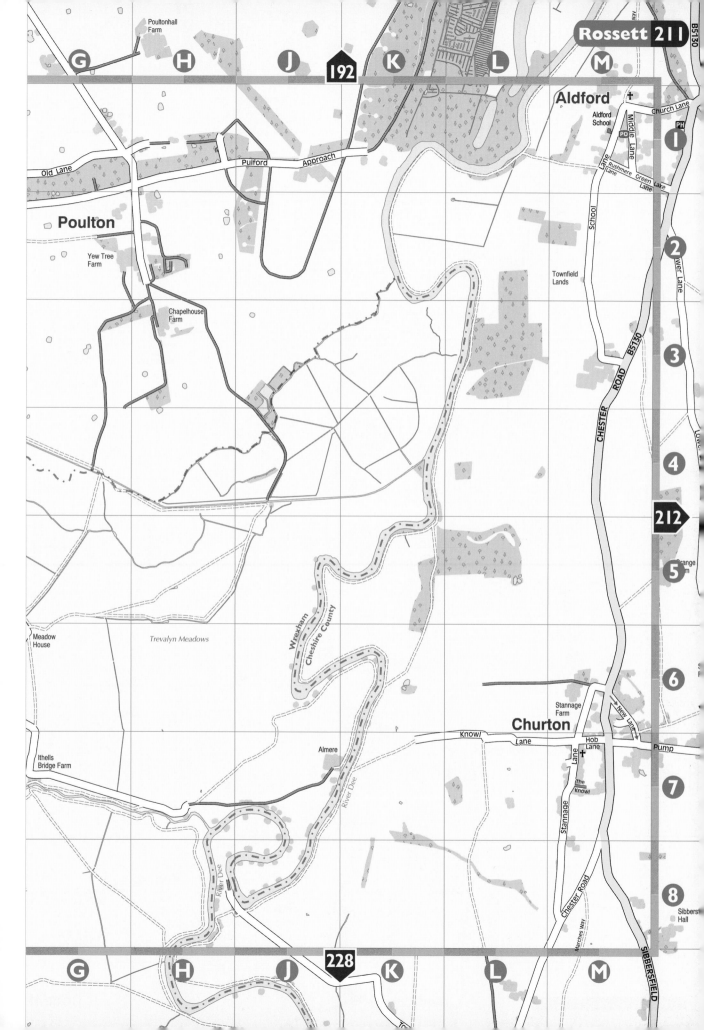

G H J **192** K L M

Aldford

Aldford
School

Church Lane

PO

Middle Lane

Rushmere
Lane

Green Lake
Lane

PH

I

Old Lane

Pulford   Approach

Poulton

Yew Tree
Farm

School Lane

Townfield
Lands

wer Lane

2

Chapelhouse
Farm

CHESTER ROAD

B5130

3

Lowe

4

212

5

Orange
m

Wrexham
Cheshire County

Meadow
House

Trevalyn Meadows

6

Stannage
Farm

New Lane

Churton

Ithells
Bridge Farm

Almere

River Dee

Know!   Lane

Hob
Lane

Stannage Lane

Pump

7

The
Knowl

River Dee

8

Chester Road

Marches Way

Sibberst
Hall

SIBBERSFIELD

G H J **228** K L M

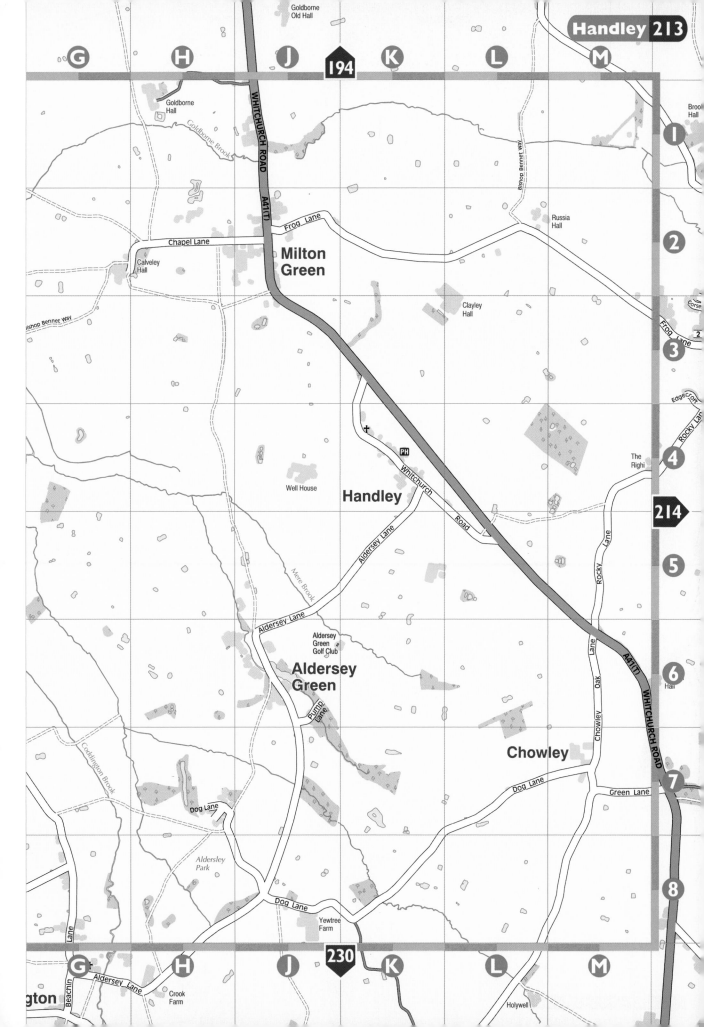

Goldborne
Old Hall

G **H** **J** 194 **K** **L** **M**

Goldborne
Hall

Brool
Hall

I

Goldborne Brook

WHITCHURCH ROAD

Frog Lane

Chapel Lane

2

Milton
Green

Calveley
Hall

Russia
Hall

A41(T)

Corse

Frog Lane

2

Clayley
Hall

Bishop Bennet Way

3

Bishop Bennet Way

Edgecroft

Rocky Lan

4

The
Righi

PH

Whitchurch

Handley

Well House

Road

Aldersey Lane

214

Mere Brook

5

Rocky

Aldersey Lane

Lane

Aldersey Lane

Aldersey
Green
Golf Club

Oak

6

Hall

**Aldersey
Green**

Lane

Chowley

Pump
Lane

Coddington Brook

Chowley

A41(T)

WHITCHURCH ROAD

Dog Lane

Dog Lane

Green Lane

7

Dog Lane

Aldersley
Park

8

Dog Lane

Yewtree
Farm

G **H** **J** 230 **K** **L** **M**

ngton

Beachin

Aldersey Lane

Lane

Crook
Farm

Holywell

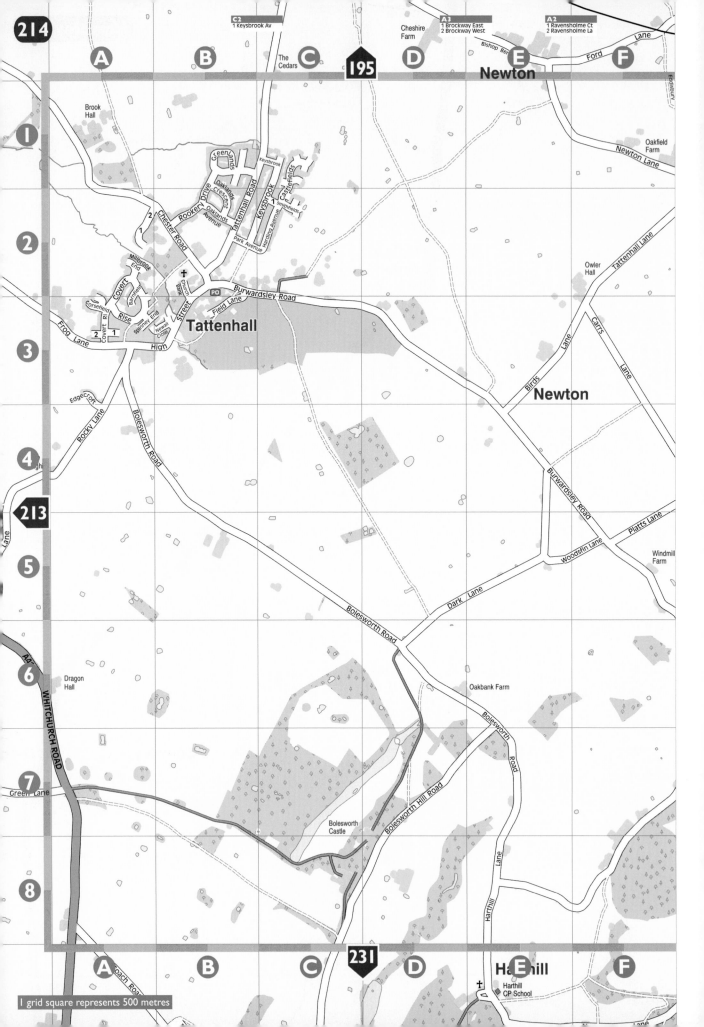

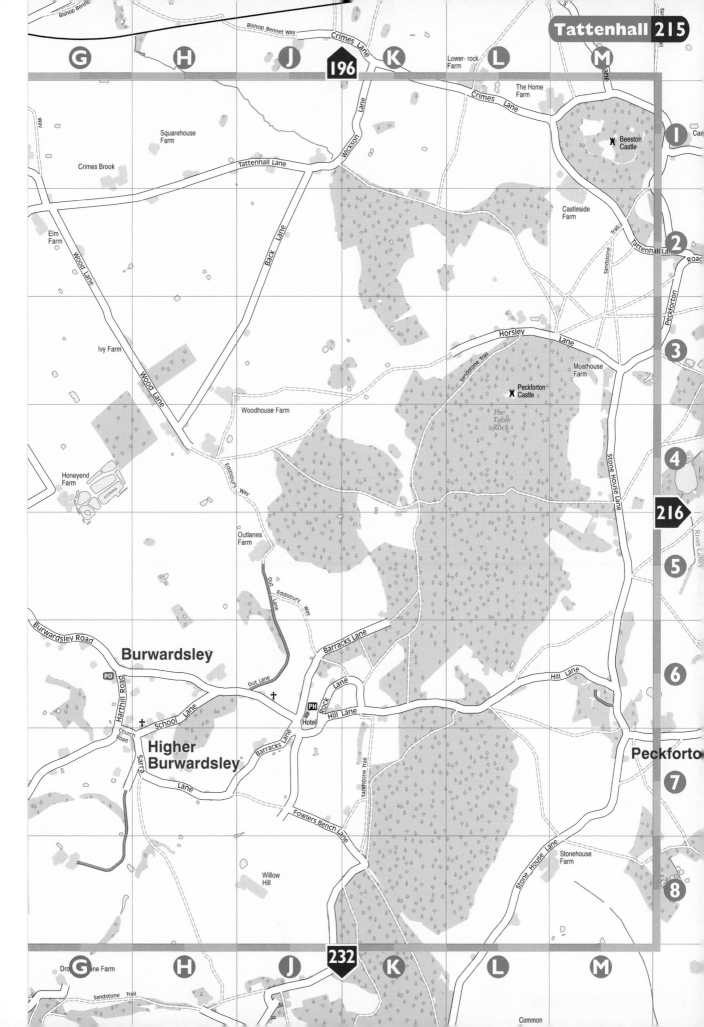

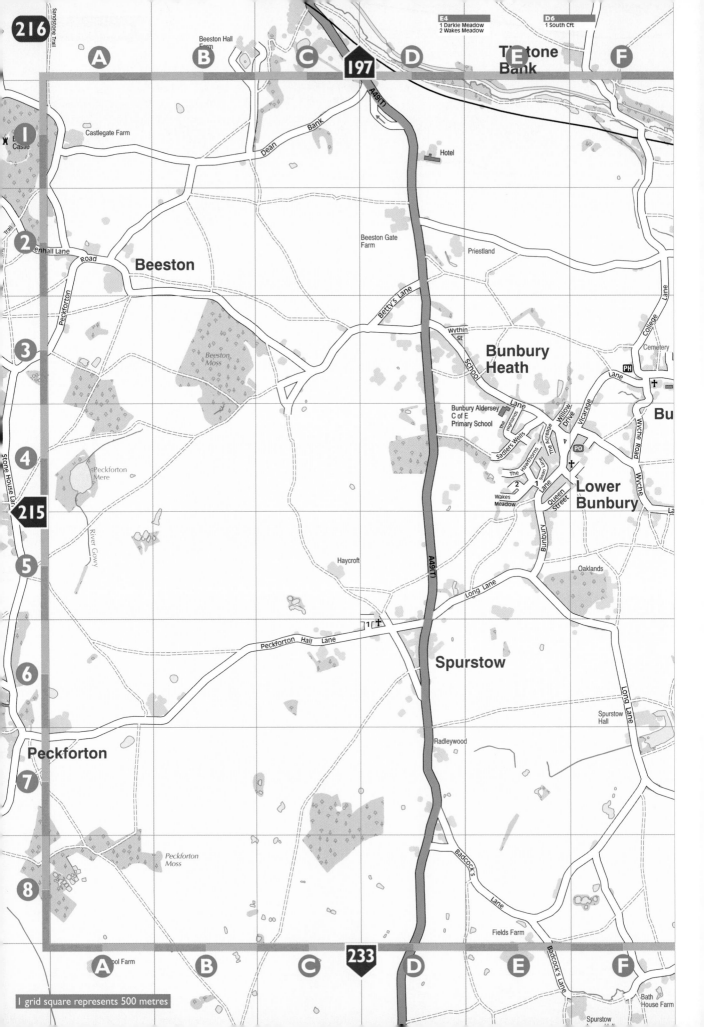

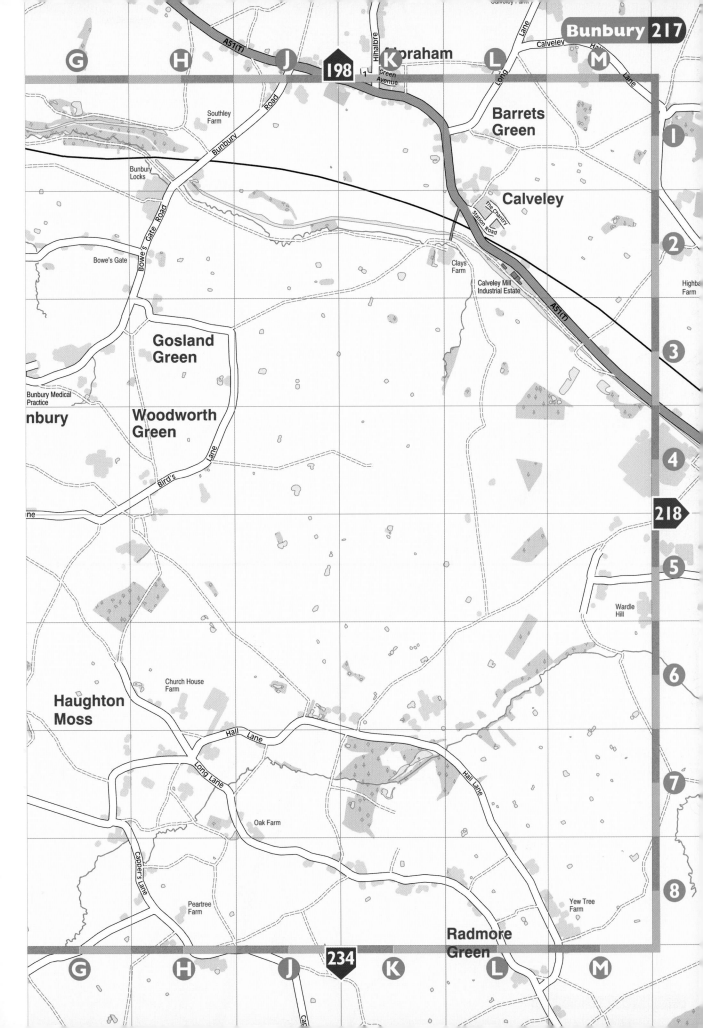

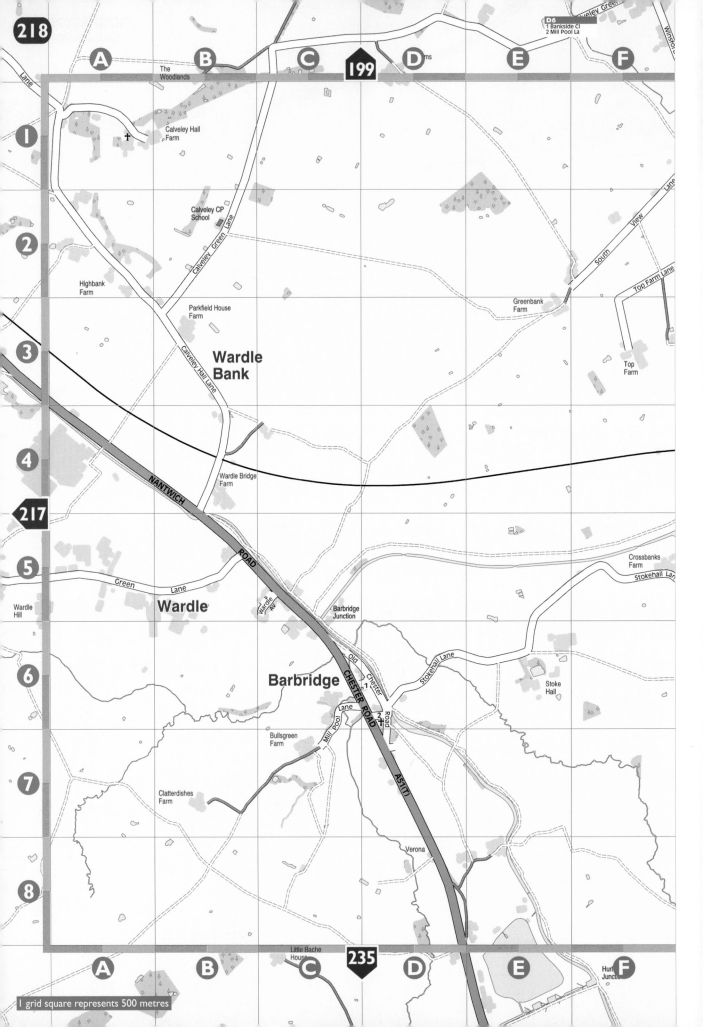

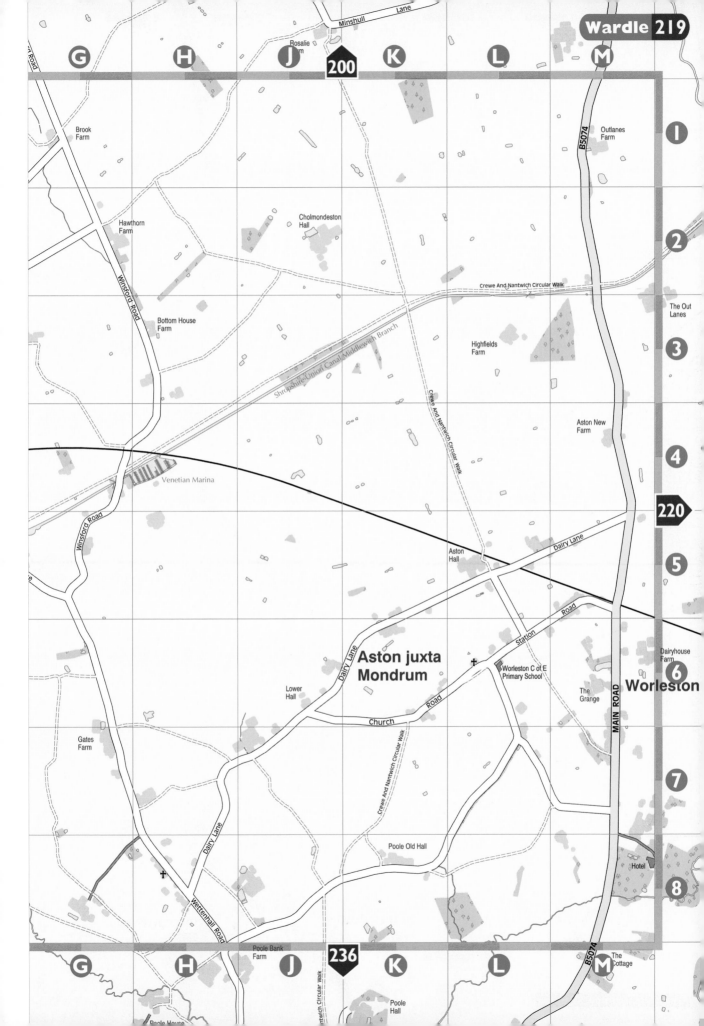

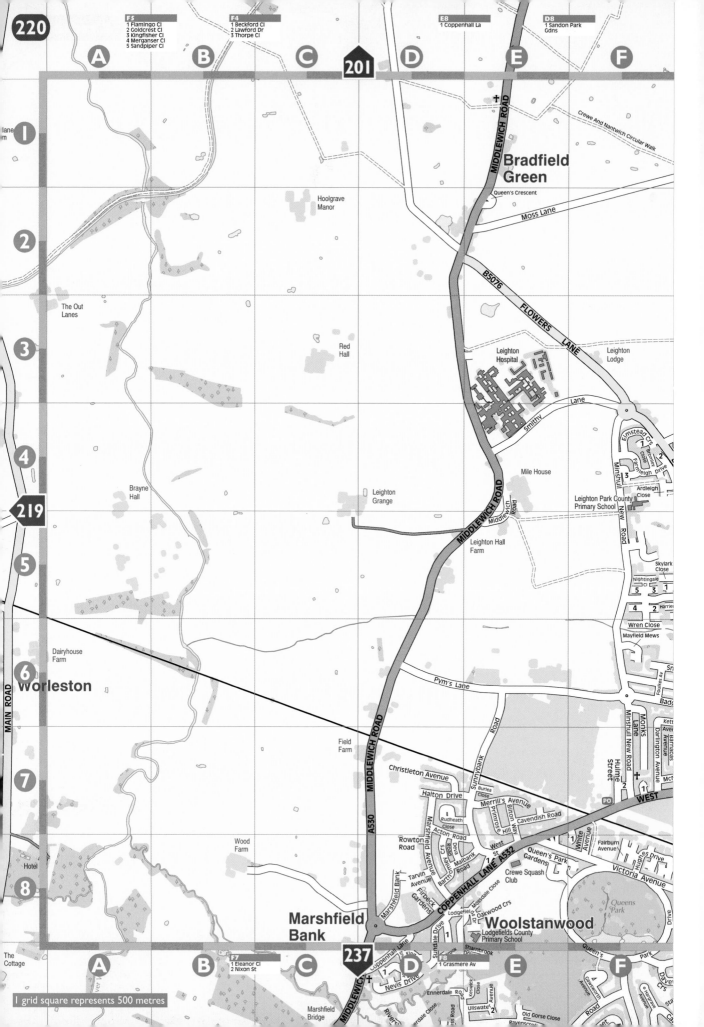

220

A   B   C   **201**   D   E   F

1

2

Hoolgrave Manor

The Out Lanes

3

Red Hall

4

219

Brayne Hall

Leighton Grange

5

Dairyhouse Farm

6 Worleston

Field Farm

7

Wood Farm

8

Hotel

The Cottage

Marshfield Bank

237

A   B   **F7**
1 Eleanor Cl
2 Nixon St   C   D   E   F

Woolstanwood

Bradfield Green

Queen's Crescent

Moss Lane

MIDDLEWICH ROAD

B5076 FLOWERS LANE

Crewe And Nantwich Circular Walk

Leighton Hospital

Leighton Lodge

Smithy Lane

Mile House

Leighton Park County Primary School

Elmstead Crs

Bromley Close

Farmleigh Drive

Ardleigh Close

New Road

Minshull New Road

Skylark Close

Nightingale Cl

Wren Close

Mayfield Mews

MIDDLEWICH ROAD

Leighton Hall Farm

Pym's Lane

Monks Lane

Hulme Street

Darlington Avenue

Barnacas Avenue

A530

Christleton Avenue

Halton Drive

Merrill's Avenue

Cavendish Road

Rudheath Close

Bilton Way

Primrose Hill

Sunnybank Road

Burlea Close

Acton Road

Rowton Road

Malbank Road

Tarvin Avenue

Marshfield Avenue

Marshfield Bank

COPPENHALL LANE A532

Crewe Squash Club

Queen's Park Gardens

White Avenue

Fairburn Avenue

Victoria Avenue

Queens Park

WEST

PO

Oakwood Crs

Lodgefields County Primary School

Sundale Drive

Sharnbrook Road

Crook St

Mossdale Close

Nevis Drive

Ennerdale Rd

Ullswater Rd

Keswick Close

Grasmere Av

Marshfield Bridge

Main Road

1 grid square represents 500 metres

G4
1 Barrows Cl
2 Becconsall Cl
3 Bodnant Cl
4 Gillow Cl
5 Highgate Cl
6 Leighton Vw

G7
1 Monk St

G8
1 Morgan Cl
2 Probert Cl

H4
1 Holbury Cl
2 Hove Cl
3 Hurn Cl
4 Melrose Dr
5 Parkstone Dr
6 Ryde Cl
7 Selsey Cl

H8
1 Saunders St

202

Lane Ends

Moss Farm

Spring Farm

Moss Farm

Bottoms Farm

Oaktree Farm

Groby Road

Crewe And Nantwich Circular Walk

Crewe And Nantwich Circular Walk

Aysgarth Avenue

Coppenhall Moss

Chapel La

Kent's Lane

Warmingham Road

Waldron's Lane

Moss Bridge

Barrows Green

Thorn Tree Drive

Simpson Court

Bleasdale Road

Rydal Mount

Moss Lane

Parkers Road

Breughton Road

Groby Farm

Moss Lane

Beconsall Drive

Heckerd

Healey Close

Lyceum Cl Lyceum

Carrington Way

Mablins Lane CP School

Wareham Drive

Somerley Cl

Hayling Cl

Groby Road

B5076

BRADFIELD

Merlin Way

Kestrel Dr

Falcon Drive

Bude

Cromer Dr

Seaton Close

Conway Close

Bidvale Wy

Stoneley Av

Stoneley Road

Coppenhall Moss

Maw Green

ROAD

Cliffe Road

NORTH STREET B5076

Castlemere Drive

Coppenhall

Remer St

Monks Coppenhall County Primary School

Foxes Hollow

222

Rigby Av

Mossford Av

Nuttield Av

Hazel Gv

Remer Street

Acer Cl

Maw Green

CW1

Thornyf Farm

Frank Bott Avenue

Selworthy Drive

Sandown Rd

Lindfield Cl

Kempton Av

Cheltenham

The Haven

Hawthorn Grove

Lime Road

Cherry Tree Road

Almond

Sydney Rd

Wheelman Road

Railton Av

Windsor Avenue

McLaren Street

Bailey Close

Greenway

Stamp Av

Ash Road

Prunus Road

Elm Drive

Sorbus Drive

Acacia Cl

Avenue

Rochester

Rolls

Frank

Sandway Road

Ryebank Avenue

Junior School

Holland Street

Abington

Evans Street

Lime St

Crossway

Sherborne

Sycamore Avenue

Pyrus Av

Plane Tree Drive

Herbert

Westbourne Avenue

Underwood Industrial Estate

Ellis Street

Birchnur

Reid St

Princess

Broad St Co Infant Sch

Sanborne Road

Hospital St

Charlesworth Street

Coppenhall County High School

Greendale Gardens

Timbrell Avenue

Brooklands Grove

Kinloch Close

Mt Pleasant

Dutton Way

Coppenhall Cem

Singleton

Elm Drive

Coppenhall Leisure Centre

Micklewright Av

Fallowfield

Badger Avenue

Crewe Cemetery

Ridgway Street

Micklewright Av Mellor St

B5076

Newhall Street

Hillside

Birch Cl

19 CREWE

18

Broom St

Newcastle St

Underwood West County Junior & Infant School

Glover Street

Goulden Street

Walker Street

Chell Street

Ford Ford

Victoria Community County High School

Ridgway Street

Audley St Audley St

Henry

Spring Gardens Street

Coleridge Way

Daxton

Heron Cl

STREET

Oxford

Derby St

Stafford St

Rose Ter

Alban

Cassen St

Primary School

Furber St

Villiers Russell Close

Queen

Poplar Gv

Beech

Oak Tree

Lansdowne Road

Coleridge Road

Cormorant

Bentley

7

Grosvenor Medical Centre

A532

Adelaide St

Delamere St

Meredith St

Secondary Sch

Market St

Sheppard Close

Mary St

Byron Cl

Chestnut

Wordsworth Drive

Burns Drive

Swinburne

Kipling

Eliot

8

Richard Moon Street

Samuel street

Bright Street

Richard St

West Avenue

Heathfield Av

Paul's St

Holt St

Victoria Community High Sch

Gal & Gifts

Victoria Street

Earnswood Medical Cen

English Touring Crewe & Nantwich Thtr Borough Council

Heath St

Brierley Business Cen

Brierley Primary School

March Street

Barrie Gv

Conrad

Hungerford Medical Centre

Primary Sch

Shelley

Scott

Tennyson Av

Byron

HUNGERFORD ROAD

The Valley

Coppenhall Gv

Coppenhall Heyes

Castle St

Bus Stn

Chester square

The Health Centre

Chester St

Earle St Co

Police Stn

Forge St

Tower

King St

Vincent Surrey

Richmond

Earle St

2 EARLE ST

Macon Business Park

The Old Surg

Gresty Ter

Buxton

Lea

Lynbrook Rd

Holmlea

A532 HUNGERFORD ROAD

Springfield

Renaissance

238

Wistaston Road

Alton Street

Collins St

Britten Road Lewis street

Earle St

Apollo Cinema Club

Eaton High

Vernon Wy

Bulkeley St

Macon

CRE GR

Mancheste Metrop University

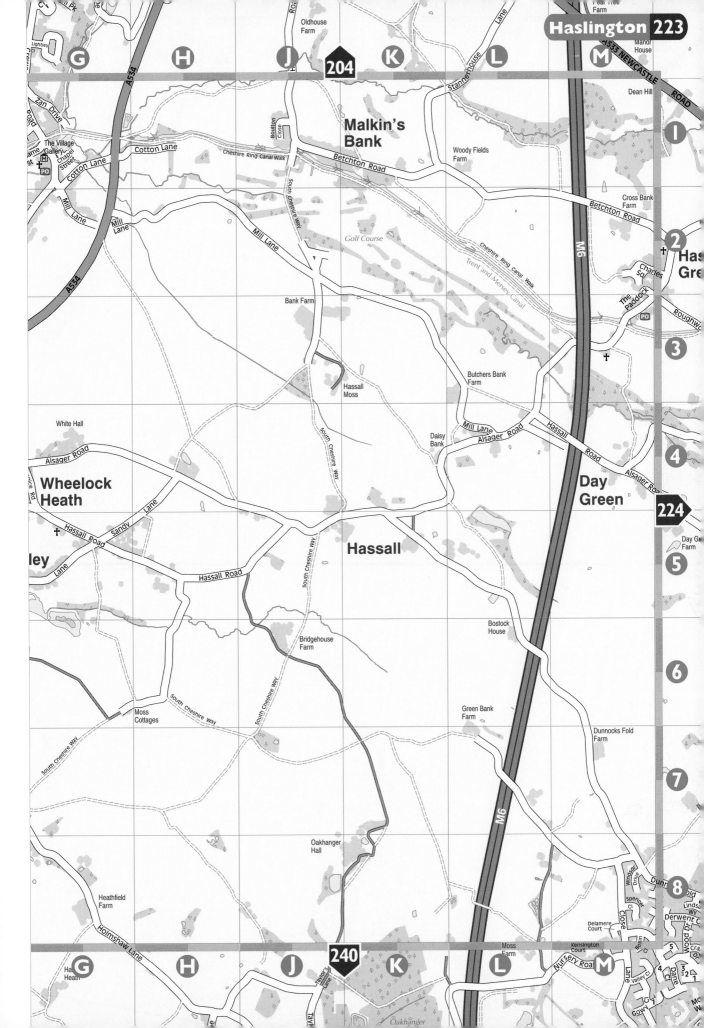

Oldhouse Farm

Stannerhouse Lane

A534

G **H** **J** 204 **K** **L** **M** A535 NEWCASTLE ROAD

Pear Tree Farm

Manor House

Dean Hill

I

Zan Drive

Lightley Cl

The Village Gallery

M PO

Chapel Street

Cotton Lane

Cotton Lane

Boulton Close

Cheshire Ring Canal Walk

Malkin's Bank

Betchton Road

Woody Fields Farm

Betchton Road

Cross Bank Farm

2 Has Gre

Mill Lane

Mill Lane

Mill Lane

South Cheshire Way

Golf Course

Cheshire Ring Canal Walk

Trent and Mersey Canal

M6

Charles Sq

The Paddock

PO

Roughw

3

Bank Farm

Hassall Moss

Butchers Bank Farm

Daisy Bank

Mill Lane

Alsager Road

Hassall Road

4

White Hall

Alsager Road

Wheelock Heath

Sandy Lane

Hassall Road

Day Green

Alsager Ro

224

Day G Farm

5

nce Rd

Lane

Hassall Road

Hassall Road

South Cheshire Way

South Cheshire Way

Hassall

ley

Bostock House

6

Bridgehouse Farm

South Cheshire Way

South Cheshire Way

Green Bank Farm

Dunnocks Fold Farm

7

Moss Cottages

South Cheshire Way

Oakhanger Hall

Windsor Drive

Dunn

8

Heathfield Farm

Spencer Cl

Delamere Court

Derwent

Lindsa WY

Kensington Court

5

Holmshaw Lane

Ha Heath

G **H** **J** 240 **K** **L** Moss Farm Nursery Roa **M** Dane Lane

Valley Cl

Gow

Oakhanger

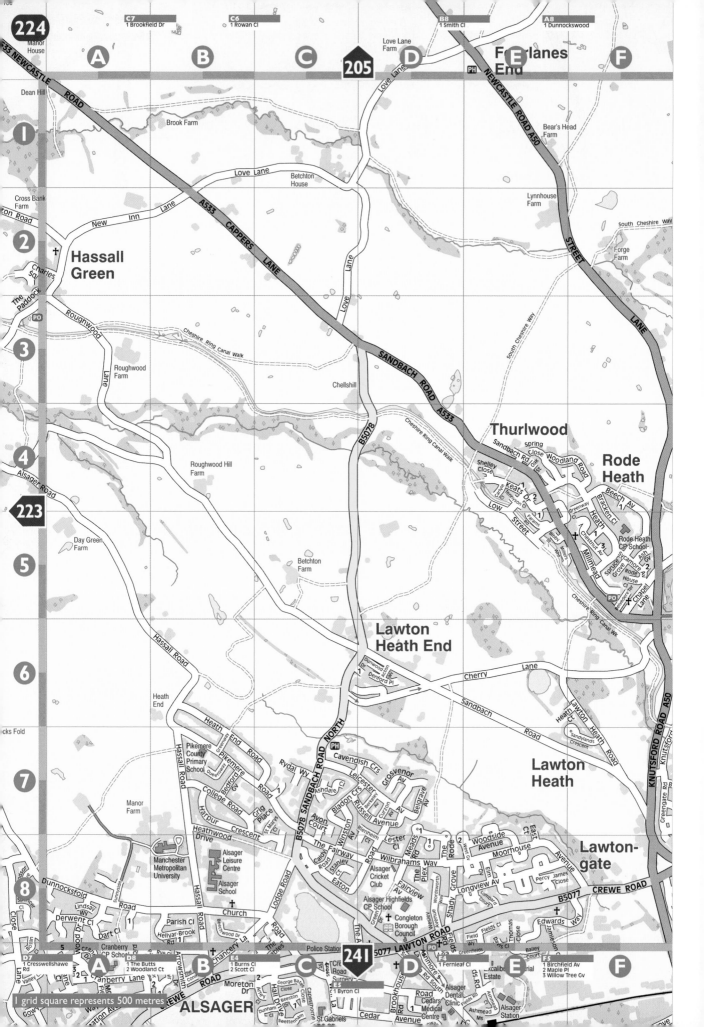

G H J **206** K L M

Chance Hall Lane

Great Moreton
Hall (Hotel)

1

L8
1 The Spinney

M5
1 Hollinshead Cl

Chance
Hall

Higher
Smallwood

CONGLETON ROAD

Cheshire

2

South Cheshire Way

Cuttleford

Little Moreton
Hall (NT)

Boden Hall

Walkers
Lane

3

Pump
Farm

Chance Hall Lane

Moor's
Farm

Boarded
Barn

Townsend
Farm

Rode
Mill

Church Lane

Holehouse Lane

Moorson
Avenue

Station
Road

4

226

A34

Stone Chair Lane

Station Road

Barnbridge Close

Barberycroft

Foundry
Lane

1

Cinderhill
Lane Surg

Spring

Townsend
Lane

Pool Side

Rode
Pool

Rode
Hall

Barber
Drive

Wavertree AV

Drenfell Road

Mead
AV
Lane

5

Margery AV

Cinder-Hill

Alma
Cl

The Mount

Bank
Farm

Church Lane

NORTH

**Scholar
Green**

Scholar Green
CP School

6

Brick House

Portland
Drive

Little-moss

CONGLETON ROAD

Nursery Rd

Little Moss Lane

Moss
Lane

**Hall
Green**

7

Hall o' Lee

Church Lawton
Gate CP School

Meadow
Wy

Barnwood
AV

Cherry Tree
Avenue

Ashbank
Farm

Trent & Mersey Canal

Cheshire Ring Canal Wk

Little
Close

Bleeding
Wolf
Lane

Moss
House

Brattswood Drive

Woodgate AV

Brown Road

Grove
AV

Lawton
Coppice

1

Woodside

Moss
Lane

Knowsley Lane

8

**Church
Lawton**

The
Grove

Liverpool
Road West

Grove Park

Elmwood

Crosswood

LIVERPOOL

Liverpool
Road West

ROAD

Lawton
Hall

Knowsley Lane

Dairylands
Road

LINLEY LANE

G H J **242** K L M

ST

Lawton
Avenue

**Red
Bull**

Cheshire Ring Canal Wk

LC

A50

LIVERPOOL

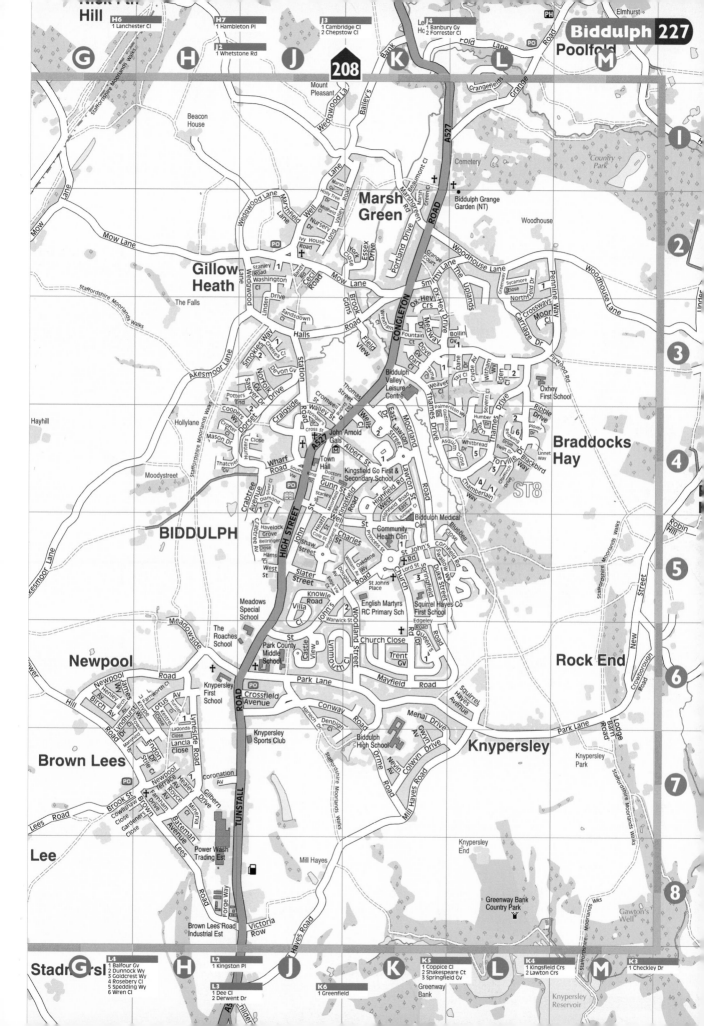

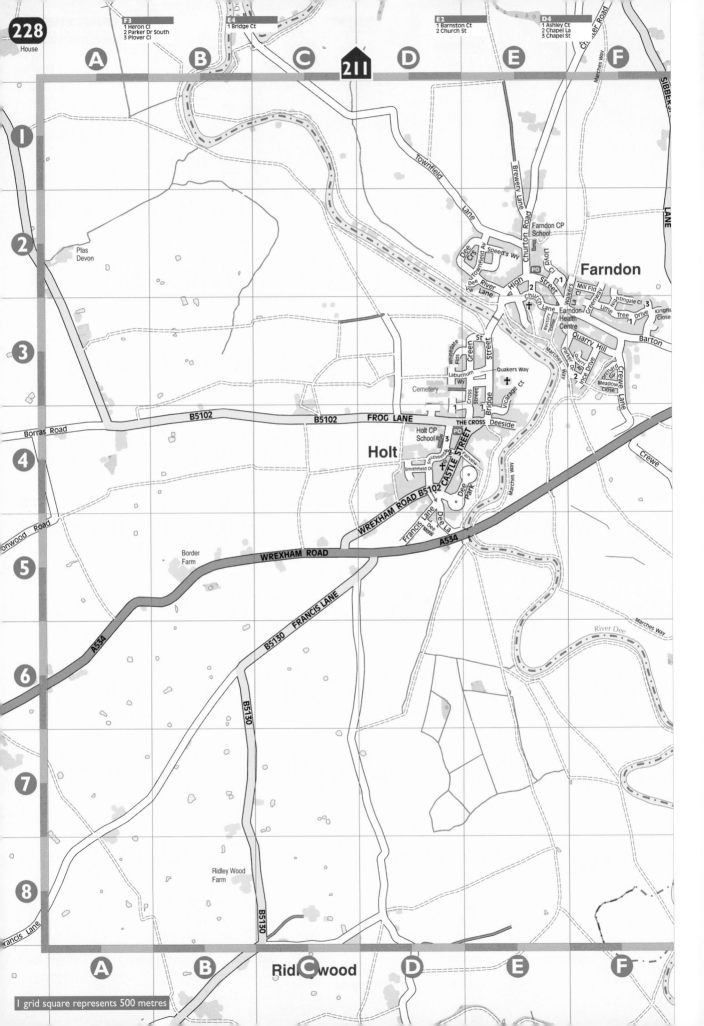

211

Plas
Devon

Farndon

Farndon CP School

Dee Crs

Townfield Av

speed's Wy

Dee River Vw

Dee La

High Street

Churton Road

Brewery Lane

Lloyd Cl

PO

Walkers La

Mill Fld

Farndon Health Centre

Nightingale Cl

Greenway

Lime Tree Drive

Kingfis
Close

Barton

Church Lane

Rectory La

Marches Way

Parker Dr

Quarry Hill

Quarry Hill

Ince Drive

Crewe Lane

Orchard Av

Meadow Close

Green Street

St Street

Whitegate Flds

Laburnum Wy

Quakers Way

Cemetery

Vicarage Ct

Cross Street

Bridge Street

THE CROSS

Deeside

Borras Road

B5102

B5102

FROG LANE

Holt CP School

Holt

PO

CASTLE STREET

Smithfield

Fairview

Smithfield Dr

Dee Park

WREXHAM ROAD B5102

Francis Lane

Dee La

Dee Mdw

Marches Way

A534

Crewe

Border Farm

WREXHAM ROAD

A534

FRANCIS LANE

B5130

River Dee

Marches Way

A534

B5130

Ridley Wood Farm

B5130

Ridley wood

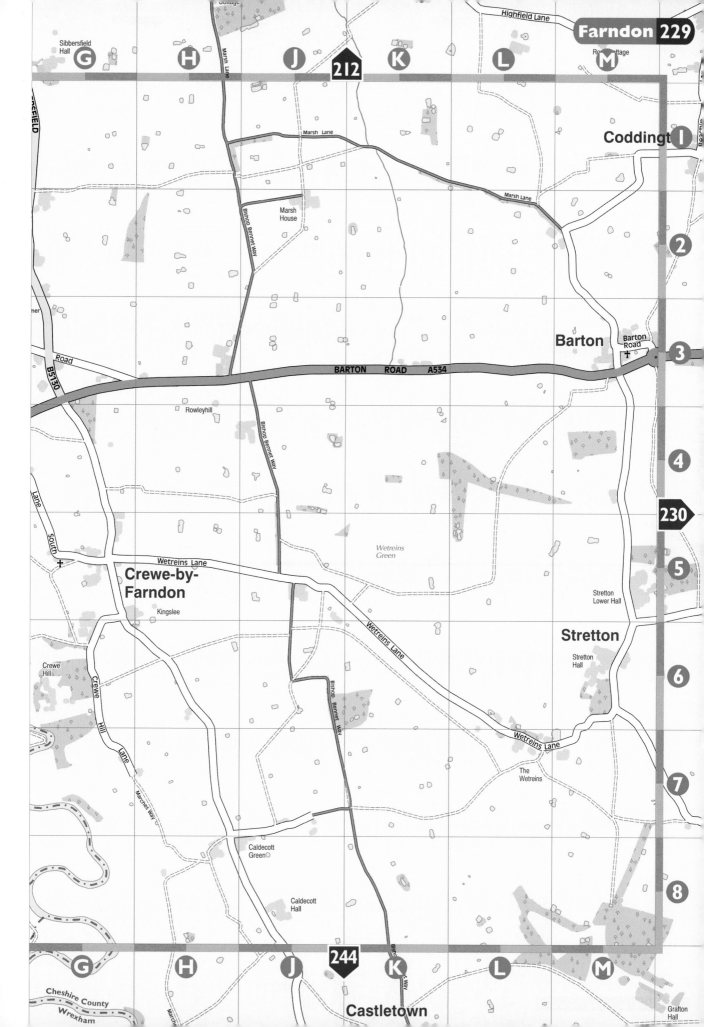

Sibbersfield
Hall **G**

H

Marsh Lane

J

212

K

L

M

Highfield Lane

Ro _Cottage_

Coddingt I

Marsh Lane

2

Marsh House

Marsh Lane

Bishop Bennet Way

Barton

Barton Road

3

Road

B5130

BARTON ROAD A534

Rowleyhill

Bishop Bennet Way

4

230

Lane

South

Wetreins Lane

Crewe-by-Farndon

Kingslee

Wetreins Green

Stretton Lower Hall

5

Stretton

Stretton Hall

6

Crewe Hill

Crewe Hill Lane

Wetreins Lane

Wetreins Lane

Bishop Bennet Way

The Wetreins

7

Marches Way

Caldecott Green

Caldecott Hall

8

G

H

J

244

t Way

K

Bishop

L

M

Grafton Hall

Cheshire County
Wrexham

Castletown

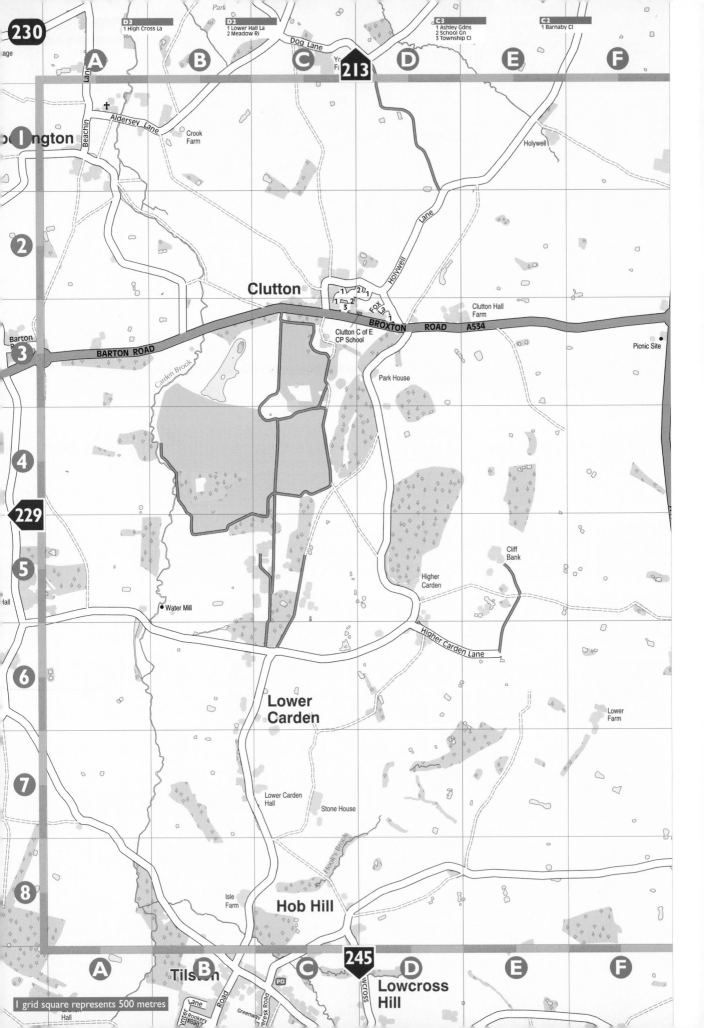

230

D3
1 High Cross La

D2
1 Lower Hall La
2 Meadow Ri

C3
1 Ashley Gdns
2 School Gn
3 Township Cl

C2
1 Barnaby Cl

A   B   C   D   E   F

Dog Lane

213

Park

Aldersey Lane

Crook Farm

Holywell

ington

2

Clutton

Holywell Lane

Clutton Hall Farm

Barton P

3

BARTON ROAD

BROXTON   ROAD   A534

Picnic Site

Carden Brook

Clutton C of E CP School

Fox La

Park House

4

229

Higher Carden

Cliff Bank

5

Hall

Water Mill

6

Lower Carden

Higher Carden Lane

Lower Farm

7

Lower Carden Hall

Stone House

Hook's Brook

8

Isle Farm

Hob Hill

A   B   C   D   E   F

Tilston

245

Lowcross Hill

PO

Greenway Road

Rookery Road

Hall

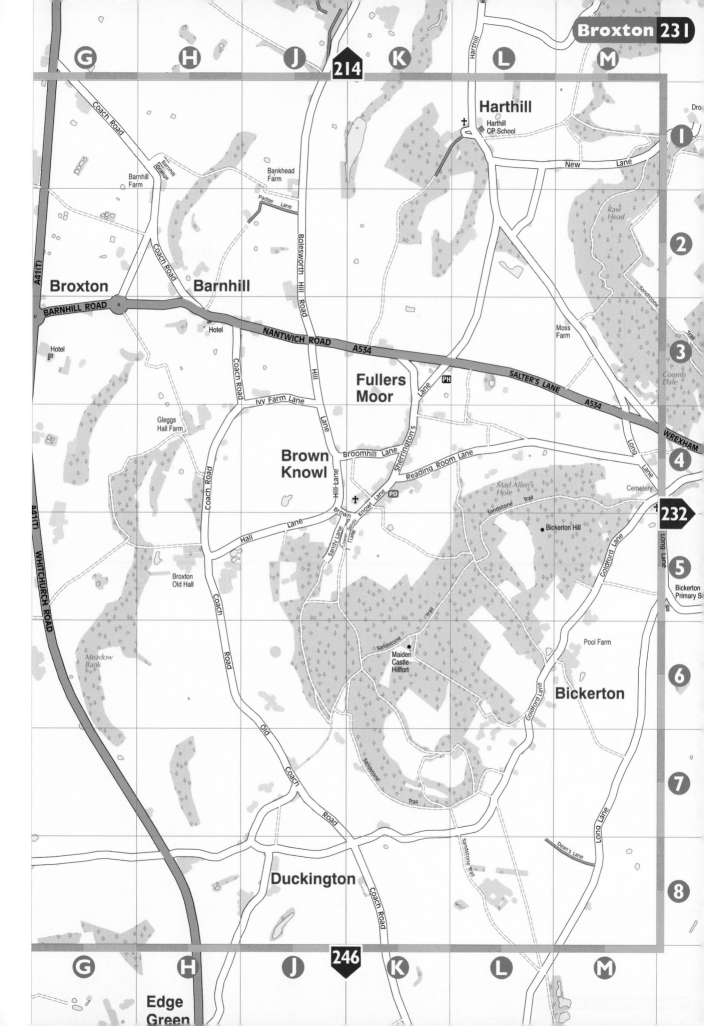

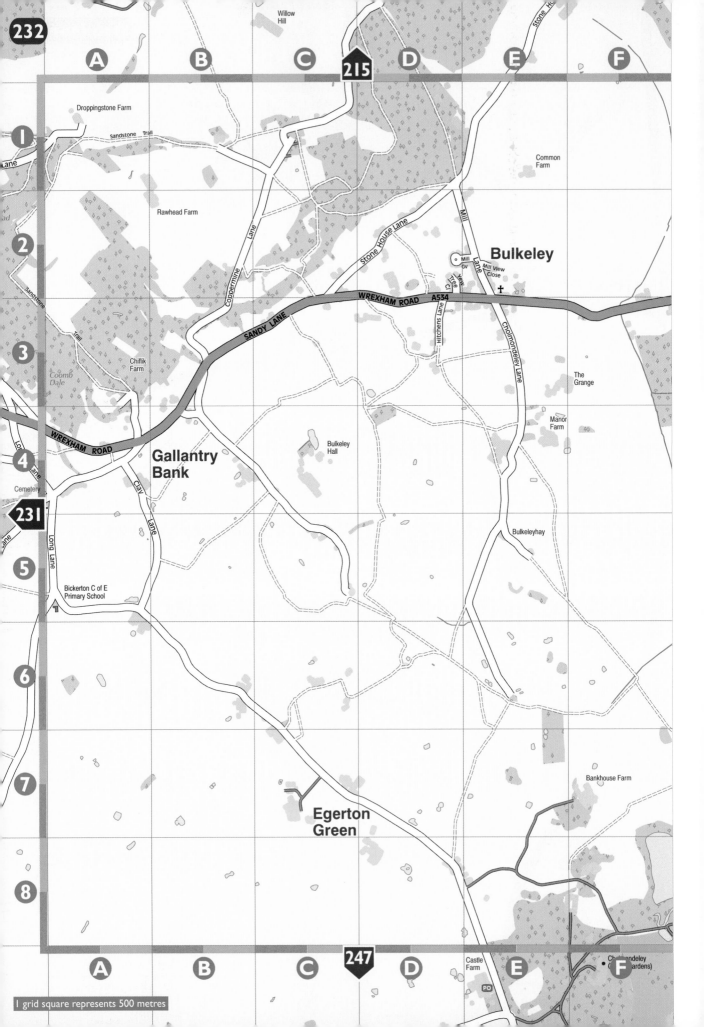

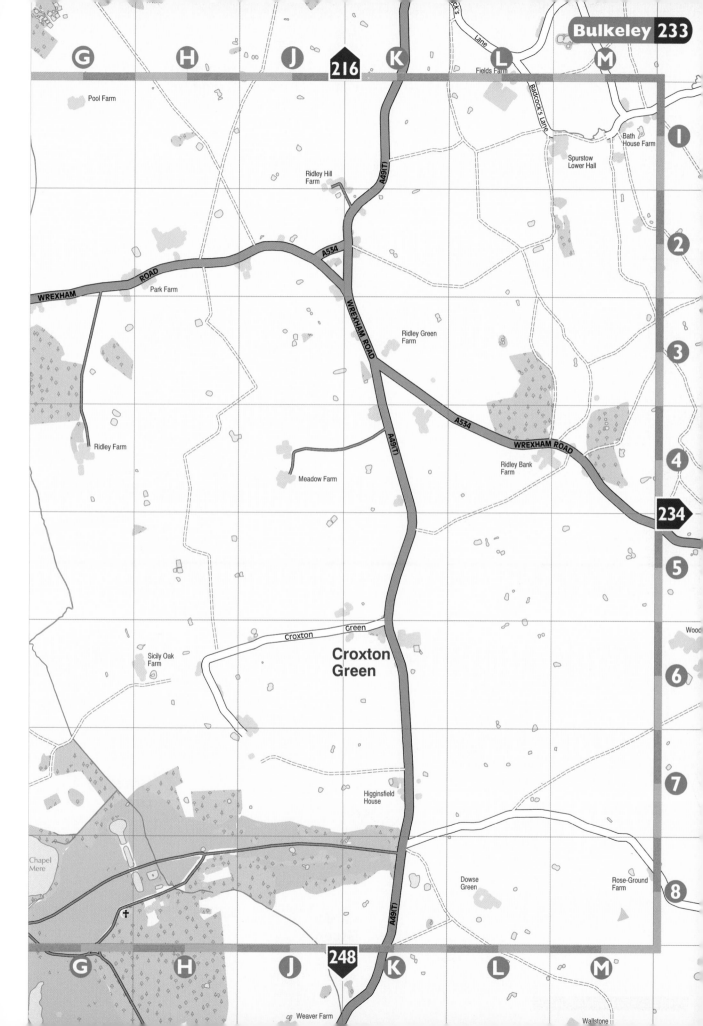

Pool Farm

Ridley Hill Farm

Fields Farm

Bath House Farm

Spurstow Lower Hall

WREXHAM ROAD

Park Farm

A534

WREXHAM ROAD

Ridley Green Farm

Ridley Farm

A49(T)

Meadow Farm

A534

WREXHAM ROAD

Ridley Bank Farm

Croxton Green

Croxton Green

Sicily Oak Farm

Wood

Higginsfield House

Chapel Mere

A49(T)

Dowse Green

Rose-Ground Farm

Wallstone

Weaver Farm

G H J **216** K L M

I 2 3 4 **234** 5 6 7 8

G H J **248** K L M

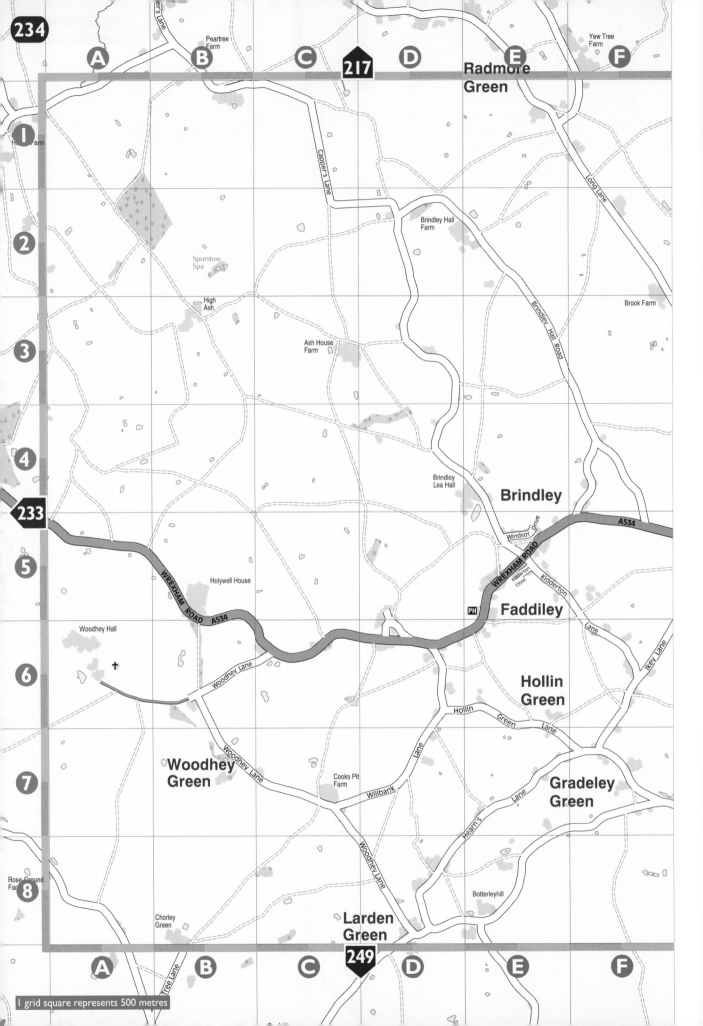

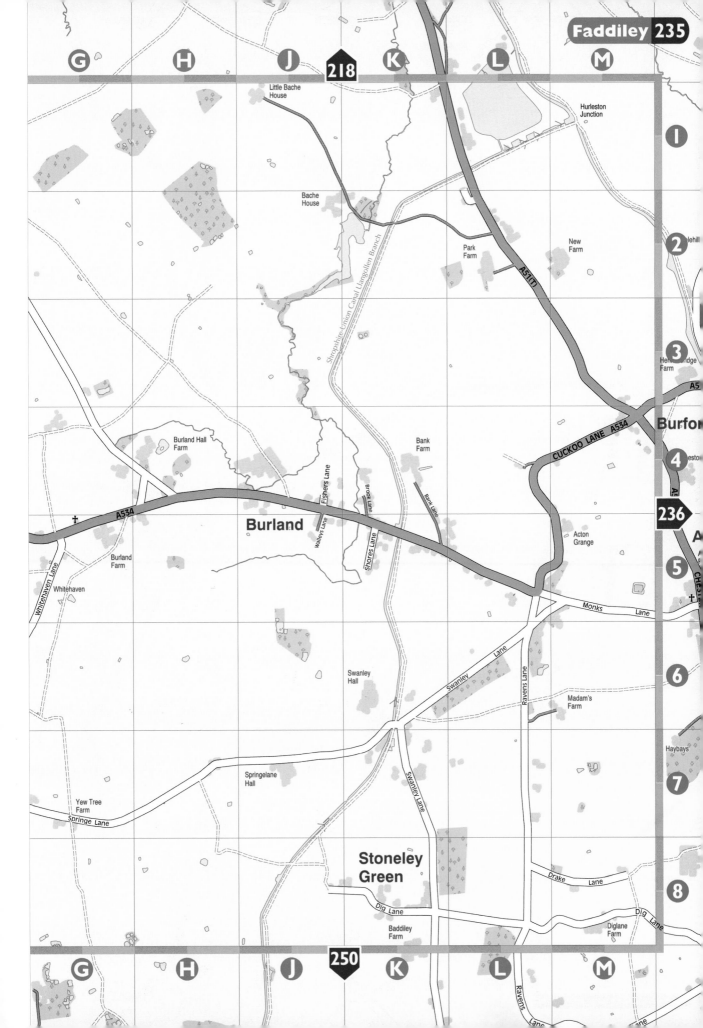

G H J **218** K L M

I
2
3
4
236
5
6
7
8

Little Bache House

Hurleston Junction

Bache House

Shropshire-Union Canal Llangollen Branch

Park Farm

New Farm

A51(T)

dehill

Henhull Bridge Farm

A5

Burland Hall Farm

Bank Farm

Burfor

CUCKOO LANE A534

cheston

A534

Burland

Fishers Lane

Brook Lane

Bank Lane

Acton Grange

Whitehaven Lane

Burland Farm

Whitehaven

Walley's Lane

Shores Lane

Monks Lane

Swanley Hall

Swanley Lane

Ravens Lane

Madam's Farm

Haybays

Springelane Hall

Yew Tree Farm

Springe Lane

Swanley Lane

Stoneley Green

Drake Lane

Dig Lane

Baddiley Farm

Diglane Farm

Dig Lane

Ravens Lane

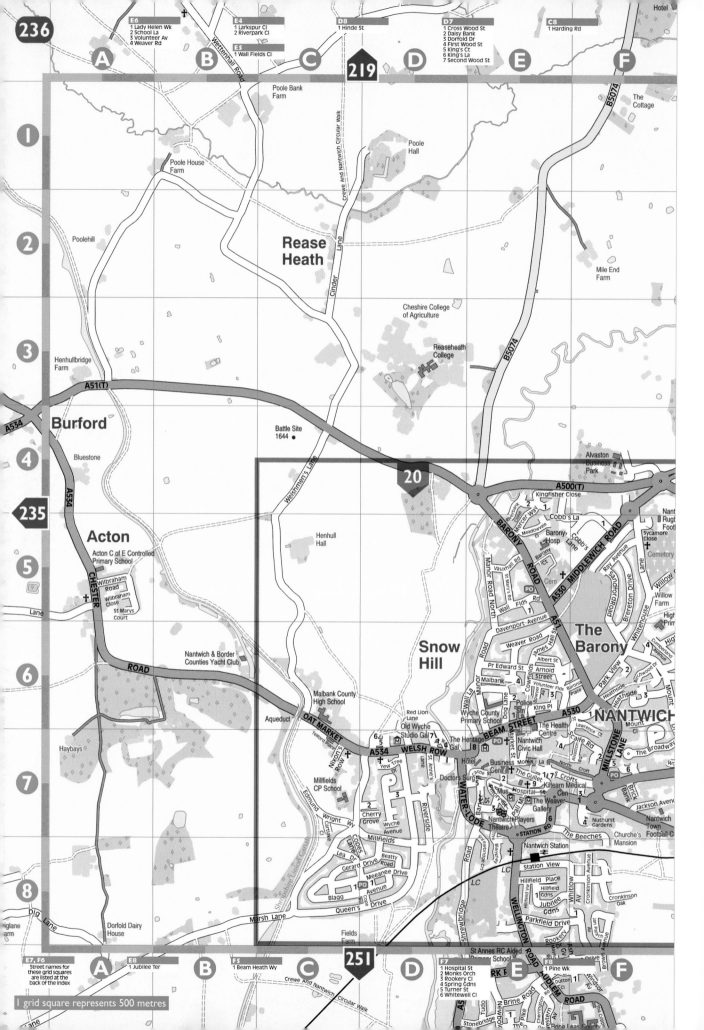

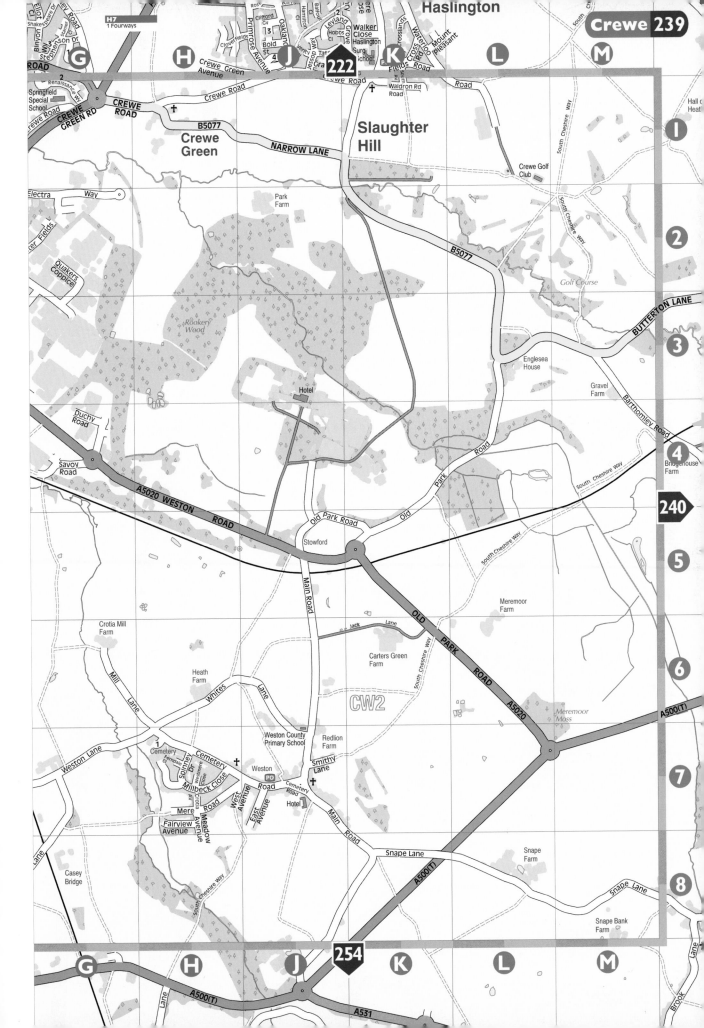

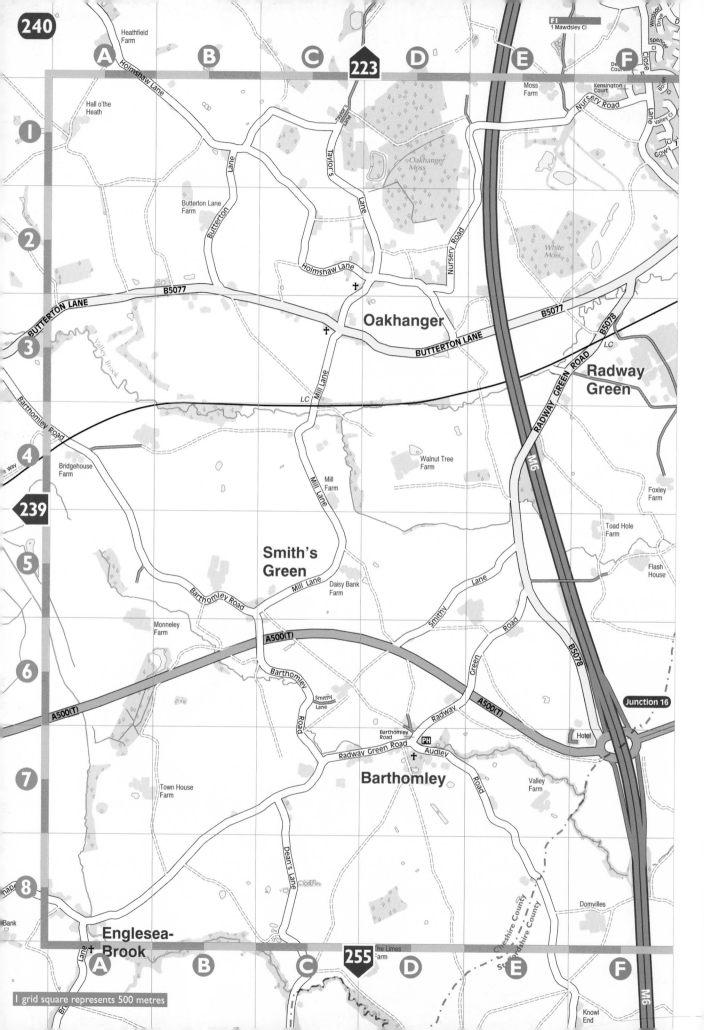

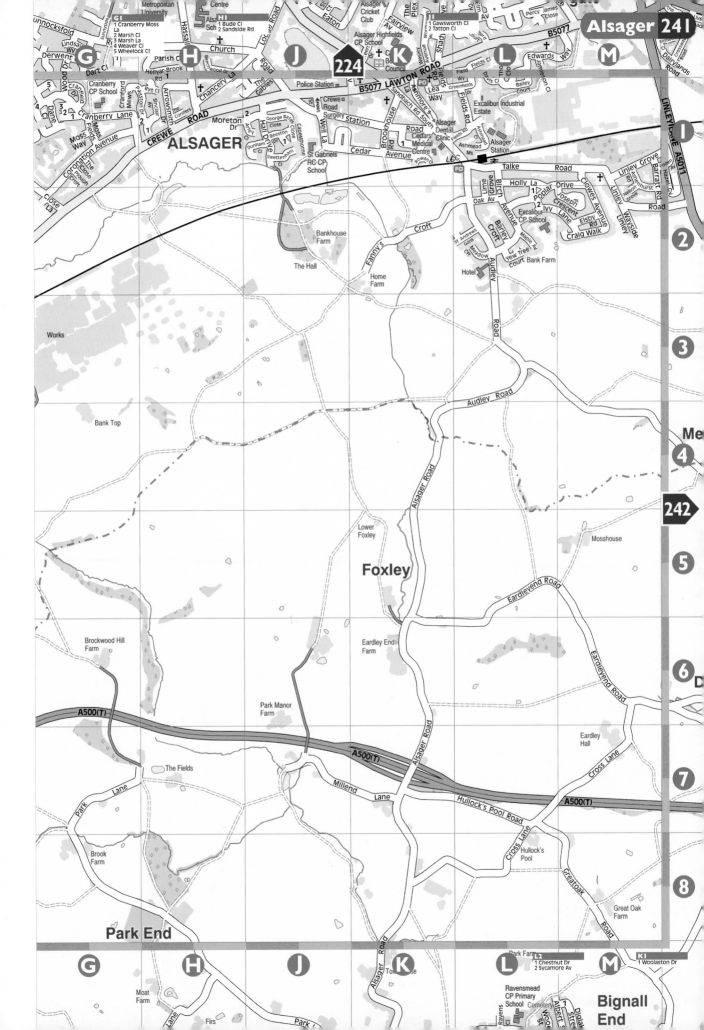

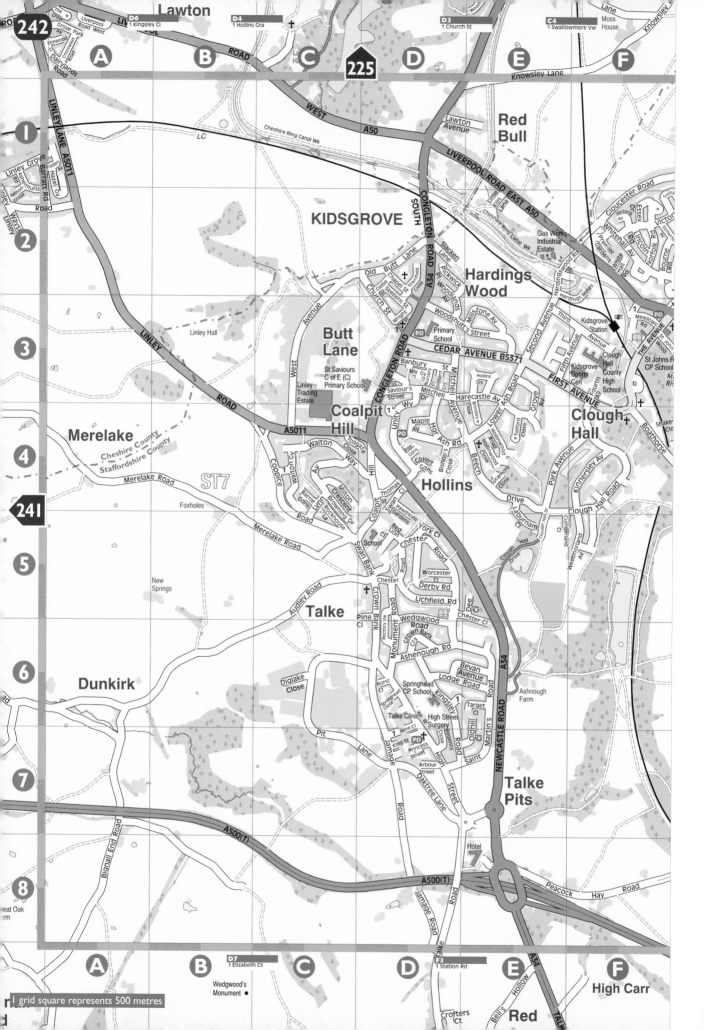

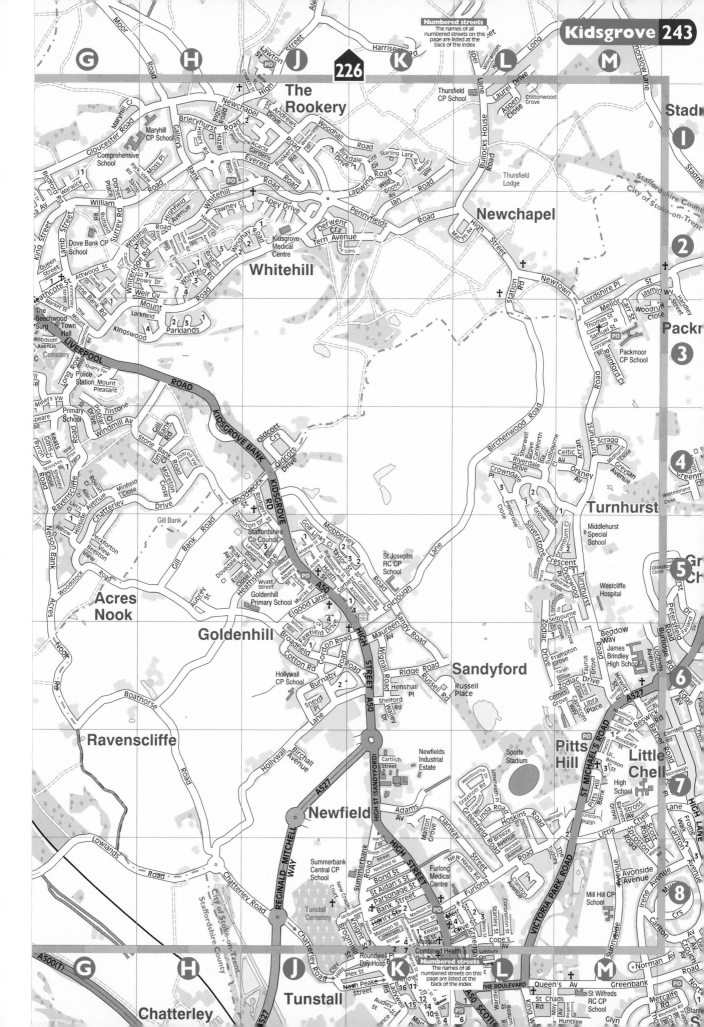

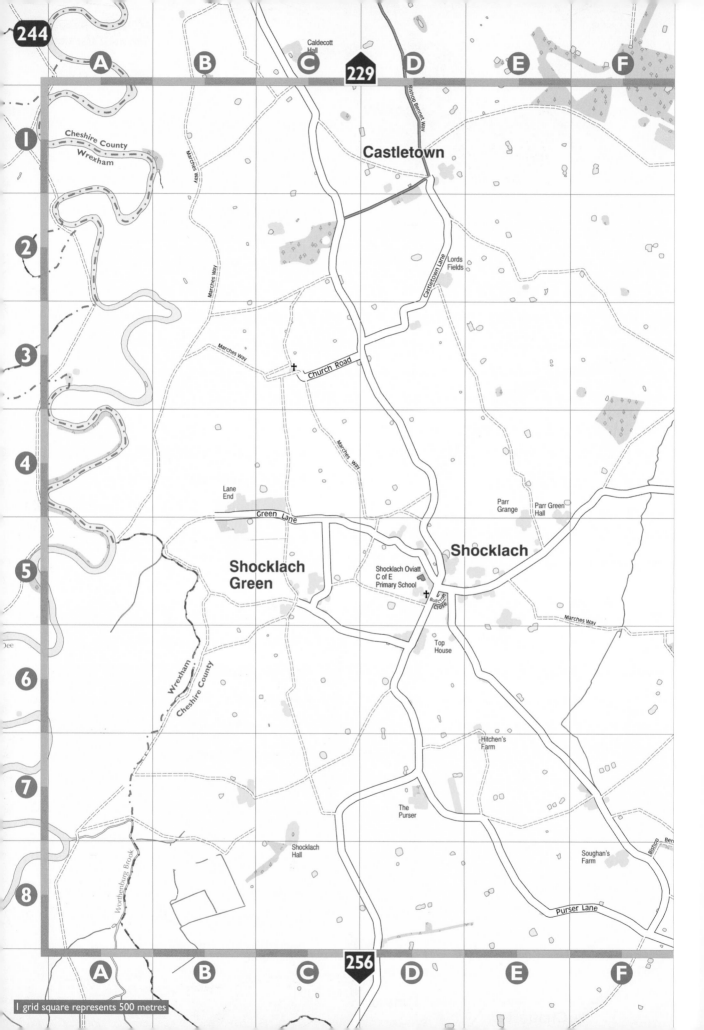

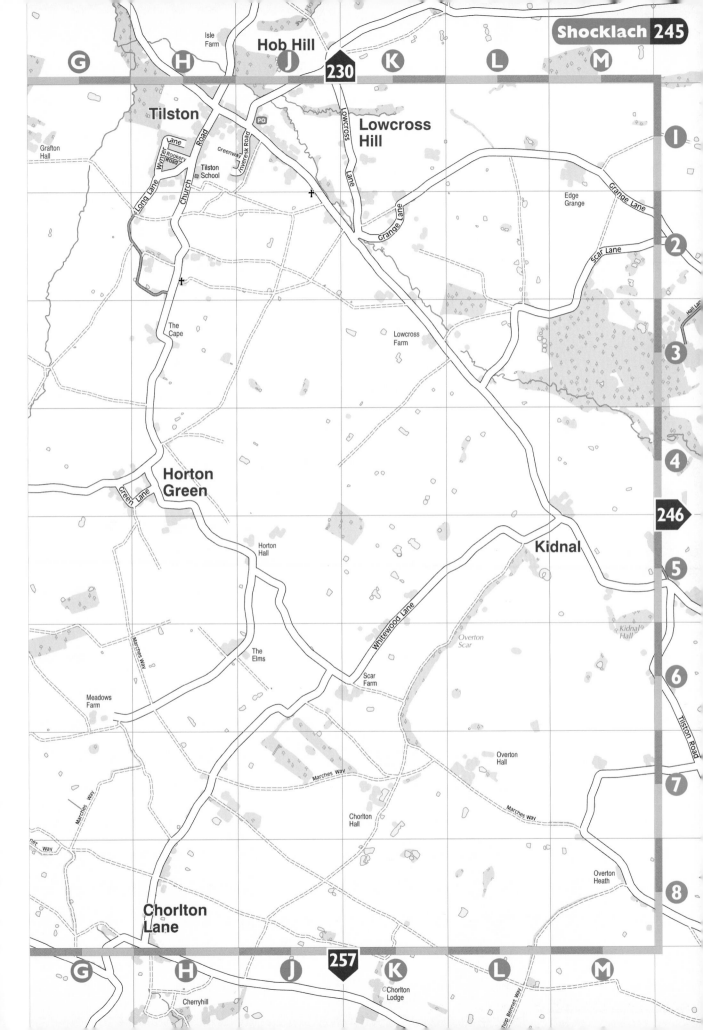

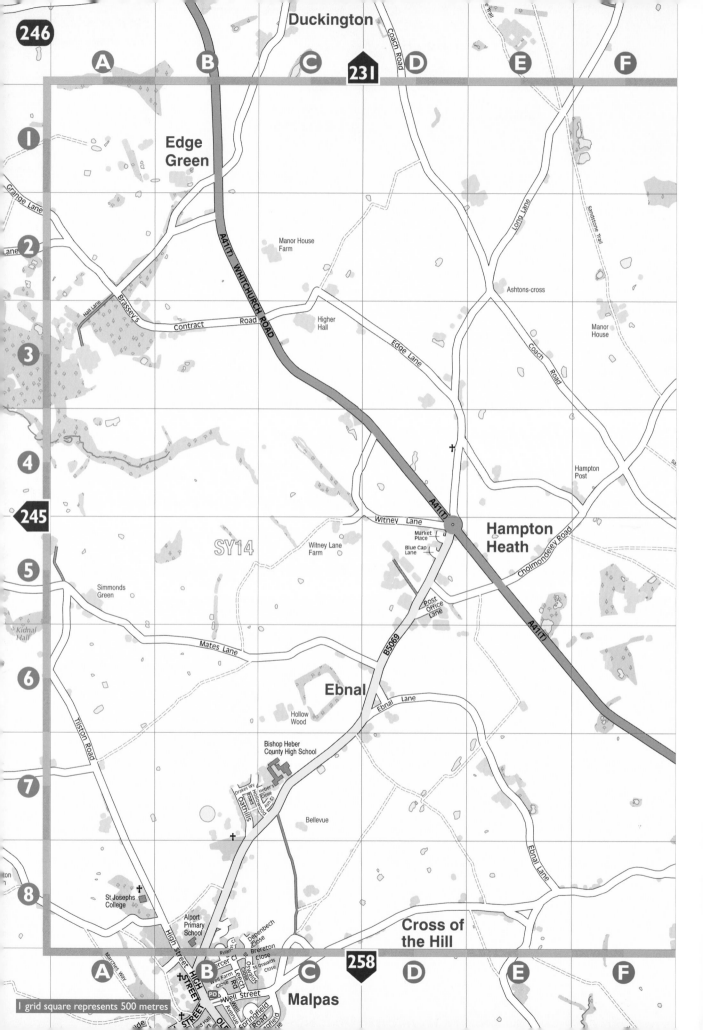

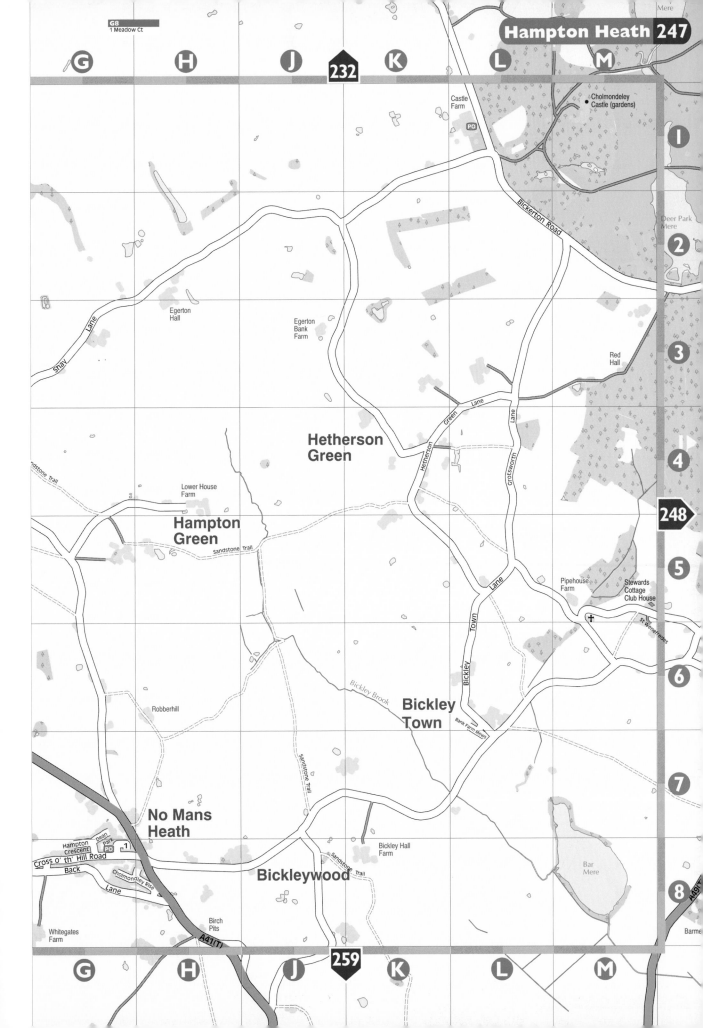

G8
1 Meadow Ct

G H J **232** K L M

Castle
Farm

PO

● Cholmondeley
Castle (gardens)

Bickerton Road

Deer Park
Mere

I

2

Egerton
Hall

Egerton
Bank
Farm

Red
Hall

3

Shav Lane

Sandstone Trail

Hetherson
Green

Hetherson Green Lane

Lane

Grotsworth Lane

I

4

Lower House
Farm

Sandstone Trail

248

Hampton
Green

Pipehouse
Farm

Stewards
Cottage
Club House

5

St Wenefredes

✝

6

Bickley Town Lane

Robberhill

Bickley Brook

Bickley
Town

Bank Farm Mews

7

Sandstone Trail

No Mans
Heath

Bar
Mere

Hampton
Crescent

Dean
Park
PO 1

Cross o' th' Hill Road

Back

Cholmondley Rise

Lane

Bickley Hall
Farm

Sandstone Trail

Bickleywood

8

A49(T)

Whitegates
Farm

Birch
Pits

A41(T)

Barme

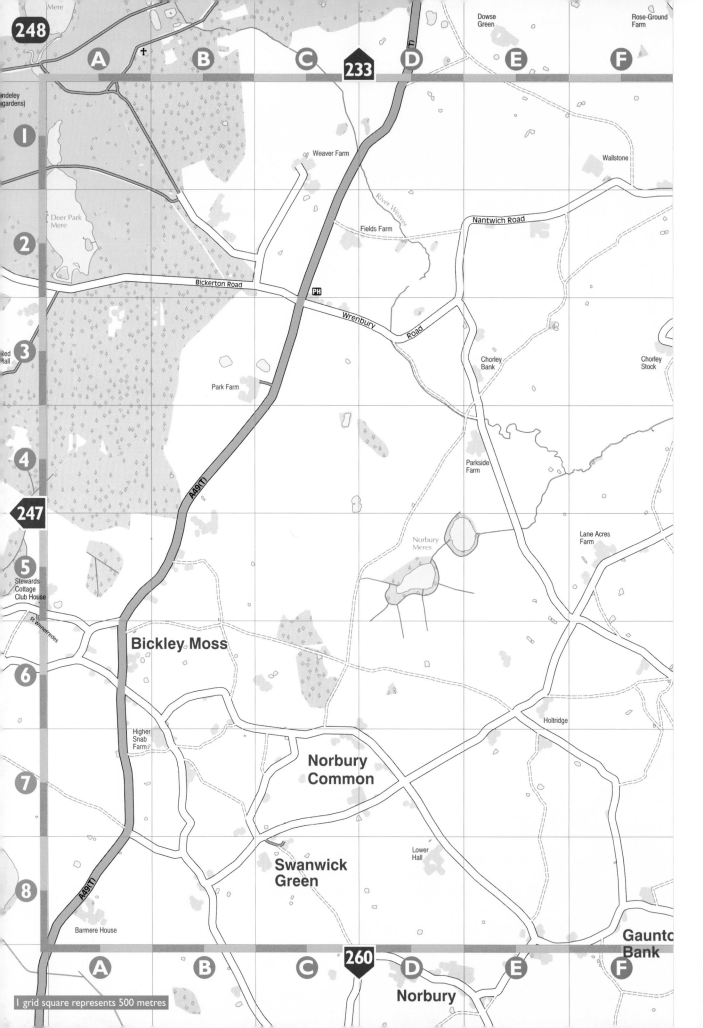

A   B   C   **233**   D   E   F

(ndeley gardens)

I

Mere

Dowse Green

Rose-Ground Farm

Wallstone

Weaver Farm

River Weaver

Nantwich Road

Deer Park Mere

2

Fields Farm

Bickerton Road

PH

Wrenbury Road

Red Hall

3

Park Farm

Chorley Bank

Chorley Stock

4

A49(T)

Parkside Farm

247

Lane Acres Farm

5

Stewards Cottage Club House

Norbury Meres

St Wenefredes

Bickley Moss

6

Higher Snab Farm

Holtridge

Norbury Common

7

Lower Hall

Swanwick Green

A49(T)

8

Barmere House

Gaunto Bank

A   B   C   **260**   D   E   F

Norbury

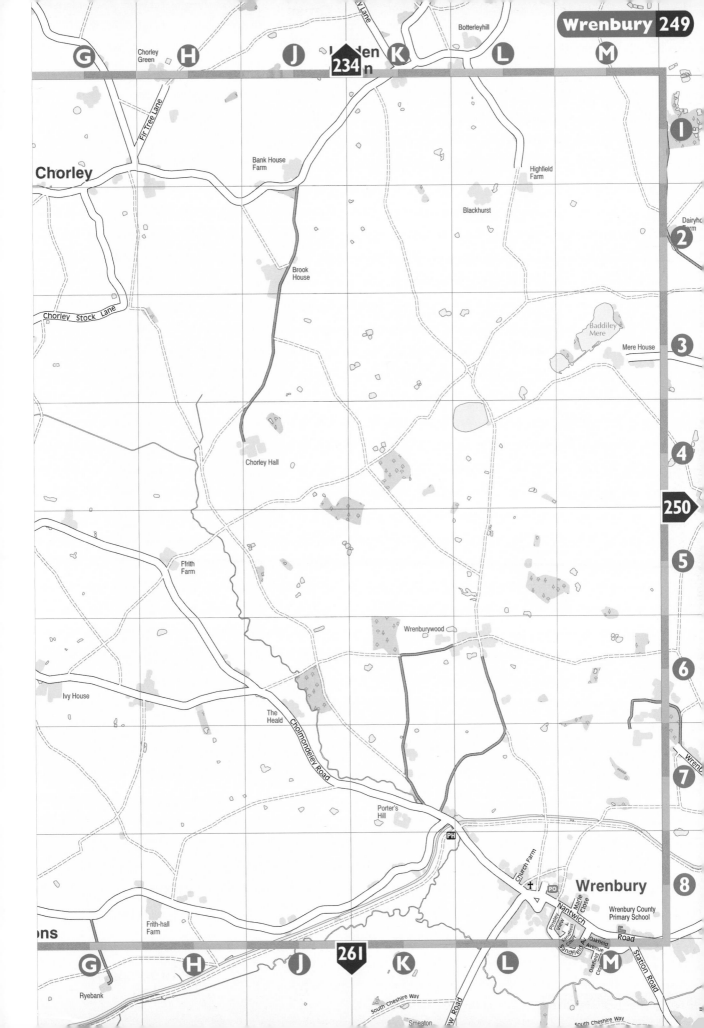

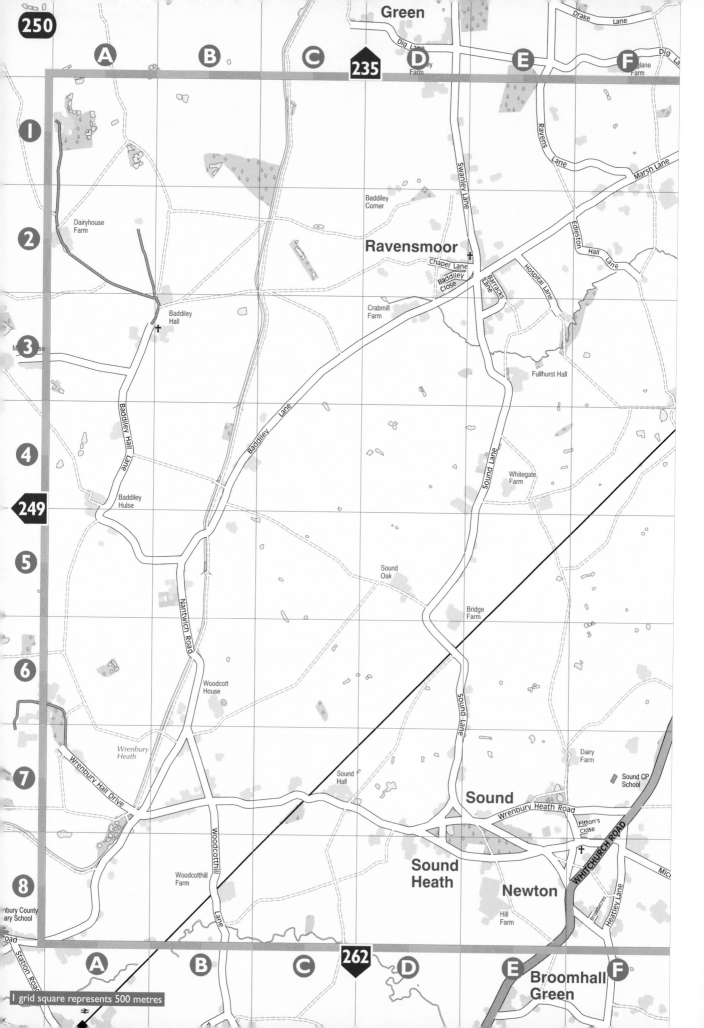

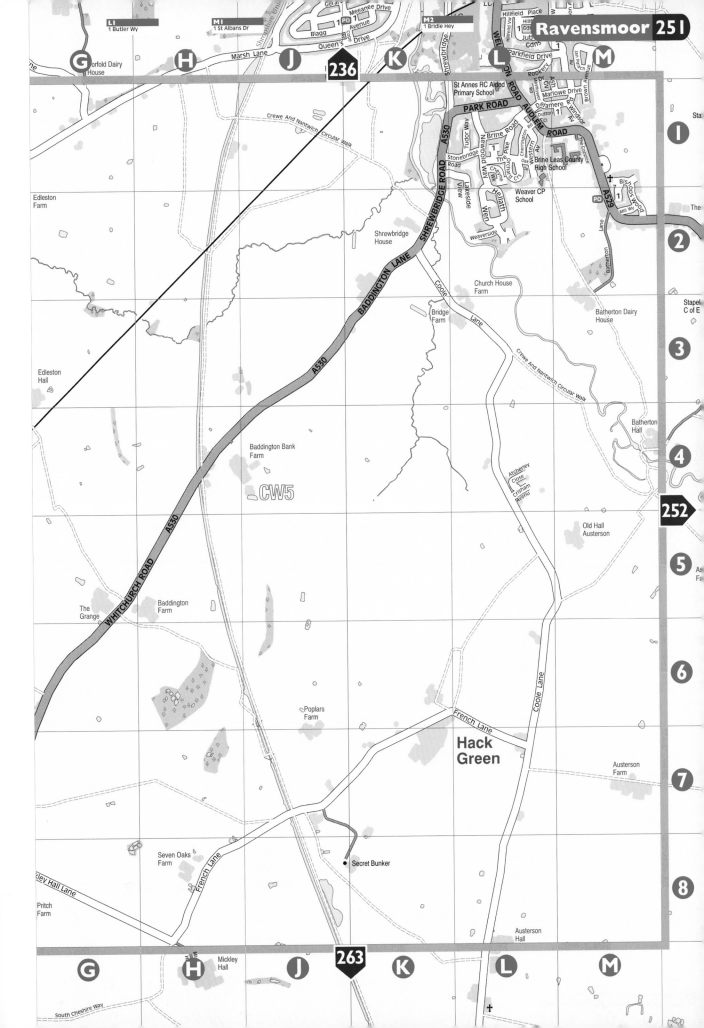

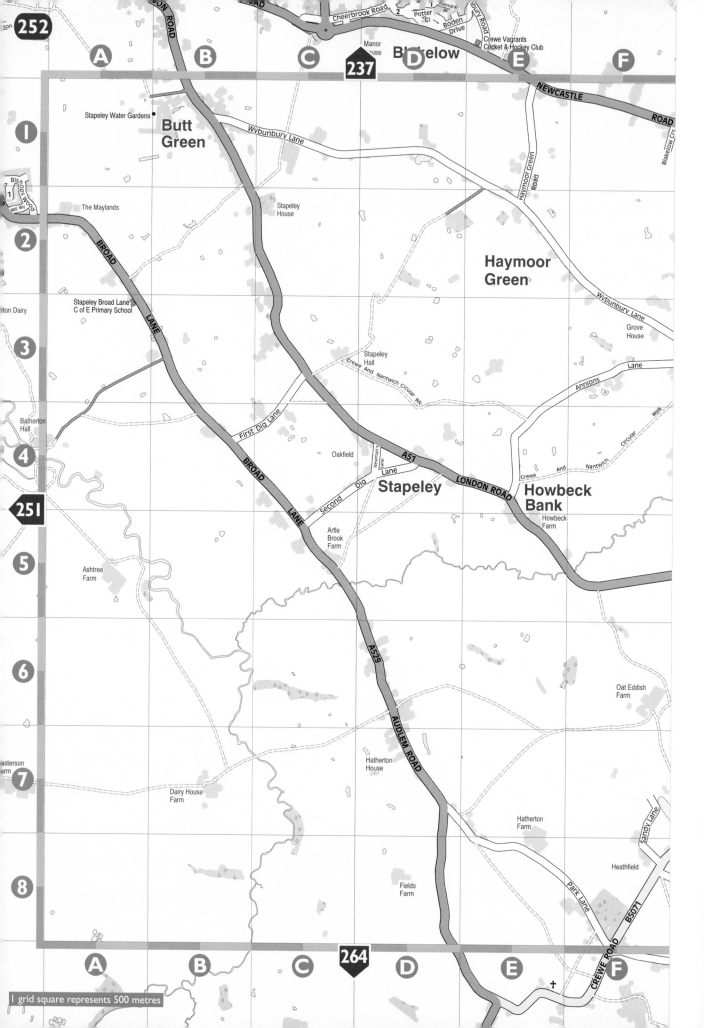

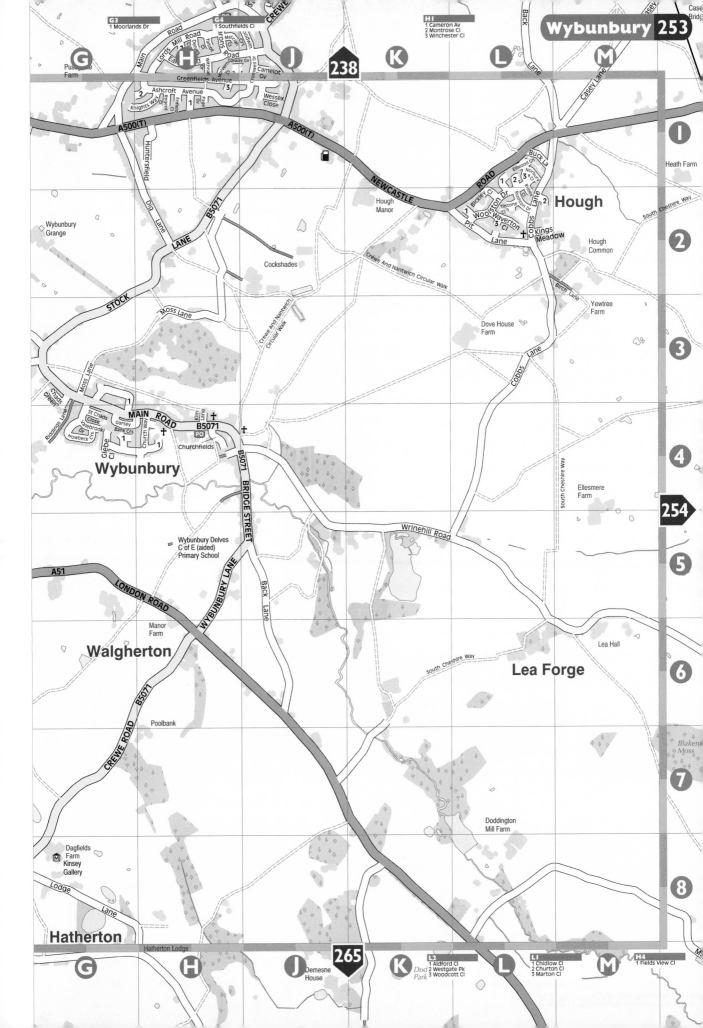

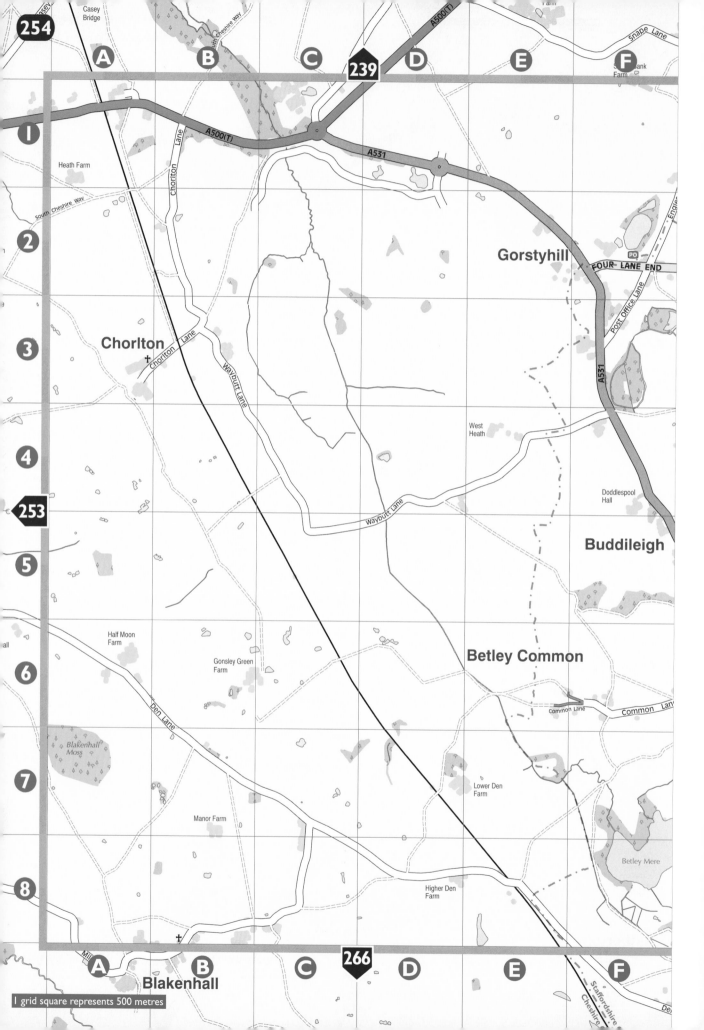

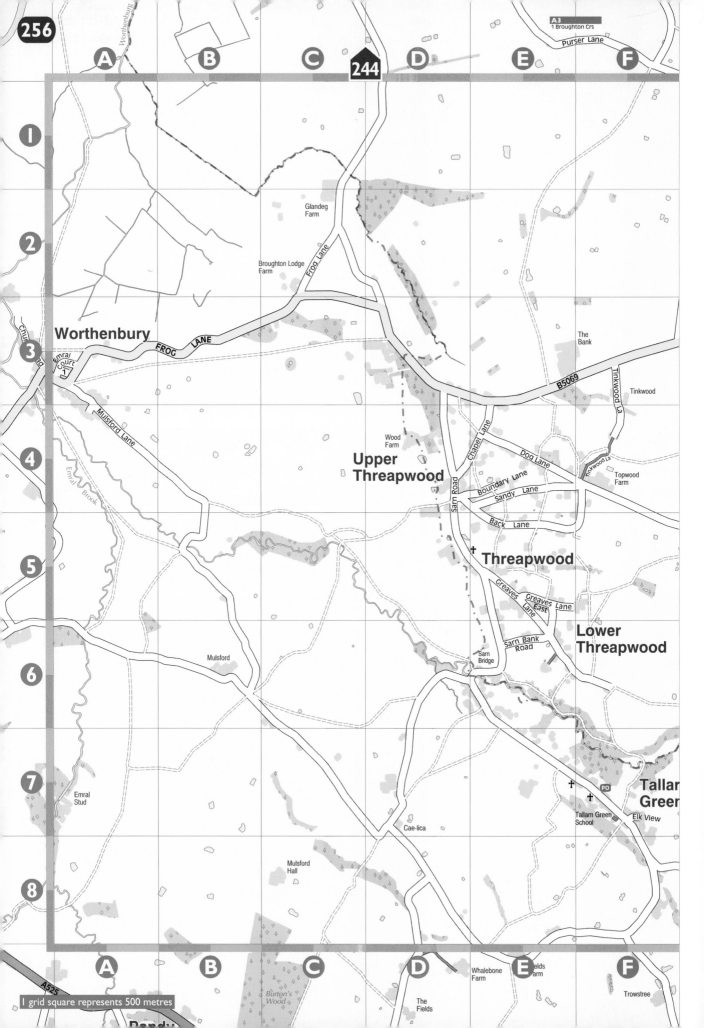

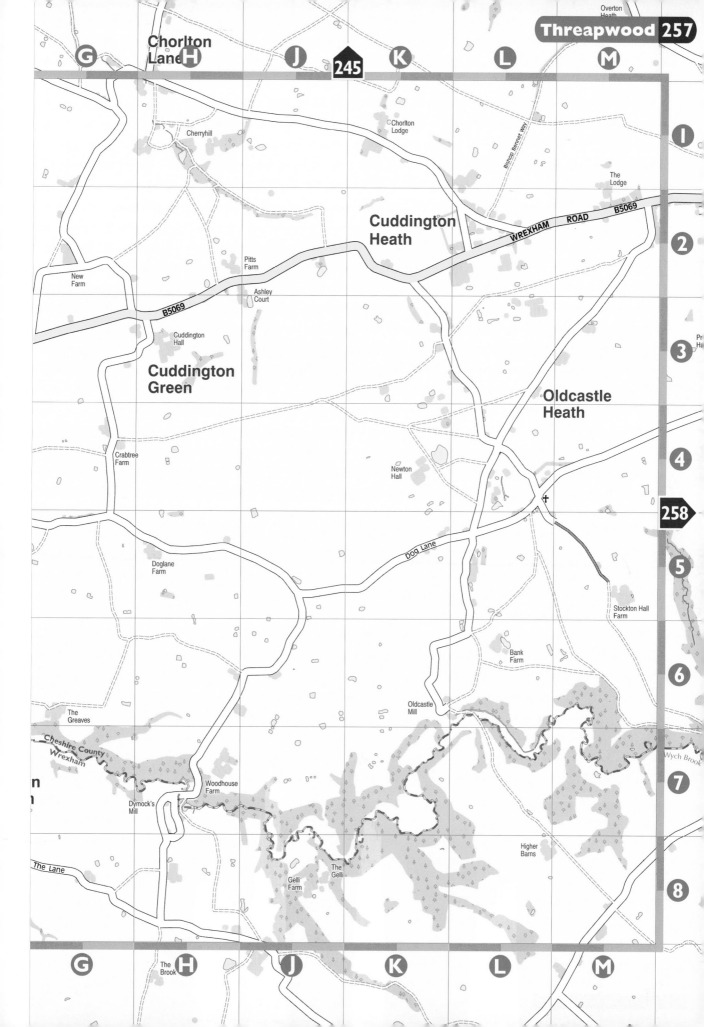

G H J 245 K L M

Chorlton Lane

Overton Heath

Cherryhill

Chorlton Lodge

The Lodge

Bishop Bennet Way

Cuddington Heath

WREXHAM ROAD B5069

Pitts Farm

New Farm

B5069

Ashley Court

Cuddington Hall

Cuddington Green

Oldcastle Heath

Crabtree Farm

Newton Hall

Dog Lane

Doglane Farm

Stockton Hall Farm

Bank Farm

The Greaves

Oldcastle Mill

Cheshire County

Wrexham

Wych Brook

Woodhouse Farm

Dymock's Mill

Higher Barns

The Lane

Gelli Farm

The Gelli

The Brook

G H J K L M

I

2

3

4

258

5

6

7

8

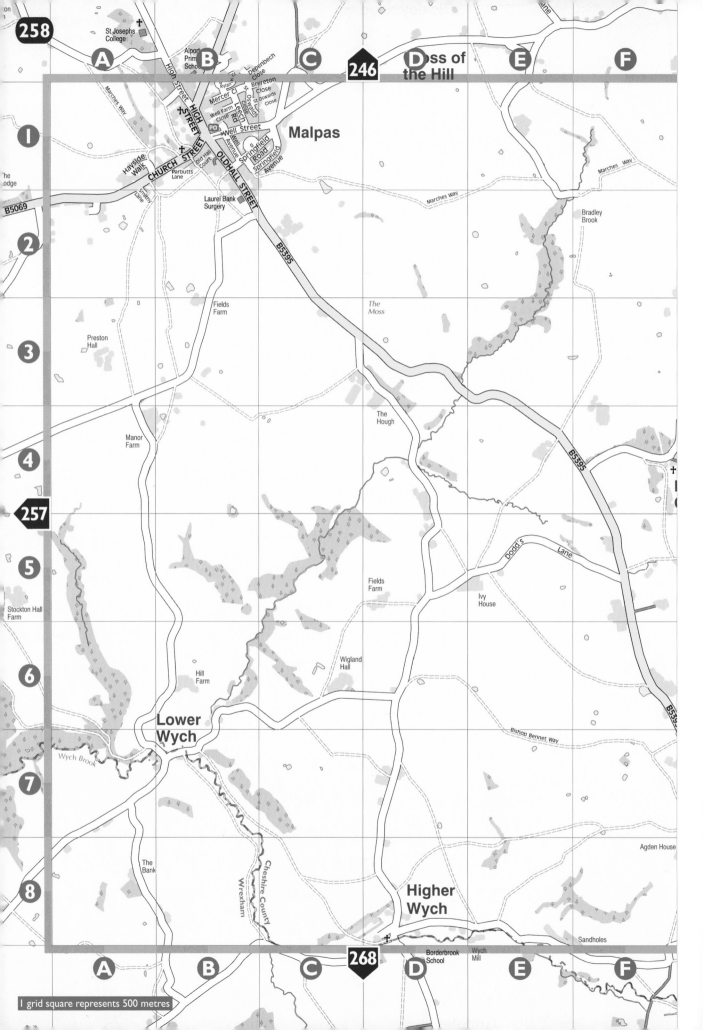

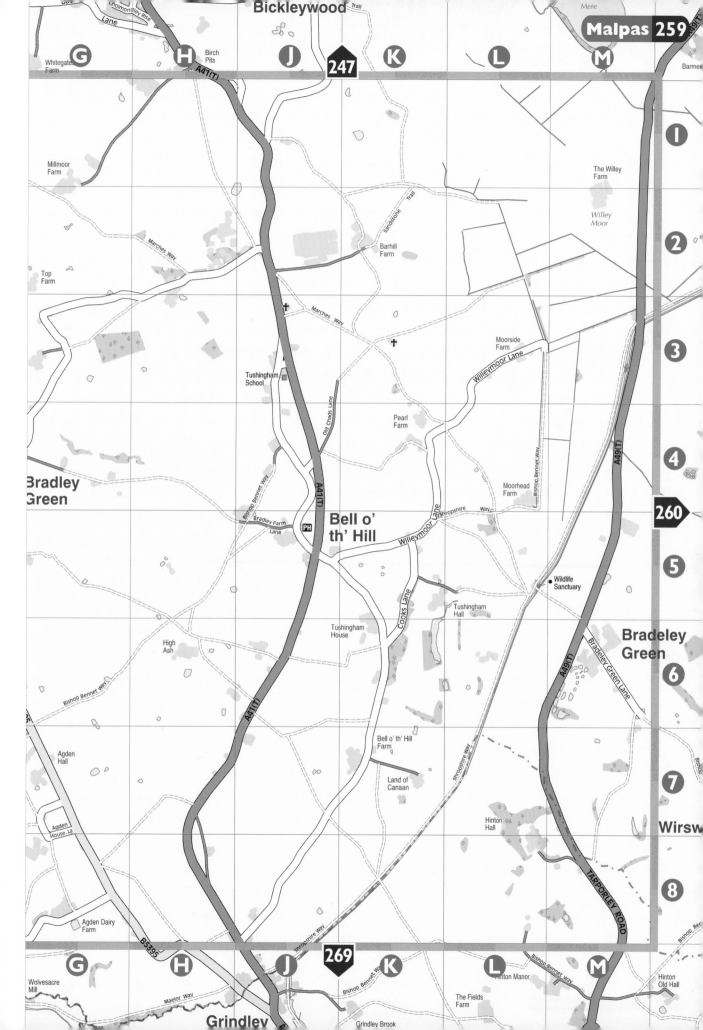

A49(T)

Barmer House
A
B
C
248
D
E
F
Gaunt
Bank

I

Willey

2

Handley
Park

Hurst
Green

Norbury

Shropshire Union Canal (Llangollen Branch)

Steer
Bridge

3

A49(T)

Hadley
Hall

Lane

4

Wirswall Road

Marbury

School

School
Close

PH

Quoisley

Quoisley
Meres

✝

South Cheshire Way

259

Big
Mere

Bank
Farm

5

Deemster
Manor

South Cheshire Way

**Bradeley
Green**

6

Heath Lane

Fox Hall

Bishop Bennet Way

Wood
Farm

Wicksted
Hall

7

Wicksted
Old Hall

South Cheshire Way

Oss Mere

Wirswall

Bishop Bennet Way

8

PORLEY ROAD

Mile Bank Road

Chinnel
Farm

Cheshire County
Shropshire County

Hinton
Old Hall
A
B
Lower House
Farm
C
270
D
E
F

1 grid square represents 500 metres

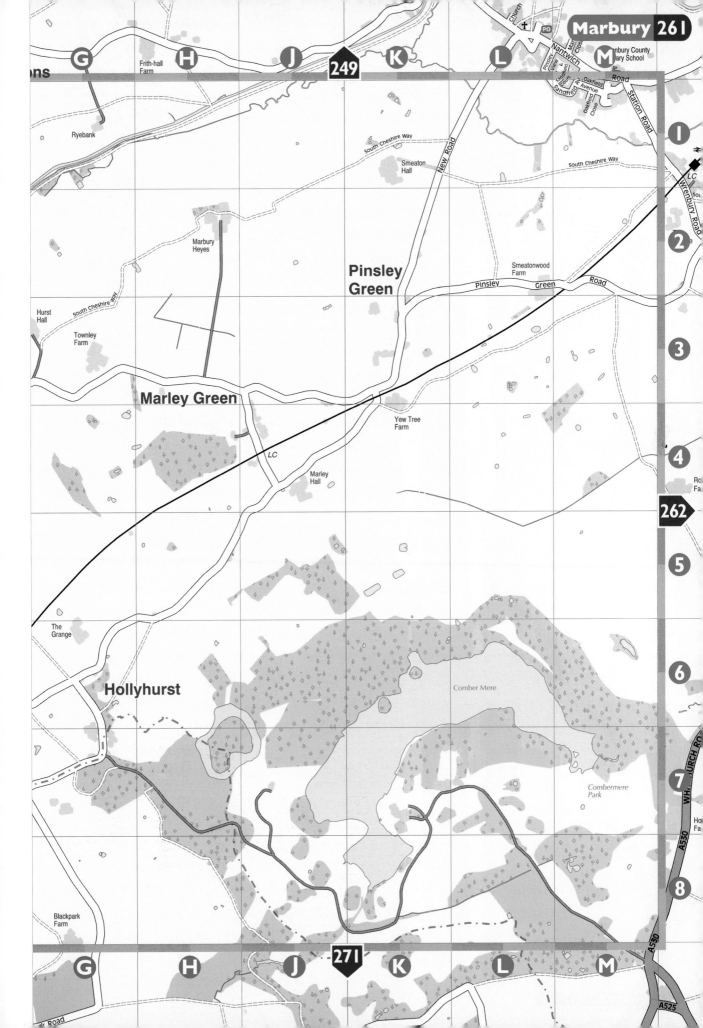

G   H   J   249   K   L   M

Church

PO

Nantwich

Pinsley View

Sandfield Court

Oakfield Avenue

Oakfield Close

Station Road

Wrenbury County Primary School

Road

I

Wrenbury Road

LC

2

South Cheshire Way

New Road

Smeaton Hall

South Cheshire Way

Frith-hall Farm

Ryebank

Marbury Heyes

Pinsley Green

Smeatonwood Farm

Pinsley   Green   Road

3

Hurst Hall

South Cheshire Way

Townley Farm

Marley Green

LC

Yew Tree Farm

4

262

Ro Fa

Marley Hall

5

The Grange

6

Hollyhurst

Comber Mere

Combermere Park

7

WHITCHURCH RO

A530

Ho Fa

8

Blackpark Farm

A530

G   H   J   271   K   L   M

A525

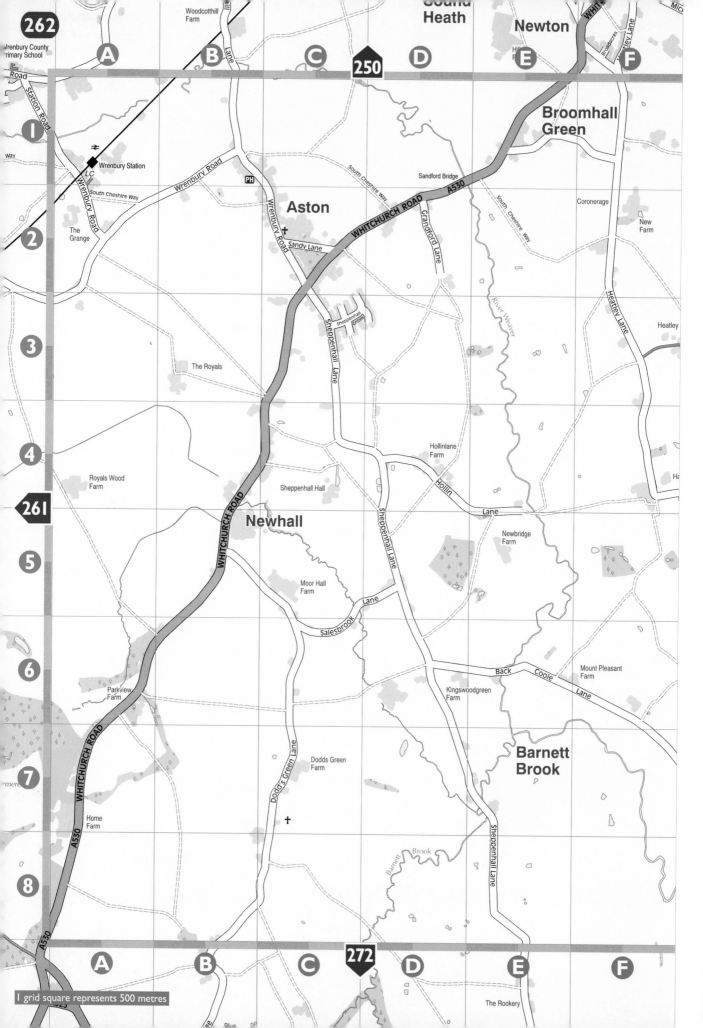

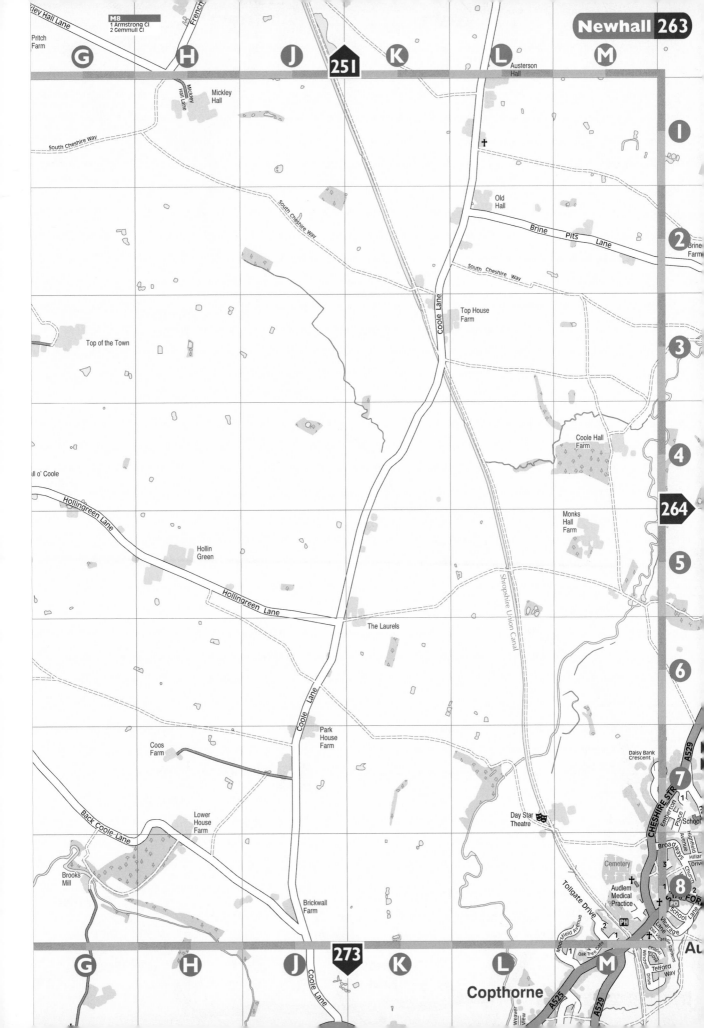

Copthorne

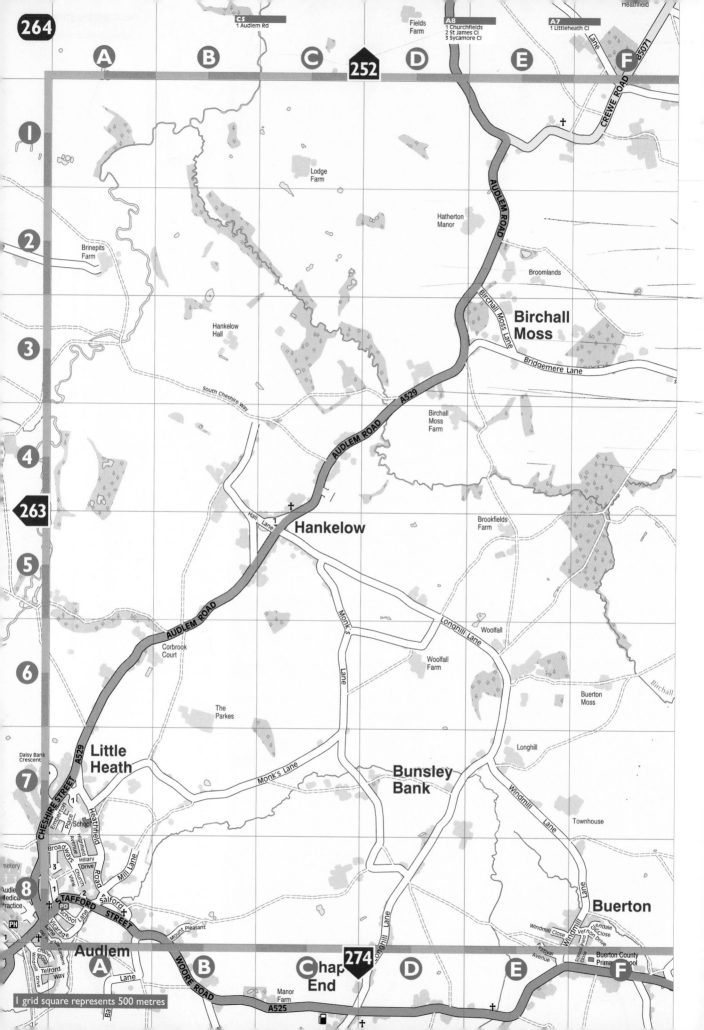

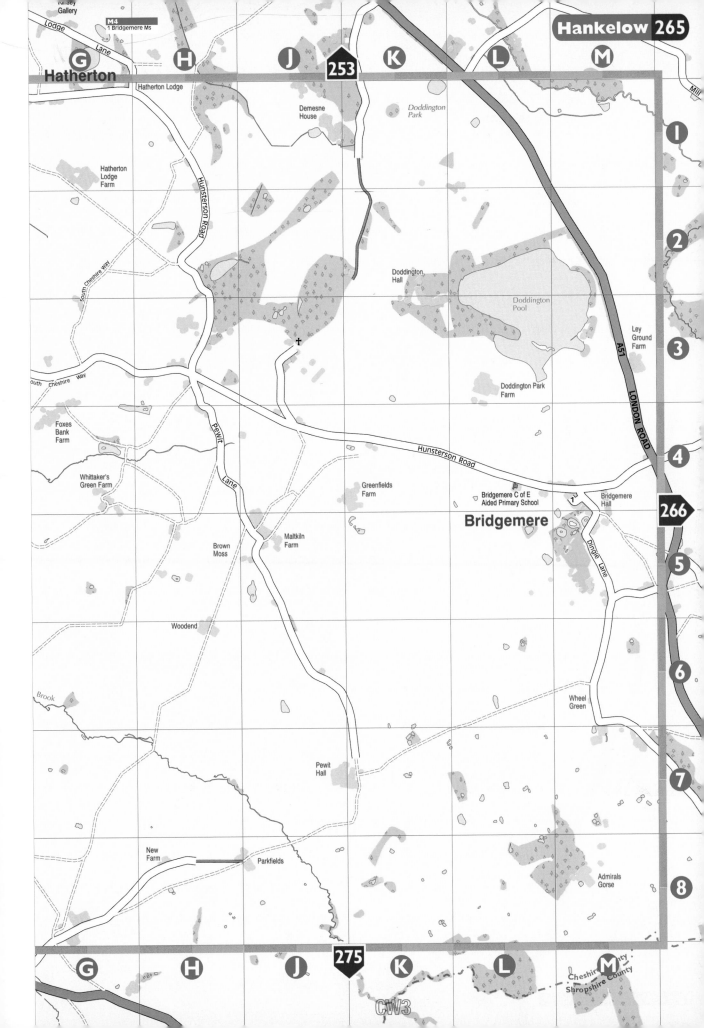

Hatherton

Hatherton Lodge

Hatherton Lodge Farm

Kinsey Gallery

Lodge Lane

M4
1 Bridgemere Ms

Hunterson Road

South Cheshire Way

South Cheshire Way

Foxes Bank Farm

Whittaker's Green Farm

Pewit Lane

Brown Moss

Woodend

Brook

New Farm

Parkfields

Demesne House

Doddington Park

Doddington Hall

Doddington Pool

Doddington Park Farm

Greenfields Farm

Maltkiln Farm

Pewit Hall

Bridgemere

Bridgemere C of E Aided Primary School

Bridgemere Hall

Dingle Lane

Wheel Green

Admirals Gorse

Ley Ground Farm

A51 LONDON ROAD

Mill

Cheshire County
Shropshire County

G H J K L M

253

266

275

CW3

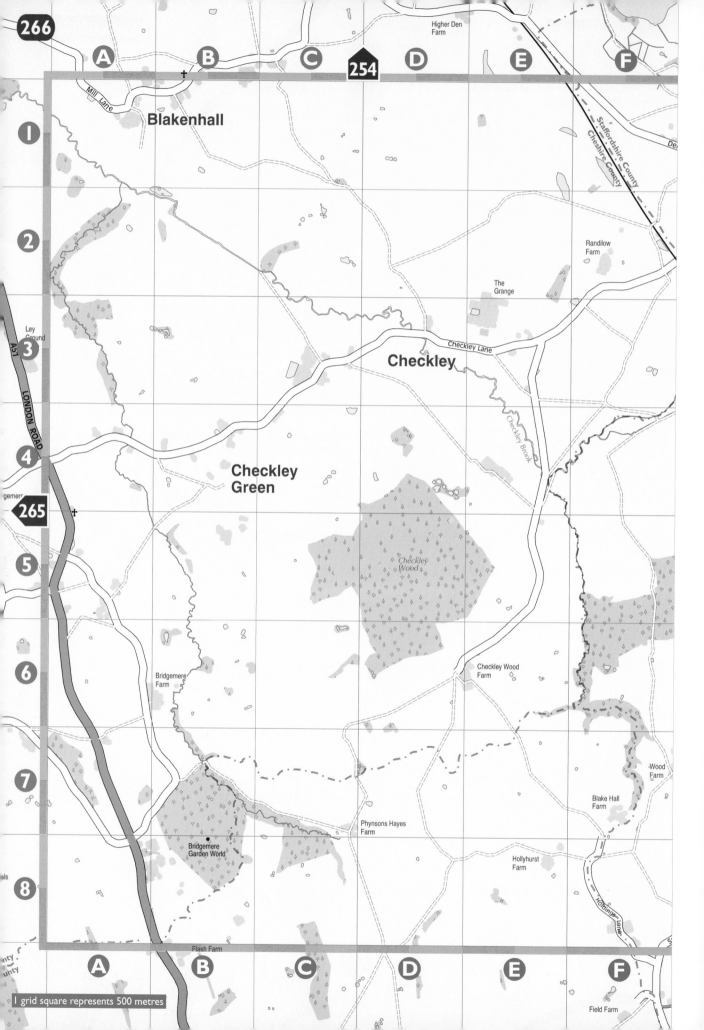

266

A   B   C   **254**   D   E   F

Higher Den Farm

Mill Lane

Blakenhall

Staffordshire County
Cheshire County

Den

1

Randilow Farm

2

The Grange

Ley Ground

Checkley Lane

A51

LONDON ROAD

3

Checkley

Checkley Brook

4

Checkley Green

265

Checkley Wood

5

6

Bridgemere Farm

Checkley Wood Farm

Wood Farm

7

Phynsons Hayes Farm

Blake Hall Farm

Bridgemere Garden World

Hollyhurst Farm

Holbine Lane

8

Flash Farm

A   B   C   D   E   F

Field Farm

1 grid square represents 500 metres

Ravenshall

K5
1 Fern Dene
2 Heather Gld

K6
1 Charles Cotton Dr

L4
1 Park Cl

G Cracow **H** Moss

J

255

K

L

M

I

Wrinehill

Cracow Moss

Old Road

Lane

2

A531

MAIN ROAD

Bowseywood Farm

3

Heighley Lane

Heighley Castle Way

KEELE ROAD

Wrinehill Hall

Lower Thornhill

Bowsey Wood Road

Woodland Hills

Hidden Hills

Madeley Manor

4

Meac Cour Scho

Higher Thornhill

College Close

1

Windy Arbour

Holm Oak Drive

Woodside Close

3 1 3 4
2 5

Beck Road

Salisbury C

Little Madeley

5

Arbour Close

New Road

Beech Brook

Greenmeadows Road

1

Police Station

A525 NEWCASTLE ROAD

Middle Madeley

PO

Mill Lane

6

Wrinehill Wood

Apple Croft

2 1

Pear Tree Drive

Primrose Dell

The Bridle Path

Beresford Dale

7

Plover Field

Furnace Lane

Staffordshire County Council

Pecan Place

6

Bower End

Moss Lane

Morningside

Cherry Hill

Merlin Green

3

Madeley High School

Waterside Close

Middle Madeley

Bower End Lane

Moor Hall

Bramble Lea

Birch Dale

2

The Holbon

Pastoral Close

Knightley

Hungerford La

6

John Offley Road

Hungerford H Farm

Izaac Walton Way

+

Madeley

Sir John Offley C of E Primary School

Vicarage Lane

Castle Lane

Nethersey Hey Lane

7

Red Lane

Station Road

BAR HILL

Field House

Bar Hill House Farm

8

M5
1 Daltry Wy
2 Elkington Rl
3 Garners Wk
4 Heron Cl
5 Kingfisher Cl
6 Lindops La

L6
1 Grayling Willows
2 Laverock Gv
3 River Lea Ms

L5
1 Lynam Wy
2 Roseberry Dr
3 Thornhill Dr

G Onneley Golf Club **H**

J

K

L

Main Road

M

Hotel

PH

Hey House

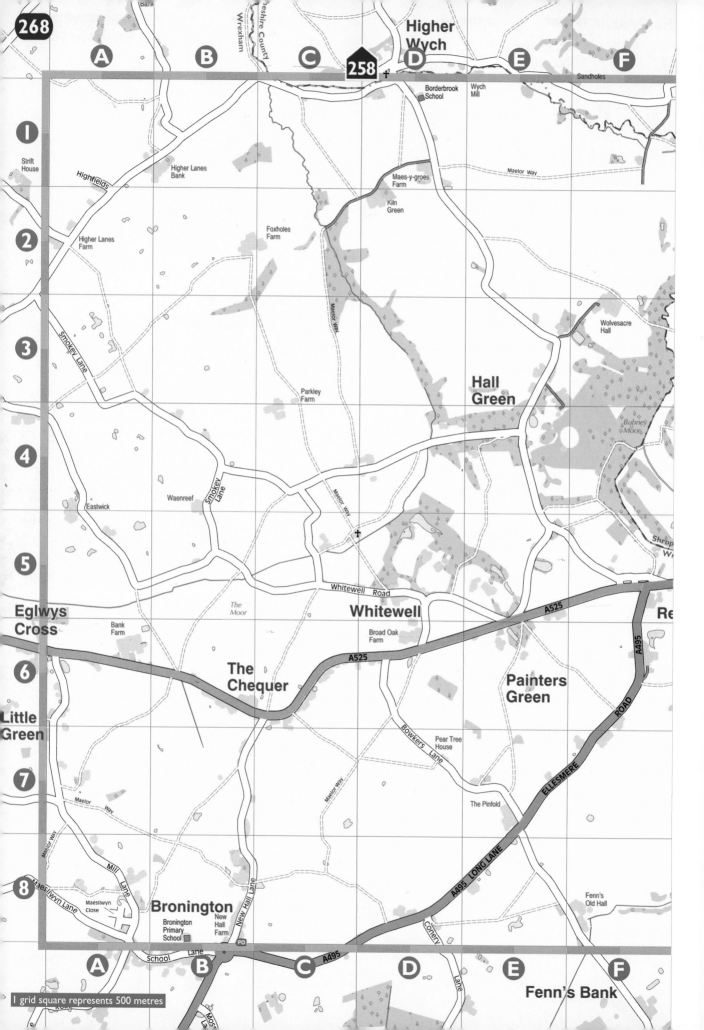

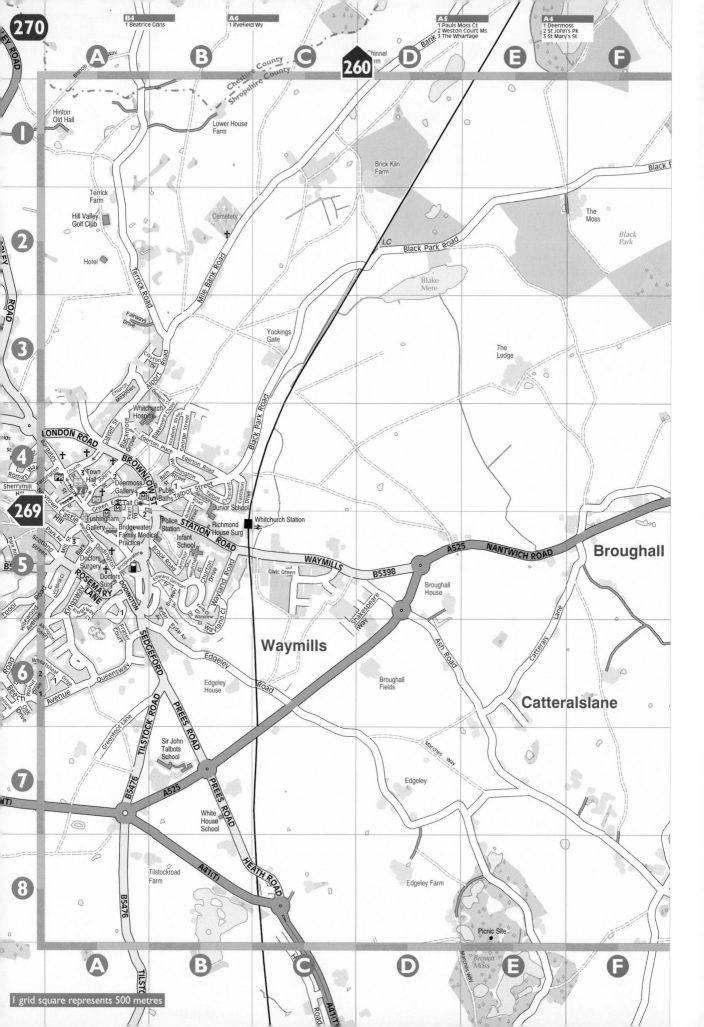

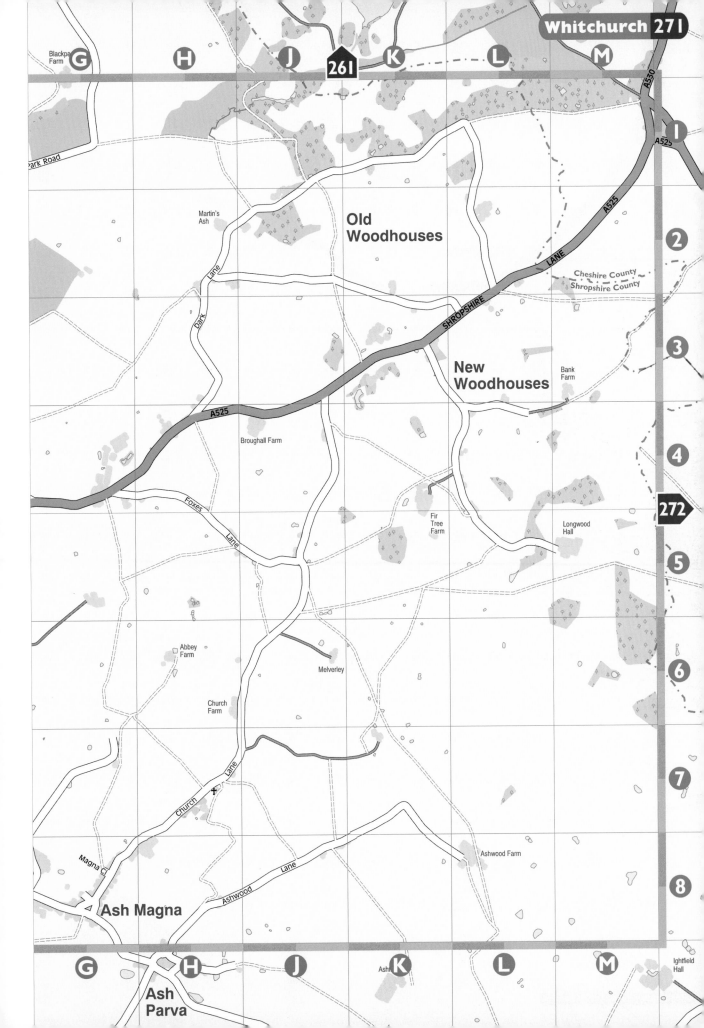

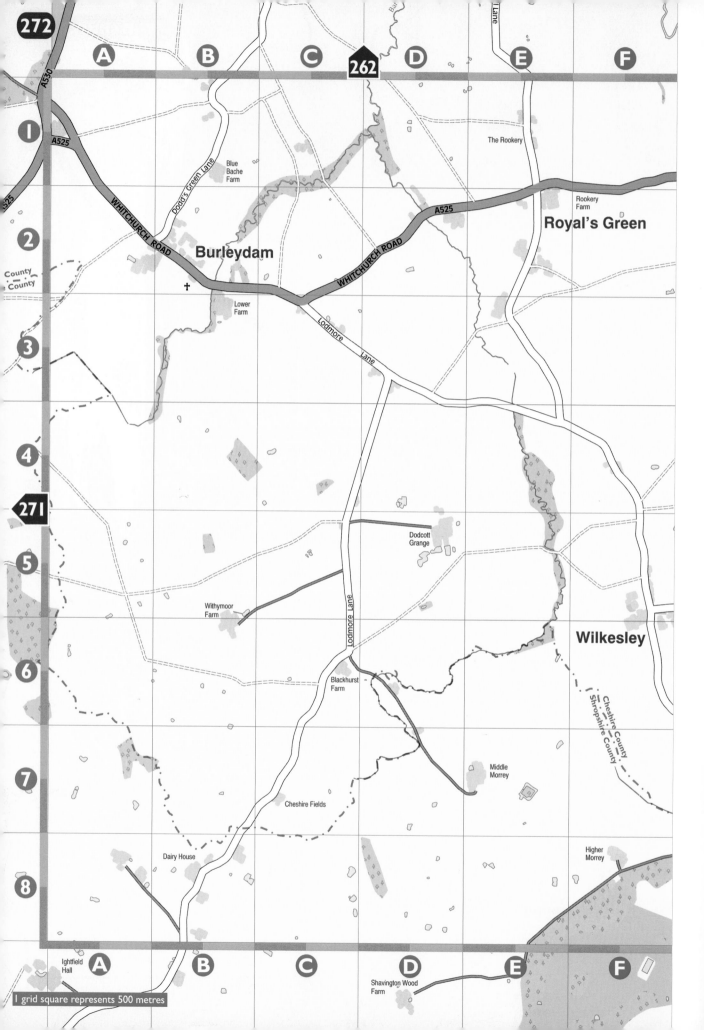

A   **B**   **C**   262   **D**   **E**   **F**

A530

A525

1

A525

WHITCHURCH ROAD

Dodd's Green Lane

Blue
Bache
Farm

The Rookery

A525

Rookery
Farm

Royal's Green

2

County
e County

Burleydam

WHITCHURCH ROAD

✝

Lower
Farm

Lodmore   Lane

3

4

271

Dodcott
Grange

5

Withymoor
Farm

Lodmore Lane

Wilkesley

6

Blackhurst
Farm

Cheshire County
Shropshire County

7

Cheshire Fields

Middle
Morrey

Dairy House

Higher
Morrey

8

Ightfield
Hall

Shavington Wood
Farm

I grid square represents 500 metres

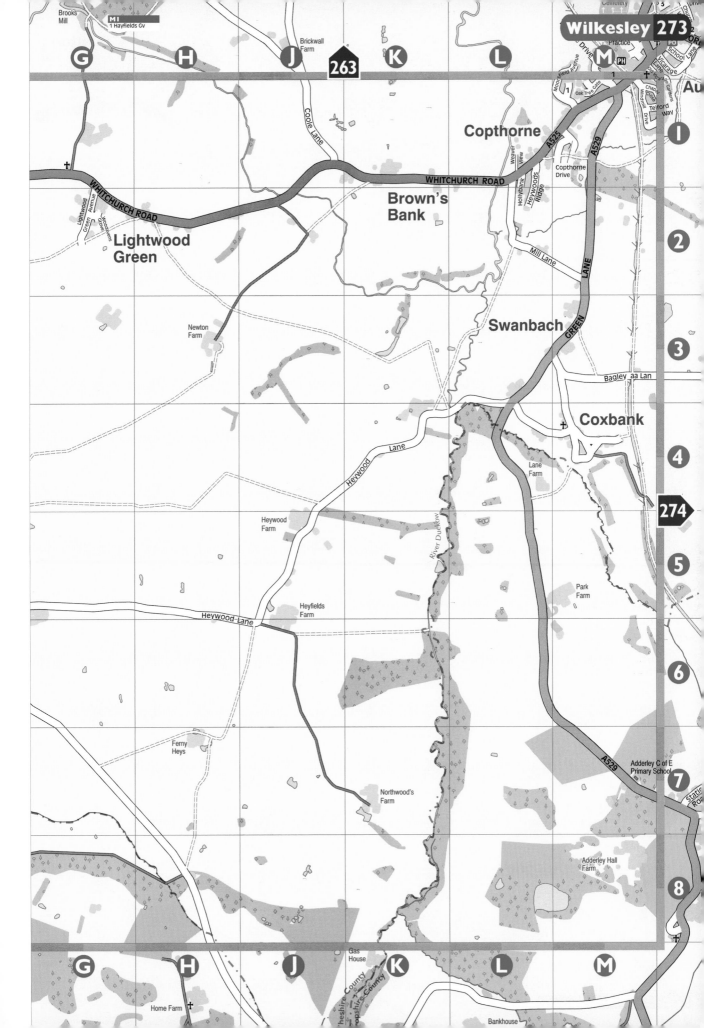

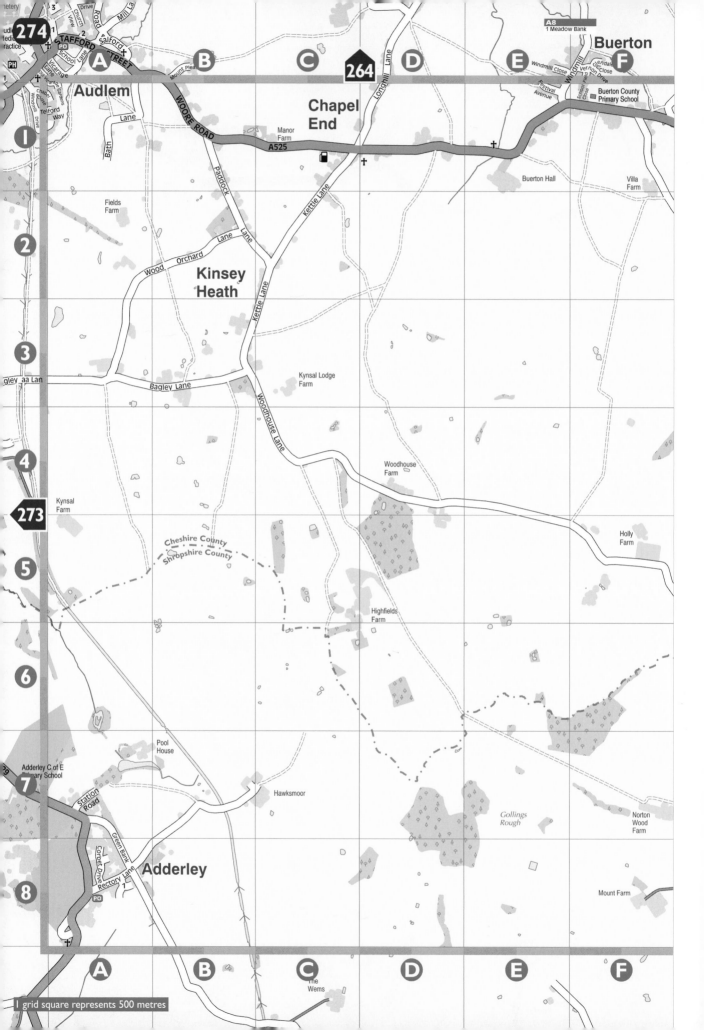

Audlem

Chapel
End

Buerton

Manor
Farm

A525

Buerton County
Primary School

1 Meadow Bank

Windmill Close

Festival
Avenue

Buerton Hall

Villa
Farm

Fields
Farm

Wood Orchard Lane

Paddock Lane

Kettle Lane

Kinsey
Heath

Kynsal Lodge
Farm

Bagley Lane

Woodhouse Lane

Woodhouse
Farm

Kynsal
Farm

Cheshire County
Shropshire County

Holly
Farm

Highfields
Farm

Adderley C. of E
Primary School

Pool
House

Hawksmoor

Gollings
Rough

Norton
Wood
Farm

Station Road

Green Bank

Corbet Drive

Rectory Lane

Adderley

Mount Farm

The Wems

G · H · J · 265 · K · L · M

I
2
3
4
5
6
7
8

CW3

A525 WOORE ROAD

The Grange

Fields Farm

Gorsey Bank Farm

Cheshire County
Shropshire County

Admirals

Woore Hall

Three Wells

Hankins Heys Lane

Canridden Wood

College Fields

Hankins Heys Lane

Hankins Heys

Mere Farm

Bellaport Road

Bellaport Home Farm

Bellaport Old Hall

Poplar Lane

The Grove

Bellaport Road

Bearstone

G · H · J · K · L · M

Bearstone Road

Bellaport Lodge

Abbot's Meads	145 H8	Brooklands	269 L3
Acres Nook	243 G5	Brookvale	74 B7
Acton	236 A5	Broomedge	59 K3
Acton Bridge	127 L1	Broomhall Green	262 E1
Adderley	274 A8	Broomhill	147 M4
Adlington	86 B7	Broughall	270 F5
Adswood	46 D7	Broughton	190 C1
Alderley Edge	110 C2	Brownedge	181 M8
Aldersey Green	213 J6	Brown Heath	171 H6
Aldford	211 M1	Brown Knowl	231 J4
Allgreave	188 C2	Brown Lees	227 G7
Allostock	156 F1	Brownlow	206 E5
Alpraham	198 D8	Brownlow Heath	206 D7
Alsager	241 H1	Brown's Bank	273 K2
Altrincham	42 F7	Broxton	231 G2
Alvanley	124 C4	Bruche	37 M5
Anderton	103 J8	Bruera	193 K6
Antrobus	77 K8	Bryn	128 B6
Appleton	7 H1	Bucklow Hill	80 B1
Appleton Park	56 D7	Buckoak	124 F7
Appleton Thorn	57 G8	Buddileigh	254 F5
Arclid	205 H3	Budworth Heath	104 B3
Arclid Green	205 H4	Buerton	264 F8
Arley	78 B5	Buglawton	185 H7
Arley Green	78 E6	Bulkeley	232 E2
Arthill	60 B4	Bunbury	216 F4
Ashley	61 L7	Bunbury Heath	216 E3
Ashley Heath	61 K4	Bunsley Bank	264 D7
Ash Magna	271 G8	Burford	236 A4
Ashton	148 F5	Burland	235 J5
Ashton Heath	100 D2	Burleydam	272 B2
Ashton-in-Makerfield	22 D1	Burton	118 D2
Aspull Common	24 B3	Burton	172 F8
Astbury	207 H4	Burtonwood	27 G6
Astle	135 K4	Burwardsley	215 G6
Astmoor	73 L1	Butley Town	112 C4
Aston	100 D3	Butt Green	252 B1
Aston	166 B1	Butt Lane	242 C3
Aston	262 C2	Byley	156 A5
Aston juxta Mondrum	219 K6	Cadishead	31 J8
Audlem	274 A1	Cale Green	46 F6
Backford	121 H8	Callands	36 D2
Backford Cross	120 F5	Calrofold	139 J2
Balderton	191 K3	Calveley	217 L2
Ball o' Ditton	6 D1	Capenhurst	120 B4
Balterley	255 J3	Carr Green	40 F6
Balterley Green	255 H2	Carrington Moss	41 M1
Balterley Heath	255 G3	Castlefields	73 M2
The Banks	49 K8	Castletown	244 D1
The Bank	226 B5	Catteralslane	270 E6
Barbridge	218 C6	Chadkirk	48 B4
Barnett Brook	262 E7	Chapel End	274 C1
Barnhill	231 H2	Cheadle	45 L7
Barnton	129 G1	Cheadle Heath	46 A5
The Barony	21 G4	Cheadle Hulme	65 G4
Barrets Green	217 L1	Checkley	266 D3
Barrowmore Estate	147 L6	Checkley Green	266 B4
Barrow's Green	34 D8	Chelford	135 H1
Barrows Green	220 F3	Chemistry	269 K5
Barthomley	240 D7	The Chequer	268 B6
Barton	229 M3	Cherry Tree	48 F2
Bate Heath	104 F1	Chester	17 K6
Bath Vale	208 B1	Childer Thornton	94 B4
Bearstone	275 M8	Cholmondeston	199 L8
Beechwood	73 L7	Chorley	249 G1
Beeston	216 A2	Choriton	254 A3
Belgrave	191 L6	Choriton Lane	245 H8
Bell o' th' Hill	259 J5	Chowley	213 L7
Benchill	44 C8	Christleton	170 E4
Betchton Heath	204 E7	Church Lawton	225 H8
Betley	255 G6	Church Minshull	201 H7
Betley Common	254 E6	Churton	211 L6
Bewsey	4 B1	Cinnamon Brow	29 G8
Bickerton	231 M6	Clark Green	113 G1
Bickley Moss	248 A6	Clifton	73 K8
Bickley Town	247 K6	Clifton	178 E3
Bickleywood	247 J8	Clive Green	178 E6
Biddulph	227 H5	Clock Face	34 D1
Big Mancot	166 E2	Clotton	173 K8
Birchall Moss	264 E3	Clotton Common	173 K6
Birch Heath	197 H4	Cloud Side	209 H1
Birchwood	29 L8	Clough Hall	242 F4
Blackbrook	37 L2	Clutton	230 B2
Blackden Heath	158 B1	Coalpit Hill	242 C4
Blacon	144 F8	Cobbs	56 D4
Blakelow	237 K8	Coddington	229 M1
Blakenhall	266 A1	Cold Moss Heath	204 C7
Bold Heath	34 C4	Collins Green	26 D3
Bollington	113 H5	Comberbach	103 K5
Bollington Cross	112 D5	Commonside	126 C4
Booth Bank	60 B5	Common Side	175 K1
Booth Green	86 B5	Compstall	49 G1
Boothsdale	173 K1	Congleton	207 K3
Boots Green	133 G7	Congleton Edge	208 D2
Bosley	186 D4	Cooksongreen	126 F3
Bostock Green	154 C5	Coppenhall	221 K5
Bowdon	60 F3	Coppenhall Moss	221 K3
Bowgreen	61 G3	Copthorne	273 L1
Braddocks Hay	227 M4	Cotebrook	174 F5
Bradeley Green	259 M6	Coxbank	273 M4
Bradfield Green	220 E1	Cracow Moss	255 H8
Bradley	99 L5	Cranage	157 G6
Bradley Green	258 F4	Crewe	19 J1
Bradley Mount	112 D5	Crewe-by-Farndon	229 G5
Bradwall Green	181 H8	Crewe Green	239 H1
Bramhall	65 M5	Croft	29 H4
Bramhall Moor	66 B2	Cronton	33 H7
Bramhall Park	65 J3	Cross Lane	201 K6
Brassey Green	196 D6	Cross o' th' Hill	246 D8
Bredbury	47 M1	Cross Town	107 H2
Bredbury Green	48 A2	Crowton	127 H3
Brereton Green	181 M7	Cross Wood	53 K2
Brereton Heath	182 E6	Croxton Green	233 J6
Bretton	167 L8	Cuddington	127 L8
Brickhouses	204 E4	Cuddington Green	257 H3
Bridgemere	265 L5	Cuddington Heath	257 K2
Bridgemont	89 L2	Cuerdley Cross	54 A1
Bridge Trafford	147 G2	Culcheth	30 A1
Brindley	234 E4	Dale Brow	112 A7
Broadheath	42 C5	Dales Green	226 C7
Broadoak	210 A2	Dallam	36 F3
Broken Cross	130 F5	Danebank	68 D2
Broken Cross	137 K4	Danebridge	188 B5
Bronington	268 B8	Dane in Shaw	208 C3
Brook Bottom	68 E3	Daresbury	75 H2
Brookhouse	139 K1	Darland	210 D4
Brookhouse Green	206 A5	Davenham	154 A2
Brooklands	43 H2	Davenport	46 E8

Davenport	182 E5	Hassall	223 K5
Davenport Green	62 F2	Hassall Green	224 A2
Davenport Green	109 M1	Hatchmere	126 D8
Day Green	223 M4	Hatherton	253 G2
Dean Row	84 F4	Hatton	75 M3
Deansgreen	59 H4	Hatton Heath	194 A3
Delamere	150 D6	Haughton Moss	217 G6
Didsbury	45 H1	Havannah	184 F6
Disley	68 B6	Hawarden	166 D2
Ditton	52 B5	Hawk Green	67 L1
Dobs Hill	166 A8	Haymoor Green	252 E2
Dodleston	191 G5	Hazel Grove	67 G3
Doe Green	54 C1	Heald Green	64 A3
Dones Green	102 B5	Heath	9 G8
Duckington	231 J8	Heatley	40 D7
Duddon	173 G6	Heaton Mersey	45 L1
Duddon Common	173 J5	Heaton Norris	2 A3
Dudlows Green	56 E7	Heaviley	47 G6
Dunham Town	41 K8	Hebden Green	176 F5
Dunham Woodhouses	41 H8	Helsby	98 C8
Dunhum-On-The-Hill	123 L6	Henbury	137 H4
Dunkirk	120 E5	Hermitage Green	28 B4
Dunkirk	242 A6	Hetherson Green	247 J4
Dutton	75 G8	Higher Burwardsley	215 H7
Earlestown	26 F1	Higher Disley	68 D7
East Didsbury	45 K3	Higherfence	139 G4
Eaton	185 G4	Higher Hurdsfield	138 F2
Eaton	198 A1	Higher Marston	104 C7
Ebnal	246 C6	Higher Poynton	87 H2
Eccleston	192 E3	Higher Runcorn	9 G5
Edge Green	22 F1	Higher Shurlach	130 E7
Edge Green	246 B1	Higher Walton	55 L5
Edgeley	46 D5	Higher Whitley	76 E7
Egerton Green	232 C7	Higher Wincham	105 H7
Ellesmere Port	10 C6	Higher Wych	258 D8
Elton	97 G8	High Lane	67 L5
Elton Green	123 G2	Highlane	161 J5
Elworth	203 M6	High Legh	59 H7
Englesea-brook	240 A8	Hightown	208 A2
Ettiley Heath	203 K7	Hillcliffe	56 C5
Faddiley	234 E5	Hinderton	92 A3
Fanshowe	136 C8	Hob Hill	230 C8
Farndon	228 F2	Hockley	87 G1
Farnworth	53 G1	Hodgehill	159 L4
Fearnhead	38 A2	The Hollands	209 J8
Feldy	79 G8	Hollinfare	40 A1
Fernilee	115 L3	Hollin Green	234 E6
Fiddler's Ferry	54 C3	Hollins	242 D4
Finney Green	84 C2	Hollins Green	40 D4
Fivecrosses	99 J7	Hollinsgreen	180 C8
Foggbrook	47 M5	Hollowmoor Heath	148 A6
Fourlanes End	205 L8	Hollyhurst	261 G6
Fowley Common	25 J7	Holmes Chapel	181 H3
Foxley	241 K5	Holt	228 D4
Foxwist Green	152 F6	Hood Manor	36 C7
Frandley	103 G1	Hoofield	196 A2
Frodsham	99 K5	Hoo Green	79 L2
Fullers Moor	231 K3	Hoole	170 A1
Fulshaw Park	84 A7	Hoole Bank	146 C5
Furness Vale	89 J1	Hooton	93 M3
Gallantry Bank	232 B4	Hope Green	86 D3
Garden City	142 E5	Horton Green	245 H4
Gatesheath	194 F7	Horwich End	89 L7
Gatley	45 G8	Hough	110 D3
Gauntons Bank	248 F8	Hough	253 M2
Gawsworth	161 L4	Hough Green	52 A3
Gemini	36 D1	Houghton Green	28 E7
Gibb Hill	103 K3	Howbeck Bank	252 E2
Gillbent	64 F6	Howbeck Bank	252 E4
Gillow Heath	227 H2	Howley	5 M7
Ginclough	113 L6	Hulme	37 H1
Glazebrook	31 G6	Hulme Walfield	184 B5
Glazebury	25 H6	Huntington	169 M6
Golborne	23 H5	Hunt's Cross	50 B6
Goldenhill	243 H6	Hurdsfield	15 L3
Goostrey	157 K3	Huxley	196 A5
Gorse Covert	30 B6	Huyton Quarry	32 B2
Gorstage	128 B6	Illidge Green	205 H1
Gorstella	191 G3	Ince	97 G6
Gorstyhill	254 E2	Irlam	31 M3
Gosland Green	217 H3	Jodrell Bank	158 D3
Gowhole	69 L8	Keckwick	54 F8
Gradeley Green	234 E7	Kelsall	149 J8
Grange	9 M8	Kenyon	24 A8
Grappenhall	57 H2	Kerridge	113 G6
Gravel	178 B4	Kerridge-end	139 J2
Great Barrow	147 K6	Kettleshulme	88 E8
Great Budworth	104 B5	Key Green	185 L8
Great Moor	47 J6	Kidnal	245 L5
Great Sankey	36 B6	Kidsgrove	242 C2
Great Sutton	94 D7	Kingsley	126 D2
Great Warford	109 H5	Kingsway	7 G4
Greenbank	12 B4	Kingswood	36 A1
Greendale	111 J5	Kinnerton Green	190 A5
Greenlooms	171 M8	Kinsey Heath	274 B2
Gresty Green	238 D4	Kitt's Moss	65 K7
Grindley Brook	269 H1	Knolls Green	82 E8
Guilden Sutton	146 F7	Knotbury	165 M7
Gurnett	138 F8	Knowl Bank	255 L5
Hack Green	251 L7	Knutsford	107 J3
Hague Bar	68 F4	Knypersley	227 L2
Hale	61 M2	Lacey Green	84 B3
Hale	71 K2	Lach Dennis	131 K7
Hale Bank	52 B8	Lache	168 E7
Halebarns	62 D4	Lane Ends	49 K3
Halewood	50 F4	Lane Ends	68 E8
Hall Green	225 L7	Lane Ends	221 L1
Hall Green	268 E3	Lane Head	23 M6
Hallowsgate	149 H8	Langley	163 J1
Halton	73 M4	Larden Green	234 C8
Halton Brook	73 K3	Latchford	56 C1
Halton View	7 M3	Lately Common	25 J3
Hampton Green	247 H5	Lavister	210 B3
Hampton Heath	246 E5	Lawton-gate	224 F8
Handbridge	17 K9	Lawton Heath	224 E7
Handforth	64 C8	Lawton Heath End	224 D6
Hand Green	197 H6	Lea by Backford	121 G8
Handley	213 K4	Lea Forge	253 L2
Hankelow	264 C5	Lea Green	201 C4
Hapsford	123 L3	Ledsham	119 M2
Harden Park	110 B1	Ley Hey Park	48 C5
Hardings Wood	242 E2	Lightwood Green	273 G2
Hardley	195 G3	Lindow End	109 G2
Harriseahead	226 D7	Lingley Green	35 J5
Hartford	128 E8	Lingley Mere	35 K4
Hartfordbeach	129 H6	Little Barrow	147 L3
Harthill	231 L1	Little Bollington	60 C2
Haslington	222 D8		

Little Budworth	175 M5
Little Chell	243 M7
Little Heath	170 E4
Little Heath	264 A7
Little Leigh	102 C7
Little Madeley	267 M5
Little Mancot	166 E2
Little Moor	47 K4
Little Neston	91 K6
Littler	176 F2
Little Stanney	121 L3
Little Sutton	93 M6
Littleton	170 D3
Little Town	29 H2
Locking Stumps	29 H8
Longbarn	38 C3
Longford	37 H3
Long Green	147 M3
Longmoss	137 J4
Lostock Gralam	131 H2
Lostock Green	131 H4
Lowcross Hill	245 K1
Lower Bredbury	47 J2
Lower Bunbury	216 F4
Lower Carden	230 C6
Lower Heath	184 D6
Lower House	6 D5
Lowerhouse	112 E4
Lower Kinnerton	190 C3
Lower Peover	132 E3
Lower Pexhill	137 G8
Lower Stretton	76 E4
Lower Threapwood	256 F6
Lower Walton	56 A4
Lower Whitley	102 D1
Lower Withington	158 F4
Lower Wych	258 B6
Low Leighton	69 K4
Lowton	23 K4
Lowton Common	24 A4
Lowton Heath	23 J6
Lowton St Mary's	24 A5
Lugsdale	7 L6
Lunts Heath	34 A7
Lyme Green	162 D2
Lymm	58 E1
Macclesfield	15 J4
Macclesfield Forest	140 B7
Madeley	267 L6
Malkin's Bank	223 K1
Malpas	258 C1
Mancot Royal	166 F1
Manley	125 G8
Manley Common	125 J7
Manor Park	179 G4
Marbury	260 D4
Marford	210 A7
Marley Green	261 H3
Marple	48 E6
Marple Bridge	49 H5
Marpleridge	67 M2
Marshfield Bank	220 C8
Marsh Green	98 F4
Marsh Green	227 K2
The Marsh	207 J3
Marston	130 C1
Marthall	108 E8
Martinscroft	38 D5
Martin's Moss	205 M6
Marton	160 C8
Marton Green	152 D8
Maw Green	221 M5
Meadowbank	153 K7
Mellor	49 L6
Mere	80 B4
Mere Heath	153 M3
Merelake	242 A4
Mickle Trafford	146 E4
Middle Madeley	267 M5
Middlewich	179 K3
Middlewood	67 H7
Midway	86 D2
Mill Brow	49 L4
Milners Heath	194 C2
Milton Green	213 J2
Mobberley	81 L5
Mobberley	108 B1
Mollington	144 D3
Monk's Heath	136 B3
Moore	55 G6
Moorside	91 J5
The Moor	166 E3
Morley	83 J3
Morley Green	83 H3
Moss Bank	53 K4
Mossbrow	40 D5
Moss End	104 C2
Moss Houses	161 M2
Moss Lane	138 B8
Mossley	208 B5
Moss Nook	63 M4
Moston	145 K3
Moston Green	203 H5
Mottram St Andrew	111 G3
Mouldsworth	149 G1
Moulton	153 M5
Mount Pleasant	226 B6
Mow Cop	226 C5
Nantwich	21 H6
Ness	92 B7
Nessholt	91 L8
Neston	91 K5
Nether Alderley	110 A6
Netherton	98 F6
Newall Green	44 A8
Newchapel	243 L2
Newchurch Common	152 C5
Newfield	243 J7
Newhall	262 B5
New Horwich	89 L6
New Lane End	29 G2
New Mills	69 H4
New Pale	125 K6
Newpool	227 G6
Newsbank	183 L3
Newton	125 L2
Newton	145 L7
Newton	195 L8

Place	Ref
Newton	214 E5
Newton	250 E8
Newtonia	179 H4
Newton-Le-Willows	27 K1
Newton Park	27 M2
Newtown	69 H7
Newtown	99 K3
Newtown	209 H6
New Woodhouses	271 L3
Nick i'th' Hill	208 A8
No Mans Heath	247 H7
Noonsun	108 E3
Norbury	260 D1
Norbury Common	248 C7
Norbury Moor	66 E3
Norcott Brook	76 C6
Norley	126 F6
Northern Moor	43 M3
North Rode	185 L2
Northwich	13 J6
Norton	74 C3
Nova Scotia	152 C7
Oakgrove	162 C5
Oakhanger	240 D3
Oakmere	151 H5
Oakwood	29 M8
Occlestone Green	202 B2
Offerton	47 L5
Offerton Green	48 A6
Oglet	70 D4
Old Boston	22 B5
Oldcastle Heath	257 L3
Oldfield Brow	42 B7
Old Warren	166 E8
Old Woodhouses	271 K2
Ollerton	107 L6
Orford	37 K3
Oscroft	172 F2
Oughtrington	40 A8
Over	177 H4
Over Knutsford	107 J4
Over Peover	134 A4
Overpool	94 F5
Over Tabley	80 A7
Overton	99 H5
Paddington	38 A5
Paddockhill	83 G8
Padgate	37 M3
Painters Green	268 E6
Palacefields	73 M7
Park End	241 G8
Parkgate	91 J3
Parkgate	134 B4
Partington	40 F2
Peckforton	215 M7
Peel Hall	63 M2
Penketh	35 K8
Pennington	24 D1
Pentre	142 E7
Peover Heath	134 D5
Pewterspear	76 F1
Pickmere	104 F6
Picton	146 C1
Pinsley Green	261 K2
Piper's Ash	146 C8
Pitts Hill	243 M7
Plemstall	147 H3
Plumley	105 M8
Pocket Nook	24 C4
Poolfold	208 F8
Portwood	3 J1
Pott Shrigley	113 K1
Poulton	211 G2
Pownall Park	83 M4
Poynton	112 A5
Prestbury	112 A5
Preston Brook	74 F7
Preston on the Hill	75 G6
Puddinglake	156 A4
Puddington	118 E5
Pulford	210 C2
Quarrybank	174 C5
Queensferry	142 D6
Queen's Park	17 L7
Quoisley	260 B4
Radmore Green	217 L8
Radway Green	240 F3
Rainhill	33 K1
Rainhill Stoops	33 L2
Rainow	113 K7
Rainowlow	113 K5
Ravenscliffe	243 G7
Ravenshall	255 G8
Ravensmoor	250 D2
Rease Heath	236 C2
Redbrook	268 F5
Red Bull	242 E1
Reddish	40 A7
Rhuddall Heath	197 L3
Risley	29 L6
Rixton	39 M2
Rock End	227 M6
Rocksavage	73 H7
Rodeheath	185 H1
Rode Heath	224 F4
Romiley	48 D2
The Rookery	243 J1
Rosehill	61 J3
Rossett	210 C5
Rostherne	80 E1
Roundthorn	43 L7
Row-of-trees	109 J1
Rowton	170 F7
Rowton Moor	170 F6
Royal's Green	272 E2
Rudheath	130 D6
Rudheath Woods	156 D2
Ruloe	127 J5
Runcorn	9 K5
Rushgreen	39 M7
Rushton	175 K7
Saighton	193 M3
Sale	42 E1
Salterswall	177 G1
Saltney	168 C7
Sandbach	204 A4
Sandbach Heath	204 D6
Sandiway	152 B1
Sandlow Green	182 A3
Sandycroft	167 G2
Sandyford	243 L6
Sankey Bridges	36 C8
Saughall	144 B3
Scholar Green	225 K6
School Green	177 H7
Sealand	143 L6
Sharston	44 F7
Shavington	238 C8
Shaw Heath	2 E9
Shaw Heath	107 K1
Shell Green	53 L2
Shocklach	244 D5
Shocklach Green	244 B5
Shotton	142 B7
Shotwick	119 G8
Siddington	160 A1
Siddington Heath	159 M3
Simm's Cross	7 K5
Sinderland Green	41 K3
Skellorn Green	86 D4
Slaughter Hill	239 K1
Smallwood	205 M7
Smethwick Green	205 M1
Smiths Green	159 G2
Smith's Green	240 C5
Smithy Green	65 H4
Smithy Green	132 E2
Snow Hill	20 D5
Somerford	182 F5
Sound	250 E7
Sound Heath	250 D8
Southgate	73 L5
Speke	70 E1
Spen Green	206 B6
Sproston Green	180 D2
Spurstow	216 D6
Stamford Bridge	147 J8
Stanley Green	64 E7
Stanlow	96 B7
Stapeley	252 D4
Statham	39 K8
Stepping Hill	47 K8
Stoak	121 M5
Stockport	2 B3
Stockton Heath	56 C3
Stoneley Green	235 K8
Stretton	76 E2
Stretton	229 M6
Strines	68 C3
Stud Green	203 H3
Styal	63 M8
Sutton Green	120 B1
Sutton Lane Ends	162 F2
Sutton Manor	34 A2
Sutton Weaver	100 B1
Swanbach	273 L3
Swan Green	132 D5
Swanwick Green	248 C8
Swettenham	182 E1
Sworton Heath	58 F7
Sydney	222 A7
Tabley Hill	106 D1
Talke	242 C5
Talke Pits	242 E7
Tallarn Green	256 F7
Tarbock Green	32 C8
Tarporley	197 K2
Tarvin	172 C1
Tarvin Sands	172 C1
Tattenhall	214 B3
Tatton Dale	80 D3
Taxal	89 J8
Thelwall	57 L1
Thornsett	69 L2
Thorns Green	62 C7
Thornton-le-Moors	122 D3
Threapwood	256 E5
Thurlwood	224 E4
Tilston	245 H1
Tilstone Bank	197 L8
Tilstone Fearnall	197 L6
Timbersbrook	208 D2
Timperley	43 G5
Tirley Garth	174 B3
Tiverton	197 J7
Torkington	67 H2
Tower Hill	113 J8
Town End	33 J6
Town Fields	177 K5
Town of Lowton	23 G7
Town Park	74 B3
Trevalyn	210 D6
Turnhurst	243 M4
Twemlow Green	158 B7
Twiss Green	24 E7
Two Mills	119 L5
Tytherington	112 D8
Upper Threapwood	256 C4
Upton	52 B2
Upton	145 K6
Upton Heath	145 M4
Upton Rocks	52 E1
Utkinton	174 A5
Vicarscross	170 E1
Vulcan Village	27 J4
Wades Green	200 F7
Wain Lee	226 F8
Walgherton	253 G6
Walker Barn	139 M4
Walley's Green	201 M5
Warburton	40 A4
Warburton Green	62 C6
Wardle	218 B5
Wardle Bank	218 B3
Wardsend	87 G3
Wargrave	27 J3
Warmingham	202 E5
Warren	161 L3
Warrington	4 E4
Waterside	89 L1
Waverton	171 H8
Waymills	270 C6
Way's Green	177 L4
Weaverham	128 F4
Weetwood Common	173 J3
Well Green	62 D1
Wells Green	237 M5
Wervin	122 A8
West Bank	52 F7
Westbrook	36 A3
West Heath	206 F1
Weston	8 E9
Weston	72 F6
Weston	137 M5
Weston Point	8 A7
Westy	37 M7
Wettenhall	199 M5
Wettenhall Green	199 L6
Whaley Bridge	89 J5
Wharton	177 M1
Wharton Green	154 B8
Wheelock	222 F2
Wheelock Heath	223 G4
Whirley Grove	137 L1
Whisterfield	159 L1
Whiston	32 E1
Whiston Cross	32 D1
Whiston Lane Ends	32 C2
Whitby	121 H1
Whitbyheath	120 F3
Whitchurch	269 L5
Whitefield Lane End	32 B4
Whitegate	153 G5
Whitehill	243 J2
Whiteley Green	112 E2
Whitemore	208 D6
Whitewell	268 C5
Whitley Reed	77 J3
Widnes	6 E6
Wildboarclough	164 D6
Wilderspool	56 C2
Wilkesley	272 F6
Willaston	93 H4
Willaston	237 J7
Willington Corner	173 L2
Willow Green	102 B7
Wilmslow	84 B6
Wilmslow Park	84 D5
Wimbolds Trafford	122 F6
Wincham	130 D1
Wincle	187 M4
Windle Hill	92 C5
Windlehurst	67 L3
Windmill Hill	74 C2
Windy Arbor	32 D4
Windyharbour	159 J3
Winnington	12 C2
Winsford	177 K2
Winterley	222 F5
Winwick	28 B8
Winwick Quay	28 B8
Wirswall	260 A7
Wistaston	237 K3
Wistaston Green	237 K2
Withington Green	158 E1
Wolverham	95 J8
Woodbank	119 L6
Woodend	68 C4
Woodford	85 K2
Woodhey Green	234 B7
Woodhouse Green	209 J2
Woodhouse Park	63 J3
Woodhouses	42 B2
Woodhouses	98 E8
Wood Lanes	87 C4
Woodside	149 J3
Woodside	200 A6
Woods Moor	66 B1
Woodworth Green	217 H4
Woolstanwood	220 E8
Woolston	38 C5
Woolton	50 A3
Worleston	219 M6
Wornish Nook	184 A3
Worthenbury	256 A3
Wrenbury	249 M8
Wrights Green	57 G7
Wrinehill	267 J3
Wybunbury	253 G4
Wythenshawe	63 H1

USING THE STREET INDEX

Street names are listed alphabetically. Each street name is followed by its postal town or area locality, the Postcode District, the page number, and the reference to the square in which the name is found.

Example: **Abbey Pl** *CW/HAS* CW1......221 K6 ▣

Some entries are followed by a number in a blue box. This number indicates the location of the street within the referenced grid square. The full street name is listed at the side of the map page.

GENERAL ABBREVIATIONS

Abbr.	Meaning	Abbr.	Meaning	Abbr.	Meaning	Abbr.	Meaning	Abbr.	Meaning
ACC	ACCESS	CTYD	COURTYARD	HLS	HILLS	MWY	MOTORWAY	SE	SOUTH EAST
ALY	ALLEY	CUTT	CUTTINGS	HO	HOUSE	N	NORTH	SER	SERVICE AREA
AP	APPROACH	CV	COVE	HOL	HOLLOW	NE	NORTH EAST	SH	SHORE
AR	ARCADE	CYN	CANYON	HOSP	HOSPITAL	NW	NORTH WEST	SHOP	SHOPPING
ASS	ASSOCIATION	DEPT	DEPARTMENT	HRB	HARBOUR	O/P	OVERPASS	SKWY	SKYWAY
AV	AVENUE	DL	DALE	HTH	HEATH	OFF	OFFICE	SMT	SUMMIT
BCH	BEACH	DM	DAM	HTS	HEIGHTS	ORCH	ORCHARD	SOC	SOCIETY
BLDS	BUILDINGS	DR	DRIVE	HVN	HAVEN	OV	OVAL	SP	SPUR
BND	BEND	DRO	DROVE	HWY	HIGHWAY	PAL	PALACE	SPR	SPRING
BNK	BANK	DRY	DRIVEWAY	IMP	IMPERIAL	PAS	PASSAGE	SQ	SQUARE
BR	BRIDGE	DWGS	DWELLINGS	IN	INLET	PAV	PAVILION	ST	STREET
BRK	BROOK	E	EAST	IND EST	INDUSTRIAL ESTATE	PDE	PARADE	STN	STATION
BTM	BOTTOM	EMB	EMBANKMENT	INF	INFIRMARY	PH	PUBLIC HOUSE	STR	STREAM
BUS	BUSINESS	EMBY	EMBASSY	INFO	INFORMATION	PK	PARK	STRD	STRAND
BVD	BOULEVARD	ESP	ESPLANADE	INT	INTERCHANGE	PKWY	PARKWAY	SW	SOUTH WEST
BY	BYPASS	EST	ESTATE	IS	ISLAND	PL	PLACE	TDG	TRADING
CATH	CATHEDRAL	EX	EXCHANGE	JCT	JUNCTION	PLN	PLAIN	TER	TERRACE
CEM	CEMETERY	EXPY	EXPRESSWAY	JTY	JETTY	PLNS	PLAINS	THWY	THROUGHWAY
CEN	CENTRE	EXT	EXTENSION	KG	KING	PLZ	PLAZA	TNL	TUNNEL
CFT	CROFT	F/O	FLYOVER	KNL	KNOLL	POL	POLICE STATION	TOLL	TOLLWAY
CH	CHURCH	FC	FOOTBALL CLUB	L	LAKE	PR	PRINCE	TPK	TURNPIKE
CHA	CHASE	FK	FORK	LA	LANE	PREC	PRECINCT	TR	TRACK
CHYD	CHURCHYARD	FLD	FIELD	LDG	LODGE	PREP	PREPARATORY	TRL	TRAIL
CIR	CIRCLE	FLDS	FIELDS	LGT	LIGHT	PRIM	PRIMARY	TWR	TOWER
CIRC	CIRCUS	FLS	FALLS	LK	LOCK	PROM	PROMENADE	U/P	UNDERPASS
CL	CLOSE	FLS	FLATS	LKS	LAKES	PRS	PRINCESS	UNI	UNIVERSITY
CLFS	CLIFFS	FM	FARM	LNDG	LANDING	PRT	PORT	UPR	UPPER
CMP	CAMP	FT	FORT	LTL	LITTLE	PT	POINT	V	VALE
CNR	CORNER	FWY	FREEWAY	LWR	LOWER	PTH	PATH	VA	VALLEY
CO	COUNTY	FY	FERRY	MAG	MAGISTRATE	PZ	PIAZZA	VIAD	VIADUCT
COLL	COLLEGE	GA	GATE	MAN	MANSIONS	QD	QUADRANT	VIL	VILLA
COM	COMMON	GAL	GALLERY	MD	MEAD	QU	QUEEN	VIS	VISTA
COMM	COMMISSION	GDN	GARDEN	MDW	MEADOWS	QY	QUAY	VLG	VILLAGE
CON	CONVENT	GDNS	GARDENS	MEM	MEMORIAL	R	RIVER	VLS	VILLAS
COT	COTTAGE	GLD	GLADE	MKT	MARKET	RBT	ROUNDABOUT	VW	VIEW
COTS	COTTAGES	GLN	GLEN	MKTS	MARKETS	RD	ROAD	W	WEST
CP	CAPE	GN	GREEN	ML	MALL	RDG	RIDGE	WD	WOOD
CPS	COPSE	GND	GROUND	ML	MILL	REP	REPUBLIC	WHF	WHARF
CR	CREEK	GRA	GRANGE	MNR	MANOR	RES	RESERVOIR	WK	WALK
CREM	CREMATORIUM	GRG	GARAGE	MS	MEWS	RFC	RUGBY FOOTBALL CLUB	WKS	WALKS
CRS	CRESCENT	GT	GREAT	MSN	MISSION	RI	RISE	WLS	WELLS
CSWY	CAUSEWAY	GTWY	GATEWAY	MT	MOUNT	RP	RAMP	WY	WAY
CT	COURT	GV	GROVE	MTN	MOUNTAIN	RW	ROW	YD	YARD
CTRL	CENTRAL	HGR	HIGHER	MTS	MOUNTAINS	S	SOUTH	YHA	YOUTH HOSTEL
CTS	COURTS	HL	HILL	MUS	MUSEUM	SCH	SCHOOL		

POSTCODE TOWNS AND AREA ABBREVIATIONS

AIMK .... Ashton-in-Makerfield
ALL/GAR .... Allerton/Garston
ALS/KID .... Alsager/Kidsgrove
ALT .... Altrincham
AUD/MAD/W ...... Audlem/Madeley/Woore
BEB .... Bebington
BIDD .... Biddulph
BNG/LEV .... Burnage/Levenshulme
BRAM/HZG .... Bramhall/Hazel Grove
BURS/TUN .... Burslem/Tunstall
BUX .... Buxton
CCHDY .... Chorlton-cum-Hardy
CH/BCN .... Chester/Blacon
CHD/CHDH .... Cheadle (Gtr. Man)/Cheadle Hulme
CHF/WBR .... Chapel-en-le-Frith/Whaley Bridge
CHNE .... Chester northeast
CHSE .... Chester southeast
CHSW/BR .... Chester southwest/Broughton
CONG .... Congleton
CQ .... Connah's Quay
CW/HAS .... Crewe/Haslington
CW/SHV .... Crewe/Shavington
DID/WITH .... Didsbury/Withington
EDGY/DAV .... Edgeley/Davenport
END/WER .... Endon/Werrington
EP .... Ellesmere Port
FLINT .... Flint
FROD/HEL .... Frodsham/Helsby
GLSP .... Glossop
GOL/RIS/CUL ...... Golborne/Risley/Culcheth
GTS/LS .... Great Sutton/Little Sutton
HALE/TIMP .... Hale/Timperley
HES .... Heswall
HLWD .... Halewood
HOLMCH .... Holmes Chapel
HTNM .... Heaton Moor
HUY .... Huyton
HYDE .... Hyde
IRL .... Irlam
KNUT .... Knutsford
LEEK .... Leek
LEIGH .... Leigh
LYMM .... Lymm
MALPAS .... Malpas
MANAIR .... Manchester Airport
MCFLDN .... Macclesfield north
MCFLDS .... Macclesfield south
MKTDR .... Market Drayton
MOLD/BUCK .... Mold/Buckley
MPL/ROM .... Marple/Romiley
MWCH .... Middlewich
NANT .... Nantwich
NEWLW .... Newton-le-Willows
NEWUL .... Newcastle-under-Lyme
NM/HAY .... New Mills/Hayfield
NSTN .... Neston
NTHLY .... Netherley
NTHM/RTH .... Northern Moor/Roundthorn
NWCHE .... Northwich east
NWCHW .... Northwich west
OFTN .... Offerton
PART .... Partington
POY/DIS .... Poynton/Disley
PS/BROM .... Port Sunlight/Bromborough
RAIN/WH .... Rainhill/Whiston
RDSH .... Reddish
RNFD/HAY .... Rainford/Haydock
RUNC .... Runcorn
SALE .... Sale
SBCH .... Sandbach
SPK/HALE .... Speke/Hale
STHEL .... St Helens
STKP .... Stockport
TPLY/KEL .... Tarporley/Kelsall
TYLD .... Tyldesley
WARR .... Warrington
WARRN/WOL .... Warrington north/Woolston
WARRS .... Warrington south
WARRW/BUR .... Warrington west/Burtonwood
WDN .... Widnes
WHITCH .... Whitchurch
WILM/AE .... Wilmslow/Alderley Edge
WLTN .... Woolton
WRX/GR/LL .... Wrexham/Gresford/Llay
WRXS/E .... Wrexham south & east
WSFD .... Winsford
WYTH/NTH .... Wythenshawe/Northenden

Abb - Anc

Index - streets

A

Abberley Rd *WLTN* L25 .... 50 D5
Abbey Cl *ALT* WA14 .... 61 G3
GOL/RIS/CU WA3 .... 29 G4
NWCHW CW8 .... 153 G5
WDN WA8 .... 52 C4
WSFD CW7 .... 177 K6
Abbey Ct *WLTN* L25 .... 50 B2
Abbey Flds *CW/SHV* CW2 .... 237 K4
Abbey Gn *CH/BCN* CH1 .... 16 F4
Abbey Gv *STKP* SK1 .... 3 L7
Abbey Hey *RUNC* WA7 .... 74 C4
Abbey La *NWCHW* CW8 .... 129 H7
NWCHW CW8 .... 150 E7
Abbey Pl *CW/HAS* CW1 .... 221 K6
Abbey Rd *CHD/CHDH* SK8 .... 46 A7
GOL/RIS/CU WA3 .... 24 C4
MCFLDN SK10 .... 138 B2
SBCH CW11 .... 203 L6
WDN WA8 .... 52 B4
Abbey Sq *CH/BCN* CH1 .... 16 F4
Abbey St *CH/BCN* CH1 .... 17 G4
Abbey Wy *NWCHW* CW8 .... 129 H8
Abbeyway North
RNFD/HAY WA11 .... 22 A5
Abbeyway South
RNFD/HAY WA11 .... 22 A6
Abbeywood Gv *RAIN/WH* L35 .... 32 F2
Abbotsbury Cl *CW/SHV* CW2 .... 238 B4
POY/DIS SK12 .... 66 D7
Abbots Cl *MCFLDN* SK10 .... 138 B2
Abbot's Dr *CH/BCN* CH1 .... 145 J8
Abbotsfield Cl *WARRS* WA4 .... 56 E6
Abbotsford Cl
GOL/RIS/CU WA3 .... 23 K3
Abbotsford Gv *ALT* WA14 .... 42 E4
Abbot's Gra *CHNE* CH2 .... 16 E1
Abbots Hall Av *STHEL* WA9 .... 34 D1
Abbots Knoll *CH/BCN* CH1 .... 145 J8
Abbotsleigh Dr *BRAM/HZG* SK7 .... 65 M2
Abbots Ms *EP* CH65 .... 10 D5
Abbot's Nook *CHNE* CH2 .... 16 F2
Abbots Pk *CH/BCN* CH1 .... 145 J8
Abbots Wy *NSTN* CH64 .... 91 K3
NWCHW CW8 .... 129 H8
Abbott's Cl *CONG* CW12 .... 208 B4
RUNC WA7 .... 9 H7
Abbotts Rd *CHSE* CH3 .... 171 H7
Abbotts Wy *WSFD* CW7 .... 177 G2
Aber Av *OFTN* SK2 .... 47 J8
Aberdare Cl *WARRW/BUR* WA5 .... 36 E3
Aberdaron Dr *CH/BCN* CH1 .... 168 E1
Aberdeen Crs *EDGY/DAV* SK3 .... 2 C8
Aberdeen Gv *EDGY/DAV* SK3 .... 2 D7
Aberfeldy Cl *HOLMCH* CW4 .... 181 H2
Aberford Rd *NTHM/RTH* M23 .... 44 A7
Abergele St *OFTN* SK2 .... 46 F6
Aber Las *FLINT* CH6 .... 116 B8
Aber Rd *CHD/CHDH* SK8 .... 46 A6
Abingdon Av *WARR* WA1 .... 38 E5
Abingdon Cl *MCFLDN* SK10 .... 137 M4
Abingdon Crs *CHSW/BR* CH4 .... 168 F6
Abingdon Gv *HLWD* L26 .... 51 G3
Abingdon Rd *BRAM/HZG* SK7 .... 65 L2
Abington Cl *CW/HAS* CW1 .... 221 H6
Abington Rd *SALE* M33 .... 43 J1
Abstone Cl *WARR* WA1 .... 38 C5
Acacia Av *CHD/CHDH* SK8 .... 65 G2
HALE/TIMP WA15 .... 61 M1
KNUT WA16 .... 106 E3
WARR WA1 .... 38 D4
WDN WA8 .... 53 H1
WILM/AE SK9 .... 83 M7
Acacia Cl *CHNE* CH2 .... 123 J1
Acacia Crs *CW/HAS* CW1 .... 221 L6
Acacia Dr *GTS/LS* CH66 .... 120 F3
HALE/TIMP WA15 .... 61 M1
SBCH CW11 .... 203 L5
Acacia Gdns *ALS/KID* ST7 .... 243 J1
Acacia Gv *RUNC* WA7 .... 9 M7
Academy St *WARR* WA1 .... 5 H7
Academy Wy *WARR* WA1 .... 5 G8
Acer Av *CW/HAS* CW1 .... 221 L5
Achilles Av *WARRN/WOL* WA2 .... 37 H2
Ackerley Cl *WARRN/WOL* WA2 .... 37 M1
Ackers La *WARRS* WA4 .... 56 E3
Ackers Rd *WARRS* WA4 .... 56 E2
Ack La East *BRAM/HZG* SK7 .... 65 J5
BRAM/HZG SK7 .... 65 M3
Ack La West *CHD/CHDH* SK8 .... 65 H5
Ackworth Dr *NTHM/RTH* M23 .... 44 A6
Acorn Av *CHD/CHDH* SK8 .... 45 L6
Acorn Bank Cl *CW/SHV* CW2 .... 238 B5
Acorn Cl *LEIGH* WN7 .... 24 F1
NWCHW CW8 .... 151 M2
WSFD CW7 .... 178 A4
Acorn Dr *EP* CH65 .... 121 H3
Acorn La *CONG* CW12 .... 208 E1
Acorn St *NEWLW* WA12 .... 27 J1
A Ct *AIMK* WN4 .... 22 B2
The Acreage *HOLMCH* CW4 .... 157 L3
TPLY/KEL CW6 .... 216 E4
Acrefield *SALE* M33 .... 43 G1
Acrefield Pk *WLTN* L25 .... 50 A1
Acrefield Rd *WDN* WA8 .... 52 B3
WLTN L25 .... 50 A1
Acre Gn *HLWD* L26 .... 51 G6
Acre La *CHD/CHDH* SK8 .... 65 H6
Acre Rd *GTS/LS* CH66 .... 94 D7
Acres Ct *WYTH/NTH* M22 .... 44 D8
Acres Crs *FROD/HEL* WA6 .... 126 B2
Acresfield Rd *HALE/TIMP* WA15 .... 43 G4
Acres La *CHNE* CH2 .... 146 A4
Acres Nook Rd *BURS/TUN* ST6 .... 243 G5
Acres Rd *CHD/CHDH* SK8 .... 45 G7
Acre St *MPL/ROM* SK6 .... 48 B2
Acreville Gv *GOL/RIS/CU* WA3 .... 25 J5
Acton Av *WARRS* WA4 .... 76 D1
Acton La *NWCHW* CW8 .... 127 M1
Acton Rd *CW/SHV* CW2 .... 220 D7
WARRW/BUR WA5 .... 26 E6
Acton Wy *ALS/KID* ST7 .... 224 D8
Adam Av *GTS/LS* CH66 .... 94 C8
GTS/LS CH66 .... 120 C1
Adam Cl *CHD/CHDH* SK8 .... 46 B8
GTS/LS CH66 .... 94 D8
Adams Av *BURS/TUN* ST6 .... 243 K7
Adams Cl *NEWLW* WA12 .... 27 K2
POY/DIS SK12 .... 86 E2
Adams Hl *KNUT* WA16 .... 107 G3
Adamson Ct *WARRS* WA4 .... 57 H2
Adamson Gdns
DID/WITH M20 .... 44 F1
Adamson St *AIMK* WN4 .... 22 A1
WARRS WA4 .... 56 B1
Adam St *WARRN/WOL* WA2 .... 5 J2
Adcroft St *STKP* SK1 .... 3 H9
Adder Hl *CHSE* CH3 .... 170 B5
Addingham Av *WDN* WA8 .... 52 C5
Addison Cl *CW/SHV* CW2 .... 237 M4
Addison Rd *HALE/TIMP* WA15 .... 61 L2
Addison Sq *WDN* WA8 .... 6 F2
Adelaide Rd *BRAM/HZG* SK7 .... 65 L6
CH/BCN CH1 .... 144 D8
EDGY/DAV SK3 .... 2 B8
Adelaide St *CW/HAS* CW1 .... 18 E2
MCFLDN SK10 .... 15 J3
Adela Rd *RUNC* WA7 .... 8 E3
Adey Rd *LYMM* WA13 .... 40 A7
Adfalent La *NSTN* CH64 .... 93 G5
Adlington Cl *HALE/TIMP* WA15 .... 43 K6
POY/DIS SK12 .... 86 F2
Adlington Ct *GOL/RIS/CU* WA3 .... 29 M6
GOL/RIS/CU WA3 .... 29 M6
Adlington Dr *NWCHE* CW9 .... 13 K9
SBCH CW11 .... 204 C5
Adlington Pk *MCFLDN* SK10 .... 86 C3
Adlington Rd *CW/SHV* CW2 .... 237 M1
RUNC WA7 .... 74 D2
WILM/AE SK9 .... 84 E5
Adlington St *MCFLDS* SK11 .... 14 E4
Admirals Rd *GOL/RIS/CU* WA3 .... 38 E1
Adria Rd *DID/WITH* M20 .... 45 J1
Adshall Rd *CHD/CHDH* SK8 .... 46 A7
Adshead Cl *WYTH/NTH* M22 .... 63 H1
Adshead Ct *MCFLDN* SK10 .... 113 H4
Adswood Gv *EDGY/DAV* SK3 .... 46 D6
Adswood La East *OFTN* SK2 .... 46 F6
Adswood La West
EDGY/DAV SK3 .... 46 E6
Adswood Old Hall Rd
CHD/CHDH SK8 .... 46 D8
Adswood Rd *CHD/CHDH* SK8 .... 46 C8
EDGY/DAV SK3 .... 46 D7
Adswood Ter *EDGY/DAV* SK3 .... 46 E6
Adwell Cl *GOL/RIS/CU* WA3 .... 24 A4
Adwy Wynt *FLINT* CH6 .... 116 B8
Aegean Rd *ALT* WA14 .... 42 A6
Afton *WDN* WA8 .... 52 A2
Agden Brow *LYMM* WA13 .... 59 K4
Agden House La *WHITCH* SY13 .... 259 G7
Agden La *LYMM* WA13 .... 59 L5
Agecroft Rd *MPL/ROM* SK6 .... 48 A3
NWCHE CW9 .... 130 C5
Agnes St *STHEL* WA9 .... 34 C1
Aimson Rd *HALE/TIMP* WA15 .... 43 J5
Ainley Cl *RUNC* WA7 .... 74 A7
Ainley Rd *WYTH/NTH* M22 .... 63 K1
Ainscough Rd *GOL/RIS/CU* WA3 .... 38 E1
Ainsdale Cl *BRAM/HZG* SK7 .... 66 A5
WARRW/BUR WA5 .... 35 M8
Ainsdale Dr *CHD/CHDH* SK8 .... 64 B3
SALE M33 .... 42 E2
Ainsworth La *NWCHW* CW8 .... 101 G8
Ainsworth Rd *NWCHW* CW8 .... 128 E3
Aintree Av *SALE* M33 .... 42 C1
Aintree Cl *BRAM/HZG* SK7 .... 66 F2
Aintree Gv *EDGY/DAV* SK3 .... 46 E6
GTS/LS CH66 .... 120 D1
Airdrie Cl *PS/BROM* CH62 .... 93 K1
Aire *WDN* WA8 .... 52 B2
Aire Cl *EP* CH65 .... 10 A3
Airedale Cl *CHD/CHDH* SK8 .... 45 J6
WARRW/BUR WA5 .... 35 M5
Airedale Ct *ALT* WA14 .... 42 E7
Airfield Vw *CHSW/BR* CH4 .... 167 H6
Aitchison Rd *NWCHE* CW9 .... 131 G2
Ajax Av *WARRN/WOL* WA2 .... 37 H2
Akesmoor Dr *OFTN* SK2 .... 47 J6
Akesmoor La *BIDD* ST8 .... 226 F5
Alamein Crs *WARRN/WOL* WA2 .... 5 H2
Alamein Dr *MPL/ROM* SK6 .... 48 E2
WSFD CW7 .... 177 K4
Alamein Rd *NWCHW* CW8 .... 102 F8
Alan Dr *HALE/TIMP* WA15 .... 62 A4
MPL/ROM SK6 .... 48 E6
Alan Rd *HTNM* SK4 .... 46 A1
Alan St *NWCHE* CW9 .... 13 M3
Alban St *CW/HAS* CW1 .... 18 E2
Albany Crs *LYMM* WA13 .... 39 K8
Albany Gdns *GTS/LS* CH66 .... 94 C5
Albany Gv *LYMM* WA13 .... 39 J8
Albany Rd *BRAM/HZG* SK7 .... 65 L8
LYMM WA13 .... 58 C1
WILM/AE SK9 .... 83 M7
Albany St *BURS/TUN* ST6 .... 243 J5
Albany Ter *RUNC* WA7 .... 9 G3
Alberta St *STKP* SK1 .... 3 H7
Albert Av *FLINT* CH6 .... 116 B7
Albert Cl *CHD/CHDH* SK8 .... 65 G2
Albert Ct *ALT* WA14 .... 42 D8
Albert Dr *NSTN* CH64 .... 91 K4
WARRW/BUR WA5 .... 35 K6
Albert Hill St *DID/WITH* M20 .... 45 H1
Albert Pl *ALT* WA14 .... 42 D7
NWCHE CW9 .... 13 M2
Albert Rd *CHD/CHDH* SK8 .... 65 G2
HALE/TIMP WA15 .... 61 L1
HTNM SK4 .... 46 B1
MCFLDN SK10 .... 112 E4
WARRS WA4 .... 57 G2
WDN WA8 .... 7 L2
WILM/AE SK9 .... 84 A6
Albert Rd East
HALE/TIMP WA15 .... 61 L1
Albert Sq *ALT* WA14 .... 61 K1
Albert St *AIMK* WN4 .... 22 B1
BIDD ST8 .... 227 K4
BRAM/HZG SK7 .... 66 D1
CH/BCN CH1 .... 17 J3
CW/HAS CW1 .... 18 F2
EDGY/DAV SK3 .... 2 D6
IRL M44 .... 31 L6
KNUT WA16 .... 106 F2
MCFLDS SK11 .... 14 E5
NANT CW5 .... 20 F4
RUNC WA7 .... 9 G3
Albion Cl *HTNM* SK4 .... 2 E1
Albion Pl *BRAM/HZG* SK7 .... 66 D1
CH/BCN CH1 .... 17 G7
Albion Rd *NM/HAY* SK22 .... 69 J5
NWCHE CW9 .... 13 K1
Albion St *CH/BCN* CH1 .... 17 G6
CW/SHV CW2 .... 18 A5
Albury Dr *BNG/LEV* M19 .... 45 K2
Alcester Av *EDGY/DAV* SK3 .... 45 M5
Alcester Rd *CHD/CHDH* SK8 .... 45 H8
SALE M33 .... 43 H2
Alcock St *RUNC* WA7 .... 9 H1
Aldcliffe *GOL/RIS/CU* WA3 .... 23 M5
Alder Av *CQ* CH5 .... 166 A1
HUY L36 .... 32 A4
POY/DIS SK12 .... 86 F1
WDN WA8 .... 53 G1
Alderbank Rd *WARRW/BUR* WA5 .... 36 A6
Alder Cl *ALS/KID* ST7 .... 243 G4
LEIGH WN7 .... 24 F2
Alder Crs *WARRN/WOL* WA2 .... 5 J1
Aldercroft Av *WYTH/NTH* M22 .... 63 J2
Alderdale Dr *MPL/ROM* SK6 .... 67 L5
Alderdale Gv *WILM/AE* SK9 .... 83 L7
Alderdale Rd *CHD/CHDH* SK8 .... 46 C8
Alder Dr *GTS/LS* CH66 .... 120 F3
HALE/TIMP WA15 .... 43 K7
Alderfield Dr *SPK/HALE* L24 .... 71 G2
Alder Gv *CHNE* CH2 .... 146 B8
EDGY/DAV SK3 .... 2 A7
Alderhay La *ALS/KID* ST7 .... 226 C8
Alder La *FROD/HEL* WA6 .... 98 D1
WARRN/WOL WA2 .... 37 H4
WARRW/BUR WA5 .... 27 G5
WDN WA8 .... 32 F8
Alderley Av *GOL/RIS/CU* WA3 .... 23 K5
Alderley Cl *BRAM/HZG* SK7 .... 66 F4
POY/DIS SK12 .... 86 F2
SBCH CW11 .... 204 D5
Alderley La *LEIGH* WN7 .... 25 H2
Alderley Ldg *WILM/AE* SK9 .... 84 A7
Alderley Pl *CH/BCN* CH1 .... 144 E6
Alderley Rd *MCFLDN* SK10 .... 110 F2
MCFLDN SK10 .... 137 K1
MCFLDS SK11 .... 135 H2
NWCHW CW8 .... 12 D2
SALE M33 .... 43 L2
WARRS WA4 .... 38 D8
WILM/AE SK9 .... 84 A8
Alderney Cl *EP* CH65 .... 121 J3
MCFLDN SK10 .... 137 M4
Alder Ri *CHF/WBR* SK23 .... 89 K4
Alder Rd *CHD/CHDH* SK8 .... 45 K7
GOL/RIS/CU WA3 .... 23 M4
NWCHW CW8 .... 128 D4
WARR WA1 .... 38 D5
Alder Root La *WARRN/WOL* WA2 .... 27 K5
Alders Av *WYTH/NTH* M22 .... 44 C7
Aldersey Cl *RUNC* WA7 .... 74 D3
Aldersey La *CHSE* CH3 .... 230 A1
Aldersey Rd *CW/SHV* CW2 .... 237 M1
Aldersgate *NM/HAY* SK22 .... 69 H4
Aldersgate Av *RUNC* WA7 .... 74 D5
Aldersgate Dr *HLWD* L26 .... 51 G6
Aldersgate Rd *CHD/CHDH* SK8 .... 65 J7
OFTN SK2 .... 47 H6
Aldersgreen Av *MPL/ROM* SK6 .... 67 M5
Alders Rd *POY/DIS* SK12 .... 68 A5
WYTH/NTH M22 .... 44 C7
Alder St *NEWLW* WA12 .... 27 J1
Alders Wy *MCFLDN* SK10 .... 111 L6
Alderton Dr *AIMK* WN4 .... 22 A1
Alderton Gv *WSFD* CW7 .... 153 M8
Alderue Av *WYTH/NTH* M22 .... 44 D6
Alder Wood Av *SPK/HALE* L24 .... 70 E1
Aldewood Cl *GOL/RIS/CU* WA3 .... 30 A6
Aldfield Rd *NTHM/RTH* M23 .... 43 L3
Aldford Cl *CW/SHV* CW2 .... 253 L2
DID/WITH M20 .... 45 J1
Aldford Pl *WILM/AE* SK9 .... 109 M2
Aldford Rd *CHNE* CH2 .... 145 M6
Aldgate *EP* CH65 .... 10 B8
Aldington Dr *MWCH* CW10 .... 179 K7
Aldridge Dr *WARRW/BUR* WA5 .... 26 F5
Aldwick Av *DID/WITH* M20 .... 45 J1
Aldwyn Crs *BRAM/HZG* SK7 .... 66 C2
Aled Wy *CHSW/BR* CH4 .... 168 D7
Alexander Dr *HALE/TIMP* WA15 .... 43 G6
WDN WA8 .... 6 A5
Alexander Gv *RUNC* WA7 .... 9 L4
Alexandra Cl *EDGY/DAV* SK3 .... 46 C6
Alexandra Gv *IRL* M44 .... 31 M4
Alexandra Rd *HTNM* SK4 .... 2 B2
MWCH CW10 .... 179 K6
SALE M33 .... 43 K1
WARRS WA4 .... 56 F2
Alexandra St *CQ* CH5 .... 142 B6
EP CH65 .... 10 E4
WARR WA1 .... 37 L5
WDN WA8 .... 7 G7
WSFD CW7 .... 177 J3
Alforde St *WDN* WA8 .... 7 H7
Alfred Cl *WDN* WA8 .... 7 J5
Alfred Rd *GOL/RIS/CU* WA3 .... 24 A4
Alfred St *IRL* M44 .... 31 L6
NEWLW WA12 .... 27 L1
NWCHW CW8 .... 12 E6
WDN WA8 .... 7 J5
Alfreton Rd *OFTN* SK2 .... 47 K6
Alfriston Dr *NTHM/RTH* M23 .... 44 A2
Algernon St *RUNC* WA7 .... 8 E1
WARR WA1 .... 5 L4
WARRS WA4 .... 56 C3
Algreave Rd *EDGY/DAV* SK3 .... 46 A4
Alice Ct *WDN* WA8 .... 53 G8
Alison Dr *MCFLDN* SK10 .... 15 L3
Alkington Gdns *WHITCH* SY13 .... 269 M6
Alkington Rd *WHITCH* SY13 .... 269 L8
Allandale *ALT* WA14 .... 42 B8
Allans Cl *CQ* CH5 .... 142 C7
NSTN CH64 .... 91 L6
Allansford Av *CHSE* CH3 .... 171 G8
Allans Meadow *NSTN* CH64 .... 91 L6
Allanson Rd *WYTH/NTH* M22 .... 44 E3
Allcard St *WARRW/BUR* WA5 .... 4 D2
Alldis St *OFTN* SK2 .... 47 H7
Allen Av *GOL/RIS/CU* WA3 .... 25 J8
Allenby Rd *IRL* M44 .... 31 K8
Allendale *RUNC* WA7 .... 74 B6
Allendale Av *RAIN/WH* L35 .... 33 K1
Allen Dr *NWCHE* CW9 .... 153 M2
Allen Rd *RUNC* WA7 .... 8 B8
Allen St *MCFLDS* SK11 .... 15 J7
WARRN/WOL WA2 .... 4 F5
Allerby Wy *GOL/RIS/CU* WA3 .... 23 L4
Allerdean Wk *HTNM* SK4 .... 45 M1
Allerton Rd *WDN* WA8 .... 7 K2
WLTN L25 .... 50 A2
Allgreave Cl *MWCH* CW10 .... 179 J6
SALE M33 .... 43 K3
Allington La *CHSW/BR* CH4 .... 17 J9
Allington Pl *CHSW/BR* CH4 .... 17 J9
Allotment Rd *IRL* M44 .... 31 K6
All Saints Dr *WARRS* WA4 .... 57 L1
All Saints' Rd *HTNM* SK4 .... 2 D1
SPK/HALE L24 .... 70 C1
Allscott Wy *AIMK* WN4 .... 22 C1
Allt Goch *FLINT* CH6 .... 116 A6
Alma Av *CW/HAS* CW1 .... 221 J6
Alma Cl *ALS/KID* ST7 .... 225 L5
MCFLDS SK11 .... 14 B6
Alma La *WILM/AE* SK9 .... 84 A6
Alma Rd *BRAM/HZG* SK7 .... 67 G4
SALE M33 .... 42 E2
Alma St *CHSE* CH3 .... 17 M4
NEWLW WA12 .... 27 H1
Almeda Rd *SPK/HALE* L24 .... 71 G2
Almer Dr *WARRW/BUR* WA5 .... 36 C7
Almond Av *CW/HAS* CW1 .... 221 K6
RUNC WA7 .... 9 L7
Almond Cl *EDGY/DAV* SK3 .... 2 A7
HLWD L26 .... 50 E5
Almond Dr *WARRW/BUR* WA5 .... 26 F6
Almond Gv *WARR* WA1 .... 38 B5
Almond Tree Rd
CHD/CHDH SK8 .... 65 G3
Alness Dr *RAIN/WH* L35 .... 33 K2
Alnwick Dr *EP* CH65 .... 121 K2
Alpine Rd *STKP* SK1 .... 3 K5
Alpine St *NEWLW* WA12 .... 27 G1
Alport Rd *WHITCH* SY13 .... 270 A3
Alpraham Crs *CHNE* CH2 .... 145 L6
Alsager Rd *SBCH* CW11 .... 223 M4
Alsfeld Wy *NM/HAY* SK22 .... 69 G4
Alstead Av *HALE/TIMP* WA15 .... 62 A1
Alston Av *SALE* M33 .... 42 F1
Alston Cl *BRAM/HZG* SK7 .... 66 A3
Alstone Dr *ALT* WA14 .... 42 A6
Alt *WDN* WA8 .... 52 B2
Altair Av *WYTH/NTH* M22 .... 63 K4
Altcar Wk *WYTH/NTH* M22 .... 63 J2
Alton Dr *MCFLDN* SK10 .... 15 L1
Alton Rd *WILM/AE* SK9 .... 83 M4
Altrincham Rd *NTHM/RTH* M23 .... 43 K5
WILM/AE SK9 .... 63 J8
WILM/AE SK9 .... 83 J2
WYTH/NTH M22 .... 44 D6
Alt Wk *WSFD* CW7 .... 178 A2
Alumbrook Av *HOLMCH* CW4 .... 181 J1
Alum Ct *HOLMCH* CW4 .... 181 J3
Alun Crs *CHSW/BR* CH4 .... 169 G6
Alundale Rd *WSFD* CW7 .... 177 J1
Alvanley Cl *SALE* M33 .... 43 H3
Alvanley Crs *EDGY/DAV* SK3 .... 46 C6
Alvanley Dr *FROD/HEL* WA6 .... 124 C2
Alvanley Ri *NWCHE* CW9 .... 13 J7
Alvanley Rd *FROD/HEL* WA6 .... 124 C2
GTS/LS CH66 .... 94 E8
Alvanley Vw *CHNE* CH2 .... 123 H1
Alvaston Av *HTNM* SK4 .... 46 B1
Alvaston Rd *NANT* CW5 .... 21 G6
Alverstone Cl
WARRW/BUR WA5 .... 35 J5
Alverton Cl *WDN* WA8 .... 6 B5
Alveston Cl *MCFLDN* SK10 .... 137 M3
Alveston Dr *WILM/AE* SK9 .... 84 C4
Alvington Gv *BRAM/HZG* SK7 .... 66 A3
Alvis Rd *CQ* CH5 .... 167 H1
Alwain Gn *SPK/HALE* L24 .... 70 F2
Alwinton Av *HTNM* SK4 .... 45 L1
Alwyn Cl *LEIGH* WN7 .... 24 F3
Alwyn Gdns *CHNE* CH2 .... 145 L4
Alyndale Rd *CHSW/BR* CH4 .... 168 D6
Alyn Dr *WRX/GR/LL* LL12 .... 210 B5
Alyn Rd *CHNE* CH2 .... 146 F3
Ambassador Dr *HLWD* L26 .... 51 G3
Amberleigh Cl *WARRS* WA4 .... 77 H1
Amberley Dr *HALE/TIMP* WA15 .... 62 B4
NTHM/RTH M23 .... 44 A7
Amberley Rd *MCFLDS* SK11 .... 14 A8
Amberwood Dr *NTHM/RTH* M23 .... 43 K6
Ambleside *CHNE* CH2 .... 145 M6
Ambleside Av
HALE/TIMP WA15 .... 43 J7
Ambleside Cl *CW/SHV* CW2 .... 237 L2
MCFLDS SK11 .... 137 M6
WSFD CW7 .... 177 J1
Ambleside Ct *CONG* CW12 .... 207 G2
Ambleside Crs
WARRN/WOL WA2 .... 37 J1
Ambleside Rd *EP* CH65 .... 121 J2
Ambrose Pl *BURS/TUN* ST6 .... 243 M5
Ambuscade Cl *CW/HAS* CW1 .... 19 J2
Amelia Cl *WDN* WA8 .... 34 B8
Amelia St *WARRN/WOL* WA2 .... 5 J2
Amersham Cl *MCFLDN* SK10 .... 138 C1
Amis Gv *GOL/RIS/CU* WA3 .... 23 L4
Amlwch Av *OFTN* SK2 .... 47 K6
Amy St *CW/SHV* CW2 .... 18 E5
Ancaster St *BURS/TUN* ST6 .... 243 K5
The Anchorage *CHSE* CH3 .... 171 G7
LYMM WA13 .... 58 D1
NSTN CH64 .... 91 J5
Anchor Cl *RUNC* WA7 .... 74 D6
WHITCH SY13 .... 270 B5

Ancoats Rd *KNUT* WA16...... 108 E4
Anderson Cl *CW/HAS* CW1 ..... 19 M3
  RAIN/WH L35 .... 33 K3
  WARRN/WOL WA2 .... 38 B2
Anderson St *MCFLDS* SK11 ..... 14 E5
Andertons La *MCFLDS* SK11 .... 137 H4
Anderton Wy *WILM/AE* SK9 .... 84 D1
Andover Wl *WARRN/WOL* WA2 .. 37 L3
Andover Wy *WLTN* L25 ...... 50 D4
Andrew Cl *WDN* WA8 .... 52 C4
Andrew Crs *CHSW/BR* CH4 ..... 17 K8
Andrew Gv *MCFLDN* SK10 ...... 139 C5
Andrew La *MPL/ROM* SK6 ...... 67 L3
Andrew's Cl *CHSE* CH3 .... 172 B2
Andrew St *BURS/TUN* ST6 ...... 243 J5
  HTNM SK4 .... 2 E4
Anfield Rd *CHD/CHDH* SK8 ..... 64 F2
Angel St *BRAM/HZG* SK7 .... 66 D1
Anglesea Av *WILM/AE* SK9 ..... 46 F6
Anglesey Cl *EP* CH65 .... 121 J5
Anglesey Dr *POY/DIS* SK12 ..... 66 E6
Anglesey Gv *CHD/CHDH* SK8.... 45 M6
Anglesey Water *POY/DIS* SK12.. 66 E6
Angus Gv *MWCH* CW10 .... 179 K2
Ankers Knowl La *MCFLDN* SK10.. 140 D4
Ankers La *MCFLDS* SK11 .... 140 D5
Annable Rd *IRL* M44 .... 31 M4
  MPL/ROM SK6 .... 47 K1
Annan Cl *CONG* CW12 .... 208 A3
Ann Cl *GTS/LS* CH66 .... 94 D5
Anne Ct *ALS/KID* ST7 .... 242 D7
Anne St *BURS/TUN* ST6 .... 243 J5
  STHEL WA9 .... 34 D1
Anne's Wy *CHSW/BR* CH4 ...... 17 K7
Annette Av *NEWLW* WA12 ...... 22 A7
Annie St *WARRN/WOL* WA2 ..... 5 J4
Annions La *NANT* CW5 .... 252 F3
Annis Cl *WILM/AE* SK9 .... 110 B2
Annis Rd *WILM/AE* SK9 .... 110 B2
Ann St *NWCHE* CW9 .... 130 D3
  RUNC WA7 .... 9 J1
Ann St West *WDN* WA8 .... 7 J1
Ansdell Rd *WDN* WA8 .... 7 K1
Ansley Gv *HTNM* SK4 .... 46 B1
Anson Cl *BRAM/HZG* SK7 ...... 65 M7
  WARRN/WOL WA2 .... 37 L2
Anson Rd *POY/DIS* SK12 .... 87 H1
  WILM/AE SK9 .... 84 E3
Anthony Dr *NWCHE* CW9 ...... 153 M5
Antons Ct *HLWD* L26 .... 50 F6
Antons Rd *HLWD* L26 .... 50 F6
Antony Rd *WARRS* WA4 .... 56 B3
Antrim Cl *BNG/LEV* M19 .... 45 K2
Antrim Dr *GTS/LS* CH66 .... 120 F2
Antrim Rd *WARRN/WOL* WA2 ... 37 G2
Antrobus St *CONG* CW12 .... 207 L1
Anvil Cl *CH/BCN* CH1 .... 144 A3
Appleby Av *HALE/TIMP* WA15... 43 J7
Appleby Cl *EDGY/DAV* SK3 ..... 46 D7
  MCFLDS SK11 .... 137 M7
  WDN WA8 .... 52 C4
Appleby Dr *CO* CH5 .... 166 C2
Appleby Rd *CHD/CHDH* SK8 .... 45 H8
  NTHLY L27 .... 32 A8
  WARRN/WOL WA2 .... 37 J1
Apple Cft *AUD/MAD/W* CW3 .... 267 K5
Applecross Cl
  GOL/RIS/CU WA3 .... 30 A6
Appledale Dr *GTS/LS* CH66 .... 121 G4
Apple Dell Av
  GOL/RIS/CU WA3 .... 23 J3
Appledore Cl *SPK/HALE* L24 .... 50 B8
Appledore Dr *NTHM/RTH* M23 .. 43 K5
Appledore Gv *ALS/KID* ST7 ..... 243 L4
Applefield *NWCHW* CW8 .... 12 C5
Appleford *WARRS* WA4 .... 56 E5
Apple Market St *NWCHE* CW9 .. 13 G2
Appleton Cl *CHSW/BR* CH4 .... 169 K5
Appleton Dr *EP* CH65 .... 120 F1
Appleton Gv *SALE* M33 .... 42 E2
Appleton Rd *CHNE* CH2 .... 145 L7
  HALE/TIMP WA15 .... 61 L3
  WDN WA8 .... 7 J2
Appleton Village *WDN* WA8 .... 7 H2
Apple Tree Gv *GTS/LS* CH66 .... 120 F4
Appletree Gv *WARRN/WOL* WA2.. 37 M2
Apple Tree Rd *NM/HAY* SK22 ... 69 J2
Applewood Av *CO* CH5 .... 142 F5
Appleyards La *CHSW/BR* CH4.... 17 H9
  CHSW/BR CH4 .... 169 K5
April Ri *MCFLDN* SK10 .... 111 L6
Apsley Cl *ALT* WA14 .... 61 H3
Apsley Gv *ALT* WA14 .... 61 H3
Apsley Wy *STKP* SK1 .... 3 H5
Aragon Wy *MPL/ROM* SK6 ..... 48 F6
Aran Cl *SPK/HALE* L24 .... 71 K2
Arbour Cl *AUD/MAD/W* CW3 .... 267 L5
  MCFLDN SK10 .... 138 D1
  NWCHW CW8 .... 130 C4
Arbour Crs *MCFLDN* SK10 ...... 138 D1
Arbour Ms *MCFLDN* SK10 ...... 138 D1
Arbour St *ALS/KID* ST7 .... 242 D7
Arbury Av *EDGY/DAV* SK3 ...... 45 M5
Arbury La *WARRN/WOL* WA2 .... 28 C6
Arcadia Av *SALE* M33 .... 43 G3
Archer Av *WARRS* WA4 .... 56 E2
Archer Cl *MCFLDN* SK10 .... 112 E5
Archer St *LEIGH* WN7 .... 25 H2
  OFTN SK2 .... 47 J7
Archers Wy *CH/BCN* CH1 ...... 16 A3
Arclid Cl *GTS/LS* CH66 .... 120 E3
Arclid Dr *WILM/AE* SK9 .... 84 E2
Arden *WDN* WA8 .... 52 A2
Ardenbrook Ri *MCFLDN* SK10... 111 L6
Arden Cl *CHSE* CH3 .... 172 C1
  GOL/RIS/CU WA3 .... 30 B6
Arden Ct *BRAM/HZG* SK7 ...... 65 K3
  CONG CW12 .... 208 B5
Arden Dr *NSTN* CH64 .... 91 L6
Ardenfield Dr *WYTH/NTH* M22 .. 63 L2
Arden Lodge Rd
  NTHM/RTH M23 .... 43 K5
Ardens Meadow *TPLY/KEL* CW6.. 197 J4
Arden St *NM/HAY* SK22 .... 69 J5
Arderne Av *CW/SHV* CW2 ...... 18 A7
Arderne Rd *HALE/TIMP* WA15... 43 G4

Ardern Gv *STKP* SK1 .... 3 H8
Ardern Lea *FROD/HEL* WA6 .... 124 D3
Ardleigh Cl *CW/HAS* CW1 ...... 220 F4
Ardwick Rd *SPK/HALE* L24 ..... 70 F1
Argosy Dr *MANAIR* M90 .... 62 F5
Argyle St *BRAM/HZG* SK7 ...... 66 E2
Argyll Av *CHSW/BR* CH4 .... 16 B9
Argyll Cl *MCFLDN* SK10 .... 14 A3
Argyll Rd *CHD/CHDH* SK8 ...... 45 M7
Aries Cl *BURS/TUN* ST6 .... 243 M6
Arkenshaw Rd *GOL/RIS/CU* WA3.. 29 G5
Arkenstone Cl *WDN* WA8 ...... 52 C2
Arkle Av *WILM/AE* SK9 .... 64 E8
Arklow Dr *SPK/HALE* L24 ...... 71 K2
Arkwright St *WSFD* CW7 .... 177 G4
Arkwright Cl *RUNC* WA7 .... 73 M1
Arkwright Dr *MPL/ROM* SK6 .... 49 G6
Arkwright Rd *MPL/ROM* SK6 .... 49 G6
  RUNC WA7 .... 73 M1
Arley Av *WARRS* WA4 .... 56 D3
Arley Cl *WILM/AE* SK9 .... 84 F7
  ALT WA14 .... 42 D4
  CHNE CH2 .... 145 M6
  MCFLDS SK11 .... 14 A8
Arley Dr *SALE* M33 .... 43 G2
Arley End *KNUT* WA16 .... 59 J8
Arley Gv *EDGY/DAV* SK3 .... 46 D8
Arley Mere Cl *CW/HAS* CW1 .... 64 F1
Arley Mossend La *NWCHE* CW9.. 104 D2
Arley Pl *CW/SHV* CW2 .... 238 A4
Arley Rd *NWCHE* CW9 .... 77 L4
  NWCHE CW9 .... 130 C3
  WARRS WA4 .... 57 J8
Arley Wk *SBCH* CW11 .... 203 K7
Arlington Cl *CW/SHV* CW2 ...... 238 C4
Arlington Crs *WILM/AE* SK9 .... 83 L7
Arlington Dr *GOL/RIS/CU* WA3 .. 24 C4
  LEIGH WN7 .... 24 C4
  MCFLDS SK11 .... 14 A6
  OFTN SK2 .... 66 A1
  POY/DIS SK12 .... 86 D1
  WARRW/BUR WA5 .... 35 L8
Arlington Rd *CHD/CHDH* SK8 ... 45 J8
Arlington Wy *WILM/AE* SK9 .... 83 L7
Armadale Cl *EDGY/DAV* SK3 .... 46 E8
Armett St *MCFLDS* SK11 .... 14 F7
Armistead Wy *HOLMCH* CW4 ... 157 G7
Armitage Rd *ALT* WA14 .... 61 K1
Armitstead Rd *SBCH* CW11 ..... 222 F1
Armour Av *WARRN/WOL* WA2 .. 37 M2
Armoury Bank *AIMK* WN4 ...... 22 B1
Armoury St *EDGY/DAV* SK3 ..... 2 F7
Armscot Cl *WLTN* L25 .... 50 B5
Armscot Pl *WLTN* L25 .... 50 B5
Armstrong Cl
  AUD/MAD/W CW3 .... 263 M8
  GOL/RIS/CU WA3 .... 29 K8
Armthorpe Dr *GTS/LS* CH66 .... 94 B7
Arncliffe Dr *NTHM/RTH* M23 ... 63 G1
  WARRW/BUR WA5 .... 26 F6
Arncliffe Rd *WLTN* L25 .... 50 D3
Arndale *RUNC* WA7 .... 73 L7
Arnfield Rd *EDGY/DAV* SK3 ..... 46 D7
Arnhem Crs *WARRN/WOL* WA2.. 5 H2
Arnhem Wy *CHSE* CH3 .... 170 B7
Arnold Pl *WDN* WA8 .... 52 C5
Arnold's Crs *CHSW/BR* CH4 .... 190 A1
Arnold St *EDGY/DAV* SK3 ...... 2 E9
  NANT CW5 .... 20 F4
Arnside Av *BRAM/HZG* SK7 ..... 66 C2
  CONG CW12 .... 207 G2
Arnside Cl *CHD/CHDH* SK8 ..... 45 H8
  MPL/ROM SK6 .... 67 L4
  WSFD CW7 .... 177 K2
Arnside Gv *WARRS* WA4 .... 56 B2
Arpley Rd *WARR* WA1 .... 5 G9
Arpley St *WARR* WA1 .... 4 E7
Arradon Ct *CHNE* CH2 .... 145 L7
Arran Av *EP* CH65 .... 121 J3
  SALE M33 .... 43 J1
Arran Cl *HOLMCH* CW4 .... 181 J3
  WARRN/WOL WA2 .... 38 A2
  FROD/HEL WA6 .... 99 J5
Arran Dr *ALS/KID* ST7 .... 243 M4
Arrivals Wy *MANAIR* M90 ...... 63 H5
Arron Pl *CW/SHV* CW2 .... 237 K1
Arrowcroft Rd *CHSE* CH3 ...... 146 F7
Arrowsmith Dr *ALS/KID* ST7 ... 241 H1
Arrow St *LEIGH* WN7 .... 25 H1
Arthill La *ALT* WA14 .... 60 D3
Arthog Dr *HALE/TIMP* WA15.... 61 M4
Arthog Rd *DID/WITH* M20 ..... 45 J2
  HALE/TIMP WA15 .... 61 M4
Arthur Av *EP* CH65 .... 10 F4
Arthur St *BURS/TUN* ST6 ...... 243 J8
  CH/BCN CH1 .... 16 B3
  CW/SHV CW2 .... 19 H7
  NWCHE CW9 .... 131 G2
  RUNC WA7 .... 8 F3
  WARRN/WOL WA2 .... 4 E5
Artists La *MCFLDN* SK10 .... 110 B6
Artle Rd *CW/SHV* CW2 .... 238 C4
Arundale Av *BRAM/HZG* SK7 ... 66 D4
Arundel Cl *CW/SHV* CW2 ...... 237 L4
  HALE/TIMP WA15 .... 62 C3
  KNUT WA16 .... 107 G4
  MCFLDN SK10 .... 15 L1
Arundel Gv *OFTN* SK2 .... 47 M1
Arundel Rd *CHD/CHDH* SK8 .... 65 G5
Ascol Dr *NWCHE* CW9 .... 131 J1
Ascot Av *RUNC* WA7 .... 73 H6
  SALE M33 .... 43 J4
Ascot Cl *CONG* CW12 .... 184 D8
  MCFLDN SK10 .... 138 C1
  WARR WA1 .... 38 E5
  WARRS WA4 .... 57 J2
Ascot Dr *CHD/CHDH* SK8 ...... 67 G2
  GTS/LS CH66 .... 120 D1
Ash Av *ALT* WA14 .... 42 A7
  CHD/CHDH SK8 .... 45 L1
  IRL M44 .... 31 K7
  NEWLW WA12 .... 27 J1
Ashbank *NWCHE* CW9 .... 130 D5
Ashberry Cl *WILM/AE* SK9 ..... 84 D1
Ashberry Dr *WARRS* WA4 ...... 57 H7
Ashbourne Av *MCFLDN* SK10... 45 M6

  RUNC WA7 .... 73 H6
Ashbourne Cl *GTS/LS* CH66 .... 120 E4
Ashbourne Crs *SALE* M33 ...... 43 K2
Ashbourne Dr *MPL/ROM* SK6 ... 67 L6
Ashbourne Ms
  MCFLDN SK10 .... 137 M4
Ashbourne Rd *BRAM/HZG* SK7.. 66 D1
  WARRW/BUR WA5 .... 36 B7
Ashbrook Av *RUNC* WA7 .... 73 M8
  RUNC WA7 .... 99 M1
Ashbrook Cl *CHD/CHDH* SK8 ... 64 B3
Ashbrook Crs *WARRN/WOL* WA2.. 37 K4
Ashbrook Dr *MCFLDN* SK10 .... 112 A6
Ashbrook Rd *MCFLDN* SK10 .... 110 F6
  MCFLDN SK10 .... 112 F5
Ashburn Gv *HTNM* SK4 .... 2 B2
Ashburn Rd *HTNM* SK4 .... 2 B2
Ashburton Rd *EDGY/DAV* SK3... 46 B8
Ashbury Cl *RUNC* WA7 .... 74 D2
Ashby Dr *SBCH* CW11 .... 203 J7
Ashby Pl *CHNE* CH2 .... 17 K1
  CHNE CH2 .... 145 L8
Ash Cl *GTS/LS* CH66 .... 120 F3
  HOLMCH CW4 .... 157 K6
  MALPAS SY14 .... 246 C7
  TPLY/KEL CW6 .... 197 K2
Ashcott Av *HTNM* SK4 .... 44 D8
Ashcroft *WILM/AE* SK9 .... 83 M7
Ashcroft Av *CW/SHV* CW2 ..... 253 H1
Ashcroft Rd *LYMM* WA13 ...... 40 B8
Ashdale Cl *ALS/KID* ST7 .... 224 C7
Ashdale Dr *CHD/CHDH* SK8 .... 64 B2
Ashdene Rd *WILM/AE* SK9 ..... 83 M7
Ashdown Gv *HLWD* L26 .... 51 G2
Ashdown La *GOL/RIS/CU* WA3 .. 30 A7
Ashdown Rd *HTNM* SK4 .... 2 B1
  KNUT WA16 .... 107 M6
Ashenhurst Rd *ALS/KID* ST7 ... 241 M1
Ashenough Rd *ALS/KID* ST7 .... 242 D6
Ashfield *RAIN/WH* L35 .... 33 K1
  WILM/AE SK9 .... 83 M8
Ashfield Cl *WILM/AE* SK9 ...... 84 A8
Ashfield Crs *CH/BCN* CH1 ...... 144 D7
  CHD/CHDH SK8 .... 45 K6
  CO CH5 .... 166 D2
Ashfield Dr *MCFLDN* SK10 ..... 14 B2
Ashfield Gv *EDGY/DAV* SK3 .... 46 F8
  IRL M44 .... 31 L6
  MPL/ROM SK6 .... 49 H3
Ashfield Rd *CHD/CHDH* SK8 .... 45 K6
  CO CH5 .... 142 B6
  EDGY/DAV SK3 .... 46 F8
  HALE/TIMP WA15 .... 61 L1
Ashfield Rd North *EP* CH65 .... 10 E7
Ashfield St *MWCH* CW10 ...... 179 K5
Ashford Cl *HLWD* L26 .... 50 E5
  WILM/AE SK9 .... 64 C8
Ashford Rd *WILM/AE* SK9 ...... 84 A8
Ashgate Av *WYTH/NTH* M22 ... 44 B8
Ashgate La *NWCHW* CW9 ..... 104 F7
Ash Gv *ALS/KID* ST7 .... 224 F5
  ALT WA14 .... 61 J3
  CHD/CHDH SK8 .... 64 B4
  CHSW/BR CH4 .... 169 H7
  CO CH5 .... 142 B6
  GTS/LS CH66 .... 94 C6
  HALE/TIMP WA15 .... 42 F5
  KNUT WA16 .... 107 K3
  MCFLDS SK11 .... 138 C7
  MPL/ROM SK6 .... 48 E7
  MWCH CW10 .... 179 K5
  NWCHW CW8 .... 128 E5
  RUNC WA7 .... 9 M7
  WARRS WA4 .... 56 D1
Ashgrove *WSFD* CW7 .... 177 K4
Ash Hay La *CHNE* CH2 .... 146 C3
Ash House La *NWCHW* CW8 ... 102 C5
Ashlands *FROD/HEL* WA6 ...... 99 J5
Ashlands Rd *HALE/TIMP* WA15.. 42 F5
Ash La *CO* CH5 .... 166 D3
  HALE/TIMP WA15 .... 62 C3
  SALE M33 .... 56 E4
  WDN WA8 .... 51 M4
Ash Lawn Cl *CHNE* CH2 .... 145 J8
Ashlea Cl *CO* CH5 .... 166 C2
Ashlea Dr *NANT* CW5 .... 237 L7
Ashleigh Cl *CHSW/BR* CH4 ..... 168 E6
Ashleigh Rd *HALE/TIMP* WA15.. 43 H4
Ashley Cl *CW/HAS* CW1 .... 222 D7
  RAIN/WH L35 .... 33 K2
Ashley Ct *WRXS/E* LL13 .... 228 D4
Ashley Dr *BRAM/HZG* SK7 ..... 65 J6
  NWCHW CW9 .... 129 G6
  SALE M33 .... 42 E2
Ashley Gdns *MALPAS* SY14 .... 230 C3
  MPL/ROM SK6 .... 67 K4
Ashley Gra *NWCHE* CW9 ...... 153 L1
Ashley Meadow *CW/HAS* CW1.. 222 D7
Ashleymill La *ALT* WA14 .... 61 K4
Ashley Mill La North *ALT* WA14.. 61 K4
Ashley Rd *ALT* WA14 .... 61 K1
  HALE/TIMP WA15 .... 61 L2
  KNUT WA16 .... 80 D4
  OFTN SK2 .... 47 J4
  RUNC WA7 .... 73 K2
  WILM/AE SK9 .... 84 B3
Ashley Wy *WDN* WA8 .... 7 H8
Ashley Wy West *WDN* WA8 .... 6 F7
Ashmead *ALS/KID* ST7 .... 241 L4
Ashmeade *HALE/TIMP* WA15... 62 B3
Ashmeade Ms *ALS/KID* ST7 .... 241 L1
Ashmoor Rd *WYTH/NTH* M22 .. 63 K3
Ashmore Av *EDGY/DAV* SK3 .... 45 M5
Ashmore Cl *GOL/RIS/CU* WA3 .. 39 G1
  MWCH CW10 .... 179 K5
Ashmore's La *ALS/KID* ST7 ..... 241 K1
Ashmuir Cl *CH/BCN* CH1 ...... 168 D1
  CW/HAS CW1 .... 221 H6
Ash Rd *CHNE* CH2 .... 123 J7
  CW/HAS CW1 .... 221 K6
  GOL/RIS/CU WA3 .... 40 A2
  LYMM WA13 .... 58 C1
  NWCHW CW8 .... 151 M2

  PART M31 .... 40 D1
  POY/DIS SK12 .... 86 F1
  WARRN/WOL WA2 .... 28 B6
  WARRW/BUR WA5 .... 35 M8
  WHITCH SY13 .... 270 D6
Ashstead *SALE* M33 .... 43 J3
Ash St *BRAM/HZG* SK7 .... 66 D1
  EDGY/DAV SK3 .... 46 B4
  GOL/RIS/CU WA3 .... 23 H2
  NWCHE CW9 .... 13 K1
Ash Ter *MCFLDS* SK11 .... 138 C8
Ashton Av *ALT* WA14 .... 42 E6
  MCFLDN SK10 .... 137 K3
  RAIN/WH L35 .... 33 J2
Ashton Cl *CONG* CW12 .... 208 B3
  FROD/HEL WA6 .... 99 J3
  MWCH CW10 .... 179 K7
  NWCHE CW9 .... 129 L8
  PS/BROM CH62 .... 93 L1
  RUNC WA7 .... 72 F6
Ashton Dr *FROD/HEL* WA6 ..... 99 J3
  FROD/HEL WA6 .... 99 J2
  WLTN L25 .... 50 B5
Ashton Heath *AIMK* WN4 ...... 22 C2
Ashton La *CHSE* CH3 .... 148 E6
Ashton Pl *BRAM/HZG* SK7 ..... 66 F3
Ashton Rd *FROD/HEL* WA6 ..... 149 K1
  GOL/RIS/CU WA3 .... 22 F2
  NEWLW WA12 .... 22 C6
  PART M31 .... 41 J1
Ashton St *WARRN/WOL* WA2.... 5 G5
Ashtree Cl *MCFLDN* SK10 ...... 112 C4
  NSTN CH64 .... 91 M5
Ashtree Cft *NSTN* CH64 .... 93 C5
Ashtree Dr *NSTN* CH64 .... 92 A6
Ashtree Farm Ct *NSTN* CH64 ... 93 G4
Ashurst Dr *EDGY/DAV* SK3 ..... 46 B7
Ashurst Rd *WYTH/NTH* M22 ... 63 M1
Ash Vw *CW/SHV* CW2 .... 238 B5
Ashville Ct *CW/SHV* CW2 ...... 238 B5
Ashville Rd *RUNC* WA7 .... 99 L1
Ashway Clough North
  OFTN SK2 .... 47 K7
Ashway Clough South
  OFTN SK2 .... 47 K7
Ashwell Av *GOL/RIS/CU* WA3 ... 23 K3
Ashwell Rd *NTHM/RTH* M23 ... 44 B5
Ashwood *ALT* WA14 .... 61 H4
Ashwood Av *AIMK* WN4 .... 22 A2
  GOL/RIS/CU WA3 .... 23 K4
  SALE M33 .... 42 E1
  WARR WA1 .... 37 L5
Ashwood Cl *GTS/LS* CH66 ..... 120 D3
  NWCHW CW8 .... 103 H8
Ashwood Crs *CHNE* CH2 ...... 170 B1
Ashwood Crs *MPL/ROM* SK6 ... 48 F5
  NWCHW CW8 .... 129 H1
Ashwood La *CHNE* CH2 .... 122 A7
  WHITCH SY13 .... 271 H8
Ashwood Rd *POY/DIS* SK12 .... 68 D6
Ashworth Cl *ALT* WA14 .... 61 H3
Ashworth Pk *KNUT* WA16 ...... 106 F4
Askern Av *WYTH/NTH* M22 .... 63 K1
Askrigg Av *GTS/LS* CH66 .... 94 B7
Aspen Cl *ALS/KID* ST7 .... 243 L1
  GTS/LS CH66 .... 120 E3
  HALE/TIMP WA15 .... 43 L7
Aspen Gv *CH/BCN* CH1 .... 144 B5
  WARR WA1 .... 38 A5
The Aspens *NWCHW* CW8 ..... 127 K7
Aspen Wy *CHNE* CH2 .... 146 B8
  MPL/ROM SK6 .... 48 F5
  NWCHW CW8 .... 128 E5
  WARR WA1 .... 68 A5
Aspenwood *AIMK* WN4 .... 22 A2
Aspen Wd *MPL/ROM* SK6 ..... 48 E5
Aspinall Cl *WARRN/WOL* WA2 .. 38 A1
Aspull Cl *GOL/RIS/CU* WA3 ..... 29 J8
Aspull Common *LEIGH* WN7 ... 24 C3
Asquith Cl *BIDD* ST8 .... 227 K4
  CW/HAS CW1 .... 222 C7
Assheton Wk *SPK/HALE* L24 ... 71 L2
Astbury Cl *ALS/KID* ST7 .... 243 J1
  GOL/RIS/CU WA3 .... 24 B4
  HALE/TIMP WA15 .... 42 E6
Astbury Dr *EDGY/DAV* SK3 ..... 46 D6
Astbury Dr *NWCHW* CW8 ..... 103 G8
Astbury Lane Ends *CONG* CW12.. 207 L4
Astbury St *CONG* CW12 .... 207 J2
Aster Crs *RUNC* WA7 .... 73 M8
Astle Cl *MWCH* CW10 .... 179 J5
Astle Ct *MCFLDS* SK11 .... 135 G1
Astle La *MCFLDN* SK10 .... 135 L4
Astley Cl *KNUT* WA16 .... 107 J5
  WARRS WA4 .... 56 B1
  WDN WA8 .... 52 C1
Astley St *IRL* M44 .... 31 L4
Astley St *HTNM* SK4 .... 2 E5
Astmoor Bridge La *RUNC* WA7.. 73 M2
Astmoor Rd *RUNC* WA7 .... 9 M1
  RUNC WA7 .... 73 K1
Aston Av *GOL/RIS/CU* WA3 ..... 29 M7
  WSFD CW7 .... 177 H2
Aston Ct *WARR* WA1 .... 38 C3
Aston Fields Rd *RUNC* WA7 .... 74 D8
Aston Gn *RUNC* WA7 .... 74 E6
Aston Hl *CO* CH5 .... 166 B1
Aston La *RUNC* WA7 .... 100 B1
Aston La North *RUNC* WA7 .... 100 B1
Aston La South *RUNC* WA7 .... 100 E3
Aston Md *CO* CH5 .... 166 B1
Aston Park Rd *CO* CH5 .... 142 A8
Aston Rd *CO* CH5 .... 142 B8
Aston Wy *MWCH* CW10 .... 179 L3
Aston Wy *WARRS* WA4 .... 56 F4
Atcherley Rd *NANT* CW5 .... 251 L4
Athelbrae Cl *NWCHW* CW8 .... 12 F5
Athens St *STKP* SK1 .... 3 K6
Atherleigh Wy *LEIGH* WN7 .... 24 C1
Atherton La *IRL* M44 .... 31 L7
Atherton Rd *EP* CH65 .... 94 F6
Atherton St *EDGY/DAV* SK3 .... 46 B6
Athey St *MCFLDS* SK11 .... 14 E6
Athlone Rd *CHD/CHDH* SK8 .... 46 A7
Athey St *MCFLDS* SK11 .... 14 E6
Atholl Av *CW/SHV* CW2 .... 18 A3
Atholl Cl *MCFLDN* SK10 .... 14 A3
Athol Rd *BRAM/HZG* SK7 ..... 65 K7
Athol St *HTNM* SK4 .... 2 D2

Atis Cft *FLINT* CH6 .... 116 C7
Atkinson St *OFTN* SK2 .... 3 K9
Atlanta Av *MANAIR* M90 .... 63 G4
Atlantic St *ALT* WA14 .... 42 A6
Atlow Dr *NTHM/RTH* M23 ..... 44 B7
Attenbury's La *ALT* WA14 ...... 52 C2
Attlee Av *MCFLDN* SK10 .... 25 H8
Attlee Rd *HUY* L36 .... 32 A1
Attwood Cl *CW/HAS* CW1 ...... 222 C8
Attwood Rd *HALE/TIMP* WA15.. 43 H7
Attwood St *ALS/KID* ST7 .... 243 G2
Atwood Rd *DID/WITH* M20 .... 45 J1
Aubourn Cl *WDN* WA8 .... 52 C1
Aubrey St *BURS/TUN* ST6 ...... 243 H5
Auckery Av *GTS/LS* CH66 ...... 120 D1
Auckland St *CH/BCN* CH1 ...... 144 C3
Audie Murphy Rd
  WARRW/BUR WA5 .... 36 B6
Audlem Cl *RUNC* WA7 .... 73 M8
Audlem Dr *NWCHE* CW9 ...... 13 K8
Audlem Rd *AUD/MAD/W* CW3 .. 264 B6
  AUD/MAD/W CW3 .... 264 C5
  NANT CW5 .... 251 L1
Audrey Crs *CHSW/BR* CH4 ..... 169 K6
Audrey Rd *ALS/KID* ST7 .... 241 L4
  ALS/KID ST7 .... 242 C5
  CW/SHV CW2 .... 240 D7
Audrey St *CW/HAS* CW1 .... 19 H1
Audre Cl *WARRW/BUR* WA5 .... 35 K6
Aughton Wy *CHSW/BR* CH4 .... 167 K8
Augusta Dr *MCFLDN* SK10 ..... 138 B1
Austell Rd *WYTH/NTH* M22 .... 63 K3
Austen Cl *SBCH* CW11 .... 203 K6
Austin Cl *WSFD* CW7 .... 177 K1
Austins Hl *CHSE* CH3 .... 172 C4
Austin St *NWCHE* CW9 .... 130 D2
Austral Av *WARR* WA1 .... 38 B5
Australia La *WARRS* WA4 ...... 57 J3
Autumn Av *KNUT* WA16 .... 107 J2
Avalon Dr *DID/WITH* M20 ..... 45 J4
Avebury Cl *GOL/RIS/CU* WA3 ... 23 L4
  WDN WA8 .... 53 L1
Avebury Rd *NTHM/RTH* M23 ... 44 A7
Aveley Av *WARR* WA1 .... 38 B5
Avenue St *STKP* SK1 .... 3 H5
The Avenue *ALS/KID* ST7 ...... 224 C8
  ALS/KID ST7 .... 242 F3
  CHD/CHDH SK8 .... 64 A3
  CHSE CH3 .... 147 M5
  CO CH5 .... 166 C4
  HALE/TIMP WA15 .... 61 M4
  HLWD L26 .... 50 E5
  KNUT WA16 .... 59 J7
  LYMM WA13 .... 58 C3
  MPL/ROM SK6 .... 47 K1
  NEWLW WA12 .... 22 C8
  NWCHE CW9 .... 103 K4
  NWCHE CW9 .... 130 B1
  SALE M33 .... 42 D1
  SBCH CW11 .... 203 L4
  TPLY/KEL CW6 .... 197 K3
  WILM/AE SK9 .... 110 A3
Averham Cl *AIMK* WN4 .... 22 B3
Avery Cl *WARRN/WOL* WA2 .... 37 L2
Aviemore Dr *WARRN/WOL* WA2.. 38 A1
Avocet Cl *NEWLW* WA12 ...... 22 C8
  WARRN/WOL WA2 .... 27 J6
Avocet Dr *ALT* WA14 .... 42 B4
  WSFD CW7 .... 177 K6
Avon *WDN* WA8 .... 52 A2
Avon Av *WARRW/BUR* WA5 .... 35 L8
Avon Cl *ALS/KID* ST7 .... 243 L1
  MCFLDN SK10 .... 14 A1
  MPL/ROM SK6 .... 48 E7
Avon Ct *ALS/KID* ST7 .... 224 C7
Avondale *EP* CH65 .... 121 H2
Avondale Av *BRAM/HZG* SK7 ... 66 F2
Avondale Dr *WDN* WA8 .... 52 B3
Avondale Ri *WILM/AE* SK9 ..... 84 D6
Avondale Rd *BRAM/HZG* SK7 ... 66 F2
  EDGY/DAV SK3 .... 2 A8
Avon Dr *CONG* CW12 .... 207 M3
  CW/HAS CW1 .... 222 A7
Avonlea Cl *CHSW/BR* CH4 ..... 168 E8
Avonlea Rd *SALE* M33 .... 42 D3
Avon Rd *CHD/CHDH* SK8 ...... 64 B5
  GOL/RIS/CU WA3 .... 30 A2
  HALE/TIMP WA15 .... 61 L4
Avonside Av *BURS/TUN* ST6 ... 243 M8
Avonside Wy *MCFLDS* SK11 .... 138 C7
Avon St *EDGY/DAV* SK3 .... 46 B5
Avro Wy *MANAIR* M90 .... 62 F5
Aylesbury Cl *GTS/LS* CH66 ..... 120 C1
  MCFLDN SK10 .... 138 D1
Aylesby Cl *KNUT* WA16 .... 107 H3
Aylin St *DR* SALE* M33 .... 43 H1
Ayr Cl *BRAM/HZG* SK7 .... 67 G2
Ayrshire Cl *MWCH* CW10 ...... 179 K2
Ayrshire Wy *CONG* CW12 ...... 208 A3
Aysgarth Av *CHD/CHDH* SK8 ... 45 J6
  CW/HAS CW1 .... 221 H3
Aysgarth Cl *SALE* M33 .... 42 D1
Ayshford Cl *ALT* WA14 .... 42 B6
Azalea Gv *HLWD* L26 .... 50 D2
  RUNC WA7 .... 73 L1

B

Babbacombe Rd *OFTN* SK2 .... 47 J6
  WARRW/BUR WA5 .... 35 L8
Babbage Rd *CO* CH5 .... 143 G8
Bache Av *CHNE* CH2 .... 145 J7
Bache Dr *CHNE* CH2 .... 145 K7
Bachefield Av *CHSE* CH3 ...... 169 M6
Bache Hall Ct *CHNE* CH2 ...... 145 J7
Bachelor's La *CHSE* CH3 ...... 170 A4
Back Adcroft St *STKP* SK1 ..... 3 H9
Back Booth St *NEWLW* WA12 .. 27 G1
Back Bridge St *NEWLW* WA12 .. 27 H1
  NM/HAY SK22 .... 69 J3
Back Brook Pl *WARRS* WA4 .... 56 E1

Back Chapel St
  BRAM/HZG SK7 .... 66 E1 🔢
Back Coole La *NANT* CW5 .. 262 E6
Back Crosland Ter
  FROD/HEL WA6 .... 124 B2
Back Cross La *NEWLW* WA12 .. 22 B8 🔢
Back Eastford Rd
  WARRS WA4 .... 56 A3 🔢
Back Eddisbury Rd
  MCFLDN SK10 .... 139 J5
Backford Cl *RUNC* WA7 .... 74 C7 🔢
Backford Gdns *GTS/LS* CH66 .. 120 F5 🔢
Back Forshaw St
  WARRN/WOL WA2 .... 5 J3
Back Heathcote St
  ALS/KID ST7 .... 243 C2 🔢
Back High St *RUNC* WA7 .... 9 G2
Back La *ALT* WA14 .... 41 H7
  AUD/MAD/W CW3 .... 255 H4
  CHSE CH3 .... 215 J2
  CONG CW12 .... 183 L7
  CONG CW12 .... 184 F2
  CW/SHV CW2 .... 238 E8
  FROD/HEL WA6 .... 124 C2
  HALE/TIMP WA15 .... 61 M7
  KNUT WA16 .... 59 M7
  KNUT WA16 .... 132 B5
  MALPAS SY14 .... 247 G8
  MALPAS SY14 .... 256 E5
  NANT CW5 .... 253 J5
  NWCHE CW9 .... 78 D5
  SBCH CW11 .... 181 H5
  SBCH CW11 .... 205 K5
  TPLY/KEL CW6 .... 173 G6
  TPLY/KEL CW6 .... 198 C5
  WARRS WA4 .... 76 D8
  WARRW/BUR WA5 .... 26 D5
  WARRW/BUR WA5 .... 54 A2
  TPLY/KEL CW6 .... 197 H2
Back Lawrence St
  NEWLW WA12 .... 27 G1 🔢
Back Legh St *NEWLW* WA12 .. 27 G1 🔢
Back Market St
  NEWLW WA12 .... 22 A8
Back Massie St
  CHD/CHDH SK8 .... 45 K6 🔢
Back Paradise St
  MCFLDN SK11 .... 14 F6 🔢
Back Queen St *CH/BCN* CH1 .. 17 H4
Back Union Rd *NM/HAY* SK22 .. 69 J5
Back Wallgate *MCFLDS* SK11 .. 15 G5
Back Water St *STKP* SK1 .... 3 H3 🔢
Badcock's La *TPLY/KEL* CW6 .. 233 L1
Baddiley Cl *NANT* CW5 ...... 250 D2
Baddiley Hall La *NANT* CW5 .. 250 A4
Baddiley La *NANT* CW5 ...... 250 B4
Baddington La *NANT* CW5 .... 251 K3
Badger Av *CW/HAS* CW1 ...... 220 F6
Badger Bait *NSTN* CH64 ...... 91 M6
Badger Rd *RUNC* WA7 .... 74 A5
Badger Rd *MCFLDN* SK10 ...... 112 A5
  MCFLDN SK10 .... 138 D2
Badgers Cl *CHSE* CH3 .... 170 E5
  GTS/LS CH66 .... 120 F4 🔢
  WSFD CW7 .... 177 G3 🔢
Badgers Pk *NTH* CH64 .... 91 M6
Badgersrake La *GTS/LS* CH66 .. 93 K8
Badgers Set *NWCHW* CW8 .... 127 K7
Badgers Wk *CHNE* CH2 ...... 145 L2
  WYTH/NTH M22 .... 63 L3
Bag La *NWCHW* CW8 .... 127 J5
Bagley La *AUD/MAD/W* CW3 .. 273 M3
Bagmere Cl *SBCH* CW11 ...... 181 M7
  SBCH CW11 .... 203 M5 🔢
Bagmere La *SBCH* CW11 ...... 182 B7
Bagnall Cl *WARRW/BUR* WA5 .. 36 C7
Bagot Av *WARRW/BUR* WA5 .. 4 D1
Bagstock Av *POY/DIS* SK12 .. 86 E2
Baguley Av *WDN* WA8 .... 52 A7
Baguley Crs *EDGY/DAV* SK3 .. 46 D6
Baguley La *SALE* M33 .... 43 L1 🔢
Bailey Av *EP* CH65 .... 94 F6
Bailey Cl *CW/HAS* CW1 ...... 221 J5
Bailey Ct *ALS/KID* ST7 ...... 241 M1
Bailey Crs *CONG* CW12 ...... 185 G8
  SBCH CW11 .... 204 D6
Bailey La *MANAIR* M90 ...... 63 H3
  PART M31 .... 31 M8
Bailey's Bank *BIDD* ST8 .... 227 K1
Baileys *WDN* WA8 .... 34 A7
Baileys La *HLWD* L26 .... 51 C4
  SPK/HALE L24 .... 71 L3
Bailey Wk *ALT* WA14 .... 61 J4
Bainbridge Av *GOL/RIS/CU* WA3 .. 23 M4
Baines Av *IRL* M44 .... 31 M3
Baker Dr *GTS/LS* CH66 ...... 120 E1
Baker Rd *RUNC* WA7 .... 8 B8
Baker's La *KNUT* WA16 ...... 132 C6
  WSFD CW7 .... 177 L2
Baker St *HALE/TIMP* WA15 .. 43 H5 🔢
  HTNM SK4 .... 2 E1
  MCFLDS SK11 .... 14 E7
Baker Wy *CHSE* CH3 .... 148 E5
  CHSE CH3 .... 170 E5
Bakestonedale Rd
  MCFLDN SK10 .... 113 K1
Bakewell Cl *GTS/LS* CH66 .. 120 E4
Bakewell Rd *BRAM/HZG* SK7 .. 66 E4
  WARRW/BUR WA5 .... 27 C5
Bakewell St *EDGY/DAV* SK3 .. 2 D8
Bala Cl *WARRW/BUR* WA5 .... 36 E2 🔢
Baldock Cl *WARRS* WA4 ...... 57 J1
Baldock Rd *DID/WITH* M20 .. 45 K1
Balfour Cl *CW/HAS* CW1 .... 222 C4
Balfour Gv *BIDD* ST8 .... 227 L4 🔢
Balfour Rd *ALT* WA14 .... 42 D5
Balfour St *RUNC* WA7 .... 8 F4
Balham Cl *WDN* WA8 .... 34 A8
Ballantyne Wy
  GOL/RIS/CU WA3 .... 23 L4 🔢
Ballater Crs *GOL/RIS/CU* WA3 .. 170 B2
Ballater Dr *WARRN/WOL* WA2 .. 28 E8
Balliol Cl *MCFLDS* SK11 .... 162 F1
Ball La *FROD/HEL* WA6 ...... 126 D1
Balmer Rd *NTHM/RTH* M23 .. 44 A7
Balmoral Av *CHD/CHDH* SK8 .. 65 G3
  CW/SHV CW2 .... 238 B3

  GOL/RIS/CU WA3 .... 23 K3
  NWCHE CW9 .... 13 J9
Balmoral Cl *KNUT* WA16 .... 107 H3
  WSFD CW7 .... 177 J1
Balmoral Dr *ALT* WA14 ...... 42 F4
  FROD/HEL WA6 .... 98 B8
  HOLMCH WA4 .... 181 H2
  MPL/ROM SK6 .... 67 L5
  POY/DIS SK12 .... 86 D1
Balmoral Gdns *EP* CH65 .... 121 K1
Balmoral Gv *BRAM/HZG* SK7 .. 66 F1
Balmoral Pk *CH/BCN* CH1 .. 16 D1
  CH/BCN CH1 .... 145 H8
Balmoral Pl *NANT* CW5 ...... 237 K8
Balmoral Rd *HALE/TIMP* WA15 .. 42 E8
  HTNM SK4 .... 46 A1
  WARRS WA4 .... 56 F2
  WDN WA8 .... 34 A8
Balmoral Wy *WILM/AE* SK9 .. 84 A6
Balniel St *STHEL* WA9 ...... 34 D1
Balsham Cl *WLTN* L25 .... 50 C5
Balshaw Av *IRL* M44 .... 31 M2
Baltic Rd *ALT* WA14 .... 42 A6
Bamber Av *SALE* M33 .... 43 L1
Bamford Cl *CHD/CHDH* SK8 .. 64 D4
  MCFLDN SK10 .... 113 G5 🔢
  RUNC WA7 .... 9 M9
  RUNC WA7 .... 73 J6
Bamford Gdns
  HALE/TIMP WA15 .... 43 K6 🔢
Bamford Gv *DID/WITH* M20 .. 45 G1
Bamford Rd *DID/WITH* M20 .. 45 G1
Bamford St *MCFLDN* SK10 .. 15 K3 🔢
  STKP SK1 .... 3 G7
Bampton Cl *STKP* SK1 ...... 47 H5 🔢
Bampton Rd *WYTH/NTH* M22 .. 63 J3
Banastre Dr *NEWLW* WA12 .. 27 M1
Banbury Av *WLTN* L25 ...... 50 C2
Banbury Cl *LEIGH* WN7 ...... 24 E3
  MCFLDN SK10 .... 138 E2
Banbury Dr *ALT* WA14 ...... 42 E4
  WARRW/BUR WA5 .... 36 C8
Banbury Gv *BIDD* ST8 ...... 227 J4 🔢
Banbury Rd *NTHM/RTH* M23 .. 43 M7
Banbury St *ALS/KID* ST7 .. 242 D3
  STKP SK1 .... 3 G6
Bancroft *NWCHW* CW8 .... 101 L8
Bancroft Av *CHD/CHDH* SK8 .. 65 G3
Bancroft Cl *MPL/ROM* SK6 .. 47 L1 🔢
  WLTN L25 .... 50 B1
Bancroft Rd *HALE/TIMP* WA15 .. 62 A1
  WDN WA8 .... 53 K2
Bandon Cl *SPK/HALE* L24 .. 71 K2 🔢
Bangor Cl *GTS/LS* CH66 .... 120 F4 🔢
Bangor Rd *CHD/CHDH* SK8 .. 45 M6
Bank Cl *CHNE* CH2 .... 145 L7
  MCFLDN SK11 .... 15 K7
  MCFLDN SK11 .... 92 A6
Bankes' La *RUNC* WA7 .... 72 E6
Bank Farm Ms *MALPAS* SY14 .. 247 L6
Bankfield Av *HTNM* SK4 ...... 46 A2
  WARRN/WOL WA2 .... 38 B2
Barnes Av *HTNM* SK4 .... 46 A2
Bank Gdns *WARRW/BUR* WA5 .. 35 L8 🔢
Bankhall La *HALE/TIMP* WA15 .. 61 L4
Bankhall Rd *HTNM* SK4 ...... 46 A2
Bankhey *NSTN* CH64 .... 91 M7
Bank House La *FROD/HEL* WA6 .. 98 C8
  SBCH CW11 .... 206 A5
Banklands Cl *IRL* M44 ...... 31 K7 🔢
Bank La *CONG* CW12 .... 185 H3
  MCFLDN SK10 .... 114 C6
  NANT CW5 .... 235 K4
Bank Mellor Rd *NM/HAY* SK22 .. 69 J5 🔢
Bank Pas *GOL/RIS/CU* WA3 .. 23 G3
Bank Rd *MPL/ROM* SK6 ...... 48 A1
Banks Cl *CONG* CW12 .... 207 J1 🔢
Bankside *HALE/TIMP* WA15 .. 62 D6
Bank Side *NWCHW* CW8 ...... 128 C3
Bankside *RUNC* WA7 .... 74 E5
Bankside Cl *MPL/ROM* SK6 .. 49 J5 🔢
  NANT CW5 .... 218 D6 🔢
  WILM/AE SK9 .... 84 D2 🔢
Bankside Rd *DID/WITH* M20 .. 45 H5
Banks La *STKP* SK1 .... 3 M8
Banks Rd *CQ* CH5 .... 166 D3
  ALS/KID ST7 .... 226 C8
  BURS/TUN ST6 .... 243 K8
  CHD/CHDH SK8 .... 45 L6
  GOL/RIS/CU WA3 .... 23 G3
  GOL/RIS/CU WA3 .... 31 G7
  MCFLDS SK11 .... 15 K7
  MCFLDS SK11 .... 15 H7
  NEWLW WA12 .... 26 F1
  WARR WA1 .... 5 G7
  WDN WA8 .... 53 G8
The Bank *ALS/KID* ST7 ...... 226 B5
Bank Vw *HOLMCH* WA4 .... 157 L4
Banky Flds *CONG* CW12 ...... 207 J2
Banky Fields Crs *CONG* CW12 .. 207 J3
Banner Hey *RAIN/WH* L35 .... 32 D3
Bann St *EDGY/DAV* SK3 ...... 2 E7
Bannister Dr *CHD/CHDH* SK8 .. 64 F2
Bannister St *OFTN* SK2 ...... 3 H9
Bann St *EDGY/DAV* SK3 ...... 2 E7
Banstead Av *WYTH/NTH* M22 .. 44 D5
Barbara St *WA9* WA9 .... 34 E1 🔢
Barbauld St *WARR* WA1 ...... 5 G7
Barber Dr *ALS/KID* ST7 .... 225 L5
Barber Pl *BURS/TUN* ST6 .... 243 M6
Barber Rd *BURS/TUN* ST6 .. 243 M6
Barberry Cl *ALT* WA14 ...... 42 B4
Barber's La *NWCHE* CW9 .... 77 L4
  NWCHE CW9 .... 77 L4
Barber St *MCFLDS* SK11 .... 15 J8
Barbondale Cl
  WARRW/BUR WA5 .... 35 M5
Barcheston Rd *CHD/CHDH* SK8 .. 45 K8
Barclay Rd *POY/DIS* SK12 .. 86 E2
Bardale Gv *AIMK* WN4 ...... 22 A1
Bardell Cl *POY/DIS* SK12 .. 86 D2 🔢
Bardley Crs *HUY* L36 .... 32 A5
Bardney Av *GOL/RIS/CU* WA3 .. 22 F2

Bardon Rd *NTHM/RTH* M23 .. 43 M6
Bardsea Av *WYTH/NTH* M22 .. 63 K3 🔢
Bardsey Cl *EP* CH65 .... 121 J3 🔢
Bardsley Av *WARRW/BUR* WA5 .. 36 F2
Bardsley St *HTNM* SK4 ...... 2 D1
Barfold Cl *OFTN* SK2 .... 48 D1
Barford Cl *WARRW/BUR* WA5 .. 36 B3
Barford Dr *GOL/RIS/CU* WA3 .. 24 A4
  WILM/AE SK9 .... 84 C3
Barford Gra *NSTN* CH64 .... 93 H4
Barford Rd *SPK/HALE* L24 .. 50 B6
Bargates *WHITCH* SY13 ...... 269 M4
Barham Ct *GOL/RIS/CU* WA3 .. 29 K8
Barington Dr *RUNC* WA7 .... 74 E5
Baristow Cl *CHNE* CH2 ...... 17 G1
Barker Rd *MPL/ROM* SK6 .... 47 M1
Barker's Hollow Rd *WARRS* WA4 .. 75 C6
Barker St *CW/SHV* CW2 ...... 19 G9
  NANT CW5 .... 20 E7
Bark HI *WHITCH* SY13 ...... 270 A5
Barkhill Rd *CHSE* CH3 ...... 170 B1 🔢
Barley Castle Cl *WARRS* WA4 .. 77 H1
Barleycastle La *WARRS* WA4 .. 57 K7
Barleycorn Cl *SALE* M33 .... 44 A1 🔢
Barley Cft *ALS/KID* ST7 .... 241 L2
  CHD/CHDH SK8 .... 64 F4
  CHSE CH3 .... 170 A5
Barleycroft Ter *ALS/KID* ST7 .. 225 H5
Barley Dr *BRAM/HZG* SK7 .. 65 L5 🔢
Barley Mow Cl *NTHM/RTH* M23 .. 120 C2
Barley Rd *WARRS* WA4 ...... 57 J1
Barleywood Cl *CW/SHV* CW2 .. 238 B4 🔢
Barlow Crs *MPL/ROM* SK6 .. 48 F8
Barlow Dr *WSFD* CW7 .... 176 F4
Barlow Fold Rd *MPL/ROM* SK6 .. 48 F7
Barlow Gv *STHEL* WA9 ...... 26 A2 🔢
Barlow HI *MCFLDS* SK11 .... 187 M3
Barlow Rd *ALT* WA14 .... 42 B4
  NWCHE CW9 .... 153 M5
  WILM/AE SK9 .... 84 B3
Barlow's La South
  BRAM/HZG SK7 .... 66 C1
Barlow Wy *SBCH* CW11 ...... 66 C1
Barlow Wood Dr *MPL/ROM* SK6 .. 68 B1
Barmouth Cl *WARRW/BUR* WA5 .. 36 E2
Barnabas Av *CW/HAS* CW1 .. 220 F7
Barnaby Cl *MALPAS* SY14 .. 230 C2 🔢
Barnaby Rd *POY/DIS* SK12 .. 86 D2
Barnack Cl *WARR* WA1 ...... 38 A4
Barnacre Av *NTHM/RTH* M23 .. 62 F1
Barnacre Dr *NSTN* CH64 .... 91 H2
Barnard Av *HTNM* SK4 ...... 46 B2
Barnard Cl *MCFLDS* SK11 .. 137 M6
Barnard St *WARRW/BUR* WA5 .. 55 K1
Barnbridge Cl *ALS/KID* ST7 .. 225 L5
Barnbrook Cl *WSFD* CW7 .. 177 G3
Barnclose Rd *WYTH/NTH* M22 .. 63 K3
Barn Cft *FROD/HEL* WA6 .... 98 C8
Barncroft *RUNC* WA7 .... 74 D5
Barncroft Cl *MCFLDS* SK11 .. 135 G1
Barncroft Gdns
  WYTH/NTH M22 .... 44 C7 🔢
Barn Croft Rd *HLWD* L26 .. 51 C5
Barnes Av *HTNM* SK4 .... 46 A2
Barnes Cl *CH/BCN* CH1 ...... 144 F6 🔢
  CW/HAS CW1 .... 222 C8 🔢
  WARRW/BUR WA5 .... 36 A7
  WDN WA8 .... 53 K2 🔢
Barnes Rd *WDN* WA8 .... 53 L1
Barneston Rd *WDN* WA8 .... 53 J2
Barnett Av *NEWLW* WA12 .. 26 E1
Barnett Gv *BURS/TUN* ST6 .. 243 M7
Barnett St *MCFLDS* SK11 .. 14 D6 🔢
Barnfield Av *MPL/ROM* SK6 .. 48 D1
  RUNC WA7 .... 74 D6
Barnfield Cl *GTS/LS* CH66 .. 120 C2 🔢
  WHITCH SY13 .... 269 L4 🔢
  WARR WA1 .... 38 C5
Barnfield Rd *MCFLDN* SK10 .. 112 F5
Barnfield Rd East *EDGY/DAV* SK3 .. 46 F8
Barnfield Rd West
  EDGY/DAV SK3 .... 46 E8
Barngate Rd *CHD/CHDH* SK8 .. 45 G6
Barnham Ct *CW/HAS* CW1 .. 222 D7
Barnhill Gra *CHSE* CH3 ...... 231 H1
Barnhill Rd *CHSE* CH3 ...... 231 G3
Barnhouse La *CHSE* CH3 .. 147 L5
  CHSE CH3 .... 148 A3
Barn La *GOL/RIS/CU* WA3 .. 22 F5
Barn Meadow *NWCHW* CW8 .. 12 E1
Barn Rd *CONG* CW12 .... 184 C8
Barnsfold Rd *MPL/ROM* SK6 .. 67 M1
Barnside Wy *MCFLDN* SK10 .. 138 C1 🔢
  NWCHE CW9 .... 153 M4
Barns La *LYMM* WA13 .... 41 G6
Barnsley St *STKP* SK1 ...... 3 K7
Barns Pl *HALE/TIMP* WA15 .. 62 C4
Barnstaple Wy
  WARRW/BUR WA5 .... 35 L8
Barnston Ct *CHSE* CH3 ...... 228 E2 🔢
Barn St *WDN* WA8 .... 7 G9
Barnswood Cl *WARRS* WA4 .. 57 J8
Barnton Cl *GOL/RIS/CU* WA3 .. 23 K5 🔢
Barn Wy *NEWLW* WA12 ...... 27 H1
Barnwell Av *GOL/RIS/CU* WA3 .. 24 D8
Barnwell Cl *CW/SHV* CW2 .. 238 B4
Baron Cl *WARR* WA1 .... 38 A4
Baron Gn *CHD/CHDH* SK8 .. 64 D5
Baronia Pl *NANT* CW5 ...... 21 G5
Barons Cl *FLINT* CH6 ...... 116 A6
  WDN WA8 .... 53 H1
Barons Quay Rd *NWCHE* CW9 .. 13 H1
Barons Rd *CW/SHV* CW2 .... 238 B8
Barony Rd *NANT* CW5 .... 20 F2
Barony Wy *CHSW/BR* CH4 .. 168 E8
Barrack HI *MPL/ROM* SK6 .. 48 A2
Barrack Hall Cl *MPL/ROM* SK6 .. 48 A1
Barracks La *CHSE* CH3 ...... 215 J7
  MCFLDN SK10 .... 15 L6
  NANT CW5 .... 250 E2
Barrastitch La *NWCHW* CW8 .. 127 L6
Barratt Rd *ALS/KID* ST7 .. 241 M1

Barrel Well HI *CHSE* CH3 .. 17 M5
Barrie Gdns *ALS/KID* ST7 .. 242 C4
Barrie Gv *CW/HAS* CW1 ...... 19 K3
Barrington Av *CHD/CHDH* SK8 .. 65 G3
Barrington Dr *MWCH* CW10 .. 179 J5
Barrington Rd *ALT* WA14 .. 42 D6
Barrow Av *WARRN/WOL* WA2 .. 5 K1
Barrowdale Rd *GOL/RIS/CU* WA3 .. 23 H4
Barrowfield Rd *WYTH/NTH* M22 .. 63 G2
Barrow Hall La
  WARRW/BUR WA5 .... 35 L6 🔢
Barrow La *CHSE* CH3 .... 147 K7
  CHSE CH3 .... 148 B8
  GOL/RIS/CU WA3 .... 28 C2
  HALE/TIMP WA15 .... 62 B5
  NWCHE CW9 .... 102 F2
Barrow Meadow
  CHD/CHDH SK8 .... 64 E4
Barrow's Brow *KNUT* WA16 .. 132 E5
Barrows Cl *CW/HAS* CW1 .. 221 G4
Barrow's Green La *WDN* WA8 .. 34 B8 🔢
Barrow's Rw *WDN* WA8 ...... 34 B8
Barrule Av *BRAM/HZG* SK7 .. 66 E3 🔢
Barrule Cl *WARRS* WA4 ...... 56 D5 🔢
Barrymore Av *WARRS* WA4 .. 37 M8
Barrymore Crs *NWCHE* CW9 .. 103 J4
Barrymore Rd *NWCHW* CW8 .. 128 E3
  RUNC WA7 .... 9 K9
  WARRS WA4 .... 37 M8
Barsbank Cl *LYMM* WA13 .... 58 C1 🔢
Barsbank La *LYMM* WA13 .... 58 C1 🔢
Barshaw Gdns *WARRS* WA4 .. 76 E1 🔢
The Bars *CH/BCN* CH1 ...... 17 J5
Barston Av *EP* CH65 .... 94 F7
Bartholomew Cl *RAIN/WH* L35 .. 33 L3
Bartholomew Wy
  CHSW/BR CH4 .... 169 J6
Barthomley Crs *CW/HAS* CW1 .. 221 G4 🔢
Barthomley Rd *ALS/KID* ST7 .. 255 M2
  CW/HAS CW1 .... 239 M3
  CW/SHV CW2 .... 240 C6
Bartlegate *RUNC* WA7 ...... 74 B7 🔢
Bartlet Cl *CQ* CH5 .... 142 F6 🔢
Bartley Rd *WYTH/NTH* M22 .. 44 C4
Barton Av *WARRS* WA4 ...... 56 F2
Barton Cl *WSFD* CW7 .... 177 M3
  WILM/AE SK9 .... 84 D2
Barton Ct *CHSE* CH3 .... 228 F3
  CONG CW12 .... 207 M2
  HTNM SK4 .... 45 J3
  MALPAS SY14 .... 229 J3
Bartons Pl *NWCHE* CW9 ...... 13 M1
Barton St *GOL/RIS/CU* WA3 .. 23 C4
  MCFLDS SK11 .... 14 F8
Barwood Av *ALS/KID* ST7 .. 225 G7
Basford Rd *CW/SHV* CW2 .... 238 D4
Basford Wy *WSFD* CW7 ...... 177 H3
Basil St *HTNM* SK4 .... 2 D1
Basle Cl *BRAM/HZG* SK7 .... 65 L1
Baslow Dr *BRAM/HZG* SK7 .. 66 F4
  CHD/CHDH SK8 .... 64 C4
Bateman Av *BIDD* ST8 ...... 227 H7
Batemans Ct *CW/SHV* CW2 .. 238 B4 🔢
Batemill Cl *ALS/KID* ST7 .. 137 M3 🔢
Batemill La *MCFLDS* SK11 .. 134 D6
Batemill Rd *NM/HAY* SK22 .. 69 K2
Bates La *FROD/HEL* WA6 .... 98 D8
  FROD/HEL WA6 .... 124 D1
Bate's Mill La *TPLY/KEL* CW6 .. 196 E8
Bateson St *STKP* SK1 ...... 3 J4
Bath Cl *BRAM/HZG* SK7 ...... 67 G2
Bath Crs *CHD/CHDH* SK8 .... 65 H6
Batherton Cl *WDN* WA8 ...... 7 J7
Batherton La *NANT* CW5 .... 251 M2
Bathfields Crs *WHITCH* SY13 .. 269 L4
Bath La *AUD/MAD/W* CW3 .. 274 A1
Bath St *ALT* WA14 .... 61 K2
  CH/BCN CH1 .... 17 J5
  SBCH CW11 .... 204 C6
  WARR WA1 .... 4 F6
  WHITCH SY13 .... 269 M6
Bathwood Dr *NSTN* CH64 .. 91 L7 🔢
Batterbee Ct *CW/HAS* CW1 .. 222 D7
Battersbay Gv *BRAM/HZG* SK7 .. 66 E2
Battersby La *WARRN/WOL* WA2 .. 5 J4
Battersea Ct *WDN* WA8 ...... 52 F1 🔢
Battersea Rd *HTNM* SK4 .... 45 L3
Battery La *WARR* WA1 ...... 38 F1
Bawtry Ct *WARRN/WOL* WA2 .. 37 L3
Baxter Cl *RUNC* WA7 .... 74 D5 🔢
Baxter Gdns *NTHM/RTH* M23 .. 44 A5
Baxter St *WARRW/BUR* WA5 .. 4 B7
Baycliffe *LYMM* WA13 ...... 58 D2
Baycliffe Cl *RUNC* WA7 ...... 73 K7
Baycroft Cl *NTHM/RTH* M23 .. 44 A3
Bayley Rd *NANT* CW5 .... 237 K7
Bayswater Cl *RUNC* WA7 .... 54 F8
Baytree Cl *GTS/LS* CH66 .. 120 F3
Bayvil Cl *RUNC* WA7 .... 74 E5
Bazley Rd *WYTH/NTH* M22 .. 44 D3
Beach Gv *NWCHW* CW8 .... 12 B6
Beachin La *CHSE* CH3 ...... 212 F7
  MALPAS SY14 .... 230 A1
Beach Rd *NWCHW* CW8 .... 12 B6
  NWCHW CW8 .... 129 H6
Beacomfold *MPL/ROM* SK6 .. 49 H1
Beacon Dr *NTHM/RTH* M23 .. 63 G2 🔢
Beacon Rd *MPL/ROM* SK6 .. 48 A3
Beaconsfield Crs *WDN* WA8 .. 34 B8 🔢
Beaconsfield Gv *WDN* WA8 .. 34 B8 🔢
Beaconsfield Rd *ALT* WA14 .. 42 D5
  CQ CH5 .... 142 A6 🔢
  RUNC WA7 .... 8 D6
  WDN WA8 .... 53 H1
Beaconsfield St *CHSE* CH3 .. 17 K5
Beacon Vw *MPL/ROM* SK6 .. 48 A3
Beadnell Dr *WARRW/BUR* WA5 .. 54 E1
Beaford Dr *WYTH/NTH* M22 .. 63 K4
Beagle Point *WSFD* CW7 .... 177 G3
Beal Cl *HTNM* SK4 .... 45 K1 🔢
Beam Heath Wy *NANT* CW5 .. 21 G2
Beaminster Rd *HTNM* SK4 .. 45 M1
Beamish Cl *WARRS* WA4 .... 76 D1
Beamont St *WDN* WA8 ...... 53 G8 🔢

Beamsley Dr *WYTH/NTH* M22 .. 63 H2 🔢
Beam St *NANT* CW5 .... 20 E6
Bean Leach Dr *OFTN* SK2 .. 47 N6 🔢
Bean Leach Dr *OFTN* SK2 .. 47 M6
Bean Leach Rd *BRAM/HZG* SK7 .. 47 L8
Beard Crs *NM/HAY* SK22 .... 69 K4
Beardsmore Dr
  GOL/RIS/CU WA3 .... 23 L4
Bearhurst La *MCFLDS* SK11 .. 136 F7
Beasley Cl *GTS/LS* CH66 .. 120 D1
Beathwaite Dr *BRAM/HZG* SK7 .. 65 J3
Beat La *MCFLDS* SK11 ...... 209 K4
Beatrice Av *CHD/CHDH* SK8 .. 64 F2
Beatrice Gdns *WHITCH* SY13 .. 270 B4 🔢
Beatrice St *WARRS* WA4 .... 56 D1 🔢
Beatty Av *WARRN/WOL* WA2 .. 37 J3
Beatty Cl *RAIN/WH* L35 .... 32 D3
Beatty Dr *CONG* CW12 ...... 185 G8
Beatty Rd *NANT* CW5 .... 20 C8
Beaufort Av *SALE* M33 ...... 43 J1 🔢
Beaufort Cha *WILM/AE* SK9 .. 84 F3
Beaufort Cl *RUNC* WA7 ...... 9 J9
  WARRW/BUR WA5 .... 36 A7
  WDN WA8 .... 52 A4 🔢
  WILM/AE SK9 .... 110 B2
Beaufort Rd *OFTN* SK2 ...... 47 K8
  SALE M33 .... 43 J1
Beaufort St *WARRW/BUR* WA5 .. 4 A8
Beaulieu Av *WSFD* CW7 .... 177 M2
Beaumaris Crs *BRAM/HZG* SK7 .. 66 C4
Beaumaris Dr *EP* CH65 ...... 121 K2
Beaumont Cl *BIDD* ST8 ...... 227 K2
  CHSW/BR CH4 .... 168 E6 🔢
  CW/SHV CW2 .... 237 M4
Beauty Bank *NWCHW* CW8 .. 152 E7
  WSFD CW7 .... 200 A1 🔢
Beauvale Av *OFTN* SK2 ...... 47 J5
Beaverbrook Av
  GOL/RIS/CU WA3 .... 25 H8
Beaver Rd *DID/WITH* M20 .. 45 H1
Bebbington Rd *SALE* M33 .. 43 M2 🔢
Beccles Rd *SALE* M33 ...... 43 H3
Becconsall Cl *CW/HAS* CW1 .. 221 G4
Becconsall Dr *CW/HAS* CW1 .. 221 G4
Bechers *ALS/KID* ST7 ...... 242 B1
Beckenham Gv *WSFD* CW7 .. 177 G3 🔢
Beckett Av *WSFD* CW7 ...... 178 D4
Beckett's La *CHSE* CH3 .... 170 A4
Beckfield Rd *NTHM/RTH* M23 .. 44 A7
Beck La *MCFLDN* SK10 ...... 137 L2
Beck Rd *AUD/MAD/W* CW3 .. 267 M5
Beckton Gdns *WYTH/NTH* M22 .. 63 J1
Becontree Dr *NTHM/RTH* M23 .. 43 K6
Beddow Wy *BURS/TUN* ST6 .. 243 M6
Bedells La *WILM/AE* SK9 .. 84 A6
Bedford Av *EP* CH65 .... 121 G2
  SALE M33 .... 43 G2
Bedford Av East *EP* CH65 .. 121 H2
Bedford Cl *HUY* L36 .... 32 A1
Bedford Ct *CW/SHV* CW2 .. 19 G9
Bedford Dr *HALE/TIMP* WA15 .. 43 J6
Bedford Gdns *CW/SHV* CW2 .. 18 E9
Bedford Gn *IRL* M44 .... 31 J6
Bedford Pl *CW/SHV* CW2 .... 18 E9
Bedford Ri *WSFD* CW7 ...... 177 J6
Bedford Rd *CW/SHV* CW2 .. 243 G1
  MCFLDS SK11 .... 14 D7
Bedford St *CW/SHV* CW2 .. 18 F9
  WARRS WA4 .... 56 C4
Bedward Rw *CH/BCN* CH1 .. 16 E5
Beech Av *ALS/KID* ST7 .... 224 F4
  BRAM/HZG SK7 .... 66 E3
  CHD/CHDH SK8 .... 65 H7
  EDGY/DAV SK3 .... 46 F6 🔢
  FROD/HEL WA6 .... 98 C8
  GOL/RIS/CU WA3 .... 23 M5
  GOL/RIS/CU WA3 .... 30 A1
  KNUT WA16 .... 81 L6
  MPL/ROM SK6 .... 48 D6
  NM/HAY SK22 .... 69 J5
  WARRW/BUR WA5 .... 54 C1
  WHITCH SY13 .... 269 M6
  WYTH/NTH M22 .... 44 D4
Beech Bank *MCFLDN* SK10 .. 15 G2
Beech Cl *CONG* CW12 .... 184 B8
  HOLMCH WA4 .... 157 K8
  KNUT WA16 .... 107 M6
  NEWLW WA12 .... 27 J2
  NWCHW CW8 .... 151 M2 🔢
  WILM/AE SK9 .... 110 B1
Beech Cottages
  WILM/AE SK9 .... 110 A4 🔢
Beech Crs *LEIGH* WN7 ...... 24 E1
  POY/DIS SK12 .... 66 E8
Beech Cft *AUD/MAD/W* CW3 .. 267 L5
Beechcroft Av *CW/SHV* CW2 .. 238 B5
Beechcroft Dr *EP* CH65 .... 121 H1
Beech Dr *ALS/KID* ST7 ...... 242 E4
  CW/SHV CW2 .... 237 L2
  KNUT WA16 .... 107 H2
  LEIGH WN7 .... 24 F2
The Beeches *CHNE* CH2 .... 145 M6
  FROD/HEL WA6 .... 98 C8
  NANT CW5 .... 20 F7
  WHITCH SY13 .... 269 M4
Beech Farm Dr *MCFLDN* SK10 .. 15 G1
Beechfield *ALT* WA14 ...... 61 J1 🔢
  NWCHW CW8 .... 153 L4
  SALE M33 .... 42 F2 🔢
Beechfield Av *WILM/AE* SK9 .. 83 L7
Beechfield Cl *LEIGH* WN7 .. 24 F1
  MWCH CW10 .... 179 H2
Beechfield Gdns *NWCHW* CW8 .. 129 H6
Beechfield Rd *CHD/CHDH* SK8 .. 65 H4
  EDGY/DAV SK3 .... 10 D7
  EP CH65 .... 121 H1
  WARRS WA4 .... 57 C3
  WILM/AE SK9 .... 110 B4
Beechfields *WSFD* CW7 .... 178 B4 🔢
Beech Gv *CHNE* CH2 .... 170 A1
  CW/HAS CW1 .... 19 K2
  GTS/LS CH66 .... 121 G4
  LEIGH WN7 .... 24 E2
  LYMM WA13 .... 58 E2

MCFLDS SK11 ....138 E7
NWCHW CW8 ....128 D4
SBCH CW11 ....204 D6
WARR WA1 ....38 A5
WILM/AE SK9 ....84 A6
WSFD CW7 ....177 K5
Beech Hall Dr MCFLDN SK10 ..138 C2
Beech Heyes CI NWCHW CW8 .. 128 E4 [1]
Beech Heyes Dr
  NWCHW CW8 ....128 E4 [2]
Beech Hey La NSTN CH64 ....93 H3
Beechlands Av CHSE CH3 ....170 A3 [1]
Beech La FROD/HEL WA6 ....126 D5
  MCFLDN SK10 ....15 C2
  MPL/ROM SK6 ....48 C2
  NWCHW CW8 ....129 C1
  TPLY/KEL CW6 ....175 H6
  WILM/AE SK9 ....84 A6
Beech Ms OFTN SK2 ....47 C7
Beechmill Dr GOL/RIS/CU WA3 ... 29 K1
Beechmoore WARRS WA4 ....55 H7
Beechpark Av WYTH/NTH M22... 44 C5
Beech Ri CHF/WBR SK23 ....89 J7
  NWCHW CW8 ....127 H2
Beech Rd CHD/CHDH SK8 ....65 H5
  CHF/WBR SK23 ....89 L5
  CQ CH5 ....166 A1
  EDGY/DAV SK3 ....46 E6
  GOL/RIS/CU WA3 ....23 G3
  HALE/TIMP WA15 ....61 L1
  MPL/ROM SK6 ....67 M5 [1]
  RUNC WA7 ....9 M7
  RUNC WA7 ....74 B8
  TPLY/KEL CW6 ....175 K3
  WARRS WA4 ....56 C4
  WILM/AE SK9 ....110 B1
Beech St MWCH CW10 ....179 C2
Beech St West CW/HAS CW1 ...18 E3 [1]
Beech Tree CI NANT CW5.......237 K7
Beechtree Farm CI KNUT WA16 ... 59 H5
Beechtree La KNUT WA16 ....59 H5
Beechurst Rd CHD/CHDH SK8... 46 B7
Beech View Rd FROD/HEL WA6 .. 126 C3
Beech Wk LEIGH WN7 ....24 E2
Beechway CHNE CH2 ....145 J6 [1]
  MCFLDN SK10 ....113 C5
  MPL/ROM SK6 ....67 M5
  WILM/AE SK9 ....83 M7
Beechways WARRS WA4 ....56 D7
Beechways Dr NSTN CH64 ....91 K4
Beechwood ALT WA14 ....61 H3 [1]
  KNUT WA16 ....107 J2
Beechwood Av AIMK WN4 ....22 A2 [1]
  HLWD L26 ....50 E5
  MPL/ROM SK6 ....48 C2
  NEWLW WA12 ....22 D8
  NWCHW CW8 ....129 C6
  RUNC WA7 ....73 M7
  RUNC WA7 ....73 K7
  WARR WA1 ....37 L4
  WARRW/BUR WA5 ....36 D3
Beechwood Dr ALS/KID ST7 ... 224 B8
  CONG CW12 ....184 F4
  GTS/LS CH66 ....120 D3
  MPL/ROM SK6 ....49 C6
  NWCHW CW9 ....104 F6
  WILM/AE SK9 ....84 E1 [1]
Beechwood Gv
  CHD/CHDH SK8 ....65 G4 [1]
Beechwood La GOL/RIS/CU WA3 .. 24 D8
Beechwood Ms MCFLDN SK10 ... 14 F1
Beechwood Rd CHSW/BR CH4 .. 168 D7
Beecroft CI WARRW/BUR WA5 ... 36 D3
Benham CI SALE M33 ....42 C1 [1]
Beeston Av HALE/TIMP WA15... 42 F6
Beeston Brow MCFLDN SK10 ... 113 H5
Beeston CI GOL/RIS/CU WA3 .... 29 K8 [1]
  HOLMCH CW4 ....181 C1
  MCFLDN SK10 ....113 J3 [1]
  MWCH CW10 ....179 K7
Beeston Dr ALS/KID ST7 ....241 J1
  KNUT WA16 ....107 G4
  WSFD CW7 ....177 J5
Beeston Gn GTS/LS CH66 ....94 E7 [1]
Beeston Gv EDGY/DAV SK3 ....46 E7
Beeston Mt MCFLDN SK10 ....113 H3
Beeston Rd CHSW/BR CH4 ....190 B1
  CHSW/BR CH4 ....190 A5
  WILM/AE SK9 ....64 D7 [1]
Beeston St NWCHW CW8 ....12 F4
Beeston Ter MCFLDS SK11.......137 L6
Beeston Vw ALS/KID ST7 ....243 G5
  CHSW/BR CH4 ....169 L5
Beggarman's La KNUT WA16 ... 107 G5
Begley CI MPL/ROM SK6 ....47 M3
Belfield CI DID/WITH M20 ....45 H1 [1]
Belfry CI WILM/AE SK9 ....84 D4
Belfry Dr MCFLDN SK10 ....112 C8
Belgrave Av ALS/KID ST7 ....224 D7
  CHSW/BR CH4 ....168 E6
  CHSW/BR CH4 ....191 M5
  CHSW/BR CH4 ....192 C6
  CONG CW12 ....207 J1
  MPL/ROM SK6 ....48 F6 [1]
  WARR WA1 ....37 M5
Belgrave CI CHSW/BR CH4 ....191 C6
  LEIGH WN7 ....24 C4 [1]
  WDN WA8 ....53 L1 [1]
Belgrave Crs OFTN SK2 ....47 G8
Belgrave Dr EP CH65 ....94 F7
Belgrave PI CHSW/BR CH4 ....17 H9
Belgrave Rd ALT WA14 ....61 J1
  CHSE CH3 ....170 B4
  CW/SHV CW2 ....18 C4
  IRL M44 ....31 K7
  MCFLDS SK11 ....138 C8
  NWCHW CW9 ....130 A8
Belgrave St CH/BCN CH1 ....17 J3
Belgravia Gdns
  HALE/TIMP WA15 ....61 L4
Bellaport Rd MKTDR TF9 ....275 G8
Bellard Dr CHNE CH2 ....146 A8
Bell Av MCFLDS SK11 ....162 F1
Bellcroft WYTH/NTH M22 ....44 E4 [1]
Belldale CI HTNM SK4 ....46 A2
Bellemonte Rd
  FROD/HEL WA6 ....99 H6 [1]
Belleville Av WYTH/NTH M22 ... 63 L4 [1]

Bellevue La CHSE CH3 ....146 D8
Belle Vue Ter SBCH CW11 ....204 B6
Bellfield Av CHD/CHDH SK8 .... 65 H3 [1]
Bellhouse La WARRS WA4 ....55 K5
  WARRS WA4 ....57 J3
Bell House Rd WDN WA8 ....7 M3
Bellingham Dr RUNC WA7 ....9 H7
Bell La RAIN/WH L35 ....34 A2
  WARRS WA4 ....38 E8
  WARRS WA4 ....57 L1
Bell Meadow Ct TPLY/KEL CW6 .. 197 J2
Bellringer Ct BIDD ST8 ....227 J5
Belmont Av GOL/RIS/CU WA3 .... 23 J3
  MCFLDN SK10 ....137 J3
  SBCH CW11 ....203 M5
  WARRS WA4 ....56 F1
Belmont CI HTNM SK4 ....2 D2
Belmont Crs WARRW/BUR WA5 ... 35 M6
Belmont Dr CHSW/BR CH4 ....168 B6
  MPL/ROM SK6 ....49 H3
Belmont Rd BRAM/HZG SK7 .... 65 L7
  CHD/CHDH SK8 ....45 H6
  HALE/TIMP WA15 ....61 L2
  NWCHW CW9 ....103 M3
  NWCHW CW9 ....130 C5
  WDN WA8 ....53 K2
Belmont St HTNM SK4 ....2 D2
Belmont Wy HTNM SK4 ....2 E2
Belper Rd HTNM SK4 ....45 M3
Belsay Dr NTHM/RTH M23 ....44 A8
Belstone Av HTNM SK4 ....63 G1
Belstone CI BRAM/HZG SK7 .... 65 M2
Belton CI WHITCH SY13 ....269 L5
Belton Rd WHITCH SY13 ....269 L6
Belvedere CI CQ CH5 ....142 D7 [1]
  FROD/HEL WA6 ....99 J3
Belvedere Dr CH/BCN CH1 ....144 E8
  MPL/ROM SK6 ....47 J1
Belvedere Rd AIMK WN4 ....22 C1
  NEWLW WA12 ....22 B8
Belvedere Ter ALS/KID ST7 .... 224 F5
Belvoir Av BRAM/HZG SK7 ....66 E4
Belvoir Rd WARRS WA4 ....56 B4
  WDN WA8 ....7 K2
Bembridge CI WARRW/BUR WA5 .. 35 J5
  WDN WA8 ....33 M8
Bembridge Dr MWCH CW10 ... 179 J4
Bempton CI OFTN SK2 ....48 A7 [1]
Bemrose Av ALT WA14 ....42 C6
Benbrook Wy MCFLDS SK11 ... 161 L3
Benchill Court Rd
  WYTH/NTH M22 ....44 E8
Benchill Dr WYTH/NTH M22 .... 44 D7
Benchill Rd WYTH/NTH M22 .... 44 C6
Bendee Av NSTN CH64 ....92 A5
Bendee Rd NSTN CH64 ....91 M5
Bengal St EDGY/DAV SK3 ....2 E8
Bennet CI NSTN CH64 ....93 G4
Bennet Rd NWCHE CW9 ....130 D6
Bennett Av WARR WA1 ....37 M6
Bennett CI CW/HAS CW1 ....19 K3
  EDGY/DAV SK3 ....2 A7
Bennett Randle CI SBCH CW11...203 L5
Bennett's La CQ CH5 ....166 B2
  MCFLDS SK11 ....186 E6
  WDN WA8 ....53 L3
Bennett St EDGY/DAV SK3 ....2 A7
  WARR WA1 ....5 H7
Benson Rd GOL/RIS/CU WA3 .... 38 D2
Benson St BURS/TUN ST6 ....243 M7
Bentham Av WARRN/WOL WA2 ... 37 J1
Bentham Rd GOL/RIS/CU WA3 ... 30 A2
Bentinck Av ALT WA14 ....42 C8
Bentinck St RUNC WA7 ....8 E1
Bent La CONG CW12 ....206 F3
  GOL/RIS/CU WA3 ....30 A2
  LYMM WA13 ....40 C6
  NWCHW CW8 ....127 H3
Bentley Dr CW/HAS CW1 ....222 A7
Bentley Gv WSFD CW7 ....177 J6
Bentley's Farm La WARRS WA4 ... 76 E1
Benton Dr CHNE CW2 ....145 J8 [1]
  MPL/ROM SK6 ....49 J4
Bents Av MPL/ROM SK6 ....47 M1
Bentside Rd POY/DIS SK12 .... 68 D7
Benty Heath La NSTN CH64 .... 93 C1
Beresford DI AUD/MAD/W CW3 .. 267 K5
Beresford St WARR WA1 ....37 L5 [1]
Berisford CI HALE/TIMP WA15 ... 42 E5
Berkeley Av ALS/KID ST7 ....224 D7
Berkeley CI LEIGH WN7 ....24 C4
  OFTN SK2 ....47 J4
Berkeley Crs CW/SHV CW2 .... 238 A4
Berkeley Ri WSFD CW7 ....177 C4
Berkeley Rd BRAM/HZG SK7 .... 66 F1
Berkley Dr CHSW/BR CH4 ....169 K6
Berkshire CI MCFLDN SK10 .... 137 L2 [1]
Berkshire Dr CONG CW12 ....184 D8 [1]
  IRL M44 ....31 J7
  WARR WA1 ....38 D5
Berlin Rd EDGY/DAV SK3 ....46 D6
Bernard Av WARRS WA4 ....56 D4
Berne CI BRAM/HZG SK7 ....46 E8
Bernisdale Rd KNUT WA16 ....81 M8
Bernsdale CI CQ CH5 ....166 F1
Berrington Av WLTN L25 ....50 A2 [1]
Berrington Gv AIMK WN4 ....22 A1
Berristall Rd MCFLDN SK10 .... 113 K8
Berry CI GTS/LS CH66 ....120 C1
  WILM/AE SK9 ....84 A7
Berrycroft La MPL/ROM SK6 .... 48 A1
Berry Dr GTS/LS CH66 ....94 C8
Berry Rd WDN WA8 ....6 A3
Berrystead NWCHW CW8 ....129 H8
Berrywood Dr RAIN/WH L35 ... 32 F2
Bertram St NEWLW WA12 ....26 F1
Berwick Av HTNM SK4 ....45 L2 [1]
  WARR WA1 ....38 E6 [1]
Berwick Ct HOLMCH CW4 ....181 H2 [1]
Berwick Gdns GTS/LS CH66 .... 94 B6
Berwick Gv GTS/LS CH66 ....94 B6
Berwick Rd GTS/LS CH66 ....94 A6
Berwyn Av CHD/CHDH SK8 .... 46 B7
Berwyn CI GTS/LS CH66 ....94 A6
Bessancourt HOLMCH CW4 .... 181 J1
Bessemer Rd IRL M44 ....31 M6
Beswick Rd BURS/TUN ST6 ....243 M6

Beswicks La WILM/AE SK9 ....109 J1
Beswicks Rd NWCHW CW8 ....12 F1
Betchton CI SBCH CW11 ....204 C5
Betchworth Crs RUNC WA7 ....73 K6
Betchton Rd SBCH CW11 ....223 J1
Betjeman CI WARRS WA4 ....37 M8 [1]
Betjeman Wy CW/HAS CW1 .... 19 L1
Betley Hall Gdns
  AUD/MAD/W CW3 ....255 G6
Betnor Av STKP SK1 ....3 M6
Betony CI HLWD L26 ....50 E3
Betsyfield Dr GOL/RIS/CU WA3 ... 29 G5
Bettison Av LEIGH WN7 ....25 J1
Betty's La TPLY/KEL CW6 ....216 D3
Bevan CI WARRW/BUR WA5 .... 36 D6
Bevan PI AUD/MAD/W CW3 .... 267 L6
Bevan Av WARRS WA4 ....56 D4
Beverley Rd OFTN SK2 ....47 J4
  WARR/BUR WA5 ....36 C6
Beverley Wy GTS/LS CH66.......94 B5
  MCFLDN SK10 ....112 C8
Bevin Av GOL/RIS/CU WA3 ....25 H8
Bevyl Rd NSTN CH64 ....91 H2
Bewley Ct CHSE CH3 ....170 A5
Bewsey Farm CI
  WARRW/BUR WA5 ....36 D5 [1]
Bewsey Park CI
  WARRW/BUR WA5 ....4 C2
Bewsey Rd WARR WA1 ....5 G6
  WARRN/WOL WA2 ....4 F5
Bexhill Av HALE/TIMP WA15 .... 42 F6 [1]
  WARRN/WOL WA2 ....28 B8
Bexhill CI SPK/HALE L24 ....50 B8
Bexhill Rd EDGY/DAV SK3 ....46 E8
Bexington Dr CW/HAS CW1 .... 221 H4
Bexton CI WARRN/WOL WA2 .... 28 B8
Bexton La KNUT WA16 ....106 F5
Bexton Rd KNUT WA16 ....106 F4
Bibby Av WARR WA1 ....37 L6
Bibby's La MCFLDN SK10 ....139 G3
Bibby St ALS/KID ST7 ....224 E5
Bibury Av WYTH/NTH M22 .... 63 H1
Bickerton Av FROD/HEL WA6 ... 99 K5
Bickerton CI GOL/RIS/CU WA3 ... 29 K8 [2]
Bickerton Dr BRAM/HZG SK7 ... 66 A3
  MALPAS SY14 ....247 L2
Bickerton Rd ALT WA14 ....42 B7
Bickley CI NWCHE CW9 ....129 L8
  RUNC WA7 ....9 L5
  WARRN/WOL WA2 ....37 M1
Bickley Town La MALPAS SY14 ... 247 L6
Bicknell CI WARRW/BUR WA5 ... 36 B4 [1]
Bida La CONG CW12 ....208 B4
Biddall CI NTHM/RTH M23 .... 44 B6
Biddulph Av WYTH/NTH M22 .... 63 J1
Biddulph Common Rd
  BIDD ST8 ....209 G5
Biddulph Park Rd BIDD ST8 .... 209 H7
Biddulph Rd ALS/KID ST7 ....226 E6
  BIDD ST8 ....208 D7
  CONG CW12 ....208 B3
Bideford Dr NTHM/RTH M23 ... 43 M5 [1]
Bideford Rd OFTN SK2 ....47 J3
  WARRW/BUR WA5 ....35 L8
Bidston CI CHNE CW2 ....145 K7
Bidston Dr WILM/AE SK9 ....84 E2 [1]
Bidston Gn GTS/LS CH66 ....94 D8 [1]
Bidvale Wy CW/HAS CW1 ....221 L4
Big Field La TPLY/KEL CW6 .... 174 B5
Biggin St WARRN/WOL WA2 .... 37 L3 [1]
Bignall End Rd ALS/KID ST7 .... 242 A8
Billington Av NEWLW WA12 .... 22 B6
Billington CI
  WARRW/BUR WA5 ....35 L4 [1]
Billington Rd WDN WA8 ....33 H8 [1]
Bilson Dr EDGY/DAV SK3 ....46 B5
Bilton CI WDN WA8 ....53 L2
Bilton Wy CW/SHV CW2 ....220 E7
Bingham Dr NTHM/RTH M23 ... 43 M6 [1]
Bings Rd CHF/WBR SK23 ....89 L5
Bingswood Av CHF/WBR SK23... 89 L5
Binney Rd NWCHE CW9 ....13 L3
Binyon Wy CW/HAS CW1 ....222 A4
Birchall Av BURS/TUN ST6 ....243 J7
  GOL/RIS/CU WA3 ....24 D8
Birchall Moss La NANT CW5 .... 264 C2
Birchall St GOL/RIS/CU WA3 .... 29 G5
Birch Av ALS/KID ST7 ....241 L1
  BIDD ST8 ....227 G6
  CW/HAS CW1 ....19 L2
  IRL M44 ....31 K7
  MCFLDN SK10 ....14 B3
  MPL/ROM SK6 ....67 M5
  SALE M33 ....43 H1 [1]
  WARRN/WOL WA2 ....28 A8
  WILM/AE SK9 ....83 M6
  WSFD CW7 ....178 A3
Birch Brook Rd LYMM WA13 .... 40 B7
Birch CI CW/HAS CW1 ....19 L1
  HOLMCH CW4 ....181 K1
Birch Ct CONG CW12 ....206 F1
Birchdale ALT WA14 ....61 J2
Birch DI AUD/MAD/W CW3 .... 267 L6
Birchdale Av CHD/CHDH SK8 ... 64 B2
Birchdale Crs WARRS WA4 ....56 C4
Birchdale Rd WARR WA4 ....38 A5
  WARRS WA4 ....56 C5
Birch Dr BRAM/HZG SK7 ....66 C2
Birchen CI HLWD L26 ....51 G5
Birchenwood Rd
  BURS/TUN ST6 ....243 J4
Birches Croft Dr MCFLDN SK10 ... 137 M3
Birches La NWCHE CW9 ....131 G3
The Birches CHSW/BR CH4 .... 190 B1
  CW/SHV CW2 ....238 C4
Birchfield Av ALS/KID ST7 ....224 F5 [1]
  WDN WA8 ....7 H1
Birchfield Crs CQ CH5 ....166 B1 [1]
Birchfield Rd EDGY/DAV SK3 .... 46 A5

LYMM WA13 ....40 B8
  WARRW/BUR WA5 ....36 B7
  WDN WA8 ....7 H2
  WDN WA8 ....34 A8
  WDN WA8 ....53 C1 [1]
Birchfields HALE/TIMP WA15 ... 61 M3
Birch Fold HOLMCH CW4 ....157 H3
Birchgate CI MCFLDN SK10 .... 137 L3 [1]
Birch Gv GTS/LS CH66 ....121 G3
  HALE/TIMP WA15 ....43 L7
  KNUT WA16 ....107 K2
  NWCHE CW9 ....104 F7
  WARR WA1 ....131 H5
  WARRS WA4 ....56 D1 [2]
Birch Heath La CHSE CH3 ....170 E4
Birch Heath Rd TPLY/KEL CW6... 197 H4
Birch HI FROD/HEL WA6 ....125 J4
Birchinall CI MCFLDS SK11 .... 14 A8
Birchin CI NANT CW5 ....21 J4
Birchin La NANT CW5 ....21 H4
Birch La CW/SHV CW2 ....253 M2
  MWCH CW10 ....178 F2
Birchmuir CI CW/HAS CW1 .... 221 H6
Birch Ri CHNE CH2 ....145 K6
  CQ CH5 ....166 B3
Birch Rd CHD/CHDH SK8 ....45 G7
  CHSW/BR CH4 ....168 F7
  CONG CW12 ....206 F1
  GOL/RIS/CU WA3 ....40 B2
  PART M31 ....40 D1
  PART M31 ....41 M1
  POY/DIS SK12 ....86 F2
  RUNC WA7 ....9 K6
  WDN WA8 ....53 C1
Birch Tree Av BRAM/HZG SK7 ... 67 G3
Birch Tree CI ALT WA14 ....61 J3
Birch Tree Dr WYTH/NTH M22 ... 63 K1 [1]
  HOLMCH CW4 ....157 J4
  WARRS WA4 ....76 F6
Birch Tree Rd
  GOL/RIS/CU WA3 ....23 M4 [1]
Birchvale Av MPL/ROM SK6 .... 48 D1
Birchway BRAM/HZG SK7 ....65 K5
Birch Wy MCFLDN SK10 ....111 L6
  MPL/ROM SK6 ....67 M5
Birchyards WARRS WA4 ....56 E7
Birchwood Bvd
  GOL/RIS/CU WA3 ....38 D2
Birchwood CI CHNE CH2 ....123 J1 [2]
  GTS/LS CH66 ....120 D3 [2]
  LEIGH WN7 ....24 F1
Birchwood Dr KNUT WA16 ....132 D5
  NANT CW5 ....21 H5
  WILM/AE SK9 ....84 D4
Birchwood Park Av
  GOL/RIS/CU WA3 ....38 D2
Birchwood Wy GOL/RIS/CU WA3 .. 29 M8
Bird Hall Av CHD/CHDH SK8 .... 46 C4
Bird Hall La CHD/CHDH SK8 .... 46 B5
Bird Hall Rd CHD/CHDH SK8 .... 46 B7
Birdlip Dr NTHM/RTH M23 .... 63 G1
Birds La CHSE CH3 ....214 E3
  TPLY/KEL CW6 ....217 H4
Birkdale Av WARRS WA4 ....36 A7
  MCFLDN SK10 ....112 C8
Birkdale CI BRAM/HZG SK7 .... 66 A7
Birkdale Ct NWCHE CW9 ....13 L2
Birkdale Dr ALS/KID ST7 ....243 J1
  SALE M33 ....42 E2
Birkdale Gdns WSFD CW7 ....177 G2 [1]
  WARRW/BUR WA5 ....35 M8
  WDN WA8 ....34 B7
Birkenhead Rd NSTN CH64 .... 92 E3
Birkenhead St NWCHE CW9 .... 130 C4
Birkett Av EP CH65 ....121 J2
Birkin CI KNUT WA16 ....81 K8 [1]
Birkinheath La ALT WA14 ....61 H8
Birkworth Ct OFTN SK2 ....47 K6 [2]
Birley CI HALE/TIMP WA15 ....42 F5
Birley Pk DID/WITH M20 ....44 F1
Birley St NEWLW WA12 ....22 D8
Birling Dr NTHM/RTH M23 .... 44 B8
Birnam Dr WLTN L35 ....33 K2 [2]
Birstall Ct RUNC WA7 ....73 K5
Birtles CI CHD/CHDH SK8 ....45 M7
  SBCH CW11 ....204 B8
Birtles La MCFLDN SK10 ....136 D3
Birtlespool Rd CHD/CHDH SK8 ... 45 M8
Birtles Rd MCFLDN SK10 ....137 K3
  WARRN/WOL WA2 ....37 J3
Birtwistle Rd NWCHE CW9 ....130 D6
Bisham Pk RUNC WA7 ....74 D2
Bishop Bennet Wy CHSE CH3... 195 L8
  CHSE CH3 ....229 J2
  MALPAS SY14 ....244 F8
  MALPAS SY14 ....257 L1
  WHITCH SY13 ....259 L4
  WHITCH SY13 ....259 L4
Bishopdale WARRW/BUR WA5... 35 M5
Bishopdale Dr RAIN/WH L35 .... 33 K2
Bishop Dr RAIN/WH L35 ....32 D1
Bishopgates Dr NWCHE CW9 ... 129 L8 [2]
Bishop Rd MCFLDN SK10 ....113 C5
Bishop's CI ALS/KID ST7 ....242 D4
  ALT WA14 ....61 H3
  CHD/CHDH SK8 ....46 A7
Bishops Ct CHSW/BR CH4 ....167 J8
  WARRN/WOL WA2 ....27 M8
  WLTN L25 ....50 B2 [1]
Bishops Gdns EP CH65 ....10 B7
Bishop St CHNE CH2 ....17 L1
  STKP SK1 ....3 J5
Bishops Wd NANT CW5 ....251 M1
Bishopton Dr MCFLDS SK11 .... 137 M4
Bisley Av NTHM/RTH M23 ....43 M6
Bispham Rd
  WARRW/BUR WA5 ....36 B8 [1]
Bittern CI POY/DIS SK12 ....86 A1
  RUNC WA7 ....74 D4
  WARRN/WOL WA2 ....37 K1 [1]
Bittern Gv MCFLDN SK10 ....14 B2
Blackacres CI SBCH CW11 ....203 M6
Blackberry CI ALT WA14 ....42 B4 [1]

Blackberry Gv HLWD L26 ....50 D2 [1]
Blackbird Wy BIDD ST8 ....227 L4
Blackboards La GTS/LS CH66 ... 94 A5
Blackbrook Av CQ CH5 ....166 C2
  WARRN/WOL WA2 ....37 M2
Blackbrook CI
  GOL/RIS/CU WA3 ....23 M4 [2]
Blackburn CI
  WARRN/WOL WA2 ....38 C2 [1]
Blackburne Av WDN WA8 ....52 B7
Blackburne Dr WLTN L25 ....50 D5
Blackcarr Rd NTHM/RTH M23 ... 44 B7
Blackcroft NWCHW CW8 ....129 C2
Blackden La HOLMCH CW4 .... 134 A8
  KNUT WA16 ....134 A5
  MCFLDS SK11 ....159 M4
Black Denton's PI WDN WA8 .... 7 M3
Black Diamond St CH/BCN CH1 ... 17 H2
Blackdown CI GTS/LS CH66 .... 94 A1 [1]
Blackeys La NSTN CH64 ....91 L4
Black Firs La CONG CW12 ....183 L5
Black Friars CH/BCN CH1 ....16 F7
Blackheath La RUNC WA7 ....54 E8
Blackhill La KNUT WA16 ....106 F4
Blackhurst Brow MCFLDN SK10 ... 111 H1
Blackhurst St WARR WA1 ....5 H7
Black La MCFLDN SK10 ....15 J3
Blackledge CI
  WARRN/WOL WA2 ....38 A1 [1]
Blackley CI MCFLDN SK10 ....112 B8
  WARRS WA4 ....56 D1
Black Lion La GTS/LS CH66 .... 94 B6
Blacklock Hall Rd SPK/HALE L24 ... 70 C1
Blackmore Gv WHITCH SY13 ... 270 A4
Black Moss Rd ALT WA14 ....41 L5
Black Park Rd WHITCH SY13 ... 270 C4
Black Rd MCFLDS SK11 ....15 K8
Blackshaw CI CONG CW12 ....208 B3
Blackshaw Dr WARRW/BUR WA5... 36 B3
Blackshaw La WILM/AE SK9 .... 109 M3
Blackshaw St EDGY/DAV SK3 ... 2 F7 [1]
  MCFLDS SK11 ....14 F7
Blackstone Rd OFTN SK2 ....47 K7
Blackthorn CI CHSE CH3 ....170 A7 [1]
  CHSW/BR CH4 ....190 B1 [1]
Blackthorne Av GTS/LS CH66 ... 121 C4
Blackthorne Dr SALE M33 ....42 D2
Blackwell CI MWCH CW10 ....179 K6 [1]
Blackwood Dr NTHM/RTH M23 ... 43 K4
Blacon Av CH/BCN CH1 ....144 F7
Blacon Hall Rd CH/BCN CH1 ... 144 F7
Blacon Point Rd CH/BCN CH1 ... 168 D1
Bladen CI CHD/CHDH SK8 ....46 A8
Bladon CI NWCHE CW9 ....129 L8 [3]
Bladon Crs ALS/KID ST7 ....224 C7
Blagg Av NANT CW5 ....20 B9
Blair CI BRAM/HZG SK7 ....66 C4
  SALE M33 ....42 C3
Blair Dr WDN WA8 ....52 B1
Blairgowrie Dr MCFLDN SK10 ... 112 B8
Blakeacre CI HLWD L26 ....50 F6 [1]
Blakeacre Rd HLWD L26 ....50 F6
Blake CI CH/BCN CH1 ....144 F6
  CW/SHV CW2 ....237 M3 [1]
Blakeden La WSFD CW7 ....176 D3
Blake Dr OFTN SK2 ....47 L5
Blake La NWCHW CW8 ....152 A2
Blakeley La KNUT WA16 ....82 E5
Blakelow Bank MCFLDS SK11 ... 15 M8
Blakelow CI MWCH CW10 ....179 H5
Blakelow Crs NANT CW5 ....252 F1
Blakelow Rd MCFLDS SK11 .... 15 M8
Blakemere Av SALE M33 ....43 L1 [2]
Blakemere CI WHITCH SY13 ... 270 B4
Blakemere Ct EP CH65 ....10 E4
Blakemere La FROD/HEL WA6 ... 126 D8
Blakemere Wy SBCH CW11 ....203 M4
Blake St CONG CW12 ....207 J1 [2]
Blandford Dr MCFLDN SK10 .... 137 M4 [3]
  NWCHW CW9 ....153 L1
Blandford Rd HTNM SK4 ....45 M2
  WARRW/BUR WA5 ....36 B7
The Blankney NANT CW5 ....20 C7
Blantern Rd CHSW/BR CH4 .... 190 A5
Blantyre St RUNC WA7 ....72 F1
Blaven CI EDGY/DAV SK3 ....46 F7
Blay CI WLTN L25 ....50 D4
Blaze HI MCFLDN SK10 ....113 K4
Blazemoss Bank OFTN SK2 .... 47 K7
Bleak Hey Rd WYTH/NTH M22 ... 63 M2
Bleasdale Rd CW/HAS CW1 .... 221 H3
  NEWLW WA12 ....22 B8
  WYTH/NTH M22 ....63 G2
Bleatarn Rd STKP SK1 ....47 L5
Bleeding Wolf La ALS/KID ST7 ... 225 J7
Blenheim CI ALT WA14 ....61 K2
  CQ CH5 ....166 A3
  CW/SHV CW2 ....237 L4 [1]
  MCFLDN SK10 ....14 B3
  NWCHE CW9 ....129 M8
  POY/DIS SK12 ....66 F8 [1]
  WARRN/WOL WA2 ....37 M2 [1]
  WILM/AE SK9 ....84 D5
Blenheim CI ALS/KID ST7 ....224 C7
Blenheim Gdns WSFD CW7 .... 177 J5
Blenheim Rd AIMK WN4 ....22 D2
  CHD/CHDH SK8 ....65 H2
Blenheim Wy SPK/HALE L24 ... 70 B1
Bletchley Rd HTNM SK4 ....45 L3
Bloomsbury Gv
  HALE/TIMP WA15 ....43 G6
Bloomsbury La
  HALE/TIMP WA15 ....43 G6
Bloomsbury Wy WDN WA8 .... 52 D1 [1]
Bloom St EDGY/DAV SK3 ....2 E8
Blossom Hts NWCHW CW8 .... 12 C5
Blossoms Hey CHD/CHDH SK8... 64 E3
Blossoms La BRAM/HZG SK7 ... 65 J5
Blossoms St OFTN SK2 ....46 F5 [1]
Bluebell CI BIDD ST8 ....227 L5
  CHSE CH3 ....170 B6
  MCFLDN SK10 ....138 D1 [1]
  NWCHW CW8 ....129 L3
Bluebell Ct RUNC WA7 ....73 M8 [1]
Bluebell Gv CHD/CHDH SK8 .... 45 K8

Bluebell La MCFLDN SK10 138 C1
Bluebell Ms MCFLDN SK10 138 D1 2
Bluebell Wy WILM/AE SK9 84 C3
Blueberry Rd ALT WA14 61 G2
Blue Cap La MALPAS SY14 246 D5
Bluecoat St WARRN/WOL WA2 5 G3
Blue Hatch FROD/HEL WA6 99 J4
Bluestone Dr HTNM SK4 45 L1
Blundell's La RAIN/WH L35 33 G3
Blyth Cl HALE/TIMP WA15 43 K6
MCFLDN SK10 137 L3 2
RUNC WA7 74 D7
Blythe Av BRAM/HZG SK7 65 J6
CONG CW12 207 G2
WDN WA8 34 B7 1
The Blythings TPLY/KEL CW6 197 J1 1
Boathorse Rd ALS/KID ST7 242 F4
BURS/TUN ST6 243 G6
Boathouse La NSTN CH64 91 H2
Boat La WYTH/NTH M22 44 E3
Boat Stage LYMM WA13 58 E1
Bob's La IRL M44 31 K8
Boddens Hill Rd HTNM SK4 46 A3
Bodden St GOL/RIS/CU WA3 24 A3
Boden Dr NANT CW5 237 K8
Boden St MCFLDS SK11 15 H5
Bodiam Ct EP CH65 121 L2
Bodlondeb FLINT CH6 116 B8 1
Bodmin Av MCFLDN SK10 137 L3
Bodmin Cl RUNC WA7 74 B6 2
Bodmin Dr BRAM/HZG SK7 65 L5
Bodmin Wy HLWD L26 50 E4
Bodnant Cl CW/HAS CW1 221 G4 3
Bognor Cl SPK/HALE L24 50 B8 1
Bognor Rd EDGY/DAV SK3 46 E8
Bohars TPLY/KEL CW6 197 K4
Bolam Cl NTHM/RTH M23 43 M3
Bolderstone Pl OFTN SK2 47 L8
Bold La WARRW/BUR WA5 26 C5
Bold Pl CH/BCN CH1 17 H4
Bold Sq CH/BCN CH1 17 J4
Bold St ALT WA14 61 K1
CW/HAS CW1 222 C8
RUNC WA7 9 J1
SBCH CW11 204 B6
WARR WA1 4 F7
WDN WA8 7 G7
Bolesworth Hill Rd CHSE CH3 214 D7
CHSE CH3 231 J2
Bolesworth Rd CHNE CH2 145 M6
CHSE CH3 214 A4
Boleyn Cl CH/BCN CH1 144 E6
Boleyn Ct RUNC WA7 74 C1
Bollin Av ALT WA14 61 H4
WSFD CW7 178 B2
Bollinbarn MCFLDN SK10 14 C1
Bollinbarn Dr MCFLDN SK10 14 B1
MCFLDN SK10 138 A2
Bollinbrook Rd MCFLDN SK10 14 C2
Bollin Cl ALS/KID ST7 240 F1
GOL/RIS/CU WA3 30 A2
LYMM WA13 40 A8
SBCH CW11 203 L5
WSFD CW7 178 B2
Bollin Dr ALT WA14 42 E4
CONG CW12 207 M3
LYMM WA13 39 M8
SALE M33 43 H2
Bollin Gv BIDD ST8 227 L3
MCFLDN SK10 111 M5
Bollington Av NWCHE CW9 13 L8
Bollington La MCFLDN SK10 135 M2
Bollington Rd MCFLDN SK10 112 D6
Bollinhead La MCFLDS SK11 163 K2
Bollin Hl WILM/AE SK9 84 A4
Bollin Ms MCFLDN SK10 112 A5 1
Bollin Sq ALT WA14 61 H3 2
Bollin Wk WILM/AE SK9 84 B5
Bollinway HALE/TIMP WA15 62 A4
Bollin Wy MCFLDN SK10 112 A7
Bollinwood Cha WILM/AE SK9 84 D5
Bolshaw Farm La
CHD/CHDH SK8 64 C6
Bolshaw Rd CHD/CHDH SK8 64 B6
Bolton Av BNG/LEV M19 45 K2
CHD/CHDH SK8 65 H6
WARRS WA4 37 M8 2
Bolton Cl GOL/RIS/CU WA3 24 B4
POY/DIS SK12 66 D8
Bombay Rd EDGY/DAV SK3 46 C5
Bomish La MCFLDS SK11 134 D8
Bonar Cl EDGY/DAV SK3 2 A7 1
Bonar Rd EDGY/DAV SK3 2 A8
Boncarn Dr NTHM/RTH M23 44 A8
Bond Cl WARRW/BUR WA5 36 D8
Bond St BURS/TUN ST6 243 K8
MCFLDS SK11 14 E7
NWCHW CW8 129 K3
Bongs Rd OFTN SK2 47 M5
Bonington Ri MPL/ROM SK6 49 H4
Bonis Crs OFTN SK2 47 J8
Bonis Hall La MCFLDN SK10 112 A2
Bonnywell Rd LEIGH WN7 24 F1
Bonville Cha ALT WA14 42 A8
Bonville Rd ALT WA14 42 A7
Booth Av CHSE CH3 148 E5
SBCH CW11 204 D6
TPLY/KEL CW6 175 M5
Boothbank La ALT WA14 60 A6
Booth Bed La HOLMCH CW4 157 J3
KNUT WA16 133 H8
KNUT WA16 157 J1
Boothby St MCFLDN SK10 14 E4 1
OFTN SK2 47 J8
Boothfield Rd WYTH/NTH M22 44 C6
Boothfields KNUT WA16 107 J2
Booth La MWCH CW10 179 K5
Booth Rd ALT WA14 42 C8
NWCHW CW8 129 G8
WILM/AE SK9 84 A3
Boothsdale TPLY/KEL CW6 173 L1
Booths Hill Cl LYMM WA13 58 D2 1
Booth's Hill La LYMM WA13 58 C1
Booth's Hill Rd LYMM WA13 58 C1
Booth's La LYMM WA13 58 B2
WARRS WA4 76 E6
Boothsmere Cl SBCH CW11 203 M4
Booth St CONG CW12 207 J2
EDGY/DAV SK3 2 F9
NEWLW WA12 27 G1 5
WARRW/BUR WA5 4 A9
Border Wy CHSE CH3 170 C3
Bordley Wk NTHM/RTH M23 43 L3
Bordon Rd EDGY/DAV SK3 46 B5
Borough Gv FLINT CH6 116 B6
Borough Rd CONG CW12 207 M1
HALE/TIMP WA15 42 E8
Borron Rd NEWLW WA12 22 B7
Borron St STKP SK1 3 K3
Borrowdale Av CHD/CHDH SK8 45 H8
WARRN/WOL WA2 37 H1
Borrowdale Cl CW/SHV CW2 237 L1 1
FROD/HEL WA6 99 K4
Borrowdale Rd OFTN SK2 47 H5
WDN WA8 52 C4
Borth Av OFTN SK2 47 J5
Boscombe Dr BRAM/HZG SK7 66 C2
Bosden Av BRAM/HZG SK7 66 E1
Bosden Cl WILM/AE SK9 64 D7
Bosden Fold STKP SK1 3 G7
Bosdenfold Rd BRAM/HZG SK7 66 E1
Bosden Hall Rd BRAM/HZG SK7 66 E1
Bosley Cl MWCH CW10 179 J6
WILM/AE SK9 84 D2
Bosley Dr POY/DIS SK12 87 G1 1
Bosley Gv BURS/TUN ST6 243 J5
Bosley Rd EDGY/DAV SK3 46 A4
Bosley Vw CONG CW12 208 B3
Bossington Cl OFTN SK2 47 J4
Bostock Gn EP CH65 94 F7
Bostock Rd MCFLDS SK11 137 L5
MWCH CW10 154 D8
WSFD CW7 154 A8
Bostock St WARRW/BUR WA5 4 B5
Boston Av RUNC WA7 9 K6
Boston Cl BRAM/HZG SK7 65 K5
GOL/RIS/CU WA3 24 F8
Boswell Av WARRS WA4 56 B2
Botany Rd SPK/HALE L24 50 C8
Boteler Av WARRW/BUR WA5 4 C3
Bottoms La CHSW/BR CH4 17 K8
Boughton CHSE CH3 17 L5
Boughton Hall Av CHSE CH3 170 A3
Boughton Hall Dr CHSE CH3 170 B3
Boulder Dr NTHM/RTH M23 63 G2
The Boulevard
BRAM/HZG SK7 66 E2 1
CHSW/BR CH4 190 C1
EP CH65 94 F8
Boulting Av WARRW/BUR WA5 36 F2
Boulton Cl SBCH CW11 223 J1
Boundary Dr WLTN L25 50 D5
Boundary Farm Rd HLWD L26 50 D6
Boundary Gv SALE M33 43 M2 2
Boundary La CHSW/BR CH4 168 D7
CONG CW12 208 A4
KNUT WA16 134 D5
MALPAS SY14 256 E4
MCFLDS SK11 159 K5
Boundary La North
NWCHW CW8 151 M2
Boundary La South
NWCHW CW8 151 M2
Boundary Pk NSTN CH64 91 K4
Boundary Rd CHD/CHDH SK8 45 M6
Boundary St NWCHE CW9 130 D2
Bourne Av GOL/RIS/CU WA3 23 K4
Bourne Cl NWCHW CW8 128 E5
Bournemouth Cl RUNC WA7 74 D6 1
Bourne Rd ALS/KID ST7 242 F2
Bourne St ALS/KID ST7 226 C5
WILM/AE SK9 83 M6
Bourton Rd WLTN L25 50 B6
Bouverie St CH/BCN CH1 16 E2
Bowden Cl CONG CW12 183 M8
GOL/RIS/CU WA3 24 F8
LEIGH WN7 25 H2 1
Bowden Crs NM/HAY SK22 69 K4
Bowden Dr NWCHE CW9 130 C4
Bowden La MPL/ROM SK6 48 E5
Bowden St BRAM/HZG SK7 66 E1 2
Bowden View La KNUT WA16 79 M2
Bowdon Cl WARR WA1 37 M4 1
Bowdon Ri ALT WA14 61 K2
Bowdon Rd ALT WA14 61 J1
Bowdon St EDGY/DAV SK3 2 E8 1
Bowen Cl BRAM/HZG SK7 65 M7 1
WDN WA8 33 K8 1
Bowen Cooke Av CW/HAS CW1 18 A1
CW/HAS CW1 221 G6
Bowen St CW/SHV CW2 18 A5
Bower Av BRAM/HZG SK7 66 D3
HTNM SK4 2 B2
Bower Crs WARRS WA4 76 D2
Bower End La
AUD/MAD/W CW3 267 K6
Bowerfield Av BRAM/HZG SK7 66 D4
Bowerfield Crs BRAM/HZG SK7 66 E4
Bowerfold La HTNM SK4 2 B3
Bower Rd HALE/TIMP WA15 61 L3
Bower St WDN WA8 7 L2
Bowery Av CHD/CHDH SK8 64 F6
Bowe's Gate Rd TPLY/KEL CW6 217 H2
Bowfell Cl BEB CH63 93 K1 1
Bowfell Dr MPL/ROM SK6 67 L4
Bow Green Rd ALT WA14 61 G3
Bowhill La AUD/MAD/W CW3 255 J6
Bowkers Cft SBCH CW11 222 F4
Bowkers La WHITCH SY13 268 D6
Bowland Av GOL/RIS/CU WA3 23 J3 2
STHEL WA9 34 A1
Bowland Cl GOL/RIS/CU WA3 30 B7 1
OFTN SK2 47 L7
RUNC WA7 73 L7 1
Bowland Cft CW/HAS CW1 221 H3 1
Bowland Ri WSFD CW7 177 H5
Bowland Rd NTHM/RTH M23 43 M6
Bow La ALT WA14 61 G4
Bowley Av WYTH/NTH M22 63 G2
Bowling Green Ct NANT CW5 20 F6 1
NWCHW CW8 12 F1
Bowman Av WARRS WA4 38 A7
Bowmere Cl TPLY/KEL CW6 197 K3
Bowmere Dr WSFD CW7 177 J4
Bowmere Rd TPLY/KEL CW6 197 K3
Bowmont Cl CHD/CHDH SK8 46 A8
Bowness Av CHD/CHDH SK8 65 H3
IRL M44 31 K8
WARRN/WOL WA2 37 J2
WSFD CW7 177 K2
Bowness Cl HOLMCH CW4 181 G1
Bowness Ct CONG CW12 207 G3
Bowness Rd CW/SHV CW2 237 K1
Bowood Ct WARRN/WOL WA2 28 A8 1
Bowring Dr NSTN CH64 91 H3
Bow Rd LEIGH WN7 25 H1
Bowsey Wood Rd
AUD/MAD/W CW3 267 K3
Bow St EDGY/DAV SK3 2 A7
Bowyer Av NANT CW5 20 F5
Boxgrove Cl WDN WA8 53 H1 1
Boxhill Dr NTHM/RTH M23 44 A3 1
Box La CONG CW12 206 F1
Boxmoor Cl CHSW/BR CH4 169 G7
Box Tree Ms MCFLDS SK11 14 A6
Boydell Av WARRS WA4 57 H2 2
Boydell Wy CHSW/BR CH4 191 G5
Boyle Av WARRN/WOL WA2 37 L3
Brabant Rd CHD/CHDH SK8 65 H2
Brabyns Av MPL/ROM SK6 48 D1
Brabyns Brow MPL/ROM SK6 49 G5
Bracadale Dr EDGY/DAV SK3 46 E7
Bracken Cl ALS/KID ST7 224 F4
CHSW/BR CH4 190 C1
GOL/RIS/CU WA3 29 J7
MCFLDN SK10 137 M3 3
MPL/ROM SK6 49 J5
Brackendale CHNE CH2 123 H1
RUNC WA7 73 K4
Brackendale Rd CQ CH5 166 D1
Bracken Dr NTHM/RTH M23 44 B7
Brackenfield Wy WSFD CW7 177 G4 1
Brackenlea Pl EDGY/DAV SK3 46 D7 1
Bracken Rd GTS/LS CH66 94 E8
Bracken Wy FROD/HEL WA6 99 J6
KNUT WA16 107 G4
NWCHE CW9 103 J5
NWCHE CW9 130 C1
NWCHW CW8 129 H1
Brackenwood Cl CW/SHV CW2 238 B4
Brackenwood Dr
CHD/CHDH SK8 45 K8 2
Brackenwood Gv
RAIN/WH L35 32 F1 1
Brackenwood Ms
WILM/AE SK9 84 E4 2
Brackley Av IRL M44 31 K6
Brackley St RUNC WA7 8 E1
WARRS WA4 56 C3
Bradburn Rd IRL M44 31 L5
Bradburns La NWCHW CW8 129 H6
Bradbury Av ALT WA14 42 A7 1
Bradbury Gdns CONG CW12 207 M3 1
Bradbury Rd WSFD CW7 178 A1
Bradda Mt BRAM/HZG SK7 65 M2
Braddan Av SALE M33 43 J1 2
Braddon Cl NWCHE CW9 129 M8
Bradeley Green La
WHITCH SY13 259 M6
Bradeley Hall Rd CW/HAS CW1 222 B7
Bradeley Rd CW/HAS CW1 222 C8
Bradfield Rd CW/HAS CW1 221 G4
Bradford La MCFLDN SK10 110 A6
Bradford Rd WSFD CW7 153 L6
Bradford St CHSW/BR CH4 17 H9
Bradgate Av CHD/CHDH SK8 64 D3
Bradgate Cl WYTH/NTH M22 44 E4
Bradgate Rd ALT WA14 42 A7
SALE M33 43 H2 1
Bradlegh Rd NEWLW WA12 27 J2
Bradley Bvd WARRW/BUR WA5 36 B6
Bradley Cl HALE/TIMP WA15 42 E5
MWCH CW10 179 H5
Bradley Farm La WHITCH SY13 259 J5
Bradley Fold RAIN/WH L35 32 A4
Bradley La FROD/HEL WA6 99 K6
WARRW/BUR WA5 26 F2
Bradley St MCFLDS SK11 15 K8 1
Bradley Wy WDN WA8 7 L3
Bradnor Rd WYTH/NTH M22 44 D5
Bradshaw Av CHSW/BR CH4 168 B5
Bradshaw Crs MPL/ROM SK6 49 G5 1
Bradshaw Hall La
CHD/CHDH SK8 64 D4
Bradshaw La LYMM WA13 59 K1
WARRS WA4 57 H1
Bradshaw Rd MPL/ROM SK6 48 F5
Bradshaw St WDN WA8 7 H1 1
Bradwall Rd SBCH CW11 204 B3
Bradwall St SBCH CW11 204 B5
Bradwell Cl EP CH65 95 G8
Bradwell Dr CHD/CHDH SK8 64 C5
Bradwell Gv CONG CW12 207 M2
Bradwell Rd BRAM/HZG SK7 66 E4
GOL/RIS/CU WA3 23 L5
Braemar Av NWCHE CW9 130 C5
Braemar Cl CHSE CH3 170 C1
CW/SHV CW2 237 L4 2
HOLMCH CW4 181 J2
RAIN/WH L35 32 F1 2
WARRN/WOL WA2 38 A1 2
Braemar Dr SALE M33 42 C2
Braemar Rd BRAM/HZG SK7 66 F1
Braeside Av CQ CH5 166 C2
Braeside Cl GTS/LS CH66 94 C7 1
MCFLDS SK11 15 L8
OFTN SK2 47 M7
Braidwood Av KNUT WA16 107 J1 1
Brains La TPLY/KEL CW6 198 A7
Braintree Rd WYTH/NTH M22 63 L4
Braithwaite Cl RAIN/WH L35 33 J1 1
RUNC WA7 73 K7 1
Braithwaite Rd GOL/RIS/CU WA3 23 K3
Brakeley La NWCHW CW8 102 D8
Brakenwood Ms WARRS WA4 57 J3 1
Brakespeare St BURS/TUN ST6 243 J5
The Brake ALS/KID ST7 226 B5
Brake Village ALS/KID ST7 226 B5
Bramall Cl SBCH CW11 204 C5
Bramble Cl CHSE CH3 170 A5
MCFLDN SK10 138 B2
MWCH CW10 179 L2
WARRW/BUR WA5 54 E1
WSFD CW7 177 J1 2
Bramble Lea AUD/MAD/W CW3 267 L6
The Brambles CQ CH5 142 B6
CW/HAS CW1 222 B8
NWCHE CW9 130 C1
Bramble Wy RUNC WA7 73 L8 1
Brambling Cl OFTN SK2 48 A8
RUNC WA7 73 L7 2
Brambling Pk HLWD L26 50 E3
Brambling Wy
GOL/RIS/CU WA3 23 L4 3
Bramcote Av NTHM/RTH M23 44 B6 1
Bramhall Cl HALE/TIMP WA15 43 K6 2
SALE M33 43 L1
SPK/HALE L24 70 E2 1
WSFD CW7 177 H3
Bramhall Dr HOLMCH CW4 181 G1
PS/BROM CH62 93 M1
Bramhall La EDGY/DAV SK3 46 F7
Bramhall La South
BRAM/HZG SK7 65 L6
OFTN SK2 46 F6
Bramhall Moor La
BRAM/HZG SK7 66 B3
Bramhall Park Rd
BRAM/HZG SK7 65 J3
Bramhall Rd CW/SHV CW2 237 M2
Bramhalls Pk NWCHE CW9 129 J1
Bramhall St WARRW/BUR WA5 4 B7
Bramham Rd MPL/ROM SK6 48 F8
Bramley Cl BRAM/HZG SK7 65 L6 1
GTS/LS CH66 120 F4 3
WILM/AE SK9 83 K8
Bramley Ct TPLY/KEL CW6 149 K7
Bramley Crs HTNM SK4 46 B2 1
Bramley Dr BRAM/HZG SK7 65 L6 2
Bramley Rd BRAM/HZG SK7 65 L6
Brampton Av MCFLDN SK10 14 A2 1
Brampton Ct STHEL WA9 26 B1 1
Brampton Rd BRAM/HZG SK7 65 M2
Bramshill Cl GOL/RIS/CU WA3 30 A6
Bramway BRAM/HZG SK7 65 J5
MPL/ROM SK6 67 M5
Bramwell St STKP SK1 3 L7
Brancaster Dr GOL/RIS/CU WA3 24 A5
Brancepeth Ct EP CH65 121 K1
Branden Dr KNUT WA16 107 H3
Brandon WDN WA8 52 A2
Brandon Av CHD/CHDH SK8 64 B3
WYTH/NTH M22 44 C4 1
Brandon Cl WILM/AE SK9 84 D2 2
Brandon Gv WRX/GR/LL LL12 210 B5 1
Brandreth Cl RAIN/WH L35 33 J1 2
Brandwood Av
WARRN/WOL WA2 37 H2 3
Branfield Av CHD/CHDH SK8 64 D3
Branksome Dr CHD/CHDH SK8 64 D3
Branksome Rd HTNM SK4 46 B3
Bransdale Cl WARRW/BUR WA5 35 L5
Bransdale Wy MCFLDS SK11 137 M5
Bransford Cl AIMK WN4 22 C2
Branson Wk HALE/TIMP WA15 43 J6
Brantfield Ct
WARRN/WOL WA2 37 L2 2
Brantwood Rd
CHD/CHDH SK8 64 F3 2
Brassey's Contract Rd
MALPAS SY14 246 A2
Brassey St CHSE CH3 17 M5
Brassey Wy NANT CW5 237 K7 1
Brassington St
AUD/MAD/W CW3 255 G6 1
Brathay Cl WARRN/WOL WA2 37 J1
Brattswood Dr ALS/KID ST7 224 F7
Bray Cl CHD/CHDH SK8 64 E2
CW/HAS CW1 19 K2
RUNC WA7 73 K6
Braydon Cl WLTN L25 50 C6 1
Brayford Rd WYTH/NTH M22 63 K3 2
Bray Rd CHSW/BR CH4 168 F6 2
SPK/HALE L24 50 C8
Braystan Gdns
CHD/CHDH SK8 45 H6 1
Braystones Cl ALS/KID ST7 243 L4 2
Brayton Av DID/WITH M20 45 J2
Breach House La KNUT WA16 81 M2
Bread St MCFLDS SK11 14 E7
Breaston Av LEIGH WN7 25 H1
Breck Rd WDN WA8 7 K2
The Breck GTS/LS CH66 94 E5
Brecon Av CHD/CHDH SK8 64 E3
Brecon Cl POY/DIS SK12 66 F8 2
Brecon Dr GTS/LS CH66 120 E3
Brecon Wy CW/SHV CW2 238 A5
WSFD CW7 177 J5
Bredbury Gn MPL/ROM SK6 48 A3
Bredon Cl GTS/LS CH66 94 A6
Breeze Av BURS/TUN ST6 243 L8
Breezehill Cl NSTN CH64 91 L4
Breezehill Pk NSTN CH64 91 M4
Breezehill Rd NSTN CH64 91 M4
Brenchley Dr NTHM/RTH M23 44 A2 2
Brencon Av SALE M33 43 J3
Brendall Cl OFTN SK2 48 A7
Brendon Av
WARRN/WOL WA2 37 G1 1
Brendor Rd WLTN L25 50 B3
Brennus Pl CH/BCN CH1 16 E4
Brent Cl POY/DIS SK12 66 B8
Brentfield WDN WA8 6 B1
Brent Moor Rd BRAM/HZG SK7 66 A1
Brentnall Cl
WARRW/BUR WA5 36 C7 1
Brentnall St STKP SK1 3 G9
Brent Rd HTNM SK4 2 B5
NTHM/RTH M23 44 A2
Brent Wy HLWD L26 50 F6
Brentwood Av ALT WA14 42 E5
IRL M44 31 K6
Brentwood Crs ALT WA14 42 E6 2
Brentwood Dr CHD/CHDH SK8 45 H7
Brentwood Rd CH/BCN CH1 144 E7
Brereton Cl ALT WA14 61 J3
CW/SHV CW2 237 L2
MALPAS SY14 258 B1
RUNC WA7 74 A4 1
SBCH CW11 204 C5
Brereton Ct CONG CW12 182 F6
Brereton Dr NANT CW5 21 H3
Brereton Gv IRL M44 31 L6
Brereton Heath La CONG CW12 182 D6
Brereton La HOLMCH CW4 180 C2
Brereton Rd NWCHW CW8 129 G8
WILM/AE SK9 84 E1
Breton Cl CHNE CH2 145 L7
Bretton Dr CHSW/BR CH4 190 B1
Bretton La CHSW/BR CH4 167 M7
Bretton Rd CHSW/BR CH4 167 L8
Brett St WYTH/NTH M22 44 E3 1
WYTH/NTH M22 44 E3 1
Brewer's Gn BRAM/HZG SK7 66 D1 3
Brewery La CHSE CH3 228 E1
Brewery St ALT WA14 42 D8
STKP SK1 3 H3
Brian Av WARRN/WOL WA2 37 K4
WARRS WA4 56 E3
Briar Av BRAM/HZG SK7 66 F2
GOL/RIS/CU WA3 40 B2
Briar Cl KNUT WA16 107 G1
Briar Crs WYTH/NTH M22 44 E7
Briardale Cl CW/SHV CW2 237 M4
Briardale Gdns GTS/LS CH66 94 C6 1
Briardale Rd GTS/LS CH66 94 C6
NSTN CH64 93 G4
Briardene Gdns
WYTH/NTH M22 44 E8 2
Briarfield Av WDN WA8 52 A3
Briarfield Rd CHD/CHDH SK8 65 H1
EP CH65 10 D7
HALE/TIMP WA15 43 J6
Briarlands Av SALE M33 42 F2
Briarlands Cl BRAM/HZG SK7 65 K6 1
Briar La NWCHW CW8 128 E5
Briar Rd GOL/RIS/CU WA3 23 H4
Briars Cl RAIN/WH L35 33 K3
Briars Mt HTNM SK4 46 A2
Briars Pk CHD/CHDH SK8 65 J3
Briarstead Cl BRAM/HZG SK7 65 K5 1
Briarswood ALS/KID ST7 243 H3 1
Briarswood Cl RAIN/WH L35 32 F2 2
Briarwood RUNC WA7 74 B3
WILM/AE SK9 84 C5
Briarwood Av MCFLDS SK11 138 D7
NTHM/RTH M23 43 K4
WARR WA1 37 L5
Briarwood Crs MPL/ROM SK6 48 F8
Brick Bank NANT CW5 21 H7
Brick Bank La HOLMCH CW4 157 H3
Brickbridge Rd MPL/ROM SK6 49 G7
Brickfields HUY L36 32 A3
Brickhill La HALE/TIMP WA15 62 B8
Brickhurst Wy WARR WA1 38 B4
Brickkiln La ALT WA14 60 C1
Brick Kiln La MWCH CW10 154 B5
Brickkiln Rw ALT WA14 61 J3
Brick St NEWLW WA12 26 F1
Bridge Av WARRS WA4 37 M8
Bridge Cl CW/SHV CW2 238 A5
LYMM WA13 59 H1 1
PART M31 41 G1
Bridge Ct NSTN CH64 91 L5 1
WRXS/E LL13 228 E4 1
Bridgedown TPLY/KEL CW6 197 J3 1
Bridge Dr CHD/CHDH SK8 45 K8
CHSE CH3 170 D5
WILM/AE SK9 84 D1
Bridge End Dr MCFLDN SK10 112 A5
Bridge End La MCFLDN SK10 112 A5
Bridgefield Av WILM/AE SK9 84 C3
Bridgefield St STKP SK1 2 F5
Bridge Gn MCFLDN SK10 112 A5
Bridge Gv HALE/TIMP WA15 42 F5
Bridge La BRAM/HZG SK7 65 M3
FROD/HEL WA6 99 J3
NWCHW CW8 151 M1
WARR WA1 38 C6
WARRS WA4 56 E5
Bridgeman Rd CH/BCN CH1 168 E1
Bridgeman St
WARRW/BUR WA5 36 D8 1
Bridge Meadow GTS/LS CH66 120 F2
Bridgemere Cl SBCH CW11 203 M4 1
Bridgemere La NANT CW5 264 E3
Bridgemere Ms NANT CW5 265 M4 1
Bridgemere Wy NWCHE CW9 129 L8
Bridgend Cl CHD/CHDH SK8 46 B8
WDN WA8 52 D1
Bridge Rd HALE/TIMP WA15 43 J5
STHEL WA9 34 D2
WARR WA1 38 C5
Bridge Rw CONG CW12 184 E8
Bridges Rd EP CH65 11 L8
Bridge St CH/BCN CH1 17 G6
CHF/WBR SK23 89 L5
CHSW/BR CH4 168 D5
CONG CW12 207 K2
CQ CH5 142 A5
GOL/RIS/CU WA3 23 G5 1
MCFLDS SK11 14 F6
NANT CW5 253 J4
NEWLW WA12 23 G5
NEWLW WA12 27 H1
NM/HAY SK22 69 J3
NSTN CH64 91 L5
NWCHE CW9 130 E2
RUNC WA7 9 J2
STKP SK1 3 G4
WARR WA1 5 G7
WRXS/E LL13 228 E4
Bridge Vw CQ CH5 142 F5
Bridge View Cl WDN WA8 53 G8 2
Bridgewater Av WARRS WA4 37 M8
Bridgewater Cl CONG CW12 208 B3
Bridgewater Dr CHSE CH3 170 C2
Bridgewater Ms WARRS WA4 56 C4 1
Bridgewater Pl WSFD CW7 177 G3 3
Bridgewater Rd ALT WA14 42 D5
Bridgewater St LYMM WA13 58 E1 1
RUNC WA7 9 G1
WHITCH SY13 270 A5
Bridgewater Wy HUY L36 32 A4
Bridgeway East RUNC WA7 74 C2
Bridgeway West RUNC WA7 74 B2
Bridgewood Dr GTS/LS CH66 120 C2
Bridgfield Cl MPL/ROM SK6 67 L5 1
Bridle Hey NANT CW5 251 M2 1
Bridlemere Ct WARR WA1 37 L4 1

The Bridle Pth
AUD/MAD/W CW3 .... 267 K5
Bridle Rd BRAM/HZG SK7 .... 85 M1
CW/SHV CW2 .... 18 D5
Bridle Wy BRAM/HZG SK7 .... 85 M2
GTS/LS CH66 .... 120 D1
Brien St ALT WA14 .... 42 D6
Brierley Rd CONG CW12 .... 208 B3
Brierley St CW/HAS CW1 .... 19 H3
WARRW/BUR WA5 .... 4 D5
Briers Cl WARRN/WOL WA2 .. 37 M1
Brierton Dr WYTH/NTH M22 .. 63 H3 ◆
Brieryhurst Rd ALS/KID ST7 .. 243 H1
Briggs Av CW/SHV CW2 .... 238 D3
Briggs Cl SALE M33 .... 42 C3
Brighton Crs MCFLDS SK11 .. 163 H1 ◆
Brighton Rd HTNM SK4 .... 2 A5
HUY L36 .... 32 B1 ◆
Brighton St WARRW/BUR WA5 .. 4 B4
Brights Av ALS/KID ST7 .... 243 H2
Bright St CW/HAS CW1 .... 18 D3
Brightwell Cl
WARRW/BUR WA5 .... 35 L7 ◆
Brignall Gv GOL/RIS/CU WA3 .. 23 K3 ◆
Brimelow Crs
WARRW/BUR WA5 .... 54 L1 ◆
Brimelow St MPL/ROM SK6 .. 47 J1 ◆
Brimscombe Av
WYTH/NTH M22 .... 63 J2 ◆
Brindley Av MPL/ROM SK6 .. 48 F7
WARRS WA4 .... 37 M8
WSFD CW7 .... 177 H2
Brindley Cl ALS/KID ST7 .... 242 E3
Brindley Hall Rd NANT CW5 .. 234 E3
Brindley La SBCH CW11 .... 181 J8
Brindley Pk SBCH CW11 .... 222 F1
Brindley Rd RUNC WA7 .... 73 M1
Brindley Wy CONG CW12 .. 208 B3
MCFLDS SK11 .... 162 C1
Brinell Dr IRL M44 .... 31 M7
Brine Pits La NANT CW5 .... 263 L2
Brine Rd NANT CW5 .... 251 L1
Brinkburn Rd BRAM/HZG SK7 .. 67 G1
Brinkshaw Av WYTH/NTH M22 .. 63 L2
Brinksway EDGY/DAV SK3 .... 2 A7
Brinnington Rd STKP SK1 .... 3 L1
Brinton Cl WDN WA8 .... 6 B5
Briony Av HALE/TIMP WA15 .. 62 C2
Brisbane Cl BRAM/HZG SK7 .. 65 M7
Brisbane Rd CH/BCN CH1 .. 144 C8 ◆
Bristol Av RUNC WA7 .... 74 E6
Bristol Cl CH/BCN CH1 .... 144 C8 ◆
Bristol Dr GTS/LS CH66 .... 120 E3
Bristow Ct WARRW/BUR WA5 .. 36 A4
Brittania Dr NWCHE CW9 .. 130 E5 ◆
Brittania Gdns FROD/HEL WA6 .. 124 B3
Brittania Rd FROD/HEL WA6 .. 124 B2
Brixham Av CHD/CHDH SK8 .. 64 F5
Broadacre NWCHE CW9 .... 103 K5
Broadacres NANT CW5 .... 250 F8
Broadbent Av WARRS WA4 .. 37 M8
Broadcar Rd MCFLDS SK11 .. 139 J6
Broadfield Rd BURS/TUN ST6 .. 243 J6
Broadfields RUNC WA7 .... 74 C4
Broad Hey MPL/ROM SK6 .. 48 D1
Broad Hey Cl WLTN L25 .... 50 B1
Broadheys La KNUT WA16 .. 58 D6
Broadhey Vw NM/HAY WA22 .. 69 H3
Broad Hill Cl BRAM/HZG SK7 .. 66 A2
Broadhurst Av GOL/RIS/CU WA3 .. 29 M2
WARRW/BUR WA5 .... 36 D8 ◆
Broadhurst La CONG CW12 .. 207 J1
Broadhurst St EDGY/DAV SK3 .. 46 E5
Broadlake NSTN CH64 .... 92 F4
Broadland Gdns GTS/LS CH66 .. 120 F2
Broadland Rd GTS/LS CH66 .. 120 F2
Broad La HALE/TIMP WA15 .. 62 B4
HOLMCH CW4 .... 180 D4
NANT CW5 .... 252 B4
WARRS WA4 .... 57 H4
WARRW/BUR WA5 .... 26 D4
Broadleigh Wy CW/SHV CW2 .. 238 C4
Broadley Av GOL/RIS/CU WA3 .. 23 J5 ◆
WYTH/NTH M22 .... 44 D8 ◆
Broadmead CHSE CH3 .... 170 C2
Broad Oak Av CHSW/BR CH4 .. 190 B1
WARRW/BUR WA5 .... 35 L8
Broadoak Av WYTH/NTH M22 .. 44 C7 ◆
Broadoak Dr WYTH/NTH M22 .. 44 D7 ◆
Broad Oak La DID/WITH M20 .. 45 J4
Broadoak La KNUT WA16 .... 59 K7
KNUT WA16 .... 81 L6
Broadoak Rd BRAM/HZG SK7 .. 65 M2
WYTH/NTH M22 .... 44 C8
Broadoaks WRX/GR/LL LL12 .. 210 C4
Broad St CW/HAS CW1 .... 18 E1
Broadwalk MCFLDS SK10 .. 112 A7
Broad Wk WILM/AE SK9 .... 83 M4
Broadway BRAM/HZG SK7 .. 65 M2
CHD/CHDH SK8 .... 45 J8
HALE/TIMP WA15 .... 62 A3
NWCHW CW8 .... 129 H1
OFTN SK2 .... 47 J5
WDN WA8 .... 52 A3
WILM/AE SK9 .... 84 B6
Broadway Av CHD/CHDH SK8 .. 45 K7
Broadways AUD/MAD/W CW3 .. 263 M8
The Broadway NANT CW5 .. 21 H6
Broadway West CHNE CH2 .. 145 K7
Broadwell Dr LEIGH WN7 .. 24 E3
Broadwood Ct MPL/ROM SK6 .. 67 M5
Broady Ct CW/SHV CW2 .... 18 F7
Brock Dr CHD/CHDH SK8 .... 65 C4
Brock Hollow SBCH CW11 .. 203 M8
Brockhurst St NWCHE CW9 .. 13 H2
Brockhurst Wy NWCHE CW9 .. 13 J7
Brocklebank Dr NWCHW CW8 .. 12 F5
Brocklehurst Av MCFLDS SK10 .. 15 K2
Brocklehurst Dr MCFLDS SK10 .. 112 A5
Brocklehurst Wy MCFLDS SK10 .. 138 D1
Brock Rd GOL/RIS/CU WA3 .. 38 D1
Brock St MCFLDS SK10 .... 15 H6
Brockway East CHSE CH3 .. 214 A3 ◆
Brockway West CHSE CH3 .. 214 A3 ◆
Brodie Cl CHNE CH2 .... 145 J3

Brogden Av GOL/RIS/CU WA3 .. 24 E8
Brogden Dr CHD/CHDH SK8 .. 45 H7 ◆
Brogden Gv SALE M33 .... 43 G1 ◆
Broken Banks MCFLDS SK11 .. 15 H7
Broken Cross MCFLDS SK11 .. 137 L4
Bromleigh Av CHD/CHDH SK8 .. 45 H6
Bromley Av GOL/RIS/CU WA3 .. 23 K5
Bromley Cl WARRN/WOL WA1 .. 220 F4
WARRN/WOL WA2 .... 37 M1
Bromley Dr HOLMCH CW4 .. 181 J2
Bromley Rd CONG CW12 .... 207 L2
MCFLDS SK10 .... 137 L4
SALE M33 .... 43 J2
Brompton Gdns
WARRW/BUR WA5 .... 4 A2
Brompton Rd HTNM SK4 .... 46 A2 ◆
Brompton Wy GTS/LS CH66 .. 120 E3
Bronington Cl WYTH/NTH M22 .. 44 E1
Bron Llwyn FLINT CH6 .... 116 A8
Brookash Rd WYTH/NTH M22 .. 64 A4
Brook Av CW/SHV CW2 .... 238 C1
HALE/TIMP WA15 .... 42 E6
WARRS WA4 .... 37 M7
WARRS WA4 .... 56 E3
WILM/AE SK9 .... 84 D1
Brook Bottom Rd NM/HAY SK22 .. 68 F3
Brook Cl CW/HAS CW1 .... 19 L5
HALE/TIMP WA15 .... 42 E6
WARRS WA4 .... 33 J6
Brookcot Rd NTHM/RTH M23 .. 43 M5
Brookcroft Av
WYTH/NTH M22 .... 44 D7 ◆
Brookcroft Rd WYTH/NTH M22 .. 44 D7 ◆
Brookdale RAIN/WH L35 .... 52 A1
Brookdale Av KNUT WA16 .. 107 J2 ◆
MPL/ROM SK6 .... 49 G8
Brookdale Cl MPL/ROM SK6 .. 47 M1 ◆
Brookdale Pl CH/BCN CH1 .. 17 H3 ◆
Brookdale Ri BRAM/HZG SK7 .. 65 M2
Brookdale Rd BRAM/HZG SK7 .. 65 M3
CHD/CHDH SK8 .... 44 F7
Brookdale Wy CHSE CH3 .. 171 H7
Brook Dr MPL/ROM SK6 .. 48 F8
TPLY/KEL CW6 .... 149 K8
WARRS WA4 .... 36 A7
Brooke Av CHNE CH2 .... 145 M4
Brooke Dr WILM/AE SK9 .. 84 D8 ◆
Brookes Av CHSW/BR CH4 .. 190 B1
Brooke Wy WILM/AE SK9 .. 64 D8 ◆
Brook Farm Cl PART M31 .. 40 E2 ◆
Brookfield CW/HAS CW1 .. 222 D7 ◆
WHITCH SY13 .... 269 L4
Brookfield Av HALE/TIMP WA15 .. 42 F5
POY/DIS SK12 .... 86 C1
RUNC WA7 .... 73 L2
STKP SK1 .... 3 K9
Brookfield Cl LYMM WA13 .. 58 D1
STKP SK1 .... 3 K9
TPLY/KEL CW6 .... 197 K4
Brookfield Crs CHD/CHDH SK8 .. 45 K7
HOLMCH CW4 .... 157 M3
Brookfield Dr ALS/KID ST7 .. 224 C7 ◆
HALE/TIMP WA15 .... 43 G5
HOLMCH CW4 .... 181 H1
Brookfield Gdns
WYTH/NTH M22 .... 44 C6 ◆
Brookfield La MCFLDS SK11 .. 15 L7
Brookfield Pk WARRS WA4 .. 57 G2 ◆
Brookfield Rd CHD/CHDH SK8 .. 45 L7
GOL/RIS/CU WA3 .... 24 C8
LYMM WA13 .... 58 D1
NWCHE CW9 .... 103 K4
Brookfield St NEWLW WA12 .. 27 H1
Brook Furlong FROD/HEL WA6 .. 98 E2
Brook Gdns BIDD ST8 .... 227 K2
Brookhead Dr CHD/CHDH SK8 .. 46 A7
Brook Hey NSTN CH64 .... 91 H2
Brookhouse Cl
MCFLDS SK10 .... 137 M3 ◆
Brook House Dr CW/SHV CW2 .. 238 C4
Brookhouse La CONG CW12 .. 208 A1
CW/HAS CW1 .... 201 K6
TPLY/KEL CW6 .... 172 D6
WARRS WA4 .... 102 B2
Brookhouse Rd ALS/KID ST7 .. 241 K1
SBCH CW11 .... 204 B6
Brookland Av CW/HAS CW1 .. 237 M4
Brookland Dr SBCH CW11 .. 204 D6
Brookland La STHEL WA9 .. 26 A2
Brookland Rd
BURS/TUN ST6 .... 243 M7 ◆
LEIGH WN7 .... 24 E1
MCFLDS SK11 .... 14 C7
Brooklands Av AIMK WN4 .. 22 D2 ◆
Brooklands Crs SALE M33 .. 43 H1
Brooklands Dr HOLMCH CW4 .. 157 M4
NWCHE CW9 .... 130 A8 ◆
Brooklands Gdns NSTN CH64 .. 91 J3
Brooklands Gv CW/HAS CW1 .. 221 G6
Brooklands Rd BRAM/HZG SK7 .. 66 E3
CONG CW12 .... 206 F1
NSTN CH64 .... 91 J3
NTHM/RTH M23 .... 43 J4
SALE M33 .... 43 H1
Brooklands Station Ap
SALE M33 .... 43 G1 ◆
Brookland St WARR WA1 .. 37 L3 ◆
Brook La CHNE CH2 .... 17 G1
CHSW/BR CH4 .... 167 J4
CONG CW12 .... 206 E7
GOL/RIS/CU WA3 .... 39 G4
HALE/TIMP WA15 .... 42 E6
KNUT WA16 .... 107 H3
NANT CW5 .... 235 K4
NSTN CH64 .... 91 J2
NWCHE CW9 .... 130 D5
WILM/AE SK9 .... 109 M1
Brookledge La MCFLDS SK10 .. 86 C7
Brookleigh Av CO CH5 .... 166 D2 ◆
Brooklyn Crs CHD/CHDH SK8 .. 45 K7
Brooklyn Dr EP CH65 .... 94 F7
LYMM WA13 .... 39 L8
Brook Lynn Av GOL/RIS/CU WA3 .. 23 M3
Brooklyn Rd CHD/CHDH SK8 .. 45 K7 ◆
OFTN SK2 .... 47 J6

Brooklyn St CW/SHV CW2 .. 18 F7
Brookmere Cl SBCH CW11 .. 203 L4 ◆
Brook Pl CW/BCN CH1 .... 17 H3
WARRS WA4 .... 56 E1 ◆
Brook Rd CHD/CHDH SK8 .. 45 M6
CO CH5 .... 142 A6
GTS/LS CH66 .... 94 D7
LYMM WA13 .... 39 K8
TPLY/KEL CW6 .... 197 K4
WHITCH SY13 .... 270 B5
Brooks Av BRAM/HZG SK7 .. 66 D1
Brooks Dr HALE/TIMP WA15 .. 62 D4
NTHM/RTH M23 .... 43 K5
Brook Side CHSE CH3 .... 148 E5
CHSE CH3 .... 170 A4 ◆
CO CH5 .... 142 F5 ◆
FROD/HEL WA6 .... 126 C2
NWCHW CW8 .... 151 M1 ◆
Brookside Av LYMM WA13 .. 39 J8
MCFLDS SK11 .... 162 F1
OFTN SK2 .... 47 L6
POY/DIS SK12 .... 86 E1
WARRS WA4 .... 56 D3
WARRW/BUR WA5 .... 36 A7
Brookside Cl CHD/CHDH SK8 .. 45 M4
Brookside La MPL/ROM SK6 .. 67 L5
Brookside Rd CHD/CHDH SK8 .. 45 G5
CONG CW12 .... 207 K1 ◆
FROD/HEL WA6 .... 99 G4
SALE M33 .... 43 G2
Brookside Ter CHNE CH2 .. 145 K8
Brook Slack TPLY/KEL CW6 .. 175 K3
Brooks La MCFLDS SK11 .. 186 D2
MWCH CW10 .... 179 K4
Brooks St AIMK WN4 .... 22 C2 ◆
Brook St BIDD ST8 .... 227 C7
BRAM/HZG SK7 .... 66 E2 ◆
CH/BCN CH1 .... 17 H3
CHD/CHDH SK8 .... 45 M6
CONG CW12 .... 207 M1
CW/SHV CW2 .... 19 G6
GOL/RIS/CU WA3 .... 23 G5
KNUT WA16 .... 107 G3
MCFLDS SK11 .... 15 J6
NSTN CH64 .... 91 L4
NWCHW CW9 .... 13 K1
NWCHW CW9 .... 130 E2
RUNC WA7 .... 9 G1 ◆
Brook Street Br CHNE CH2 .. 17 K2
Brookthorn Cl OFTN SK2 .. 47 M7 ◆
Brookvale Av North RUNC WA7 .. 74 B7
Brookvale Av South RUNC WA7 .. 74 B6
Brookvale Cl WARRW/BUR WA5 .. 26 F6
Brookway HALE/TIMP WA15 .. 42 F6
Brook Wy NWCHW CW8 .. 129 H8
WARRW/BUR WA5 .... 36 A7
Brook Well NSTN CH64 .... 91 L7
Brookwood Av SALE M33 .. 42 E1
Brookwood Cl WARRS WA4 .. 56 B4
Broom Av WARRS WA4 .... 56 E6
Broom Crs CHSE CH3 .... 172 B3
Broome Ct RUNC WA7 .... 74 B7 ◆
Broomehouse Av IRL M44 .. 31 L4
Broomfield Cl MCFLDS SK11 .. 135 C1
WILM/AE SK9 .... 84 E4 ◆
Broomfield Crs EDGY/DAV SK3 .. 46 C7
Broomfield La HALE/TIMP WA15 .. 61 C8
NWCHW CW8 .... 102 F8
Broomfields Rd WARRS WA4 .. 56 D5
Broomheath La CHSE CH3 .. 172 C5
Broomhill Dr BRAM/HZG SK7 .. 65 K6
Broomhill La CHSE CH3 .. 147 L4
CHSE CH3 .... 231 J4
Broomhill St BURS/TUN ST6 .. 243 J8
Broom La KNUT WA16 .... 132 C2
Broom Rd HALE/TIMP WA15 .. 61 L1
PART M31 .... 40 F2 ◆
Broom's La TPLY/KEL CW6 .. 149 K7
Broom St CW/HAS CW1 .. 18 B1
Broom Wy HLWD L26 .... 50 D5
Broomwood Rd
HALE/TIMP WA15 .... 43 J7
Broseley Av DID/WITH M20 .. 45 K1 ◆
GOL/RIS/CU WA3 .... 24 D7
Broseley La GOL/RIS/CU WA3 .. 24 D7
Brough St West MCFLDS SK11 .. 14 D7
Broughton Av GOL/RIS/CU WA3 .. 23 K5
Broughton Crs WRXS/E LL13 .. 256 A3 ◆
Broughton Hall Rd
CHSW/BR CH4 .... 190 C1
Broughton La CW/SHV CW2 .. 237 M4
Broughton Mills Rd
CHSW/BR CH4 .... 167 M6
Broughton Rd CW/HAS CW1 .. 221 J3
MCFLDS SK10 .... 86 C7
Broughville Dr DID/WITH M20 .. 45 J4
Brow La NWCHE CW9 .... 77 K7
Browmere Dr GOL/RIS/CU WA3 .. 29 G5
Brown Av ALS/KID ST7 .... 225 G8
NANT CW5 .... 251 M1
Brown Heath Rd CHSE CH3 .. 171 G5
Brownhill Dr WARR WA1 .. 37 M4
Brownhills Rd TPLY/KEL CW6 .. 175 H6
Browning Av WDN WA8 .. 6 B5
Browning Cl CH/BCN CH1 .. 144 F6
SBCH CW11 .... 203 L5 ◆
Browning Dr EP CH65 .... 94 F8
Browning Gv ALS/KID ST7 .. 242 C4
Browning St CW/HAS CW1 .. 18 E3
Browning Wy WSFD CW7 .. 176 F5
Brown Knowl La CHSE CH3 .. 231 J4
Brown La CHD/CHDH SK8 .. 64 C1
Brown Lees CW/SHV CW2 .. 18 B9
Brown Lees Rd ALS/KID ST7 .. 226 H7
BIDD ST8 .... 227 H7
Brownley Court Rd
WYTH/NTH M22 .... 44 D7 ③
Brownley Rd WYTH/NTH M22 .. 44 D7 ③
WYTH/NTH M22 .... 63 L2
Brownlow Cl POY/DIS SK12 .. 86 E2
Brownlow St WHITCH SY13 .. 270 A4
Brown's La CHSW/BR CH4 .. 16 F9
WILM/AE SK9 .... 84 E4
Brown St ALT WA14 .... 61 K1
CONG CW12 .... 207 L1

MCFLDS SK11 .... 14 F7
STKP SK1 .... 2 F4 ◆
WDN WA8 .... 53 K5
WILM/AE SK9 .... 110 A3 ③
Brownwood Cl SALE M33 .. 43 J3 ◆
Brownwood Cl SALE M33 .. 43 J3
Brows Av NTHM/RTH M23 .. 44 A2
The Brow FROD/HEL WA6 .. 126 C2
Broxton Av MWCH CW10 .. 179 K6
Broxton Cl ALT WA14 .... 52 C1 ◆
Broxton Dr CW/SHV CW2 .. 18 A7
Broxton Rd GTS/LS CH66 .. 94 E7
MALPAS SY14 .... 230 D3
Bruce Av WARRN/WOL WA2 .. 37 K3
Bruce Dr GTS/LS CH66 .... 94 C8
Bruche Av WARR WA1 .... 37 M5
Bruche Dr WARR WA1 .... 37 M4
The Bruen CHSE CH3 .... 172 C1 ◆
Bruera Av EP CH65 .... 94 F3
Brundage Wy CHD/CHDH SK8 .. 63 K2
Brundrett St STKP SK1 .... 3 K7
Brunel Rd MCFLDS SK11 .. 162 C1
Brunner Gv NANT CW5 .... 21 K7
Brunner Pl WSFD CW7 .. 177 G4
Brunner Rd WDN WA8 .... 7 G4
Brunstead Cl NTHM/RTH M23 .. 43 K5
Brunswick Crs GTS/LS CH66 .. 120 E1
Brunswick Rd ALT WA14 .. 42 D5
Brunswick St CONG CW12 .. 207 M1
MCFLDN SK10 .... 15 H4
STHEL WA9 .... 26 B1
SALE M33 .... 43 G2
Bruntleigh Av WARRS WA4 .. 57 G1 ③
Bruntwood Av CHD/CHDH SK8 .. 64 A3
Bruntwood La CHD/CHDH SK8 .. 45 L8
CHD/CHDH SK8 .... 64 E3
Brussels Rd EDGY/DAV SK3 .. 46 D6
Bryant Av WARRS WA4 .. 37 M8
Brydges Rd MPL/ROM SK6 .. 48 E7
Bryndale Gv SALE M33 .. 42 F3
Bryn Estyn Av WHITCH SY13 .. 269 M4
Bryn Gwyn FLINT CH6 .... 116 B8
Bryn Helig FLINT CH6 .... 116 B8 ③
Brynlow Dr MWCH CW10 .. 179 H4
Brynmore Dr MCFLDS SK11 .. 15 L6
Brynn St WDN WA8 .... 7 J3
Bryn Onnen FLINT CH6 .. 116 B8
Bryn Rd FLINT CH6 .... 116 A7
Bryn Siriol FLINT CH6 .... 116 B7
Brynton Cl MCFLDS SK10 .. 14 F2
Brynton Rd MCFLDS SK10 .. 14 F2
Bryone Dr OFTN SK2 .... 47 H7
Buchan Cl WARRW/BUR WA5 .. 36 A3 ③
Buchan Gv CW/SHV CW2 .. 18 C6
Buckbean Wy HOLMCH CW4 .. 157 L3 ◆
Buckfast Cl CHD/CHDH SK8 .. 65 H5
HALE/TIMP WA15 .... 62 B2
MCFLDN SK10 .... 14 D1
POY/DIS SK12 .... 66 D8
WARRW/BUR WA5 .... 54 E2 ③
Buckfast Ct RUNC WA7 .. 74 E1
Buckfast Wy MWCH CW10 .. 179 H5
Buckingham Av CHSE CH3 .. 170 A2
WDN WA8 .... 34 A8
Buckingham Cl CW/SHV CW2 .. 237 L2
NWCHE CW9 .... 129 L8
WARRW/BUR WA5 .... 36 C8
WSFD CW7 .... 177 J5 ③
Buckingham Dr KNUT WA16 .. 107 H5
NWCHE CW9 .... 129 L8
WARRW/BUR WA5 .... 36 C8
WSFD CW7 .... 177 J5 ③
Buckingham Gdns EP CH65 .. 121 K2 ③
Buckingham Rd ALT WA14 .. 42 F3
CHD/CHDH SK8 .... 64 F2
IRL M44 .... 31 J6
POY/DIS SK12 .... 66 D8
WILM/AE SK9 .... 83 M6
Buckingham Wy
HALE/TIMP WA15 .... 43 G6
Buckland Cl WDN WA8 .. 6 A6
Buck La CW/SHV CW2 .... 253 L1
Buckley Av MWCH CW10 .. 155 M5
Buckley Cl MWCH CW10 .. 179 H4 ③
Buckley Dr MPL/ROM SK6 .. 48 E7
Buckley St MCFLDS SK11 .. 14 F7
WARRN/WOL WA2 .... 37 K4
Bucklow Av KNUT WA16 .. 82 A8
PART M31 .... 31 M8
Bucklow Dr WYTH/NTH M22 .. 44 A8
Bucklow Gdns LYMM WA13 .. 40 A8
Bucklowhill La KNUT WA16 .. 80 A2
Bucklow Vw ALT WA14 .. 61 G1
Buckthorn Cl HALE/TIMP WA15 .. 43 L7
Buckton St WARR WA1 .. 5 L3
Buckwood Cl BRAM/HZG SK7 .. 67 G1
Bude Cl ALS/KID ST7 .... 241 H1 ③
BRAM/HZG SK7 .... 65 M5
CW/HAS CW1 .... 221 H4
Bude Rd WDN WA8 .... 52 B1 ③
Budworth Av STHEL WA9 .. 34 B1
WARRS WA4 .... 37 M8
WDN WA8 .... 6 A1
Budworth Cl RUNC WA7 .. 73 K5
SBCH CW11 .... 203 L5 ③
Budworth Dr WLTN L25 .. 50 C2 ③
Budworth Heath La
NWCHE CW9 .... 104 B3
Budworth La CHNE CH2 .. 144 F6
Budworth La NWCHE CW9 .. 103 M5
Budworth Rd GTS/LS CH66 .. 120 E2
KNUT WA16 .... 105 K2
NWCHE CW9 .... 104 C3
SALE M33 .... 43 L1
Buerton Ap CHSE CH3 .... 193 M6
Buggen La NSTN CH64 .. 91 K4
Buildwas Rd NSTN CH64 .. 91 L2
Bulford La CHD/CHDH SK8 .. 45 L6
POY/DIS SK12 .... 86 E1
WILM/AE SK9 .... 84 C1
Bulkeley St CHSE CH3 .. 170 A3
CW/HAS CW1 .... 19 K5
EP CH65 .... 121 H1 ③
Bullcroft Cl MALPAS SY14 .. 244 D5
Bull Hl HLWD L26 .... 50 E3 ③
Bull Hl NSTN CH64 .... 91 M6
Bull-hill-lane MCFLDN SK10 .. 139 K2
Bull Hill La MCFLDN SK10 .. 139 K3

Bullocks House Rd ALS/KID ST7 .. 243 L1
Bullocks La MCFLDN SK11 .. 162 E1
Bullock St OFTN SK2 .... 46 F5 ③
Bumper's La CH/BCN CH1 .. 168 E4
Bunbury Cl CHNE CH2 .. 122 A5
MWCH CW10 .... 179 J7
NWCHE CW9 .... 13 K8
Bunbury Dr RUNC WA7 .. 73 J6
Bunbury La TPLY/KEL CW6 .. 216 C5
Bunbury Rd TPLY/KEL CW6 .. 217 H1
Bunce La MCFLDS SK11 .. 184 A1
Bunce St CH/BCN CH1 .. 16 F7
Bunkershill Rd MPL/ROM SK6 .. 48 B3
Bunting Cl GOL/RIS/CU WA3 .. 23 L4 ③
Bunting Ct HLWD L26 .... 50 D2
Buntingford Rd WARRS WA4 .. 57 J1 ③
Bunts La CONG CW12 .... 207 L3
Burbage Rd NTHM/RTH M23 .. 63 G2
Burdett Rd GTS/LS CH66 .. 120 E2
Burdon Av WYTH/NTH M22 .. 44 E8
Burfield Dr WARRS WA4 .. 56 C6
Burford Av BRAM/HZG SK7 .. 65 J7
Burford Cl WILM/AE SK9 .. 83 L7
Burford Gv SALE M33 .... 42 E3
Burford La HALE/TIMP WA15 .. 59 J2
Burgamot La NWCHE CW9 .. 103 J4
Burganey Ct CHSW/BR CH4 .. 210 C2
Burgess Av WARRS WA4 .. 56 B1
Burland Cl RUNC WA7 .... 8 F4
Burlea Cl CW/SHV CW2 .. 220 E7
Burlea Dr CW/SHV CW2 .. 238 B7
Burleigh Cl BRAM/HZG SK7 .. 66 A3
Burlescombe Cl ALT WA14 .. 42 B6 ③
Burley Av GOL/RIS/CU WA3 .. 23 K3
Burley Ct HTNM SK4 .... 2 A3 ③
Burley La WARRS WA4 .. 57 J8
Burlidge Rd CHSW/BR CH4 .. 168 F6
Burlington Cl HTNM SK4 .. 45 L2 ③
Burlington Dr EDGY/DAV SK3 .. 46 F8
Burlington Gdns
EDGY/DAV SK3 .... 46 F8 ②
Burlington Ms EDGY/DAV SK3 .. 46 F8
Burlington Rd ALT WA14 .. 42 D7
Burnaby Rd BURS/TUN ST6 .. 243 J6
Burnage Av SPK/HALE L24 .. 70 C2
Burnage La HTNM SK4 .. 45 K2
Burnell Rd EP CH65 .... 95 L8
Burnet Cl WARRN/WOL WA2 .. 38 C2
Burnfell GOL/RIS/CU WA3 .. 23 L5 ③
Burnham Cl CHD/CHDH SK8 .. 64 F2 ③
GOL/RIS/CU WA3 .... 24 E8 ③
WARRW/BUR WA5 .... 35 M7
WDN WA8 .... 52 C1 ③
Burnham Rd CHSW/BR CH4 .. 168 F6
Burnsall Av GOL/RIS/CU WA3 .. 23 M4
Burnsall Dr WDN WA8 .... 52 C1
Burns Av CHD/CHDH SK8 .. 65 H5
ALS/KID ST7 .... 243 G4
GTS/LS CH66 .... 94 E8
RAIN/WH L35 .... 32 E1
Burns Crs OFTN SK2 .... 47 L5 ③
WDN WA8 .... 6 F4
Burns Dr CW/HAS CW1 .. 19 L3
Burns Gv HUY L36 .... 32 A3
WARRN/WOL WA2 .... 37 J2
Burnside HALE/TIMP WA15 .. 62 D5
Burnside Av WARRS WA4 .. 56 D3
Burnside Rd MPL/ROM SK6 .. 47 M1 ③
WILM/AE SK9 .... 84 C6
Burnside Rd CHD/CHDH SK8 .. 45 G7
Burns Rd CONG CW12 .... 208 A2
STHEL WA9 .... 34 A1
Burns Wy CW/HAS CW1 .. 144 E6
Burnt Acre MCFLDS SK11 .. 135 H1
Burnwood Gv ALS/KID ST7 .. 243 H2 ③
Burran Rd WYTH/NTH M22 .. 63 K4
Burrough Cl GOL/RIS/CU WA3 .. 38 F1
Burrows Hl NWCHW CW8 .. 129 H5
Burrows La FROD/HEL WA6 .. 124 D3
The Burrows NWCHW CW8 .. 127 K7
Bursar Cl NEWLW WA12 .. 22 D8
Burslam St CONG CW12 .. 207 L2
Burton Av HALE/TIMP WA15 .. 43 G3
TPLY/KEL CW6 .... 197 J1
WDN WA8 .... 52 F1 ③
Burton Dr POY/DIS SK12 .. 66 D8
Burton Gn GTS/LS CH66 .. 94 D8 ②
Burton La CW/HAS CW1 .. 221 H3 ②
Burton La TPLY/KEL CW6 .. 172 F6
Burton Rd CH/BCN CH1 .. 144 C7
NSTN CH64 .... 91 L6
WARRN/WOL WA2 .... 37 K3
Burton St HTNM SK4 .... 2 E1
Burtonwood Rd
WARRW/BUR WA5 .... 36 A4
Burwardsley Rd CHSE CH3 .. 214 B2
Burwardsley Wy NWCHE CW9 .. 129 L8
Burway Dr WHITCH SY13 .. 270 B5
Burwell Gv NTHM/RTH M23 .. 43 M5 ②
Bury St RDSH SK5 .... 3 G1
Bushell Cl NSTN CH64 .. 91 M4
Bushell Rd NSTN CH64 .. 91 M4
Bushel's Dr STHEL WA9 .. 34 D2
Bushey Dr NTHM/RTH M23 .. 44 A7
Bush Rd CHSE CH3 .... 170 E5
WDN WA8 .... 52 F7
Butcher La NTHM/RTH M23 .. 43 K5
Butler St CO CH5 .... 142 B7
Butler Wy NANT CW5 .... 251 L1 ③
Butley Cl MCFLDN SK10 .. 138 D1
MWCH CW10 .... 179 H7
Butley La MCFLDN SK10 .. 111 M2
Butley St BRAM/HZG SK7 .. 66 E2
Butterbache Rd CHSE CH3 .. 170 A6
Butterbur Cl CHSE CH3 .. 170 A6
Buttercup Dr EDGY/DAV SK3 .. 46 D7 ②
Butterfield Cl EDGY/DAV SK3 .. 46 D7
Buttermarket St WARR WA1 .. 5 J6 ③
Buttermere Av EP CH65 .. 121 J1
WARRN/WOL WA2 .... 37 J1

WYTH/NTH M22 ....63 J2 🔲
Buttermere CI *FROD/HEL* WA6 .. 99 K4 🔲
Buttermere Ct *CONG* CW12 ....207 G2
Buttermere Dr *CW/HAS* CW1 .. 221 H3 🔲
HALE/TIMP WA15..............62 C6
WILM/AE SK9 ....108 F5
Buttermere Gv *RUNC* WA7 ......73 K6
Buttermere Rd *CHD/CHDH* SK8 .. 64 B1
PART M31 ....40 E1
WSFD CW7 ....177 J2
Butterton La *CW/HAS* CW1 ....239 M3
Butterhouse La
HALE/TIMP WA15 ....62 E2
Button La *NTHM/RTH* M23 ......43 M2
Butts Av *LEIGH* WN7 ....25 H1
Butts St *LEIGH* WN7 ....25 G1
The Butts *ALS/KID* ST7 ....224 D8 🔲
AUD/MAD/W CW3 ....255 G7
Buxton Av *CW/HAS* CW1 ....19 K4
Buxton CI *WARRW/BUR* WA5 .....36 M4
Buxton Crs *SALE* M33 ....43 K3
Buxton La *MPL/ROM* SK6 ....48 E7
Buxton New Rd *MCFLDN* SK10 .. 139 J4 🔲
Buxton Old Rd *CONG* CW12 ....184 F8
MCFLDN SK11 ....139 C5
POY/DIS SK12 ....68 D6
Buxton Rd *BRAM/HZG* SK7 ....66 F3
CHF/WBR SK23 ....89 L3
CONG CW12 ....184 F8
MCFLDN SK10 ....15 K5
MCFLDS SK11 ....15 H5 🔲
NM/HAY SK22 ....69 H6
OFTN SK2 ....47 J8 🔲
OFTN SK2 ....69 H2
Buxton Rd West *POY/DIS* SK12 .. 68 A6
Buxton St *BRAM/HZG* SK7 ....66 F3
CHD/CHDH SK8 ....45 G7 🔲
Byfield Rd *WYTH/NTH* M22 ......44 C8
Byland CI *CHD/CHDH* SK8 ....65 H6
Byland CI *WDN* WA8 ....34 C7
Bylands CI *POY/DIS* SK12 ......66 D8 🔲
Byley La *MWCH* CW10 ....156 A8
MWCH CW10 ....179 L2
Byng Av *IRL* M44 ....31 J8
By-pass Rd *CHSE* CH3 ....172 B1
Byre CI *SALE* M33 ....44 A1
Byrom La *GOL/RIS/CU* WA3 ......23 M2
Byrom St *ALT* WA14 ....61 K1
Byron Av *RAIN/WH* L35 ....2 F2
Byron CI *ALS/KID* ST7 ....224 E5 🔲
CH/BCN CH1 ....144 E6
CW/HAS CW1 ....19 L4
MWCH CW10 ....179 K7
SBCH CW11 ....203 M4
Byron CI *ALS/KID* ST7 ....243 G4
WARRN/WOL WA2 ....37 J2 🔲
Byron Dr *CHD/CHDH* SK8 ....45 M6 🔲
Byron's La *MCFLDS* SK11 ....15 J9
MCFLDS SK11 ....138 E7
Byrons St *MCFLDS* SK11 ....15 H9
Byron St *RUNC* WA7 ....8 F4
Byron Wy *CW/SHV* CW2..........237 M3
Bython CI *CHSE* CH3 ....170 E5 🔲

C

Cabot CI *WARRW/BUR* WA5 ......36 C3 🔲
Cadnam Dr *WYTH/NTH* M22 ......63 M1
Cadnant CI *CH/BCN* CH1 ....168 D1
Cadshaw CI *GOL/RIS/CU* WA3 .....29 K7
Cae Bychan *FLINT* CH6 ....116 B8
Cae Derw *FLINT* CH6 ....116 B7
Cae Hir *FLINT* CH6 ....116 B7
Caerleon CI *WSFD* CW7 ....177 G4
Caernarvon Av *WSFD* CW7 ....177 H5 🔲
Caernarvon CI *CO* CH5 ....142 B7
Caernarvon Ct *EP* CH65 ....121 K2 🔲
Caernarvon Dr *BRAM/HZG* SK7 ...66 C3
Caernarvon Rd *CW/SHV* CW2 ....237 L4
Caesar Av *FLINT* CH6 ....116 C7
Cairns Crs *CH/BCN* CH1 ....144 D8
Cairo St *WARR* WA1 ....5 G7
Caister Wy *WSFD* CW7 ....177 J5 🔲
Caistor St *STKP* SK1 ....3 L2
Caithness CI *NTHM/RTH* M23 ....44 A8 🔲
Calamine CI *MCFLDS* SK11 ....15 J8
Calcutta CI *EDGY/DAV* SK3 ....46 C5
Caldbeck Av
WARRN/WOL WA2 ....37 K2 🔲
Caldecott Crs *WHITCH* SY13 ....269 L5
Calder Av *CW/HAS* CW1 ....222 A7
IRL M44 ....31 M3
WYTH/NTH M22 ....44 D4
Calderbrook Dr *CHD/CHDH* SK8 ...66 A6 🔲
Calder CI *MCFLDN* SK10 ....112 F4
POY/DIS SK12 ....86 D2
WDN WA8 ....53 M1
Calder Dr *RAIN/WH* L35 ....33 H1
Calderfield CI *WARRS* WA4 ....56 B4
Calder Wy *GTS/LS* CH66 ....94 C7 🔲
Caldey Rd *NTHM/RTH* M23 ....43 L7
Caldicott CI *WSFD* CW7 ....177 J5
Caldwell Av *WDN* WA8 ....7 G6
Caldwell's Gate La *NWCHE* CW9 .. 78 A3
Caldy CI *CHNE* CH2 ....145 K7
Caldy Dr *GTS/LS* CH66 ....94 D8
Caldy Rd *ALS/KID* ST7 ....224 C8
WILM/AE SK9 ....84 D1
Caldy Valley Rd *CHSE* CH3......170 B4
Caldy Wy *WSFD* CW7 ....177 H3
Caldywood Dr *RAIN/WH* L35 .....32 K1
Cale Gn *EDGY/DAV* SK3 ....46 F6
Cale Rd *NM/HAY* SK22 ....69 K4
Cale St *OFTN* SK2 ....47 G5
California CI *WARRW/BUR* WA5 ...36 C4
Callands Rd *WARRW/BUR* WA5 ...36 D2
Calmington La *RUNC* WA7 ....54 F8
Calow Dr *LEIGH* WN7 ....25 J1
Calrofold La *MCFLDN* SK10 .....139 J3 🔲
Calstock CI *WARRW/BUR* WA5 ....54 E1 🔲
Calve Croft Rd *WYTH/NTH* M22 ..63 L3
Calveley Green La
TPLY/KEL CW6 ....218 E7 🔲
Calveley Hall La *TPLY/KEL* CW6 .. 198 E2 🔲
TPLY/KEL CW6 ....218 B3

Calveley Rd *MCFLDN* SK10 .....137 M3 🔲
Calverhall Wy *AIMK* WN4.........22 A1
Calverley CI *WILM/AE* SK9 ....84 C4 🔲
Calverly CI *RUNC* WA7 ....74 C7 🔲
Calver Rd *WARRN/WOL* WA2 .....27 M8
WARRN/WOL WA2 ....37 G1
Camberley Av *BRAM/HZG* SK7 ...66 C5
Camberley Dr *WLTN* L25 ....50 C4
Camborne Av *MCFLDN* SK10 ....137 L4
WLTN L25 ....50 C4
Camborne CI *CONG* CW12 ......207 L4
RUNC WA7 ....74 C6 🔲
Cambourne Rd
WARRW/BUR WA5 ....26 F6
Cambo Wk *HTNM* SK4 ....45 M1
Cambrian Av *CHSE* CH3 ....170 B2
Cambrian Rd *CH/BCN* CH1 ....16 D3
EDGY/DAV SK3 ....2 B8
Cambrian Wy *CQ* CH5 ....166 A2
WLTN L25 ....50 B1
Cambridge Av *MCFLDS* SK11 ....14 D8
WILM/AE SK9 ....83 M5
WSFD CW7 ....177 G4
Cambridge CI *BIDD* ST8 ....227 J5 🔲
SALE M33 ....42 D1 🔲
WARRS WA4 ....56 B5 🔲
Cambridge Dr *HLWD* L26 ....50 F4 🔲
Cambridge Gdns *FROD/HEL* WA6 .. 98 D8
WARRS WA4 ....56 C6
Cambridge Rd *CHD/CHDH* SK8 ...45 H6
CHNE CH2 ....145 M7
EP CH65 ....10 F8
HALE/TIMP WA15 ....61 L2
MCFLDS SK11 ....14 D8
Cambridge St *OFTN* SK2 ....47 G6
RUNC WA7 ....9 L2
WDN WA8 ....7 J6
Camden Ct *RUNC* WA7 ....74 D5 🔲
Camden St *EP* CH65 ....10 A7
Camden St *CW/HAS* CW1 ....19 H5 🔲
Camelot Gv *CW/SHV* CW2........238 C8
Cameron Av *CW/SHV* CW2 ......253 H1 🔲
RUNC WA7 ....8 D7
Cameron Ct *WARRN/WOL* WA2 ...28 A8
Cameron Rd *WDN* WA8 ....7 G5
Camm St *CW/SHV* CW2 ....19 G7
Campbell Av *RUNC* WA7 ....9 G7
Campbell CI *CONG* CW12 ....185 G8
CW/HAS CW1 ....222 C8
WRX/GR/LL LL12 ....210 B5
Campbell Crs *WARRW/BUR* WA5 .. 35 M4
Campbell Rd *SALE* M33 ....42 F1
Campden Wy *WILM/AE* SK9 ......64 D8
Camphill Rd *WLTN* L25 ....50 A5
Campion CI *CHSE* CH3 ....170 A6
GOL/RIS/CU WA3 ....29 J8 🔲
Camp Rd *WLTN* L25 ....50 B3
Campsey Ash *WDN* WA8 ....52 F1
Camrose CI *RUNC* WA7 ....73 J6
Camsley La *LYMM* WA13 ....58 B1
Cam St *WLTN* L25 ....50 A3 🔲
Canaan *GOL/RIS/CU* WA3.........24 C4
Canada CI *WARRN/WOL* WA2 .....38 A2
Canada St *OFTN* SK2 ....47 G6
Canadian Av *CHNE* CH2 ....146 A8
Canal Reach *RUNC* WA7 ....74 C2
Canal Rd *ALT* WA14 ....42 E5
CONG CW12 ....207 M3
Canal Side *CH/BCN* CH1 ....17 H4
Canalside *EP* CH65 ....11 H5
Canal Side *MCFLDS* SK11 ....15 L7
NWCHW CW8 ....129 H2
WARRS WA4 ....55 J7
WARRS WA4 ....57 J3
WARRS WA4 ....74 F6
Canal St *CH/BCN* CH1 ....16 E4
CHF/WBR SK23 ....89 L5
CONG CW12 ....207 L2
MCFLDN SK10 ....15 J5
MPL/ROM SK6 ....49 G6 🔲
NEWLW WA12 ....26 F2
RUNC WA7 ....9 K2
STKP SK1 ....3 H7
Canal Ter *MWCH* CW10 ....179 K4
Canal Wk *MCFLDN* SK10 ....112 F6
Canberra Rd *BRAM/HZG* SK7 ....65 L7
Canberra Sq *WARRN/WOL* WA2 ...37 K2
Candahar Wy *CH/BCN* CH1 ......144 D8 🔲
Candelan Wy *KNUT* WA16 ....59 J8
Candleford PI *OFTN* SK2 ....47 L8
Candleston CI *WARRW/BUR* WA5 .. 36 E3
Canford CI *CW/HAS* CW1 ....221 H4
WARRW/BUR WA5 ....36 C6
Canley CI *STKP* SK1 ....3 H8
Cannell St *RUNC* WA7 ....74 A6
Cannell St *WARRW/BUR* WA5 ....36 D8 🔲
Canning St *CH/BCN* CH1 ....16 F4 🔲
HTNM SK4 ....2 F3
Cann La *NWCHE* CW9 ....79 G7
NWCHE CW9 ....104 F1
WARRS WA4 ....56 F8
Cannock CI *GTS/LS* CH66 ....120 E4
Cannon St *EP* CH65 ....10 B7
STHEL WA9 ....34 C1
Canon CI *ALT* WA14 ....61 H3
Canons Rd *WARRW/BUR* WA5 ....36 D6
Canon St *RUNC* WA7 ....8 F1
Canterbury Av
GOL/RIS/CU WA3 ....23 K3 🔲
Canterbury CI *GTS/LS* CH66 ....120 E4 🔲
Canterbury Pk *DID/WITH* M20 ...4 F4 🔲
Canterbury Rd *CH/BCN* CH1 ....144 F7
HALE/TIMP WA15 ....61 L2
STKP SK1 ....3 L6
WDN WA8 ....52 C5
Canterbury St *WARRS* WA4 ....5 J9 🔲
Cantley CI *RUNC* WA7 ....73 K6 🔲
Canton St *MCFLDS* SK11 ....15 H9
Canute PI *KNUT* WA16 ....107 G2 🔲
Capeland CI *CW/HAS* CW1 ....168 E7 🔲
Capenhurst Av *CW/SHV* CW2 ...237 M1
WARRN/WOL WA2 ....38 A2
Capenhurst CI *NTHM/RTH* M23 ..43 M8
Capenhurst La *CH/BCN* CH1 ....120 A5

EP CH65 ....121 G1
Capesthorne CI *ALS/KID* ST7 ...241 J1
BRAM/HZG SK7 ....66 F4 🔲
HOLMCH CW4 ....181 H1 🔲
NWCHE CW9 ....129 M8
SBCH CW11 ....204 C5
WDN WA8 ....6 D4
Capesthorne Rd *BRAM/HZG* SK7 .. 66 F4 🔲
CHSE CH3 ....171 H7
CW/SHV CW2 ....237 L2
HALE/TIMP WA15 ....43 K6
MPL/ROM SK6 ....67 L5
WARRN/WOL WA2 ....37 L2
WILM/AE SK9 ....83 L7
Capesthorne Wy *MCFLDS* SK11 .. 15 L6
Capper CI *ALS/KID* ST7 ....243 G2
Cappers La *SBCH* CW11 ....224 B2
TPLY/KEL CW6 ....217 H8
Capricorn Wy *BURS/TUN* ST6 ...243 M1 🔲
Capton CI *BRAM/HZG* SK7 ....66 A2
Carden Av *WSFD* CW7 ....177 H3
Carden CI *GOL/RIS/CU* WA3 .....29 K8 🔲
Cardew Av *WYTH/NTH* M22 ......44 B2
Cardiff St *GTS/LS* CH66 ....120 F2
Cardigan CI *WARRS* WA4 ....14 B5
WARRW/BUR WA5 ....36 D2
Carey St *WDN* WA8 ....7 H4
Carisbrook Av *MCFLDN* SK10 ...15 K2
Carisbrook Dr *WSFD* CW7 ....177 J5
Carisbrooke Av *BRAM/HZG* SK7 .. 65 K3
Carisbrooke CI *CW/SHV* CW2 ....237 L4
Carkington Rd *MCFLDS* SK11 ...50 C3
Carleton Rd *POY/DIS* SK12 ......67 J8
Carlile St *EDGY/DAV* SK3 ....2 E8
Carlines Av *CQ* CH5 ....166 A2
Carlin Ga *HALE/TIMP* WA15 .....43 G6
Carling Dr *WYTH/NTH* M22 ......63 L2
Carlingford CI *EDGY/DAV* SK3 ...46 E7 🔲
Carlingford Rd *WARRS* WA4 .....56 B4
Carlisle CI *KNUT* WA16 ....82 A8
MCFLDS SK11 ....137 M7
MPL/ROM SK6 ....48 A3
WSFD CW7 ....177 G3
Carlisle Dr *ALT* WA14 ....42 E4 🔲
Carlisle Rd *CH/BCN* CH1 ....144 E7
Carlisle St *CW/SHV* CW2 ....18 D8
WARRS WA4 ....56 C4 🔲
WILM/AE SK9 ....110 A4
Carloon Dr *NTHM/RTH* M23 ......44 B3
Carloon Rd *NTHM/RTH* M23 ......44 B3
Carlow CI *SPK/HALE* L24 ....71 J2
Carlow Dr *WYTH/NTH* M22 ....63 L2
Carlton Av *BRAM/HZG* SK7 ......65 K7 🔲
CHD/CHDH SK8 ....64 F1
CHSW/BR CH4 ....168 D6
MPL/ROM SK6 ....48 D1
RUNC WA7 ....73 K2
WILM/AE SK9 ....84 C2
Carlton CI *CHNE* CH2 ....146 E4
NSTN CH64 ....91 J2
Carlton Dr *HALE/TIMP* WA15 ....62 F7
Carlton Crs *GTS/LS* CH66 ....94 E4
STKP SK1 ....3 K4
Carlton Dr *CHD/CHDH* SK8 ......45 G6 🔲
Carlton PI *BRAM/HZG* SK7 ....66 F3 🔲
CHNE CH2 ....146 A8
Carlton Rd *GOL/RIS/CU* WA3 ....23 K3
HALE/TIMP WA15 ....62 B2
HTNM SK4 ....46 A2
LYMM WA13 ....40 B7
NWCHE CW9 ....13 K4
Carlton St *WARRS* WA4 ....56 C4 🔲
WDN WA8 ....7 H4
Carlton Wy *GOL/RIS/CU* WA3 ....31 J7
Carlyle CI *ALS/KID* ST7 ....224 E4
Carlyle Crs *GTS/LS* CH66 ....94 E8
Carlyon Wy *HLWD* L26 ....50 E4 🔲
Carmarthen CI
WARRW/BUR WA5 ....36 D2
WSFD CW7 ....177 J5 🔲
Carmel CI *CH/BCN* CH1 ....168 D1
Carmel Ct *WDN* WA8 ....34 B8 🔲
Carmel Ms *WILM/AE* SK9 ....84 B2
Carmenna Dr *BRAM/HZG* SK7 ...66 M5
Carmichael CI *PART* M31 ....40 E1
Carmichael St *EDGY/DAV* SK3 ...2 C9
Carnaby CI *HUY* L36 ....32 A4 🔲
Carnarvon Ct *STKP* SK1 ....3 K7
Carnarvon St *WARRS* WA4 ....56 D1
Carnegie CI *MCFLDN* SK10 ......14 A2 🔲
SALE M33 ....42 D1 🔲
Carnforth Dr *SALE* M33 ....43 G1 🔲
Carnforth Gv *ALS/KID* ST7 ......243 L4
Carnforth Rd *CHD/CHDH* SK8 ...46 B8
Carnoustie CI *WILM/AE* SK9 .....84 D2 🔲
Carnoustie Dr *CHD/CHDH* SK8 ..64 C3
MCFLDN SK10 ....112 C7
Caroline St *EDGY/DAV* SK3 ......2 D9
IRL M44 ....31 L4
WDN WA8 ....7 J7 🔲
Carol St *WARRS* WA4 ....56 D1
Carpenter Gv *WARRN/WOL* WA2 .. 38 A3
Carr Brow *MPL/ROM* SK6 ....68 A5
Carr CI *STKP* SK1 ....3 L7
Carrfield Av *EDGY/DAV* SK3 .....47 G8
HALE/TIMP WA15 ....43 H6
Carrgreen La *LYMM* WA13 ....40 F6
Carriage Dr *BIDD* ST8 ....227 L3
Carrick Dr *EP* CH65 ....121 H2
Carrick Rd *CHSW/BR* CH4 ....16 B8
Carrington Field St *OFTN* SK2 ...46 F5
Carrington La *GOL/RIS/CU* WA3 ..24 A5
LEIGH WN7 ....24 E4
SPK/HALE L24 ....71 K2
Carrington St *WARRS* WA4 ....4 D3
WDN WA8 ....7 H8
Catherine Dr *CO* CH5 ....166 A2 🔲
Catherine Rd *ALT* WA14 ....61 J1
MPL/ROM SK6 ....47 M3
Catherine St *BRAM/HZG* SK7 ....47 L8
CH/BCN CH1 ....16 D4
CW/SHV CW2 ....19 G8
MCFLDS SK11 ....14 F5
WARRW/BUR WA5 ....4 D3
WDN WA8 ....7 H8
Catkin Rd *HLWD* L26 ....50 D2
Catterall Av *WARRN/WOL* WA2 ..37 K2 🔲
Catterals La *WHITCH* SY13 ......270 E6
SALE M33 ....43 J6
Catterick Av *DID/WITH* M20 .....45 J1
Catterick CI *HLWD* L26 ....50 F4 🔲
Catterick Rd *DID/WITH* M20 .....45 J1

Carrwood *HALE/TIMP* WA15 .....62 B5
KNUT WA16 ....107 J3
Carr Wood Av *BRAM/HZG* SK7 ...65 L4
Carr Wood Rd *BRAM/HZG* SK7 ...65 K3
Carrwood Rd *WILM/AE* SK9 ......83 M5
Carsdale Rd *WYTH/NTH* M22 ....63 L5
Carstairs Av *EDGY/DAV* SK3 .....47 K8
Cartbridge La *HLWD* L26 ....50 F3
Carter Av *TPLY/KEL* CW6 ....149 K8 🔲
Carter La *MCFLDS* SK11 ....109 G8
Carter St *CH/BCN* CH1 ....17 J3
Cartier CI *WARRW/BUR* WA5 .....36 C3 🔲
Cartlake CI *NANT* CW5 ....20 B7
Cartledge CI *NWCHW* CW8 .....152 A1 🔲
Cartlich St *BURS/TUN* ST6 ....243 K7
Cartmel Av *WARRN/WOL* WA2 ...37 J1 🔲
Cartmel CI *BRAM/HZG* SK7 ......66 C1
CHD/CHDH SK8 ....64 C1
HOLMCH CW4 ....181 G1
MCFLDN SK10 ....138 B2
WARRW/BUR WA5 ....36 E2 🔲
WSFD CW7 ....177 K2 🔲
Cartmel Dr *GTS/LS* CH66 ....120 F2
HALE/TIMP WA15 ....43 K6
Cartmell CI *RUNC* WA7 ....73 H6
Cartridge CI *WYTH/NTH* M22 ....63 M1 🔲
Cartridge La *WARRS* WA4 ....57 K6
Cartwright Rd *CW/HAS* CW1 ....222 D6
Cartwright St *RUNC* WA7 ....9 L3
WARRW/BUR WA5 ....4 B5
Carver Av *HOLMCH* CW4 ....157 G6
Carver CI *WSFD* CW7 ....154 A8 🔲
Carver Dr *MPL/ROM* SK6 ....48 E7
Carver Rd *HALE/TIMP* WA15 .....61 L2
MPL/ROM SK6 ....48 E7
Casey La *GTS/LS* CH66 ....94 B7
Cashmere Rd *EDGY/DAV* SK3 ...46 C5
Caspian Av *WARRN/WOL* WA2 ...42 A6
Cassia Green La *NWCHW* CW8 ..152 B6
WSFD CW7 ....152 D7
Cassley Rd *SPK/HALE* L24 ....71 G1
Casson St *CW/HAS* CW1 ....18 D2
Castillon Dr *WHITCH* SY13 ......270 B4
Castle Bank *NWCHW* CW8 ....12 F5
Castle CI *CHSW/BR* CH4 ....167 H6
CHSW/BR CH4 ....210 D2
TPLY/KEL CW6 ....149 K8
Castle Ct *NWCHW* CW8 ....12 E4
Castle Croft Rd *CHSW/BR* CH4 ..169 H7
Castle Dr *CH/BCN* CH1 ....16 F8
EP CH65 ....121 G1
Castle Dyke St *FLINT* CH6 ....116 B5
Castle Edge Rd *NM/HAY* SK22 ...69 G2
Castle Farm La *OFTN* SK2 ....47 J7 🔲
Castlefield Av South *NTHM/RTH* M23 .. 73 M3
Castlefields Av East *RUNC* WA7 ...74 A3 🔲
Castlefields *CHSE* CH3 ....214 C2
Castlefields Av East *RUNC* WA7 ...74 A3 🔲
Castlefields Av North
RUNC WA7 ....74 A2 🔲
Castlefields Av South
RUNC WA7 ....74 A4 🔲
Castleford Dr *MCFLDN* SK10 ....111 L6
Castlegate *MCFLDN* SK10 ....111 L6
Castlegate Ms *MCFLDN* SK10 ...111 M6 🔲
Castle Gn *WARRW/BUR* WA5 .....36 A2
Castlehill *CHSW/BR* CH4 ....210 C2 🔲
Castle HI *MCFLDN* SK10 ....111 L6
NEWLW WA12 ....22 E8
WHITCH SY13 ....270 D4
Castle Hill St *CO* CH5 ....142 B8 🔲
Castle Inn Rd *CONG* CW12 ......208 C3
Castle La *AUD/MAD/W* CW3 .....267 L7
Castlemead Wk *NWCHE* CW9 ...129 L8
Castlemere Dr *CW/HAS* CW1 ....221 J5
Castle Mill La *HALE/TIMP* WA15 ..61 M6 🔲
HALE/TIMP WA15 ....62 B3
HALE/TIMP WA15 ....82 E1
Castle Ri *CO* CH5 ....166 D4
MCFLDN SK10 ....111 M6
RUNC WA7 ....73 K2
Castle Shaw Rd *OFTN* SK2 ....47 K7
Castle St *CH/BCN* CH1 ....16 F7
CW/HAS CW1 ....18 E3
EDGY/DAV SK3 ....2 D8
FLINT CH6 ....116 B5
MCFLDS SK11 ....15 G5
NANT CW5 ....20 E6
NWCHW CW8 ....12 F5
WDN WA8 ....53 K7
WRXS/E LL13 ....228 D4
Castletown La *CHSE* CH3 ....244 D2
Castle Vw *BIDD* ST8 ....227 J6
Castleview Rd *ALS/KID* ST7 .....243 H1
Castle Wy *CHSW/BR* CH4 ....191 G6
Castleway *HALE/TIMP* WA15 ....62 C5
Castlewood Gdns *OFTN* SK2 ....47 J7 🔲
Castner Av *RUNC* WA7 ....8 D7
Catchpenny La *MCFLDS* SK11 ..158 E1 🔲
Catford CI *WDN* WA8 ....52 C2
Catford Gn *SPK/HALE* L24 ......70 F1
Catford Rd *NTHM/RTH* M23 ......43 M7
Catfoss CI *WARRN/WOL* WA2 ....37 J2
Catherine CI *CW/HAS* CW1 ......221 H4

Catterwood Dr
MPL/ROM SK6 ....49 H2 🔲
Caughall Rd *CHNE* CH2 ....145 L4
Caunce Av *GOL/RIS/CU* WA3 ....23 G5
Causeway Av *WARRS* WA4 ......56 C1 🔲
The Causeway *ALT* WA14 ....42 D8
Cavalier Dr *CH/BCN* CH1 ....144 E6
Cavan CI *EDGY/DAV* SK3 ....45 M5
Cavell CI *WLTN* L25 ....50 A3
Cavell Dr *EP* CH65 ....95 G8
Cavendish Av *GOL/RIS/CU* WA3 ..29 L7
Cavendish CI *MCFLDN* SK10 ....138 D1 🔲
WARRW/BUR WA5 ....36 D5
WSFD CW7 ....177 G4
Cavendish Crs *ALS/KID* ST7 ....224 C7
Cavendish Farm Rd *RUNC* WA7 ..72 F7
Cavendish Gdns *EP* CH65 ....95 G8
Cavendish Ms *WILM/AE* SK9 ....84 A7
Cavendish Rd *ALT* WA14 ....61 J1
BRAM/HZG SK7 ....66 E3
CHSW/BR CH4 ....169 H5
CW/SHV CW2 ....220 E7
HTNM SK4 ....45 M2
Cavendish St *RUNC* WA7 ....8 F3 🔲
Cavendish Wy *HOLMCH* CW4 ...180 F2
Caversham CI *WARRS* WA4 ......56 D5
Cawdor Dr *CHSE* CH3 ....170 A2
Cawdor St *RUNC* WA7 ....8 E1 🔲
WARRS WA4 ....56 C4
Cawfield Av *WDN* WA8 ....6 B3
Cawley Av *GOL/RIS/CU* WA3 ....24 E8
Cawley La *MCFLDN* SK10 ....86 E5
Cawley St *MCFLDS* SK11 ....15 J6 🔲
RUNC WA7 ....9 G5
Cawood CI *GTS/LS* CH66 ....94 B7
Cawthorne Av *WARRS* WA4 .....57 G2
Caxton CI *WDN* WA8 ....52 C1 🔲
Caxton Rd *RAIN/WH* L35 ....33 L3
C' Ct *AIMK* WN4 ....22 B2
Caxton Rd *RAIN/WH* L35 ....33 L3
The Ceal *MPL/ROM* SK6 ....49 H2
Cecil Av *SALE* M33 ....43 L3
Cecil Rd *BIDD* ST8 ....227 J2
HALE/TIMP WA15 ....61 L2
Cecil St *CHSE* CH3 ....170 A3
Cedab Rd *EP* CH65 ....10 F6
Cedar Av *ALS/KID* ST7 ....241 K1
ALS/KID ST7 ....242 D3
ALT WA14 ....42 C8
BRAM/HZG SK7 ....66 E2
CQ CH5 ....143 G5
GOL/RIS/CU WA3 ....23 M5
GTS/LS CH66 ....94 C5
RUNC WA7 ....9 M8
WDN WA8 ....53 H1
Cedar CI *HOLMCH* CW4 ....157 K8
MWCH CW10 ....179 L6
NWCHE CW9 ....131 G1
POY/DIS SK12 ....86 E1 🔲
SBCH CW11 ....204 C7
Cedar Ct *CONG* CW12 ....207 M4
GOL/RIS/CU WA3 ....29 M2
NANT CW5 ....237 K6
Cedar Crs *NEWLW* WA12 ....27 K2
Cedardale Dr *GTS/LS* CH66 .....120 F3
Cedardale Pk *WDN* WA8 ....34 E8
Cedar Dr *CHNE* CH2 ....146 B8
NWCHW CW8 ....103 G8
Cedarfield Rd *LYMM* WA13 ....40 B7
Cedar Gdns *CO* CH5 ....166 A1
Cedar Gv *CHNE* CH2 ....146 B8
MCFLDS SK11 ....138 D7
NANT CW5 ....21 K6
NSTN CH64 ....91 M4
WARR WA4 ....38 A5
WARRS WA4 ....56 D1 🔲
WSFD CW7 ....178 A3
Cedar Ms *CH/BCN* CH1 ....144 E8
Cedar Pk *CHSE* CH3 ....170 C2
Cedar Rd *CHD/CHDH* SK8 ....45 G7
HALE/TIMP WA15 ....61 L1
MPL/ROM SK6 ....48 E8
OFTN SK2 ....47 H8
PART M31 ....40 E1
RAIN/WH L35 ....32 D1
WARRW/BUR WA5 ....35 M6 🔲
Cedars Rd *WYTH/NTH* M22 ....63 K1
Cedar St *NEWLW* WA12 ....27 J2
Cedar Wy *CW/SHV* CW2..........238 B5
Cedarway *MCFLDN* SK10 ....113 G4
Cedarways *WARRS* WA4 ....56 D7 🔲
Cedarwood *NWCHW* CW8 ....127 K6
Cedarwood Av *WYTH/NTH* M22 ..46 A3 🔲
Cedarwood Ct *TPLY/KEL* CW6 ..197 J1
Celandine CI *CHSE* CH3 ....170 A5
Celtic Av *ALS/KID* ST7 ....243 M4
Celtic St *CQ* CH5 ....142 A5
STKP SK1 ....3 K7
Celyn Crs *CHSW/BR* CH4 ....168 D7
Cement PI *CH/BCN* CH1 ....17 H4 🔲
Cemetery Rd *CW/SHV* CW2 .....239 H7
Cemlyn PI *CH/BCN* CH1 ....168 E1
Central Av *EP* CH65 ....10 E9
LEIGH WN7 ....25 J1 🔲
SALE M33 ....42 D3
SPK/HALE L24 ....71 G3
WARRN/WOL WA2 ....5 J1
WARRS WA4 ....56 B1
Central Dr *BRAM/HZG* SK7 ......65 K2
CHD/CHDH SK8 ....64 B2
CQ CH5 ....142 B7
MPL/ROM SK6 ....48 C1 🔲
NWCHW CW8 ....129 L5
Central Expy *RUNC* WA7 ....73 K4
Central Gv *NWCHE* CW9 ....130 D6 🔲
Central Rd *MANAIR* M90 ....63 J2
NWCHE CW9 ....130 D5
PART M31 ....40 F1
WARRS WA4 ....56 B1
Central St *ALS/KID* ST7 ....226 B6
Central Wy *ALT* WA14 ....42 D8
NEWLW WA12 ....27 L2
SPK/HALE L24 ....70 E2
WARRN/WOL WA2 ....5 G5
Centre Ct *LEIGH* WN7 ....24 B3 🔲

Centre Park Sq *WARR* WA1 .... 4 F9
Centurion Cl *GOL/RIS/CU* WA3 ... 29 K8
Chadkirk Rd *MPL/ROM* SK6 .... 48 B3
Chadvil Rd *CHD/CHDH* SK8 .... 45 J7
Chadwell Rd *OFTN* SK2 .... 47 L5
Chadwick Av *GOL/RIS/CU* WA3... 29 H5
  WARRS WA4 .... 56 E3
Chadwick Cl *WILM/AE* SK9 .... 84 C3
Chadwick Pl *GOL/RIS/CU* WA3 ..... 29 L7
Chadwick Rd *MWCH* CW10 .... 179 J6
  RUNC WA7 .... 73 L1
Chadwick St *MPL/ROM* SK6 .... 48 F7
  STKP SK1 .... 3 G8
Chadwick Ter *MCFLDN* SK10 .... 15 K2
Chaffinch Cl *CONG* CW12 .... 207 L3
  GOL/RIS/CU WA3 .... 38 F1
  WYTH/NTH M22 .... 44 F7
Chaffinch Dr *BIDD* ST8 .... 227 L4
Chaffinch Gld *HLWD* L26 .... 50 E5
Chaffinch Wy *WSFD* CW7 .... 177 K6
Chain Maker's Rw
  CHSW BR CH4 .... 168 E5
Chalfield Av *GTS/LS* CH66 .... 94 C7
Chalfield Cl *CW/SHV* CW2 .... 238 B5
  GTS/LS CH66 .... 94 C7
Chalfont Cl *WARRS* WA4 .... 56 E6
Chalford Rd *NTHM/RTH* M23 .... 63 G1
Chalgrave Cl *WDN* WA8 .... 53 L1
Challinor St *CHSE* CH3 .... 170 A3
Chamber Brook La
  FROD/HEL WA6 .... 126 C2
Chamberlain Ct *CW/HAS* CW1 .. 222 C7
Chamberlain Wy *BIDD* ST8 .... 227 L4
Chambers St *CW/SHV* CW2 .... 19 G8
Chance Hall La *ALS/KID* ST7 ..... 225 H3
Chancel La *WILM/AE* SK9 .... 84 B4
Chancellor Rd *RUNC* WA7 .... 54 D7
Chancel Ms *STKP* SK1 .... 3 J5
Chancery La *ALS/KID* ST7 .... 241 H1
  MCFLDN SK10 .... 113 H5
Chandler Wy *GOL/RIS/CU* WA3... 23 L4
Chandley St *CHD/CHDH* SK8 .... 45 K6
Chandos Cl *CHSW/BR* CH4 .... 169 L6
Change La *NSTN* CH64 .... 93 H4
Chantler Av *WARRS* WA4 .... 37 L8
Chantry Av *NWCHW* CW8 .... 129 H8
Chantry Cl *POY/DIS* SK12 .... 68 E7
Chantry Ct *MCFLDS* SK11 .... 138 D7
Chantry Fold *POY/DIS* SK12 .... 68 D6
Chantry Rd *POY/DIS* SK12 .... 68 D6
The Chantry *TPLY/KEL* CW6 .... 217 L2
Chapel Av *FROD/HEL* WA6 .... 126 C2
Chapel Bank *ALS/KID* ST7 .... 226 D5
Chapel Cl *ALS/KID* ST7 .... 226 B6
  AUD/MAD/W CW3 .... 273 M1
  CH/BCN CH1 .... 144 A3
  CHSE CH3 .... 171 G7
  NWCHW CW9 .... 103 K5
  WSFD CW7 .... 199 M7
Chapel Ct *ALT* WA14 .... 42 D8
  NWCHW CW9 .... 13 H4
Chapel Cft *MCFLDS* SK11 .... 135 H1
Chapel Cross Rd
  WARRN/WOL WA2 .... 38 A2
Chapel Dr *HALE/TIMP* WA15 .... 62 C5
Chapelfields *FROD/HEL* WA6 .... 99 G4
Chapel House La *NSTN* CH64 ...... 119 G5
Chapel La *ALS/KID* ST7 .... 224 F5
  ALS/KID ST7 .... 226 E8
  CHSE CH3 .... 170 A3
  CHSE CH3 .... 193 G8
  CHSE CH3 .... 193 K5
  CHSE CH3 .... 213 H2
  CW/HAS CW1 .... 221 K3
  FROD/HEL WA6 .... 124 F8
  FROD/HEL WA6 .... 126 C2
  GOL/RIS/CU WA3 .... 39 M3
  HALE/TIMP WA15 .... 62 C5
  KNUT WA16 .... 80 B1
  KNUT WA16 .... 156 E1
  MALPAS SY14 .... 256 E4
  MCFLDN SK10 .... 113 L7
  MCFLDS SK11 .... 159 K3
  NANT CW5 .... 250 D2
  NWCHE CW9 .... 153 L4
  NWCHW CW8 .... 127 K1
  PART M31 .... 40 F1
  RAIN/WH L35 .... 33 M2
  TPLY/KEL CW6 .... 173 L2
  WARRS WA4 .... 56 C4
  WARRS WA4 .... 77 H1
  WARRS WA4 .... 102 A5
  WARRW/BUR WA5 .... 26 F6
  WDN WA8 .... 33 J7
  WILM/AE SK9 .... 83 M6
  WRX/GR/LL LL12 .... 210 C5
  WRXS/E LL13 .... 228 D4
Chapelmere Cl *SBCH* CW11 ...... 203 L5
Chapelmere Ct *CW/HAS* CW1 ... 221 J5
Chapel Ms *EP* CH65 .... 10 C9
  EP CH65 .... 95 H8
Chapel Pl *AIMK* WN4 .... 22 B1
Chapel Rd *CHF/WBR* SK23 .... 89 M7
  KNUT WA16 .... 107 M6
  WARRW/BUR WA5 .... 54 E1
  WILM/AE SK9 .... 110 A3
  WSFD CW7 .... 177 M2
  WYTH/NTH M22 .... 44 D4
Chapel St *AIMK* WN4 .... 22 B1
  ALS/KID ST7 .... 226 B6
  ALS/KID ST7 .... 242 D2
  BRAM/HZG SK7 .... 66 E1
  CHD/CHDH SK8 .... 45 K7
  CHF/WBR SK23 .... 89 L4
  CHSE CH3 .... 17 K4
  CONG CW12 .... 207 K2
  CW/SHV CW2 .... 19 G6
  HTNM SK4 .... 45 K2
  MCFLDN SK10 .... 113 H4
  MCFLDS SK11 .... 135 H1
  NEWLW WA12 .... 27 L1
  NM/HAY SK22 .... 69 H6
  NWCHE CW9 .... 130 C1
  NWCHE CW9 .... 153 L4
  NWCHW CW8 .... 12 E4
  NWCHW CW8 .... 128 C3
  SBCH CW11 .... 204 B6

  SBCH CW11 .... 223 G1
  WDN WA8 .... 7 G7
  WILM/AE SK9 .... 110 A3
  WRXS/E LL13 .... 228 D4
Chapel Street (Lon Y Capel)
  FLINT CH6 .... 116 A6
Chapel Wks *CHD/CHDH* SK8 ..... 65 H6
Chapman Cl *WDN* WA8 .... 33 K8
Charcoal Rd *ALT* WA14 .... 60 E1
Charcoal Woods *ALT* WA14 .... 61 G1
Chard Dr *WYTH/NTH* M22 .... 63 K3
Chardin Av *MPL/ROM* SK6... .... 49 J4
Charity La *MCFLDS* SK11 .... 139 M4
Charlcote Crs *CW/SHV* CW2 ...... 238 C4
Charlecote Rd *POY/DIS* SK12 ...... 66 F8
Charles Av *MPL/ROM* SK6 .... 48 C5
  NWCHE CW9 .... 153 M2
  WARRW/BUR WA5 .... 35 M6
Charles Cotton Dr
  AUD/MAD/W CW3 .... 267 K6
Charles Crs *CHSW/BR* CH4 .... 17 K8
Charles Dr *FLINT* CH6 .... 116 B7
Charles Rd *CHNE* CH2 .... 145 H4
Charles Sq *SBCH* CW11 .... 223 M2
Charles St *BIDD* ST8 .... 227 J5
  BRAM/HZG SK7 .... 66 D1
  CH/BCN CH1 .... 17 H3
  CHNE CH2 .... 17 L2
  CW/HAS CW1 .... 18 F3
  IRL M44 .... 31 L6
  STKP SK1 .... 3 J9
  WDN WA8 .... 18 D4
Charleston Cl *GTS/LS* CH66 ...... 120 D1
  SALE M33 .... 42 D2
Charlestown Rd East *OFTN* SK2 .. 66 A1
Charlestown Rd West
  EDGY/DAV SK3 .... 65 M1
Charlesworth Ct *SBCH* CW11 ... 204 C6
Charlesworth Crs
  CHF/WBR SK23 .... 89 K1
Charlesworth Rd *CHF/WBR* SK23.. 89 K1
  CW/HAS CW1 .... 221 K6
  STKP SK1 .... 3 G9
Charlock Cl *LEIGH* WN7 .... 24 F1
Charlock Sq *ALT* WA14 .... 42 B4
Charlotte St *BURS/TUN* ST6 ...... 243 J5
  CH/BCN CH1 .... 16 D4
  CHD/CHDH SK8 .... 45 K7
  MCFLDS SK11 .... 15 H6
  STKP SK1 .... 3 L2
Charlotte St West
  MCFLDS SK11 .... 14 F5
Charlton Cl *RUNC* WA7 .... 74 A1
Charlton Rd *MCFLDN* SK10 .... 14 D5
  WARRS WA4 .... 56 F1
Charminster Cl
  WARRW/BUR WA5 .... 36 B7
Charmouth Wk *WYTH/NTH* M22 .. 63 M1
Charnock Av *NEWLW* WA12 ...... 26 F1
Charnock Rd *GOL/RIS/CU* WA3.... 29 M1
Charnville Rd *CHD/CHDH* SK8..... 44 F8
Charnwood *ALS/KID* ST7 .... 243 H3
Charnwood Cl
  GOL/RIS/CU WA3 .... 30 B7
  MCFLDN SK10 .... 14 A3
Charnwood Crs
  BRAM/HZG SK7 .... 66 D4
Charter Av *WARRW/BUR* WA5 ..... 37 G4
Charter Cl *SALE* M33 .... 42 D1
Charter Crs *GTS/LS* CH66 .... 120 E1
Charterhall Dr *CHNE* CH2 .... 17 L4
Charterhouse Rd *WLTN* L25 ...... 50 B3
Charter Rd *HALE/TIMP* WA15 ..... 42 E8
  MCFLDN SK10 .... 113 G3
Charter Wy *MCFLDN* SK10 .... 138 E1
Chartley Gv *MWCH* CW10 .... 179 K2
Chartwell Dr *NTHM/RTH* M23..... 43 K5
Chartwell Gv *HLWD* L26 .... 51 G3
Chartwell Pk *SBCH* CW11 .... 204 A8
Chase Briar Wd
  CHD/CHDH SK8 .... 65 H3
Chase Dr *GTS/LS* CH66 .... 120 E2
Chasefield *ALT* WA14 .... 61 G2
Chaser Ct *CH/BCN* CH1 .... 168 D1
Chase Wy *GTS/LS* CH66 .... 120 D2
Chatburn Av *GOL/RIS/CU* WA3 .. 23 J3
Chatburn Cl *GOL/RIS/CU* WA3 ... 29 M2
Chatcombe Rd *WYTH/NTH* M22... 63 G2
Chatfield Dr *GOL/RIS/CU* WA3 ..... 38 E1
Chatham St *EDGY/DAV* SK3 .... 2 C8
  MCFLDS SK11 .... 15 G5
Chatham Wy *CW/HAS* CW1 ...... 222 C7
Chatswood Av *OFTN* SK2 .... 46 F6
Chatsworth Av *GOL/RIS/CU* WA3.. 24 B7
  MCFLDS SK11 .... 137 L6
Chatsworth Cl *CW/SHV* CW2 ... 238 A4
  GTS/LS CH66 .... 94 C7
  HALE/TIMP WA15 .... 43 J7
  NWCHE CW9 .... 13 J9
Chatsworth Dr *CHNE* CH2 .... 146 A7
  CW/HAS CW1 .... 222 C7
  WDN WA8 .... 52 C1
Chatsworth Rd *BRAM/HZG* SK7... 66 F3
  MPL/ROM SK6 .... 67 M6
  WILM/AE SK9 .... 83 L8
Chatters Pk *RUNC* WA7 .... 74 E2
Chatterley Dr *ALS/KID* ST7 ...... 243 G5
Chatterley Rd *BURS/TUN* ST6.... 243 J8
Chatterton Dr *RUNC* WA7 .... 74 E4
Chatwell Gdns *WARRS* WA4 ...... 56 F7
Chaucer Cl *CH/BCN* CH1 .... 144 E6
Chaucer Gv *SBCH* CW11 .... 203 J4
Chaucer Pl *WARRS* WA4 .... 37 M8
Chaucer St *RUNC* WA7 .... 9 G4
Cheadle La *KNUT* WA16 .... 132 A3
Cheadle Old Rd *EDGY/DAV* SK3... 46 D5
Cheadle Rd *CHD/CHDH* SK8 ...... 45 L8
Cheadle Wd *CHD/CHDH* SK8 ..... 64 E4
Cheam Rd *HALE/TIMP* WA15...... 42 F7
Checkley Dr *BIDD* ST8 .... 227 K3
Checkley La *AUD/MAD/W* CW3 .. 261 M8
Cheddar Gv *WARRW/BUR* WA5.. 26 F5
Chedlee Dr *CHD/CHDH* SK8 ...... 64 E3
Chedlin Dr *NTHM/RTH* M23 ...... 44 A8
Chedworth Dr *NTHM/RTH* M23... 44 B8
  WDN WA8 .... 33 J8

Cheerbrook Rd *NANT* CW5 ...... 237 J8
Cheese Hill La *NWCHW* CW8 .... 127 H8
Chelford Av *GOL/RIS/CU* WA3 .... 23 K5
Chelford Cl *CH/BCN* CH1 .... 168 F2
  HALE/TIMP WA15 .... 42 E6
Chelford Gv *EDGY/DAV* SK3...... 46 D7
Chelford La *KNUT* WA16 .... 134 C3
Chelford Rd *CONG* CW12 .... 183 L8
  HOLMCH CW4 .... 158 B5
  KNUT WA16 .... 107 H4
  MCFLDN SK10 .... 109 J7
  MCFLDN SK10 .... 111 H7
  MCFLDS SK11 .... 135 J3
  SALE M33 .... 43 L2
  WILM/AE SK9 .... 64 D7
Chell St *CW/HAS* CW1 .... 18 C1
Chelmarsh Av *AIMK* WN4 .... 22 C1
Chelmsford Rd *EDGY/DAV* SK3 .... 2 B8
Chelsea Cl *BIDD* ST8 .... 227 J3
Chelston Dr *CHD/CHDH* SK8 ..... 64 C6
Cheltenham Cl *MCFLDN* SK10.... 112 C8
  WARRW/BUR WA5 .... 36 A4
Cheltenham Crs *CW/HAS* CW1 ... 221 H5
  RUNC WA7 .... 73 H6
Cheltenham Dr *NEWLW* WA12 ... 22 C7
Cheltenham Rd *EDGY/DAV* SK3... 46 A5
  EP CH65 .... 121 K1
Chemical St *NEWLW* WA12 ...... 27 H1
Chemistry *WHITCH* SY13 .... 269 K5
Chemistry La *CQ* CH5 .... 142 E8
Chemistry Rd *SPK/HALE* L24 ...... 50 C7
Chepstow Av *SALE* M33 .... 42 C1
Chepstow Cl *BIDD* ST8 .... 227 J3
  MCFLDN SK10 .... 112 C8
  WARRW/BUR WA5 .... 36 E1
  WSFD CW7 .... 177 M5
Chepstow Dr *BRAM/HZG* SK7 ...... 67 G2
Cherington Cl
  NTHM/RTH M23 .... 44 B2
  WILM/AE SK9 .... 84 F1
Cherington Crs *MCFLDS* SK11 ..... 14 C7
Cherington Rd *CHD/CHDH* SK8 .... 45 J8
Cheriton Cl *HLWD* L26 .... 50 E4
Cheriton Ri *OFTN* SK2 .... 48 A6
Cheriton Wy *CW/SHV* CW2 ...... 238 A4
Cherrington Rd *NANT* CW5 ...... 251 L1
Cherry Blossom Rd
  RUNC WA7 .... 73 M7
Cherry Cl *NSTN* CH64 .... 92 C4
Cherry Cnr *LYMM* WA13 .... 58 A6
Cherry Crs *WSFD* CW7 .... 177 J4
Cherrycroft *MPL/ROM* SK6 .... 48 E3
Cherry Dale Rd *CHSW/BR* CH4 .. 190 A1
Cherryfields Rd *MCFLDS* SK11 .. 137 M5
Cherry Gv *GTS/LS* CH66 .... 121 G3
  NANT CW5 .... 20 C7
Cherry Grove Rd *CHSE* CH3 ...... 170 A3
Cherry Hl *AUD/MAD/W* CW3 .... 267 L6
Cherry La *ALS/KID* ST7 .... 224 E6
  CONG CW12 .... 208 A4
  LYMM WA13 .... 58 B4
  NWCHW CW8 .... 128 C4
  NWCHW CW8 .... 151 M2
  SALE M33 .... 42 C2
Cherry Orchard Cl
  BRAM/HZG SK7 .... 65 K3
Cherry Orchard Rd *CQ* CH5....... 166 D7
Cherry Rd *CHSE* CH3 .... 170 A3
Cherrysutton *WDN* WA8 .... 52 B1
Cherry Tree Av *ALS/KID* ST7 ...... 225 G7
  LYMM WA13 .... 58 D2
  NWCHW CW8 .... 103 G8
  POY/DIS SK12 .... 86 F1
  RUNC WA7 .... 9 L6
  WARRW/BUR WA5 .... 35 M8
Cherry Tree Ct *OFTN* SK2 .... 47 J8
Cherry Tree Dr *BRAM/HZG* SK7... 67 G4
  STHEL WA9 .... 26 A2
Cherry Tree La *ALT* WA14 .... 60 E6
  MPL/ROM SK6 .... 48 E2
  OFTN SK2 .... 47 J7
Cherry Tree Rd *CHD/CHDH* SK8 .. 64 F3
  CW/HAS CW1 .... 221 K6
  GOL/RIS/CU WA3 .... 23 M4
  NTHM/RTH M23 .... 43 M3
Cherry V *WLTN* L25 .... 50 B1
Cherry Wk *CHD/CHDH* SK8 ...... 65 J4
  KNUT WA16 .... 132 D5
Cherrywood Crs
  NWCHW CW8 .... 103 H8
  WARRN/WOL WA2 .... 37 K2
Cheryl Ct *NWCHW* CW8 .... 128 A4
Cheryl Dr *WDN* WA8 .... 53 K3
Cheshire Cl *NEWLW* WA12 ...... 27 L1
Cheshire Ring Canal Wk
  ALS/KID ST7 .... 224 D4
  ALS/KID ST7 .... 226 A3
  ALS/KID ST7 .... 242 E2
  ALT WA14 .... 41 L7
  MCFLDN SK10 .... 87 L4
  MPL/ROM SK6 .... 48 F4
  MWCH CW10 .... 154 D4
  MWCH CW10 .... 179 J2
  NWCHW CW8 .... 129 J2
  SBCH CW11 .... 222 D1
  WARRS WA4 .... 55 J6
  WARRS WA4 .... 75 J2
  WARRS WA4 .... 101 K4
Cheshire Rd *PART* M31 .... 40 D2
Cheshire St *AUD/MAD/W* CW3 .. 263 M8
Cheshyre Dr *RUNC* WA7 .... 73 M7
Cheshyre's La *RUNC* WA7 .... 8 D9
  RUNC WA7 .... 72 C6
Chessington Cl *WARRS* WA4 ...... 56 D5
Chester Ap *CHSW/BR* CH4 ...... 192 D1
Chester Av *GOL/RIS/CU* WA3 ...... 23 K4
  HALE/TIMP WA15 .... 61 M7

  SALE M33 .... 42 B3
  WHITCH SY13 .... 269 L4
Chester Cl *ALS/KID* ST7 .... 242 D5
  CQ CH5 .... 142 B7
  IRL M44 .... 31 K7
  RUNC WA7 .... 73 M2
  WILM/AE SK9 .... 84 C2
Chester Dr *AIMK* WN4 .... 22 D2
Chesterfield Cl *WSFD* CW7 ...... 176 F3
Chestergate *EDGY/DAV* SK3 .... 2 D6
  MCFLDN SK10 .... 14 F4
  STKP SK1 .... 2 F5
Chester High Rd *NSTN* CH64 ..... 92 A2
Chester La *WSFD* CW7 .... 176 F2
Chester New Rd *WARRS* WA4 .... 55 M5
Chester Rd *ALS/KID* ST7 .... 242 D5
  ALT WA14 .... 60 D6
  BRAM/HZG SK7 .... 66 B3
  BRAM/HZG SK7 .... 85 K2
  BRAM/HZG SK7 .... 85 M1
  CHSE CH3 .... 170 A6
  CHSE CH3 .... 194 E7
  CHSE CH3 .... 211 M8
  CHSE CH3 .... 214 B2
  CHSW/BR CH4 .... 167 G7
  CQ CH5 .... 166 B8
  EP CH65 .... 121 G1
  FLINT CH6 .... 116 D7
  FROD/HEL WA6 .... 98 F6
  FROD/HEL WA6 .... 124 B2
  GTS/LS CH66 .... 94 C7
  GTS/LS CH66 .... 121 G3
  HOLMCH CW4 .... 181 H2
  KNUT WA16 .... 80 B6
  KNUT WA16 .... 105 L7
  MCFLDS SK11 .... 14 D5
  MWCH CW10 .... 179 C2
  NANT CW5 .... 218 C6
  NANT CW5 .... 236 A5
  NSTN CH64 .... 91 L5
  NWCHW CW8 .... 12 E4
  NWCHW CW8 .... 128 E8
  NWCHW CW8 .... 151 K3
  POY/DIS SK12 .... 66 B8
  RUNC WA7 .... 74 E7
  TPLY/KEL CW6 .... 149 G7
  TPLY/KEL CW6 .... 149 M6
  WARRS WA4 .... 56 F3
  WARRS WA4 .... 56 A4
  WARRS WA4 .... 75 H2
  WHITCH SY13 .... 269 M3
  WRX/GR/LL LL12 .... 210 B5
  WSFD CW7 .... 176 F2
Chester Road (East) *CQ* CH5 .... 142 D7
Chester Road Roman Rd
  KNUT WA16 .... 106 A3
Chester Road (West) *CQ* CH5 .... 142 D7
Chester Sq *CW/HAS* CW1 .... 18 E4
Chester St *CHSW/BR* CH4 .... 168 F5
  CW/HAS CW1 .... 18 F4
  EDGY/DAV SK3 .... 2 C6
  FLINT CH6 .... 116 B5
Chester Street (Heol Caer)
  FLINT CH6 .... 116 A5
Chesterton Cl *MWCH* CW10 ...... 179 L7
Chesterton Dr *CW/SHV* CW2...... 237 M3
Chesterton Gv *SBCH* CW11 ...... 203 K7
Chesterton Rd *NTHM/RTH* M23 ... 43 K4
Chester Wks *MPL/ROM* SK6 ...... 48 A3
Chester Wy *NWCHW* CW9 .... 13 G3
  NWCHE CW9 .... 13 J2
  NWCHE CW9 .... 130 C3
Chestnut Av *ALS/KID* ST7 .... 224 F5
  CHD/CHDH SK8 .... 45 L7
  CW/SHV CW2 .... 238 C7
  GTS/LS CH66 .... 120 F3
  IRL M44 .... 31 K7
  LEIGH WN7 .... 24 F1
  MCFLDN SK10 .... 15 J1
  WARRW/BUR WA5 .... 35 M6
  WDN WA8 .... 53 H2
Chestnut Cl *CHNE* CH2 .... 170 A1
  MWCH CW10 .... 179 H2
  NM/HAY SK22 .... 69 L3
  NWCHW CW8 .... 151 M2
  TPLY/KEL CW6 .... 197 K2
  WHITCH SY13 .... 269 M6
  WILM/AE SK9 .... 84 E4
Chestnut Dr *ALS/KID* ST7 .... 241 L2
  CONG CW12 .... 183 M8
  HOLMCH CW4 .... 181 K1
  LEIGH WN7 .... 24 F1
  POY/DIS SK12 .... 86 F1
  SALE M33 .... 42 D3
Chestnut Dr South *LEIGH* WN7 ... 24 F1
Chestnut Gv *CQ* CH5 .... 166 C2
  CW/HAS CW1 .... 19 J2
  GOL/RIS/CU WA3 .... 23 M4
  NWCHW CW8 .... 103 H8
  WSFD CW7 .... 177 J4
Chestnut La *LEIGH* WN7 .... 24 F1

Chichester Rd *MPL/ROM* SK6 ..... 48 C2
Chichester St *CH/BCN* CH1 .... 16 E3
Chidlow Cl *CW/SHV* CW2 .... 253 L1
  WDN WA8 .... 53 G7
Chidwall Rd *WYTH/NTH* M22 ...... 63 K2
Chigwell Cl *WYTH/NTH* M22 ...... 44 E7
Childer Crs *GTS/LS* CH66 .... 94 B5
Childer Gdns *GTS/LS* CH66 .... 94 B5
Child's La *CONG* CW12 .... 206 E6
Childwall Rd *GTS/LS* CH66 .... 94 E4
Chilham Cl *WSFD* CW7 .... 177 J5
Chilham Pl *MCFLDS* SK11 .... 137 M6
Chilington Av *WDN* WA8 .... 6 C5
Chilmark Dr *NTHM/RTH* M23 ...... 44 A6
Chiltern Av *MCFLDS* SK11 .... 14 A7
  WARRN/WOL WA2 .... 37 G3
Chiltern Cl *AIMK* WN4 .... 22 C2
  BRAM/HZG SK7 .... 66 B3
  CHSW/BR CH4 .... 169 H7
  NWCHW CW8 .... 152 A2
Chiltern Crs *WARRN/WOL* WA2 ... 37 G1
Chiltern Dr *HALE/TIMP* WA15 ..... 61 M2
  OFTN SK2 .... 47 K8
Chiltern Gdns *SALE* M33 .... 43 J4
Chiltern Rd *GOL/RIS/CU* WA3 ...... 37 G1
  STHEL WA9 .... 26 A1
  WARRN/WOL WA2 .... 37 G3
Chiltern Wy *WSFD* CW7 .... 177 H5
Chilton Dr *GTS/LS* CH66 .... 120 F2
Chilwell Cl *WDN* WA8 .... 33 K8
Chilworth Cl *CW/SHV* CW2 ...... 238 C4
China La *WARRS* WA4 .... 56 C2
The Chines *NWCHW* CW8 .... 127 K7
Chinley Cl *BRAM/HZG* SK7 .... 65 L1
  HTNM SK4 .... 46 B1
  SALE M33 .... 43 K1
Chippenham Av *OFTN* SK2 .... 47 K5
Chippingdall Cl
  WARRW/BUR WA5 .... 36 C7
Chipstead Cl *NWCHW* CW8 ...... 129 G8
Chirk Cl *CHNE* CH2 .... 145 M6
Chirk Pl *WSFD* CW7 .... 177 J5
Chiseldon Av *WYTH/NTH* M22 .... 63 L2
Chiswick Cl *RUNC* WA7 .... 74 D5
Chiswick Gdns *WARRS* WA4 ...... 56 F6
Chiswick Rd *DID/WITH* M20 ...... 45 J3
Chisworth Cl *BRAM/HZG* SK7 ...... 65 L1
Chokeberry Cl *ALT* WA14 .... 42 B4
Chollerton Cl *KNUT* WA16 .... 59 J8
Cholmondeley Av *ALT* WA14 ...... 42 E4
Cholmondeley La *MALPAS* SY14... 232 E3
Cholmondeley Rd *EP* CH65 .... 94 F8
  MALPAS SY14 .... 246 E5
  NANT CW5 .... 246 A1
  RUNC WA7 .... 73 K7
Cholmondeley St
  MCFLDS SK11 .... 15 C8
  WDN WA8 .... 53 C8
Cholmondley Ri *MALPAS* SY14 ... 247 G8
Chorley Hall Cl *WILM/AE* SK9 .... 109 M3
Chorley Hall La *WILM/AE* SK9 ... 109 M3
Chorley Rd *SALE* M33 .... 43 L2
Chorley's La *WDN* WA8 .... 53 K1
Chorley Stock La *NANT* CW5..... 249 G3
Chorley St *WARRN/WOL* WA2 .... 22 C6
Chorlton Cl *RUNC* WA7 .... 74 D3
Chorlton Dr *CHD/CHDH* SK8 ...... 45 L6
Chorlton La *CW/SHV* CW2 ...... 254 A3
Chowley Oak La *CHSE* CH3 ...... 213 M7
Chretien Rd *WYTH/NTH* M22 ...... 44 D2
Chrimes Dr *NWCHW* CW8 .... 150 F6
Christchurch Av *CW/SHV* CW2 ...... 18 A9
Christie Cl *GTS/LS* CH66 .... 94 A3
Christie St *STKP* SK1 .... 3 K8
  WDN WA8 .... 53 K3
Christleton Av *CW/SHV* CW2 ...... 220 D7
  NWCHW CW9 .... 130 A8
Christleton Ct *RUNC* WA7 .... 54 C8
Christleton Dr *GTS/LS* CH66 ...... 94 E6
Christleton Rd *CHSE* CH3 .... 170 A3
Chudleigh Cl *ALT* WA14 .... 42 B6
  BRAM/HZG SK7 .... 66 A1
  HLWD L26 .... 50 E3
Church Bank *CHSE* CH3 .... 214 B2
Church Bk *CHF/WBR* SK23 .... 89 K5
Church Brow *ALT* WA14 .... 61 H2
Church Cl *BIDD* ST8 .... 227 K6
  NWCHW CW9 .... 128 D3
Church College Cl *CH/BCN* CH1 ... 16 E1
Church Ct *CHSE* CH3 .... 148 F4
Church Cft *CHSW/BR* CH4 ...... 191 C6
Church Dr *NEWLW* WA12 .... 27 J3
  WARRN/WOL WA2 .... 38 A7
Church End *SPK/HALE* L24 .... 71 K3
Church Farm *NANT* CW5 .... 249 L8
Churchfield Rd *FROD/HEL* WA6 ... 99 J5
Churchfields *ALT* WA14 .... 61 H3
  AUD/MAD/W CW3 .... 264 A5
  FROD/HEL WA6 .... 98 C3
  GOL/RIS/CU WA3 .... 29 H5
  KNUT WA16 .... 107 J2
  NANT CW5 .... 253 H4
  NWCHW CW9 .... 129 H1
  NWCHW CW8 .... 152 B2
  WDN WA8 .... 34 B7
Churchgate *STKP* SK1 .... 3 G5
Church Gn *LYMM* WA13 .... 40 B4
Church Gv *BRAM/HZG* SK7 .... 66 E2
Church Hall Cl *CH/BCN* CH1 ...... 144 F8
Church Hl *KNUT* WA16 .... 107 G2
Church La *ALS/KID* ST7 .... 225 H4
  ALS/KID ST7 .... 226 E5
  AUD/MAD/W CW3 .... 255 K7
  BRAM/HZG SK7 .... 85 J2
  CHNE CH2 .... 121 H8
  CHNE CH2 .... 121 J8
  CHNE CH2 .... 122 A5
  CHNE CH2 .... 145 K5

CHSE CH3 .... 146 F8
CHSE CH3 .... 211 M1
CHSE CH3 .... 228 E3
CONG CW12 .... 185 K3
CQ CH5 .... 166 D4
CW/SHV CW2 .... 237 L5
GOL/RIS/CU WA3 .... 23 K5
GOL/RIS/CU WA3 .... 29 M1
GTS/LS CH66 .... 94 D8
KNUT WA16 .... 82 B7
MCFLDN SK10 .... 113 L8
MCFLDS SK11 .... 137 H4
MCFLDS SK11 .... 161 K4
MCFLDS SK11 .... 162 F1
MPL/ROM SK6 .... 48 E6
MPL/ROM SK6 .... 48 C2
MPL/ROM SK6 .... 49 G7
NANT CW5 .... 20 E7
NM/HAY SK22 .... 69 J4
NSTN CH64 .... 91 L5
NWCHW CW8 .... 128 D3
SBCH CW11 .... 204 E6
SBCH CW11 .... 205 M7
WARRS WA4 .... 57 H3
WHITCH SY13 .... 271 H7
WILM/AE SK9 .... 110 A2
Churchley Cl EDGY/DAV SK3 .... 46 A6
Churchley Rd EDGY/DAV SK3 .... 46 A5 ⬛
Church Mdw NWCHW CW8 .... 102 D8 ⬛
WHITCH SY13 .... 270 A3
Church Meadow Wk
WDN WA8 .... 52 B7 ⬛
Churchmere Cl CW/HAS CW1 .... 221 J5 ⬛
Church Ms KNUT WA16 .... 107 H2 ⬛
MCFLDN SK10 .... 113 G4 ⬛
NWCHE CW9 .... 104 F3
Church Pde EP CH65 .... 10 F5 ⬛
Church Ri NWCHW CW8 .... 152 B2
Church Rd ALS/KID ST7 .... 224 B8
BIDD ST8 .... 227 K5
CH/BCN CH1 .... 144 A2 ⬛
CHD/CHDH SK8 .... 45 G7
CHD/CHDH SK8 .... 65 H5
CHSE CH3 .... 148 F5
CHSE CH3 .... 215 C7
CHSE CH3 .... 244 C3
CHSW/BR CH4 .... 167 J8
CHSW/BR CH4 .... 192 E2
FROD/HEL WA6 .... 99 J5
HLWD L26 .... 50 F3
HTNM SK4 .... 2 D3
LYMM WA13 .... 58 D2
MALPAS SY14 .... 245 H2
MPL/ROM SK6 .... 49 L6
NANT CW5 .... 219 K6
NM/HAY SK22 .... 69 J5
NWCHE CW9 .... 13 K1
NWCHW CW8 .... 102 D8
NWCHW CW8 .... 129 H2
SPK/HALE L24 .... 71 L4
WILM/AE SK9 .... 83 L8
WILM/AE SK9 .... 84 D1
WLTN L25 .... 50 A1
WYTH/NTH M22 .... 44 D3
Church Rd South WLTN L25 .... 50 A2
Churchside MCFLDS SK11 .... 15 H5
Churchston Av BRAM/HZG SK7 .... 66 A2
Church St ALS/KID ST7 .... 226 B8
ALS/KID ST7 .... 226 C6
ALS/KID ST7 .... 242 D3 ⬛
ALT WA14 .... 42 D7
CH/BCN CH1 .... 17 H2 ⬛
CH/BCN CH1 .... 17 H2 ⬛
CHD/CHDH SK8 .... 45 K6 ⬛
CHSE CH3 .... 172 C2
CHSE CH3 .... 228 E2 ⬛
EP CH65 .... 10 F5 ⬛
FROD/HEL WA6 .... 99 H4
GOL/RIS/CU WA3 .... 23 H3 ⬛
HTNM SK4 .... 2 E2
MALPAS SY14 .... 258 A3
MCFLDN SK10 .... 15 G5
MCFLDN SK10 .... 113 H4
MPL/ROM SK6 .... 48 F6 ⬛
MPL/ROM SK6 .... 49 G7 ⬛
NEWLW WA12 .... 22 E8
NWCHE CW9 .... 104 A4
NWCHE CW9 .... 104 E7
NWCHE CW9 .... 153 M4 ⬛
NWCHE CW9 .... 154 A1
NWCHW CW8 .... 128 C3
RUNC WA7 .... 9 G1
SBCH CW11 .... 204 B6
TPLY/KEL CW6 .... 149 J8
WARR WA1 .... 5 K6
WDN WA8 .... 53 G7
WHITCH SY13 .... 270 A4
WILM/AE SK9 .... 84 B5
WILM/AE SK9 .... 177 L3
Church Street (Heol-yr-eglwys)
FLINT CH6 .... 116 A6
Church St North TPLY/KEL CW6 .... 149 K7
Church St West MCFLDS SK11 .... 14 F5
Church Ter WILM/AE SK9 .... 64 D8
Church Vw AUD/MAD/W CW3 .... 264 A8
CQ CH5 .... 166 F1
FROD/HEL WA6 .... 126 B2
KNUT WA16 .... 107 G2
LYMM WA13 .... 40 B8
Church Wks CHSE CH3 .... 170 C4
Churchward Cl CHNE CH2 .... 145 M8
Churchway MCFLDN SK10 .... 137 L2
Church Wy CH/BCN CH1 .... 144 E7 ⬛
FROD/HEL WA6 .... 124 D3
NANT CW5 .... 253 H4
Churchway Rd SPK/HALE L24 .... 71 G2
Churchwood Rd DID/WITH M20 .... 45 H1
Churchwood Wy LYMM WA13 .... 58 F1
Churton Av SALE M33 .... 42 E1
Churton Cl CW/SHV CW2 .... 253 L1 ⬛
NWCHE CW9 .... 129 L8 ⬛
Churton Dr WHITCH SY13 .... 270 B5
Churton Rd CHSE CH3 .... 228 E2
Churton St CHSE CH3 .... 170 A2

Cicely Mill La KNUT WA16 .... 80 C1
Cinder Cl CHSE CH3 .... 146 F7
Cinder Hl NWCHW CW8 .... 152 L6
Cinder-hill La ALS/KID ST7 .... 225 L6
Cinder La CHSE CH3 .... 146 F8
KNUT WA16 .... 134 C5
MCFLDS SK11 .... 134 E3
NANT CW5 .... 236 C2
NWCHE CW9 .... 131 G4
WARRS WA4 .... 57 M4
Cinnamon La WARRN/WOL WA2 .... 37 M1
Cinnamon La North
WARRN/WOL WA2 .... 28 F8
Circle Av NANT CW5 .... 237 L7
The Circle CW/SHV CW2 .... 238 D3
KNUT WA16 .... 80 C2
Circular Dr CHSW/BR CH4 .... 168 E8
City Rd CH/BCN CH1 .... 17 J4
City Walls Rd CH/BCN CH1 .... 16 E5
Civic Gn WHITCH SY13 .... 270 C5
Civic Wy EP CH65 .... 10 D7
WDN WA8 .... 179 J3
Clair Av CQ CH5 .... 167 G1
Clamhunger La KNUT WA16 .... 80 C5
Clandon Av BURS/TUN ST6 .... 243 L8
Clanfield Av WDN8 .... 52 C1
Clanway St BURS/TUN ST6 .... 243 K7
Clapgate MPL/ROM SK6 .... 48 A3 ⬛
Clap Gate Crs WDN SK8 .... 52 B7
Clap Gates Crs WARRW/BUR WA5 .... 4 E3
Clap Gates Rd WARRW/BUR WA5 .... 4 B8
Clare Av CHNE CH2 .... 17 M1
WILM/AE SK9 .... 84 C1
Clare Dr CW/SHV CW2 .... 237 M3
EP CH65 .... 121 H3
MCFLDN SK10 .... 138 C1
Claremont Av ALT WA14 .... 42 D4
Claremont Av NWCHE CW9 .... 153 M1 ⬛
CQ CH5 .... 142 E6
MPL/ROM SK6 .... 48 C6
WDN WA8 .... 34 C8 ⬛
Claremont Dr ALT WA14 .... 42 D4
WDN WA8 .... 34 B8
Claremont Gv DID/WITH M20 .... 45 G1
HALE/TIMP WA15 .... 61 L1
Claremont Rd CHD/CHDH SK8 .... 65 G4
CW/SHV CW2 .... 18 C8
GOL/RIS/CU WA3 .... 24 D8
OFTN SK2 .... 47 H8
WARR WA1 .... 9 K3
Clarence Av CHSE CH3 .... 170 B2
WARRW/BUR WA5 .... 35 K6 ⬛
WDN WA8 .... 34 A8
Clarence Ct WARR WA1 .... 84 A6
Clarence Gv CW/HAS CW1 .... 18 C2 ⬛
Clarence Rd HALE/TIMP WA15 .... 61 M1
MCFLDN SK10 .... 113 G4
WARRS WA4 .... 57 H2
Clarence St CQ CH5 .... 142 B7 ⬛
GOL/RIS/CU WA3 .... 23 G3
RUNC WA7 .... 8 F1
WARR WA1 .... 37 L5
Clarence Ter RUNC WA7 .... 9 C1
Clarendon Av HALE/TIMP WA15 .... 42 E7
HTNM SK4 .... 46 B1 ⬛
Clarendon Cl CHSW/BR CH4 .... 169 L6
RUNC WA7 .... 74 D5
Clarendon Ct WARRN/WOL WA2 .... 27 M8
Clarendon Dr MCFLDN SK10 .... 139 C3
Clarendon Rd BRAM/HZG SK7 .... 66 F1
IRL M44 .... 31 L5
Clarendon St RDSH SK5 .... 3 G1
Clare Pl WARR WA1 .... 177 J5
Clares Farm Cl WARR WA1 .... 38 F5 ⬛
Clare St ALS/KID ST7 .... 226 C6
ALS/KID ST7 .... 226 E8
Clarke Av GOL/RIS/CU WA3 .... 24 F8
WARRS WA4 .... 56 D2
Clarke Crs HALE/TIMP WA15 .... 62 B1
Clarke La MCFLDN SK10 .... 112 F7
MCFLDS SK11 .... 139 L4
Clarke Ter MCFLDS SK11 .... 15 G9
Clary Meadow NWCHW CW8 .... 12 F1
NWCHW CW8 .... 129 L3
Claude St WARR WA1 .... 5 K4
Claughton Av CW/SHV CW2 .... 238 D3
Claverton Cl RUNC WA7 .... 73 H6 ⬛
Claverton Rd NTHM/RTH M23 .... 43 L8
Claydon Ct HLWD L26 .... 51 G3
Clay Heyes MCFLDS SK11 .... 135 G1
Clayhill Gn GTS/LS CH66 .... 94 C5
Clay La CQ CH5 .... 142 C8
CW/HAS CW1 .... 222 D6
HALE/TIMP WA15 .... 43 J8
KNUT WA16 .... 134 A4
MALPAS SY14 .... 232 A4
NTHM/RTH M23 .... 43 M8
SBCH CW11 .... 203 G8
WARRW/BUR WA5 .... 26 E6
WILM/AE SK9 .... 64 C7
WILM/AE SK9 .... 83 J8
WSFD CW7 .... 152 B8
Claypit Rd CHSW/BR CH4 .... 169 H7
Claypits La CHSE CH3 .... 170 F8
Claypit St WHITCH SY13 .... 270 A4
Clayton Av CONG CW12 .... 184 F7
DID/WITH M20 .... 45 H1
GOL/RIS/CU WA3 .... 23 L4
Clayton Crs RUNC WA7 .... 8 E4
Clayton Dr WHITCH SY13 .... 270 A3
Clayton Rd GOL/RIS/CU WA3 .... 29 M6
Cleaver Ms MCFLDS SK11 .... 138 C3 ⬛
Cleave Rd CH/BCN CH1 .... 144 E8 ⬛
Cledford Crs MWCH CW10 .... 179 K6
Cledford La MWCH CW10 .... 179 M5
Cleethorpes Rd RUNC WA7 .... 74 C5
Cleeve Rd NTHM/RTH M23 .... 44 A7
Cleeve Wy CHD/CHDH SK8 .... 65 H6
Clegg St WARRN/WOL WA2 .... 5 H3
Clegg St MPL/ROM SK6 .... 47 M1 ⬛
Clelland St WARRS WA4 .... 56 C1 ⬛

Clement Rd MPL/ROM SK6 .... 49 H5
Clement St HTNM SK4 .... 2 E2
Clemley La TPLY/KEL CW6 .... 149 K6
Clerewood Av CHD/CHDH SK8 .... 64 B5
Clevedon Cl MCFLDS SK11 .... 14 B7
Cleveland Dr GOL/RIS/CU WA3 .... 23 K4
GTS/LS CH66 .... 94 A6
Cleveland Gv CQ CH5 .... 142 E6 ⬛
Cleveland Rd HALE/TIMP WA15 .... 61 M1
WARRN/WOL WA2 .... 37 H1
Cleveland Wy WSFD CW7 .... 177 H5
Cleveleys Av CHD/CHDH SK8 .... 64 B3
WDN WA8 .... 53 K1
Cleveleys Rd
WARRW/BUR WA5 .... 36 B8 ⬛
Cleves Cl CH/BCN CH1 .... 144 D6
Clifden Dr WYTH/NTH M22 .... 63 L2
Cliffe Rd CH/HAS CW1 .... 221 H5
NSTN CH64 .... 91 M7
Cliffe St WARR WA1 .... 4 D6
WDN WA8 .... 7 L2
Cliff La LYMM WA13 .... 58 B6
MCFLDN SK10 .... 139 H2
NWCHW CW8 .... 101 J8
WARRS WA4 .... 57 M5
WARRS WA4 .... 57 K2
Cliffmere Cl CHD/CHDH SK8 .... 64 F1
Clifford Av HALE/TIMP WA15 .... 43 C6
Clifford Dr CHSW/BR CH4 .... 168 F7
Clifford Gv CW/HAS CW1 .... 222 C8
Clifford Pl WSFD CW7 .... 177 J5 ⬛
Clifford Rd MCFLDS SK11 .... 14 B6
POY/DIS SK12 .... 66 C8
WARRW/BUR WA5 .... 36 A8
WILM/AE SK9 .... 83 M6
Cliff Rd NWCHW CW8 .... 101 K8
WILM/AE SK9 .... 84 B4
Cliff Side WILM/AE SK9 .... 84 B4
Clifton Av CHD/CHDH SK8 .... 64 A2
CW/SHV CW2 .... 29 K1
GOL/RIS/CU WA3 .... 29 K1
HALE/TIMP WA15 .... 42 E7
HLWD L26 .... 50 E3
PS/BROM CH62 .... 93 L1
Clifton Cl WARR WA1 .... 38 C5
Clifton Crs FROD/HEL WA6 .... 99 J3
Clifton Dr CH/BCN CH1 .... 168 E1
CHD/CHDH SK8 .... 44 F7
CHD/CHDH SK8 .... 64 A2
MPL/ROM SK6 .... 48 F5
NWCHE CW9 .... 13 J9
WILM/AE SK9 .... 83 L8
Clifton Gdns EP CH65 .... 121 J1 ⬛
Clifton La RUNC WA7 .... 99 L1
Cliftonmill Mdw
GOL/RIS/CU WA3 .... 22 F4 ⬛
Clifton Park Rd OFTN SK2 .... 47 G7
Clifton Rd LEIGH WN7 .... 24 E2
RUNC WA7 .... 9 H8
RUNC WA7 .... 73 J6
SALE M33 .... 43 H1 ⬛
SBCH CW11 .... 205 K5
Clifton St CW/SHV CW2 .... 18 D6
WARRS WA4 .... 5 K9
WILM/AE SK9 .... 110 A3
Cliftonville Rd WARR WA1 .... 38 C6
Clinton Cl WDN WA8 .... 52 A4
Clinton Vw WDN WA8 .... 52 A4
Clitheroe Rd NWCHW CW8 .... 128 D3
Clive Av WARRN/WOL WA2 .... 37 J3
Clive Back La WSFD CW7 .... 178 C5
Cliveden Rd CHSW/BR CH4 .... 168 F7
Clivegreen La WSFD CW7 .... 178 C4
Clive St WSFD CW7 .... 178 C4
Clive St BURS/TUN ST6 .... 243 L8
Clock Face Rd WDN WA8 .... 34 E5
Cloister Rd HTNM SK4 .... 45 K2
The Cloisters CHD/CHDH SK8 .... 46 A7 ⬛
Clos Coed CQ CH5 .... 142 E8
The Close ALS/KID ST7 .... 241 G1
ALT WA14 .... 42 C7
CH/BCN CH1 .... 144 A3
CQ CH5 .... 166 B3
MPL/ROM SK6 .... 49 G3
NWCHW CW8 .... 12 C6
Cloud Vw CONG CW12 .... 208 A2
Clough Av MPL/ROM SK6 .... 49 J6
SALE M33 .... 42 D3
WARRN/WOL WA2 .... 37 H2 ⬛
WILM/AE SK9 .... 84 B2
Clough Bank MCFLDN SK10 .... 112 F5
Clough Hall Dr ALS/KID ST7 .... 242 F5
Clough Hall Rd ALS/KID ST7 .... 242 E5
Clough La NWCHW CW8 .... 12 C7
Clough Rd SPK/HALE L24 .... 50 D8
WSFD CW7 .... 177 L3
Clough Side MPL/ROM SK6 .... 49 J5
Cloughside POY/DIS SK12 .... 68 E6
The Clough RUNC WA7 .... 74 B7
Clovelly Av WARRW/BUR WA5 .... 35 L5 ⬛
Clovelly Gv RUNC WA7 .... 74 B7
Clovelly Rd OFTN SK2 .... 47 J4
Clover Av CHD/CHDH SK8 .... 46 D7 ⬛
FROD/HEL WA6 .... 99 K5
HLWD L26 .... 50 D2
Clover Ct RUNC WA7 .... 74 B7 ⬛
Cloverdale CHD/CHDH SK8 .... 12 B5
Cloverdale Rd MCFLDS SK11 .... 138 B7 ⬛
Clover Dr WILM/AE SK9 .... 84 D3
Clover Dr WSFD CW7 .... 177 K1
Cloverfield Gdns GTS/LS CH66 .... 94 D5
Cloverfields CW/HAS CW1 .... 222 B8
Cloverfields La CHSW/BR CH4 .... 168 F7
Cloverley Dr HALE/TIMP WA15 .... 43 G8
Clover Pl CHSW/BR CH4 .... 168 F7
Clover Rd HALE/TIMP WA15 .... 43 G7
MPL/ROM SK6 .... 48 E1 ⬛
Clowes Av ALS/KID ST7 .... 241 M1
Clowes St MCFLDS SK11 .... 14 D6
Clumber Cl POY/DIS SK12 .... 86 E1
Clumber Rd POY/DIS SK12 .... 86 E1
Clutha Rd EDGY/DAV SK3 .... 46 F8

CHD/CHDH SK8 .... 64 E3
Combermere Cl
CHD/CHDH SK8 .... 45 M8 ⬛
Comber Wy KNUT WA16 .... 107 G4
Comboy Dr NWCHE CW9 .... 130 C6
Combs Cl NM/HAY SK22 .... 69 G4
Comfrey Gv HLWD L26 .... 50 E2 ⬛
Commercial Av CHD/CHDH SK8 .... 64 E7
Commercial Rd BRAM/HZG SK7 .... 66 F5
BRAM/HZG SK7 .... 15 H4
Common Farm La
MCFLDS SK11 .... 134 E3
Commonhall St CH/BCN CH1 .... 16 F6
Common La AUD/MAD/W CW3 .... 254 E6
CHSE CH3 .... 171 G8
FROD/HEL WA6 .... 123 K3
GOL/RIS/CU WA3 .... 24 D8
MCFLDS SK11 .... 134 E3
NWCHE CW9 .... 131 L7
TPLY/KEL CW6 .... 173 J5
WARRS WA4 .... 56 E2
WARRS WA4 .... 76 E4
WSFD CW7 .... 152 C7
Common Rd NEWLW WA12 .... 26 E1
Commonside FROD/HEL WA6 .... 125 G3
Commons MI SBCH CW11 .... 204 B5
The Commons SBCH CW11 .... 204 B6
Common St NEWLW WA12 .... 26 E1
Commonwealth Cl
WSFD CW7 .... 177 J6 ⬛
Company's Cl RUNC WA7 .... 72 F6 ⬛
Compass Cl RUNC WA7 .... 74 D7
Compstall Rd MPL/ROM SK6 .... 48 D2
Compton Dr NTHM/RTH M23 .... 63 G2 ⬛
Compton Pl CHSW/BR CH4 .... 169 G6 ⬛
EP CH65 .... 10 D7
Compton Wy HLWD L26 .... 50 E6
Concorde Pl
WARRN/WOL WA2 .... 37 K2 ⬛
Condliffe Cl SBCH CW11 .... 204 B5
Conery Cl FROD/HEL WA6 .... 98 C8
Conery La WHITCH SY13 .... 268 D8
Coney Gv NTHM/RTH M23 .... 44 A5
RUNC WA7 .... 74 B7 ⬛
Congleton Cl WILM/AE SK9 .... 110 A4
Congleton Edge Rd
CONG CW12 .... 208 B7
Congleton La MCFLDS SK11 .... 135 H4
Congleton Rd ALS/KID ST7 .... 226 E4
ALS/KID ST7 .... 242 D3
BIDD ST8 .... 227 K3
CHSW/BR CH4 .... 167 J8
CONG CW12 .... 158 F7
CONG CW12 .... 184 D5
CONG CW12 .... 206 E7
CONG CW12 .... 225 L1
MCFLDN SK10 .... 110 A6
MCFLDS SK11 .... 138 A8
MCFLDS SK11 .... 160 C8
MCFLDS SK11 .... 161 K5
SBCH CW11 .... 204 B5
SBCH CW11 .... 204 C4
SBCH CW11 .... 205 M7
Congleton Rd North
ALS/KID ST7 .... 225 L8
Congleton Rd South
ALS/KID ST7 .... 242 D2
Conifer Cl GTS/LS CH66 .... 121 G4
Conifer Gv WARRW/BUR WA5 .... 35 M5
The Conifers ALS/KID ST7 .... 241 H1
Coniston Av CONG CW12 .... 206 F2
SALE M33 .... 43 J2
WARRW/BUR WA5 .... 35 K8
WSFD CW7 .... 177 J2 ⬛
Coniston Cl GTS/LS CH66 .... 94 A3
NANT CW5 .... 21 J4
RUNC WA7 .... 73 K6
WILM/AE SK9 .... 109 C5 ⬛
Coniston Dr FROD/HEL WA6 .... 99 K4
HOLMCH CW4 .... 180 F1
WILM/AE SK9 .... 64 C8
Coniston Rd CHD/CHDH SK8 .... 45 H6
CHNE CH2 .... 145 M7
MPL/ROM SK6 .... 67 K4
NSTN CH64 .... 91 L6
PART M31 .... 31 J8
Coniston Wk HALE/TIMP WA15 .... 43 K7
Coniston Wy MCFLDS SK11 .... 137 M7
Conleach Rd SPK/HALE L24 .... 70 E1
WARR WA1 .... 37 L5
Connaught Av CQ CH5 .... 142 B6 ⬛
Connaught Cl WILM/AE SK9 .... 84 C4 ⬛
Connaught Dr NEWLW WA12 .... 27 J2
Connell Rd NTHM/RTH M23 .... 44 A6 ⬛
Connor Wy CHD/CHDH SK8 .... 44 F8
Conrad Cl CW/HAS CW1 .... 19 K3
Conroy Wy NEWLW WA12 .... 27 J3
Consett Av NTHM/RTH M23 .... 44 A6
Consort Cl MCFLDN SK10 .... 112 C6
Consort Pl ALT WA14 .... 61 H1
Constable Dr MPL/ROM SK6 .... 49 H4
WILM/AE SK9 .... 84 C4
Constables Cl RUNC WA7 .... 74 A3 ⬛
Constance Rd PART M31 .... 31 J4
Constance Wy WDN WA8 .... 53 G7 ⬛
Consul St WYTH/NTH M22 .... 44 E3 ⬛
Convamore Rd
BRAM/HZG SK7 .... 65 K5 ⬛
Conway Av IRL M44 .... 31 M4
WARRW/BUR WA5 .... 36 F2
WSFD CW7 .... 177 J5 ⬛
Conway Cl CHSW/BR CH4 .... 168 D7
CW/HAS CW1 .... 221 J4
KNUT WA16 .... 107 G4
WARRW/BUR WA5 .... 35 M6 ⬛
Conway Crs MCFLDN SK10 .... 15 L2
Conway Dr BRAM/HZG SK7 .... 66 C3
HALE/TIMP WA15 .... 43 H8 ⬛
NEWLW WA12 .... 27 L1
Conway Rd BIDD ST8 .... 227 J6
CHD/CHDH SK8 .... 64 E2
SALE M33 .... 43 K1
Coogee Av WARRW/BUR WA5 .... 35 L5 ⬛
Cooke's La NWCHE CW9 .... 130 F6
Cooke St BRAM/HZG SK7 .... 66 D1
Cook's Br WRX/GR/LL LL12 .... 210 E7
Cooks La WHITCH SY13 .... 259 K6
Cooksmere La SBCH CW11 .... 203 M3

Cook St EDGY/DAV SK3 .... 2 E6
EP CH65 .... 10 F6
Coole La AUD/MAD/W CW3 ...... 263 J7
AUD/MAD/W CW3 .... 273 J1
NANT CW5 .... 251 K2
Coombe Dr RUNC WA7 .... 8 F7
Coombes Av MPL/ROM SK6 ...... 48 F7
Coombes St OFTN SK2 .... 47 H7
Co-operative St BRAM/HZG SK7 .. 66 E1
Cooper Av NEWLW WA12 .... 26 F1
WARRN/WOL WA2 .... 37 H2
Coope Rd MCFLDN SK10 ...... 112 E5
Coopers Cft CHSE CH3 .... 170 A5
Cooper St BRAM/HZG SK7 ...... 66 F1
CONG CW12 .... 207 L1
RUNC WA7 .... 9 G1
STKP SK1 .... 3 H9
WDN WA8 .... 7 J2
Coopers Wy BIDD ST8 .... 227 H4
Cope Av NANT CW5 .... 20 C9
Copeland Gv RUNC WA7 .... 73 L7
Copeland Rd WARRS WA4 .... 56 B2
Cope's Av BURS/TUN ST6 .... 243 L8
Copes La NANT CW5 .... 20 B7
Copeswood Cl
CHSW/BR CH4 .... 190 C1
Cop Meadow MCFLDS SK11 ...... 162 F2
Coppenhall Heyes
WYTH/NTH M22 .... 44 E3
Copperbeech Cl
WYTH/NTH M22 .... 44 E3
Copperfield Cl
GOL/RIS/CU WA3 .... 29 J7
POY/DIS SK12 .... 86 D2
Copperfields TPLY/KEL CW6 ...... 197 K2
WILM/AE SK9 .... 84 C4
Copperhill Cl CONG CW12 ...... 208 B5
Coppermine La MALPAS SY14 ...... 232 B3
Copper St MCFLDS SK11 .... 15 K8
Copperwood Dr RAIN/WH L35 ...... 32 E2
Coppice Av SALE M33 .... 42 D2
Coppice Cl BIDD ST8 .... 227 K5
NANT CW5 .... 237 K6
Coppice Dr MWCH CW10 .... 179 L6
POY/DIS SK12 .... 87 H1
WYTH/NTH M22 .... 44 D3
Coppice Gn CHNE CH2 .... 97 J8
WARRN/BUR WA5 .... 36 B2
Coppice La POY/DIS SK12 ...... 68 A6
RAIN/WH L35 .... 32 B5
Coppice Ri MCFLDS SK11 ...... 138 D7
Coppice Rd ALS/KID ST7 ...... 242 C4
NANT CW5 .... 237 K6
POY/DIS SK12 .... 87 H1
SBCH CW11 .... 222 F4
The Coppice CHF/WBR SK23 ...... 89 M7
HALE/TIMP WA15 .... 62 B4
NANT CW5 .... 251 M1
NWCHE CW9 .... 130 C1
NWCHW CW8 .... 127 J7
SBCH CW11 .... 203 L5
Coppice Wy WILM/AE SK9 ...... 84 E1
Coppins Cl CHSE CH3 .... 170 A2
FROD/HEL WA6 .... 124 B1
The Coppins
WARRN/WOL WA2 .... 37 J2
WILM/AE SK9 .... 83 L8
Copse Av WYTH/NTH M22 ...... 63 L1
The Copse HALE/TIMP WA15 ...... 62 D5
MPL/ROM SK6 .... 49 J4
NEWLW WA12 .... 22 A8
RUNC WA7 .... 74 A6
WRX/GR/LL LL12 .... 210 A5
Copthorne Cl CONG CW12 ...... 207 M2
Copthorne Dr
AUD/MAD/W CW3 .... 273 M1
Coral Av CHD/CHDH SK8 ...... 65 G3
Coral Rd CHD/CHDH SK8 ...... 65 G3
Corbar Rd RUNC WA7 .... 47 G7
Corbet Av WARRN/WOL WA2 ...... 5 G1
Corbet Cl MKTDR TF9 .... 274 A8
Corbet St WARRN/WOL WA2 ...... 5 G1
Corcoran Dr MPL/ROM SK6 ...... 48 F2
Corda Av WYTH/NTH M22 ...... 44 D4
Corfe Crs BRAM/HZG SK7 ...... 66 D3
Corfe Wy WSFD CW7 .... 177 J5
Corks La POY/DIS SK12 ...... 68 E7
Corley Av EDGY/DAV SK3 ...... 45 M5
Cormorant Cl CW/HAS CW1 ...... 19 M3
Cormorant Dr RUNC WA7 ...... 8 D3
Cornbrook Rd MCFLDS SK11 .. 138 C8
Corner Cft CHSE CH3 .... 170 A2
Cornerhouse La WDN WA8 ...... 52 D1
The Corners NWCHW CW8 ...... 128 C5
Cornfield Cl GTS/LS CH66 ...... 120 C7
MCFLDN SK10 .... 138 C1
SALE M33 .... 43 M1
Cornfield Dr WYTH/NTH M22 ...... 63 J1
Cornfield Rd BIDD ST8 ...... 227 K5
MPL/ROM SK6 .... 48 E1
Cornforth Wy WDN WA8 ...... 52 F1
Corn Hey Rd SALE M33 .... 42 C2
Cornishway WYTH/NTH M22 ...... 63 K4
Cornubia Rd WDN WA8 .... 7 M6
Cornwall Av RUNC WA7 ...... 9 G3
Cornwall Cl CONG CW12 ...... 208 A4
MCFLDN SK10 .... 137 L3
MPL/ROM SK6 .... 67 L5
Cornwall Gv CW/HAS CW1 ...... 18 C2
Cornwall Rd CHD/CHDH SK8 .. 64 B4
CHNE CH2 .... 145 L5
CQ CH5 .... 142 B8
IRL M44 .... 31 K7
WDN WA8 .... 53 H1
Cornwall St CH/BCN CH1 ...... 17 G2
WARR WA1 .... 37 L5
Cornwell Cl WILM/AE SK9 ...... 84 D4
Coronation Av ALS/KID ST7 ...... 241 G1
BIDD ST8 .... 227 H7
GOL/RIS/CU WA3 .... 25 J5
WARRS WA4 .... 57 J2
WSFD CW7 .... 177 J3
Coronation Crs CW/HAS CW1 .. 221 L6

SBCH CW11 .... 204 A7
Coronation Dr FROD/HEL WA6 .. 99 K3
NEWLW WA12 .... 27 L3
RAIN/WH L35 .... 32 C1
RNFD/HAY WA11 .... 22 A5
WARRW/BUR WA5 .... 35 M8
WDN WA8 .... 52 B4
Coronation Gv NWCHW CW8 .. 102 F8
Coronation Rd
CHSW/BR CH4 .... 190 B1
CONG CW12 .... 207 M2
EP CH65 .... 95 J8
MWCH CW10 .... 179 K6
RUNC WA7 .... 9 J4
WARR WA1 .... 74 F6
Coronation St BURS/TUN ST6 .. 243 L8
CHSW/BR CH4 .... 168 F5
CW/HAS CW1 .... 19 H1
MCFLDS SK11 .... 15 J9
Coroner's La ALT WA14 .... 34 A7
Coronet Av NWCHE CW9 ...... 129 M8
Coronet Wy WDN WA8 .... 52 B4
Corporation St FLINT CH6 ...... 116 A5
STKP SK1 .... 3 H4
Correction Brow POY/DIS SK12 .. 67 J6
Corridor Rd EP CH65 .... 96 B7
Corsham St HLWD L26 .... 50 E6
Corwen Cl WARRW/BUR WA5 .. 36 E3
Cosham Rd WYTH/NTH M22 .. 63 M1
Cossack Av WARRN/WOL WA2 .. 37 J3
Cotebrook Dr CHNE CH2 ...... 145 L5
Cotebrook Rd NWCHE CW9 .. 130 C5
Cotefield Cl MPL/ROM SK6 ...... 48 F7
Cotefield Rd WYTH/NTH M22 .. 63 H2
Cote Green La MPL/ROM SK6 .. 49 H3
Cote Green Rd MPL/ROM SK6 .. 49 H3
Cote La RUNC WA7 .... 73 M6
Cotes Pl CH/BCN CH1 .... 168 E1
Cotgreaves Cl CHSW/BR CH4 .. 169 H7
Cotman Dr MPL/ROM SK6 ...... 49 J4
Cotswold Av BRAM/HZG SK7 .. 66 B3
GOL/RIS/CU WA3 .... 23 K6
Cotswold Cl CHNE CH2 ...... 145 M6
MCFLDN SK10 .... 137 L3
NWCHW CW8 .... 152 A2
Cotswold Gv STHEL WA9 ...... 26 A1
Cotswold Rd HTNM SK4 ...... 2 D2
WARRN/WOL WA2 .... 37 H1
Cotswolds Cresent HLWD L26 .. 50 E5
Cotswold Wy WSFD CW7 ...... 177 H5
Cottage Cl NSTN CH64 .... 91 L5
Cottage Gdns MPL/ROM SK6 .. 47 K1
Cottage La CQ CH5 .... 166 D2
MCFLDN SK10 .... 15 M6
Cottage Rd CHSW/BR CH4 .. 169 H7
Cottage St MCFLDS SK11 ...... 14 D5
Cottam Crs MPL/ROM SK6 ...... 49 H5
Cottam Dr WARRN/WOL WA2 .. 38 A5
Cotterdale Cl WARRW/BUR WA5 .. 35 M5
Cotterill Cl SALE M33 .... 43 J3
Cotterill RUNC WA7 .... 73 K4
Cotterill St WARR WA1 .... 5 J5
CW/SHV CW2 .... 19 G8
Cottesmore Gdns
HALE/TIMP WA15 .... 62 C4
Cottesmore Wy
GOL/RIS/CU WA3 .... 23 H5
Cotton La CHSE CH3 .... 171 J2
RUNC WA7 .... 73 K4
SBCH CW11 .... 223 H1
Cotton Rd BURS/TUN ST6 ...... 243 J6
Cotton Tree St HTNM SK4 ...... 2 E5
Cottonwood Gv ALS/KID ST7 .. 243 L1
Cottrell Rd HALE/TIMP WA15 .. 62 D5
Coulton Rd WDN WA8 .... 53 L1
Council Av AIMK WN4 ...... 22 B1
Councillor La CHD/CHDH SK8 .. 45 M6
CHD/CHDH SK8 .... 46 B8
Countess Av CHD/CHDH SK8 .. 64 E7
Countess Cl MCFLDS SK11 .. 137 M5
Countess Rd DID/WITH M20 .. 45 H1
Countess St OFTN SK2 .... 47 G7
County Av CH/BCN CH1 ...... 145 J8
Counting House Rd
POY/DIS SK12 .... 68 E7
Court Av HLWD L26 .... 51 G3
Courthill St STKP SK1 .... 3 K7
Courtney Gn WILM/AE SK9 .. 84 D2
Courtney Pl ALT WA14 .... 61 G3
Courtney Rd CHSW/BR CH4 .. 168 E3
The Court MWCH CW10 ...... 179 K5
Cousens Wy CH/BCN CH1 .. 145 H8
Covell Rd POY/DIS SK12 ...... 66 D7
Covent Gdn STKP SK1 .... 3 G6
Coventry Av EDGY/DAV SK3 .. 45 M5
GTS/LS CH66 .... 120 E4
Coverdale Av RAIN/WH L35 .. 33 K2
Coverdale Cl WARRW/BUR WA5 .. 35 M5
Coverdale Fold SBCH CW11 .. 203 K1
Covert Cl WSFD CW7 .... 177 H4
Covert Gdns ALS/KID ST7 .. 242 D4
Covert Ri CHSE CH3 .... 214 A3
Covert Rd WYTH/NTH M22 .. 44 E7
The Cove HALE/TIMP WA15 .. 61 M1
Covington Pl WILM/AE SK9 .. 84 B6
Cowanway WDN WA8 .... 33 M8
Cowbrook La MCFLDS SK11 .. 162 B6
Cowburn Dr NM/HAY SK22 .. 69 J3
Cowdell St WARRN/WOL WA2 .. 5 H2
Cowfields NANT CW5 .... 20 F5
Cowhey Cl CHSW/BR CH4 .. 169 H7
Cow Hey La RUNC WA7 ...... 73 G7
Cow La BRAM/HZG SK7 ...... 47 K8
CHSE CH3 .... 195 L2
FROD/HEL WA6 .... 127 G7
HALE/TIMP WA15 .... 61 M7
MCFLDN SK10 .... 113 K8
MCFLDS SK11 .... 15 H9
MWCH CW10 .... 179 H3
NANT CW5 .... 21 G5
NM/HAY SK22 .... 69 H4
NWCHE CW9 .... 13 H6
NWCHW CW8 .... 128 D3
NWCHW CW9 .... 129 L5
TPLY/KEL CW6 .... 174 B5
Crescent Wy EDGY/DAV SK3 .. 47 G7
Cressbrook Rd WARRS WA4 .. 56 C4
Cresswell Av NM/HAY SK22 .. 69 J4

Cox La WRX/GR/LL LL12 ...... 210 C8
Coxton Rd WYTH/NTH M22 .. 63 L3
Coylton Av RAIN/WH L35 ...... 33 K2
Crab La WARRN/WOL WA2 .. 38 A1
Crabmill Cl WARRN/WOL WA2 .. 38 A1
Crabmill La FROD/HEL WA6 .. 126 E6
SBCH CW11 .... 202 E4
Crabtree Av BIDD ST8 ...... 227 J5
HALE/TIMP WA15 .... 62 D5
POY/DIS SK12 .... 68 E7
Crabtree Fold RUNC WA7 ...... 74 C4
Crabtree Gv CW/HAS CW1 .. 221 L6
Crabtree La KNUT WA16 ...... 59 G5
Crabwall Pl CH/BCN CH1 ...... 144 F7
Cracow Moss
AUD/MAD/W CW3 .... 267 G1
Craddock St SALE M33 ...... 43 J4
Cradley WDN WA8 .... 52 C2
Cragside Wy WILM/AE SK9 .. 84 C6
Craig Cl HTNM SK4 .... 46 B3
MCFLDS SK11 .... 138 B7
Craig Dr CHF/WBR SK23 ...... 89 L6
Craig Gdns GTS/LS CH66 ...... 94 E5
Craig Rd CONG CW12 .... 184 F8
HTNM SK4 .... 46 B3
MCFLDS SK11 .... 138 B7
Craigside BIDD ST8 .... 227 J4
Craig Wk ALS/KID ST7 ...... 241 M2
Craigweil Dr DID/WITH M20 .. 45 J1
Craithie Rd CHSE CH3 ...... 170 A2
Crampton Dr HALE/TIMP WA15 .. 62 C4
Cranage Cl RUNC WA7 ...... 73 K5
Cranage La NWCHW CW9 .. 130 D3
Cranage Rd CW/SHV CW2 .. 18 A6
Cranberry Cl ALT WA14 ...... 42 B4
Cranberry La ALS/KID ST7 .. 241 G1
Cranberry Moss La
ALS/KID ST7 .... 241 G1
Cranborne Av WARRS WA4 .. 56 B3
Cranborne Rd CW/HAS CW1 .. 19 G1
CW/HAS CW1 .... 221 K6
Cranbourne Av CHD/CHDH SK8 .. 65 H2
Cranbourne Cl HALE/TIMP WA15 .. 43 G6
Crandon Dr DID/WITH M20 .. 45 J4
Cranebrook Cl CW/HAS CW1 .. 221 G4
Cranesbill Cl WYTH/NTH M22 .. 63 J3
Cranfield Dr ALS/KID ST7 .. 241 G1
Cranford Av KNUT WA16 ...... 106 F3
MCFLDN SK10 .... 15 M7
Cranford Ct CHSW/BR CH4 .. 169 G7
Cranford Dr IRL M44 .... 31 M1
Cranford Gdns MPL/ROM SK6 .. 48 F5
Cranford Ms ALS/KID ST7 .. 241 G1
Cranford Rd WILM/AE SK9 .. 84 A3
Cranford Sq KNUT WA16 ...... 106 F3
Cranham Av GOL/RIS/CU WA3 .. 23 L5
Cranham Rd WYTH/NTH M22 .. 63 G2
Cranleigh Cl WARRS WA4 ...... 56 B5
Cranleigh Ct CH/BCN CH1 .. 145 H8
Cranleigh Dr BRAM/HZG SK7 .. 67 G4
CHD/CHDH SK8 .... 65 J8
SALE M33 .... 43 J3
Cranmere Cl NWCHE CW9 .. 130 A8
Cranmere Dr SALE M33 ...... 42 D2
Cranshaw Av STHEL WA9 .. 34 D1
Cranshaw La WDN WA8 ...... 34 D1
Cranston Dr DID/WITH M20 .. 45 H4
SALE M33 .... 43 L1
Cranston Gv CHD/CHDH SK8 .. 64 F7
Cranswick Gn GTS/LS CH66 .. 94 C7
Crantock Cl HLWD L26 ...... 50 F4
Crantock Dr CHD/CHDH SK8 .. 64 C4
Cranwell Av GOL/RIS/CU WA3 .. 24 F8
Crauford Rd CONG CW12 ...... 184 F4
Craven Av GOL/RIS/CU WA3 .. 23 L5
Craven Ct WARRN/WOL WA2 .. 27 M8
Craven Dr ALT WA14 .... 42 C4
Craven Rd ALT WA14 .... 42 C5
RAIN/WH L35 .... 33 G2
Cravenwood Rd HLWD L26 .. 50 F5
Crawford Av WDN WA8 ...... 52 B3
Crawford Pl RUNC WA7 ...... 73 H6
Crawford's Wk CHNE CH2 .. 17 L2
Crawley Av WARRN/WOL WA2 .. 37 L3
WYTH/NTH M22 .... 63 K1
Crawley Cl WLTN L25 .... 50 D4
Crawley Gv OFTN SK2 ...... 47 H6
Crayford Av CONG CW12 .. 185 G2
Creden Av WYTH/NTH M22 .. 63 L1
Crediton Cl ALT WA14 ...... 42 B6
Cresanne Cl MWCH CW10 .. 179 K5
Crescent Av EDGY/DAV SK3 .. 47 G7
Crescent Dr CHF/WBR SK23 .. 89 K2
FROD/HEL WA6 .... 124 B1
Crescent Pk HTNM SK4 ...... 2 A5
HTNM SK4 .... 2 A5
Crescent Rd ALT WA14 ...... 42 A6
CHD/CHDH SK8 .... 45 J6
CONG CW12 .... 207 J2
EP CH65 .... 11 G6
HALE/TIMP WA15 .... 61 L2
HOLMCH CW4 .... 156 F6
KNUT WA16 .... 80 B1
STKP SK1 .... 3 L2
WILM/AE SK9 .... 110 B2
The Crescent ALT WA14 ...... 42 A7
CHD/CHDH SK8 .... 45 K6
CHNE CH2 .... 145 M8
CONG CW12 .... 207 J2
EDGY/DAV SK3 .... 47 G8
EP CH65 .... 11 G6
HALE/TIMP WA15 .... 42 F5
HUY L36 .... 32 A2
KNUT WA16 .... 80 B1
LYMM WA13 .... 58 F2
MCFLDN SK10 .... 15 K3
MCFLDN SK10 .... 111 G2
MWCH CW10 .... 179 H3
NANT CW5 .... 21 G5
NM/HAY SK22 .... 69 H4
NWCHE CW9 .... 13 H6
NWCHW CW8 .... 128 D3
NWCHW CW9 .... 129 L5
TPLY/KEL CW6 .... 174 B5

Cresswell Cl
WARRW/BUR WA5 .... 36 D2
Cresswellshawe Rd
ALS/KID ST7 .... 224 D7
Cresswell St NM/HAY SK22 .. 69 J4
Cresta Dr RUNC WA7 ...... 72 F6
Crew Av MCFLDN SK10 ...... 15 H3
Crewe and Nantwich
Cicular Wk
NANT CW5 .... 252 C3
Crewe and Nantwich
Circular Wk CW/HAS CW1 .. 201 J6
Crewe And Nantwich
Circular Wk CW/HAS CW1 .. 220 F1
CW/HAS CW1 .... 221 L2
CW/SHV CW2 .... 253 K2
Crewe and Nantwich
Circular Wk NANT CW5 .. 219 L2
NANT CW5 .... 251 L3
Crewe And Nantwich
Circular Wk NANT CW5 .. 252 E4
SBCH CW11 .... 222 B2
Crewe Green Av CW/HAS CW1 .. 222 B8
Crewe Green Rd CW/HAS CW1 .. 239 C1
Crewe Hill La CHSE CH3 ...... 229 G6
Crewe La CHSE CH3 .... 228 F3
Crewe La South CHSE CH3 .. 228 F4
Crewe Rd ALS/KID ST7 ...... 224 F8
ALS/KID ST7 .... 241 H1
CW/HAS CW1 .... 19 K7
CW/HAS CW1 .... 239 H1
CW/SHV CW2 .... 238 C8
NANT CW5 .... 21 L6
NANT CW5 .... 237 K6
NANT CW5 .... 264 F1
NTHM/RTH M23 .... 43 L4
SBCH CW11 .... 204 B6
SBCH CW11 .... 222 F2
Crewe St CH/BCN CH1 ...... 17 J3
CW/HAS CW1 .... 19 G4
Crewood Common Rd
FROD/HEL WA6 .... 127 G1
Crib La TPLY/KEL CW6 ...... 196 F5
Criccieth Ct EP CH65 .... 121 K2
Criccieth Rd EDGY/DAV SK3 .. 46 A5
Criftin Cl GTS/LS CH66 ...... 120 C2
Crimes La CHSE CH3 ...... 196 C8
Cringle Dr CHD/CHDH SK8 .. 45 J8
Cringles Dr RAIN/WH L35 ...... 32 A5
Crisham Av NANT CW5 ...... 251 L4
Crispin Rd WYTH/NTH M22 .. 63 L4
Critchley Rd SPK/HALE L24 .. 71 G2
Croasdale Dr RUNC WA7 ...... 73 L7
Crocus St NWCHW CW8 ...... 129 H1
Croes Atti La FLINT CH6 ...... 116 C7
Croesmere Dr GTS/LS CH66 .. 120 D2
Croft Av GOL/RIS/CU WA3 .. 22 F2
Croft Cl CHSE CH3 .... 171 G7
CONG CW12 .... 207 M2
HALE/TIMP WA15 .... 62 C6
TPLY/KEL CW6 .... 174 B5
Croften Dr NSTN CH64 ...... 91 L7
Crofter Cl BIDD ST8 .... 227 H4
Crofters Cl CW/SHV CW2 .. 238 E4
GTS/LS CH66 .... 120 E3
Crofters Ct HOLMCH CW4 .. 157 G8
Crofters Gn WILM/AE SK9 .. 83 M6
Crofters Heath GTS/LS CH66 .. 120 E3
Crofters Lea NWCHW CW8 .. 12 C4
Crofters Pk CQ CH5 .... 167 G1
The Crofters SALE M33 ...... 43 M1
Crofters Wy CH/BCN CH1 .. 143 M4
CQ CH5 .... 166 E2
Croft Gdns WARRS WA4 ...... 57 G5
Croftlands Rd WYTH/NTH M22 .. 44 E8
Croft La CHSW/BR CH4 ...... 190 F5
KNUT WA16 .... 107 H4
Crofton Av HALE/TIMP WA15 .. 43 G4
Crofton Cl WARRS WA4 ...... 57 J7
Crofton Gdns
GOL/RIS/CU WA3 .... 29 L1
Crofton Rd RUNC WA7 ...... 8 C5
Croft Rd CHD/CHDH SK8 .. 65 J6
SALE M33 .... 43 L2
WILM/AE SK9 .... 83 L8
Croftside WARR WA1 .... 38 F5
Croftside Wy WILM/AE SK9 .. 84 C6
Croft St GOL/RIS/CU WA3 .. 23 G4
WDN WA8 .... 7 H8
The Croft CHNE CH2 .... 145 K7
RUNC WA7 .... 73 L3
Cromar Crs WRX/GR/LL LL12 .. 210 C8
Cromar Rd BRAM/HZG SK7 .. 66 F1
Crombie Av WYTH/NTH M22 .. 44 B4
Cromdale Av BRAM/HZG SK7 .. 66 F1
Cromdale Wy WARRW/BUR WA5 .. 35 M5
Cromer Dr CW/HAS CW1 .. 221 H4
Cromer Rd CHD/CHDH SK8 .. 45 L6
SALE M33 .... 43 J1
Cromer St STKP SK1 .... 3 K4
Cromer Wy HLWD L26 ...... 50 F4
Cromford Ms CHF/WBR SK23 .. 89 L7
Cromley Rd MPL/ROM SK6 .. 67 L5
OFTN SK2 .... 66 A1
Crompton Cl MPL/ROM SK6 .. 48 E1
Crompton Rd MCFLDS SK11 .. 14 E8
Cromwell Av CHD/CHDH SK8 .. 45 G6
MPL/ROM SK6 .... 48 G5
WARRW/BUR WA5 .... 36 C4
Cromwell Av South
WARRW/BUR WA5 .... 36 C2
Cromwell Dr CW/SHV CW2 .. 253 J1
Cromwell Rd BRAM/HZG SK7 .. 65 K6
EP CH65 .... 10 F7
IRL M44 .... 31 K7
NWCHW CW8 .... 12 C3
Cromwell St BIDD ST8 ...... 227 H4
HTNM SK4 .... 2 D2
WDN WA8 .... 7 G9
Cronkinson Av NANT CW5 .. 21 G8
Cronkinson Oak NANT CW5 .. 21 G8
Cronton La RAIN/WH L35 ...... 33 L3
WDN WA8 .... 33 H4
WDN WA8 .... 33 J4
Cronton Park Cl WDN WA8 .. 33 J6

Cronton Rd RAIN/WH L35 ...... 32 B5
Cronulla Dr WARRW/BUR WA5 .. 35 K5
Crooked La CHSE CH3 ...... 196 B1
Crookedyard Rd MCFLDS SK11 .. 139 L5
Crookenden Cl CHNE CH2 .. 145 J3
Crookenden Rd CHNE CH2 .. 145 J3
Crookilley Wy STKP SK1 ...... 3 K2
Crook La WSFD CW7 ...... 178 A2
Crook St CH/BCN CH1 ...... 16 F5
Croppers Rd WARRN/WOL WA2 .. 37 M1
Crosby Av WARRW/BUR WA5 .. 37 G4
Crosby Gv NSTN CH64 ...... 93 H3
Crosby St OFTN SK2 .... 46 F5
Crosfield St WARR WA1 ...... 4 E6
Crossacres Rd WYTH/NTH M22 .. 44 F8
Crossall St MCFLDS SK11 ...... 15 G7
Crossfield Av BIDD ST8 ...... 227 J6
GOL/RIS/CU WA3 .... 29 M2
LYMM WA13 .... 58 F1
WSFD CW7 .... 177 K5
Crossfield Gv MPL/ROM SK6 .. 49 H3
OFTN SK2 .... 47 H8
Crossfield Rd HALE/TIMP WA15 .. 42 D2
MCFLDN SK10 .... 112 E6
WILM/AE SK9 .... 64 D8
Crossfields CHSE CH3 ...... 172 B2
Crossgate Av WYTH/NTH M22 .. 44 D6
Crossgate Ms HTNM SK4 .. 45 L2
Crossgates WDN WA8 ...... 53 M1
Cross Gn CHNE CH2 ...... 145 L6
Cross Gv HALE/TIMP WA15 .. 42 F4
Cross Hey CHSW/BR CH4 .. 17 K8
Cross Hillocks La RAIN/WH L35 .. 51 L1
Crosslands CONG CW12 ...... 208 A3
CW/HAS CW1 .... 222 D8
Cross La ALS/KID ST7 ...... 241 L8
CONG CW12 .... 158 E8
CONG CW12 .... 208 A4
FROD/HEL WA6 .... 98 B4
GOL/RIS/CU WA3 .... 29 K5
HOLMCH CW4 .... 158 C7
MPL/ROM SK6 .... 48 E7
MWCH CW10 .... 179 K6
NEWLW WA12 .... 27 H1
NSTN CH64 .... 91 L7
SBCH CW11 .... 204 C7
SBCH CW11 .... 205 M4
WARRS WA4 .... 57 G2
WILM/AE SK9 .... 84 F4
Cross La East PART M31 .. 40 F2
Cross La CHSE CH3 .... 172 C4
Cross La South CHSE CH3 .. 29 K5
Cross La West PART M31 .. 40 E2
Crossley Av GTS/LS CH66 .. 94 E6
Crossley Crs CHNE CH2 ...... 146 B7
Cross St WARR WA1 .... 5 J5
Crossmoor Crs MPL/ROM SK6 .. 48 C2
Crossmoor Gv MPL/ROM SK6 .. 48 C2
Cross O' Th' Hill Rd
MALPAS SY14 .... 247 G8
Cross Rd CHD/CHDH SK8 .. 64 B5
CW/HAS CW1 .... 222 D8
Cross St ALS/KID ST7 ...... 241 J1
BIDD ST8 .... 227 J4
CHNE CH2 .... 17 J3
CW/HAS CW1 .... 222 D8
CW/HAS CW1 .... 19 G5
GOL/RIS/CU WA3 .... 23 G5
MCFLDS SK11 .... 15 H8
NM/HAY SK22 .... 69 J4
NSTN CH64 .... 91 L4
NWCHE CW9 .... 130 H1
NWCHW CW8 .... 129 H1
RUNC WA7 .... 9 G1
WARRN/WOL WA2 .... 37 J3
WDN WA8 .... 7 K3
WRXS/E LL13 .... 228 E2
The Cross LYMM WA13 ...... 58 E1
WRXS/E LL13 .... 228 D4
Crosstree La CQ CH5 ...... 166 D3
Cross Tree Ri CQ CH5 ...... 166 D4
Crosswaite Rd OFTN SK2 .. 47 K6
Crossway BRAM/HZG SK7 .. 65 L7
CW/HAS CW1 .... 221 K6
DID/WITH M20 .... 45 L1
OFTN SK2 .... 47 G8
WDN WA8 .... 6 A4
Crossways BIDD ST8 ...... 227 L3
CQ CH5 .... 142 E7
Crossways Rd ALS/KID ST7 .. 225 G8
Cross Wood St NANT CW5 .. 20 D6
Croston Cl WDN WA8 ...... 33 J8
WILM/AE SK9 .... 110 C3
Crotia Av CW/SHV CW2 ...... 239 H1
Croton St HTNM SK4 ...... 45 L2
Crouch La CONG CW12 ...... 185 K8
Crouchley La LYMM WA13 .. 58 F3
Croughton Rd CHNE CH2 .. 121 M4
CHNE CH2 .... 122 A5
GTS/LS CH66 .... 94 F4
Crowborough Rd BIDD ST8 .. 227 M6
Crowder's La NWCHE CW9 .. 131 H4
Crowe Av WARRN/WOL WA2 .. 37 H1
Crowland Gdns
CHD/CHDH SK8 .... 65 H3
Crowland Rd NTHM/RTH M23 .. 62 F1
Crow La East NEWLW WA12 .. 22 A8
Crow La West NEWLW WA12 .. 22 A8
Crowley La NWCHE CW9 ...... 77 M1
Crowley Rd HALE/TIMP WA15 .. 43 H6
Crown Av WDN WA8 ...... 52 B4
Crown Bank ALS/KID ST7 .. 242 C4
SBCH CW11 .... 204 B6
Crown Bank Crs ALS/KID ST7 .. 242 C4
Crown Ct BRAM/HZG SK7 .. 66 D1
Crowndale Pl BURS/TUN ST6 .. 243 L4
Crownest La BURS/TUN ST6 .. 243 J7
Crown Fields Cl NEWLW WA12 .. 22 B7
Crown Gdns NEWLW WA12 .. 22 B8
Crown Ga RUNC WA7 ...... 73 M5
Crown Gn LYMM WA13 ...... 59 H1
Crown La KNUT WA16 ...... 132 D4
Crown Park Dr NEWLW WA12 .. 22 B8

Crown Passages
  HALE/TIMP WA15 ...... 61 L2
Crown St MPL/ROM SK6 ...... 67 M1
  NEWLW WA12 ...... 27 G1
  NWCHE CW9 ...... 13 H1
  WARR WA1 ...... 5 C6
Crown St West MCFLDS SK11 ...... 14 E6
Crowsdale PI OFTN SK2 ...... 47 L8
Crowthorn Dr
  NTHM/RTH M23 ...... 63 G2 ☐
Crowton Av SALE M33 ...... 42 D2 ☐
Crowton Vw FROD/HEL WA6 ...... 127 C6
Crow Wood La WDN WA8 ...... 53 K2
Crow Wood PI WDN WA8 ...... 53 K1 ☐
Crow Wood Rd GOL/RIS/CU WA3.. 23 K3
Croxton CI MPL/ROM SK6 ...... 48 E7
  SALE M33 ...... 42 D2 ☐
Croxton Gn MALPAS SY14 ...... 233 J6
Croxton La MWCH CW10 ...... 155 G7
Croxton Wy NWCHW CW8 ...... 129 G8 ☐
Croyde CI WYTH/NTH M22 ...... 63 M5
Croyde Rd SPK/HALE L24 ...... 71 C1
Crum HI NWCHE CW9 ...... 13 J2
Crummock Rd CHD/CHDH SK8 .. 64 B1 ☐
Cruttenden Rd OFTN SK2 ...... 47 J8
Cryers La CHNE CH2 ...... 122 F4
Cuckoo La NANT CW5 ...... 235 M4
  NSTN CH64 ...... 92 B5
Cuckstoolpit HI MCFLDN SK10 ...... 15 J5
Cuddington Crs EDGY/DAV SK3 ...... 46 D6
Cuddington La NWCHW CW8 ...... 151 J1
Cuerdley Gn WDN WA8 ...... 54 A2
Cuerdley Rd WARRW/BUR WA5 ...... 54 C1
Cuerdon Dr WARRS WA4 ...... 57 K3
Culbert Av DID/WITH M20 ...... 45 J1 ☐
Culbin CI GOL/RIS/CU WA3 ...... 30 A6 ☐
Culchetch Av MPL/ROM SK6 ...... 48 F6 ☐
Culcheth Hall Dr
  GOL/RIS/CU WA3 ...... 24 F8
Culcheth Rd ALT WA14 ...... 61 K1
Culford CI RUNC WA7 ...... 74 D3 ☐
Culland St CW/SHV CW2 ...... 18 F8
Cullen Rd RUNC WA7 ...... 8 B8
Culmere Rd WYTH/NTH M22 ...... 63 K3
Culver Rd EDGY/DAV SK3 ...... 46 D7
Cumber CI WILM/AE SK9 ...... 83 K8
Cumber Dr WILM/AE SK9 ...... 83 K8
Cumberland Av IRL M44 ...... 31 J7
  NANT CW5 ...... 21 H4
Cumberland Dr ALT WA14 ...... 61 H1
  MCFLDN SK10 ...... 113 H4 ☐
Cumberland Gv GTS/LS CH66 ...... 120 C1
Cumberland Rd CONG CW12 ...... 207 C3
  PART M31 ...... 40 D2
  SALE M33 ...... 43 J2
Cumberland St MCFLDN SK10 ...... 14 E4
  MCFLDS SK11 ...... 14 D5
  WARRS WA4 ...... 56 C1
Cumber La RAIN/WH L35 ...... 32 F1
  WILM/AE SK9 ...... 83 K8
Cumbermere Dr SBCH CW11 ...... 203 L5
Cumbers Dr NSTN CH64 ...... 92 A7
Cumbers La NSTN CH64 ...... 92 A7
Cumbrae Dr EP CH65 ...... 121 J3
Cuncliffe St SALE M33 ...... 43 J1
Cundiff CI MCFLDS SK11 ...... 15 K8 ☐
Cunliffe Av NEWLW WA12 ...... 22 B7
Cunliffe CI RUNC WA7 ...... 74 A5
Cunliffe St EDGY/DAV SK3 ...... 2 B7
Cunningham CI
  WARRW/BUR WA5 ...... 35 M7 ☐
Cunningham Dr RUNC WA7 ...... 8 D6
  WYTH/NTH M22 ...... 64 A4
Cunningham Rd WDN WA8 ...... 6 B5
Cuppin St CH/BCN CH1 ...... 16 F6
Curate St STKP SK1 ...... 3 K6
Curlender Wy SPK/HALE L24 ...... 71 L2
Curlew CI GOL/RIS/CU WA3 ...... 23 K4 ☐
  WSFD CW7 ...... 177 J7 ☐
Curlew Gv GOL/RIS/CU WA3 ...... 38 E1
Currans Rd WARRW/WOL WA2 ...... 37 G2 ☐
Curtis Rd HTNM SK4 ...... 46 A2
Curzon Av ALS/KID ST7 ...... 224 D7
  WARRS WA4 ...... 56 C1
Curzon CI CHSW/BR CH4 ...... 16 B8
Curzon Dr HALE/TIMP WA15 ...... 43 H6
Curzon Gn OFTN SK2 ...... 47 K4
Curzon Gv WSFD CW7 ...... 177 M3 ☐
Curzon Ms WILM/AE SK9 ...... 84 A6
Curzon Pk North CHSW/BR CH4 .. 16 C8
Curzon Pk South
  CHSW/BR CH4 ...... 169 C5
Curzon Rd CHD/CHDH SK8 ...... 64 B5
  OFTN SK2 ...... 47 K5
  POY/DIS SK12 ...... 86 E2
Curzon St CHSW/BR CH4 ...... 168 F5
  RUNC WA7 ...... 9 G5
Cutgate Rd NTHM/RTH M23 ...... 43 L3 ☐
Cuthbert Rd CHD/CHDH SK8 ...... 45 L6
Cwm Eithion FLINT CH6 ...... 116 B8
Cwrt Onnen CO CH5 ...... 166 E3 ☐
Cygnet CI GTS/LS CH66 ...... 94 D8
Cygnet St WARR WA1 ...... 56 A1
Cyman CI CH/BCN CH1 ...... 168 D1
Cymbal Ct RDSH SK5 ...... 3 G1
Cynthia Av WARR WA1 ...... 38 B5
Cynthia Dr MPL/ROM SK6 ...... 48 F7
Cynthia Rd RUNC WA7 ...... 8 E4
Cypress Av GTS/LS CH66 ...... 120 F3
  WDN WA8 ...... 53 H1
Cypress CI EDGY/DAV SK3 ...... 2 A7
  WARR WA1 ...... 38 E5 ☐
Cypress Rd RUNC WA7 ...... 9 M9
Cypress Wy MPL/ROM SK6 ...... 68 C1
Cyril Bell CI LYMM WA13 ...... 58 F1
Cyril St WARRN/WOL WA2 ...... 5 H3

D

Dacre's Bridge La RAIN/WH L35... 32 D5
Daffodil CI WDN WA8 ...... 34 E8
Dagnall Av WARRW/BUR WA5 ...... 36 F2
Daine Av NTHM/RTH M23 ...... 44 B3
Daintry St MCFLDS SK11 ...... 15 J6

Daintry Ter MCFLDN SK10 ...... 15 J6
Dairy Farm CI LYMM WA13 ...... 58 F1
Dairyground Rd BRAM/HZG SK7 .. 65 L5
Dairyhouse La ALT WA14 ...... 42 B5
Dairy House La BRAM/HZG SK7 .. 85 H1
Dairy House Rd CHD/CHDH SK8 .. 65 H7
Dairy House Wy CW/SHV CW2 ...... 237 M2
Dairylands Rd ALS/KID ST7 ...... 225 G8
Dairy La NANT CW5 ...... 219 H8
Daisy Av NEWLW WA12 ...... 27 J2
Daisy Bank NANT CW5 ...... 20 C7
Daisy Bank Crs
  AUD/MAD/W CW3 ...... 263 M7
Daisybank Dr CONG CW12 ...... 184 D7
  SBCH CW11 ...... 204 C6
Daisy Bank Rd LYMM WA13 ...... 58 F1
  WYTH/NTH M22 ...... 64 A3
Daisy Bank Rd LYMM WA13 ...... 58 F1
  WARRW/BUR WA5 ...... 35 M8 ☐
Daisyfield CI WYTH/NTH M22 ...... 63 J3 ☐
Daisy La WRX/GR/LL LL12 ...... 210 E8
Daisy Ms EDGY/DAV SK3 ...... 46 D8
Daisy Mill Bank CI
  GOL/RIS/CU WA3 ...... 29 L1
Daisy St OFTN SK2 ...... 46 F5 ☐
Daisy Wy MPL/ROM SK6 ...... 67 M5
Dakins Rd LEIGH WN7 ...... 25 H2
Dalby CI GOL/RIS/CU WA3 ...... 30 B7
Dalby Gv STKP SK1 ...... 3 K5
Dale Av BRAM/HZG SK7 ...... 65 M4
  GTS/LS CH66 ...... 94 C6
Dale CI WARRW/BUR WA5 ...... 4 A9
  WARRW/BUR WA5 ...... 36 D8
  WDN WA8 ...... 52 A4
Dale Ct MWCH CW10 ...... 179 K5
Dale Crs CONG CW12 ...... 207 M2
Dalecroft FROD/HEL WA6 ...... 123 L3
Dale Dr CHNE CH2 ...... 145 K4
  EP CH65 ...... 94 F7
Dalefords La NWCHW CW8 ...... 152 B4
Dale Gv CONG CW12 ...... 208 A2
  HALE/TIMP WA15 ...... 42 F5
  IRL M44 ...... 31 L6
Dale Head Rd MCFLDN SK10 ... 111 M8
Dale Hey GTS/LS CH66 ...... 93 L2
Dale La WARRS WA4 ...... 56 E5
Dale PI CONG CW12 ...... 207 M2
Dale Rd CO CH5 ...... 142 A8
  GOL/RIS/CU WA3 ...... 23 G5
  MPL/ROM SK6 ...... 48 E5
  NM/HAY SK22 ...... 69 J5
Dalesford CI LEIGH WN7 ...... 24 C4
Dalesford Crs MCFLDS SK11 ...... 137 M4 ☐
Dales Green Rd ALS/KID ST7 ...... 226 C7
Daleside CHNE CH2 ...... 145 K4
Dales Rw HUY L36 ...... 32 B2
Dale St CHSE CH3 ...... 170 A3
  EDGY/DAV SK3 ...... 46 D5
  MCFLDN SK10 ...... 15 K5
  RUNC WA7 ...... 9 G5
The Dale NSTN CH64 ...... 91 K6
  TPLY/KEL CW6 ...... 197 J6
  WARRW/BUR WA5 ...... 35 M7
Dale Vw ALS/KID ST7 ...... 226 C7
  NEWLW WA12 ...... 22 E8
Dalewood Crs CHNE CH2 ...... 123 G1 ☐
Dalewood Gdns RAIN/WH L35 .. 32 F2 ☐
Dallam La WARRN/WOL WA2 ...... 4 F5
Dallimore Rd NTHM/RTH M23 ...... 43 L6
Dalmahoy CI WSFD CW7 ...... 177 J2 ☐
  DID/WITH M20 ...... 45 J2 ☐
Dalston Dr BRAM/HZG SK7 ...... 65 J7
Dalton Av WARRW/BUR WA5 ...... 4 D2
Dalton Bank WARR WA1 ...... 5 K5
Dalton CI CH/BCN CH1 ...... 168 E1
Dalton Ct RUNC WA7 ...... 73 L1
  SBCH CW11 ...... 203 L5
Dalton St GOL/RIS/CU WA3 ...... 29 L6
  RUNC WA7 ...... 73 K2
Dalton Wy MWCH CW10 ...... 179 K3
Daltry Wy ALS/MAD/W CW3 .. 267 M5 ☐
Dalveen Dr HALE/TIMP WA15 .. 42 F5 ☐
Dalwood CI RUNC WA7 ...... 74 E5
Dame Hollow CHD/CHDH SK8 .. 64 D5 ☐
Dameny Ct BRAM/HZG SK7 ...... 65 L4
Damery Rd BRAM/HZG SK7 ...... 65 J3
Dam Head La GOL/RIS/CU WA3 .. 30 F8
Damhead La NSTN CH64 ...... 92 E5
Damian Dr NEWLW WA12 ...... 22 A7 ☐
Dam La GOL/RIS/CU WA3 ...... 22 F1
  GOL/RIS/CU WA3 ...... 28 F5
  KNUT WA16 ...... 108 C1
  WARR WA1 ...... 38 D5
Dams La KNUT WA16 ...... 132 D7
Damson La KNUT WA16 ...... 82 B8
Dam Wood Rd SPK/HALE L24 ...... 48 C6
Dan Bank MPL/ROM SK6 ...... 48 C6
Danby CI RUNC WA7 ...... 73 K6 ☐
  WARRW/BUR WA5 ...... 36 F2
Danby Fold RAIN/WH L35 ...... 33 H1 ☐
Dane Av EDGY/DAV SK3 ...... 46 A4 ☐
  PART M31 ...... 31 M8
Dane Bank Av CONG CW12 ...... 184 E8
  CW/SHV CW2 ...... 18 A8
Dane Bank Dr POY/DIS SK12 ...... 68 D6
Danebank Rd LYMM WA13 ...... 39 L8
Dane Bank Rd NWCHE CW9 ...... 13 L4
Danebank Rd East LYMM WA13... 39 L8
Dane CI ALS/KID ST7 ...... 241 G1
  BRAM/HZG SK7 ...... 65 K2
  CHSW/BR CH4 ...... 168 F7
  SBCH CW11 ...... 203 L5
Dane Dr BIDD ST8 ...... 227 L3
  WILM/AE SK9 ...... 83 G6
Danefield Ct CHD/CHDH SK8 .. 64 D4 ☐
Danefield Rd HOLMCH CW4 ...... 157 J8
  NWCHE CW9 ...... 13 L4
Dane Gdns ALS/KID ST7 ...... 243 J2
Dane Gv CHNE CH2 ...... 146 F4
Dane Hill CI POY/DIS SK12 ...... 68 D6
Danesbury Ri CHD/CHDH SK8 .. 45 K7 ☐
Danescroft WDN WA8 ...... 52 B1
Danes Sq MCFLDS SK11 ...... 138 D7 ☐
Dane St CONG CW12 ...... 207 J1
  MWCH CW10 ...... 179 K2
  NWCHE CW9 ...... 13 H3

Daneswell Rd SPK/HALE L24 ...... 71 G2 ☐
Dane Valley Wy HOLMCH CW4 .. 156 C8
Daniel Adamson Av
  PART M31 ...... 40 D1 ☐
Daniel CI GOL/RIS/CU WA3 ...... 30 A8
Daniell Wy CHSE CH3 ...... 170 A5
Daniel's La STKP SK1 ...... 3 G4 ☐
Daniel St BRAM/HZG SK7 ...... 66 E2 ☐
Dans Rd WDN WA8 ...... 53 L2
Dappleheath Rd CW/SHV CW2 ... 18 B9
Darby CI NSTN CH64 ...... 91 L8
Darden CI HTNM SK4 ...... 45 L1
Daresbury CI EDGY/DAV SK3 .. 46 D7 ☐
  HOLMCH CW4 ...... 181 G1
  SALE M33 ...... 43 M1 ☐
Daresbury Expy RUNC WA7 ...... 8 F2
Daresbury La WARRS WA4 ...... 75 C1
Daresbury La WARRS WA4 ...... 75 K2
Darian Av WYTH/NTH M22 ...... 63 K4
Daric CI LEIGH WN7 ...... 24 C3
Dark Ark La CHSE CH3 ...... 149 J1
Darkie Meadow
  TPLY/KEL CW6 ...... 216 E4 ☐
Dark La CHSE CH3 ...... 214 D5
  FROD/HEL WA6 ...... 126 B3
  MCFLDS SK11 ...... 137 C4
  MCFLDS SK11 ...... 161 M1
  NWCHE CW9 ...... 104 C5
  WARRS WA4 ...... 76 D7
  WHITCH SY13 ...... 271 H3
Darland CI WRX/GR/LL LL12 ...... 210 C4
Darland La WRX/GR/LL LL12 ...... 210 C4
  WRX/GR/LL LL12 ...... 210 E4
Darley Av CHD/CHDH SK8 ...... 45 H7
  CW/SHV CW2 ...... 18 A6
  WARRW/WOL WA2 ...... 37 L1
Darley CI WDN WA8 ...... 52 B1
Darley Rd BRAM/HZG SK7 ...... 66 F5
Darlington Av CW/HAS CW1 ...... 220 F7
Darlington Crs CH/BCN CH1 ...... 144 A3
Darlington St MWCH CW10 ...... 179 J3
Darnaway CI GOL/RIS/CU WA3 ...... 30 B6
Darnbrook Dr
  WYTH/NTH M22 ...... 63 H3 ☐
Darnhall School La WSFD CW7 ... 177 J7
Dart CI ALS/KID ST7 ...... 224 A8
  BIDD ST8 ...... 227 K3
Dartington CI BRAM/HZG SK7 .. 65 M1
  NTHM/RTH M23 ...... 43 K6
Dartnall CI POY/DIS SK12 ...... 68 A6
Darwick Dr HUY L36 ...... 32 A4
Darwin Gv BRAM/HZG SK7 ...... 65 L6
Darwin Rd CH/BCN CH1 ...... 144 C5
Darwin St NWCHW CW8 ...... 12 E5
Daten Av GOL/RIS/CU WA3 ...... 29 M6
Dauncey CI CHNE CH2 ...... 145 J3 ☐
Davehall Av WILM/AE SK9 ...... 84 A5
Davenfield Gv DID/WITH M20 .. 45 H1 ☐
Davenham Av WARR WA1 ...... 37 L4
Davenham Ct NWCHE CW9 ...... 154 A1
Davenham Crs CW/SHV CW2 ...... 237 M1
Davenham Rd NWCHE CW9 ...... 154 E1
  WILM/AE SK9 ...... 84 D8 ☐
Davenham Wy MWCH CW10 ...... 179 K7
Davenport CW/SHV CW2 ...... 238 C4
  NANT CW5 ...... 20 E4
  WARRS WA4 ...... 37 M7
  WILM/AE SK9 ...... 83 L8
Davenport La KNUT WA16 ...... 82 C6
  MCFLDS SK11 ...... 160 A7
  SBCH CW11 ...... 205 J7
Davenport Park La CONG CW12.. 182 D2
Davenport Park Rd OFTN SK2 .. 47 G7
Davenport Rd BRAM/HZG SK7 .. 65 K3
Davenport Rw RUNC WA7 ...... 73 K4 ☐
Davenport St CONG CW12 ...... 207 J1
  CW/HAS CW1 ...... 221 J6
  MCFLDN SK10 ...... 15 J5
Daven Rd CONG CW12 ...... 207 M3
Daveylands WILM/AE SK9 ...... 84 D6
Davey La WILM/AE SK9 ...... 110 A2
David Rd LYMM WA13 ...... 58 C1
David's Av WARRW/BUR WA5 .. 36 B7
Davidson Av CONG CW12 ...... 185 G7
David St NWCHW CW8 ...... 12 F4
Davids Wk WLTN L25 ...... 50 C1 ☐
Davies Av CHD/CHDH SK8 ...... 64 B6
  NEWLW WA12 ...... 22 C8
  WARRS WA4 ...... 37 M8
Davies CI WDN WA8 ...... 53 G8
Davies Rd MPL/ROM SK6 ...... 47 K1 ☐
  PART M31 ...... 41 G1
Davies Wy LYMM WA13 ...... 58 D1
Davis CI ALS/KID ST7 ...... 224 E8
Davy Av GOL/RIS/CU WA3 ...... 29 L7
Davy Rd RUNC WA7 ...... 73 L1
Dawley CI AIMK WN4 ...... 22 A1
Dawlish Av CHD/CHDH SK8 ...... 64 F4
Dawlish CI BRAM/HZG SK7 ...... 65 L5
  GOL/RIS/CU WA3 ...... 40 B2 ☐
  WLTN L25 ...... 50 C4
Dawn CI NSTN CH64 ...... 91 M7
Dawn Gdns EP CH65 ...... 95 H8
Dawpool CI CHNE CH2 ...... 145 K7
Dawson Dr CH/BCN CH1 ...... 16 F1
Dawson Rd ALT WA14 ...... 42 D5
  CHD/CHDH SK8 ...... 64 D4
  MCFLDN SK10 ...... 113 G5 ☐
  MCFLDS SK11 ...... 137 M5
Dawson St STKP SK1 ...... 3 L2
Daylesford CI CHD/CHDH SK8... 45 J8
Daylesford Crs CHD/CHDH SK8.. 45 K8
Daylesford Rd CHD/CHDH SK8.. 45 K8
Deacon CI ALT WA14 ...... 61 H1
  GOL/RIS/CU WA3 ...... 23 G5 ☐
Deacon Ct WLTN L25 ...... 50 B2 ☐
Deacon Rd WDN WA8 ...... 7 J3
  WILM/AE SK9 ...... 84 C3
Deacons CI STKP SK1 ...... 3 J5
Deakin's Rd WSFD CW7 ...... 153 M8
Dean Bank TPLY/KEL CW6 ...... 216 C1
Dean CI MCFLDN SK10 ...... 113 C5
  PART M31 ...... 31 M8
  SBCH CW11 ...... 203 L4
  WDN WA8 ...... 7 J4
  WILM/AE SK9 ...... 84 C3
Dean Ct GOL/RIS/CU WA3 ...... 23 G5 ☐
Dean Crs WARRN/WOL WA2 ...... 37 H2 ☐

Dean Dr ALT WA14 ...... 61 H3
  WILM/AE SK9 ...... 84 C3
Deane Av CHD/CHDH SK8 ...... 45 M7
  HALE/TIMP WA15 ...... 43 G7
Deanery Wy STKP SK1 ...... 3 G4
Dean La ALS/KID ST7 ...... 225 H3
Dean Meadow NEWLW WA12 ...... 22 C8 ☐
Dean Moor Rd BRAM/HZG SK7 .. 66 A2
Dean Pk MALPAS SY14 ...... 247 K6
Dean Rd GOL/RIS/CU WA3 ...... 23 C5
  IRL M44 ...... 31 L6
Dean Row Rd WILM/AE SK9 ...... 84 C3
Deans CI CHNE CH2 ...... 145 K6 ☐
  CHSE CH3 ...... 172 B5 ☐
Deansfield Wy CHNE CH2 ...... 123 C1
Deansgate EP CH65 ...... 10 B7
Deansgate La HALE/TIMP WA15... 42 E5
Dean's La CW/SHV CW2 ...... 240 C8
  CW/SHV CW2 ...... 255 J2
  MALPAS SY14 ...... 231 M8
  SBCH CW11 ...... 203 L6
  WARRS WA4 ...... 57 M1
Deans Rd EP CH65 ...... 121 M1
Dean St MWCH CW10 ...... 179 J2
  NWCHE CW9 ...... 130 C4
  WDN WA8 ...... 7 J4
  WSFD CW7 ...... 177 J4 ☐
Deans Wy CHSE CH3 ...... 172 B2
  CHSW/BR CH4 ...... 190 A4
Deansway WDN WA8 ...... 52 C4
Deanwater CI GOL/RIS/CU WA3 .. 23 L6
Deanwater Ct CHD/CHDH SK8 .. 64 D5 ☐
Dean Wy STHEL WA9 ...... 34 B1
Deanway WILM/AE SK9 ...... 84 C4
Dean Wood CI RAIN/WH L35 ...... 32 F2 ☐
Debra CI GTS/LS CH66 ...... 94 E8
Debra Rd GTS/LS CH66 ...... 120 C1
Dee Av HALE/TIMP WA15 ...... 43 K7
Dee Banks CHSE CH3 ...... 17 M9
Dee CI ALS/KID ST7 ...... 242 C7
  BIDD ST8 ...... 227 L3 ☐
  SBCH CW11 ...... 203 L4
Dee Crs CHSE CH3 ...... 228 E2
Dee Fords Av CHSE CH3 ...... 170 A3
Dee Hills Pk CHSE CH3 ...... 17 K5
  CHSE CH3 ...... 17 K5
  WRXS/E LL13 ...... 228 D4
Dee Mdw WRXS/E LL13 ...... 228 D5
Dee Pk WRXS/E LL13 ...... 228 D4
Deepdale LEIGH WN7 ...... 25 J1 ☐
Deep DI WARRW/BUR WA5 ...... 35 M6
Deepdale Av WDN WA8 ...... 52 C1
Deepdale Dr RAIN/WH L35 ...... 33 K1
Deepwood Gv RAIN/WH L35 ...... 32 E2 ☐
Deeracre Av OFTN SK2 ...... 47 J6
Deermoss WHITCH SY13 ...... 270 A4 ☐
Dee Rd CHNE CH2 ...... 146 F3
  CO CH5 ...... 142 F5
  RAIN/WH L35 ...... 33 H1
Deer Park Ct RUNC WA7 ...... 73 M6 ☐
Deerwood CI GTS/LS CH66 ...... 94 D5 ☐
Deerwood Crs GTS/LS CH66 ...... 94 D5
  MCFLDN SK10 ...... 137 K8 ☐
Dee Vw CHSE CH3 ...... 228 E2
Dee Wy WSFD CW7 ...... 178 A2 ☐
Deiniol's Rd CO CH5 ...... 166 E2 ☐
Deirdre Av WDN WA8 ...... 7 H3
De Lacy Rw RUNC WA7 ...... 74 A2
Delafield CI WARRN/WOL WA2 .. 37 M1
Delaford CI EDGY/DAV SK3 ...... 46 E8 ☐
Delahays Dr HALE/TIMP WA15 .. 62 A2
Delahays Rd HALE/TIMP WA15... 62 B2
Delamere Av CHD/CHDH SK8 .. 45 H7
  CONG CW12 ...... 206 F1
  FROD/HEL WA6 ...... 126 B6
  NANT CW5 ...... 251 L1
  OFTN SK2 ...... 47 H8
  WDN WA8 ...... 52 C3
Delamere CI BRAM/HZG SK7 ...... 65 J7
  SBCH CW11 ...... 203 M4
Delamere Dr GTS/LS CH66 ...... 94 E8
  MCFLDN SK10 ...... 15 M1
Delamere La CHSE CH3 ...... 149 J2
Delamere Park Wy East
  NWCHW CW8 ...... 127 K7
Delamere Park Wy West
  NWCHW CW8 ...... 127 K7
Delamere Ri WSFD CW7 ...... 177 H3 ☐
Delamere Rd BRAM/HZG SK7 .. 65 H7
  CHD/CHDH SK8 ...... 45 H7
  CONG CW12 ...... 206 F1
  FROD/HEL WA6 ...... 126 B6
  NANT CW5 ...... 251 L1
  OFTN SK2 ...... 47 H8
  WDN WA8 ...... 52 C3
Delamere St CH/BCN CH1 ...... 16 F3
  CW/HAS CW1 ...... 221 J6
  WARRW/BUR WA5 ...... 4 B6
  WSFD CW7 ...... 177 G3
Delamere Wy FROD/HEL WA6 ...... 99 J7
  FROD/HEL WA6 ...... 150 B1
  WARRS WA4 ...... 76 A5
Delamer Rd ALT WA14 ...... 61 J1
Delamore's Acre NSTN CH64 ...... 91 K8
Delenty Dr GOL/RIS/CU WA3 ...... 29 K8
Delery Dr WARR WA1 ...... 37 L4
Delf La SPK/HALE L24 ...... 50 D7
Delfur Rd BRAM/HZG SK7 ...... 65 K6
Delhi Rd IRL M44 ...... 31 M4
Delhi Rd WARRN/WOL WA2 ...... 38 A2
Dell CI ALS/KID ST7 ...... 242 C7
Dell Side MPL/ROM SK6 ...... 47 L1
The Dell CHSE CH3 ...... 146 F7 ☐
  NWCHW CW8 ...... 127 J8
  TPLY/KEL CW6 ...... 197 J8
Delmar Rd KNUT WA16 ...... 107 J3
Delphfields Rd WARRS WA4 ...... 56 C5
Delphield RUNC WA7 ...... 74 D4
Delph La WARRN/WOL WA2 ...... 28 E6
  WARRS WA4 ...... 75 C1
Delta CI CHSW/BR CH4 ...... 168 B6 ☐

Delves Av WARRW/BUR WA5 ...... 4 C2
Delves CI CW/SHV CW2 ...... 238 B8
Delves Wk CHSE CH3 ...... 170 B5
Delvine Dr CHNE CH2 ...... 145 K6
Delwood Gdns
  WYTH/NTH M22 ...... 44 D8 ☐
Demage CI BIDD ST8 ...... 227 J6
Demage La CH/BCN CH1 ...... 120 D1
  CHNE CH2 ...... 145 K4
Demmings Rd CHD/CHDH SK8 .. 45 M7
Denbigh CI BIDD ST8 ...... 227 J6
  BRAM/HZG SK7 ...... 66 C4
  FROD/HEL WA6 ...... 124 A3
Denbigh Crs MWCH CW10 ...... 179 J5
Denbigh Dr WSFD CW7 ...... 177 H5
Denbigh Gdns EP CH65 ...... 121 J1 ☐
Denbigh St CH/BCN CH1 ...... 16 D2
  HTNM SK4 ...... 12 D4
Denbury Av WARRS WA4 ...... 56 F2
Denbury Dr ALT WA14 ...... 42 B7 ☐
Denbury Gn BRAM/HZG SK7 ...... 66 A2
Dene CT WARRS WA4 ...... 2 A3
Dene Dr WSFD CW7 ...... 177 K4
Denefield CI MPL/ROM SK6 ...... 49 H3 ☐
  WARRW/BUR WA5 ...... 35 M8 ☐
Denehurst CI
  WARRW/BUR WA5 ...... 35 M8 ☐
Denehurst Park Wy
  NWCHW CW8 ...... 127 K7
Dene Pk DID/WITH M20 ...... 45 C2
Dene Rd West DID/WITH M20.... 44 F1
Denesgate WSFD CW7 ...... 177 K4 ☐
Deneside Av CW/HAS CW1 ...... 221 J6
Deneside Crs BRAM/HZG SK7 .. 66 F1
Denesway SALE M33 ...... 42 E1 ☐
Deneway BRAM/HZG SK7 ...... 65 J5
  HTNM SK4 ...... 2 A3
  MPL/ROM SK6 ...... 67 M5
Deneway CI HTNM SK4 ...... 2 A3
Deneway Ms HTNM SK4 ...... 2 A3
Denford CI CHSW/BR CH4 ...... 167 J8 ☐
Denford PI ALS/KID ST7 ...... 224 D6
Denhall CI CHNE CH2 ...... 145 L7
Denhall La NSTN CH64 ...... 118 A2
Denham Av WARRW/BUR WA5... 36 B7
Denham Dr BRAM/HZG SK7 ...... 65 K5
Denholm Rd DID/WITH M20 ...... 45 J4 ☐
Denise Av WARRW/BUR WA5 ...... 35 L7
Denison Rd BRAM/HZG SK7 ...... 66 E4
Den La NANT CW5 ...... 254 A6
Denmark St HALE/TIMP WA15 .. 42 D8
Dennett CI WARR WA1 ...... 38 E6
Dennis Dr CHSW/BR CH4 ...... 169 H6
Dennison Rd CHD/CHDH SK8 .. 65 G4
Dennis Rd WDN WA8 ...... 7 L6
Densham Av WARRN/WOL WA2... 37 H2
Denshaw CI BNG/LEV M19 ...... 45 L1
Denson Dr CQ CH5 ...... 166 A2
Denson Rd HALE/TIMP WA15 .. 43 H4
Denston CI CW/SHV CW2 ...... 18 C9
Denstone Av SALE M33 ...... 42 E1 ☐
Denstone CI WLTN L25 ...... 50 B4 ☐
Denstone Dr CHSW/BR CH4 ...... 169 G8
Dentith Dr CH/BCN CH1 ...... 144 B8
Denton CI WSFD CW7 ...... 177 J3 ☐
Denton Dr NWCHE CW9 ...... 130 C3
Denton St WDN WA8 ...... 7 L3
Denver Av CW/SHV CW2 ...... 18 D6
Denver Dr HALE/TIMP WA15 .. 43 J7 ☐
Denver Rd WARRS WA4 ...... 57 G3
Denville Crs WYTH/NTH M22 ...... 63 L1
Depenbech CI MALPAS SY14 .... 246 B8
Depleach Rd CHD/CHDH SK8 .. 45 K7 ☐
Depmore La FROD/HEL WA6 .... 126 A2
Deptford Av NTHM/RTH M23 .. 63 G1 ☐
De Quincey Rd ALT WA14 ...... 42 D3
Derby CI IRL M44 ...... 31 J7
  NEWLW WA12 ...... 27 H1 ☐
Derby Ct SALE M33 ...... 43 J1 ☐
Derby Dr WARR WA1 ...... 37 M5
Derby PI CHNE CH2 ...... 17 K1
Derby Rd ALS/KID ST7 ...... 242 D5
  GOL/RIS/CU WA3 ...... 23 J3
  NM/HAY SK22 ...... 69 K3
  WARRS WA4 ...... 56 C4
  WDN WA8 ...... 34 D8
Derby Rw NEWLW WA12 ...... 27 K4
Derbyshire Hill Rd STHEL WA9.. 26 A1
Derbyshire Rd PART M31 ...... 40 E2 ☐
  POY/DIS SK12 ...... 67 K7
Derbyshire Rd South SALE M33.. 43 K1
Derby St ALT WA14 ...... 42 F7
  CONG CW12 ...... 207 K1 ☐
  CW/HAS CW1 ...... 18 C1
  EDGY/DAV SK3 ...... 2 D8
  HUY L36 ...... 32 A2
  MPL/ROM SK6 ...... 48 F7
  NEWLW WA12 ...... 27 H1
Derek Av WARRN/WOL WA2 ...... 37 K3
Derrington Av CW/SHV CW2.... 18 F6
Derry Av WYTH/NTH M22 ...... 44 B8
Derwen Rd EDGY/DAV SK3 ...... 46 E5
Derwent Av GOL/RIS/CU WA3 .. 23 J6
  HALE/TIMP WA15 ...... 43 K7 ☐
  WSFD CW7 ...... 178 A2 ☐
Derwent CI ALS/KID ST7 ...... 224 A8
  GOL/RIS/CU WA3 ...... 30 A2 ☐
  HOLMCH CW4 ...... 181 G1
  LEIGH WN7 ...... 24 E1 ☐
  MCFLDS SK11 ...... 14 A9
  NANT CW5 ...... 237 K6
  PART M31 ...... 31 M8
  RAIN/WH L35 ...... 33 H1
Derwent Crs ALS/KID ST7 ...... 243 J2
Derwent Dr BIDD ST8 ...... 227 L3 ☐
  BRAM/HZG SK7 ...... 65 J7 ☐
  CONG CW12 ...... 207 M3
  GTS/LS CH66 ...... 94 B2
  SALE M33 ...... 43 G2
  WILM/AE SK9 ...... 84 C7
Derwent Rd CHNE CH2 ...... 145 M7
  MPL/ROM SK6 ...... 67 L4
  WARRS WA4 ...... 56 A2
  WDN WA8 ...... 52 C3

Desoto Rd WDN WA8 .... 52 E7
Desoto Rd East WDN WA8 .... 6 E9
Deva Av CHSW/BR CH4 .... 168 D6
Deva Cl BRAM/HZG SK7 .... 66 D3
　FLINT CH6 .... 116 C7
　POY/DIS SK12 .... 66 B8
Deva La CHNE CH2 .... 145 J6
Deva Link CH/BCN CH1 .... 16 A2
Deva Rd CW/SHV CW2 .... 220 D8
Devisdale Rd ALT WA14 .... 42 B8
Devon Cl MCFLDN SK10 .... 137 M2
　MWCH CW10 .... 179 L2
Devon Gv BIDD ST8 .... 227 J3
Devon Pl CONG CW12 .... 184 E8
　WDN WA8 .... 53 G1 [2]
Devon Rd CHNE CH2 .... 145 M7
　IRL M44 .... 31 K7
　PART M31 .... 40 E2 [1]
Devonshire Dr WILM/AE SK9 .... 110 B2
Devonshire Gdns NEWLW WA12 .... 27 J2
Devonshire Park Rd OFTN SK2 .... 47 G7
Devonshire Pl CHSW/BR CH4 .... 17 J9
　RUNC WA7 .... 9 C1
Devonshire Rd ALT WA14 .... 42 C6
　BRAM/HZG SK7 .... 66 F4
　CHSW/BR CH4 .... 167 J8
　HTNM SK4 .... 46 B2
　WARR WA1 .... 37 M4
Dewar Ct RUNC WA7 .... 75 L1
De Warenne Cl WHITCH SY13 .... 270 B5
Dewar St GOL/RIS/CU WA3 .... 29 L7
Dewes Ct CW/HAS CW1 .... 18 D2
Dewhurst Rd GOL/RIS/CU WA3 .... 38 D2
Dewint Av MPL/ROM SK6 .... 49 H4
Dial Cl CONG CW12 .... 209 G3
Dial Park Rd OFTN SK2 .... 47 K8
Dial Rd HALE/TIMP WA15 .... 62 C4
　OFTN SK2 .... 47 J7
Dialstone La OFTN SK2 .... 47 J5
Dial St WARR WA1 .... 4 F5
Diamond Av ALS/KID ST7 .... 243 H2
Diamond Cl BIDD ST8 .... 227 J4
Diamond Cl OFTN SK2 .... 47 G6
Diamond Ter MPL/ROM SK6 .... 67 M1
Dickens Cl CHD/CHDH SK8 .... 65 H7 [1]
　SBCH CW11 .... 203 K6
Dickens La POY/DIS SK12 .... 86 E1
Dickenson St WARRN/WOL WA2 .... 5 J3
Dickson Cl WDN WA8 .... 7 J4
Dicksons Dr CHNE CH2 .... 145 K7
Dickson St WDN WA8 .... 7 H4
Didcot Cl WLTN L25 .... 50 D4
Didcot Rd WYTH/NTH M22 .... 63 J3
Didsbury Pk DID/WITH M20 .... 45 H2
Didsbury Rd HTNM SK4 .... 45 L2
Dierdens Ter MWCH CW10 .... 179 J3
Dierden St WSFD CW7 .... 178 B3
Diglake Cl ALS/KID ST7 .... 242 C6
Diglands Mn NM/HAY SK22 .... 69 K3
Dig La FROD/HEL WA6 .... 99 J5
　NANT CW5 .... 253 H2
　WARRN/WOL WA2 .... 29 G8
Diglee Rd CHF/WBR SK23 .... 89 J1
Dilworth Cl OFTN SK2 .... 47 L7
Dinas Cl CH/BCN CH1 .... 168 D1
Dingle Av NEWLW WA12 .... 26 F2
　WILM/AE SK9 .... 109 L1
Dingle Bank CHSW/BR CH4 .... 16 E9
Dingle Bank Cl LYMM WA13 .... 58 E1
Dingle Bank Rd BRAM/HZG SK7 .... 65 K2
Dingle Cl MCFLDN SK10 .... 138 B1
　MPL/ROM SK6 .... 48 D2
Dingle Gv CHD/CHDH SK8 .... 44 F6
Dingle La BIDD ST8 .... 209 K7
　NANT CW5 .... 265 M5
　SBCH CW11 .... 204 C6
　TPLY/KEL CW6 .... 149 L6
　WARRS WA4 .... 56 F6
　WSFD CW7 .... 177 G3 [2]
The Dingle BRAM/HZG SK7 .... 65 J3
　CW/HAS CW1 .... 222 D7
　LYMM WA13 .... 58 E1 [1]
Dingle Wy NWCHW CW8 .... 127 L7 [1]
Dingleway WARRS WA4 .... 56 D4
Dinmor Rd WYTH/NTH M22 .... 63 J3
Diploma Dr MWCH CW10 .... 179 J2
Dirty Mile CO CH5 .... 166 A8
Distaff Rd POY/DIS SK12 .... 66 B8
Ditchfield La KNUT WA16 .... 59 H8
Ditchfield Pl WDN WA8 .... 52 B4
Ditchfield Rd WARRW/BUR WA5 .... 54 E1
　WDN WA8 .... 52 A4
Ditton Rd WDN WA8 .... 6 F8
Dixon Av NEWLW WA12 .... 22 C7
Dixon Rd RNFD/HAY WA11 .... 22 A4
　SALE M33 .... 43 K2
Dixon Dr MCFLDS SK11 .... 134 F1
Dixon St IRL M44 .... 31 L4
　WARR WA1 .... 4 F1
Dobb Hedge Cl
　HALE/TIMP WA15 .... 62 C6
Dobbinetts La HALE/TIMP WA15 .... 62 D1
　NTHM/RTH M23 .... 43 J3
Dobell's Rd NWCHW CW8 .... 13 H7
Dobers La FROD/HEL WA6 .... 125 J1
Dock Rd CQ CH5 .... 142 A4
　NWCHE CW9 .... 13 H4
　WDN WA8 .... 52 F7
　WDN WA8 .... 53 G7
Dock St EP CH65 .... 10 F4
　WDN WA8 .... 53 C7
Dock Yard Rd EP CH65 .... 11 H6
Doctors Cl BIDD ST8 .... 227 J4
Doddington Cl SBCH CW11 .... 204 C4
Doddington Rd CW/SHV CW2 .... 18 A6
Dodd's Green La WHITCH SY13 .... 272 B2
Dodd's La CONG CW12 .... 207 J3
　MALPAS SY14 .... 258 C3
Doddswood Dr CONG CW12 .... 184 F8 [1]
Dodge Fold OFTN SK2 .... 47 K1
Dodge Hl HTNM SK4 .... 2 F3
Dodgsley Dr FROD/HEL WA6 .... 126 C3
Dodington WHITCH SY13 .... 270 A5
Dodleston La CHSW/BR CH4 .... 191 G7
Dog La CHSE CH3 .... 213 J8
　HOLMCH CW4 .... 181 L5

MALPAS SY14 .... 256 E4
NANT CW5 .... 20 E5
TPLY/KEL CW6 .... 149 H7
Dogmore La TPLY/KEL CW6 .... 198 C5
Dolphin Crs GTS/LS CH66 .... 120 E2
Dombey Rd POY/DIS SK12 .... 86 D2
Domestic Ap MANAIR M90 .... 63 J6
Dominic Cl NTHM/RTH M23 .... 43 L3 [2]
Domville RAIN/WH L35 .... 32 E2
Domville Cl LYMM WA13 .... 58 E1
Donagh Rd MCFLDN SK10 .... 137 M2
Dona St STKP SK1 .... 3 K7
Donkey La WILM/AE SK9 .... 84 A7
Donne Pl CH/BCN CH1 .... 145 G6
Donnington Av CHD/CHDH SK8 .... 45 M6
Donnington Cl LEIGH WN7 .... 24 D3
Donnington Wy
　CHSW/BR CH4 .... 168 F5 [2]
Dood's La WARRS WA4 .... 57 H7
Doodson Av IRL M44 .... 31 M2
Dooley La MPL/ROM SK6 .... 48 B5
Dooley's Grig MCFLDS SK11 .... 158 F3
Dooley's La WILM/AE SK9 .... 83 H2
Dorac Av CHD/CHDH SK8 .... 64 C6
Dorchester Cl ALS/KID ST7 .... 243 G1 [1]
　HALE/TIMP WA15 .... 62 C1 [1]
　WILM/AE SK9 .... 84 D4 [1]
Dorchester Ct CHD/CHDH SK8 .... 65 H3
　SALE M33 .... 43 H2
Dorchester Dr NTHM/RTH M23 .... 43 L3
Dorchester Pk RUNC WA7 .... 74 D1
Dorchester Rd BRAM/HZG SK7 .... 66 B3
　CHSW/BR CH4 .... 168 F7
　WARRW/BUR WA5 .... 36 B7
Dorchester Wy MCFLDN SK10 .... 138 C1
　WARRW/BUR WA5 .... 26 F8 [1]
Doreen Av CONG CW12 .... 208 B4 [1]
Dorfield Cl MPL/ROM SK6 .... 47 L1 [1]
Dorfold Cl SBCH CW11 .... 204 C5
Dorfold Dr NANT CW5 .... 20 C7
Dorfold Wy CHNE CH2 .... 145 L6 [1]
Doric Av FROD/HEL WA6 .... 99 J5
　MPL/ROM SK6 .... 47 K1
Doris Rd EDGY/DAV SK3 ....
Dorking St STKP SK1 .... 3 M9 [1]
Dorland Gv OFTN SK2 .... 47 H5 [1]
Dormer Cl CHSE CH3 .... 171 G7
Dorney Cl WARRS WA4 .... 56 E6
Dornoch Ct HOLMCH CW4 .... 181 H2
Dorothea St WARRN/WOL WA2 .... 5 J2
Dorothy Rd BRAM/HZG SK7 .... 66 F1
Dorric Wy CW/HAS CW1 .... 221 J5
Dorrington Cl RUNC WA7 .... 74 D4 [1]
Dorrington Rd EDGY/DAV SK3 .... 46 A5
Dorrit Cl POY/DIS SK12 .... 86 E2
Dorset Av BRAM/HZG SK7 .... 65 K3
　CHD/CHDH SK8 .... 46 C8
Dorset Cl CONG CW12 .... 184 E8
Dorset Dr BIDD ST8 .... 227 J4
Dorset Pl ALS/KID ST7 .... 243 G1
　CHNE CH2 .... 146 A7
Dorset Rd ALT WA14 .... 42 B8
　CHNE CH2 .... 145 M5
　HUY L36 .... 32 A1
　IRL M44 .... 31 K6
Dorset Wy WARR WA1 .... 38 A4
Douglas Av BIDD ST8 .... 227 J5
　STHEL WA9 .... 26 B6
Douglas Cl NWCHW CW8 .... 12 B9
　WDN WA8 .... 53 M1
Douglas La WSFD CW7 .... 200 A6
Douglas Pl CHSW/BR CH4 .... 168 E6
Douglas Rd BRAM/HZG SK7 .... 66 E1
　EDGY/DAV SK3 .... 46 E8
Dounrey Cl WARRN/WOL WA2 .... 38 A2
Douthwaite Dr MPL/ROM SK6 .... 48 E3
Dove Cl CHNE CH2 .... 97 J8
　EP CH65 ....
　FROD/HEL WA6 .... 98 C7 [1]
　GOL/RIS/CU WA3 .... 29 M8
　SBCH CW11 .... 204 A4
Dovecote Cl CW/SHV CW2 .... 238 B4
Dovecote Gn
　WARRW/BUR WA5 .... 36 A3 [1]
Dove Ct WLTN L25 .... 50 B1 [1]
Dovedale Cl BURS/TUN ST6 .... 243 H5
　CONG CW12 .... 185 G8 [1]
　MPL/ROM SK6 ....
　WARRN/WOL WA2 .... 37 L1 [1]
Dovedale Rd OFTN SK2 .... 47 K5
Dove Gv BIDD ST8 .... 227 J5
Dove Pl WSFD CW7 .... 178 B2 [1]
Dover Cl RUNC WA7 .... 74 E6
　WSFD CW7 .... 177 H6
Dover Dr EP CH65 .... 121 K2
Dover Rd CHSW/BR CH4 .... 169 G7
　MCFLDN SK10 .... 15 L1
　WARRS WA4 .... 57 G1
Dover St GOL/RIS/CU WA3 .... 23 G2
　RUNC WA7 .... 9 J1
Doward St WDN WA8 .... 7 L1
Dowland Ct NTHM/RTH M23 .... 43 M2 [1]
Downes Cl MCFLDS SK11 .... 14 B2
Downesway WILM/AE SK9 .... 109 M3
Downham Av
　GOL/RIS/CU WA3 .... 29 M2 [1]
Downham Cha
　HALE/TIMP WA15 .... 43 H6 [1]
Downham Pl CH/BCN CH1 .... 144 E8
Downham Wk NTHM/RTH M23 .... 43 K4
Downing Cl MCFLDS SK11 .... 162 F1
Downs Dr ALT WA14 .... 42 E4
Downs End KNUT WA16 .... 107 J3
Downsfield Rd CHSW/BR CH4 .... 168 F8
Downside WDN WA8 .... 52 B1
Downs Rd RUNC WA7 .... 9 H5
Downway La STHEL WA9 .... 26 A3
Doyle Av RAIN/WH L35 .... 32 D2
Dragon La RAIN/WH L35 .... 32 D2
Dragon's La MWCH CW10 .... 202 B2
　SBCH CW11 .... 203 G3
Dragon Yd WDN WA8 .... 34 B8 [1]
Drake Av IRL M44 .... 31 L6
Drake Cl RAIN/WH L35 .... 32 E2 [1]
　WARRW/BUR WA5 .... 36 D3 [1]

Drake La NANT CW5 .... 235 L8
Drakelow La MWCH CW10 .... 155 L4
Drake Rd ALT WA14 .... 42 B4
　NSTN CH64 .... 91 L3
Drakes Wy MALPAS SY14 .... 246 B7
Drayford Cl NTHM/RTH M23 .... 43 M2 [1]
Drayton Av CHD/CHDH SK8 .... 64 B5
Drayton Cl RUNC WA7 .... 8 E4
　SALE M33 .... 42 D2
Drayton Crs CW/HAS CW1 .... 19 L2
Drayton Gv HALE/TIMP WA15 .... 43 G8
Drenfell Rd NWCHE CW9 .... 13 H3
Drill Field Rd NWCHE CW9 .... 13 H5
The Drive CHD/CHDH SK8 .... 46 C8
　DID/WITH M20 .... 45 J1
　HALE/TIMP WA15 .... 62 D4
　HOLMCH CW4 .... 181 J2
　LEIGH WN7 .... 24 F1 [1]
　LYMM WA13 .... 59 K3
　MPL/ROM SK6 .... 47 K1
　MPL/ROM SK6 .... 48 E6
　SALE M33 .... 42 E3
Drive Wy RAIN/WH L35 .... 32 E2
Driveway RAIN/WH L35 .... 32 F2 [1]
Dronfield Rd WYTH/NTH M22 .... 44 D4
Drovers Wy SBCH CW11 .... 204 A7
Druid Cl AIMK WN4 .... 22 C2 [1]
Drumber La ALS/KID ST7 .... 226 B4
Drumble Fld MCFLDS SK11 .... 135 G1
Drumburn Cl BURS/TUN ST6 .... 243 M5
Drummond Av GTS/LS CH66 .... 94 C8
Drummond Ct WDN WA8 .... 53 K2 [1]
Drummond St
　BURS/TUN ST6 .... 243 K5 [1]
Drummond Wy
　MCFLDN SK10 .... 137 L3 [1]
Druridge Dr WARRW/BUR WA5 .... 35 M8
Drury Cl CW/HAS CW1 .... 19 L2
Drury La CQ CH5 .... 166 A7
　CW/HAS CW1 .... 202 D8
　KNUT WA16 .... 107 G2
Dryden Av CHD/CHDH SK8 .... 45 L6
Dryden Cl CW/SHV CW2 .... 238 A4 [1]
　MPL/ROM SK6 .... 48 F8
　RAIN/WH L35 .... 32 E1
Dryden Pl WARRN/WOL WA2 .... 37 J2
Dryhurst Dr POY/DIS SK12 .... 68 D6
Dryhurst La POY/DIS SK12 .... 68 D6
Dublin Cft GTS/LS CH66 .... 120 E3
Duchy Rd CW/HAS CW1 .... 239 G4
Duchy St EDGY/DAV SK3 .... 2 D9
Duckers La CQ CH5 .... 166 E2
Duck La CHSE CH3 .... 148 F5
Duckworth Gv
　WARRN/WOL WA2 .... 38 A3
Duddon Cl TPLY/KEL CW6 .... 173 G6
Duddon Hook La
　TPLY/KEL CW6 .... 172 F6
Duddon Rd TPLY/KEL CW6 .... 173 H7
Dudleston Rd GTS/LS CH66 .... 94 B6
Dudley Av RUNC WA7 .... 73 K2
Dudley Crs PS/BROM CH62 .... 94 B1
Dudley Rd EP CH65 .... 10 D8
　HALE/TIMP WA15 .... 43 H5
　IRL M44 .... 31 K8
Dudley St WARRN/WOL WA2 .... 5 H2
Dudlow Green Rd WARRS WA4 .... 56 D7
Duke Av CHD/CHDH SK8 .... 64 F6
　GOL/RIS/CU WA3 .... 25 J5
Duke Cl RUNC WA7 .... 8 E2
Dukefield St WYTH/NTH M22 .... 44 E4 [1]
Duke's Crs SBCH CW11 .... 204 A4
Duke St AIMK WN4 .... 22 C1
　BIDD ST8 .... 227 K5
　CH/BCN CH1 .... 17 G7
　CW/SHV CW2 .... 18 E5
　FLINT CH6 .... 116 A6
　GOL/RIS/CU WA3 .... 23 G3
　MCFLDS SK11 .... 15 G6
　NEWLW WA12 .... 27 H1 [1]
　STKP SK1 .... 2 F6
　WILM/AE SK9 .... 110 B2
Dukesway CHD/CHDH SK8 .... 145 L5
Dukes St CHNE CH2 .... 184 E8
Dulas Ct CHNE CH2 .... 145 L4
Dulverton Av CHSE CH3 .... 170 C2 [1]
Dulwich Cl SALE M33 .... 42 D1
Dumbah La MCFLDN SK10 .... 112 C6
Dumbers MCFLDS SK11 .... 187 G2
Dunacre Wy HLWD L26 .... 50 F5
Dunbar Av NTHM/RTH M23 .... 63 G1
Dunbar Cl GTS/LS CH66 .... 94 C7
　HOLMCH CW4 .... 181 H2
Dunbeath Av RAIN/WH L35 .... 33 K3
Dunbeath Cl RAIN/WH L35 .... 33 K3
Dunblane Av HTNM SK4 .... 2 C3
Duncan Av NEWLW WA12 .... 22 C7
　RUNC WA7 .... 9 L4
Duncansby Crs
　WARRW/BUR WA5 .... 35 L6 [2]
Duncan St WARRN/WOL WA2 .... 5 K2
Duncombe Cl BRAM/HZG SK7 .... 66 A1 [1]
Dundalk La WDN WA8 .... 6 B4
Dundalk Rd WDN WA8 .... 6 B4
Dundas St CQ CH5 .... 142 D7
Dundee Cl WARRN/WOL WA2 .... 28 E8
Dundonald Av WARRS WA4 .... 56 C3 [1]
Dundonald Rd CHD/CHDH SK8 .... 65 G5
　DID/WITH M20 .... 45 J1
Dundonald St OFTN SK2 .... 47 G7
Dundrennan Cl POY/DIS SK12 .... 66 D7 [1]
Dunelm Dr NTHM/RTH M23 .... 43 K3
Dungeon La SPK/HALE L24 .... 70 F3
The Downs ALT WA14 .... 61 K1
　CHD/CHDH SK8 .... 64 D1
　NWCHW CW8 .... 127 K7
Dunham Av GOL/RIS/CU WA3 .... 22 F3 [1]
　SBCH CW11 .... 204 C6
Dunham Crs CW/SHV CW2 .... 238 B4
Dunham Gv LEIGH WN7 .... 24 F4
Dunham Lawn ALT WA14 .... 42 B8 [1]
Dunham Ms ALT WA14 .... 42 C8
Dunham Rd ALT WA14 .... 42 B8
　LYMM WA13 .... 40 E5
　NWCHE CW9 .... 129 M8

PART M31 .... 41 K1
Dunham Wy CHNE CH2 .... 145 M6 [2]
Dunkeld Rd NTHM/RTH M23 .... 43 M2
Dunkery Rd WYTH/NTH M22 .... 63 K3
Dunkirk Dr EP CH65 .... 121 G3
Dunkirk Cl CH/BCN CH1 .... 120 C4
　GTS/LS CH66 .... 121 G3
Dunley Cl GOL/RIS/CU WA3 .... 30 A6 [1]
Dunlin Av NEWLW WA12 .... 22 C8 [1]
Dunlin Cl OFTN SK2 .... 48 A7
　POY/DIS SK12 .... 66 A8
　RUNC WA7 .... 73 M7
　WARRN/WOL WA2 .... 37 L1
Dunlop Rd SPK/HALE L24 .... 70 B2
Dunlop St WARRS WA4 .... 56 B1 [1]
Dunmail Gv RUNC WA7 .... 73 L8 [1]
Dunmore Cl CHD/CHDH SK8 .... 45 M6
Dunmore Crs GTS/LS CH66 .... 94 B6
Dunmore Rd CHD/CHDH SK8 .... 45 M6
　GTS/LS CH66 .... 94 B6
Dunmow Ct OFTN SK2 .... 47 L7
Dunmow WARRS WA4 .... 57 J1
Dunmow Wy WLTN L25 .... 50 C4
Dunning St BURS/TUN ST6 .... 243 K8 [1]
Dunnisher Rd NTHM/RTH M23 .... 44 B8
Dunnock Cl OFTN SK2 .... 48 A7
　WARRN/WOL WA2 .... 37 L1 [1]
Dunnockfold Rd ALS/KID ST7 .... 223 M8
Dunnockswood ALS/KID ST7 .... 224 A8
Dunnock Wy BIDD ST8 .... 227 L4 [1]
Dunn's Rake CHSE CH3 .... 148 F5
Dunollie Rd SALE M33 .... 43 L1
Dunoon Cl HOLMCH CW4 .... 181 H2
Dunraven Rd NSTN CH64 .... 92 A5
Dunscar Cl GOL/RIS/CU WA3 .... 29 K7
Dunsdale Dr AIMK WN4 .... 22 C1
Dunsfold Dr NTHM/RTH M23 .... 43 K4
Dunsford WDN WA8 .... 53 H1 [1]
Dunstall Rd WYTH/NTH M22 .... 44 E7
Dunstan La NSTN CH64 .... 118 E2
Dunster Cl BRAM/HZG SK7 .... 66 C3
　NWCHE CW9 .... 130 A8 [1]
Dunster Rd MCFLDN SK10 .... 15 L2
Dunvegan Rd BRAM/HZG SK7 .... 66 F3
Dunwood Dr ALS/KID ST7 .... 224 D6
Durban Av CHSE CH3 .... 170 D5
Durham Av MCFLDN SK10 .... 137 M2
　MPL/ROM SK6 .... 48 A3 [2]
　WARR WA1 .... 38 E5 [2]
Durham Dr IRL M44 .... 31 J6
Durham Rd CH/BCN CH1 .... 144 F7
　WDN WA8 .... 53 H1 [2]
　WILM/AE SK9 .... 64 D7 [2]
Durley Av HALE/TIMP WA15 .... 43 H5
Durlston Cl WDN WA8 .... 52 C2
Durrell Wy GOL/RIS/CU WA3 .... 23 L4
Dursley RAIN/WH L35 .... 32 F2
Dutton Cl NANT CW5 .... 251 L1
Dutton Gn EP CH65 .... 121 M1
Dutton Gv LEIGH WN7 .... 25 J2 [1]
Dutton La FROD/HEL WA6 .... 127 H6
Dutton's La TPLY/KEL CW6 .... 149 J7
Dutton St WARR WA1 .... 5 J7
Dutton Wy CW/HAS CW1 .... 221 H6
Duxford Ct WARRN/WOL WA2 .... 37 L3 [1]
Dyar Ter CHSW/BR CH4 .... 129 K3
Dye House La NM/HAY SK22 .... 69 J4
Dye La MPL/ROM SK6 .... 48 B2
Dyers Cl LYMM WA13 .... 40 A8 [1]
Dyers La LYMM WA13 .... 40 A8
Dyer St GOL/RIS/CU WA3 .... 22 F4
Dyfed Dr CQ CH5 .... 142 D8
Dykin Cl WDN WA8 .... 53 L1
Dykin Rd WDN WA8 .... 53 K1
Dymchurch Rd SPK/HALE L24 .... 50 B8
Dysart St OFTN SK2 .... 47 H7
Dyserth Rd CH/BCN CH1 .... 168 D1
Dystelegh Rd POY/DIS SK12 .... 68 E7

E

Eadie Gv CW/HAS CW1 .... 221 G5
Eaglais Wy MCFLDN SK10 .... 137 M2
Eagland Pl CONG CW12 .... 184 E8
Eagle Brow LYMM WA13 .... 58 D1
Eagle La GTS/LS CH66 .... 94 D5
Eaglesfield NWCHW CW8 .... 129 J8
Eagles Wy RUNC WA7 .... 73 L6
Ealing Rd WARRW/BUR WA5 .... 36 A7
Eanleywood La RUNC WA7 .... 74 C5
Eardley Crs CONG CW12 .... 184 D8
Eardleyend Rd ALS/KID ST7 .... 241 L5
Eardswick Cl CHNE CH2 .... 17 G1
Eardswick La CW/HAS CW1 .... 201 K7
Eardswick Rd MWCH CW10 .... 179 K6
Earle Cl NEWLW WA12 .... 26 F1
Earle Crs NSTN CH64 .... 91 K3
Earle Dr NSTN CH64 .... 91 K4
Earle Rd BRAM/HZG SK7 .... 65 L2
　WDN WA8 .... 7 L6
Earle's Crs CQ CH5 .... 166 E1
Earles La NWCHE CW9 .... 104 E6
　TPLY/KEL CW6 .... 149 J7
Earle St CW/HAS CW1 .... 19 G3
　NEWLW WA12 .... 26 F2
Earl Rd CHD/CHDH SK8 .... 64 F7
　WILM/AE SK9 .... 65 G5
Earls Gdns EP CH65 .... 10 C7
Earls Oak CHNE CH2 .... 145 K5
Earls Rd CW/SHV CW2 .... 238 B8
Earl St EDGY/DAV SK3 .... 2 C8
　FLINT CH6 .... 116 A5
　WARRN/WOL WA2 .... 5 H2
Earlsway CHSW/BR CH4 .... 16 B9
　MCFLDS SK11 .... 137 L6
Earls Wy NWCHE CW9 .... 129 M8
　RUNC WA7 .... 73 L5 [1]
Earlwood Gdns RAIN/WH L35 .... 32 E2 [1]
Earnshaw Av STKP SK1 .... 3 M6
Easby Cl CHD/CHDH SK8 .... 65 H6
　POY/DIS SK12 .... 66 D7
Easenhall Cl WDN WA8 .... 34 B8
East Av CHD/CHDH SK8 .... 64 D4

CW/SHV CW2 .... 239 J7
GOL/RIS/CU WA3 .... 23 J3
LEIGH WN7 .... 25 J1
MCFLDN SK10 .... 112 E5
NWCHE CW9 .... 130 D6
WARRN/WOL WA2 .... 5 J1
WARRS WA4 .... 56 D3
WARRW/BUR WA5 .... 36 A8
Eastbury Cl WDN WA8 .... 34 C7
Eastcott Cl CONG CW12 .... 183 M8
Eastdale Pl ALT WA14 .... 42 D5 [1]
Eastdale Rd WARR WA1 .... 38 A5
East Dam Wood Rd
　SPK/HALE L24 .... 70 F2
East Downs Rd ALT WA14 .... 61 J2
　CHD/CHDH SK8 .... 64 F2
East Dr BIDD ST8 .... 227 K4
　MPL/ROM SK6 .... 67 M1
East Dudley St WSFD CW7 .... 177 M3
Easter Ct WARRW/BUR WA5 .... 36 B2
Eastern Av SPK/HALE L24 .... 70 F2
Eastern Pathway CHSW/BR CH4 .... 17 J8
Eastern Rd NANT CW5 .... 237 L7
Eastfields Gv CH/BCN CH1 .... 144 A4
Eastford Rd WARRS WA4 .... 56 A3
East Front RAIN/WH L35 .... 32 E3
Eastgate Rd HOLMCH CW4 .... 181 K1
　RUNC WA7 .... 54 E8
Eastgate St CH/BCN CH1 .... 17 G5
East Gn CQ CH5 .... 143 G6
Eastham Gn SPK/HALE L24 .... 50 B8 [1]
Eastham Rake GTS/LS CH66 .... 93 J7
East Lancashire Rd
　GOL/RIS/CU WA3 .... 23 H6
East La NWCHW CW8 .... 152 A1
　RUNC WA7 .... 73 M5
East Lawns SPK/HALE L24 .... 71 G1
Eastleigh Crs LEIGH WN7 .... 25 H1 [1]
Eastleigh Rd CHD/CHDH SK8 .... 64 B3
East Mains SPK/HALE L24 .... 71 G1
East Millwood Rd SPK/HALE L24 .... 51 G8
Easton Dr CHD/CHDH SK8 .... 46 A7
East Over MPL/ROM SK6 .... 48 A4
East Park Rd MCFLDS SK11 .... 138 B7
East Rd MANAIR M90 .... 63 J5
　MWCH CW10 .... 179 H3
　SPK/HALE L24 .... 51 H7
East St WDN WA8 .... 53 L8 [1]
East V MPL/ROM SK6 .... 49 G7
East Vw WARRS WA4 .... 57 H2
Eastward Av WILM/AE SK9 .... 83 M6
Eastway GTS/LS CH66 .... 94 D5
　SALE M33 .... 42 F3
　WDN WA8 .... 6 A3
Eastwell Rd AIMK WN4 .... 22 A1
Eastwood FROD/HEL WA6 .... 74 C3
Eastwood Av NEWLW WA12 .... 27 M1 [1]
Eastwood Rd WARRW/BUR WA5 .... 26 F5
Eaton Av CHSW/BR CH4 .... 169 K5
Eaton Bank CONG CW12 .... 184 F7
Eaton Cl CHD/CHDH SK8 .... 64 F1
　CHSW/BR CH4 .... 167 J8
　POY/DIS SK12 .... 87 G1
　SBCH CW11 .... 204 C5
　WRX/GR/LL LL12 .... 210 C5
Eaton Crs NWCHE CW9 .... 153 L2
Eaton Dr HALE/TIMP WA15 .... 43 G4
　MWCH CW10 .... 179 H4
　WILM/AE SK9 .... 109 M4
Eaton Gv CHSW/BR CH4 .... 168 E7
Eaton La HOLMCH CW4 .... 157 J3
　MCFLDS SK11 .... 138 D7
　NWCHE CW9 .... 153 K2
　TPLY/KEL CW6 .... 175 G6
　TPLY/KEL CW6 .... 197 L4
Eaton Ms CHSW/BR CH4 .... 169 K5
Eaton Rd ALS/KID ST7 .... 224 C8
　ALT WA14 .... 61 J3
　CHSW/BR CH4 .... 17 H9
　TPLY/KEL CW6 .... 197 K3
　WSFD CW7 .... 199 J5
Eaton St CW/SHV CW2 .... 18 F4
　RUNC WA7 .... 9 G3
Eaton Vw NWCHE CW9 .... 153 L4
Eaves Brow Rd GOL/RIS/CU WA3 .... 29 H5
Eaves Knoll Rd NM/HAY SK22 .... 69 G3
Ebbdale Cl STKP SK1 .... 3 J8
Ebnal La MALPAS SY14 .... 248 D6
Ebor Rd WYTH/NTH M22 .... 44 E8 [1]
Ebury Pl CHSW/BR CH4 .... 17 G9
Ecclesbridge Rd MPL/ROM SK6 .... 48 F8
Eccles Cl CHF/WBR SK23 .... 89 K4
Eccles Gv STHEL WA9 .... 34 E1
Eccles Rd CHF/WBR SK23 .... 89 M7
Eccleston Av CHSW/BR CH4 .... 169 K6
　GTS/LS CH66 .... 94 F1
Eccleston Cl GOL/RIS/CU WA3 .... 29 J7 [1]
Eccleston Dr RUNC WA7 .... 9 M5
Eccleston Rd CHSW/BR CH4 .... 190 A5
　EDGY/DAV SK3 .... 46 B8
Eccups La WILM/AE SK9 .... 83 J1
Echo Cl CHSW/BR CH4 .... 168 E8
Eckersley Cl NTHM/RTH M23 .... 43 M6
Ecton Av MCFLDN SK10 .... 139 G5
Ecton Cl WSFD CW7 .... 154 A8
Edale Cl ALT WA14 .... 61 J3
　BRAM/HZG SK7 .... 66 E3
　BURS/TUN ST6 .... 243 J5
　CHD/CHDH SK8 .... 64 D5
Edale Dr TPLY/KEL CW6 .... 149 L6
Edale Gv SALE M33 .... 42 E2
Eddisbury Hl NWCHW CW8 .... 150 C5
Eddisbury Rd GTS/LS CH66 .... 120 F2
Eddisbury Ter MCFLDS SK11 .... 15 L6
Eddisbury Wy CHSE CH3 .... 149 J1
　CHSE CH3 .... 195 M8
　CHSE CH3 .... 215 J5
　NWCHE CW9 .... 153 L1
Edelsten St WARRW/BUR WA5 .... 4 C7
Eden Av GOL/RIS/CU WA3 .... 25 J8
　MPL/ROM SK6 .... 67 L3
　WSFD CW7 .... 177 M2
Edenbridge Gdns WARRS WA4 .... 76 E1
Edenbridge Rd CHD/CHDH SK8 .... 46 B8
Eden Cl ALS/KID ST7 .... 243 H2
　BIDD ST8 .... 227 L3
　GTS/LS CH66 .... 94 C7

RAIN/WH L35 .... 33 H2
STKP SK1 .... 3 J7
WILM/AE SK9 .... 83 L7
Edendale *WDN* WA8 ...... 52 B2
Edendale Dr *WYTH/NTH* M22 ... 63 K3
Eden Dr *MCFLDN* SK10 .... 15 M3
Edenhall Cl *KNUT* WA16 .. 108 A1
Edenfield Rd *KNUT* WA16 . 108 A1
Edenhall Cl *HOLMCH* CW4 . 181 G1
Edenhall Dr *WLTN* L25 .... 50 D2
Edenhurst Av *HALE/TIMP* WA15 . 43 H7
Edenhurst Rd *OFTN* SK2 .. 47 H6
Eden Pl *CHD/CHDH* SK8 ... 45 K6
Edensor Dr *HALE/TIMP* WA15 . 62 C1
Edgars Dr *WARRN/WOL* WA2 . 38 A2
Edgecroft *CHSE* CH3 ...... 214 A3
Edge Green La *GOL/RIS/CU* WA3 . 22 F2
Edge Green Rd *GOL/RIS/CU* WA3 . 22 F3
Edge Gv *CHNE* CH2 .... 17 M4
Edgehill Cha *WILM/AE* SK9 . 84 E5
Edge La *MALPAS* SY14 .... 246 D3
Edgeley Fold *EDGY/DAV* SK3 . 46 C5
Edgeley Rd *BIDD* ST8 ..... 227 K6
EDGY/DAV SK3 .... 46 C5
WHITCH SY13 .... 270 B6
Edgemoor *ALT* WA14 .... 61 G2
Edgerley La *CHSE* CH3 .... 212 C6
Edgerley Pl *AIMK* WN4 .... 22 A1
Edgerton Rd *GOL/RIS/CU* WA3 . 23 L4
Edge View Ct *BIDD* ST8 ... 227 J5
Edge View La *KNUT* WA16 . 109 H2
Edgeview Rd *CONG* CW12 .. 208 B5
Edgeway *MCFLDS* SK11 .... 137 J4
WILM/AE SK9 .... 84 B7
Edgewell La *TPLY/KEL* CW6 . 198 A1
Edgewood Dr *CW/SHV* CW2 . 238 A5
Edgeworth Rd
GOL/RIS/CU WA3 .... 22 F3
Edgworth St *WARR* WA1 ... 4 F6
Edinburgh Cl *WARRN/WOL* WA2 . 4 A3
Edinburgh Dr *HUY* L36 .... 32 A4
MCFLDN SK10 .... 14 A3
Edinburgh Rd *CONG* CW12 . 207 M2
CW/SHV CW2 .... 237 L4
WDN WA8 .... 52 A4
Edinburgh Wy *CHSW/BR* CH4 . 17 K7
Edison Rd *RUNC* WA7 ...... 73 K1
Edith St *RUNC* WA7 .... 8 F1
Edleston Hall La *NANT* CW5 . 250 E2
Edleston Rd *CW/SHV* CW2 . 1 K7
Edmonton Rd *SALE* M33 .... 42 D1
Edmonton Dr *EDGY/DAV* SK3 . 47 G8
Edmund Cl *HTNM* SK4 ...... 2 E1
Edmund Wright Wy *NANT* CW5 . 20 A7
Edna St *CHNE* CH2 .... 17 L2
Edward Av *MPL/ROM* SK6 .. 47 L1
Edward Gdns *WARR* WA1 .. 38 F6
Edward German Dr
WHITCH SY13 .... 270 B5
Edward Rd *WARRW/BUR* WA5 . 35 K6
Edwards Av *CW/SHV* CW2 .. 258 C7
Edwards Cl *CW/SHV* CW2 .. 238 B7
MPL/ROM SK6 .... 48 E7
Edward's La *SPK/HALE* L24 . 50 B6
Edward St *CHSW/BR* CH4 .. 169 G6
Edward St *CW/SHV* CW2 ... 19 G8
EP CH65 .... 10 E4
MCFLDS SK11 .... 14 D6
MPL/ROM SK6 .... 49 G3
NWCHE CW9 .... 130 C4
STKP SK1 .... 3 G7
WDN WA8 .... 53 K3
Edwards Wy *ALS/KID* ST7 .. 224 E4
MPL/ROM SK6 .... 48 E7
WDN WA8 .... 52 C4
Edwin Dr *FLINT* CH6 .... 116 B7
Edwin St *STKP* SK1 .... 3 M7
WDN WA8 .... 53 K3
Egdon Cl *WDN* WA8 .... 53 L2
Egerton *KNUT* WA16 .... 59 J7
Egerton Av *LYMM* WA13 ... 40 C4
NWCHW CW8 .... 129 C8
WARR WA1 .... 37 L5
Egerton Dr *CHNE* CH2 ..... 145 K7
Egerton Moss
HALE/TIMP WA15 .... 61 L7
Egerton Pl *WHITCH* SY13 . 270 A4
Egerton Rd *CH/BCN* CH1 .. 144 D7
EDGY/DAV SK3 .... 47 G8
HALE/TIMP WA15 .... 62 A1
LYMM WA13 .... 58 C2
WHITCH SY13 .... 270 B4
WILM/AE SK9 .... 84 B4
Egerton Sq *KNUT* WA16 ... 107 G2
Egerton St *CH/BCN* CH1 ... 17 J3
EP CH65 .... 10 E5
RUNC WA7 .... 8 F1
WARR WA1 .... 5 K6
WARRS WA4 .... 56 C3
Egerton Wk *CHSW/BR* CH4 . 191 C6
Eggbridge La *CHSE* CH3 ... 174 A3
Eglington Av *RAIN/WH* L35 . 32 D3
Egremont Cl *NTHLY* L27 ... 37 J7
Egremont Gv *EDGY/DAV* SK3 . 46 B4
Egremont Rd *NTHLY* L27 .. 32 A8
Egypt St *WARR* WA1 .... 4 F7
WDN WA8 .... 6 F6
Eisenhower Dr
WARRW/BUR WA5 .... 36 B7
Elaine Cl *GTS/LS* CH66 .... 94 C4
WDN WA8 .... 7 L2
Elaine St *WARR* WA1 .... 5 M3
Elandor Rd *SBCH* CW11 ... 203 K5
Elcho Rd *ALT* WA14 .... 61 H1
Elcombe Av *GOL/RIS/CU* WA3 . 23 L5
Elderberry Wy *WILM/AE* SK9 . 84 E4
Elder Cl *OFTN* SK2 .... 47 K4
Eldercroft *HALE/TIMP* WA15 . 61 L7
Elder Dr *CHSW/BR* CH4 .... 168 E7
Eldon Rd *EDGY/DAV* SK3 ... 2 B9
MCFLDN SK10 .... 137 L4
Eldon St *WARR* WA1 .... 5 K6
Eldon Ter *NSTN* CH64 ...... 91 L5
Eleanor Cl *CW/HAS* CW1 .. 220 F7
Eleanor St *EP* CH65 .... 10 F5
WDN WA8 .... 7 H7
Electricity St *CW/SHV* CW2 . 18 F5
Elf Mill Cl *EDGY/DAV* SK3 . 46 E6

Elgar Cl *EP* CH65 .... 120 F1
Elgin Av *DID/WITH* M20 .. 45 K1
HOLMCH CW4 .... 181 H2
WARRS WA4 .... 56 A2
Elgin Cl *CHSE* CH3 .... 170 A1
Elgol Cl *RUNC* WA7 .... 8 E7
Elgood La *BURS/TUN* ST6 . 243 J5
Eliot Ct *CW/HAS* CW1 ..... 222 B8
Elizabethan Wy *NWCHE* CW9 . 130 E6
STKP SK1 .... 3 H8
Elizabeth Cl *POY/DIS* SK12 . 68 D7
Elizabeth Ct *ALS/KID* ST7 . 242 D7
HTNM SK4 .... 2 A3
WDN WA8 .... 7 J7
Elizabeth Crs *CHSW/BR* CH4 . 17 K7
Elizabeth Dr *WARR* WA1 .. 38 A4
Elizabeth St *CONG* CW12 . 207 J2
CW/HAS CW1 .... 18 D1
LEIGH WN7 .... 25 H1
MCFLDS SK11 .... 15 G6
STHEL WA9 .... 34 E1
WHITCH SY13 .... 270 B4
Elkan Cl *WDN* WA8 .... 53 L1
Elkan Rd *WDN* WA8 .... 53 K1
Elkington Ri
AUD/MAD/W CW3 ...... 267 M5
Elkstone Cl *BURS/TUN* ST6 . 243 L8
Elk Vw *MALPAS* SY14 ...... 256 F7
Ella Gv *KNUT* WA16 .... 107 H2
Elland Dr *GTS/LS* CH66 ... 94 C7
Ellen Brook Rd *WYTH/NTH* M22 . 63 K4
Ellen St *HTNM* SK4 .... 2 D1
WARRW/BUR WA5 .... 4 D3
Ellerby Cl *RUNC* WA7 ...... 74 E5
Ellerton Av *GTS/LS* CH66 . 94 C7
Ellerton Cl *WDN* WA8 ..... 52 D1
Ellesmere Av *CHNE* CH2 .. 145 K7
CHSW/BR CH4 .... 167 K8
MPL/ROM SK6 .... 48 F6
Ellesmere Cl *SBCH* CW11 . 203 L4
Ellesmere Dr *CHD/CHDH* SK8 . 46 A7
Ellesmere Rd *ALT* WA14 ... 42 D6
EDGY/DAV SK3 .... 46 A5
GOL/RIS/CU WA3 .... 24 E8
NWCHE CW9 .... 130 A8
WARRS WA4 .... 56 B3
WHITCH SY13 .... 268 E7
Ellesmere St *RUNC* WA7 ... 9 J2
WARR WA1 .... 5 J7
Ellesworth Cl *WARRW/BUR* WA5 . 34 B5
Ellingham Wy *NWCHE* CW9 . 153 L1
Elliot St *WDN* WA8 .... 7 J4
Elliott Av *GOL/RIS/CU* WA3 . 23 H3
WARR WA1 .... 37 L5
Ellis Ashton St *HUY* L36 .. 32 A2
Ellis La *FROD/HEL* WA6 .... 99 K3
Ellison St *WARRS* WA4 .... 56 D3
Ellis St *CW/HAS* CW1 ..... 221 H6
WDN WA8 .... 6 F7
Ellon Av *RAIN/WH* L35 .... 33 K2
Elloway Rd *SPK/HALE* L24 . 71 G1
Ellwood Gn *CW/SHV* CW2 . 253 L1
Ellwood Rd *STKP* SK1 ..... 3 M6
Elm Av *GOL/RIS/CU* WA3 .. 23 G3
WDN WA8 .... 53 H2
Elm Beds Rd *POY/DIS* SK12 . 87 J2
Elm Cl *ALS/KID* ST7 ...... 243 H4
CW/SHV CW2 .... 237 L2
POY/DIS SK12 .... 86 F1
TPLY/KEL CW6 .... 197 K2
WHITCH SY13 .... 269 M6
Elm Crs *WILM/AE* SK9 ..... 110 B2
Elm Cft *CO* CH5 .... 166 E2
Elmdale Rd *CHD/CHDH* SK8 . 64 B2
Elm Dr *CW/HAS* CW1 ...... 221 L6
HOLMCH CW4 .... 157 K8
MCFLDN SK10 .... 15 K1
Elmfield Av *WYTH/NTH* M22 . 44 E4
Elmfield Dr *MPL/ROM* SK6 . 48 E6
Elmfield Rd *EDGY/DAV* SK3 . 46 F7
WILM/AE SK9 .... 110 B3
Elm Gv *ALS/KID* ST7 ...... 224 B8
CHSW/BR CH4 .... 168 E7
DID/WITH M20 .... 45 H1
GTS/LS CH66 .... 121 G3
WARR WA1 .... 37 M5
WDN WA8 .... 7 J2
WILM/AE SK9 .... 110 A2
WSFD CW7 .... 178 A3
Elmley Cl *OFTN* SK2 .... 48 A7
Elmore Cl *HOLMCH* CW4 .. 181 H1
RUNC WA7 .... 74 D3
Elmridge Dr *HALE/TIMP* WA15 . 62 C4
Elm Ri *FROD/HEL* WA6 ..... 99 J3
MCFLDN SK10 .... 111 L6
Elm Rd *CHD/CHDH* SK8 .... 45 G7
CONG CW12 .... 207 H1
CO CH5 .... 166 A4
GOL/RIS/CU WA3 .... 40 A2
HALE/TIMP WA15 .... 61 L1
MPL/ROM SK6 .... 67 M5
MWCH CW10 .... 179 K5
NSTN CH64 .... 92 F4
NWCHW CW8 .... 128 D5
RUNC WA7 .... 9 M6
WARRN/WOL WA2 .... 28 B4
WARRW/BUR WA5 .... 35 M8
Elm Rd South *EDGY/DAV* SK3 . 46 A5
Elmsett Cl *WARRW/BUR* WA5 . 35 L7
Elmsleigh Rd *CHD/CHDH* SK8 . 64 A2
Elmsmere Rd *DID/WITH* M20 . 45 K1
Elm Sq *CHSW/BR* CH4 ..... 168 F6
Elmstead Crs *CW/HAS* CW1 . 220 F4
Elmstead Rd *MCFLDS* SK11 . 135 G1
Elmsted Cl *CHD/CHDH* SK8 . 65 H1
The Elms *GOL/RIS/CU* WA3 . 23 M4
MCFLDN SK10 .... 137 L4
Elm St *EP* CH65 .... 10 E5
HUY L36 .... 32 A2
LEIGH WN7 .... 24 F1
NWCHE CW9 .... 13 M1
Elmsway *BRAM/HZG* SK7 .. 65 H6
HALE/TIMP WA15 .... 62 B4
MCFLDN SK10 .... 113 G5

MPL/ROM SK6 .... 67 L6
Elmswood Av *RAIN/WH* L35 . 33 K2
Elm Tree Av *LYMM* WA13 .. 58 D2
WARR WA1 .... 37 M4
Elm Tree Dr *WYTH/NTH* M22 . 63 K1
Elm Tree La *SBCH* CW11 .. 203 K4
Elm Tree Rd *GOL/RIS/CU* WA3 . 23 M5
LYMM WA13 .... 58 D2
MPL/ROM SK6 .... 47 J1
Elmwood *RUNC* WA7 ...... 74 C3
Elmwood Av *AIMK* WN4 ... 22 A2
CHNE CH2 .... 145 M8
Elmwood Cl *ALS/KID* ST7 . 224 F8
CO CH5 .... 142 B8
Elmwood Gv *WSFD* CW7 .. 177 M4
WSFD CW7 .... 178 A4
Elmwood Rd *NWCHW* CW8 . 103 H8
Elnor Av *CHF/WBR* SK23 .. 89 L7
Elnor La *CHF/WBR* SK23 .. 89 M7
Elsby Rd *ALS/KID* ST7 .... 241 M2
Elsinore Av *IRL* M44 ...... 31 M3
Elston Av *NEWLW* WA12 .. 22 B7
Elstree Av *CHSE* CH3 ..... 170 B1
Elstree Gv *EDGY/DAV* SK3 . 2 C7
Elswick Av *BRAM/HZG* SK7 . 65 L5
Eltham Av *OFTN* SK2 ...... 47 J7
Eltham Cl *AIMK* WN4 ...... 22 D1
WDN WA8 .... 53 L1
Elton Av *GOL/RIS/CU* WA3 . 23 L5
GOL/RIS/CU WA3 .... 29 J8
PS/BROM CH62 .... 93 L1
WILM/AE SK9 .... 84 E3
Elton Crossings Rd *SBCH* CW11 . 203 K6
Elton Dr *BRAM/HZG* SK7 .. 66 D4
Elton La *FROD/HEL* WA6 ... 97 L8
SBCH CW11 .... 222 D3
Elton Lordship La
FROD/HEL WA6 .... 98 A5
Elton Rd *ALT* WA14 .... 42 D2
SBCH CW11 .... 203 J7
Elton Ter *BURS/TUN* ST6 .. 243 J5
Elverston St *WYTH/NTH* M22 . 44 B3
Elvington Cl *RUNC* WA7 ... 99 M1
Elway Rd *AIMK* WN4 .... 22 C1
Elworth Av *WDN* WA8 ..... 34 A7
Elworth Rd *SBCH* CW11 ... 203 K6
Elworth St *SBCH* CW11 ... 204 A5
Elworthy Av *HLWD* L26 .... 50 F3
Elwyn Av *WYTH/NTH* M22 . 44 D5
Elwyn Dr *HLWD* L26 .... 50 F4
Ely Cl *GTS/LS* CH66 ...... 120 E4
Ely Pk *RUNC* WA7 .... 74 E2
Embassy Cl *CH/BCN* CH1 .. 144 C7
Emberton Pl *AUD/MAD/W* CW3 . 264 A7
Embleton Ct *RUNC* WA7 ... 73 K7
Embridge Cswy *BUX* SK17 . 115 H7
Emerald Rd *WYTH/NTH* M22 . 63 M5
Emery Cl *ALT* WA14 .... 42 D5
Emery St *WDN* WA8 .... 7 H6
Emlyn Gv *CHD/CHDH* SK8 .. 46 A6
Emmett St *NWCHW* CW8 .. 129 H1
Empress Av *WYTH/NTH* M22 . 48 F7
Empress Dr *CW/SHV* CW2 . 18 C6
Emral Ct *WRXS/E* LL13 .... 256 A5
Emslie Ct *WARR* WA1 ...... 91 J4
Emsworth Dr *SALE* M33 ... 43 J3
Enderby Rd *CH/BCN* CH1 .. 16 E2
Endon Av *MCFLDN* SK10 .. 113 G5
Endon Dr *BIDD* ST8 .... 227 H7
Endsleigh Cl *CHNE* CH2 .. 145 L4
Endsleigh Gdns *CHNE* CH2 . 145 L4
Enfield Cl *CW/SHV* CW2 .. 253 H1
Enfield Park Rd
WARRN/WOL WA2 .... 28 E8
Enfield Rd *EP* CH65 .... 10 D7
Enford Av *WYTH/NTH* M22 . 63 G2
Englefield Av *CHSW/BR* CH4 . 168 D6
Englefield Cl *CW/HAS* CW1 . 221 G4
Englefield Dr *FLINT* CH6 .. 116 C7
Englesea Brook La *CW/SHV* CW2 . 254 F2
Englesea Gv *CW/SHV* CW2 . 18 B9
Ennerdale *CHNE* CH2 ..... 145 M7
MCFLDS SK11 .... 137 M7
Ennerdale Av *WARRN/WOL* WA2 . 37 H1
WILM/AE SK9 .... 108 F5
WSFD CW7 .... 177 K1
Ennerdale Dr *CONG* CW12 . 207 H2
FROD/HEL WA6 .... 99 J4
HALE/TIMP WA15 .... 43 G4
Ennerdale Rd *CHD/CHDH* SK8 . 64 B1
CW/SHV CW2 .... 237 L1
PART M31 .... 40 E1
STKP SK1 .... 3 L9
Ennis Cl *NTHM/RTH* M23 .. 43 L1
SPK/HALE L24 .... 71 K2
Enstone Rd *WLTN* L25 ..... 50 B6
Enticott Rd *IRL* M44 ...... 31 J7
Entwistle Gv *LEIGH* WN7 .. 25 J1
Enville Rd *ALT* WA14 ...... 61 J1
Enville St *WARRS* WA4 .... 5 J9
Epping Av *WARR* WA1 ..... 34 B1
Epping Cl *RAIN/WH* L35 ... 33 K2
Epping Dr *WARR* WA1 ..... 38 D4
Epsom Cl *CHD/CHDH* SK8 . 64 E8
SALE M33 .... 42 C2
WILM/AE SK9 .... 64 E8
Epsom Cl *BRAM/HZG* SK7 . 66 F2
Epsom Gdns *WARRS* WA4 . 56 E5
Eric Av *WARR* WA1 .... 37 L4
Eric Bullows Cl *WYTH/NTH* M22 . 63 J3
Eric St *WDN* WA8 .... 7 L2
Erindale Crs *FROD/HEL* WA6 . 99 C6
Ermine Rd *CHNE* CH2 ..... 145 L8
Ernest St *CHD/CHDH* SK8 . 45 G7
CW/SHV CW2 .... 18 B4
OFTN SK2 .... 47 G6
Ernocroft La *MPL/ROM* SK6 . 49 L1
Ernocroft Rd *MPL/ROM* SK6 . 49 H3
Erringden Cl *OFTN* SK2 ... 47 L6
Errington Av *EP* CH65 ..... 10 E5
Errol Av *WYTH/NTH* M22 .. 44 C8
Errwood Cl *SPK/HALE* L24 . 71 L2
Erskine La *PART* M31 ...... 40 F1
Erskine St *MPL/ROM* SK6 . 49 H2
Erwood St *WARRN/WOL* WA2 . 4 F4

Eryngo St *STKP* SK1 .... 3 K6
Esher Dr *SALE* M33 .... 43 H4
Eskdale *CHD/CHDH* SK8 ... 45 J8
EP CH65 .... 121 H1
Eskdale Av *WYTH/NTH* M22 . 63 J7
Eskdale Dr *HALE/TIMP* WA15 . 43 J5
WSFD CW7 .... 177 J2
Esk Rd *WSFD* CW7 .... 178 A2
Esonwood Rd *RAIN/WH* L35 . 32 D1
Essex Av *DID/WITH* M20 .. 45 J2
Essex Dr *ALS/KID* ST7 .... 242 F2
Essex Gdns *IRL* M44 ...... 31 J8
Essex Rd *CHNE* CH2 ...... 146 A7
Esthers La *NWCHW* CW8 .. 128 D4
Esther St *WDN* WA8 .... 7 K3
Estuary Vw *CO* CH5 ...... 166 A2
Etchells Rd *CHD/CHDH* SK8 . 64 D3
Etchells St *STKP* SK1 ..... 3 G5
Ethelda Dr *CHNE* CH2 ..... 146 A7
Etherow Av *MPL/ROM* SK6 . 48 E2
Etherow Cl *SBCH* CW11 ... 203 L5
Eton Rd *EP* CH65 .... 95 K8
Eton St *LEIGH* WN7 .... 24 F1
Ettiley Av *SBCH* CW11 .... 203 J7
Ettrick Pk *CHSE* CH3 ..... 170 A2
Euclid Av *WARRS* WA4 .... 57 H2
Europa Bvd *WARRW/BUR* WA5 . 36 B1
Europa Wy *EDGY/DAV* SK3 . 46 F4
EP CH65 .... 10 F6
Eustace St *WARRN/WOL* WA2 . 4 E5
Evansleigh Dr *CO* CH5 .... 167 G1
Evans Pl *WARRS* WA4 ..... 56 D1
Evans Rd *SPK/HALE* L24 .. 50 C7
Evans St *CW/HAS* CW1 .... 221 J6
FLINT CH6 .... 116 A5
Eva Rd *EDGY/DAV* SK3 .... 46 A5
Eva St *SBCH* CW11 .... 203 K4
Evelyn St *WARRW/BUR* WA5 . 36 D8
Everdon Cl *WSFD* CW7 ... 177 M1
Everest Cl *ALS/KID* ST7 .. 243 J1
Everglade Cl *MCFLDS* SK11 . 138 B7
Everite Rd *WDN* WA8 ...... 52 B2
Eversley *WDN* WA8 .... 52 B2
Eversley Cl *FROD/HEL* WA6 . 99 J6
WARRS WA4 .... 56 F7
Eversley Ct *CHNE* CH2 ... 145 J8
Eversley Pk *CHNE* CH2 ... 145 J8
Eversley Rd *DID/WITH* M20 . 45 G1
Evesham Av *HTNM* SK4 .... 46 B1
NTHM/RTH M23 .... 43 K5
Evesham Cl *LEIGH* WN7 ... 24 D3
MCFLDN SK10 .... 112 E8
WARRS WA4 .... 56 C4
Evesham Drive *WILM/AE* SK9 . 84 C2
Evesham Rd *CHD/CHDH* SK8 . 46 B8
Eveside Cl *CHD/CHDH* SK8 . 46 B8
Ewart St *CHSW/BR* CH4 ... 168 B5
Ewloe Ct *EP* CH65 .... 121 K2
Ewrin La *MCFLDN* SK10 ... 114 C7
Exbourne Cl *WYTH/NTH* M22 . 63 J3
Excalibur Wy *IRL* M44 .... 31 M5
Exchange Cl *MCFLDS* SK11 . 15 G5
Exchange Pl *RAIN/WH* L35 . 33 J1
Exchange St *EDGY/DAV* SK3 . 2 F6
MCFLDS SK11 .... 15 G5
Exeley *RAIN/WH* L35 ...... 32 E2
Exeter Cl *CHD/CHDH* SK8 . 64 F4
Exeter Pl *CH/BCN* CH1 ... 144 F7
Exeter Rd *EP* CH65 .... 10 E7
Exit Rd West *MANAIR* M90 . 63 H5
Exmouth Crs *RUNC* WA7 .. 74 E6
Exmouth Wy
WARRW/BUR WA5 ...... 26 F6
Exton Pk *CH/BCN* CH1 .... 16 E1
Eyam Gv *OFTN* SK2 .... 47 K8
Eyam Rd *BRAM/HZG* SK7 .. 66 E4
Eyebrook Rd *ALT* WA14 ... 61 G3

F

Factory La *POY/DIS* SK12 . 68 E5
WARR WA1 .... 4 E8
WDN WA8 .... 53 H1
Factory Rd *CQ* CH5 .... 142 F8
Fairacre Dr *MWCH* CW10 .. 179 K6
Fairacres Rd *MPL/ROM* SK6 . 67 L4
Fairbourne Av *WILM/AE* SK9 . 83 M8
Fairbourne Cl
WARRW/BUR WA5 ...... 36 E1
WILM/AE SK9 .... 83 M8
Fairbourne Dr *HALE/TIMP* WA15 . 43 H2
WILM/AE SK9 .... 83 M8
Fairbrook *CW/SHV* CW2 .. 237 L2
Fairbrother Crs
WARRN/WOL WA2 ...... 37 K2
Fairburn Av *CW/SHV* CW2 . 220 F8
Fairburn Cl *WDN* WA8 .... 53 L1
Fairclough Av *WARR* WA1 . 5 J1
Fairclough Rd *RAIN/WH* L35 . 33 H1
Fairclough St *NEWLW* WA12 . 27 H1
WARRW/BUR WA5 ...... 26 E6
Fairfax Av *HALE/TIMP* WA15 . 43 G6
Fairfax Cl *MPL/ROM* SK6 .. 48 D5
Fairfax Dr *RUNC* WA7 ..... 73 K2
WILM/AE SK9 .... 83 M8
Fairfield Av *CHD/CHDH* SK8 . 64 F7
EP CH65 .... 121 G2
MCFLDN SK10 .... 113 G5
SBCH CW11 .... 204 A7
Fairfield Gdns *WARRS* WA4 . 56 E2
Fairfield Rd *CHSW/BR* CH4 . 168 F6
Fairfield St *WARR* WA1 .... 5 K4
Fairford Rd *CHSW/BR* CH4 . 168 F6
Fairford Wy *WILM/AE* SK9 . 84 D5

Fairhaven Cl *BRAM/HZG* SK7 . 65 M4
WARRW/BUR WA5 ...... 36 B8
Fairhaven Rd *NSTN* CH64 .. 91 K3
Fairholme Av *DID/WITH* M20 . 144 B3
Fairholme Rd *HTNM* SK4 .. 2 B2
WDN WA8 .... 154 A4
Fairlands Rd *SALE* M33 ... 42 F2
Fairlawn *HTNM* SK4 .... 2 C2
Fairlea Av *DID/WITH* M20 . 45 J2
Fairlie Dr *HALE/TIMP* WA15 . 43 H4
RAIN/WH L35 .... 33 K2
Fair Md *KNUT* WA16 ...... 107 H4
Fairmeadow *CHSW/BR* CH4 . 210 D2
Fairmead Rd *NTHM/RTH* M23 . 44 C3
Fairmile Dr *DID/WITH* M20 . 45 J4
Fairoak Ct *RUNC* WA7 .... 100 F1
Fairoak La *RUNC* WA7 ..... 100 F1
Fairview *WRXS/E* LL13 .... 228 D4
Fairview Av *ALS/KID* ST7 . 224 D8
CW/SHV CW2 .... 239 H7
Fairview Cl *MPL/ROM* SK6 . 48 F5
Fair View Cl *NWCHW* CW8 . 128 F1
Fairview Dr *MPL/ROM* SK6 . 48 F5
Fairview Rd *GTS/LS* CH66 . 121 G2
HALE/TIMP WA15 .... 43 J7
MCFLDS SK11 .... 14 B9
Fairway *BRAM/HZG* SK7 ... 65 K6
CHD/CHDH SK8 .... 45 H8
CO CH5 .... 167 G1
Fairway Av *NTHM/RTH* M23 . 43 K5
Fairway Dr *SALE* M33 ..... 42 E2
Fairways *FROD/HEL* WA6 .. 99 K5
WARRS WA4 .... 56 D7
Fairways Cl *WLTN* L25 .... 50 B4
Fairways Dr *GTS/LS* CH66 . 94 D5
WHITCH SY13 .... 270 A3
The Fairways *WSFD* CW7 .. 177 G2
The Fairway *ALS/KID* ST7 . 224 C8
OFTN SK2 .... 47 K5
Fairwood Rd *NTHM/RTH* M23 . 43 K5
Fairy La *SALE* M33 .... 44 B1
Fairywell Cl *WILM/AE* SK9 . 84 D3
Fairywell Dr *SALE* M33 .... 43 G3
Fairywell Rd *HALE/TIMP* WA15 . 43 H5
Falcon Cl *MWCH* CW10 ... 179 K6
NM/HAY SK22 .... 69 K4
WSFD CW7 .... 177 K6
Falcondale Rd
WARRN/WOL WA2 ...... 28 B6
Falcon Dr *CW/HAS* CW1 .. 221 H4
Falconers Gv *WARRW/BUR* WA5 . 36 B2
Falcon Rd *GTS/LS* CH66 .. 120 F1
Falcons Wy *RUNC* WA7 ... 73 L6
Fallibroome Cl *MCFLDN* SK10 . 137 L4
Fallibroome Rd *MCFLDN* SK10 . 137 L4
Fallowfield *RUNC* WA7 .... 73 K3
Fallowfield Cl *WSFD* CW7 . 176 F3
Fallowfield Ct *CW/HAS* CW1 . 221 G6
Fallowfield Gv
WARRN/WOL WA2 ...... 38 B3
Fallows Wy *RAIN/WH* L35 . 32 C3
Falls Gv *CHD/CHDH* SK8 .. 64 A1
Falmer Dr *WYTH/NTH* M22 . 63 H3
Falmouth Cl *MCFLDN* SK10 . 137 L4
Falmouth Dr *WARRW/BUR* WA5 . 54 E1
Falmouth Pl *RUNC* WA7 .. 74 E6
Falmouth Rd *CONG* CW12 . 207 L4
CW/HAS CW1 .... 221 G6
Falstone Cl *GOL/RIS/CU* WA3 . 30 B6
Falstone Dr *RUNC* WA7 ... 74 E4
Falterley Rd *NTHM/RTH* M23 . 43 L4
Fancroft Rd *WYTH/NTH* M22 . 44 C7
Fanner's La *KNUT* WA16 .. 58 C7
Fanny's Cft *ALS/KID* ST7 . 241 K2
Fanshawe La *MCFLDS* SK11 . 136 D8
Faraday Rd *EP* CH65 ...... 10 A9
Faraday St *GOL/RIS/CU* WA3 . 29 L7
Farams Rd *ALS/KID* ST7 .. 224 E5
Farbailey Cl *CHSW/BR* CH4 . 168 H7
Farcroft *NTHM/RTH* M23 .. 43 M4
Farden Dr *NTHM/RTH* M23 . 43 K4
Farefield Av *GOL/RIS/CU* WA3 . 22 F2
Farfields Cl *MCFLDS* SK11 . 161 L3
Faringdon Cl *WLTN* L25 ... 50 B6
Faringdon Rd *WARRN/WOL* WA2 . 28 B6
Farlands Dr *DID/WITH* M20 . 45 H5
Farley Cl *MWCH* CW10 .... 179 H4
Farley Ct *CHD/CHDH* SK8 . 45 M8
Farley Rd *SALE* M33 ...... 43 J2
Farm Cl *NWCHW* CW8 ..... 128 D3
Farmdale Dr *CHNE* CH2 ... 123 G1
Farmer Cl *CW/SHV* CW2 .. 18 A3
Farmer Cl *NTHM/RTH* M23 . 44 A1
Farmers Heath *GTS/LS* CH66 . 120 D2
Farmer's La *WARRW/BUR* WA5 . 27 G6
Farmer St *HTNM* SK4 ..... 2 D1
Farmfield Cl *CO* CH5 ...... 142 B7
Farmfield Dr *MCFLDN* SK10 . 138 B1
Farm La *MCFLDS* SK11 .... 158 E3
POY/DIS SK12 .... 68 A3
WARRS WA4 .... 56 E4
Farmleigh Dr *CW/HAS* CW1 . 220 F4
Farmleigh Gdns
WARRW/BUR WA5 ...... 36 C6
Farm Rd *CQ* CH5 .... 142 E5
NWCHE CW9 .... 130 E5
NWCHW CW8 .... 128 D3
NWCHW CW8 .... 150 F4
STHEL WA9 .... 34 D1
Farmside *WARRW/BUR* WA5 . 4 B3
Farmstead Wy *GTS/LS* CH66 . 120 E3
Farm Wk *ALT* WA14 .... 60 E2
Farm Wy *NEWLW* WA12 ... 27 L3
Farnborough Gv *HLWD* L26 . 50 F3
Farndale *WDN* WA8 .... 34 A7
Farndale Cl *CW/SHV* CW2 . 238 A6
WARRW/BUR WA5 ...... 35 M5
Farndale Gv *AIMK* WN4 ... 22 C2
Farndon Av *BRAM/HZG* SK7 . 47 M8
Farndon Cl *CHSW/BR* CH4 . 167 J8
NWCHW CW8 .... 152 A1
SALE M33 .... 43 L1
Farndon Dr *HALE/TIMP* WA15 . 43 G6
Farndon Rd *GTS/LS* CH66 . 94 E6
Farne Cl *EP* CH65 .... 121 J4
Farnham Av *MCFLDS* SK11 . 14 A8
Farnham Cl *CHD/CHDH* SK8 . 65 G5

WARRS WA4 .... 56 E5
Farnham Dr BIDD ST8 .... 227 H7
Farnhill Cl RUNC WA7 .... 74 D4
Farnley Cl RUNC WA7 .... 74 D3
Farnworth Cl BIDD ST8 .... 227 H6
WDN WA8 .... 34 B8
Farnworth Rd
WARRW/BUR WA5 .... 35 K8
Farnworth St WARRW WA8 .... 34 B8
Farrant St WDN WA8 .... 7 K4
Farrell Rd WARRS WA4 .... 56 C4
Farrell St WARR WA1 .... 5 L6
Far Ridings MPL/ROM SK6 .... 48 D1
Farr St EDGY/DAV SK3 .... 2 C7
Farthing Cl WLTN L25 .... 50 A5
Farwood Cl MCFLDN SK10 .... 137 M3
Faulkner Dr HALE/TIMP WA15 .... 43 H8
MWCH CW10 .... 179 L6
Faulkners Cl CHSW/BR CH4 .... 190 A5
Faulkners La CHSE CH3 .... 170 D5
KNUT WA16 .... 108 E1
Faulkner St CHNE CH2 .... 17 L1
Fawborough Rd
NTHM/RTH M23 .... 43 M3
Fawfield Dr BURS/TUN ST6 .... 243 J6
Fawley Gv WYTH/NTH M22 .... 44 D8
Fawley Rd RAIN/WH L35 .... 33 L3
Fawns Keep WILM/AE SK9 .... 84 D5
Fawns Leap NWCHW CW8 .... 127 L7
Faywood Dr MPL/ROM SK6 .... 49 G6
Fearnham Cl LEIGH WN7 .... 24 E5
Fearnhead La WARRN/WOL WA2 .... 38 C1
Feathers La CH/BCN CH1 .... 16 F6
Feathers St FLINT CH6 .... 116 A5
Feeny St STHEL WA9 .... 34 B2
Feilden Ct STHEL WA9 .... 34 B2
Feilden Rd NTHM/RTH M23 .... 43 M2
Felix Rd NWCHW CW8 .... 12 E3
Fellpark Rd NTHM/RTH M23 .... 44 A2
Fellwood Gv RAIN/WH L35 .... 32 E2
Felskirk Rd WYTH/NTH M22 .... 63 J4
Felsted Av WLTN L25 .... 50 C2
Felton Av WYTH/NTH M22 .... 63 J1
Fence Av MCFLDN SK10 .... 15 J4
Fence La CONG CW12 .... 226 C1
Fence St OFTN SK2 .... 47 K8
Fenham Dr WARRW/BUR WA5 .... 35 J8
Fennel St WARR WA1 .... 5 J6
Fenside Rd WYTH/NTH M22 .... 44 E7
Fenton Av OFTN SK2 .... 47 J8
Fenton Cl CONG CW12 .... 208 A3
SPK/HALE L24 .... 70 C1
WDN WA8 .... 52 C1
Fenton Gn SPK/HALE L24 .... 70 D2
Fenwick Dr HTNM SK4 .... 45 L1
Fenwick La RUNC WA7 .... 73 K6
Fenwick Rd GTS/LS CH66 .... 120 E2
Ferguson Av GTS/LS CH66 .... 94 E6
Ferguson Dr
WARRN/WOL WA2 .... 37 K3
Ferma La CHSE CH3 .... 147 K6
Fern Av NEWLW WA12 .... 27 K2
Fernbank Cl WARRS WA1 .... 19 M5
GOL/RIS/CU WA3 .... 29 L8
WSFD WA7 .... 178 B3
Fern Bank Dr NTHM/RTH M23 .... 43 L4
Fernbank Ri MCFLDN SK10 .... 113 H4
Fern Cl GOL/RIS/CU WA3 .... 29 K8
MPL/ROM SK6 .... 48 F6
Fern Ct CW/HAS CW1 .... 19 K5
Fern Crs CONG CW12 .... 208 A2
Ferndale Av CHNE CH2 .... 123 C1
OFTN SK2 .... 47 H8
Ferndale Cl CW/SHV CW2 .... 239 H7
SBCH CW11 .... 204 C7
WARR WA1 .... 38 C5
WDN WA8 .... 34 E5
Ferndale Crs MCFLDS SK11 .... 137 L5
Ferndale Rd SALE M33 .... 43 H7
Fern Dene AUD/MAD/W CW3 .... 267 K5
Ferndown Rd NTHM/RTH M23 .... 43 K4
Ferney Pl BURS/TUN ST6 .... 243 J6
Fern Gv CQ CH5 .... 166 A1
Fernhill MPL/ROM SK6 .... 49 H6
Fernhill Rd CH/BCN CH1 .... 144 E6
Fernhurst RUNC WA7 .... 73 K4
Fernilee Cl NM/HAY SK22 .... 69 J3
Fern Lea CHD/CHDH SK8 .... 64 B3
Fernlea HALE/TIMP WA15 .... 61 M3
Fern Lea Dr MCFLDS SK11 .... 14 E8
Fernleaf Cl ALS/KID ST7 .... 224 F4
Fernlea Rd NWCHE CW9 .... 104 B6
Fernleigh NWCHW CW8 .... 12 A5
Fernleigh Cl WSFD CW7 .... 177 G3
Ferney Rd OFTN SK2 .... 47 H6
Fernone WILM/AE SK9 .... 84 D1
Fern Rd EP CH65 .... 121 G2
Fernside Rd CQ CH5 .... 142 A8
Fern Vw HALE/TIMP WA15 .... 43 L7
Fern Wy NWCHW CW8 .... 128 C3
Fernwood MPL/ROM SK6 .... 49 J5
Fernwood Dr HLWD L26 .... 50 F4
Fernwood Gv WILM/AE SK9 .... 84 C4
Ferrous Wy IRL M44 .... 31 M6
Ferry Cl CQ CH5 .... 143 G6
Ferry La CH/BCN CH1 .... 168 C3
WARRS WA4 .... 38 E8
Festival Av AUD/MAD/W CW3 .... 264 E8
WARRN/WOL WA2 .... 37 K2
Festival Crs WARRN/WOL WA2 .... 37 K2
Festival Dr MCFLDN SK10 .... 110 F6
Festival Hl CONG CW12 .... 207 M2
Festival Rd EP CH65 .... 94 F7
Festival Wy RUNC WA7 .... 9 L6
Fford Cledwen
(Cledwen Road)
CHSW/BR CH4 .... 167 K7
Fford Glyndwr FLINT CH6 .... 116 B7
Fford Y Fran FLINT CH6 .... 116 B8
Fford Llewelyn FLINT CH6 .... 116 B7
Fiddlers Ferry Rd WDN WA8 .... 53 K4
Fiddlers La CH/BCN CH1 .... 144 B2
Field Av CW/SHV CW2 .... 237 M3
Fieldbank Rd MCFLDN SK10 .... 14 C4
Field Cl BRAM/HZG SK7 .... 65 K8

MCFLDN SK10 .... 112 F5
MPL/ROM SK6 .... 48 D7
NWCHW CW8 .... 12 B5
Fieldfare WSFD CW7 .... 178 A4
Fieldfare Cl GOL/RIS/CU WA3 .... 23 K4
GOL/RIS/CU WA3 .... 29 M8
Fieldgate WDN WA8 .... 52 B6
Fieldhead Ms WILM/AE SK9 .... 84 E4
Field Hey La NSTN CH64 .... 93 H3
Field House La MPL/ROM SK6 .... 49 G6
Fielding Av POY/DIS SK12 .... 86 E2
Field La CHSE CH3 .... 172 B2
CHSE CH3 .... 214 B3
CW/SHV CW2 .... 237 K2
WARRS WA4 .... 56 C6
Field Rd STHEL WA9 .... 34 D1
Fields Cl ALS/KID ST7 .... 224 E8
Fields Dr SBCH CW11 .... 204 A7
Fieldsend Dr LEIGH WN7 .... 24 C4
Fieldside CQ CH5 .... 166 C3
TPLY/KEL CW6 .... 173 H6
Field Side Cl KNUT WA16 .... 82 A8
Fields Rd ALS/KID ST7 .... 241 K1
CONG CW12 .... 207 L4
CW/HAS CW1 .... 222 D8
The Fields NANT CW5 .... 237 K7
Fields St MPL/ROM SK6 .... 47 M1
Fields View La NANT CW5 .... 253 H4
Fieldsway RUNC WA7 .... 73 G6
Fieldvale Rd SALE M33 .... 42 E3
Field Vw BIDD ST8 .... 227 K3
Field View Dr MCFLDS SK11 .... 138 E7
Fieldview Dr WARRN/WOL WA2 .... 37 J3
Field Wy ALS/KID ST7 .... 224 E8
Fieldway CH/BCN CH1 .... 144 A2
CHNE CH2 .... 145 L8
FROD/HEL WA6 .... 99 J3
GTS/LS CH66 .... 94 B5
NWCHW CW8 .... 128 C3
WDN WA8 .... 53 L2
Fife Rd WARR WA1 .... 37 L5
Fifth Av ALS/KID ST7 .... 242 E3
FLINT CH6 .... 116 A7
RUNC WA7 .... 73 M5
Fildes Cl WARRW/BUR WA5 .... 36 C7
Filey Rd OFTN SK2 .... 47 J5
Filkin's La CHSE CH3 .... 170 A3
Finchale Dr HALE/TIMP WA15 .... 62 B3
Finch Cl STHEL WA9 .... 34 D1
Finchdale Gdns
GOL/RIS/CU WA3 .... 24 B4
Finchett Dr CH/BCN CH1 .... 16 C2
Finch La HLWD L26 .... 51 H6
Finchley Rd HALE/TIMP WA15 .... 61 L1
Findlay Cl NEWLW WA12 .... 27 J2
Findon Rd NTHM/RTH M23 .... 44 A6
Finger House La WDN WA8 .... 34 D3
Finger Post La FROD/HEL WA6 .... 126 F7
Finland Rd EDGY/DAV SK3 .... 46 D5
Finlan Rd WDN WA8 .... 6 F7
Finlay Av WARRW/BUR WA5 .... 54 E1
Finlow Hill La MCFLDN SK10 .... 110 D6
Finney Cl WILM/AE SK9 .... 84 C2
Finney Dr WILM/AE SK9 .... 84 C2
Finney La CHD/CHDH SK8 .... 64 C3
WYTH/NTH M22 .... 64 A4
Finney's La MWCH CW10 .... 179 H2
Finningley Ct
WARRN/WOL WA2 .... 37 L3
Finsbury Pk WDN WA8 .... 34 C7
Finsbury Wk WSFD CW7 .... 177 G3
Fir Avennue HLWD L26 .... 51 C4
Fir Av BRAM/HZG SK7 .... 65 L4
Firbank CHNE CH2 .... 123 J1
Firbank Cl RUNC WA7 .... 74 D5
Firbank Rd NTHM/RTH M23 .... 43 K6
Firbeck Av CQ CH5 .... 166 C2
Fir Cl HLWD L26 .... 51 C4
POY/DIS SK12 .... 86 E1
TPLY/KEL CW6 .... 197 K2
Firdale Rd NWCHW CW8 .... 12 A5
Firemans Sq CH/BCN CH1 .... 16 F4
Firethorne Rd HLWD L26 .... 50 D2
Fir Gv MCFLDS SK11 .... 138 C7
NWCHW CW8 .... 128 E4
WARR WA1 .... 37 M5
Fir La NWCHW CW8 .... 152 A2
Firman Cl WARRW/BUR WA5 .... 36 B4
Fir Rd BRAM/HZG SK7 .... 65 L3
MPL/ROM SK6 .... 48 E8
Firs Gv CHD/CHDH SK8 .... 45 G8
Firs La WARRS WA4 .... 56 B6
Firs Rd CHD/CHDH SK8 .... 64 A1
First Av ALS/KID ST7 .... 242 E5
CQ CH5 .... 142 F5
CW/HAS CW1 .... 19 K8
FLINT CH6 .... 116 A7
MCFLDN SK10 .... 86 D3
SBCH CW11 .... 204 A7
First Dig La NANT CW5 .... 252 B4
The Firs ALT WA14 .... 61 H2
WHITCH SY13 .... 269 M4
Fir St HTNM SK4 .... 2 E4
IRL M44 .... 31 J6
WDN WA8 .... 7 L1
First Wood St NANT CW5 .... 20 D5
Firs Wy SALE M33 .... 42 C1
Firswood Mt CHD/CHDH SK8 .... 45 G8
Firth Flds NWCHE CW9 .... 153 M2
Firth Fields Cl NWCHE CW9 .... 153 M2
Fir Tree Av CHSW/BR CH4 .... 169 H7
GOL/RIS/CU WA3 .... 23 M4
KNUT WA16 .... 107 J4
Firtree Av WARR WA1 .... 38 M8
Firtree Cl NWCHW CW8 .... 103 H8
Fir Tree Cl WARRS WA4 .... 76 D3
Firtree Gv GTS/LS CH66 .... 121 G4
Fir Tree La CHSE CH3 .... 170 E3
NANT CW5 .... 249 H1
Firvale Av CHD/CHDH SK8 .... 64 B3
Firwood Cl OFTN SK2 .... 47 J4
Firwood Rd BIDD ST8 .... 227 L3
Fisher Av RAIN/WH L35 .... 32 D2

WARRN/WOL WA2 .... 37 H3
Fisherfield Dr GOL/RIS/CU WA3 .... 30 A6
Fishermans Cl CW/HAS CW1 .... 222 F5
Fisher Pl RAIN/WH L35 .... 32 D2
Fisher Rd CH/BCN CH1 .... 144 E8
Fishers Gn TPLY/KEL CW6 .... 174 B7
Fishers La NWCHE CW9 .... 235 J4
Fisher St RUNC WA7 .... 9 K1
Fishpool Rd NWCHW CW8 .... 174 F1
TPLY/KEL CW6 .... 174 F2
Fistral Av CHD/CHDH SK8 .... 64 C4
Fitton's Cl NANT CW5 .... 250 F7
Fitton St NWCHE CW9 .... 130 F2
Fitz Cl MCFLDN SK10 .... 138 D1
Fitz Crs MCFLDN SK10 .... 138 D1
Fitzherbert St WARRN/WOL WA2 .... 5 H2
Fitzwalter Rd WARR WA1 .... 38 D5
Fitzwilliam Av MCFLDS SK11 .... 162 F1
Five Ashes Rd CHSW/BR CH4 .... 169 H7
Flagcroft Dr NTHM/RTH M23 .... 43 M6
Flagg Wood Av MPL/ROM SK6 .... 48 D5
Flag La CW/SHV CW2 .... 18 E5
NSTN CH64 .... 91 M5
Flag La North CHNE CH2 .... 145 L4
Flamingo Cl CW/HAS CW1 .... 220 F5
Flamstead Av NTHM/RTH M23 .... 43 L6
Flander Cl WDN WA8 .... 52 C2
Flashes La CHNE CH2 .... 92 B7
Flash La MCFLDN SK10 .... 112 D5
NWCHE CW9 .... 77 M7
Flat La SBCH CW11 .... 204 B6
TPLY/KEL CW6 .... 149 J8
Flatt La EP CH65 .... 10 C7
Flatts La CHF/WBR SK23 .... 88 F8
Flaxcroft Rd WYTH/NTH M22 .... 63 K2
Flaxley Cl GOL/RIS/CU WA3 .... 30 A7
Flaxmere Dr CHSE CH3 .... 170 B4
Fleet Av STHEL WA9 .... 26 B2
Fleet St EP CH65 .... 10 F5
Fleetwood Cl WARRW/BUR WA5 .... 36 B8
Fleetwood Wk RUNC WA7 .... 74 C5
Fleming Rd SPK/HALE L24 .... 50 C6
WYTH/NTH M22 .... 63 K3
Fleming St EP CH65 .... 10 F5
Flers Av WARRS WA4 .... 56 C1
Fletcher Dr ALT WA14 .... 61 J3
POY/DIS SK12 .... 67 M6
Fletcher Gv NWCHE CW9 .... 130 C6
Fletchers La LYMM WA13 .... 39 M8
Fletcher St CW/HAS CW1 .... 18 D1
STKP SK1 .... 3 G5
WARRS WA4 .... 56 B1
Fletsand Rd WILM/AE SK9 .... 84 C6
Flint Cl BRAM/HZG SK7 .... 64 A6
NSTN CH64 .... 91 K6
Flint Ct EP CH65 .... 121 K2
Flint Dr NSTN CH64 .... 91 L5
Flint Gv IRL M44 .... 31 J6
Flint Meadow NSTN CH64 .... 91 L5
Flint St EDGY/DAV SK3 .... 2 F9
MCFLDN SK10 .... 15 K5
Flittogate La KNUT WA16 .... 105 K3
Flixton Dr CW/SHV CW2 .... 18 A8
Floatshall Rd NTHM/RTH M23 .... 43 M6
Floats Rd NTHM/RTH M23 .... 43 L6
Flora St AIMK WN4 .... 22 B2
Florence St HTNM SK4 .... 2 F3
WARRS WA4 .... 56 D1
Florida Cl WARRW/BUR WA5 .... 36 C5
Florist St EDGY/DAV SK3 .... 46 D5
Flowers La CW/HAS CW1 .... 220 E3
Flower St NWCHW CW8 .... 12 E5
Flowery Fld OFTN SK2 .... 66 A1
Fluin La FROD/HEL WA6 .... 99 J4
Foden Av ALS/KID ST7 .... 241 M1
Foden La BRAM/HZG SK7 .... 85 K1
WILM/AE SK9 .... 109 J2
Foden St MCFLDN SK10 .... 15 G3
Fogg's La WARRS WA4 .... 77 G6
Fold La BIDD ST8 .... 208 E8
MCFLDN SK11 .... 186 D2
Fold Ms BRAM/HZG SK7 .... 66 E1
Folds La CHF/WBR SK23 .... 115 M2
Fold St GOL/RIS/CU WA3 .... 23 G3
The Fold MCFLDN SK10 .... 112 A4
Fol Hollow CONG CW12 .... 207 H3
Folkestone Cl MCFLDN SK10 .... 138 B2
Folkstone Wy RUNC WA7 .... 74 C5
Folly La WARRW/BUR WA5 .... 4 D2
Fonthill Gv SALE M33 .... 42 F3
Forbes Cl GOL/RIS/CU WA3 .... 29 L8
SALE M33 .... 43 K2
STKP SK1 .... 3 L7
Forbes Pk BRAM/HZG SK7 .... 65 K5
Forbes Rd STKP SK1 .... 3 L6
Fordbank Cl DID/WITH M20 .... 45 G2
Ford Cl CW/HAS CW1 .... 18 D1
Fordington Rd
WARRW/BUR WA5 .... 36 B7
Fordland Cl GOL/RIS/CU WA3 .... 23 L3
Ford La CHSE CH3 .... 195 M8
CW/HAS CW1 .... 18 D1
WYTH/NTH M22 .... 44 E3
Ford Ldg DID/WITH M20 .... 45 H2
Fords La ALS/KID ST7 .... 226 D6
BRAM/HZG SK7 .... 65 K6
Ford St EDGY/DAV SK3 .... 2 C6
WARR WA1 .... 5 L4
Foregate St CH/BCN CH1 .... 17 H5
Foreland Cl WARRW/BUR WA5 .... 35 J5
Forest Av HOLMCH CW4 .... 157 J3
Forest Cl MCFLDN SK10 .... 113 L7
NWCHW CW8 .... 151 M1
Forest Dr CHSW/BR CH4 .... 190 B1
HALE/TIMP WA15 .... 42 F6
MCFLDS SK11 .... 163 J1
SALE M33 .... 42 E2
Forester Av KNUT WA16 .... 107 J2
Foresters Cl FROD/HEL WA6 .... 127 G6
Forest Gdns PART M31 .... 40 D1
Forest Gate La TPLY/KEL CW6 .... 149 L5
Forest La FROD/HEL WA6 .... 126 C6
Forest Rd CW/SHV CW2 .... 13 K1
Forest Rd GTS/LS CH66 .... 94 E5

WSFD CW7 .... 177 H4
Forest St CH/BCN CH1 .... 17 J5
NWCHW CW8 .... 128 C4
Forge Cl WDN WA8 .... 33 J7
Forge Flds SBCH CW11 .... 222 F1
Forge La CONG CW12 .... 207 H1
Forge Rd CHF/WBR SK23 .... 89 L5
GTS/LS CH66 .... 94 C6
WARRW/BUR WA5 .... 35 M7
Forge St CW/HAS CW1 .... 19 G4
Forge Wy BIDD ST8 .... 227 H8
CHSW/BR CH4 .... 168 F8
Formby Cl WARRW/BUR WA5 .... 35 M8
Formby Dr CHD/CHDH SK8 .... 64 B4
Forrester Cl BIDD ST8 .... 227 J4
Forrest Wy WARRW/BUR WA5 .... 55 L1
Forshaw's La WARRW/BUR WA5 .... 26 E4
Forshaw St WARRN/WOL WA2 .... 5 J3
Forster Av NWCHW CW8 .... 128 E4
Forster St GOL/RIS/CU WA3 .... 23 C3
WARRN/WOL WA2 .... 5 H3
Fortescue Rd OFTN SK2 .... 47 K5
Fortyacre Dr MPL/ROM SK6 .... 47 L1
Forty Acre La HOLMCH CW4 .... 158 D7
Foscarn Dr NTHM/RTH M23 .... 44 B7
Foster Rd CONG CW12 .... 185 G7
Foster St WDN WA8 .... 7 K2
Fothergill St WARR WA1 .... 5 M3
Foulkes Av CW/HAS CW1 .... 220 F6
Foundry Bank CONG CW12 .... 207 L2
Foundry La ALS/KID ST7 .... 225 M5
SBCH CW11 .... 203 K5
WDN WA8 .... 52 B7
Foundry St MCFLDN SK10 .... 113 H4
NEWLW WA12 .... 27 H1
WARRN/WOL WA2 .... 5 C5
Fountain Cl HALE/TIMP WA15 .... 62 B1
Fountain Ct BIDD ST8 .... 227 K3
Fountain La FROD/HEL WA6 .... 99 G4
NWCHW CW9 .... 153 M2
Fountains Cl MWCH CW10 .... 179 G3
RUNC WA7 .... 74 C7
Fountains Rd CHD/CHDH SK8 .... 65 H6
Fountain St CONG CW12 .... 207 K2
MCFLDN SK10 .... 15 J5
Fountains Wk GOL/RIS/CU WA3 .... 24 B4
Fouracres Rd NTHM/RTH M23 .... 43 M7
Four Lanes End CW/SHV CW2 .... 254 F2
Fourseasons Cl CW/SHV CW2 .... 238 B4
Fourth Av ALS/KID ST7 .... 242 F3
CQ CH5 .... 142 E2
CW/HAS CW1 .... 19 M9
FLINT CH6 .... 116 A7
RUNC WA7 .... 73 M5
Fourways CW/SHV CW2 .... 239 H7
Fowey Cl MCFLDN SK10 .... 137 K3
Fowler Cl CH/BCN CH1 .... 144 D8
Fowlers-bench La CHSE CH3 .... 215 J7
Fowler St MCFLDN SK10 .... 15 G3
Fowley Common La
GOL/RIS/CU WA3 .... 25 H7
Fownhope Av SALE M33 .... 42 F1
Fownhope Rd SALE M33 .... 42 F1
Foxall Wy GTS/LS CH66 .... 120 D2
Fox Bench Cl CHD/CHDH SK8 .... 65 J6
Fox Cl HALE/TIMP WA15 .... 42 F6
Foxcote WDN WA8 .... 52 B2
Foxcote Cl CH/BCN CH1 .... 144 D7
Fox Cover CHSE CH3 .... 146 F7
Fox Cover La CHNE CH2 .... 146 B4
Foxcovert La KNUT WA16 .... 132 E5
Foxes Cl CQ CH5 .... 166 L1
Foxes Fold NWCHW CW8 .... 12 E1
Foxes Hey NWCHW CW8 .... 127 K7
Foxes Hollow CW/HAS CW1 .... 222 E7
Foxes La WHITCH SY13 .... 271 H4
Foxes Wk CHSE CH3 .... 170 A5
Foxfield Cl WARRN/WOL WA2 .... 37 L1
Foxfield La WSFD CW7 .... 176 F3
Foxfield Rd NTHM/RTH M23 .... 63 G1
Fox Gdns ALS/KID ST7 .... 242 D4
LYMM WA13 .... 39 J8
Foxglove Av HLWD L26 .... 50 E3
Foxglove Cl CHSE CH3 .... 170 A6
CW/SHV CW2 .... 238 B5
MCFLDN SK10 .... 113 J4
Foxglove Ct FROD/HEL WA6 .... 99 J4
Foxglove Dr ALT WA14 .... 42 C4
Foxglove Wy NSTN CH64 .... 91 L7
Fox Gv KNUT WA16 .... 107 J3
Foxhall Rd HALE/TIMP WA15 .... 42 E6
Foxhill ALT WA14 .... 42 A7
Fox Hl TPLY/KEL CW6 .... 149 K8
Foxhill Cha OFTN SK2 .... 48 A7
Foxhill Ct TPLY/KEL CW6 .... 197 K3
Foxhill Gv FROD/HEL WA6 .... 98 D8
Foxhill La HLWD L26 .... 50 F2
Foxhills Cl WARRS WA4 .... 76 D1
Fox Hunter Cl CHSE CH3 .... 148 F5
Foxlair Rd WYTH/NTH M22 .... 63 H1
Foxland Rd CHD/CHDH SK8 .... 45 H8
Fox La CHSE CH3 .... 171 G7
MALPAS SY14 .... 230 D5
Fox Lea CH/BCN CH1 .... 144 A4
Foxlea NWCHE CW9 .... 103 J5
Foxleigh HLWD L26 .... 50 D3
Foxley Cl LYMM WA13 .... 59 C2
Foxley Heath WDN WA8 .... 6 E4
Fox's Bank La RAIN/WH L35 .... 32 F5
WDN WA8 .... 32 F5
Fox's Dr CQ CH5 .... 142 F6
Foxshaw Cl RAIN/WH L35 .... 32 D3
Fox St EDGY/DAV SK3 .... 2 C8
RUNC WA7 .... 9 G4
WARRW/BUR WA5 .... 4 A6
Foxwist Cl CHNE CH2 .... 17 L1
Foxwist Gn NWCHW CW8 .... 150 A3
Foxwood Dr KNUT WA16 .... 134 A4
Foy St AIMK WN4 .... 22 B1
Framingham Rd SALE M33 .... 43 J8
Frampton Gv BURS/TUN ST6 .... 243 L6
Frances Av CHD/CHDH SK8 .... 45 G6
Frances James Leech St
EDGY/DAV SK3 .... 2 F7
Frances St CHD/CHDH SK8 .... 45 L1
CW/SHV CW2 .... 19 G8
IRL M44 .... 31 L7

MCFLDS SK11 .... 14 D5
Francis Cl WDN WA8 .... 52 C4
Francis Ct CH/BCN CH1 .... 17 J4
Francis La WRXS/E LL13 .... 228 D5
Francis Rd FROD/HEL WA6 .... 99 J3
IRL M44 .... 31 M4
WARRS WA4 .... 56 B3
Francis St BURS/TUN ST6 .... 243 M7
CH/BCN CH1 .... 17 J3
Frank Bott Av CW/HAS CW1 .... 221 G5
Franklin Cl WARRW/BUR WA5 .... 36 C4
Franklyn Av CW/SHV CW2 .... 18 C6
Frank Perkins Wy IRL M44 .... 31 M5
Frank St WDN WA8 .... 7 M3
Frank Webb Av CW/HAS CW1 .... 221 G6
Fraser Av SALE M33 .... 43 L1
Fraser Ct CHSW/BR CH4 .... 17 H9
WHITCH SY13 .... 270 A6
Fraser Rd WARRW/BUR WA5 .... 35 K6
Frawley Av NEWLW WA12 .... 22 B7
Freckleton Cl
WARRW/BUR WA5 .... 36 B8
Frederick St WARRS WA4 .... 56 D1
WDN WA8 .... 7 J3
Fredric Pl RUNC WA7 .... 9 J1
Free Green La KNUT WA16 .... 132 F3
Freemantle St EDGY/DAV SK3 .... 2 B7
French La NANT CW5 .... 251 H8
French St WDN WA8 .... 53 K3
Frensham Wy WLTN L25 .... 50 D4
Freshfield CHD/CHDH SK8 .... 64 A2
Freshfield Cl MPL/ROM SK6 .... 49 H3
Freshfield Dr MCFLDN SK10 .... 138 C1
Freshfield Rd HTNM SK4 .... 45 M2
Freshfields CW/SHV CW2 .... 238 A5
KNUT WA16 .... 106 E1
NWCHE CW9 .... 103 J5
Freshfields Dr WARRN/WOL WA2 .... 38 B3
Freshmeadow La
FROD/HEL WA6 .... 124 A2
Freshpool Wy WYTH/NTH M22 .... 44 E6
Freshwater WARRW/BUR WA5 .... 35 K5
Freshwater
WARRW/BUR WA5 .... 35 K5
Frewland Av EDGY/DAV SK3 .... 46 F8
Friars Av WARRW/BUR WA5 .... 35 L7
Friars Cl ALT WA14 .... 61 H3
MCFLDN SK10 .... 113 K7
WILM/AE SK9 .... 83 L4
Friars Ct CQ CH5 .... 166 C4
Friars Ga WARR WA1 .... 5 C8
Friars La WARR WA1 .... 5 C8
Friars Wy MCFLDN SK10 .... 137 L2
Frida Crs NWCHW CW8 .... 12 E6
Friends La WARRW/BUR WA5 .... 35 K6
Frieston Rd ALT WA14 .... 42 F3
Frimley Gdns WYTH/NTH M22 .... 63 K1
Frinton Cl SALE M33 .... 42 F3
Frith Av NWCHW CW8 .... 150 D4
Frith Ter MCFLDS SK11 .... 138 D8
Frobisher Ct
WARRW/BUR WA5 .... 36 D4
Frobisher Rd NSTN CH64 .... 91 L4
Froda Av FROD/HEL WA6 .... 99 H5
Frodsham Av HTNM SK4 .... 2 A2
Frodsham Rd FROD/HEL WA6 .... 124 C3
SALE M33 .... 43 L2
Frodsham St CH/BCN CH1 .... 17 G5
Froghall La KNUT WA16 .... 59 L5
LYMM WA13 .... 59 K4
WARR WA1 .... 4 D5
WARRN/WOL WA2 .... 4 E5
WARRW/BUR WA5 .... 4 C6
Frog La CHSE CH3 .... 213 J2
KNUT WA16 .... 105 G3
MALPAS SY14 .... 256 C2
WRXS/E LL13 .... 228 D4
Frome Av NSTN SK2 .... 47 J3
Frome Ct EP CH65 .... 10 D7
Frome Wy WLTN L25 .... 50 D3
Front St SBCH CW11 .... 204 B6
Frosts Ms EP CH65 .... 10 D5
Fryer Rd NWCHE CW9 .... 131 G1
Fuchsia Cl GTS/LS CH66 .... 120 F3
Fulbeck WDN WA8 .... 52 C2
Fulbeck Cl CW/SHV CW2 .... 238 B4
Fulbrook Dr CHD/CHDH SK8 .... 65 G6
Fuller Dr CW/SHV CW2 .... 238 A4
Fuller St BURS/TUN ST6 .... 243 L8
Fullerton Rd HTNM SK4 .... 46 B2
NWCHW CW8 .... 129 G8
Fulmar Cl POY/DIS SK12 .... 66 A8
Fulmar Dr OFTN SK2 .... 47 M7
SALE M33 .... 42 C2
Fulmards Cl WILM/AE SK9 .... 84 C5
Fulshaw Ct WILM/AE SK9 .... 84 A5
Fulshaw Pk WILM/AE SK9 .... 84 A4
Fulshaw Pk South WILM/AE SK9 .... 83 M8
Fulstone Ms OFTN SK2 .... 47 M8
Fulton Gv NWCHE CW9 .... 153 M1
Fulwood Gdns GTS/LS CH66 .... 94 C6
Fulwood Ms GTS/LS CH66 .... 94 C6
Fulwood Rd GOL/RIS/CU WA3 .... 23 L6
GTS/LS CH66 .... 94 C6
Furber St CW/HAS CW1 .... 18 F2
Furlong Rd BURS/TUN ST6 .... 243 L8
WYTH/NTH M22 .... 63 H1
Furnace La AUD/MAD/W CW3 .... 267 K5
Furne Rd CH/BCN CH1 .... 144 E8
Furness Cl HOLMCH CW4 .... 181 C1
POY/DIS SK12 .... 66 C8
WSFD CW7 .... 177 G8
Furness Gv HTNM SK4 .... 46 A3
Furness Lodge Cl
CHF/WBR SK23 .... 69 K8
Furness Rd CHD/CHDH SK8 .... 65 K6
Furnivall St SBCH CW11 .... 204 B5
Furnival St CW/SHV CW2 .... 18 F8
The Furrows GTS/LS CH66 .... 120 F4
Fylde Av CHD/CHDH SK8 .... 64 C4
Fylde Rd HTNM SK4 .... 46 A2
Fytton Cl MCFLDS SK11 .... 161 K3

G

Gable Av *WILM/AE* SK9........ 84 A5
Gables Cl *WARRN/WOL* WA2 .... 37 M1
The Gables *ALS/KID* ST7 .... 241 J1
Gable St *NEWLW* WA12............ 27 G1
Gabriel Bank *NWCHW* CW8 .... 127 G3
Gadbrook Pk *NWCHE* CW9 .... 130 D7
Gadbrook Rd *NWCHE* CW9 .... 130 D6
Gaddum Rd *ALT* WA14 .... 61 G3
DID/WITH M20 .... 45 J1
Gail Av *HTNM* SK4.................... 2 C3
Gail Cl *WILM/AE* SK9 .... 110 B2
Gainford Av *CHD/CHDH* SK8 .... 45 H8
Gainford Cl *WDN* WA8 .... 52 C1
Gainsborough Av
MPL/ROM SK6 .... 49 H4
Gainsborough Cl
WILM/AE SK9 .... 84 D4
Gainsborough Ct *WDN* WA8 .. 52 B3
Gainsborough Dr
CHD/CHDH SK8 .... 45 M6
Gainsborough Rd *CW/SHV* CW2.. 18 C6
WARRS WA4 .... 56 B2
Gairloch Cl *WARRN/WOL* WA2 .. 28 F8
Gaisgill Ct *WDN* WA8 .... 52 C3
Gala Cl *CHSW/BR* CH4 .... 190 C1
Galbraith Cl *CONG* CW12 ...... 207 J2
Galbraith Rd *DID/WITH* M20 .... 45 J2
Gale Av *WARRW/BUR* WA5 ...... 36 F3
Galion Wy *WDN* WA8 .... 33 M8
Galleys Bank *ALS/KID* ST7 .... 243 H1
Galloway St *HOLMCH* CW4 .... 181 J2
Gallowsclough La
FROD/HEL WA6 .... 126 F8
NWCHW CW8 .... 151 G1
Galston Av *RAIN/WH* L35........ 33 K2
Galway Gv *CW/SHV* CW2 ...... 238 B8
Game St *SBCH* CW11 .... 222 F1
Gamford La *WRX/GR/LL* LL12 .. 210 D5
Ganton Cl *WDN* WA8 .... 34 B8
Ganworth Cl *SPK/HALE* L24 .... 70 E2
Ganworth Rd *SPK/HALE* L24 .... 70 E2
Garage Rd *SPK/HALE* L24 ...... 50 F7
Garbett St *BURS/TUN* ST6 .... 243 J5
Garden Ct *CH/BCN* CH1 .... 16 F4
Gardeners Cl *BIDD* ST8.......... 227 G7
Garden La *ALT* WA14.............. 42 D7
CH/BCN CH1 .... 16 D2
Garden Rd *KNUT* WA16 .... 106 F1
Garden St *MCFLDN* SK10 .... 15 J3
MCFLDN SK10 .... 112 F4
OFTN SK2 .... 47 J7
WLTN L25 .... 50 A2
Garden Wy *CQ* CH5 .... 142 A6
Garfield St *STKP* SK1 .... 3 J3
Garfit St *MWCH* CW10 .... 179 J2
Garland Rd *WYTH/NTH* M22 .... 63 L1
Garner Av *HALE/TIMP* WA15 .... 43 C3
Garner Cl *ALT* WA14 .... 61 K2
Garner's La *EDGY/DAV* SK3 .... 46 F7
Garner St *WARRN/WOL* WA2 .... 5 K2
Garners Wk
AUD/MAD/W CW3 .... 267 M5
Garnett Av *WARRS* WA4 .... 37 M8
Garnetts La *WDN* WA8 .... 72 A1
Garnett St *STKP* SK1 .... 3 C6
Garrett Fld *GOL/RIS/CU* WA3 .... 29 K7
Garrett Wk *EDGY/DAV* SK3 .... 2 A8
Garrick Gdns *WYTH/NTH* M22 .. 44 D8
Garrigill Cl *WDN* WA8 .... 34 B7
Garsdale Av *RAIN/WH* L35 .... 33 K2
Garsdale Cl *WARRW/BUR* WA5 .. 35 M5
Garside Av *GOL/RIS/CU* WA3 .. 23 K5
Garston Cl *HTNM* SK4 .... 2 A2
Garswood St *AIMK* WN4 .... 22 B1
Garth Av *HALE/TIMP* WA15 .... 42 E6
Garth Dr *CHNE* CH2 .... 145 J7
Garth Ganol *FLINT* CH6 .... 116 B8
Garthland Rd *BRAM/HZG* SK7 .. 66 F1
Garthorp Rd *NTHM/RTH* M23 .. 43 L3
Garth Rd *MPL/ROM* SK6 .... 49 C6
OFTN SK2 .... 47 J5
WYTH/NTH M22 .... 44 D8
Garton Dr *GOL/RIS/CU* WA3 .. 23 L3
Gartons La *STHEL* WA9............ 34 C1
Garven Pl *WARR* WA1 .... 4 F7
Garway *WLTN* L25 .... 50 C1
Garwood Cl *WARRW/BUR* WA5.. 36 B4
Gaskell Av *KNUT* WA16 .... 106 F2
WARRS WA4 .... 57 G1
Gaskell Rd *ALT* WA14 .... 42 D6
Gaskell St *WARRS* WA4 .... 56 C3
Gaskill Rd *SPK/HALE* L24 ...... 50 D8
Gas Rd *MCFLDS* SK11 .... 15 H5
Gas St *HTNM* SK4 .... 2 E5
Gateacre Vale Rd *WLTN* L25 .. 50 B1
Gateacre Wk *NTHM/RTH* M23 .. 43 L5
Gatefield St *CW/HAS* CW1 ...... 18 E3
Gatesheath Dr *CHNE* CH2 .... 145 K5
Gatesheath La *CHSE* CH3 .... 194 E7
Gate Warth St
WARRW/BUR WA5 .... 36 D8
Gateway *CW/HAS* CW1 .... 19 L7
Gathill Cl *CHD/CHDH* SK8 .... 64 F3
Gatley Gn *CHD/CHDH* SK8 .... 45 G7
Gatley Rd *CHD/CHDH* SK8 .... 45 J7
SALE M33 .... 43 J8
Gatwick Av *NTHM/RTH* M23 .. 44 B6
Gaunts Wy *RUNC* WA7 .... 73 L4
Gavin Rd *WDN* WA8 .... 52 B5
Gawend La *MCFLDS* SK11 .... 162 C2
Gawer Pk *CH/BCN* CH1 .... 145 J8
Gawsworth Av *CW/SHV* CW2 .. 237 M1
DID/WITH M20 .... 45 J3
Gawsworth Cl *ALS/KID* ST7 .. 241 J1
BRAM/HZG SK7 .... 65 L2
EDGY/DAV SK3 .... 46 D7
HALE/TIMP WA15................ 43 K6
HOLMCH CW4...................... 181 H1
POY/DIS SK12 .... 86 F2
Gawsworth Dr *SBCH* CW11 .. 204 C4
Gawsworth Ms
CHD/CHDH SK8 .... 45 H7
Gawsworth Rd *GOL/RIS/CU* WA3 .. 22 F3
GTS/LS CH66 .... 94 E8

MCFLDS SK11 .... 137 K8
SALE M33 .... 43 L2
Gayhurst Av
WARRN/WOL WA2 .... 37 M2
Gaymoore Cl *CHNE* CH2 .... 16 F2
Gayton Cl *CHNE* CH2 .... 145 L7
Gee St *EDGY/DAV* SK3 .... 2 B3
Gemini Gv *BURS/TUN* ST6 .... 243 L6
Gemmull Cl
AUD/MAD/W CW3 .... 263 M8
General St *WARR* WA1 .... 5 J6
Geneva Rd *BRAM/HZG* SK7 .... 65 K1
WSFD CW7 .... 177 J3
George Bates Cl *ALS/KID* ST7 .. 241 J1
George Mann Cl *WYTH/NTH* M22.. 63 J3
George Richards Wy *ALT* WA14 .. 42 C5
Georges Crs *WARRS* WA4 ...... 57 H2
George's La *NWCHE* CW9 .... 104 D3
George's Rd *HTNM* SK4 .... 2 D4
SALE M33 .... 43 H1
George's Rd West *POY/DIS* SK12 .. 86 D1
George St *CH/BCN* CH1 .... 16 F4
CHF/WBR SK23 .... 89 L5
EP CH65 .... 10 E4
KNUT WA16 .... 106 F2
MCFLDS SK11 .... 15 H6
MPL/ROM SK6 .... 49 H2
NEWLW WA12 .... 22 A8
NWCHW CW8 .... 129 H1
SBCH CW11 .... 203 L4
STKP SK1 .... 3 J5
WHITCH SY13 .... 270 B4
WILM/AE SK9 .... 110 A3
WSFD CW7 .... 177 L3
George St East *STKP* SK1 .... 3 M7
George St West *MCFLDS* SK11 .. 14 F5
STKP SK1 .... 3 L8
George Vi Av *MWCH* CW10 .... 179 J7
George Vi Cl *MWCH* CW10 .... 179 K6
Georgian Cl *HLWD* L26 .... 50 F6
Gerard Dr *NANT* CW5 .... 20 B8
Gerard St *AIMK* WN4 .... 22 B1
Germander Cl *HLWD* L26 .... 50 E3
Gerneth Cl *SPK/HALE* L24 ...... 50 C8
Gerneth Rd *SPK/HALE* L24 .... 70 B1
Gerosa Av *WARRN/WOL* WA2 .. 28 B4
Gerrard Av *GTS/LS* CH66 .... 94 C8
HALE/TIMP WA15.................. 43 C4
WARRW/BUR WA5 .... 4 C2
Gerrard Dr *NWCHW* CW8 .... 128 D3
Gerrard Rd *GOL/RIS/CU* WA3 .. 29 C5
Gerrards Av *CHSE* CH3 .... 170 A3
Gerrard's La *HLWD* L26 .... 50 F6
Gerrard St *WDN* WA8 .... 7 J5
Giantswood La *CONG* CW12 .. 183 M3
Gibb Hl *NWCHW* CW9 .... 103 K3
Gibb La *MPL/ROM* SK6 .... 49 L7
Gibbon Av *WYTH/NTH* M22 .... 63 K2
Gibbon Dr *NWCHE* CW9 ...... 131 G1
Gib La *NTHM/RTH* M23............ 44 C4
Gibsmere Cl *HALE/TIMP* WA15 .. 43 K6
Gibson Crs *SBCH* CW11 .... 203 K6
Gibson St *WARR* WA1 .... 5 K7
WARRS WA4 .... 56 D3
Gibson Wy *ALT* WA14 .... 42 C4
Gibwood Rd *WYTH/NTH* M22 .. 44 C4
Gigg La *WARRS* WA4 .... 38 E8
WARRS WA4 .... 55 H7
Gig La *WARR* WA1 .... 38 D4
Gilbern Dr *BIDD* ST8 .... 227 H7
Gilbert Cl *ALS/KID* ST7 .... 243 G2
Gilbert Rd *HALE/TIMP* WA15 .. 61 L3
Gilbert St *BURS/TUN* ST6 ...... 243 J5
Gilchrist Av *MCFLDS* SK11 .... 137 L5
Gilchrist Rd *IRL* M44 .... 31 L6
Gilderdale Cl *GOL/RIS/CU* WA3 .. 30 B7
Gillan Cl *RUNC* WA7 .... 74 C7
Gill Bank Rd *ALS/KID* ST7 .... 243 H4
BURS/TUN ST6 .... 243 H5
Gill Bent Rd *CHD/CHDH* SK8 .. 65 G6
Gillbrook Rd *DID/WITH* M20 .. 45 H1
Gillow Cl *CW/HAS* CW1 .... 221 G4
Gill St *STKP* SK12 .... 3 L1
Gillwood Dr *MPL/ROM* SK6 .... 47 M3
Gilmore St *EDGY/DAV* SK3 ...... 2 F7
Giltbrook Cl *WDN* WA8 .... 52 F1
Gilwell Cl *WARRS* WA4 .... 57 G2
Gilwell Dr *NTHM/RTH* M23 .... 43 M8
Gingerbread La *NANT* CW5 .... 21 K6
Gipsy La *CH/BCN* CH1 .... 144 F2
OFTN SK2 .... 47 J6
Girton Cl *EP* CH65 .... 11 G9
Girton Rd *EP* CH65 .... 11 G9
Girvin Dr *NSTN* CH64 .... 91 L6
Gisburn Av *GOL/RIS/CU* WA3.. 22 F2
Gladeside Rd *WYTH/NTH* M22 .. 44 C8
The Glade *HTNM* SK4.............. 46 A3
Gladewood Cl *WILM/AE* SK9 .. 84 C4
Gladstone Av *CH/BCN* CH1 .... 16 C4
Gladstone Gv *BIDD* ST8 .... 227 K4
HTNM SK4 .... 46 A1
Gladstone Rd *ALT* WA14........ 42 D6
CH/BCN CH1 .... 16 D2
CHSW/BR CH4 .... 190 B1
NSTN CH64 .... 91 L4
Gladstone St *CQ* CH5 .... 142 A6
CQ CH5 .... 142 D7
CW/HAS CW1 .... 18 F3
NANT CW5 .... 237 K6
NWCHW CW8 .... 12 C5
OFTN SK2 .... 47 J8
WARRN/WOL WA2 .... 4 E5
WDN WA8 .... 7 J4
WSFD CW7 .... 177 K5
Gladstone Ter *CQ* CH5 .... 166 F1
Gladstone Wy *CQ* CH5 .... 166 D2
Glaisdale Cl *AIMK* WN4 .... 22 C1
CW/SHV CW2 .... 238 A6
Glamis Cl *CHSE* CH3 .... 170 A2
CW/SHV CW2 .... 237 L4
Glan Aber Pk *CHSW/BR* CH4 .. 169 G5
Glandon Dr *CHD/CHDH* SK8 .. 65 J5
Glan Gors *FLINT* CH6 .... 116 B8
Glanvor Rd *EDGY/DAV* SK3 .... 2 A8
Glan Y Fferi (Ferry Bank)
CQ CH5 .... 142 C6
Glastonbury Av *CHD/CHDH* SK8.. 65 J6

CHNE CH2 .... 145 M5
SALE M33 .... 43 L3
HALE/TIMP WA15................ 62 B2
Glastonbury Cl *RUNC* WA7 .... 74 E1
Glastonbury Dr *MWCH* CW10 .. 179 H3
POY/DIS SK12 .... 66 D7
Glazebrook La *GOL/RIS/CU* WA3 .. 31 G6
Glazebrook St *WARR* WA1 .... 5 L5
Glazebury Dr *NTHM/RTH* M23 .. 44 B7
Glaziers La *GOL/RIS/CU* WA3 .. 29 K2
Gleadmere *WDN* WA8 .... 52 C2
Gleave Av *MCFLDN* SK10 .... 113 H4
Gleave Rd *NWCHW* CW8 .... 50 A7
WARRW/BUR WA5 .... 26 F6
Glebe Av *AIMK* WN4 .... 22 B2
WARRS WA4 .... 57 J3
Glebe Cl *NANT* CW5.............. 253 G4
Glebecroft Av *CHNE* CH2 .... 123 G1
Glebeland *GOL/RIS/CU* WA3 .. 29 L1
Glebelands Rd *KNUT* WA16 .. 107 G3
NTHM/RTH M23 .... 43 M6
Glebe La *WDN* WA8 .... 34 A7
Glebe Mdw *CHNE* CH2 .... 146 F3
Glebe Rd *NWCHW* CW8 ...... 128 A8
Glebe St *ALS/KID* ST7 .... 242 D2
STKP SK1 .... 3 K6
The Glebe *RUNC* WA7 .... 73 L3
Gleggs Cl *CHSE* CH3 .... 170 B5
Glegg St *MCFLDN* SK10 .... 15 J6
Glenathol Rd *GTS/LS* CH66 .. 94 C8
Glenbourne Pk *BRAM/HZG* SK7 .. 65 K7
Glenby Av *WYTH/NTH* M22 .... 63 M1
Glen Cl *GOL/RIS/CU* WA3 ...... 40 B2
Glencoe Dr *SALE* M33 .... 42 F8
Glencourse Rd *WDN* WA8 ...... 34 A7
Glendale Av *CHNE* CH2 .... 123 G1
CQ CH5 .... 166 F1
Glendale Cl *AUD/MAD/W* CW3 .. 264 F8
CW/SHV CW2 .... 237 K1
Glendene Av *BRAM/HZG* SK7 .. 65 K7
Glendyke Rd *GTS/LS* CH66 .... 94 C8
Gleneagles Cl *BRAM/HZG* SK7 .. 66 A5
CHSE CH3 .... 170 B1
WILM/AE SK9 .... 84 D4
Gleneagles Dr *HOLMCH* CW4 .. 181 H2
MCFLDN SK10 .... 112 C8
WDN WA8 .... 34 A7
WSFD CW7 .... 177 J2
Gleneagles Rd *CHD/CHDH* SK8 .. 64 C3
GTS/LS CH66 .... 94 C8
Glenesk Ct *CQ* CH5 .... 142 F6
Glenesk Rd *GTS/LS* CH66 ...... 94 C8
Glenfield Av *ALT* WA14 .... 42 B8
Glenfield Dr *POY/DIS* SK12 .... 86 D1
Glenholme Rd *BRAM/HZG* SK7 .. 65 K5
Glenlea Dr *DID/WITH* M20 ...... 45 H2
Glenmaye Rd *GTS/LS* CH66 .. 94 C8
Glenmere Rd *DID/WITH* M20 .. 45 J4
Glenmoor Rd *STKP* SK1 .... 3 J6
Glenn Pl *WDN* WA8 .... 6 B3
Glenorchy Cl *HOLMCH* CW4 .. 181 J2
Glen Ri *HALE/TIMP* WA15 ...... 43 C7
Glen Rd *GTS/LS* CH66 .... 94 C8
Glenside Cl *CH/BCN* CH1 .... 144 D7
Glenside Dr *WILM/AE* SK9 ...... 84 C6
The Glen *CH/BCN* CH1 .... 144 E7
RUNC WA7 .... 73 M6
Glenthorn Gv *SALE* M33 .... 43 H1
Glenton Pk *NSTN* CH64 .... 91 M6
Glenville Cl *RUNC* WA7 .... 73 H6
WLTN L25 .... 50 B1
Glenwood Cl *GTS/LS* CH66 .... 94 C6
Glenwood Gdns *GTS/LS* CH66 .. 94 C6
Glenwood Gv *OFTN* SK2 .... 66 B1
Glenwood Rd *GTS/LS* CH66 .... 94 C6
Gleyve *KNUT* WA16 .... 59 J7
Glossop Rd *MPL/ROM* SK6 .... 49 J3
Gloucester Av *CQ* CH5 .... 142 B6
GOL/RIS/CU WA3 .... 29 H5
MPL/ROM SK6 .... 48 F6
Gloucester Cl *GTS/LS* CH66 .. 120 F4
MCFLDN SK10 .... 112 E8
WARR WA1 .... 38 D5
Gloucester Rd *ALS/KID* ST7 .. 242 F2
CHD/CHDH SK8 .... 64 C5
HUY L36 .... 32 A1
KNUT WA16 .... 106 F4
POY/DIS SK12 .... 66 D8
WDN WA8 .... 53 H1
Gloucester St *CH/BCN* CH1 .. 17 G2
EDGY/DAV SK3 .... 2 D9
Glover Rd *GOL/RIS/CU* WA3 .. 29 J7
Glovers Loom *CHSE* CH3 .... 170 B5
Glover St *CW/HAS* CW1 .... 18 B1
NEWLW WA12 .... 27 J7
Glyn Av *HALE/TIMP* WA15 ...... 62 A2
Glynnedale Pk *CQ* CH5 .... 166 A3
Glynne St *CQ* CH5 .... 142 D7
Glynne Wy *CQ* CH5 .... 166 D4
Goathland Wy *MCFLDS* SK11 .. 15 H9
MCFLDS SK11 .... 138 D7
Goddard Av *RUNC* WA7 .... 73 L1
Goddard St *CW/HAS* CW1 ...... 18 C2
Godfrey St *WARRN/WOL* WA2 .. 5 L3
Godscroft La *FROD/HEL* WA6 .. 98 E6
Godshill Cl *WARRW/BUR* WA5 .. 35 K5
Godstow *RUNC* WA7 .... 54 E8
Godward Rd *NM/HAY* SK22 .... 69 H4
Golborne Dale Rd *NEWLW* WA12 .. 23 G8
Golborne La *KNUT* WA16 ...... 78 F1
Golborne Rd *GOL/RIS/CU* WA3 .. 23 J4
WARRN/WOL WA2 .... 28 A5
Golborne St *NEWLW* WA12 .... 22 E8
WARR WA1 .... 4 F6
Goldcliffe Cl *WARRW/BUR* WA5 .. 36 D2
Goldcrest Cl *CW/HAS* CW1 .... 220 F5
RUNC WA7 .... 73 M7
WSFD CW7 .... 177 J2
WYTH/NTH M22 .... 44 F7
Goldcrest Ms *HLWD* L26 .... 50 E3
Goldcrest Wy *BIDD* ST8 .... 227 L4
Goldfinch Cl *CONG* CW12 .... 207 L3
HLWD L26 .... 50 E3
Goldfinch Farm Rd
SPK/HALE L24...................... 70 C1
Goldfinch La *GOL/RIS/CU* WA3 .. 29 L8
Goldford La *MALPAS* SY14 .... 231 L6

Goldie Av *WYTH/NTH* M22 .... 63 M3
Goldsmith Dr *SBCH* CW11 .... 203 K6
Goldsworth Fold
RAIN/WH L35 .... 33 H1
Golf Links Cl *BURS/TUN* ST6 .. 243 J5
Golf Rd *HALE/TIMP* WA15 ...... 61 M1
Gonsley Cl *CHNE* CH3 .... 17 G1
Gonville Av *MCFLDS* SK11 .... 162 F1
Gooch Dr *NEWLW* WA12 .... 27 K2
Goodall St *MCFLDS* SK11 ...... 15 K7
Goodfellow St *BURS/TUN* ST6 .. 243 J5
Goodlass Rd *SPK/HALE* L24 .. 50 A7
Goodridge Av *WYTH/NTH* M22 .. 63 J3
Goodrington Rd *WILM/AE* SK9 .. 84 E2
Goodwin Crs *CW/SHV* CW2 .. 238 C8
Goodwood Av *NTHM/RTH* M23 .. 43 K4
Goodwood Cl *CH/BCN* CH1 .... 16 B4
NWCHW CW8 .... 129 H1
Goodwood Crs
HALE/TIMP WA15................ 43 J6
Goodwood Gv *GTS/LS* CH66 .. 120 D1
Goodwood Ri *MWCH* CW10 .. 179 G2
Goodwood Rd *MPL/ROM* SK6 .. 48 E7
Gooseberry La *RUNC* WA7 .... 74 D3
TPLY/KEL WA3 .... 173 L1
Goosebrook Cl *NWCHE* CW9 .. 103 J4
Goosebrook La *NWCHE* CW9 .. 102 F2
Goose Gn *ALT* WA14 .... 42 D8
Goose La *WARRS* WA4 .... 76 A2
Goostrey Cl *WILM/AE* SK9 .... 84 E3
Goostrey La *HOLMCH* CW4 .. 157 G5
WARRS WA4 .... 158 A6
Gordale Cl *CONG* CW12 ...... 185 G7
WARRW/BUR WA5 .... 35 M5
Gordon Av *BRAM/HZG* SK7 .... 66 D1
WARR WA1 .... 38 B5
Gordon La *CHNE* CH2 .... 121 H7
Gordon Rd *BURS/TUN* ST6 .... 243 J6
Gordon St *HTNM* SK4 .... 2 F3
Gore La *KNUT* WA16 .... 109 H1
Gorse Av *MPL/ROM* SK6 .... 48 E6
Gorse Bank Rd *HALE/TIMP* WA15.. 62 C5
Gorse La *FROD/HEL* WA6 ...... 127 G6
Gorse Covert *NWCHE* CW9 .. 130 C5
Gorse Covert Rd
GOL/RIS/CU WA3 .... 30 A7
Gorsefield *CHSE* CH3 .... 214 A3
Gorsefield Hey *WILM/AE* SK9 .. 84 E4
Gorselands *CHD/CHDH* SK8 .. 65 H7
Gorse La *CONG* CW12 .... 207 L5
Gorse Sq *PART* M31 .... 40 D1
Gorse Stacks *CH/BCN* CH1 .... 17 G4
The Gorse *ALT* WA14 .... 61 H4
Gorse Wy *CHSE* CH3 .... 170 A4
Gorsewood Rd *RUNC* WA7 .... 74 D6
Gorsey Av *WYTH/NTH* M22 .... 44 C8
Gorsey Bank Crs *NANT* CW5 .. 253 G4
Gorsey Bank Rd *EDGY/DAV* SK3 .. 46 B4
Gorsey Brow *MPL/ROM* SK6 .. 48 E7
STKP SK1 .... 3 J6
Gorsey Dr *WYTH/NTH* M22 .... 44 C8
Gorsey La *ALT* WA14 .... 42 B7
LYMM WA13 .... 41 G6
WARRN/WOL WA2 .... 5 L2
WDN WA8 .... 53 L4
Gorsey Mount St *STKP* SK1 ...... 3 J5
Gorsey Rd *WILM/AE* SK9 ...... 83 M5
WYTH/NTH M22 .... 44 C8
Gorseywell La *RUNC* WA7 .... 74 F6
Gorstage La *NWCHW* CW8 .. 128 B7
Gorstons La *NSTN* CH64 .... 92 A6
Gorston Wk *WYTH/NTH* M22 .. 63 J4
Gosberryhole La *CONG* CW12 .. 209 G2
Gosforth Pl *CHNE* CH2 .... 17 L1
Gosling Rd *GOL/RIS/CU* WA3 .. 29 H5
Gosport Cl *WARRN/WOL* WA2 .. 37 L3
Goss St *CH/BCN* CH1 .... 16 F5
Gotherage Cl *MPL/ROM* SK6 .. 48 E2
Gotherage La *MPL/ROM* SK6 .. 48 E2
Gothic Cl *MPL/ROM* SK6 .... 48 E2
Gough Av *WARRN/WOL* WA2 .. 37 H2
Gough's La *KNUT* WA16 .... 107 H5
Gough St *EDGY/DAV* SK3 .... 2 D6
Goulden St *CW/HAS* CW1 ...... 18 B1
WARRW/BUR WA5 .... 4 B5
Goulders Ct *RUNC* WA7 .... 74 B7
Gourham Dr *CHD/CHDH* SK8 .. 64 F3
Govan St *WYTH/NTH* M22 ...... 44 E3
Gower Av *BRAM/HZG* SK7 ...... 66 C1
Gowy Cl *ALS/KID* ST7 .... 240 F1
SBCH CW11 .... 203 L4
WILM/AE SK9 .... 84 E3
Gowy Crs *CHSE* CH3 .... 172 B3
Gowy Rd *CHNE* CH2 .... 146 F3
Goyt Av *MPL/ROM* SK6 .... 47 M1
Goyt Crs *MPL/ROM* SK6 .... 47 M1
STKP SK1 .... 3 L1
Goyt Pl *CHF/WBR* SK23 .... 89 L5
Goyt Rd *CHF/WBR* SK23 .... 89 L6
MPL/ROM SK6 .... 48 F8
NM/HAY SK22 .... 69 J6
POY/DIS SK12 .... 68 D7
Goyt Valley Rd *MPL/ROM* SK6 .. 47 M1
Goyt Vw *NM/HAY* SK22 .... 69 H6
Goyt Wy *MPL/ROM* SK6 .... 49 H7
MPL/ROM SK6 .... 69 J6
Grace Av *WARRN/WOL* WA2 .. 37 H4
Grace Cl *CW/HAS* CW1 .... 222 C8
Grace Rd *EP* CH65 .... 10 E5
Gradwell St *EDGY/DAV* SK3 .... 2 E7
Grafton Cl *MCFLDS* SK11 ...... 17 G2
Grafton Rd *EP* CH65 .... 10 E5
Grafton St *ALT* WA14 .... 42 D8
HTNM SK4 .... 2 F2
NEWLW WA12 .... 27 H1
WDN WA8 .... 4 B4
Graham Av *GTS/LS* CH66 ...... 94 D7
Graham Cl *WDN* WA8 .... 52 C3
Graham Crs *IRL* M44 .... 31 J8
Graham Dr *HLWD* L26 .... 51 G4
POY/DIS SK12 .... 68 C5
Graham Rd *CH/BCN* CH1 .... 144 E8
STKP SK1 .... 3 M7
WDN WA8 .... 52 C4

Grainger's Rd *NWCHE* CW9 .... 13 H9
Gralam Cl *SALE* M33 .... 43 L3
Graley Cl *HLWD* L26 .... 50 F6
Grammar School Rd
LYMM WA13 .... 58 F2
WARRS WA4 .... 56 F1
Grampian Wy *GOL/RIS/CU* WA3 .. 23 K8
NSTN CH64 .... 91 L7
WSFD CW7 .... 177 G5
Granary Wy *SALE* M33 .... 42 F7
Granby Cl *RUNC* WA7 .... 74 C7
Granby Rd *CHD/CHDH* SK8 .... 65 H4
HALE/TIMP WA15................ 43 G3
OFTN SK2 .... 47 H7
WARRS WA4 .... 56 B4
Grandford La *NANT* CW5 ...... 262 C2
Granford Cl *ALT* WA14 .... 42 D5
Grange Av *CHD/CHDH* SK8 .... 64 F1
HALE/TIMP WA15................ 43 H5
HALE/TIMP WA15................ 62 A2
NWCHW CW8 .... 129 C1
WARRS WA4 .... 37 L8
WLTN L25 .... 50 D5
Grangebrook Dr *WSFD* CW7 .. 177 J1
Grange Cl *CW/HAS* CW1 .... 19 K5
GOL/RIS/CU WA3 .... 23 J4
SBCH CW11 .... 203 M5
Grange Ct *BIDD* ST8 .... 227 K2
Grange Crs *GTS/LS* CH66 ...... 94 A3
Grange Dr *NWCHW* CW8 ...... 129 G6
WARRW/BUR WA5 .... 36 A8
WDN WA8 .... 6 B3
Grangefields *BIDD* ST8 .... 227 L1
Grangelands *MCFLDN* SK10 .. 137 M2
Grange La *DID/WITH* M20 ...... 45 H2
MALPAS SY14 .... 245 K2
NWCHW CW8 .... 150 C5
NWCHW CW8 .... 153 G5
WSFD CW7 .... 177 J2
Grange Lea *MWCH* CW10 .... 179 H3
Grangemoor *RUNC* WA7 .... 73 K5
Grange Park Av *CHD/CHDH* SK8.. 45 K7
RUNC WA7 .... 9 L3
WILM/AE SK9 .... 84 A4
Grange Park Rd *CHD/CHDH* SK8 .. 45 K7
RUNC WA7 .... 9 L3
Grange Pl *IRL* M44 .... 31 K7
Grange Rd *ALT* WA14 .... 61 J3
BIDD ST8 .... 227 L1
BRAM/HZG SK7 .... 65 M1
CHNE CH2 .... 145 K8
CHSE CH3 .... 170 B2
CQ CH5 .... 142 B8
EP CH65 .... 10 E8
HALE/TIMP WA15................ 43 H5
MCFLDS SK11 .... 14 F8
NWCHE CW9 .... 130 D6
NWCHW CW8 .... 129 G1
RUNC WA7 .... 151 M2
RUNC WA7 .... 9 L3
Grangeside *CHNE* CH2 .... 145 K5
Grange St *LEIGH* WN7 .... 24 C1
The Grange *NWCHW* CW8 .... 129 H7
Grangeway *RUNC* WA7 .... 9 L8
Grange Wy *SBCH* CW11 ...... 203 M5
Grangeway *WILM/AE* SK9 ...... 64 D8
Grangewood Dr *KNUT* WA16 .. 134 F1
Granston Cl *WARRW/BUR* WA5 .. 36 E2
Granstone Cl *BURS/TUN* ST6 .. 243 L6
Grant Cl *WARRW/BUR* WA5 .... 36 D3
Grant Dr *CQ* CH5 .... 166 A2
Grantham Av *WARR* WA1 ...... 37 L5
WARRS WA4 .... 56 B4
Grantham Cl *NWCHE* CW9 .... 130 C5
Grantham Rd *HTNM* SK4 .... 2 F4
Grant Rd *WARRW/BUR* WA5 .. 36 B6
Granville Dr *GTS/LS* CH66 ...... 94 B5
Granville Gdns *DID/WITH* M20 .. 45 G2
Granville Rd *CH/BCN* CH1 ...... 16 C2
CHD/CHDH SK8 .... 46 C7
HALE/TIMP WA15................ 43 J6
NWCHE CW9 .... 13 J9
WILM/AE SK9 .... 83 M7
Granville Sq *WSFD* CW7 .... 177 K4
Granville St *RUNC* WA7 .... 9 H1
WARR WA1 .... 5 L4
WSFD CW7 .... 177 K4
Grapes St *MCFLDS* SK11 .... 15 H7
Grappenhall La *WARRS* WA4 .. 57 K6
Grappenhall Rd *EP* CH65 ...... 120 F1
WARRS WA4 .... 56 D3
Grasmere Av *CONG* CW12 .... 206 F2
CW/SHV CW2 .... 220 F8
WARRN/WOL WA2 .... 37 K1
Grasmere Cl *WSFD* CW7 ...... 177 K2
Grasmere Crs *BRAM/HZG* SK7 .. 65 L4
MPL/ROM SK6 .... 67 L3
Grasmere Dr *HOLMCH* CW4 .. 181 G1
RUNC WA7 .... 73 K7
Grasmere Rd *CHD/CHDH* SK8 .. 64 B1
CHNE CH2 .... 145 M7
EP CH65 .... 121 J2
FROD/HEL WA6 .... 99 J4
HALE/TIMP WA15................ 43 J6
LYMM WA13 .... 39 M8
NSTN CH64 .... 91 L6
PART M31 .... 40 E1
SALE M33 .... 43 J2
WILM/AE SK9 .... 110 A3
Grason Av *WILM/AE* SK9 .... 84 C3
Grassfield Wy *KNUT* WA16 .... 107 G5
Grassholme Dr *OFTN* SK2 ...... 48 A7
Grassington Crs *WLTN* L25 .... 50 D2
Gratrix La *SALE* M33 .... 43 M1
Gravel La *ALS/KID* ST7 .... 83 L8
Grave Oak La *GOL/RIS/CU* WA3 .. 25 H3
Graveyard La *KNUT* WA16 ...... 82 F7
Graylag Cl *RUNC* WA7 .... 73 M7
Grayling Willows
AUD/MAD/W CW3 .... 267 L6
Graymarsh Dr *POY/DIS* SK12 .. 86 E2
Graysands Rd *HALE/TIMP* WA15 .. 61 M1
Gray's La *ALS/KID* ST7 .... 226 B5
Grayshott Rd *BURS/TUN* ST6 .. 243 L7
Greasby Dr *GTS/LS* CH66 ...... 94 E8
Great Ashfield *WDN* WA8 ...... 52 D1
Great Egerton St *STKP* SK1 ...... 2 F4

Greatfield Rd WYTH/NTH M22 44 B8
Great King St MCFLDS SK11 14 E5
Great Moor St OFTN SK2 47 H7
Greatoak Rd ALS/KID ST7 241 M8
Great Portwood St STKP SK1 3 H3
Great Queen St MCFLDS SK11 14 E5
Great Riding RUNC WA7 74 C5
Great Underbank STKP SK1 2 F5
Greave Rd STKP SK1 47 J4
Greaves La MALPAS SY14 256 E5
Greaves La East MALPAS SY14 256 E5
Greaves Rd WILM/AE SK9 83 K5
Grebe Cl KNUT WA16 107 H1
POY/DIS SK12 66 B8
Greeba Av WARRS WA4 56 B1
Greeba Rd NTHM/RTH M23 43 L6
Greek St EDGY/DAV SK3 2 F8
RUNC WA7 8 F1
Green Acre Cl KNUT WA16 107 H4
Greenacre Cl WLTN L25 50 C4
Greenacre Rd CHSW/BR CH4 168 F8
WLTN L25 50 C4
Greenacres FROD/HEL WA6 99 J6
SBCH CW11 204 A5
TPLY/KEL CW6 173 G6
Greenacres Cl
GOL/RIS/CU WA3 24 B4
Greenacres Rd CONG CW12 206 F2
The Greenacres LYMM WA13 40 A8
Greenall Av WARRW/BUR WA5 35 K8
Greenall Rd NWCHE CW9 13 L2
Greenall's Av WARRS WA4 56 C3
Green Av NWCHE CW9 153 L1
NWCHW CW8 129 G1
TPLY/KEL CW6 198 D8
Greenbank CHSW/BR CH4 169 L7
Green Bank MKTDR TF9 274 A7
Greenbank Av CHD/CHDH SK8 45 G7
GTS/LS CH66 94 C5
HTNM SK4 45 L2
Greenbank Cl NANT CW5 237 K7
Greenbank Crs MPL/ROM SK6 48 F7
Greenbank Dr MCFLDN SK10 113 G4
Greenbank Gdns WARRS WA4 56 F2
Greenbank La NWCHW CW8 12 B6
Greenbank Rd CHD/CHDH SK8 45 G6
CHNE CH2 146 A8
CQ CH5 142 A7
MPL/ROM SK6 49 H3
WARRS WA4 56 F2
Greenbank St WARRS WA4 56 C2
Greenbeech Cl MPL/ROM SK6 48 E5
Green Bridge Cl RUNC WA7 74 A3
Greenbridge Rd RUNC WA7 74 B2
Greenbrow Rd NTHM/RTH M23 62 F1
Green Cl CHD/CHDH SK8 45 G6
Green Coppice RUNC WA7 74 C4
Green Ct GOL/RIS/CU WA3 24 B3
Green Cts ALT WA14 61 H1
Green Cft MPL/ROM SK6 48 D1
Greendale Dr MWCH CW10 179 H5
Greendale Gdns CW/HAS CW1 19 K1
Greendale La MCFLDN SK10 111 K4
Green Dr ALS/KID ST7 224 D8
HALE/TIMP WA15 43 G5
WILM/AE SK9 84 D2
Green End WHITCH SY13 270 A5
Greene's Rd RAIN/WH L35 32 D2
Greenfield BIDD ST8 227 K6
Greenfield Av CHSW/BR CH4 190 A5
Greenfield Cl EDGY/DAV SK3 46 E6
HALE/TIMP WA15 43 J6
NM/HAY SK22 69 G4
Greenfield Crs CHNE CH2 146 B7
CHSE CH3 171 H6
Greenfield Gdns CHNE CH2 123 H1
Greenfield La CHNE CH2 146 A7
FROD/HEL WA6 99 H3
Greenfield Rd BURS/TUN ST6 243 L7
CHSE CH3 171 H7
CHSW/BR CH4 167 J8
CONG CW12 207 H1
GTS/LS CH66 94 B5
MCFLDN SK10 113 G5
Greenfields CHNE CH2 145 M3
WHITCH SY13 269 M4
WSFD CW7 178 B3
Greenfields Av CW/SHV CW2 238 B8
WARRS WA4 56 D4
Greenfields Cl NEWLW WA12 22 C8
NSTN CH64 91 M7
WARR WA1 38 C5
Greenfields Cft NSTN CH64 91 L7
Greenfields Dr ALS/KID ST7 241 K1
NSTN CH64 91 L8
Greenfields La CHSE CH3 170 F7
Greenfields Ri WHITCH SY13 269 L4
Greenfield Wy NWCHW CW8 128 A8
Greenfinch Cl HLWD L26 50 E3
Greenfold Wy LEIGH WN7 25 H2
Greenfoot La WHITCH SY13 270 A7
Greenford Cl CHD/CHDH SK8 46 B8
Green Gables Cl
CHD/CHDH SK8 64 B3
Greengate HALE/TIMP WA15 62 D5
Greengate Rd ALS/KID ST7 224 F7
Greengates Crs NSTN CH64 91 L7
Greengates St BURS/TUN ST6 243 L8
Greenhalgh St HTNM SK4 2 F3
Green Hall Ms WILM/AE SK9 84 B6
Greenham Rd NTHM/RTH M23 43 M2
Greenhill Av CQ CH5 166 A3
Greenhill La WARRS WA4 76 A7
Greenhill Rd HALE/TIMP WA15 43 J6
Greenhills Cl MCFLDS SK11 15 K7
Green Hill St EDGY/DAV SK3 2 C9
Green Hill Ter EDGY/DAV SK3 2 C9
Greenhill Wk POY/DIS SK12 68 D6
Greenhouse Farm Rd
RUNC WA7 74 B6
Greenhythe Rd CHD/CHDH SK8 64 C6
Green Jones Brow
WARRW/BUR WA5 26 F6
Green Lake La CHSE CH3 211 M1
Greenland Cl TPLY/KEL CW6 197 K3
Greenlands CHSE CH3 214 B1
Green La AUD/MAD/W CW3 273 M3
BRAM/HZG SK7 66 D1
CH/BCN CH1 144 C6
CHNE CH2 146 C1
CHSE CH3 170 B2
CHSE CH3 213 M7
CHSW/BR CH4 168 E7
CHSW/BR CH4 190 A6
CQ CH5 142 B7
EP CH65 95 J8
GOL/RIS/CU WA3 24 A2
GTS/LS CH66 94 D8
HALE/TIMP WA15 43 H8
HALE/TIMP WA15 62 B1
HTNM SK4 2 B4
IRL M44 31 K7
KNUT WA16 80 D8
KNUT WA16 105 L6
KNUT WA16 134 D3
MALPAS SY14 244 C4
MALPAS SY14 245 G4
MCFLDN SK10 113 H3
MPL/ROM SK6 48 B3
NANT CW5 218 A5
NANT CW5 237 L7
NWCHE CW9 104 F8
NWCHE CW9 153 M1
POY/DIS SK12 67 J8
POY/DIS SK12 68 D7
SBCH CW11 203 G4
TPLY/KEL CW6 149 K8
WARR WA1 38 A4
WARRN/WOL WA2 28 A5
WARRS WA4 56 F7
WARRW/BUR WA5 26 E5
WDN WA8 6 C2
WILM/AE SK9 84 B5
WILM/AE SK9 109 M4
Green Lane Cl WARRN/WOL WA2 28 A5
Green La East CQ CH5 143 K5
Green La North
HALE/TIMP WA15 43 H8
Green Lane (West) CQ CH5 143 H1
Greenlaw Cl NWCHE CW9 13 K8
Green Lawns Dr
GTS/LS CH66 120 F4
Greenlea Cl EP CH65 121 H2
Green Mdw CQ CH5 166 A4
MPL/ROM SK6 48 F5
Green Meadows Dr
MPL/ROM SK6 48 F5
Greenmeadows Rd
AUD/MAD/W CW3 267 L5
Green Meadows Wk
WYTH/NTH M22 63 L3
Greenoak Dr SALE M33 43 J3
Green Oaks Pth WDN WA8 7 M4
Green Oaks Wy WDN WA8 7 L4
Greenore Dr SPK/HALE L24 71 K2
Green Pk NWCHW CW8 128 E5
Greenpark Rd WYTH/NTH M22 44 D3
Green Pastures HTNM SK4 45 L3
Green Rd PART M31 40 E1
Greensbridge La HLWD L26 51 H3
Greenshall La POY/DIS SK12 68 F6
Greenshank Cl NEWLW WA12 22 C8
Greenside Av FROD/HEL WA6 99 K5
Greenside Cl ALS/KID ST7 243 G5
Greenside Ct NWCHE CW9 131 K7
Greenside Dr ALT WA14 61 L3
IRL M44 31 M3
NWCHE CW9 131 G4
Green Strawberry EP CH65 121 G4
Green St EDGY/DAV SK3 46 F6
KNUT WA16 107 G2
MCFLDN SK10 15 J6
SBCH CW11 204 B5
WARRW/BUR WA5 4 C7
WILM/AE SK9 110 A3
WRXS/E LL13 228 E3
Greensway CHSW/BR CH4 16 A9
The Green CHD/CHDH SK8 64 F4
CHSE CH3 172 F2
CHSW/BR CH4 190 B5
EP CH65 121 H2
HTNM SK4 2 A3
MPL/ROM SK6 68 A1
MWCH CW10 179 K6
NSTN CH64 91 K4
NSTN CH64 91 M6
NWCHW CW8 129 H7
RUNC WA7 73 M3
WILM/AE SK9 84 E1
Green Tree Gdns MPL/ROM SK6 48 B2
Greenvale Dr CHD/CHDH SK8 45 J6
Green Vw LYMM WA13 40 B7
Greenview Dr DID/WITH M20 45 J4
Green Villa Pk WILM/AE SK9 83 L8
Greenville Rd NSTN CH64 91 M3
Green Wk ALT WA14 61 G1
CHD/CHDH SK8 45 G6
HALE/TIMP WA15 42 F5
NWCHW CW8 128 A8
Green Wy CH/BCN CH1 144 A3
Greenway ALS/KID ST7 224 B7
ALT WA14 42 A7
BRAM/HZG SK7 65 K6
CHSE CH3 228 F3
CONG CW12 207 H1
CW/HAS CW1 221 K6
MALPAS SY14 245 H1
MPL/ROM SK6 48 E3
WARR WA1 37 M5
WARRS WA4 56 D5
WARRW/BUR WA5 35 L5
WILM/AE SK9 84 A6
WYTH/NTH M22 44 E4
Greenway Cl ALS/KID ST7 224 F5
FROD/HEL WA6 124 B1
SALE M33 42 D1
Greenway Dr NWCHE CW9 130 C5
Greenway Rd BIDD ST8 227 L2
CHD/CHDH SK8 64 C6
HALE/TIMP WA15 42 F4
RUNC WA7 8 F5
SPK/HALE L24 71 G1
WDN WA8 7 J1
Greenway St CHSW/BR CH4 17 G8
Greenwood Av
CHSW/BR CH4 169 K5
CONG CW12 207 M1
OFTN SK2 47 J6
Greenwood Cl GOL/RIS/CU WA3 29 M2
HALE/TIMP WA15 43 K7
NWCHW CW8 128 D3
Greenwood Crs
WARRN/WOL WA2 37 K2
Greenwood Dr NEWLW WA12 27 K2
WILM/AE SK9 84 D4
Greenwood Rd LYMM WA13 58 E2
WYTH/NTH M22 44 B8
Greenwood St ALT WA14 42 D8
Greg Av MCFLDN SK10 112 E5
Greg Ms WILM/AE SK9 84 B2
Gregory Av MPL/ROM SK6 48 B3
Gregory Cl WARRW/BUR WA5 36 C5
Gregson Rd WDN WA8 7 M3
Grendale Av BRAM/HZG SK7 66 E3
STKP SK1 3 M6
Grenfell Cl NSTN CH64 91 J3
Grenfell Pk NSTN CH64 91 J3
Grenfell St WDN WA8 7 J5
Grenville Cl CW/HAS CW1 222 C7
Grenville Rd BRAM/HZG SK7 66 C1
Grenville St EDGY/DAV SK3 2 C7
Gresford Av CHNE CH2 17 J1
Gresford Cl RAIN/WH L35 32 F1
WARRW/BUR WA5 36 D2
Gresty Av WYTH/NTH M22 63 M3
Gresty Green Rd CW/SHV CW2 238 D4
Gresty La CW/SHV CW2 238 B6
Gresty Rd CW/SHV CW2 19 H8
Gresty Ter CW/HAS CW1 19 K5
Greta Av CHD/CHDH SK8 64 C6
Greville Dr WSFD CW7 178 A3
Grey Friars CH/BCN CH1 16 E6
Greyfriars Rd WYTH/NTH M22 63 H2
Greyhound Farm Rd
SPK/HALE L24 70 C1
Greyhound Park Rd
CH/BCN CH1 168 F1
Greyhound Rd MCFLDN SK10 111 H7
Greylands Rd DID/WITH M20 45 J4
Greymist Av WARR WA1 38 C5
Grey Rd ALT WA14 42 C7
Greysan Av ALS/KID ST7 243 M4
Greystoke Av HALE/TIMP WA15 43 K6
SALE M33 43 H1
Greystoke Dr WILM/AE SK9 110 A2
Greystoke Rd MCFLDN SK10 15 L1
Greystoke St STKP SK1 3 K6
Greystone Pk CW/HAS CW1 19 H3
Greystone Rd WARRW/BUR WA5 35 M8
Greystones GTS/LS CH66 94 D8
Greystones Rd CHSE CH3 170 C3
Grey St WARR WA1 5 J5
Grice St WARRS WA4 56 C3
Grid La MPL/ROM SK6 49 L3
Griffin Cl CH/BCN CH1 144 F7
NM/HAY SK22 69 J6
WARRW/BUR WA5 26 E6
Griffin Ms WDN WA8 53 H1
Griffith Av GOL/RIS/CU WA3 29 L7
Griffiths Ct CQ CH5 142 A7
Griffiths Dr NWCHE CW9 130 C6
Griffiths Rd NWCHE CW9 130 E4
Griffiths St WARRS WA4 37 M8
Grig Pl ALS/KID ST7 224 C7
Grimsditch La WARRS WA4 76 A6
Grimshaw Av MCFLDN SK10 113 G5
Grimshaw La MCFLDN SK10 113 G5
Grimshaw St GOL/RIS/CU WA3 23 G3
STKP SK1 3 K5
Grimstead Cl NTHM/RTH M23 43 L6
Grindley Bank CHNE CH2 146 F4
Grindley Gdns EP CH65 121 J2
Grisedale Av
WARRN/WOL WA2 37 H1
Grisedale Cl RUNC WA7 73 L7
Grisedale Wy MCFLDS SK11 138 A7
Gritstone Trail MCFLDS SK11 163 L3
MCFLDS SK11 187 J8
POY/DIS SK12 88 C5
Grizedale WDN WA8 52 B2
Grizedale Cl CW/SHV CW2 237 K2
Groarke Dr WARRW/BUR WA5 35 K7
Groby Rd ALT WA14 42 C8
CW/HAS CW1 221 K2
Groomscroft CQ CH5 166 B4
Groomsdale La CQ CH5 166 B4
Grosvenor Av ALS/KID ST7 224 D7
GOL/RIS/CU WA3 23 K4
NWCHW CW8 129 G8
WARR WA1 37 L5
Grosvenor Cl
WARRW/BUR WA5 36 C7
WILM/AE SK9 84 A8
Grosvenor Ct WSFD CW7 177 J5
Grosvenor Crs WRX/GR/LL LL12 210 B5
Grosvenor Dr POY/DIS SK12 86 C1
Grosvenor Gdns NEWLW WA12 27 H2
WYTH/NTH M22 44 E6
Grosvenor Park Rd
CH/BCN CH1 17 J5
Grosvenor Park Ter
CH/BCN CH1 17 J6
Grosvenor Pl BURS/TUN ST6 243 K8
CH/BCN CH1 17 G7
Grosvenor Rd ALT WA14 42 E6
CH/BCN CH1 16 F7
CHD/CHDH SK8 46 C8
CHSE CH3 172 A2
CHSW/BR CH4 16 E9
CONG CW12 207 G1
CQ CH5 142 B7
HTNM SK4 46 B1
HTNM SK4 46 A1
MPL/ROM SK6 48 F5
WDN WA8 34 B8
Grosvenor Rbt CH/BCN CH1 16 F7
Grosvenor St
BRAM/HZG SK7 66 D1
CH/BCN CH1 16 F7
CW/HAS CW1 18 C2
MCFLDN SK10 14 E4
RUNC WA7 9 K1
STKP SK1 3 G8
WSFD CW7 177 L4
Grotsworth La MALPAS SY14 247 L4
Grotto La KNUT WA16 134 A4
Grounds St WARRN/WOL WA2 5 H3
Grove Av ALS/KID ST7 225 G8
ALS/KID ST7 242 E4
CHSE CH3 170 B1
LYMM WA13 58 C1
NWCHE CW9 131 G1
WILM/AE SK9 84 A5
Grove Cl WSFD CW7 177 H4
Grove Gdns CHSE CH3 170 E2
Grove La CHD/CHDH SK8 65 H7
DID/WITH M20 45 H2
HALE/TIMP WA15 43 G6
HALE/TIMP WA15 62 A1
Grovemount NWCHE CW9 153 M2
Grove Pk KNUT WA16 107 G3
Grove Park Av ALS/KID ST7 225 G8
Grove Ri LYMM WA13 58 E1
Grove Rd CH/BCN CH1 120 F7
HALE/TIMP WA15 61 L1
The Groves CH/BCN CH1 17 H6
EP CH65 121 G4
Grove St BRAM/HZG SK7 66 E1
NM/HAY SK22 69 H5
RUNC WA7 8 F1
WARRS WA4 5 K9
WILM/AE SK9 84 B5
The Grove ALS/KID ST7 225 G8
CHD/CHDH SK8 65 G6
DID/WITH M20 45 H3
EDGY/DAV SK3 46 E5
GOL/RIS/CU WA3 23 K3
LYMM WA13 58 E1
SALE M33 43 H1
WARRW/BUR WA5 35 M8
WHITCH SY13 269 M3
Grove Wy WILM/AE SK9 84 B5
Grovewood Gdns RAIN/WH L35 32 E1
Grovewood Ms MCFLDS SK11 14 F8
Grub La TPLY/KEL CW6 149 J7
Grundey St BRAM/HZG SK7 66 E2
Grundy Cl WDN WA8 52 F1
Grundy St GOL/RIS/CU WA3 23 G5
HTNM SK4 45 L2
Guardian St WARRW/BUR WA5 4 D5
Guernsey Cl WARRS WA4 56 D4
Guernsey Dr EP CH65 121 J3
Guernsey Rd WDN WA8 53 L1
Guests Slack FROD/HEL WA6 126 B3
Guest St WDN WA8 7 G7
Guilden Gn CHSE CH3 146 E7
Guilden Sutton La CHSE CH3 146 C8
Guildford Av CHD/CHDH SK8 65 G6
Guildford Cl CHSW/BR CH4 168 F6
STKP SK1 3 M9
WARRN/WOL WA2 38 A3
Guillemot Cl CW/HAS CW1 19 M2
Guillemot Wy HLWD L26 50 E3
Gullane Cl MCFLDN SK10 112 B8
Gull Cl POY/DIS SK12 86 B1
The Gullet NANT CW5 20 F6
Gunco La MCFLDN SK10 112 C4
MCFLDS SK11 15 J9
Gunn Gv NSTN CH64 91 M4
Gunn St BIDD ST8 227 J4
Gun St WRX/GR/LL LL12 210 B5
Gutterscroft CW/HAS CW1 222 D7
Gutticar Rd WDN WA8 52 B4
Guy La CHSE CH3 171 H7
Guywood La MPL/ROM SK6 48 C1
Gwenbury Av STKP SK1 3 M6
Gwyn Av BIDD ST8 227 K6
Gwynedd Dr FLINT CH6 116 A6

H

Hackberry Cl ALT WA14 42 B4
Hacked Way La MCFLDS SK11 140 A6
Haddon Cl CW/SHV CW2 238 B5
HOLMCH CW4 181 H1
MCFLDS SK11 138 B7
MPL/ROM SK6 67 L6
WILM/AE SK9 109 M2
Haddon Dr WDN WA8 52 C1
Haddon Gv HALE/TIMP WA15 42 F5
SALE M33 43 G1
Haddon La NSTN CH64 92 B8
Haddon Rd BRAM/HZG SK7 66 E3
CHD/CHDH SK8 64 C5
GOL/RIS/CU WA3 23 K3
NSTN CH64 118 D2
Hadfield Gv WLTN L25 50 C1
Hadfield St NWCHE CW9 13 L1
Hadleigh Cl WARRW/BUR WA5 35 K7
Hadley Cl CHD/CHDH SK8 64 F3
Hadlow La NSTN CH64 92 F5
Hadlow Rd NSTN CH64 92 F6
Hadrian Dr CH/BCN CH1 144 E6
Hadrian Wy NWCHW CW8 152 B2
Hafod Cl CH/BCN CH1 168 D1
Hag Bank La POY/DIS SK12 68 D5
Haguebar Rd NM/HAY SK22 68 F4
Hague Bush Cl
GOL/RIS/CU WA3 23 L3
Hague Fold Rd NM/HAY SK22 68 F4
Haig Av IRL M44 31 J8
WARRW/BUR WA5 36 A8
Haig Rd KNUT WA16 81 J8
WDN WA8 7 G3
Haileybury Rd WLTN L25 50 B4
Hailsham Cl BURS/TUN ST6 243 L7
Hale Av POY/DIS SK12 86 D2
Hale Bank Rd WDN WA8 51 L7
Hale Cl LEIGH WN7 25 H2
Hale Dr SPK/HALE L24 70 F2
Hale Gate Rd WDN WA8 71 M1
Hale Gv WARRW/BUR WA5 36 A6
Hale Low Rd HALE/TIMP WA15 61 M1
Hale Rd HALE/TIMP WA15 61 L1
HTNM SK4 2 A2
SPK/HALE L24 70 C1
WDN WA8 6 A5
Hale St WARRN/WOL WA2 5 G3
Hale Vw RUNC WA7 8 D6
Hale View Rd FROD/HEL WA6 98 C8
HUY L36 32 A2
Halewood Av GOL/RIS/CU WA3 22 F3
Halewood Dr WLTN L25 50 B2
Halewood Pl WLTN L25 50 C1
Halewood Rd WLTN L25 50 B1
Halewood Wy WLTN L25 50 C2
Haley Rd North
WARRW/BUR WA5 26 E6
Haley Rd South
WARRW/BUR WA5 26 E6
Halfacre La WARRS WA4 57 L1
Halfacre Rd WYTH/NTH M22 44 C8
Half Moon La OFTN SK2 47 L6
Half St MCFLDS SK11 15 H9
Halifax Cl WARRN/WOL WA2 37 K2
Halkett Cl CHSW/BR CH4 168 E7
Halkyn Rd CHNE CH2 17 J1
Halkyn St FLINT CH6 116 A6
Hallam St OFTN SK2 47 G6
Hallas Gv NTHM/RTH M23 44 B3
Hallastone Rd FROD/HEL WA6 98 B8
Hall Av HALE/TIMP WA15 42 F5
WDN WA8 52 A3
Halla-way WARRS WA4 56 E1
Hall Cl MCFLDN SK10 112 D8
Hallcroft PART M31 31 M8
Hallcroft Pl WARRS WA4 57 G2
Hall Dr ALS/KID ST7 241 J1
NANT CW5 237 J6
NWCHE CW9 104 B6
WARRS WA4 56 D6
Hallefield Crs MCFLDN SK10 15 K6
Hallefield Dr MCFLDN SK10 15 J6
Hallefield Rd MCFLDS SK11 15 K6
Hallfield Dr CHNE CH2 123 H1
Hallfield Gv BURS/TUN ST6 243 L7
Hallfield Pk GTS/LS CH66 94 D8
Hallfields Rd CHSE CH3 172 C2
WARRN/WOL WA2 5 L1
Hallgate Dr CHD/CHDH SK8 64 A2
Hallgate Rd STKP SK1 3 M7
Hallgreen La CONG CW12 183 K4
Hall Gv MCFLDN SK10 138 D1
Hall Hl MCFLDN SK10 112 E5
Halliday Cl GOL/RIS/CU WA3 38 F1
Halliwell's Brow KNUT WA16 79 H1
Hall La AUD/MAD/W CW3 264 B5
CHSE CH3 231 J5
HUY L36 32 A2
KNUT WA16 82 C8
KNUT WA16 105 H3
MALPAS SY14 246 A3
MCFLDS SK11 162 F1
NTHM/RTH M23 44 B6
NWCHE CW9 102 F5
NWCHE CW9 104 E8
PART M31 31 M8
RAIN/WH L35 33 J3
SBCH CW11 202 E8
SBCH CW11 203 H7
STHEL WA9 26 A8
TPLY/KEL CW6 149 K6
TPLY/KEL CW6 174 C7
TPLY/KEL CW6 217 H7
WARRS WA4 57 H4
WARRS WA4 75 K2
WARRS WA4 76 D4
WARRW/BUR WA5 27 H4
WDN WA8 33 K6
WSFD CW7 199 M2
The Hall La TPLY/KEL CW6 198 B1
Hall Meadow CHD/CHDH SK8 64 E3
Hall Moss La BRAM/HZG SK7 65 H8
Hall Nook WARRW/BUR WA5 35 M8
Hall O'shaw St CW/HAS CW1 19 J3
Hallows Av WARRN/WOL WA2 37 K4
Hallows Cl TPLY/KEL CW6 149 J8
Hallows Dr TPLY/KEL CW6 149 J8
Hall Rd ALT WA14 61 J3
BRAM/HZG SK7 65 K3
WARR WA1 38 D5
WILM/AE SK9 84 E1
WILM/AE SK9 84 A5
Hallsgreen La CHNE CH2 122 F5
Hallshaw Av CW/HAS CW1 19 K2
Hallside Pk KNUT WA16 107 J3
Halls Rd ALS/KID ST7 226 C6
BIDD ST8 227 J3
Hall St CHD/CHDH SK8 45 K6
MCFLDS SK11 14 E5
NM/HAY SK22 69 H4
STHEL WA9 34 E1
STKP SK1 3 K6
WARR WA1 5 J7
Hall Ter WARRW/BUR WA5 35 L5
Hallwood Cl RUNC WA7 73 H6
Hallwood Dr GTS/LS CH66 93 J8
Hallwood Link Rd RUNC WA7 73 L6
Hallwood Park Av RUNC WA7 73 L6
Hallwood Rd NTHM/RTH M23 44 A6
WILM/AE SK9 84 E1
Hall Wood Rd WILM/AE SK9 84 D2
Hallworthy Cl LEIGH WN7 24 B3
Halsall Av WARRN/WOL WA2 37 K4
Halsall Cl RUNC WA7 74 C7
Halsnead Av RAIN/WH L35 32 C3
Halstead Gv CHD/CHDH SK8 44 F7
Halstone Av WILM/AE SK9 83 L8
Halton Brook Av RUNC WA7 73 K3
Halton Brow RUNC WA7 73 L3
Halton Ct RUNC WA7 73 K2
Halton Crs GTS/LS CH66 120 F2
Halton Dr CW/SHV CW2 220 D7
HALE/TIMP WA15 43 H3
Halton Hey RAIN/WH L35 32 D3
Halton Link Rd RUNC WA7 73 L4
Halton Lodge Av RUNC WA7 73 K5
Halton Rd CHNE CH2 145 M6
GTS/LS CH66 120 E3
RUNC WA7 9 K2
WARRW/BUR WA5 35 M6
Halton Station Rd RUNC WA7 99 M1
Halton View Rd WDN WA8 7 M2
Halton Wy GTS/LS CH66 120 E3
Hambledon Cl GTS/LS CH66 94 A6
Hamble Dr WARRW/BUR WA5 54 F1
Hambleton Cl WDN WA8 52 C1
Hambleton Dr NTHM/RTH M23 44 A8

Hambleton Pl BIDD ST8 .... 227 H7 2
Hambleton Rd CHD/CHDH SK8...... 64 C4
Hambleton Wy WSFD CW7 .... 177 G5
Hambletts Hollow
  FROD/HEL WA6 .... 126 F6
Hamble Wy MCFLDN SK10........ 137 L3
Hamilton Av CQ CH5 .... 167 G1
  IRL M44 .... 31 K8
Hamilton Cl CW/HAS CW1 ...... 222 C8
  MCFLDN SK10 .... 139 G4 4
  NSTN CH64 .... 91 H2
Hamilton Crs HTNM SK4 .... 46 B3 4
Hamilton Pl CHD/CHDH CH1 .... 16 F5
Hamilton Sq HTNM SK4 .... 2 E2
Hamilton St CHNE CH2 .... 17 L1
Hammersley St STHEL WA9 .... 34 C1 2
Hammond St CW/SHV CW2 .... 18 E6
Hamnett Ct GOL/RIS/CU WA3 ..... 38 E1 2
Hamon Rd HALE/TIMP WA15 ...... 42 B6
Hampden Rd SALE M33 .... 43 G1 2
Hampshire Cl CONG CW12 .... 184 D8 2
Hampshire Pl PART M31 .... 40 D2
Hampson Av
  GOL/RIS/CU WA3 .... 29 M1 2
Hampson Crs WILM/AE SK9 .... 64 C8
Hampson St STKP SK1 .... 3 M8
Hampstead Ct WSFD CW7 .... 177 G4 2
Hampstead Dr OFTN SK2 .... 47 J7
Hampstead La OFTN SK2 .... 47 J7
Hampton Av CQ CH5 .... 142 E8
Hampton Cl NSTN CH64 .... 91 L6 2
  WDN WA8 .... 53 L1 2
Hampton Crs MALPAS SY14 ..... 247 G8
  NSTN CH64 .... 91 L7
Hampton Dr WARRW/BUR WA5 ... 36 C8
  WDN WA8 .... 33 J7
Hampton Gdns EP CH65 .... 10 A7
Hampton Gv ALT WA14 .... 42 E5
  CHD/CHDH SK8 .... 64 E2 2
Hampton Rd CHSW/BR CH4 ...... 168 F6
  IRL M44 .... 31 K8
Hams Cl BIDD ST8 .... 227 J5
Hamsterley Cl GOL/RIS/CU WA3.. 30 B6
Hanbury Cl CW/SHV CW2 .... 238 B5
Hancock Rd CONG CW12 .... 184 F8
Handbridge CHSW/BR CH4 .... 17 G8
Handforth Cl WARRS WA4 .... 38 C8
Handforth La RUNC WA7 .... 73 K6 2
Handforth Rd CW/SHV CW2 ...... 237 L1
  WILM/AE SK9 .... 84 E3
Hand La LEIGH WN7 .... 24 E3
Handley Cl EDGY/DAV SK3 .... 46 C7
Handley Hl WSFD CW7 .... 177 H4
Handley Rd BRAM/HZG SK7 ...... 65 L1
Hand St MCFLDS SK11 .... 14 D5
Hangman's La NWCHW CW9 .... 131 J5
Hankelow Cl CHNE CH2 .... 17 G1
  MWCH CW10 .... 179 J6
Hankey St RUNC WA7 .... 8 F2
Hankins Heys La
  AUD/MAD/W CW3 .... 275 G3
Hankinson Ct PART M31 .... 40 F2 2
  WDN WA8 .... 52 C3
Hanley Cl POY/DIS SK12 .... 68 D7
  WDN WA8 .... 52 C3
Hanley Rd WDN WA8 .... 52 C3
Hannesburg Gdns
  NTHM/RTH M23 .... 43 M8 2
Hannet Rd WYTH/NTH M22 .... 63 K3
Hanns Hall Rd NSTN CH64 .... 92 C4
Hanover Dr WSFD CW7 .... 177 K6 2
Hanover Rd ALT WA14 .... 42 B5
Hanover St WARR WA1 .... 4 E8
Hanson Ms STKP SK1 .... 3 L4
Hanwell Cl LEIGH WN7 .... 24 D3
Hapsford Cl GOL/RIS/CU WA3 .... 29 J8
Hapsford La CHNE CH2 .... 97 K8
  FROD/HEL WA6 .... 123 L3
Hapton Pl HTNM SK4 .... 2 E2 2
Harbbour Cl CHNE CH2 .... 145 L5 2
Harbord St WARR WA1 .... 5 K8
Harbour La MCFLDS SK11 .... 161 J3
Harbury Crs WYTH/NTH M22 ..... 44 C7 2
Harcourt Cl GOL/RIS/CU WA3 .... 38 E1
Harcourt Rd ALT WA14 .... 42 D6
Hardberry Pl OFTN SK2 .... 47 L6 2
Hardcastle Rd EDGY/DAV SK3.... 46 D5
Harden Pk WILM/AE SK9 .... 110 A1
Hardie Cl STHEL WA9 .... 34 A1 2
Hardie Rd HUY L36 .... 32 A1
Harding Av CHNE CH3 .... 214 C2
  WARRN/WOL WA2 .... 37 K3
Harding Rd CHNE CH2 .... 145 H4
  NANT CW5.......................... 20 B8
Hardings Meadow ALS/KID ST7 .. 242 E2 2
Harding St STKP SK1 .... 3 M6
Hardingswood Rd ALS/KID ST7 .. 242 E2
Hardman Av MPL/ROM SK6 ...... 48 A1 2
Hardman St EDGY/DAV SK3 .... 2 D7
Hardwick Cl MPL/ROM SK6 .... 67 M6
Hardwick Dr MCFLDS SK11 ..... 138 B7
Hardwicke Rd POY/DIS SK12 ..... 66 F8
Hardwick Rd PART M31 .... 41 G1
  RUNC WA7 .... 73 K1
Hardy Cl CW/SHV CW2 .... 237 M4 2
  GTS/LS CH66 .... 120 F1
Hardy Dr BRAM/HZG SK7 .... 65 K5
  HALE/TIMP WA15 .... 42 F5
  WARRN/WOL WA2 .... 5 H4
Harebell Cl CHSE CH3 .... 170 A6
Harecastle Av ALS/KID ST7 ..... 242 D3
Harefield Cl DID/WITH M20 .... 45 G2
  WILM/AE SK9 .... 84 A7
Harefield Gn SPK/HALE L24 .... 70 D1 2
Harefield Rd SPK/HALE L24 ..... 70 D1
  WILM/AE SK9 .... 64 E8 2
Hare La CHSE CH3 .... 146 C8
Hare's La FROD/HEL WA6 .... 98 E4
Harewood Av GTS/LS CH66 ...... 94 C6
Harfield Gdns GTS/LS CH66 ..... 94 C7
Harford Cl BRAM/HZG SK7 ..... 66 A3 2
Hargate Dr HALE/TIMP WA15 ..... 62 A3

Hargrave Av CW/SHV CW2 ...... 237 M1
Hargrave Dr GTS/LS CH66 .... 94 E7
Hargreaves Ct WDN WA8 .... 53 K3 2
Hargreaves Rd
  HALE/TIMP WA15.................. 43 J6
  NWCHE CW9 .... 130 C4
Harington Cl CHNE CH2 .... 145 J3
Harington Rd CHNE CH2 .... 145 J4
Harland Dr AIMK WN4 .... 22 C2
Harlech Cl WARRW/BUR WA5 .... 36 E2
Harlech Dr BIDD ST8 .... 227 J6
  BRAM/HZG SK7 .... 66 C3
Harlech Wy EP CH65 .... 121 K1
Harleen Gv OFTN SK2 .... 47 K5
Harling Rd WYTH/NTH M22...... 44 D5
Harlow Cl WARRS WA4 .... 57 J1
Harlyn Av BRAM/HZG SK7 .... 65 M5
Harlyn Cl HLWD L26 .... 50 E6
Harlyn Gdns
  WARRW/BUR WA5 .... 54 D1 2
The Harn GTS/LS CH66 .... 120 C1 2
Harold St STKP SK1 .... 3 M8
Harper Cl GTS/LS CH66 .... 94 D8
Harper Gv CONG CW12 .... 184 E8
Harper Rd WYTH/NTH M22 .... 44 E5
Harpers Rd WARRN/WOL WA2 ... 38 A3
Harptree Cl RAIN/WH L35 .... 32 E1
Harpur Cl MCFLDS SK11 .... 15 H8
Harpur Crs ALS/KID ST7 .... 224 B7
Harrier Cl CW/HAS CW1 .... 220 F5
Harrier Dr HLWD L26 .... 50 E3
Harriet St IRL M44 .... 31 L7
Harrington Dr MCFLDS SK11 .... 161 K3
Harrington Rd ALT WA14 .... 42 B7
Harris Cl CW/HAS CW1 .... 221 H3
Harriseahead La ALS/KID ST7 ... 226 D8
Harrison Dr HOLMCH CW4 ...... 157 H3
Harrison Gv CQ CH5 .... 167 G1
Harrisons Pl NWCHW CW8 .... 12 F3
Harrison St WDN WA8 .... 52 B6
Harrison Wy NEWLW WA12 ...... 22 C8
Harrogate St NWCHE CW9 ..... 131 G2
Harrop La MCFLDN SK10 .... 86 E7
Harrop Rd HALE/TIMP WA15...... 61 M2
  MCFLDN SK10....................... 113 J4
  RUNC WA7 .... 9 J5
Harrop St STKP SK1 .... 3 J9
Harrow Cl CW/SHV CW2 .... 18 A9
  WARRS WA4 .... 56 E6
Harrow Crs LEIGH WN7 .... 24 F1
Harrow Dr RUNC WA7 .... 73 L2
  SALE M33 .... 43 G2
Harrow Rd EP CH65 .... 95 K8
  SALE M33 .... 43 G2
Harrow Wy NWCHE CW9 .... 153 L1 2
Harry Rowley Cl
  WYTH/NTH M22 .... 63 J2 4
Harrytown MPL/ROM SK6 .... 48 A2
Hart Av SALE M33 .... 43 M1 2
Hartford Av WILM/AE SK9 .... 83 M7 2
Hartford Br NWCHE CW9 .... 153 K1
Hartford Cl SBCH CW11 .... 204 C5
Hartford Dr EP CH65 .... 94 F8
Hartford Gdns HALE/TIMP WA15 .. 43 K7
Hartford Rd NWCHE CW9 .... 153 L2
  SALE M33 .... 42 D3
Hartford Wy CH/BCN CH1 .... 16 A4
Harthill La CHSE CH3 .... 214 E8
Harthill Rd CH/BCN CH1 .... 144 E6
  CHSE CH3 .... 215 G6
Hartington Dr BRAM/HZG SK7 ... 66 E4
Hartington Rd ALT WA14 .... 42 D5
  BRAM/HZG SK7 .... 65 L6
  CHD/CHDH SK8 .... 64 D4 2
  MPL/ROM SK6 .... 67 L6
  OFTN SK2 .... 47 G8
Hartland Cl OFTN SK2 .... 47 J4 2
  POY/DIS SK12 .... 66 D7 2
  WDN WA8 .... 34 A7
Hartley Cl LYMM WA13 .... 58 F1 2
Hartley Gn MCFLDN SK10 ...... 112 F4 4
Hartley Rd ALT WA14 .... 42 C7
Hartley St EDGY/DAV SK3 .... 2 C8
Hart St ALT WA14 .... 42 D7
Hartswell Cl GOL/RIS/CU WA3 .. 23 G2 2
Hartwood Cl WARRS WA4 .... 76 E1
Harvard Cl RUNC WA7 .... 74 D2 2
Harvard Ct WARRN/WOL WA2 .. 37 G1 2
Harvest Cl NWCHE CW9 .... 153 M4 2
  SALE M33 .... 44 A1 2
Harvest Rd MCFLDN SK10 ...... 138 C1
Harvey Av NANT CW5 .... 21 J5
  NEWLW WA12 .... 26 F1 2
Harvey Cl GOL/RIS/CU WA3 ..... 24 B3 2
  WARRN/WOL WA2 .... 37 H1 2
Harvey La GOL/RIS/CU WA3 ..... 22 F3
Harvey Rd CONG CW12 .... 185 G7
Harvey St STKP SK1 .... 3 G5
Harwood Gdns WARRS WA4 ..... 57 G2
Harwood Rd HTNM SK4 .... 45 L2
Harwoods Cl WRX/GR/LL LL12 .. 210 D6
Harwood's La WRX/GR/LL LL12 . 210 D6
Harwood St HTNM SK4 .... 2 E2 2
Haryngton Av WARRW/BUR WA5 .. 4 C2
Haseley Cl POY/DIS SK12 .... 66 E7
Haselhurst Wk
  NTHM/RTH M23 .... 43 M2 2
Haslam Rd EDGY/DAV SK3....... 46 E6
Haslemere RAIN/WH L35 .... 32 F1
Haslemere Av HALE/TIMP WA15 .. 62 C6
Haslemere Dr CHD/CHDH SK8 .. 65 G3
  WARRW/BUR WA5 .... 35 K8
Haslemere Wy CW/HAS CW1 .. 221 K6 2
Haslin Crs CHSE CH3............... 170 D5
Haslington Rd WYTH/NTH M22 .. 63 L2
Hassall Cross La SBCH CW11 ... 222 F4
Hassall Rd ALS/KID ST7 .... 224 B6
  SBCH CW11 .... 204 C8
Hassals La CHNE CH2 .... 146 F1
Hastings Av WARRN/WOL WA2 .. 28 B8
Hastings Cl CHD/CHDH SK8...... 65 J2
  STKP SK1 .... 3 M9 2
Hastings Dr HUY L36 .... 32 A4

Hastings Dr HUY L36 .... 32 A4
Hasty La HALE/TIMP WA15 .... 62 F5
  MANAIR M90......................... 62 F4
Hatchery Rd WARRS WA4 .... 57 H8
Hatchett Rd WYTH/NTH M22 ..... 63 L3
Hatchmere Cl
  HALE/TIMP WA15.................. 43 K6 2
  SBCH CW11 .... 203 M5 2
  WARRW/BUR WA5 .... 4 B5
Hatchmere Dr CHSE CH3......... 170 B4
Hatfield Ct HOLMCH CW4 .... 181 G1
Hatfield Gdns WARRS WA4 .... 56 E8
Hathaway Dr MCFLDS SK11 ..... 138 C7
Hathaway Gdns MPL/ROM SK6 .. 47 L1
Hatherlow MPL/ROM SK6 .... 48 A2
Hatherlow La BRAM/HZG SK7 ... 66 D2
Hatherton Av NWCHE CW9 .... 129 M8 3
Hatherton Wy CHNE CH2 .... 16 F2
Hatley La FROD/HEL WA6 .... 98 F5
Hatton Av PS/BROM CH62 .... 93 L1
Hatton La NWCHW CW8 .... 12 C7
  WARRS WA4 .... 76 B3
Hatton Rd MCFLDS SK11 .... 14 F7
  STKP SK1 .... 2 F4
Haughton Dr WYTH/NTH M22 .. 44 D3 2
Havannah La CONG CW12 ...... 184 F6
  STHEL WA9 .... 26 B1
Havannah St CONG CW12 ...... 184 F8
Haveley Rd WYTH/NTH M22 ..... 44 C7
Havelock Gv BIDD ST8 .... 227 J5
Haven Cl BRAM/HZG SK7 .... 66 B3
The Haven CW/HAS CW1 .... 221 K5
  HALE/TIMP WA15 .... 61 M1
Havergal St RUNC WA7 .... 8 F4
Haverton Dr WYTH/NTH M22 .... 63 H2 2
Havisham Cl GOL/RIS/CU WA3 .. 29 K7
Hawarden Br CQ CH5 .... 142 C5
Hawarden Gdns EP CH65 .... 121 K2 2
Hawarden Rd ALT WA14 .... 42 D6
Hawarden Wy CQ CH5 .... 166 E2
Hawdraw Gn OFTN SK2 .... 47 L6 2
Hawes Cl OFTN SK2 .... 47 G6
Hawes St BURS/TUN ST6 .... 243 K8
Haweswater Av
  CW/HAS CW1 .... 221 H3 2
Haweswater Cl RUNC WA7 .... 74 A7
Haweswater Dr WSFD CW7 ...... 177 K2 2
Hawick Cl GTS/LS CH66 .... 94 A7 2
Hawke Gn HUY L36 .... 32 A5
Hawker Cl CHSW/BR CH4 .... 167 J8
Hawk Green Rd MPL/ROM SK6 .. 67 M1
Hawkins La MCFLDN SK10...... 139 K1
Hawkins Rd NSTN CH64 .... 91 M3
Hawkins Vw CHSE CH3 .... 147 L6
Hawkridge Dr NTHM/RTH M23 .. 43 M2
Hawk Rd NM/HAY SK22 .... 69 K4
Hawks Ct RUNC WA7 .... 73 L6
Hawkshaw Cl GOL/RIS/CU WA3 .. 29 J8
Hawkshead Cl RUNC WA7 .... 74 A7 2
Hawkshead Rd
  WARRW/BUR WA5 .... 26 E6
Hawkshead Wy WSFD CW7 .... 177 K2
Hawkstone Gv
  FROD/HEL WA6 .... 98 C8 2
Hawk St SBCH CW11 .... 204 B6 2
Hawkswick Dr NTHM/RTH M23 .. 44 A1
Hawley Dr HALE/TIMP WA15 ..... 62 B4
Hawley La HALE/TIMP WA15..... 62 B4
Hawley's La WARRN/WOL WA2 .. 37 G3
Haworth Av CONG CW12 .... 184 F7
Haworth Cl MCFLDS SK11 ...... 138 B7 2
Hawthorn Av HALE/TIMP WA15 .. 42 F5
  MPL/ROM SK6 .... 48 D6
  NEWLW WA12 .... 27 J1
  RUNC WA7 .... 9 H4
  WDN WA8 .... 53 H2 2
  WILM/AE SK9 .... 84 A5
Hawthorn Cl CQ CH5 .... 166 B1
  HALE/TIMP WA15.................. 42 F5
  HOLMCH CW4 .... 181 G1
  WSFD CW7 .... 177 J1 2
Hawthorne Av GOL/RIS/CU WA3 .. 25 J7
  HLWD L26 .... 50 E6
  WARR WA1 .... 38 B5
  WARRW/BUR WA5 .... 35 M6
Hawthorne Cl CONG CW12 ..... 184 A8
Hawthorne Dr NSTN CH64 .... 93 H3
  SBCH CW11 .... 204 C6
Hawthorne Gv POY/DIS SK12 ... 67 J8
  WARR WA1 .... 37 M5 2
  WSFD CW7 .... 178 A3 2
Hawthorne Rd FROD/HEL WA6 .. 99 J7
  WARRS WA4 .... 56 C4 2
Hawthorne St WARRW/BUR WA5 .. 4 E1
Hawthorn Gdns ALS/KID ST7 ... 242 D4
Hawthorn Gv BRAM/HZG SK7 ... 65 J6
  CW/HAS CW1 .... 221 K5
  HTNM SK4 .... 46 B1
  NWCHW CW8 .... 102 F8 2
  WARRS WA4 .... 56 D3 2
  WILM/AE SK9 .... 84 B5
Hawthorn La CW/SHV CW2 .... 237 M2 2
  WILM/AE SK9 .... 84 A5 2
Hawthorn Pk WILM/AE SK9 ..... 84 A5 2
Hawthorn Ri MCFLDN SK10 .... 111 L6
Hawthorn Rd CHD/CHDH SK8 ... 45 G7
  CHSE CH3 .... 170 C5
  CHSW/BR CH4 .... 168 F7
  GTS/LS CH66 .... 94 C6
  HALE/TIMP WA15 .... 61 L1
  HTNM SK4 .... 45 L2
  KNUT WA16 .... 131 M1 4
  LYMM WA13 .... 58 C1 2
  MCFLDN SK10 .... 112 F4
  NSTN CH64 .... 91 H2
  NWCHW CW8 .... 128 C4
The Hawthorns NWCHW CW8 ... 12 B5
  TPLY/KEL CW6 .... 197 K3 2
  TPLY/KEL CW6 .... 216 C2
Hawthorn St WILM/AE SK9 ...... 84 A6
Hawthorn Vls HOLMCH CW4 ... 181 J1
Hawthorn Wk NWCHE CW9 .... 130 C1 2
  WILM/AE SK9 .... 84 A5 2

Hawthorn Wy MCFLDN SK10 .... 15 K1
Haybarn Rd NTHM/RTH M23 .... 44 B5
Hayburn Rd OFTN SK2 .... 47 J2 2
Haycastle Cl WARRW/BUR WA5 .. 36 E3
Hay Cft CHD/CHDH SK8 .... 64 E4
Haycroft Cl GTS/LS CH66 .... 120 D2
Haydock Av SALE M33 .... 138 C1 2
Haydock Dr BRAM/HZG SK7 ..... 66 F2
  HALE/TIMP WA15 .... 43 H7
Haydock Park Gdns
  NEWLW WA12 .... 22 B3
Haydock St AIMK WN4 .... 22 B2 2
  NEWLW WA12 .... 22 A8
  WARRN/WOL WA2 .... 5 G5
Haydon Wy CQ CH5 .... 142 F6 2
Hayes Crs FROD/HEL WA6 .... 99 H3
Hayes Dr NWCHW CW8 .... 129 H1
Hayes Pk CH/BCN CH1 .... 16 E1
Haye's Rd IRL M44 .... 31 L7
Hayfield Cl MCFLDN SK10 ...... 138 B1 2
Hayfield Rd NM/HAY SK22 .... 69 L3
  WARR WA1 .... 38 C4
Hayfields KNUT WA16 .... 107 J2
Hayfields Gv
  AUD/MAD/W CW3 .... 273 M1 2
Hayfield Wk HALE/TIMP WA15 .. 43 J6 2
Hayhead Cl ALS/KID ST7 .... 243 H2
Hayhurst Av MWCH CW10....... 179 J3
Hayhurst Cl NWCHE CW9 .... 13 H3
Hayle Cl MCFLDN SK10 .... 137 K3 2
Hayling Cl CW/HAS CW1 .... 221 H4
Haymakers Cl CHSW/BR CH4 .. 168 F8 2
Haymakers Wy CH/BCN CH1 ... 144 A4
Hayman Av LEIGH WN7 .... 24 D2
Haymoor Green Rd NANT CW5 .. 252 E2
Hayside Wk MALPAS SY14 ..... 258 A1
Haythorp Av WYTH/NTH M22 ... 63 L1
Hayton St KNUT WA16 .... 106 F3
Haywood Cl GOL/RIS/CU WA3 .. 23 L3 2
Haywood Crs RUNC WA7 .... 74 D2 2
Hazel Av CHD/CHDH SK8 .... 45 L7
  MCFLDS SK11 .... 138 A7
  MPL/ROM SK6 .... 48 D2
  RUNC WA7 .... 9 J7
  SALE M33 .... 43 H1 2
Hazelbadge Cl POY/DIS SK12 ... 66 C8 2
Hazelbadge Rd POY/DIS SK12 .. 66 C8
Hazelborough Cl
  GOL/RIS/CU WA3 .... 30 B6
Hazel Cl ALS/KID ST7 .... 243 H1
  GTS/LS CH66 .... 120 F3
  MPL/ROM SK6 .... 48 E8
Hazelcroft WILM/AE SK9 .... 110 A4
Hazel Dr LYMM WA13 .... 58 F2
  NWCHW CW8 .... 128 D5
  OFTN SK2 .... 47 K6
  POY/DIS SK12 .... 86 F1
  WSFD CW7 .... 177 J4
  WYTH/NTH M22 .... 44 A4
Hazel Gv ALS/KID ST7 .... 242 A1
Hazelhurst Dr MCFLDN SK10 .. 113 G4
Hazelhurst Rd BURS/TUN ST6 .. 243 M6
Hazelmere Cl NWCHW CW8 ..... 12 A8
Hazel Rd ALT WA14 .... 42 D7
  CHD/CHDH SK8 .... 65 H3
  CHSW/BR CH4 .... 168 F7
Hazelshaw La SBCH CW11 ..... 182 A8
Hazel St BRAM/HZG SK7 .... 66 E1 2
Hazelton Cl LEIGH WN7 .... 24 E3 2
Hazelwell SALE M33 .... 43 H1
Hazelwood Cl HLWD L26 .... 50 D2 3
Hazelwood Gv HLWD L26 .... 50 D2
Hazelwood Ms WARRS WA4 ..... 57 J3 2
Hazelwood Rd BRAM/HZG SK7 .. 66 E4
  HALE/TIMP WA15 .... 61 L2
  NWCHW CW8 .... 103 H8
  OFTN SK2 .... 47 G8
  WARR WA1 .... 38 A4
Hazlehurst Gv AIMK WN4 .... 22 C1
Hazlehurst Rd FROD/HEL WA6 .. 99 J7
Hazlemere Av MCFLDS SK11 .... 14 A8
Hazlemere Av MCFLDS SK11 .... 45 L1
Headland Cl GOL/RIS/CU WA3 .. 23 L6
Headlands Rd BRAM/HZG SK7 .. 65 M3
The Headlands CH/BCN CH1 .... 17 J5
Headworth Cl NWCHE CW9 ..... 13 G9
Heald Cl ALT WA14 .... 61 J2
Heald Gv CHD/CHDH SK8 .... 64 A3
Heald St NEWLW WA12 .... 26 F1
  STKP SK1 .... 3 J3
Healey Av BIDD ST8 .... 227 H7
Healey Cl CW/HAS CW1 .... 221 G4
  NTHM/RTH M23 .... 44 A2
Health St CQ CH5 .... 142 B6 2
Heapy St MCFLDS SK11 .... 15 J8
Hearn's La NANT CW5 .... 234 E8
Heath Av ALS/KID ST7 .... 224 F5
  GTS/LS CH66 .... 121 G3
  SBCH CW11 .... 204 E6
Heathbank Rd CHD/CHDH SK8 .. 64 F4
  EDGY/DAV SK3 .... 46 B5
  CHSE CH3 .... 172 B3
Heath Cl CHSE CH3 .... 170 B4
Heathcote Av HTNM SK4 .... 2 A1
Heathcote Gdns
  NWCHE CW9 .... 130 D1 2
Heathcote Rd ALS/KID ST7 ..... 242 F3
  ALS/KID ST7 .... 224 E6
Heath Crs EDGY/DAV SK3 .... 46 F7
Heath Dr CHSE CH3 .... 172 B3
  RUNC WA7 .... 9 G8
Heath End Rd ALS/KID ST7 .... 224 D6
Heather Av IRL M44 .... 31 K6
Heather Brae NEWLW WA12 .... 22 A8
Heather Cl GOL/RIS/CU WA3 .... 29 K7
  GTS/LS CH66 .... 120 F1
  MCFLDS SK11 .... 162 C1
  RUNC WA7 .... 73 J7
Heather Ct CHSE CH3 .... 170 A4
Heatherfield Ct WILM/AE SK9 .. 84 E4

Heather Gld
  AUD/MAD/W CW3 .... 267 K5 2
Heather Rd ALT WA14 .... 61 L3
Heatherside ALS/KID ST7 .... 226 C1
The Heathers OFTN SK2 .... 47 H8 2
Heather Wy MPL/ROM SK6 ...... 48 E7
Heatherways TPLY/KEL CW6 ... 197 J1
Heath Farm La PART M31 .... 41 G1
Heathfield WILM/AE SK9 .... 84 A7
Heathfield Av CHD/CHDH SK8 .. 45 H7
  CW/HAS CW1 .... 18 D3
Heathfield Cl CONG CW12 ..... 206 F1
  NANT CW5........................... 21 H4
  SALE M33 .... 43 M1
Heathfield Pk WARRS WA4 ...... 57 G2
  WDN WA8 .... 52 D1
Heathfield Rd
  AUD/MAD/W CW3 .... 264 A1
  EP CH65 .... 10 D7
  OFTN SK2 .... 46 F6
Heathfields Cl CHNE CH2 .... 17 G1
Heathfield Sq KNUT WA16 ..... 106 F2 2
Heathgate Av SPK/HALE L24 ... 71 G2
Heath Gn TPLY/KEL CW6 .... 174 C8
Heath Gv GTS/LS CH66............ 94 B5
Heathlands Rd GTS/LS CH66.... 94 B5
Heathland Ter EDGY/DAV SK3 .. 46 E5
Heath La CHNE CH2 .... 121 L5
  CHSE CH3 .... 147 L6
  CHSE CH3 .... 170 A4
  GOL/RIS/CU WA3 .... 23 K6
  GOL/RIS/CU WA3 .... 29 G2
  GTS/LS CH66 .... 94 B5
  KNUT WA16 .... 58 D8
  KNUT WA16 .... 132 F5
  NSTN CH64 .... 93 J4
  NWCHE CW9 .... 102 B5
  NWCHE CW9 .... 104 A3
  WHITCH SY13 .... 260 E6
Heathmoor Av GOL/RIS/CU WA3 .. 23 K6
Heath Park Gv RUNC WA7 .... 8 F7
Heath Rd AIMK WN4 .... 22 B2
  ALT WA14 .... 61 K2
  CHNE CH2 .... 145 K5
  CONG CW12 .... 207 G2
  EDGY/DAV SK3 .... 46 F6
  HALE/TIMP WA15.................. 42 F4
  MCFLDN SK10 .... 112 C6
  NWCHW CW8 .... 128 E3
  RUNC WA7 .... 9 J7
  SBCH CW11 .... 204 D6
  WARRW/BUR WA5 .... 35 M7
  WDN WA8 .... 6 B1
  WHITCH SY13 .... 270 B8
Heath Road Crs RUNC WA7 ...... 9 J5
Heath Rd South RUNC WA7 ...... 9 G9
Heathside NANT CW5............... 21 G5
Heathside La BURS/TUN ST6 .. 243 H5
Heathside Park Rd
  EDGY/DAV SK3 .... 45 M5
Heaths La TPLY/KEL CW6 .... 174 C2
Heath St AIMK WN4 .... 22 C2 2
  BIDD ST8 .... 227 J5
  BURS/TUN ST6 .... 243 J5
  CW/HAS CW1 .... 19 G3
  GOL/RIS/CU WA3 .... 23 G4
  WARRS WA4 .... 56 C4
Heathview Rd WDN WA8 .... 52 A8
Heath Wy TPLY/KEL CW6......... 197 K4
Heathwood Dr ALS/KID ST7 .... 224 B7
Heathwood Gv WARR WA1 .... 38 B5
Heatley Cl LYMM WA13 .... 40 A8 2
Heatley La NANT CW5 .... 250 F8
Heaton Av BRAM/HZG SK7 ...... 65 K1
  LEIGH WN7 .... 24 C2
Heaton Cl LYMM WA13 .... 70 F1
Heaton Ct GOL/RIS/CU WA3 .... 29 M6
Heaton La HTNM SK4 .... 2 D5
Heaton Moor Rd HTNM SK4 ..... 46 B1
Heaton Rd HTNM SK4 .... 2 B1
Heaton Sq WSFD CW7 .... 177 J4 2
Heaton St EDGY/DAV SK3 .... 47 G6
Heaviley Gv OFTN SK2 .... 47 G6
Heaward Cl CW/SHV CW2 ...... 238 B8 2
Hebden Av GOL/RIS/CU WA3 .... 25 H8
Heber's Cl MALPAS SY14 .... 246 C7
Heber St GOL/RIS/CU WA3...... 22 F2
Hedge Hey RUNC WA7 .... 74 A3
Hedge Rw RUNC WA7 .... 10 D3
Hedgerow Dr NWCHE CW9 .... 130 C1 2
Hedingham Cl HLWD L26......... 51 G3
  MCFLDN SK10 .... 137 M4 2
Hefferston Grange Dr
  NWCHW CW8 .... 128 A5
Hefferston Ri NWCHW CW8 .... 128 A5
Heighley Castle Wy
  AUD/MAD/W CW3 .... 267 L3
Heighley La AUD/MAD/W CW3 .. 267 L1
The Heights FROD/HEL WA6 .... 98 C3 2
Helena Cl KNUT WA16 .... 107 J2
Helen St GOL/RIS/CU WA3....... 22 F2
Hellath Wen NANT CW5 .... 251 L2
Hell Nook GOL/RIS/CU WA3..... 22 E3
Hellyar-brook Rd ALS/KID ST7 .. 224 B8
Helmsdale Cl CW/HAS CW1 .... 221 H6 2
Helmsdale La WARRW/BUR WA5 .. 36 C6
Helmsley Cl WARRW/BUR WA5 .. 4 B2
Helmsley Rd HLWD L26 .... 50 F5
Helsby Av PS/BROM CH62 .... 93 M1
Helsby Rd FROD/HEL WA6 ...... 124 C3
  SALE M33 .... 43 L2
Helsby St WARR WA1 .... 5 M4
Helston Av HLWD L26 .... 50 F3
Helston Cl BRAM/HZG SK7 ...... 65 M5 2
  RUNC WA7 .... 74 B7
  WARRW/BUR WA5 .... 35 L7 2
Helston Gv CHD/CHDH SK8 ..... 64 C4
Helton Cl HOLMCH CW4.......... 181 G1
Hemingford Cl GTS/LS CH66 ... 120 D2 2
Hemingway Vw FROD/HEL WA6 .. 124 B2
Hemmingshaw La SBCH CW11 .. 205 H4
Hemming St NWCHW CW8 ..... 129 K3 2
Hempcroft Rd HALE/TIMP WA15 .. 43 J7
Hempshaw La STKP SK1 .... 3 K8
Hemsworth Av GTS/LS CH66 .... 94 C7 2
Henbury Cl MWCH CW10......... 179 J5
Henbury La CHD/CHDH SK8 .... 64 F6
Henbury Pl RUNC WA7............. 73 H6

Henbury Ri MCFLDS SK11 .... 137 J4
Henbury Rd WILM/AE SK9 .... 64 D8 🯅
Henbury St OFTN SK2 .... 47 J8
Henderson Cl WARRW/BUR WA5 .. 35 K6
Henderson Rd HUY L36 .... 32 A1
  WDN WA8 .... 6 F4
Henderson St MCFLDS SK11 .... 14 F6
Hendham Cl BRAM/HZG SK7 .. 66 A2 🯅
Hendham Dr ALT WA14 ...... 42 B6
Hendon Cl CW/HAS CW1 ...... 19 L1
Hendon Dr EDGY/DAV SK3 .... 46 A5 🯅
Henley Av BIDD ST8 .... 227 C6
  CHD/CHDH SK8 .... 64 F2
  IRL M44 .... 31 L6
Henley Cl NSTN CH64 .... 91 L6
  WARRS WA4 .... 56 F6
Henley Ct RUNC WA7 .... 73 K2 🯅
Henley Dr HALE/TIMP WA15 ..... 42 F5
  WSFD CW7 .... 177 M3 🯆
Henley Mnr GOL/RIS/CU WA3 .. 24 D8
Henley Rd CHSW/BR CH4 ...... 168 F6
  NSTN CH64 .... 91 L6
Henrietta St CQ CH5 .... 142 B6
Henry Pl CH/BCN CH1 .... 17 C3
Henry St BURS/TUN ST6 ...... 243 K8
  CW/HAS CW1 .... 19 H2
  CW/HAS CW1 .... 222 D8
  LEIGH WN7 .... 25 C1
  LYMM WA13 .... 58 E1 🯅
  STKP SK1 .... 3 L7
  TPLY/KEL CW6 .... 197 J2 🯅
  WARR WA1 .... 4 E7
  WDN WA8 .... 7 M2 🯅
Henry Taylor St WARRS WA4 .. 37 M8
Henry Wood Ct CHSW/BR CH4 .. 168 E6
Henshall Av WARRS WA4 ...... 37 M8
Henshall Dr SBCH CW11 ...... 204 D4 🯆
Henshall Hall Dr CONG CW12 .. 208 B3
Henshall La ALT WA14 .... 41 J5
Henshall Rd MCFLDS SK10 .... 112 C5
Henshall St CH/BCN CH1 .... 16 E2
Henshaw La MCFLDS SK11 .... 160 E1
Henson Gv HALE/TIMP WA15 .. 43 C8
Heol-y-bryn FLINT CH6 ...... 116 B8 🯅
Hepherd St WARRW/BUR WA5 .. 36 D8 🯈
Hepley Rd POY/DIS SK12 ...... 87 C1
Hepple Cl HTNM SK4 .... 45 M1 🯅
Hepworth Cl GOL/RIS/CU WA3 .. 22 F2 🯆
Herald Pk CW/HAS CW1 ...... 19 J6
Heralds Cl WDN WA8 .... 52 B4
Heralds Gn WARRW/BUR WA5 .. 26 E6 🯈
Herdman St CW/SHV CW2 .... 19 C7
Hereford Av GOL/RIS/CU WA3 .. 23 H4 🯅
  GTS/LS CH66 .... 120 E4
Hereford Cl AIMK WN4 ...... 22 C2 🯈
  WARR WA1 .... 38 D5 🯅
Hereford Dr WILM/AE SK9 .... 84 E1
Hereford Rd CHD/CHDH SK8 .. 46 A8 🯅
Hereford Pl CH/BCN CH1 .... 145 C8 🯅
Hereford Wy MWCH CW10 .... 179 K2
Hereward Rd CHSE CH3 ...... 170 B3
Heritage Gdns DID/WITH M20 .. 45 H2
Herle Dr WYTH/NTH M22 .... 63 J3 🯅
Hermitage Av MPL/ROM SK6 .. 48 F2
Hermitage Ct CH/BCN CH1 .. 144 A4
Hermitage Dr HOLMCH CW4 .. 157 K8
Hermitage Gdns
  MPL/ROM SK6 .... 48 F2 🯅
Hermitage Green La
  WARRW/WOL WA2 .... 28 A4
Hermitage La HOLMCH CW4 .. 157 J4
Hermitage Rd CH/BCN CH1 .. 144 A4
  HALE/TIMP WA15 .... 62 A1
Heronbrook WHITCH SY13 .... 269 K4
Heron Cl AUD/MAD/W CW3 .. 267 M5 🯅
  CHSE CH3 .... 228 F3 🯅
  CHSW/BR CH4 .... 167 H8
  KNUT WA16 .... 107 H1
  RUNC WA7 .... 74 D4 🯅
  WSFD CW7 .... 177 K7 🯅
Heron Ct HLWD L26 .... 50 E3
  NSTN CH64 .... 91 J5
Heron Crs CW/HAS CW1 ...... 19 M2
Heron Dr POY/DIS SK12 ...... 86 A1
Heron Pl CHNE CH2 .... 16 F2
Heron St EDGY/DAV SK3 ...... 2 D8
Herons Wy CHSW/BR CH4 .... 192 B1
  RUNC WA7 .... 54 F8 🯅
Herrick Cl CW/SHV CW2 ...... 238 A4
Hertford Cl CONG CW12 .... 184 E8
  HLWD L26 .... 50 F5
  WARR WA1 .... 38 E5
Hertford Gv IRL M44 .... 31 J6
Hesketh Av DID/WITH M20 .. 45 C1
Hesketh Cl WARRW/BUR WA5 .. 35 M8
Hesketh Cft CW/HAS CW1 .. 221 C4
Hesketh Dr NWCHE CW9 .... 131 C1
Hesketh Meadow La
  GOL/RIS/CU WA3 .... 24 A4
Hesketh Rd SALE M33 ...... 42 F1 🯅
  SPK/HALE L24 .... 71 L2
Hesketh St North
  WARRW/BUR WA5 .... 36 D8 🯅
Hesketh St HTNM SK4 ...... 2 E3 🯅
  WARRW/BUR WA5 .... 36 D8 🯉
Heskin Cl RAIN/WH L35 ...... 33 H1
Hesnall Cl GOL/RIS/CU WA3 .. 25 J4
Heswall Av DID/WITH M20 .. 29 L1
Heswall Rd GTS/LS CH66 .... 94 C5 🯅
Hetherson Green La
  MALPAS SY14 .... 247 K4
Hever Dr HLWD L26 .... 51 C3
Hewetson Crs MCFLDS SK11 .. 137 L5
Hewitt Dr WSFD CW7 .... 178 D4
Hewitt Gv NWCHE CW9 ...... 104 F7
Hewitt St BURS/TUN ST6 .... 243 M6
  CHNE CH2 .... 17 M2
  CW/SHV CW2 .... 19 H8
  NWCHE CW9 .... 130 D2
  WARRS WA4 .... 56 C1
Hexham Cl OFTN SK2 .... 47 J7 🯅
Hexham Wy MCFLDS SK10 .... 112 C8

Heybridge La MCFLDN SK10 .... 112 B5
Heybrook Rd NTHM/RTH M23 .. 44 B7
Heyes Av HALE/TIMP WA15 .... 43 H5 🯅
Heyes Dr HALE/TIMP WA15 .... 43 H5
  LYMM WA13 .... 58 C2
Heyes Farm Rd MCFLDS SK11 .. 137 L4 🯅
Heyes La HALE/TIMP WA15 .... 43 H4
  WARRS WA4 .... 56 E4
  WILM/AE SK9 .... 110 B2
Heyes Mt RAIN/WH L35 ...... 33 J2
Heyes Pk NWCHW CW8 ...... 128 F8
Heyes Rd WDN WA8 .... 52 C4
The Heyes WLTN L25 .... 50 B2
Heyeswood La NWCHW CW8 .. 129 C8
Heyfield Park Rd
  GTS/LS CH66 .... 94 B5 🯅
Heyland Rd NTHM/RTH M23 .. 44 A6
Hey Lock Cl NEWLW WA12 .... 27 J4 🯅
Heyridge Dr WYTH/NTH M22 .. 44 D3
Heys Av MPL/ROM SK6 ...... 48 E1
  NTHM/RTH M23 .... 44 A3
Heysbank Rd POY/DIS SK12 .. 68 D7
Heyscroft Rd HTNM SK4 .... 46 A2
  WLTN L25 .... 50 B2
Heysham Cl RUNC WA7 ...... 74 C6
Heysham Rd NTHLY L27 ...... 32 A8 🯅
Hey Shoot La GOL/RIS/CU WA3 .. 25 J7
Heys La MPL/ROM SK6 ...... 48 E1
Heysoms Av NWCHW CW8 .. 12 C5
Heysoms Cl NWCHW CW8 .. 12 C5 🯅
The Heys RUNC WA7 .... 73 L3 🯅
Heywood Av GOL/RIS/CU WA3 .. 23 H3
Hey Wood Cl NEWLW WA12 .. 27 J4 🯆
Heywood Cl WILM/AE SK9 .... 110 B2
Heywood Gdns RAIN/WH L35 .. 32 E2
Heywood La AUD/MAD/W CW3 .. 273 K4
  WHITCH SY13 .... 273 H5
Heywood Rd GTS/LS CH66 .... 94 D7
  SALE M33 .... 43 H1
  WILM/AE SK9 .... 110 B2
Heywoods Rdg
  AUD/MAD/W CW3 .... 273 L2
The Heywoods CHNE CH2 .... 145 J8
Heyworth Av MPL/ROM SK6 .. 48 D1
Hibbert La MPL/ROM SK6 .... 48 F7
Hibbert St NM/HAY SK22 .... 69 H6 🯆
  WDN WA8 .... 7 J4
Hibel Rd MCFLDN SK10 ...... 15 C4
Hickhurst La TPLY/KEL CW6 .. 198 B1
Hickmore Heys CHSE CH3 .... 146 F8 🯅
Hickory Cl WARR WA1 ...... 38 E5
Hickson St NWCHW CW8 .... 129 H1
Hickton Dr ALT WA14 ...... 42 B6
Hidcote Cl CW/SHV CW2 .... 238 B4 🯅
Hidden Hills AUD/MAD/W CW3 .. 267 L4
Hield Brow NWCHE CW9 .... 104 C5
Hield Gv NWCHE CW9 ...... 104 C5
Hield La NWCHE CW9 ...... 104 C5
Higginbotham Gn
  MCFLDS SK11 .... 15 J9 🯆
Higham Av WARRW/BUR WA5 .. 36 F3
High Bank ALT WA14 .... 42 D7
High Bank Cl IRL M44 ...... 31 K6
Highbank Dr NWCHW CW8 .. 129 H1
Highbank Dr DID/WITH M20 .. 45 H4
Highbank Rd FROD/HEL WA6 .. 126 C2
  NWCHW CW8 .... 12 D5
High Bank Side STKP SK1 .... 3 G5
High Bent Av CHD/CHDH SK8 .. 65 G6
Highcliffe Av CH/BCN CH1 .. 145 H8
High Crest Av CHD/CHDH SK8 .. 44 F7
Highcroft CQ CH5 .... 142 A7
Highcroft Av CONG CW12 .... 207 M2
Highcroft Rd MPL/ROM SK6 .. 48 C1
High Cross La MALPAS SY14 .. 230 D3 🯅
Highdales Rd NTHM/RTH M23 .. 44 B7
High Elm Dr HALE/TIMP WA15 .. 62 C4
High Elm Rd HALE/TIMP WA15 .. 62 C4
High Elms CHD/CHDH SK8 .... 65 H7
Higher Ash Rd ALS/KID ST7 .. 242 D4
Higher Ashton WDN WA8 .... 52 F1
Higher Barlow Rw STKP SK1 .. 3 H7
Higher Bents La
  MPL/ROM SK6 .... 47 M1 🯈
Higher Bury St HTNM SK4 .... 2 C3
Higher Carden La MALPAS SY14 .. 230 D6
Higher Downs ALT WA14 .... 61 J1
  KNUT WA16 .... 107 J3
Higher Fence Rd MCFLDS SK10 .. 15 M2 🯅
Higher Heyes Dr
  FROD/HEL WA6 .... 126 B4
Higher Hillgate STKP SK1 .... 3 H7
Higher La CHF/WBR SK23 .. 114 D1 🯅
  LYMM WA13 .... 59 G3
  LYMM WA13 .... 59 J3
  MCFLDN SK10 .... 113 H6
  POY/DIS SK12 .... 88 E4
  WARRS WA4 .... 101 J1
Higher Rd HLWD L26 .... 50 E5
  SPK/HALE L24 .... 51 H7
High Fld ALT WA14 .... 60 B2
Highfield CHNE CH2 .... 97 H8
  CQ CH5 .... 166 C4 🯅
  MCFLDN SK10 .... 112 A7
  SALE M33 .... 43 J1
Highfield Av ALS/KID ST7 .... 243 H2 🯅
  AUD/MAD/W CW3 .... 264 A7
  GOL/RIS/CU WA3 .... 22 F4 🯆
  LEIGH WN7 .... 25 J1
  MPL/ROM SK6 .... 48 D2
  NWCHE CW9 .... 131 G1 🯅
  WARRS WA4 .... 56 D8
  WARRW/BUR WA5 .... 36 A7
Highfield Cl EDGY/DAV SK3 .. 46 F8
  NSTN CH64 .... 91 L4
Highfield Crs WDN WA8 ...... 7 G1
Highfield Dr LYMM WA13 .... 58 C2
  MCFLDN SK10 .... 14 B2
  NANT CW5 .... 21 H4
Highfield Est WILM/AE SK9 .. 84 C3
Highfield Pk HTNM SK4 ...... 45 K8 🯅
Highfield Pkwy BRAM/HZG SK7 .. 65 K8
Highfield Rd BRAM/HZG SK7 .. 65 M1
  CH/BCN CH1 .... 144 D7

CHD/CHDH SK8 .... 64 F3
  CONG CW12 .... 207 L3
  GTS/LS CH66 .... 94 B6
  HALE/TIMP WA15 .... 43 H7
  HALE/TIMP WA15 .... 62 A2
  LYMM WA13 .... 58 C2
  MPL/ROM SK6 .... 48 F6 🯅
  NTH CH64 .... 91 L4
  NWCHW CW8 .... 13 C3
  POY/DIS SK12 .... 66 A8 🯅
  WDN WA8 .... 6 F2
Highfield Rd East BIDD ST8 .. 227 K5
Highfield Rd North EP CH65 .. 10 E7
Highfield Rd West BIDD ST8 .. 227 K4
Highfields WHITCH SY13 .... 268 A1
Highfields Av WHITCH SY13 .. 269 M6
Highfield St EDGY/DAV SK3 .... 2 A7
Highfield Ter NM/HAY SK22 .. 69 K4
Highgate Cl CW/HAS CW1 .. 221 C4 🯅
High Gates Cl WARRW/BUR WA5 .. 4 A3
High Grove Rd CHD/CHDH SK8 .. 45 J7
High Hill Rd NM/HAY SK22 .. 69 K3
Highland Av CQ CH5 .... 166 A1
Highlands Av WHITCH SY13 .. 269 M6
Highlands Rd OFTN SK2 .... 47 M6
  RUNC WA7 .... 8 F8
The Highlands TPLY/KEL CW6 .. 216 E4
Highland Wy KNUT WA16 .... 107 C5
High Lea CHD/CHDH SK8 .... 45 J7
High Lee Rd NM/HAY SK22 .. 69 G4
High Lowe Av CONG CW12 .. 185 G8
Highmarsh Crs NEWLW WA12 .. 27 J5
High Meadow CHD/CHDH SK8 .. 64 E4 🯅
High Mdw MPL/ROM SK6 .... 48 C1
Highoaks Rd WLTN L25 ...... 50 B3
High Pk CQ CH5 .... 166 C3
High St ALS/KID ST7 ...... 226 D5
  ALS/KID ST7 .... 242 D7
  ALS/KID ST7 .... 243 L2
  ALT WA14 .... 42 D8
  BIDD ST8 .... 227 J5
  BRAM/HZG SK7 .... 66 F2
  BURS/TUN ST6 .... 243 K8
  BURS/TUN ST6 .... 243 K6
  CHD/CHDH SK8 .... 45 K6
  CHSE CH3 .... 172 B2
  CHSE CH3 .... 214 A3
  CHSE CH3 .... 228 E2
  CW/SHV CW2 .... 19 C5
  FROD/HEL WA6 .... 99 H3
  FROD/HEL WA6 .... 126 F6
  GOL/RIS/CU WA3 .... 23 G4
  MALPAS SY14 .... 246 B8
  MCFLDN SK10 .... 113 H4
  MCFLDS SK11 .... 15 H9
  NEWLW WA12 .... 22 D8
  NM/HAY SK22 .... 69 J4
  NSTN CH64 .... 91 L5
  NWCHE CW9 .... 104 A5
  NWCHW CW8 .... 128 C3
  RUNC WA7 .... 8 F2
  SBCH CW11 .... 204 B6
  SPK/HALE L24 .... 71 K3
  STKP SK1 .... 3 G5
  TPLY/KEL CW6 .... 173 K8
  TPLY/KEL CW6 .... 197 J3
  WARR WA1 .... 5 J5
  WHITCH SY13 .... 270 A4
  WLTN L25 .... 50 A2
  WSFD CW7 .... 177 J3
High Street (Sandyford)
  BURS/TUN ST6 .... 243 K7
Hightown CW/HAS CW1 ...... 18 E2
  MWCH CW10 .... 179 H7
  SBCH CW11 .... 204 B6 🯅
Hightree Dr MCFLDS SK11 .. 137 H4
High Vw ALS/KID ST7 ...... 226 B7
  FROD/HEL WA6 .... 98 C8
The Highway CQ CH5 .... 166 A3
High Wood Fold MPL/ROM SK6 .. 49 J4
Highwood Rd WARRS WA4 .. 56 C5
Higifield Av SALE M33 ...... 43 J1
Hignett Av MPL/ROM SK6 .. 47 M2
Higson Av MPL/ROM SK6 .... 48 F3
Hilary Av CHD/CHDH SK8 .... 64 D4
  GOL/RIS/CU WA3 .... 23 K3
Hilary Cl CHSE CH3 .... 170 B3
  HTNM SK4 .... 2 C3
  WARRW/BUR WA5 .... 35 K6
  WDN WA8 .... 53 L1
Hilary Rd WYTH/NTH M22 .. 63 H3
Hilbre Bank TPLY/KEL CW6 .. 198 D8
Hilbre Dr EP CH65 .... 121 J3
Hilda Av CHD/CHDH SK8 .... 45 L7
Hilden Rd WARRW/BUR WA5 .. 37 L3
Hillary Av CONG CW12 ...... 208 A2
Hillary Dr AUD/MAD/W CW3 .. 264 A8
Hillary Rd ALS/KID ST7 .... 243 H1
Hillberry Crs WARRS WA4 .. 56 B1
Hillbrook Rd BRAM/HZG SK7 .. 65 K6
Hill Cl NSTN CH64 .... 91 J7 🯅
Hill Cliffe Rd WARRS WA4 .. 56 B4 🯅
Hill Ct NSTN CH64 .... 92 A7
Hill Ct NSTN CH64 .... 92 B7
Hill Court Ms MPL/ROM SK6 .. 48 B2 🯆
Hillcourt Rd MPL/ROM SK6 .. 67 L5
Hillcrest Av HOLMCH CW4 .. 181 H1
Hill Crest Av NM/HAY SK22 .. 69 J4
Hillcrest Av HUY L36 ...... 32 A2
Hill Crest Av NM/HAY SK22 .. 69 J4
Hillcrest Dr GTS/LS CH66 .. 94 A6 🯉
Hillcrest Rd BRAM/HZG SK7 .. 65 M3
  GTS/LS CH66 .... 94 B6
  MCFLDN SK10 .... 112 A7
  MCFLDS SK11 .... 138 A8 🯅
  OFTN SK2 .... 47 J6
  TPLY/KEL CW6 .... 149 L6

Hillsden Ri CONG CW12 ...... 207 M2 🯈
  POY/DIS SK12 .... 86 F1
Hodder Bank OFTN SK2 ...... 47 L7
Hodgehill La MCFLDS SK11 .. 159 L8
Hodge La NWCHW CW8 .... 128 D2 🯅
Hodgkinson Av
  WARRW/BUR WA5 .... 36 F3
Hodgson Dr HALE/TIMP WA15 .. 43 G4 🯆
Hodnet Dr AIMK WN4 ...... 22 C1
Hogarth Rd MPL/ROM SK6 .. 49 H4
Hoghton Rd SPK/HALE L24 .. 71 L3
Hogshead La NWCHW CW8 .. 151 J4
Holbein Cl CHSW/BR CH4 .. 169 K6
Holborn Ct WDN WA8 ...... 52 F1
Holborn St STKP SK1 ...... 3 C6 🯅
The Holborn AUD/MAD/W CW3 .. 267 L6
Holbrook Cl WARRW/BUR WA5.. 35 L7
Holbury Cl CW/HAS CW1 .. 221 H4 🯅
Holcet Dr ALT WA14 ...... 42 B7 🯈
Holcombe Av GOL/RIS/CU WA3 .. 23 J4
Holcombe Cl ALT WA14 .... 42 B6 🯆
Holcombe Dr MCFLDN SK10 .. 138 D3 🯆
Holcroft La GOL/RIS/CU WA3 .. 30 C1
Holdings La AUD/MAD/W CW3 .. 266 F8
Hole House Fold
  MPL/ROM SK6 .... 48 B2 🯈
Holehouse La ALS/KID ST7 .. 225 K4
  MCFLDN SK10 .... 112 C2
  MCFLDS SK11 .... 139 J8
Hole House La NWCHW CW8 .. 102 E8
Holes La WARR WA1 .... 131 G5
  WARRW/BUR WA5 .... 4 C1
Holford Av NWCHE CW9 .... 131 C1
Holford Crs KNUT WA16 .... 107 C3
Holford St CONG CW12 .... 207 K1
Holford Wy NEWLW WA12 .. 27 M1 🯅
Holgrave Cl KNUT WA16 .... 59 J8
Holiday La OFTN SK2 ...... 47 M6 🯅
Holker Cl POY/DIS SK12 .... 66 F8
Holkham Cl WDN WA8 ...... 6 E3
Holland Cl SBCH CW11 .... 204 C7
Holland Rd BRAM/HZG SK7 .. 65 L5
  HLWD L26 .... 50 E6
  SPK/HALE L24 .... 70 E2
Hollands La TPLY/KEL CW6 .. 149 J7
Hollands Pl MCFLDS SK11 .. 15 L7 🯈
Hollands Rd NWCHE CW9 .. 13 H5
Holland St CW/HAS CW1 .. 21 H6
  MCFLDS SK11 .... 14 F7 🯆
Holland Wy HLWD L26 ...... 50 E6
Hollies Dr MPL/ROM SK6 .. 49 G7
Hollies La WILM/AE SK9 .... 84 F5
Hollies Rd HLWD L26 ...... 50 F5
The Hollies DID/WITH M20 .. 45 K7
  NWCHE CW9 .... 153 L4 🯅
Holliney Av WYTH/NTH M22 .. 63 M3
Holliney Rd WYTH/NTH M22 .. 63 M3
Hollingford Pl KNUT WA16 .. 106 F4
Hollin Green La NANT CW5 .. 234 D6
Hollingreen La NANT CW5 .. 263 G4
Hollingwood Cl AIMK WN4 .. 22 A1 🯅
Hollingworth Dr MPL/ROM SK6 .. 67 M1
Hollin La MCFLDS SK11 .... 163 H4
  NANT 262 D4
  WILM/AE SK9 .... 84 C4 🯅
Hollin Rd MCFLDN SK10 .... 113 C5
Hollins Crs ALS/KID ST7 .... 242 E4
Hollins Dr WARRN/WOL WA2 .. 28 A6
Hollins Gra ALS/KID ST7 .... 242 D4 🯅
Hollins Green Rd MPL/ROM SK6 .. 48 F6
Hollinshead Cl ALS/KID ST7 .. 225 M5 🯅
Hollins Hl TPLY/KEL CW6 .. 174 E3
Hollins La MPL/ROM SK6 .... 48 F6
  NWCHE CW9 .... 77 M8
  WARRN/WOL WA2 .... 27 L6
Hollins Mt MPL/ROM SK6 .. 49 H4
Hollins Rd MCFLDS SK11 .... 15 L9
Hollinwood Cl ALS/KID ST7 .. 242 E4
Hollinwood La MPL/ROM SK6 .. 68 B2
Hollinwood Rd ALS/KID ST7 .. 242 E4
Holloway RUNC WA7 .... 8 F4
Hollow Dr WARRS WA4 .... 56 E3
Hollow La FROD/HEL WA6 .. 126 A1
  KNUT WA16 .... 107 H3
Hollow Oak La NWCHW CW8 .. 127 K8
Hollowood Rd MALPAS SY14 .. 246 B7
The Hollows CHD/CHDH SK8 .. 64 C3 🯅
The Hollow ALS/KID ST7 .. 226 B7
Holly Av CHD/CHDH SK8 .... 45 K7
  NEWLW WA12 .... 27 K1
Hollybank AUD/MAD/W CW3 .. 273 L2
Holly Bank SALE M33 ...... 43 J1
Hollybank WARRS WA4 ...... 55 G7
Hollybank Rd RUNC WA7 .. 73 M4
Holly Bank Rd WILM/AE SK9 .. 84 B3
Hollybush Crs NANT CW5 .. 237 K2
Holly Bush La GOL/RIS/CU WA3 .. 23 L3 🯅
Hollybush Sq GOL/RIS/CU WA3 .. 23 L3 🯆
Holly Cl CHNE CH2 .... 146 F4
  HALE/TIMP WA15 .... 43 G6
  SPK/HALE L24 .... 71 K3
Holly Ct FROD/HEL WA6 .... 98 C7
Hollycroft Av WYTH/NTH M22 .. 44 D6 🯅
Holly Dr WSFD CW7 .... 177 K4
Hollyfield Rd EP CH65 ...... 10 D7 🯅
Holly Gra ALT WA14 ...... 61 K2 🯅
  BRAM/HZG SK7 .... 65 M1
Holly Gv CQ CH5 .... 166 B1
  KNUT WA16 .... 105 M1
  WARR WA1 .... 38 A5
Holly Heath Cl SBCH CW11 .. 204 C7
Hollyhedge Court Rd
  WYTH/NTH M22 .... 44 E7
Holly Hedge La WARRS WA4 .. 55 K6
Hollyhedge Rd NTHM/RTH M23 .. 44 B7
  WYTH/NTH M22 .... 44 C7
Holly Hey RAIN/WH L35 .... 32 D3
Hollyhey Dr NTHM/RTH M23 .. 44 B3
Holly La ALS/KID ST7 ...... 226 E7
  ALS/KID ST7 .... 241 L1
  WILM/AE SK9 .... 63 L7
Holly Mt CW/SHV CW2 ...... 238 C7
Hollymount Av OFTN SK2 .. 47 J7 🯈
Hollymount Dr OFTN SK2 .. 47 J7
Hollymount Gdns OFTN SK2 .. 47 J7
Hollymount Rd OFTN SK2 .. 47 J7

296 Hol - Kel

Holly Rd BRAM/HZG SK7 .... 65 L7
CHSW/BR CH4 .... 168 F7 2
EP CH65 .... 10 F7
GOL/RIS/CU WA3 .... 23 J4
LYMM WA13 .... 40 B7 1
MCFLDS SK11 .... 14 D6
MPL/ROM SK6 .... 67 L5
NWCHW CW8 .... 128 C4
POY/DIS SK12 .... 86 E1
WARRW/BUR WA5 .... 35 L7
Holly Rd North WILM/AE SK9 .... 84 A6
Holly Rd South WILM/AE SK9 .... 84 B7
Holly St STKP SK1 .... 3 K6
Holly Ter WARRW/BUR WA5 .... 35 M7
Hollythorn Av CHD/CHDH SK8 .... 65 J5 4
Holly Tree Dr BIDD ST8 .... 227 J2
KNUT WA16 .... 132 D5
Hollytree Rd KNUT WA16 .... 131 M1
WLTN L25 .... 50 B1
Holly Wk NWCHW CW8 .... 12 A5
Hollywall La BURS/TUN ST6 .... 243 L7
Hollyway WYTH/NTH M22 .... 44 E4
Hollywell Rd MPL/ROM SK6 .... 49 L4
Holmcrofts NSTN CH64 .... 91 L7
Holm Dr CHNE CH2 .... 123 J1
Holme Beech Gv OFTN SK2 .... 47 J4 4
Holme Cl CHSE CH3 .... 170 C5
Holme Rd DID/WITH M20 .... 44 F1
Holmes Chapel Rd CONG CW12 .... 183 C7
HOLMCH CW4 .... 182 A3
KNUT WA16 .... 107 H7
MCFLDS SK11 .... 134 F7
MWCH CW10 .... 179 M2
NWCHW CW8 .... 131 M8
SBCH CW11 .... 204 E4
Holmes Ct GOL/RIS/CU WA3 .... 29 J8 3
Holmes St CHD/CHDH SK8 .... 45 L6 4
EDGY/DAV SK3 .... 2 F9
Holme St CHSE CH3 .... 171 L1
Holmesville Av CONG CW12 .... 207 H2
Holmfield Av RUNC WA7 .... 9 L3
Holmfield Cl HTNM SK4 .... 2 C1
Holmfield Dr CHD/CHDH SK8 .... 65 H4
GTS/LS CH66 .... 120 D1
Holmlea Dr CW/HAS CW1 .... 19 L5
Holmlea Wy MCFLDN SK10 .... 111 K6
Holm Oak Dr AUD/MAD/W CW3 .... 267 L7
Holm Oak Wy GTS/LS CH66 .... 120 E4
Holmsfield Rd WARR WA1 .... 5 M7
Holmshaw La CW/HAS CW1 .... 222 F6
Holmwood AV HTNM SK4 .... 44 E4
Holmwood Dr EP CH65 .... 121 H2 5
Holt Hey NSTN CH64 .... 92 A7
Holt La RUNC WA7 .... 73 M4
Holt's La WILM/AE SK9 .... 83 M1
Holt St ALT WA14 .... 42 C5
CW/HAS CW1 .... 18 D3
STKP SK1 .... 3 H8
Holtswell Cl GOL/RIS/CU WA3 .... 23 L3 4
Holwick Rd NTHM/RTH M23 .... 43 M2
Holyhead Cl WARRW/BUR WA5 .... 36 D1
Holyrood Av WDN WA8 .... 34 A8
Holyrood Dr CW/SHV CW2 .... 237 L4
Holyrood Wy CHSE CH3 .... 170 B1
Holywell Cl NSTN CH64 .... 91 H3
Holywell La CHSE CH3 .... 230 D2
Home Farm Av MCFLDN SK10 .... 137 M3 4
Homelands Cl SALE M33 .... 42 F2 3
Homelands Rd SALE M33 .... 42 F2
Home Pk CH/BCN CH1 .... 144 F3
Homer Dr MPL/ROM SK6 .... 49 H4
Homestead Cl HUY L36 .... 32 A1 1
Homestead Crs BNG/LEV M19 .... 45 K1
Homestead Rd POY/DIS SK12 .... 68 C6
Homeway FROD/HEL WA6 .... 124 B2 2
Homewood Av
   WYTH/NTH M22 .... 44 D3 5
Homewood Crs NWCHW CW8 .... 129 H4
Honey Flds TPLY/KEL CW6 .... 197 J3
Honey Hall Rd HLWD L26 .... 50 E6
Honeysuckle Cl
   CHSW/BR CH4 .... 190 C1 5
   GTS/LS CH66 .... 120 C2 2
   HLWD L26 .... 50 D2 2
   NTHM/RTH M23 .... 43 K3
   WDN WA8 .... 34 B8 4
Honford Rd WYTH/NTH M22 .... 44 B8
Hong Kong Av MANAIR M90 .... 63 G4
Honister Av WARRN/WOL WA2 .... 37 J2
Honister Cl NTHLY L27 .... 51 C1
Honister Gv RUNC WA7 .... 73 L7
Honiton Wy ALT WA14 .... 42 A6
   WARRW/BUR WA5 .... 35 L3
Hood Gv LEIGH WN7 .... 25 H1
Hood La WARRW/BUR WA5 .... 36 C7
Hood La North
   WARRW/BUR WA5 .... 36 C6
Hood Rd WDN WA8 .... 6 F3
Hoofield La CHSE CH3 .... 196 A4
Hoogreen La KNUT WA16 .... 79 K3
Hooker St NWCHW CW8 .... 12 E5
Hookstone Dr GTS/LS CH66 .... 94 C6
Hoole Cl CHD/CHDH SK8 .... 46 A7
Hoole Gdns CHNE CH2 .... 170 B1
Hoole La CHNE CH2 .... 17 M4
   CHSE CH3 .... 17 L4
Hoole Rd CHNE CH2 .... 17 L1
Hoole Wy CH/BCN CH1 .... 17 H3
Hoole Way Rbt CH/BCN CH1 .... 17 H3
Hooleyhey La MCFLDN SK10 .... 140 C2
Hooley Range HTNM SK4 .... 46 B1
Hoolpool La FROD/HEL WA6 .... 97 M7
Hooper St STKP SK1 .... 2 F6
Hooten La LEIGH WN7 .... 25 J1
Hooton Gn GTS/LS CH66 .... 94 A2
Hooton La GTS/LS CH66 .... 94 B3
Hooton Rd NSTN CH64 .... 93 H5
Hooton Wy GTS/LS CH66 .... 93 K8 2
Hope Av WILM/AE SK9 .... 84 C1
Hope Carr La LEIGH WN7 .... 25 H1
Hope Carr Rd LEIGH WN7 .... 25 H1
Hope Carr Wy LEIGH WN7 .... 25 H2
Hope Cft GTS/LS CH66 .... 120 F2
Hope Farm Rd GTS/LS CH66 .... 120 E3
Hopefield Rd LYMM WA13 .... 40 B8
Hope Green Wy POY/DIS SK12 .... 86 D2 2
Hope La GOL/RIS/CU WA3 .... 25 L2

MCFLDN SK10 .... 86 E3
Hope Rd CHSW/BR CH4 .... 190 B1
SALE M33 .... 43 L1 2
Hopes Carr STKP SK1 .... 3 H6
Hope St BRAM/HZG SK7 .... 66 D2
CHSW/BR CH4 .... 168 F6
CW/SHV CW2 .... 19 C8
HTNM SK4 .... 2 D5
MCFLDN SK10 .... 15 J5
NEWLW WA12 .... 27 H1
NWCHW CW8 .... 12 F4
SBCH CW11 .... 204 B6
Hope St West MCFLDN SK10 .... 14 E4
Hope Ter EDGY/DAV SK3 .... 2 F8 3
Hopkins Cl CONG CW12 .... 207 H1
Hopkins Fld ALT WA14 .... 61 H3
Hopton Av WYTH/NTH M22 .... 63 L1
Hopwood Cl GOL/RIS/CU WA3 .... 23 M4 1
Hopwood St WARR WA1 .... 5 J5
Horbury Gdns GTS/LS CH66 .... 94 C7
Hornbeam Av GTS/LS CH66 .... 120 F3
Hornbeam Cl
   HALE/TIMP WA15 .... 43 L7 2
   RUNC WA7 .... 74 C4
Hornbeam Crs AIMK WN4 .... 22 B1
Hornbeam Dr NWCHW CW8 .... 128 E8
Hornbeam Rd HLWD L26 .... 51 C5
Hornby Dr NANT CW5 .... 21 J6
Hornby La WARRN/WOL WA2 .... 28 A6
Horncastle Cl
   GOL/RIS/CU WA3 .... 23 M4 3
Hornsea Rd OFTN SK2 .... 48 A7
Horridge Av NEWLW WA12 .... 22 C7
Horrocks La WARR WA1 .... 5 G7
Horrocks Rd CHNE CH2 .... 145 L7
Horsemarket St WARR WA1 .... 5 G6
Horseshoe Cl FROD/HEL WA6 .... 126 B2 1
Horseshoe Crs
   WARRN/WOL WA2 .... 37 L1 3
Horseshoe Dr MCFLDS SK11 .... 14 D6
Horseshoe La WILM/AE SK9 .... 110 A2
Horsham Av BRAM/HZG SK7 .... 66 C3 1
Horsley La TPLY/KEL CW6 .... 215 L3
Horstone Crs GTS/LS CH66 .... 120 F2
Horstone Gdns GTS/LS CH66 .... 120 F2
Horstone Rd GTS/LS CH66 .... 120 F2
Horton St OFTN SK2 .... 46 F5
Hoseley La WRX/GR/LL LL12 .... 210 A8
Hoskins La BURS/TUN ST6 .... 243 L7
Hospital La NANT CW5 .... 250 E2
Hospital St CW/HAS CW1 .... 221 K6
   NANT CW5 .... 20 F7
Hospital Wy RUNC WA7 .... 73 M5
Hostock Cl RAIN/WH L35 .... 32 D2 3
Hotel Rd MANAIR M90 .... 63 J5
Hotel St NEWLW WA12 .... 27 H1 7
Hothershall Cl CW/HAS CW1 .... 221 H3 3
Hough Cl MCFLDN SK10 .... 113 K7
Hough Gn CHSW/BR CH4 .... 169 G6
   HALE/TIMP WA15 .... 61 L7
Hough Green Rd WDN WA8 .... 52 A2
Hough La FROD/HEL WA6 .... 126 F7
   WILM/AE SK9 .... 84 D7
Houghley Cl MCFLDN SK10 .... 138 C2
Hough's La WARRS WA4 .... 56 A6
Houghton Cl CHNE CH2 .... 17 M3
   NEWLW WA12 .... 27 H1 1
   WDN WA8 .... 7 M1
Houghton Cft WDN WA8 .... 33 J6
Houghton St NEWLW WA12 .... 27 H1 1
   RAIN/WH L35 .... 33 J1 1
   WARRN/WOL WA2 .... 5 G4
   WDN WA8 .... 53 K2
Houldsworth Av ALT WA14 .... 42 E5 1
Houndings La SBCH CW11 .... 204 B7
Housesteads Dr CHNE CH2 .... 17 M2
Housman Cl CH/BCN CH1 .... 145 C7
Hove Cl CW/HAS CW1 .... 221 H4 4
The Hove RUNC WA7 .... 74 D6
Howard Av CHD/CHDH SK8 .... 65 G3
Howard Cl MPL/ROM SK6 .... 48 A2
Howard Dr HALE/TIMP WA15 .... 62 A3
Howard Rd CHSW/BR CH4 .... 168 D6
   GOL/RIS/CU WA3 .... 29 M6
   WYTH/NTH M22 .... 44 D3 3
Howard St CW/HAS CW1 .... 221 M6
   STKP SK1 .... 3 G3
Howards Wy NSTN CH64 .... 92 A6
Howarth Dr IRL M44 .... 31 M3 1
Howbeck Crs NANT CW5 .... 253 G4
Howden Rd NM/HAY SK22 .... 69 J3
Howells Av GTS/LS CH66 .... 120 C1
Howe Rd CHSW/BR CH4 .... 169 H5
Howe St MCFLDN SK10 .... 15 L2
Howey Hl CONG CW12 .... 207 K3
   FROD/HEL WA6 .... 99 G5
Howey Ri FROD/HEL WA6 .... 99 G5
Howley La WARR WA1 .... 5 J7
Howson Rd WARRN/WOL WA2 .... 37 J2
Howty Cl WILM/AE SK9 .... 84 D3
Hoylake Cl LEIGH WN7 .... 24 D2
   RUNC WA7 .... 74 C6
Hoylake Rd EDGY/DAV SK3 .... 46 A4
   SALE M33 .... 43 M2
Hoyle St WARRW/BUR WA5 .... 4 D3
Hubert Dr MWCH CW10 .... 179 J4
Hucclecote Av
   WYTH/NTH M22 .... 63 J2 3
Hucklow Av NTHM/RTH M23 .... 63 G2
Hudson Cl WARRW/BUR WA5 .... 36 D4
Hughes Av WARRN/WOL WA2 .... 37 K2
Hughes Dr CW/SHV CW2 .... 220 F8
Hughes Pl WARRN/WOL WA2 .... 37 K2 2
Hughes St WARRS WA4 .... 56 C1
Hugh St CHSW/BR CH4 .... 168 F7
Hulley Rd MCFLDN SK10 .... 138 C1
Hullock's Pool Rd ALS/KID ST7 .... 241 L7
Hulme Hall Av CHD/CHDH SK8 .... 65 G4
Hulme Hall Cl CHD/CHDH SK8 .... 65 G3 2
Hulme Hall La CHD/CHDH SK8 .... 65 G4
Hulme Hall La KNUT WA16 .... 132 A5
Hulme Hall Rd CHD/CHDH SK8 .... 65 G2
Hulme La SALE M33 .... 43 K1
Hulme Sq MCFLDS SK11 .... 138 C7

Hulme St CW/HAS CW1 .... 220 F7
STKP SK1 .... 3 L9
Hulseheath La KNUT WA16 .... 80 A1
Hulse La NWCHW CW9 .... 131 L6
Hulton Cl CONG CW12 .... 208 B3
Humber Cl WDN WA8 .... 53 M1
Humber Dr BIDD ST8 .... 227 L4
Humber Rd GTS/LS CH66 .... 120 F2
   WARRN/WOL WA2 .... 37 L2
Hume St WARR WA1 .... 5 L4
Humphrey's Cl RUNC WA7 .... 74 D5 3
Hungerford Av CW/HAS CW1 .... 19 K5
Hungerford La
   AUD/MAD/W CW3 .... 267 M6
Hungerford Pl SBCH CW11 .... 204 A7
Hungerford Rd CW/HAS CW1 .... 19 K4
Hungerford Ter CW/HAS CW1 .... 19 M5
Hunsterson Rd NANT CW5 .... 265 H1
Hunston Rd SALE M33 .... 42 F1
Hunt Cl WARRW/BUR WA5 .... 36 B4 4
Hunter Av CW/SHV CW2 .... 238 D5
Hunter Rd MANAIR M90 .... 37 H2
Hunters Cl BIDD ST8 .... 227 J4
   WILM/AE SK9 .... 84 F3 1
Hunters Ct FROD/HEL WA6 .... 98 D8
   RUNC WA7 .... 73 L6 2
Hunter's Crs CHSE CH3 .... 172 B3
Hunter's Dr CHSE CH3 .... 172 B3
Huntersfield CW/SHV CW2 .... 253 H1
Hunters Fld NWCHW CW8 .... 12 C4
Hunters Hl FROD/HEL WA6 .... 126 C3
   NWCHW CW8 .... 128 C3 2
Hunters Ms WILM/AE SK9 .... 84 C5
Hunters Ri WSFD CW7 .... 177 J3
Hunter St CH/BCN CH1 .... 16 F5
Hunters Wk CH/BCN CH1 .... 16 F5 3
Hunters Wy NSTN CH64 .... 91 J4
Huntley Av EDGY/DAV SK3 .... 46 B5
Huntley St WARRW/BUR WA5 .... 36 C8
Huntly Cha WILM/AE SK9 .... 84 C6
Hunts Cl CHSE CH3 .... 170 B3
Hunts Cross Av WLTN L25 .... 50 B1
Huntsham Cl ALT WA14 .... 42 B6 3
Hunts La WARRS WA4 .... 56 F2
Huntsman Dr IRL M44 .... 31 M5
Hurdsfield Cl MWCH CW10 .... 179 J5 1
   OFTN SK2 .... 47 J8
Hurdsfield Rd MCFLDN SK10 .... 15 K3
Hurford Av EP CH65 .... 94 F8
Hurlbote Cl WILM/AE SK9 .... 64 D7 3
Hurlbutts Dr CQ CH5 .... 142 D6
Hurlestone Cl CHNE CH2 .... 146 F3 1
Hurley Cl WARRW/BUR WA5 .... 36 C7
Hurley Dr CHD/CHDH SK8 .... 64 E2 2
Hurn Cl CW/HAS CW1 .... 221 H4 8
   SALE M33 .... 42 C1
Hurst Av CHD/CHDH SK8 .... 65 J6
   SALE M33 .... 42 C1
Hurst Cl ALS/KID ST7 .... 242 D6
Hurstfold Av BNG/LEV M19 .... 45 K1
Hursthead Rd CHD/CHDH SK8 .... 65 H5
Hurst La GOL/RIS/CU WA3 .... 25 H5
   MCFLDN SK10 .... 113 G4
Hurst Lea Rd NM/HAY SK22 .... 69 J5 1
Hurst Mill La GOL/RIS/CU WA3 .... 25 J4
Hurst Park Dr HUY L36 .... 32 A1
Hurst St LEIGH WN7 .... 25 H1
   WDN WA8 .... 53 G8 1
Hurstvale Av CHD/CHDH SK8 .... 64 B3 2
Hurstwood CHSE CH3 .... 171 G8
Hurstwood Rd OFTN SK2 .... 47 M8 2
Hutchins' Cl MWCH CW10 .... 179 L6 1
Hutchinson St WDN WA8 .... 7 G1
Huttfield Rd SPK/HALE L24 .... 51 G8 1
Hutton Dr CONG CW12 .... 208 A2
Huxley Av BRAM/HZG SK7 .... 65 L5
   MCFLDN SK10 .... 14 B1
Huxley Dr BRAM/HZG SK7 .... 65 L5
Huxley La CHSE CH3 .... 196 A5
Huxley St ALT WA14 .... 42 D5
   NWCHW CW8 .... 12 E5
Huxton Gn BRAM/HZG SK7 .... 66 A6
Hyacinth Cl EDGY/DAV SK3 .... 46 D7 3
Hyde Bank Rd NM/HAY SK22 .... 69 J4
Hyde Cl EP CH65 .... 94 F8
   RUNC WA7 .... 73 K6 1
Hyldavale Av CHD/CHDH SK8 .... 45 H6
Hylton Cl EP CH65 .... 121 L2
Hylton Dr CHD/CHDH SK8 .... 65 J4
Hythe Av CW/HAS CW1 .... 221 H4
Hythe Rd EDGY/DAV SK3 .... 46 B4

I

Ian Rd ALS/KID ST7 .... 243 H4
Ikey La NANT CW5 .... 234 F6
Ilex Av WARRN/WOL WA2 .... 28 B6
Ilfracombe Rd OFTN SK2 .... 47 K4
Imperial Av CH/BCN CH1 .... 144 C8
Imperial Ms EP CH65 .... 10 D5
Ince Av PS/BROM CH62 .... 93 L1
Ince Cl HTNM SK4 .... 2 E2
Ince Dr CHSE CH3 .... 228 F3
Ince La CHNE CH2 .... 97 H8
   CHNE CH2 .... 122 F8
Ince Orchards CHNE CH2 .... 97 H8
Ince St HTNM SK4 .... 2 E2 1
Ingersley Rd MCFLDN SK10 .... 113 H4
Ingham Cl CHSE CH3 .... 170 A3
Ingham Rd ALT WA14 .... 42 D4
   WDN WA8 .... 33 M8
Ingle Dr OFTN SK2 .... 47 J5
Inglenook Rd
   WARRW/BUR WA5 .... 35 M8 8
Ingle Rd CHD/CHDH SK8 .... 46 A6
Inglesham Cl LEIGH WN7 .... 24 E3 3
   NTHM/RTH M23 .... 44 B6
Ingleton Cl CHD/CHDH SK8 .... 46 J6 8
   HOLMCH CW4 .... 181 G1
   NEWLW WA12 .... 22 B8 2
Ingleton Gv RUNC WA7 .... 73 K7
Ingleton Rd EDGY/DAV SK3 .... 2 A8
Inglewood Av MWCH CW10 .... 179 K7
Inglewood Cl
   GOL/RIS/CU WA3 .... 30 B6 1
Ingram Dr HTNM SK4 .... 45 L1

Inman Av STHEL WA9 .... 26 B2
Inner Central Rd SPK/HALE L24 .... 50 F7
Inner South Rd SPK/HALE L24 .... 50 F8
Inner West Rd SPK/HALE L24 .... 50 E8
Innisfree Cl GTS/LS CH66 .... 94 C7 2
Insall Rd WARRN/WOL WA2 .... 37 M2
Intack La NWCHE CW8 .... 105 G7
Intake Cl NSTN CH64 .... 93 G4 2
International Ap MANAIR M90 .... 63 J5 1
Inveresk Rd MALPAS SY14 .... 245 J1
Ion Pth WSFD CW7 .... 178 C3
Irby Cl GTS/LS CH66 .... 94 E8
Ireland Rd SPK/HALE L24 .... 71 L3
Ireland St WARRN/WOL WA2 .... 5 G1
   WDN WA8 .... 53 K2
Irene Av BURS/TUN ST6 .... 243 M8
Iris Cl WDN WA8 .... 52 C2
Ironbridge Dr HOLMCH CW4 .... 181 J2
Irons La CHSE CH3 .... 147 M5
Irvin Dr WYTH/NTH M22 .... 64 A4
Irving Cl OFTN SK2 .... 66 A1
Irving's Crs CHSW/BR CH4 .... 168 D6
Irwell La RUNC WA7 .... 9 K1
Irwell Ri MCFLDN SK10 .... 112 F5
Irwell Rd WARRS WA4 .... 56 B2
Irwell St WDN WA8 .... 53 G8
Irwin Dr WILM/AE SK9 .... 64 C7
Irwin Rd ALT WA14 .... 42 C4
Isabella Ct CHSW/BR CH4 .... 168 E6 2
Isherwood Cl WARRN/WOL WA2 .... 37 M1
Isherwood Dr MPL/ROM SK6 .... 48 D6
Isis Cl CONG CW12 .... 207 M3
Islay Cl EP CH65 .... 121 J4
Islington Rd OFTN SK2 .... 47 J8
Ivanhoe Av GOL/RIS/CU WA3 .... 23 K3
Iveagh Cl RUNC WA7 .... 74 C1
Iver Cl WDN WA8 .... 33 J6
Iver Rd CHNE CH2 .... 145 L5
Ivy Av NEWLW WA12 .... 27 J2
Ivy Ct CHSW/BR CH4 .... 210 D2
Ivy Dr NWCHW CW8 .... 152 A2
Ivy Farm Cl NSTN CH64 .... 91 M6
Ivy Farm Gdns
   GOL/RIS/CU WA3 .... 24 D8 1
Ivy Farm La CHSE CH3 .... 231 J4
Ivy Gdns CONG CW12 .... 207 J2
Ivy House Rd BIDD ST8 .... 227 J2
   GOL/RIS/CU WA3 .... 23 K3 2
Ivy La ALS/KID ST7 .... 241 L2
   MCFLDS SK11 .... 14 A8
Ivy Meade Rd MCFLDS SK11 .... 137 M6
Ivy Ms CHNE CH2 .... 146 A7
Ivy Rd GOL/RIS/CU WA3 .... 23 H4
   MCFLDS SK11 .... 14 A7
   POY/DIS SK12 .... 86 E1
   WARR WA1 .... 38 E5
Ivy St RUNC WA7 .... 9 G4
Izaac Walton Wy
   AUD/MAD/W CW3 .... 267 L7

J

Jack Brady Cl NTHM/RTH M23 .... 43 L8
Jack La CW/SHV CW2 .... 239 K6
   MWCH CW10 .... 154 B7 1
Jackson Av GOL/RIS/CU WA3 .... 29 L1
   NANT CW5 .... 21 H7
   WARR WA1 .... 37 M5
Jackson Cl RAIN/WH L35 .... 33 K3
Jackson La MCFLDN SK10 .... 113 G5
Jackson Rd CONG CW12 .... 184 E7
Jacksons Edge Rd POY/DIS SK12 .... 68 A5
Jackson's La BRAM/HZG SK7 .... 66 B4
Jackson St CHD/CHDH SK8 .... 45 L6
   MCFLDS SK11 .... 15 H9
   WARRW/BUR WA5 .... 26 E6
Jacqueline St BURS/TUN ST6 .... 243 J8
Jamage Rd ALS/KID ST7 .... 242 D7
James Av GTS/LS CH66 .... 120 C1
James Cl WDN WA8 .... 53 L8
James Ct WLTN L25 .... 50 B2
James Hall St NANT CW5 .... 20 F4
James Rd WLTN L25 .... 50 B2
James St CH/BCN CH1 .... 17 H3
   EDGY/DAV SK3 .... 2 E9
   MCFLDS SK11 .... 15 G7
   NWCHE CW9 .... 130 C4
   STHEL WA9 .... 34 D1
   WARR WA1 .... 5 H6
James Wy BIDD ST8 .... 227 G6
Jamieson Cl ALS/KID ST7 .... 224 E8
   CHSE CH3 .... 170 A2 2
Jan Palach Av NANT CW5 .... 21 G9
Jarman MCFLDS SK11 .... 138 B8
Jasmine Cl NTHM/RTH M23 .... 43 L3 2
Jasmin Wy ALS/KID ST7 .... 243 M2
Jaycean Av BURS/TUN ST6 .... 243 L8
Jay Cl GOL/RIS/CU WA3 .... 30 A3
Jays Cl RUNC WA7 .... 74 E5
Jayton Av DID/WITH M20 .... 45 H4
Jean Av LEIGH WN7 .... 24 E2
Jedburgh Av GTS/LS CH66 .... 94 A6
Jefferson St BURS/TUN ST6 .... 243 K8
Jellicoe Av IRL M44 .... 31 L6 3
Jennet's La GOL/RIS/CU WA3 .... 25 J3
Jennings St EDGY/DAV SK3 .... 46 B5
Jenny La BRAM/HZG SK7 .... 85 L1
Jepson St OFTN SK2 .... 47 G6
Jersey Av EP CH65 .... 121 J3
Jersey St STHEL WA9 .... 34 C1
Jervis Cl WARRN/WOL WA2 .... 38 A1
Jesmond Crs CW/SHV CW2 .... 18 C7
Jesmond Gv CHD/CHDH SK8 .... 65 H4 8
Jesmond Rd CH/BCN CH1 .... 16 C3
Jessop Dr MPL/ROM SK6 .... 48 F4
Jessop Wy CW/HAS CW1 .... 222 D1
Jeudwine Cl WLTN L25 .... 50 B4
Jockey St WARRN/WOL WA2 .... 5 G1
Jodrell Cl HOLMCH CW4 .... 181 G1
Jodrell Meadow CHF/WBR SK23 .... 89 K4
Jodrell Rd CHF/WBR SK23 .... 89 K4
Jodrell St MCFLDS SK11 .... 15 J7

NM/HAY SK22 .... 69 H5
Jodrell Vw ALS/KID ST7 .... 243 H4
Johannesburg Gdns
   NTHM/RTH M23 .... 43 M8 3
John Av GOL/RIS/CU WA3 .... 29 L1
John Brunner Crs NWCHW CW8 .... 12 E6
John Fryer Av NWCHE CW9 .... 105 G7
John Nicholas Crs EP CH65 .... 10 F6 1
   EP CH65 .... 11 G5 1
John Offley Rd
   AUD/MAD/W CW3 .... 267 K6
John Rd LYMM WA13 .... 58 C1
Johns Av RUNC WA7 .... 8 F5
Johns Cl MCFLDN SK10 .... 113 K7
Johnson Av NEWLW WA12 .... 22 B7
Johnson Cl CONG CW12 .... 208 B3
Johnsons Cl CHSW/BR CH4 .... 169 H7 2
Johnson's La WDN WA8 .... 53 L4
Johnson St CHF/WBR SK23 .... 89 L4 2
John's Pl MPL/ROM SK6 .... 48 C2 3
John Steet MPL/ROM SK6 .... 48 C2 2
John St ALT WA14 .... 42 D8 2
   BIDD ST8 .... 227 J5
   BRAM/HZG SK7 .... 66 D1 11
   CW/HAS CW1 .... 18 E2
   EP CH65 .... 10 D5
   GOL/RIS/CU WA3 .... 23 G4
   IRL M44 .... 31 L7
   MCFLDN SK10 .... 113 H4 13
   MCFLDS SK11 .... 15 H8
   MPL/ROM SK6 .... 49 G7
   MPL/ROM SK6 .... 49 H2
   STKP SK1 .... 3 G7
   TPLY/KEL CW6 .... 174 B5
   WARRN/WOL WA2 .... 5 G5
   WSFD CW7 .... 177 J3 4
Jonathan's Wy CH/BCN CH1 .... 144 E7
Jones's La MWCH CW10 .... 180 C5
Jones Sq STKP SK1 .... 3 H9
Jonson St NSTN CH64 .... 91 J3
Jordangate MCFLDN SK10 .... 15 G4
Joseph Crs ALS/KID ST7 .... 241 L2
Joseph Johnson Ms
   WYTH/NTH M22 .... 44 E3 2
Joseph St MPL/ROM SK6 .... 49 G6 3
   WDN WA8 .... 7 L1
Joules Ct STKP SK1 .... 3 H6
Joule St GOL/RIS/CU WA3 .... 29 M7
Joyce Av WSFD CW7 .... 177 J2 2
Joy La STHEL WA9 .... 34 C2
   WARRW/BUR WA5 .... 26 D8
Jubilee Av CW/SHV CW2 .... 18 C5
   WARR WA1 .... 37 M4
   WARRW/BUR WA5 .... 35 L8 2
Jubilee Cl BIDD ST8 .... 227 K5
Jubilee Gdns NANT CW5 .... 20 F9
   NM/HAY SK22 .... 69 J5
Jubilee Gv LYMM WA13 .... 39 J8
Jubilee Rd CONG CW12 .... 207 L2
Jubilee St CQ CH5 .... 142 B6
   NM/HAY SK22 .... 69 J5
Jubilee Ter NANT CW5 .... 20 F8
Jubilee Wy WDN WA8 .... 6 C2
Jubits La WDN WA8 .... 34 A4
Judy La MCFLDS SK11 .... 163 G2
Julian Wy WDN WA8 .... 33 M8
Julius Cl FLINT CH6 .... 116 C7
Jumper La MCFLDN SK10 .... 113 L6
Junction La NEWLW WA12 .... 27 H1 2
Junction Rd OFTN SK2 .... 3 G9
   STKP SK1 .... 3 G9
June Av HTNM SK4 .... 46 B2 2
Juniper Dr GTS/LS CH66 .... 120 E3
Juniper Gv GTS/LS CH66 .... 120 F3
Juniper La GOL/RIS/CU WA3 .... 39 G4
Juniper Ri MCFLDN SK10 .... 137 L3 3
Jupiter Dr CH/BCN CH1 .... 144 E6
Jurby Ct WARRN/WOL WA2 .... 37 M3 1
   WARRN/WOL WA2 .... 37 L3 3
Justice St MCFLDN SK10 .... 15 G2

K

Kaleyards CH/BCN CH1 .... 17 G4
Kane Cl GOL/RIS/CU WA3 .... 24 A3
Karen Cl WARRW/BUR WA5 .... 26 F6
Karen Wy GTS/LS CH66 .... 120 D1
Katherine Rd OFTN SK2 .... 47 J7
Kay Av MPL/ROM SK6 .... 47 K1
Kaye Av GOL/RIS/CU WA3 .... 29 M1
Kay La LYMM WA13 .... 59 J4
Kay's Av STKP SK1 .... 3 L6
Kays Wood Rd MPL/ROM SK6 .... 48 D6
Kearsley Av CQ CH5 .... 166 A3
Keats Av RAIN/WH L35 .... 32 F1
Keats Cl GTS/LS CH66 .... 120 E4 3
   WDN WA8 .... 6 E4
Keats Dr ALS/KID ST7 .... 224 E4
   CW/SHV CW2 .... 238 A4 4
   MCFLDN SK10 .... 137 L3
Keats Gdns ALS/KID ST7 .... 243 L4
Keats Gv WARRN/WOL WA2 .... 37 J2
Keats La NWCHE CW9 .... 105 G7
Keble St WDN WA8 .... 7 J6
Keckwick La RUNC WA7 .... 75 H2 1
   WARRS WA4 .... 75 H2 1
Kedleston Gn OFTN SK2 .... 47 K5
Keele Crs MCFLDS SK11 .... 14 C8
Keele St BURS/TUN ST6 .... 243 K8
Keepers La KNUT WA16 .... 107 K1 1
Keepers La NWCHE CW9 .... 128 E4
   NWCHW CW8 .... 128 E4
Keith Av WARRW/BUR WA5 .... 35 L6
Keith Dr EDGY/DAV SK3 .... 46 B5
Kelbrook Ct WSFD CW7 .... 47 L7
Kelburn Ct GOL/RIS/CU WA3 .... 29 M6
Kelby Av NTHM/RTH M23 .... 44 B5
Kelfield Av NTHM/RTH M23 .... 43 M3
Kelmscott GTS/LS CH66 .... 120 D2
Kelsall Av PS/BROM CH62 .... 93 L1
Kelsall Cl GOL/RIS/CU WA3 .... 38 C1
   PS/BROM CH62 .... 93 L1
   WDN WA8 .... 6 B1
Kelsall Crs EDGY/DAV SK3 .... 46 D6 3
Kelsall Dr HALE/TIMP WA15 .... 43 J6

Kelsall Rd CHD/CHDH SK8 ...... 46 A7
   CHSE CH3 .... 148 C8
Kelsall St CONG CW12 .... 207 L1
Kelsborrow CI NWCHE CW9 .... 153 L1
Kelsborrow Wy TPLY/KEL CW6 .. 149 K8
Kelso Wy MCFLDN SK10 .... 112 C8
Kelvin CI GOL/RIS/CU WA3 ...... 29 K6
Kelvin Gv CHNE CH2 .... 145 L8
Kelvindale Dr HALE/TIMP WA15 .. 43 J5
Kelvin St GOL/RIS/CU WA3 ...... 29 K6
Kemberton Dr WDN WA8 .... 34 A7
Kemble Av NTHM/RTH M23 ...... 44 C3
Kemble CI CW/SHV CW2 .... 238 B4
Kemmel Av WARRS WA4 .... 56 C2
   WYTH/NTH M22 .... 44 F7
Kemp Rd MPL/ROM SK6 .... 49 J4
Kempsell Wy HLWD L26 .... 51 C5
Kempsford CI NTHM/RTH M23 .. 44 B6
Kempton Av CW/HAS CW1 ...... 221 J5
   SALE M33 .... 42 D1
Kempton CI BRAM/HZG SK7 .... 67 G2
   CH/BCN CH1 .... 16 C3
   NEWLW WA12 .... 22 D7
   RUNC WA7 .... 73 J6
Kempton Wy MCFLDN SK10 .... 112 C8
Kendal Av SALE M33 .... 43 J1
   WARRN/WOL WA2 .... 37 J2
Kendal CI CHNE CH2 .... 146 A6
   GTS/LS CH66 .... 120 D2
   HALE/TIMP WA15 .... 43 K7
Kendal Ct CONG CW12 .... 207 L2
Kendal Dr BRAM/HZG SK7 ...... 65 J7
   CHD/CHDH SK8 .... 45 J8
   GTS/LS CH66 .... 120 D2
   RAIN/WH L35 .... 33 C1
Kendal Ri RUNC WA7 .... 73 K7
Kendal Rd MCFLDS SK11 .... 137 M6
   WDN WA8 .... 52 C3
Kendrick CI NWCHW CW8 ...... 128 D3
Kendricks Fold RAIN/WH L35 .. 33 H1
Kendrick St WARR WA1 .... 4 E6
Kenilworth Av CHD/CHDH SK8 .. 65 G1
   KNUT WA16 .... 107 J2
   RUNC WA7 .... 9 H7
   WILM/AE SK9 .... 84 D1
Kenilworth CI CW/SHV CW2 .... 238 A5
   MCFLDS SK11 .... 137 M6
   MPL/ROM SK6 .... 48 F4
Kenilworth Ct EP CH65 .... 121 L2
Kenilworth Dr BRAM/HZG SK7 .. 66 D4
   WARR WA1 .... 37 M4
Kenilworth Gdns NEWLW WA12 .. 27 J2
Kenilworth Rd EDGY/DAV SK3 .. 45 M5
   GOL/RIS/CU WA3 .... 23 L5
   MCFLDS SK11 .... 137 M7
   NSTN CH64 .... 91 L6
Kenley Av WDN WA8 .... 33 K7
Kenmare Bank NWCHW CW9 .. 13 K8
Kenmore Gv IRL M44 .... 31 K6
Kenmore Rd SALE M33 .... 42 C3
   WYTH/NTH M22 .... 44 C5
Kennedy Av MCFLDN SK10 ...... 137 M3
Kennedy CI CHNE CH2 .... 146 A7
Kennedy Dr CQ CH5 .... 166 D2
Kennedy Wy HTNM SK4 .... 2 B4
Kennel La NWCHW CW8 .... 151 M1
Kennelwood Rd NWCHE CW9 .. 103 J5
Kennerley Rd OFTN SK2 .... 47 G7
Kennerley's La WILM/AE SK9 .. 84 C2
Kennet CI WILM/AE SK9 .... 84 D2
Kenneth Rd WDN WA8 .... 52 C4
Kennett Rd NTHM/RTH M23 .... 63 C1
Kennet Wy MCFLDS SK11 ...... 137 M4
Kenninghall Rd WYTH/NTH M22 .. 63 K1
Kennington Crs CQ CH5 .... 142 D8
Kensington Av WARRS WA4 .... 57 J2
Kensington CI ALS/KID ST7 .... 240 F1
   BURS/TUN ST6 .... 243 L8
   WILM/AE SK9 .... 84 A6
   WSFD CW7 .... 177 J5
Kensington Dr NANT CW5 ...... 237 K8
Kensington Gdns
   HALE/TIMP WA15 .... 61 M3
Kensington Gn CHSW/BR CH4 .. 168 F8
Kensington Gv ALT WA14 .... 42 E4
Kensington Rd EDGY/DAV SK3 .. 46 B5
   EP CH65 .... 10 B8
Kensington Wy NWCHE CW9 .. 153 L1
Kent Av CHD/CHDH SK8 .... 46 C8
   CQ CH5 .... 142 B7
   MCFLDN SK10 .... 112 C6
Kent CI WHITCH SY13 .... 270 B5
Kent Dr CONG CW12 .... 184 D8
Kent Gv RUNC WA7 .... 9 K4
Kentmere Av WSFD CW7 .... 177 K2
Kentmere CI CHD/CHDH SK8 .. 64 B1
Kentmere PI
   WARRN/WOL WA2 .... 37 G1
Kentmere Rd HALE/TIMP WA15 .. 43 J6
Kentmore CI HTNM SK4 .... 45 L2
Kenton Rd HLWD L26 .... 50 F5
Kentridge Dr GTS/LS CH66 .... 120 D1
Kent Rd CHNE CH2 .... 145 M7
   EDGY/DAV SK3 .... 46 B4
   IRL M44 .... 31 J7
   PART M31 .... 40 E2
   WARRW/BUR WA5 .... 36 C8
Kent's Green La CW/HAS CW1 .. 222 E5
Kent's La CW/HAS CW1 .... 221 J3
Kentstone Av HTNM SK4 .... 45 K1
Kent St WARRS WA4 .... 5 J9
   WDN WA8 .... 7 J3
Kentwell Dr MCFLDN SK10 .... 138 C2
Kenview CI WDN WA8 .... 52 A8
Kenwick CI GTS/LS CH66 ...... 120 C1
Kenwood Av BRAM/HZG SK7 .. 65 K7
   CHD/CHDH SK8 .... 45 G6
   HALE/TIMP WA15 .... 43 H7
Kenworthy La WYTH/NTH M22 .. 44 D2
Kenworthy St BURS/TUN ST6 .. 243 L8
Kenyon Av SALE M33 .... 43 L2
   WARRW/BUR WA5 .... 35 L7
Kenyon La GOL/RIS/CU WA3 .. 23 M6
Kepwick Dr MPL/ROM SK6 ...... 63 L3
Kerfoot CI WYTH/NTH M22 ...... 44 E4
Kerfoot St WARRN/WOL WA2 .... 4 F2

Keristal Av CHSE CH3 .... 170 A5
Kerne CI NTHM/RTH M23 .... 44 A3
Kerridge CI MWCH CW10 .... 179 H4
Kerridge Rd MCFLDN SK10 .... 139 H1
Kerris CI WYTH/NTH M22 .... 63 L3
Kersal CI HALE/TIMP WA15 ...... 43 J5
Kershaw Av SALE M33 .... 43 K2
Kershaw Gv MCFLDS SK11 ...... 14 C5
Kershaw Rd WDN WA8 .... 6 B2
Kershaw Wy NEWLW WA12 ...... 22 C7
Kestral Gv HLWD L26 .... 50 D3
Kestrel Av KNUT WA16 .... 107 H1
Kestrel CI BIDD ST8 .... 227 H6
   CONG CW12 .... 207 L3
   NANT CW5 .... 20 C6
   MWCH CW10 .... 179 K7
   WSFD CW7 .... 177 J7
Kestrel Dr CW/HAS CW1 .... 221 H5
Kestrel La GOL/RIS/CU WA3 .... 29 L3
Kestrel Rd NWCHW CW8 .... 12 B5
Kestrels Wy RUNC WA7 .... 73 M6
Keswick Av CHD/CHDH SK8 .... 64 B1
   MCFLDS SK11 .... 137 M7
   WARRN/WOL WA2 .... 37 J2
Keswick CI CHNE CH2 .... 146 A7
   CW/SHV CW2 .... 237 L1
   IRL M44 .... 31 K8
   MCFLDS SK11 .... 137 M7
   WDN WA8 .... 52 C3
   WSFD CW7 .... 177 K2
Keswick Ct CONG CW12 .... 207 G3
Keswick Crs WARRN/WOL WA2 .. 37 J2
Keswick Dr BRAM/HZG SK7 .... 65 J7
   FROD/HEL WA6 .... 99 H4
Keswick Rd HALE/TIMP WA15 .. 43 K6
   MPL/ROM SK6 .... 67 L4
Ketland CI CQ CH5 .... 142 C6
Ketland PI CQ CH5 .... 142 C6
Kettell Av CW/HAS CW1 .... 220 F6
Kettle La AUD/MAD/W CW3 .... 274 C3
Kettleshulme Wy POY/DIS SK12 .. 87 G2
Kew Dr CHD/CHDH SK8 .... 64 E2
Keyes CI GOL/RIS/CU WA3 ...... 29 M8
Keyes Gdns GOL/RIS/CU WA3 .. 29 M8
Keysbrook CHSE CH3 .... 214 C2
Keysbrook Av CHSE CH3 .... 214 C2
Kidderton CI NANT CW5 .... 234 E5
Kidderton La NANT CW5 .... 234 E5
Kidsgrove Bank ALS/KID ST7 .. 243 H4
Kidsgrove Rd BURS/TUN ST6 .. 243 J4
Kilbuck La RNFD/HAY WA11 .... 22 A4
Kilburn CI CHD/CHDH SK8 ...... 64 B5
Kilburn Rd EDGY/DAV SK3 .... 2 B9
Kildare CI SPK/HALE L24 .... 71 K2
Kildonan Rd WARRS WA4 .... 57 C2
Kilford CI WARRW/BUR WA5 .... 36 E2
Killingworth La
   GOL/RIS/CU WA3 .... 30 B7
Killins La CQ CH5 .... 142 A6
Kilmorey Pk CHNE CH2 .... 17 L1
Kilmorey Park Av CHNE CH2 .... 17 K1
Kilmorey Park Rd CHNE CH2 .... 17 K1
Kilmory Av WLTN L25 .... 50 C2
Kiln Cft MPL/ROM SK6 .... 47 M3
Kilncroft RUNC WA7 .... 74 B7
Kiln Croft La WILM/AE SK9 ...... 64 E8
Kiln La NANT CW5 .... 253 H4
Kilsby Dr WDN WA8 .... 53 L2
Kilshaw Rd WARRW/BUR WA5 .. 26 F8
Kilsyth CI WARRN/WOL WA2 .... 28 F8
Kilworth Av SALE M33 .... 42 F8
Kimberley Av MPL/ROM SK6 .... 48 B2
Kimberley Dr WARRS WA4 ...... 56 C3
Kimberley PI AIMK WN4 .... 22 C1
Kimberley St EDGY/DAV SK3 .... 46 B4
   WARRW/BUR WA5 .... 4 A6
Kinburn Rd BNG/LEV M19 ...... 45 K2
Kinder Dr CW/SHV CW2 .... 237 K1
   MPL/ROM SK6 .... 49 G6
Kinder Gv MPL/ROM SK6 .... 48 E2
Kinder St EDGY/DAV SK3 .... 2 E9
Kinderton CI KNUT WA16 .... 59 J8
Kinderton CI MWCH CW10 .... 179 J3
King Edward Dr FLINT CH6 .... 116 A7
King Edward Rd KNUT WA16 .. 106 F2
   MCFLDN SK10 .... 14 F4
King Edward St CQ CH5 .... 142 B6
   MCFLDN SK10 .... 14 F4
   MWCH CW10 .... 179 J4
   WARR WA1 .... 37 L5
Kingfisher CI
   AUD/MAD/W CW3 .... 267 M5
   CHSE CH3 .... 228 F3
   CONG CW12 .... 207 L3
   CW/HAS CW1 .... 220 F5
   GOL/RIS/CU WA3 .... 29 M8
   NANT CW5 .... 20 F1
   RUNC WA7 .... 73 M7
Kingfisher Dr WSFD CW7 ...... 177 K6
Kingfisher Gv NWCHE CW9 .... 104 F7
Kingfisher Rd OFTN SK2 .... 47 J6
King George Av NWCHW CW9 .. 13 L4
King George CI AIMK WN4 ...... 22 B1
King George Crs WARR WA1 .... 37 L5
King George Rd
   RNFD/HAY WA11 .... 22 A5
King George St CQ CH5 .... 142 A6
Kingham CI WLTN L25 .... 50 C2
King James Ct RUNC WA7 ...... 73 L1
King PI NANT CW5 .... 20 F5
King's Acre ALT WA14 .... 61 C3
Kings Av CHD/CHDH SK8 .... 45 G8
   FLINT CH6 .... 116 B7
   GOL/RIS/CU WA3 .... 23 K4
Kingsbridge CI MPL/ROM SK6 .. 48 E5
Kingsbury CI WARRS WA4 ...... 56 F4
King's CI BRAM/HZG SK7 .... 65 M2
   CHSW/BR CH4 .... 168 F7
   WILM/AE SK9 .... 84 A5
King's Ct NANT CW5 .... 20 C6
   RDSH SK5 .... 3 G2
King's Crs MWCH CW10 .... 179 J2
King's Crs East CHSE CH3 ...... 170 A3
King's Crs West CHSE CH3 ...... 170 A3
Kingsdale Av RAIN/WH L35 .... 33 K1
Kingsdale Rd WARRW/BUR WA5 .. 35 M5

Kingsdown Rd WYTH/NTH M22 .. 63 J3
Kings Dr CHD/CHDH SK8 .... 65 G1
   CW/SHV CW2 .... 237 L4
   FROD/HEL WA6 .... 99 H4
   HTNM SK4 .... 46 A1
   MPL/ROM SK6 .... 49 J4
   WLTN L25 .... 50 B2
Kingsfield Ct CHSW/BR CH4 .. 192 C1
Kingsfield Crs BIDD ST8 .... 227 K4
Kingsfield Dr DID/WITH M20 .. 45 J2
Kingsfield Rd BIDD ST8 .... 227 J5
Kingsgate Rd WYTH/NTH M22 .. 63 J3
Kingshead CI RUNC WA7 .... 74 A2
Kingsholme Rd WYTH/NTH M22 .. 63 J2
Kingsland Rd EDGY/DAV SK3 .. 46 A5
King's La MWCH CW10 .... 156 E5
   NANT CW5 .... 20 C6
   TPLY/KEL CW6 .... 175 K8
   WILM/AE SK9 .... 84 C2
Kingsley Av PS/BROM CH62 .... 93 L1
Kingsley CI ALS/KID ST7 .... 242 D6
   CHSE CH3 .... 170 B4
   CONG CW12 .... 208 A1
   CQ CH5 .... 142 F5
   CW/HAS CW1 .... 222 C8
   EP CH65 .... 10 F7
   FROD/HEL WA6 .... 99 K6
   HALE/TIMP WA15 .... 43 H5
   NWCHW CW8 .... 127 H5
   RUNC WA7 .... 9 H4
   WYTH/NTH M22 .... 44 A4
Kingsley Crs RUNC WA7 .... 9 H5
Kingsley Dr NWCHE CW9 .... 13 J8
   WARRS WA4 .... 56 C5
Kingsley Gdns CHSE CH3 ...... 170 A4
Kingsley Rd ALS/KID ST7 ...... 242 D6
   CHSE CH3 .... 170 B4
   CONG CW12 .... 208 A1
   POY/DIS SK12 .... 66 D8
Kirklands SALE M33 .... 43 G2
Kirkman Fold RAIN/WH L35 .... 33 H1
Kirkstall CI MCFLDN SK10 ...... 14 D1
Kirkstall Rd CHD/CHDH SK8 .... 65 K5
Kirkstone Av WARRN/WOL WA2 .. 37 J1
Kirkstone Crs NWCHW CW8 .... 74 A8
Kirkwall CI CHSE CH3 .... 170 A2
Kirkwood CI CHSE CH3 .... 170 A2
Kishfield La CHF/WBR SK23 .... 89 G7
Kitchener Av IRL M44 .... 31 J8
Kitchen St CH/BCN CH1 .... 16 D6
Kite CI ALS/KID ST7 .... 243 K1
Kitfield Av MWCH CW10 .... 179 J5
Kitt's Moss La BRAM/HZG SK7 .. 65 K6
Kiveton Dr AIMK WN4 .... 22 C2
Knightley AUD/MAD/W CW3 .. 267 M7
Knight Rd WARRW/BUR WA5 .. 26 F6
Knightsbridge STKP SK1 .... 3 G3
Knightsbridge Av
   NWCHE CW9 .... 153 L1
   WARRS WA4 .... 57 J1
Knightsbridge CI WILM/AE SK9 .. 84 D3
Knight's CI MCFLDS SK11 ...... 15 J7
Knights Gn FLINT CH6 .... 116 A6
Knights La TPLY/KEL CW6 ...... 174 D3
Knights Meadow WSFD CW7 .. 177 J1
Knight St BURS/TUN ST6 ...... 243 L8
   DID/WITH M20 .... 45 H2
   MCFLDS SK11 .... 15 J7
Knights Wy CW/SHV CW2 ...... 253 C1
Knightwake Rd NM/HAY SK22 .. 69 G4
Knole Av POY/DIS SK12 .... 66 F8
Knoll St NM/HAY SK22 .... 69 H4
Knottingley Dr GTS/LS CH66 .. 94 C7
Knotty La CONG CW12 .... 209 C4
Knotty Ms WLTN L25 .... 50 F3
Knowe Av WYTH/NTH M22 ...... 63 K3
The Knowe NSTN CH64 .... 93 C4
Knowlbank Rd ALS/KID ST7 .. 255 M6
Knowle CI GTS/LS CH66 .... 120 C1
Knowle Pk WILM/AE SK9 .... 84 C1
Knowle Rd BIDD ST8 .... 227 J5
   MPL/ROM SK6 .... 49 K6
Knowles St WDN WA8 .... 7 L1
Knowl Hey Rd HLWD L26 .... 51 G6
Knowl La CHSE CH3 .... 211 L7
The Knowl CHSE CH3 .... 211 M7
Knowsley Av GOL/RIS/CU WA3 .. 23 H3
Knowsley Crs STKP SK1 .... 3 M8
Knowsley Dr LEIGH WN7 .... 24 D2
   WDN WA8 .... 51 J4
Knowsley La ALS/KID ST7 ...... 225 L8
Knowsley Rd BRAM/HZG SK7 .. 66 F4
   CHNE CH2 .... 146 A8
   MCFLDS SK11 .... 138 C7
   RAIN/WH L35 .... 33 K2
   STKP SK1 .... 3 M8
Knutsford Old Rd WARRS WA4 .. 57 C2
Knutsford Rd ALS/KID ST7 .... 224 F7
   HOLMCH CW4 .... 156 F5
   KNUT WA16 .... 107 K1
   MCFLDS SK11 .... 134 F1
   NWCHE CW9 .... 77 C7
   WARRS WA4 .... 5 H9
   WILM/AE SK9 .... 109 L1
Knutsford Wy CH/BCN CH1 .. 168 F2
Knypersley Av OFTN SK2 .... 47 J5
Knype Wy BIDD ST8 .... 227 H6
Kohima Crs CHSE CH3 .... 170 B7
Kronsbec Av GTS/LS CH66 ...... 94 D6
Kylemore Wy HLWD L26 .... 50 E8
Kyle Rd BRAM/HZG SK7 .... 66 F3
Kynaston Dr CHSW/BR CH4 .. 168 C5

Kintore Av BRAM/HZG SK7 ...... 66 F2
Kintore CI WSFD CW7 .... 178 A2
Kintore Dr WARRW/BUR WA5 .. 35 K6
Kipling Av HUY L36 .... 32 A3
   WARRN/WOL WA2 .... 37 J3
Kipling CI OFTN SK2 .... 47 M6
Kipling Crs WDN WA8 .... 6 F4
Kipling Gv STHEL WA9 .... 34 A1
Kipling Rd CH/BCN CH1 .... 144 F7
Kipling Wy CW/HAS CW1 ...... 19 M3
Kirby CI CHNE CH2 .... 145 K7
Kirkacre Av NEWLW WA12 ...... 27 J4
Kirkbeck LEIGH WN7 .... 25 J1
Kirkbride CI NTHLY L27 .... 32 A8
Kirkby Av SALE M33 .... 43 J2
Kirkby Dr SALE M33 .... 43 K2
Kirkby Rd WARRN/WOL WA2 .. 29 M1
Kirkcaldy Av WARRW/BUR WA5 .. 35 K6
Kirkfell Dr HALE/TIMP WA15 .. 43 H5
Kirkham CI GOL/RIS/CU WA3 .. 23 L6
Kirkham CI WARRW/BUR WA5 .. 36 B8
Kirkham Rd CHD/CHDH SK8 .. 64 C4
   LEIGH WN7 .... 24 D2
   WDN WA8 .... 53 J7
Lacey Ct WDN WA8 .... 7 J7
Lacey Gn WILM/AE SK9 .... 84 B3
Lacey Gv WILM/AE SK9 .... 84 C3
Lacey St WDN WA8 .... 7 H7
Lache Hall Crs CHSW/BR CH4 .. 168 F8
Lache La CHSW/BR CH4 .... 191 J3
Lache Park Av CHSW/BR CH4 .. 169 C6
Lacy St STKP SK1 .... 3 G7
Ladies Mile KNUT WA16 .... 106 F2
Ladies Wk NSTN CH64 .... 91 L4
Ladybarn Av GOL/RIS/CU WA3 .. 22 F5
Ladybarn Crs BRAM/HZG SK7 .. 65 M6
Ladybower CHD/CHDH SK8 .... 65 J1
Ladybridge Ri CHD/CHDH SK8 .. 65 J1
Ladybridge Rd CHD/CHDH SK8 .. 65 J1
Ladybrook Av HALE/TIMP WA15 .. 43 H5
Ladybrook Rd BRAM/HZG SK7 .. 65 J1
Ladycroft CI WARR WA1 .... 38 E5
Ladyfield St WILM/AE SK9 ...... 84 B5
Ladyfield Ter WILM/AE SK9 .... 84 B5
Ladygates AUD/MAD/W CW3 .. 255 C6
Lady Helen Wk NANT CW5 ...... 20 F5
Lady La GOL/RIS/CU WA3 .... 29 J3
   KNUT WA16 .... 82 C5
Ladypit Rd CHF/WBR SK23 ...... 69 M8
Ladypool SPK/HALE L24 .... 71 J3
Ladys CI POY/DIS SK12 .... 66 E8
Ladysmith Av AIMK WN4 .... 22 C1
Ladysmith Rd DID/WITH M20 .. 45 J2
Ladysmith St EDGY/DAV SK3 .. 46 E5
Ladythorn Av MPL/ROM SK6 .. 49 C7
Ladythorn Crs BRAM/HZG SK7 .. 65 M6
Ladythorn Gv BRAM/HZG SK7 .. 65 M6
Ladythorn Rd BRAM/HZG SK7 .. 65 M6
Ladywell CI BRAM/HZG SK7 .... 66 A2
Lady Wk WARRW/BUR WA5 .... 36 C3
Lagonda CI BIDD ST8 .... 227 H7
Lagos Gv WSFD CW7 .... 177 L2
Laidon Av CW/SHV CW2 .... 238 A4
Laira St WARRN/WOL WA2 .... 5 J3
Laithwaite CI STHEL WA9 .... 34 B1
Lake House CI NWCHW CW8 .. 128 C3
Lakelands CI MCFLDS SK10 .... 15 L5
Lake La WARRS WA4 .... 76 F7
Lakenheath Rd HLWD L26 ...... 50 E6
Lakeside AUD/MAD/W CW3 .. 255 C6
   CHSW/BR CH4 .... 192 B2
   MCFLDS SK11 .... 186 D4
Lakeside CI WDN WA8 .... 53 L5
Lakeside Dr POY/DIS SK12 ...... 66 E7
   WARR WA1 .... 56 A1
Lakeside Gn OFTN SK2 .... 47 J6
Lakeside Rd LYMM WA13 .... 58 D3
Lakeside Vw NANT CW5 .... 251 L1
Lakes Rd MPL/ROM SK6 .... 49 C6
Lake St OFTN SK2 .... 47 H7
   RAIN/WH L35 .... 32 E3
Lake Vw CONG CW12 .... 207 H2
Lakewood CHSW/BR CH4 ...... 192 B2
Laleham Gn BRAM/HZG SK7 .. 65 L1
Laleston CI WDN WA8 .... 6 C5
Lamberton Dr NTHM/RTH M23 .. 43 M4
Lambert's La CONG CW12 ...... 207 M4
Lamb La GTS/LS CH66 .... 129 C8
Lamb La ALT WA14 .... 61 K7
Lamborne Gv MWCH CW10 .... 179 J3
Lambourn AUD/MAD/W CW3 .. 33 J7
Lambourn CI POY/DIS SK12 .... 66 D8
Lambourn Dr CW/HAS CW1 .. 221 H3
Lambourne CI GTS/LS CH66 .. 120 F4
   WYTH/NTH M22 .... 63 K4
Lambsickle CI RUNC WA7 ...... 72 F6
Lambsickle La RUNC WA7 ...... 72 F6
Lambs La WARR WA1 .... 38 A4
Lamb St ALS/KID ST7 .... 243 C2
Lamerton CI
   WARRW/BUR WA5 .... 35 K2
Lampeter CI
   WARRW/BUR WA5 .... 36 E2
Lampits La CHSE CH3 .... 147 L6
Lamport CI WDN WA8 .... 53 L1
Lampton CI ALT WA14 .... 42 D5
Lanark Av WYTH/NTH M22 ...... 44 D4
Lanark CI BRAM/HZG SK7 ...... 67 C2
Lancashire HI RDSH SK5 .... 3 C3
Lancashire La PART M31 .... 40 E2
Lancaster Av GOL/RIS/CU WA3 .. 23 J4
   RAIN/WH L35 .... 32 D1
   RAIN/WH L35 .... 52 A2
   RUNC WA7 .... 8 D7
Lancaster CI BRAM/HZG SK7 .. 66 D4
   MPL/ROM SK6 .... 48 A3
   WARRN/WOL WA2 .... 37 M2
   WSFD CW7 .... 177 K6
Lancaster Dr CHSE CH3 .... 170 B2
Lancaster Flds CW/HAS CW1 .. 19 M8
Lancaster Pk CHSW/BR CH4 .. 190 A4
Lancaster Rd DID/WITH M20 .. 45 J2
   IRL M44 .... 31 J7
   WDN WA8 .... 53 C1
   WILM/AE SK9 .... 84 E3
Lancaster St STKP SK1 .... 3 J3
   WARRW/BUR WA5 .... 4 D8
Lancelot Rd WYTH/NTH M22 .. 63 M2
Lancelyn Dr WILM/AE SK9 ...... 84 C4
Lancer Ct RUNC WA7 .... 73 L1
Lancers Cft GTS/LS CH66 ...... 120 E3
Lancia CI BIDD ST8 .... 227 H7
Lancing Av DID/WITH M20 ...... 45 K1
   WARRN/WOL WA2 .... 28 A8
Lancing CI WLTN L25 .... 50 D3
Lancing Rd EP CH65 .... 11 G9
Lancing Wy WLTN L25 .... 50 D3
Land Cut La GOL/RIS/CU WA3 .. 38 D1
Lander CI WARRW/BUR WA5 .. 36 D5
Landkey CI NTHM/RTH M23 .... 43 M2
Land La WILM/AE SK9 .... 84 C6
Landor CI GOL/RIS/CU WA3 .... 23 L4
Landrake Gv BURS/TUN ST6 .. 243 L5
Landscape Dene FROD/HEL WA6 .. 98 G7
   WARRS WA4 .... 56 B3
Landseer Av NSTN CH64 .... 91 M5
Landseer Dr MCFLDN SK10 .... 137 L4
   MPL/ROM SK6 .... 49 H5
Landside LEIGH WN7 .... 24 F7
Landswood Pk NWCHW CW8 .. 129 H8

L

Laburnam CI ALS/KID ST7 ...... 242 E4
Laburnam Av CW/SHV CW2 .... 237 L2
   WARR WA1 .... 38 C5
Laburnum CI CONG CW12 .... 183 M8
   HALE/TIMP WA15 .... 43 H7
Laburnum Crs NWCHW CW8 .. 129 H1
Laburnum Farm CI
   NSTN CH64 .... 92 A7
Laburnum Gv CHSW/BR CH4 .. 168 E6
   CW/HAS CW1 .... 221 K6
   GTS/LS CH66 .... 121 C4
   NWCHW CW8 .... 128 C3
   RUNC WA7 .... 9 K7
Laburnum La HALE/TIMP WA15 .. 61 L4
   WARRW/BUR WA5 .... 35 J6
   MCFLDS SK11 .... 138 C7
Laburnum Rd GOL/RIS/CU WA3 .. 23 M4
   IRL M44 .... 31 K7
   MCFLDS SK11 .... 138 C7
Laburnum St AIMK WN4 .... 22 B2
Lacey Av WILM/AE SK9 .... 84 B4

Lane Ends *MPL/ROM* SK6 .... 48 D1
Lane Head Av *GOL/RIS/CU* WA3 .... 23 L4
Lanehead Rd *CHF/WBR* SK23 .... 89 J7
Laneside Dr *BRAM/HZG* SK7 .... 66 A3
Laneside Rd *DID/WITH* M20 .... 45 J4
  NM/HAY SK22 .... 69 L5
The Lane *MALPAS* SY14 .... 257 G8
Langbar *RAIN/WH* L35 .... 32 E2
Langcliffe Cl *GOL/RIS/CU* WA3 .... 29 L1
Langdale Av *GOL/RIS/CU* WA3 .... 23 J3
  LYMM WA13 .... 58 F1
Langdale Cl *CHD/CHDH* SK8 .... 64 C1
  HALE/TIMP WA15 .... 42 E7
  MCFLDS SK11 .... 137 M7
  MPL/ROM SK6 .... 67 L4
  WARRN/WOL WA2 .... 37 L1
  WDN WA8 .... 52 C4
  WSFD CW7 .... 177 K2
Langdale Ct *CONG* CW12 .... 207 G3
Langdale Rd *BRAM/HZG* SK7 .... 65 J7
  CW/SHV CW2 .... 237 K1
  PART M31 .... 40 E1
  RUNC WA7 .... 9 J4
  SALE M33 .... 42 E3
Langdale Wy *FROD/HEL* WA6 .... 99 J3
Langfield *GOL/RIS/CU* WA3 .... 23 L5
Langford *SPK/HALE* L24 .... 71 J3
Langford Ct *CHSE* CH3 .... 172 C2
Langford Dr *LEIGH* WN7 .... 24 E2
Langford Rd *NWCHE* CW9 .... 131 G1
Langford St *MCFLDS* SK11 .... 14 E5
Langford Wy *WARRS* WA4 .... 57 K8
Langham Gv *HALE/TIMP* WA15 .... 43 H4
Langham Rd *ALT* WA14 .... 61 J2
  HTNM SK4 .... 46 B3
Langland Cl *WARRW/BUR* WA5 .... 4 B3
Langley Av *BRAM/HZG* SK7 .... 66 B3
Langley Cl *GOL/RIS/CU* WA3 .... 23 J3
  SBCH CW11 .... 204 C4
Langley Dr *WILM/AE* SK9 .... 84 E1
Langley Hall Cl *MCFLDS* SK11 .... 139 H8
Langley Rd *MCFLDS* SK11 .... 163 H1
  NWCHE CW9 .... 13 K7
Langport Dr *CHSE* CH3 .... 170 C2
Langston Gn *BRAM/HZG* SK7 .... 66 A3
  WDN WA8 .... 52 B1
Langton Gn *WARR* WA1 .... 38 D5
Langwell Cl *GOL/RIS/CU* WA3 .... 30 A7
Lanreath Cl *MCFLDN* SK10 .... 137 K3
Lansbury Rd *HUY* L36 .... 32 A2
Lansdown Cl *BRAM/HZG* SK7 .... 65 J5
Lansdowne *FROD/HEL* WA6 .... 99 K6
  GOL/RIS/CU WA3 .... 29 L2
Lansdowne Av *MPL/ROM* SK6 .... 48 D2
Lansdowne Gv
  CHSW/BR CH4 .... 169 G5
Lansdowne Rd *ALT* WA14 .... 42 D6
  CHSE CH3 .... 171 K1
  CW/HAS CW1 .... 19 L3
Lansdowne St *MCFLDN* SK10 .... 15 K3
Lansdown Rd *BRAM/HZG* SK7 .... 190 B1
Lantern Vw *NM/HAY* SK22 .... 69 H3
Lapwing Cl *GOL/RIS/CU* WA3 .... 23 K4
  WSFD CW7 .... 177 J7
Lapwing Ct *HLWD* L26 .... 50 E3
Lapwing Dr *RUNC* WA7 .... 74 A6
Lapwing La *MCFLDS* SK11 .... 135 H5
  WARRS WA4 .... 54 F5
Lapwing Rd *ALS/KID* ST7 .... 243 K2
Larch Av *CHD/CHDH* SK8 .... 65 G3
  CQ CH5 .... 142 B8
  CW/SHV CW2 .... 238 F7
  MCFLDS SK11 .... 138 A7
  NEWLW WA12 .... 27 J2
  WARRW/BUR WA5 .... 35 L7
  WDN WA8 .... 53 H2
Larch Cl *ALS/KID* ST7 .... 243 G4
  GOL/RIS/CU WA3 .... 23 M6
  MPL/ROM SK6 .... 48 C1
  NTHM/RTH M23 .... 43 J4
  NWCHW CW8 .... 128 D5
  POY/DIS SK12 .... 86 F1
  RUNC WA7 .... 9 M8
Larchdale Cl *GTS/LS* CH66 .... 120 F4
Larchfields *CH/BCN* CH1 .... 144 A4
Larch Ri *MCFLDS* SK10 .... 111 K6
Larch Rd *CW/SHV* CW2 .... 237 L2
  PART M31 .... 40 E1
  RUNC WA7 .... 9 M9
Larchtree Cl *NWCHW* CW8 .... 103 H8
Larchway *BRAM/HZG* SK7 .... 65 J5
  CHSW/BR CH4 .... 168 E6
Larchway *MPL/ROM* SK6 .... 67 M5
Larchways *WARRS* WA4 .... 56 D7
Larchwood Dr *WILM/AE* SK9 .... 84 E4
Lark Av *ALS/KID* ST7 .... 243 K1
Larkfield *ALS/KID* ST7 .... 243 G3
Larkfield Av *WARR* WA1 .... 37 M5
Lark Hall Cl *MCFLDS* SK10 .... 139 G4
Lark Hall Crs *MCFLDS* SK10 .... 139 G5
Lark Hall Rd *MCFLDS* SK10 .... 139 G5
Larkhill Cl *HALE/TIMP* WA15 .... 43 H6
Lark Hill Rd *EDGY/DAV* SK3 .... 2 B7
Larkhill Vw *EDGY/DAV* SK3 .... 46 C7
Larkspur Cl *CHSW/BR* CH4 .... 168 F8
  LEIGH WN7 .... 24 F1
  NANT CW5 .... 20 F1
  RUNC WA7 .... 73 M8
Larkstoke Cl *WARRS* WA4 .... 56 F6
Larkswood Dr *OFTN* SK2 .... 47 M7
Larne Av *EDGY/DAV* SK3 .... 46 B5
Larne Dr *CHSW/BR* CH4 .... 167 K8
Larwood Av *HTNM* SK4 .... 46 A3
Laskey La *WARRS* WA4 .... 38 F8
Latchford St *WARRS* WA4 .... 57 G1
Latebrook Cl *BURS/TUN* ST6 .... 243 J5
Latham Av *FROD/HEL* WA6 .... 124 B3
  NEWLW WA12 .... 22 C8
  RUNC WA7 .... 9 L4
Latham Rd *SBCH* CW11 .... 204 A7
Latham St *WSFD* CW7 .... 177 J3
Lathom Av *WARRN/WOL* WA2 .... 37 H4
Lathom Gv *SALE* M33 .... 43 L1
Lathom Rd *IRL* M44 .... 31 M4
Lathom Wy *MCFLDN* SK10 .... 15 L1
Launceston Cl *RUNC* WA7 .... 74 C6

Launceston Dr
  BRAM/HZG SK7 .... 65 M5
  WARRW/BUR WA5 .... 177 H5
Laura St *CW/SHV* CW2 .... 19 H9
Laurel Av *CHD/CHDH* SK8 .... 45 K7
  NEWLW WA12 .... 27 K2
  WARR WA1 .... 38 D5
Laurel Bank *WARRS* WA4 .... 57 J3
  WDN WA8 .... 53 G1
  WSFD CW7 .... 177 K4
Laurel Cl *MWCH* CW10 .... 179 H2
  NWCHW CW8 .... 103 G8
  SBCH CW11 .... 204 C7
Laurel Dr *ALS/KID* ST7 .... 243 L1
  CW/SHV CW2 .... 237 M2
  EP CH65 .... 121 H2
  HALE/TIMP WA15 .... 43 H8
  NSTN CH64 .... 93 H3
Laurel Gv *CHNE* CH2 .... 170 A1
  GOL/RIS/CU WA3 .... 23 K4
Laurel Pk *TPLY/KEL* CW6 .... 173 G6
Laurels Farm Ct *CHNE* CH2 .... 123 H1
Laurel St *HTNM* SK4 .... 2 E4
Laurel Wk *PART* M31 .... 40 E2
Laurelwood Dr *GTS/LS* CH66 .... 120 E4
Laureston Av *CW/HAS* CW1 .... 19 M3
Lausanne Rd *BRAM/HZG* SK7 .... 65 L1
  RUNC WA7 .... 9 M5
Lavender Cl *NTHM/RTH* M23 .... 43 L3
Lavender Ct *CQ* CH5 .... 142 B6
Lavender Dr *NWCHE* CW9 .... 130 E6
Lavenders Brow *STKP* SK1 .... 3 H5
Lavenham Cl *WARRW/BUR* WA5 .... 66 E4
  MCFLDN SK10 .... 138 C2
Laverock Gv
  AUD/MAD/W CW3 .... 267 M5
Lavington Cl *CHD/CHDH* SK8 .... 46 A6
Lavister Av *BNG/LEV* M19 .... 45 K1
Lavister Cl *NWCHE* CW9 .... 129 M8
Lavister Wks *WRX/GR/LL* LL12 .... 210 C3
Lawford Dr *CW/HAS* CW1 .... 220 F4
Lawn Av *WARR* WA1 .... 37 M4
Lawn Dr *CHNE* CH2 .... 145 K5
  HALE/TIMP WA15 .... 42 E6
Lawnsdale *NWCHW* CW8 .... 123 K1
Lawnswood Gv *CHNE* CH2 .... 123 H1
Lawrence Av *NWCHE* CW9 .... 153 L4
Lawrence Av West
  MWCH CW10 .... 179 J3
Lawrence Cl *HOLMCH* CW4 .... 157 G7
  SBCH CW11 .... 203 K6
Lawrence Pl *POY/DIS* SK12 .... 86 D2
Lawrence Rd *ALT* WA14 .... 42 C6
  BRAM/HZG SK7 .... 66 E1
Lawrence St *CQ* CH5 .... 167 G1
  CW/HAS CW1 .... 18 F4
  NEWLW WA12 .... 27 G1
  STKP SK1 .... 2 F6
Laws Gdns *CHSE* CH3 .... 170 A4
Lawson Av *CHD/CHDH* SK8 .... 45 H7
  CW/SHV CW2 .... 237 J5
  WARR WA1 .... 38 E5
Law St *CHNE* CH2 .... 17 L2
Lawton Av *ALS/KID* ST7 .... 242 D1
  BRAM/HZG SK7 .... 65 L4
Lawton Cl *GOL/RIS/CU* WA3 .... 29 L1
  MPL/ROM SK6 .... 48 C1
Lawton Coppice *ALS/KID* ST7 .... 225 L8
Lawton Crs *BIDD* ST8 .... 227 K4
Lawton Heath Rd *ALS/KID* ST7 .... 224 F6
Lawton Moor Rd
  NTHM/RTH M23 .... 44 A3
Lawton Rd *ALS/KID* ST7 .... 241 K1
  RAIN/WH L35 .... 33 K2
Lawton St *ALS/KID* ST7 .... 226 C8
  BIDD ST8 .... 227 K4
  CONG CW12 .... 207 L2
  CW/SHV CW2 .... 18 F6
Lawton Wy *SBCH* CW11 .... 203 L5
Laxey Av *WARR* WA1 .... 38 D6
Laxton Cl *GTS/LS* CH66 .... 120 F4
Laxton Rd *WLTN* L25 .... 50 C6
Laxton Wy *MWCH* CW10 .... 179 J2
Layland Av *GOL/RIS/CU* WA3 .... 24 E8
Layton Cl *GOL/RIS/CU* WA3 .... 23 M6
  STKP SK1 .... 3 J7
  WLTN L25 .... 50 C2
Layton Dr *MPL/ROM* SK6 .... 48 C1
Layton Rd *MPL/ROM* SK6 .... 48 C1
Lea Av *CW/HAS* CW1 .... 19 L4
Lea Bank *MCFLDS* SK11 .... 14 B5
Leaches La *CQ* CH5 .... 166 E1
Lea Cl *SBCH* CW11 .... 204 C7
Leacroft Rd *GOL/RIS/CU* WA3 .... 30 A6
Lea Cross Gv *WDN* WA8 .... 52 C1
Leadbeaters Rd *MCFLDS* SK11 .... 15 L7
Leader Williams Rd *IRL* M44 .... 31 M3
Leadgate La *CHSE* CH3 .... 195 M2
  NANT CW5 .... 20 B8
Leadsmithy St *MWCH* CW10 .... 179 J3
Leadworks La *CH/BCN* CH1 .... 17 J4
Leafield Dr *CHD/CHDH* SK8 .... 64 F6
Leafield Rd *POY/DIS* SK12 .... 68 C6
  WLTN L25 .... 50 B6
Leaf La *WSFD* CW7 .... 178 A2
Lea Hall Pk *CH/BCN* CH1 .... 145 G1
Leahurst Cl *CHNE* CH2 .... 145 M8
Lea La *CHSE* CH3 .... 212 B1
Leamington Av *NEWLW* WA12 .... 27 J3
Leamington Cl *NSTN* CH64 .... 91 L6
  WARRW/BUR WA5 .... 36 A4
Leamington Rd *CONG* CW12 .... 206 F1
  MCFLDN SK10 .... 137 M3
Leamington St *CW/SHV* CW2 .... 237 M4
Lea Rd *CHD/CHDH* SK8 .... 64 B3
Leas Cl *GTS/LS* CH66 .... 94 C7
Leaside *RUNC* WA7 .... 73 K3
Leaside Wy *WILM/AE* SK9 .... 84 C6
Leas Pas *MWCH* CW10 .... 179 H3
The Leas *HALE/TIMP* WA15 .... 62 B1
Lea St *NM/HAY* SK22 .... 69 G4
Leatham Gv *GOL/RIS/CU* WA3 .... 38 E1
Leather's La *HLWD* L26 .... 50 F5

  CH/BCN CH1 .... 144 F7
  HLWD L26 .... 50 E6
Lichfield St *MWCH* CW10 .... 179 K2
Lichfield Wk *MPL/ROM* SK6 .... 48 A3
Lickers La *RAIN/WH* L35 .... 32 E2
Lidgetts La *MCFLDN* SK10 .... 113 J8
Liebig St *WDN* WA8 .... 7 J5
Liffey Av *WYTH/NTH* M22 .... 63 L1
Light Alders La *POY/DIS* SK12 .... 68 A5
Lightburne Av *LEIGH* WN7 .... 24 E1
Lightburn St *RUNC* WA7 .... 8 F5
Lightfoot Dr *HALE/TIMP* WA15 .... 61 M3
Lightfoot Cl *TPLY/KEL* CW6 .... 173 L2
Lightfoot St *CHNE* CH2 .... 17 K2
Lighthorne Av *EDGY/DAV* SK3 .... 45 H3
Lighthorne Gv *EDGY/DAV* SK3 .... 45 J5
Lighthorne Rd *EDGY/DAV* SK3 .... 45 M5
Lightley Cl *SBCH* CW11 .... 204 A5
Light Oaks Rd *GOL/RIS/CU* WA3 .... 25 J6
Lightwood Green Av
  AUD/MAD/W CW3 .... 273 G2
Lilac Av *KNUT* WA16 .... 106 C3
  WARRW/BUR WA5 .... 36 A7
Lilac Crs *RUNC* WA7 .... 9 L6
Lilac Dr *CH/BCN* CH1 .... 12 D5
Lilac Gv *GTS/LS* CH66 .... 121 G4
  WARRS WA4 .... 56 E3
Lilac St *OFTN* SK2 .... 46 F6
Lilford Av *WARRW/BUR* WA5 .... 35 M6
Lilford Dr *WARRW/BUR* WA5 .... 4 D3
Lilford Sq *MCFLDS* SK11 .... 138 D7
Lilford St *WARRW/BUR* WA5 .... 4 D3
Lily Av *NEWLW* WA12 .... 27 J2
Lily Cl *EDGY/DAV* SK3 .... 46 D7
Lily La *MWCH* CW10 .... 156 A6
Lily Pl *AIMK* WN4 .... 22 C2
Limbrick Rd *ALS/KID* ST7 .... 255 M3
Lime Av *FROD/HEL* WA6 .... 99 J4
  NM/HAY SK22 .... 69 K3
  NWCHE CW9 .... 13 H8
  WDN WA8 .... 128 D4
Lime Cl *GOL/RIS/CU* WA3 .... 40 A2
  MWCH CW10 .... 179 H2
  SBCH CW11 .... 204 A5
  TPLY/KEL CW6 .... 197 K2
Limefield Av *LYMM* WA13 .... 58 F2
Lime Gv *ALS/KID* ST7 .... 241 L2
  CHD/CHDH SK8 .... 45 K6
  CHNE CH2 .... 17 M1
  CHNE CH2 .... 123 C1
  CHSW/BR CH4 .... 168 D6
  CW/SHV CW2 .... 238 C8
  GOL/RIS/CU WA3 .... 23 K6
  HALE/TIMP WA15 .... 43 H6
  MCFLDS SK10 .... 15 K5
  RUNC WA7 .... 9 L6
  WSFD CW7 .... 178 A3
Limeheath Pl *BURS/TUN* ST6 .... 243 L7
Lime Kiln La *ALS/KID* ST7 .... 242 E2
  MPL/ROM SK6 .... 49 G7
Limekiln La *WARRW/BUR* WA5 .... 35 L1
Limes La *WARRS* WA4 .... 76 C5
The Limes *GOL/RIS/CU* WA3 .... 24 D8
  WRX/GR/LL LL12 .... 210 E3
Lime St *CW/HAS* CW1 .... 221 J6
  EP CH65 .... 10 E4
Lime Tree Av *CW/HAS* CW1 .... 221 K5
  EP CH65 .... 10 E4
Lime Tree Cl *GTS/LS* CH66 .... 121 G4
Lime Tree Dr *CHSE* CH3 .... 228 F3
Limetree La *KNUT* WA16 .... 59 K6
Limeways *WARRS* WA4 .... 56 E7
Limewood Crs *NWCHW* CW8 .... 103 H8
Limewood Gv *NWCHW* CW8 .... 103 H8
Linbeck Gv *GOL/RIS/CU* WA3 .... 23 J3
Lincoln Av *CHD/CHDH* SK8 .... 64 B5
  GOL/RIS/CU WA3 .... 23 K3
  IRL M44 .... 31 J8
Lincoln Cl *GOL/RIS/CU* WA3 .... 24 C4
  HUY L36 .... 32 B1
  MCFLDN SK10 .... 113 K7
  RUNC WA7 .... 73 H5
  WARR WA1 .... 38 E6
Lincoln Dr *AIMK* WN4 .... 22 C2
  CHNE CH2 .... 146 A7
  HALE/TIMP WA15 .... 43 H7
Lincoln Ri *MPL/ROM* SK6 .... 48 A3
Lincoln Rd *ALS/KID* ST7 .... 242 F2
  CH/BCN CH1 .... 144 F7
  CQ CH5 .... 166 A2
  GTS/LS CH66 .... 120 D1
  WILM/AE SK9 .... 84 E3
Lincoln Sq *WDN* WA8 .... 53 H2
Lincoln St *CW/HAS* CW1 .... 18 D2
Lincoln Wy *RAIN/WH* L35 .... 33 K3
Lincombe Hey *WYTH/NTH* M22 .... 112 C5
Lincombe Rd *WYTH/NTH* M22 .... 63 J1
Linda Dr *BRAM/HZG* SK7 .... 66 D3
Lindale Cl *CONG* CW12 .... 185 G7
Linda Rd *BURS/TUN* ST6 .... 243 L7
Lindbury Av *OFTN* SK2 .... 47 J5
Linden Av *HALE/TIMP* WA15 .... 42 E7
  WHITCH SY13 .... 269 M5
Linden Ct *CONG* CW12 .... 208 A4
  GTS/LS CH66 .... 120 F4
  LYMM WA13 .... 39 M8
  WARR WA1 .... 38 D5
Linden Dr *BIDD* ST8 .... 227 J3
  CHNE CH2 .... 146 F3
  CW/HAS CW1 .... 19 L5
  FROD/HEL WA6 .... 124 D3
Linden Gv *BRAM/HZG* SK7 .... 65 K8
  CHNE CH2 .... 146 A8
  CHSW/BR CH4 .... 168 D6
  OFTN SK2 .... 47 J5
Linden Rd *CHD/CHDH* SK8 .... 65 G1
Linden Wy *MPL/ROM* SK6 .... 68 A5
  WDN WA8 .... 33 M8
Lindfield *WARRS* WA4 .... 55 H7
Lindfield Est North
  WILM/AE SK9 .... 84 A6

Lindfield Est South
  WILM/AE SK9 .... 83 M6
Lindi Av *WARRS* WA4 .... 57 H3
Lindisfarne Av *EP* CH65 .... 121 J3
  GOL/RIS/CU WA3 .... 24 C3
  SALE M33 .... 43 H3
Lindisfarne Cl *MWCH* CW10 .... 179 H3
Lindley Av *WARRS* WA4 .... 37 M8
Lindop Cl *KNUT* WA16 .... 107 J2
Lindop Rd *HALE/TIMP* WA15 .... 61 M3
Lindops La
  AUD/MAD/W CW3 .... 267 M5
Lindow Ct *MPL/ROM* SK6 .... 47 K1
Lindow Fold Dr *WILM/AE* SK9 .... 83 K8
Lindow La *WILM/AE* SK9 .... 83 L6
Lindow St *SALE* M33 .... 43 M1
Lindrick Cl *MCFLDN* SK10 .... 112 C8
Lindrum Av *MCFLDS* SK11 .... 162 D2
Lindsay Av *CHD/CHDH* SK8 .... 65 H5
Lindsay St *STHEL* WA9 .... 34 E1
Lindsay Wk *NWCHW* CW8 .... 128 A8
Lindsay Wy *ALS/KID* ST7 .... 224 A8
Lindsell Rd *ALT* WA14 .... 42 C4
Lindsgate Dr
  HALE/TIMP WA15 .... 43 H5
Lindsworth Cl
  WARRW/BUR WA5 .... 36 C6
Lindwall Cl *NTHM/RTH* M23 .... 44 B2
Linear Vw *NEWLW* WA12 .... 27 J4
Linehan Cl *HTNM* SK4 .... 45 K2
Linen Hall Pl *CH/BCN* CH1 .... 16 F6
Lines Rd *IRL* M44 .... 31 M4
Lingard Rd *WYTH/NTH* M22 .... 44 D3
Lingdale Rd *CHD/CHDH* SK8 .... 64 F2
Lingfield Av *BRAM/HZG* SK7 .... 66 F2
  SALE M33 .... 42 B2
Lingfield Cl *MCFLDN* SK10 .... 112 C8
Lingfield Dr *CW/HAS* CW1 .... 221 J5
Lingfield Rd *RUNC* WA7 .... 8 D6
Lingley Green Av
  WARRW/BUR WA5 .... 35 J6
Lingley Rd *WARRW/BUR* WA5 .... 35 K6
Linglongs Av *CHF/WBR* SK23 .... 89 J7
Linglongs Rd *CHF/WBR* SK23 .... 89 J7
Lingmell Gdns *HOLMCH* CW4 .... 180 F1
Lings Wk *WYTH/NTH* M22 .... 63 L3
Lingwell Av *WDN* WA8 .... 52 D2
Lingwood Rd *WARRW/BUR* WA5 .... 35 L6
Linhope Cl *HTNM* SK4 .... 45 L1
Link Rd *HUY* L36 .... 32 B3
  SALE M33 .... 42 D2
Links Av *GTS/LS* CH66 .... 94 C5
Linkside Av *WARRN/WOL* WA2 .... 28 B6
Linkside Wy *GTS/LS* CH66 .... 120 F4
Links Rd *MPL/ROM* SK6 .... 48 F8
  WILM/AE SK9 .... 109 L1
Linksway *CHD/CHDH* SK8 .... 45 G8
  CHNE CH2 .... 145 J5
  CONG CW12 .... 207 L4
Linksway Cl *CONG* CW12 .... 207 M4
The Link *WILM/AE* SK9 .... 84 D1
Linkway *RUNC* WA7 .... 9 L7
Linley Gv *ALS/KID* ST7 .... 241 M1
Linley La *ALS/KID* ST7 .... 242 A1
Linley Rd *ALS/KID* ST7 .... 241 M2
  CHD/CHDH SK8 .... 65 H4
Linnards La *NWCHE* CW9 .... 104 F7
Linner Rd *SPK/HALE* L24 .... 70 D1
Linnet Cl *NEWLW* WA12 .... 27 J1
  OFTN SK2 .... 47 M7
  WARRN/WOL WA2 .... 37 K1
  WSFD CW7 .... 178 A4
Linnet Gv *GOL/RIS/CU* WA3 .... 38 E1
  MCFLDN SK10 .... 14 A2
Linnett Cl *CW/HAS* CW1 .... 221 G5
Linnet Wy *BIDD* ST8 .... 227 L4
Linney Rd *BRAM/HZG* SK7 .... 65 K2
Linton Av *GOL/RIS/CU* WA3 .... 22 F2
Linwood Cl *RUNC* WA7 .... 74 C7
Linwood Gv *RAIN/WH* L35 .... 32 E2
Linwood Wy *BURS/TUN* ST6 .... 243 L7
Lion St *CONG* CW12 .... 207 G2
Lisburn Av *SALE* M33 .... 43 G1
Lisburne Av *OFTN* SK2 .... 47 K6
Lisburne Cl *OFTN* SK2 .... 47 K6
Liskeard Cl *RUNC* WA7 .... 74 B6
Liskeard Dr *BRAM/HZG* SK7 .... 65 K5
Lismore Av *EDGY/DAV* SK3 .... 46 B5
Lisson Gv *HALE/TIMP* WA15 .... 61 L2
Lister Cl *MWCH* CW10 .... 179 K6
Lister Rd *RUNC* WA7 .... 9 L1
Litherland Av *WYTH/NTH* M22 .... 63 L2
Litherland Rd *SALE* M33 .... 43 L1
Little Abbey Gtwy
  CH/BCN CH1 .... 16 F4
Little Aston Cl *MCFLDN* SK10 .... 112 C8
Littlebrook Cl *CHD/CHDH* SK8 .... 46 C8
Little Brook Rd *SALE* M33 .... 42 C3
Little Chell La *BURS/TUN* ST6 .... 243 M7
Littlecote Gdns *WARRS* WA4 .... 76 D1
Littledale Rd *WARRW/BUR* WA5 .... 35 M5
Littledales La *NWCHW* CW8 .... 128 D7
Little Egerton St *STKP* SK1 .... 2 F4
Littlegate *RUNC* WA7 .... 9 M8
Little Gn *GTS/LS* CH66 .... 120 D1
Littleheath
  AUD/MAD/W CW3 .... 264 A7
Little Heath La *ALT* WA14 .... 41 K7
Little Heath Rd *CHSE* CH3 .... 170 E3
  SPK/HALE L24 .... 70 E2
Little La *NSTN* CH64 .... 91 H3
Little Meadow Cl *MCFLDN* SK10 .... 112 B5
Little Meadow Rd *ALT* WA14 .... 61 H3
Little Moss La *ALS/KID* ST7 .... 225 L7
Little Moss La *ALS/KID* ST7 .... 225 L7
Littler La *WSFD* CW7 .... 176 F3
Little Roodee *CQ* CH5 .... 167 H5
Little St John St *CH/BCN* CH1 .... 17 H6
Little Stanney La *CHNE* CH2 .... 121 L4
Littlestone Cl *WDN* WA8 .... 34 A8
Little St *CONG* CW12 .... 207 K2
  MCFLDN SK10 .... 14 F4
Littleton Cl *NWCHE* CW9 .... 129 L8
  WARRW/BUR WA5 .... 36 D8
Littleton La *CHSE* CH3 .... 170 D2

Little Underbank *STKP* SK1 .... 3 G5
Little Wissage *GTS/LS* CH66 .... 120 F2 ◨
Littlewood Rd *WYTH/NTH* M22 .... 44 A8
Littondale Av *RAIN/WH* L35 .... 33 K2 ◨
Littondale Cl *CONG* CW12 .... 184 F7
Liverpool Rd *ALS/KID* ST7 .... 243 G3
  CH/BCN CH1 .... 120 F5
  CHNE CH2 .... 16 F2
  IRL M44 .... 31 M4
  NSTN CH64 .... 91 M2
  WARRW/BUR WA5 .... 4 D7
  WDN WA8 .... 6 E3
  WHITCH SY13 .... 269 M6
Liverpool Rd East *ALS/KID* ST7 .... 242 D1
Liverpool Rd West *ALS/KID* ST7 .... 225 G8
Liverpool Rw *NEWLW* WA12 .... 27 K4
Liverpool St *NWCHE* CW9 .... 130 C4
Livingstone Cl *MCFLDS* SK10 .. 137 M4◨
Livingstone Rd *CH65* 36 D5
Livingstone Rd *EP* CH65 .... 170 C4
Livingstone Wy *MWCH* CW10 .. 179 K6◨
Llanberis Rd *EDGY/DAV* SK3 .... 2 B8
Llandaff Cl *GTS/LS* CH66 .... 120 E3
Llandovery Cl *WSFD* CW7 .... 177 H5 ◨
Llanfair Rd *EDGY/DAV* SK3 .... 2 B8
Llewellyn St *CO* CH5 .... 142 A6
Lloyd Av *CHD/CHDH* SK8 .... 45 G6
Lloyd Cl *CHSE* CH3 .... 228 C2
Lloyd Crs *NEWLW* WA12 .... 26 F1
Lloyd Dr *EP* CH65 .... 121 K3
Lloyd Gdns *ALT* WA14 .... 61 K1◨
Lloyd Pl *CH/BCN* CH1 .... 144 E8
Lloyd Sq *ALT* WA14 .... 42 D8◨
Lloyd St *ALT* WA14 .... 42 D8
  FLINT CH6 .... 116 B5◨
  HTNM SK4 .... 2 D1
Llyndir La *WRX/GR/LL* LL12 .... 210 B3
Llys Cadnant (Cadnant Court)
  CHSW/BR CH4 .... 167 K7◨
Llys Caer *CHSW/BR* CH4 .... 190 A1◨
Loachbrook Av *CONG* CW12 .... 207 G2◨
Lobelia Gv *RUNC* WA7 .... 73 M8◨
Lochinvar Av *GTS/LS* CH66 .... 93 M6
Lochleven Cl *CW/SHV* CW2 .... 238 A5
Lochmaben Cl *HOLMCH* CW4 .. 181 H2◨
Lochmaddy Cl *BRAM/HZG* SK7 .. 66 F3◨
Loch St *RUNC* WA7 .... 9 G1
Locker Av *WARRN/WOL* WA2 .... 37 H2
Lockerbie Cl *HOLMCH* CW4 .... 181 J2
  WARRN/WOL WA2 .... 28 E8
Lockett Cl *WDN* WA8 .... 53 G2
Lockett St *WARRS* WA4 .... 56 F1
Lockgate East *RUNC* WA7 .... 74 C2
Lockgate West *RUNC* WA7 .... 74 C2
Locking Stumps La
  WARRN/WOL WA2 .... 38 B1
Lockitt St *CW/SHV* CW2 .... 19 C6
Lock La *PART* M31 .... 40 D1
Lock Rd *ALT* WA14 .... 42 C6
  WARR WA1 .... 37 M5
Lockside *MPL/ROM* SK6 .... 49 C6
Locksley Cl *HTNM* SK4 .... 2 B3
Lockton La *WARRW/BUR* WA5 .... 4 B2
Lodge Barn Rd *BIDD* ST8 .... 227 M6
Lodge Brow *MCFLDN* SK10 .... 113 C3
Lodge Cl *LYMM* WA13 .... 40 B8
Lodge Ct *HTNM* SK4 .... 45 M2
Lodge Dr *GOL/RIS/CU* WA3 .... 29 M1
  NWCHE CW9 .... 153 M5◨
  WSFD CW7 .... 178 A3
Lodge Farm Cl *BRAM/HZG* SK7 .. 65 L2
Lodgefields Dr *CW/SHV* CW2 .... 220 D8
Lodge Hollow *FROD/HEL* WA6 .. 124 B1◨
Lodge La *CH/BCN* CH1 .... 144 A2
  MWCH CW10 .... 179 L2
  NANT CW5 .... 253 C6
  NEWLW WA12 .... 22 B3
  NWCHE CW9 .... 78 A6
  NWCHE CW9 .... 131 C2
  NWCHW CW8 .... 129 H8
  RUNC WA7 .... 73 L4
  WARRS WA4 .... 101 J4
  WARRW/BUR WA5 .... 4 B2
  WDN WA8 .... 33 H8
Lodge Rd *ALS/KID* ST7 .... 224 C8
  ALS/KID ST7 .... 242 D6
  KNUT WA16 .... 107 J1
  SBCH CW11 .... 203 L7
Lodmore La *WHITCH* SY13 .... 272 C6
Lofthouse Ga *WDN* WA8 .... 52 F1
Logwood Rd *HUY* L36 .... 32 A4
Lomas Cl *BNG/LEV* M19 .... 45 L1◨
Lomas Sq *MCFLDS* SK11 .... 138 D7◨
Lomas St *EDGY/DAV* SK3 .... 2 D9
Lomax Rd *NANT* CW5 .... 237 K6◨
Lombard Ct *ALS/KID* ST7 .... 224 E8
Lomond Av *HALE/TIMP* WA15 .... 62 A1
Lomond Gv *EP* CH65 .... 120 F1
Lomond Wy *WYTH/NTH* M22 .... 63 M2
London *STKP* SK1 .... 3 G6
London Rd *FROD/HEL* WA6 .... 99 H4
  KNUT WA16 .... 156 E1
  MCFLDN SK10 .... 86 C4
  MCFLDN SK10 .... 112 C6
  MCFLDS SK11 .... 162 D1
  NANT CW5 .... 21 J8
  NWCHE CW9 .... 13 H9
  OFTN SK2 .... 47 K8
  SBCH CW11 .... 203 K4
  WARRS WA4 .... 56 D8
  WHITCH SY13 .... 269 M4
  WILM/AE SK9 .... 110 A3
London Rd North *POY/DIS* SK12 .. 66 E8
London Rd South *POY/DIS* SK12 .. 86 D2
London Road Ter
  MCFLDS SK11 .... 138 D7◨
London Rw *NEWLW* WA12 .... 27 K4
London Sq *STKP* SK1 .... 3 G6
Loney St *MCFLDS* SK11 .... 14 E6
Long Acre *NWCHW* CW8 .... 127 K8
  NWCHW CW8 .... 128 C5
Longacres Rd *NSTN* CH64 .... 91 J2
Longacre St *MCFLDS* SK11 .... 14 E5
Longbarn Bvd *WARRN/WOL* WA2.. 38 C2
Long Barn La *WARR* WA1.... 38 D4
  WARRN/WOL WA2 .... 38 B2

Longburgh Cl *CHNE* CH2 .... 17 M2
Longbutt La *LYMM* WA13 .... 58 F2
Longbutts La *MCFLDS* SK11 .... 161 L3
Longcroft Dr *ALT* WA14 .... 42 B8
Longcroft Gv *NTHM/RTH* M23 .... 44 A5
Longdale Dr *CH/BCN* CH1 .... 144 C7
Longden La *MCFLDS* SK11 .... 139 C6
Longden St *MCFLDS* SK11 .... 15 K6
Longdin St *WARRS* WA4 .... 56 F1
Longdown Rd *CONG* CW12 .... 183 M8
Longfield Av *CHD/CHDH* SK8 .... 64 C5
  CHNE CH2 .... 145 L5◨
  HALE/TIMP WA15 .... 43 J6
Longfield Rd *NTHM/RTH* M23 .... 43 M4
  WARRN/WOL WA2 .... 37 J3
Longford St *CW/SHV* CW2 .... 19 C8◨
  WARRN/WOL WA2 .... 5 G2
Long Grain Pl *OFTN* SK2 .... 47 K7
Longham Cl *BRAM/HZG* SK7 .... 65 J3
Long Hey *HALE/TIMP* WA15 .... 62 A1
  RAIN/WH L35 .... 32 D2
Longhey Rd *WYTH/NTH* M22 .... 44 D7
Long Hl *CHF/WBR* SK23 .... 115 M5
Longhill La *AUD/MAD/AV* CW3 .. 264 D5
Longhope Rd *WYTH/NTH* M22 .... 63 H1
Longhorn Cl *MWCH* CW10 .... 179 K3◨
Longhurst La *MPL/ROM* SK6 .... 49 H5
Longlands Dr *NM/HAY* SK22.... 69 H4◨
Longlands Rd *NM/HAY* SK22.... 69 H4
Long La *ALS/KID* ST7 .... 226 E8
  CH/BCN CH1 .... 144 B2
  CHNE CH2 .... 145 L4
  CHSE CH3 .... 194 C1
  CONG CW12 .... 159 C6
  KNUT WA16 .... 133 J5
  MALPAS SY14 .... 231 M4
  MALPAS SY14 .... 245 H2
  MALPAS SY14 .... 246 E2
  MCFLDN SK10 .... 113 H1
  MWCH CW10 .... 179 J4
Long La South *MWCH* CW10 .... 179 J5
Longlevens Rd *WYTH/NTH* M22 .... 63 J2
Longley Av *TPLY/KEL* CW6 .... 149 K6
Longley La *WYTH/NTH* M22 .... 44 D4
Longlooms Rd *EP* CH65 .... 121 K3
Long Marl Dr *WILM/AE* SK9 .... 64 F8
Longmead Av *BRAM/HZG* SK7 .. 66 E5
Longmeade Gdns *WILM/AE* SK9.. 64 F5
Longmeadow *CHD/CHDH* SK8 .... 65 J5
  NWCHW CW8 .... 128 C3
Longmere Av *WYTH/NTH* M22 .. 63 K1◨
Longmoss Cl *MWCH* CW10 .... 179 H4◨
Longnor Rd *BRAM/HZG* SK7 .... 66 E5
  CHD/CHDH SK8 .... 64 D5
Longridge *KNUT* WA16 .... 107 K2
Long Rw *ALS/KID* ST7 .... 243 G3
Longshaw St *WARRW/BUR* WA5 .. 36 F4
Long Shoot Rd *MCFLDS* SK11 .. 158 E2
Longshut La *STKP* SK1 .... 3 G9
Longshut La West *OFTN* SK2.... 3 G9
Longsides Rd *HALE/TIMP* WA15.... 62 C5
Longsight La *CHD/CHDH* SK8 .... 64 F7
Longsight St *HTNM* SK4 .... 2 C4
Long Spinney *RUNC* WA7 .... 74 C4
Longster Trail *CHSE* CH3 .... 146 E8
  FROD/HEL WA6 .... 124 C1
Longstone La *TPLY/KEL* CW6 .... 151 K8
Longton Av *GOL/RIS/CU* WA3 .... 23 J4
Long Valley Rd *ALS/KID* ST7 .... 227 J2
Longview Av *ALS/KID* ST7 .... 224 D8
Long View Dr *HUY* L36 .... 32 A1
Longwood Av *WYTH/NTH* M22 .. 47 H6◨
Longwood Rd *WARRS* WA4 .... 56 E7
  WYTH/NTH M22 .... 63 L1
Longworth Wy *WLTN* L25 .... 50 A1
Lon Odyn (Kiln Close)
  FLINT CH6 .... 116 A6◨
Lonsdale Av *LEIGH* WN7 .... 24 D2
Lonsdale Cl *WDN* WA8 .... 52 C4
Lonsdale Rd *HLWD* L26 .... 50 E6◨
Looe Cl *WDN* WA8 .... 6 C1
The Looms *NSTN* CH64 .... 91 H2
Loonies Ct *STKP* SK1 .... 3 G7◨
Lord Nelson St *WARR* WA1 .... 5 J7
Lordship La *FROD/HEL* WA6 .... 97 M6
Lordshire Pl *ALS/KID* ST7 .... 243 M3
Lords La *GOL/RIS/CU* WA3 .... 29 J3
Lords Mill Rd *CW/SHV* CW2 .... 238 B3
Lord's St *IRL* M44 .... 31 J7
Lord St *BIDD* ST8 .... 227 K5
  CHSE CH3 .... 17 M5
  CW/SHV CW2 .... 19 C6
  GOL/RIS/CU WA3 .... 29 C4
  MCFLDN SK10 .... 113 H4
  MCFLDS SK11 .... 15 H8
  NEWLW WA12 .... 27 L1◨
  RUNC WA7 .... 8 F1
  STKP SK1 .... 3 H6
  WARRS WA4 .... 5 H9
Lorgill Cl *EDGY/DAV* SK3 .... 46 F5◨
Lorland Rd *EDGY/DAV* SK3 .... 46 B5
Lorna Gv *CHD/CHDH* SK8 .... 44 F6
Lorna Rd *CHD/CHDH* SK8 .... 65 H2
Lorraine Rd *HALE/TIMP* WA15 .... 43 G7
Lorraine St *ALS/KID* ST7 .... 243 M3◨
Lostock Av *BRAM/HZG* SK7 .... 66 B3
  POY/DIS SK12 .... 66 B8
Lostock Gn *NWCHE* CW9 .... 131 C3
Lostock Hall Rd *POY/DIS* SK12 .. 86 C2
Lostock Rd *POY/DIS* SK12 .... 86 C2
Lostock Wy *WILM/AE* SK9 .... 64 D8
Lottery St *EDGY/DAV* SK3 .... 2 C5
Lotus Av *BIDD* ST8 .... 227 H6
Loughborough Cl *SALE* M33 .. 42 D1◨
Louise St *CH/BCN* CH1 .... 16 D3
Loushers La *WARRS* WA4 .... 56 D2
Lovage Cl *WARRN/WOL* WA2 .. 38 C3◨
Lovat Dr *KNUT* WA16 .... 107 H1

Love La *HTNM* SK4 .... 2 E3
  NANT CW5 .... 20 E7
  SBCH CW11 .... 224 B1
Lovel Rd *SPK/HALE* L24 .... 70 D2
Lovel Ter *WDN* WA8 .... 52 B7
Lovel Wy *SPK/HALE* L24 .... 70 D1
Lovely La *WARRW/BUR* WA5 .... 4 B5
Love St *CH/BCN* CH1 .... 17 H5
Lowcross La *MCFLDS* SK11 .... 245 K1
Lowe Av *CONG* CW12 .... 207 L2
  WARRS WA4 .... 37 M8
Lowe Crs *NWCHE* CW9 .... 77 J8
Lower Gv *KNUT* WA16 .... 107 H2
Lower Appleton Rd *WDN* WA8 .. 7 K2◨
Lower Ash Rd *ALS/KID* ST7 .... 242 E4
Lower Aston Hall La *CO* CH5 .. 166 B1
Lower Bank St *MCFLDS* SK11 .... 15 J7◨
Lower Bridge St *CH/BCN* CH1 .... 17 G6
Lower Bury St *HTNM* SK4 .... 2 C4
Lower Carrs *STKP* SK1 .... 3 H6
Lower Church St *WDN* WA8 .... 53 G7
Lower Darwin St *NWCHW* CW8 .. 12 F6
Lower Exchange St
  MCFLDS SK11 .... 15 G6
Lowerfield Dr *OFTN* SK2 .... 47 M7
Lower Field Rd *CHSW/BR* CH4 .. 169 G7
Lowerfield Rd *MCFLDN* SK10 .... 15 J2
Lower Fold *MPL/ROM* SK6 .... 49 H5
Lower Greenshall La
  POY/DIS SK12 .... 68 E5
Lower Hague *NM/HAY* SK22 .... 68 E4
Lower Haigh St *WSFD* CW7 .... 177 J3
Lower Hall La *MALPAS* SY14 .... 230 D2◨
Lower Heath *CONG* CW12 .... 184 E8
Lower Heath Av *CONG* CW12 .... 184 F8
Lower High St *ALS/KID* ST7 .... 226 D5
Lower Hillgate *STKP* SK1 .... 3 H6
Lower House La *WDN* WA8 .... 6 F6
Lower La *CHSE* CH3 .... 212 A2
  TPLY/KEL CW6 .... 198 A1
Lowerlea *POY/DIS* SK12 .... 68 C6
Lower Macclesfield Rd
  CHF/WBR SK23 .... 89 K6
Lower Meadow Rd
  WILM/AE SK9 .... 64 E8
Lower Mersey St *EP* CH65 .... 10 F3
Lower Moat Cl *HTNM* SK4 .... 2 E1
Lower Mumforth St
  FLINT CH6 .... 116 B5◨
Lower Park Crs *POY/DIS* SK12 .. 66 B6
Lower Park Rd *CHSW/BR* CH4 .. 17 J7
  POY/DIS SK12 .... 66 B7
Lower Rake La *FROD/HEL* WA6 .. 98 F8
Lower Robin Hood La
  FROD/HEL WA6 .... 124 B1
Lower Sandy La *CHSE* CH3 .... 231 J5
Lower Strines Rd *MPL/ROM* SK6.. 49 C7
Lower Sydney St *FLINT* CH6 .. 116 B5◨
Lower Wash La *WARRS* WA4 .... 56 E1
Lowes La *MCFLDS* SK11 .... 161 L3
The Lowes *ALT* WA14 .... 61 L8
Lowe St *GOL/RIS/CU* WA3 .... 23 G4
  MCFLDS SK11 .... 15 H7
  STKP SK1 .... 3 G6
Loweswater Cl
  WARRN/WOL WA2 .... 37 H1
Loweswater Rd
  CHD/CHDH SK8 .... 64 B1◨
Lowfield Gdns *GOL/RIS/CU* WA3 .. 23 J5
Lowfield Gv *OFTN* SK2 .... 46 F5
Lowfield Rd *EDGY/DAV* SK3 .... 46 B8
Lowfields Av *PS/BROM* CH62 .... 93 K1
Lowfields Cl *PS/BROM* CH62 .... 93 L1◨
Low Hl *FROD/HEL* WA6 .... 123 K7
Lowick Cl *BRAM/HZG* SK7 .... 66 D2
Lowland Rd *OFTN* SK2 .... 47 H8
Lowlands Rd *BURS/TUN* ST6 .. 243 G8
  RUNC WA7 .... 8 F7
Lowland Wy *KNUT* WA16 .... 107 G5
Low Lea Rd *MPL/ROM* SK6 .... 49 H8
Low Leighton Rd *NM/HAY* SK22.. 69 K5
Low Meadow *CHF/WBR* SK23 .. 89 K4
Lowndes Cl *CW/SHV* CW2 .... 221 G4
Lowndes La *OFTN* SK2 .... 47 H4
Lownorth Rd *WYTH/NTH* M22 .. 63 L4
Lowry Cl *WARRW/BUR* WA5 .... 36 D6
Lowry Dr *MPL/ROM* SK6 .... 49 H4◨
Low St *ALS/KID* ST7 .... 224 E4
Lowther Av *GOL/RIS/CU* WA3 .. 24 F8
  HALE/TIMP WA15 .... 43 G6
Lowther Dr *RAIN/WH* L35 .... 33 H1
Lowther St *MCFLDN* SK10 .... 113 H4
Lowton Gdns *GOL/RIS/CU* WA3 .. 23 H7
Lowton Rd *GOL/RIS/CU* WA3 .... 23 H3
  SALE M33 .... 42 D2
Low Wood Rd *BRAM/HZG* SK7 .. 65 J3
Loxdale Dr *EP* CH65 .... 94 F8
Loxley Cl *WARRW/BUR* WA5 .... 36 A4
Loyola Hey *RAIN/WH* L35 .... 33 L4
Lucerne Cl *CHSE* CH3 .... 170 B6
Lucerne Rd *BRAM/HZG* SK7 .... 65 L1
Lucy St *EDGY/DAV* SK3 .... 2 E8
Ludford Gv *SALE* M33 .... 42 F2
Ludford St *CW/SHV* CW2 .... 18 F2
Ludlow Cl *CW/SHV* CW2 .... 19 K6
Ludlow Cl *MCFLDN* SK10 .... 15 K1
  WSFD CW7 .... 177 H5
Ludlow Crs *RUNC* WA7 .... 9 J7
Ludlow Dr *EP* CH65 .... 121 L1
Ludlow Rd *CH/BCN* CH1 .... 145 G7
  STKP SK1 .... 47 J4
Ludwell Cl *CHSW/BR* CH4 .... 169 H7
Lugano Rd *BRAM/HZG* SK7 .... 65 L1
Lugsdale Rd *WDN* WA8 .... 53 H2
Lullington Cl *WYTH/NTH* M22 .... 63 J3◨
Lulworth Cl *WSFD* CW7 .... 177 H5
Lulworth Gdns
  NTHM/RTH M23 .... 43 M4◨
Lulworth Gv *BURS/TUN* ST6 .. 243 L6◨
Lumb Brook Rd *WARRS* WA4 .... 56 E4
Lumb Cl *BRAM/HZG* SK7 .... 65 L6
Lumber La *WARRW/BUR* WA5 .. 26 E4
Lumb La *BRAM/HZG* SK7 .... 65 L6
Lumley Pl *CH/BCN* CH1 .... 17 H6◨
Lumley Rd *CHNE* CH2 .... 145 J8
  MCFLDS SK11 .... 137 M5

Lundy Dr *EP* CH65 .... 121 J4
Lune Cl *CONG* CW12 .... 208 A3
Lunedale Gn *OFTN* SK2 .... 47 L6
Lunehurst *GOL/RIS/CU* WA3 .... 23 L4◨
Lunt Av *CW/SHV* CW2 .... 18 D8
  RAIN/WH L35 .... 32 E1
Lunt's Heath Rd *WDN* WA8 .... 34 A7
Lupin Dr *CHSE* CH3 .... 170 B6
Lupus Gv *GTS/LS* CH66 .... 120 F1
Lurgan Av *SALE* M33 .... 43 J1◨
Lutener St *ALT* WA14 .... 42 C4◨
Luther Gv *STHEL* WA9 .... 26 B2
Luther Rd *KNUT* WA16 .... 107 H2
Luton Dr *NTHM/RTH* M23 .... 44 A8◨
Luton St *WDN* WA8 .... 7 H7◨
Lutyens Cl *MCFLDN* SK10 .. 137 M4◨
Lyceum Cl *CW/HAS* CW1 .... 221 G4
Lyceum Wy *CW/HAS* CW1 .... 221 G4
Lychgate *WARRS* WA4 .... 55 M5◨
Lycroft Cl *RUNC* WA7 .... 73 H6
Lydbury Cl *WARRW/BUR* WA5 .. 36 D2
Lydd Cl *SPK/HALE* L24 .... 50 B8
Lydden Rd *EP* CH65 .... 10 D4
Lydgate Cl *CW/SHV* CW2 .... 237 M4
Lydgate Rd *SALE* M33 .... 43 J3
Lydiate La *NSTN* CH64 .... 92 E4
  WLTN L25 .... 50 D2
Lydiate La *WILM/AE* SK9 .... 110 A4
Lydney Av *CHD/CHDH* SK8 .... 64 A1
Lydstep Ct *WARRW/BUR* WA5 .. 36 E2◨
Lydyett La *NWCHW* CW8 .... 129 H1
Lyme Av *MCFLDS* SK11 .... 138 D7
  WILM/AE SK9 .... 84 B3
Lyme Cv *ALT* WA14 .... 42 C8
  LYMM WA13 .... 58 C2
  MPL/ROM SK6 .... 48 F7
  MPL/ROM SK6 .... 48 D7
Lyme Rd *BRAM/HZG* SK7 .... 66 E3
  POY/DIS SK12 .... 66 B7
Lyme St *BRAM/HZG* SK7 .. 66 D1◨◨
  MCFLDS SK11 .... 45 L2
Lyme Vw *MCFLDS* SK11 .... 162 D2
Lymewood Dr *POY/DIS* SK12 .... 68 A8
  WILM/AE SK9 .... 84 E4◨
Lymington Dr *NTHM/RTH* M23 .... 43 K4
Lymm Cl *EDGY/DAV* SK3 .... 46 D6◨
Lymmhay La *LYMM* WA13 .... 39 L8
Lymmington Av *LYMM* WA13 .... 58 C1
Lymm Rd *LYMM* WA13 .... 59 M3
Lynalls Cl *CONG* CW12 .... 206 F1
Lynam Wy *AUD/MAD/AV* CW3 .. 267 L5◨
Lynbrook Rd *CW/HAS* CW1 .... 19 L4
Lyncastle Rd *WARRS* WA4 .... 57 K8
Lyncombe Cl *CHD/CHDH* SK8 .. 65 H6◨
Lyndale Av *WARRN/WOL* WA2 .. 37 K4
Lyndale Ct *WSFD* CW7 .... 178 A1
Lyndene Gdns *CHD/CHDH* SK8 .. 45 H6◨
Lyndene Rd *WYTH/NTH* M22 .... 44 D7
Lyndhurst Av *BRAM/HZG* SK7 .. 66 C6
  SALE M33 .... 42 F1◨
Lyndhurst Cl *WILM/AE* SK9 .... 83 K7◨
Lyndhurst Dr *BIDD* ST8 .... 227 G7
  HALE/TIMP WA15 .... 62 A2
Loweswater Gv *RUNC* WA7 .... 9 L6
Lyndon Cl *IRL* M44 .... 31 M3
Lyndor Cl *WLTN* L25 .... 50 B3
Lyndor Rd *WLTN* L25 .... 50 B3
Lyneal Av *GTS/LS* CH66 .... 120 C2
Lyneham *RAIN/WH* L35 .... 32 F2
Lyneside Rd *BIDD* ST8 .... 227 H6
Lyngard Cl *WILM/AE* SK9 .... 84 D3
Lyngate Cl *STKP* SK1 .... 3 J7
Lynham Av *WARRW/BUR* WA5 .. 36 B7◨
Lynmouth Cl *BIDD* ST8 .... 227 J6
Lynmouth Gv *BURS/TUN* ST6 .. 243 L5
Lynn Av *ALS/KID* ST7 .... 242 C4
Lynn Cl *RUNC* WA7 .... 9 L9
Lynndene *GTS/LS* CH66 .... 94 D5
Lynnwood Rd *BNG/LEV* M19.... 45 L2
Lynthorpe Av *IRL* M44 .... 31 K6
Lynton Av *IRL* M44 .... 31 L6
  WARRW/BUR WA5 .... 35 L8
Lynton Crs *WDN* WA8 .... 6 C1
Lynton Dr *MPL/ROM* SK6 .... 67 L4
Lynton Gdns *WARRS* WA4 .... 56 D8
Lynton Gv *CW/HAS* CW1 .... 222 D7
  HALE/TIMP WA15 .... 42 F7
Lynton La *WILM/AE* SK9 .... 110 A2
Lynton Ms *WILM/AE* SK9 .... 110 A2◨
Lynton Park Rd *CHD/CHDH* SK8 .. 64 F4
Lynton Pl *CHSW/BR* CH4 .... 167 H8
Lynton Rd *CHD/CHDH* SK8.... 64 F4
  HUY L36 .... 32 B1
Lyntonvale Av *CHD/CHDH* SK8 .. 45 G6
Lynton St *CW/SHV* CW2 .... 238 A4◨
Lynwood *HALE/TIMP* WA15 .... 62 A4
Lynwood Av *GOL/RIS/CU* WA3 .. 23 L6
  WARRS WA4 .... 56 C5
Lynwood Rd *CH/BCN* CH1 .... 144 A7
Lyon's La *WARRS* WA4 .... 57 K1
Lyons Rd *WARRW/BUR* WA5 .... 35 M8
Lyon St *CW/SHV* CW2 .... 17 H3
  CW/HAS CW1 .... 19 H4
  MCFLDS SK11 .... 14 F6
  WARRS WA4 .... 56 F1
Lyster Cl *GOL/RIS/CU* WA3 .... 38 F1
Lytham Dr *BRAM/HZG* SK7 .... 66 A5
Lytham Rd *CHD/CHDH* SK8 .... 64 B3
  WDN WA8 .... 53 H2
Lytham St *EDGY/DAV* SK3 .... 46 F6◨
Lytherton Av *IRL* M44 .... 31 K8
Lythgoes La *WARRN/WOL* WA2.. 5 H4

M

Mableden Cl *CHD/CHDH* SK8.... 64 D4
Mablins La *CW/HAS* CW1 .... 221 H4
Macarthur Rd
  WARRW/BUR WA5 .... 36 B6◨
Macclesfield Rd *BRAM/HZG* SK7 .. 66 F4
  CHF/WBR SK23 .... 89 J6
  CONG CW12 .... 184 F6
  HOLMCH CW4 .... 181 K1
  MCFLDN SK10 .... 112 A7
  MCFLDN SK10 .... 114 B5
  MCFLDN SK10 .... 137 M1
  WILM/AE SK9 .... 84 C6
Macdermott Rd *WDN* WA8 .... 52 C1◨
Macdonald Rd *IRL* M44 .... 31 L5
Mackets Cl *WLTN* L25 .... 50 C3
Macket's La *WLTN* L25 .... 50 C3
Macon Ct *CW/HAS* CW1 .... 19 J6
Macon Wy *CW/HAS* CW1 .... 19 J6
Maddocks Hl *WARRS* WA6 .... 126 F7
Madeley Cl *ALT* WA14 .... 61 L4◨
  CHSW/BR CH4 .... 167 J8
Madeley St *BURS/TUN* ST6 .. 243 K8
  CW/SHV CW2 .... 18 F7
Madeline Mckenna Ct
  WDN WA8 .... 52 C1◨
Madison Av *CHD/CHDH* SK8 .... 65 G2
Madison St *BURS/TUN* ST6 .. 243 K8
Madras Rd *EDGY/DAV* SK3 .... 46 C5◨
Madron Av *MCFLDN* SK10 .. 137 M3
Maelor Wy *WHITCH* SY13 .... 268 A7
Maes Alaw *FLINT* CH6 .... 116 B7
Maes Gwyn *FLINT* CH6 .... 116 A7
Maes-hyfryd *FLINT* CH6 .... 116 A7
Maesllwyn Cl *WHITCH* SY13 .... 268 A8
Maes Teg *FLINT* CH6 .... 116 A8
Maes-y-dre Av *FLINT* CH6 .... 116 B7
Mafeking Pl *AIMK* WN4 .... 22 C3
Magdala Pl *NWCHE* CW9 .... 130 C4
Magdalen Ct *CW/SHV* CW2 .... 18 A9
Magda Rd *OFTN* SK2 .... 47 J7
Magenta Av *IRL* M44 .... 31 L6
Mag La *LYMM* WA13 .... 58 F5
Magna Cl *WHITCH* SY13 .... 271 G8
Magnolia Cl *GTS/LS* CH66 .... 120 F3
  HLWD L26 .... 50 D2
  WARR WA1 .... 38 E5◨
Magnolia Dr *RUNC* WA7 .... 73 M8◨
Magnolia Ri *MCFLDS* SK10 .... 111 K6
Magpie Crs *ALS/KID* ST7 .... 243 H2◨
Mahood St *EDGY/DAV* SK3 .... 2 D9
Maidenhills *MWCH* CW10 .... 179 K4
Maidstone Cl *MCFLDN* SK10 .. 138 D2◨
Maidstone Rd *HTNM* SK4 .... 45 K1
Maidwell Cl *WSFD* CW7 .... 154 M4
Main Dr *RAIN/WH* L35 .... 32 E3
Main Front *RAIN/WH* L35 .... 32 E3
Main La *GOL/RIS/CU* WA3 .... 28 E1
Main Rd *AUD/MAD/AV* CW3 .... 255 G6
  CHSW/BR CH4 .... 167 H8
  CW/SHV CW2 .... 238 B8
  HOLMCH CW4 .... 157 J4
  MCFLDS SK11 .... 139 J8
  NANT CW5 .... 219 M7
  NANT CW5 .... 253 C4
  NWCHE CW9 .... 153 L4
Main St *CHSE* CH3 .... 147 K7
  FROD/HEL WA6 .... 99 G4
  RUNC WA7 .... 73 M4
Maintree Crs *SPK/HALE* L24 .... 51 C8
Mainwaring Dr *CHSW/BR* CH4 .. 168 C5
  WILM/AE SK9 .... 84 D4
Mainwaring Rd *KNUT* WA16 .. 134 A4
Mainwaring Ter
  NTHM/RTH M23 .... 44 A2◨
Mainwood Rd *HALE/TIMP* WA15 .. 43 J7
Mairesfield Av *WARRS* WA4 .... 57 K2
Maismore Rd *NTHM/RTH* M23 .. 63 C3
Maisterson Ct *NANT* CW5 .... 20 C7
Maitland St *STKP* SK1 .... 3 L9
Maitland Wy *CH/BCN* CH1 .... 144 C7
Maitland-wood Cl *NWCHE* CW9 .. 130 D5
Major Cross St *WDN* WA8 .... 7 H6◨
Makepeace Cl *CHSE* CH3 .... 170 C1◨
Makerfield Dr *NEWLW* WA12 .... 22 A7
Malaga Av *MANAIR* M90 .... 63 H5◨
Malam Dr *NWCHE* CW9 .... 130 C6
Malbank *NANT* CW5 .... 20 E5
Malbank Rd *CW/SHV* CW2 .... 220 D8
Malcolm Av *WARRN/WOL* WA2 .. 37 K3
Malcolm St *RUNC* WA7 .... 9 K3
Malden Gv *NTHM/RTH* M23 .... 44 A5◨
Maldon Cl *HLWD* L26 .... 50 F6
  OFTN SK2 .... 48 A7
Malgam Dr *DID/WITH* M20 .... 45 H4◨
Malham Ct *OFTN* SK2 .... 47 K6◨
Malhamdale Av *RAIN/WH* L35 .. 33 K2
Malham Cl *SPK/HALE* L24 .... 71 K2
Maliston Rd *WARRW/BUR* WA5 .. 36 B7
Mallaig Cl *HOLMCH* CW4 .... 181 J2
Mallard Cl *HLWD* L26 .... 50 E3
  KNUT WA16 .... 107 G2◨
  OFTN SK2 .... 48 A7
  RUNC WA7 .... 73 M7◨
  WARRN/WOL WA2 .... 37 K1
Mallard Crs *POY/DIS* SK12 .... 66 A8
Mallard Gn *ALT* WA14 .... 42 B4◨
Mallard La *GOL/RIS/CU* WA3 .... 38 F1
Mallards Reach
  MPL/ROM SK6 .... 48 B2◨
Mallard Wy *WSFD* CW7 .... 177 K6◨
Malling Rd *NTHM/RTH* M23 .... 44 A8
Mallory Cl *CW/HAS* CW1 .... 19 M1
Mallory Cl *CONG* CW12 .... 206 F1
Mallory Rd *EP* CH65 .... 10 B9
Mallory Wk *CHSW/BR* CH4 .... 191 H5
Mallow Cl *CHSE* CH3 .... 170 A6◨
Mallowdale Rd *OFTN* SK2 .... 47 L6
Malmesbury Cl *MWCH* CW10 .. 179 H3◨
  POY/DIS SK12 .... 66 D8
Malmesbury Pk *RUNC* WA7 .... 74 D1
Malmesbury Rd *CHD/CHDH* SK8 .. 64 A6
Malpas Cl *CHD/CHDH* SK8 .... 46 A8◨
  NWCHE CW9 .... 13 M4
  WILM/AE SK9 .... 84 D3
Malpas Dr *ALT* WA14 .... 42 E4◨
  WARRW/BUR WA5 .... 36 C8
Malpas Rd *EP* CH65 .... 94 F8
  NWCHE CW9 .... 13 M4
  RUNC WA7 .... 73 M4
Malpas Wy *WARRW/BUR* WA5 .. 36 C8◨
Malsham Rd *NTHM/RTH* M23 .. 43 M2◨

Maltby Rd *NTHM/RTH* M23 .... 43 M6 ⓵
Malt Kiln Rd *KNUT* WA16 .... 105 M8
Maltmans Rd *LYMM* WA13 .... 58 D1
Malton Av *GOL/RIS/CU* WA3 .... 23 L5
Malton Cl *WDN* WA8 .... 33 J7
Malton Dr *ALT* WA14 .... 42 A6
  BRAM/HZG SK7 .... 66 D5
Malton Gv *BURS/TUN* ST6 .... 243 K8
Malton Rd *WLTN* L25 .... 50 C3
Malt St *KNUT* WA16 .... 107 G2
Malvern Av *CHD/CHDH* SK8 .... 44 F7
  EP CH65 .... 121 J1
Malvern Cl *CONG* CW12 .... 206 F1
  CW/SHV CW2 .... 238 B8
  HTNM SK4 .... 2 D2
  WARRW/BUR WA5 .... 36 A4
Malvern Dr *ALT* WA14 .... 42 B7
  MCFLDN SK10 .... 112 E8
Malvern Rd *CH/BCN* CH1 .... 145 C8
  KNUT WA16 .... 106 F4
Malvern Ter *LEIGH* WN7 .... 24 F1 ⓵
Malvern Wy *CO* CH5 .... 177 G4
Manchester Br *CW/HAS* CW1 .... 19 J4
Manchester New Rd *PART* M31 .... 40 F1
Manchester Rd *ALT* WA14 .... 42 D5
  CHD/CHDH SK8 .... 45 K4
  CONG CW12 .... 184 E7
  GOL/RIS/CU WA3 .... 39 L4
  KNUT WA16 .... 80 E8
  MCFLDN SK10 .... 112 C6
  NWCHE CW9 .... 13 M3
  PART M31 .... 31 M8 ⓵
  WARR WA1 .... 5 L5
  WARR WA1 .... 39 C5 ⓵
  WILM/AE SK9 .... 84 C4
Manchester Rw *NEWLW* WA12 .... 27 K4 ⓵
Mancot La *CO* CH5 .... 166 D1
Mancot Royal Cl *CO* CH5 .... 166 D1 ⓵
Mancot Wy *CO* CH5 .... 166 E1
Mancroft Cl *WARR* WA1 .... 38 E5 ⓵
Mandalay Gdns
  MPL/ROM SK6 .... 48 D5 ⓵
Mandarin Gn *ALT* WA14 .... 42 B4 ⓵
Manifold Cl *SBCH* CW11 .... 203 M4
Manifold Dr *MPL/ROM* SK6 .... 67 M6
Manley Av *GOL/RIS/CU* WA3 .... 22 F2
Manley Cl *HOLMCH* CW4 .... 181 G1
  NWCHE CW9 .... 13 J8
  NWCHE CW9 .... 77 J8
Manley Ct *CO* CH5 .... 142 B5
Manley Gdns *WARRW/BUR* WA5 .... 4 C6
Manley Gv *BRAM/HZG* SK7 .... 65 L6 ⓵
Manley La *FROD/HEL* WA6 .... 123 L7
Manley Rd *FROD/HEL* WA6 .... 124 D4
  HUY L36 .... 32 A4
  MCFLDS SK11 .... 138 A7 ⓵
  SALE M33 .... 42 E3
Manley Vw *CHNE* CH2 .... 123 J1
Manna Dr *CHNE* CH2 .... 123 J1 ⓵
Mannings La *CHNE* CH2 .... 146 B6
Mannings La South
  CHNE CH2 .... 146 A7 ⓵
Manning St *CW/SHV* CW2 .... 19 H9
Manora Rd *NWCHE* CW9 .... 13 K3
Manor Av *CW/SHV* CW2 .... 238 A3
  GOL/RIS/CU WA3 .... 23 J4
  HOLMCH CW4 .... 157 M3
  NWCHE CW9 .... 104 B6
  RAIN/WH L35 .... 33 J2
  SALE M33 .... 42 D1
Manor Cl *CHD/CHDH* SK8 .... 65 J4
  CHSE CH3 .... 147 L6
  CHSW/BR CH4 .... 167 J5
  CONG CW12 .... 208 B3
  NSTN CH64 .... 91 J5
  WARR WA1 .... 38 D5
  WILM/AE SK9 .... 83 L4
Manor Ct *CW/SHV* CW2 .... 238 B3
  GOL/RIS/CU WA3 .... 23 J4
Manor Crs *CHSW/BR* CH4 .... 167 J4
  KNUT WA16 .... 107 H2
  MCFLDN SK10 .... 138 D1
  MWCH CW10 .... 179 J5
  WLTN L25 .... 50 B3
Manor Dr *CHSE* CH3 .... 170 B3
  NWCHE CW9 .... 130 C5
  NWCHW CW8 .... 129 H2
Manor Farm Cl *CHNE* CH2 .... 146 E4
Manor Farm Crs *CH/BCN* CH1 .... 120 B4
Manor Farm Rd *RUNC* WA7 .... 54 D8
Manor Fell *RUNC* WA7 .... 74 B6
Manorfield Cl *CH/BCN* CH1 .... 120 A4
Manor Flds *MWCH* CW10 .... 179 J3
Manor Gdns *WILM/AE* SK9 .... 84 D5 ⓵
Manor Gv *LEIGH* WN7 .... 25 J1
  NWCHW CW8 .... 12 B7
Manor Hill Rd *MPL/ROM* SK6 .... 48 F5
Manorial Rd *NSTN* CH64 .... 91 J4
Manorial Rd South *NSTN* CH64 .... 91 J4
Manor La *CHSW/BR* CH4 .... 167 H5
  CO CH5 .... 167 G6
  GTS/LS CH66 .... 120 F1
  HOLMCH CW4 .... 181 K2
  KNUT WA16 .... 107 L6
  MWCH CW10 .... 179 J4 ⓵
  NWCHE CW9 .... 154 D2
  WRX/GR/LL LL12 .... 210 B6
Manor Pk *CHSE* CH3 .... 147 L6
Manor Park Av *RUNC* WA7 .... 54 C8
Manor Park Dr *GTS/LS* CH66 .... 120 F2
Manor Pk North *KNUT* WA16 .... 107 J2
Manor Park Rd *CONG* CW12 .... 185 K2
Manor Pk South *KNUT* WA16 .... 107 H3
Manor Rd *ALS/KID* ST7 .... 226 D5
  CHD/CHDH SK8 .... 65 J3
  CHF/WBR SK23 .... 89 L7
  CHSW/BR CH4 .... 169 H7
  CO CH5 .... 143 C6
  FROD/HEL WA6 .... 99 J3
  HALE/TIMP WA15 .... 42 E8
  LYMM WA13 .... 58 E2
  MPL/ROM SK6 .... 48 F5
  NANT CW5 .... 20 E5
  NWCHW CW8 .... 151 M2
  RNFD/HAY WA11 .... 22 A5
  RUNC WA7 .... 73 K2
  SBCH CW11 .... 204 D6
  WDN WA8 .... 52 B3

  WILM/AE SK9 .... 83 L4
  WLTN L25 .... 50 B3
Manor Rd North *NANT* CW5 .... 20 E2
Manor Sq *WSFD* CW7 .... 177 G4 ⓵
Manor St *GOL/RIS/CU* WA3 .... 23 H3 ⓵
  NWCHW CW8 .... 12 C6
Manor Wy *CW/SHV* CW2 .... 238 B3 ⓵
  SBCH CW11 .... 204 E6
Manorwood Dr *RAIN/WH* L35 .... 32 E2
Manse Field Rd *FROD/HEL* WA6 .... 126 B3
Manse Gdns *NEWLW* WA12 .... 22 D8
Mansell Cl *WDN* WA8 .... 34 C7 ⓵
Mansell Dr *HLWD* L26 .... 50 E6
Mansfield Cl *GOL/RIS/CU* WA3 .... 30 A8
Mansfield Dr *BIDD* ST8 .... 227 G7
Mansfield Rd *EP* CH65 .... 121 G2
Mansion Dr *KNUT* WA16 .... 107 H2
Manston Dr *CHD/CHDH* SK8 .... 65 G2
Manston Rd *WARRW/BUR* WA5 .... 54 F1
Manuel Perez Rd
  WARRW/BUR WA5 .... 36 B6 ⓵
Manvers St *HTNM* SK4 .... 2 F1
Manx Rd *WARRS* WA4 .... 56 B1
Maori Dr *FROD/HEL* WA6 .... 99 G4
Maple Av *ALS/KID* ST7 .... 241 L2
  ALS/KID ST7 .... 242 D4
  CHD/CHDH SK8 .... 64 F2
  GOL/RIS/CU WA3 .... 23 M5
  GTS/LS CH66 .... 94 C6
  HALE/TIMP WA15 .... 43 L7
  MCFLDS SK11 .... 138 D7
  MPL/ROM SK6 .... 48 F8
  NEWLW WA12 .... 27 K2
  POY/DIS SK12 .... 69 G6
  POY/DIS SK12 .... 86 F1
  RUNC WA7 .... 9 M6
  WDN WA8 .... 7 K2
Maple Cl *CONG* CW12 .... 183 M8
  HOLMCH CW4 .... 157 K8
  OFTN SK2 .... 47 H6
  RAIN/WH L35 .... 32 E1
  SBCH CW11 .... 181 M7
  SBCH CW11 .... 204 C6
Maple Ct *WSFD* CW7 .... 178 A1 ⓵
Maple Crs *WARRW/BUR* WA5 .... 35 M8
Maplecroft *STKP* SK1 .... 3 M8
Maple Gv *CHNE* CH2 .... 146 B8
  CHSW/BR CH4 .... 168 D7
  CW/HAS CW1 .... 221 L6
  GTS/LS CH66 .... 121 G3
  NWCHW CW8 .... 12 A5
  NWCHW CW8 .... 103 H8 ⓵
  WARRS WA4 .... 56 D1
  WILM/AE SK9 .... 178 A3
Maple La *NWCHW* CW8 .... 151 M2
Maple Ms *NTHM/RTH* M23 .... 43 J4
Maple Pl *ALS/KID* ST7 .... 224 F5 ⓵
Maple Rd *BRAM/HZG* SK7 .... 65 L7
  NTHM/RTH M23 .... 43 J4
  PART M31 .... 40 E1
  WARR WA1 .... 38 E5
  WARRN/WOL WA2 .... 28 B6
  WILM/AE SK9 .... 110 B2
Maple Rd West *NTHM/RTH* M23 .... 43 J4
The Maples *WSFD* CW7 .... 178 A1 ⓵
Mapleton Dr *RUNC* WA7 .... 99 M1
Mapleton Ms *NTHM/RTH* M23 .... 43 J4
Maplewood Gv *CH/BCN* CH1 .... 144 B4
Maplewood Rd *WILM/AE* SK9 .... 84 K4
Mapley Av *WYTH/NTH* M22 .... 44 D4
Maplin Dr *OFTN* SK2 .... 48 A7
Mapplewell Crs
  WARRW/BUR WA5 .... 36 A6
Marbury Gdns *EP* CH65 .... 94 F6
Marbury La *NWCHE* CW9 .... 103 L2
Marbury Rd *CHSE* CH3 .... 170 C2
  NWCHE CW9 .... 103 K6
  WILM/AE SK9 .... 84 B3 ⓵
Marbury St *WARRS* WA4 .... 5 J9
March Av *HTNM* SK4 .... 46 B2 ⓵
Marchbank Dr *CHD/CHDH* SK8 .... 45 J6
Marches Wy *CH/BCN* CH1 .... 17 G4
  CHSE CH3 .... 192 F8
  CHSE CH3 .... 244 B3
  MALPAS SY14 .... 244 F5
  MALPAS SY14 .... 258 F1 ⓵
  WHITCH SY13 .... 269 J3
March St *CW/HAS* CW1 .... 19 H3
Marchwiel Rd *EP* CH65 .... 11 H9
Marcien Wy *WDN* WA8 .... 52 F1
Marcliff St *HTNM* SK4 .... 46 B2
Marcross Cl *WARRW/BUR* WA5 .... 36 B3
Mardale Cl *CONG* CW12 .... 185 G7
  NTHLY L27 .... 51 L1 ⓵
Mardale Crs *LYMM* WA13 .... 58 F1
Mardale Dr *CHD/CHDH* SK8 .... 45 H6
Mardale Rd *NTHLY* L27 .... 51 G1
Marden Rd *NTHM/RTH* M23 .... 44 A7
Mardon Cl *KNUT* WA16 .... 81 K8
Marford Dr *WYTH/NTH* M22 .... 44 D6 ⓵
Marford Crs *SALE* M33 .... 42 F2
Marford Hl *WRX/GR/LL* LL12 .... 210 A8
Margaret Av *WARR* WA1 .... 38 B5
Margaret's La *GTS/LS* CH66 .... 94 A5
Margaret St *STHEL* WA9 .... 34 E1 ⓵
Margery Av *ALS/KID* ST7 .... 225 L5
Marian *FLINT* CH6 .... 116 B8
Marian Av *NEWLW* WA12 .... 26 E1
Marian Cl *RAIN/WH* L35 .... 33 J2
Marian Dr *CHSE* CH3 .... 170 B4
  RAIN/WH L35 .... 33 H2
Marie Cl *NANT* CW5 .... 249 M8
Marie Dr *WARRS* WA4 .... 57 K2
Marigold Cl *MCFLDS* SK11 .... 137 M5
Marina Av *WARRW/BUR* WA5 .... 36 B8
Marina Cl *WILM/AE* SK9 .... 64 D7
Marina Dr *CHNE* CH2 .... 145 L5
  CO CH5 .... 142 B6
  EP CH65 .... 10 E8 ⓵
  MPL/ROM SK6 .... 48 C5
  WARRN/WOL WA2 .... 37 J3
Marina Gv *RUNC* WA7 .... 9 K3
Marina La *RUNC* WA7 .... 74 E5 ⓵

Marina Village *RUNC* WA7 .... 74 E5 ⓵
Marine Av *PART* M31 .... 40 D1
Mariner Cl *RUNC* WA7 .... 74 D6
Marion Dr *RUNC* WA7 .... 72 F6
Maritime Cl *NEWLW* WA12 .... 22 C7 ⓵
Mark Av *GTS/LS* CH66 .... 94 C8
Mark Cl *CHNE* CH2 .... 17 M3
Market Pl *MALPAS* SY14 .... 246 D5
  MCFLDN SK10 .... 15 G4
  MCFLDN SK10 .... 113 H4 ⓵
  STKP SK1 .... 3 G4
  WSFD CW7 .... 177 M3
Market Sq *CW/HAS* CW1 .... 18 F4
Market St *ALS/KID* ST7 .... 243 G3
  ALT WA14 .... 42 D8 ⓵
  CHF/WBR SK23 .... 89 L5
  CONG CW12 .... 207 K2
  CW/HAS CW1 .... 19 G1
  CW/HAS CW1 .... 19 G4
  EP CH65 .... 10 D9
  NANT CW5 .... 20 E6
  NEWLW WA12 .... 22 A8
  NM/HAY SK22 .... 69 H5
  NWCHE CW9 .... 13 K2
  POY/DIS SK12 .... 68 D6
  WDN WA8 .... 7 H6
Markfield Crs *WLTN* L25 .... 50 D3
Marland Av *CHD/CHDH* SK8 .... 64 F2
Marlborough Av *CHD/CHDH* SK8 .... 65 H3
  CO CH5 .... 166 A4
  WILM/AE SK9 .... 110 B2
  WSFD CW7 .... 177 J1
Marlborough Cl
  CW/SHV CW2 .... 237 L4 ⓵
  MCFLDN SK10 .... 112 D8
  MPL/ROM SK6 .... 48 D5 ⓵
Marlborough Crs *WARRS* WA4 .... 56 F2
  WDN WA8 .... 34 A7 ⓵
Marlborough Dr
  FROD/HEL WA6 .... 124 D2 ⓵
  MCFLDN SK10 .... 112 D8
  EP CH65 .... 121 K1
Marlborough Rd *ALT* WA14 .... 61 K2
  GOL/RIS/CU WA3 .... 23 E5 ⓵
  SPK/HALE L24 .... 70 D2 ⓵
Marl Cft *CHSE* CH3 .... 170 B5
Marlcroft Av *HTNM* SK4 .... 46 B2 ⓵
Marldon Pl *BURS/TUN* ST6 .... 243 J6 ⓵
Marl Edge *MCFLDN* SK10 .... 112 A7 ⓵
Marley Av *CW/HAS* CW1 .... 221 H6
Marley Cl *HALE/TIMP* WA15 .... 42 F5
  RAIN/WH L35 .... 33 L3 ⓵
Marleyer Ri *MPL/ROM* SK6 .... 48 A4
Marley Rd *POY/DIS* SK12 .... 86 E2
Marley Wy *CHSW/BR* CH4 .... 168 E5
Marlfield Rd *HALE/TIMP* WA15 .... 62 D5
  WARRS WA4 .... 57 G2
Marl Heys *CHNE* CH2 .... 145 L5 ⓵
Marlhill Cl *OFTN* SK2 .... 47 L7
Marling Cl *FROD/HEL* WA6 .... 99 K6
Marling Pk *WDN* WA8 .... 52 B3
Marlow Av *CHNE* CH2 .... 145 M5
Marlow Cl *CHD/CHDH* SK8 .... 64 F2 ⓵
  GOL/RIS/CU WA3 .... 29 J7 ⓵
Marlow Dr *ALT* WA14 .... 60 F2
  WILM/AE SK9 .... 64 C7
Marlowe Cl *CH/BCN* CH1 .... 145 G7
  CW/SHV CW2 .... 238 A4 ⓵
  SBCH CW11 .... 203 K7
  WDN WA8 .... 6 E3
Marlowe Ct *MCFLDS* SK11 .... 138 C7 ⓵
Marlowe Dr *NANT* CW5 .... 251 L1
Marlowe Rd *NSTN* CH64 .... 91 L4 ⓵
  NWCHE CW9 .... 130 C5
Marlowe Wks *MPL/ROM* SK6 .... 47 L2
Marlston Av *CHSW/BR* CH4 .... 169 G6
Marlston Pl *RUNC* WA7 .... 73 H6
Marmion Cl *GOL/RIS/CU* WA3 .... 23 L3
Marne Av *WYTH/NTH* M22 .... 44 E7
Marnel Dr *CO* CH5 .... 142 E8
Maroon Rd *WYTH/NTH* M22 .... 63 M5
Marple Crs *CW/SHV* CW2 .... 237 L2
Marple Hall Dr *MPL/ROM* SK6 .... 48 D5
Marple Old Rd *OFTN* SK2 .... 48 A6
Marple Rd *NWCHE* CW9 .... 130 C5
  OFTN SK2 .... 47 K5
Marquis Dr *CHD/CHDH* SK8 .... 64 D5
Marrick Av *CHD/CHDH* SK8 .... 45 J7
Marriott Rd *MCFLDN* SK11 .... 222 F1 ⓵
Marriott St *STKP* SK1 .... 3 H8
Marron Av *WARRN/WOL* WA2 .... 37 H2
Marsden Av *WARRS* WA4 .... 38 A4
Marsden Dr *HALE/TIMP* WA15 .... 43 J6
Marsden Rd *HLWD* L26 .... 50 F6
  MPL/ROM SK6 .... 48 C1
Marsden Ter *MCFLDS* SK11 .... 14 F6 ⓵
Marshall Av *WARRW/BUR* WA5 .... 36 F1
Marshall La *NWCHW* CW8 .... 12 D6
Marshall Rd *WARR* WA1 .... 38 D5
Marshalls Ct *NWCHW* CW8 .... 12 A9
Marsham Dr *MPL/ROM* SK6 .... 49 G7 ⓵
Marsh Av *ALS/KID* ST7 .... 243 K2
Marsh Cl *ALS/KID* ST7 .... 241 G1 ⓵
  EDGY/DAV SK3 .... 46 D6 ⓵
Marshfield Bank *CW/SHV* CW2 .... 220 D7
Marshfield La *BIDD* ST8 .... 227 J2
Marshfield Rd *HALE/TIMP* WA15 .... 43 J7
Marshgate *WDN* WA8 .... 52 B6
Marshgate Pl *FROD/HEL* WA6 .... 99 J2
Marsh Green Cl *BIDD* ST8 .... 227 K2
Marshgreen Rd *BIDD* ST8 .... 227 K1
Marsh Green Rd *SBCH* CW11 .... 203 K4
Marsh Gv *BIDD* ST8 .... 227 J1
Marsh Hall Rd *WDN* WA8 .... 34 B8
Marsh House La
  WARRN/WOL WA2 .... 5 K3
Marshlands Rd *NSTN* CH64 .... 91 L7
Marsh La *ALS/KID* ST7 .... 241 G1 ⓵
  CHNE CH2 .... 97 G6
  CHNE CH2 .... 123 H1
  CHSE CH3 .... 212 B8
  FLINT CH6 .... 116 B5
  FROD/HEL WA6 .... 99 G4
  FROD/HEL WA6 .... 127 G6
  HOLMCH CW4 .... 181 G1
  KNUT WA16 .... 80 F1
  NANT CW5 .... 250 F1

  NM/HAY SK22 .... 69 K6
  RUNC WA7 .... 73 M1 ⓵
  WARRS WA4 .... 101 K1
  WARRS WA4 .... 102 A3
  WARRW/BUR WA5 .... 54 C2
Marsh Rd *WARRS* WA4 .... 57 H8
Marsh St *WARR* WA1 .... 5 M3
  WDN WA8 .... 7 G1
Marsh Vw *CO* CH5 .... 142 A5
Marsland Av *HALE/TIMP* WA15 .... 43 H4
Marsland Rd *HALE/TIMP* WA15 .... 43 H6
  MPL/ROM SK6 .... 48 D5
  SALE M33 .... 43 K1 ⓵
Marsland St *BRAM/HZG* SK7 .... 66 D2 ⓵
  STKP SK1 .... 3 H2
Marsland Ter *STKP* SK1 .... 3 M8
Marson St *WARRN/WOL* WA2 .... 4 F5
Marston Cl *PS/BROM* CH62 .... 93 L1
Marston La *NWCHE* CW9 .... 104 C6
Martens Rd *IRL* M44 .... 31 L7
Marthall Dr *SALE* M33 .... 43 L2
Marthall La *KNUT* WA16 .... 108 A6
Martham Cl *WARRS* WA4 .... 57 G1
Martham Dr *OFTN* SK2 .... 48 A6
Martin Av *NEWLW* WA12 .... 22 B7
  WARRN/WOL WA2 .... 37 K3
Martin Cl *CHNE* CH2 .... 145 J4
  OFTN SK2 .... 47 M7
  RUNC WA7 .... 74 A5
Martindale Gv *RUNC* WA7 .... 73 K7
Martin Dr *CHNE* CH2 .... 145 J4 ⓵
  FROD/HEL WA6 .... 99 H4
Martinscroft Rd
  NTHM/RTH M23 .... 44 B7 ⓵
Martinsfields *NWCHW* CW8 .... 101 M7
Martin's La *CHSE* CH3 .... 171 M4
Martland Av *GOL/RIS/CU* WA3 .... 23 K5
Martlet Av *POY/DIS* SK12 .... 68 C5
Martock *RAIN/WH* L35 .... 33 K3
Martock Av *WYTH/NTH* M22 .... 63 L1 ⓵
Marton Av *CHD/CHDH* SK8 .... 45 J2
Marton Cl *CONG* CW12 .... 184 E7
  CW/SHV CW2 .... 253 L1 ⓵
  GOL/RIS/CU WA3 .... 23 E8 ⓵
  SPK/HALE L24 .... 70 D2 ⓵
Marton Gn *EDGY/DAV* SK3 .... 46 D7
  SPK/HALE L24 .... 70 D2 ⓵
Marton Hall La *MCFLDN* SK10 .... 184 A1
Marton La *MCFLDS* SK11 .... 160 D5
  MCFLDS SK11 .... 184 F1
Marton Rd *CHSW/BR* CH4 .... 190 C1
Marwood Cl *ALT* WA14 .... 42 B6 ⓵
Marwood Dr *NTHM/RTH* M23 .... 62 F1 ⓵
Maryfield Cl *GOL/RIS/CU* WA3 .... 23 C5 ⓵
Maryhill Cl *ALS/KID* ST7 .... 243 G1
Maryhill Rd *RUNC* WA7 .... 9 G7
Marylon Dr *WYTH/NTH* M22 .... 44 E3 ⓵
Marys Ga *CW/SHV* CW2 .... 237 L4
Mary St *CHD/CHDH* SK8 .... 45 K6
  CW/HAS CW1 .... 19 H3
  STHEL WA9 .... 34 E1 ⓵
  STKP SK1 .... 3 J4
  WDN WA8 .... 53 K5
Masefield Av *WDN* WA8 .... 6 F5
Masefield Dr *CH/BCN* CH1 .... 144 E6
  CW/HAS CW1 .... 19 L4
  HTNM SK4 .... 46 A2 ⓵
Masefield Wy *SBCH* CW11 .... 203 K7 ⓵
Maskery Pl *CONG* CW12 .... 207 K1 ⓵
Mason Av *WARR* WA1 .... 37 L4
  WDN WA8 .... 34 A8
Mason Cl *GTS/LS* CH66 .... 120 D2
Mason Dr *BIDD* ST8 .... 227 H4
Masons La *MCFLDN* SK10 .... 15 L2
Mason St *CHNE* CH2 .... 16 F3
  RUNC WA7 .... 9 L1
  WARR WA1 .... 5 K7
  WLTN L25 .... 50 A2
Massey Av *LYMM* WA13 .... 58 A2
  NWCHW CW8 .... 129 C8
  WARRW/BUR WA5 .... 36 F2
  WSFD CW7 .... 177 M3
Massey Brook La *LYMM* WA13 .... 58 B2
Masseyfield Rd *RUNC* WA7 .... 74 A7
Massey Rd *HALE/TIMP* WA15 .... 42 E8 ⓵
Massey St *STKP* SK1 .... 3 G6
  WILM/AE SK9 .... 110 A3 ⓵
Massey Wk *WYTH/NTH* M22 .... 63 M3
Massie St *CHD/CHDH* SK8 .... 45 K6
Mates La *MALPAS* SY14 .... 246 B6
Mather Av *CHNE* CH2 .... 23 L6
  RUNC WA7 .... 8 B8
Mather Cl *MWCH* CW10 .... 179 J4
Mather Dr *NWCHE* CW9 .... 103 J4
  NWCHE CW9 .... 130 D5
Mathers Cl *WARRN/WOL* WA2 .... 29 C8 ⓵
Mathieson Rd *WDN* WA8 .... 7 J5
Matlock Cl *WARRW/BUR* WA5 .... 36 A3 ⓵
Matlock Dr *BRAM/HZG* SK7 .... 66 E4
Matlock Rd *CHD/CHDH* SK8 .... 64 C5
Matterdale Cl *FROD/HEL* WA6 .... 99 K5
Matthew Cl *CHNE* CH2 .... 17 M3
Matthews Pl *CONG* CW12 .... 208 A2 ⓵
Matthews St *WARR* WA1 .... 5 L3
Matthew St *MPL/ROM* SK6 .... 49 G6 ⓵
Matty's La *FROD/HEL* WA6 .... 99 G5
Mauldeth Cl *HTNM* SK4 .... 46 A1
Mauldeth Rd *HTNM* SK4 .... 45 M1
Maureen Av *BURS/TUN* ST6 .... 243 K6
Maveen Gv *OFTN* SK2 .... 47 G8
Mavor Ct *CW/HAS* CW1 .... 18 D3
Mawdsley Av *WARR* WA1 .... 38 E5
Mawdsley Cl *ALS/KID* ST7 .... 240 F1 ⓵
Maw Green Rd *CW/HAS* CW1 .... 221 M5
Maw La *CW/HAS* CW1 .... 222 C4
Maxfield Cl *MCFLDS* SK11 .... 137 M4 ⓵
Maxwell Av *CO* CH5 .... 166 D1
  OFTN SK2 .... 47 J7
Maxwell Cl *EP* CH65 .... 121 G2
Maxwell St *CW/SHV* CW2 .... 18 F6
  GOL/RIS/CU WA3 .... 29 L6
May Av *CHD/CHDH* SK8 .... 65 H6
  HTNM SK4 .... 2 A4 ⓵
Mayberry Gv *WARRN/WOL* WA2 .... 38 A3
Maydor Av *CHSW/BR* CH4 .... 168 C5
Mayer St *OFTN* SK2 .... 47 J5 ⓵
Mayfair Cl *POY/DIS* SK12 .... 66 E8 ⓵

  WARRW/BUR WA5 .... 35 K5
Mayfair Dr *NWCHE* CW9 .... 153 L1
  SALE M33 .... 42 E2
Mayfair Gv *WDN* WA8 .... 6 B2
Mayfair Rd *WYTH/NTH* M22 .... 44 E8
  WDN WA8 .... 52 B3
Mayfield Av *MCFLDS* SK11 .... 138 C7
  HOLMCH CW4 .... 181 K1
Mayfield Cl *HALE/TIMP* WA15 .... 43 H6
Mayfield Dr *GOL/RIS/CU* WA3 .... 24 C4
  LEIGH WN7 .... 24 C4
  NWCHW CW8 .... 128 A8
Mayfield Gv *NWCHW* CW8 .... 128 A8
  WILM/AE SK9 .... 83 L7 ⓵
Mayfield Ms *CW/HAS* CW1 .... 220 F6
Mayfield Rd *BIDD* ST8 .... 227 K6
  BRAM/HZG SK7 .... 65 L8
  CH/BCN CH1 .... 144 D7
  HALE/TIMP WA15 .... 43 H6
  KNUT WA16 .... 81 M8
  MPL/ROM SK6 .... 49 H3
  NWCHE CW9 .... 13 M3
  WARRS WA4 .... 57 G2
Mayfield St *AIMK* WN4 .... 22 A1 ⓵
Mayfield Ter *MCFLDS* SK11 .... 138 C7 ⓵
Mayfield Vw *LYMM* WA13 .... 58 E2
Mayflower Av *SPK/HALE* L24 .... 50 A6
Mayflower Rd *NANT* CW5 .... 20 F9
Mayhurst Av *CCHDY* M21 .... 44 D1 ⓵
Mayor's Rd *HALE/TIMP* WA15 .... 42 E8
May Rd *CHD/CHDH* SK8 .... 65 C6
May St *GOL/RIS/CU* WA3 .... 23 J2
Maythorn Av *GOL/RIS/CU* WA3 .... 29 G5
Maytree Av *CHSE* CH3 .... 170 D2
Maywood Av *CHD/CHDH* SK8 .... 64 F5
Maywood Dr *DID/WITH* M20 .... 45 H4
Mc Carthy Cl *GOL/RIS/CU* WA3 .... 39 G1
Mc Clellan Pl *WDN* WA8 .... 7 J3
Mcgarva Wy *EP* CH65 .... 95 J8 ⓵
Mcgough Cl *STHEL* WA9 .... 34 A1 ⓵
Mckee Av *WARRN/WOL* WA2 .... 37 H2
Mc Kinley St *BURS/TUN* ST6 .... 243 K8 ⓵
Mclaren St *CW/HAS* CW1 .... 221 H5
Mcminnis Av *STHEL* WA9 .... 26 A3
Mcneill Av *CW/HAS* CW1 .... 220 F7
Mead Av *ALS/KID* ST7 .... 225 L5
Mead Cl *KNUT* WA16 .... 106 F4
The Meade *WILM/AE* SK9 .... 84 B4
Meadow Av *CONG* CW12 .... 207 J3
  CW/SHV CW2 .... 239 H7
  HALE/TIMP WA15 .... 62 B1
  HOLMCH CW4 .... 157 J3
  STHEL WA9 .... 34 G3 ⓵
  WARRS WA4 .... 56 A2
Meadow Bank *HALE/TIMP* WA15 .... 43 C5
  HTNM SK4 .... 46 B2 ⓵
  MKTDR TF9 .... 274 A8 ⓵
  MPL/ROM SK6 .... 47 M1 ⓵
  TPLY/KEL CW6 .... 149 K8 ⓵
Meadowbank Gdns
  GOL/RIS/CU WA3 .... 25 J5 ⓵
Meadow Brow *WILM/AE* SK9 .... 110 A2
Meadow Cl *CHF/WBR* SK23 .... 89 J4
  CHSE CH3 .... 172 B2
  CHSE CH3 .... 228 F3
  CW/SHV CW2 .... 238 D7
  FROD/HEL WA6 .... 124 B3 ⓵
  HALE/TIMP WA15 .... 62 B1
  HOLMCH CW4 .... 157 L3
  LEIGH WN7 .... 24 E2
  MPL/ROM SK6 .... 67 M4
  NSTN CH64 .... 91 J6
  NSTN CH64 .... 92 F4 ⓵
  NWCHW CW8 .... 128 A8 ⓵
  WDN WA8 .... 52 D1
  WILM/AE SK9 .... 83 L8
  WSFD CW7 .... 177 J1 ⓵
Meadow Ct *CH/BCN* CH1 .... 144 F3
  MALPAS SY14 .... 247 G8 ⓵
Meadow Cft *ALS/KID* ST7 .... 241 L2
  BRAM/HZG SK7 .... 66 E1
Meadowcroft *CH/BCN* CH1 .... 144 A3
  CHSW/BR CH4 .... 190 A5
Meadow Cft *NSTN* CH64 .... 92 F4
Meadowcroft *WHITCH* SY13 .... 269 L4 ⓵
Meadow Dr *CW/SHV* CW2 .... 237 M5
  KNUT WA16 .... 106 F4
  MCFLDN SK10 .... 112 B5
  NWCHW CW8 .... 129 G1
Meadowfield *CHF/WBR* SK23 .... 89 J4
  TPLY/KEL CW6 .... 197 J3
Meadow Field Rd
  CHSW/BR CH4 .... 169 G7 ⓵
Meadow Ga *NWCHE* CW9 .... 104 F7
Meadowgate Cl *SBCH* CW11 .... 203 K7
Meadow Gv *NWCHE* CW9 .... 13 L9
  WSFD CW7 .... 153 L7
Meadow Hey Cl *WLTN* L25 .... 50 B1 ⓵
Meadow La *CHSE* CH3 .... 170 A7
  EP CH65 .... 11 G6
  NSTN CH64 .... 92 E3
  NWCHE CW9 .... 103 J5
  NWCHE CW9 .... 153 M5
  POY/DIS SK12 .... 68 D6
  WARRN/WOL WA2 .... 38 A2
Meadow Ri *MALPAS* SY14 .... 230 D2 ⓵
  WSFD CW7 .... 177 G3 ⓵
Meadow Rd *CHSW/BR* CH4 .... 167 H8
  NWCHW CW8 .... 128 E4
Meadows Gn *GOL/RIS/CU* WA3 .... 23 L7
Meadowside *BIDD* ST8 .... 227 H6
  BRAM/HZG SK7 .... 65 J2 ⓵
  CHF/WBR SK23 .... 89 K4
  CO CH5 .... 166 A3
  MCFLDN SK10 .... 87 H4 ⓵
  NM/HAY SK22 .... 69 G6
  NWCHW CW8 .... 12 C4
Meadowside Av *WYTH/NTH* M22 .... 44 E8
Meadowside La *CH/BCN* CH1 .... 226 B5
  CHSW/BR CH4 .... 17 J9
Meadows La *CH/BCN* CH1 .... 144 A4
  CHSW/BR CH4 .... 17 J8
Meadows Pl *CHSW/BR* CH4 .... 17 J8
Meadows Rd *ALS/KID* ST7 .... 242 F3 ⓵
  CHD/CHDH SK8 .... 64 F4
The Meadows *CO* CH5 .... 142 B7
  FLINT CH6 .... 116 A6
  IRL M44 .... 31 K6
  NSTN CH64 .... 91 M6

RAIN/WH L35 .... 33 J2
Meadow St NM/HAY SK22 ... 69 J4
NWCHE CW9 .... 13 J2
OFTN SK2 .... 47 J7
Meadowsway CHNE CH2 ... 145 K4
Meadowsweet Rd
KNUT WA16 .... 107 M1
Meadowvale CI NANT CW5 ... 20 F2
Meadow Vw CHNE CH2 ... 123 C1
CQ CH5 .... 143 G6
MWCH CW10 .... 179 H2
Meadow View Dr
FROD/HEL WA6 .... 99 G5
Meadow View Rd WHITCH SY13 ... 269 M5
Meadow Wy ALS/KID ST7 ... 225 C7
HALE/TIMP WA15 ... 62 B1
MCFLDN SK10 .... 15 J2
WILM/AE SK9 .... 83 L8
Mead Rd WARR WA1 ... 38 A4
Meadscroft Dr WILM/AE SK9 ... 109 M3
Meads Rd WHITCH SY13 ... 224 D8
Meadway BRAM/HZG SK7 ... 65 L7
GOL/RIS/CU WA3 ... 23 K4
GTS/LS CH66 .... 94 B5
MCFLDN SK10 .... 112 A7
MPL/ROM SK6 .... 49 K6
POY/DIS SK12 .... 66 B7
RUNC WA7 .... 73 K3
SALE M33 .... 42 E2
WDN WA8 .... 52 A3
Meadway CI SALE M33 ... 42 E1
Meadway Rd CHD/CHDH SK8 ... 65 H1
Meakin CI CONG CW12 ... 208 D3
Mealhouse Brow STKP SK1 ... 3 G5
Meal St HTNM SK4 ... 2 E1
NM/HAY SK22 ... 69 J4
Mechanics' La CQ CH5 ... 142 E8
Meddings CI WILM/AE SK9 ... 110 A4
Medina Av CW7 ... 177 M2
Medina CI CHD/CHDH SK8 ... 46 B8
Medina Wy ALS/KID ST7 ... 243 H2
Medlar CI CHSW/BR CH4 ... 168 F7
Medway CI LEIGH WN7 ... 24 C4
WARRN/WOL WA2 ... 37 L2
WILM/AE SK9 ... 84 D2
Medway Crs ALT WA14 ... 42 C6
Medway Dr BIDD ST8 ... 227 K3
Medway Rd GOL/RIS/CU WA3 ... 30 A2
Meeanee Dr NANT CW5 ... 20 B8
Meerbrook Rd EDGY/DAV SK3 ... 46 A4
Mee St MCFLDS SK11 ... 138 E7
Meeting La WARRN/BUR WA5 ... 35 K7
Meg La MCFLDN SK10 ... 137 L4
MCFLDS SK11 ... 137 L4
Meir St BURS/TUN ST6 ... 243 K8
Melbecks Wk NTHM/RTH M23 ... 43 M2
Melbourne Av MANAIR M90 ... 63 C4
Melbourne Gv CW/HAS CW1 ... 222 C7
Melbourne Rd BRAM/HZG SK7 ... 65 L6
CH/BCN CH1 ... 144 D8
Melbreck Av CQ CH5 ... 166 A3
Melbury Ct GOL/RIS/CU WA3 ... 29 M6
Melbury Rd CHD/CHDH SK8 ... 65 H6
Melchett Crs NWCHE CW9 ... 130 D5
Melford CI CW/SHV CW2 ... 238 C4
Melford Dr MCFLDN SK10 ... 138 C2
RUNC WA7 ... 9 L5
Melford Rd BRAM/HZG SK7 ... 66 F3
Meliden Crs NTHM/RTH M23 ... 63 L2
Meliden Gv FROD/HEL WA6 ... 124 A3
Melkridge CI CHNE CH2 ... 170 A1
Melksham CI MCFLDS SK11 ... 14 B7
Melling CI LEIGH WN7 ... 24 F3
Mellington Av DID/WITH M20 ... 45 J4
Mellock CI NSTN CH64 ... 91 M6
Mellock La NSTN CH64 ... 91 M5
Mellor CI RAIN/WH L35 ... 32 A5
RUNC WA7 ... 74 D4
Mellor Ct OFTN SK2 ... 47 L5
Mellor Crs KNUT WA16 ... 106 E3
Mellor CI CHD/CHDH SK8 ... 65 H3
NM/HAY SK22 ... 69 J1
Mellors Bank ALS/KID ST7 ... 226 C6
Mellor St ALS/KID ST7 ... 243 M3
CW/HAS CW1 ... 19 C1
Melrose Av CHSE CH3 ... 170 B2
CQ CH5 ... 142 F6
DID/WITH M20 ... 45 J1
EDGY/DAV SK3 ... 45 M5
SALE M33 ... 43 H1
WARRS WA4 ... 56 D4
Melrose Crs EDGY/DAV SK3 ... 46 D8
HALE/TIMP WA15 ... 62 B3
POY/DIS SK12 ... 67 K7
Melrose Dr CW/HAS CW1 ... 221 H4
GTS/LS CH66 ... 120 F4
Melsomby Rd NTHM/RTH M23 ... 44 A2
Meltham CI HTNM SK4 ... 45 L3
Meltham Rd HTNM SK4 ... 45 L3
Melton Av WARRS WA4 ... 56 B4
Melton CI CONG CW12 ... 206 F1
Melton Dr CONG CW12 ... 206 F1
Melton Rd RUNC WA7 ... 73 H6
Melverly Dr CH/BCN CH1 ... 144 C8
Melville Rd IRL M44 ... 31 J7
Melvin Av WYTH/NTH M22 ... 44 E8
Menai Dr BIDD ST8 ... 227 K6
Menai Gv CHD/CHDH SK8 ... 46 A6
Menai Rd EDGY/DAV SK3 ... 46 E6
Mendip Av WARRN/WOL WA2 ... 37 H1
WYTH/NTH M22 ... 44 F8
Mendip CI CHD/CHDH SK8 ... 64 B5
GTS/LS CH66 ... 120 E1
HLWD L26 ... 50 E5
HTNM SK4 ... 2 E1
WSFD CW7 ... 177 H4
Menin Av WARRS WA4 ... 56 C1
Menlow CI WARRS WA4 ... 57 J3
Mentmore Gdns WARRS WA4 ... 56 F7
Mentone Crs WYTH/NTH M22 ... 44 E8
Mentone Rd MANAIR M90 ... 46 B1
Meols CI GTS/LS CH66 ... 94 E8
Mercer CI MALPAS SY14 ... 258 B1
Mercer St NEWLW WA12 ... 22 D8
WARRW/BUR WA5 ... 26 E6
Mercer Wy CHSW/BR CH4 ... 168 F6

Merchants Crs GOL/RIS/CU WA3 ... 23 L3
Mercian CI CW/SHV CW2 ... 238 B8
Mercian Wy EDGY/DAV SK3 ... 2 D9
Mercury Ct CH/BCN CH1 ... 168 E2
Mere Bank NWCHE CW9 ... 154 A4
Merebank Rd CW/SHV CW2 ... 18 C9
Merebrook Rd MCFLDS SK11 ... 137 M4
Mere Brook Wk CW/SHV CW2 ... 238 C3
Mere CI CW/HAS CW1 ... 222 D8
GTS/LS CH66 ... 120 D2
KNUT WA16 ... 105 C5
SALE M33 ... 43 M1
Mere Crs NWCHW CW8 ... 150 F6
Merecroft CHSE CH3 ... 171 C8
Meredith Av WARRS WA4 ... 57 H2
Meredith St CW/HAS CW1 ... 18 E2
Merefield Rd HALE/TIMP WA15 ... 43 J7
Merehaven CI KNUT WA16 ... 104 F5
Mereheath La NANT CW5 ... 80 D5
Mereheath Pk KNUT WA16 ... 106 F1
Merelake Rd ALS/KID ST7 ... 242 A4
Mere La KNUT WA16 ... 104 F6
NWCHW CW8 ... 152 A2
Merepool CI MPL/ROM SK6 ... 48 D5
Mere Rd CW/SHV CW2 ... 239 H7
NEWLW WA12 ... 22 F8
NWCHE CW9 ... 104 B6
WARRN/WOL WA2 ... 38 A2
Mereside Av CONG CW12 ... 207 L2
Mereside CI CHD/CHDH SK8 ... 45 M8
MCFLDN SK10 ... 14 A2
Mereside Gdns CHF/WBR SK23 ... 89 K6
Mereside Rd KNUT WA16 ... 80 C3
Mere St CW/HAS CW1 ... 222 D8
Merevale CI RUNC WA7 ... 73 L6
Merewood Av WYTH/NTH M22 ... 44 D6
Merewood CI WARRN/WOL WA2 ... 37 K1
Mereworth Dr NWCHE CW9 ... 13 G9
Merganser CI CW/HAS CW1 ... 220 F5
Meriton Rd WILM/AE SK9 ... 64 C8
Merlin Av KNUT WA16 ... 107 H1
Merlin CI OFTN SK2 ... 48 A6
RUNC WA7 ... 74 A4
WSFD CW7 ... 178 A4
Merlin Ct HLWD L26 ... 50 D3
Merlin Gn AUD/MAD/W CW3 ... 267 L6
Merlin Wy ALS/KID ST7 ... 243 K1
CW/HAS CW1 ... 221 G4
Merrick Av WYTH/NTH M22 ... 44 E8
Merrick CI WARRN/WOL WA2 ... 37 L2
The Merridale HALE/TIMP WA15 ... 61 M4
Merriden Rd MCFLDN SK10 ... 14 D1
Merrill's Av CW/SHV CW2 ... 220 E7
Merriman Rd KNUT WA16 ... 107 J1
Merrivale Rd CW/SHV CW2 ... 238 A4
WLTN L25 ... 35 J1
Merrybent CI OFTN SK2 ... 47 K8
Merrydale CI MCFLDN SK10 ... 137 M3
Merryman's La WILM/AE SK9 ... 109 H5
Mersey Crs DID/WITH M20 ... 44 D1
Mersey Mdw DID/WITH M20 ... 44 F1
Mersey Rd DID/WITH M20 ... 44 F1
HTNM SK4 ... 45 M2
RUNC WA7 ... 9 G1
WDN WA8 ... 53 G8
Mersey Sq STKP SK1 ... 2 F5
Mersey St RUNC WA7 ... 9 H1
STHEL WA9 ... 26 A1
STKP SK1 ... 3 K3
WARR WA1 ... 5 H8
Merseyton Rd EP CH65 ... 10 D2
Mersey View Rd WDN WA8 ... 52 B8
Mersey View South Rd
RUNC WA7 ... 8 A8
Mersey Wk WARRS WA4 ... 37 M7
Mersey Wy WARRW/BUR WA5 ... 36 C8
Mersham Ct WDN WA8 ... 33 M8
Merston Dr DID/WITH M20 ... 45 J5
Merstone CI HLWD L26 ... 51 C5
Merton Av BRAM/HZG SK7 ... 66 F4
Merton CI NSTN CH64 ... 91 L7
Merton Dr CHSW/BR CH4 ... 169 G8
Merton Gv HALE/TIMP WA15 ... 43 H6
Merton Rd EDGY/DAV SK3 ... 46 B3
GTS/LS CH66 ... 120 E1
POY/DIS SK12 ... 66 B8
PS/BROM CH62 ... 94 B1
Mertoun Rd WARRS WA4 ... 56 B3
Mervyn Rd NWCHW CW8 ... 128 E3
Merwood Av CHD/CHDH SK8 ... 64 D4
Messuage La CONG CW12 ... 159 G8
Meteor Crs WARRN/WOL WA2 ... 37 K2
Mevagissey Rd RUNC WA7 ... 74 C7
Mevril Rd CHF/WBR SK23 ... 89 L7
The Mews CHD/CHDH SK8 ... 129 H2
NWCHW CW8 ... 129 H2
TPLY/KEL CW6 ... 197 J4
Meyer St EDGY/DAV SK3 ... 46 F6
Meynell CI CW/SHV CW2 ... 238 A3
Meynell Dr LEIGH WN7 ... 24 F2
Meynell PI CH/BCN CH1 ... 145 G7
Micawber Rd POY/DIS SK12 ... 86 E2
Micklegate CHNE CH2 ... 146 E4
RUNC WA7 ... 74 D5
Micklehurst Gn OFTN SK2 ... 47 L7
Micklewright Av CW/HAS CW1 ... 19 G1
Mickley Hall La NANT CW5 ... 263 H1
Middlecroft CHSE CH3 ... 146 E7
Middlefields CHD/CHDH SK8 ... 46 B8
Middle Hillgate STKP SK1 ... 3 H6
Middlehills MCFLDS SK11 ... 139 G6
Middlehurst Av NWCHW CW8 ... 128 E4
Middlehurst Rd WARRS WA4 ... 57 G2
Middle La CHSE CH3 ... 211 M1
CONG CW12 ... 185 J8
FROD/HEL WA6 ... 125 M3
Middle Rd SPK/HALE L24 ... 50 F7
Middleton Av FROD/HEL WA6 ... 99 H5
KNUT WA16 ... 107 H3
Middlewich Rd CW/HAS CW1 ... 220 E5
CW/SHV CW2 ... 237 J1
HOLMCH CW4 ... 156 E6
MWCH CW10 ... 201 L4
NANT CW5 ... 21 G3
NWCHE CW9 ... 13 M2

SBCH CW11 .... 203 L6
CW7 .... 178 C3
Middlewich St CW/HAS CW1 ... 19 G1
Middlewood
GOL/RIS/CU WA3 ... 23 M4
Middlewood Dr HTNM SK4 ... 46 A3
Middlewood Rd MPL/ROM SK6 ... 67 K5
POY/DIS SK12 ... 67 C8
Middlewood Wy MCFLDN SK10 ... 87 C6
Midfield CI BIDD ST8 ... 227 J2
Midhurst CI ALS/KID ST7 ... 243 M4
CHD/CHDH SK8 ... 64 F4
Midland Rd BRAM/HZG SK7 ... 65 L1
Midland Ter NM/HAY SK22 ... 69 J5
Midland Wk BRAM/HZG SK7 ... 65 L1
Midland Wy WARR WA1 ... 4 E5
Midway CHD/CHDH SK8 ... 65 H7
Midwood St WDN WA8 ... 7 J3
Milborne CI CHNE CH2 ... 145 L7
Milburn Av NTHM/RTH M23 ... 44 B2
Mile Bank Rd WHITCH SY13 ... 260 D8
Mile End La OFTN SK2 ... 47 J5
Miles CI GOL/RIS/CU WA3 ... 38 F1
Milford CI CW/SHV CW2 ... 238 B4
Milford Gdns WARRS WA4 ... 56 D8
Milford Gv OFTN SK2 ... 47 J5
Milk St CONG CW12 ... 207 K1
Millar Crs WDN WA8 ... 7 G6
Millbank LYMM WA13 ... 58 L1
Mill Bank NSTN CH64 ... 92 A7
Millbank CI MCFLDS SK11 ... 135 C1
Millbank Dr MCFLDN SK10 ... 137 M3
Millbeck CI CW/SHV CW2 ... 239 H7
Millbrook End NTHM/RTH M23 ... 63 C1
Millbrook La CHSW/BR CH4 ... 3 G7
Mill Brow MPL/ROM SK6 ... 49 K4
WDN WA8 ... 7 M2
Mill Brow Rd MPL/ROM SK6 ... 49 L4
Millbuck Wy SBCH CW11 ... 203 J6
Mill CI CHNE CH2 ... 145 K6
EP CH65 ... 121 J3
KNUT WA16 ... 81 K8
WARRN/WOL WA2 ... 28 E8
Mill Cft FLINT CH6 ... 116 C7
Millcroft Rd WLTN L25 ... 50 C3
Milldale Rd LEIGH WN7 ... 24 B3
Millend La ALS/KID ST7 ... 241 J7
Millers CI CHSE CH3 ... 171 C8
SALE M33 ... 44 A1
Millersdale Gv RUNC WA7 ... 73 K7
Millers La LYMM WA13 ... 40 B7
Millers Meadow MCFLDN SK10 ... 5 K9
Miller St WARRS WA4 ... 5 K9
Millers Vw ALS/KID ST7 ... 243 G4
Millers Whf ALS/KID ST7 ... 224 E5
Milley La KNUT WA16 ... 105 J5
Mill Farm CI WARRN/WOL WA2 ... 37 L1
Mill Field CI CHSE CH3 ... 228 F2
Millfield La CHSE CH3 ... 193 M3
Millfield Rd WDN WA8 ... 7 L1
Millfields NANT CW5 ... 20 C8
Millgate STKP SK1 ... 3 G4
Millgate La DID/WITH M20 ... 45 G4
Mill Gn CONG CW12 ... 207 K1
... 92 F4
Mill Green La WDN WA8 ... 34 D7
Mill Gv ALS/KID ST7 ... 242 D3
MALPAS SY14 ... 232 D2
Mill Hey RAIN/WH L35 ... 33 L3
Mill Hill Av POY/DIS SK12 ... 66 D5
Mill Hill Dr SBCH CW11 ... 204 A8
Mill Hill Hollow POY/DIS SK12 ... 66 D5
Mill Hill La SBCH CW11 ... 204 A8
Millhouse Av NTHM/RTH M23 ... 44 A8
WARRS WA4 ... 56 D3
Millhouse La GOL/RIS/CU WA3 ... 29 C6
The Millingford HOLMCH CW4 ... 181 J2
Millingford Av GOL/RIS/CU WA3 ... 22 F2
Millingford Gv AIMK WN4 ... 22 B1
Millington CI RUNC WA7 ... 73 M8
Millington Hall La ALT WA14 ... 60 B7
Millington La ALT WA14 ... 60 B6
Mill La ALS/KID ST7 ... 226 A5
AUD/MAD/W CW3 ... 264 A8
AUD/MAD/W CW3 ... 267 M5
AUD/MAD/W CW3 ... 273 L2
BRAM/HZG SK7 ... 66 F4
CHD/CHDH SK8 ... 45 K6
CHD/CHDH SK8 ... 65 H1
CHNE CH2 ... 145 K7
CHSE CH3 ... 147 L7
CHSE CH3 ... 171 L2
CHSE CH3 ... 172 C1
CHSE CH3 ... 195 J3
CONG CW12 ... 183 L3
CONG CW12 ... 208 C4
CQ CH5 ... 142 A6
CW/SHV CW2 ... 239 G6
CW/SHV CW2 ... 240 C5
FROD/HEL WA6 ... 99 L2
FROD/HEL WA6 ... 126 D1
GTS/LS CH66 ... 94 D8
HALE/TIMP WA15 ... 62 B1
HOLMCH CW4 ... 157 L3
HOLMCH CW4 ... 181 L3
HOLMCH CW4 ... 182 A4
KNUT WA16 ... 82 B8
KNUT WA16 ... 134 D3
LYMM WA13 ... 40 C7
MALPAS SY14 ... 232 D2
MCFLDN SK10 ... 85 L6
MCFLDN SK10 ... 85 H8
MCFLDN SK10 ... 113 J4
MCFLDS SK11 ... 15 H7
MCFLDS SK11 ... 135 L6
MWCH CW10 ... 179 H3
NANT CW5 ... 266 A1
NEWLW WA12 ... 27 L1
NSTN CH64 ... 92 C7
NSTN CH64 ... 118 C3
NWCHW CW8 ... 127 M7
RAIN/WH L35 ... 33 J3
SBCH CW11 ... 203 J3

SBCH CW11 .... 223 G2
TPLY/KEL CW6 .... 172 F5
TPLY/KEL CW6 .... 173 J3
TPLY/KEL CW6 .... 176 A4
TPLY/KEL CW6 .... 198 B2
WARRN/WOL WA2 .... 27 L7
WARRN/WOL WA2 .... 28 E8
WARRN/WOL WA2 .... 37 G1
WARRS WA4 .... 55 L5
WARRS WA4 .... 56 D3
WDN WA8 .... 33 K7
WDN WA8 .... 34 C8
WDN WA8 .... 34 D7
WHITCH SY13 .... 268 A8
WILM/AE SK9 .... 108 F6
WSFD CW7 .... 153 J6
WYTH/NTH M22 .... 44 E3
Millmead ALS/KID ST7 ... 224 F5
Mill Meadow NEWLW WA12 ... 27 L7
Millom Av NTHM/RTH M23 ... 44 B3
Millom PI CHD/CHDH SK8 ... 64 B1
Mill Park Dr PS/BROM CH62 ... 93 L1
Mill Pool La NANT CW5 ... 218 D6
Millrace Dr CW/SHV CW2 ... 238 B4
Mill Ri ALS/KID ST7 ... 242 F3
Mill Rd MCFLDS SK11 ... 15 J8
Mill Rw SBCH CW11 ... 204 C6
Millstone Av ALS/KID ST7 ... 242 E3
Millstone CI POY/DIS SK12 ... 66 F7
Millstone La NANT CW5 ... 20 C6
Millstone Pas MCFLDS SK11 ... 15 J8
Mill St AIMK WN4 ... 22 C2
ALT WA14 ... 42 E7
BRAM/HZG SK7 ... 66 D1
CHSW/BR CH4 ... 17 H8
CONG CW12 ... 19 G5
GOL/RIS/CU WA3 ... 23 G4
MCFLDS SK11 ... 15 G5
NANT CW5 ...
NSTN CH64 ... 91 L4
WHITCH SY13 ... 270 A5
WILM/AE SK9 ... 84 B5
WLTN L25 ... 50 A2
Mills Wy CW/HAS CW1 ... 221 H4
Mill View CI MALPAS SY14 ... 232 E2
Mill View Rd CQ CH5 ... 142 A6
Millway CHSE CH3 ... 171 H7
HALE/TIMP WA15 ... 62 C5
Mill Wy NANT CW5 ... 251 M2
Millway Rd SPK/HALE L24 ... 51 G8
Millwood CHD/CHDH SK8 ... 64 E4
Millwood CI ALS/KID ST7 ... 243 C4
Millwood Gdns RAIN/WH L35 ... 32 F2
Millwood Rd SPK/HALE L24 ... 70 E1
Milne CI CW/SHV CW2 ... 237 M4
Milner Av NWCHW CW8 ... 12 B6
Milner Rd WARRW/BUR WA5 ... 4 D7
Milnes Av LEIGH WN7 ... 24 F2
Milnthorpe Rd
WARRW/BUR WA5 ... 26 E6
Milton Av IRL M44 ... 31 L6
NEWLW WA12 ... 27 H1
RAIN/WH L35 ... 32 E1
WDN WA8 ... 6 E5
Milton CI MPL/ROM SK6 ... 48 F8
MWCH CW10 ... 179 K7
NWCHE CW9 ... 105 C7
RAIN/WH L35 ... 32 E1
Milton Crs ALS/KID ST7 ... 242 C4
CHD/CHDH SK8 ... 45 J7
Milton Dr CW/SHV CW2 ... 237 M4
HALE/TIMP WA15 ... 43 G3
POY/DIS SK12 ... 66 D8
Milton Gv FROD/HEL WA6 ... 124 A3
WARRS WA4 ... 56 D2
Milton Rd CH/BCN CH1 ... 144 F6
EP CH65 ... 95 K8
GOL/RIS/CU WA3 ... 23 K5
WDN WA8 ... 7 G5
Milton Rough NWCHW CW8 ... 127 L2
Milton St CH/BCN CH1 ... 17 H4
STHEL WA9 ... 34 A2
WDN WA8 ... 53 G7
Milton Wy SBCH CW11 ... 203 K6
Milvain Dr WARRN/WOL WA2 ... 37 J3
Milverton Dr CHD/CHDH SK8 ... 65 H7
Min Awel FLINT CH6 ... 116 B8
Miners Wy SPK/HALE L24 ... 71 C1
WDN WA8 ... 7 H7
Minerva Av CH/BCN CH1 ... 168 D2
Minerva CI BIDD ST8 ... 227 H7
WARRS WA4 ... 56 D2
Minfield CI ALS/KID ST7 ... 243 C4
Minn-end-lane MCFLDS SK11 ... 187 C6
Minor Av MCFLDS SK11 ... 162 D2
Minshull CI NANT CW5 ... 200 C8
WSFD CW7 ... 200 A7
Minshull New Rd CW/HAS CW1 ... 220 F6
Minshull St KNUT WA16 ... 107 C2
Minster CI CW/SHV CW2 ... 237 K7
Minster Ct ALT WA14 ... 61 C4
CHD/CHDH SK8 ... 46 A7
Minster Dr ALT WA14 ... 61 C4
Minton CI CONG CW12 ... 208 D3
Minton Wy WDN WA8 ... 34 B7
Mirfield CI HTNM SK4 ... 46 B2
Mirfield CI GOL/RIS/CU WA3 ... 23 K5
HLWD L26 ... 50 F7
Mirion St CW/HAS CW1 ... 19 H3
Misty CI WDN WA8 ... 52 C2
Mitchell Av ALS/KID ST7 ... 242 D3
WARRW/BUR WA5 ... 26 E7
Mitchell CI CHD/CHDH SK8 ... 44 F6
Mitchell Rd ALS/KID ST7 ... 242 D3
Mitchell St AIMK WN4 ... 22 C2
GOL/RIS/CU WA3 ... 23 G5
WARRS WA4 ... 56 C4
Mithril CI RAIN/WH L35 ... 53 L1
Mitre CI RAIN/WH L35 ... 32 D3
Moat Av WYTH/NTH M22 ... 44 C8
Moat Gdns WYTH/NTH M22 ... 44 C8
Moat House Dr CW/SHV CW2 ... 18 B8
Moat La GOL/RIS/CU WA3 ... 39 L3
Moat Rd WYTH/NTH M22 ... 44 C8
Mobberley CI WARRS WA4 ... 57 L1
Mobberley Rd BURS/TUN ST6 ... 243 J7

KNUT WA16 .... 81 L2
KNUT WA16 .... 107 H2
WILM/AE SK9 .... 83 J3
Modbury CI BRAM/HZG SK7 ... 66 A3
Moelfre Dr CHD/CHDH SK8 ... 65 J5
Moel Parc FLINT CH6 ... 116 B8
Moggie La MCFLDN SK10 ... 86 F3
Mollington Ct CH/BCN CH1 ... 144 E3
Mollington Rd WYTH/NTH M22 ... 63 L4
Molly Pitcher Wy
WARRW/BUR WA5 ... 36 B7
Molly Potts CI KNUT WA16 ... 107 H4
Molyneux La WARRW/BUR WA5 ... 4 D1
Mona Av CHD/CHDH SK8 ... 64 D3
Monaco Dr WYTH/NTH M22 ... 44 D2
Monarch CI IRL M44 ... 31 L6
Monarch Dr NWCHE CW9 ... 12 F8
Mond Rd WDN WA8 ... 7 G5
Mond St NWCHW CW8 ... 129 H2
Money Ash Rd HALE/TIMP WA15 ... 61 K1
Monfa Av EDGY/DAV SK3 ... 47 G8
Monica Dr WDN WA8 ... 34 A7
Monica Rd WLTN L25 ... 50 B3
Monica Ter AIMK WN4 ... 22 B2
Monks Gv EP CH65 ... 10 D6
Monk's La AUD/MAD/W CW3 ... 264 C2
CW/HAS CW1 ... 220 F6
NANT CW5 ... 20 F6
NANT CW5 ... 235 M5
Monks Orch NANT CW5 ... 21 G6
Monks St WARRW/BUR WA5 ... 4 B5
Monk St CW/HAS CW1 ... 18 B2
Monks Wy NWCHW CW8 ... 129 H8
WLTN L25 ... 50 B2
Monkswood CI
WARRW/BUR WA5 ... 36 E2
Monmouth CI WARR WA1 ... 38 E5
Monmouth Crs AIMK WN4 ... 22 C2
Monmouth Rd CHD/CHDH SK8 ... 65 H3
Monroe CI WARR WA1 ... 38 B5
Monsal Av EDGY/DAV SK3 ... 47 K5
Monsall CI MCFLDS SK11 ... 15 M4
Monsall Dr MCFLDS SK11 ... 15 M7
Montagu Rd OFTN SK2 ... 47 K5
Montagu St MPL/ROM SK6 ... 49 H2
Montclare Crs WARRS WA4 ... 56 E3
Montcliffe CI GOL/RIS/CU WA3 ... 29 J7
Montgomery Rd WDN WA8 ... 6 A6
Montgomery Wy WSFD CW7 ... 177 H5
Mont Morency Rd KNUT WA16 ... 81 K8
Montpelier Av RUNC WA7 ... 72 F6
Montpellior Rd
WYTH/NTH M22 ... 63 K2
Montrose Av EDGY/DAV SK3 ... 66 A1
Montrose CI CW/SHV CW2 ... 253 H1
MCFLDN SK10 ... 14 A3
WARRN/WOL WA2 ... 28 F8
Montrose Ct HOLMCH CW4 ... 181 H2
Monument Rd ALS/KID ST7 ... 242 D6
Moody St CONG CW12 ... 207 L3
Moor CI BIDD ST8 ... 227 L3
Moorcroft KNUT WA16 ... 131 M1
Moorcroft Av CHSE CH3 ... 170 B3
Moorcroft Crs CHSE CH3 ... 146 E3
Moorcroft Rd NTHM/RTH M23 ... 43 M3
Moordale Rd KNUT WA16 ... 107 H2
Moorditch La FROD/HEL WA6 ... 98 B3
Moore Av STHEL WA9 ... 26 A1
WARRS WA4 ... 57 K1
Moore CI WDN WA8 ... 53 K2
Moore Gv LYMM WA13 ... 40 B7
Moore La WARRS WA4 ... 55 H5
Moor End WYTH/NTH M22 ... 44 D6
Mooreway RAIN/WH L35 ... 33 L3
Moorfield Av BIDD ST8 ... 227 J4
Moorfield Ct CQ CH5 ... 166 B3
Moorfield Crs GOL/RIS/CU WA3 ... 24 A5
Moorfield Dr NSTN CH64 ... 91 J2
WILM/AE SK9 ... 83 L7
Moorfield Gv SALE M33 ... 43 K1
Moorfield Rd CQ CH5 ... 166 B3
WDN WA8 ... 34 D8
Moorfields NANT CW5 ... 237 G5
Moorhead La SBCH CW11 ... 205 J1
Moorhill Rd MCFLDS SK11 ... 138 C8
Moorhouse Av ALS/KID ST7 ... 224 E8
Moorhouse CI CHNE CH2 ... 145 K7
Mooring CI RUNC WA7 ... 74 D6
Moorings CONG CW12 ... 207 L3
Moorings CI NSTN CH64 ... 91 H3
The Moorings MWCH CW10 ... 179 J3
POY/DIS SK12 ... 68 E6
Moorland Av SALE M33 ... 43 J1
Moorland Dr CHD/CHDH SK8 ... 64 F4
RUNC WA7 ... 74 E5
Moorland Rd ALS/KID ST7 ... 226 D5
BIDD ST8 ... 227 K4
DID/WITH M20 ... 45 H1
GTS/LS CH66 ... 94 E4
OFTN SK2 ... 47 G8
Moorlands Av LEIGH WN7 ... 24 F1
NWCHW CW8 ... 128 A8
Moorlands CI MCFLDN SK10 ... 138 C1
Moorlands Dr NANT CW5 ... 253 C3
Moorlands Pk NWCHW CW8 ... 128 A8
Moor La BRAM/HZG SK7 ... 85 K1
CHSE CH3 ... 171 C4
CHSW/BR CH4 ... 190 C6
CQ CH5 ... 166 E4
FROD/HEL WA6 ... 99 H4
FROD/HEL WA6 ... 123 L3
NTHM/RTH M23 ... 44 A2
WDN WA8 ... 6 F7
WILM/AE SK9 ... 83 J7
Moor La South WDN WA8 ... 6 F7
Moor Nook SALE M33 ... 43 K1
Moor Park Rd DID/WITH M20 ... 45 J4
Moor-park Wy NWCHE CW9 ... 129 M8
Moor Rd NTHM/RTH M23 ... 43 L4
Moorsfield Av
AUD/MAD/W CW3 ... 273 M1
Moorside KNUT WA16 ... 107 C2
Moorside Av NSTN CH64 ... 91 J4
Moorside CI WDN WA8 ... 6 F6
Moorside La MCFLDN SK10 ... 87 L8
NSTN CH64 ... 91 J5
Moorside Rd HTNM SK4 ... 46 A2

Moors La *WSFD* CW7 .... 177 J7
Moorson Av *ALS/KID* ST7 .... 225 M4
Moor Top Pl *HTNM* SK4 .... 46 B1
Moorwood Dr *SALE* M33 .... 42 E1
Moran Cl *WILM/AE* SK9 .... 84 D2
Moran Crs *MCFLDS* SK11 .... 14 D7
Moran Rd *MCFLDS* SK11 .... 14 D7
Morcott La *SPK/HALE* L24 .... 71 K7
Morden Av *AIMK* WN4 .... 22 B1
Moresby Cl *RUNC* WA7 .... 74 E5
Moresby Dr *DID/WITH* M20 .... 45 H4
Moreton Av *BRAM/HZG* SK7 .... 65 L7
 SALE M33 .... 42 F1
Moreton Cl *ALS/KID* ST7 .... 243 H4
 GOL/RIS/CU WA3 .... 22 F3
Moreton Dr *ALS/KID* ST7 .... 241 H1
 HOLMCH WA4 .... 181 H1
 LEIGH WN7 .... 24 E3
 POY/DIS SK12 .... 66 F8
 SBCH CW11 .... 204 C5
 WILM/AE SK9 .... 84 E1
Moreton La *OFTN* SK2 .... 47 J5
Moreton Rd *CW/SHV* CW2 .... 237 M2
Moreton St *NWCHW* CW8 .... 12 D2
Moreville Cl *NWCHE* CW9 .... 153 L1
Morgan Av *WARRN/WOL* WA2 .... 37 J2
Morgan Cl *CH/BCN* CH1 .... 144 F7
 CW/SHV CW2 .... 18 A3
Morland Av *NSTN* CH64 .... 91 M5
Morley Br *FROD/HEL* WA6 .... 123 J8
Morley Cl *CHNE* CH2 .... 146 F4
Morley Dr *CONG* CW12 .... 208 A3
Morley Green Rd *WILM/AE* SK9 .... 83 J3
Morley Rd *RUNC* WA7 .... 9 C5
 WARRS WA4 .... 56 A3
Morley's La *TYLD* M29 .... 25 M1
Morley St *WARR* WA1 .... 5 K5
Mornant Av *NWCHW* CW8 .... 153 C1
Morningside *AV* CW3 .... 267 L6
Morningside Dr *DID/WITH* M20 .... 45 J4
Mornington Av
 CHD/CHDH 45 K8
 EP CH65 .... 10 F8
Mornington Cl *SBCH* CW11 .... 203 K5
Mornington Rd *CHD/CHDH* SK8 .... 45 K8
Morphany La *WARRS* WA4 .... 75 L6
Morrell Rd *WYTH/NTH* M22 .... 44 D4
Morreys La *TPLY/KEL* CW6 .... 149 M6
Morris Av *WARRS* WA4 .... 37 M8
Morris Dr *NWCHW* CW8 .... 128 D3
Morrison Cl *WARRW/BUR* WA5 .... 36 A7
Morris Pk *NWCHW* CW8 .... 129 H8
Mort Av *WARRS* WA4 .... 38 A3
Mortimer Av *WARRN/WOL* WA2 .... 5 H1
Mortimer Dr *SBCH* CW11 .... 204 C7
Mortlake Cl *WDN* WA8 .... 52 C1
Mortlake Crs *CHSE* CH3 .... 170 A3
Morton Av *FROD/HEL* WA6 .... 124 B3
Morton Cl *WARRW/BUR* WA5 .... 36 C4
Morton Dr *MCFLDS* SK11 .... 162 F1
Morton Rd *CH/BCN* CH1 .... 144 E8
 RUNC WA7 .... 74 D4
Morval Crs *RUNC* WA7 .... 9 M5
Morven Av *BRAM/HZG* SK7 .... 66 F1
Morven Cl *WARRN/WOL* WA2 .... 37 L1
Morven Dr *NTHM/RTH* M23 .... 44 A7
Moscow Rd *EDGY/DAV* SK3 .... 46 D5
Moscow Rd East *EDGY/DAV* SK3 .... 46 D5
Mosedale Cl *NTHM/RTH* M23 .... 43 L4
Mosedale Gv *RUNC* WA7 .... 73 L7
Moseldene Rd *OFTN* SK2 .... 47 K7
Moseley Av *WARRS* WA4 .... 38 A4
Moseley Rd *CHD/CHDH* SK8 .... 64 F1
Moseley St *EDGY/DAV* SK3 .... 2 E8
Mosley Cl *HALE/TIMP* WA15 .... 42 F5
Mosley Rd *HALE/TIMP* WA15 .... 43 H6
Mossack Av *WYTH/NTH* M22 .... 63 K3
Moss Bank *CH/BCN* CH1 .... 16 E1
 CHD/CHDH SK8 .... 65 J7
 WSFD CW7 .... 177 H5
Moss Bank Rd *WDN* WA8 .... 53 K5
Moss Bower Rd *MCFLDS* SK11 .... 138 C8
Moss Brow *MCFLDN* SK10 .... 112 E5
Moss Brow La *KNUT* WA16 .... 58 D8
Moss Cl *NSTN* CH64 .... 93 C4
 WARRS WA4 .... 56 E2
Moss Cft *CW/HAS* CW1 .... 221 C4
Mossdale Cl *CW/SHV* CW2 .... 220 E8
 WARRW/BUR WA5 .... 36 A5
Mossdale Dr *RAIN/WH* L35 .... 33 K1
Mossdale Rd *NTHM/RTH* M23 .... 43 M3
 SALE M33 .... 42 E3
Moss Dr *MWCH* CW10 .... 179 K6
Mossfield Cl *HTNM* SK4 .... 46 B4
Mossfield Crs *ALS/KID* ST7 .... 243 H2
Mossfield Rd *HALE/TIMP* WA15 .... 43 K6
Moss Flds *ALS/KID* ST7 .... 241 C1
Mossford Av *CW/HAS* CW1 .... 221 H5
Moss Ga *GOL/RIS/CU* WA3 .... 29 C1
Moss Gn *WRX/GR/LL* LL12 .... 210 C5
Moss Green Wy *STHEL* WA9 .... 26 A6
Moss Gv *CHSW/BR* CH4 .... 168 D6
 LYMM WA13 .... 40 B8
Mossgrove Rd *HALE/TIMP* WA15 .... 42 F6
Mosshall La *WARRS* WA4 .... 76 F3
Moss Hey Dr *NTHM/RTH* M23 .... 44 B3
Mosslands Cl *GTS/LS* CH66 .... 120 C2
Moss La *ALS/KID* ST7 .... 225 L8
 AUD/MAD/W CW3 .... 267 K6
 BRAM/HZG SK7 .... 65 J7
 CONG CW12 .... 182 F7
 CONG CW12 .... 184 E6
 CW/HAS CW1 .... 220 E2
 CW/HAS CW1 .... 221 G4
 CW/HAS CW1 .... 221 J1
 FROD/HEL WA6 .... 124 F8
 FROD/HEL WA6 .... 127 G7
 GOL/RIS/CU WA3 .... 23 H7
 GOL/RIS/CU WA3 .... 25 K7
 GOL/RIS/CU WA3 .... 30 F7
 HALE/TIMP WA15 .... 42 F5
 IRL M44 .... 31 K7
 KNUT WA16 .... 59 L6
 KNUT WA16 .... 78 C1
 KNUT WA16 .... 80 D8
 KNUT WA16 .... 108 B8
 KNUT WA16 .... 108 F1
 LYMM WA13 .... 40 E3

LYMM WA13 .... 41 H4
MCFLDN SK10 .... 111 G2
MCFLDN SK11 .... 112 E4
MCFLDS SK11 .... 138 B7
MCFLDS SK11 .... 159 K2
MWCH CW10 .... 156 B5
NANT CW5 .... 253 H3
NWCHE CW9 .... 104 E6
NWCHE CW9 .... 131 J5
NWCHW CW8 .... 12 D4
NWCHW CW8 .... 151 M1
PART M31 .... 41 G1
SALE M33 .... 42 D1
SBCH CW11 .... 203 J5
STHEL WA9 .... 26 A3
TPLY/KEL CW6 .... 197 H2
WARRS WA4 .... 55 G6
WILM/AE SK9 .... 63 K7
WILM/AE SK9 .... 110 B3
Mossley Ct *CONG* CW12 .... 207 M4
 CQ CH5 .... 166 C4
Mossley Garth Cl *CONG* CW12 .... 208 A3
Mossmere Rd *CHD/CHDH* SK8 .... 46 A8
Moss Pl *ALS/KID* ST7 .... 243 H1
 IRL M44 .... 31 H2
 NWCHW CW8 .... 12 D2
 WARRS WA4 .... 57 G1
 WILM/AE SK9 .... 110 C2
Moss Rose *WILM/AE* SK9 .... 110 B2
Moss Side La *GOL/RIS/CU* WA3 .... 39 L1
 NWCHE CW9 .... 77 J5
 WARRS WA4 .... 54 E5
Moss Side Rd *IRL* M44 .... 31 K6
Moss Sq *CW/HAS* CW1 .... 19 G4
 MCFLDS SK11 .... 138 D8
Moss St *NWCHW* CW8 .... 128 D3
 WDN WA8 .... 53 K5
The Moss *NWCHE* CW9 .... 103 K5
Mossvale *GTS/LS* CH66 .... 94 D4
Moss View Rd *MCFLDS* SK11 .... 138 A3
 PART M31 .... 41 G1
Moss Wy *ALS/KID* ST7 .... 241 C1
Mosswood Pk *DID/WITH* M20 .... 45 H4
Mosswood Rd *WILM/AE* SK9 .... 84 E3
Moston Gv *LYMM* WA13 .... 58 D1
Moston Rd *CHNE* CH2 .... 145 K4
 SBCH CW11 .... 203 J7
Mostyn Av *CHD/CHDH* SK8 .... 64 E2
 NSTN CH64 .... 91 H7
Mostyn Pl *CH/BCN* CH1 .... 144 E6
Mostyn Sq *CO* CH5 .... 142 A6
Motcombe Farm Rd
 CHD/CHDH SK8 .... 64 B3
Motcombe Gv *CHD/CHDH* SK8 .... 64 A1
Motcombe Rd *CHD/CHDH* SK8 .... 64 B2
Mottershead Rd *WDN* WA8 .... 7 G5
 WYTH/NTH M22 .... 44 B8
Mottram Cl *CHD/CHDH* SK8 .... 46 A7
 WARRS WA4 .... 57 H1
Mottram Dr *HALE/TIMP* WA15 .... 43 G7
Mottram Fold *STKP* SK1 .... 3 G7
Mottram Rd *SALE* M33 .... 43 L1
 WARRS WA4 .... 110 B3
Mottram St *STKP* SK1 .... 3 G7
Moughland La *RUNC* WA7 .... 9 C6
Moulders La *WARR* WA1 .... 5 H4
Mouldsworth Cl *NWCHE* CW9 .... 129 L8
Moulton Cl *KNUT* WA16 .... 107 L3
 NWCHE CW9 .... 129 L8
 RUNC WA7 .... 73 M8
Mountain St *STKP* SK1 .... 3 K4
Mountain Vw *CHSW/BR* CH4 .... 168 E6
 FROD/HEL WA6 .... 124 B1
 WRX/GR/LL LL12 .... 210 D6
Mountbatten Wy *CONG* CW12 .... 207 K1
Mount Cl *NANT* CW5 .... 21 H5
Mount Dr *MPL/ROM* SK6 .... 48 F7
 NANT CW5 .... 21 H5
Mount Farm Wy *GTS/LS* CH66 .... 120 C2
Mountfield Rd *BRAM/HZG* SK7 .... 65 L7
 CQ CH5 .... 166 B1
 EDGY/DAV SK3 .... 46 C5
Mount Gv *WYTH/NTH* M22 .... 44 F7
Mount Pk *WLTN* L25 .... 50 A1
Mount Park Ct *WLTN* L25 .... 50 A1
Mount Pl *CHSE* CH3 .... 17 L4
Mount Pleasant *ALS/KID* ST7 .... 243 H3
 AUD/MAD/W CW3 .... 264 B8
 BRAM/HZG SK7 .... 66 D1
 CHNE CH2 .... 97 G8
 CW/HAS CW1 .... 221 H6
 CW/HAS CW1 .... 222 D8
 MCFLDN SK10 .... 113 H3
 WDN WA8 .... 7 K1
 WILM/AE SK9 .... 84 B3
Mount Pleasant Av
 FLINT CH6 .... 116 A7
 STHEL WA9 .... 26 A1
Mount Pleasant Dr *WSFD* CW7 .... 177 G5
Mount Pleasant Rd
 ALS/KID ST7 .... 226 B5
 NWCHE CW9 .... 153 M2
Mount Pleasant *CHSW/BR* CH4 .... 168 F5
Mount Rd *ALS/KID* ST7 .... 243 H3
 HTNM SK4 .... 2 B3
 RUNC WA7 .... 73 M4
Mount St *WDN* WA8 .... 7 K1
 WLTN L25 .... 50 A2
Mount Ter *MCFLDS* SK11 .... 15 L5
The Mount *ALS/KID* ST7 .... 225 L5
 ALS/KID ST7 .... 243 H3
 ALT WA14 .... 42 D7
 CHSE CH3 .... 17 M5
 CONG CW12 .... 207 G2
 HALE/TIMP WA15 .... 62 C4
 NWCHE CW9 .... 104 A5
Mount Wy *CHSE* CH3 .... 171 G8
Mourne Cl *GTS/LS* CH66 .... 94 A6
Mowbray Av *SALE* M33 .... 43 J3
Mowbray St *STKP* SK1 .... 3 H7
Mow Cop Rd *ALS/KID* ST7 .... 226 C6
Mowcroft La *WARRW/BUR* WA5 .... 54 B1
Mow La *ALS/KID* ST7 .... 226 A7
 ALS/KID ST7 .... 227 G2
 CONG CW12 .... 207 M8
Mowpen Brow *KNUT* WA16 .... 59 H6

Moxon Av *WARRS* WA4 .... 37 M7
Moyles Cl *WDN* WA8 .... 52 D2
Mudhouse La *NSTN* CH64 .... 118 F2
Mudhurst La *POY/DIS* SK12 .... 88 E3
Muirfield Cl *NWCHE* CW9 .... 13 K8
 WARRN/WOL WA2 .... 38 A1
 WSFD CW7 .... 84 D4
Muirfield Dr *MCFLDN* SK10 .... 112 C8
 WSFD CW7 .... 177 J2
Muir Rd *CH/BCN* CH1 .... 168 E1
Mulberry Av *GOL/RIS/CU* WA3 .... 23 M5
Mulberry Cl *CHD/CHDH* SK8 .... 64 C5
 CHNE CH2 .... 123 J1
 WARR WA1 .... 38 E6
Mulberry Gdns *SBCH* CW11 .... 203 K5
Mulberry Ms *HTNM* SK4 .... 2 E1
Mulberry Mount St
 EDGY/DAV SK3 .... 2 F8
Mulberry Ri *NWCHW* CW8 .... 12 B5
Mulberry Rd *CW/SHV* CW2 .... 237 L2
Mulcaster Ct *CW/HAS* CW1 .... 222 D7
Mullacre Rd *WYTH/NTH* M22 .... 44 D6
Mullein Cl *GOL/RIS/CU* WA3 .... 23 K4
Mullins Av *NEWLW* WA12 .... 22 C7
Mullion Cl *HLWD* L26 .... 50 E4
 RUNC WA7 .... 74 B6
Mullion Dr *HALE/TIMP* WA15 .... 42 E5
Mullion Gv *WARRN/WOL* WA2 .... 38 A3
Mulsford La *MALPAS* SY14 .... 256 A4
Munro Av *WYTH/NTH* M22 .... 63 M2
Murdishaw Av *RUNC* WA7 .... 74 C7
Muriel Cl *WARRW/BUR* WA5 .... 35 K6
Murieston Rd *HALE/TIMP* WA15 .... 61 L2
Murray Cl *MCFLDN* SK10 .... 14 A2
Murrayfield *MCFLDN* SK10 .... 112 A7
Murrayfield Dr *NANT* CW5 .... 237 K7
Murray St *BURS/TUN* ST6 .... 243 J5
Musbury Av *CHD/CHDH* SK8 .... 65 H2
Museum St *WARR* WA1 .... 5 J7
Musgrave Rd *WYTH/NTH* M22 .... 63 K1
Mustard La *GOL/RIS/CU* WA3 .... 29 H4
Muter Av *WYTH/NTH* M22 .... 63 M2
Myddleton La *WARRN/WOL* WA2 .... 36 B2
Myrica Cl *CHNE* CH2 .... 170 B1
Myrtle Av *CHSW/BR* CH4 .... 190 A5
 NEWLW WA12 .... 27 J2
 WARRS WA4 .... 56 D1
Myrtle Gv *CHNE* CH2 .... 170 A1
 WARRS WA4 .... 56 D1
Myrtle Rd *PART* M31 .... 40 D2
Myrtle St *CW/SHV* CW2 .... 18 F6
 EDGY/DAV SK3 .... 46 B4
 EP CH65 .... 10 E3
Mythorne Av *IRL* M44 .... 40 C1

N

Nabbs Cl *ALS/KID* ST7 .... 243 H2
Nabbswood Rd *ALS/KID* ST7 .... 243 H2
Nab La *MCFLDN* SK10 .... 113 J3
Nab La *MCFLDN* SK10 .... 113 J3
Nairn Av *HOLMCH* CW4 .... 181 H2
Nairn Cl *WARRN/WOL* WA2 .... 38 A1
Nancy Vw *MCFLDN* SK10 .... 113 H4
Nangreave Rd *OFTN* SK2 .... 47 G6
Nan Nook Rd *NTHM/RTH* M23 .... 43 M5
Nansen Cl *WARRW/BUR* WA5 .... 36 D5
Nansen Rd *CHD/CHDH* SK8 .... 45 C8
Nansmoss La *WILM/AE* SK9 .... 83 K3
Nantwich Rd *ALS/KID* ST7 .... 255 L3
 CHSE CH3 .... 231 J3
 CW/SHV CW2 .... 18 C9
 GTS/LS CH66 .... 120 F1
 MALPAS SY14 .... 248 E2
 MWCH CW10 .... 179 H3
 MWCH CW10 .... 201 M3
 NANT CW5 .... 218 A4
 NANT CW5 .... 237 J2
 NANT CW5 .... 249 L8
 TPLY/KEL CW6 .... 197 J4
 WHITCH SY13 .... 270 E5
Naomi Cl *CH/BCN* CH1 .... 144 D7
Napier Rd *CHNE* CH2 .... 145 J4
 HTNM SK4 .... 46 B1
Napier St *BRAM/HZG* SK7 .... 66 D1
 WARR WA1 .... 5 J7
Naples Rd *EDGY/DAV* SK3 .... 46 B6
Nares Cl *WARRW/BUR* WA5 .... 36 C3
Narrow La *CW/HAS* CW1 .... 239 J1
 MCFLDN SK10 .... 87 G3
 WRX/GR/LL LL12 .... 210 E4
The Narrows *ALT* WA14 .... 42 C8
Naseby Rd *CONG* CW12 .... 207 G1
Nathans Rd *WYTH/NTH* M22 .... 44 C8
Nat La *WSFD* CW7 .... 177 M2
Navigation Cl *RUNC* WA7 .... 74 D6
Navigation Rd *ALT* WA14 .... 42 D5
 HALE/TIMP WA15 .... 42 E6
 NWCHW CW8 .... 13 G4
Navigation St *WARR* WA1 .... 5 L7
Naylor Av *GOL/RIS/CU* WA3 .... 23 H4
Naylor Ct *NWCHE* CW9 .... 13 H3
Naylor Rd *WDN* WA8 .... 53 K3
Naylor St *BURS/TUN* ST6 .... 243 M7
 WARR WA1 .... 5 H6
Neal Av *CHD/CHDH* SK8 .... 64 A4
Nearbrook Rd *WYTH/NTH* M22 .... 44 C8
Nearcroft Rd *NTHM/RTH* M23 .... 44 A5
Nearmaker Av
 WYTH/NTH M22 .... 44 C8
Nearmaker Rd *WYTH/NTH* M22 .... 44 C8
Neasham Cl *HLWD* L26 .... 50 F4
Neath Av *WYTH/NTH* M22 .... 44 D5
Neath Cl *POY/DIS* SK12 .... 66 D7
Needham Cl *RUNC* WA7 .... 73 K2
Needham Dr *HOLMCH* CW4 .... 157 C7
Needhams Bank *SBCH* CW11 .... 203 J6
Needhams Wharf Cl
 MCFLDN SK10 .... 15 M2
 MCFLDN SK10 .... 139 G3
Neills Rd *STHEL* WA9 .... 26 B6
Neil St *WDN* WA8 .... 7 K1
Nelson Av *POY/DIS* SK12 .... 87 G1
 RAIN/WH L35 .... 32 E2
Nelson Bank *ALS/KID* ST7 .... 243 G5
Nelson Cl *POY/DIS* SK12 .... 87 G1

Nelson Dr *IRL* M44 .... 31 L6
Nelson Gv *ALS/KID* ST7 .... 241 M2
Nelson Pl *RAIN/WH* L35 .... 32 E2
Nelson Rd *EP* CH65 .... 10 E4
 GOL/RIS/CU WA3 .... 29 K8
Nelson St *BRAM/HZG* SK7 .... 47 M8
 CH/BCN CH1 .... 17 J3
 CONG CW12 .... 207 G2
 CQ CH5 .... 142 B6
 CW/SHV CW2 .... 18 F7
 MCFLDS SK11 .... 15 G7
 NEWLW WA12 .... 27 G1
 RUNC WA7 .... 9 H2
 WDN WA8 .... 7 G9
Nemos Cl *RUNC* WA7 .... 74 C2
Neptune Cl *RUNC* WA7 .... 74 D5
Nesfield Ct *SBCH* CW11 .... 222 E5
Nesfield Dr *CW/HAS* CW1 .... 222 F5
Nesfield Rd *NTHM/RTH* M23 .... 43 M2
Nessina Gv *CW/SHV* CW2 .... 237 M4
Neston Av *SALE* M33 .... 43 L2
Neston Dr *CHNE* CH2 .... 145 K7
Neston Gn *GTS/LS* CH66 .... 94 D8
Neston Gv *EDGY/DAV* SK3 .... 46 D7
Neston Rd *NSTN* CH64 .... 91 M7
Neston Wy *WILM/AE* SK9 .... 84 D1
Nethercote Av
 NTHM/RTH M23 .... 44 B6
Nethercroft Rd
 HALE/TIMP WA15 .... 43 J7
Netherfield *WDN* WA8 .... 6 B4
Netherfields *WILM/AE* SK9 .... 110 A4
Nether Fold *MCFLDN* SK10 .... 112 A4
Nether Lea *HOLMCH* CW4 .... 157 J4
Netherlea Ct *HOLMCH* CW4 .... 157 J4
Netherley Rd *RAIN/WH* L35 .... 32 C8
Netherpool Rd *GTS/LS* CH66 .... 94 F4
Netherset Hey La
 AUD/MAD/W CW3 .... 267 M7
Netherton Dr *FROD/HEL* WA6 .... 99 G5
Netherwood Rd *WYTH/NTH* M22 .... 44 C6
Netley Rd *NTHM/RTH* M23 .... 44 A8
Nettlebarn Rd *WYTH/NTH* M22 .... 44 C7
Neufchatel Cl *WHITCH* SY13 .... 270 B5
Neumann St *NWCHE* CW9 .... 13 L2
Nevada St *WARRW/BUR* WA5 .... 36 B4
Nevendon Dr *NTHM/RTH* M23 .... 43 M8
Neville Av *STHEL* WA9 .... 26 B2
 WARRN/WOL WA2 .... 37 K3
Neville Crs *WARRW/BUR* WA5 .... 55 G1
Neville Dr *CHSE* CH3 .... 170 B3
Neville St *BRAM/HZG* SK7 .... 66 B1
 CW/SHV CW2 .... 18 F9
 NEWLW WA12 .... 22 A8
Nevill Rd *BRAM/HZG* SK7 .... 65 L2
Nevin Av *BIDD* ST8 .... 227 K7
 CHD/CHDH SK8 .... 64 E3
Nevin Cl *BRAM/HZG* SK7 .... 66 A5
Nevin Rd *CH/BCN* CH1 .... 168 D1
Nevis Dr *CW/SHV* CW2 .... 237 K1
Newall Cl *CHSE* CH3 .... 214 B3
Newall Crs *WSFD* CW7 .... 178 A3
Newall Rd *NTHM/RTH* M23 .... 62 F1
New Bank Rd *WDN* WA8 .... 52 B3
New Barn Av *AIMK* WN4 .... 22 C1
New Barnet *WDN* WA8 .... 33 M8
New Barn La *LEIGH* WN7 .... 24 E2
New Beech Rd *HTNM* SK4 .... 45 L2
Newberry Gv *EDGY/DAV* SK3 .... 46 D7
Newbold Wy *NANT* CW5 .... 251 L1
Newborough Cl
 WARRW/BUR WA5 .... 36 D2
Newboult Rd *CHD/CHDH* SK8 .... 45 L6
Newbourne Cl
 BRAM/HZG SK7 .... 66 D1
Newbridge Cl *RUNC* WA7 .... 74 C6
 WARRW/BUR WA5 .... 36 C2
New Bridge La *STKP* SK1 .... 3 J5
New Bridge Rd *EP* CH65 .... 95 M8
Newbrook Av *CCHDY* M21 .... 44 D1
Newburgh Cl *RUNC* WA7 .... 74 D3
Newbury Av *CW/HAS* CW1 .... 221 J5
 WDN WA8 .... 52 F1
Newbury Cl *CHD/CHDH* SK8 .... 65 G6
 WDN WA8 .... 52 F1
Newbury Rd *CHD/CHDH* SK8 .... 64 C5
 CHSW/BR CH4 .... 168 F6
Newby Ct *CONG* CW12 .... 207 G3
Newby Dr *ALT* WA14 .... 42 D6
 CHD/CHDH SK8 .... 45 G7
 SALE M33 .... 43 K1
Newby Rd *BRAM/HZG* SK7 .... 66 C2
 HTNM SK4 .... 2 A4
Newcastle Rd *ALS/KID* ST7 .... 242 E7
 AUD/MAD/W CW3 .... 267 M5
 CONG CW12 .... 206 F6
 CW/SHV CW2 .... 253 K1
 NANT CW5 .... 21 L8
 SBCH CW11 .... 204 F1
Newcastle Rd North
 SBCH CW11 .... 181 L6
Newcastle Rd South
 SBCH CW11 .... 181 M7
Newcastle St *CW/HAS* CW1 .... 18 B1
New Chapel Rd *BURS/TUN* ST6 .... 243 J8
New Chester Rd *PS/BROM* CH62 .... 94 A1
Newchurch La *GOL/RIS/CU* WA3 .... 29 M2
Newcombe Av
 WARRN/WOL WA2 .... 37 L4
New Crane Ms *CW/HAS* CW1 .... 16 D5
New Crane St *CH/BCN* CH1 .... 16 D4
Newcroft Dr *EDGY/DAV* SK3 .... 46 D6
New Cut La *WARR* WA1 .... 38 B6
Newdigate St *CW/HAS* CW1 .... 18 F2
New Farm Ct *CHSE* CH3 .... 147 L7
Newfield Dr *CW/HAS* CW1 .... 19 J1
Newfield Rd *LYMM* WA13 .... 58 D1
Newfield Ter *FROD/HEL* WA6 .... 124 B2
New Forest Rd *NTHM/RTH* M23 .... 43 J4
Newgate *MCFLDS* SK11 .... 15 G6

Newgate Rd *SALE* M33 .... 42 B3
 WILM/AE SK9 .... 83 K5
Newgate St *CH/BCN* CH1 .... 17 G6
New Grosvenor Rd *EP* CH65 .... 10 D4
New Hall Av *WYTH/NTH* M22 .... 64 B5
Newhall Ct *CHNE* CH2 .... 145 L6
Newhall Dr *GOL/RIS/CU* WA3 .... 29 L3
New Hall La *GOL/RIS/CU* WA3 .... 29 L3
 WHITCH SY13 .... 268 B3
Newhall Rd *CHNE* CH2 .... 145 L6
New Hall St *MCFLDN* SK10 .... 14 F3
New Hall Rd *SALE* M33 .... 43 M1
Newham Cl *MCFLDS* SK11 .... 162 F1
Newhaven Cl *CHD/CHDH* SK8 .... 65 J2
New Hayes Rd *BURS/TUN* ST6 .... 243 K8
Newhey Av *WYTH/NTH* M22 .... 44 D7
New Hey Rd *CHD/CHDH* SK8 .... 45 L7
Newhey Rd *WYTH/NTH* M22 .... 44 D7
New Horwich Rd *CHF/WBR* SK23 .... 89 L5
New Hutte La *HLWD* L26 .... 50 F6
Newington Ct *ALT* WA14 .... 61 H1
Newland Ct *WDN* WA8 .... 52 C1
Newlands Av *BRAM/HZG* SK7 .... 65 L4
 CHD/CHDH SK8 .... 65 G5
 IRL M44 .... 31 M1
Newlands Cl *CHD/CHDH* SK8 .... 65 G5
 FROD/HEL WA6 .... 99 J6
 GOL/RIS/CU WA3 .... 23 J4
Newlands Dr *DID/WITH* M20 .... 45 J4
 LEIGH WN7 .... 24 F1
 LEIGH WN7 .... 24 F1
 MCFLDN SK10 .... 137 L5
 NTHM/RTH M23 .... 43 L4
 WARRS WA4 .... 56 F2
New La *CHSE* CH3 .... 211 M6
 CHSE CH3 .... 231 M1
 GOL/RIS/CU WA3 .... 29 G5
 WARRS WA4 .... 57 H7
 WSFD CW7 .... 177 M8
Newlyn Av *CONG* CW12 .... 207 M4
 MCFLDN SK10 .... 137 L3
Newlyn Cl *BRAM/HZG* SK7 .... 66 D3
 RUNC WA7 .... 74 B6
Newlyn Dr *AIMK* WN4 .... 22 B2
 MPL/ROM SK6 .... 48 A1
 SALE M33 .... 43 M1
Newlyn Gdns *WARRW/BUR* WA5 .... 54 D1
New Manchester Rd *WARR* WA1 .... 38 A3
Newman Cl *CONG* CW12 .... 207 H1
New Manor Rd *WARRS* WA4 .... 75 H6
Newman's La *NANT* CW5 .... 252 D4
Newman St *WARRS* WA4 .... 56 F1
Newmarket Cl *ALT* WA14 .... 42 B2
 MCFLDN SK10 .... 112 C8
New Mill Stile *WLTN* L25 .... 50 A1
Newmoore La *RUNC* WA7 .... 54 F8
New Moor La *BRAM/HZG* SK7 .... 66 D1
New Moss Rd *IRL* M44 .... 31 K6
Newnham Dr *EP* CH65 .... 95 J8
New Pale Rd *FROD/HEL* WA6 .... 125 H4
New Park Rd *CQ* CH5 .... 142 A8
New Platt La *HOLMCH* CW4 .... 156 E3
Newpool Rd *BIDD* ST8 .... 227 G6
Newpool Ter *BIDD* ST8 .... 227 H7
Newquay Cl *RUNC* WA7 .... 74 B6
Newquay Ct *CONG* CW12 .... 207 L2
Newquay Dr *BRAM/HZG* SK7 .... 65 M5
 MCFLDN SK10 .... 137 K4
New Rd *AUD/MAD/W* CW3 .... 267 L5
 CHF/WBR SK23 .... 89 L6
 CHF/WBR SK23 .... 89 M3
 CONG CW12 .... 183 J5
 CONG CW12 .... 207 G2
 CQ CH5 .... 226 B1
 CQ CH5 .... 166 B8
 GTS/LS CH66 .... 94 A4
 KNUT WA16 .... 80 E1
 LYMM WA13 .... 58 E1
 MCFLDN SK10 .... 112 A5
 NANT CW5 .... 261 K1
 NWCHW CW9 .... 77 K3
 SBCH CW11 .... 205 M2
 TPLY/KEL CW6 .... 173 H6
 WARRS WA4 .... 5 J9
 WSFD CW7 .... 177 L2
New Roskell Sq *FLINT* CH6 .... 116 B5
Newry Ct *CHNE* CH2 .... 145 K8
Newry Pk *CHNE* CH2 .... 145 K8
Newry Pk East *CHNE* CH2 .... 145 K8
New School La *GTS/LS* CH66 .... 94 B4
Newsham Cl *WDN* WA8 .... 33 H8
Newsham Rd *HUY* L36 .... 32 A4
Newsholme Cl
 GOL/RIS/CU WA3 .... 29 L3
Newstead Gv *MPL/ROM* SK6 .... 47 L1
Newstead Gv *POY/DIS* SK12 .... 66 D7
Newstead Ter *HALE/TIMP* WA15 .... 42 F5
New St *ALT* WA14 .... 42 C8
 BIDD ST8 .... 227 M6
 CONG CW12 .... 207 G2
 CW/HAS CW1 .... 222 C7
 NM/HAY SK22 .... 69 J5
 NSTN CH64 .... 91 L7
 RUNC WA7 .... 9 G3
 SBCH CW11 .... 203 K5
 WILM/AE SK9 .... 83 L7
Newton Av *GOL/RIS/CU* WA3 .... 29 L7
Newton Bank *MWCH* CW10 .... 179 H3
Newton Gv *WARRN/WOL* WA2 .... 37 M3
Newton Hall Dr *CHNE* CH2 .... 145 M7
Newton Hall La *KNUT* WA16 .... 82 E6
Newton Hall Ms *MWCH* CW10 .... 179 L4
Newton Heath *MWCH* CW10 .... 179 H3
Newton Hollow
 FROD/HEL WA6 .... 125 H4
Newton La *CHNE* CH2 .... 145 L7
 CHSE CH3 .... 195 M7
 CHSE CH3 .... 214 F1
 NEWLW WA12 .... 22 E6
 WARRS WA4 .... 75 J4
Newton Park Dr *NEWLW* WA12 .... 27 M2

Newton Park Vw *CHNE* CH2.... 145 K7
Newton Rd *ALT* WA14 .... 42 E5 ⑤
  EP CH65 .... 10 F7
  GOL/RIS/CU WA3 .... 23 H7
  STHEL WA9 .... 26 A1
  WARRN/WOL WA2 .... 27 M4
  WILM/AE SK9 .... 84 A3
Newtons Crs *CW/HAS* CW1 .... 222 E5
Newtons Gv *CW/HAS* CW1 ..... 222 E5
Newtons La *CW/HAS* CW1 ..... 222 E5
Newton St *CW/HAS* CW1 ...... 19 G2
  EDGY/DAV SK3 .... 2 E8
  MCFLDS SK11 .... 14 F7
Newtown *ALS/KID* ST7 .... 243 L2
  NSTN CH64 .... 91 M6
  WHITCH SY13 .... 269 M4
New Warrington Rd
  NWCHW CW9 .... 130 B3
New Zealand Rd *STKP* SK1 .... 3 K4
Niagara St *OFTN* SK2 .... 47 G6
Nicholas Av *NWCHE* CW9 ..... 130 C6
Nicholas Ct *CH/BCN* CH1 ..... 16 E6
Nicholas Rd *WDN* WA8 .... 52 C4
Nicholas St *CH/BCN* CH1 ..... 16 E5
Nicholas Street Ms *CH/BCN* CH1 .. 16 E6
Nicholls St *WARRS* WA4 ...... 57 H2
Nicholson Av *MCFLDN* SK10 ... 15 J2
Nicholson Rd *MCFLDN* SK10 ... 15 J2
Nicholson St *HTNM* SK4 ...... 2 F3
  WARR WA1 .... 4 D6
Nickleby Rd *POY/DIS* SK12 .... 86 E1
Nick Olson CI *CHNE* CH2 ..... 146 K4
Nicol Av *GOL/RIS/CU* WA3 .... 38 F3
Nidderdale Av *RAIN/WH* L35 .. 33 K1 ①
Nidderdale CI *CONG* CW12 .... 185 G7 ①
Niddries Av *NWCHE* CW9 ..... 153 M5
Niddries La *NWCHE* CW9 ..... 153 L5
Nield Ct *CHNE* CH2 .... 145 K5
Nield's Brow *ALT* WA14 ...... 61 J2 ⑥
Nields Wy *MPL/ROM* SK6 ..... 49 K8
Nigel Gresley CI
  CW/HAS CW1 .... 222 A8 ①
Nightingale CI *CHSE* CH3 ..... 228 F3
  CW/HAS CW1 .... 220 F5
  GOL/RIS/CU WA3 .... 29 M8 ②
  MWCH CW10 .... 179 K6
  RUNC WA7 .... 73 L7
  WILM/AE SK9 .... 84 B3
Nightingale Ct *WSFD* CW7 .... 177 K6 ⑤
Nightingale Gdns
  NTHM/RTH M23 .... 44 A3 ②
Nile St *CW/SHV* CW2 .... 18 F7
Ninfield Rd *NTHM/RTH* M23 .. 44 B8
Nisbet Av *WYTH/NTH* M22 .... 63 L1
Nixon Dr *WSFD* CW7 .... 177 G2
Nixon Rd *NWCHW* CW8 ...... 151 M1
Nixon's Rw *NANT* CW5 .... 20 D6
Nixon St *CW/HAS* CW1 .... 220 F7 ③
  EDGY/DAV SK3 .... 2 F8
  MCFLDS SK11 .... 14 D4
Noahs Ark La *KNUT* WA16 .... 108 L3
Noble CI *GOL/RIS/CU* WA3 .... 38 E1
Nook La *GOL/RIS/CU* WA3 .... 23 H4
  NWCHE CW9 .... 77 L6
  WARRN/WOL WA2 .... 38 B2
  WARRS WA4 .... 57 G1
The Nook *CHNE* CH2 .... 145 L8
  CHSE CH3 .... 146 C8
  CHSW/BR CH4 .... 168 E6
  CQ CH5 .... 166 D2
  WLTN L25 .... 50 B1
Nora St *WARR* WA1 .... 5 K7
Norbreck Av *CHD/CHDH* SK8 . 46 A6
  CW/SHV CW2 .... 18 D8
Norbreck CI *WARRW/BUR* WA5. 36 A8
Norbreck Crs *WARRW/BUR* WA5. 36 A8
Norbury Av *MPL/ROM* SK6 ... 48 E6
  WARRN/WOL WA2 .... 37 K4 ①
Norbury CI *CW/SHV* CW2 .... 253 L1
  KNUT WA16 .... 107 J1
Norbury Crs *BRAM/HZG* SK7 . 66 D2
Norbury Dr *CONG* CW12 ..... 184 E8
  MPL/ROM SK6 .... 48 F6
  MWCH CW10 .... 179 H4
Norbury Fold *RAIN/WH* L35 ... 33 L3 ②
Norbury Gv *BRAM/HZG* SK7 .. 66 D2 ①
Norbury Hollow Rd
  BRAM/HZG SK7 .... 67 H4
Norbury St *MCFLDS* SK11 .... 14 E7
  NWCHE CW9 .... 13 M2
  STKP SK1 .... 3 G6
Norcott Av *WARRS* WA4 ..... 56 D2
Norcott Dr *WARRW/BUR* WA5 . 26 F6 ①
Norcross CI *OFTN* SK2 .... 47 K7
Norden CI *GOL/RIS/CU* WA3 .. 29 J7
Norfolk CI *IRL* M44 .... 31 J1
Norfolk Dr *WARRW/BUR* WA5 . 35 L6
Norfolk Gv *BIDD* ST8 .... 227 J3
Norfolk PI *WDN* WA8 .... 52 C4
Norfolk Rd *ALS/KID* ST7 ..... 242 F7
  CHNE CH2 .... 145 M8 ①
  CONG CW12 .... 184 E8
  EP CH65 .... 10 E8
Norfolk St *RUNC* WA7 .... 9 K1
Norgate St *DID/WITH* M20 ... 45 H1 ①
Norgrove CI *RUNC* WA7 ...... 74 D4
Norland's La *RAIN/WH* L35 ... 33 L4
  WDN WA8 .... 33 L5
Norland St *WDN* WA8 .... 53 K3 ⑤
Norleane Crs *RUNC* WA7 ..... 9 J7
Norleigh Rd *WYTH/NTH* M22 . 44 D4
Norley Av *EP* CH65 .... 94 F6
  PS/BROM CH62 .... 93 L1
Norley La *FROD/HEL* WA6 .... 126 F6
Norley PI *HLWD* L26 .... 50 E6
Norley Rd *FROD/HEL* WA6 ... 125 M2
  NWCHW CW8 .... 130 F3
Norman Av *BRAM/HZG* SK7 .. 66 C1 ①
  NEWLW WA12 .... 27 L1
  RNFD/HAY WA11 .... 22 A5
Normanby Cha *ALT* WA14 .... 61 H4
Normanby Rd *WARRW/BUR* WA5. 4 A4
Norman CI *GTS/LS* CH66 ..... 120 F4
Norman Dr *WSFD* CW7 .... 177 J6 ②
Normandy Av *WSFD* CW7 .... 177 K4
Normandy Rd *CHNE* CH2 ..... 145 J3

Norman Rd *ALT* WA14 .... 42 C6
  RUNC WA7 .... 9 G5
Norman's La *WARRS* WA4 .... 76 F8
Norman's PI *ALT* WA14 ...... 42 B6
Norman St *CQ* CH5 .... 142 B8
  WARRN/WOL WA2 .... 5 H4
Normanton Rd *EDGY/DAV* SK3. 46 A5
Norman Wy *CH/BCN* CH1 ..... 144 E7 ②
Norreys Av *WARRW/BUR* WA5 . 4 D1
Norris Av *HTNM* SK4 .... 2 A4
Norris Hill Dr *HTNM* SK4 .... 2 A3
Norris Rd *CH/BCN* CH1 ...... 144 E7
  SALE M33 .... 43 J2
Norris St *WARRN/WOL* WA2 .. 5 K1
  WARRN/WOL WA2 .... 5 G1
North Av *SPK/HALE* L24 ..... 50 A6
  WARRN/WOL WA2 .... 5 G1
North Brook Rd *TPLY/KEL* CW6. 174 B5
Northbury Rd *GTS/LS* CH66 .. 120 E3
Northcliffe Rd *OFTN* SK2 .... 47 J4
Northcombe Rd
  EDGY/DAV SK3 .... 46 E7 ⑦
Northcote Rd *BRAM/HZG* SK7 . 65 M5
North Cft *NANT* CW5 .... 20 F6
Northdale Rd *WARR* WA1 .... 38 A4
North Downs *KNUT* WA16 .... 107 J3
North Downs Rd *CHD/CHDH* SK8. 64 F1
North Dr *KNUT* WA16 .... 59 J8
  NWCHE CW9 .... 130 E5
  SALE M33 .... 43 L1
Northenden Rd *CHD/CHDH* SK8. 45 G6
  SALE M33 .... 43 L1
North End La *HLWD* L26 ..... 50 E1
Northern La *RAIN/WH* L35 ... 52 A1
Northern Pathway
  CHSW/BR CH4 .... 17 J8
Northern Ri *GTS/LS* CH66 .... 94 E8
Northern Rd *SPK/HALE* L24 .. 50 E8 ②
Northfield CI *STHEL* WA9 .... 34 D1 ③
Northfield Dr *BIDD* ST8 ..... 227 J3
  WILM/AE SK9 .... 84 D4
Northfield PI *CW/SHV* CW2 .. 238 C7
Northfields *KNUT* WA16 ..... 107 J1
North Front *RAIN/WH* L35 ... 32 E3
Northgate CI *CW/SHV* CW2 .. 238 D7
Northgate Av *CHNE* CH2 .... 17 G2
  MCFLDN SK10 .... 14 F3
Northgate Rd *EDGY/DAV* SK3. 2 A7
Northgate St *CH/BCN* CH1 ... 16 F4
North Gn *CQ* CH5 .... 143 G6
North Harvey St *STKP* SK1 .. 3 H5
North Linkside Rd *WLTN* L25 . 50 C3
North Manor Wy *WLTN* L25 .. 50 C5
Northmead *MCFLDN* SK10 ... 112 A7
Northolt Ct *WARRN/WOL* WA2. 37 L3 ③
Northolt Rd *NTHM/RTH* M23 . 43 M3
North Pde *NSTN* CH64 .... 91 G2
  SALE M33 .... 43 K2 ②
  SPK/HALE L24 .... 70 E1
North Park Brook Rd
  WARRW/BUR WA5 .... 36 E3
North Park Rd *BRAM/HZG* SK7. 65 L1 ①
North PI *STKP* SK1 .... 3 G5
North Rd *EP* CH65 .... 94 E1
  HALE/TIMP WA15 .... 62 A4
  MANAIR M90 .... 63 J6
  SPK/HALE L24 .... 50 F7
North Stafford St *CW/HAS* CW1. 19 H3
North St *ALS/KID* ST7 ...... 226 B6
  CHSE CH3 .... 170 A3
  CHSW/BR CH4 .... 168 B5
  CONG CW12 .... 207 K1
  CQ CH5 .... 142 B7
  CQ CH5 .... 167 G1
  CW/HAS CW1 .... 221 J5
Northumberland Rd
  PART M31 .... 40 E2 ①
North Vale Rd *HALE/TIMP* WA15. 42 F6
North Vw *HUY* L36 .... 32 A2
Northward Rd *WILM/AE* SK9 . 83 M6
Northway *CHSW/BR* CH4 ..... 16 B9
North Wy *CW/SHV* CW2 ..... 238 D7
  HOLMCH CW4 .... 181 J1
Northway *LYMM* WA13 ...... 39 K8 ②
  NWCHW CW8 .... 129 K3
  RUNC WA7 .... 73 M4
  WARRN/WOL WA2 .... 37 H2
  WDN WA8 .... 6 A3
Northwich Rd *KNUT* WA16 ... 106 B3
  KNUT WA16 .... 156 D2
  NWCHE CW9 .... 103 K2
  NWCHW CW8 .... 128 D3 ③
  RUNC WA7 .... 74 C7
  WARRS WA4 .... 76 F5
  WARRS WA4 .... 101 K4
Northwood Av
  CHD/CHDH SK8 .... 65 G1 ⑤
  MWCH CW10 .... 179 L2
  NEWLW WA12 .... 27 M1 ⑤
Northwood La *KNUT* WA16 .. 78 F3
Northwood Rd *RUNC* WA7 ... 73 L2
Norton Av *CHSW/BR* CH4 .... 168 D4
  WARRW/BUR WA5 .... 35 L7
Norton Ga *RUNC* WA7 .... 74 C4
Norton Gv *HTNM* SK4 .... 46 B3 ③
Norton HI *RUNC* WA7 .... 74 C2
Norton La *RUNC* WA7 .... 74 C4
Norton Rd *CHSE* CH3 .... 170 C2
Norton's La *CHSE* CH3 ...... 148 B1
  TPLY/KEL CW6 .... 149 M5
Norton Station Rd *RUNC* WA7. 74 D4
Norton Vw *RUNC* WA7 ...... 74 D4
Norton Village *RUNC* WA7 ... 74 D4
Norton Wy *SBCH* CW11 ..... 203 K5
Nortonwood La *RUNC* WA7 .. 74 C3
Norview Dr *DID/WITH* M20 .. 45 H5
Norville *GTS/LS* CH66 .... 94 D5
Norweb Wy *LEIGH* WN7 ..... 25 H1
Norwell Rd *WYTH/NTH* M22 . 44 E7
Norwich Av *AIMK* WN4 ...... 22 D2
  GOL/RIS/CU WA3 .... 23 K4
Norwich Dr *GTS/LS* CH66 ... 120 E4
Norwood Av *BRAM/HZG* SK7 . 65 K7 ③
  GOL/RIS/CU WA3 .... 23 L5
  MPL/ROM SK6 .... 67 K5
Norwood Dr *CHSW/BR* CH4 .. 169 H7
  HALE/TIMP WA15 .... 43 K7
Norwood Rd *CHD/CHDH* SK8 . 45 H6
  OFTN SK2 .... 47 H8

Nottingham CI *WARR* WA1 ... 38 D6
Nuffield Rd *WYTH/NTH* M22 . 44 E8
Nun House CI *WSFD* CW7 .... 178 B3 ③
Nun House Dr *WSFD* CW7 .... 178 B3
Nunsmere CI *WSFD* CW7 .... 178 B3 ③
Nun's Rd *CH/BCN* CH1 ...... 16 E6
Nursery Av *HALE/TIMP* WA15. 61 L4
Nursery CI *ALS/KID* ST7 .... 242 D3
  OFTN SK2 .... 47 K5
  WDN WA8 .... 53 K1
  WLTN L25 .... 50 C4
Nursery Dr *BIDD* ST8 .... 227 J2
  POY/DIS SK12 .... 66 D8
Nursery La *CONG* CW12 ..... 207 L2
  EDGY/DAV SK3 .... 46 A5
  MCFLDN SK10 .... 109 K7
  MCFLDS SK11 .... 160 A1
  WILM/AE SK9 .... 83 M6
Nursery Rd *ALS/KID* ST7 .... 225 L7
  CHD/CHDH SK8 .... 64 F3
  CW/HAS CW1 .... 240 D2
  HTNM SK4 .... 2 A3
  MCFLDN SK10 .... 112 E5 ⑧
  NWCHW CW8 .... 129 H1
The Nursery *NWCHW* CW8 .. 12 A6
Nutfield Av *CW/HAS* CW1 ... 221 H5
Nuthurst Gdns *NANT* CW5 .. 21 G7
Nuttall Gv *GOL/RIS/CU* WA3 . 29 J8
Nuttall St *IRL* M44 .... 31 L6

O

Oak Av *ALS/KID* ST7 .... 241 L2
  CHD/CHDH SK8 .... 64 C7
  GOL/RIS/CU WA3 .... 23 H4
  HTNM SK4 .... 46 B2
  IRL M44 .... 31 K7
  MCFLDS SK11 .... 138 A7
  MPL/ROM SK6 .... 48 C2
  NEWLW WA12 .... 27 J1
  POY/DIS SK12 .... 69 G6
  WILM/AE SK9 .... 83 M7
  WSFD CW7 .... 177 K5
Oak Bank CI *NANT* CW5 ..... 237 L8
Oak Bank Dr *MCFLDN* SK10 . 113 H8
Oak Bank La *CHNE* CH2 ..... 146 C5
Oak CI *RAIN/WH* L35 .... 32 E1
  WILM/AE SK9 .... 83 M6
Oakdale Av *FROD/HEL* WA6 .. 99 K6
  WARRS WA4 .... 56 C5
Oakdale CI *CHSW/BR* CH4 ... 190 B1 ⑧
  DID/WITH M20 .... 45 J3
Oakdale Dr *CHD/CHDH* SK8 . 64 B2
Oakdene Av *CHD/CHDH* SK8 . 64 B5
  GTS/LS CH66 .... 94 C7
  WARR WA1 .... 38 C5
Oakdene Crs *MPL/ROM* SK6 . 48 F5
Oakdene Gdns *MPL/ROM* SK6. 48 F5
Oakdene Rd *HALE/TIMP* WA15. 43 H4
  MPL/ROM SK6 .... 48 F5
Oakdene Wy *BIDD* ST8 ...... 227 K5
Oak Dr *BRAM/HZG* SK7 ...... 65 J5
  CHSW/BR CH4 .... 190 A5
  MPL/ROM SK6 .... 48 D6 ④
  MWCH CW10 .... 179 K5
  RUNC WA7 .... 9 M8
  WHITCH SY13 .... 269 M6
Oakenbank La *MCFLDN* SK10. 113 L4
Oakenclough CI *WILM/AE* SK9. 84 D2 ⑦
Oakfield Av *CHD/CHDH* SK8 . 45 L6
  CHNE CH2 .... 145 L4
  GOL/RIS/CU WA3 .... 22 F3
  KNUT WA16 .... 107 J1
  NANT CW5 .... 261 M1
Oakfield CI *BRAM/HZG* SK7 .. 65 L8
  NANT CW5 .... 261 M1
  WILM/AE SK9 .... 110 B4
Oakfield Dr *CHNE* CH2 ...... 145 L4
  SALE M33 .... 54 A4
Oakfield Ri *HOLMCH* CW4 ... 181 H1
Oakfield Rd *CH/BCN* CH1 .... 144 C8
  CQ CH5 .... 166 A3
  EDGY/DAV SK3 .... 46 F7
  GTS/LS CH66 .... 93 L4
  HALE/TIMP WA15 .... 42 E7
  MANAIR M90 .... 131 M1
  POY/DIS SK12 .... 66 F8
  WILM/AE SK9 .... 110 B2
Oakfield St *HALE/TIMP* WA15. 42 E7
Oak Gv *CHD/CHDH* SK8 ..... 45 L7
  EP CH65 .... 121 G1
  NANT CW5 .... 251 L1
  POY/DIS SK12 .... 66 D8
Oakhead Rd *RAIN/WH* L35 .. 32 E1
Oakhill CI *MCFLDN* SK10 .... 112 B8 ①
Oak House La *WSFD* CW7 ... 177 H4 ⑤
Oakhurst Cha *WILM/AE* SK9 . 110 A2
Oakhurst Dr *CHD/CHDH* SK8 . 46 B7
  CW/SHV CW2 .... 238 B5
Oakland Av *CW/HAS* CW1 ... 222 C8
  OFTN SK2 .... 47 J6
Oaklands *CHSE* CH3 .... 146 F7
  RAIN/WH L35 .... 33 J1 ⑧
Oaklands Av *CHD/CHDH* SK8. 65 G2
  MPL/ROM SK6 .... 49 J4 ⑨
Oaklands Crs *CHSE* CH3 ..... 214 B1
Oaklands Dr *BRAM/HZG* SK7. 66 D2
  LYMM WA13 .... 58 D2
Oaklands Rd *GOL/RIS/CU* WA3. 23 L5
  KNUT WA16 .... 107 M6
Oakland St *WARR* WA1 ...... 37 L5
  WDN WA8 .... 53 G8
Oak La *MCFLDN* SK10 .... 113 G6
  MCFLDS SK11 .... 160 C7
  NWCHW CW8 .... 151 M2
  WILM/AE SK9 .... 83 M6
Oaklea Av *CHNE* CH2 .... 145 M8
Oak Lea Av *WILM/AE* SK9.... 84 A7
Oakleigh Av *HALE/TIMP* WA15. 43 K8
Oakleigh Ct *CONG* CW12 .... 206 F1
Oakleigh Ri *NWCHW* CW8 ... 12 E1
Oakleigh Rd *CHD/CHDH* SK8 . 64 E4

Oakley CI *SBCH* CW11 .... 204 A4
Oakley Rd *CQ* CH5 .... 166 E2
Oakley St *CW/HAS* CW1 ..... 18 F2
Oak Meadow *NWCHW* CW8 . 128 E5
Oakmere CI *SBCH* CW11 .... 203 M5
  WYTH/NTH M22 .... 44 D8 ③
Oakmere Dr *CHSE* CH3 ...... 170 B4
  GTS/LS CH66 .... 120 F4
  WARRW/BUR WA5 .... 54 F1
Oakmere Rd *CHD/CHDH* SK8. 45 M8 ⑧
  WILM/AE SK9 .... 64 D7 ⑤
  WSFD CW7 .... 176 F3
Oakmere St *RUNC* WA7 ..... 9 G3
Oak Ms *WILM/AE* SK9 .... 84 C3
Oakmoor Rd *NTHM/RTH* M23. 44 A6
Oak Rd *CHD/CHDH* SK8 ..... 45 L6
  CHSW/BR CH4 .... 168 F6
  GTS/LS CH66 .... 93 L3
  HALE/TIMP WA15 .... 61 L1
  LYMM WA13 .... 58 C1
  MCFLDN SK10 .... 111 H7
  MCFLDS SK11 .... 135 C2
  PART M31 .... 40 D2
  RAIN/WH L35 .... 32 E1
  WARRW/BUR WA5 .... 54 F1
Oaks CI *STHEL* WA9 .... 34 D1 ④
The Oaks Dr *CHNE* CH2 ..... 145 J5
Oaks PI *WDN* WA8 .... 7 G6
The Oaks *CHD/CHDH* SK8 ... 64 A2
Oakston Av *RAIN/WH* L35 ... 33 K2 ⑧
Oak St *ALS/KID* ST7 .... 224 E4
  BRAM/HZG SK7 .... 66 D1
  CW/SHV CW2 .... 19 G5
  EDGY/DAV SK3 .... 46 B4
  EP CH65 .... 10 E3 ⑧
  GOL/RIS/CU WA3 .... 29 G5
  LEIGH WN7 .... 24 F1
  NWCHE CW9 .... 13 K1
  SBCH CW11 .... 203 K4
Oak Tree CI *CQ* CH5 .... 142 A8 ②
  CW/HAS CW1 .... 19 L2
Oaktree CI *NWCHW* CW8 ... 103 H8 ⑧
Oak Tree CI *OFTN* SK2 ...... 47 K4 ⑧
Oaktree CI *TPLY/KEL* CW6 ... 197 K2
Oak Tree Ct *CHD/CHDH* SK8 . 45 K6
Oaktree Ct *CHNE* CH2 ...... 170 A1 ②
Oak Tree Dr *CW/HAS* CW1 .. 19 L2
Oaktree La *ALS/KID* ST7 .... 242 D7
Oak Tree La *MWCH* CW10 .. 156 D5
Oak Vw *KNUT* WA16 .... 107 J3
  MCFLDS SK11 .... 160 C7
  SPK/HALE L24 .... 71 G1
Oakway *DID/WITH* M20 ..... 45 J4 ⑦
Oakways *WARRS* WA4 .... 56 D7
Oakwood Av *AIMK* WN4 .... 22 A2
  CHD/CHDH SK8 .... 45 H7
  WARR WA1 .... 5 M3
  WILM/AE SK9 .... 83 L6
Oakwood Ct *ALT* WA14 ..... 61 H4 ④
Oakwood Crs *CW/SHV* CW2 . 220 E8
  SBCH CW11 .... 204 E6
Oakwood Dr *LEIGH* WN7 .... 24 E3
  MCFLDN SK10 .... 112 C6
Oakwood Ga *GOL/RIS/CU* WA3. 29 K8
  NWCHW CW8 .... 129 C2
  SBCH CW11 .... 203 H4
Oak Wood Rd *KNUT* WA16 .. 79 M2
Oakwood Rd *MPL/ROM* SK6 . 48 C2
  POY/DIS SK12 .... 68 D6 ⑧
Oakworth Dr *HUY* L36 ...... 32 A5
Oatfield CI *WHITCH* SY13 ... 269 M6 ③
Oathills *MALPAS* SY14 ...... 246 B7
Oathills CI *TPLY/KEL* CW6 ... 197 K3
Oathills Dr *TPLY/KEL* CW6 ... 197 K3
Oatlands *WILM/AE* SK9 ..... 110 B4
Oatlands Rd *WYTH/NTH* M22. 63 J2
Oat Market *NANT* CW5 ...... 20 D6
Oat St *STKP* SK1 .... 3 J9
Oban Crs *EDGY/DAV* SK3 .... 46 D8
Oban Dr *SALE* M33 .... 43 L1
Oban Gv *WARRN/WOL* WA2 . 38 A1
Obelisk Wy *CONG* CW12 .... 207 J1
Occlestone CI *SALE* M33 .... 43 L3 ⑧
Ocean St *ALT* WA14 .... 42 B6
Offerton Dr *OFTN* SK2 ...... 47 K5
Offerton Fold *OFTN* SK2 .... 47 J5 ⑥
Offerton Gn *OFTN* SK2 ..... 47 M6
Offerton La *OFTN* SK2 ...... 47 M7
Offerton Rd *BRAM/HZG* SK7 . 67 C4
  OFTN SK2 .... 48 A8
Offerton St *STKP* SK1 ...... 3 L3
Offley Av *SBCH* CW11 ...... 204 B5
Offley Rd *SBCH* CW11 ...... 204 B5
Ogden Gv *CHD/CHDH* SK8 .. 44 F8 ⑧
Ogden Rd *BRAM/HZG* SK7 ... 65 K7
Ogden St *DID/WITH* M20 ... 45 H1 ①
Oglet La *SPK/HALE* L24 ..... 70 C2
Oil Sites Rd *EP* CH65 .... 11 C5
Okell Dr *HLWD* L26 .... 50 E2 ③
Okell St *RUNC* WA7 .... 9 G3
Old Bank La *MPL/ROM* SK6 . 48 F4 ②
Old Boston *RNFD/HAY* WA11 . 22 A5
Oldbridge Rd *SPK/HALE* L24. 70 F1
Old Butt La *ALS/KID* ST7 .... 242 D2
Old Chads La *WHITCH* SY13 . 259 J4
Old Chapel St *EDGY/DAV* SK3. 2 D9
Old Cherry La *LYMM* WA13 .. 58 A6 ⑤
Old Chester Rd *FROD/HEL* WA6. 94 D7 ⑤
  GTS/LS CH66 .... 94 D7 ①
  NANT CW5 .... 218 C6
  WARRS WA4 .... 55 M5
Old Church St *EP* CH65 ..... 10 F4 ⑧
Old Coach Rd *MALPAS* SY14 . 231 J6
  TPLY/KEL CW6 .... 149 K7
Old Colliery Rd *RAIN/WH* L35. 32 D7
Oldcott Crs *ALS/KID* ST7 .... 243 J4
Oldcott Dr *ALS/KID* ST7 ..... 243 J4
The Old Ctyd *WYTH/NTH* M22. 44 F7 ⑧
Old Croft Ms *STHEL* WA9 ... 34 A1
Old Distillery Rd *SPK/HALE* L24. 50 B7
Old Farm CI *NSTN* CH64 .... 93 G4
Old Farm Dr *OFTN* SK2 ..... 47 M6 ①
Oldfield Crs *CHSW/BR* CH4 .. 168 F7
Oldfield Dr *CHSE* CH3 ...... 170 C2

HALE/TIMP WA15 .... 42 F6
  KNUT WA16 .... 82 A8
Oldfield Rd *ALT* WA14 ...... 42 A7
  EP CH65 .... 10 D8
  LYMM WA13 .... 39 H8
  SBCH CW11 .... 199 H5
Old Gardens St *STKP* SK1 ... 3 H7
The Old Gdn *HALE/TIMP* WA15. 43 H5 ①
Oldgate *WDN* WA8 .... 52 C6
Old Gate CI *MWCH* CW10 ... 179 H5
Old Gorse CI *CW/SHV* CW2 .. 237 L1
Old Hall *RAIN/WH* L35 ...... 32 E4
Old Hall Av *CHF/WBR* SK23 . 89 L8
Old Hall CI *WARRS* WA4 .... 56 A4
Old Hall Ct *CHSE* CH3 ...... 148 F5
  MALPAS SY14 .... 258 B1
Old Hall Crs *WILM/AE* SK9 .. 84 E1 ③
Old Hall Dr *AIMK* WN4 ...... 22 A2
  EP CH65 .... 95 H8
  OFTN SK2 .... 47 L6
Old Hall Gdns *CHNE* CH2 ... 17 K1
Old Hall La *BRAM/HZG* SK7 . 85 K3
  CHNE CH2 .... 123 H1
  KNUT WA16 .... 105 L1
  MPL/ROM SK6 .... 49 J7
Old Hall Pk *CHSE* CH3 ...... 146 F7
Old Hall PI *CH/BCN* CH1 .... 16 F6 ③
Old Hall Rd *CHD/CHDH* SK8 . 45 G6
  CQ CH5 .... 166 A3
  NWCHE CW9 .... 13 J8
  WARRW/BUR WA5 .... 36 D4
Oldhall St *MALPAS* SY14 .... 258 B1
Old Hall St *MCFLDN* SK10 .. 15 G2 ③
Oldham Av *STKP* SK1 .... 3 M6
Oldhams HI *NWCHW* CW8 .. 13 G1
Oldham's Ri *MCFLDN* SK10 . 112 C8 ①
Oldham St *MCFLDN* SK10 ... 113 H4
  WARRS WA4 .... 56 B1
Old Higher Rd *WDN* WA8 ... 51 K7
Oldhill CI *ALS/KID* ST7 ..... 242 F7
Old Hutte La *SPK/HALE* L24. 51 G7
Oldknow Rd *MPL/ROM* SK6 . 49 G6
Old La *CHSW/BR* CH4 .... 210 D2
  NWCHE CW9 .... 103 J1
  NWCHE CW9 .... 154 D2
  NWCHW CW8 .... 127 M2
  RAIN/WH L35 .... 33 H2
Old Liverpool Rd
  WARRW/BUR WA5 .... 4 C8
Old Market PI *KNUT* WA16 .. 107 G2 ④
Old Meadow La
  HALE/TIMP WA15 .... 62 B1
Old Mill La *BRAM/HZG* SK7 . 67 C4
  MCFLDS SK11 .... 15 J8
  WARRS WA4 .... 102 F1
Old Mill Rd *SBCH* CW11 .... 204 C6
Old Moss La *GOL/RIS/CU* WA3. 25 K6
  TPLY/KEL CW6 .... 172 D6
Old Oak St *DID/WITH* M20 .. 45 H1
Old Orch *NWCHE* CW9 ...... 77 J8
  RAIN/WH L35 .... 32 E3
  WILM/AE SK9 .... 84 A5
The Old Orch
  HALE/TIMP WA15 .... 43 H4 ①
The Old Paddock *HOLMCH* CW4. 157 M4
Old Park La *NSTN* CH64 ..... 239 K5
  CW/SHV CW2 .... 239 K5
Old Pearl La *CHSE* CH3 ..... 170 B3
The Old Quarry *WLTN* L25 .. 50 A2
Old Quay CI *NSTN* CH64 .... 91 J5 ⑧
Old Quay La *NSTN* CH64 .... 91 K5
Old Quay St *RUNC* WA7 ..... 9 K1
Old Rectory Gdns
  CHD/CHDH SK8 .... 45 K7 ②
Old Rd *AUD/MAD/W* CW3 ... 267 G1
  CHD/CHDH SK8 .... 45 M6
  CHF/WBR SK23 .... 89 L8
  HTNM SK4 .... 2 F1
  NWCHE CW9 .... 129 K1
  WARRS WA4 .... 5 H9
  WILM/AE SK9 .... 84 D1
Old School CI *NSTN* CH64 .. 91 M7
Old School House La
  WARRN/WOL WA2 .... 28 A5
Old School PI *AIMK* WN4 ... 22 A1 ⑧
Old Seals Wy *CH/BCN* CH1 . 16 B2
Old Smithy La *LYMM* WA13 . 58 C2
Old Stack Yd *CHSE* CH3 .... 147 L7
Old Upton La *WDN* WA8 .... 33 L8
Old Vicarage Gdns
  AUD/MAD/W CW3 .... 263 M8
Old Vicarage Rd *NSTN* CH64. 93 G4
Old Wargrave Rd *NEWLW* WA12. 27 H1
Old Warrington Rd
  NWCHE CW9 .... 130 A2
Oldwood Rd *NTHM/RTH* M23. 63 L1
Old Wool La *CHD/CHDH* SK8. 45 M8
Old Wrexham Rd
  CHSW/BR CH4 .... 169 J5
O'leary St *WARRN/WOL* WA2. 5 K2
Olive Dr *NSTN* CH64 .... 91 L4
Oliver CI *MCFLDN* SK10 .... 112 F4 ③
Oliver La *GTS/LS* CH66 ..... 94 D8
Olive Rd *HALE/TIMP* WA15 .. 43 G4
  NSTN CH64 .... 91 L4
Oliver St *EDGY/DAV* SK3 .... 3 G8
  WARRN/WOL WA2 .... 5 G4
Ollerbarrow Rd
  HALE/TIMP WA15 .... 61 L2
Ollersett Av *NM/HAY* SK22 . 69 J4
Ollersett La *NM/HAY* SK22 . 69 K4
Ollershaw La *NWCHE* CW9 . 104 C8
Ollerton CI *WARRS* WA4 .... 57 H1
Ollerton Rd *WILM/AE* SK9 .. 64 D7 ③
Olney Av *WYTH/NTH* M22 .. 44 D6
One Oak La *WILM/AE* SK9 .. 84 F5
Onslow Rd *CH/BCN* CH1 .... 144 D7 ④
  EDGY/DAV SK3 .... 2 A8
Onston La *NWCHW* CW8 .... 127 L3
Openfields CI *HLWD* L26 .... 50 E2 ③
Openshaw La *IRL* M44 ...... 31 L6 ②
Orange Gv *WARRN/WOL* WA2. 37 L2
Orchard Av *CHF/WBR* SK23 . 89 K5
  LYMM WA13 .... 58 F1
  NWCHW CW8 .... 101 L8
  PART M31 .... 31 M8
Orchard Brow *GOL/RIS/CU* WA3. 40 A2
Orchard CI *CHD/CHDH* SK8 . 65 J5 ⑧

CHNE CH2 .... 145 K7
CQ CH5 .... 166 D1
FROD/HEL WA6 .... 99 G6
GTS/LS CH66 .... 120 F3
HOLMCH SK11 .... 157 L3
MCFLDS SK11 .... 14 D8
MWCH CW10 .... 179 J5
NWCHE CW9 .... 105 C6
NWCHW CW8 .... 128 D3
NWCHW CW8 .... 129 H1
POY/DIS SK12 .... 86 E1
RAIN/WH L35 .... 32 E3
WILM/AE SK9 .... 83 M7
WSFD CW7 .... 177 K5
Orchard Ct CW/HAS CW1 .... 222 D7
OFTN SK2 .... 47 K6
Orchard Crs ALS/KID ST7 .... 242 D3
MCFLDN SK10 .... 109 M6
NANT CW5 .... 251 L1
Orchard Cft CHSE CH3 .... 146 E7
Orchard Dene NWCHW CW8 .... 127 K7
Orchard Dr HALE/TIMP WA15 .... 62 A1
NSTN CH64 .... 91 L7
NWCHW CW8 .... 102 D7
WILM/AE SK9 .... 84 E1
Orchard Gn WILM/AE SK9 .... 110 B3
Orchard Gv CHSE CH3 .... 228 F3
Orchard La GTS/LS CH66 .... 94 A4
Orchard Park La CHNE CH2 .... 97 H8
Orchard Pl FROD/HEL WA6 .... 98 C8
HALE WA15 .... 43 H5
Orchard Ri NWCHE CW9 .... 153 L4
Orchard Rd CHF/WBR SK23 .... 89 K5
EP CH65 .... 121 G2
HALE/TIMP WA15 .... 42 E7
LYMM WA13 .... 40 B7
MPL/ROM SK6 .... 49 H2
Orchard Rd East
WYTH/NTH M22 .... 44 D2
Orchard Rd West
WYTH/NTH M22 .... 44 D2
The Orchards CW/SHV CW2 .... 238 C8
KNUT WA16 .... 104 F6
Orchard St AIMK WN4 .... 22 C1
CH/BCN CH1 .... 16 D3
CW/HAS CW1 .... 18 E2
NANT CW5 .... 237 K6
NWCHE CW9 .... 13 L2
STKP SK1 .... 3 H5
WARR WA1 .... 5 J6
WARRN/WOL WA2 .... 38 A2
WARRS WA4 .... 56 C4
The Orchard FROD/HEL WA6 .... 124 A2
Orchard V EDGY/DAV SK3 .... 46 C6
Orchard Wy TPLY/KEL CW6 .... 149 K7
WDN WA8 .... 52 A1
Orchid Cl CHSE CH3 .... 170 A6
IRL M44 .... 31 L4
Orchil Cl GTS/LS CH66 .... 94 A6
Ordnance Av GOL/RIS/CU WA3 .... 29 M8
Ordsall SBCH CW11 .... 222 F1
Orford Av POY/DIS SK12 .... 68 D6
WARRN/WOL WA2 .... 5 J2
Orford Cl MPL/ROM SK6 .... 67 L5
Orford Gn WARRN/WOL WA2 .... 37 K3
Orford La WARRN/WOL WA2 .... 5 H3
Orford St WARR WA1 .... 5 H6
Oriel Cl OFTN SK2 .... 47 H6
Orient Dr WLTN L25 .... 50 B1
Orkney Av ALS/KID ST7 .... 243 M4
Orkney Cl EP CH65 .... 121 J3
NTHM/RTH M23 .... 44 A8
WDN WA8 .... 53 L1
Orme Cl MCFLDN SK10 .... 112 A4
MCFLDN SK10 .... 138 D1
Orme Crs MCFLDN SK10 .... 138 D1
Orme Rd BIDD ST8 .... 227 K7
Ormerod Cl MPL/ROM SK6 .... 47 M3
SBCH CW11 .... 204 C7
Orme St STKP SK1 .... 3 L3
WILM/AE SK9 .... 110 A3
Ormonde Rd CHNE CH2 .... 145 J8
Ormonde St CH/BCN CH1 .... 17 J3
Ormsby Cl EDGY/DAV SK3 .... 46 E8
Orms Gill Pl OFTN SK2 .... 47 L6
Orphanage St HTNM SK4 .... 2 F2
Orrell Cl WARRW/BUR WA5 .... 36 A6
Orrishmere Rd CHD/CHDH SK8 .... 64 F4
Orton Av NTHM/RTH M23 .... 44 A3
Orton Cl WSFD CW7 .... 154 M3
Orton Rd NTHM/RTH M23 .... 44 D6
Orwell Av WYTH/NTH M22 .... 44 D6
Orwell Cl STHEL WA9 .... 34 A1
WILM/AE SK9 .... 84 D2
Osborne Av WARRN/WOL WA2 .... 37 K3
Osborne Cl SBCH CW11 .... 203 K7
Osborne Gv CHD/CHDH SK8 .... 64 A1
CW/SHV CW2 .... 238 C8
Osborne Rd GOL/RIS/CU WA3 .... 23 L5
HALE/TIMP WA15 .... 42 E7
OFTN SK2 .... 46 F5
WARRS WA4 .... 56 B3
Osborne St MPL/ROM SK6 .... 47 J1
Osbourne Cl WILM/AE SK9 .... 84 D6
Osbourne Pl ALT WA14 .... 42 D8
Osier Cl CHNE CH2 .... 123 J1
Osmere Cl WHITCH SY13 .... 270 B3
Ostler's La KNUT WA16 .... 82 D4
Otley Gv EDGY/DAV SK3 .... 46 D8
Ottawa Cl NTHM/RTH M23 .... 43 M8
Otterburn Pl OFTN SK2 .... 47 K6
Otters Bank WSFD CW7 .... 177 C3
Otterspool Rd MPL/ROM SK6 .... 48 B5
Oughtrington Crs LYMM WA13 .... 59 H1
Oughtrington La LYMM WA13 .... 59 G2
Oughtrington Vw LYMM WA13 .... 40 B8
Oulton Av CHNE CH2 .... 145 L6
Oulton Dr CONG CW12 .... 206 F1
Oulton Mill La TPLY/KEL CW6 .... 175 G5

Oulton Pl CH/BCN CH1 .... 17 G4
Oundle Pl WLTN L25 .... 50 B5
Ousel Nest NWCHW CW8 .... 127 K8
Outer Central Rd SPK/HALE L24 .... 50 E7
Out La CHSE CH3 .... 215 J5
WLTN L25 .... 50 B2
Outram Cl MPL/ROM SK6 .... 48 F8
Outwood Dr CHD/CHDH SK8 .... 64 A4
Outwood La MANAIR M90 .... 63 J4
Outwood La West
MANAIR M90 .... 63 H4
Outwood Rd CHD/CHDH SK8 .... 64 B4
The Oval CHD/CHDH SK8 .... 64 B4
EP CH65 .... 121 J1
WYTH/NTH M22 .... 64 A4
Ovenhouse La MCFLDN SK10 .... 112 E6
Oven La MCFLDS SK11 .... 140 D7
Overdale La MCFLDN SK10 .... 151 K3
Overdale Rd MPL/ROM SK6 .... 47 M3
NSTN CH64 .... 93 G3
POY/DIS SK12 .... 68 F6
Overdene Rd WSFD CW7 .... 177 K4
Overfields KNUT WA16 .... 107 J1
Over Hall Dr WSFD CW7 .... 177 J5
Overhill Dr WILM/AE SK9 .... 84 E5
Overhill La WILM/AE SK9 .... 84 E5
Overhill Rd WILM/AE SK9 .... 84 D5
Overlea Av CQ CH5 .... 166 C2
Overlea Dr CQ CH5 .... 166 C2
Overleigh Ct CHSW/BR CH4 .... 17 G9
Overleigh Rd CHSW/BR CH4 .... 169 J5
Overpool Gdns GTS/LS CH66 .... 120 F1
Overpool Rd EP CH65 .... 94 F7
GTS/LS CH66 .... 94 E6
Over Rd NANT CW5 .... 200 F4
Overton Cl CONG CW12 .... 207 J1
MWCH CW10 .... 179 H4
Overton Crs BRAM/HZG SK7 .... 47 L8
SALE M33 .... 42 D2
Overton Dr FROD/HEL WA6 .... 99 J6
Overton Rd BIDD ST8 .... 208 F7
CONG CW12 .... 208 F5
WYTH/NTH M22 .... 44 D7
Overway WSFD CW7 .... 177 L3
Overwood Av CH/BCN CH1 .... 144 E4
Overwood La CH/BCN CH1 .... 144 C8
Overwood Pl BURS/TUN ST6 .... 243 M5
Overwood Rd WYTH/NTH M22 .... 44 D7
Ovington Cl RUNC WA7 .... 73 M8 ⑩
Owen Cl CH/BCN CH1 .... 144 E6
Owen Dr SPK/HALE L24 .... 70 B2
Owen Rd RAIN/WH L35 .... 33 J2
Owen St CW/SHV CW2 .... 18 E7
EDGY/DAV SK3 .... 2 D6
NWCHE CW9 .... 13 M2
WARRN/WOL WA2 .... 4 F3
Owley Wood Rd NWCHW CW8 .... 128 E3
Oxborough Cl WDN WA8 .... 33 M8
Oxbridge Cl SALE M33 .... 42 D1
Oxenham Rd WARRN/WOL WA2 .... 37 G1
Oxenhurst Gn OFTN SK2 .... 47 L7
Oxford Cl GTS/LS CH66 .... 120 E4
Oxford Dr HLWD L26 .... 50 F4
Oxford Gv IRL M44 .... 31 J6
Oxford Rd ALT WA14 .... 61 K1
CHSW/BR CH4 .... 168 F6
MCFLDS SK11 .... 14 D5
RUNC WA7 .... 9 G5
Oxford St CW/HAS CW1 .... 18 C2
NEWLW WA12 .... 27 H1
WARRS WA4 .... 5 K9
WDN WA8 .... 7 J6
Oxford Wy HTNM SK4 .... 2 D1
Ox-hey Crs BIDD ST8 .... 227 K3
Ox-hey Dr BIDD ST8 .... 227 K3
Oxheys RUNC WA7 .... 74 C4
Ox La RAIN/WH L35 .... 32 C6
Oxmead Cl WARRN/WOL WA2 .... 38 B3
Oxmoor Cl RUNC WA7 .... 74 A7
Oxney Cl MCFLDN SK10 .... 137 M4
Oxton Av WYTH/NTH M22 .... 44 C8
Oxton Cl WDN WA8 .... 33 J8
Oxton Gn GTS/LS CH66 .... 94 D8 ④

P

Packsaddle Pk MCFLDN SK10 .... 111 L7
Padarn Cl CHSW/BR CH4 .... 168 D7
Padden Brook MPL/ROM SK6 .... 48 B2
Paddington Bank WARR WA1 .... 37 M6
Paddock Brow MCFLDN SK10 .... 112 A7
Paddock Cha POY/DIS SK12 .... 66 F2
Paddock Cl CHF/WBR SK23 .... 88 F8
Paddock Dr NSTN CH64 .... 91 K2
Paddock Gv STHEL WA9 .... 34 D1
Paddock Hl KNUT WA16 .... 109 G1
Paddock La AUD/MAD/W CW3 .... 274 B1
CHF/WBR SK23 .... 88 F8
CHF/WBR SK23 .... 89 M7
LYMM WA13 .... 40 D5
LYMM WA13 .... 41 G7
Paddock Ri RUNC WA7 .... 73 L8
Paddock Rd CHSW/BR CH4 .... 192 E3
The Paddocks EDGY/DAV SK3 .... 47 G7
MCFLDN SK10 .... 112 A7
MCFLDN SK10 .... 152 B6
The Paddock BRAM/HZG SK7 .... 65 K3
CHD/CHDH SK8 .... 45 L7
CHF/WBR SK23 .... 89 M6
CHNE CH2 .... 123 G1
CHSW/BR CH4 .... 16 C9
CQ CH5 .... 166 D2
FROD/HEL WA6 .... 124 C2
GTS/LS CH66 .... 120 D1
HALE/TIMP WA15 .... 43 H8
LYMM WA13 .... 59 J1
NANT CW5 .... 237 K6
NWCHW CW8 .... 129 J8
SBCH CW11 .... 223 M3
TPLY/KEL CW6 .... 197 K3
Paddock Vw NWCHW CW10 .... 179 J2
Paddock Wk NWCHW CW8 .... 127 K7
Paddock Wy CHSW/BR CH4 .... 190 A5
Padgate La WARR WA1 .... 37 L5

Padgbury Cl CONG CW12 .... 207 G3
Padgbury La CONG CW12 .... 206 F2
Padge La CHSE CH3 .... 231 J2
Padston Dr ALS/KID ST7 .... 241 G1
Padstow Cl CW/HAS CW1 .... 221 J4
HLWD L26 .... 50 E3
MCFLDN SK10 .... 137 L4
WARRW/BUR WA5 .... 54 E1
Padstow Dr BRAM/HZG SK7 .... 65 M5
Padworth Pl CW/HAS CW1 .... 221 H3
Page Gv CW/SHV CW2 .... 253 H1
Page La WDN WA8 .... 7 M3
Paignton Cl HUY L36 .... 32 B1
WARRW/BUR WA5 .... 35 L8
Painswick Rd GTS/LS CH66 .... 120 E2
WYTH/NTH M22 .... 63 H3
Palace Ar AIMK WN4 .... 22 B1
Palace Fields Av RUNC WA7 .... 74 A5
Palace Hey NSTN CH64 .... 92 A7
Palatine Cl CH/BCN CH1 .... 144 D6
IRL M44 .... 31 M3
Palatine Dr DID/WITH M20 .... 44 F1
WYTH/NTH M22 .... 44 D3
Palgrave Cl CH/BCN CH1 .... 145 G7
Palin Dr WARRW/BUR WA5 .... 35 M6
Pall Ml NANT CW5 .... 20 E7
Palliser Cl GOL/RIS/CU WA3 .... 39 C1
Palma Av MANAIR M90 .... 63 G4
Palmer Av CHD/CHDH SK8 .... 45 M6
Palmer Crs WARRW/BUR WA5 .... 36 A4
Palmer Rd SBCH CW11 .... 204 C7
Palmerston Cl CW/HAS CW1 .... 222 C7
Palmerston Cl CH/BCN CH1 .... 145 H8
Palmerston Rd MCFLDS SK11 .... 14 A6
OFTN SK2 .... 66 A1
Palmerston St MCFLDN SK10 .... 113 C4
Palm Gv GTS/LS CH66 .... 121 G3
WLTN L25 .... 50 B3
Palmyra Sq North WARR WA1 .... 4 F7
Palmyra Sq South WARR WA1 .... 4 F7
Panfield Rd WYTH/NTH M22 .... 44 C8
Pangbourne Cl EDGY/DAV SK3 .... 46 C6
WARRS WA4 .... 56 E6
Panton Pl CHNE CH2 .... 17 M1
Panton Rd CHNE CH2 .... 17 M1
Parade Crs SPK/HALE L24 .... 70 E2
Parade Rd MANAIR M90 .... 63 J5
The Parade CH/BCN CH1 .... 144 E7
NSTN CH64 .... 91 H3
Paradise La NANT CW5 .... 200 D5
RAIN/WH L35 .... 32 D2
Paradise St MCFLDS SK11 .... 14 F6
Paragon Cl WDN WA8 .... 34 B7
Parish Cl ALS/KID ST7 .... 224 B8
Park Av ALS/KID ST7 .... 242 E4
ALT WA14 .... 42 E4
BRAM/HZG SK7 .... 65 J7
CH/BCN CH1 .... 144 A2
CHD/CHDH SK8 .... 64 F3
CHF/WBR SK23 .... 89 K1
CHSE CH3 .... 214 B2
CHSW/BR CH4 .... 168 E6
CQ CH5 .... 142 C6
CQ CH5 .... 166 D2
EDGY/DAV SK3 .... 45 M5
FLINT 116 A6
GOL/RIS/CU WA3 .... 22 F2
HALE/TIMP WA15 .... 61 M3
LYMM WA13 .... 59 K4
MCFLDS SK11 .... 14 F8
MPL/ROM SK6 .... 48 C1
MWCH CW10 .... 179 J3
NANT CW5 .... 237 J7
NANT CW5 .... 251 L1
NEWLW WA12 .... 22 F5
NM/HAY SK22 .... 69 J5
NSTN CH64 .... 93 H4
NWCHW CW8 .... 129 K3
PART M31 .... 41 G1
POY/DIS SK12 .... 67 M6
RUNC WA7 .... 8 F7
TPLY/KEL CW6 .... 175 L4
TPLY/KEL CW6 .... 197 J2
WARRN/WOL WA2 .... 37 K3
WARRW/BUR WA5 .... 35 J5
WARRW/BUR WA5 .... 35 L6
WDN WA8 .... 7 K2
WHITCH SY13 .... 269 M5
WILM/AE SK9 .... 83 M5
Park Av North NEWLW WA12 .... 27 L1
Park Av South NEWLW WA12 .... 27 J2
Park Bank CONG CW12 .... 207 M2
Park Bvd WARR WA1 .... 5 G9
Park Brook Rd MCFLDS SK11 .... 14 A6
Parkbrook Rd NTHM/RTH M23 .... 44 B5
Park Cl ALT WA14 .... 42 F4
AUD/MAD/W CW3 .... 267 L4
CHSE CH3 .... 172 B2
Park Ct RUNC WA7 .... 9 G7
WRX/GR/LL LL12 .... 210 B5
Park Crs CHF/WBR SK23 .... 89 K1
NWCHW CW8 .... 127 M8
WARRS WA4 .... 56 D6
WILM/AE SK9 .... 84 B3
Parkdale Rd WARR WA1 .... 38 A5
Park Dr CHNE CH2 .... 146 A8
CW/SHV CW2 .... 237 M3
EP CH65 .... 121 H1
HALE/TIMP WA15 .... 43 G5
HALE/TIMP WA15 .... 61 M3
HTNM SK4 .... 46 B2
Park Dr South CHNE CH2 .... 170 A1
Parkend Dr LEIGH WN7 .... 24 D2
Parkend Rd NTHM/RTH M23 .... 44 A7
Parker Av NWCHW CW8 .... 129 G6
Parker Dr CHSE CH3 .... 228 E3
Parker Dr South CHSE CH3 .... 228 F3
Parkers Ct RUNC WA7 .... 73 L6
Parkers Rd CW/HAS CW1 .... 221 G4
Parker St MCFLDS SK11 .... 15 J6
RUNC WA7 .... 9 J1
WARR WA1 .... 4 E8
Park Est CW/SHV CW2 .... 238 D7
Parkett Heyes Rd
MCFLDS SK11 .... 137 L5
Park Farm Vw
BURS/TUN ST6 .... 243 K5
Parkfield CW/HAS CW1 .... 221 G4
Parkfield Av MPL/ROM SK6 .... 48 A8
WARRS WA4 .... 56 D5
Parkfield Dr EP CH65 .... 121 G2
FROD/HEL WA6 .... 124 B1
Parkfield Rd ALT WA14 .... 42 C8
CHD/CHDH SK8 .... 64 F3
CHSW/BR CH4 .... 190 C1
KNUT WA16 .... 107 H4
NWCHW CW9 .... 13 M3

Parkfields La WARRN/WOL WA2 .... 37 M2
Parkgate KNUT WA16 .... 107 J1
Parkgate Av KNUT WA16 .... 134 A4
Parkgate Dr OFTN SK2 .... 47 H8
Parkgate La KNUT WA16 .... 81 J8
Parkgate Rd CH/BCN CH1 .... 16 F2
CH/BCN CH1 .... 145 J8
GTS/LS CH66 .... 119 J2
MCFLDS SK11 .... 138 C8
NSTN CH64 .... 91 J4
WARRS WA4 .... 56 D3
Park Gates Av CHD/CHDH SK8 .... 65 J3
Park Gates Dr CHD/CHDH SK8 .... 65 J3
Parkgate Wy RUNC WA7 .... 74 C5
Park Gn MCFLDS SK11 .... 15 H7
Park Hill Cl NM/HAY SK22 .... 69 J3
Park Hill Rd HALE/TIMP WA15 .... 62 A3
Park House Dr MCFLDN SK10 .... 112 A4
SBCH CW11 .... 204 D6
Park House La MCFLDN SK10 .... 112 A4
Parkland Av NM/HAY SK22 .... 69 J3
Parkland Cl WARRS WA4 .... 57 H8
Parkland Dr CHNE CH2 .... 123 H1
Parklands ALS/KID ST7 .... 243 H3
GTS/LS CH66 .... 94 D7
WDN WA8 .... 52 C1
Parklands Dr SALE M33 .... 42 D2
Parklands Gdns GTS/LS CH66 .... 94 D6
Parklands Rd NTHM/RTH M23 .... 43 M5
The Parklands CONG CW12 .... 208 A2
Parklands Vw POY/DIS SK12 .... 66 D6
Parklands Wy POY/DIS SK12 .... 66 D6
Park La ALS/KID ST7 .... 241 G7
ALT WA14 .... 60 B2
BIDD ST8 .... 227 J6
CHSE CH3 .... 195 L1
CONG CW12 .... 207 M2
FROD/HEL WA6 .... 99 H4
HALE/TIMP WA15 .... 62 A3
KNUT WA16 .... 104 E4
MCFLDS SK11 .... 14 E8
MCFLDS SK11 .... 15 H7
NANT CW5 .... 252 F8
NWCHE CW9 .... 153 M5
NWCHW CW8 .... 129 H8
POY/DIS SK12 .... 66 E8
SBCH CW11 .... 203 M6
STKP SK1 .... 3 M7
WARRS WA4 .... 55 M7
Parklea GTS/LS CH66 .... 94 D6
Park Lodge Cl CHD/CHDH SK8 .... 45 L8
Park Mount Cl MCFLDS SK11 .... 14 B9
Park Mount Dr MCFLDS SK11 .... 14 C9
Park Pl HTNM SK4 .... 45 M2
Park Ri MPL/ROM SK6 .... 48 C1
Park Rd ALT WA14 .... 61 G2
CHD/CHDH SK8 .... 44 F6
CHD/CHDH SK8 .... 45 L6
CHD/CHDH SK8 .... 65 J3
CHF/WBR SK23 .... 89 K6
CHNE CH2 .... 122 E3
CONG CW12 .... 207 L2
CW/HAS CW1 .... 222 D7
EP CH65 .... 10 E9
EP CH65 .... 95 J8
HALE/TIMP WA15 .... 42 F4
HALE/TIMP WA15 .... 61 M3
LYMM WA13 .... 40 C4
LYMM WA13 .... 59 K4
MCFLDS SK11 .... 14 F8
MPL/ROM SK6 .... 48 C1
MWCH CW10 .... 179 J3
NANT CW5 .... 237 J7
NANT CW5 .... 251 L1
NEWLW WA12 .... 22 F5
NM/HAY SK22 .... 69 J5
NSTN CH64 .... 93 H4
NWCHW CW8 .... 129 K3
PART M31 .... 41 G1
POY/DIS SK12 .... 67 M6
RUNC WA7 .... 8 F7
TPLY/KEL CW6 .... 175 L4
TPLY/KEL CW6 .... 197 J2
WARRN/WOL WA2 .... 37 K3
WARRW/BUR WA5 .... 35 J5
WARRW/BUR WA5 .... 35 L6
WDN WA8 .... 7 K2
WHITCH SY13 .... 269 M5
WILM/AE SK9 .... 83 M5
Park Rd North NEWLW WA12 .... 27 L1
Park Rd South NEWLW WA12 .... 27 K2
Park Rd West CHSW/BR CH4 .... 16 A9
Park Rw RUNC WA7 .... 45 M3
Parkside Av STHEL WA9 .... 34 B1
Parkside Rd MPL/ROM SK6 .... 67 K4
Parkside La MPL/ROM SK6 .... 49 J6
Parkside Rd NEWLW WA12 .... 22 F5
SALE M33 .... 43 K1
Parkside Wk BRAM/HZG SK7 .... 65 L1
The Parks RNFD/HAY WA11 .... 33 J2
Parkstone Dr CW/HAS CW1 .... 221 H4
Park St CH/BCN CH1 .... 17 G6
MCFLDS SK11 .... 113 H4
MCFLDS SK11 .... 15 H7
MPL/ROM SK6 .... 47 M1
NSTN CH64 .... 91 L4
NWCHW CW8 .... 12 E4
STKP SK1 .... 3 G4
Parksway WARR WA1 .... 38 C3
The Park CHSE CH3 .... 170 E4
WARRW/BUR WA5 .... 54 D1
Park Vale Rd MCFLDS SK11 .... 14 E8
Park Vw AIMK WN4 .... 22 B2
EDGY/DAV SK3 .... 45 M5
HOLMCH SK11 .... 181 J1
NM/HAY SK22 .... 69 J3
WILM/AE SK9 .... 84 B6
Park View Ri NM/HAY SK22 .... 69 J3
Park View Rd ALS/KID ST7 .... 243 G1
Park Wk CHNE CH2 .... 145 K8
Park Wy CH/BCN CH1 .... 144 A3
Parkway BRAM/HZG SK7 .... 65 J3
CQ CH5 .... 142 D2
EDGY/DAV SK3 .... 45 M5
HOLMCH SK11 .... 181 J1
NM/HAY SK22 .... 69 J3
WILM/AE SK9 .... 84 B6
Parkwood Cl LYMM WA13 .... 58 D2

Parkwood Rd NTHM/RTH M23 .... 44 C5
RAIN/WH L35 .... 32 E2
Parliament St NWCHW CW8 .... 12 D4
Parliament Wy GTS/LS CH66 .... 120 F4
Parlington Ct WDN WA8 .... 52 C5
Parndon Dr OFTN SK2 .... 47 J5
Parnell Av WYTH/NTH M22 .... 44 D4
Parren Av RAIN/WH L35 .... 32 C3
Parrs Mount Ms HTNM SK4 .... 45 M2
Parr St MCFLDS SK11 .... 14 E6
WARR WA1 .... 5 H8
WDN WA8 .... 7 L2
Parrs Wood Av DID/WITH M20 .... 45 J3
Parrs Wood La DID/WITH M20 .... 45 K3
Parrs Wood Rd DID/WITH M20 .... 45 H4
Parrs Wood View WARRS WA4 .... 57 G3
Parry Dr WARRS WA4 .... 57 L1
Parsonage Gdns MPL/ROM SK6 .... 49 G5
Parsonage Rd WDN WA8 .... 53 G8
Parsonage St BURS/TUN ST6 .... 243 K8
HTNM SK4 .... 2 E4
MCFLDS SK11 .... 15 H7
Parsonage Wy CHD/CHDH SK8 .... 46 A7
WARRW/BUR WA5 .... 36 A7
Parsons La CHNE CH2 .... 145 H5
Parson St CONG CW12 .... 207 J2
Partridge Av NTHM/RTH M23 .... 44 B6
Partridge Cl CONG CW12 .... 207 L3
GOL/RIS/CU WA3 .... 29 L8
WSFD CW7 .... 177 K7
Partridge Wy NWCHE CW9 .... 104 F7
Parvey La MCFLDS SK11 .... 162 E3
Paston Rd WYTH/NTH M22 .... 44 D5
Pastoral St MCFLDN SK10 .... 138 C1
TPLY/KEL CW6 .... 149 J8
WLTN L25 .... 50 B3
Pasture Cl ALS/KID ST7 .... 243 H5
Pasture Dr GOL/RIS/CU WA3 .... 29 G5
Pasturefield Cl SALE M33 .... 43 M1
Pasture Field Rd
WYTH/NTH M22 .... 63 M3
Pasture La WARRN/WOL WA2 .... 38 B3
Patch Croft Rd WYTH/NTH M22 .... 63 M3
Patch La BRAM/HZG SK7 .... 65 K7
Patmos La KNUT WA16 .... 131 M4
Patrivale Cl WARR WA1 .... 37 M5
Patten La WARR WA1 .... 5 G7
Patterdale Av WARRN/WOL WA2 .... 37 J2
Patterdale Cl CW/SHV CW2 .... 237 K1
Patterdale Rd OFTN SK2 .... 47 H6
PART M31 .... 40 E1
WYTH/NTH M22 .... 44 E4
Patterson St NEWLW WA12 .... 22 B8
Paul Cl WARRW/BUR WA5 .... 35 K6
Paulden Av NTHM/RTH M23 .... 44 B6
Paulden Rd NWCHE CW9 .... 131 G2
Pauls Moss Ct WHITCH SY13 .... 270 A5
Paul St WARRN/WOL WA2 .... 4 E5
Pavement La WYTH/NTH M22 .... 44 E4
The Pavilions NWCHE CW9 .... 153 L2
Paxford Pl WILM/AE SK9 .... 84 A7
Payne Cl WARRW/BUR WA5 .... 36 D6
Paythorne Cl
GOL/RIS/CU WA3 .... 29 K1
Paythorne Gn OFTN SK2 .... 47 L7
Peacefield MPL/ROM SK6 .... 48 E7
Peach Fld CHSE CH3 .... 170 B5
Peach La NANT CW5 .... 237 L3
Peacock Av CHD/CHDH SK8 .... 64 B6
WARR WA1 .... 37 L6
WSFD CW7 .... 177 J6
Peacock Hay Rd ALS/KID ST7 .... 242 E8
Peacock La KNUT WA16 .... 59 J6
Peak Bank MPL/ROM SK6 .... 48 C2
Peak Dale Av BURS/TUN ST6 .... 243 H5
Peakdale Av CHD/CHDH SK8 .... 64 A3
Peakdale Rd MPL/ROM SK6 .... 49 G8
Peak Rd NM/HAY SK22 .... 69 K4
Peak St STKP SK1 .... 3 J5
Pearle St MCFLDN SK10 .... 15 C3
Pearl La CHSE CH3 .... 170 D5
Pearl St BRAM/HZG SK7 .... 47 L8
MCFLDN SK10 .... 112 A5
Pearl Yd WHITCH SY13 .... 270 A5
Pearson Av WARRS WA4 .... 56 D2
Pearson Cl PART M31 .... 41 G1
Pearson St MCFLDS SK11 .... 15 K7
RDSH SK5 .... 3 G1
Pear Tree Av CW/HAS CW1 .... 221 H5
RUNC WA7 .... 9 M8
Pear Tree Cl CQ CH5 .... 142 A3
Peartree Cl FROD/HEL WA6 .... 99 K3
Pear Tree Cl MPL/ROM SK6 .... 49 H4
Peartree Cl SBCH CW11 .... 204 E6
Pear Tree Dr AUD/MAD/W CW3 .... 267 K5
NWCHE CW9 .... 104 F6
Pear Tree La NWCHW CW8 .... 101 K8
WHITCH SY13 .... 269 L3
Peartree Pl WARRS WA4 .... 5 J9
Pear Tree Wy CHNE CH2 .... 145 M7
GTS/LS CH66 .... 120 E3
Pearwood Cl TPLY/KEL CW6 .... 197 K3
Peaslake Cl MPL/ROM SK6 .... 48 D2
Peasley Cl WARRN/WOL WA2 .... 38 B3
Peckfield Cl RUNC WA7 .... 74 A7
SBCH CW11 .... 203 L5
Peckforton Cl CHD/CHDH SK8 .... 45 L6
Peckforton Dr GTS/LS CH66 .... 73 M8 ⑪
Peckforton Hall La
TPLY/KEL CW6 .... 216 C6
Peckforton Rd TPLY/KEL CW6 .... 216 A3
Peckforton Wy CHNE CH2 .... 145 L5
Peckmill Cl WILM/AE SK9 .... 84 E2
Peck Mill La FROD/HEL WA6 .... 124 A5
Pedley Hl MCFLDN SK10 .... 86 F5
MCFLDN SK10 .... 113 L8
Pedley House La KNUT WA16 .... 108 E3
Pedley La CONG CW12 .... 185 L8
KNUT WA16 .... 108 C5
Pedley St CW/SHV CW2 .... 19 H7
Peebles Cl GTS/LS CH66 .... 93 M6
Peel Av ALT WA14 .... 61 K2
Peel Cl RAIN/WH L35 .... 32 E1
WARR WA1 .... 38 D6

Peel Crs CHSE CH3 148 E5
Peel Dr CONG CW12 207 H5
Peelgate Dr CHD/CHDH SK8 64 A2 2
Peel Hall La CHSE CH3 148 E5
Peel Hall Rd WYTH/NTH M22 63 M1
Peel House La WDN WA8 53 H1
Peel La CONG CW12 207 J5
Peel Rd HALE/TIMP WA15 61 L1
Peel St CW/HAS CW1 18 C2
MCFLDS SK11 15 G8
NEWLW WA12 27 G1
OFTN SK2 46 F6
RUNC WA7 8 F1
Peerswood Ct NSTN CH64 91 L7 2
Peewit Cl WSFD CW7 177 K7 3
Peggie's La MCFLDN SK10 112 D1
Pelham Cl CW/HAS CW1 222 C7
Pelham Rd WARRS WA4 57 J1
Pemberton Cl NSTN CH64 93 G4
Pemberton Rd CH/BCN CH1 16 F4 3
Pembrey Wy WLTN L25 50 D4 1
Pembroke Cl CHSW/BR CH4 169 L6
CQ CH5 142 D8 1
Pembroke Dr EP CH65 121 G1
Pembroke Gdns WARRS WA4 56 D8
Pembroke Gv IRL M44 31 J6
Pembroke Rd MCFLDS SK11 137 M5
Pembroke Wy WSFD CW7 177 H5 3
Pembury Cl WYTH/NTH M22 63 J1 1
Penare Gorran Hvn
RUNC WA7 74 C6 1
Penarth Rd WYTH/NTH M22 44 D4
Penbrook Cl CW/SHV CW2 237 K1
Pencarrow Cl DID/WITH M20 44 F1
Pendeen Cl WYTH/NTH M22 63 L3
Pendennis Rd HTNM SK4 2 B2
Pendine Cl WARRW/BUR WA5 36 C2
Pendlebury Rd CHD/CHDH SK8 45 G6
Pendlebury St WARRS WA4 56 F1
Pendle Gdns GOL/RIS/CU WA3 29 L1
Pendle Rd GOL/RIS/CU WA3 23 J3
Pendleton Gn HLWD L26 50 E5
Penfold Cl CH/BCN CH1 120 B4
Penfold Hey CHNE CH2 145 K5
Penfolds RUNC WA7 73 K3
Penfold Wy CHSW/BR CH4 191 G5
Pengrove Cl BURS/TUN ST6 243 L4
Penhale Ms BRAM/HZG SK7 65 M5 3
Penistone Dr GTS/LS CH66 94 B7
Penketh Av WARRW/BUR WA5 4 C1
Penketh Gn SPK/HALE L24 50 E8 3
Penketh Rd WARRW/BUR WA5 36 A8
Penketh's La RUNC WA7 9 H1
Penkford La WARRW/BUR WA5 26 D3
Penkmans La FROD/HEL WA6 99 J6
Penlan Dr CQ CH5 166 C2
Penlington Ct NANT CW5 21 H5
Penmann Cl HLWD L26 50 F5 1
Penmann Crs HLWD L26 50 F5
Penmark Cl WARRW/BUR WA5 36 C2
Penmere Gv SALE M33 42 E3
Penmon Cl CH/BCN CH1 168 D1
Penmoor Cha BRAM/HZG SK7 66 B3
Pennant Cl GOL/RIS/CU WA3 39 G1
Penn Gn CHD/CHDH SK8 65 H3
Penn House Cl BRAM/HZG SK7 65 L5
Pennine Dr ALT WA14 42 B7
Pennine La GOL/RIS/CU WA3 23 J3
Pennine Rd BRAM/HZG SK7 66 B3
WARRN/WOL WA2 37 L2
Pennine Wy BIDD ST8 227 L2
WSFD CW7 177 H4
Pennington Av LEIGH WN7 24 E1
Pennington Gdns LEIGH WN7 24 E1
Pennington Gn GTS/LS CH66 120 C1
Pennington La
WARRW/BUR WA5 26 C1
Pennington Rd LEIGH WN7 24 F1
Penningtons La MCFLDS SK11 137 L7
Penn La RUNC WA7 8 E4
Penny Bank Cl
CHSW/BR CH4 190 A1 3
Pennyfields Rd ALS/KID ST7 243 K2
Penny La MCFLDN SK10 139 K1
RAIN/WH L35 33 G5
RDSH SK5 3 G2
RNFD/HAY WA11 22 A5
WARRW/BUR WA5 26 D4
Pennymoor Dr ALT WA14 42 B6
Pennypleck La NWCHE CW9 78 A2
Penny's La NWCHE CW9 130 E5
Penrhos Av CHD/CHDH SK8 44 F8
Penrhyn Av CHD/CHDH SK8 64 E3
Penrhyn Crs BRAM/HZG SK7 66 C4
RUNC WA7 9 J8
Penrhyn Dr BRAM/HZG SK7 66 C3
Penrhyn Rd EDGY/DAV SK3 2 A8
NWCHW CW8 12 D3
Penrith Av MCFLDS SK11 137 M7
SALE M33 43 J2
WARRN/WOL WA2 37 J2 3
Penrith Cl FROD/HEL WA6 99 K4
PART M31 31 L8
Penrith Ct CONG CW12 207 G2
Penrose Gdns WARRW/BUR WA5 54 D1
Penroy Av DID/WITH M20 44 D1
Penry Av IRL M44 31 L6
Penryn Av SALE M33 43 J3
Penryn Cl WARRW/BUR WA5 35 L8
Pensarn Gdns
WARRW/BUR WA5 36 D2 3
Pensby Av CHNE CH2 145 K7
Pensby Dr GTS/LS CH66 94 D8
Pensford Rd NTHM/RTH M23 62 F1
Penshaw Ct RUNC WA7 73 L5
Pentland Av WARRN/WOL WA2 37 H1
Pentland Cl BRAM/HZG SK7 66 B3
CHSE CH3 170 A2
WSFD CW7 177 H4 2
Pentland Pl WARRN/WOL WA2 37 H1 3
Pentre Cl CHSE CH3 148 F5
Pentre La CHSE CH3 148 F5
Pentwyn Gv NTHM/RTH M23 44 B5 3
Penzance Cl MCFLDN SK10 137 L4 3
Peover La CONG CW12 185 L5
MCFLDS SK11 134 F4
Peover Rd WILM/AE SK9 64 E7
Pepler Av NTHM/RTH M23 44 B2
Pepper Rd BRAM/HZG SK7 66 B2
The Peppers LYMM WA13 58 F1
Pepper St CH/BCN CH1 17 G6
CHSE CH3 170 D4
KNUT WA16 81 M3
LYMM WA13 58 E1
MCFLDS SK11 134 E2
MCFLDS SK11 137 H4
MWCH CW10 179 J3
SPK/HALE L24 71 K3
WARRS WA4 77 G1
WHITCH SY13 270 A4
Percival Cl CHNE CH2 145 J4
Percival La KNUT WA16 134 B1
RUNC WA7 8 D2
Percival Rd CHNE CH2 145 J4
EP CH65 10 D6
Percival St WARR WA1 5 J7
Percy James Cl ALS/KID ST7 224 E8
Percy Rd CHSW/BR CH4 17 H9
Percy St NWCHE CW9 13 J2
STKP SK1 3 G4
WARRW/BUR WA5 4 B6
Peregrine Cl WSFD CW7 177 K7
Peregrine Rd OFTN SK2 47 M8
Perimeter Rd CHNE CH2 97 J7
Perkins St BURS/TUN ST6 243 J5
Perrey St RUNC WA7 9 K2
Perrin Av RUNC WA7 8 D7
Perrins Rd WARRW/BUR WA5 26 F6
Perry Rd HALE/TIMP WA15 43 H6
Perth Cl BRAM/HZG SK7 65 L7
HOLMCH CW4 181 H2
WARRN/WOL WA2 28 F8
Peterborough Cl
GTS/LS CH66 120 F5 3
MCFLDN SK10 14 A1
Peter House Rd MCFLDS SK11 162 F1
Peter Salem Dr
WARRW/BUR WA5 36 B6
Petersburg Rd EDGY/DAV SK3 46 C6
Peters Cl MCFLDN SK10 112 A5
Petersfield Dr NTHM/RTH M23 43 K5
Petersfield Gdns
GOL/RIS/CU WA3 24 E8 3
Petersgate RUNC WA7 74 D5
Petersham Dr WARRS WA4 56 E7
Peterstone Cl
WARRW/BUR WA5 36 D2 4
Peter St AIMK WN4 22 C1
ALT WA14 61 K1
BRAM/HZG SK7 66 D1
GOL/RIS/CU WA3 23 G4 3
MCFLDS SK11 14 E8
NWCHE CW9 13 M1
STKP SK1 3 J3
Peter St West MCFLDS SK11 14 E6 1
Peterswood Cl WYTH/NTH M22 63 H1
Petheridge Dr
WYTH/NTH M22 63 H3 3
Petrel Av POY/DIS SK12 66 A8
Petrel Cl EDGY/DAV SK3 46 D6
WSFD CW7 177 K7
Petunia Cl MCFLDS SK11 138 B7
Petworth Av WARRN/WOL WA2 37 H1
Petworth Cl CW/SHV CW2 238 B4
SPK/HALE L24 50 B8
WYTH/NTH M22 44 E7
Pevensey Dr KNUT WA16 107 G4
Peveril Av NM/HAY SK22 69 J3 3
Peveril Cl WARRS WA4 56 D4 2
Peveril Dr BRAM/HZG SK7 66 F4
Peveril Gdns POY/DIS SK12 69 G6
Peveril Ms POY/DIS SK12 69 G6 1
Peveril Rd ALT WA14 42 C5
Pewit La NANT CW5 265 H4
Pewsey Rd WYTH/NTH M22 63 M1
Pewterspear Green Rd
WARRS WA4 76 D1
Pewterspear La WARRS WA4 56 D8
Pexall Rd CONG CW12 185 J1
Pexhill Dr MCFLDN SK10 137 L5
Pexhill Rd MCFLDN SK10 137 L4 1
MCFLDS SK11 160 C2
Pheasant Cl GOL/RIS/CU WA3 29 M8
Pheasant Dr NWCHE CW9 104 F7
Pheasant Fld SPK/HALE L24 71 J2
Pheasant Gv HLWD L26 50 E3
Pheasant Ri ALT WA14 61 K3
Pheasant Wk KNUT WA16 59 J8
Pheasant Wy WSFD CW7 177 K7
Philip Dr SALE M33 43 H2
Philip Rd WDN WA8 52 B4
Philips Dr WARRW/BUR WA5 35 L6
Philips La GTS/LS CH66 94 C8
Philip St CQ CH5 167 G2
Phillips Rd CH/BCN CH1 168 D1
Phillip St CHNE CH2 17 K2
Phipps' La WARRW/BUR WA5 26 E5
Phoenix Av WARRW/BUR WA5 36 F2 1
Phoenix Cl ALS/KID ST7 243 J2 1
Phoenix St CQ CH5 167 G2
Physics Rd SPK/HALE L24 50 C7
Phythian Crs WARRW/BUR WA5 35 M8
Piccadilly STKP SK1 3 G6
Pichael Nook WARRS WA4 38 A8
Pickenham Cl MCFLDS SK11 137 M6
Pickering Cl HALE/TIMP WA15 43 G5
Pickering Crs WARRS WA4 57 K1
Pickering Rd WDN WA8 52 B7
Pickerings Cl RUNC WA7 73 J6
Pickering St CHNE CH2 17 K1
Pickford's Brow STKP SK1 3 G5 2
Pickford St MCFLDS SK11 15 H6
Pickmere Cl EDGY/DAV SK3 46 C6
SALE M33 43 M2
SBCH CW11 203 M5
Pickmere Dr CHSE CH3 170 B4 1
PS/BROM CH62 93 M1
RUNC WA7 74 C7
Pickmere Gdns
CHD/CHDH SK8 45 M7 1
Pickmere La KNUT WA16 105 G6
Pickmere Rd WILM/AE SK9 64 D7
Pickmere St WARRW/BUR WA5 4 B7
Pickwick Cl SBCH CW11 204 C4
Pickwick Pl ALS/KID ST7 242 D2
Pickwick Rd POY/DIS SK12 86 D1
Picow Farm Rd RUNC WA7 8 B6
Picow St RUNC WA7 8 F4
Picton Av EP CH65 10 F8
RUNC WA7 9 K4
Picton Cl GOL/RIS/CU WA3 29 J8
NWCHE CW9 129 M8 3
PS/BROM CH62 93 K1
Picton Dr WILM/AE SK9 84 E3
WSFD CW7 177 H2
Picton Gorse La CHNE CH2 146 B4
Picton La CHNE CH2 122 A5
Pierce St CQ CH5 142 D7 3
MCFLDS SK11 14 E5
Pierpoint Ct CH/BCN CH1 16 F6 1
Pierpoint St NEWLW WA12 23 G5
WARRW/BUR WA5 4 D3
Pigot Pl WARRS WA4 37 M7 2
Pike La FROD/HEL WA6 126 A1
Pikemere Rd ALS/KID ST7 224 B7
Pikenall La NWCHW CW8 127 J1
Pike Rd MCFLDN SK10 114 A6
Pike St WARRS WA4 56 C3
The Pike NANT CW5 251 L1
Pilgrim Cl WARRN/WOL WA2 28 A6 1
Pillar Box La SBCH CW11 204 A1
Pillmoss La WARRS WA4 76 A3
Pillory St NANT CW5 20 E7
Pimblett St GOL/RIS/CU WA3 23 G5 4
Pimlico Rd RUNC WA7 8 D4
Pimmcroft Wy SALE M33 43 M1
Pine Av NEWLW WA12 27 J2
WDN WA8 7 K1
Pine Cl ALS/KID ST7 242 C5
MCFLDN SK10 15 M2
MPL/ROM SK6 48 E8
RAIN/WH L35 32 E1
Pinedale Cl GTS/LS CH66 120 F4
Pine Gdns CHNE CH2 145 J6
Pine Gv CHNE CH2 146 B8
GOL/RIS/CU WA3 23 J4 1
GTS/LS CH66 121 G3
SBCH CW11 204 C6
WARR WA1 38 A5
WSFD CW7 178 A3
Pinehey NSTN CH64 91 K3
Pinehurst MCFLDN SK10 111 L6 1
Pinellas RUNC WA7 9 K1
Pine Rd BRAM/HZG SK7 65 M4
MCFLDN SK10 15 M3
POY/DIS SK12 86 F1 1
RUNC WA7 9 M8
The Pines LEIGH WN7 24 F1 2
Pine St EDGY/DAV SK3 2 C6
Pine Tree Cl CHSW/BR CH4 190 B1
Pinetree Cl NWCHW CW8 103 H8
Pine Trees KNUT WA16 81 M4
Pine Wk NANT CW5 21 G9
Pineways WARRS WA4 56 D7
Pinewood AIMK WN4 22 A2
ALT WA14 61 G2
Pinewood Av WARR WA1 37 L5 1
Pinewood Cl CHNE CH2 123 J1
Pinewood Ct ALT WA14 61 L3
CW/SHV CW2 238 B5 3
HALE/TIMP WA15 61 L3
Pinewood Rd WARRW/BUR WA5 26 F5
WILM/AE SK9 84 E4
Pinfold Cl HALE/TIMP WA15 62 D5 2
Pinfold Ct CHSW/BR CH4 169 L6
Pinfold Dr CHD/CHDH SK8 65 G3 1
Pinfold La CHSW/BR CH4 169 K6
KNUT WA16 108 D5
KNUT WA16 132 B1
MANAIR M90 62 F6
MWCH CW10 179 H3 3
TPLY/KEL CW6 175 L5
Pinfold Rd WLTN L25 50 C5
Pinfold St MCFLDS SK11 14 F5
Pinfold Wy NWCHW CW8 128 D3 1
Pingard's La NWCHW CW8 127 J6
Pingate Dr CHD/CHDH SK8 65 G6
Pingate La CHD/CHDH SK8 65 G6
Pingate La South
CHD/CHDH SK8 65 G6
Pingot Av NTHM/RTH M23 44 B2
Pingot Cft CHSE CH3 170 B5
Pingot Rd NM/HAY SK22 69 L4
Pinmill Brow FROD/HEL WA6 99 H5
Pinmill Cl FROD/HEL WA6 99 H5
Pinners Brow WARRN/WOL WA2 5 G4
Pinners Fold RUNC WA7 74 B3
Pinnington Rd RAIN/WH L35 32 E1
Pinsley Green Rd NANT CW5 261 L2
Pinsley Vw NANT CW5 249 L8
Pintail Av EDGY/DAV SK3 46 D6
Pintail Pl WSFD CW7 177 K6 3
Pipe La WARR WA1 38 B3
Piperhill Av WYTH/NTH M22 44 D3
Pipers Ash WSFD CW7 177 G3 2
Pipers La CHNE CH2 146 B8
NSTN CH64 118 F4
The Pipers GOL/RIS/CU WA3 23 M4
Pipit Av NEWLW WA12 27 J1
Pipit Cl HLWD L26 50 E2 1
Pipit La GOL/RIS/CU WA3 38 E1
Pippin Cl MWCH CW10 179 J5
Pippins Cl CQ CH5 142 A7
Pippits Rw RUNC WA7 73 L8 3
Pirie Cl CONG CW12 185 G8 2
Pirie Rd CONG CW12 185 G7
Pitchcombe Rd WYTH/NTH M22 63 H2
Pitfield Gdns NTHM/RTH M23 43 M5
Pit La ALS/KID ST7 242 C7
CW/SHV CW2 253 L2
WDN WA8 34 A8
Pit Pl WLTN L25 50 A2
Pitt La MCFLDS SK11 159 H3
Pitts Cl CHSE CH3 172 C2 1
Pitts Heath La RUNC WA7 74 D1
Pitts Hill Bank BURS/TUN ST6 243 M7
Pitt St EDGY/DAV SK3 2 D8
MCFLDS SK11 15 H9
WARRW/BUR WA5 4 D4
WDN WA8 53 G7
Place Rd ALT WA14 42 C6 1
Plaistow Ct RUNC WA7 73 L5
Plane Tree Cl MPL/ROM SK6 48 D7
Plane Tree Dr CW/HAS CW1 221 L6
Plane Tree Gv
RNFD/HAY WA11 22 A5 2
Planetree Rd HALE/TIMP WA15 62 A2
Plane Tree Rd PART M31 40 D1
Plantagenet Cl WSFD CW7 177 K6 3
Plantation Cl RUNC WA7 74 A3
Plantation Dr GTS/LS CH66 94 E5
Plant La SBCH CW11 203 G3
Plant St SBCH CW11 204 A5
Plas Newton La CHNE CH2 145 M6
Platt Av SBCH CW11 204 A5
Platts La CHSE CH3 171 K5
CHSE CH3 193 L7
CHSE CH3 214 F5
Platt St CHD/CHDH SK8 45 L6
Pleachway HTNM SK4 45 M2
Pleasance Wy NEWLW WA12 22 D8 2
Pleasant St MCFLDN SK10 15 L3 1
NWCHW CW8 12 E4
Pleasant Wy CHD/CHDH SK8 65 J6
Pleck Rd EP CH65 121 G2
Plemstall Cl CHNE CH2 146 F4
Plemstall La CHNE CH2 147 G3
Plemstall Wy CHNE CH2 146 F3
The Plex ALS/KID ST7 224 D8
Plinston Av WARRS WA4 37 M8
Plough Cft ALS/KID ST7 241 G1
Plough La CHSE CH3 170 F5
CQ CH5 142 B8
Ploughmans Wy GTS/LS CH66 120 E4
MCFLDN SK10 138 B1
Plover Av WSFD CW7 177 K7
Plover Cl CHSE CH3 228 F3 3
NEWLW WA12 27 J1
Plover Dr ALT WA14 42 B4 3
BIDD ST8 227 L4
RUNC WA7 74 D4
Plover Fld AUD/MAD/W CW3 267 K6
Plovers La FROD/HEL WA6 98 C7
Plover Wy GOL/RIS/CU WA3 23 L4
Plowden Rd WYTH/NTH M22 63 H2
Plowley Cl DID/WITH M20 45 H2
Pluckington Rd HUY L36 32 B2
Plucksbridge Rd MPL/ROM SK6 68 A1
Plumley Cl EDGY/DAV SK3 46 F7 2
Plumley Gdns RAIN/WH L35 52 A3
Plumley Moor Rd KNUT WA16 105 L7
Plumley Rd WILM/AE SK9 64 D7 3
Plumpstons La
FROD/HEL WA6 99 H3 1
Plumtre Av WARRW/BUR WA5 4 D1
Plymouth Cl RUNC WA7 74 E6
Plymouth Dr BRAM/HZG SK7 65 L5
Plymouth Gv EDGY/DAV SK3 46 B5 2
Plymouth St CQ CH5 142 A6
Poachers' La WARRS WA4 56 F1
Pochard Av WSFD CW7 177 K6
Pochard Dr ALT WA14 42 B5
POY/DIS SK12 66 A8
Pochard Ri RUNC WA7 74 D4
Pochin Wy MWCH CW10 179 L3
Pocket Nook La
GOL/RIS/CU WA3 24 A4
Pocklington Ct
WARRN/WOL WA2 37 M3 2
Pocklington Dr NTHM/RTH M23 43 M5
Podsmead Rd WYTH/NTH M22 63 H2
Poise Brook Dr OFTN SK2 47 M7 2
Poise Brook Rd OFTN SK2 47 M7
Poise Cl BRAM/HZG SK7 67 G1
Poleacre Dr WDN WA8 52 D2
Pole La NWCHE CW9 103 L3
Police St ALT WA14 42 D7 1
Pollard Sq PART M31 41 G1 1
Pollen Cl SALE M33 43 J2
Pollen Rd ALT WA14 42 C6
Pollit Cft MPL/ROM SK6 47 M3
Pollitt Crs STHEL WA9 34 C1
Polperro Cl MCFLDN SK10 137 K3 1
WARRW/BUR WA5 54 E1 3
Pond St GOL/RIS/CU WA3 24 A4
Pond Wk STHEL WA9 26 A3
Poolcroft SALE M33 43 M1
Poole Av WARRN/WOL WA2 37 H2 3
Poole Cl BRAM/HZG SK7 65 K3
Poole Crs WARRN/WOL WA2 37 H2 2
Poole Hall La GTS/LS CH66 94 E4
Poole Hall Rd EP CH65 94 F4
Poole La CHNE CH2 122 E2
Pool End Cl MCFLDN SK10 112 D8
Pool End Rd MCFLDN SK10 112 D8
Pooles La SBCH CW11 206 A5
Poole St WSFD CW7 177 L3
Poolford La HOLMCH CW4 180 E2
Pool House Rd POY/DIS SK12 67 J7
Pool La CHNE CH2 96 F7
CHSE CH3 148 C8
LYMM WA13 39 J8
NWCHW CW8 152 B2
RUNC WA7 9 J1
SBCH CW11 222 F5
WARRS WA4 56 A3
Pool Rd GOL/RIS/CU WA3 40 A1
Pool Side ALS/KID ST7 225 H4
Poolside AUD/MAD/W CW3 267 L6
Poolside Rd RUNC WA7 9 J4
Pools Platt La NWCHE CW9 77 L5
Pool St MCFLDS SK11 15 J8
WDN WA8 7 K6
Pooltown Rd EP CH65 94 F6
Poplar Av ALT WA14 42 D6
CQ CH5 142 B8
GOL/RIS/CU WA3 29 M1
NEWLW WA12 27 K1
NM/HAY SK22 69 K3
NWCHE CW9 153 M4
RUNC WA7 9 M8
WARRW/BUR WA5 35 L8
WILM/AE SK9 83 L7
Poplar Cl CHD/CHDH SK8 45 H7 3
CONG CW12 184 A8
EP CH65 95 H8
NWCHW CW8 152 A1 2
RUNC WA7 9 M9
WHITCH SY13 269 L5 1
WSFD CW7 177 H4
Poplar Dr ALS/KID ST7 241 L2
ALS/KID ST7 243 G4
MWCH CW10 179 K5
Poplar Gv CHNE CH2 123 G1
CW/HAS CW1 19 K2
IRL M44 31 K6
MCFLDN SK10 113 G4
OFTN SK2 47 J8
SALE M33 43 H1
Poplar La MKTDR TF9 275 M6
Poplar Rd BNG/LEV M19 45 K1
CHSW/BR CH4 168 F7
MCFLDS SK11 14 F8
NWCHW CW8 128 D4
Poplars Av WARRN/WOL WA2 28 A8
The Poplars LEIGH WN7 24 C4
LYMM WA13 39 K8 3
Poplar St GOL/RIS/CU WA3 23 H3 3
HTNM SK4 45 L2
LEIGH WN7 24 F1 3
Poplar Wy MPL/ROM SK6 68 A5
Poppy Cl NTHM/RTH M23 43 L3 2
Porlock Cl STKP SK1 47 J4
WARRW/BUR WA5 35 L8
Porlock Rd NTHM/RTH M23 44 B6
Porter Av NEWLW WA12 22 C7
Porter Cl RAIN/WH L35 33 K3
Porter Dr NWCHE CW9 130 C6
Porters Cft CHSE CH3 146 F7 3
Porter St RUNC WA7 9 M2
Porter Wy NWCHE CW9 130 C5
Portford Cl MCFLDN SK10 137 M3
Porthcawl Cl WDN WA8 52 C1
Porthleven Dr NTHM/RTH M23 43 L6
Porthleven Rd RUNC WA7 74 B7
Portland Cl BRAM/HZG SK7 66 B3
Portland Dr ALS/KID ST7 225 L6
BIDD ST8 227 K2
Portland Gv CW/HAS CW1 222 C7
Portland Pl FROD/HEL WA6 98 C8 3
Portland Rd ALT WA14 61 J1
NM/HAY SK22 69 K3 1
Portland St RUNC WA7 8 E1
Portloe Av HLWD L26 50 F3
Portloe Rd CHD/CHDH SK8 64 B5
Portmarnock Cl
MCFLDN SK10 138 B1 3
Portola Cl WARRS WA4 57 J2
Portrea Cl EDGY/DAV SK3 46 E7
Portree Dr HOLMCH CW4 181 H2
Portrush Cl MCFLDN SK10 112 C8 3
Portrush Rd WYTH/NTH M22 63 L2
Portsmouth Pl RUNC WA7 74 E6 2
Port St STKP SK1 2 E4
Portway WYTH/NTH M22 63 H2
Portwood Pl RDSH SK5 3 G3
Posnett St EDGY/DAV SK3 2 A7
Post Office La CW/SHV CW2 254 F3
FROD/HEL WA6 126 D7
MALPAS SY14 246 D5
RUNC WA7 8 A8
Post Office Pl NWCHE CW9 13 J1
Post Office St ALT WA14 42 D7
Potter Cl NANT CW5 237 K8
Potters End BIDD ST8 227 H3
Potters La WDN WA8 51 M8
Pottery La RAIN/WH L35 32 C1
Poulton Cl HLWD L26 50 D6
Poulton Crs WARR WA1 38 D4
Poulton Dr WDN WA8 6 A5 1
Pound Rd GTS/LS CH66 94 C5
Poundswick La WYTH/NTH M22 63 K1
Povey Rd WARRN/WOL WA2 37 K3 3
Powderham Cl
BURS/TUN ST6 243 L4 3
Powell Av GOL/RIS/CU WA3 29 L8
Powell's Orch CHSW/BR CH4 16 F9
Powell St WARRS WA4 56 F1
Powey La CH/BCN CH1 120 B7
Powicke Dr MPL/ROM SK6 47 M3
Powicke Wk MPL/ROM SK6 47 M3
Pownall Av BRAM/HZG SK7 65 M6
Pownall Rd ALT WA14 61 K1
CHD/CHDH SK8 65 G3
WILM/AE SK9 83 M4
Pownall Sq MCFLDS SK11 14 E5
Pownall St BRAM/HZG SK7 66 D1 14
MCFLDN SK10 15 G3
Powy Dr ALS/KID ST7 243 G2
Powys Cl CQ CH5 142 D8
Powys St WARRW/BUR WA5 4 C7
Poynings Dr WYTH/NTH M22 63 J3 3
Poynton Cl WARRS WA4 57 H1
Poynton St MCFLDS SK11 14 E5 3
Pratchitts Rw NANT CW5 20 F7
Preece Cl WDN WA8 52 D1
Preece Ct CW/HAS CW1 18 D2
Preesall Av CHD/CHDH SK8 64 B4
Prees Rd WHITCH SY13 270 B6
Premier Gdns ALS/KID ST7 242 F2
Prenton Gn SPK/HALE L24 70 E1 1
Prenton Pl CHSW/BR CH4 17 J9
Prescot Rd HALE/TIMP WA15 61 M2
WDN WA8 6 B2 2
WDN WA8 32 F7
Prescot St CHNE CH2 17 L2
Prescott Av GOL/RIS/CU WA3 22 F2 3
Prescott Rd WILM/AE SK9 84 B3
Prescott St GOL/RIS/CU WA3 23 G3 3
WARRS WA4 56 E1
Prestbury Av HALE/TIMP WA15 42 E6
Prestbury Cl NWCHE CW9 129 M8 1
OFTN SK2 47 K8
Prestbury Dr MPL/ROM SK6 47 L1
WARRS WA4 57 K1
Prestbury La MCFLDN SK10 112 B5
Prestbury Rd MCFLDN SK10 14 E4
MCFLDN SK10 110 F6
WILM/AE SK9 84 E7
Preston Av IRL M44 31 M5
Preston on the Hl WARRS WA4 74 F6
Preston St STHEL WA9 34 A2 1
Preston St West MCFLDS SK11 14 D8
Prestwich Av GOL/RIS/CU WA3 29 L1
Prestwich Cl OFTN SK2 3 M9
Prestwick Cl MCFLDN SK10 112 C7 1
WSFD CW7 177 J2 2
Pretoria St CHSW/BR CH4 17 H9
Price Av SBCH CW11 204 A7
Price Dr SBCH CW11 204 A7

Price Gv *STHEL* WA9 .... 26 A2
Priest Av *CHD/CHDH* SK8.... 45 C8
Priestfield Gv *EP* CH65 .... 10 D7
Priest La *MCFLDN* SK10 ...... 111 H3
Priest St *STKP* SK1 .... 46 F5
Priestway La *NSTN* CH64...... 118 E3
Priesty Ct *CONG* CW12 .... 207 K2
Priesty Flds *CONG* CW12 ...... 207 K2
Primitive St *ALS/KID* ST7 .... 226 C5
Primrose Av *CW/HAS* CW1 .... 222 C7
MCFLDN SK11 .... 14 C9
MPL/ROM SK6 .... 48 E6
Primrose Bank *ALT* WA14 .... 61 J3 ⬚
Primrose Cha *HOLMCH* CW4.. 157 K4
Primrose Cl *CHSE* CH3 .... 170 A6
RUNC WA7 .... 74 A4
WARRN/WOL WA2 .... 37 J3
WDN WA8 .... 6 C3
Primrose Dell
AUD/MAD/W CW3 .... 267 K6
Primrose Hl *CW/SHV* CW2 .... 220 E7
NWCHW CW8 .... 127 M8
TPLY/KEL CW6 .... 149 L6
Primrose La *FROD/HEL* WA6 .. 124 A3
Primrose Vw *AIMK* WN4 .... 22 B2 ⬚
Prince Albert St *CW/HAS* CW1 .. 19 C4
Prince Edward St *NANT* CW5 .... 20 E4
Prince of Wales Av *FLINT* CH6 .. 116 A6
Prince Rd *POY/DIS* SK12 ...... 67 J7
Princes Av *CH/BCN* CH1...... 17 K4
MPL/ROM SK6 .... 48 A1
NWCHW CW9 .... 13 L2
Princes Dr *FLINT* CH6 .... 116 B8
MPL/ROM SK6 .... 48 D5
SALE M33 .... 43 K1
Princes Pk *NWCHW* CW8 .... 129 G2 ⬚
Princes Hl *WDN* WA8 .... 6 C2
Princes Rd *ALT* WA14 .... 42 D6
EP CH65 .... 94 F6
MPL/ROM SK6 .... 48 A1
SALE M33 .... 43 J2
Princess Av *AIMK* WN4 .... 22 C1
CHD/CHDH SK8 .... 65 C1
RNFD/HAY WA11 .... 22 A5
WARR WA1 .... 37 M6
WARRW/BUR WA5 .... 35 L6
Princess Cl *CW/SHV* CW2 .... 237 M4
Princess Crs *MWCH* CW10 .... 179 K6
WARR WA1 .... 37 M6 ⬚
Princess Dr *CW/SHV* CW2 .... 237 L4
MCFLDN SK10 .... 112 E6
NANT CW5 .... 21 H5
SBCH CW11 .... 204 A4
Princess Gv *CW/SHV* CW2 .... 237 M4
Princess Pkwy *WYTH/NTH* M22 .. 44 C4
Princess Rd *AIMK* WN4 .... 22 B1
DID/WITH M20 .... 44 D1
KNUT WA16 .... 156 E1
LYMM WA13 .... 58 C1
WILM/AE SK9 .... 83 M7
Princess St *ALS/KID* ST7 .... 242 D7
ALT WA14 .... 42 C4
BIDD ST8 .... 227 K5
CH/BCN CH1 .... 16 F5
CONG CW12 .... 207 K2
CW/HAS CW1 .... 221 J6
KNUT WA16 .... 107 G2
MCFLDN SK10 .... 112 F5
NWCHW CW9 .... 130 E2
RUNC WA7 .... 9 C1
WARRW/BUR WA5 .... 36 D8 ⬚
WSFD WA7 .... 178 A3
Princes St *FLINT* CH6 .... 116 B6 ⬚
NEWLW WA12 .... 27 H1 ⬚
STKP SK1 .... 2 F4
WDN WA8 .... 7 H4
Princes Wy *MCFLDS* SK11 .... 137 L5
Princeway *FROD/HEL* WA6 .... 99 H4
Prince William Av *CQ* CH5 .... 167 H1
Prince William Ct *CW/HAS* CW1 .. 19 B8
Prince William Gdns *CQ* CH5 .. 166 E2 ⬚
Prinknash Rd *WYTH/NTH* M22 .. 63 K3
Prior Cl *CQ* CH5 .... 142 A8 ⬚
WLTN L25 .... 50 B2
Priorsfield Rd *WLTN* L25 ...... 50 B2
Priory Av *NWCHE* CW9 .... 129 M8
Priory Cl *CH/BCN* CH1 .... 145 J8 ⬚
CONG CW12 .... 208 B5
CW/HAS CW1 .... 221 G4
RAIN/WH L35 .... 32 C3
RUNC WA7 .... 74 A3
WSFD WA7 .... 177 J1 ⬚
Priory Dr *MCFLDN* SK10 ...... 137 L2
Priory La *MCFLDN* SK10 ...... 137 L2
Priory Pl *CH/BCN* CH1 .... 17 H5 ⬚
Priory Rd *ALT* WA14 .... 61 H4
CHD/CHDH SK8 .... 46 A7
RUNC WA7 .... 74 C2 ⬚
WILM/AE SK9 .... 83 L4
Priory St *ALT* WA14 .... 61 J4
NWCHE CW9 .... 13 J5
WARRS WA4 .... 56 B1
The Priory *NSTN* CH64 .... 91 K3
WARRN/WOL WA2 .... 28 A5
Priory Wy *NWCHW* CW8 ...... 129 H8
WLTN L25 .... 50 B2
Pritchard Dr *NWCHE* CW9 .... 153 L2
Probert Cl *CW/SHV* CW2 ...... 18 A4
Proctors Cl *WDN* WA8 .... 7 M1
Proctors La *SBCH* CW11 ...... 203 K7
Proffitts La *FROD/HEL* WA6 .. 98 E8
Promised Land La *CHSE* CH3 .. 170 C4
Prospect Av *IRL* M44 .... 31 L6
Prospect Cl *CQ* CH5 .... 166 A2 ⬚
Prospect Dr *HALE/TIMP* WA15 .. 62 D5
Prospect La *GOL/RIS/CU* WA3 .. 39 J1
Prospect Rd *IRL* M44 .... 31 L6
Prospect V *CHD/CHDH* SK8 .. 64 B3
Prosperity Wy *NWCHW* CW10 .. 179 K3
Prosser Rd *CHNE* CH2 .... 145 J3
Provan Wy *CH/BCN* CH1 ...... 144 D7
Provident St *STHEL* WA9 ...... 26 A1
Provident Wy *HALE/TIMP* WA15 .. 43 G5
Prunus Rd *CW/HAS* CW1 ...... 221 L6
The Pryors *CHSE* CH3............ 172 C1
Ptarmigan Pl *WSFD* WA7 ...... 177 K7 ⬚

Public Hall St *RUNC* WA7 ...... 9 H1
Pudding La *TPLY/KEL* CW6 .... 197 G5
Puddington La *NSTN* CH64 .... 118 D4
Puddle Bank La *CONG* CW12.. 207 M7
Puffin Av *POY/DIS* SK12........ 86 A1
Pulford Ap *CHSW/BR* CH4 .... 211 J1
Pulford Cl *NWCHE* CW9 .... 129 L8
WARR WA1 .... 73 K6
Pulford Ct *CHSW/BR* CH4 .... 210 D2
Pulford Gv *SALE* M33 .... 191 G6
Pulford Rd *CH/BCN* CH1 ...... 144 E7
EP CH65 .... 94 F8
SALE M33 .... 43 J2
Pullman Dr *NWCHE* CW9 ...... 130 C4
Pump La *CHSE* CH3 .... 212 A7
CHSE CH3 .... 213 J6
RUNC WA7 .... 73 M4
Pump Tree Ms *MCFLDS* SK11 .. 137 L5 ⬚
Purbeck Cl *WYTH/NTH* M22 .. 63 J3 ⬚
Purdy Cl *WARRW/BUR* WA5 .. 36 D3
Purley Av *NTHM/RTH* M23 .... 44 B3
Purley Dr *IRL* M44 .... 31 J7
Purser La *MALPAS* SY14 ...... 244 E8
Putney Ct *RUNC* WA7 .... 73 L5 ⬚
Pye Cl *RNFD/HAY* WA11 ...... 22 B4
Pyecroft Cl *WARRW/BUR* WA5 .. 35 K6
Pyecroft Rd *WARRW/BUR* WA5 .. 35 K6
Pyecroft St *CHSW/BR* CH4 .... 17 G9
Pymgate Dr *CHD/CHDH* SK8 .. 64 A2
Pymgate La *CHD/CHDH* SK8 .. 64 A2
Pym's La *CW/HAS* CW1 .... 220 D6
Pyrus Av *CW/HAS* CW1 .... 221 L6
Pyrus Gv *FROD/HEL* WA6 .... 98 C8 ⬚
Pytcheley Hollow
FROD/HEL WA6 .... 126 F6

Q

Quadrant Cl *RUNC* WA7 .... 74 D6 ⬚
The Quadrant *MPL/ROM* SK6 .. 48 A2
STKP SK1 .... 3 L5
Quail Cl *WARRN/WOL* WA2.... 37 K1
Quakers Coppice *CW/HAS* CW1 .. 239 G2
Quakers Wy *WRXS/E* LL13.... 228 E3
Quantock Cl *GTS/LS* CH66 .... 94 A6 ⬚
HTNM SK4 .... 2 E3
WSFD WA7 .... 177 G5 ⬚
Quarry Av *CHSE* CH3 .... 228 F3
Quarry Bank *TPLY/KEL* CW6 .. 174 D2
Quarry Bank Rd *WILM/AE* SK9 .. 83 M1
Quarry Cl *CHSW/BR* CH4 ...... 16 F9
RUNC WA7 .... 73 K3
Quarry Hl *CHSE* CH3 .... 228 F3
Quarry La *CHSE* CH3 .... 170 D5
NSTN CH64 .... 92 B3
TPLY/KEL CW6 .... 149 K8
WARRS WA4 .... 56 C6
Quarry Ri *MPL/ROM* SK6 ...... 48 B1
Quarry Rd *MPL/ROM* SK6 ...... 48 B2
NM/HAY SK22 .... 69 M1
NSTN CH64 .... 92 C3
Quarry St South *WLTN* L25 .... 50 A2
Quay Fold *WARRW/BUR* WA5 .. 4 B8
Quay Pl *RUNC* WA7 .... 74 E5
Quayside *CONG* CW12 .... 207 L3
Quay Side *FROD/HEL* WA6.... 99 K2
Quayside *NSTN* CH64 .... 91 K7
Quayside Ms *LYMM* WA13 .... 58 F1
Quayside Wy *MCFLDS* SK11.. 15 K7
The Quay *FROD/HEL* WA6 .... 99 K2
Queasybirch La *WARRS* WA4 .. 76 A4
Queenhill Rd *WYTH/NTH* M22 .. 44 E3 ⬚
Queen's Av *CH/BCN* CH1 ...... 17 K4
CH/BCN CH1 .... 167 G1 ⬚
EP CH65 .... 121 G1
FLINT CH6 .... 116 B7
GOL/RIS/CU WA3 .... 25 J5
KNUT WA16 .... 15 J2
MPL/ROM SK6 .... 48 A1
WARR WA1 .... 37 L5
WDN WA8 .... 52 B4
Queensbury Wy *WDN* WA8 .... 52 D1
Queens Cl *HTNM* SK4 .... 46 A2
MCFLDN SK10 .... 112 E6
RUNC WA7 .... 8 F5
Queens Crs *CHNE* CH2 .... 145 L5
CW/HAS CW1 .... 220 E2
WARR WA1 .... 38 A4 ⬚
Queen's Dr *BIDD* ST8 .... 227 K6
CHD/CHDH SK8 .... 65 G1
CHSW/BR CH4 .... 17 K7
FROD/HEL WA6 .... 124 B1
GOL/RIS/CU WA3 .... 23 J4
HTNM SK4 .... 46 A2
MWCH CW10 .... 179 K6
NANT CW5 .... 20 C6
NEWLW WA12 .... 22 C7
SBCH CW11 .... 204 A4
WARRS WA4 .... 56 F2
Queens Gdns *EP* CH65 .... 10 C7
Queensgate *BRAM/HZG* SK7 .. 65 L7
CHS CH3 .... 12 E3
Queen's Park Dr *CW/SHV* CW2 .. 237 M1
Queen's Park Gdns
CW/SHV CW2 .... 220 E8
Queen's Park Rd *CHSW/BR* CH4 .. 17 H8
Queen's Park Vw *CHSW/BR* CH4 .. 17 H8
Queens Pl *CH/BCN* CH1 ...... 17 H4
Queen's Rd *BRAM/HZG* SK7 .. 66 C2
CH/BCN CH1 .... 17 K3
CHD/CHDH SK8 .... 45 M8
CHD/CHDH SK8 .... 64 F1
CHSE CH3 .... 170 B2
CQ CH5 .... 142 F5
GTS/LS CH66 .... 94 C5
HALE/TIMP WA15 .... 61 L1
MPL/ROM SK6 .... 48 A1
RNFD/HAY WA11 .... 22 A5
RUNC WA7 .... 8 F4
WHITCH SY13 .... 270 B5
Queen St *ALS/KID* ST7 .... 243 G2
CH/BCN CH1 .... 17 H4
CHD/CHDH SK8 .... 45 L8

WDN WA8 .... 53 L1
CQ CH5 .... 142 D7
CW/HAS CW1 .... 221 J6
CW/SHV CW2 .... 238 C8
EP CH65 .... 10 F4
FLINT CH6 .... 116 B6 ⬚
GOL/RIS/CU WA3 .... 23 H4 ⬚
KNUT WA16 .... 106 F2
MCFLDN SK10 .... 15 H4
MCFLDN SK10 .... 113 H4
MPL/ROM SK6 .... 48 F6 ⬚
MWCH CW10 .... 179 J3 ⬚
NEWLW WA12 .... 27 H1
NWCHE CW9 .... 13 H4
RUNC WA7 .... 9 G1
TPLY/KEL CW6 .... 216 E4
Queensway *ALS/KID* ST7 .... 224 B7
BNG/LEV M19 .... 45 K2
CHD/CHDH SK8 .... 64 C4
CHNE CH2 .... 145 M7
CQ CH5 .... 142 A6
CW/HAS CW1 .... 19 G4
FROD/HEL WA6 .... 99 H5
IRL M44 .... 31 M2
KNUT WA16 .... 106 E1
POY/DIS SK12 .... 86 D1
RUNC WA7 .... 8 F1
WDN WA8 .... 6 D7
WDN WA8 .... 53 G7 ⬚
WHITCH SY13 .... 270 A6
WSFD WA7 .... 177 K4
Queen Victoria St *MCFLDS* SK11 .. 15 G5
The Quillet *NSTN* CH64 .... 91 M5
Quinn St *WDN* WA8 .... 7 J6
Quinta Rd *CONG* CW12........ 207 G3
Quintbridge Cl *HLWD* L26 .... 50 E5

R

Raby Cl *WDN* WA8 .... 53 K2
Raby Gdns *NSTN* CH64 .... 91 L4
Raby Park Cl *NSTN* CH64 .... 91 L4
Raby Park Rd *NSTN* CH64 .... 91 L4
Racecourse La *TPLY/KEL* CW6 .. 175 G2
Racecourse Pk *WILM/AE* SK9 .. 83 M6 ⬚
Racefield Cl *LYMM* WA13 .... 58 F1 ⬚
Racefield Rd *ALT* WA14 .... 42 C8
KNUT WA16 .... 106 F3
The Race *WILM/AE* SK9 .... 84 D2
Rackhouse Rd *NTHM/RTH* M23 .. 44 B3
Radbroke Cl *SBCH* CW11 .... 204 D4 ⬚
Radcliffe Av *GOL/RIS/CU* WA3 .. 29 L1
Radcliffe Rd *MCFLDN* SK10 .. 162 D5
SBCH CW11 .... 222 F1
Raddel La *WARRS* WA4 .... 76 C7
Radford Cl *CQ* CH5 .... 142 A5 ⬚
OFTN SK2 .... 47 K5
WDN WA8 .... 52 C5
Radlet Dr *HALE/TIMP* WA15 .. 43 G4
Radlett Cl *WARRW/BUR* WA5 .. 54 C1
Radley Cl *SALE* M33 .... 42 D1 ⬚
Radley La *WARRN/WOL* WA2 .. 37 K1
Radnor Cl *CONG* CW12 .... 207 H1
CQ CH5 .... 142 D8 ⬚
HLWD L26 .... 50 D6
SBCH CW11 .... 203 L5
Radnor Dr *CHSW/BR* CH4 .... 169 G7
WDN WA8 .... 52 C5
Radnormere Dr *CHD/CHDH* SK8.. 45 M8
Radnor St *WARRW/BUR* WA5 .. 4 B8
Radway Gn *GTS/LS* CH66...... 94 E7
Radway Green Rd
CW/SHV CW2 .... 240 C7
Raeburn Av *NSTN* CH64........ 91 M5
Raeburn Dr *MPL/ROM* SK6 .... 49 H4 ⬚
Rae St *EDGY/DAV* SK3 .... 2 B7
Raglan Ct *GOL/RIS/CU* WA3.. 29 M6
Raglan Dr *ALT* WA14 .... 42 E4 ⬚
Raglan Rd *MCFLDN* SK10 .... 15 M1
SALE M33 .... 42 F1
Ragley Cl *POY/DIS* SK12 ...... 66 F8 ⬚
Railton Av *CW/HAS* CW1 ...... 221 G5
RAIN/WH L35 .... 33 K2
Railton Cl *RAIN/WH* L35 .... 33 K3 ⬚
Railway Bri Rd *EDGY/DAV* SK3 .. 2 F7
GOL/RIS/CU WA3 .... 23 H3 ⬚
Railway St *ALT* WA14 .... 42 D8
CW/SHV CW2 .... 19 H7
HTNM SK4 .... 2 D5
NEWLW WA12 .... 27 H1
Rainbow Cl *MWCH* CW10 .... 179 H5
WDN WA8 .... 52 C1
Rainbow Dr *HLWD* L26 .... 50 E4
Rainbow St *CW/HAS* CW1 .... 19 H4
Rainford Av *HALE/TIMP* WA15 .. 43 G7
Rainford Cl *ALS/KID* ST7 .... 243 M3
Rainow Rd *EDGY/DAV* SK3 .... 46 C6 ⬚
MCFLDN SK10 .... 139 C2
Rainow Vw *MCFLDN* SK10 .... 113 J3 ⬚
Rake La *CHNE* CH2 .... 121 K7
CHSE CH3 .... 171 G4
CHSW/BR CH4 .... 192 A4
CQ CH5 .... 166 F5
FROD/HEL WA6 .... 98 B8
FROD/HEL WA6 .... 123 K5
The Rake *NSTN* CH64 .... 118 D3
Rake Wy *CH/BCN* CH1 .... 144 A4
Raleigh Av *RAIN/WH* L35 .... 18 D2 ⬚
Raleigh Cl *WARRW/BUR* WA5 .. 36 D3
Raleigh Rd *NSTN* CH64 .... 91 L3 ⬚
Ramillies Av *CHD/CHDH* SK8 .. 65 H3
Ramp Rd East *MANAIR* M90 .. 63 J5
Ramp Rd South *MANAIR* M90 .. 63 H5
Ramp Rd West *MANAIR* M90.. 63 H5
Ramps Ga *NWCHW* CW8 .... 152 A2 ⬚
Ramsay Cl *GOL/RIS/CU* WA3 .. 38 E1 ⬚
Ramsbottom St *CW/HAS* CW1 .. 18 D2 ⬚
Ramsbrook La *SPK/HALE* L24 .. 50 C8 ⬚
Ramsbrook Rd *SPK/HALE* L24 .. 50 C8
Ramsdale Rd *BRAM/HZG* SK7 .. 65 L4
Ramsden Ct *CHSW/BR* CH4 .. 168 F8 ⬚
Ramsey Cl *AIMK* WN4 .... 22 B2 ⬚
RAIN/WH L35 .... 32 E1 ⬚

Ramsey Rd *EP* CH65 .... 121 J3
Ramsfield Rd *SPK/HALE* L24 .. 51 G8
Ramsgill Cl *NTHM/RTH* M23 .. 43 L3
Ramsons Cl *HLWD* L26 .... 50 E3 ⬚
Randle Meadow *GTS/LS* CH66 .. 120 F2
Randolph Pl *EDGY/DAV* SK3 .. 2 F9
Rangemoor Cl
GOL/RIS/CU WA3 .... 30 A6 ⬚
Rangemore Av *WYTH/NTH* M22 .. 44 D4
Range Rd *EDGY/DAV* SK3...... 46 E6
Rannoch Cl *FROD/HEL* WA6.. 99 J5
Ranulph Ct *FROD/HEL* WA6.. 99 J5
Ranworth Cl *GOL/RIS/CU* WA3 .. 23 L4
Ranworth Dr *GOL/RIS/CU* WA3 .. 23 L5
Ranworth Rd
WARRW/BUR WA5 .... 35 L6 ⬚
Rappax Rd *HALE/TIMP* WA15 .. 62 A4
Ratcliffe St *STKP* SK1 .... 3 G8 ⬚
Rathbone Pk *TPLY/KEL* CW6 .. 197 K2 ⬚
Rathlin Cl *WDN* WA8 .... 53 L1
Rathmell Cl *GOL/RIS/CU* WA3 .. 29 L1 ⬚
Rathmel Rd *NTHM/RTH* M23 .. 43 M2 ⬚
Rathvale Dr *WYTH/NTH* M22 .. 63 J4 ⬚
Raven Cl *SBCH* CW11 .... 204 A4
Ravenfield Cl *HLWD* L26 ...... 50 E4 ⬚
Ravenfield Dr *WDN* WA8 ...... 38 A2 ⬚
Ravenho La *MCFLDN* SK10 .. 139 K1
Ravenhurst Ct *GOL/RIS/CU* WA3 .. 29 M7
Ravenna Av *NTHM/RTH* M23 .. 43 K5 ⬚
Ravenoak Park Rd
CHD/CHDH SK8 .... 65 H4
Ravenoak Rd *CHD/CHDH* SK8 .. 65 H3 ⬚
CHD/CHDH SK8 .... 65 J3 ⬚
EDGY/DAV SK3 .... 47 G8
Raven Rd *HALE/TIMP* WA15 .. 43 H3
Ravenscar Crs *WYTH/NTH* M22 .. 63 K4
Ravenscliffe Rd *ALS/KID* ST7 .. 243 C4
Ravenscroft *HOLMCH* CW4.... 181 C1
Ravenscroft Cl *SBCH* CW11 .. 204 C5
Ravenscroft Rd *CW/SHV* CW2 .. 237 L1
Ravensdale Cl
WARRN/WOL WA2 .... 37 K1 ⬚
Ravensfield *NWCHW* CW8 .... 127 K8 ⬚
Ravensholme Cl *CHSE* CH3 .. 214 A2 ⬚
Ravensholme La *CHSE* CH3 .. 214 A2 ⬚
Ravens La *NANT* CW5 .... 250 E1
Ravenswood *NWCHW* CW8 .. 129 H8
Ravenswood Av *HTNM* SK4 .. 46 A3 ⬚
Ravenswood Dr
CHD/CHDH SK8 .... 65 H4 ⬚
Ravenswood Rd *WILM/AE* SK9 .. 83 L8
Ravenwood Dr
HALE/TIMP WA15 .... 62 D5
Rawcliffe Cl *WDN* WA8 .... 33 M8 ⬚
Rawdon Cl *RUNC* WA7 .... 74 A5
Rawlings Cl *GOL/RIS/CU* WA3 .. 38 F1
Rawlinson Crs *HLWD* L26 .... 51 H4 ⬚
Rawpool Gdns *NTHM/RTH* M23 .. 44 A5
Rawson Rd *CH/BCN* CH1 ...... 168 C1
Ray Av *NANT* CW5 .... 21 G2
Raydale Cl *GOL/RIS/CU* WA3 .. 23 L3 ⬚
Rayleigh Av *NWCHE* CW9 .... 154 A4
Rayleigh Wy *MCFLDN* SK10 .. 137 L3 ⬚
Raymond Av *WARRS* WA4 .... 56 D2
Raymond Rd *NTHM/RTH* M23 .. 44 B2
Raymond St *CH/BCN* CH1 .... 16 E4
Raymond Wy *NSTN* CH64 .... 92 A5
Rayner St *STKP* SK1 .... 3 L8
Raynham Av *DID/WITH* M20 .. 45 H1
Readesdale Av *CW/SHV* CW2 .. 237 M2
Reade's La *CONG* CW12 ...... 208 E4
CONG CW12 .... 208 B4
Reading Room La *CHSE* CH3 .. 231 K4
Reaper Cl *WARRW/BUR* WA5.. 36 D6
Reay St *WDN* WA8 .... 7 L1
Rectors La *CQ* CH5 .... 142 F8
Rectory Av *GOL/RIS/CU* WA3 .. 23 K5
Rectory Cl *CHSE* CH3 .... 228 E3
CW/SHV CW2 .... 237 L4
FLINT CH6 .... 116 A7
NANT CW5 .... 20 F6
WARRN/WOL WA2 .... 28 A6
Rectory Dr *HLWD* L26 .... 50 F3
Rectory Flds *STKP* SK1 .... 3 J5
Rectory Gn *STKP* SK1 .... 3 J5
Rectory La *CH/BCN* CH1 ...... 119 M3
CQ CH5 .... 166 D4
LYMM WA13 .... 58 E2
MKTDR TF9 .... 274 A8
WARRN/WOL WA2 .... 28 A6
Rectory Rd *ALS/KID* ST7 .... 242 D6
Redacre *POY/DIS* SK12.......... 66 F6
Red Bank Av *NEWLW* WA12.. 27 M3
Redbourne Av *HLWD* L26 .... 50 F6
Redbourne Dr *WDN* WA8 ...... 33 H8
Redbrook Rd *HALE/TIMP* WA15 .. 43 K6
PART M31 .... 40 E2
Redbrook Wy *MCFLDN* SK10 .. 86 C7
Red Brow La *WARRS* WA4 .... 74 F4
Redburn Rd *NTHM/RTH* M23 .. 44 B5
Redcar Cl *BRAM/HZG* SK7 .... 67 G3
Red Cow Yd *KNUT* WA16 .... 107 G2 ⬚
Reddish Av *CHF/WBR* SK23 .. 89 J6
Reddish Crs *LYMM* WA13 .... 39 M8
Reddish La *CHF/WBR* SK23 .. 89 K6
LYMM WA13 .... 39 M8
Reddish Rd *CHF/WBR* SK23 .. 89 K6
Reddy La *ALT* WA14 .... 60 B4
Redesdale Cl *SBCH* CW11 .... 203 M5 ⬚
WARRN/WOL WA2 .... 37 L2 ⬚
Redesmere Cl *HALE/TIMP* WA15 .. 43 K6
NWCHE CW9 .... 13 K8
Redesmere Dr *CHD/CHDH* SK8 .. 45 M8
WILM/AE SK9 .... 109 M3
Redesmere Rd *MCFLDS* SK11 .. 160 B1
WILM/AE SK9 .... 64 D7
Redfern Av *CONG* CW12 ...... 184 F8
SALE M33 .... 43 J3
Redford Dr *BRAM/HZG* SK7 .. 66 A2
Redgate La *NWCHW* CW8 .... 12 C5
Redhill Dr *MPL/ROM* SK6 .... 47 K1
Redhill Rd *CHSW/BR* CH4 .... 168 F5 ⬚
TPLY/KEL CW6 .... 149 J7
Redhills Ms *EP* CH65 .... 10 D5
Red House La *ALT* WA14 ...... 41 H4
Redhouse La *POY/DIS* SK12 .. 68 E6

Redland Cl *CHSW/BR* CH4 .... 169 G5
CHS CH3 .... 195 K6
FROD/HEL WA6 .... 99 J4
POY/DIS SK12 .... 68 B7
SBCH CW11 .... 203 J6
WARRS WA4 .... 56 C5
WARRS WA4 .... 102 C3
Red Lion Cl *ALS/KID* ST7 .... 242 D5
Red Lion La *GTS/LS* CH66.... 94 C5
NANT CW5 .... 20 C5
Redmain Gv *GOL/RIS/CU* WA3 .. 23 L4
Redmayne Cl *NEWLW* WA12 .. 22 B8 ⬚
Redmoor La *NM/HAY* SK22 .. 69 H6
Red Pike *GTS/LS* CH66 .... 94 D5
Redpoll Gv *HLWD* L26 .... 50 F3
Redpoll La *GOL/RIS/CU* WA3 .. 29 L8 ⬚
Redruth Av *MCFLDN* SK10 .... 137 L3 ⬚
Redruth Cl *RUNC* WA7 .... 74 C6
Redshank Av *WSFD* WA7 ...... 177 J7
Redshank Cl *NEWLW* WA12 .. 22 C8 ⬚
Redshank La *GOL/RIS/CU* WA3 .. 29 M8
Redshaw Cl *MWCH* CW10 .... 179 J6 ⬚
Redstart Cl *GOL/RIS/CU* WA3 .. 23 L4 ⬚
Redstone Dr *WSFD* WA7 ...... 177 G3 ⬚
Red Stone Hl *FROD/HEL* WA6 .. 98 B8
Redstone Rd *BNG/LEV* M19 .. 45 K1
Redvales Ct *GOL/RIS/CU* WA3 .. 29 J8 ⬚
Redvers Av *GTS/LS* CH66 .... 94 A2
Redway La *MCFLDN* SK10 .... 113 H5
Redwing Dr *BIDD* ST8 .... 227 L4
Redwing Wy *HLWD* L26 .... 50 D2
Redwood Cl *CHSW/BR* CH4 .. 168 E6
NWCHW CW8 .... 103 H8
WARR WA1 .... 38 E6
Redwood Dr *CHNE* CH2 .... 97 J8
GTS/LS CH66 .... 120 F3
MPL/ROM SK6 .... 47 M1 ⬚
Reece Cl *CHNE* CH2 .... 146 E4
Reedgate La *NWCHW* CW9 .. 77 L3
Reed La *NWCHE* CW9 .... 77 H7
Reedshaw Bank *OFTN* SK2 .. 47 K7 ⬚
Reedsmere Cl *WARRS* WA4 .. 56 E2 ⬚
Reedsmere Wk *NWCHE* CW9 .. 103 K4
Rees Crs *HOLMCH* CW4 ...... 157 J8
Reeve Cl *OFTN* SK2 .... 47 M7
Reeves Rd *CHSE* CH3 .... 170 B4
Reeve St *GOL/RIS/CU* WA3 .. 24 B4
Reevey Av *BRAM/HZG* SK7 .. 66 C2
Regal Cl *GTS/LS* CH66 .... 120 E1
NWCHE CW9 .... 129 L8
Regency Cl *ALS/KID* ST7 .... 242 D7
Regency Ct *CHNE* CH2 .... 146 E4
Regency Pk *WILM/AE* SK9 .... 83 M7 ⬚
Regency Wy *NWCHE* CW9 .... 129 L8
Regent Av *MCFLDS* SK11 .... 14 D8
WARR WA1 .... 38 A4
Regent Cl *BRAM/HZG* SK7 .... 65 K8
CHD/CHDH SK8 .... 46 C8
CW/SHV CW2 .... 253 H1
WILM/AE SK9 .... 83 M7
Regent Rd *ALT* WA14 .... 42 D8 ⬚
OFTN SK2 .... 47 G6
WDN WA8 .... 7 J2
Regents Cl *CHSE* CH3 .... 170 B2
Regents Ga *NANT* CW5 .... 21 J7
Regent St *NEWLW* WA12 .... 27 G1
NWCHE CW9 .... 153 M4
RUNC WA7 .... 9 G5
WARR WA1 .... 4 F7
Reginald Mitchell Wy
BURS/TUN ST6 .... 243 J8
Reid Av *WARRW/BUR* WA5 .. 36 F4 ⬚
Reid Ct *GTS/LS* CH66 .... 94 C5
Reid St *CW/HAS* CW1 .... 221 L6
Reigate Cl *WLTN* L25 .... 50 C2
Remer St *CW/HAS* CW1 ...... 221 K5
Rena Cl *HTNM* SK4 .... 2 A3
Renaissance Ct
CW/HAS CW1 .... 222 A8 ⬚
Renaissance Wy *CW/HAS* CW1 .. 239 G1
Rendel Cl *NEWLW* WA12 ...... 27 K2
Rendlesham Cl *GOL/RIS/CU* WA3 .. 30 B6
Renfrew Cl *MCFLDN* SK10 .... 137 M2
Renown Cl *WARR WN SPK/HALE* L24 .. 50 A6
Renown Wy *SPK/HALE* L24 .. 50 A6
Renshaw St *NWCHE* CW9 .... 130 D2
Rensherds Pl *KNUT* WA16 .... 59 J7
Renton Av *RUNC* WA7 .... 73 K2
Renton Cl *KNUT* WA16 .... 59 J8
Renton Rd *WYTH/NTH* M22 .. 44 D8
Repton Cl *CW/HAS* CW1 ...... 222 D7
Repton Dr *CW/HAS* CW1 ...... 222 D7
Repton Rd *EP* CH65 .... 95 K8
Reservoir Rd *CHF/WBR* SK23 .. 89 K5
EDGY/DAV SK3 .... 46 B5 ⬚
EDGY/DAV SK3 .... 46 D6 ⬚
The Retreat *CW/HAS* CW1 .... 221 J6 ⬚
MPL/ROM SK6 .... 48 B3
Revesby Cl *WDN* WA8 .... 52 D2 ⬚
Reveton Gn *BRAM/HZG* SK7 .. 66 A2 ⬚
Reynolds Av *GOL/RIS/CU* WA3 .. 29 L7
STHEL WA9 .... 26 B2
Reynolds Dr *MPL/ROM* SK6 .. 49 H4 ⬚
Reynold's La *SBCH* CW11 .... 204 E5
Reynolds Ms *WILM/AE* SK9 .. 84 E4 ⬚
Reynolds St *WARRN/WOL* WA2 .. 56 F1
Reynolds Wy *WLTN* L25 ...... 50 A2
Rhoden St *CW/HAS* CW1 ...... 222 A6
Rhodes Cl *CW/HAS* CW1 ...... 222 D8
Rhodes St *WARRN/WOL* WA2 .. 56 F1
Rhona Dr *WARRW/BUR* WA5 .. 35 L6 ⬚
Rhos Av *CHD/CHDH* SK8 ...... 64 F3
Rhos Dr *BRAM/HZG* SK7 ...... 66 D3
Rhoswen *FLINT* CH6 .... 116 B8 ⬚
Rhuddlan Ct *EP* CH65 .... 121 K2
Rhuddlan Rd *CH/BCN* CH1 .. 144 D8
Rhum Cl *EP* CH65 .... 121 J3
Rhyl St *WDN* WA8 .... 6 F7 ⬚
Ribble Av *RAIN/WH* L35 .... 33 J1
WSFD WA7 .... 178 B3
Ribble Cl *GOL/RIS/CU* WA3 .. 29 M2
WDN WA8 .... 53 M1
Ribble Dr *BIDD* ST8 .... 227 L4
Ribble Pl *WSFD* WA7 .... 178 B3 ⬚
Ribble St *CW/HAS* CW1 .... 55 L1
Ribblesdale *EP* CH65 .... 121 G1
Ribblesdale Av *CONG* CW12 .. 185 G7

Ribchester Gdns
GOL/RIS/CU WA3 .... 30 A1
Ribchester Wy RAIN/WH L35 .... 32 A5
Richard Moon St CW/HAS CW1 .. 18 C3
Richards Cft CHSE CH3 .... 170 A5 🗓
SBCH CW11 .... 203 K6 🗓
Richardson Cl CW/SHV CW2 .... 238 D7
SBCH CW11 .... 203 K6 🗓
Richardson St STKP SK1 .... 47 G5
WARRN/WOL WA3 .... 5 L3
Richard St CW/HAS CW1 .... 18 D3
NWCHE CW9 .... 130 C5
STKP SK1 .... 3 H3
Richbell Cl IRL M44 .... 31 L5
Richmond Av RUNC WA7 .... 73 L2
WARRS WA4 .... 37 M8
WILM/AE SK9 .... 64 D7
Richmond Cl GOL/RIS/CU WA3 .. 24 D8
LYMM WA13 .... 40 B8 🗓
SALE M33 .... 43 M1 🗓
SBCH CW11 .... 203 L5 🗓
Richmond Crs CHSE CH3 .... 170 C3
Richmond Dr LYMM WA13 .... 40 B8
NWCHE CW9 .... 130 A8
Richmond Gdns NEWLW WA12 .. 2 C7 🗓
Richmond Gn ALT WA14 .... 61 H2
Richmond Gv CHD/CHDH SK8 ... 64 F2
Richmond HI KNUT WA16 ...... 107 H3 🗓
MCFLDS SK11 .... 15 K8
Richmond Hill Rd
CHD/CHDH SK8 .... 45 J7
Richmond PI MCFLDS SK11 ...... 15 K9
Richmond Rd ALT WA14 .... 42 D7
CW/HAS CW1 .... 19 J3
HTNM SK4 .... 45 M2 🗓
MPL/ROM SK6 .... 48 C1
Richmond St WARRS WA4 .... 57 G1
WDN WA8 .... 7 L2
Richmond Wy HUY L36 .... 32 A5
Ricroft Rd MPL/ROM SK6 .... 49 H1
Ridding Av WYTH/NTH M22 .... 63 L1 🗓
Ridding Cl OFTN SK2 .... 47 K6
Ridding La RUNC WA7 .... 74 B7
Riddings La NANT CW5 .... 253 G4
NWCHW CW8 .... 129 G8
Riddings Rd HALE/TIMP WA15 .. 43 G4
HALE/TIMP WA15 .... 61 M3
Ridge Av HALE/TIMP WA15 ..... 62 C6
MPL/ROM SK6 .... 49 G8
Ridgeborne Cl
WARRW/BUR WA5 .... 36 D2
Ridge Cl MPL/ROM SK6 .... 48 E2
Ridge Crs MPL/ROM SK6 .... 67 M1
Ridge End Fold MPL/ROM SK6 .. 68 A3
Ridge HI MCFLDS SK11 .... 163 C5
TPLY/KEL CW6 .... 174 B7
Ridgemont Av HTNM SK4 ...... 46 B2
Ridge Pk BRAM/HZG SK7 .... 65 K6
Ridge Rd BURS/TUN ST6 ...... 243 K6
MPL/ROM SK6 .... 49 G8
The Ridge NWCHW CW8 .... 150 D5
Ridgetor Rd WLTN L25 .... 50 A1
Ridge Vw MCFLDS SK11 .... 138 C7
Ridgeway GOL/RIS/CU WA3 .... 23 L5
WILM/AE SK9 .... 84 F5
Ridgeway Cl GTS/LS CH66 .... 120 C2
Ridgeway Gdns LYMM WA13 ... 58 D1
Ridgeway Rd HALE/TIMP WA15 . 43 J7
The Ridgeway CHSE CH3 ...... 172 C1
CQ CH5 .... 166 B2
FROD/HEL WA6 .... 125 C2
POY/DIS SK12 .... 68 C5
RUNC WA7 .... 74 D6
WDN WA8 .... 33 J6
WLTN L25 .... 50 A1
Ridgewell Av
GOL/RIS/CU WA3 .... 23 K4 🗓
Ridgmont Rd BRAM/HZG SK7 .. 65 L8
Ridgway St CW/HAS CW1 ...... 19 G1
WARRN/WOL WA3 .... 5 L2
The Ridgway MPL/ROM SK6 ... 48 A3
Riding Fold HLWD L26 .... 50 D2 🗓
The Ridings CH/BCN CH1 ..... 144 A3
Ridley Cl CW/SHV CW2 .... 253 L1
WARRW/BUR WA5 .... 36 C8
Ridley Dr ALT WA14 .... 42 E3 🗓
WARRW/BUR WA5 .... 36 C8
Ridley Gv SALE M33 .... 43 M1
Ridley Rd MCFLDN SK10 ..... 112 E4 🗓
Rigby Av CW/HAS CW1 .... 221 C5
Rigby Rd ALS/KID ST7 .... 243 H1
Rigbys La AIMK WN4 .... 22 D1
Rigby St AIMK WN4 .... 22 A1
ALT WA14 .... 61 K1 🗓
GOL/RIS/CU WA3 .... 23 G4 🗓
Rigg St CW/HAS CW1 .... 18 D2
Riley Cl SALE M33 .... 42 B3
SBCH CW11 .... 203 K7
Riley Dr RUNC WA7 .... 9 H6
Riley Wood Cl MPL/ROM SK6 .. 47 M3 🗓
Rilshaw La WSFD CW7 .... 178 A4
Rilston Av GOL/RIS/CU WA3 ... 29 K1
Rimington Av
GOL/RIS/CU WA3 .... 23 J3 🗓
Rimington Cl GOL/RIS/CU WA3 . 29 L1 🗓
CW/SHV CW2 .... 238 A5
Rimsdale Cl CHD/CHDH SK8 ... 64 A1
CW/SHV CW2 .... 238 A5
Ringley Av GOL/RIS/CU WA3 ... 22 F3
Ringmer Dr WYTH/NTH M22 ... 63 J3 🗓
Ringmore Rd BRAM/HZG SK7 .. 66 A2
Ring-o-bells La POY/DIS SK12 .. 68 D6
Ring Rd CHNE CH2 .... 146 B8
CHSE CH3 .... 170 C3
Ringsfield Rd SPK/HALE L24 .. 71 G1 🗓
Ringstead Cl WILM/AE SK9 .... 84 D3 🗓
Ringstead Dr WILM/AE SK9 ... 84 D3
Ringstone Wy CHF/WBR SK23 . 89 K4
Ringway CHSE CH3 .... 171 H7
GTS/LS CH66 .... 94 E8
NSTN CH64 .... 91 M2
Ringway Gv SALE M33 .... 43 L2
Ringway Rd MANAIR M90 ...... 63 J5
RUNC WA7 .... 73 K2
WYTH/NTH M22 .... 63 L5
Ringway Rd West MANAIR M90 . 63 J4
Ringwood Av BRAM/HZG SK7 .. 66 B3
Ringwood Cl GOL/RIS/CU WA3 . 30 B7
Ripley Av CHD/CHDH SK8 ..... 65 H7
OFTN SK2 .... 47 H8

Ripley Cl BRAM/HZG SK7 ...... 66 E4
Ripley St WARRW/BUR WA5 ..... 4 B4
Ripon Av GOL/RIS/CU WA3 ..... 23 K4
Ripon Cl HALE/TIMP WA15 .... 62 C3
HUY L36 .... 32 A1
MCFLDN SK10 .... 138 C1
NEWLW WA12 .... 22 C7 🗓
Ripon Dr AIMK WN4 .... 22 D2
CW/SHV CW2 .... 238 A4
Rippleton Rd WYTH/NTH M22 .. 44 E8
Rippon Av GTS/LS CH66 ...... 94 C7
Riseley St MCFLDN SK10 ...... 14 E4
Rishworth Ct OFTN SK2 .... 47 K7
Rising Sun Rd MCFLDS SK11 .. 138 A8
Risley Gv GOL/RIS/CU WA3 .... 29 M6
Rissington Av NTHM/RTH M23 . 44 B6
Rivacre Brow GTS/LS CH66 ... 94 E5
Rivacre Rd EP CH65 .... 94 C2
GTS/LS CH66 .... 94 C4
Riva Rd BNG/LEV M19 .... 45 K2 🗓
Riverbank Cl MCFLDN SK10 .. 112 F4
NANT CW5 .... 20 E2
Riverdale Dr BURS/TUN ST6 .. 243 L4
Riverdane Rd CONG CW12 .... 184 F8
River La CHSE CH3 .... 228 E2
CHSW/BR CH4 .... 16 F9
PART M31 .... 31 M8
River Lea Ms
AUD/MAD/W CW3 .... 267 L6 🗓
Rivermead Av HALE/TIMP WA15 . 62 A8
Riverpark Cl NANT CW5 .... 20 F1
River Rd WARRS WA4 .... 56 C2
Riversdale FROD/HEL WA6 ..... 99 J3
WARR WA1 .... 56 C2
Riversdale Rd CHD/CHDH SK8 . 45 J7 🗓
RUNC WA7 .... 10 D8
Riverside FROD/HEL WA6 ...... 99 J3
Riverside NANT CW5 .... 20 D8
NWCHE CW9 .... 13 K9
Riverside Cl WARR WA1 .... 5 K8
Riverside St MCFLDS SK11 .... 139 J8
Riverside Crs HOLMCH CW4 .. 157 J8
Riverside Dr NWCHW CW8 ..... 12 E6
Riverside Gv CW/SHV CW2 ... 237 K1
Riverside Pk CQ CH5 .... 142 F6
Riverside Wk NSTN CH64 ..... 91 K7
Riversmead CHSE CH3 .... 170 A7
Riverston Dr NTHM/RTH M23 .. 43 K5
River St CONG CW12 .... 207 K1
MCFLDS SK11 .... 15 J8
STKP SK1 .... 3 L2
WILM/AE SK9 .... 84 B4
Riverton Rd DID/WITH M20 ... 45 H5
River Vw WSFD CW7 .... 177 J5
Riverview Rd NSTN CH64 ..... 91 M7
Rivington Av GOL/RIS/CU WA3 . 23 J3
Rivington Gv IRL M44 .... 31 K6
Rivington Rd EP CH65 .... 10 D8
HALE/TIMP WA15 .... 61 M2
RUNC WA7 .... 100 F1
Rixton Av WARRW/BUR WA5 ..... 4 B1
The Roaches MCFLDS SK11 ... 138 B7 🗓
Roachill Cl ALT WA14 .... 42 B7
Road Beta MWCH CW10 ...... 179 K4
Road Five WSFD CW7 .... 178 C2
Road Four WSFD CW7 .... 178 B2
Road One WSFD CW7 .... 154 B8
Roadside Ct GOL/RIS/CU WA3 . 24 A4
Road St TPLY/KEL CW6 .... 197 G1
Road Three WSFD CW7 .... 178 C3
Road Two WSFD CW7 .... 178 B2
Roan Cl MCFLDS SK11 .... 15 L6
Roan House Wy MCFLDS SK11 . 15 L6
Roan Ms MCFLDS SK11 .... 15 L6
Roan Wy WILM/AE SK9 ...... 110 B4
Roaring Gate La
HALE/TIMP WA15 .... 62 L1
Robert Moffat KNUT WA16 .... 59 J7
Robert Owen Gdns
WYTH/NTH M22 .... 44 D4 🗓
Robert Salt Ct ALT WA14 ..... 42 E6 🗓
Roberts Ct RUNC WA7 .... 73 L6
Robertscroft Cl
WYTH/NTH M22 .... 44 C8 🗓
Roberts Dr NWCHE CW9 ..... 130 C6
Roberts Rd CW/HAS CW1 ...... 19 M1
Robert St BURS/TUN ST6 .... 243 K8 🗓
NWCHW CW8 .... 12 F6
RUNC WA7 .... 9 L2
WARRW/BUR WA5 .... 4 C5
WDN WA8 .... 7 K3
Robeson Wy WYTH/NTH M22 .. 44 F6
Robin Cl MCFLDN SK10 ...... 113 L7 🗓
RUNC WA7 .... 74 D5
SBCH CW11 .... 204 A4
Robin Crs MCFLDS SK11 ..... 162 D2
Robin Cft MPL/ROM SK6 ...... 47 K1
Robin Hood Av MCFLDS SK11 . 138 C7
Robin Hood La FROD/HEL WA6 . 124 B2
Robin La MCFLDS SK11 ...... 135 G1
MCFLDS SK11 .... 162 D2
Robinsbay Rd WYTH/NTH M22 . 63 L5
Robins Cl BRAM/HZG SK7 ..... 65 L3
Robins Cft GTS/LS CH66 ..... 120 F2
Robin's La BRAM/HZG SK7 .... 65 K5
GOL/RIS/CU WA3 .... 29 K2
Robinsons Cft CHSE CH3 .... 170 B5
Robinson Rd EDGY/DAV SK3 ... 2 D9
Robinsway ALT WA14 .... 61 J3 🗓
Robins Wy MCFLDS SK10 .... 113 C5 🗓
Robinswood Rd WYTH/NTH M22 . 63 K3
Rob La NEWLW WA12 .... 22 E8
Robson St WARR WA1 .... 74 D7
Roby Gv WARRW/BUR WA5 .... 36 A6 🗓
Roche Gdns CHD/CHDH SK8 ... 65 H6
Rochester Cl GOL/RIS/CU WA3 . 23 C4 🗓
WARRW/BUR WA5 .... 36 C7 🗓
Rochester Crs CW/HAS CW1 ... 19 L1
Rochester Dr ALT WA14 ...... 42 E3 🗓
EP CH65 .... 121 K1 🗓
Rochester Gv BRAM/HZG SK7 . 66 E1
Rochester Rd WYTH/NTH M22 . 63 K4
Rock Bank CHF/WBR SK23 .... 89 L6
Rock Dr FROD/HEL WA6 .... 99 J3
Rock Farm Cl NSTN CH64 .... 92 A6
Rock Farm Dr NSTN CH64 .... 92 A6 🗓
Rock Farm Gv NSTN CH64 .... 92 A6 🗓

Rockfield Cl WDN WA8 .... 52 D2
Rockfield Dr FROD/HEL WA6 .. 124 C2
Rockford Ldg KNUT WA16 .... 107 J3
Rockhill Rd WLTN L25 .... 50 B3
Rockhouse La ALS/KID ST7 .. 242 C4
Rockingham Cl MCFLDS SK11 .. 30 B6
Rock La CHSE CH3 .... 215 J6
WDN WA8 .... 52 E1
Rocklee Gdns NSTN CH64 ..... 92 A6
Rocklynes MPL/ROM SK6 ..... 48 B2 🗓
Rocksavage Expy RUNC WA7 .. 73 J7
Rockside ALS/KID ST7 .... 226 C6
Rock St GOL/RIS/CU WA3 .... 23 C2
NM/HAY SK22 .... 69 J5 🗓
The Rock FROD/HEL WA6 .... 124 B2
Rockwood Pk GOL/RIS/CU WA3 . 18 B5
Rocky La CHSE CH3 .... 213 M5
Rodborough Rd
NTHM/RTH M23 .... 62 F1
Roddy La FROD/HEL WA6 .... 126 D2
Rodeheath Cl WILM/AE SK9 ... 84 D5 🗓
Rode House Cl ALS/KID ST7 .. 224 F5
Rodens Cl WRX/GR/LL LL12 .. 210 C5 🗓
Rodepool Cl WILM/AE SK9 .... 84 D2 🗓
Rodger Av AUD/MAD/W CW3 . 255 C6
Rodgers Cl FROD/HEL WA6 .... 99 H3
Rodgers St BURS/TUN ST6 ... 243 J4
Rodmill Dr CHD/CHDH SK8 ... 45 G8
Rodney St MCFLDS SK11 ..... 15 C7
WARRN/WOL WA2 .... 5 C4
Roebuck St CW/HAS CW1 ..... 18 E2
Roeburn Wy WARRW/BUR WA5 .. 54 D1
Roedean Cl WLTN L25 .... 50 B4 🗓
Roehampton Dr RUNC WA7 .... 73 L5
Roehurst La WSFD CW7 ..... 177 J2
Roemarsh Ct RUNC WA7 ..... 73 L6
Roe Pk CONG CW12 .... 226 E3
Roe St MCFLDS SK11 .... 14 F6
Roewood La MCFLDS SK10 .. 139 C3
Rogate Dr NTHM/RTH M23 .... 44 A7
Roger Av MPL/ROM SK6 ...... 47 M3
Rogerson's Gn HLWD L26 .... 50 E2 🗓
Rokeby Av GOL/RIS/CU WA3 .. 23 K3
Rokeby Ct RUNC WA7 .... 54 D7
Rokeden NEWLW WA12 .... 22 D8 🗓
Roland Av RUNC WA7 .... 8 E4
Rolleston St WARRN/WOL WA2 . 4 E5
Rollins La MPL/ROM SK6 ...... 49 G3
Rolls Av CW/HAS CW1 .... 221 C6
Rolt Crs MWCH CW10 .... 179 H4
Roman Cl NEWLW WA12 ...... 27 J2
RUNC WA7 .... 73 L3
Roman Ct NSTN CH64 .... 91 M5
Roman Dr CH/BCN CH1 ...... 144 D5
Romanes St NWCHW CW8 ..... 12 E5
Roman Rd HTNM SK4 .... 2 F4
WARRS WA4 .... 56 C3 🗓
Roman Wy SBCH CW11 .... 203 L5
WHITCH SY13 .... 269 M4
Romford Wy HLWD L26 .... 50 F6 🗓
Romiley Rd GTS/LS CH66 .... 94 E6
Romiley St STKP SK1 .... 3 L3
Romney Cl WDN WA8 .... 53 K2
Romney Rd NSTN CH64 .... 91 M5
Romsey Dr CHD/CHDH SK8 ... 65 H6
Ronald Dr WARRN/WOL WA2 .. 38 B2
Ronaldshay WDN WA8 .... 53 L2 🗓
Ronaldsway HLWD L26 .... 51 G4
Ronan Rd WDN WA8 .... 52 E7
Rood HI CONG CW12 .... 207 K1
Rood La CONG CW12 .... 184 D8
Rookery Av AIMK WN4 .... 22 B2
Rookery Cl NANT CW5 .... 21 G7
SBCH CW11 .... 203 J7
Rookery Dr CHSE CH3 .... 214 B2
NANT CW5 .... 20 F9
Rookerypool Cl WILM/AE SK9 . 84 D3 🗓
Rookery Ri WSFD CW7 .... 178 A4
Rookery Rd ALS/KID ST7 .... 243 J1
MALPAS SY14 .... 245 H1
The Rookery CHSW/BR CH4 .. 190 B1
NEWLW WA12 .... 22 D8 🗓
Rook Rd WARRS WA4 .... 37 L8
Rook St CW/SHV CW2 .... 18 E7
Rookwood Av
NTHM/RTH M23 .... 43 M5 🗓
Rookwood HI BRAM/HZG SK7 .. 65 L8
Roome St WARRN/WOL WA2 .... 5 J2
Rooth St HTNM SK4 .... 2 C4
Rope Bank Av CW/SHV CW2 .. 238 A5
Rope La CW/SHV CW2 .... 238 A5
Ropers Bridge Cl RAIN/WH L35 . 32 D2
The Ropewalk NSTN CH64 .... 91 J4 🗓
Rosam Ct RUNC WA7 .... 73 L6
Roscoe Av NEWLW WA12 ..... 27 L1 🗓
WARRN/WOL WA2 .... 37 K4
Roscoe Cl RAIN/WH L35 ...... 32 A5
Roscoe Crs RUNC WA7 .... 73 H7
Roscoe Rd IRL M44 .... 31 L3
Roscoe St EDGY/DAV SK3 ...... 2 D7
Roseacre Dr CHD/CHDH SK8 .. 64 C3
Rose Av IRL M44 .... 31 L3
Rose Bank LYMM WA13 .... 58 E1
MCFLDN SK10 .... 112 F5 🗓
Rosebank Cl WSFD CW7 ..... 177 M4 🗓
Rosebank Rd IRL M44 .... 40 C1

WARRS WA4 .... 56 E2
WARRW/BUR WA5 .... 36 C2
Rosemary Cl CHSW/BR CH4 .. 190 C1 🗓
WARRW/BUR WA5 .... 36 C2
Rosemary Dr NEWLW WA12 ... 27 M1
Rosemary La STKP SK1 .... 3 J2
WHITCH SY13 .... 270 A5
Rosemere Dr GTS/LS CH66 .. 120 F5
Rosemoor Gdns WARRS WA4 .. 56 F7
Roseneath BRAM/HZG SK7 ... 65 K3
Rose St RDSH SK5 .... 3 C1
CW/SHV CW2 .... 238 A4
Rose Ter CW/HAS CW1 .... 18 E1
Rose V CHD/CHDH SK8 .... 64 B3
Rose View Av WDN WA8 ...... 53 C2
Roseville Dr CONG CW12 .... 208 B4
Roseway BRAM/HZG SK7 ..... 65 M2
Rosewood Av CHNE CH2 .... 145 K7
FROD/HEL WA6 .... 99 K5 🗓
HTNM SK4 .... 46 A3
WARR WA1 .... 37 L5 🗓
Rosewood Cl CW/HAS CW1 .. 221 L6 🗓
Rosewood Gdns
CHD/CHDH SK8 .... 44 F6 🗓
Rosewood Gv CH/BCN CH1 .. 144 B4 🗓
Rosgill Cl HTNM SK4 .... 45 L2 🗓
Roskell Rd WLTN L25 .... 50 C5
Roslyn Rd EDGY/DAV SK3 .... 46 E7
Rossall Crs LEIGH WN7 .... 25 C1
Rossall Dr BRAM/HZG SK7 ... 65 M6
Rossall Gv GTS/LS CH66 ..... 94 D6
Rossall Rd WARRW/BUR WA5 .. 36 B8
WDN WA8 .... 53 K2
Ross Av EDGY/DAV SK3 .... 46 C7
Rossbank Rd EP CH65 .... 10 A4
Rosscliffe Rd EP CH65 .... 10 A4
Ross Cl WARRW/BUR WA5 ..... 36 D4
Rossendale Dr
GOL/RIS/CU WA3 .... 30 A7 🗓
Rossendale Rd CHD/CHDH SK8 . 64 C4
Rosset Cl NWCHE CW9 ...... 129 L8
Rosett Av HALE/TIMP WA15 .. 43 G4
WYTH/NTH M22 .... 63 K3
Rossett Cl WARRW/BUR WA5 .. 36 C2 🗓
Rossett Gv ALS/KID ST7 .... 243 M4 🗓
Rossett Pk WRX/GR/LL LL12 . 210 D4
Rossett Rd WRX/GR/LL LL12 . 210 D5
Rossfield Rd EP CH65 .... 10 A4
Rosslare Rd WYTH/NTH M22 .. 63 L2
Rosslyn Cl RUNC WA7 .... 167 C2
Rosslyn Gv HALE/TIMP WA15 . 43 C6
Rosslyn La NWCHW CW8 .... 152 A1
Rosslyn Rd CHD/CHDH SK8 .. 64 D3
CHSE CH3 .... 170 B1
Rossmill La HALE/TIMP WA15 . 62 A7
Rossmore Gdns GTS/LS CH66 . 94 D6
Rossmore Rd East EP CH65 .. 94 F5
Rossmore Rd West GTS/LS CH66 . 94 D5
Rossmount Rd EP CH65 ...... 10 A5
Ross Rd EP CH65 .... 10 B6
Ross St WDN WA8 .... 52 B8
Rosswood Rd EP CH65 .... 10 B5
Rostherne Av GOL/RIS/CU WA3 . 23 C6
GTS/LS CH66 .... 94 E8
MPL/ROM SK6 .... 67 L4
Rostherne Cl WARRW/BUR WA5 . 36 D8
Rostherne La ALT WA14 ...... 60 D7
Rostherne Rd EDGY/DAV SK3 .. 46 F7
SALE M33 .... 43 M1
WILM/AE SK9 .... 83 L7
Rostherne St ALT WA14 ...... 61 K1 🗓
Rostherne Wy SBCH CW11 .. 203 M5
Rosthernmere Rd
CHD/CHDH SK8 .... 45 M8
Rostrevor Rd EDGY/DAV SK3 .. 46 E8
Rothay Dr WARRW/BUR WA5 .. 54 D1
Rothbury Cl RUNC WA7 .... 73 L6 🗓
Rothbury Ct STHEL WA9 ..... 34 B2 🗓
Rotherby Rd WYTH/NTH M22 . 63 L4
Rotherdale Av HALE/TIMP WA15 . 43 K7
Rother Dr EP CH65 .... 10 A3
Rotherwood Rd WILM/AE SK9 . 83 K7
Rothesay Crs SALE M33 ..... 42 C2
Rothesay Dr CHSW/BR CH4 .. 16 B9
Rothley Av WYTH/NTH M22 ... 44 D7
Rothwell Rd GOL/RIS/CU WA3 . 23 J3
Rottingdene Dr
WYTH/NTH M22 .... 63 J3 🗓
Rough Bank CONG CW12 .... 208 E4
Roughey Gdns WYTH/NTH M22 . 44 C8
Rough Heys La MCFLDS SK11 . 137 C4
Roughlea Av GOL/RIS/CU WA3 . 29 L1 🗓
Roughley Av WARRW/BUR WA5 . 36 D8 🗓
Roughlyn Crs CHSW/BR CH4 . 191 L3
Roughwood La SBCH CW11 .. 224 D5
The Roundabout WDN WA8 ... 33 K6
Roundcroft MPL/ROM SK6 ... 48 D1
Round Gdns MCFLDN SK10 .. 113 G4
Roundhey CHD/CHDH SK8 ... 64 B4
Round Hill Meadow CHSE CH3 . 170 B5
Round Meadow MCFLDS SK10 . 113 K7 🗓
Round Thorn GOL/RIS/CU WA3 . 29 C5
Roundthorn Rd NTHM/RTH M23 . 43 M6
Roundthorn Wk
NTHM/RTH M23 .... 43 M6 🗓
Round Wy NM/HAY SK22 ..... 69 H4
Roundwood Dr WARRN/WOL WA2 . 44 D5
Roundy La MCFLDN SK10 ..... 86 F7
Rousdale Cl WDN WA8 .... 7 K2 🗓
Rowan Av GOL/RIS/CU WA3 .. 23 M5
SALE M33 .... 43 J2
Rowan Cl ALS/KID ST7 ...... 224 C6 🗓
ALS/KID ST7 .... 241 K1 🗓
ALS/KID ST7 .... 243 C4 🗓
MWCH CW10 .... 179 L6
RUNC WA7 .... 9 L8
SBCH CW11 .... 203 M6
Rowan Dr CHD/CHDH SK8 .... 65 J4
Rowan Pk CHSE CH3 .... 170 C5
Rowan Pl CHNE CH2 .... 146 B8
Rowan Ri NWCHW CW8 ...... 129 C1
Rowan Rd CQ CH5 .... 166 A1

NWCHW CW8 .... 128 C4
Rowanside MCFLDN SK10 ... 111 L6
Rowanside Dr WILM/AE SK9 .. 84 E4 🗓
The Rowans CHSW/BR CH4 .. 190 B1
Rowan Tree Dr SALE M33 .... 43 H3
Rowan Wy MCFLDN SK10 .... 15 J2
Rowarth Rd NTHM/RTH M23 .. 62 F2
Rowcliffe Av CHSW/BR CH4 .. 169 G8
Rowden Crs CQ CH5 .... 142 A6
Rowden St CQ CH5 .... 142 A6
Rowfield Dr NTHM/RTH M23 .. 62 F1 🗓
Rowland Cl WARRN/WOL WA2 . 38 A1
Rowlandsway WYTH/NTH M22 . 63 K2
Rowley Bank La KNUT WA16 .. 79 J3
Rowley Rd BRAM/HZG SK7 ... 66 E4 🗓
Rowley's Cl CQ CH5 .... 142 C6
Rowley Wy KNUT WA16 ...... 107 H5
Rowson Dr IRL M44 .... 31 K6
Rowthorn Cl WDN WA8 .... 6 C5
Rowton Bridge Rd CHSE CH3 . 170 E5
Rowton Cl NWCHE CW9 ..... 129 M8
Rowton La CHSE CH3 .... 170 F6
Rowton Rd CW/SHV CW2 .... 220 D8
Roxborough Cl
WARRW/BUR WA5 .... 27 C6 🗓
Roxborough Wk WLTN L25 .... 50 C1
Roxburgh Cl MCFLDN SK10 .. 14 A3
Roxburgh Rd GTS/LS CH66 .. 93 M6
Roxby Wy KNUT WA16 .... 107 C5
Roxholme Wk WYTH/NTH M22 . 63 J4
Royal Av WDN WA8 .... 52 B4
Royal Gdns ALT WA14 .... 60 F2
NWCHE CW9 .... 153 L1
Royal George St EDGY/DAV SK3 . 2 F8
Royal La TPLY/KEL CW6 ..... 198 A1
Royal Mdw MCFLDN SK10 ... 14 A3
Royal Oak Rd NTHM/RTH M23 . 43 M5
Royal Oak Yd STKP SK1 .... 3 C5
Royal POY/DIS SK12 .... 68 D7
Royalthorn Dr
WYTH/NTH M22 .... 44 C6 🗓
Royalthorn Rd WYTH/NTH M22 . 44 D6
Royce Av BIDD ST8 .... 227 H7
HALE/TIMP WA15 .... 42 F7
Royce Cl CW/HAS CW1 ...... 221 C5
Royden Av IRL M44 .... 31 M4 🗓
RUNC WA7 .... 8 F6
Royds Cl NWCHW CW8 ...... 129 H7
Roylance Dr MWCH CW10 ... 179 J4
Royle Cl OFTN SK2 .... 47 C7
Royleen Cl FROD/HEL WA6 ... 99 K6
Royle Green Rd WYTH/NTH M22 . 44 F7
Royle's Pl NWCHW CW8 ...... 12 C6
Royle St CONG CW12 .... 207 K1
NWCHE CW9 .... 13 M3
OFTN SK2 .... 47 C7
WSFD CW7 .... 177 J3
Royon Dr EDGY/DAV SK3 ..... 46 B5
Royston Av WARR WA1 .... 37 M5
Royston Cl GOL/RIS/CU WA3 . 23 L4 🗓
GTS/LS CH66 .... 120 F2
Royton Av SALE M33 .... 43 K2
Rozel Crs WARRW/BUR WA5 .. 36 B8
Ruabon Rd DID/WITH M20 ... 45 J2
Rubens Cl MPL/ROM SK6 .... 49 J4
Rudd Av STHEL WA9 .... 26 A2
Ruddpark Rd WYTH/NTH M22 . 63 K3
Rudgate RAIN/WH L35 .... 32 C2
Rudheath Cl CW/SHV CW2 .. 220 D7
Rudloe Ct WARRN/WOL WA2 .. 37 M3
Rudstone Cl GTS/LS CH66 ... 94 B7
Rudyard Cl MCFLDS SK11 .... 14 C9
Rudyard Gv SALE M33 .... 42 E2
Rufford Cl CW/SHV CW2 .... 238 A4
WDN WA8 .... 52 C2 🗓
Rugby Cl MCFLDN SK10 .... 112 E8
Rugby Dr MCFLDN SK10 .... 138 E1
SALE M33 .... 43 C2
Rugby Rd EP CH65 .... 121 J1
LEIGH WN7 .... 24 F1
Ruislip Cl WLTN L25 .... 50 C2
Ruislip Ct WARRN/WOL WA2 .. 37 M3
Runcorn Docks Rd RUNC WA7 . 8 D3
Runcorn Rd NWCHW CW8 ... 102 C6
WARRS WA4 .... 55 G8
Runcorn Spur Rd RUNC WA7 ... 9 K4
Runger La MANAIR M90 ...... 62 F5
Runnymede WARR WA1 .... 38 C5
Runnymede Cl EDGY/DAV SK3 . 46 C5
Rupert St BIDD ST8 .... 227 J4
Ruscar Cl HLWD L26 .... 50 E2 🗓
Ruscoe Av SBCH CW11 ...... 203 L6
Ruscolm Cl WARRW/BUR WA5 . 35 K5 🗓
Rushey Cl HALE/TIMP WA15 .. 62 D5
Rushey Rd WYTH/NTH M22 ... 44 C7
Rushfield Crs RUNC WA7 ..... 74 B7
Rushfield Rd CHD/CHDH SK8 . 65 G6
CHSW/BR CH4 .... 169 H7
Rush Gdns LYMM WA13 .... 40 A8
Rushgreen Rd LYMM WA13 ... 39 M8
Rushmere Cl MCFLDN SK10 .. 112 F2
Rushmere La CHSE CH3 ..... 211 M1
Rushmore Gv WARR WA1 ..... 38 A5
Rusholme Cl HLWD L26 ...... 51 G6 🗓
Rushside Rd CHD/CHDH SK8 . 64 F6
Rushton Av NEWLW WA12 .... 22 B8
Rushton Cl MPL/ROM SK6 ... 49 C7 🗓
NWCHE CW9 .... 130 C5
WDN WA8 .... 52 F1
Rushton Dr BRAM/HZG SK7 .. 65 K1
CHNE CH2 .... 145 L5
CW/SHV CW2 .... 253 L5
MPL/ROM SK6 .... 48 F8
MPL/ROM SK6 .... 48 C1
MWCH CW10 .... 179 J5
Rushton Fold MCFLDN SK10 . 111 G2
Rushton La TPLY/KEL CW6 .. 175 J7
Rushton Pl WLTN L25 .... 50 A2
Rushton Rd CHD/CHDH SK8 .. 65 G6 🗓
EDGY/DAV SK3 .... 46 B5
Rushton St DID/WITH M20 ... 45 H2 🗓
Rushyfield Crs MPL/ROM SK6 . 48 D1
Rushy Vw NEWLW WA12 ...... 22 A8
Ruskin Av NEWLW WA12 ..... 22 B8
WARRN/WOL WA2 .... 37 J2 🗓
Ruskin Ct KNUT WA16 ...... 107 G2
Ruskin Dr EP CH65 .... 121 K1

Ruskin Gdns MPL/ROM SK6...... 48 A1
Ruskin Gv MPL/ROM SK6...... 48 A1
Ruskin Rd CONG CW12...... 207 L2
CW/SHV CW2 ...... 18 E8
Ruskin Wy KNUT WA16 ...... 107 G1
Russell Av ALS/KID ST7...... 224 C7
MPL/ROM SK6 ...... 67 L5
Russell Cl CONG CW12 ...... 207 M4
Russell Dr CW/HAS CW1 ...... 222 C7
Russell Pl BURS/TUN ST6 ...... 243 L6
Russell Rd BURS/TUN ST6 ...... 243 K6
HUY L36 ...... 32 B2
PART M31 ...... 41 G1
RUNC WA7 ...... 8 C5
WSFD CW7 ...... 177 J4
Russell St SK2 ...... 47 G6
Russet Cl MWCH CW10 ...... 179 H2
Russet Rd NWCHW CW8 ...... 128 D4
Ruthin Av CHD/CHDH SK8 ...... 64 E2
Ruthin Cl WARRN/WOL WA2 ...... 36 E1
Rutland Av GOL/RIS/CU WA3 ...... 23 K5
HLWD L26 ...... 50 F4
WARRS WA4 ...... 56 B4
Rutland Cl CHD/CHDH SK8 ...... 45 H6
CONG CW12 ...... 184 E8
SBCH CW11 ...... 203 J3
Rutland Dr MWCH CW10 ...... 179 J5
NWCHW CW8 ...... 128 C3
Rutland Pl CHNE CH2 ...... 146 A7
Rutland Rd ALS/KID ST7 ...... 243 G2
ALT WA14 ...... 42 D6
BRAM/HZG SK7 ...... 66 E4
IRL M44 ...... 31 K7
MCFLDN SK11 ...... 138 C8
PART M31 ...... 40 E2
Rutland St RUNC WA7 ...... 8 F2
Rutter Av WARRW/BUR WA5 ...... 36 F2
Rutter's La BRAM/HZG SK7 ...... 66 C2
Ryburn Rd MCFLDS SK11 ...... 138 K1
Rycot Rd SPK/HALE L24 ...... 50 C8
Rydal Av BRAM/HZG SK7 ...... 66 C1
MPL/ROM SK6 ...... 67 L4
WARRS WA4 ...... 56 A2
WHITCH SY13 ...... 270 B6
Rydal Cl CHD/CHDH SK8 ...... 45 H8
EP CH65 ...... 121 J2
HOLMCH CW4 ...... 181 H2
NSTN CH64 ...... 91 M6
WSFD CW7 ...... 177 K1
Rydal Ct CONG CW12 ...... 207 G2
Rydal Dr HALE/TIMP WA15 ...... 62 D4
Rydal Gv CHSW/BR CH4...... 169 G6
FROD/HEL WA6 ...... 124 B3
RUNC WA7 ...... 9 K7
Rydal Mt CW/HAS CW1 ...... 221 H3
Rydal Rd NEWLW WA12 ...... 27 J1
Rydal Wy ALS/KID ST7 ...... 224 C7
WDN WA8 ...... 52 C4
Ryde Av HTNM SK4 ...... 46 B2
Ryde Cl CW/HAS CW1 ...... 221 H4
Ryder Av ALT WA14 ...... 42 E5
Ryder Gv LEIGH WN7 ...... 25 J2
Ryder Rd WARR WA1 ...... 38 C4
WDN WA8 ...... 34 B8
Ryders St NWCHW CW8 ...... 12 E3
Ryebank Av CW/HAS CW1 ...... 221 H5
Ryebank Wy MCFLDS SK10 ...... 138 C1
Ryebrook Gv BURS/TUN ST6 ...... 243 M5
Ryeburn Av WYTH/NTH M22 ...... 63 K1
Rye Cl ALS/KID ST7 ...... 241 H1
Ryecroft CHNE CH2 ...... 123 H1
Ryecroft Av GOL/RIS/CU WA3...... 23 L3
Ryecroft Cl MWCH CW10 ...... 179 H5
Ryecroft Gv NTHM/RTH M23 ...... 44 A5
Ryecroft La CHSE CH3 ...... 172 B6
KNUT WA16 ...... 81 L8
TPLY/KEL CW6 ...... 172 E6
Ryedale Cl HTNM SK4 ...... 46 B2
Ryefield Cl HALE/TIMP WA15 ...... 43 J7
Ryefield Rd SALE M33 ...... 55 J7
Ryefield Wy WHITCH SY13 ...... 270 A6
Ryeland St CW/HAS CW1 ...... 142 A5
Rylands Cl MALPAS SY14 ...... 258 M1
Rylands St WARR WA1 ...... 17 K5
WDN WA8 ...... 7 J4
Ryles Cl MCFLDS SK11 ...... 138 C7
Ryles Crs MCFLDS SK11 ...... 138 C7
Ryle's Park Rd MCFLDS SK11 ...... 138 C7
Ryle St MCFLDS SK11 ...... 15 G8
Ryleys La WILM/AE SK9 ...... 109 M3
Rylstone Av CCHDY M21 ...... 44 D1

S

Sabre Cl RUNC WA7 ...... 74 D5
Sack La NWCHE CW9 ...... 78 F6
Saddleback Dr MCFLDN SK10 ...... 111 M5
Saddlers Ri RUNC WA7 ...... 74 C4
Saddlewood Av BNG/LEV M19 ...... 45 K2
Sadler Cl WSFD CW7 ...... 177 K3
Sadler Rd WSFD CW7 ...... 177 K3
Sadler's Cl HOLMCH CW4 ...... 181 H1
Sadlers La TPLY/KEL CW6 ...... 175 G3
Sadler St WDN WA8 ...... 7 L2
Sadlers Wls TPLY/KEL CW6 ...... 216 E4
Saffron Cl GOL/RIS/CU WA3 ...... 23 L4
WARRN/WOL WA2 ...... 38 B3
Sagars Rd WILM/AE SK9 ...... 64 C8
Sage Cl WARRN/WOL WA2 ...... 38 C2
Saighton La CHSE CH3 ...... 193 M2
St Aidan's St BURS/TUN ST6 ...... 243 K8
St Alban Rd WARRW/BUR WA5 ...... 35 L7
St Albans Crs ALT WA14 ...... 42 C4
St Albans Dr RUNC WA7 ...... 251 M1
St Albans Pl NM/HAY SK22 ...... 69 J5
St Albans St NM/HAY SK22 ...... 69 J4
St Aldates MPL/ROM SK6 ...... 47 M2
St Alkmond Meadow
WHITCH SY13 ...... 269 M4
St Ambrose Rd WDN WA8 ...... 7 M2
St Andrew's Av CW/SHV CW2 ...... 18 F9
HALE/TIMP WA15...... 42 E4
St Andrews Cl MPL/ROM SK6...... 48 B3
St Andrews Cl NWCHE CW9 ...... 130 E5
WARRN/WOL WA2 ...... 29 G8

St Andrews Dr ALS/KID ST7...... 243 J1
HOLMCH CW4 ...... 181 H2
St Andrews Gdns ALS/KID ST7 ...... 243 L2
St Andrews Rd CHD/CHDH SK8 ...... 64 C3
EP CH65 ...... 121 K1
MCFLDS SK11 ...... 14 D7
St Anne's Av MWCH CW10...... 179 J4
WARRS WA4 ...... 57 H2
St Annes Av East WARRS WA4 ...... 57 H2
St Anne's La NANT CW5 ...... 20 D6
St Anne's Rd WDN WA8 ...... 53 H2
St Ann St CH/BCN CH1 ...... 17 G3
St Ann's Rd BRAM/HZG SK7 ...... 66 C3
MWCH CW10 ...... 179 H3
St Ann's Rd North
CHD/CHDH SK8 ...... 64 B3
St Ann's Rd South
CHD/CHDH SK8 ...... 64 C3
St Ann's Sq CHD/CHDH SK8 ...... 64 C4
St Anns St SALE M33 ...... 54 E7
St Asaph Dr WARRW/BUR WA5... 36 D2
St Asaph Rd GTS/LS CH66 ...... 120 E4
St Augustine's Av
WARRS WA4 ...... 37 M8
St Augustine's Rd
EDGY/DAV SK3 ...... 46 B4
St Austell Av WARRW/BUR WA5 ...... 54 E1
St Austell Av MCFLDN SK10 ...... 137 K3
St Austell Cl RUNC WA7 ...... 74 B6
St Austell Dr CHD/CHDH SK8... 64 B4
St Austins La WARR WA1 ...... 17 H5
St Barnabas Ct MCFLDS SK11 ...... 15 H9
St Barnabas Pl WARRW/BUR WA5 ... 4 B5
St Bartholomews Ct CQ CH5 ...... 143 L6
St Bede's Av NWCHW CW8 ...... 128 D3
St Bees Cl CHD/CHDH SK8 ...... 64 B1
St Benedicts Cl WARR WA5 ...... 5 H3
St Brannocks Rd CHD/CHDH SK8...... 65 H5
St Brides Cl WARRW/BUR WA5 ...... 54 E1
St Bridget's Cl
WARRN/WOL WA2 ...... 37 M1
St Catherine Dr NWCHW CW8...... 128 F8
St Catherine's Cl FLINT CH6 ...... 116 A6
St Chad's Av MPL/ROM SK6 ...... 48 C2
St Chads Cl NANT CW5 ...... 253 G4
St Chad's Flds WSFD CW7 ...... 177 J7
St Chad's Gv MPL/ROM SK6 ...... 48 C2
St Chad's Rd CH/BCN CH1 ...... 144 F8
St Christophers Cl CHNE CH2 ...... 145 J4
St Christopher's Dr
MPL/ROM SK6 ...... 48 A2
St Clairs St CW/SHV CW2 ...... 19 H9
St Crewood Cl CW/SHV CW2 ...... 238 B5
St David's Av MPL/ROM SK6...... 48 B2
St Davids Cl FLINT CH6 ...... 116 B8
SALE M33 ...... 43 G1
St David's Cl CQ CH5 ...... 142 B6
GTS/LS CH66 ...... 120 F4
WARRW/BUR WA5 ...... 36 E2
St David's Rd BRAM/HZG SK7 ...... 66 C3
St David's Ter CHSW/BR CH4 ...... 168 C5
St Elmo Cl OFTN SK2 ...... 47 K5
St Elmo Pk POY/DIS SK12 ...... 67 J8
St Elphins Cl WARR WA1 ...... 5 K6
St Ethelwold's St CQ CH5 ...... 142 B8
St Gabriel's Av HUY L36 ...... 32 A2
St Georges Av GTS/LS CH66 ...... 120 F4
HALE/TIMP WA15 ...... 43 G4
St George's Cl KNUT WA16 ...... 107 J4
WARRS WA4 ...... 76 E1
St George's Ct ALT WA14 ...... 42 B5
St George's Crs CHSE CH3 ...... 171 G7
CHSW/BR CH4 ...... 17 J8
HALE/TIMP WA15 ...... 43 G4
St George's Pl MCFLDS SK11 ...... 15 H8
St Georges Rd NM/HAY SK22 ...... 69 J4
WSFD CW7 ...... 177 J4
St George's St MCFLDS SK11 ...... 15 H7
St Helens Cl GOL/RIS/CU WA3 ...... 40 B1
St Helens Linkway RAIN/WH L35 ...... 33 M3
St Helens Rd LEIGH WN7 ...... 24 C3
NWCHE CW9 ...... 13 K2
St Hilda's Dr FROD/HEL WA6 ...... 99 J3
St Hilda's Rd WYTH/NTH M22 ...... 44 D3
St Hugh's Cl ALT WA14 ...... 42 E4
St Ives Av CHD/CHDH SK8 ...... 46 A1
St Ives Cl MCFLDN SK10 ...... 137 L3
St Ives Crs SALE M33 ...... 43 G3
St Ives Wy CQ CH5 ...... 167 G1
HLWD L26 ...... 50 F4
St James Av CHNE CH2 ...... 145 M6
CONG CW12 ...... 207 J2
MCFLDS SK11 ...... 161 L2
St James Cl
AUD/MAD/W CW3 ...... 264 A8
St James Ct HALE/TIMP WA15 ...... 42 E8
St James Dr SALE M33 ...... 43 G1
WILM/AE SK9 ...... 84 A6
St James Mt RAIN/WH L35 ...... 33 J2
St James's Gv ALT WA14 ...... 42 F3
St James St CH/BCN CH1 ...... 17 H3
St James Ter WSFD CW7 ...... 177 G4
St John Av WARRS WA4 ...... 56 B2
St John's Av KNUT WA16 ...... 106 F3
NWCHE CW9 ...... 130 F1
St John's Brow RUNC WA7 ...... 9 J1
St John's Cl MPL/ROM SK6 ...... 48 B2
NWCHE CW9 ...... 130 D5
St Johns Dr WSFD CW7 ...... 177 G4
St John's Pk WHITCH SY13 ...... 270 A4
St Johns Pl BIDD ST8 ...... 227 K5
St John's Rear Rd CHSW/BR CH4... 17 J8
St John's Rd ALT WA14 ...... 61 J1
BIDD ST8 ...... 227 J6
BRAM/HZG SK7 ...... 66 B3
CHSW/BR CH4 ...... 17 J7
CONG CW12 ...... 184 F7
HTNM SK4 ...... 45 L2
KNUT WA16 ...... 106 F3
MCFLDS SK11 ...... 14 F7
WILM/AE SK9 ...... 109 L1
St John's St RUNC WA7 ...... 9 J1
WHITCH SY13 ...... 270 A4
St John St CH/BCN CH1 ...... 17 H3
NEWLW WA12 ...... 27 L1

St John's Wy NWCHW CW8 ...... 152 A2
SBCH CW11 ...... 204 E6
St John's Wd ALS/KID ST7 ...... 242 F1
St Joseph's Cl
WARRW/BUR WA5 ...... 35 L7
St Joseph St BURS/TUN ST6 ...... 243 K5
St Josephs Wy NANT CW5 ...... 21 J7
St Katherines Wy WARR WA1 ...... 5 L6
St Kilda Cl EP CH65 ...... 121 J3
St Lawrence Ct NANT CW5 ...... 21 G5
St Lawrence Rd FROD/HEL WA6 ...... 99 H5
St Leonards Dr HALE/TIMP WA15... 42 F6
St Lesmo Rd EDGY/DAV SK3 ...... 46 B4
St Luke's Av GOL/RIS/CU WA3 ...... 23 K4
St Luke's Crs WDN WA8 ...... 34 B8
St Luke's Wy FROD/HEL WA6 ...... 99 H3
St Margaret's Av
WARRN/WOL WA2 ...... 37 K3
St Margarets Ct
AUD/MAD/W CW3 ...... 255 G6
St Margaret's Rd ALT WA14 ...... 42 C8
CHD/CHDH SK8 ...... 46 A6
St Mark's Av WARRN/WOL WA2 ...... 2 A4
St Marks Crs GTS/LS CH66 ...... 120 F5
St Marks Rd CHSW/BR CH4 ...... 168 F6
St Martin's Av HTNM SK4...... 2 A4
St Martins Dr GTS/LS CH66 ...... 120 D2
St Martins La RUNC WA7 ...... 74 D5
St Martin's Rd ALS/KID ST7 ...... 242 E7
MPL/ROM SK6 ...... 49 G6
St Martin's Wy CH/BCN CH1 ...... 16 E4
St Mary's Av NWCHW CW8 ...... 128 D3
STKP SK1 ...... 3 J3
WARRS WA4 ...... 56 C6
St Marys Cl NANT CW5 ...... 236 A5
WLTN L25 ...... 50 A2
St Mary's Dr CHD/CHDH SK8 ...... 45 M6
NWCHW CW8 ...... 153 G4
St Mary's Hl CH/BCN CH1 ...... 17 G7
St Mary's Pl WLTN L25 ...... 50 A2
St Mary's Rd ALT WA14 ...... 61 H2
CHSW/BR CH4 ...... 191 G5
NANT CW5 ...... 20 E3
NM/HAY SK22 ...... 69 H4
POY/DIS SK12 ...... 68 D7
RUNC WA7 ...... 73 M3
WARRW/BUR WA5 ...... 35 M7
WDN WA8 ...... 53 G8
St Mary's St CW/HAS CW1 ...... 18 E3
WHITCH SY13 ...... 270 A4
St Mary's Wy CHSW/BR CH4 ...... 167 J7
STKP SK1 ...... 3 J3
St Matthews Cl RUNC WA7 ...... 222 D8
WARRS WA4 ...... 56 D5
St Matthew's Rd EDGY/DAV SK3 ...... 2 D8
St Mawes Cl WDN WA8 ...... 6 C1
St Mawgan Ct
WARRN/WOL WA2 ...... 37 M2
St Michael's Av BRAM/HZG SK7 ...... 65 L5
St Michaels Cl NWCHW CW8 ...... 102 D7
WDN WA8 ...... 52 C5
St Michael's Rd BURS/TUN ST6... 243 M7
STHEL WA9 ...... 34 A1
WDN WA8 ...... 52 C5
St Michael's Wy MWCH CW10 ...... 179 J3
St Monicas Cl WARRS WA4 ...... 56 D5
St Nicholas Rd GOL/RIS/CU WA3 ...... 24 A3
RAIN/WH L35 ...... 32 C3
St Olave St CH/BCN CH1 ...... 17 G7
St Oswalds Cl MALPAS SY14 ...... 258 B1
WARRN/WOL WA2 ...... 28 B6
St Oswald's Crs SBCH CW11 ...... 181 M7
St Oswalds Rd AIMK WN4 ...... 22 A2
St Oswalds Wy CH/BCN CH1 ...... 17 G2
St Paul's Cl CW/HAS CW1 ...... 18 E3
St Pauls Gdns GTS/LS CH66 ...... 94 B5
St Paul's Rd MCFLDN SK10 ...... 15 J6
WDN WA8 ...... 7 H6
St Paul's St CW/HAS CW1 ...... 18 E3
STKP SK1 ...... 3 K2
St Peter's Av KNUT WA16 ...... 106 F3
St Peter's Cl LYMM WA13 ...... 40 A8
St Peter's Dr TPLY/KEL CW6 ...... 175 M5
St Petersgate STKP SK1 ...... 3 G5
St Peter's Ri SBCH CW11 ...... 203 L5
St Peters Rd CONG CW12 ...... 207 L3
St Peter's Sq STKP SK1 ...... 2 F5
St Peters Wy CHNE CH2 ...... 146 F4
WARRN/WOL WA2 ...... 5 H4
St Saviour's Rd OFTN SK2 ...... 47 J7
St Saviour's St ALS/KID ST7 ...... 242 D3
Saintsbridge Rd
WYTH/NTH M22 ...... 63 J2
St Simons Cl OFTN SK2 ...... 47 J4
St Stephen Rd
WARRW/BUR WA5 ...... 35 M7
St Stephen's Av
WARRN/WOL WA2 ...... 37 H1
St Stephens Ct SBCH CW11 ...... 203 K5
St Thomas Cl WDN WA8 ...... 6 C2
St Thomas Pl STKP SK1 ...... 3 G8
St Thomas St ALS/KID ST7 ...... 226 D5
St Thomas' Vw EP CH65 ...... 95 H8
St Vincent Dr NWCHW CW8 ...... 128 F8
St Vincent Rd
WARRW/BUR WA5 ...... 35 M7
St Vincent St HALE/TIMP WA15 ...... 42 D8
St Wenefredes MALPAS SY14 ...... 247 M5
St Werburgh St CH/BCN CH1 ...... 17 G5
St Wilfrid's Dr WARRS WA4 ...... 56 C5
Salander Crs CW/SHV CW2 ...... 238 A5
Salcombe Cl NANT CW5 ...... 21 J7
Salcombe Rd OFTN SK2 ...... 47 J4
Sale Heys Rd SALE M33 ...... 42 F1
Sale Rd NTHM/RTH M23 ...... 44 A2
Salesbrook La NANT CW5 ...... 262 C6
Salford NTHM/RTH M23 ...... 44 A8
Salisbury Av CHSW/BR CH4 ...... 168 D6
CW/SHV CW2 ...... 18 E9
Salisbury Cl AUD/MAD/W CW3 ...... 267 M5
GTS/LS CH66 ...... 120 F4
Salisbury Pl MCFLDN SK10 ...... 112 E8
Salisbury Rd ALT WA14 ...... 42 D5
WHITCH SY13 ...... 270 B4
Salisbury St CH/BCN CH1 ...... 16 D1

CQ CH5 ...... 142 B6
GOL/RIS/CU WA3 ...... 23 G4
RUNC WA7 ...... 9 G4
WARR WA1 ...... 5 L5
WDN WA8 ...... 7 J4
Salkeld St NWCHE CW9 ...... 13 M3
Salop Pl ALS/KID ST7 ...... 243 G1
Saltash Cl HLWD L26 ...... 50 E4
RUNC WA7 ...... 74 B6
WYTH/NTH M22 ...... 63 K3
Saltdene Rd WYTH/NTH M22 ...... 63 J3
Saltersgate GTS/LS CH66 ...... 120 F2
Salter's La CHNE CH2 ...... 146 C4
CHSE CH3 ...... 231 L3
MCFLDS SK11 ...... 159 H4
Salthill Dr WYTH/NTH M22 ...... 63 L2
Salt Line Wy SBCH CW11 ...... 203 K6
Saltney Ferry Rd
CHSW/BR CH4 ...... 168 B5
Salton Gdns WARRW/BUR WA5 ...... 4 B2
Saltrush Rd WYTH/NTH M22 ...... 63 K2
Saltwood Dr RUNC WA7 ...... 74 C7
Saltworks Cl FROD/HEL WA6 ...... 99 K2
Salusbury St FLINT CH6 ...... 116 B5
Salvin Cl AIMK WN4 ...... 22 D1
Samlesbury Cl DID/WITH M20 ...... 44 F1
Samuel St ALS/KID ST7 ...... 243 M3
CH/BCN CH1 ...... 17 J3
CW/HAS CW1 ...... 18 D2
HTNM SK4 ...... 2 D1
MCFLDS SK11 ...... 15 G6
WARRW/BUR WA5 ...... 4 A8
Sanbec Gdns WDN WA8 ...... 33 K7
Sandacre Rd NTHM/RTH M23 ...... 44 B5
Sandalwood RUNC WA7 ...... 74 C3
Sandalwood Cl
WARRN/WOL WA2 ...... 37 K2
Sandbach Rd ALS/KID ST7 ...... 224 E4
CONG CW12 ...... 206 F1
SALE M33 ...... 43 M1
SBCH CW11 ...... 224 D3
Sandbach Rd North
ALS/KID ST7 ...... 224 C7
Sandbach Rd South
ALS/KID ST7 ...... 241 K1
Sandby Dr MPL/ROM SK6 ...... 49 H4
Sanderling Rd OFTN SK2 ...... 48 A7
Sanders Hey Cl RUNC WA7 ...... 74 C7
Sanderson Cl
WARRW/BUR WA5 ...... 35 K6
Sanders Sq MCFLDS SK11 ...... 138 D7
Sandfield Av NANT CW5 ...... 261 M1
Sandfield Cl GOL/RIS/CU WA3 ...... 23 M4
Sandfield Ct FROD/HEL WA6 ...... 99 H4
NANT CW5 ...... 261 M1
Sandfield Crs GOL/RIS/CU WA3 ...... 25 J5
Sandfield La NWCHW CW8 ...... 127 L3
NWCHW CW8 ...... 129 J8
Sandfields FROD/HEL WA6 ...... 99 H4
Sandford Br NANT CW5 ...... 262 D1
Sandford Rd NANT CW5 ...... 21 G3
SALE M33 ...... 43 M1
Sandgate Cl SPK/HALE L24 ...... 50 B8
Sandgate Rd MCFLDN SK10 ...... 138 F2
Sandham Rd SPK/HALE L24 ...... 71 G1
Sandheys NSTN CH64 ...... 91 J3
Sandhill La MPL/ROM SK6 ...... 49 L3
Sandhill Wk WYTH/NTH M22 ...... 63 H2
Sandhole La KNUT WA16 ...... 134 D1
NWCHW CW8 ...... 127 H5
Sandhurst Av CW/SHV CW2 ...... 18 A9
Sandhurst Dr WILM/AE SK9 ...... 84 C3
Sandhurst Rd DID/WITH M20 ...... 45 H2
HLWD L26 ...... 51 G6
OFTN SK2 ...... 47 H7
Sandhurst St WARRS WA4 ...... 56 F1
Sandicroft Cl GOL/RIS/CU WA3 ...... 29 J7
Sandiford Rd HOLMCH CW4 ...... 181 J1
Sandilands Rd NTHM/RTH M23 ...... 43 K4
Sandileigh CHNE CH2 ...... 145 L8
Sandileigh Av CHD/CHDH SK8 ...... 46 A6
HALE/TIMP WA15 ...... 61 M1
KNUT WA16 ...... 106 F2
Sandileigh Dr HALE/TIMP WA15 ...... 61 M1
Sandiway BRAM/HZG SK7 ...... 65 L2
KNUT WA16 ...... 107 H2
MPL/ROM SK6 ...... 47 M1
RAIN/WH L35 ...... 32 D2
Sandiway Av WDN WA8 ...... 52 A3
Sandiway Cl NWCHW CW8 ...... 103 G2
Sandiway Pk NWCHW CW8 ...... 128 E8
Sandiway Pl ALT WA14 ...... 42 D7
Sandiway Rd ALT WA14 ...... 42 D6
CW/HAS CW1 ...... 221 G6
WILM/AE SK9 ...... 64 D7
Sand La MCFLDN SK10 ...... 109 M7
Sandle Bridge La KNUT WA16 ...... 108 E2
Sandle Bridge Ri WILM/AE SK9 ...... 108 F5
Sandon Crs NSTN CH64 ...... 91 L7
Sandon Park Gdns
CW/SHV CW2 ...... 220 D8
Sandon Pl WDN WA8 ...... 53 K3
Sandon Rd CHNE CH2 ...... 145 K8
Sandown Cl CW/HAS CW1 ...... 19 G4
MWCH CW10 ...... 179 J4
RUNC WA7 ...... 73 J6
WILM/AE SK9 ...... 84 D7
Sandown Crs NWCHW CW8 ...... 152 A2
Sandown Dr HALE/TIMP WA15 ...... 62 D6
SALE M33 ...... 43 K8
Sandown Pl MCFLDS SK11 ...... 137 M5
Sandown Rd BRAM/HZG SK7 ...... 67 G3
CQ CH5 ...... 142 A8
CW/HAS CW1 ...... 221 J6
EDGY/DAV SK3 ...... 46 D6
Sandpiper Cl CW/HAS CW1 ...... 220 F5
NEWLW WA12 ...... 27 G8
Sandpiper Ct CHSW/BR CH4 ...... 192 B2
Sandpiper Dr EDGY/DAV SK3 ...... 46 D6
Sandpiper Gv HLWD L26 ...... 50 E3
Sandra Dr NEWLW WA12 ...... 27 K1
Sandringham Av CHSE CH3 ...... 170 A2
FROD/HEL WA6 ...... 124 B1
Sandringham Cl ALT WA14 ...... 60 F3

NWCHE CW9 ...... 129 L8
WSFD CW7 ...... 177 J1
Sandringham Dr CW/SHV CW2 ...... 237 G3
HTNM SK4 ...... 46 A3
POY/DIS SK12 ...... 86 D7
WARRW/BUR WA5 ...... 36 C8
Sandringham Gdns EP CH65 ...... 121 K2
Sandringham Rd
BRAM/HZG SK7 ...... 66 F2
CHD/CHDH SK8 ...... 65 G1
MCFLDN SK10 ...... 15 L3
MPL/ROM SK6 ...... 47 J1
WDN WA8 ...... 33 M8
Sandringham Wy
WILM/AE SK9 ...... 84 A6
Sandrock Rd CHSE CH3 ...... 170 E5
Sandsdown Cl BIDD ST8 ...... 227 J3
Sandside Rd ALS/KID ST7 ...... 241 H1
Sands Rd ALS/KID ST7 ...... 226 E6
Sandstone Cl RAIN/WH L35 ...... 33 J3
Sandstone Trail FROD/HEL WA6... 124 F2
MALPAS SY14 ...... 231 K6
MALPAS SY14 ...... 246 F4
NWCHW CW8 ...... 150 A3
TPLY/KEL CW6 ...... 197 G8
TPLY/KEL CW6 ...... 215 M2
Sandwich Dr MCFLDN SK10 ...... 138 C1
Sandy Brow La GOL/RIS/CU WA3... 28 E2
Sandy Cl MCFLDN SK10 ...... 112 F5
Sandyhill Pl WSFD CW7 ...... 177 K6
Sandyhill Rd WSFD CW7 ...... 177 K5
Sandylands Crs ALS/KID ST7 ...... 224 F7
Sandylands Pk CW/SHV CW2 ...... 237 K5
Sandy La CHSE CH3 ...... 170 A4
CHSE CH3 ...... 172 C1
CHSE CH3 ...... 193 J1
CHSE CH3 ...... 231 J5
CHSW/BR CH4 ...... 168 D6
CHSW/BR CH4 ...... 190 A6
CONG CW12 ...... 182 E1
CONG CW12 ...... 206 E6
CONG CW12 ...... 206 D1
CONG CW12 ...... 207 H2
CQ CH5 ...... 142 F5
FROD/HEL WA6 ...... 124 B2
GOL/RIS/CU WA3 ...... 24 A2
GOL/RIS/CU WA3 ...... 29 G3
HOLMCH CW4 ...... 157 J3
KNUT WA16 ...... 132 E6
KNUT WA16 ...... 133 J1
LYMM WA13 ...... 40 B7
MALPAS SY14 ...... 232 B3
MALPAS SY14 ...... 256 E4
MCFLDN SK10 ...... 137 J2
MPL/ROM SK6 ...... 48 C1
NANT CW5 ...... 252 F8
NANT CW5 ...... 262 C2
NEWLW WA12 ...... 22 F4
NSTN CH64 ...... 92 A6
NTHM/RTH M23 ...... 43 K5
NWCHW CW8 ...... 128 B1
NWCHW CW8 ...... 152 C6
RDSH SK5 ...... 2 F1
RUNC WA7 ...... 8 B8
RUNC WA7 ...... 74 E6
SBCH CW11 ...... 203 K7
SBCH CW11 ...... 225 G5
WARRN/WOL WA2 ...... 37 H1
WARRS WA4 ...... 56 D4
WARRW/BUR WA5 ...... 36 A8
WDN WA8 ...... 33 L8
WDN WA8 ...... 35 H6
WILM/AE SK9 ...... 83 K4
Sandy La West
WARRN/WOL WA2 ...... 37 G1
Sandy Moor La RUNC WA7 ...... 74 D1
Sandymoor La RUNC WA7 ...... 74 D1
Sandy Rd BIDD ST8 ...... 227 J2
BURS/TUN ST6 ...... 243 K5
Sandy Wy CQ CH5 ...... 166 A3
Sankey La WARRW/BUR WA5 ...... 75 M4
Sankey St GOL/RIS/CU WA3 ...... 23 G3
NEWLW WA12 ...... 27 G1
WARR WA1 ...... 4 E7
WDN WA8 ...... 7 G9
Sankey Wy WARRW/BUR WA5 ...... 4 A7
Santon Dr GOL/RIS/CU WA3 ...... 23 L4
Sapling Cl SALE M33 ...... 42 D2
Sapling La TPLY/KEL CW6 ...... 197 L1
Sargent Rd MPL/ROM SK6 ...... 47 K2
Sarn Av WYTH/NTH M22 ...... 44 D8
Sarn Bank Rd MALPAS SY14 ...... 256 E6
Sarn Br MALPAS SY14 ...... 256 E6
Sarn Rd MALPAS SY14 ...... 256 D4
Sarra La CHSE CH3 ...... 215 H7
Sarsfield Av GOL/RIS/CU WA3 ...... 23 K4
Saughall Cl NWCHE CW9 ...... 129 L8
Saughall Hey CH/BCN CH1 ...... 144 A3
Saughall Rd CH/BCN CH1 ...... 16 C1
Saundersfoot Cl
WARRW/BUR WA5 ...... 36 E2
Saunders St CW/HAS CW1 ...... 18 D3
Saville Av WARRW/BUR WA5 ...... 36 E2
Saville Rd CHD/CHDH SK8 ...... 45 H6
Saville St MCFLDS SK11 ...... 15 K8
Savoy Rd CW/HAS CW1 ...... 239 G4
Sawley Av GOL/RIS/CU WA3 ...... 23 K3
Sawley Cl GOL/RIS/CU WA3...... 30 A2
RUNC WA7 ...... 74 E5
Sawley Dr CHD/CHDH SK8 ...... 65 H6
Sawpit St LYMM WA13 ...... 41 G5
Sawyer Dr BIDD ST8 ...... 227 J3
Saxfield Dr NTHM/RTH M23 ...... 44 C6
Saxon Crossway WSFD CW7 ...... 177 H3
Saxon Rd RUNC WA7 ...... 9 L3
Saxons La NWCHW CW8 ...... 12 C6
Saxon Ter WDN WA8 ...... 7 K3
Saxon Wy CH/BCN CH1 ...... 144 E6
GTS/LS CH66 ...... 120 F4
Sayce St WDN WA8 ...... 7 J3
Scafell Av WARRN/WOL WA2 ...... 37 J1
Scafell Cl BEB CH63 ...... 93 K1
MPL/ROM SK6 ...... 67 L4
NTHLY L27 ...... 51 G1
Scaife Rd NANT CW5 ...... 21 G6
Scaliot Cl NM/HAY SK22 ...... 69 H4
Scarisbrick Av DID/WITH M20 ...... 45 K1

Scar La MALPAS SY14 .....245 M2
Sceptre Cl NEWLW WA12 .....27 G1
Schofield Gdns LEIGH WN7 .....24 E1
Schofield St LEIGH WN7 .....24 E1
Scholars Green La LYMM WA13 .....58 F1
School Av NSTN CH64 .....91 M6
School Bank FROD/HEL WA6 .....127 G6
  WARR WA1 .....5 J6
School Brow MPL/ROM SK6 .....48 A2
School Cl KNUT WA16 .....106 E3
  POY/DIS SK12 .....86 F1
  WHITCH SY13 .....260 E4
School Ct EDGY/DAV SK3 .....46 F6
School Crs CW/HAS CW1 .....19 K4
School Dr NWCHW CW8 .....129 G1
School Field Cl
  AUD/MAD/W CW3 .....274 F1
School Gn MALPAS SY14 .....230 C3
School La ALT WA14 .....41 K8
  AUD/MAD/W CW3 .....264 A8
  AUD/MAD/W CW3 .....266 F6
  CHD/CHDH SK8 .....65 G4
  CHNE CH2 .....123 C1
  CHNE CH2 .....146 E4
  CHSE CH3 .....146 E7
  CHSE CH3 .....211 M2
  CHSE CH3 .....215 H7
  CONG CW11 .....184 D4
  CONG CW12 .....207 H4
  DID/WITH M20 .....45 J1
  FROD/HEL WA6 .....99 J5
  FROD/HEL WA6 .....125 G7
  FROD/HEL WA6 .....126 D7
  GOL/RIS/CU WA3 .....30 C7
  GOL/RIS/CU WA3 .....40 A2
  GTS/LS CH66 .....93 M3
  HUY L36 .....32 A2
  IRL M44 .....31 K7
  IRL M44 .....31 M2
  KNUT WA16 .....105 J2
  KNUT WA16 .....134 A1
  MCFLDN SK10 .....110 F6
  MCFLDS SK11 .....136 F6
  MCFLDS SK11 .....160 C7
  MPL/ROM SK6 .....49 H1
  NANT CW5 .....20 E5
  NSTN CH64 .....91 H3
  NSTN CH64 .....91 M6
  NSTN CH64 .....92 B2
  NWCHE CW9 .....103 H1
  NWCHE CW9 .....104 D8
  NWCHE CW9 .....131 G2
  NWCHE CW9 .....153 L4
  NWCHW CW8 .....129 J8
  NWCHW CW8 .....152 A2
  POY/DIS SK12 .....68 F8
  POY/DIS SK12 .....86 F1
  RAIN/WH L35 .....33 M3
  RUNC WA7 .....75 M4
  SBCH CW11 .....181 M7
  SBCH CW11 .....202 D5
  SBCH CW11 .....203 K5
  SBCH CW11 .....204 E6
  SBCH CW11 .....205 M7
  TPLY/KEL CW6 .....216 D3
  WARRS WA4 .....76 E6
  WDN WA8 .....34 E5
  WHITCH SY13 .....260 E4
  WLTN L25 .....50 A3
School Rd EP CH65 .....10 C7
  HALE/TIMP WA15 .....61 M1
  NWCHE CW9 .....130 D6
  WARRN/WOL WA2 .....37 J3
  WILM/AE SK9 .....64 D8
  WSFD CW7 .....153 K7
  WSFD CW7 .....178 A2
School Rd North NWCHE CW9 .....130 E6
School Rd South NWCHE CW9 .....130 E6
Schools HI CHD/CHDH SK8 .....64 D1
School St BRAM/HZG SK7 .....66 E2
  CHNE CH2 .....17 K1
  CW/HAS CW1 .....222 D7
  GOL/RIS/CU WA3 .....23 G4
  NEWLW WA12 .....27 H1
  WARRS WA4 .....5 H9
School Wy NWCHE CW9 .....13 J2
  SPK/HALE L24 .....70 B1
  WDN WA8 .....53 K1
Schooner Cl RUNC WA7 .....74 D6
Science Rd SPK/HALE L24 .....50 C8
Scilly Cl EP CH65 .....121 J3
Scotch Hall La NWCHE CW9 .....102 F1
Scotland Rd WARR WA1 .....5 G6
Scotland St WHITCH SY13 .....269 M5
Scots Rd CQ CH5 .....166 D2
Scott Av CW/HAS CW1 .....19 M3
  HUY L36 .....32 A4
  RAIN/WH L35 .....32 F1
  WDN WA8 .....6 E4
Scott Cl ALS/KID ST7 .....224 E4
  MCFLDN SK10 .....139 C5
  SBCH CW11 .....203 K6
Scott Dr MPL/ROM SK6 .....49 H4
Scotthope Cl MCFLDS SK11 .....137 M6
Scotton Av GTS/LS CH66 .....94 B7
Scott Rd BURS/TUN ST6 .....243 M7
  GOL/RIS/CU WA3 .....23 K3
  MCFLDN SK10 .....112 A5
Scotts Av STHEL WA9 .....34 A1
Scott St WARRN/WOL WA2 .....5 H4
Scout Dr NTHM/RTH M23 .....43 M8
Scragg St ALS/KID ST7 .....243 M4
Scroggins La PART M31 .....31 J1
Sea Bank MWCH CW10 .....179 K3
Seabury St WARRS WA4 .....57 C1
Seacombe Dr GTS/LS CH66 .....120 E1
Seacombe Gv EDGY/DAV SK3 .....46 B4
Seaford Cl RUNC WA7 .....74 D3
Seaford Pl WARRN/WOL WA2 .....28 A8
Seagull Cl CW/HAS CW1 .....19 M2
Seahill Rd CH/BCN CH1 .....143 M4
Sealand Av CQ CH5 .....142 F5
Sealand Cl SALE M33 .....37 L5
  WARRN/WOL WA2 .....37 L5
Sealand Rd CH/BCN CH1 .....16 A3
  CQ CH5 .....143 H1
  NTHM/RTH M23 .....43 M2
Sea La RUNC WA7 .....73 K2

Seal Rd BRAM/HZG SK7 .....65 M4
Seamon's Dr ALT WA14 .....42 A6
Seamon's Rd ALT WA14 .....42 A6
Seathwaite Grove Cl RUNC WA7 .....73 L7
Seaton Cl BRAM/HZG SK7 .....66 D3
  CW/HAS CW1 .....221 H4
Seaton Pk RUNC WA7 .....74 E1
Seaton St WSFD CW7 .....178 D3
Sea Vw NSTN CH64 .....91 L8
Seaville St CHSE CH3 .....17 K4
Secker Av WARRS WA4 .....56 D2
Secker Cl WARRS WA4 .....56 D2
Second Av ALS/KID ST7 .....242 E3
  CQ CH5 .....142 F1
  CW/HAS CW1 .....19 L9
  FLINT CH6 .....116 A7
  MCFLDN SK10 .....86 D3
  NWR WA7 .....73 M4
  SBCH CW11 .....204 A7
Second Dig La CW/HAS CW5 .....252 C5
Second Wood St NANT CW5 .....20 D5
Sedbergh Cl HOLMCH CW4 .....181 G1
Sedbergh Gv RUNC WA7 .....73 L7
Sedburgh Cl SALE M33 .....42 D1
Seddon Rd ALT WA14 .....61 K2
Seddon St MWCH CW10 .....179 J2
Sedgefield Cl MCFLDN SK10 .....112 C8
Sedgefield Rd CH/BCN CH1 .....16 C3
Sedgeford WHITCH SY13 .....270 A6
Sedgeford Cl WILM/AE SK9 .....84 D3
Sedgemoor Cl CHD/CHDH SK8 .....65 H2
Sedgewick Crs
  WARRW/BUR WA5 .....26 E6
Sedgmere Av CW/HAS CW1 .....221 G4
Sedum Cl CHSE CH3 .....170 A6
Sefton Av CONG CW12 .....208 A3
  WDN WA8 .....53 G1
Sefton Dr WILM/AE SK9 .....84 C2
Sefton Rd CHNE CH2 .....146 A8
Sefton St NEWLW WA12 .....26 F1
Selborne RAIN/WH L35 .....32 F2
Selbourne Dr BURS/TUN ST6 .....243 L5
  RUNC WA7 .....54 E8
Selby Cl POY/DIS SK12 .....66 D7
  RUNC WA7 .....54 E8
Selby Gdns CHD/CHDH SK8 .....65 J6
Selby Gn GTS/LS CH66 .....94 B7
Selby St WARRW/BUR WA5 .....4 A7
Selkirk Av WARRS WA4 .....57 G1
Selkirk Cl GTS/LS CH66 .....93 M7
  MCFLDN SK10 .....137 M2
Selkirk Dr CHSW/BR CH4 .....169 G5
  HOLMCH CW4 .....181 H7
Selkirk Rd CHSW/BR CH4 .....16 B9
Seller St CH/BCN CH1 .....17 J4
Selsdon Ct CHSW/BR CH4 .....169 J5
  SALE M33 .....42 F1
Selsey Av EDGY/DAV SK3 .....45 M5
Selsey Cl CW/HAS CW1 .....221 H4
Selsey Dr DID/WITH M20 .....45 J4
Selside Rd NTHLY L27 .....51 G1
Selstead Rd WYTH/NTH M22 .....63 J3
Selworth Cl HALE/TIMP WA15 .....42 E6
  WARRS WA4 .....57 K1
Selworthy Dr CW/HAS CW1 .....221 H5
Selwyn Cl WDN WA8 .....53 K1
Selwyn Dr CHD/CHDH SK8 .....65 J5
  MCFLDS SK11 .....162 F1
Semper Cl CONG CW12 .....185 G8
Seneschal Ct RUNC WA7 .....73 L6
Senna La NWCHE CW9 .....103 H4
Sennen Cl RUNC WA7 .....74 B7
Sens Cl CH/BCN CH1 .....16 E3
Sephton Av GOL/RIS/CU WA3 .....29 L1
Serenity La CQ CH5 .....166 B8
Sergeant York Loop
  WARRW/BUR WA5 .....36 B7
Serin Cl NEWLW WA12 .....27 J1
  OFTN SK2 .....47 M8
The Serpentine CHSW/BR CH4 .....16 C9
Service St HTNM SK4 .....46 B4
Servite Cl EP CH65 .....94 F6
Sett Valley Trail NM/HAY SK22 .....69 M2
Sevenoaks Cl MCFLDN SK10 .....14 C1
Sevenoaks Rd CHD/CHDH SK8 .....45 H6
Seven Sisters La KNUT WA16 .....107 J8
Seven Stiles Dr MPL/ROM SK6 .....48 E5
Severn Cl ALT WA14 .....42 C6
  BIDD ST8 .....227 L4
  CONG CW12 .....207 M3
  WARRN/WOL WA2 .....37 L2
  WDN WA8 .....53 M1
Severn Dr BRAM/HZG SK7 .....65 J6
Severn Rd GOL/RIS/CU WA3 .....29 M2
  RAIN/WH L35 .....33 H1
Severnvale EP CH65 .....121 G1
Sewell St RUNC WA7 .....9 K3
Sextant Cl RUNC WA7 .....74 D6
Sexton Av STHEL WA9 .....42 F6
Seymour Cha KNUT WA16 .....107 G4
Seymour Dr GTS/LS CH66 .....94 E6
  WARR WA1 .....38 A5
Seymour Gv HALE/TIMP WA15 .....43 G7
  MPL/ROM SK6 .....48 E6
Seymour Rd CHD/CHDH SK8 .....65 G4
  OFTN SK2 .....47 H6
Sgt York Loop
  WARRW/BUR WA5 .....36 B6
Shackerley Av CONG CW12 .....207 M1
Shackleton Cl WARRW/BUR WA5 .....36 D4
Shadewood Crs WARRS WA4 .....57 F2
Shadewood Rd MCFLDS SK11 .....14 A9
Shadowmoss Rd
  WYTH/NTH M22 .....63 L4
Shady Brook La NWCHW CW8 .....128 C3
Shady Gv ALS/KID ST7 .....224 D8
Shady La NTHM/RTH M23 .....43 K5
Shady Oak Rd OFTN SK2 .....47 M6
Shaftesbury Av CHD/CHDH SK8 .....65 H3
  CHSE CH3 .....170 D4
  HALE/TIMP WA15 .....43 H7
  WARRW/BUR WA5 .....54 C2
Shaftesbury Rd EDGY/DAV SK3 .....46 A6
Shaftesbury Wy
  WARRW/BUR WA5 .....26 F5

Shakespeare Dr CHD/CHDH SK8 .....45 M6
  CW/HAS CW1 .....222 A8
Shakespeare Gv
  WARRN/WOL WA2 .....37 H2
Shakespeare Rd MPL/ROM SK6 .....47 L1
  NSTN CH64 .....91 L3
  STHEL WA8 .....34 A2
  WDN WA8 .....7 G1
Shakespeare Wy WHITCH SY13 .....270 C6
Shalcombe Cl HLWD L26 .....51 G5
Shalford Dr WYTH/NTH M22 .....63 K4
Shallacres EP CH65 .....94 F5
Shallcross Av CHF/WBR SK23 .....89 L8
Shallcross Mill Rd
  CHF/WBR SK23 .....89 L7
Shallcross Rd CHF/WBR SK23 .....89 L8
Shandon Av WYTH/NTH M22 .....44 D3
Shanklin Cl WARRW/BUR WA5 .....35 J6
Shannon Cl CHSW/BR CH4 .....168 E7
  NANT CW5 .....237 K7
Shannon Dr BURS/TUN ST6 .....243 H5
Shannon Rd WYTH/NTH M22 .....63 L1
Shap Av HALE/TIMP WA15 .....43 K7
Shargate Cl WILM/AE SK9 .....84 C3
Sharnbrook Dr CW/SHV CW2 .....237 L1
Sharon Park Cl WARRS WA4 .....57 J3
Sharples St HTNM SK4 .....2 E1
Sharpley St MCFLDN SK10 .....14 E2
Sharps Dr WHITCH SY13 .....269 L5
Sharp St WARRN/WOL WA2 .....5 H3
  WDN WA8 .....7 H4
Sharrington Dr NTHM/RTH M23 .....43 L6
Sharston Crs KNUT WA16 .....107 H3
Sharston Rd WYTH/NTH M22 .....44 E5
Shavington Av CHNE CH2 .....145 M8
Shavington Wy NWCHE CW9 .....129 L8
Shawbury Gv SALE M33 .....42 F2
Shawbury Rd NTHM/RTH M23 .....44 B8
Shaw Cl GTS/LS CH66 .....94 E8
Shawcross La WYTH/NTH M22 .....44 F4
Shawcross St STKP SK1 .....3 H8
Shawdene Rd WYTH/NTH M22 .....44 C4
Shaw Dr KNUT WA16 .....107 J1
Shawell Ct WDN WA8 .....53 L2
Shaw Entry WDN WA8 .....33 G5
Shaw Heath EDGY/DAV SK3 .....2 F8
Shaw Rd South
  EDGY/DAV SK3 .....46 F5
Shaw's Av WARRN/WOL WA2 .....5 H1
Shaws La MCFLDN SK10 .....111 J4
  WSFD CW7 .....153 M8
Shaw's Rd ALT WA14 .....42 D8
Shaw St BIDD ST8 .....227 J5
  GOL/RIS/CU WA3 .....30 A1
  MCFLDS SK11 .....14 F5
  RUNC WA7 .....8 F3
  WARRN/WOL WA2 .....5 G4
Shay Av HALE/TIMP WA15 .....62 E3
Shayfield Av WYTH/NTH M22 .....44 D7
Shayfield Cl WYTH/NTH M22 .....44 D7
Shayfield Rd WYTH/NTH M22 .....44 D7
Shay La CHSE CH3 .....172 E1
  HALE/TIMP WA15 .....62 D3
  MALPAS SY14 .....247 G3
Shay's La TPLY/KEL CW6 .....151 L8
Sheaf Cl CHSE CH3 .....172 C2
Shearbrook La HOLMCH CW4 .....157 K3
Sheardhall Av POY/DIS SK12 .....68 E7
Shearwater Rd OFTN SK2 .....47 M7
Sheath St NWCHE CW9 .....13 H2
Shed La CHSE CH3 .....170 A2
Sheepfield Cl GTS/LS CH66 .....94 C5
Sheerwater Cl WARR WA1 .....37 M5
Sheffield Cl WARRW/BUR WA5 .....36 C7
Sheffield St HTNM SK4 .....2 F1
Sheiling Ct ALT WA14 .....42 C8
The Sheilings
  GOL/RIS/CU WA3 .....23 M4
Shelagh Av WDN WA8 .....7 H3
Shelbourne Ms MCFLDN SK10 .....137 M4
Shelburne Dr CW/HAS CW1 .....222 C7
Sheldon Av CHSE CH3 .....170 B2
  CONG CW12 .....208 A3
Sheldon Cl PART M31 .....40 F1
Sheldon Rd BRAM/HZG SK7 .....66 E5
  POY/DIS SK12 .....87 J2
Sheldrake Gv NSTN CH64 .....91 L7
Sheldrake Rd ALT WA14 .....42 B4
Sheldwich Cl LEIGH WN7 .....24 F1
  LEIGH WN7 .....24 F1
Shelford Rd BURS/TUN ST6 .....243 K6
Shelley Av NWCHE CW9 .....104 F7
Shelley Cl ALS/KID ST7 .....224 E4
  ALS/KID ST7 .....243 G4
  CW/HAS CW1 .....19 L3
  MWCH CW10 .....179 L2
Shelley Ct CHD/CHDH SK8 .....65 G3
  SBCH CW11 .....203 K6
Shelley Dr CW/SHV CW2 .....237 M3
Shelley Gv WARRS WA4 .....37 M8
Shelley Pl RAIN/WH L35 .....32 F1
Shelley Rd CH/BCN CH1 .....144 F7
  WDN WA8 .....7 G2
Shelley St STHEL WA9 .....34 B2
Shellow La MCFLDS SK11 .....161 J7
Shellway Rd EP CH65 .....122 A1
Shelton Cl WDN WA8 .....53 M1
Shenhurst Cl WILM/AE SK9 .....83 L8
Shentonfield Rd
  WYTH/NTH M22 .....44 E6
Shenton Park Av SALE M33 .....42 C5
Shepcroft La WARRS WA4 .....76 C2
Shepherds Fold Dr WSFD CW7 .....177 J1
Shepherd's La CHNE CH2 .....145 K7
Shepherd St BIDD ST8 .....227 J5
Shepley Cl BRAM/HZG SK7 .....66 D4
Shepley Dr BRAM/HZG SK7 .....66 D3
Shepley La MPL/ROM SK6 .....48 F8
Sheppard Cl CW/HAS CW1 .....19 H3
Sheppenhall Gv NANT CW5 .....262 C3
Sheppenhall La NANT CW5 .....262 C3
Shepperton Ct WARRS WA4 .....56 D6
Shepsides Cl GTS/LS CH66 .....120 C1
Shepton Dr NTHM/RTH M23 .....63 C2
Shepton Rd GTS/LS CH66 .....120 E2
  NTHM/RTH M23 .....43 M7
Sheraton Rd CHSE CH3 .....171 H7

Sherborne Av WLTN L25 .....50 D4
Sherborne Rd RUNC WA7 .....74 F1
Sherborne Rd CW/HAS CW1 .....221 K6
  EDGY/DAV SK3 .....46 A5
Sherbourne Av CHSW/BR CH4 .....169 H7
Sherbourne Cl CHD/CHDH SK8 .....65 H6
Sherbourne Rd EP CH65 .....121 J3
  MCFLDS SK11 .....137 M5
Sherbourne Wy
  WARRW/BUR WA5 .....26 F6
Sherbrook Cl SALE M33 .....42 F1
Sherbrooke Rd POY/DIS SK12 .....68 D6
Sherbrook Ri WILM/AE SK9 .....84 C6
Sherford Cl BRAM/HZG SK7 .....66 A2
Sheridan Av GOL/RIS/CU WA3 .....23 K5
Sheridan Cl CW/HAS CW1 .....221 H3
Sheri Dr NEWLW WA12 .....27 K2
Sheringham Cl
  CHSW/BR CH4 .....168 E7
Sheringham Dr CW/HAS CW1 .....221 H5
Sheringham Rd
  WARRW/BUR WA5 .....35 L6
Sherman Dr RAIN/WH L35 .....33 K3
Sherratt Cl CONG CW12 .....207 L2
Sherrington's La CHSE CH3 .....231 K4
Sherrymill Hl WHITCH SY13 .....269 M4
Sherway Dr HALE/TIMP WA15 .....43 J6
Sherwin St CW/SHV CW2 .....18 F8
Sherwood Av HTNM SK4 .....46 A3
Sherwood Cl MPL/ROM SK6 .....48 F8
  WDN WA8 .....52 C3
Sherwood Crs
  WARRW/BUR WA5 .....26 E6
  LEIGH WN7 .....25 H2
Sherwood Rd CH/BCN CH1 .....144 E7
  MCFLDS SK11 .....138 D7
  NWCHE CW10 .....179 L6
Shetland Cl WARRN/WOL WA2 .....28 E8
  WDN WA8 .....53 L1
Shetland Dr EP CH65 .....121 J3
Shevington Cl WDN WA8 .....53 L1
Shevington Gdns
  NTHM/RTH M23 .....44 B3
Shield St EDGY/DAV SK3 .....2 E1
Shiers Dr CHD/CHDH SK8 .....45 L8
Shiggins Cl WARRW/BUR WA5 .....36 D6
Shillingford Cl WARRS WA4 .....56 E7
Shilton Cl MWCH CW10 .....179 L6
  NWCHE CW9 .....154 B1
Shipgate St CH/BCN CH1 .....17 G7
Ship St FROD/HEL WA6 .....99 J2
Shipton Cl WARRW/BUR WA5 .....36 B3
  WDN WA8 .....52 D1
Shiredale Cl CHD/CHDH SK8 .....46 B8
Shirley Av CHD/CHDH SK8 .....64 C6
  MPL/ROM SK6 .....48 E8
Shirley Cl BRAM/HZG SK7 .....66 C2
Shirley Dr WARRS WA4 .....57 G2
Shirley Gv EDGY/DAV SK3 .....46 E7
Shirleys Cl MCFLDN SK10 .....112 A6
Shirleys Dr MCFLDN SK10 .....112 A6
Shocklach Rd CHNE CH2 .....145 M6
Shone Av WYTH/NTH M22 .....63 M2
Shones Cft NSTN CH64 .....92 A7
Shop La TPLY/KEL CW6 .....175 M2
Shordley Cl WRX/GR/LL L12 .....210 C5
Shoreham Dr WARRW/BUR WA5 .....55 G1
Shores Green Dr NWCHE CW9 .....104 F7
Shores La NANT CW5 .....235 K5
Short Cl NEWLW WA12 .....26 E1
Shortland Crs BNG/LEV M19 .....45 K1
Short St BRAM/HZG SK7 .....66 E2
  GOL/RIS/CU WA3 .....23 H3
  HTNM SK4 .....2 E1
  NEWLW WA12 .....26 E1
  WDN WA8 .....53 G7
Short St East HTNM SK4 .....2 F2
Shorwell Cl WARRW/BUR WA5 .....35 J5
Shorwell Gv BURS/TUN ST6 .....243 L4
Shotwick La CH/BCN CH1 .....119 H8
Shotwick Rd CQ CH5 .....118 E8
Shrewbridge Crs NANT CW5 .....20 E7
Shrewbridge Rd NANT CW5 .....20 D9
Shrewsbury Gdns
  CHD/CHDH SK8 .....65 J6
Shrewsbury Rd SALE M33 .....43 G2
Shrewsbury St WARRS WA4 .....56 D1
Shrewsbury Wy
  CHSW/BR CH4 .....168 F6
Shrigley Cl WILM/AE SK9 .....84 D3
Shrigley Ri MCFLDN SK10 .....113 J3
Shrigley Rd MCFLDN SK10 .....87 H8
  POY/DIS SK12 .....87 J2
Shropshire Cl MWCH CW10 .....179 J4
  WARR WA1 .....38 E6
Shropshire La WHITCH SY13 .....271 K3
Shropshire Rd EP CH65 .....121 M1
Shropshire Wy WHITCH SY13 .....259 K5
  WHITCH SY13 .....269 J8
Shuldham Cl KNUT WA16 .....59 J8
Shurlach Rd NWCHE CW9 .....130 D7
Shutley La NWCHW CW8 .....102 D7
Sibbersfield La CHSE CH3 .....211 M8
Sibell St CH/BCN CH1 .....17 J3
Sibley Rd HTNM SK4 .....46 B1
Sidcup Rd NTHM/RTH M23 .....43 M7
Siddall St NWCHE CW9 .....13 M2
Siddeley Cl CHSW/BR CH4 .....167 J8
Siddeley Dr NEWLW WA12 .....26 F1
Siddington Av EDGY/DAV SK3 .....46 C6
  NWCHE CW9 .....130 A8
Siddington Bank MCFLDS SK11 .....159 M1
Siddington Rd POY/DIS SK12 .....86 F2
  WILM/AE SK9 .....64 D7
Siddorn St WSFD CW7 .....177 L3
Siddow Common LEIGH WN7 .....25 G1
Side Av ALT WA14 .....61 J3
Side End La CHF/WBR SK23 .....114 F1
Side La TPLY/KEL CW6 .....172 E6
Sidlaw Cl GTS/LS CH66 .....94 B7
Sidmouth Cl WARRW/BUR WA5 .....35 L3
Sidmouth Gv CHD/CHDH SK8 .....64 F5
Sidney Rd NSTN CH64 .....91 M3
Siemens Rd IRL M44 .....31 L7
Sienna Cl IRL M44 .....31 L3
Silcock St GOL/RIS/CU WA3 .....23 G4
Silk Hl CHF/WBR SK23 .....89 M4

Silk Mill St KNUT WA16 .....107 G2
The Silk Rd MCFLDN SK10 .....15 H4
  MCFLDN SK10 .....112 C6
  MCFLDS SK11 .....15 H5
Silkstone Crs RUNC WA7 .....74 B5
Silk St CONG CW12 .....207 G2
Silsden Av GTS/LS CH66 .....24 B4
  SALE M33 .....42 D2
Silverbirch Cft
  CHSW/BR CH4 .....190 B1
Silverbirch Wy GTS/LS CH66 .....120 F4
Silver Cl BIDD ST8 .....227 J4
Silverdale NWCHW CW8 .....12 D4
Silverdale Cl FROD/HEL WA6 .....99 J5
  MPL/ROM SK6 .....67 L4
Silverdale Rd CHD/CHDH SK8 .....45 H8
  NEWLW WA12 .....22 B8
  WARRS WA4 .....56 B2
Silvergate Ct CONG CW12 .....207 L4
Silver La GOL/RIS/CU WA3 .....30 A5
Silvermine Cl ALS/KID ST7 .....243 H2
Silverne Dr EP CH65 .....121 G2
Silverstone Crs BURS/TUN ST6 .....243 L5
Silver St MCFLDN SK10 .....113 H4
  WARRN/WOL WA2 .....5 G4
Silverwood ALS/KID ST7 .....243 H3
Simkin Av WARRS WA4 .....57 M8
Simons Cl RAIN/WH L35 .....32 C4
  SALE M33 .....43 G1
Simonside WDN WA8 .....52 C2
Simons La FROD/HEL WA6 .....99 H6
Simonstone Rd CHSW/BR CH4 .....167 K8
Simonsway NTHM/RTH M23 .....63 G1
  WYTH/NTH M22 .....63 H1
Simonswood Cl
  MWCH CW10 .....179 H4
Simpson Ct CW/HAS CW1 .....221 G3
Simpson La MCFLDN SK10 .....87 K5
Simpson Rd CHNE CH2 .....145 J4
Simpson St EDGY/DAV SK3 .....2 F8
  WILM/AE SK9 .....83 M8
Simpsons Wy CHSW/BR CH4 .....190 B1
Sinclair Av ALS/KID ST7 .....241 H1
  WARRN/WOL WA2 .....37 H2
  WDN WA8 .....6 F4
Sinderland La ALT WA14 .....41 J3
  LYMM WA13 .....41 H4
Sinderland Rd ALT WA14 .....41 J3
  PART M31 .....41 J1
Singapore Av MANAIR M90 .....63 G4
Singleton Av CW/HAS CW1 .....221 J6
Singleton Rd EP CH65 .....94 F8
Siskin Cl NEWLW WA12 .....27 J1
Siskin Rd OFTN SK2 .....47 M8
Sitch La NM/HAY SK22 .....69 M1
Six Acre Gdns WARRS WA4 .....55 G7
Six Acre La RUNC WA7 .....55 G7
Sixth Av CQ CH5 .....142 E3
  FLINT CH6 .....116 A7
Skeath Cl SBCH CW11 .....204 D6
Skeffington RAIN/WH L35 .....32 E2
Skellern St ALS/KID ST7 .....242 D2
Skellorn Green La MCFLDN SK10 .....86 F4
Skelton Rd ALT WA14 .....42 A4
Skiddaw Cl RUNC WA7 .....74 A8
Skip's La CHSE CH3 .....170 E5
Skipton Cl BRAM/HZG SK7 .....66 C4
Skipton Dr GTS/LS CH66 .....94 C8
Skipton Rd HUY L36 .....32 B3
Skye Cl EP CH65 .....121 J3
  WDN WA8 .....53 L1
Skye Cft MPL/ROM SK6 .....48 D1
Skylark Cl CW/HAS CW1 .....220 F5
Slacken La ALS/KID ST7 .....242 D2
Slack La CQ CH5 .....166 B7
Slack St MCFLDS SK11 .....15 J9
  MCFLDN SK10 .....138 F2
Slade La KNUT WA16 .....81 M5
  MCFLDN SK10 .....110 C7
Slade St NWCHE CW9 .....13 M2
Slag La GOL/RIS/CU WA3 .....23 M2
Slaidburn Crs
  GOL/RIS/CU WA3 .....22 F2
Slater St BIDD ST8 .....227 J5
  MCFLDS SK11 .....14 E8
  WARRS WA4 .....5 K9
Sleddale Cl OFTN SK2 .....47 K7
Sledmoor Rd NTHM/RTH M23 .....43 M3
Sleeper's Wy MCFLDS SK11 .....139 L5
Simmonds Cl NWCHE CW9 .....153 L5
Slutchers La WARR WA1 .....4 F9
Small Av WARRN/WOL WA2 .....37 J2
Smallbrook Rd WHITCH SY13 .....269 L5
Small Crs WARRN/WOL WA2 .....37 J2
Small La KNUT WA16 .....81 M4
Smallman Rd CW/SHV CW2 .....18 D9
Smallshaw Cl AIMK WN4 .....22 A3
Smethwick La SBCH CW11 .....182 E8
Smith Child St BURS/TUN ST6 .....243 M3
Smith Cl ALS/KID ST7 .....224 B8
Smith Crs WARRN/WOL WA2 .....37 K4
Smith Dr WARRN/WOL WA2 .....37 K4
Smithfield Dr WRXS/E LL13 .....228 D4
Smithfield La SBCH CW11 .....204 C6
Smithfields CHSE CH3 .....214 C2
Smithfield St WRXS/E LL13 .....228 D4
Smith Gv CW/HAS CW1 .....220 F6
Smithills Cl GOL/RIS/CU WA3 .....29 K7
Smith La KNUT WA16 .....81 L3
  MCFLDN SK10 .....114 A7
Smith Rd WDN WA8 .....52 C3
Smith's La NWCHW CW8 .....128 C3
Smiths Lawn WILM/AE SK9 .....84 A7
Smith St CHD/CHDH SK8 .....45 M6
  MCFLDS SK11 .....15 H9
  WARR WA1 .....5 H7
Smithy Bank WSFD CW7 .....200 A1
Smithy Brow GOL/RIS/CU WA3 .....28 F5
  MCFLDN SK10 .....113 J4
Smithy Cl CH/BCN CH1 .....144 A3
  NSTN CH64 .....92 A8
  WDN WA8 .....33 J6
Smithy La ALT WA14 .....60 D1
  BIDD ST8 .....227 K2
  CHSE CH3 .....148 F2
  CONG CW12 .....184 B5
  CW/HAS CW1 .....220 E4

CW/SHV CW2 ... 239 J7
CW/SHV CW2 ... 240 D6
FROD/HEL WA6 ... 98 C7
FROD/HEL WA6 ... 126 B2
GOL/RIS/CU WA3 ... 29 C5
MALPAS SY14 ... 258 A2
MCFLDN SK10 ... 111 J2
MCFLDN SK10 ... 113 L7
MCFLDS SK11 ... 186 E6
MPL/ROM SK6 ... 49 M3
NSTN CH64 ... 93 G4
NWCHE CW9 ... 104 A4
NWCHE CW9 ... 131 G2
NWCHW CW8 ... 102 B6
NWCHW CW8 ... 128 A7
PART M31 ... 40 F1
TPLY/KEL CW6 ... 174 B6
WDN WA8 ... 33 J7
Smithy Pathway
  CHSW/BR CH4 ... 168 F8 [8]
Smithy St BRAM/HZG SK7 ... 66 D1 [13]
The Smithy WRX/GR/LL LL12 ... 210 B5 [8]
Smithy Wk SBCH CW11 ... 222 F1
Smokehall La NWCHE CW9 ... 153 M6
Smokey La WHITCH SY13 ... 268 B4
Smokies Wy BIDD ST8 ... 227 J3
Smyth Rd WDN WA8 ... 53 K2
Snab La NSTN CH64 ... 91 M8
Snabwood Cl NSTN CH64 ... 91 L7
Snape La CW/SHV CW2 ... 239 K8
Snape Rd CW/SHV CW2 ... 238 D4
  MCFLDN SK10 ... 138 E2
Snelson La KNUT WA16 ... 134 D1
  KNUT WA16 ... 134 C1
Sneyd Pl BURS/TUN ST6 ... 243 J6
Snipe Cl POY/DIS SK12 ... 86 A1
Snowberry Cl WDN WA8 ... 34 E8
Snowdon Cl GTS/LS CH66 ... 94 A6
  WARRW/BUR WA5 ... 35 L6 [7]
Snowdon Cresent
  CHSW/BR CH4 ... 169 G7 [2]
Snowdon Dr CW/SHV CW2 ... 237 K1
Snowdonia Wy WSFD CW7 ... 177 H5 [1]
Snowdon St NWCHW CW8 ... 128 C1
Snowdrop Cl RUNC WA7 ... 73 M8
Snow HI MCFLDS SK11 ... 15 J8
Soane Cl AIMK WN4 ... 22 D1
Solly Crs CONG CW12 ... 207 G2
Solvay Rd NWCHW CW8 ... 129 K2
Solway Cl WARRN/WOL WA2 ... 28 F8
Solway Gv RUNC WA7 ... 73 K7
Solway Rd WYTH/NTH M22 ... 44 E8
Somerby Dr WYTH/NTH M22 ... 63 J3 [11]
Somerford Av CW/SHV CW2 ... 18 A6
Somerford Cl SBCH CW11 ... 204 C4 [1]
Somerford Rd CHSW/BR CH4 ... 167 J8
Somerley Cl CW/HAS CW1 ... 221 H4
Somerset Av ALS/KID ST7 ... 242 F2
Somerset Cl CONG CW12 ... 184 D8
  IRL M44 ... 31 K6 [1]
Somerset Rd ALT WA14 ... 42 D6 [1]
  CHNE CH2 ... 145 M7
Somerset St CHNE CH2 ... 17 G2
Somerset Wy WARR WA1 ... 38 B4
Somerton Av SALE M33 ... 43 J1 [1]
  WYTH/NTH M22 ... 63 J1 [1]
Somerton Rd MCFLDS SK11 ... 137 M6
Somerville Cl KNUT WA16 ... 59 J8
  NSTN CH64 ... 91 L7
Somerville Crs EP CH65 ... 95 J8
Somerville Gdns
  HALE/TIMP WA15 ... 42 F5 [1]
Somerville Rd WDN WA8 ... 6 B5
Somerville St CW/SHV CW2 ... 18 D8
Soot HI NWCHW CW8 ... 129 J1
Sorbus Cl CHNE CH2 ... 123 J1 [1]
Sorbus Dr CW/HAS CW1 ... 221 L6
Sorrel Cl CHSE CH3 ... 170 A6
  WARRN/WOL WA2 ... 38 C2
Sossmoss La MCFLDN SK10 ... 109 K6
Soudan Rd OFTN SK2 ... 47 G6
Sound La NANT CW5 ... 250 D6
Souter's La CH/BCN CH1 ... 17 H6
South Acre Rd MCFLDS SK11 ... 139 C5
  WILM/AE SK9 ... 84 D1
Southampton Wy RUNC WA7 ... 74 E6 [1]
South Av CHNE CH2 ... 17 J2
  CW/HAS CW1 ... 222 D8
  LEIGH WN7 ... 25 J1
  WARRN/WOL WA2 ... 5 H2
  WARRS WA4 ... 56 C3
South Bank CH/BCN CH1 ... 145 J8
  CQ CH5 ... 142 B8 [2]
Southbank NWCHE CW9 ... 104 A5
Southbank Av CW/SHV CW2 ... 238 C7
South Bank Cl WILM/AE SK9 ... 110 E3
South Bank Rd CW CONG CW12 ... 207 M2
South Bank Ter RUNC WA7 ... 72 C1
South Cheshire Wy
  ALS/KID ST7 ... 224 E3
  CW/SHV CW2 ... 253 M2
  NANT CW5 ... 253 K6
  NANT CW5 ... 262 A2
  WHITCH SY13 ... 260 D7
South Cl TPLY/KEL CW6 ... 197 J2
  WILM/AE SK9 ... 83 M6
South Crescent Rd
  CHSW/BR CH4 ... 17 J7
South Cft TPLY/KEL CW6 ... 216 D6 [1]
South Crofts NANT CW5 ... 20 F6
South Dl WARRW/BUR WA5 ... 35 M7
Southdale Rd WARR WA1 ... 38 A5
Southdown Cl CHD/CHDH SK8 ... 64 F4 [1]
Southdown Crs CHD/CHDH SK8 ... 64 F4 [1]
South Downs KNUT WA16 ... 107 J3
South Downs Dr ALT WA14 ... 61 K4
South Downs Rd ALT WA14 ... 61 J3
South Dr CHD/CHDH SK8 ... 45 G8
  HALE/TIMP WA15 ... 43 G5
  KNUT WA16 ... 132 A1
  NWCHE CW9 ... 130 C4
Southern Cl BRAM/HZG SK7 ... 65 M2
Southern Crs BRAM/HZG SK7 ... 65 M3
Southern Rd SPK/HALE L24 ... 70 E2 [8]
Southern St WARRS WA4 ... 56 C3
Southey Cl SBCH CW11 ... 203 K7 [8]

WDN WA8 ... 6 E4
Southfield MCFLDN SK10 ... 112 A8
Southfield Rd GTS/LS CH66 ... 94 C6 [2]
Southfields KNUT WA16 ... 107 J1
Southfields Av
  WARRW/BUR WA5 ... 35 M6 [3]
Southfields Cl NANT CW5 ... 253 C4 [1]
Southfields Dr
  HALE/TIMP WA15 ... 43 H5 [9]
South Front RAIN/WH L35 ... 32 E4
South Gn CO CH5 ... 143 C6
South Gv SALE M33 ... 43 H1
  WILM/AE SK9 ... 110 A3 [9]
South Hill Rd FROD/HEL WA6 ... 124 C1
Southlands HOLMCH CW4 ... 181 J3
Southlands Av
  WARRW/BUR WA5 ... 54 F1 [9]
Southlands Ms RUNC WA7 ... 8 F6
Southlands Rd CONG CW12 ... 208 A3
Southlands Vw HOLMCH CW4 ... 157 L3
South La WDN WA8 ... 34 E7
South Manor Wy WLTN L25 ... 50 C3
South Md POY/DIS SK12 ... 66 B7
South Meade HALE/TIMP WA15 ... 43 C5
South Meadway MPL/ROM SK6... 67 M5
Southmoor Rd NTHM/RTH M23 ... 43 M5
South Oak La WILM/AE SK9 ... 83 M6
South Pde BRAM/HZG SK7 ... 65 M2
  RUNC WA7 ... 8 A8
  SPK/HALE L24 ... 70 E2
South Park Dr POY/DIS SK12 ... 66 E8
South Park Rd CHD/CHDH SK8... 45 H6
  MCFLDS SK11 ... 14 F7
South Pier Rd EP CH65 ... 11 G3
Southpool Cl BRAM/HZG SK7 ... 66 A2 [3]
Southport St STHEL WA9 ... 26 A1
South Rd ALT WA14 ... 61 J2
  EP CH65 ... 121 J1 [8]
  SPK/HALE L24 ... 51 C8
  CHSE CH3 ... 170 A3
  CW/SHV CW2 ... 19 H8
  WDN WA8 ... 7 J4
  WILM/AE SK9 ... 110 A3
South View MCFLDS SK11 ... 161 K2
South View Gdns
  CHD/CHDH SK8 ... 64 C1
South View La WSFD CW7 ... 218 F2
South Vw CH/BCN CH1 ... 16 C4
  WSFD CW7 ... 177 G4 [8]
South Wy CH/BCN CH1 ... 144 E8
Southway ALT WA14 ... 42 E6 [1]
  RUNC WA7 ... 73 L5
  WDN WA8 ... 6 A4
Southway Av WARRS WA4 ... 56 D5
Southwell Cl GOL/RIS/CU WA3 ... 23 J4 [8]
  MPL/ROM SK6 ... 48 A3
South West Av MCFLDN SK10 ... 112 F5
Southwick Rd NTHM/RTH M23 ... 44 A2
Southwood Av RUNC WA7 ... 74 C2 [8]
Southwood Rd OFTN SK2 ... 47 M8
Southworth Av
  WARRW/BUR WA5 ... 36 F4
Southworth La
  WARRN/WOL WA2 ... 28 D5
Southworth Rd NEWLW WA12 ... 22 F8
Sovereign Cl GOL/RIS/CU WA3 ... 23 L5 [8]
  NWCHE CW9 ... 130 E6
  RUNC WA7 ... 74 D5 [3]
Sovereign Ct GOL/RIS/CU WA3 .. 29 J8 [8]
Sovereign Wy CHD/CHDH SK8 ... 64 C7
Spalding Dr NTHM/RTH M23 ... 63 G2 [8]
Sparkford Av NTHM/RTH M23 ... 43 K3
Spark Hall Cl WARRS WA4 ... 76 E2
Spark La RUNC WA7 ... 73 M3
  SBCH CW11 ... 205 J3
Spark Rd NTHM/RTH M23 ... 43 M5
Sparks Cl CHSE CH3 ... 170 B5 [8]
Sparrowbutts Gv
  ALS/KID ST7 ... 243 J2 [8]
Sparrowhawk Cl HLWD L26 ... 50 E3 [8]
  RUNC WA7 ... 74 A5
Sparrow La KNUT WA16... 107 H3
Sparthfield Rd HTNM SK4 ... 2 C2
Spath La HTNM SK4 ... 2 C2
Spath La East CHD/CHDH SK8 ... 65 H7
Spath Rd DID/WITH M20 ... 45 G1
Spath Wk CHD/CHDH SK8 ... 65 H7
Spawell Cl GOL/RIS/CU WA3 ... 23 L3
Speakman Av NEWLW WA12 ... 22 B7
Speakman St RUNC WA7 ... 8 F1
Spedding Wy BIDD ST8 ... 227 L4 [8]
Speed's Wy CHSE CH3 ... 228 E2
Speedwell Cl CHSE CH3 ... 170 F4 [8]
  GOL/RIS/CU WA3 ... 23 L4 [10]
Speke Bvd SPK/HALE L24 ... 50 C8
Speke Church Rd SPK/HALE L24 .. 70 B1
Speke Hall Av SPK/HALE L24 ... 50 B8
Speke Hall Rd SPK/HALE L24 ... 50 B7
  WLTN L25 ... 50 B6
Speke Rd HLWD L26 ... 51 H6
  WDN WA8 ... 51 M5
  WLTN L25 ... 50 B3
Speke Town La SPK/HALE L24 ... 50 B8
Spencer Brook MCFLDN SK10... 111 M6
Spencer Cl ALS/KID ST7 ... 223 M8
  CW/SHV CW2 ... 238 A4
  WDN WA8 ... 6 E3 [8]
Spencer St NWCHW CW8 ... 12 F5
Spenlow LEIGH WN7 ... 25 J1
Spenlow Cl MCFLDN SK10 ... 86 E3
Spennymoor Ct RUNC WA7 ... 73 L5 [8]
Spenser Rd NSTN CH64 ... 91 L6 [2]
Spey Cl ALT WA14 ... 42 C6 [8]
  WSFD CW7 ... 177 M2
Spey Dr ALS/KID ST7 ... 243 J2
Spindus Rd SPK/HALE L24 ... 70 A1
Spink La KNUT WA16 ... 105 L6
Spinnerbottom NM/HAY SK22... 69 M2
Spinner Crs NWCHE CW9 ... 103 K5 [8]
Spinners La POY/DIS SK12 ... 66 B8
Spinners Wy MCFLDN SK10 ... 112 F5

Spinney Av HOLMCH CW4 ... 157 M3
  WDN WA8 ... 52 A3
Spinney Cl WSFD CW7 ... 178 A4 [8]
Spinney Dr CW/SHV CW2 ... 239 H7
  GTS/LS CH66 ... 120 D2
  SALE M33 ... 42 D1
Spinney End CHSE CH3 ... 214 A3
Spinney Gdns WARRS WA4 ... 57 H8
Spinney La KNUT WA16 ... 106 E2
Spinney Md MCFLDN SK10 ... 15 K1
The Spinney ALS/KID ST7 ... 225 L8 [8]
  CHD/CHDH SK8 ... 64 E1
  FROD/HEL WA6 ... 126 E7
  NANT CW5 ... 237 K6 [2]
  NSTN CH64 ... 91 K4
  NWCHW CW8 ... 127 K7
  SBCH CW11 ... 204 C6
Spion Kop AIMK WN4 ... 22 A1
Spirewood Gdns
  MPL/ROM SK6 ... 48 A3 [3]
Spital Wk CHSE CH3 ... 17 M5
Spodegreen La ALT WA14 ... 60 C4
Spout La KNUT WA16 ... 82 B8
Spragg St CONG CW12 ... 207 L1
Spring Av GTS/LS CH66 ... 94 C6
Spring Bank ALS/KID ST7 ... 226 A5
Springbank MCFLDN SK10 ... 112 E5
Springbank Cl RUNC WA7 ... 73 H6
Springbank Crs WSFD CW7 ... 177 H7
Spring Bank Pl EDGY/DAV SK3 ... 2 F7 [8]
Spring Bank Rd NM/HAY SK22 ... 69 J4
Springbourne FROD/HEL WA6 ... 99 K6
Spring Cl ALS/KID ST7 ... 224 E4
Springcroft NSTN CH64 ... 91 J3
Springdale Gdns DID/WITH M20 ... 45 G1
Springe La NANT CW5 ... 235 G7
Springfield Av
  BRAM/HZG SK7 ... 66 D1 [13]
  FROD/HEL WA6 ... 124 B1
  GOL/RIS/CU WA3 ... 22 F4 [8]
  LYMM WA13 ... 40 B7
  MALPAS SY14 ... 258 B1
  MPL/ROM SK6 ... 48 F6 [8]
  WARR WA1 ... 37 M4
  WARRS WA4 ... 57 H1
Springfield Cl CHSW/BR CH4 ... 190 A5
Springfield Crs NWCHW CW8 ... 129 G1 [8]
Springfield Dr CHNE CH2 ... 145 L8
  CW/SHV CW2 ... 237 M5
  WILM/AE SK9 ... 83 K7
Springfield Gv BIDD ST8 ... 227 K5 [8]
Springfield La IRL M44 ... 31 M2
Springfield Rd ALT WA14 ... 42 D7
  BIDD ST8 ... 227 K5
  CHD/CHDH SK8 ... 45 H7
  KNUT WA16 ... 81 M8
  MALPAS SY14 ... 258 B1
  MCFLDS SK11 ... 137 M4
  WDN WA8 ... 52 A4
Springfields CHNE CH2 ... 146 E4
  KNUT WA16 ... 107 J1 [8]
  MCFLDN SK10 ... 112 A5
  NWCHW CW8 ... 127 K8 [8]
Springfields Dr CONG CW12 ... 207 K1 [8]
Spring Gdns BRAM/HZG SK7 ... 66 D1
  CW/HAS CW1 ... 19 J2
  GTS/LS CH66 ... 94 C6
  HALE/TIMP WA15 ... 43 J7
  MCFLDN SK10 ... 15 G2
  NANT CW5 ... 21 G7
  STKP SK1 ... 3 J6
Springhead Cl ALS/KID ST7 ... 242 D6
Springhill MCFLDN SK10 ... 139 G3
Spring HI TPLY/KEL CW6 ... 197 J4
Springholm Dr WARRS WA4 ... 76 D1
Spring La CHSE CH3 ... 212 D6
  GOL/RIS/CU WA3 ... 29 H6
  LYMM WA13 ... 59 L1
Spring Meadow NWCHW CW8 ... 12 E1
Springmount
  GOL/RIS/CU WA3 ... 23 L5 [8]
Spring Mt NM/HAY SK22 ... 69 J4 [8]
Spring Rd ALT WA14 ... 61 K2
  POY/DIS SK12 ... 86 F2
The Springs ALT WA14 ... 61 H2
Spring St CONG CW12 ... 207 L2
  CQ CH5 ... 142 A5
  WDN WA8 ... 7 H8
  WILM/AE SK9 ... 84 A5
Spring V BRAM/HZG SK7 ... 66 E2 [8]
Springwell Cl CW/SHV CW2... 238 C4
Springwood Av NANT CW5 ... 107 J1
Springwood Cl CH/BCN CH1 ... 144 C8
Springwood Crs MPL/ROM SK6 ... 48 E2
Springwood La MPL/ROM SK6... 48 F2
Springwood Wy MCFLDN SK10 ... 112 D7
Sprink La CONG CW12 ... 185 K7
Sproston Rd BURS/TUN ST6 ... 243 M7
Sproston Wy NWCHE CW9 ... 129 L8 [8]
Spruce Cl GOL/RIS/CU WA3 ... 23 M5
  WARR WA1 ... 38 E5
Spruce Gv ALS/KID ST7 ... 224 F5
Spuley La MCFLDN SK10 ... 113 K1
Spunhill Av GTS/LS CH66 ... 120 C1
Spurling Rd WARRW/BUR WA5... 26 F6
Spurston Cl KNUT WA16 ... 59 J8 [8]
Square St MCFLDS SK11 ... 15 J9 [8]
The Square CHSE CH3 ... 170 E4
  HTNM SK4 ... 2 A2
  NSTN CH64 ... 91 H3
Squires Wy WDN WA8 ... 7 G4
Squirrel Cl NWCHW CW8 ... 12 B5
Squirrel La ALT WA14 ... 42 C4
Squirrel Hayes Av BIDD ST8 ... 227 L6
Squirrels Cha MCFLDN SK10 ... 111 M7 [8]
Squirrel's Jump WILM/AE SK9... 110 B3
Stable La CHSE CH3 ... 149 G1
  TPLY/KEL CW6 ... 174 F3
The Stablings WILM/AE SK9 ... 84 A7
Stadium Wy CH/BCN CH1 ... 16 B7
Stadmorslow La ALS/KID ST7 ... 226 F8
Stafford Cl MCFLDN SK10 ... 137 M2 [8]
Stafford Rd CQ CH5 ... 142 F5 [8]
  WARRS WA4 ... 56 C2

Staffordshire Moorlands Wks
  BIDD ST8 ... 208 D8
  CONG CW12 ... 227 G1
Staffordshire Wy ALS/KID ST7 ... 226 E4
Stafford St AUD/MAD/W CW3 ... 264 A8
  CW/HAS CW1 ... 18 E2
  NM/HAY SK22 ... 69 J3
Stage La LYMM WA15 ... 40 D8
Stags Leap WHITCH SY13 ... 269 L4
Stainburne Rd OFTN SK2 ... 47 K6
Staines Cl WARRS WA4 ... 56 E7
Stainmoor Ct OFTN SK2 ... 47 K6 [8]
Stainmore Cl GOL/RIS/CU WA3 ... 30 B6
Stainton Cl HLWD L26 ... 50 E4 [8]
Staithes Rd WYTH/NTH M22 ... 63 K4
Stalbridge Rd CW/SHV CW2 ... 18 F7
Stalmine Av CHD/CHDH SK8 ... 64 B3 [1]
Stamford Av ALT WA14 ... 42 A6
  CW/SHV CW2 ... 18 E6
Stamford Cl MCFLDS SK11 ... 138 C8
  NWCHE CW9 ... 12 F9
Stamford Ct LYMM WA13 ... 58 F1 [3]
Stamford La CHSE CH3 ... 171 H2
Stamford New Rd ALT WA14 ... 42 D8
Stamford Park Rd
  HALE/TIMP WA15 ... 61 J1
Stamford Rd ALT WA14 ... 60 B2
  ALT WA14 ... 61 H2
  CH/BCN CH1 ... 144 E6
  MCFLDS SK11 ... 138 C7 [8]
  WILM/AE SK9 ... 84 A3
  WILM/AE SK9 ... 110 A3
Stamford St ALT WA14 ... 42 D7
  EP CH65 ... 10 F9
Stamford Wy ALT WA14 ... 42 D7
Stamp Av CW/HAS CW1 ... 221 K6
Stancliffe Rd WYTH/NTH M22 ... 44 E7
Stancross Rd NTHM/RTH M23 ... 43 J3
Standford Dr NWCHE CW9 ... 13 J9
Stanford Crs WLTN L25 ... 50 D4
Stanhope Av CW/HAS CW1 ... 19 K6
Stanhope Cl WILM/AE SK9 ... 84 D2 [2]
Stanhope Rd ALT WA14 ... 61 G2
Stanier Cl CW/HAS CW1 ... 222 A8
Stanlaw Rd EP CH65 ... 10 F9
Stanley Av BRAM/HZG SK7 ... 66 D1 [2]
  MPL/ROM SK6 ... 48 D5
  WARRS WA4 ... 56 F2
  WARRW/BUR WA5 ... 35 K5
Stanley Cl NWCHW CW8 ... 129 G8
  WDN WA8 ... 7 L1
Stanley Ct ALS/KID ST7 ... 224 C8
Stanley Dr CHD/CHDH SK8 ... 64 D6
  HALE/TIMP WA15 ... 43 G7
Stanley Gv NWCHE CW9 ... 130 E2
Stanley Hall La POY/DIS SK12 ... 68 C5
Stanley Mt SALE M33 ... 43 G1
Stanley Park Ct
  CHSW/BR CH4 ... 168 E7 [2]
Stanley Park Dr CHSW/BR CH4 .. 168 E7
Stanley Pl CH/BCN CH1 ... 16 E5
  CQ CH5 ... 142 A7 [8]
  WARRS WA4 ... 56 F2 [8]
Stanley Place Ms CH/BCN CH1 .. 16 E6 [8]
Stanley Rd BIDD ST8 ... 227 J4
  CHD/CHDH SK8 ... 64 D6
  EP CH65 ... 10 E3
  KNUT WA16 ... 106 F2
Stanley St BIDD ST8 ... 227 J4
  BURS/TUN ST6 ... 243 L8
  CH/BCN CH1 ... 16 E5
  CW/HAS CW1 ... 18 E3
  NEWLW WA12 ... 27 G1 [8]
  NWCHE CW9 ... 130 C4 [2]
  RUNC WA7 ... 9 J1
  STKP SK1 ... 3 J4
  WARR WA1 ... 5 M4
Stannage La CHSE CH3 ... 211 M7
Stanner Cl WARRW/BUR WA5 ... 36 D2 [8]
Stannerhouse La SBCH CW11... 223 L1
Stanneybrook Cl
  FROD/HEL WA6 ... 127 G6 [8]
Stanney Cl PS/BROM CH62 ... 93 L1
Stanneylands Cl WILM/AE SK9 ... 84 C7 [8]
Stanneylands Dr WILM/AE SK9 ... 84 B2
Stanneylands Rd WILM/AE SK9 ... 64 B8
Stanney La EP CH65 ... 121 J1
Stanney Mill La CHNE CH2 ... 121 M3
Stanney Mill Rd EP CH65 ... 121 M2
Stanney Woods Av EP CH65 ... 121 J3
Stansbury Pl OFTN SK2 ... 47 L6 [8]
Stansfield Av WARR WA1 ... 37 M6 [8]
Stansfield Cl LEIGH WN7 ... 25 J2 [8]
Stanstead Av
  WARRW/BUR WA5 ... 54 F1 [2]
Stanthorne Av CW/SHV CW2 ... 237 M1
Stanton Cl NSTN CH64 ... 91 M4 [8]
Stanton Dr CHNE CH2 ... 145 K7
Stanton Rd WARRS WA4 ... 57 K1
Stanway Dr HALE/TIMP WA15 ... 61 M1
Stanwood Gdns RAIN/WH L35 ... 32 E1
Stapeley Gdns HLWD L26 ... 51 G6 [8]
Stapeley Ter NANT CW5 ... 21 J7
Stapleford Cl NTHM/RTH M23 ... 43 M8
Stapleton Av SPK/HALE L24 ... 70 D1
Stapleton Rd MCFLDN SK10 ... 138 B2
Stapley Cl RUNC WA7 ... 8 E4
Starbeck Dr GTS/LS CH66 ... 94 B6
Starkey Gv WARRS WA4 ... 37 M8 [8]
Star La LYMM WA13 ... 39 J8
  MCFLDS SK11 ... 138 D8
Starling Cl ALS/KID ST7 ... 243 K1 [8]
  RUNC WA7 ... 74 D5
Start La CHF/WBR SK23 ... 89 J5
Stash Gv NTHM/RTH M23 ... 44 B5
Statham Av LYMM WA13 ... 58 C1
  WARRN/WOL WA2 ... 37 J2
Statham Cl LYMM WA13 ... 58 D1
Statham Dr LYMM WA13 ... 58 D1
Statham La LYMM WA13 ... 39 H7
Statham St MCFLDS SK11 ... 14 F7
Station Av FROD/HEL WA6 ... 98 B8
  GTS/LS CH66 ... 94 C5
Station Cl NSTN CH64 ... 91 M5 [8]
Station Gn GTS/LS CH66 ... 94 C5
Station HI NWCHW CW8 ... 127 M2 [8]
Station La CHNE CH2 ... 146 F4

CQ CH5 ... 166 C4
Station Rd ALS/KID ST7 ... 225 L5
  ALS/KID ST7 ... 226 B4
  ALS/KID ST7 ... 241 J1
  ALS/KID ST7 ... 242 F5 [8]
  ALS/KID ST7 ... 243 L3
  ALT WA14 ... 41 H7
  AUD/MAD/W CW3 ... 267 L7
  BIDD ST8 ... 227 J3
  CH/BCN CH1 ... 17 J2
  CH/BCN CH1 ... 145 H1
  CHD/CHDH SK8 ... 65 H2 [2]
  CHF/WBR SK23 ... 69 K8
  CHNE CH2 ... 97 C7
  CHSE CH3 ... 149 G1
  CONG CW12 ... 186 A2
  CQ CH5 ... 142 D7
  CQ CH5 ... 166 C4
  CQ CH5 ... 167 G2
  EDGY/DAV SK3 ... 2 E7
  EP CH65 ... 10 F6
  GTS/LS CH66 ... 94 C6
  HOLMCH CW4 ... 158 A4
  HOLMCH CW4 ... 181 K2
  HTNM SK4 ... 45 L3
  IRL M44 ... 31 L5
  KNUT WA16 ... 81 M5
  MCFLDS SK11 ... 135 G2
  MKTDR TF9 ... 274 A7
  MPL/ROM SK6 ... 48 F6
  MPL/ROM SK6 ... 68 C3
  NANT CW5 ... 20 F7
  NANT CW5 ... 219 L6
  NANT CW5 ... 261 M1
  NM/HAY SK22 ... 69 H5
  NSTN CH64 ... 91 L3
  NSTN CH64 ... 91 J4
  NSTN CH64 ... 118 A2
  NWCHE CW9 ... 13 L1
  NWCHE CW9 ... 131 G2
  NWCHW CW8 ... 127 J2
  NWCHW CW8 ... 128 A3
  NWCHW CW8 ... 150 D4
  RAIN/WH L35 ... 33 J1
  RUNC WA7 ... 8 F2
  SBCH CW11 ... 203 K5
  TPLY/KEL CW6 ... 217 L2
  WARRS WA4 ... 56 E2
  WARRW/BUR WA5 ... 35 M7
  WARRW/BUR WA5 ... 54 D1
  WHITCH SY13 ... 270 B5
  WILM/AE SK9 ... 84 B5
  WILM/AE SK9 ... 84 A5
  WILM/AE SK9 ... 84 D1
  WRX/GR/LL LL12 ... 210 A5
  WSFD CW7 ... 178 B3
Station Rd North
  WARRN/WOL WA2 ... 38 A2
Station Rd South
  WARRN/WOL WA2 ... 38 A3
Station St BRAM/HZG SK7 ... 66 D2
  MCFLDN SK10 ... 15 G3
  RAIN/WH L35 ... 33 J1 [8]
Station Vw CHNE CH2 ... 17 L4
  NANT CW5 ... 20 F8
Staveley Dr WSFD CW7 ... 177 K2
Stavesacre LEIGH WN7 ... 24 F1
Staveton Cl BRAM/HZG SK7 ... 65 M1
Steadings Ri KNUT WA16 ... 80 D6 [8]
Steam Mill St CHSE CH3 ... 17 K4
Stearns Cl CH/BCN CH1 ... 145 G7
Steele Rd MWCH CW10 ... 179 K7 [8]
Steele St CH/BCN CH1 ... 17 G6
Steel St WARR WA1 ... 5 M2
Steeple Ct NSTN CH64 ... 91 L5
Steeple St MCFLDN SK10 ... 15 J3
Steer Br WHITCH SY13 ... 260 C3
Stein Av GOL/RIS/CU WA3 ... 23 L4
Stelfox Av HALE/TIMP WA15... 43 J5
Stendall Rd CH/BCN CH1 ... 16 A2
Stenhills Crs RUNC WA7 ... 9 K3
Stephenson Dr WARR WA1 ... 222 A8
Stephenson Rd NEWLW WA12 ... 27 J2
Stephenson Wk WSFD CW7 ... 177 G4
Stephens Ter GTS/LS CH66 ... 94 B6
Stephen St STKP SK1 ... 3 L7
  WARR WA1 ... 5 M4
Sterling Cl WSFD CW7 ... 178 A1
Sterndale Rd EDGY/DAV SK3 ... 46 E7
  MPL/ROM SK6 ... 48 B3
Sterne Cl SBCH CW11 ... 203 K6 [8]
Stetchworth Rd WARRS WA4 ... 56 B3
Stevenage Cl MCFLDS SK11 ... 14 D7
Stevenage Dr MCFLDS SK11 ... 14 D7
Stevens St WILM/AE SK9 ... 110 A3
Steventon RUNC WA7 ... 54 E8
Steward's Av WDN WA8 ... 6 E4
Stewart Cl CW/SHV CW2 ... 18 B6
Stewerton Cl
  GOL/RIS/CU WA3 ... 22 F2 [8]
Stile Cl BIDD ST8 ... 227 H7
Stile End CHNE CH2 ... 146 F4
Stiles Av MPL/ROM SK6 ... 48 E5
The Stiles NWCHW CW8 ... 127 L7
Stirling Av BRAM/HZG SK7 ... 66 D3
  MPL/ROM SK6 ... 48 F6
Stirling Cl CHSE CH3 ... 170 A2 [8]
  EDGY/DAV SK3 ... 137 M2
  MCFLDN SK10 ... 137 M2
  WARR WA1 ... 38 E5 [8]
Stirling Rd SPK/HALE L24 ... 70 B1
Stirrup Cl WARRN/WOL WA2 ... 38 A1
Stitch La HTNM SK4 ... 2 D2
Stockdale Cl RUNC WA7 ... 74 A4
Stockham La RUNC WA7 ... 74 C7
Stockholm Rd EDGY/DAV SK3... 46 D6
Stock La NANT CW5 ... 253 G3
Stockley La WARRS WA4 ... 76 F5
Stockport Rd EDGY/DAV SK3 ... 46 A5
  HALE/TIMP WA15 ... 42 F7
  MPL/ROM SK6 ... 48 F6
  WARRS WA4 ... 57 K1
Stockport Rd West
  MPL/ROM SK6 ... 47 J1
  STKP SK1 ... 3 M3
Stocks Av CHSE CH3 ... 170 A4
Stocks HI WSFD CW7 ... 177 L5

Stocks La *CHSE* CH3 .... 170 A3
 KNUT WA16 .... 133 K2
 MCFLDN SK10 .... 113 L7
 WARRW/BUR WA5 .... 35 K7
Stockswell Rd *RAIN/WH* L35 .... 32 F8
Stockton Av *EDGY/DAV* SK3 .... 46 B4 🖪
Stockton La *WARRS* WA4 .... 56 E3
Stockton Rd *WILM/AE* SK9 .... 83 M8
Stockton Wood Rd
 SPK/HALE L24 .... 70 C1
Stoke Abbott Cl *BRAM/HZG* SK7 .. 65 L1
Stoke Cl *PS/BROM* CH62 .... 93 L1
Stoke Gdns *EP* CH65 .... 95 J8
Stokehall La *NANT* CW5 .... 218 D6
Stokes St *GOL/RIS/CU* WA3 .... 29 L7
Stokoe Av *ALT* WA14 .... 42 A6
Stoneacre Gdns *WARRS* WA4 .... 56 E3
Stoneacre Rd *WYTH/NTH* M22 .... 63 J2
Stonebank Dr *NSTN* CH64 .... 92 A6
Stone Bank La *RUNC* WA7 .... 73 M6
Stone Barn La *RUNC* WA7 .... 8 B9
Stonebridge Rd *NANT* CW5 .... 251 K1
Stone Chair La *ALS/KID* ST7 .... 225 J4
Stonechat Cl *CW/HAS* CW1 .... 221 G5 🖪
 GOL/RIS/CU WA3 .... 23 L4 🖪
 RUNC WA7 .... 73 L7 🖪
Stone Cft *CHSE* CH3 .... 170 B4
Stonecrop Cl *GOL/RIS/CU* WA3 .. 29 J8
 RUNC WA7 .... 73 M8 🖪🖪
Stonecross Dr *RAIN/WH* L35 .... 33 K3
Stone Cross La North
 GOL/RIS/CU WA3 .... 23 J5 🖪
Stone Cross La South
 GOL/RIS/CU WA3 .... 23 J6
Stonehaven Dr
 WARRN/WOL WA2 .... 38 A1
Stone Hay *RAIN/WH* L35 .... 32 D3
Stoneheads Ri *CHF/WBR* SK23 .. 89 K4
Stone Heyes La *NWCHW* CW8.. 102 F7
Stonehill Cl *WARRS* WA4 .... 56 D8
Stonehills La *RUNC* WA7 .... 9 M3
Stonehouse Gn *CONG* CW12 ... 207 K1 🖪
Stone House La *MALPAS* SY14 .. 232 D2
Stonelea *RUNC* WA7 .... 74 B2
Stoneleigh Cl *CQ* CH5 .... 142 F6 🖪
 MCFLDN SK10 .... 14 E1
Stoneleigh Gdns *WARRS* WA4.. 57 K3
Stoneley Av *CW/HAS* CW1.. 221 J5
Stoneley Rd *CW/HAS* CW1 .. 221 K5
Stone Md *MPL/ROM* SK6 .... 48 E1
Stone Mead Av
 HALE/TIMP WA15 .... 62 C5
Stonepail Cl *CHD/CHDH* SK8 .... 44 F7
Stonepail Rd *CHD/CHDH* SK8 ... 45 G7 🖪
Stone Pit Cl *GOL/RIS/CU* WA3 .. 23 L3
Stone Pit La *GOL/RIS/CU* WA3 .. 28 F2
Stone Pl *CHNE* CH2 .... 17 L1
Stone Rw *MPL/ROM* SK6 .... 49 G6
Stones Manor La *NWCHW* CW8 .. 12 A9
Stoneyfold La *MCFLDS* SK11 ... 139 C6
Stoney Holt *RUNC* WA7 .... 74 C4 🖪
Stoneyland Dr *NM/HAY* SK22 .... 69 G4
Stoney La *TPLY/KEL* CW6 .... 150 C6
 WILM/AE SK9 .... 83 M7
Stonyhurst Rd *WLTN* L25 .... 50 B3
Stony La *CONG* CW12 .... 207 J3
Stopford St *EDGY/DAV* SK3 .... 2 D8
Stopsley Cl *CONG* CW12 .... 183 M8
Store St *MCFLDN* SK10 .... 113 H4 🖪
 OFTN SK2 .... 47 J4
Storeton Dr *WYTH/NTH* M22 .... 63 L2 🖪
Stortford Dr *NTHM/RTH* M23 ..... 44 B2
Stour Av *RAIN/WH* L35 .... 33 J1
Stour Cl *ALT* WA14 .... 42 C6
Stour Ct *EP* CH65 .... 10 D4
Stourport Cl *MPL/ROM* SK6 .... 48 A3 🖪
Stourvale Rd *HLWD* L26 .... 50 F5 🖪
Stowe Cl *WLTN* L25 .... 50 B5
Stradbroke Cl *GOL/RIS/CU* WA3 .. 24 A5
Straight Length *FROD/HEL* WA6.. 98 E5
Straight Mile *CHSW/BR* CH4 .... 191 M7
Straker Av *EP* CH65 .... 94 F6
Stratfield Rd *NTHM/RTH* M23 .. 43 K3
Stratford Gdns *MPL/ROM* SK6 .. 47 M1
Stratford Rd *CH/BCN* CH1 .... 144 E8
 NSTN CH64 .... 91 K6
Stratford Wy *MCFLDS* SK11 ... 138 C7 🖪
Strathaven Cl *CW/SHV* CW2 .. 237 M1
Strathmore Cl *HOLMCH* CW4 .. 181 H2
Stratton Cl *RUNC* WA7 .... 74 B6
Stratton Pk *WDN* WA8 .... 33 M7
Stratton Rd *OFTN* SK2 .... 47 J4 🖪
 WARRW/BUR WA5 .... 36 B7
Strawberry Cl *ALT* WA14 .... 42 B5 🖪
 GOL/RIS/CU WA3 .... 29 J8
Strawberry Dr *EP* CH65 .... 121 G4
Strawberry Flds *CHSE* CH3 .. 170 B5
Strawberry La *CH/BCN* CH1 .. 120 C7
 NWCHW CW8 .... 127 M1
 WILM/AE SK9 .... 83 L6
Streamside Cl *HALE/TIMP* WA15 .. 43 H8
Stream Ter *STKP* SK1 .... 3 L5
Street Hey La *NSTN* CH64 .... 93 H2
Street La *MCFLDN* SK10 .... 86 D4
 SBCH CW11 .... 224 E2
 WARRS WA4 .... 102 C1
The Street *BUX* SK17 .... 115 L8
 CHNE CH2 .... 146 C5
 CHNE CH2 .... 146 E3
 MCFLDN SK10 .... 115 H6
Stretton Av *DID/WITH* M20 .... 45 J1
 GOL/RIS/CU WA3 .... 23 L5 🖪
Stretton Cl *PS/BROM* CH62 .. 93 L1 🖪
Stretton Rd *WARRS* WA4 .... 76 F2
Stretton Wy *NWCHE* CW9 .. 129 M8 🖪
Strickland St *CO* CH5 .... 142 B7
Strines St *MPL/ROM* SK6 .... 49 G7
Stringer Av *SBCH* CW11 .... 204 C6
Stringer Crs *WARRS* WA4 .... 37 L5
Stringer's La *CHSW/BR* CH4 .. 190 B7
Stringer St *STKP* SK1 .... 3 K4
Stromness Cl
 WARRN/WOL WA2 .... 38 B1 🖪
Stross Av *BURS/TUN* ST6 .. 243 M7

Stuart Av *IRL* M44 .... 31 M2
 WLTN L25 .... 50 C5
Stuart Cl *CHSE* CH3 .... 170 C1
Stuart Dr *MPL/ROM* SK6 .... 48 C5
 WARRS WA4 .... 56 F2
Stuart Pl *CH/BCN* CH1 .... 17 H3
Stuart Rd *RUNC* WA7 .... 54 B8
Stubbins Cl *NTHM/RTH* M23 .. 43 L3
Stubbs La *KNUT* WA16 .... 82 D8
 NWCHE CW9 .... 131 H2 🖪
Stubbs Pl *CH/BCN* CH1 .... 168 E1 🖪
Stubbs Ter *MCFLDS* SK11 .... 15 J7 🖪
Stubby La *NANT* CW5 .... 135 L3
Studland Rd *WYTH/NTH* M22 .. 63 M1
Sturgess St *NEWLW* WA12 .... 26 F1
Styal Gv *CHD/CHDH* SK8 .... 64 A1
Styal Rd *WILM/AE* SK9 .... 84 A3
Styal Vw *WILM/AE* SK9 .... 84 B2
Styperson Wy *POY/DIS* SK12 .. 86 E1 🖪
Sudbourne Cl *ALS/KID* ST7 .. 243 L4
Sudbrook Cl
 GOL/RIS/CU WA3 .... 23 L4 🖪
Sudbury Cl *WLTN* L25 .... 50 D2
Sudbury Dr *CHD/CHDH* SK8 .. 64 C5
Sudbury Rd *BRAM/HZG* SK7 .. 66 F4
Sudbury Wy *SPK/HALE* L24 .. 50 B8 🖪
Sudlow La *KNUT* WA16 .... 106 F3
Suez St *NEWLW* WA12 .... 27 G1
 WARR WA1 .... 4 F7
Suffolk Av *EP* CH65 .... 94 F7
Suffolk Cl *CONG* CW12 .... 184 D8
 MCFLDN SK10 .... 137 M3
 WARR WA1 .... 38 D6
Suffolk Dr *WILM/AE* SK9 .... 84 B3
Suffolk Pl *WDN* WA8 .... 52 C5
Suffolk Rd *ALT* WA14 .... 42 B8
Suffolk St *RUNC* WA7 .... 8 E1
Sugar La *FROD/HEL* WA6 .... 124 C7
 MCFLDN SK10 .... 86 F8
 MCFLDN SK10 .... 113 K7
Sugar Pit La *KNUT* WA16 .. 106 E1
Sulby Av *WARRS* WA4 .... 56 B1
Sulgrave Av *POY/DIS* SK12 .. 66 F8
Summerbank Rd
 BURS/TUN ST6 .... 243 K8
Summerdale Rd *CO* CH5 .... 142 A8
Summerfield *ALS/KID* ST7 .. 243 H3 🖪
Summerfield Av
 WARRW/BUR WA5 .... 36 F2
Summerfield Cl
 CHSW/BR CH4 .... 190 A1 🖪
Summerfield Dr *NWCHE* CW9.. 153 M4
Summerfield Pl *WILM/AE* SK9 .. 84 A6
Summerfield Rd *CHSE* CH3 .. 146 F7 🖪
 KNUT WA16 .... 81 M8
 WYTH/NTH M22 .... 63 J2
Summerfields *KNUT* WA16 .. 107 J1 🖪
Summerhill Rd *MCFLDN* SK10.. 111 L8
Summer La *MCFLDN* SK11 .... 73 M3
 WARRS WA4 .... 75 H6
 WARRS WA4 .... 76 A4
Summerlea *CHD/CHDH* SK8 .. 65 H4 🖪
Summers Wy *KNUT* WA16 .. 107 G5
Summertrees Rd *GTS/LS* CH66.. 120 E2
Summerville Gdns *WARRS* WA4 .. 56 F3
Summit Cl *WARRS* WA4 .... 76 B3
Sumner Cl *RAIN/WH* L35 .... 33 K3
Sumner Rd *CH/BCN* CH1 .... 144 E8
Sumpter Pathway *CHNE* CH2 .. 17 M1
Sunart Cl *CW/SHV* CW2 .... 238 B6 🖪
Sunbank La *HALE/TIMP* WA15 .. 62 D6
 HALE/TIMP WA15 .... 62 F6
Sunbeam St *NEWLW* WA12 .... 27 J1 🖪
Sunbury Cl *WILM/AE* SK9 .... 84 E2
Sunbury Crs *CHSW/BR* CH4 .. 168 F6 🖪🖪
Sunbury Gdns *WARRS* WA4 .. 56 E5
Suncroft Cl *WARR* WA1 .... 38 E5
Sundale Dr *CW/SHV* CW2 .... 237 K1
Sunderland St *MCFLDS* SK11 .. 15 H6
Sundial Rd *OFTN* SK2 .... 47 K6
Sundown *NM/HAY* SK22 .... 69 G4
Sunfield *MPL/ROM* SK6 .... 34 B8
Sunfield Cl *GTS/LS* CH66 .... 120 D1 🖪
Sunningdale Av *SALE* M33 .... 43 L1
 WDN WA8 .... 52 B3
Sunningdale Cl *NWCHE* CW9 .. 130 E5 🖪
 WARRW/BUR WA5 .... 26 F6
 WSFD CW7 .... 177 G2
Sunningdale Dr *BRAM/HZG* SK7.. 66 A5
 IRL M44 .... 31 M1
Sunningdale Rd *CHD/CHDH* SK8 .. 65 C5
 MCFLDS SK11 .... 14 B8
Sunningdale Wy *NSTN* CH64.. 91 L8
Sunny Bank *WILM/AE* SK9 .... 83 K8
Sunny Bank St *MCFLDS* SK11 .. 138 D7
Sunnybank Cl *NEWLW* WA12 .. 22 C8 🖪
Sunny Bank Rd *ALT* WA14 .... 61 J4
Sunnybank Rd *CW/SHV* CW2 .. 220 E7
Sunnydale *RAIN/WH* L35 .... 33 K1
Sunnyfield Rd *HTNM* SK4 .... 45 M1
Sunnyside *ALS/KID* ST7 .... 224 A8
 CO CH5 .... 166 D2
 WARRW/BUR WA5 .... 35 L6 🖪
Sunnyside La *RUNC* WA7 .... 54 E8
Sunset Av *WYTH/NTH* M22 .... 44 D2
Sunwell Ter *MPL/ROM* SK6 .... 48 F8 🖪
Surrey Dr *CONG* CW12 .... 184 E8
Surrey Rd *ALS/KID* ST7 .... 243 G2
 CHNE CH2 .... 146 A7
 MCFLDS SK11 .... 138 A8
Surrey St *CW/HAS* CW1 .... 19 J3
 RUNC WA7 .... 9 G3
 WARRS WA4 .... 56 D1
Surridge *KNUT* WA16 .... 59 J7
Surtees Rd *NTHM/RTH* M23 .... 44 A2
Susan Dr *WARRW/BUR* WA5 .. 35 M4
Susan St *WDN* WA8 .... 7 L1
Suspension Br *CHSW/BR* CH4 .. 17 J4
Sussex Av *MCFLDS* SK11 .... 138 A7 🖪
Sussex Cl *ALS/KID* ST7 .... 242 F2
Sussex Pl *CONG* CW12 .... 184 E7
Sussex Rd *CHNE* CH2 .... 145 M8
 EDGY/DAV SK3 .... 46 B4
 IRL M44 .... 31 J6
 PART M31 .... 40 E2 🖪
Sussex St *WDN* WA8 .... 53 K3 🖪

Sutherland Dr *MCFLDN* SK10 .. 14 A2
Sutherland Wy *CHSE* CH3 .. 170 B1
Sutton Av *GOL/RIS/CU* WA3 .. 24 E8
 NSTN CH64 .... 91 L6
Sutton Cswy *FROD/HEL* WA6 .. 99 L2
Sutton Cl *CHNE* CH2 .... 146 F4 🖪
 NWCHE CW9 .... 104 F6 🖪
 PS/BROM CH62 .... 93 L1
Sutton Dr *CHNE* CH2 .... 145 L1
Sutton Fld *NWCHE* CW8 .. 152 F5
Sutton Hall *GTS/LS* CH66 .. 94 A6
Sutton Hall Gdns *GTS/LS* CH66.. 94 A6
Sutton La *MWCH* CW10 .. 179 J5
Sutton Rd *HTNM* SK4 .... 2 B1
 POY/DIS SK12 .... 86 F2
 WILM/AE SK9 .... 109 M3
Sutton St *RUNC* WA7 .... 9 K3
 WARR WA1 .... 5 J8
Sutton Wy *EP* CH65 .... 10 A8
 EP CH65 .... 10 B9 🖪
Sutton Wood Rd *SPK/HALE* L24.. 70 C1
Swaine St *EDGY/DAV* SK3 .... 2 E6
Swale Av *RAIN/WH* L35 .... 33 J1
Swalecliff Av *NTHM/RTH* M23 .. 43 K3
Swale Cl *WILM/AE* SK9 .... 84 E2
Swaledale Av *CONG* CW12 .. 185 G7
 RAIN/WH L35 .... 33 K1
Swaledale Cl *WARRW/BUR* WA5.. 35 M5
Swale Dr *ALT* WA14 .... 42 C6
Swale Rd *EP* CH65 .... 10 A3
Swallow Cl *ALS/KID* ST7 .. 243 G2 🖪
 GOL/RIS/CU WA3 .... 29 M8 🖪
 MCFLDN SK10 .... 139 G5 🖪
Swallow Ct *WSFD* CW7 .... 177 K7
Swallow Dr *SBCH* CW11 .... 204 A4
Swallowfield Cl
 CW/SHV CW2 .... 238 A4 🖪
Swallowmore Vw
 ALS/KID ST7 .... 242 C4 🖪
Swallow St *STKP* SK1 .... 3 H9
Swallow Wk *BIDD* ST8 .... 227 K5
Swanage Av *NTHM/RTH* M23 .. 43 K3
 OFTN SK2 .... 47 K6
Swanage Cl *WARRS* WA4 .... 56 E2
Swanage Ct *WSFD* CW7 .. 177 K7 🖪
Swan Av *STHEL* WA9 .... 26 A2
Swan Bank *ALS/KID* ST7 .. 242 D4
Swan Cl *ALS/KID* ST7 .... 242 D4
 GTS/LS CH66 .... 120 C2
 POY/DIS SK12 .... 66 B8
Swan Ct *NWCHW* CW8 .. 127 L5
Swan Gv *KNUT* WA16 .. 132 D5
Swanlow Av *WSFD* CW7 .. 177 K7
Swanley La *NANT* CW5 .. 235 L6
Swanlow Dr *WSFD* CW7 .. 177 K6
Swanlow La *WSFD* CW7 .. 177 K7
Swann Gv *CHD/CHDH* SK8 .. 65 H4
Swann La *CHD/CHDH* SK8 .. 65 H3
Swann Rd *HALE/TIMP* WA15 .. 43 G3
Swanscoe Av *MCFLDN* SK10 .. 113 C5
Swanscoe Cl *MWCH* CW10 .. 179 H4 🖪
Swanscoe La *MCFLDN* SK10 .. 139 H1
Swan St *CONG* CW12 .... 207 K2
 WILM/AE SK9 .... 84 B5
Swanwick Cl *HOLMCH* CW4 .. 157 J3
Swaylands Dr *SALE* M33 .... 43 H3
Sweet Briar Crs *CW/HAS* CW1 .. 237 M1
Sweet Brier Cl *NWCHE* CW8.. 103 H8 🖪
Sweetfield Gdns *GTS/LS* CH66.. 94 D5
Sweetfield Rd *GTS/LS* CH66 .. 94 D5
Sweettooth La *SBCH* CW11 .. 204 A5
Swettenham Cl *ALS/KID* ST7 .. 241 J1
 SBCH CW11 .... 204 C5
Swettenham Rd *CONG* CW12 .. 182 F1
Swettenham St *MCFLDS* SK11 .. 15 K6
Swift Cl *ALS/KID* ST7 .... 243 H2
 CW/SHV CW2 .... 237 M3
 WARRN/WOL WA2 .... 37 L1 🖪
Swift Dr *BIDD* ST8 .... 227 L4
Swinburne Dr *CW/HAS* CW1 .. 19 M3
Swinchiard La *FLINT* CH6 .. 116 A6 🖪
Swinchiard Wk *FLINT* CH6 .. 116 A6
Swindale Av
 WARRN/WOL WA2 .... 37 H1 🖪
Swinden Ct *RUNC* WA7 .... 74 D2 🖪
Swine Market *NANT* CW5 .... 20 E6
Swineyard La *NWCHE* CW9 .. 57 M8
Swinford St *WDN* WA8 .... 53 L2 🖪
Swinley Cha *WILM/AE* SK9 .... 84 F3
Swinleys Hey *CHSE* CH3 .. 170 A5 🖪
Swinnerton St *CW/HAS* CW1 .. 19 M3
Swinton Sq *KNUT* WA16 .. 107 G2 🖪
Swireford Rd *FROD/HEL* WA6.. 124 B2
Swiss Hl *WILM/AE* SK9 .... 110 B3
Swithin Rd *WYTH/NTH* M22 .... 63 L4
Swn-y-gwynt *FLINT* CH6 .. 116 B8 🖪
Swynnerton Wy *WDN* WA8 .. 34 B7 🖪
Swythamley Cl *EDGY/DAV* SK3 .. 46 A4 🖪
Swythamley Rd *EDGY/DAV* SK3 .. 46 A4
Sycamore Av *ALS/KID* ST7 .. 224 F5
 ALS/KID ST7 .... 241 L2 🖪
 ALT WA14 .... 42 A7 🖪
 CONG CW12 .... 183 M4
 CW/HAS CW1 .... 221 K6
 GOL/RIS/CU WA3 .... 23 G3
 HLWD L26 .... 50 E6
 NEWLW WA12 .... 27 J1 🖪
 WDN WA8 .... 7 J1
 WSFD CW7 .... 177 J4
Sycamore Cl *ALS/KID* ST7 .. 242 E4
 AUD/MAD/W CW3 .... 264 A8 🖪
 BIDD ST8 .... 227 L2
 HOLMCH CW4 .... 181 J1
 NANT CW5 .... 21 H2
 NM/HAY SK22 .... 69 L3 🖪
 WILM/AE SK9 .... 84 B2
Sycamore Crs
 GOL/RIS/CU WA3 .... 40 B2 🖪
 GOL/RIS/CU WA3 .... 40 B2 🖪
 MCFLDS SK11 .... 14 B8
 NWCHW CW8 .... 103 H8
Sycamore Dr *CHSW/BR* CH4 .. 168 F8

 GTS/LS CH66 .... 120 F3
 LYMM WA13 .... 39 K8
 MWCH CW10 .... 179 K7
 RUNC WA7 .... 74 A8
Sycamore Farm Cl
 MCFLDN SK10 .... 14 A1 🖪
Sycamore Gv *CHSW/BR* CH4 .. 190 B1 🖪
 SBCH CW11 .... 204 A4
Sycamore La
 WARRW/BUR WA5 .... 36 B6 🖪
Sycamore Ri *MCFLDS* SK11 .. 14 B8
Sycamore Rd *NM/HAY* SK22 .. 69 L2
 PART M31 .... 40 D1
 RUNC WA7 .... 9 M6
Sycamore St *EDGY/DAV* SK3 .. 46 B4 🖪
Sycamore Wk *CHD/CHDH* SK8 .. 45 K6 🖪
Syddal Cl *BRAM/HZG* SK7 .. 65 K7
Syddal Crs *BRAM/HZG* SK7 .. 65 K7
Syddal Gn *BRAM/HZG* SK7 .. 65 K7
Syddall Av *CHD/CHDH* SK8 .. 64 D4
Syddal Rd *BRAM/HZG* SK7 .. 65 K7
Sydney Av *LEIGH* WN7 .... 24 D2
 MANAIR M90 .... 63 G4
Sydney Rd *BRAM/HZG* SK7 .. 65 M7
 CH/BCN CH1 .... 16 D2
 CW/HAS CW1 .... 221 L6
Sydney St *NWCHW* CW8 .. 12 B5
 OFTN SK2 .... 47 J5
 RUNC WA7 .... 8 B9
Sydney Wk *FLINT* CH6 .. 116 A5 🖪
Syers Ct *WARR* WA1 .... 37 L4
Sykes Meadow *EDGY/DAV* SK3.. 46 C6
Sylvan Av *HALE/TIMP* WA15 .. 42 F4
 SALE M33 .... 43 J1
 WILM/AE SK9 .... 83 M7
Sylvan Cl *NWCHW* CW8 .. 12 A6
Sylvan Ct *WLTN* L25 .... 50 A3
Sylvan Gv *ALT* WA14 .... 42 D7
Sylvester Av *STKP* SK1 .... 47 H6
Sylvia Crs *WARRN/WOL* WA2 .. 37 K3 🖪
Symondley Rd *MCFLDS* SK11 .. 162 F2
Synge St *WARRN/WOL* WA2 .. 5 J2
Sytch Cft *NSTN* CH64 .... 91 L4

T

Tabley Av *WDN* WA8 .... 6 A1
Tabley Cl *KNUT* WA16 .... 106 E1
 SBCH CW11 .... 203 L5
Tabley Gdns *MPL/ROM* SK6 .... 49 G8
Tabley Gv *HALE/TIMP* WA15 .. 43 G4
 KNUT WA16 .... 106 D1
 SALE M33 .... 43 L2 🖪
 WILM/AE SK9 .... 64 D7
Tabley St *NWCHE* CW9 .... 13 J1
Tabor St *MCFLDS* SK11 .. 15 K8 🖪
Tadgers La *FROD/HEL* WA6 .. 98 D3
Tadman Gv *ALT* WA14 .... 42 A6
Talbot Av *NSTN* CH64 .... 91 M6
Talbot Cl *CW/SHV* CW2 .. 238 B8
 GOL/RIS/CU WA3 .... 38 E1
 NSTN CH64 .... 91 M6
Talbot Crs *WHITCH* SY13 .. 270 B4
Talbot Gdns *NSTN* CH64 .... 91 M6
Talbot Rd *ALT* WA14 .... 61 H2
 FROD/HEL WA6 .... 123 L5
 GTS/LS CH66 .... 120 F1
 WILM/AE SK9 .... 110 B3
Talbot St *BRAM/HZG* SK7 .. 47 K8
 CH/BCN CH1 .... 17 H2
 GOL/RIS/CU WA3 .... 23 G4
 WHITCH SY13 .... 270 B4
Taliesin Av *CO* CH5 .... 142 A6
Talisman Cl *RUNC* WA7 .... 74 E3 🖪
Talke Rd *ALS/KID* ST7 .. 241 L1
Talland Cl *HLWD* L26 .... 50 E3
Tall Ash Av *CONG* CW12 .. 185 G8
Tall Trees Cl *NWCHW* CW8 .. 12 A6
Tall Trees Pl *OFTN* SK2 .... 47 J6
Talman Gv *AIMK* WN4.......... 22 D1
Tamar Cl *CONG* CW12 .. 207 M3
 MCFLDN SK10 .... 137 L3 🖪🖪
Tamar Rd *ALS/KID* ST7 .. 243 H2
Tamar Wk *WSFD* CW7 .. 178 A2 🖪
Tame Cl *BIDD* ST8 .... 227 K3
 SBCH CW11 .... 203 L4
Tamworth Cl *BRAM/HZG* SK7 .. 66 D4 🖪
Tamworth St *STKP* SK1 .... 3 L3
Tanfield Rd *DID/WITH* M20 .... 45 H5
Tanhill Cl *OFTN* SK2 .... 47 L6
Tan House La *WARRW/BUR* WA5 .. 27 G8
 WDN WA8 .... 7 M4
Tankersley Gv *WARRW/BUR* WA5.. 36 A7
Tanner's La *GOL/RIS/CU* WA3 .. 23 H4
 WARRN/WOL WA2 .... 4 F5
Tannery La *NSTN* CH64 .... 91 L4
 WARRW/BUR WA5 .... 54 C1
Tannery Wy *ALT* WA14 .... 42 E5 🖪
Tannock Rd *BRAM/HZG* SK7 .. 66 E6
Tanyard Dr *HALE/TIMP* WA15 .. 62 C6
Tanyard La *HALE/TIMP* WA15.. 61 M7
Tapley Av *POY/DIS* SK12 .. 86 E2
Taplow Cl *WARRS* WA4 .... 56 E6
Taplow Gv *CHD/CHDH* SK8 .. 64 F2
Tarbock Rd *SPK/HALE* L24 .. 50 D8
Tarbolton Crs *HALE/TIMP* WA15.. 62 C1
Target Cl *ALS/KID* ST7 .. 242 E6
Tarleton Cl *HLWD* L26 .... 50 E4 🖪
Tarn Cl *WSFD* CW7 .... 177 J1
Tarn Ct *WARR* WA1 .... 38 F5
Tarn Mt *MCFLDS* SK11 .. 138 A7
Tarnside Cl *OFTN* SK2 .... 47 M6
The Tarns *CHD/CHDH* SK8 .. 64 F8
Tarnway *GOL/RIS/CU* WA3 .. 23 M5
Tarporley Cl *EDGY/DAV* SK3 .. 46 C7 🖪
Tarporley Rd *CHSE* CH3 .. 172 C3
 GTS/LS CH66 .... 94 E8
 NWCHW CW8 .... 151 L4
 TPLY/KEL CW6 .... 172 E5

 WARRS WA4 .... 76 D4
 WARRS WA4 .... 102 C3
 WHITCH SY13 .... 259 M8
Tarran Pl *ALT* WA14 .... 42 E6
Tarrant Ct *CH/BCN* CH1 .... 144 E3
Tarvin Cf *EP* CH65 .... 95 J8 🖪
 GOL/RIS/CU WA3 .... 23 L5
 MCFLDS SK11 .... 138 E7
 MWCH CW10 .... 179 K7
 RUNC WA7 .... 73 J6
Tarvin Gv *BURS/TUN* ST6 .. 243 M6
Tarvin Rd *CHD/CHDH* SK8 .. 46 A8
 CHSE CH3 .... 170 A3
 FROD/HEL WA6 .... 124 D2
Tasman Cl *WARRW/BUR* WA5 .. 36 C4
Tate Cl *WDN* WA8 .... 52 D2 🖪
Tate Dr *CW/HAS* CW1 .... 222 C8
Tatland Dr *WYTH/NTH* M22 .. 63 M1 🖪
Tattenhall La *CHSE* CH3 .. 214 F2
 TPLY/KEL CW6 .... 215 M2
Tattenhall Rd *CHSE* CH3 .. 195 J7
Tatton Cl *ALS/KID* ST7 .. 241 J1 🖪
 BRAM/HZG SK7 .... 47 M8
 CHD/CHDH SK8 .... 46 A8
 CHSW/BR CH4 .... 168 E7 🖪
 NWCHE CW9 .... 129 M8 🖪
 WSFD CW7 .... 177 H3
Tatton Dr *SBCH* CW11 .... 204 C5
Tattonmere Gdns
 CHD/CHDH SK8 .... 46 A8
Tatton Rd *CW/SHV* CW2 .... 237 L2
 WILM/AE SK9 .... 64 E7
Tatton Stile *KNUT* WA16 .... 82 A8 🖪
Tatton St *KNUT* WA16 .... 107 G2
 STKP SK1 .... 3 G5
Taunton Cl *BRAM/HZG* SK7 .. 67 G2
Taunton Rd *HUY* L36 .... 32 B2 🖪
Taurus Gv *BURS/TUN* ST6 .. 243 M6
Tavistock Av *WARRW/BUR* WA5.. 35 L8
Tavlin Av *WARRW/BUR* WA5 .. 36 F3
Tawney Cl *ALS/KID* ST7 .. 243 H2
Tawny Ct *RUNC* WA7 .... 73 L5
Taxal Moor Rd *CHF/WBR* SK23.. 89 J3
Taxi Rd *MANAIR* M90 .... 63 H5
Taxmere Cl *SBCH* CW11 .. 203 M5
Tay Cl *BIDD* ST8 .... 227 L3
Tayfield Rd *WYTH/NTH* M22 .. 63 J2
Taylor Rd *ALT* WA14 .... 42 A7
Taylor's La *CW/HAS* CW1 .. 240 C1
 WARRW/BUR WA5 .... 54 A2 🖪
Taylors Rw *RUNC* WA7 .... 9 M3
Taylor St *BURS/TUN* ST6 .. 243 J5
 WARRS WA4 .... 56 A3
 WDN WA8 .... 7 L2
Taylors Vw *CQ* CH5 .... 142 A8 🖪
Teal Av *KNUT* WA16 .... 107 H2
 POY/DIS SK12 .... 66 A8
Teal Cl *ALT* WA14 .... 42 B4
 OFTN SK2 .... 47 M7
 WARRN/WOL WA2 .... 37 L1
 WSFD CW7 .... 177 K7
Teal Gv *GOL/RIS/CU* WA3 .. 38 F7
 HLWD L26 .... 50 E3
Tedder Dr *WYTH/NTH* M22 .. 63 M5
Tedder Sq *WDN* WA8 .... 6 A5
Teddington Cl *WARRS* WA4 .. 56 E7
Tees Ct *EP* CH65 .... 10 A3
Teesdale Cl *OFTN* SK2 .... 47 L6 🖪
Tefler Ct *MWCH* CW10 .... 179 L6
Teggsnose La *MCFLDS* SK11 .. 139 J6
Tegid Wy *CHSW/BR* CH4 .. 168 D7
Tegsnose Mt *MCFLDS* SK11 .. 139 J8 🖪
Telford Cl *ALS/KID* ST7 .. 242 E4
 CONG CW12 .... 208 B2
 WDN WA8 .... 33 K8
Telford Gdns *SBCH* CW11 .. 222 F1 🖪
Telford Pl *NANT* CW5 .... 20 B6
Telford Rd *EP* CH65 .... 95 L8
 MPL/ROM SK6 .... 49 G8
Telford Wy *AUD/MAD/W* CW3 .. 273 M1
 CHSW/BR CH4 .... 168 F6 🖪🖪
 MWCH CW10 .... 179 L3
Tempest Rd *WILM/AE* SK9 .. 110 C3
Temple Ct *GOL/RIS/CU* WA3 .. 29 L5
Templeton Cl *ALT* WA14 .... 42 B6
Tenby Cl *WARRW/BUR* WA5 .. 36 F2
Tenby Dr *CHD/CHDH* SK8 .. 65 H3
 RUNC WA7 .... 73 K7
Tenby Rd *EDGY/DAV* SK3 .. 46 B5
 MCFLDS SK11 .... 137 L6
Tenement La *CHD/CHDH* SK8 .. 65 J1
 CW/HAS CW1 .... 19 L3
Tennyson Cl *ALS/KID* ST7 .. 243 G4
 CW/SHV CW2 .... 238 A3 🖪
 HTNM SK4 .... 46 A3
 MCFLDS SK11 .... 137 L5
 NWCHE CW9 .... 130 C6 🖪
Tennyson Dr *WARRN/WOL* WA2 .. 37 J2
Tennyson Rd *CHD/CHDH* SK8 .. 45 M6
 EP CH65 .... 10 B7
 HUY L36 .... 32 A4
 WDN WA8 .... 7 G2
Tennyson St *STHEL* WA9 .... 26 A8
Tennyson Wk *CH/BCN* CH1 .. 145 G7 🖪
Tensing Cl *WARRW/BUR* WA5 .. 36 B4
Terence Av *WARR* WA1.......... 37 M5
Terminal Rd East
 MANAIR M90 .... 63 H5 🖪
Terminal Rd North *MANAIR* M90 .. 63 H5
Terminal Rd South
 MANAIR M90 .... 63 H5 🖪
Tern Av *ALS/KID* ST7 .. 243 J2
Tern Cl *ALT* WA14 .... 42 B4
 BIDD ST8 .... 227 L4
 WDN WA8 .... 34 B8 🖪
Tern Dr *POY/DIS* SK12 .... 66 B8
Terrace Rd *WDN* WA8 .... 53 G7
Terrick Rd *WHITCH* SY13 .. 270 A2
Terrig St *CQ* CH5 .... 142 B8
Tetbury Rd *WYTH/NTH* M22 .. 63 H3
Tetchill Cl *GTS/LS* CH66 .. 120 D2
 RUNC WA7 .... 74 D4
Tetton La *MWCH* CW10 .. 202 E2
Teviot Wy *RDSH* SK5.......... 3 G1
Tewit Hall Cl *SPK/HALE* L24 .. 70 C1
Tewit Hall Rd *SPK/HALE* L24 .. 70 C1

Tewkesbury Av *HALE/TIMP* WA15.. **62** C1
Tewkesbury Cl *CHD/CHDH* SK8.... **65** H6
   CHNE **145** M5
   GTS/LS CH66 .... **120** E5
   MWCH CW10 .... **179** H3
   POY/DIS SK12 .... **66** D8⑤
   WLTN L25 .... **50** C2
Tewkesbury Dr
   MCFLDN SK10 .... **112** E8⑥
Tewkesbury Rd
   EDGY/DAV SK3 .... **46** B6⑩
   GOL/RIS/CU WA3 .... **23** H4④
Thackeray Dr *CHSE* CH3 .... **170** C2
Thackery Ct *SBCH* CW11 .... **203** K6⑧
Thames Av *LEIGH* WN7 .... **24** F3
Thames Cl *CONG* CW12 .... **207** M3
Thamesdale *EP* CH65 .... **121** H1
Thames Dr *BIDD* ST8 .... **227** K3
Thames Gdns *EP* CH65 .... **121** C1
Thames Gv *GOL/RIS/CU* WA3 ..... **29** M2
Thames Side *EP* CH65 .... **121** H1
Thatcher Cl *ALT* WA14 .... **61** J4
Thatcher Gv *BIDD* ST8 .... **227** H4
Thaxted Dr *OFTN* SK2 .... **48** A7
Theatre Ct *NWCHE* CW9 .... **13** H1
Thelwall Cl *HALE/TIMP* WA15 .... **42** E6⑦
Thelwall La *WARRS* WA4 .... **56** F1
Thelwall New Rd *WARRS* WA4 ... **57** H1
Thelwall Rd *GTS/LS* CH66 .... **94** E8
   SALE M33 .... **43** L1
Theobald Rd *ALT* WA14 .... **61** K3
Thetford Cl *MCFLDN* SK10 .... **138** C1⑥
Thetford Rd *WARRW/BUR* WA5 .. **35** L6
Thewlis St *WARRW/BUR* WA5 .... **4** B7
Third Av *ALS/KID* ST7 .... **242** E3
   CW/HAS CW1 .... **19** L9
   FLINT CH6 .... **116** A7
   POY/DIS SK12 .... **86** D3
   RUNC WA7 .... **73** M5
   SBCH CW11 .... **204** A7
Thirlby Dr *WYTH/NTH* M22 .... **63** K3
Thirlemere Rd *STKP* SK1 .... **3** J1
Thirlmere *MCFLDS* SK11 .... **137** M7
Thirlmere Av
   WARRN/WOL WA2 .... **37** J1⑥
Thirlmere Cl *FROD/HEL* WA6...... **99** K4
   HOLMCH CW4 .... **181** C1
   WILM/AE SK9 .... **109** M3⑨
Thirlmere Ct *CONG* CW12 .... **207** G2
Thirlmere Dr *LYMM* WA13 .... **58** F1
Thirlmere Rd *CHNE* CH2 .... **146** A7
   CW/SHV CW2 .... **237** M3
   EP CH65 .... **121** J2
   GOL/RIS/CU WA3 .... **23** J3⑦
   NSTN CH64 .... **91** H7
   PART M31 .... **31** L8
   WYTH/NTH M22 .... **63** H2
Thirsk Av *SALE* M33 .... **54** A8
Thirsk Cl *RUNC* WA7 .... **73** J6⑧
Thirsk Wy *MCFLDN* SK10 .... **138** C1⑥
Thistle Sq *PART* M31 .... **40** E2⑨
Thistleton Cl *MCFLDS* SK11 .... **15** C9
Thistlewood Dr *WILM/AE* SK9 ... **84** D5
Thomas Brassey Cl *CHNE* CH2 ... **17** K2
Thomas Cl *ALS/KID* ST7 .... **224** E8
   CH/BCN CH1 .... **144** F1
   CHNE CH2 .... **146** F4
   EP CH65 .... **121** H2⑧
Thomas Ct *RUNC* WA7 .... **73** M5⑦
Thomasons Bridge La
   WARRS WA4 .... **55** L6
Thomas St *ALS/KID* ST7 .... **242** D4
   ALS/KID ST7 .... **243** M3
   BIDD ST8 .... **227** J3
   CW/HAS CW1 .... **19** C2
   FLINT CH6 .... **116** B5⑧
   GOL/RIS/CU WA3 .... **23** G4⑦
   HALE/TIMP WA15 .... **42** E8⑧
   MPL/ROM SK6 .... **48** A1⑧
   MPL/ROM SK6 .... **49** H2⑧
   RUNC WA7 .... **9** J1
   STKP SK1 .... **3** G9
   WDN WA8 .... **7** G7
Thomas St West *OFTN* SK2 .... **3** G9
Thompson Av *GOL/RIS/CU* WA3 .. **29** L1
Thompson Dr *WHITCH* SY13 ..... **269** L5⑤
Thompson St *GOL/RIS/CU* WA3 .. **29** L7
Thomson St *EDGY/DAV* SK3 .... **2** F8
Thoresway Rd *WILM/AE* SK9 ..... **83** M7
Thorley Cl *GOL/RIS/CU* WA3 ..... **29** M1
Thorley Dr *HALE/TIMP* WA15 .... **43** H7
Thorley Gv *CW/SHV* CW2 .... **18** B9
Thorley La *HALE/TIMP* WA15 ..... **43** H6
   HALE/TIMP WA15 .... **62** B1
   HALE/TIMP WA15 .... **62** F3
Thorley Ms *BRAM/HZG* SK7 ...... **65** M5⑤
Thornberry Cl *CH/BCN* CH1 ...... **144** B4
Thornbrook Wy *SBCH* CW11 ...... **203** K6⑦
Thornbury Av
   GOL/RIS/CU WA3 .... **23** L5⑧
Thornbury Cl *CHD/CHDH* SK8 .... **65** J3
Thornbush Cl *GOL/RIS/CU* WA3 .. **23** L3
Thorn Cl *BRAM/HZG* WA5........ **54** F1
Thorndale Gv *HALE/TIMP* WA15 .. **43** G7
Thorn Dr *WYTH/NTH* M22 .... **64** A4
Thorndyke Cl *RAIN/WH* L35 ...... **33** L3
Thorne Cl *MCFLDN* SK10 .... **112** A7⑧
Thorne Dr *GTS/LS* CH66 .... **94** B8
Thorneycroft Rd
   HALE/TIMP WA15 .... **43** H7
Thorney Dr *BRAM/HZG* SK7 ...... **65** J6⑧
Thorneyholme Dr *KNUT* WA16 ... **107** H3
Thornfield Cl *GOL/RIS/CU* WA3 .. **23** J4⑧
Thornfield Cl *CHD/CHDH* SK8 .... **65** G2
Thornfield Hey *WILM/AE* SK9 .. **84** E4⑩
Thornfield Rd *HTNM* SK4.......... **46** A1
Thornfields *CQ* CH5 .... **142** A8⑧
Thorn Gv *CHD/CHDH* SK8 .... **65** H5
   HALE/TIMP WA15 .... **61** L1⑧
Thorngrove Av *NTHM/RTH* M23 .. **43** K5
Thorngrove Dr *WILM/AE* SK9 .... **84** C6
Thorngrove Hl *WILM/AE* SK9 ..... **84** C6
Thorngrove Rd *WILM/AE* SK9 .... **84** C6
Thornham Rd *SALE* M33 .... **42** E2
Thornhill Dr
   AUD/MAD/W CW3 .... **267** L5⑥
Thornholme Rd *MPL/ROM* SK6 ... **48** F8
Thorn La *NWCHW* CW8 .... **12** A9

Thornleigh Av *PS/BROM* CH62 ... **93** M1
Thornleigh Dr *GTS/LS* CH66 ...... **94** E6
Thornleigh Rd *LYMM* WA13 .... **58** C1
Thorn Rd *BRAM/HZG* SK7 .... **65** K7
   RUNC WA7 .... **9** M8
   WARR WA1 .... **38** A4
Thornsett Rd *NM/HAY* SK22 ...... **69** K2
Thornsgreen Rd
   WYTH/NTH M22 .... **63** K4
Thornton *WDN* WA8 .... **6** C5
Thornton Av *MCFLDS* SK11 .... **138** A7
Thornton Bank
   TPLY/KEL CW6 .... **198** D8⑩
Thornton Cl *LEIGH* WN7 .... **24** F3
Thorntondale Dr
   WARRW/BUR WA5 .... **35** M5
   CW/SHV CW2 .... **238** A5⑧
   WILM/AE SK9 .... **84** D1⑧
Thornton Ga *CHD/CHDH* SK8 .... **45** G6⑧
Thornton Green La *CHNE* CW2 ... **122** E3
Thornton Rd *CHD/CHDH* SK8 .... **64** C3
   EP CH65 .... **95** L8
   WARRW/BUR WA5 .... **36** B8
Thorn Tree Dr *CW/HAS* CW1 ..... **221** G3
Thorntree Gn *WARRS* WA4 .... **57** H7
Thornway *BRAM/HZG* SK7 .... **65** J4
   MCFLDN SK10 .... **113** G5⑧
   MPL/ROM SK6 .... **67** M5
Thornwythe Gv *GTS/LS* CH66 .... **94** E8
Thornycroft *WSFD* CW7 .... **177** G3⑧
Thornycroft Cl *MCFLDS* SK11 .... **161** L3⑪
Thornycroft St *MCFLDS* SK11 ..... **15** J6⑧
Thorpe Cl *CW/HAS* CW1 .... **220** F4⑨
Thorp St *MCFLDN* SK10 .... **15** H4
Thorsby Rd *HALE/TIMP* WA15 .... **42** F7⑦
Thowler La *ALT* WA14 .... **59** M6
Threaphurst La *BRAM/HZG* SK7 .. **67** J2
Threapwood Rd
   WYTH/NTH M22 .... **63** J3
Three Fields Cl *CONG* CW12 ...... **207** G1
Threeways *NWCHW* CW8 .... **127** K8
Thresher Cl *SALE* M33 .... **43** M1⑧
Threshfield Dr *HALE/TIMP* WA15 .. **43** J5
Throstle Gv *MPL/ROM* SK6 .... **48** E7
Thurlestone Rd *BRAM/HZG* SK7 .. **66** B2
Thurlestone Rd *ALT* WA14 .... **42** B6
Thurlow *GOL/RIS/CU* WA3 .... **23** L5⑧
Thurlwood Rd *ALS/KID* ST7 .... **243** J1⑧
Thurnham Gn *WILM/AE* SK9 ..... **110** A3⑦
Thurstan Rd *CHSW/BR* CH4 ...... **168** E7
Thynne St *WARR* WA1 .... **4** E8
Tibbs Cross La *WDN* WA8 .... **34** D3
Tidal La *WARRN/WOL* WA2....... **37** M4
Tidebrook Pl *BURS/TUN* ST6 ..... **243** L5
Tideswell Cl *CHD/CHDH* SK8 ..... **64** D4⑧
Tideswell Rd *BRAM/HZG* SK7 ..... **66** E4
Tidnock Av *CONG* CW12 .... **184** D7
Tiffield Ct *WSFD* CW7 .... **154** A8⑧
Tilbury Pl *RUNC* WA7 .... **74** E6
Tildsley Crs *RUNC* WA7 .... **72** F6
Tilewright Cl *ALS/KID* ST7 .... **243** H2⑧
Tillard Av *EDGY/DAV* SK3 .... **46** B4
Tilley St *WARR* WA1 .... **5** J5
Tillhey Rd *WYTH/NTH* M22 .... **63** K2
Tilman Cl *WARRW/BUR* WA5 ..... **36** B4⑧
Tilston Av *WARRS* WA4 .... **38** A8
Tilston Cl *ALS/KID* ST7 .... **243** G4
   CW/SHV CW2 .... **253** L2
   NWCHW CW8 .... **13** K9
Tilston Rd *MALPAS* SY14 .... **246** A3
Timberfields Rd *CH/BCN* CH1 .... **144** A4
Timber La *NWCHE* CW9 .... **13** H1
Timberscombe Gdns *WARR* WA1 .. **38** E6
Timber St *MCFLDN* SK10 .... **15** L2
Timbrell Av *CW/HAS* CW1 .... **221** G6
Timmis Cl *WARRN/WOL* WA2 .... **38** A1⑧
Timmis Crs *WDN* WA8 .... **7** G3
Timperley Av *WARRS* WA4 .... **38** A8
Timperley La *LEIGH* WN7 .... **25** H2
Timperley St *WDN* WA8 .... **7** J5⑧
Timpson Rd *NTHM/RTH* M23 .... **43** L5
Tinkwood La *MALPAS* SY14 ...... **256** F4
Tinsley St *WARRS* WA4 .... **56** F1
Tintagel Cl *MCFLDN* SK10 .... **137** L4
   RUNC WA7 .... **74** C6⑧
Tintern Av *AIMK* WN4............... **22** D1
   CHNE **145** M6
Tintern Cl *POY/DIS* SK12 .... **66** D7
   WARRW/BUR WA5 .... **36** E2⑧
Tintern Dr *HALE/TIMP* WA15 ..... **62** C2
Tintern Gv *STKP* SK1 .... **3** L6
Tintern Rd *CHD/CHDH* SK8 .... **65** H6
Tipping St *ALT* WA14 .... **61** K1
   HALE/TIMP WA15...................... **61** K1
Tipton Cl *CHD/CHDH* SK8 .... **46** B8
Tipton Dr *NTHM/RTH* M23 .... **44** A2
Tiree Cl *BRAM/HZG* SK7 .... **66** F3
Tirley La *TPLY/KEL* CW6 .... **173** M1
Titchfield Rd *NSTN* CH64 .... **91** H2
Tithebarn La *HALE/TIMP* WA15 .. **62** C4
Tithebarn Rd *HALE/TIMP* WA15 .. **62** C4
The Tithings *RUNC* WA7 .... **73** L3
Tiverton Av *SALE* M33 .... **42** F1
Tiverton Cl *CHNE* CH2 .... **145** L7
   HUY L36 .... **32** B2⑧
   SBCH CW11 .... **204** C5
Tiverton Dr *SALE* M33 .... **42** F1
Tiverton Rd *HLWD* L26 .... **50** E6
Tiverton Sq *WARRW/BUR* WA5 .. **35** L8⑧
Tiviot Dl *STKP* SK1 .... **3** J1
Tiviot Wy *STKP* SK1 .... **3** J1
Tobermory Rd *CHD/CHDH* SK8 .. **64** F2
Todbrook Cl *CHF/WBR* SK23 ..... **89** G3
Toft Cl *CHSW/BR* CH4 .... **168** E7
   WDN WA8 .... **6** E3
Toft Rd *KNUT* WA16 .... **107** G3
Toftwood Av *RAIN/WH* L35 ...... **33** L3⑧
Tolland La *HALE/TIMP* WA15...... **61** M4
Tolland La *CHD/CHDH* SK8 .... **65** H5
Toll Bar Av *MCFLDS* SK11 .... **15** L6⑪
Toll Bar Rd *CHSE* CH3 .... **170** C3
   MCFLDS SK11 .... **137** M4⑪
   WARRN/WOL WA2 .... **37** G1
Tollbar St *STKP* SK1 .... **3** H7

Tollemache Dr *CW/HAS* CW1 ... **221** G4
Tollgate Cl *ALS/KID* ST7 .... **242** C4
Tollgate Dr *AUD/MAD/W* CW3 .. **263** M8
Tomkinson St *CHNE* CH2 .... **17** K2
Tom La *ALT* WA14 .... **60** C4
Tomlinson Av *WARRN/WOL* WA2 .. **37** K4
Tommy's La *CONG* CW12 .... **184** F8
   CW/HAS CW1 .... **19** J7
Tonbridge Rd *MCFLDN* SK10 .... **138** B2⑧
   SPK/HALE L24 .... **50** B8
Toogood Cl *CHNE* CH2 .... **146** F4⑧
Topcroft Cl *WYTH/NTH* M22 ..... **44** E4
Top Farm La *WSFD* CW7 .... **218** F2
Topfield Rd *WYTH/NTH* M22 ..... **63** J1
Topping Ct *GOL/RIS/CU* WA3 .... **29** H8
The Toppings *MPL/ROM* SK6 ..... **48** A1
Top Rd *BIDD* ST8 .... **209** K7
   FROD/HEL WA6 .... **99** K7
   FROD/HEL WA6 .... **126** B3
Top Station Rd *ALS/KID* ST7 ..... **226** C5
Torbay Dr *OFTN* SK2 .... **3** M9
Torcross Wy *HLWD* L26 .... **50** E6
Torkington La *BRAM/HZG* SK7 ... **67** K1
Torkington Rd *BRAM/HZG* SK7 ... **66** F2
   CHD/CHDH SK8 .... **45** H7
   WILM/AE SK9 .... **84** C6
Torkington St *EDGY/DAV* SK3 ...... **2** C9
Toronto Av *MANAIR* M90 .... **63** H5
Toronto Rd *OFTN* SK2 .... **47** G6⑧
Torquay Dr *OFTN* SK2 .... **47** H8
Torridon Gv *GTS/LS* CH66 .... **120** F1⑧
Torrin Cl *EDGY/DAV* SK3 .... **46** F7
Torrington Dr *HLWD* L26 .... **50** E6
Torrise *TPLY/KEL* CW6 .... **197** K3
Torr Rd *MCFLDS* SK11 .... **138** C8⑧
Torrs Va *NM/HAY* SK22 .... **69** J5⑧
Torr Top St *NM/HAY* SK22 .... **69** J5⑧
Torrvale Rd *NM/HAY* SK22 .... **69** H5
Torville Dr *BIDD* ST8 .... **227** L4
Totland Cl *WARRW/BUR* WA5 .... **35** J3
Totland Gv *CHNE* CH2 .... **145** L8
Totnes Av *BRAM/HZG* SK7 .... **66** A2
   HLWD L26 .... **50** F3
Totridge Cl *OFTN* SK2 .... **47** K7
Tottenham Dr *NTHM/RTH* M23 .. **43** K5
Tourney Gn *WARRW/BUR* WA5 ... **36** A2
Tours Av *NTHM/RTH* M23 .... **44** A2⑧
Tower Av *NTHM/RTH* M23 .... **43** M7
Trossach Cl *WARRN/WOL* WA2 ... **37** L2
Troutbeck Av *CONG* CW12 ...... **207** G3⑧
   WARRW/BUR WA5 .... **4** C2
Troutbeck Cl *RUNC* WA7 .... **74** A7
Troutbeck Gv *WSFD* CW7 .... **177** K2
Troutbeck Rd *CHD/CHDH* SK8 ... **64** B1
   HALE/TIMP WA15 .... **43** K7⑧
Trouthall La *KNUT* WA16 .... **131** M1
Trubshaw Pl *ALS/KID* ST7 .... **243** H1
Trueman's Ct *CO* CH5 .... **166** C4
Trueman's Wy *CO* CH5 .... **166** C3
Trumans La *GTS/LS* CH66 .... **94** C5
Truro Cl *BRAM/HZG* SK7 .... **65** M5
   CONG CW12 .... **207** L4
   GTS/LS CH66 .... **120** F4⑧⑪
   MCFLDN SK10 .... **137** L3
   RUNC WA7 .... **74** C6⑧
   WARR WA1 .... **38** B4
Tudor Av *FLINT* CH6 .... **116** A8
Tudor Cl *CO* CH5 .... **142** B7
   GTS/LS CH66 .... **120** F4
   NWCHE CW9 .... **130** E6
   WARRS WA4 .... **57** C2
   WSFD CW7 .... **177** K6⑧
Tudor Dr *MCFLDN* SK10 .... **111** K5
Tudor Gn *WILM/AE* SK9 .... **84** E3
Tudor Rd *ALT* WA14 .... **42** B5
   RUNC WA7 .... **74** B1
   WILM/AE SK9 .... **84** E3
   WLTN L25 .... **50** C5
The Tudors *BURS/TUN* ST6 ...... **243** M8
Tudor Wy *CHSE* CH3 .... **170** A5
   CONG CW12 .... **207** K3
   NANT CW5 .... **251** L1
Tue La *WDN* WA8 .... **33** H6
Tuffley Rd *NTHM/RTH* M23 .... **44** A8
Tulip Cl *EDGY/DAV* SK3 .... **46** D7
Tulip Dr *HALE/TIMP* WA15 .... **42** F6
Tulip Rd *PART* M31 .... **40** E2
Tully Av *NEWLW* WA12 .... **26** E1
Tulworth Rd *POY/DIS* SK12 .... **66** D8
Tumblewood Dr
   CHD/CHDH SK8 .... **45** L8⑧
Tunbridge Cl *CW/SHV* CW2 ..... **238** A4
   WARRW/BUR WA5 .... **36** A4
Tunnel Rd *NWCHW* CW8 .... **129** H2
Tunnicliffe Rd *MCFLDS* SK11 .... **162** F1
Tunnicliffe St *MCFLDN* SK10 ..... **15** G4⑧
Tunshill Rd *NTHM/RTH* M23 ..... **43** L3
Tunstall Rd *BIDD* ST8 .... **227** J7
   CONG **186** A8
Tunstall St *HTNM* SK4................ **2** F7
Turf La *MCFLDS* SK11 .... **162** C1
Turf Lea Rd *MPL/ROM* SK6 .... **68** B3
Turnall Rd *WDN* WA8 .... **52** B5
Turnberry Cl *LYMM* WA13 .... **39** J3
   MCFLDN SK10 .... **112** C8
   NWCHE CW9 .... **130** E5⑧
   WSFD CW7 .... **177** J2⑧
Turnberry Dr *WILM/AE* SK9 ...... **84** D4
Turnberry Rd *CHD/CHDH* SK8 ... **64** C3
Turnbury Rd *WYTH/NTH* M22 .... **44** E7
Turncliff Crs *MPL/ROM* SK6 ...... **48** D5
Turncroft La *STKP* SK1 .... **3** K6
Turner Cl *WDN* WA8 .... **52** D1⑧
Turner Rd *MPL/ROM* SK6 .... **48** F6
Turner St *MCFLDN* SK10 .... **113** H4
   NANT CW5 .... **21** C6
Turnfield Rd *CHD/CHDH* SK8 .... **64** C1
Turnhurst Rd *BURS/TUN* ST6 ... **243** M6
Turnill Dr *AIMK* WN4................ **22** B2
Turnlea Cl *BIDD* ST8 .... **227** H6
Turnock St *MCFLDS* SK11 .... **15** J7
The Turnpike *MPL/ROM* SK6 ..... **48** D5
Turnstone Av *NEWLW* WA12 ..... **22** C8
Turnstone Dr *HLWD* L26 .... **50** E3
Turnstone Rd *OFTN* SK2 .... **48** A7
Turret Hall Dr
   GOL/RIS/CU WA3 .... **23** L4⑪⑬

Trawden Gn *OFTN* SK2 .... **47** K8⑧
Treborth Rd *CH/BCN* CH1 .... **168** D1
Tree Bank Cl *RUNC* WA7 .... **9** G6
Treen Cl *MCFLDN* SK10 .... **137** K3
Tree Tops *NSTN* CH64 .... **91** L7
Treetops Cl *WARR* WA1 .... **37** M5
Tree Wy *KNUT* WA16 .... **107** G5
Trefoil Cl *CHSE* CH3 .... **170** B6
   GOL/RIS/CU WA3 .... **23** M3
Tregele Cl *CH/BCN* CH1 .... **168** D1
Trelawny Av *FLINT* CH6 .... **116** B6
Trelawny Sq *FLINT* CH6 .... **116** A5⑧
Trenance Cl *RUNC* WA7 .... **74** B7
Trenchard Dr *WYTH/NTH* M22 .. **63** M5
Trent Av *WSFD* CW7 .... **178** B3
Trent Cl *BRAM/HZG* SK7 .... **65** J6
   RAIN/WH L35 .... **33** H1
   WDN WA8 .... **34** B8
   WSFD CW7 .... **178** B3
Trentdale *EP* CH65 .... **121** H1
Trent Gv *BIDD* ST8 .... **227** K6
Trentham Av *HTNM* SK4............ **45** M1⑧
Trentham Cl *WDN* WA8 .... **34** B8⑧
Trentham St *RUNC* WA7 .... **8** E1
Trent Rd *RAIN/WH* L35 .... **33** H1
Tressel Dr *STHEL* WA9 .... **34** A1
Trevalyn Wy *WRX/GR/LL* LL12 .. **210** C5
Trevithick Cl *CW/HAS* CW1 ...... **222** A8⑧
Trevone Cl *KNUT* WA16 .... **107** C3
Trevor Av *SALE* M33 .... **42** F2
Trevor Gv *GTS/LS* CH66 .... **120** F3
Trevor Sq *STKP* SK1 .... **3** K7
The Triangle *HALE/TIMP* WA15... **43** H5
Tribune Av *ALT* WA14 .... **42** B5⑧
Trickett La *NWCHW* CW8 .... **152** A1⑧
Tricketts La *NANT* CW5 .... **237** L7
Trinity Cl *CW/SHV* CW2 .... **18** B9
Trinity Ct *GOL/RIS/CU* WA3 ...... **29** M7
Trinity Gdns *EDGY/DAV* SK3 ..... **65** M1
Trinity La *MCFLDS* SK11 .... **162** F1
Trinity Pl *CONG* CW12 .... **208** B4
   WDN WA8 .... **7** J6
Trinity Sq *MCFLDN* SK10 .... **15** L3
Trinity St *CH/BCN* CH1 .... **16** F5⑧
   MPL/ROM SK6 .... **48** F7⑧
Trispen Cl *HLWD* L26 .... **50** E4
Troon Dr *CHD/CHDH* SK8 .... **64** C3⑧
Troon Rd *NTHM/RTH* M23 .... **43** M6
   HOLMCH CW4 .... **181** C1
Troon Cl *BRAM/HZG* SK7 .... **66** A5⑧

Turrocks Cl *NSTN* CH64 .... **91** L7⑧
Turrocks Cft *NSTN* CH64 .... **91** L7
Turton Cl *GOL/RIS/CU* WA3 ...... **29** J7
Turton St *GOL/RIS/CU* WA3 ...... **23** G4
Turves Rd *CHD/CHDH* SK8 .... **64** E3
Tuscan Cl *WDN* WA8 .... **34** B7
Tuscan Rd *DID/WITH* M20 .... **45** H4
Tushingham Cl *CHSE* CH3 .... **170** D3⑧
Tuson Dr *WDN* WA8 .... **33** M8
Tutor Bank *NEWLW* WA12 .... **27** K1
Tweed Cl *ALT* WA14 .... **42** C6
Tweedsmuir Cl
   WARRN/WOL WA2 .... **29** G8⑧
Tweenbrook Av *NTHM/RTH* M23 .. **63** G1
Twemlow Av *SBCH* CW11 .... **204** B4
Twemlow La *HOLMCH* CW4 ...... **157** H6
Twenty Acre Rd
   WARRW/BUR WA5 .... **36** C4
Twigworth Rd
   WYTH/NTH M22 .... **63** J2⑦
Twining Brook Rd
   CHD/CHDH SK8 .... **65** H1
Twinnies Rd *WILM/AE* SK9 .... **84** B3
Twiss Green Dr *GOL/RIS/CU* WA3 .. **24** D8
Twiss Green La *GOL/RIS/CU* WA3 .. **24** D8
Twist Av *GOL/RIS/CU* WA3 .... **23** J4
Twoacre Av *WYTH/NTH* M22 ..... **44** C7
Two Acre Gv *GTS/LS* CH66 ...... **120** F3
Twyford Cl *DID/WITH* M20 .... **44** F1⑧
   WDN WA8 .... **34** B8
Twyford La *WDN* WA8 .... **34** D6
Tyberton Pl *SPK/HALE* L24 .... **50** C6
Tyler St *WILM/AE* SK9 .... **110** A3
Tyne Cl *WARRN/WOL* WA2 .... **37** L2⑧
Tynedale Av *CW/SHV* CW2 .... **18** D8
Tynedale Cl *MCFLDS* SK11 .... **14** E5
Tynemouth Rd *RUNC* WA7 .... **74** C6
Tynesdale *EP* CH65 .... **121** H1
Tynwald Crs *WDN* WA8 .... **33** M7
Tynwald Dr *WARRS* WA4 .... **56** C5
Tyrer Rd *NEWLW* WA12 .... **27** J3
Tyrone Cl *NTHM/RTH* M23 .... **43** K4
Tytherington Cl *MWCH* CW10 ... **179** J6⑧
Tytherington Dr *MCFLDN* SK10 .. **112** D8
Tytherington La *MCFLDN* SK10... **112** D7
Tytherington Park Rd
   MCFLDN SK10 .... **138** D2

U

Ullapool Cl *GTS/LS* CH66 .... **93** M6
Ullswater *MCFLDS* SK11 .... **137** M7
Ullswater Av *CW/SHV* CW2 ...... **237** L1
   WARRN/WOL WA2 .... **37** J1
   WSFD CW7 .... **177** J2
Ullswater Crs *CHNE* CH2 .... **146** A6
Ullswater Dr *WILM/AE* SK9 ...... **108** F5
Ullswater Gv *RUNC* WA7 .... **73** K7
Ullswater Rd *CONG* CW12 .... **207** G2
   EP CH65 .... **121** J2
   GOL/RIS/CU WA3 .... **23** J3
   STKP SK1 .... **47** H5⑧
   WILM/AE SK9 .... **64** C8
   WYTH/NTH M22 .... **63** J2
Ulverston Av *WARRN/WOL* WA2 .. **37** H1
Ulviet Ga *KNUT* WA16 .... **59** J8
Underbridge La *WARRS* WA4 ..... **55** L6
Underhill *MPL/ROM* SK6 .... **48** C1
Under Rainow Rd *CONG* CW12 .. **208** E3
The Underway *RUNC* WA7 .... **73** M4
Underwood Cl
   MCFLDN SK10 .... **137** M3⑩
Underwood Dr *EP* CH65 .... **121** H2
Underwood La *CW/HAS* CW1 ..... **18** C1
Underwood Rd *WILM/AE* SK9 ... **110** C3
Unicorn Gtwy *MCFLDN* SK10 .... **15** G4
Unicorn Pl *BURS/TUN* ST6 ...... **243** M7
Union Bank La *WDN* WA8 .... **34** B3
Union Rd *MCFLDS* SK11 .... **15** K6
   MPL/ROM SK6 .... **48** F6⑧
   NM/HAY SK22 .... **69** H5
Union St *CH/BCN* CH1 .... **17** J5
   CONG CW12 .... **207** K1
   CW/SHV CW2 .... **19** G6
   MCFLDS SK11 .... **14** F6
   RUNC WA7 .... **9** K3
   SBCH CW11 .... **204** A6
   STKP SK1 .... **3** G7
   WARR WA1 .... **5** G7
Union Ter *CH/BCN* CH1 .... **17** H4
Unity Wy *ALS/KID* ST7 .... **242** D4
   STKP SK1 .... **3** H8
Unsworth Av *GOL/RIS/CU* WA3 .. **23** K3
Unsworth Ct
   WARRN/WOL WA2 .... **37** M3⑧
Upavon Rd *WYTH/NTH* M22 ...... **63** M1
Upcast La *WILM/AE* SK9 .... **109** K1
Uplands *NWCHW* CW8 .... **127** K8
Uplands Av *BURS/TUN* ST6 ...... **243** M6
Uplands Rd *NWCHE* CW9 .... **103** K8
The Uplands *BIDD* ST8 .... **227** L2
Upper Aston Hall La *CQ* CH5 .... **166** B3
Upper Brook St *STKP* SK1 .... **3** H6
Upper Cambrian Rd
   CH/BCN CH1 .... **16** D3
Upper Downs *ALT* WA14 .... **61** J1⑧
Upper Haigh St *WSFD* CW7 ...... **177** J4
Upper Hibbert La *MPL/ROM* SK6 .. **48** F8
Upper Mersey Rd *WDN* WA8 ..... **53** C7
Upper Mersey St *EP* CH65 .... **10** F4⑧
   EP CH65 .... **121** J2
Uppermill Dr *BNG/LEV* M19 ...... **45** J7
Upper Northgate St
   CH/BCN CH1 .... **16** F2
Upper Raby Rd *NSTN* CH64 ...... **92** A2
Upton Av *CHD/CHDH* SK8 .... **65** G4⑧
Upton Cl *GOL/RIS/CU* WA3 ...... **23** K4
   SPK/HALE L24 .... **70** E1⑧
   WSFD CW7 .... **153** M8
Upton Dr *ALT* WA14 .... **42** E4
   CHNE **145** J6
   WARRW/BUR WA5 .... **35** M7
Upton Gra *WDN* WA8 .... **33** K8
Upton Gn *SPK/HALE* L24 .... **70** E1⑧
Upton La *CHNE* CH2 .... **145** J5

WDN WA8 33 M8
Upton Pk CHNE CH2 145 K6
Upton Rd GTS/LS CH66 94 D8
Upwood Rd GOL/RIS/CU WA3 23 K5
Urban Dr HALE/TIMP WA15 42 E8
Urban Rd HALE/TIMP WA15 42 E8
Ure Ct EP CH65 10 A3
Urmston Av NEWLW WA12 22 B7
Urwick Rd MPL/ROM SK6 48 B3
Utkinton La TPLY/KEL CW6 174 D6
Utkinton Rd TPLY/KEL CW6 197 J1

V

Vahler Ter RUNC WA7 9 L2
Vale Av WARRN/WOL WA2 5 H1
Valebrook Dr NANT CW5 253 G4
Vale Cl BRAM/HZG SK7 47 L8
CHSW/BR CH4 190 C1
HTNM SK4 45 M2
MPL/ROM SK6 48 F2
Vale Ct WARRS WA4 101 G1
Vale Cresent CHD/CHDH SK8 64 F2
Vale Gdns EP CH65 95 H8
FROD/HEL WA6 98 B8
Vale Head WILM/AE SK9 84 D2
Valentine Rd ALS/KID ST7 243 G3
NEWLW WA12 26 F1 2
Vale Owen Rd
WARRN/WOL WA2 37 K3 6
Vale Rd ALT WA14 61 H3
EP CH65 95 H8
HALE/TIMP WA15 43 G7
HTNM SK4 45 M3
MPL/ROM SK6 48 B4
NWCHE CW9 104 B6
NWCHW CW8 129 J8
TPLY/KEL CW6 198 A8
WILM/AE SK9 83 L4
Vale Royal Dr NWCHW CW8 153 G5
Vale Vw NWCHE CW9 130 D3 2
Valewood Av HTNM SK4 46 A3
Valiant Cl WARRN/WOL WA2 37 M2
Valley Cl ALS/KID ST7 240 F1
CHD/CHDH SK8 64 E1
KNUT WA16 107 G5
Valley Ct WARRN/WOL WA2 37 M3
Valley Dr CHNE CH2 145 J7
GTS/LS CH66 94 D7
WILM/AE SK9 84 C1
Valley La NWCHW CW8 151 M1
Valley Rd BRAM/HZG SK7 65 M3
CHD/CHDH SK8 64 E1
CW/SHV CW2 237 M3
MCFLDS SK11 138 A7
NWCHW CW8 128 C3
Valley Vw GTS/LS CH66 94 D7
NEWLW WA12 27 H3
NWCHE CW9 130 C5
Valley Wy KNUT WA16 107 G5
Vanguard Ct GOL/RIS/CU WA3 29 K8 6
Varden Gv EDGY/DAV SK3 46 D7
Varden Rd POY/DIS SK12 86 E1
Vardon Dr WILM/AE SK9 84 D6
Varey Rd CONG CW12 184 F8
Vaudrey Crs CONG CW12 207 M1
Vaudrey Dr BRAM/HZG SK7 66 E2
CHD/CHDH SK8 65 G1
HALE/TIMP WA15 43 G4
WARR WA1 38 D5
Vaughan Rd CHF/WBR SK23 89 L7
HTNM SK4 2 C1
Vaughans La CHSE CH3 170 A4
Vauxhall Cl WARRW/BUR WA5 35 M8
Vauxhall Rd NANT CW5 20 E3
Vauxhall Wy WSFD CW7 177 J6
Vawdrey Dr NTHM/RTH M23 43 M2 5
Venable's Rd CH/BCN CH1 144 F8
NWCHE CW9 13 J1
Venables Wy KNUT WA16 59 J8
MWCH CW10 179 L7
Venlow Gdns CHD/CHDH SK8 65 H3
Venns Rd WARRN/WOL WA2 5 L2
Ventnor Cl MWCH CW10 179 J4
WARRW/BUR WA5 35 K5 4
Ventnor Rd DID/WITH M20 45 J1 4
HTNM SK4 46 A2 5
Verbena Cl PART M31 40 F1
RUNC WA7 73 M8 13
Verdin Av NWCHW CW8 12 F1
Verdin Cl NWCHE CW9 153 M5 2
WSFD CW7 177 J2
Verdin Ct CW/HAS CW1 221 G4
Verdin St NWCHE CW9 130 C4
Verdure Av SALE M33 43 J3
Vere St CW/HAS CW1 18 E2
Verity Cl CW/HAS CW1 222 C8
Vermont Cl WARRW/BUR WA5 36 C5
Vernon Av CONG CW12 207 M4
GTS/LS CH66 94 A2
STKP SK1 3 L4
Vernon Cl CH/BCN CH1 144 A4
CHD/CHDH SK8 64 E3
POY/DIS SK12 86 D2
Vernon Dr AUD/MAD/W CW3 264 F8
MPL/ROM SK6 48 C5
Vernon Gv SALE M33 43 L1
Vernon Pk HALE/TIMP WA15 43 G5
Vernon Rd CH/BCN CH1 16 D4
MPL/ROM SK6 47 L1
POY/DIS SK12 86 E2
Vernon St BRAM/HZG SK7 66 D1 18
CW/HAS CW1 18 C1
MCFLDN SK10 15 L5
STKP SK1 3 G4 2
WARR WA1 5 H8
Vernon Wy CW/HAS CW1 19 G2
CW/SHV CW2 19 G5
Veronica Rd DID/WITH M20 45 J1
Veronica Wy GTS/LS CH66 94 D5
Verrill Av NTHM/RTH M23 44 C3 2
Veryan Cl HLWD L26 50 F3
Vetch Cl GOL/RIS/CU WA3 31 H7
The Vetches CHSE CH3 146 F7
Viaduct Rd ALT WA14 42 D5
Viaduct St EDGY/DAV SK3 2 E6
NEWLW WA12 27 G1
Vicarage Av CHD/CHDH SK8 65 H4
Vicarage Cl CHSE CH3 146 F7 5
SPK/HALE L24 71 L3
Vicarage Ct WRXS/E LL13 228 E4
Vicarage Gdns SBCH CW11 203 K4
Vicarage Gv WSFD CW7 177 K7
Vicarage Hl FROD/HEL WA6 98 C8 7
Vicarage La ALT WA14 61 J3
AUD/MAD/W CW3 264 A8
AUD/MAD/W CW3 267 L7
FROD/HEL WA6 98 C8
FROD/HEL WA6 99 J5
NSTN CH64 118 D2
POY/DIS SK12 66 E7
SBCH CW11 203 L4
TPLY/KEL CW6 175 M5
TPLY/KEL CW6 216 F4
Vicarage Rd AIMK WN4 22 B2
CHNE CH2 17 M1
CW/HAS CW1 222 D6
EDGY/DAV SK3 46 E6
NWCHE CW9 13 L3
WDN WA8 7 H6
Vicarage Wk NWCHE CW9 13 L4
Vicarage Wy MCFLDS SK11 137 M5
Vicar's Cl CHSE CH3 148 F5
Vicars Cross Rd CHSE CH3 170 B2
Vicar's La CH/BCN CH1 17 H6
Vickers Cl CQ CH5 166 C1
Vickers Rd WDN WA8 52 E8
Vickers Wy NWCHE CW9 13 J4
Victoria Av ALS/KID ST7 242 F2
BRAM/HZG SK7 66 E1 5
CHD/CHDH SK8 65 G2
CW/HAS CW1 222 C8 3
CW/SHV CW2 220 F8
DID/WITH M20 45 G1
HALE/TIMP WA15 42 E5
HOLMCH CW4 181 J2
MPL/ROM SK6 47 M1
WARRS WA4 57 G2
WARRW/BUR WA5 35 K6 5
WDN WA8 53 G2
Victoria Cl BRAM/HZG SK7 65 K6 3
EDGY/DAV SK3 2 F9
WHITCH SY13 270 A5
Victoria Ct CHNE CH2 16 F1
Victoria Crs CHNE CH2 16 F1
CHSW/BR CH4 17 J7
CQ CH5 142 A6 4
Victoria Dr SALE M33 43 K1
Victoria Gv WDN WA8 53 G1 5
Victoria Pk NWCHW CW8 12 F1
Victoria Park Rd
BURS/TUN ST6 243 L8
Victoria Pl RAIN/WH L35 33 J1
WARRS WA4 56 C3
Victoria Rd CH/BCN CH1 17 G3 2
CHNE CH2 16 F1
CHSW/BR CH4 168 D6
CQ CH5 142 A6
EP CH65 10 D7
HALE/TIMP WA15 43 G6
HALE/TIMP WA15 61 L2
IRL M44 31 M3
MCFLDN SK10 137 M3
NEWLW WA12 22 C8
NSTN CH64 92 A6
NWCHE CW9 13 L3
RUNC WA7 9 J2
SALE M33 43 K1
STKP SK1 3 L5
WARRS WA4 56 D3
WARRW/BUR WA5 35 L8 4
WDN WA8 7 H6
WILM/AE SK9 84 A6
WYTH/NTH M22 44 D4
Victoria Rw BIDD ST8 227 J8
Victoria Sq WSFD CW7 177 G4 7
Victoria St ALT WA14 42 D7
CW/HAS CW1 18 F3
KNUT WA16 106 F2
NM/HAY SK22 69 H6 3
NWCHE CW9 130 E2 1
RAIN/WH L35 33 J1 7
SBCH CW11 204 A5
WARR WA1 5 J6
WDN WA8 7 J6
Victoria Ter RAIN/WH L35 33 J1
Victoria Wk MCFLDN SK10 15 J4
Victory Rd BRAM/HZG SK7 65 K6
Victory Rd IRL M44 31 J8
Vienna Rd EDGY/DAV SK3 46 D6
Vienna Rd East EDGY/DAV SK3 46 D6
Viewlands Dr WILM/AE SK9 84 D2 5
View Rd RAIN/WH L35 33 J2
Villa Cl BIDD ST8 227 J6
Villa Farm SBCH CW11 205 H3
Village Cl NWCHE CW9 131 G4
RUNC WA7 74 A4 3
WARRS WA4 38 E8
Village La WARRS WA4 102 D1
Village Rd CHSE CH3 147 L7 1
CHSE CH3 170 E4
CHSE CH3 171 H8
Village St RUNC WA7 74 E2
The Village CONG CW12 207 H4
MCFLDN SK10 112 A6
NSTN CH64 118 D3
Village Wks WRX/GR/LL LL12 210 A7
Village Wy WILM/AE SK9 84 D3
Villa Rd CQ CH5 143 H6
Villars St WARR WA1 5 K7
Villdale Av OFTN SK2 47 J5
Villiers Russell Cl CW/HAS CW1 19 G2
Vincent Cl WARRW/BUR WA5 36 B4
Vincent Dr CHSW/BR CH4 169 H6
Vincent St CW/HAS CW1 19 J4
MCFLDS SK11 15 G7
Vine Bank Rd ALS/KID ST7 243 G2
Vine Cl MCFLDS SK11 138 A7
Vine Crs WARRW/BUR WA5 35 L6
Vine Gv OFTN SK2 47 J6
Vine Rd GTS/LS CH66 120 F4
Vine St BRAM/HZG SK7 66 E1 5
MCFLDN SK10 113 H4
RUNC WA7 9 G3
WDN WA8 7 H6
Vine Tree Av CW/SHV CW2 18 D8
Violet Cl GOL/RIS/CU WA3 29 J8
Violet St AIMK WN4 22 B2
OFTN SK2 46 F6
WDN WA8 7 G7
Virginia Cha CHD/CHDH SK8 64 F4
Virginia Cl NTHM/RTH M23 43 K5
Virginia Dr CH/BCN CH1 144 C7
Viscount Dr CHD/CHDH SK8 64 D5
MANAIR M90 62 F5 1
Vista Av NEWLW WA12 22 A8
Vista Rd NEWLW WA12 22 A8
RUNC WA7 9 H6
The Vista IRL M44 31 J8
Vista Wy NEWLW WA12 22 A8
Volunteer Av NANT CW5 20 F5
Volunteer Flds NANT CW5 20 F5
Volunteer St CH/BCN CH1 17 G6
FROD/HEL WA6 99 J3
Vose Cl WARRW/BUR WA5 36 D6
Vulcan Cl NEWLW WA12 27 J3
WARRN/WOL WA2 37 M2 5
Vyrnwy Rd CHSW/BR CH4 168 D6

W

Waddington Cl
GOL/RIS/CU WA3 23 M4 5
WARRN/WOL WA2 37 M3
Wadebridge Av NTHM/RTH M23 43 K5
Wade Crs NWCHW CW8 102 F8
Wades La WSFD CW7 177 K1
Wadeson Wy GOL/RIS/CU WA3 29 H5
Wade St NWCHE CW9 13 M1
Wadham Wy HALE/TIMP WA15 61 M3
Wadsworth Cl WILM/AE SK9 84 E1 2
Waggs Rd CONG CW12 207 J3
Wagg St CONG CW12 207 K2
Waine St CW/HAS CW1 19 H1
Wainwright Cl OFTN SK2 47 G5 2
Wainwright Rd ALT WA14 42 B7
Wakefield Crs MPL/ROM SK6 48 A3
Wakefield Rd GTS/LS CH66 120 E3
Wakefield St GOL/RIS/CU WA3 23 G5 2
Wakeham Cha MCFLDS SK11 137 M5
Wakes Meadow
TPLY/KEL CW6 216 E4 2
Walden Cl WARRS WA4 57 K1
Walden Crs BRAM/HZG SK7 66 C1 2
Walden Dr CH/BCN CH1 119 K4
Waldon Av CHD/CHDH SK8 45 K7
Waldon Rd MCFLDS SK11 138 A7
Waldron Rd CW/HAS CW1 239 K1
Waldron's La CW/HAS CW1 221 J3
Walfield Av CONG CW12 184 D7
Walford Av CW/SHV CW2 18 C6
Walford Rd AIMK WN4 22 C1
Walgrave Cl CONG CW12 184 A8
Walker Av STHEL WA9 34 B1
Walker Cl CW/HAS CW1 222 D8
Walker Dr MWCH CW10 179 J4
Walker La MCFLDS SK11 162 E2
Walker Rd BURS/TUN ST6 243 M8
IRL M44 31 M3 3
Walkers La ALS/KID ST7 225 H2
CHSE CH3 228 F3
GTS/LS CH66 94 C6
STHEL WA9 34 A1
TPLY/KEL CW6 197 K3
WARRW/BUR WA5 54 E1
Walker St CHNE CH2 17 K2
CW/HAS CW1 18 C1
MCFLDN SK10 14 E4
STKP SK1 2 F5
WARRN/WOL WA2 4 E5
The Walk SPK/HALE L24 70 A2
Wallace St NWCHW CW8 12 E5
WDN WA8 7 H4
Wallbank Rd BRAM/HZG SK7 66 A3
Wallcroft NSTN CH64 93 G5
Wallerscote Cl NWCHW CW8 128 E4 2
Wallerscote Rd NWCHW CW8 128 D3
Waller St MCFLDS SK11 15 J8 2
Walley Dr BURS/TUN ST6 243 K6
Walleys La NANT CW5 235 J5
Walley St BIDD ST8 227 J4
Wall Fields Cl NANT CW5 20 F3
Wall Fields Rd NANT CW5 20 E3
Wallhill La CONG CW12 206 D3
Wall Hill Wy NWCHW CW8 127 M1
Wallingford Rd WILM/AE SK9 64 C7
Wallis St CW/HAS CW1 19 H3
WARRS WA4 56 B1
Wall La NANT CW5 20 E6
Walls Av CH/BCN CH1 16 D5
Wallsend Ct WDN WA8 52 F1
Wallworth's Bank
CONG CW12 207 L2 2
Walmer Dr BRAM/HZG SK7 66 A3
Walmer Pl WSFD CW7 177 J6
Walmsley St NEWLW WA12 22 D8 2
RDSH SK5 2 F1
WDN WA8 7 M4
Walney Rd WYTH/NTH M22 44 D8
Walnut Av NWCHW CW8 128 D4
Walnut Cl CHNE CH2 145 K5 1
WARR WA1 38 E5
WILM/AE SK9 84 E4
Walnut Dr WHITCH SY13 269 M6
WSFD CW7 178 A3
Walnut Gv GTS/LS CH66 120 F3
Walnut La NWCHW CW8 129 G7
Walnut Ri CONG CW12 207 H2
Walnut Rd PART M31 40 D1
Walnut Tree La SBCH CW11 204 A1
Walnut Tree Rd EDGY/DAV SK3 46 A5
Walpole Av CQ CH5 166 A4
RAIN/WH L35 32 F1
Walpole Cl CW/HAS CW1 222 C7 1
Walpole Gv WARRN/WOL WA2 37 J2
Walpole Rd RUNC WA7 73 H6
Walpole St CH/BCN CH1 16 E2
Walsh Cl NEWLW WA12 22 C7
Walsingham Dr RUNC WA7 74 D2
Walsingham Rd
WARRW/BUR WA5 35 M7
Walters Green Crs
GOL/RIS/CU WA3 23 G2
Walter St CH/BCN CH1 17 H2
WARR WA1 37 L5 5
WDN WA8 53 K3 5
Walthall St CW/SHV CW2 18 E7
Waltham Av GOL/RIS/CU WA3 25 J5
Waltham Ct RUNC WA7 54 E8 1
Waltham Dr CHD/CHDH SK8 65 H6
Waltham Pl CHSW/BR CH4 169 G6 2
Walton Av WARRW/BUR WA5 35 L7
Walton Dr MPL/ROM SK6 48 D5
Walton Gv ALS/KID ST7 242 C4
Walton Heath Dr MCFLDN SK10 112 B8
Walton Heath Rd WARRS WA4 56 B3
Walton Lea Rd WARRS WA4 55 M5
Walton New Rd WARRS WA4 56 B4
Walton Pl CH/BCN CH1 144 E8 2
Walton Rd ALT WA14 42 B7
GOL/RIS/CU WA3 29 M1
GOL/RIS/CU WA3 29 L7
SALE M33 42 F3
WARRS WA4 56 C4
The Waltons CHSW/BR CH4 169 L6
Walton St RUNC WA7 9 H3
STKP SK1 3 H9 1
Walton Wy ALS/KID ST7 242 C4
Wandsworth Wy WDN WA8 6 F9
Wansfell Pl WARRN/WOL WA2 37 G1 7
Warbler Cl HLWD L26 50 D2
Warbreck Gv SALE M33 43 K1
Warburton Bridge Rd
GOL/RIS/CU WA3 40 A3
Warburton Cl HALE/TIMP WA15 62 D6
LYMM WA13 40 A8 4
MPL/ROM SK6 48 A3 5
Warburton Dr HALE/TIMP WA15 62 D6
Warburton La LYMM WA13 40 D4
PART M31 40 F1 3
Warburton Rd WILM/AE SK9 64 D8 5
Warburton St DID/WITH M20 45 H1 7
WARRS WA4 56 D3
Warburton Vw
GOL/RIS/CU WA3 40 A2 5
Ward Av MCFLDN SK10 113 G4
Ward Cl WARRW/BUR WA5 36 B3
Ward La POY/DIS SK12 68 E8
Wardle Av NANT CW5 218 C5
Wardle Crs MCFLDS SK11 161 K3
Wardle Ms MWCH CW10 179 J4
Wardle Rd SALE M33 43 H1
Wardle St MCFLDS SK11 15 G7 1
Wardour Cl MCFLDS SK11 137 M5 5
Wardour St WARRW/BUR WA5 4 B4
Wards La CONG CW12 208 C4
SBCH CW11 181 J7
Ward St MPL/ROM SK6 47 M1
STKP SK1 3 J9
Wareham Cl WARR WA1 38 C4
Wareham Dr CW/HAS CW1 221 H4
Warford Av POY/DIS SK12 87 G2 1
Warford Crs WILM/AE SK9 109 H5
Warford Hall Dr WILM/AE SK9 109 H6
Warford La WILM/AE SK9 109 G4
Wargrave Ms NEWLW WA12 27 J3
Wargrave Rd NEWLW WA12 27 J1
Warham St WILM/AE SK9 84 B5 3
Waring Av STHEL WA9 26 B2
WARRS WA4 37 M7
Warkick Rd CH/BCN CH1 144 F7
Warkworth Cl WDN WA8 52 C1 10
Warley Cl CHD/CHDH SK8 45 L6
Warmingham La MWCH CW10 179 K6
SBCH CW11 203 H4
Warmingham Rd CW/HAS CW1 221 J3
SBCH CW11 202 D6
Warmley Rd NTHM/RTH M23 43 K4
Warnley Cl WDN WA8 52 D1 4
Warren Av CHD/CHDH SK8 45 K7
KNUT WA16 106 E2
NWCHE CW9 131 G1 2
Warren Cl BRAM/HZG SK7 65 K2
KNUT WA16 106 F2 2
MWCH CW10 179 H5
POY/DIS SK12 66 B8
Warren Ct FROD/HEL WA6 99 K6
GTS/LS CH66 120 D1
Warren Cft RUNC WA7 74 C5
Warren Dr CHSW/BR CH4 190 A1
GTS/LS CH66 94 E5
HALE/TIMP WA15 62 D5
MCFLDS SK11 161 K3
NEWLW WA12 22 F8
WARRS WA4 56 C4
Warrener St SALE M33 43 K1
Warren Gv MCFLDS SK11 161 K3 1
Warren Hey WILM/AE SK9 84 E4 12
Warren La NWCHW CW8 129 G8
WARR WA1 38 D4
Warren Lea MPL/ROM SK6 49 H2
POY/DIS SK12 66 E7
Warren Rd CHD/CHDH SK8 65 H2 3
EDGY/DAV SK3 46 E6
WARRN/WOL WA2 37 K3
WARRS WA4 56 C5
Warren St STKP SK1 3 G4
The Warren NWCHW CW8 127 K7
Warren Wy TPLY/KEL CW6 197 K3
Warrington Av CW/HAS CW1 221 J6
EP CH65 121 H2
Warrington La LYMM WA13 59 K1
Warrington Rd AIMK WN4 22 B2
CHNE CH2 146 D5
GOL/RIS/CU WA3 28 B1
GOL/RIS/CU WA3 29 M1 4
KNUT WA16 80 B5
LYMM WA13 39 H8
NEWLW WA12 23 G6
NWCHE CW9 103 K5
NWCHW CW8 128 A8
RAIN/WH L35 33 M4
RUNC WA7 54 D8
RUNC WA7 73 L2 2
WARRS WA4 55 M6
WARRW/BUR WA5 35 K8
WDN WA8 7 L5
Warslow Dr SALE M33 43 L3
Warsop Av WYTH/NTH M22 44 E7 4
Warton Cl BRAM/HZG SK7 66 A5
WARRW/BUR WA5 55 G1 1
WLTN L25 50 C2 5
Warton Dr NTHM/RTH M23 44 A7
Warwick Av AIMK WN4 22 D2 2
NEWLW WA12 27 K2
WARRW/BUR WA5 4 C2
WARRW/BUR WA5 35 K5
Warwick Cl ALS/KID ST7 243 G2
CHD/CHDH SK8 46 A8
HUY L36 32 A1 2
KNUT WA16 107 J3
MCFLDS SK11 137 M6 4
NSTN CH64 91 L7
Warwick Ct EP CH65 121 L1
Warwick Dr BRAM/HZG SK7 66 D4
HALE/TIMP WA15 61 L3
Warwick Pl WSFD CW7 177 J6
Warwick Rd HALE/TIMP WA15 61 L3
HTNM SK4 2 A2
HUY L36 32 A1
IRL M44 31 K7
MCFLDS SK11 137 L6
MPL/ROM SK6 48 A2
Warwick St BIDD ST8 227 J5
LEIGH WN7 25 K1
Wasdale Dr CHD/CHDH SK8 64 B1 4
Wasdale Gv CW/HAS CW1 221 H3 7
Washford Dr NTHM/RTH M23 43 K4
Washington Cl BIDD ST8 227 J2
Washington Dr CQ CH5 166 A2 3
WARRW/BUR WA5 36 B6
Wash La KNUT WA16 132 D8
WARRS WA4 56 E1 3
Washway Rd ALT WA14 42 E3 3
Wasley Cl WARRN/WOL WA2 37 M1
Wastdale Rd NTHM/RTH M23 43 M8
Waste La NWCHE CW8 150 F6
NWCHW CW8 151 L1
TPLY/KEL CW6 149 L7
Watburn Rd NM/HAY SK22 69 K3
Watch La SBCH CW11 203 G6
Waterbank Rw NWCHE CW9 13 H4
Waterbridge Ct WARRS WA4 56 D4
Waterfoot La CHF/WBR SK23 89 K6 1
Waterford Av DID/WITH M20 44 D1
MPL/ROM SK6 48 E2
Waterford Dr NSTN CH64 92 A5
Waterford Wy RUNC WA7 74 C6
Watergate WHITCH SY13 270 A5
Watergate La WLTN L25 50 B2
Watergate Sq CH/BCN CH1 16 E6
Watergate St CH/BCN CH1 16 F6
Watergate Wy WLTN L25 50 B2
Waterhouse Av
MCFLDN SK10 112 F4 3
Water La RAIN/WH L35 32 D8
WILM/AE SK9 84 A5
Water-lode NANT CW5 20 D6
Waterloo Gv ALS/KID ST7 243 G3 1
Waterloo La FROD/HEL WA6 125 J3
Waterloo Rd BRAM/HZG SK7 65 M3
CHNE CH2 145 J8
CW/HAS CW1 222 D8
MPL/ROM SK6 48 E2
NWCHW CW8 12 F4
POY/DIS SK12 87 G2
RUNC WA7 8 F2 1
STKP SK1 3 H6
WDN WA8 53 G7
Waterloo St West MCFLDS SK11 14 F5
Watermead Cl EDGY/DAV SK3 46 E8
Watermeetings La
MPL/ROM SK6 48 E2
Watermill Dr MCFLDS SK11 15 L6
Watersedge FROD/HEL WA6 99 K2
Waters Edge MPL/ROM SK6 49 G4
NWCHE CW9 129 K1 1
Watersedge Cl
CHD/CHDH SK8 65 H1 1
Watersfield Cl CHD/CHDH SK8 64 F4 2
Waters Gn MCFLDS SK11 15 H5
Waterside MCFLDS SK11 15 J7 3
MPL/ROM SK6 48 F7
WARRS WA4 56 D4
Waterside Av MPL/ROM SK6 48 F7 4
Waterside Cl AUD/MAD/W CW3 267 L6
WHITCH SY13 269 M4
Waterside Dr FROD/HEL WA6 99 K2
Waterside Ms SBCH CW11 222 F1 4
Waterside Rd NM/HAY SK22 68 E5
Waterside Vw NWCHE CW9 130 E5
Waterside Wy MWCH CW10 179 H2
Waters Reach POY/DIS SK12 66 F7
Waters Reams CHSE CH3 170 B4
Water St MCFLDN SK10 113 G4
MCFLDS SK11 14 F6
NEWLW WA12 22 C8 3
NWCHE CW9 13 H4
RUNC WA7 9 H1
STKP SK1 3 H2
WDN WA8 7 G9
Water Tower Rd NSTN CH64 91 L2
Water Tower St CH/BCN CH1 16 F4
Watertower Vw CHNE CH2 17 M4
Waterway CHSE CH3 171 H7
Waterways WARRW/BUR WA5 36 D6
Waterworks Dr NEWLW WA12 22 F8 1
Waterworks La GTS/LS CH66 93 L3
WARRN/WOL WA2 28 B5
Watery La CONG CW12 207 G5
FROD/HEL WA6 99 L7
WARRN/WOL WA2 27 L6
Watford Bridge Rd
NM/HAY SK22 69 K3
Watford La NM/HAY SK22 69 J2
Watford Rd NM/HAY SK22 69 J2
Watkins Av NEWLW WA12 26 F1
Watkinson Wy WDN WA8 7 L4
Watkin St CQ CH5 167 G1
WARRN/WOL WA2 5 G2
Watling Crs CHSW/BR CH4 169 L5
Watling Dr TPLY/KEL CW6 150 C6
Watling St NWCHE CW9 13 H2
NWCHW CW8 13 G2
Watson Av AIMK WN4 22 C1 7

GOL/RIS/CU WA3 .... 22 F3
Watson's CI CHSW/BR CH4 .... 190 C1
Watson Sq STKP SK1 .... 3 H6
Watton CI WARRS WA4 .... 57 L1
Wavell Av WDN WA8 .... 52 C4
Wavell Rd WYTH/NTH M22 ...... 63 K2
Wavells Wy CHSE CH3 .... 170 B7
Waveney Dr ALT WA14 .... 42 C6
   WILM/AE SK9 .... 84 D2
Waveney Rd WYTH/NTH M22 .... 44 E8
Waverley Av WARRS WA4 .... 56 D4
Waverley CI MCFLDN SK10 ...... 139 G4
Waverley Crs WRX/GR/LL LL12 .. 210 C4
Waverley Dr CHD/CHDH SK8 .... 65 H6
Waverley Rd EDGY/DAV SK3 ...... 2 B9
   GOL/RIS/CU WA3 .... 23 K3
Waverley Ter CHE2 .... 145 L8
Waverton Ap CHSE CH3 .... 193 K6
   NWCHE CW9 .... 129 L8
Waverton Mill Quays
   CHSE CH3 .... 171 H7
Waverton Rd GTS/LS CH66 ...... 94 F3
Wavertree Av ALS/KID ST7 ...... 225 L5
   WDN WA8 .... 7 G4
Wavertree Dr MWCH CW10 ...... 179 H5
Wavertree Rd CH/BCN CH1 ...... 144 C7
Waybutt La CW/SHV CW2 .... 254 D5
Wayfarers Dr NEWLW WA12 ...... 27 L2
Wayford CI FROD/HEL WA6 ...... 99 H3
Wayland CI WHITCH SY13 .... 270 B6
Wayland Rd WHITCH SY13 .... 270 B5
Waylands Dr WLTN L25 .... 50 B5
Way's Gn WSFD CW7 .... 177 L4
Wayside CI LYMM WA13 .... 58 D2
Wayside Ct CHNE CH2 .... 146 F4
Wayside Dr POY/DIS SK12 .... 66 C8
Wayside Gdns BRAM/HZG SK7 .. 67 G2
Wayside Rd MCFLDN SK10 ...... 15 M6
Waywell St WARRN/WOL WA2 .... 37 M1
Weald Dr GTS/LS CH66 .... 94 A6
Wealstone Ct CHNE CH2 .... 145 L8
Weal Stone La CHNE CH2 .... 145 L6
Wearhead CI GOL/RIS/CU WA3 .. 23 G5
Weaste La WARRS WA4 .... 57 K2
Weates CI WDN WA8 .... 53 L1
Weathercock La CONG CW12 .... 208 E1
Weatherley Dr MPL/ROM SK6 .... 48 D6
Weaver Av RAIN/WH L35 .... 33 H1
Weaver CI ALS/KID ST7 .... 241 C1
   ALT WA14 .... 61 J5
   BIDD ST8 .... 227 K3
   SBCH CW11 .... 203 L5
Weaver Ct MCFLDS SK11 .... 14 E6
Weaver Crs FROD/HEL WA6 ...... 99 K3
Weaver Gra NWCHE CW9 .... 153 L4
Weaver Gv CHNE CH2 .... 146 F3
   STHEL WA9 .... 26 A1
Weaverhall La WSFD CW7 ...... 178 B7
Weaverham Rd NWCHW CW8 .... 152 A2
Weaver La FROD/HEL WA6 ...... 99 H2
Weaver Rd EP CH65 .... 121 J1
   FROD/HEL WA6 .... 99 K3
   GOL/RIS/CU WA3 .... 30 A2
   NANT CW5 .... 20 E5
   NWCHE CW9 .... 153 L5
   NWCHW WA8 .... 12 F4
   RUNC WA7 .... 73 G6
Weaverside NANT CW5 .... 251 L2
Weaverside Av RUNC WA7 .... 73 M8
Weavers La BRAM/HZG SK7 ...... 65 K6
Weaver St CH/BCN CH1 .... 16 F6
   WSFD CW7 .... 177 L4
Weaver Valley Rd WSFD CW7.... 177 M1
Weaver Vw NANT CW5 .... 201 G6
   NWCHW CW8 .... 128 D3
Weaver Wy NWCHE CW9 .... 13 G2
Webb Dr WARRW/BUR WA5 ...... 26 F6
Webb La STKP SK1 .... 3 K6
Webb's La MWCH CW10 .... 179 J2
Webster CI CHSW/BR CH4 ...... 190 C1
Websters La GTS/LS CH66 ...... 120 F2
Weddell CI WARRW/BUR WA5 .... 36 D5
Wedgwood Dr WDN WA8 .... 34 B8
Wedgwood La BIDD ST8 .... 227 K3
Wedgwood Rd ALS/KID ST7 .... 242 D6
   CQ CH5 .... 166 B1
Wednesbury Dr
   WARRW/BUR WA5 .... 35 M6
Weedon Av NEWLW WA12 .... 22 B7
Weighbridge Rd CQ CH5 .... 118 B7
Weir Gv ALS/KID ST7 .... 243 G2
Weir La WARR WA1 .... 38 E6
Weir St NWCHE CW9 .... 13 H5
   WARRS WA4 .... 56 A3
Welbeck Av NEWLW WA12 .... 27 K2
Welbeck CI MWCH CW10 .... 179 C3
Welburn Av WYTH/NTH M22 .... 63 L1
Welbury Rd NTHM/RTH M23 .... 43 M3
Welcroft St STKP SK1 .... 3 H7
Weldon Crs EDGY/DAV SK3 ...... 46 E8
Weldon Rd ALT WA14 .... 42 C6
Welford Av GOL/RIS/CU WA3 .... 23 J5
Welford CI WILM/AE SK9 .... 84 E4
Welkin Rd MPL/ROM SK6 .... 47 J1
Welland CI HLWD L26 .... 50 E7
   SBCH CW11 .... 203 J7
Welland Rd WILM/AE SK9 ...... 84 D2
Well Av MALPAS SY14 .... 258 B1
Well Bank SBCH CW11 .... 204 B6
Wellbank Dr HLWD L26 .... 51 G3
Well Bank La KNUT WA16 .... 154 F7
Wellbrook CI RUNC WA7 .... 74 C7
   SPK/HALE L24 .... 50 D1
Wellbrooke Gdns AIMK WN4 .... 22 C1
Wellbrook Gn SPK/HALE L24 .... 70 D1
Well CI NSTN CH64 .... 92 A8
Wellcroft CI CW/SHV CW2 .... 238 B5
Weller Av POY/DIS SK12 .... 86 D2
Weller CI POY/DIS SK12 .... 86 D2
Wellesbourne CI
   MCFLDN SK10 .... 137 M3
Wellesbourne Dr
   NTHM/RTH M23 .... 43 M5
Wellesley Av CW/HAS CW1 .... 222 C8
   EP CH65 .... 10 F8

Wellesley CI NEWLW WA12 ...... 22 B7
Welles St SBCH CW11 .... 204 B5
Well Farm CI MALPAS SY14 ...... 258 B1
Wellfield RUNC WA7 .... 74 E7
   WDN WA8 .... 34 A8
   WSFD CW7 .... 177 M2
Wellfield CI KNUT WA16 .... 105 G5
Wellfield La HALE/TIMP WA15 .. 43 J8
Wellfield Rd GOL/RIS/CU WA3 .. 24 B8
   NTHM/RTH M23 .... 44 A5
   OFTN SK2 .... 47 J6
Wellfield St WARRW/BUR WA5 .. 4 B6
Wellgreen CI HALE/TIMP WA15 .. 62 C1
Wellhouse La NWCHE CW9 ...... 104 B4
Wellington Av EP CH65 .... 10 F7
   WARRN/WOL WA2 .... 37 M2
Wellington Ga SPK/HALE L24 .. 71 L2
Wellington Gv OFTN SK2 .... 46 F5
Wellington PI ALT WA14 .... 61 K1
Wellington Rd ALS/KID ST7 .... 243 G3
   BRAM/HZG SK7 .... 67 H4
   CHSW/BR CH4 .... 190 B1
   EP CH65 .... 10 D9
   MCFLDN SK10 .... 112 F4
   NANT CW5 .... 20 E9
Wellington Rd North EP CH65 .. 10 F8
Wellington Rd South
   EDGY/DAV SK3 .... 2 F6
   STKP SK1 .... 3 G8
Wellington St BRAM/HZG SK7 .. 66 F1
   CQ CH5 .... 142 B6
   MCFLDS SK11 .... 15 G6
   NEWLW WA12 .... 27 G1
   NWCHW CW8 .... 12 F4
   RUNC WA7 .... 9 G1
   STKP SK1 .... 3 G6
   WARR WA1 .... 5 J7
   WDN WA8 .... 7 G9
Well Md MPL/ROM SK6 .... 47 L1
Wells Av CW/HAS CW1 .... 222 D7
Wells CI BIDD ST8 .... 227 K4
   CHD/CHDH SK8 .... 64 C5
   CHNE CH2 .... 146 F4
   GTS/LS CH66 .... 120 E4
   WARR WA1 .... 38 E2
Wells Dr HTNM SK4 .... 45 L2
Well St ALS/KID ST7 .... 226 D5
   BIDD ST8 .... 227 J5
   MALPAS SY14 .... 258 B1
   NM/HAY SK22 .... 69 H4
   WSFD CW7 .... 177 J3
Wellswood Dr CW/SHV CW2 .... 237 M5
Wellswood Rd GTS/LS CH66 .... 94 E5
Welsby CI WARRN/WOL WA2 .... 37 M1
Welshampton CI GTS/LS CH66 .. 120 D2
Welsh La WSFD CW7 .... 177 K6
Welshmen's La NANT CW5 ...... 20 A1
Welshpool CI NTHM/RTH M23 .. 44 B2
   WARRW/BUR WA5 .... 36 D1
Welsh Rd CH/BCN CH1 .... 119 J6
   CQ CH5 .... 142 E6
   GTS/LS CH66 .... 94 A3
Welsh Rw MCFLDN SK10 .... 110 A6
   NANT CW5 .... 20 B6
Welton Av DID/WITH M20 ...... 45 J2
Welton CI SPK/HALE L24 .... 70 D1
   WILM/AE SK9 .... 83 M8
Welton Dr WILM/AE SK9 .... 83 L8
Welton Gn SPK/HALE L24 ...... 70 D1
Welton Gv WILM/AE SK9 .... 83 L8
Welwyn CI WARRS WA4 .... 57 J1
Wemyss Rd CH/BCN CH1 .... 144 D8
Wendlebury CI LEIGH WN7 ...... 24 E3
Wendon Rd NTHM/RTH M23 .... 44 B7
Wendover Rd NTHM/RTH M23 .. 43 J5
Wenger Rd WDN WA8 .... 34 B7
Wenlock CI MCFLDN SK10 ...... 14 D1
   OFTN SK2 .... 48 A6
   WARR WA1 .... 38 A4
Wenlock Crs CQ CH5 .... 166 E1
Wenlock Dr HLWD L26 .... 50 E5
Wenlock Gdns GTS/LS CH66 .... 120 F2
Wenlock La GTS/LS CH66 ...... 120 F2
Wenlock Rd LEIGH WN7 .... 24 E2
   RUNC WA7 .... 74 A8
   SALE M33 .... 43 M3
Wenlock Wy CHSW/BR CH4 .... 168 F6
Wensley Av HLWD L26 .... 50 E5
Wensleydale Av
   CHD/CHDH SK8 .... 45 J6
   CONG CW12 .... 185 G7
   RAIN/WH L35 .... 33 K1
Wensleydale CI
   NTHM/RTH M23 .... 62 F1
   WARRW/BUR WA5 .... 35 M4
Wensley Dr BRAM/HZG SK7 .... 66 D5
Wensley Rd CHD/CHDH SK8 .... 45 J6
   GOL/RIS/CU WA3 .... 23 L5
Wentworth Av HALE/TIMP WA15.. 43 G6
   MCFLDS SK11 .... 137 M6
   WARR WA1 .... 38 B5
Wentworth CI MPL/ROM SK6 .... 48 F4
   NWCHE CW9 .... 130 E5
   WDN WA8 .... 34 A7
Wentworth Dr ALS/KID ST7 .... 243 J1
   BRAM/HZG SK7 .... 66 A5
Wentworth Gv WSFD CW7 ...... 177 G2
Wepre Dr CQ CH5 .... 142 A5
Werneth CI BRAM/HZG SK7 .... 47 L8
Werneth St STKP SK1 .... 3 M2
Wervin Rd CHNE CH2 .... 145 M3
Wesley Av ALS/KID ST7 .... 224 D8
   SBCH CW11 .... 204 B6
Wesley CI NANT CW5 .... 20 F7
   NSTN CH64 .... 91 K5

Wesley PI CW/SHV CW2 .... 19 G7
   NWCHE CW9 .... 13 K2
Wesley St BRAM/HZG SK7 ...... 66 E1
   STKP SK1 .... 3 H6
Wessenden Bank East
   OFTN SK2 .... 47 K7
Wessenden Bank West
   OFTN SK2 .... 47 K7
Wessex CI CW/SHV CW2 .... 253 J1
   WARR WA1 .... 38 E5
Wessex Dr NWCHE CW9 .... 130 C6
Westage Gdns NTHM/RTH M23 .. 44 A5
Westage La NWCHE CW9 .... 104 B4
West Av ALS/KID ST7 .... 242 C5
   ALT WA14 .... 42 A7
   CHD/CHDH SK8 .... 64 C3
   CW/HAS CW1 .... 18 D3
   CW/SHV CW2 .... 239 H7
   GOL/RIS/CU WA3 .... 23 H3
   LEIGH WN7 .... 25 J1
   MWCH CW10 .... 179 J2
   NWCHE CW9 .... 130 C6
   WARRN/WOL WA2 .... 5 H1
   WARRS WA4 .... 56 C3
West Bank CH/BCN CH1 .... 145 J8
   WILM/AE SK9 .... 110 A4
West Bank Rd MCFLDN SK10 .... 14 C3
West Bank St WDN WA8 .... 53 G7
West Bond St MCFLDS SK11 .... 14 E6
Westbourne Av CW/HAS CW1 .. 221 G6
Westbourne Dr BURS/TUN ST6 .. 243 L7
Westbourne Rd CH/BCN CH1 .. 145 G8
   WARRS WA4 .... 56 B5
Westbrook Av WARRS WA4 ...... 56 D2
   WHITCH SY13 .... 269 M4
Westbrook Centre
   WARRW/BUR WA5 .... 36 C3
Westbrook Crs
   WARRW/BUR WA5 .... 36 B3
Westbrook Dr MCFLDN SK10 .... 14 C1
Westbrook Rd FROD/HEL WA6.. 126 B2
Westbrook Wy
   WARRW/BUR WA5 .... 36 A3
Westbury Av SALE M33 .... 42 C3
Westbury CI CW/SHV CW2 ...... 238 C4
   MWCH CW10 .... 179 J4
   WARR WA1 .... 38 A4
Westbury Dr MCFLDS SK11 ...... 14 B6
Westbury Wy
   CHSW/BR CH4 .... 168 F6
West CI ALT WA14 .... 61 J3
Westcliffe Gdns WARRS WA4 .... 76 E1
Westdale Rd WARR WA1 .... 38 A5
West Downs Rd CHD/CHDH SK8 .. 64 F1
West Dr CHD/CHDH SK8 .... 45 G8
   NSTN CH64 .... 91 K6
   WARRW/BUR WA5 .... 36 B8
   WSFD CW7 .... 177 M2
West Dudley St WSFD CW7 .... 177 M3
West End CHSE CH3 .... 148 C5
West End CHD/CHDH SK8 ...... 45 G6
West End Cottages
   CONG CW12 .... 207 J2
Westenra Av EP CH65 .... 94 F6
Western Ap CHNE CH2 .... 145 L8
Western Av CH/BCN CW1 ...... 168 D1
   MCFLDS SK11 .... 138 C7
   NANT CW5 .... 251 L1
   SPK/HALE L24 .... 70 C1
Western Ct CHNE CH2 .... 145 L8
Western Dr MCFLDS SK11 ...... 138 C7
Westfield CHSW/BR CH4 .... 16 C9
Westfield Crs RUNC WA7 .... 8 E5
Westfield Dr CW/SHV CW2 .... 237 L4
   KNUT WA16 .... 106 F3
Westfield Gv NWCHW CW8 .... 102 F8
Westfield Ms RUNC WA7 .... 8 E4
Westfield Rd ALS/KID ST7 ...... 226 C5
   CHD/CHDH SK8 .... 64 F4
   NWCHE CW9 .... 13 L4
   RUNC WA7 .... 8 D5
Westfields HALE/TIMP WA15 .... 61 M4
Westfields Av MCFLDN SK10 .... 14 C2
Westford Rd WARRS WA4 ...... 56 A3
Westgate HALE/TIMP WA15 ...... 61 L2
   WILM/AE SK9 .... 84 A7
Westgate Av WSFD CW7 .... 177 C3
Westgate Pk CW/SHV CW2 .... 253 L2
West Gv ALS/KID ST7 .... 224 E8
   SBCH CW11 .... 43 H1
West Hall Ms KNUT WA16 ...... 59 J7
Westhay Crs GOL/RIS/CU WA3 .. 30 A7
Westhead Av NTHM/RTH M23 .. 43 J8
West Heath Gv LYMM WA13 .... 39 J8
Westholme CI CW/SHV CW2 .... 238 C4
Westholme CI WILM/AE SK9 .. 110 A2
West House Ct
   MCFLDN SK10 .... 137 L3
West Hyde LYMM WA13 .... 58 C1
Westland Av STKP SK1 .... 3 L6
Westlands CI NSTN CH64 ...... 91 M3
Westlands Rd MWCH CW10 .... 179 H3
The Westlands CONG CW12 .... 207 J2
West La KNUT WA16 .... 59 J6
   NWCHW CW8 .... 151 M1
   RUNC WA7 .... 73 L5
West Lorne St CW/SHV CW1 .... 16 E3
West Mains SPK/HALE L24 .... 71 G1
Westmead Dr HALE/TIMP WA15.. 43 H5
Westmere Dr CW/SHV CW2 .... 239 H7
Westminster Av CHSW/BR CH4 .. 169 H6
Westminster CI
   MPL/ROM SK6 .... 48 D5
   MWCH CW10 .... 179 H3
   SALE M33 .... 42 D1
   WARRS WA4 .... 57 J2
   WDN WA8 .... 52 B4
Westminster Crs CQ CH5 ...... 142 B7
Westminster Dr CHD/CHDH SK8 .. 65 H6
   WILM/AE SK9 .... 84 A7
Westminster Gn CHSW/BR CH4 .. 17 C9
Westminster Gv EP CH65 ...... 10 E6
Westminster PI WARR WA1 ...... 5 C6
Westminster Rd CHNE CH2 ...... 17 L2

CHSW/BR CH4 .... 190 B1
   EP CH65 .... 10 E5
   HALE/TIMP WA15 .... 62 A1
   MCFLDN SK10 .... 14 F2
Westminster St CW/SHV CW2 .. 18 F6
Westminster Ter CHSW/BR CH4.. 16 F9
Westmoreland Av ALT WA14 .... 61 H4
   WDN WA8 .... 7 J2
Westmorland CI
   MCFLDN SK10 .... 137 M2
Westmorland Rd DID/WITH M20.. 45 G2
   PART M31 .... 40 E2
   SALE M33 .... 43 J2
Westmorland Ter
   HOLMCH CW4 .... 181 H1
West Oak PI CHD/CHDH SK8 .... 64 F3
Weston CI CO CH5 .... 142 F6
   MWCH CW10 .... 179 J5
Weston Court Ms
   WHITCH SY13 .... 270 A5
Weston Crs RUNC WA7 .... 72 F6
Weston Dr CHD/CHDH SK8 ...... 46 D8
Weston Gv CHNE CH2 .... 145 L6
   WYTH/NTH M22 .... 44 E4
Weston La CW/SHV CW2 .... 238 D7
   WILM/AE SK9 .... 84 D6
West Over MPL/ROM SK6 .... 48 D5
Westover Rd WARR WA1 .... 37 M5
West Park Av POY/DIS SK12 .... 86 D6
West Park Dr GTS/LS CH66 .... 120 F4
West Park Rd BRAM/HZG SK7.. 65 K2
   STKP SK1 .... 3 L3
West Quay Rd WARRN/WOL WA2.. 36 F1
Westrees NWCHW CW8 .... 127 K7
West Rd ALT WA14 .... 61 J2
   CONG CW12 .... 207 L1
   EP CH65 .... 121 J1
   NWCHW CW8 .... 128 B4
   RUNC WA7 .... 8 A8
   SPK/HALE L24 .... 50 D7
West St ALS/KID ST7 .... 226 B6
   BIDD ST8 .... 227 J5
   CHNE CH2 .... 17 J1
   CONG CW12 .... 207 J1
   CW/HAS CW1 .... 18 D2
   CW/HAS CW1 .... 222 C7
   CW/SHV CW2 .... 220 E8
   EDGY/DAV SK3 .... 2 C6
   MCFLDS SK11 .... 14 D5
   MWCH CW10 .... 179 J3
   WARRN/WOL WA2 .... 5 H2
   WILM/AE SK9 .... 110 A3
Westune WHITCH SY13 .... 269 M6
West V NSTN CH64 .... 91 L6
West Vale Rd HALE/TIMP WA15.. 42 F7
West Vw HUY L36 .... 32 B2
   WARRN/WOL WA2 .... 38 A3
West View Av HUY L36 .... 32 B2
West View Rd FROD/HEL WA6 .. 127 G6
   WYTH/NTH M22 .... 44 E4
Westville Dr CONG CW12 ...... 207 G2
Westward Rd CHSE CH3 .... 170 A4
   WILM/AE SK9 .... 83 M6
Westway CO CH5 .... 166 E2
West Wy CW/SHV CW2 .... 238 D7
   HOLMCH CW4 .... 181 H1
   SBCH CW11 .... 203 M8
   WRX/GR/LL LL12 .... 210 C5
Westwood RUNC WA7 .... 74 C3
Westwood Av HALE/TIMP WA15 .. 42 F5
Westwood Ct NSTN CH64 ...... 91 L2
Westwood Dr SALE M33 .... 43 H2
Westwood Rd CHD/CHDH SK8 .. 64 B4
   OFTN SK2 .... 47 H8
Westy La WARRS WA4 .... 37 L8
Wetherby CI CH/BCN CH1 ...... 16 C3
   NEWLW WA12 .... 22 C7
Wetherby Dr BRAM/HZG SK7 .. 67 G2
Wetherby Wy GTS/LS CH66 .... 94 C3
Wetreins La CHSE CH3 .... 229 H5
Wettenhall Rd NANT CW5 ...... 219 H8
Wetton La NWCHW CW8 .... 101 L7
Wexford Av SPK/HALE L24 .... 71 K2
Wexwood Gv RAIN/WH L35 .... 32 F2
Weybourne CI CHSW/BR CH4 .. 168 E7
Weybridge CI WARRS WA4 ...... 56 E5
Weybridge Dr MCFLDN SK10 .. 138 B1
Wey Gates Dr HALE/TIMP WA15.. 62 C6
Weyhill Rd NTHM/RTH M23 .... 44 A8
Weyman Av RAIN/WH L35 ...... 32 E1
Weymouth CI RUNC WA7 ...... 74 E6
Weymouth Rd
   WARRW/BUR WA5 .... 26 F6
Whaddon Dr CHSW/BR CH4 .... 168 F8
Whaley La CHF/WBR SK23 ...... 89 L5
Whalley Av GOL/RIS/CU WA3 .. 25 J5
Whalley CI HALE/TIMP WA15 .. 42 F4
Whalley Gv WDN WA8 .... 53 K1
Whalley Hayes MCFLDN SK10.. 14 F4
Whalley Rd HALE/TIMP WA15 .. 62 A2
   NWCHE CW9 .... 13 J3
   OFTN SK2 .... 47 J6
Whalley St WARR WA1 .... 5 K5
Wharams Bank SBCH CW11 .... 205 M7
The Wharfage WHITCH SY13 .. 270 A5
Wharf Ct CHF/WBR SK23 .... 89 L5
Wharfdale Av CW/HAS CW1 .. 221 H3
Wharfdale CI
   WARRW/BUR WA5 .... 36 A5
Wharfe CI CONG CW12 .... 207 M3
Wharfedale RUNC WA7 .... 74 B6
Wharfedale Rd RAIN/WH L35 .. 33 K1
Wharfedale Rd CONG CW12 .... 185 G7
Wharfe La EP CH65 .... 10 A3
Wharford La RUNC WA7 .... 74 E1
Wharf La CONG CW12 .... 207 H8
Wharf St HTNM SK4 .... 2 F2
   WARR WA1 .... 5 K8

Wharton Park Rd WSFD CW7 .. 177 M2
Wharton Rd WSFD CW7 .... 177 M3
Whatcroft CI RUNC WA7 .... 73 K6
Whatcroft La NWCHE CW9 .... 154 E3
West Cft EDGY/DAV SK3 .... 46 F7
   WARRW/BUR WA5 .... 36 C6
Wheatfield CI GTS/LS CH66 .... 120 C1
Wheatfield La NWCHW CW8 .... 129 G3
Wheatfield Rd WDN WA8 .... 33 J7
Wheatlands RUNC WA7 .... 73 L3
Wheatley Av NEWLW WA12 .... 22 C7
Wheatley Rd CW/HAS CW1 .... 221 L6
Wheat Moss MCFLDS SK11 .... 135 C1
Wheatsheaf Dr WHITCH SY13 .. 269 M6
Wheatsheaf La NWCHE CW9 .. 77 H8
Wheatsheaf Rd
   CHF/WBR SK23 .... 89 L6
Wheelman Rd CW/HAS CW1 .. 221 C5
Wheelock CI ALS/KID ST7 ...... 241 C1
   WILM/AE SK9 .... 84 D3
Wheelock Dr WSFD CW7 .... 178 B3
Wheelock St MWCH CW10 ...... 179 J3
Wheelock Wy ALS/KID ST7 .... 243 H2
Wheelwright CI
   MPL/ROM SK6 .... 48 F4
Wheldon CI CHNE CH2 .... 145 L4
Whelmar Rd BIDD ST8 .... 227 L2
Whernside WDN WA8 .... 52 C2
Whernside CI HTNM SK4 .... 2 F3
Whetmorhurst Rd
   MPL/ROM SK6 .... 49 L8
Whetstone Hey GTS/LS CH66 .. 94 D7
Whetstone Rd BIDD ST8 ...... 227 J2
Whickham CI WDN WA8 .... 52 F1
Whimbrel Av NEWLW WA12 .... 27 J1
Whimbrel CI RUNC WA7 .... 73 M7
Whimbrel Pk HLWD L26 .... 50 E3
Whimbrel Rd OFTN SK2 .... 48 A7
Whinberry Rd ALT WA14 .... 42 B5
Whinchat Av NEWLW WA12 .... 22 C5
Whinchat CI OFTN SK2 .... 48 A8
Whinchat Dr GOL/RIS/CU WA3 .. 38 F1
Whinfell Gv RUNC WA7 .... 73 L7
Whipcord La CH/BCN CH1 ...... 16 C3
Whirley CI MWCH CW10 .... 179 J5
Whirley La MCFLDN SK10 ...... 136 F3
Whirley Rd MCFLDN SK10 ...... 137 H2
Whirlow Rd CW/SHV CW2 ...... 238 D5
Whisterfield La MCFLDS SK11.. 159 K1
Whiston CI WSFD CW7 .... 154 A8
Whiston St MCFLDS SK11 ...... 14 E6
Whitbarrow Rd LYMM WA13 .... 39 J8
Whitbread Dr BIDD ST8 .... 227 L4
Whitburn Rd NTHM/RTH M23 .. 44 A8
Whitby Av CHNE CH2 .... 145 K7
   WARRN/WOL WA2 .... 37 K2
Whitby CI CHD/CHDH SK8 ...... 45 J6
   CW/HAS CW1 .... 221 H4
   POY/DIS SK12 .... 66 C7
Whitby La CH/BCN CH1 .... 121 G5
Whitby Rd EP CH65 .... 10 F7
   RUNC WA7 .... 9 H5
Whitby's La WSFD CW7 .... 177 H3
Whitchurch Rd WARR WA1 .... 38 A4
Whitchurch Rd
   AUD/MAD/W WA3 .... 273 G1
   CHSE CH3 .... 170 B3
   CHSE CH3 .... 171 G8
   CHSE CH3 .... 213 K4
   CHSE CH3 .... 231 G2
   MALPAS SY14 .... 246 D4
   WHITCH SY13 .... 262 A7
Whitchurch Wy RUNC WA7 .... 73 K6
White Av CW/SHV CW2 .... 220 F8
Whitebarn Rd WILM/AE SK9 .. 110 B4
Whitebeam GTS/LS CH66 ...... 120 C2
Whitebeam CI HALE/TIMP WA15 .. 43 L7
   RUNC WA7 .... 74 C3
White Broom LYMM WA13 ...... 40 B8
Whitecarr La HALE/TIMP WA15.. 62 C1
Whitechapel St DID/WITH M20.. 45 H1
Whitecroft Av
   GOL/RIS/CU WA3 .... 23 L3
Whitecroft Heath Rd
   MCFLDS SK11 .... 159 H1
Whitecroft Rd GTS/LS CH66 .. 120 E2
   MPL/ROM SK6 .... 68 C2
Whitecross WARRW/BUR WA5 .. 4 B6
Whitefield HTNM SK4 .... 2 C1
Whitefield CI LYMM WA13 ...... 40 A8
Whitefield Gv LYMM WA13 ...... 40 A8
Whitefield La RAIN/WH L35 .... 32 A6
Whitefield Rd WARRS WA4 .... 56 B4
Whitefields CHNE CH2 .... 123 H1
White Friars CHNE CH2 .... 16 F6
Whitegate Av GOL/RIS/CU WA3 .. 29 M2
Whitegate CI MWCH CW10 .... 179 J6
Whitegate La CHSE CH3 .... 148 C5
Whitegate Rd WSFD CW7 ...... 152 F8
Whitegates CI HALE/TIMP WA15.. 43 H7
   NSTN CH64 .... 92 E3
Whitegates Crs NSTN CH64 .... 92 E4
Whitegates Rd CHD/CHDH SK8 .. 45 K7
Whitehall Av ALS/KID ST7 .... 242 F5
Whitehall CI NWCHW CW8 .... 103 G8
   WILM/AE SK9 .... 84 A7
Whitehall Dr NWCHW CW8 .... 129 J8
White Hall La SBCH CW11 ...... 202 E3
Whitehall La TPLY/KEL CW6 .. 175 K4
Whitehall PI FROD/HEL WA6 .. 99 H4
   FROD/HEL WA6 .... 99 J4
White Hall Rd ALS/KID ST7 .... 242 F2
Whitehall Rd DID/WITH M20.... 45 J2
   SALE M33 .... 43 H2
White Hart Gdns NWCHW CW8 .. 128 F8
White Hart La CW/SHV CW2 .. 237 L4
Whitehaven Gdns
   DID/WITH M20 .... 45 G2
Whitehaven La NANT CW5 .... 235 G5
Whitehaven Rd BRAM/HZG SK7.. 65 J7
Whitehill Rd ALS/KID ST7 .... 243 G1
Whitehouse Dr
   HALE/TIMP WA15 .... 62 B4
   NTHM/RTH M23 .... 44 A7
White House Dr WARR WA1 .... 38 E5
Whitehouse Expy RUNC WA7 .. 73 M7
Whitehouse La ALT WA14 ...... 41 K5

KNUT WA16 .... 105 L7
NANT CW5 .... 21 H3
Whitehouse Rd *KNUT* WA16 ...... 80 B1
Whitelea Ct *CHSE* CH3 .... 170 D4
Whitelea Rd *CHF/WBR* SK23 .. 46 D7
Whiteleas Rd *CHF/WBR* SK23 ... 115 K2
Whiteley Pl *ALT* WA14 .... 42 D6
Whitelow Rd *HTNM* SK4 .... 46 A1
Whitemere Ct *EP* CH65 .... 10 E4 **5**
Whitemore Rd *MWCH* CW10 ... 179 J6
Whiteoak Cl *MPL/ROM* SK6 .... 48 E5
White Park Cl *MWCH* CW10 ..... 179 K2
Whiteridge Rd *ALS/KID* ST7 ... 243 G2
White Rd *NM/HAY* SK22 .... 69 J3
Whitesands Rd *LYMM* WA13 ...... 39 J8
Whitesmead Cl *POY/DIS* SK12 .. 68 D7 **1**
Whites La *CW/SHV* CW2 .... 239 H6
White St *MCFLDS* SK11 .... 15 H9
WARR WA1 .... 4 E7
WARRS WA4 .... 16 E7
WDN WA8 .... 53 G7 **5**
Whitethorn Av
WARRW/BUR WA5 .... 35 M7
Whitethorn Cl *MPL/ROM* SK6 .. 48 E5 **4**
White Way Cl *CQ* CH5 .... 142 F6 **6**
Whitewell Cl *NANT* CW5 .... 21 H6
Whitewell Rd *WHITCH* SY13 .. 268 C5
Whitewood La *MALPAS* SY14 .. 245 K6
Whitfield Av *WARR* WA1 .... 37 M5
Whitfield Rd *ALS/KID* ST7 ..... 243 H1
The Whitfields *MCFLDS* SK10 .. 14 A3
Whitle Rd *NM/HAY* SK22 .... 69 J3
Whitley Av *NWCHW* CW8 ...... 129 G1 **5**
WARRS WA4 .... 38 A8
Whitley Cl *MWCH* CW10 .... 179 H5
RUNC WA7 .... 8 F6
Whitley Dr *NWCHW* CW8 ..... 129 G8 **5**
Whitley Gdns *HALE/TIMP* WA15 .. 43 H5
Whitley La *KNUT* WA16 .... 79 C5
Whitley Pl *HALE/TIMP* WA15 ... 43 H5
Whitley Rd *HTNM* SK4 .... 46 B1
Whitlow Av *ALT* WA14 .... 42 B4
GOL/RIS/CU WA3 .... 22 F3
NANT CW5 .... 21 C9
Whitlow La *NWCHE* CW9 .... 153 M4
Whitmoor Cl *RAIN/WH* L35 ..... 33 L3 **4**
Whitney Cft *MCFLDS* SK11 ..... 139 G4
Whitney Pl *WLTN* L25 .... 50 C2 **4**
Whitney Rd *WLTN* L25 .... 50 C1
Whitsand Rd *WYTH/NTH* M22 ... 44 E7
Whitson Cl *KNUT* WA16 .... 59 J8
Whitstable Pk *WDN* WA8 .... 33 L8
Whittaker Av
WARRN/WOL WA2 .... 37 K2 **4**
Whittington Gdns *NWCHE* CW9 .. 153 M3
Whittle Av *WARRW/BUR* WA5 .... 36 A5
Whittlebank Rd *NM/HAY* SK22 .... 69 K1
Whittle Cl *CQ* CH5 .... 167 G1 **3**
Whittle Hall La
WARRW/BUR WA5 .... 35 M6
Whittlewood La
GOL/RIS/CU WA3 .... 30 A7 **3**
Whitton Dr *CHNE* CH2 .... 145 L7
Whitwell Cl *WARRN/BUR* WA5 .. 35 K5
Whitworth Cl *GOL/RIS/CU* WA3 . 38 E1
Wicken St *OFTN* SK2 .... 47 J5
Wicker La *CHSE* CH3 .... 147 C8
HALE/TIMP WA15 .... 62 B4
Wicklow Av *EDGY/DAV* SK3 ... 46 B5 **3**
Wicklow Cl *GTS/LS* CH66 .... 94 A6
Wicklow Dr *WYTH/NTH* M22 .... 63 L2
Wickson La *CHSE* CH3 .... 215 K1
Wicksten Dr *RUNC* WA7 .... 9 L3
Widdale Av *RAIN/WH* L35 .... 33 K1 **5**
Widdale Cl *WARRW/BUR* WA5 .. 35 M5
Widgeon Cl *POY/DIS* SK12 .... 66 B8 **1**
Widgeon Rd *ALT* WA14 .... 42 B4
Widnes Rd *WARRW/BUR* WA5 .. 54 A2
WDN WA8 .... 7 J5
The Wiend *CHNE* CH2 .... 145 K8
Wigan Rd *AIMK* WN4 .... 22 B1
GOL/RIS/CU WA3 .... 23 H1
The Wigdale *CQ* CH5 .... 166 C4 **2**
Wight Cl *EP* CH65 .... 121 J3
Wightman Av *NEWLW* WA12 ... 22 C7 **5**
Wigmore Cl *GOL/RIS/CU* WA3 .. 30 A7 **3**
Wignall Rd *BURS/TUN* ST6 ..... 243 K6
Wigsey La *LYMM* WA13 .... 40 A3
Wigshaw Cl *LEIGH* WN7 .... 24 F3
Wigshaw La *GOL/RIS/CU* WA3 .. 29 L1
Wigwam Cl *POY/DIS* SK12 ...... 66 C8
Wilbraham Cl *NANT* CW5 ...... 236 A5
Wilbraham Rd *CONG* CW12 ... 207 M1
NANT CW5 .... 236 A5
NWCHW CW8 .... 128 C3
Wilbraham St *STHEL* WA9 .... 34 E1
Wilbrahams Wy *ALS/KID* ST7 .. 224 D8
Wilcock Rd *RNFD/HAY* WA11 ... 22 A4
Wilcote Cl *WDN* WA8 .... 34 C8
Wilcott Dr *WILM/AE* SK9 .... 83 M1
Wilcott Rd *CHD/CHDH* SK8 ..... 45 G7
Wild Arum Cl
GOL/RIS/CU WA3 .... 23 L4 **14**
Wilderhope Cl *CW/SHV* CW2 .. 238 C5
Wilderspool Cswy *WARRS* WA4 .. 5 G9
Wilderspool Crs *WARRS* WA4 ... 56 B3
Wild Goose Av *ALS/KID* ST7 ... 243 K1
Wilding Av *RUNC* WA7 .... 9 K2
Wildings Old La
GOL/RIS/CU WA3 .... 29 C4
Wilding St *CW/HAS* CW1 .... 19 K4
Wildmoor La *CHSE* CH3 .... 147 K3
Wild St *BRAM/HZG* SK7 .... 66 D2 **3**
MPL/ROM SK6 .... 47 M2
Wildwood Gv *WARR* WA1 .... 38 B5
Wilford Av *SALE* M33 .... 43 C2
Wilkin Cft *CHD/CHDH* SK8 ..... 64 E3
Wilkins La *WILM/AE* SK9 .... 63 L7
Wilkinson Av *WARR* WA1 .... 37 M6
Wilkinson St *WDN* WA8 .... 53 C7 **1**
Wilkinson St North *EP* CH65 .... 10 E5
Wilks Av *WYTH/NTH* M22 .... 63 M2
Wilks St *BURS/TUN* ST6 .... 243 L8
Willan Rd *CH/BCN* CH1 .... 144 D8

Willard St *BRAM/HZG* SK7 ...... 66 D1 **13**
Willaston Dr *HLWD* L26 .... 51 C6
Willaston Hall Gdns *NANT* CW5 .. 237 J6
Willaston Rd *NSTN* CH64 .... 92 D2
Willbank La *NANT* CW5 .... 234 D7
Willdor Gv *EDGY/DAV* SK3 ...... 46 B6 **3**
Willenhall Rd *NTHM/RTH* M23 .. 44 C2
Willeymoor La *WHITCH* SY13 .. 259 K5
William Av *BIDD* ST8 .... 227 K5
William Penn Cl
WARRW/BUR WA5 .... 35 L8 **5**
William Rd *ALS/KID* ST7 .... 243 G2
Williams Av *NEWLW* WA12 ...... 22 C7
Williams Cl *CHNE* CH2 .... 145 J8 **7**
Williamson Crs *CHF/WBR* SK23 . 89 K4 **2**
Williamson Rd *CHF/WBR* SK23 .. 89 K4
William St *CHNE* CH2 .... 17 L2
CONG CW12 .... 185 C8
DID/WITH M20 .... 45 H1
NEWLW WA12 .... 15 L5
NWCHE CW9 .... 13 M2
STKP SK1 .... 3 L9 **1**
WDN WA8 .... 7 L1
WARR WA1 .... 177 L3
Williams Wy *MCFLDS* SK11 .... 137 J4
Willington Av *PS/BROM* CH62 .. 93 L1
Willington La *TPLY/KEL* CW6 .. 149 K8
Willington Rd *CHSE* CH3 .... 172 F2
TPLY/KEL CW6 .... 173 K1
Willis Cl *RAIN/WH* L35 .... 32 D2
Willis La *RAIN/WH* L35 .... 32 D2
Willis Rd *EDGY/DAV* SK3 .... 46 E6
Willis St *WARR* WA1 .... 5 L4
Willmer Crs *ALS/KID* ST7 .... 226 B6
Willoughby Cl *WARRW/BUR* WA5 . 36 C3
Willoughby St
BURS/TUN ST6 .... 243 K5 **2**
Willow Av *CHD/CHDH* SK8 ...... 64 F2
NEWLW WA12 .... 22 D8
RAIN/WH L35 .... 32 D1
WDN WA8 .... 53 H2
Willoway Rd *CHSE* CH3 .... 170 B2 **2**
Willow Bank *CHD/CHDH* SK8 .. 65 C6
FROD/HEL WA6 .... 124 E2
NANT CW5 .... 21 H4
Willowbank Dr *MCFLDN* SK10 .. 113 J3
Willow Bank Est *NEWLW* WA12 .. 27 M1
Willowbrow Rd *BEB* CH63 .... 92 D1
Willow Cl *ALS/KID* ST7 .... 243 C5
CHNE CH2 .... 145 K4
LYMM WA13 .... 39 L8
POY/DIS SK12 .... 86 E1
RUNC WA7 .... 9 K8
WSFD CW7 .... 177 K1
Willow Ct *CHSW/BR* CH4 .... 190 A5 **2**
MPL/ROM SK6 .... 48 F7 **3**
MWCH CW10 .... 179 J2
NANT CW5 .... 21 H3
Willow Crs *CHNE* CH2 .... 146 A8
CW/SHV CW2 .... 237 M2
WARR WA1 .... 38 B4
Willowcroft Wy *ALS/KID* ST7 .. 226 E8
Willowdale *NEWLW* WA12 ...... 27 L1
Willowdale Av *CHD/CHDH* SK8 . 64 B2 **2**
Willowdale Wy *GTS/LS* CH66 .. 120 F4
Willow Dr *CH/BCN* CH1 .... 144 D7
SALE M33 .... 42 E2
SBCH CW11 .... 204 E5
TPLY/KEL CW6 .... 216 E4
WARRS WA4 .... 56 D3 **4**
WILM/AE SK9 .... 84 D1
Willowfield Gv *AIMK* WN4 .... 22 A2
Willow Gn *KNUT* WA16 .... 106 F1
NWCHW CW8 .... 128 D4
Willowgreen La *NWCHW* CW8 .. 102 B7
Willow Gv *CHNE* CH2 .... 123 C2
CHNE CH2 .... 146 B8
GOL/RIS/CU WA3 .... 23 C3
GTS/LS CH66 .... 121 C3
MPL/ROM SK6 .... 48 F7
WARR WA1 .... 38 B1
Willow Hayes *CHSE* CH3 .... 170 B6 **1**
Willowherb Cl *CHSE* CH3 .... 170 B6 **1**
Willow La *BEB* CH63 .... 92 D1
CQ CH5 .... 142 E8
HOLMCH CW4 .... 157 L3
WARRS WA4 .... 56 D3
Willow Lea *CH/BCN* CH1 .... 144 F2
Willowmead Dr *MCFLDN* SK10 .. 112 A7
Willow Rd *CHSW/BR* CH4 ...... 168 F6
MPL/ROM SK6 .... 67 M5
NEWLW WA12 .... 22 E8
PART M31 .... 40 E2
Willows Cl *CW/SHV* CW2 .... 238 B5
Willow Sq *WSFD* CW7 .... 178 A2 **3**
The Willows *FROD/HEL* WA6 ... 99 J4
NWCHE CW9 .... 104 F7
PART M31 .... 40 F1
Willow St *CONG* CW12 .... 207 L1
Willow Tree Gv *ALS/KID* ST7 .. 224 F5 **3**
Willow Tree Ms
CHD/CHDH SK8 .... 64 B3 **5**
Willow Tree Rd *ALT* WA14 .... 61 K2
Willow Wy *BRAM/HZG* SK7 ..... 65 J5
CHSW/BR CH4 .... 190 B1
DID/WITH M20 .... 45 J1
MCFLDN SK10 .... 112 A7
Wilmere La *WDN* WA8 .... 34 A6
Wilmot Av *WARRW/BUR* WA5 .. 35 M6
Wilmot Dr *GOL/RIS/CU* WA3 .... 22 F5
Wilmslow Av *GTS/LS* CH66 ..... 94 E7 **3**
Wilmslow Crs *WARRS* WA4 ..... 38 D8
Wilmslow Dr *GTS/LS* CH66 ..... 94 E7
Wilmslow Old Rd
HALE/TIMP WA15 .... 62 F6
HALE/TIMP WA15 .... 11 H5
Wilmslow Park Rd *WILM/AE* SK9 .. 84 C5
Wilmslow Rd *BRAM/HZG* SK7 .. 85 H3
CHD/CHDH SK8 .... 45 K7
CHD/CHDH SK8 .... 64 D4
DID/WITH M20 .... 45 J3
HALE/TIMP WA15 .... 62 F6
MCFLDN SK10 .... 85 C8
MCFLDN SK10 .... 111 J3
WILM/AE SK9 .... 84 D1 **4**
WILM/AE SK9 .... 110 A2
Wilsden Rd *WDN* WA8 .... 52 B3 **3**
Wilsford Cl *GOL/RIS/CU* WA3 .. 23 H3 **6**

Wilson Cl *WARRS* WA4 .... 57 K1
Wilson Crs *NWCHE* CW9 .... 131 H1
Wilson Dr *NWCHE* CW9 .... 153 M5
Wilson La *GOL/RIS/CU* WA3 .... 29 L7
Wilson Patten St *WARR* WA1 ..... 4 B4
RAIN/WH L35 .... 32 D1
Wilson St *WARRW/BUR* WA5 .... 4 E2
Wilson Wy *BURS/TUN* ST6 ..... 243 J6
Wilton Av *CHD/CHDH* SK8 ...... 64 C5
Wilton Cl *NWCHW* CW8 .... 129 L8
Wilton Crs *MCFLDS* SK11 ...... 137 L6
WILM/AE SK9 .... 109 M2
Wilton Dr *HALE/TIMP* WA15 ... 62 C4
Wilton La *GOL/RIS/CU* WA3 .... 24 A7
Wilton Rd *CQ* CH5 .... 166 D2
Wiltshire Cl *MCFLDN* SK10 .... 137 L2
WARR WA1 .... 38 D6
Wiltshire Dr *CONG* CW12 ...... 184 D8
Wiltshire Rd *PART* M31 .... 40 E2 **2**
Wilwick La *MCFLDS* SK11 ..... 137 M5
Wimbledon Dr *EDGY/DAV* SK3 .. 46 C6 **6**
Wimbledon Lawns *ALT* WA14 ... 61 J1
Wimborne Cl *CHD/CHDH* SK8 .. 46 C8 **2**
Wimbolt St *OFTN* SK2 .... 47 J8 **3**
Wincanton Av *NTHM/RTH* M23 .. 43 K4
Wincham Av *NWCHE* CW9 ..... 130 D1
Wincham La *NWCHE* CW9 ..... 130 D1
Wincham Rd *SALE* M33 .... 42 C2
Winchcombe Cl *LEIGH* WN7 ... 24 E3 **3**
Winchester Av *AIMK* WN4 .... 22 A1
EP CH65 .... 121 K1
WARRW/BUR WA5 .... 36 C7
Winchester Cl *CW/SHV* CW2 .. 253 H1 **3**
WILM/AE SK9 .... 83 L7 **1**
WLTN L25 .... 50 B5
Winchester Dr *HTNM* SK4 .... 46 B2
Winchester Pk *DID/WITH* M20 .. 44 F1
Winchester Pl *WDN* WA8 .... 52 C4 **2**
Winchester Rd *HALE/TIMP* WA15 .. 62 C3
Winchester Sq *CHSW/BR* CH4 .. 168 F8
Wincle Av *POY/DIS* SK12 .... 86 F2 **1**
Windermere Av *CHNE* CH2 ..... 146 A6
SALE M33 .... 43 K2 **2**
WARRN/WOL WA2 .... 37 J1
WDN WA8 .... 34 B8 **9**
Windermere Cl *NSTN* CH64 ..... 91 M5 **2**
Windermere Dr *CONG* CW12 .. 207 G2
WILM/AE SK9 .... 109 M3
Windermere Rd *CW/SHV* CW2 .. 237 L2
EP CH65 .... 121 J2
MPL/ROM SK6 .... 67 K3
STKP SK1 .... 3 L9
WILM/AE SK9 .... 64 C8
WSFD CW7 .... 177 J2
Windermere St *WDN* WA8 .... 34 B8
Windfield Gdns *GTS/LS* CH66 .. 94 D5
Windfields Cl *CHD/CHDH* SK8 .. 65 H1 **2**
The Windings *MWCH* CW10 ... 179 F2
Windle Ct *GOL/RIS/CU* WA3 .... 29 J8 **8**
NSTN CH64 .... 91 L2
OFTN SK2 .... 47 L7
Windlehurst Old Rd
MPL/ROM SK6 .... 67 M2
Windlehurst Rd *MPL/ROM* SK6 .. 67 K4
Windmill Av *ALS/KID* ST7 ...... 243 C5
Windmill Cl *AUD/MAD/W* CW3 .. 264 E8
WARRS WA4 .... 56 C6
Windmill Dr *AUD/MAD/W* CW3 .. 273 M1
Windmill Hill Av *RUNC* WA7 .... 74 D2
Windmill Hill Av East *RUNC* WA7 .. 74 D4
Windmill Hill Av North
RUNC WA7 .... 74 C1
Windmill Hill Av South
RUNC WA7 .... 74 D3
Windmill Hill Av West *RUNC* WA7 .. 74 C2
Windmill La *AUD/MAD/W* CW3 .. 264 E7
MCFLDN SK10 .... 113 H6
WARRS WA4 .... 56 C6
WARRW/BUR WA5 .... 35 L7
Windmill Ri *CHNE* CH2 .... 145 K5
Windmill Rd *SALE* M33 .... 43 M1 **12**
Windmill St *MCFLDS* SK11 ..... 15 J8
RUNC WA7 .... 9 K2
Windscale Rd *WARRN/WOL* WA2 .. 38 A2
Windsor Av *CHD/CHDH* SK8 ... 44 F7
CQ CH5 .... 142 B6 **6**
CW/HAS CW1 .... 221 C5
HTNM SK4 .... 46 A1 **2**
NANT CW5 .... 251 M1
NEWLW WA12 .... 27 K2
TPLY/KEL CW6 .... 197 K3 **2**
WILM/AE SK9 .... 83 M6
Windsor Cl *MCFLDN* SK10 ... 112 E6
NWCHW CW8 .... 127 M8
POY/DIS SK12 .... 66 D8
Windsor Dr *ALS/KID* ST7 ...... 223 M8
ALT WA14 .... 42 F4
CHSW/BR CH4 .... 190 A1
EP CH65 .... 121 G1
MPL/ROM SK6 .... 48 E7 **6**
NANT CW5 .... 234 E5
RNFD/HAY WA11 .... 22 A5
WARRS WA4 .... 57 H1
WSFD CW7 .... 177 J7 **8**
Windsor Gv *CHD/CHDH* SK8 ... 64 F4
MPL/ROM SK6 .... 48 E2 **6**
RUNC WA7 .... 9 K6
Windsor Pl *CONG* CW12 .... 207 M2
Windsor Rd *AIMK* WN4 .... 22 B2
BRAM/HZG SK7 .... 66 F2
CHSW/BR CH4 .... 168 F6
CW/SHV CW2 .... 237 L4
GOL/RIS/CU WA3 .... 23 J4
MPL/ROM SK6 .... 48 E2
WDN WA8 .... 34 A8
Windsor Sq *MCFLDS* SK11 .... 138 D8
Windsor St *OFTN* SK2 .... 47 G6 **3**
WARRW/BUR WA5 .... 4 B5
Windways *GTS/LS* CH66 .... 94 D5
Windy Arbor Cl *RAIN/WH* L35 .. 32 D5
Windy Arbor Rd *RAIN/WH* L35 .. 32 C4
Windy Bank Av
GOL/RIS/CU WA3 .... 23 L4 **15**
Winfield Gv *MPL/ROM* SK6 ..... 49 H3 **3**
Winfield Wy *WDN* WA8 .... 7 K4

Winfrith Rd *WARRN/WOL* WA2 .. 38 A3
Wingate Dr *DID/WITH* M20 ..... 45 J2
HALE/TIMP WA15 .... 43 G7
Wingfield Av *WILM/AE* SK9 ..... 83 L6
Wingfield Dr *WILM/AE* SK9 ..... 83 L6
Wingfield Pl *WSFD* CW7 .... 177 H6
Winghay Rd *ALS/KID* ST7 ..... 243 H2
Winhill Rd *NM/HAY* SK22 .... 69 J3 **7**
Winifred Rd *DID/WITH* M20 ..... 45 H1
OFTN SK2 .... 47 G7
Winkwell Dr *CHSW/BR* CH4 ... 169 G7
Winmarith Dr *HALE/TIMP* WA15 .. 62 D5
Winmarleigh Gdns *LEIGH* WN7 .. 24 E1
Winmarleigh St *WARR* WA1 ...... 4 E7
Winnington Av *NWCHW* CW8 .. 12 A4
Winnington Gn *OFTN* SK2 .... 47 K7
Winnington La *NWCHW* CW8 .. 129 J2
Winnington Rd *MPL/ROM* SK6 .. 48 F4
Winnington St *NWCHW* CW8 .. 12 F1
WSFD CW7 .... 177 L3
The Winnows *RUNC* WA7 .... 73 K3 **1**
Winscombe Dr *CHSE* CH3 ..... 170 C2
Winsfield Rd *BRAM/HZG* SK7 .. 66 D4
Winsford Gv *GTS/LS* CH66 .... 120 C1
Winsford Rd *WSFD* CW7 .... 199 K2
Winsford Wy *CH/BCN* CH1 .... 168 F2
Winslade Cl *BRAM/HZG* SK7 .. 66 A2 **3**
Winsley Rd *NTHM/RTH* M23 ... 43 M2
Winslow Cl *RUNC* WA7 .... 74 D4
Winstanley Cl
WARRW/BUR WA5 .... 36 C7 **7**
Winstanley Rd *NSTN* CH64 ..... 91 L7
Winster Dr *NTHLY* L27 .... 51 C1
Winster Gv *OFTN* SK2 .... 47 C6
Winston Av *ALS/KID* ST7 ...... 224 C8
NEWLW WA12 .... 27 H1
STHEL WA9 .... 26 B2
Winston Cl *MPL/ROM* SK6 ..... 48 D5
Winterbottom La *KNUT* WA16 .. 79 K5
Winterburn Gn *OFTN* SK2 .... 47 L7
Winterley Dr *HLWD* L26 .... 51 C6
Winterford La *TPLY/KEL* CW6 .. 198 B1 **1**
Winter Gv *STHEL* WA9 .... 26 B1
Winterslow Av *NTHM/RTH* M23 .. 43 K3
Winterton Wy *MCFLDS* SK11 .. 162 C1
Winton Cl *BRAM/HZG* SK7 ...... 65 J3
Winton Gv *RUNC* WA7 .... 74 D3 **3**
Winton Rd *ALT* WA14 .... 61 J2
GOL/RIS/CU WA3 .... 23 L7
Winwick La *GOL/RIS/CU* WA3 .. 23 L8
Winwick Link Rd
WARRN/WOL WA2 .... 28 B6
Winwick Rd *NEWLW* WA12 ..... 27 L2
WARRN/WOL WA2 .... 5 C4
Winwick St *WARRN/WOL* WA2 .. 5 C5
Winwick Vw *WARRW/BUR* WA5 .. 26 D3
Winwood Rd *DID/WITH* M20 ... 45 J4
Wirksmoor Rd *NM/HAY* SK22 .. 69 H5
Wirral Cl *GOL/RIS/CU* WA3 ..... 29 L1
Wirral Crs *EDGY/DAV* SK3 ..... 46 A4
NSTN CH64 .... 91 M7
Wirral Vw *CQ* CH5 .... 166 A3
Wirral Wy *NSTN* CH64 .... 91 C1
Wirswall Rd *WHITCH* SY13 .... 260 C4
Wisbech Dr *NTHM/RTH* M23 ... 43 M3 **3**
Wisenholme Cl *RUNC* WA7 ..... 73 L8
Wistaston Av *CW/SHV* CW2 ... 237 M2
Wistaston Green Cl
CW/SHV CW2 .... 237 L2 **3**
Wistaston Green Rd
CW/SHV CW2 .... 237 K2
Wistaston Pk *CW/SHV* CW2 ... 237 M3
Wistaston Rd *CW/SHV* CW2 .... 18 D5
NANT CW5 .... 237 L2
Wisterdale Cl *CW/SHV* CW2 ... 238 A5
Witham Av *WYTH/NTH* M22 .... 44 E7
Witham Cl *CW/SHV* CW2 .... 238 A4 **3**
Witham Wy *BIDD* ST8 .... 227 L3
Withenfield Rd *NTHM/RTH* M23 .. 43 M4
Withens Cl *NWCHW* CW8 ...... 128 D4 **3**
Withens Gn *OFTN* SK2 .... 47 L6
Withenshaw La *MCFLDS* SK11 .. 163 K7
Withens La *NWCHW* CW8 ..... 128 D4
Withers Av *WARRN/WOL* WA2 .. 5 L1
Wither's La *KNUT* WA16 .... 58 B8
Withington Av *GOL/RIS/CU* WA3 .. 25 C8
Withington Cl *NWCHE* CW9 .... 13 J7
SBCH CW11 .... 204 C5
Withington Rd *SPK/HALE* L24 .. 70 F1
Withinlee Rd *MCFLDN* SK10 ... 111 J6
Withins Rd *GOL/RIS/CU* WA3 .. 29 M1
Within Wy *SPK/HALE* L24 .... 71 L3
Withnall Dr *CW/SHV* CW2 ..... 238 B8
Withnell Rd *DID/WITH* M20 ..... 45 K1
Withy Cl *FROD/HEL* WA6 .... 99 J4
Withycombe Rd
WARRW/BUR WA5 .... 35 K8
Withy Cft *CHSE* CH3 .... 170 B5
Withyfold Dr *MCFLDN* SK10 .... 15 J2
Withypool Dr *OFTN* SK2 .... 47 H7
Witney Gdns *WARRS* WA4 ...... 56 F6
Witney La *MALPAS* SY14 ...... 246 D5
Wittenbury Rd *HTNM* SK4 .... 46 B2
Witton St *NWCHE* CW9 .... 13 J1
Witt Rd *WDN* WA8 .... 7 G7
Wivern Pl *NWCHE* CW9 .... 9 K1
Woburn Av *NEWLW* WA12 ...... 27 K2
Woburn Cl *MCFLDN* SK10 ...... 14 E1
NWCHE CW9 .... 12 E9
Woburn Dr *CHNE* CH2 .... 145 M5 **3**
HALE/TIMP WA15 .... 62 B2
WDN WA8 .... 33 K7
Woburn Rd *WARRN/WOL* WA2 .. 28 A3
Woking Rd *CHD/CHDH* SK8 ... 65 C6
Wold Ct *CQ* CH5 .... 166 C4
Wolsey Dr *ALT* WA14 .... 61 C3
Wolstanholme Cl *CONG* CW12 .. 207 M3
Wolverham Rd *EP* CH65 .... 11 C6
Wolverton Dr *RUNC* WA7 .... 74 D3
WILM/AE SK9 .... 84 C3
Wolvesey Rd *WSFD* CW7 .... 177 H6 **8**
Woodacre Rd *GTS/LS* CH66 .... 94 F4
Woodacres Cft *WILM/AE* SK9 .. 83 M6
Woodale Cl *WARRW/BUR* WA5 .. 35 L5
Woodall Dr *RUNC* WA7 .... 9 J5

Woodavens Gv
AUD/MAD/W CW3 .... 273 G2
Woodbank Cl *MPL/ROM* SK6 .. 47 L1 **5**
STKP SK1 .... 3 M7
STKP SK1 .... 47 J4 **6**
Woodbank Rd *EP* CH65 .... 121 K2
WARRW/BUR WA5 .... 36 A8
Woodbine Av *IRL* M44 .... 31 K8 **2**
Woodbine Crs *OFTN* SK2 .... 46 F5 **14**
Woodbine Rd *LYMM* WA13 ..... 40 B8
SALE M33 .... 43 C2
Woodbourne Rd *NM/HAY* SK22 .. 69 G7
SALE M33 .... 43 C2
Woodbridge Av *HLWD* L26 ...... 50 D2
Woodbridge Cl *WARRS* WA4 ... 56 F8
Woodbridge Gv
NTHM/RTH M23 .... 44 A3 **3**
Woodbrook *CHF/WBR* SK23 .... 89 L5
Woodbrook Rd *CHF/WBR* SK23 .. 89 L5
Woodbrook Rd *WILM/AE* SK9 .. 110 B3
Woodburn Rd *WYTH/NTH* M22 .. 44 D4
Woodchurch La *GTS/LS* CH66 .. 94 E7
Woodclose *GTS/LS* CH66 .... 94 A3
Woodcock La *ALS/KID* ST7 ... 226 C6
Woodcote Av *BRAM/HZG* SK7 .. 65 J3
EP CH65 .... 121 K2 **3**
Woodcote Cl
WARRN/WOL WA2 .... 37 K3 **7**
Woodcote Pl *SBCH* CW11 ...... 222 F4
Woodcote Rd *ALT* WA14 .... 42 D3
Woodcote Vw *WILM/AE* SK9 ... 84 F3
Woodcott Cl *CW/SHV* CW2 ... 253 L2 **3**
Woodcotthill La *NANT* CW5 ... 250 B7
Woodcroft *OFTN* SK2 .... 47 K6
Wood Edge *ALS/KID* ST7 ...... 241 C1
Woodedge *AIMK* WN4 .... 22 A1
Wood End *BRAM/HZG* SK7 ..... 65 K2
Woodend Av *SPK/HALE* L24 ... 50 C7
Woodend Cl *MWCH* CW10 .... 179 J6 **3**
GOL/RIS/CU WA3 .... 39 K2
KNUT WA16 .... 82 E4
Wood End La *ALS/KID* ST7 ..... 94 E8
Woodend La *SPK/HALE* L24 .... 50 C8
Woodend Rd *EDGY/DAV* SK3 .. 46 F8
EP CH65 .... 94 F6
WYTH/NTH M22 .... 44 D8
Woodfall Cl *NSTN* CH64 .... 92 A6
Woodfall Gv *NSTN* CH64 .... 92 A6
Woodfall La *NSTN* CH64 .... 91 M8
Woodfield *WYTH/NTH* M22 ..... 63 K1
Woodfield Av *FLINT* CH6 .... 116 F7
Woodfield Cl *CHSW/BR* CH4 .. 190 A1 **3**
Woodfield Crs *AIMK* WN4 .... 22 A2 **3**
MPL/ROM SK6 .... 47 M2 **1**
Woodfield Gv *CHNE* CH2 .... 146 B7
Woodfield Rd *ALT* WA14 .... 42 C6
CHD/CHDH SK8 .... 65 H5
Woodfield Rd North *EP* CH65 .. 10 E7
Woodfin Cft *MCFLDS* SK11 ... 135 C1
Woodford Av *GOL/RIS/CU* WA3 .. 23 K5
Woodford Cl *CW/SHV* CW2 ... 237 M2
FROD/HEL WA6 .... 124 B2 **4**
RUNC WA7 .... 73 H6 **2**
WARRS WA4 .... 57 J1
Woodford Gdns *DID/WITH* M20 .. 45 G2
Woodford La *MCFLDN* SK10 ... 85 J6
WSFD CW7 .... 177 H4
Woodford La West *WSFD* CW7 .. 177 G5
Woodford Rd *BRAM/HZG* SK7 .. 65 L7
POY/DIS SK12 .... 66 B7
WILM/AE SK9 .... 85 C4
Woodgate Av *ALS/KID* ST7 ... 224 F7
Woodgate Cl *MPL/ROM* SK6 ... 47 M1
Woodgreen La *NANT* CW5 ..... 200 C7
Woodhall Cl *BRAM/HZG* SK7 .. 85 K1
WARRW/BUR WA5 .... 36 A4
Woodhall Rd *ALS/KID* ST7 .... 243 J1
Woodham Cl *NWCHW* CW8 .... 12 B9
Woodham Gv *NSTN* CH64 ...... 91 M7 **2**
Woodhatch Rd *NTHM/RTH* M23 .. 43 M3
Woodhatch Rd *RUNC* WA7 ..... 74 D7
Woodhead Dr *HALE/TIMP* WA15 .. 61 M3
Woodhead Rd *HALE/TIMP* WA15 .. 61 M3
Woodheys *HTNM* SK4 .... 45 M1
Woodheys Dr *SALE* M33 .... 42 D3
Woodhey Cl *GOL/RIS/CU* WA3 .. 38 F1
Woodhouse End Rd
MCFLDS SK11 .... 161 L3
Woodhouse La *ALT* WA14 .... 41 H8
ALT WA14 .... 42 B3
AUD/MAD/W CW3 .... 274 C3
BIDD ST8 .... 227 L2
MCFLDS SK11 .... 161 K3
SALE M33 .... 42 C2
WYTH/NTH M22 .... 44 B7
WYTH/NTH M22 .... 63 J4
Woodhouse La East
HALE/TIMP WA15 .... 43 H3 **3**
Woodhouse Rd *WYTH/NTH* M22 .. 63 K4
Woodland Av *BRAM/HZG* SK7 .. 66 E3
CW/HAS CW1 .... 19 M5
LYMM WA13 .... 59 C2
NANT CW5 .... 21 J6
NEWLW WA12 .... 27 M1 **3**
WDN WA8 .... 34 A8
Woodland Bank *CHNE* CH2 ... 146 F3 **2**
Woodland Cl *MCFLDS* SK11 ... 135 E1
Woodland Ct *ALS/KID* ST7 .... 224 D8 **2**
Woodland Crs *CQ* CH5 .... 142 A6 **3**
Woodland Dr *LYMM* WA13 ...... 58 F2
Woodland End *MCFLDS* SK11 .. 135 C1 **3**
Woodland Gdns
CW/HAS CW1 .... 221 K6 **2**
Woodland Hills
AUD/MAD/W CW3 .... 267 L3
Woodland Rd *ALS/KID* ST7 .... 224 E4
EP CH65 .... 121 C2
HLWD L26 .... 50 E5
Woodlands Av *ALS/KID* ST7 ... 242 F8
CHD/CHDH SK8 .... 65 C4
CONG CW12 .... 184 D8
LEIGH WN7 .... 24 C5
Woodlands Cl *CHD/CHDH* SK8 .. 65 C4
NSTN CH64 .... 91 K4
TPLY/KEL CW6 .... 175 C4

Woodlands Ct CQ CH5 .... 166 C4
Woodlands Crs KNUT WA16 .... 59 J8
Woodlands Dr CHNE CH2
HOLMCH CW4 .... 157 L3
KNUT WA16 .... 107 H2
OFTN SK2 .... 47 J4
SALE M33 .... 43 J3
WARRS WA4 .... 57 K1
Woodlands Gv NWCHW CW8 .... 128 F1
Woodlands La CHSE CH3 .... 170 A2
HALE/TIMP WA15 .... 42 E7
Woodlands Park Rd OFTN SK2 .... 47 K4
Woodlands Pkwy
HALE/TIMP WA15 .... 42 E7
Woodlands Rd ALT WA14 .... 42 E7
CHSE CH3 .... 170 A6
CHSW/BR CH4 .... 169 G5
HTNM SK4 .... 45 K2
MCFLDS SK11 .... 14 E8
NM/HAY SK22 .... 69 G4
NSTN CH64 .... 91 K4
NWCHW CW8 .... 12 A9
POY/DIS SK12 .... 68 A6
WILM/AE SK9 .... 84 E1
Woodlands Rd East
NWCHW CW8 .... 12 A8
The Woodlands NWCHE CW9 .... 105 C6
NWCHW CW8 .... 12 E1
Woodland St BIDD ST8 .... 227 K5
CQ CH5 .... 142 A6
Woodlands Wy TPLY/KEL CW6 .... 197 K1
Woodland Vw GTS/LS CH66 ...... 94 B4
Wood La CHSE CH3 .... 215 C2
CHSW/BR CH4 .... 167 H8
HALE/TIMP WA15 .... 42 E7
HOLMCH CW4 .... 157 J3
HUY L36 .... 32 B2
KNUT WA16 .... 82 B3
MPL/ROM SK6 .... 48 D7
MWCH CW10 .... 180 D8
NSTN CH64 .... 91 J2
NSTN CH64 .... 118 C2
NWCHW CW8 .... 128 E4
PART M31 .... 40 E1
RUNC WA7 .... 73 M8
RUNC WA7 .... 74 C6
TPLY/KEL CW6 .... 173 K5
WARRS WA4 .... 56 E4
Wood La East MCFLDN SK10 .... 87 H4
Wood La North MCFLDN SK10 .... 87 H4
Wood La South MCFLDN SK10 .... 87 G5
Wood La West MCFLDN SK10 .... 87 G4
Woodlark CI WSFD CW7 .... 178 A4
Woodlea Av CHNE CH2 .... 145 M5
Woodlea Ct NWCHW CW8 .... 12 C4
Woodlea Dr MCFLDN SK10 ...... 112 E4
Woodley CI OFTN SK2 .... 47 K5
Woodley Fold
WARRW/BUR WA5 .... 35 M8
Woodman St STKP SK1 .... 2 F4
Wood Mt HALE/TIMP WA15 ...... 43 H7
Woodmount CI MPL/ROM SK6 .... 48 E2
Woodnoth Dr CW/SHV CW2 ..... 238 C7
Wood Orchard La
AUD/MAD/W CW3 .... 274 B2
Woodpecker CI GOL/RIS/CU WA3.. 29 M8
Woodpecker Dr HLWD L26 ...... 50 C6
NWCHE CW9 .... 129 M8
Woodridge RUNC WA7 .... 74 C3
Wood Rd HALE/TIMP WA15 ...... 43 G3
HLWD L26 .... 50 E5
SALE M33 .... 43 H3
Woodrock Rd WLTN L25 .... 50 B2
Woodrow Wy IRL M44 .... 31 M4
Woodroyd CI BRAM/HZG SK7 .... 65 K3
Woodruff CI ALS/KID ST7 ...... 243 M3
Woodruffe Gdns MPL/ROM SK6 .. 48 A4
Wood's CI KNUT WA16 .... 107 M6
Woodsfin La CHSE CH3 .... 214 E5
Woods Gv CHD/CHDH SK8 ...... 65 H5
Woodshutt's St ALS/KID ST7 .... 242 D3
Woodside ALS/KID ST7 .... 225 L8
AUD/MAD/W CW3 .... 267 L5
KNUT WA16 .... 107 H2

MCFLDS SK11 .... 160 A1
Woodside Av ALS/KID ST7 ...... 224 E8
ALS/KID ST7 .... 242 F3
CW/SHV CW2 .... 237 M2
FROD/HEL WA6 .... 99 K5
Woodside CI CQ CH5 .... 166 A3
Woodside Dr MPL/ROM SK6 .... 67 L5
SBCH CW11 .... 204 C6
Woodside Rd CH/SHV CW2 .... 237 M3
POY/DIS SK12 .... 66 E8
Woodside St NM/HAY SK22 .... 69 H6
LYMM WA13 .... 59 H5
WARRW/BUR WA5 .... 35 M6
Woods La CHD/CHDH SK8 ...... 65 H5
NWCHW CW8 .... 12 A9
Woods Moor La EDGY/DAV SK3 .. 47 G8
Woodsome CI EP CH65 .... 121 H3
Woodsome Dr EP CH65 .... 121 H3
Wood Sorrel Wy
GOL/RIS/CU WA3 .... 23 L4
Woods Rd IRL M44 .... 31 M4
The Woods ALT WA14 .... 42 E6
Woodstock Av CHD/CHDH SK8 .. 65 G5
NEWLW WA12 .... 27 K2
Woodstock CI LEIGH WN7 ...... 24 E3
Woodstock Dr MWCH CW10 .... 179 L7
Woodstock Gdns WARRS WA4 .. 56 F6
Woodstock Rd ALT WA14 ...... 42 C4
BURS/TUN ST6 .... 243 G5
Woodstock St BURS/TUN ST6.. 243 H4
Wood St ALS/KID ST7 .... 226 C5
ALT WA14 .... 42 D8
CHD/CHDH SK8 .... 45 K6
CONG CW12 .... 207 K1
CQ CH5 .... 167 G2
CW/SHV CW2 .... 19 G8
EDGY/DAV SK3 .... 2 C7
EDGY/DAV SK3 .... 2 E6
GOL/RIS/CU WA3 .... 23 H4
MCFLDS SK11 .... 15 H6
NM/HAY SK22 .... 69 H5
WARR WA1 .... 5 M5
WDN WA8 .... 7 L3
Woodthorn CI RUNC WA7 ...... 54 F8
Woodthorpe Dr
CHD/CHDH SK8 .... 65 G2
Woodvale ALT WA14 .... 61 J2
Woodvale CI
WARRN/WOL WA2 .... 37 L3
Woodvale Dr GOL/RIS/CU WA3 .. 23 L3
Woodvale Rd GTS/LS CH66 .... 94 B5
KNUT WA16 .... 107 C4
WLTN L25 .... 50 B2
Wood Vw WYTH/NTH M22 ..... 44 D3
Woodview Crs WDN WA8 ...... 52 A4
Woodview Rd WDN WA8 ...... 52 A4
Wood Ville CQ CH5 .... 166 D2
Woodville Dr MPL/ROM SK6 .... 48 E8
Woodville PI WDN WA8 .... 6 A2
Woodville Rd ALT WA14 ...... 42 C8
Woodward St NWCHW CW8 ... 128 D3
Woodward Wk CHSE CH3 ...... 172 C1
Woodwise La NTHM/RTH M23 .. 43 L3
Woolacombe CI WARRS WA4 .. 56 D1
Woolaston Dr ALS/KID ST7 .... 241 K1
Woolden Rd IRL M44 .... 31 C5
Woolley Av POY/DIS SK12 ...... 86 D1
Woolley CI FROD/HEL WA6 .... 99 K2
Woolmer CI GOL/RIS/CU WA3 ... 30 B6
Woolston Av CONG CW12 ..... 207 M2
Woolston Dr CW/SHV CW2 .... 253 L2
Woolston Grange Av WARR WA1.. 38 E4
WARRN/WOL WA2 .... 38 C2
Woolton Bvd WLTN L25 ...... 50 B3
Woolton Mt WLTN L25 .... 50 A1
Woolton Pk WLTN L25 .... 50 A1
Woolton Park CI WLTN L25 .... 50 A1
Woolton St WLTN L25 .... 50 B2
Woore Rd AUD/MAD/W CW3 ... 274 B1
Worcester Av
GOL/RIS/CU WA3 .... 23 H4
Worcester CI ALS/KID ST7 .... 242 D5

MPL/ROM SK6 .... 48 A3
WARRW/BUR WA5 .... 36 B7
Worcester PI CH/BCN CH1 .... 145 G7
Worcester Rd CHD/CHDH SK8 .. 46 A8
SALE M33 .... 42 D1
Worcester St EP CH65 .... 10 F5
Worcester Wk EP CH65 ...... 10 F5
Wordsworth Av STHEL WA9 .... 34 A1
WARRS WA4 .... 56 B1
Wordsworth CI
CW/SHV CW2 .... 237 M3
SBCH CW11 .... 203 K6
Wordsworth Crs CH/BCN CH1 .. 145 G7
Wordsworth Dr CW/HAS CW1 .. 19 L3
Wordsworth Ms
CH/BCN CH1 .... 145 G7
Wordsworth Sq CH/BCN CH1 .. 145 G7
Wordsworth Wy ALS/KID ST7 .. 224 D8
GTS/LS CH66 .... 120 E3
Works La NWCHE CW9 .... 130 E3
Worleston CI MWCH CW10 .... 179 J6
Worrall St CONG CW12 ...... 207 L1
EDGY/DAV SK3 .... 2 E9
Worsborough Av
WARRW/BUR WA5 .... 36 B7
Worsley Av CH/BCN CH1 ...... 144 A4
WARRS WA4 .... 37 M8
Worsley Crs OFTN SK2 .... 47 H5
Worsley Dr CONG CW12 ...... 208 B3
Worsley Rd WARRS WA4 ...... 56 B3
Worsley St GOL/RIS/CU WA3 ... 23 C4
WARRW/BUR WA5 .... 4 D2
Worthing CI OFTN SK2 .... 47 K6
Worthing St NWCHE CW9 .... 130 C4
Worthington Av PART M31 .... 40 F1
Worthington CI MCFLDS SK11 .. 137 H4
NANT CW5 .... 21 K7
RUNC WA7 .... 74 A5
Worthington St WHITCH SY13 .. 270 B4
Wotton Dr AIMK WN4 .... 22 D1
Wrekin Av NTHM/RTH M23 .... 63 C1
Wrekin CI WLTN L25 .... 50 B4
Wrekin Wy CHSW/BR CH4 .... 168 F6
Wrenbury Crs EDGY/DAV SK3 .. 46 C6
Wrenbury Dr CHD/CHDH SK8 .. 45 L6
Wrenhall Dr NANT CW5 ...... 250 E5
Wrenbury Heath Rd NANT CW5.. 250 E7
Wrenbury Rd MALPAS SY14 ... 248 C3
NANT CW5 .... 262 A1
Wren CI BIDD ST8 .... 227 L4
CW/HAS CW1 .... 220 F6
GOL/RIS/CU WA3 .... 29 M8
MCFLDN SK10 .... 14 A2
OFTN SK2 .... 47 M7
RUNC WA7 .... 74 A6
Wren Gv HLWD L26 .... 50 E3
Wrenmere CI SBCH CW11 .... 203 L4
Wrenshot La KNUT WA16 ..... 59 J7
Wrexham CI BIDD ST8 .... 227 K3
WARRW/BUR WA5 .... 36 E2
Wrexham Rd CHSW/BR CH4.... 169 J6
MALPAS SY14 .... 257 L2
NANT CW5 .... 234 F5
TPLY/KEL CW6 .... 233 G3
WHITCH SY13 .... 269 L5
WRXS/E LL13 .... 228 D5
Wright Av NWCHE CW9 ...... 130 C6
Wright Crs WDN WA8 .... 53 C8
Wrights Bank North OFTN SK2.. 47 K7
Wrights Bank South OFTN SK2 .. 47 L7
Wright's La SBCH CW11 ...... 204 D6
WARRW/BUR WA5 .... 35 L1
WDN WA8 .... 53 M2
Wrigley CI ALS/KID ST7 ...... 242 D3
Wrigley La MCFLDN SK10 ..... 111 H8
Wrinehill Rd NANT CW5 ...... 253 K5
Wroxham CI CHNE CH2 ...... 17 G2
FROD/HEL WA6 .... 98 B8
Wroxham Rd WARRW/BUR WA5.. 35 L6
Wyatt Gv AIMK WN4 .... 22 D1
Wyatt St BURS/TUN ST6 ...... 243 J5

Wybersley Rd MPL/ROM SK6 ... 68 A3
Wybunbury La NANT CW5 .... 252 B1
NANT CW5 .... 253 H6
Wybunbury Rd NANT CW5 ... 237 K8
Wyche Av NANT CW5 .... 20 C7
Wyche CI NWCHE CW9 ...... 130 E6
Wyche La TPLY/KEL CW6 ..... 216 F4
Wychelm Rd PART M31 ...... 40 F1
Wyche Rd TPLY/KEL CW6 ..... 216 F4
Wych-house La MWCH CW10 .. 179 J3
Wych La MCFLDN SK10 ...... 86 C7
Wychwood ALT WA14 .... 61 H3
Wychwood Av LYMM WA13 .. 58 C1
Wycliffe Av WILM/AE SK9 .... 84 A6
Wycliffe Rd GTS/LS CH66 .... 120 F1
Wycliffe St HTNM SK4 .... 2 D4
Wyedale EP CH65 .... 121 H1
Wynchgate BRAM/HZG SK7 .. 67 G1
Wyncroft CI EP CH65 .... 121 G1
WDN WA8 .... 52 C5
Wyncroft Rd WDN WA8 ..... 52 C5
Wyndham CI NANT CW5 ..... 65 L5
Wyndham Crs GTS/LS CH66 .. 120 E2
Wyndham Rd CH/BCN CH1 ... 144 C8
The Wynd TPLY/KEL CW6 .... 149 J8
Wyne CI BRAM/HZG SK7 ..... 67 G1
Wynfield Av WYTH/NTH M22 .. 63 M5
Wyngate Rd CHD/CHDH SK8 .. 64 F3
HALE/TIMP WA15 .... 61 M4
Wynnstay Rd CHSW/BR CH4 .. 167 J8
Wynter La MALPAS SY14 ..... 245 H1
Wynton CI LEIGH WN7 ...... 24 C2
Wynyard CI SALE M33 ...... 43 K2
Wynyard Rd WYTH/NTH M22 .. 63 J1
Wyrevale Gv AIMK WN4 ..... 22 C1
Wyswall CI HLWD L26 .... 50 E3
Wythburn Gv RUNC WA7 .... 73 L7
Wythburn Rd STKP SK1 ..... 47 H5
Wythenshawe Rd
NTHM/RTH M23 .... 43 L4
Wythens Rd CHD/CHDH SK8 .. 64 B4
Wythin St TPLY/KEL CW6 ..... 216 D3
Wyville CI BRAM/HZG SK7 .... 67 G2

Y

Yarcombe CI HLWD L26 ...... 50 F3
Yardington WHITCH SY13 .... 269 M4
Yardley Av WARRW/BUR WA5 .. 4 D1
Yarmouth Dr NTHM/RTH M23 .. 44 B3
Yarmouth Rd WARRW/BUR WA5.. 35 L6
Yarrow CI CHSW/BR CH4 ..... 167 H8
Yarwood Av NTHM/RTH M23 .. 43 M5
Yarwood CI NWCHW CW8 .... 13 G5
Yarwoodheath La ALT WA14 .. 60 E4
Yarwood St ALT WA14 ...... 61 K1
Yatehouse La MWCH CW10 ... 155 J7
Yates CI WARRW/BUR WA5 ... 36 C7
Yates Rd CHNE CH2 .... 122 E3
NM/HAY SK22 .... 69 J5
Yates St CW/SHV CW2 ...... 18 E7
STKP SK1 .... 3 L2
Yattendon Av
NTHM/RTH M23 .... 43 K4
Yealand Av HTNM SK4 ...... 2 C2
Yeald Brow LYMM WA13 .... 58 B1
Yeardsley Av CHF/WBR SK23 .. 89 K1
Yeardsley CI BRAM/HZG SK7 .. 65 L1
Yeardsley Gn CHF/WBR SK23 .. 89 K4
Yeardsley La CHF/WBR SK23 .. 89 K1
Yearsleys La FROD/HEL WA6 .. 127 G7
Yeld La TPLY/KEL CW6 ...... 149 L6
Yelverton CI HLWD L26 ...... 50 F3
Yeoford Dr ALT WA14 .... 42 B6
Yeoman CI BRAM/HZG SK7 ... 66 D1
Yeoman Wy GTS/LS CH66 .... 120 E3
Yeovil CI WARR WA1 .... 38 C4
Yerburgh St CHNE CH2 ...... 145 K8
Yewdale Dr GTS/LS CH66 .... 120 F3
Yewdale Rd OFTN SK2 ...... 47 H6
Yewlands NWCHW CW8 .... 127 K7
Yewlands Dr KNUT WA16 .... 107 J2

Yew St HTNM SK4 .... 46 B4
Yew Tree Av BRAM/HZG SK7 .. 66 F4
NEWLW WA12 .... 22 A8
WYTH/NTH M22 .... 44 D3
Yewtree CI NSTN CH64 ...... 91 M5
Yew Tree CI CHNE CH2 ...... 122 E3
CHSW/BR CH4 .... 190 C1
LYMM WA13 .... 39 L8
MALPAS SY14 .... 232 D2
MCFLDN SK10 .... 112 B5
MCFLDS SK11 .... 14 B9
MPL/ROM SK6 .... 48 E7
MWCH CW10 .... 179 H2
TPLY/KEL CW6 .... 175 M5
WILM/AE SK9 .... 84 D5
Yew Tree Ct ALS/KID ST7 .... 241 L2
Yew Tree Dr MPL/ROM SK6 ... 47 K1
NANT CW5 .... 20 C6
NWCHW CW8 .... 103 H8
WYTH/NTH M22 .... 44 D3
Yew Tree Gv CHD/CHDH SK8 .. 64 A1
Yewtree La NTHM/RTH M23 .. 44 B2
POY/DIS SK12 .... 86 F2
WYTH/NTH M22 .... 44 D3
Yew Tree La CONG CW12 .... 226 C2
WARRS WA4 .... 57 J7
Yew Tree Park Rd
CHD/CHDH SK8 .... 65 H6
Yewtree Rd KNUT WA16 ..... 131 M1
Yew Tree Rd CW/SHV CW2 ... 238 A4
EDGY/DAV SK3 .... 65 M1
MCFLDN SK10 .... 87 H3
WLTN L25 .... 50 C4
Yew Tree Ter ALS/KID ST7 .... 243 G4
Yew Tree Wy GOL/RIS/CU WA3.. 23 H5
MCFLDN SK10 .... 112 B6
The Yonne CH/BCN CH1 ..... 16 E5
York Av CQ CH5 .... 142 B7
GOL/RIS/CU WA3 .... 29 M2
WARRW/BUR WA5 .... 35 L5
York CI ALS/KID ST7 .... 242 D5
BIDD ST8 .... 227 K2
CHD/CHDH SK8 .... 46 A7
York Crs WILM/AE SK9 ...... 84 D5
York Dr ALT WA14 .... 61 K3
BRAM/HZG SK7 .... 67 G2
CHNE CH2 .... 146 F4
MANAIR M90 .... 62 F5
WARRS WA4 .... 57 G2
WSFD CW7 .... 177 K6
York PI RUNC WA7 .... 9 H3
York Rd AIMK WN4 .... 22 C2
ALT WA14 .... 61 J3
EP CH65 .... 10 E8
HUY L36 .... 32 A1
IRL M44 .... 31 K7
WARRS WA4 .... 57 G2
WDN WA8 .... 52 C4
York Rd South AIMK WN4 .... 22 C2
Yorkshire Rd PART M31 ..... 40 E2
York St CH/BCN CH1 .... 17 H4
DID/WITH M20 .... 45 H1
EDGY/DAV SK3 .... 2 E7
GOL/RIS/CU WA3 .... 23 G3
HALE/TIMP WA15 .... 61 L1
MCFLDN SK10 .... 15 J5
RUNC WA7 .... 9 G5
WARRS WA4 .... 5 J9
Young St BURS/TUN ST6 .... 243 M6
Yule St EDGY/DAV SK3 ...... 2 C7

Z

Zan Dr SBCH CW11 .... 223 G1
Zinnia Dr IRL M44 .... 31 L4
Zion St NWCHW CW8 .... 12 E4
Zodiac Dr BURS/TUN ST6 .... 243 M6
Zurich Gdns BRAM/HZG SK7 .. 65 L1

Index - featured places

Abbey Gate College
CHSE CH3 .... 193 L4
Abbey Gate School
CHNE CH2 .... 16 F3
The Accord Clinic
MWCH CW10 .... 179 J3
Acorn Business Park
EDGY/DAV SK3 .... 2 D5
Acorns Surgery
MWCH CW10 .... 179 J3
Acton C of E Controlled
Primary School
NANT CW5 .... 236 A5
Adderley C of E Primary
School
MKTDR TF9 .... 273 M7
Adelaide Street County
Secondary School
CW/HAS CW1 .... 18 D2
Adlington CP School
MCFLDN SK10 .... 86 E7
Adswood Clinic
EDGY/DAV SK3 .... 46 E7
Adswood Primary School
EDGY/DAV SK3 .... 46 D7
A & E Wythenshawe Hospital
NTHM/RTH M23 .... 43 M7
Aircraft Factory
CHSW/BR CH4 .... 167 K6
Alban Retail Park
WARRN/WOL WA2 .... 37 G2
Albert Road Medical Centre
WDN WA8 .... 7 K2
Alderley Edge CP School
WILM/AE SK9 .... 110 A2

Alderley Edge Cricket Club
WILM/AE SK9 .... 110 B3
Alderley Edge Golf Club
WILM/AE SK9 .... 109 L1
Alderley Edge School for Girls
WILM/AE SK9 .... 109 M2
Aldersley Green Golf Club
CHSE CH3 .... 213 J6
Alderwood CP School
SPK/HALE L24 .... 70 E1
Aldford School
CHSE CH3 .... 211 M1
The Alexandra Hospital
CHD/CHDH SK8 .... 45 K6
Alexandra Industrial Estate
WDN WA8 .... 6 F7
Alexandra Park Junior
& Infant School
WILM/AE SK9 .... 46 C5
All Hallows RC High School
MCFLDN SK10 .... 14 C6
All Saints C of E Junior School
MPL/ROM SK6 .... 48 B1
All Saints C of E Primary School
MPL/ROM SK6 .... 49 G7
Alport Primary School
MALPAS SY14 .... 246 B8
Alsager Cricket Club
ALS/KID ST7 .... 224 D8
Alsager Dental Clinic
ALS/KID ST7 .... 241 K1
Alsager Highfields CP School
ALS/KID ST7 .... 224 D8
Alsager Leisure Centre
ALS/KID ST7 .... 224 B8

Alsager School
ALS/KID ST7 .... 224 B8
Altrincham & Broadheath
CP School
ALT WA14 .... 42 C4
Altrincham C of E Primary
School
ALT WA14 .... 42 C7
Altrincham General Hospital
ALT WA14 .... 42 C8
Altrincham Grammar School
for Boys
ALT WA14 .... 61 K2
Altrincham Grammar School
for Girls
ALT WA14 .... 61 L1
Altrincham Ice Rink
ALT WA14 .... 42 D6
Altrincham Industrial Centre
ALT WA14 .... 42 A6
Altrincham Rugby Football Club
HALE/TIMP WA15 .... 43 J5
Altrincham Leisure Centre
HALE/TIMP WA15 .... 42 E7
Altrincham Preparatory School
ALT WA14 .... 61 J2
Altrincham Priory Hospital
HALE/TIMP WA15 .... 62 A4
Alvanley Primary School
FROD/HEL WA6 .... 124 D3
Alvaston Business Park
NANT CW5 .... 21 G1
Amalgamated Sports Club
POY/DIS SK12 .... 68 B6

Ambulance Station
CHNE CH2 .... 17 G2
Amphitheatre
CH/BCN CH1 .... 17 H6
Annandale Medical Centre
KNUT WA16 .... 107 J1
Antrobus C of E
Controlled School
NWCHE CW9 .... 77 J8
Apollo Cinema Bingo
& Social Club
CW/HAS CW1 .... 19 G4
Appleton Thorn Community
Primary School
WARRS WA4 .... 57 J8
Aquinas Sixth Form College
OFTN SK2 .... 47 H6
The Archways Surgery
MPL/ROM SK6 .... 48 B2
Arclid Industrial Estate
SBCH CW11 .... 205 G4
Arden Primary School
MPL/ROM SK6 .... 47 K1
Arley House
NWCHE CW9 .... 78 D6
Art Gallery
NSTN CH64 .... 91 K4
Art Theatre
NM/HAY SK22 .... 69 H5
Ashdene CP School
WILM/AE SK9 .... 83 M7
Ash Grove CP School
MCFLDS SK11 .... 138 C8
Ashley C of E Primary School
HALE/TIMP WA15 .... 61 M7

Ashley Retail Park
WDN WA8 .... 7 K6
Ashley School
WDN WA8 .... 6 B3
Ashmount Industrial Centre
FLINT CH6 .... 116 B4
Ashton Hayes County
Primary School
CHSE CH3 .... 148 E4
Astbury C of E Aided
Primary School
CONG CW12 .... 207 H4
Astbury Golf Club
CONG CW12 .... 207 L5
Astmoor County
Primary School
RUNC WA7 .... 73 M2
Aston CP School
RUNC WA7 .... 100 C3
Atherton County Infant School
EP CH65 .... 94 F7
Atlantic Business Centre
ALT WA14 .... 42 C5
Audlem Medical Practice
AUD/MAD/W CW3 .... 263 M8
Austin Rawlinson Sports Centre
SPK/HALE L24 .... 70 E1
Avondale Industrial Estate
EDGY/DAV SK3 .... 46 B4
Avondale Recreation Centre
EDGY/DAV SK3 .... 46 B5
Avondale Secondary School
EDGY/DAV SK3 .... 2 A9
Baguley Hall Primary School
NTHM/RTH M23 .... 44 A6

Baileys Business Park
  MCFLDN SK10 .... 112 F5
Bankfield High School
  WDN WA8 .... 6 A2
Bank Quay Trading Estate
  WARRW/BUR WA5 .... 4 D9
Banks Lane Primary School
  STKP SK1 .... 3 L8
Barlow Medical Centre
  DID/WITH M20 .... 45 H1
The Barlow RC High School
  DID/WITH M20 .... 45 J2
Barnton County
  Primary School
  NWCHW CW8 .... 103 G8
Barony Hospital
  NANT CW5 .... 20 F2
Barrack Hill Primary School
  MPL/ROM SK6 .... 48 A2
Barrington Medical Centre
  ALT WA14 .... 42 D6
Barrow C of E County
  Primary School
  CHSE CH3 .... 147 K6
Barrow Hall Community
  Primary School
  WARRW/BUR WA5 .... 35 K5
Beach Tennis Club
  NWCHW CW8 .... 129 H6
Beamont Community
  Junior School
  WARRN/WOL WA2 .... 5 K2
Beaver Road Junior
  & Infant School
  DID/WITH M20 .... 45 H1
Bedford Methodist
  Primary School
  LEIGH WN7 .... 25 H1
Beech House Group Practice
  BRAM/HZG SK7 .... 66 E2
Beechwood County
  Primary School
  CW/HAS CW1 .... 18 E2
Beechwood County
  Primary School
  RUNC WA7 .... 73 K7
The Beechwood Surgery
  ALS/KID ST7 .... 243 G3
Beeston Castle
  TPLY/KEL CW6 .... 215 M1
Belgrave County
  Infant School
  CHSW/BR CH4 .... 169 H7
Bell Tower
  CH/BCN CH1 .... 17 G5
Benchill Junior & Infant School
  WYTH/NTH M22 .... 44 C6
Benchill Medical Practice
  WYTH/NTH M22 .... 44 D8
The Berrisford Gallery
  WILM/AE SK9 .... 109 L1
Bethesda School
  CHD/CHDH SK8 .... 64 D1
Betley C of E Primary School
  AUD/MAD/W CW3 .... 255 H6
Bewsey Lodge Community
  Primary School
  WARRW/BUR WA5 .... 4 C3
Bewsey Old School
  WARRW/BUR WA5 .... 4 B3
Bexton CP School
  KNUT WA16 .... 106 F5
Bickerton C of E
  Primary School
  MALPAS SY14 .... 232 A5
Biddulph Community
  Health Centre
  BIDD ST8 .... 227 K5
Biddulph High School
  BIDD ST8 .... 227 K7
Biddulph Medical Centre
  BIDD ST8 .... 227 K5
Biddulph Valley Leisure Centre
  BIDD ST8 .... 227 K3
Birchwood C of E Primary
  School
  GOL/RIS/CU WA3 .... 38 F1
Birchwood Community
  High School
  GOL/RIS/CU WA3 .... 38 D1
Birchwood Medical Centre
  GOL/RIS/CU WA3 .... 38 E1
Bishop Heber County
  High School
  MALPAS SY14 .... 246 C7
Bishop Martin C of E
  Primary School
  WLTN L25 .... 50 A2
Bishops C of E High School
  CHSE CH3 .... 170 A4
Bishop Wilson C of E
  Primary School
  NSTN CH64 .... 118 D3
B & J Leisure Centre
  WILM/AE SK9 .... 84 A5
Black Cat Industrial Estate
  WDN WA8 .... 7 G8
Blackfirs County
  Primary School
  CONG CW12 .... 183 M8
Blacksheep Gallery
  CQ CH5 .... 166 E4
Blacon Clinic
  CH/BCN CH1 .... 144 E7
Blacon County High School
  CH/BCN CH1 .... 144 D8
Blacon County Infant School
  CH/BCN CH1 .... 144 E7
Blacon Hall County
  Junior School
  CH/BCN CH1 .... 144 E7
Blue Chip Business Park
  ALT WA14 .... 42 B5
Blue Planet Aquarium
  EP CH65 .... 121 K3
Boat Museum
  EP CH65 .... 11 G4

Bold Industrial Estate
  WDN WA8 .... 34 C7
Bold Street Medical Centre
  WARR WA1 .... 4 F8
Bollinbrook C of E
  Primary School
  MCFLDN SK10 .... 14 D1
Bollin CP School
  ALT WA14 .... 61 H3
Bollington Cross
  C of E Primary School
  MCFLDN SK10 .... 112 E5
Bollington Leisure Centre
  MCFLDN SK10 .... 112 E6
Bollington Medical Centre
  MCFLDN SK10 .... 112 F4
Bolshaw Primary School
  CHD/CHDH SK8 .... 64 B5
Bolton County Junior
  & Infant School
  WARRS WA4 .... 56 F1
Borderbrook School
  MALPAS SY14 .... 268 D1
Borron Road Industrial Estate
  NEWLW WA12 .... 22 C8
Boughton Health Centre
  CHSE CH3 .... 17 L4
Boughton Heath CP School
  CHSE CH3 .... 170 A4
Boughton St Pauls
  County Infant School
  CHSE CH3 .... 17 K4
Bowdon Cricket Club
  ALT WA14 .... 61 J3
Bowdon Rugby Union
  Football Club
  HALE/TIMP WA15 .... 43 J3
Bowdon Vale Cricket Club
  ALT WA14 .... 61 J4
Bowers Business Park
  WDN WA8 .... 7 K6
Brabyns School
  MPL/ROM SK6 .... 49 G3
Bradshaw Community
  Primary School
  WARRS WA4 .... 57 H2
Bradshaw Hall Infant
  & Junior School
  CHD/CHDH SK8 .... 64 E3
Bramhall Hall
  BRAM/HZG SK7 .... 65 L3
Bramhall Health Centre
  BRAM/HZG SK7 .... 65 L6
Bramhall High School
  BRAM/HZG SK7 .... 65 M4
Bramhall Park Medical Centre
  BRAM/HZG SK7 .... 65 L2
Braunhall Park Golf Course
  BRAM/HZG SK7 .... 65 K4
Bredbury Green
  Primary School
  MPL/ROM SK6 .... 47 M3
Brentwood Gallery
  & Framing Centre
  WARRS WA4 .... 56 C3
Brentwood School
  ALT WA14 .... 42 E5
Brereton C of E Aided School
  SBCH CW11 .... 181 M7
Briars Hey School
  RAIN/WH L35 .... 33 K3
Brickfield Business Centre
  NWCHE CW9 .... 130 D3
Bridge College
  OFTN SK2 .... 47 K4
Bridge Hall Primary School
  EDGY/DAV SK3 .... 46 D6
Bridge House Medical Centre
  CHD/CHDH SK8 .... 65 H1
Bridge Industrial Estate
  SPK/HALE L24 .... 50 B7
Bridgemere C of E
  Aided Primary School
  NANT CW5 .... 265 L4
Bridgewater Community
  High School
  WARRS WA4 .... 56 D6
Bridgewater Community
  High School
  WARRS WA4 .... 56 D5
Bridgewater Family
  Medical Practice
  WHITCH SY13 .... 270 A5
Brierley Business Centre
  CW/HAS CW1 .... 19 H3
Brierley County Primary
  School
  CW/HAS CW1 .... 19 H3
Brine Leas County High
  School
  NANT CW5 .... 251 L1
Broad Oak Community
  Primary School
  STHEL WA9 .... 26 A1
Broadoak High School
  PART M31 .... 40 E2
Broad Oak Primary School
  DID/WITH M20 .... 45 H4
Broad Street County
  Infant School
  CW/HAS CW1 .... 221 J6
Broken Cross County
  Primary School
  MCFLDS SK11 .... 137 L5
Broken Cross Surgery
  MCFLDN SK10 .... 137 L4
Bronington Primary School
  WHITCH SY13 .... 268 B8
Brook Acre Community
  Primary School
  WARRN/WOL WA2 .... 37 L3
Brook Dean CP School
  WILM/AE SK9 .... 64 D7
Brook Farm Residential
  Special School
  TPLY/KEL CW6 .... 197 L4
The Brookfield School
  WDN WA8 .... 53 K2

Brookfield Surgery
  LYMM WA13 .... 58 E1
Brookhead Junior School
  CHD/CHDH SK8 .... 45 M7
Brookside Infant School
  GTS/LS CH66 .... 94 D8
Brookside Primary School
  MPL/ROM SK6 .... 67 L6
Brookvale County
  Comprehensive School
  RUNC WA7 .... 74 C7
Brookvale County
  Junior School
  RUNC WA7 .... 74 B7
Brookvale Recreation Centre
  RUNC WA7 .... 74 C6
Brookway High School
  NTHM/RTH M23 .... 43 L4
Broomfields Community
  Junior School
  WARRS WA4 .... 56 E5
Broomwood CP School
  HALE/TIMP WA15 .... 43 K7
Broughton Industrial Estate
  CHSW/BR CH4 .... 167 M6
Broughton Junior
  & Infant School
  CHSW/BR CH4 .... 167 J8
Brow CP School
  RUNC WA7 .... 73 M3
Brownhall Moor
  Industrial Estate
  BRAM/HZG SK7 .... 66 B2
Brown Lees Road
  Industrial Estate
  BIDD ST8 .... 227 H8
Bruche Community
  Junior & Infant School
  WARR WA1 .... 38 A5
Bruntwood Primary School
  CHD/CHDH SK8 .... 64 E2
Brymau Five Trading Estate
  CHSW/BR CH4 .... 168 C5
Brymau Four Trading Estate
  CHSW/BR CH4 .... 168 D5
Brymau One Trading Estate
  CHSW/BR CH4 .... 168 E5
Brymau Three Trading Estate
  CHSW/BR CH4 .... 168 E5
Brymau Two Trading Estate
  CHSW/BR CH4 .... 168 E5
Budworth Sailing Club
  NWCHE CW9 .... 104 A5
Buerton County
  Primary School
  AUD/MAD/W CW3 .... 274 F1
Buglawton County
  Primary School
  CONG CW12 .... 185 G8
Buglawton Hall School
  CONG CW12 .... 185 J7
Bunbury Aldersey
  C of E Primary School
  TPLY/KEL CW6 .... 216 D4
Bunbury Medical Practice
  TPLY/KEL CW6 .... 217 G3
Burnage Rugby Club
  HTNM SK4 .... 45 L3
Burton Manor College
  NSTN CH64 .... 118 D3
Burtonwood Community
  Primary School
  WARRW/BUR WA5 .... 26 E5
Burtonwood Industrial Centre
  WARRW/BUR WA5 .... 26 E5
Business Centre
  NANT CW5 .... 20 E6
Business Centre
  WARR WA1 .... 5 C6
Business Centre
  WARRW/BUR WA5 .... 4 D4
Button Lane Primary School
  NTHM/RTH M23 .... 43 M2
Byley CP School
  MWCH CW10 .... 156 A5
Byrchall High School
  AIMK WN4 .... 22 B3
Cadishead Junior School
  IRL M44 .... 31 K6
Cadishead Recreation Centre
  IRL M44 .... 31 K7
Calderbank Surgery
  EDGY/DAV SK3 .... 46 F8
Cale Green Primary School
  EDGY/DAV SK3 .... 46 E5
Cale Green Surgery
  EDGY/DAV SK3 .... 46 F6
Callands Community
  Primary School
  WARRW/BUR WA5 .... 36 E2
Calveley CP School
  TPLY/KEL CW6 .... 218 B2
Calveley Mill Industrial Estate
  TPLY/KEL CW6 .... 217 L2
Camberley Medical Centre
  WLTN L25 .... 50 C4
Cambridge Road CP School
  EP CH65 .... 10 F8
Canalside Industrial Estate
  EP CH65 .... 11 H4
Cannon Drew Junior School
  CQ CH5 .... 166 D4
Capenhurst Grange School
  GTS/LS CH66 .... 120 E2
Capenhurst Primary School
  CH/BCN CH1 .... 120 B4
Capesthorne Hall
  MCFLDS SK11 .... 136 A6
Capital Business Centre
  BRAM/HZG SK7 .... 65 K6
Carver Theatre
  MPL/ROM SK6 .... 48 F7
Castle CP School
  ALS/KID ST7 .... 226 D6
Castlefields Health Centre
  RUNC WA7 .... 74 A2
Castle Surgery
  NWCHW CW8 .... 12 E4

Castle Tennis & Bowling Club
  NWCHW CW8 .... 12 F5
The Castle
  CH/BCN CH1 .... 16 F8
Castle View CP School
  RUNC WA7 .... 73 K4
Catalyst Museum
  WDN WA8 .... 53 G7
Causeway Medical Centre
  WARRS WA4 .... 56 B1
Cavendish School
  RUNC WA7 .... 73 H7
Cedar Cross Medical Centre
  RAIN/WH L35 .... 32 D1
Cedars Medical Centre
  ALS/KID ST7 .... 241 K1
Chaigley School
  WARRS WA4 .... 38 E8
Chantry Court
  CH/BCN CH1 .... 168 E2
Chapelfield Clinic
  WDN WA8 .... 52 B3
Chapel Museum
  ALS/KID ST7 .... 226 D6
Chapel Street Clinic
  WDN WA8 .... 7 H7
Chatfield Community
  Primary School
  GOL/RIS/CU WA3 .... 38 E1
Cheadle Cricket Club
  CHD/CHDH SK8 .... 45 J7
Cheadle Golf Course
  CHD/CHDH SK8 .... 45 L8
Cheadle Heath Clinic
  EDGY/DAV SK3 .... 46 A4
Cheadle Heath Junior
  & Infant School
  EDGY/DAV SK3 .... 46 A5
Cheadle Heath Sports Centre
  CHD/CHDH SK8 .... 46 A6
Cheadle Hulme College
  CHD/CHDH SK8 .... 65 H5
Cheadle Hulme Medical Centre
  CHD/CHDH SK8 .... 65 G4
Cheadle Hulme School
  CHD/CHDH SK8 .... 65 G4
Cheadle Medical Practice
  CHD/CHDH SK8 .... 45 K6
Cheadle Primary School
  CHD/CHDH SK8 .... 45 K6
Cheadle RC Junior
  & Infants School
  CHD/CHDH SK8 .... 64 E2
Cheadle Royal Hospital
  CHD/CHDH SK8 .... 64 C2
Cheadle Royel Shopping Centre
  CHD/CHDH SK8 .... 64 D2
Cheadle Swimming
  & Recreation Centre
  CHD/CHDH SK8 .... 45 L8
Cheadle Town Football Club
  CHD/CHDH SK8 .... 45 L7
Chelford C of E Primary School
  MCFLDS SK11 .... 134 F1
Cherry Grove County
  Primary School
  CHSE CH3 .... 170 A3
Cherry Manor Primary School
  SALE M33 .... 42 C2
Cherry Tree Community
  Primary School
  LYMM WA13 .... 58 C2
Cherry Tree Hospital
  OFTN SK2 .... 47 J7
Cheshire County Council
  CH/BCN CH1 .... 16 F4
Cheshire County Council
  CH/BCN CH1 .... 17 H6
Cheshire County Council
  CH/BCN CH1 .... 143 L1
Cheshire County Council
  CHNE CH2 .... 17 M1
Cheshire County Council
  CHNE CH2 .... 121 H8
Cheshire County Council
  CHSW/BR CH4 .... 192 B1
Cheshire County Council
  GTS/LS CH66 .... 120 F2
Cheshire County Council
  RUNC WA7 .... 74 F7
Cheshire County Council
  WILM/AE SK9 .... 84 D1
Cheshire County Council
  WILM/AE SK9 .... 84 A6
Cheshire County Officers
  Sports Club
  CHNE CH2 .... 146 A6
Cheshire Health Clinic
  SBCH CW11 .... 204 B5
Cheshire Magistrates Court
  MCFLDN SK10 .... 15 G3
Cheshire Museums
  NWCHE CW9 .... 13 G5
Chesire County Council
  WDN WA8 .... 7 J5
Chesnut Lodge Special School
  WDN WA8 .... 6 C3
Chesterbank Business Park
  CHSW/BR CH4 .... 168 D5
Chester Boughton Hall
  Cricket Club
  CHSE CH3 .... 170 B3
Chester Business Centre
  CH/BCN CH1 .... 17 H5
Chester Business Park
  CHSW/BR CH4 .... 192 C1
Chester Cathedral
  CH/BCN CH1 .... 17 G5
Chester Catholic
  Aided High School
  CHSW/BR CH4 .... 169 K6
Chester City Council
  CH/BCN CH1 .... 16 A3
Chester City Council
  CH/BCN CH1 .... 17 J5
Chester City Council
  CH/BCN CH1 .... 145 G7

Chester City Council
  CH/BCN CH1 .... 168 F3
Chester City Football Club
  CH/BCN CH1 .... 168 E3
Chester County Court
  CH/BCN CH1 .... 16 F5
Chester Figure Clinic
  CH/BCN CH1 .... 17 G5
The Chestergate Clinic
  MCFLDN SK10 .... 14 F4
Chester Golf Club
  CHSW/BR CH4 .... 16 C7
Chester Rugby Union
  Football Club
  CHSE CH3 .... 170 D2
Chester Swimming Association
  CH/BCN CH1 .... 17 J5
Chester Toy Museum
  CH/BCN CH1 .... 17 G6
Chester Visitors Centre
  CH/BCN CH1 .... 17 H5
Childer Thornton CP School
  GTS/LS CH66 .... 94 B4
Cholmondeley Castle
  MALPAS SY14 .... 247 M1
Christie Street
  Industrial Estate
  STKP SK1 .... 3 K9
Christleton County
  Primary School
  CHSE CH3 .... 170 D4
Christleton High School
  CHSE CH3 .... 170 E5
Christleton Sports Centre
  CHSE CH3 .... 170 F5
Christleton Sports Club
  CHSE CH3 .... 170 F3
Church Coppenhall
  County Junior School
  CW/HAS CW1 .... 221 H6
Church Hill Gallery
  KNUT WA16 .... 107 G3
Church Lawton Gate
  CP School
  ALS/KID ST7 .... 225 G7
Church Street Industrial Estate
  WARR WA1 .... 5 J7
Cinderhill Lane Surgery
  ALS/KID ST7 .... 225 M5
Cinnamon Brow C of E
  Primary School
  WARRN/WOL WA2 .... 37 M1
City College Manchester
  NTHM/RTH M23 .... 43 M4
City College Manchester
  NTHM/RTH M23 .... 43 K4
City College Manchester
  NTHM/RTH M23 .... 44 C3
City Walls Medical Centre
  CH/BCN CH1 .... 16 E5
Civic Centre
  CQ CH5 .... 142 A5
Civic Hall
  BRAM/HZG SK7 .... 66 C3
Civic Hall
  WSFD CW7 .... 177 K3
The Civic Hall
  MCFLDN SK10 .... 113 G4
Cledford County Junior School
  MWCH CW10 .... 179 J5
The Clinic Centre
  MCFLDS SK11 .... 138 D7
Clinic for the Handicapped
  WARRN/WOL WA2 .... 4 F5
The Clinic
  CQ CH5 .... 166 A3
Clinic & Welfare Centre
  WARR WA1 .... 38 B5
Clough Hall County
  High School
  ALS/KID ST7 .... 242 F3
Cloughwood School
  NWCHW CW8 .... 12 C9
Club House
  MCFLDN SK10 .... 112 C7
Club Houses
  WRX/GR/LL LL12 .... 210 C5
Club Theatre
  ALT WA14 .... 42 C4
Clutton C of E CP School
  MALPAS SY14 .... 230 C3
Clwydian Community
  Care NHS Trust
  CQ CH5 .... 142 A5
The Cobbs Community
  Infant School
  WARRS WA4 .... 56 E4
College
  NANT CW5 .... 21 J7
College of Law Christleton Hall
  CHSE CH3 .... 170 D4
Comberbach CP School
  NWCHE CW9 .... 103 J4
Commercial Business Centre
  RAIN/WH L35 .... 33 J1
The Commons Surgery
  SBCH CW11 .... 204 B6
Community Care for Health
  WDN WA8 .... 7 H6
Concord Business Park
  WYTH/NTH M22 .... 63 J3
Concord Business Park
  WYTH/NTH M22 .... 63 J3
Congleton Borough Council
  ALS/KID ST7 .... 224 D8
Congleton Borough Council
  CONG CW12 .... 207 L2
Congleton Business Centre
  CONG CW12 .... 207 L1
Congleton Golf Club
  CONG CW12 .... 208 G3
Congleton Leisure Centre
  CONG CW12 .... 207 L1
Congleton Town Council
  CONG CW12 .... 207 L2
Constance Industrial Estate
  WDN WA8 .... 7 H9

Coppenhall County
  High School
    CW/HAS CW1 .... 221 L6
Coppenhall Leisure Centre
    CW/HAS CW1 .... 19 J1
Cottage Crafts & Gallery
    GOL/RIS/CU WA3 .... 29 G4
Council Offices
    KNUT WA16 .... 107 G3
Council Offices
    NWCHE CW9 .... 13 H2
Countess of Chester Hospital
    CHNE CH2 .... 145 J6
County Galleries
    ALT WA14 .... 42 D8
County Hall
    CH/BCN CH1 .... 17 G7
County Primary School
    FLINT CH6 .... 116 C6
County Secondary School
    FLINT CH6 .... 116 A8
Courtyard Studio Gallery
    MCFLDN SK10 .... 136 B3
Cranberry CP School
    ALS/KID ST7 .... 241 G1
Cranford Lodge Hospital
    KNUT WA16 .... 106 F3
Cransley School
    NWCHE CW9 .... 103 L3
Crewe Alexandra
  Football Club
    CW/SHV CW2 .... 19 H8
Crewe Golf Club
    CW/HAS CW1 .... 239 L1
Crewe & Nantwich
  Borough Council
    CW/HAS CW1 .... 19 G3
Crewe Road Surgery
    ALS/KID ST7 .... 241 J1
Crewe Squash Club
    CW/SHV CW2 .... 220 E8
Crewe Vagrants Cricket
  & Hockey Club
    NANT CW5 .... 237 L8
Croft Community
  Primary School
    GOL/RIS/CU WA3 .... 29 H4
Cromdale Way Community
  Hall & Health Centre
    WARRW/BUR WA5 .... 35 L6
Cronton C of E School
    WDN WA8 .... 33 J6
Crossacres Junior
  & Infant School
    WYTH/NTH M22 .... 44 F8
Cross Clinic
    LYMM WA13 .... 58 E1
Crown Courts
    CH/BCN CH1 .... 16 F7
Crown Industrial Estate
    ALT WA14 .... 42 E5
Crown Royal Industrial Park
    STKP SK1............................. 3 J7
Crowton Christ Church
  C of E Primary School
    NWCHW CW8 .... 127 H3
Cuddington CP School
    NWCHW CW8 .... 151 M2
Culcheth Clinic
    GOL/RIS/CU WA3 .... 29 L1
Culcheth Community
  Primary School
    GOL/RIS/CU WA3 .... 25 G8
Culcheth Hall School
    ALT WA14 .... 61 J1
Culcheth High School
    GOL/RIS/CU WA3 .... 30 A1
Culcheth Sports Club
    GOL/RIS/CU WA3 .... 29 M1
The Dale Primary School
    MPL/ROM SK6 .... 48 D5
Dallam Community
  Primary School
    WARRW/BUR WA5 .... 36 F3
Danebridge Medical Centre
    NWCHE CW9 .... 13 H3
Daneside Business Park
    CONG CW12 .... 184 E8
Daneside Theatre
    CONG CW12 .... 207 K1
Dane Valley County High
  School
    CONG CW12 .... 184 F7
Daresbury CP School
    WARRS WA4 .... 75 H2
Darland County Secondary
  School
    WRX/GR/LL LL12 .... 210 C4
Darwin Street CP School
    NWCHW CW8 .... 12 E4
Daven County Primary School
    CONG CW12 .... 207 L2
Davenham C of E
  Aided Primary School
    NWCHE CW9.......................... 153 M2
Davenham Cricket Club
    NWCHE CW9 .... 153 M2
David Lewis Centre
    WILM/AE SK9 .... 109 G6
Day Star Theatre
    AUD/MAD/W CW3 .... 263 L7
Deacon Trading Estate
    NEWLW WA12 .... 27 G2
Dean Lane Medical Centre
    BRAM/HZG SK7 .... 66 D4
Dean Row County
  Junior School
    WILM/AE SK9 .... 84 E3
Dean Valley CP School
    MCFLDN SK10 .... 112 E4
Dee Banks School
    CHSE CH3 .... 170 A5
Dee Point CP School
    CH/BCN CH1...................... 168 D1
Deermoss Gallery
    WHITCH SY13 .... 270 A4
Deeside College
    CQ CH5 .... 142 F3

Deeside Community Hospital
    CQ CH5 .... 142 A8
Deeside Industrial Estate
    CQ CH5 .... 143 G3
Delamere CP School
    NWCHW CW8 .... 150 C6
Delamere Forest Golf Club
    NWCHW CW8 .... 150 E3
Delamere Forest School
    FROD/HEL WA6 .... 126 C8
Demmings Infant School
    CHD/CHDH SK8 .... 45 M7
Derwen School
    CHSW/BR CH4 .... 190 A5
Deva Business Park
    CQ CH5 .... 143 G4
Deva Industrial Park
    CQ CH5 .... 167 G1
Dial Park Primary School
    OFTN SK2 .... 47 K8
Didsbury C of E Primary
  School
    DID/WITH M20 .... 45 H1
Didsbury Cricket Club
    DID/WITH M20 .... 45 J3
Didsbury Road Primary School
    HTNM SK4 .... 45 M2
Dingle County Primary School
    CW/HAS CW1 .... 222 D6
Disley CP School
    POY/DIS SK12...................... 68 D6
District C E Primary School
    NEWLW WA12 .... 22 A8
Ditton C of E Primary School
    WDN WA8 .... 52 A3
Ditton CP School
    WDN WA8 .... 6 A3
Ditton Hall St Michaels
  RC Primary School
    WDN WA8 .... 52 C5
Ditton Medical Centre
    WDN WA8 .... 6 A4
Dodleston C of E
  County Primary School
    CHSW/BR CH4 .... 191 G5
Dorin Park School
    CHNE CH2.......................... 145 K6
Dove Bank CP School
    ALS/KID ST7 .... 243 G2
Drug Dependency Clinic
    WDN WA8 .... 7 H7
Duddon St Peters
  C of E Primary School
    TPLY/KEL CW6 .... 173 H6
Dunham on Hill CP School
    FROD/HEL WA6 .... 123 L6
Dunkirk Trading Estate
    CH/BCN CH1...................... 120 D7
Duttons Business Centre
    NWCHE CW9 .... 13 G4
Eagle Sports Club
    WARRW/BUR WA5 .... 36 B8
Earnswood Medical Centre
    CW/HAS CW1 .... 18 E3
Eaton Bank Industrial Estate
    CONG CW12 .... 184 F8
Eaton CP School
    TPLY/KEL CW6 .... 198 B1
Eaton Golf Club
    CHSE CH3 .... 171 J7
Ebbe Fonte Galleria
    WILM/AE SK9 .... 84 B5
Eccleston C of E
  Aided Primary School
    CHSW/BR CH4 .... 192 E2
Edgeley Medical Practice
    EDGY/DAV SK3 .... 2 B8
Edleston Road County
  Primary School
    CW/SHV CW2 .... 18 F7
Egerton CP School
    KNUT WA16 .... 106 F2
Ellesmere Port
  Business Centre
    EP CH65 .... 10 D8
Ellesmere Port Catholic
  High School
    EP CH65 .... 121 G1
Ellesmere Port Clinic
    EP CH65 .... 95 H8
Ellesmere Port Hospital
    EP CH65 .... 121 G2
Ellesmere Port Stadium
    EP CH65 .... 121 L1
Elmridge Primary School
    HALE/TIMP WA15 .... 62 C4
Elms Medical Centre
    CHNE CH2 .... 17 K1
Elton County Primary School
    CHNE CH2 .... 97 G8
Elworth C of E Primary School
    SBCH CW11 .... 203 L5
Elworth Hall County
  Primary School
    SBCH CW11 .... 203 L5
Elworth Mount Pleasant
  Cricket Club
    SBCH CW11 .... 203 K4
English Martyrs RC
  Primary School
    BIDD ST8............................ 227 K5
English Touring Theatre
    CW/HAS CW1 .... 19 G3
Ensor Trading Estate
    NM/HAY SK22...................... 69 J6
Epic Leisure Centre
    EP CH65 .... 95 G4
Eric Moore Health Centre
    WARRN/WOL WA2 .... 4 F5
Etchells Primary School
    CHD/CHDH SK8 .... 64 C3
Europa Business Park
    EDGY/DAV SK3 .... 46 B6
Evelyn Street Community
  Primary School
    WARRW/BUR WA5.................. 4 A4
Everite Road Industrial Estate
    WDN WA8 .... 52 B5

Excalibur CP School
    ALS/KID ST7 .... 241 L2
Excalibur Industrial Estate
    ALS/KID ST7 .... 241 L1
Express Industrial Estate
    WDN WA8 .... 52 A5
Expressway Business Park
    CQ CH5 .... 142 E7
Eyton Place Practice
    FLINT CH6 .... 116 A4
Fairfield C of E School
    WARR WA1 .... 5 K4
Fairfield County High School
    WDN WA8 .... 53 J1
Fairfield County
  Junior & Infant School
    WDN WA8 .... 7 K1
Fairhill Industrial Estate
    IRL M44.............................. 31 M1
Fairway Primary School
    OFTN SK2 .... 47 L5
Fairway Trading Estate
    WDN WA8 .... 6 D8
Fallibroome High School
    MCFLDN SK10 .... 137 L2
Farndon CP School
    CHSE CH3 .... 228 E2
Farndon Health Centre
    CHSE CH3 .... 228 E3
Farnworth C of E
  Junior & Infant School
    WDN WA8 .... 34 A8
Fearnhead Cross
  Medical Centre
    WARRN/WOL WA2 .... 37 M2
Fire Station
    CH/BCN CH1........................ 17 G3
Firs School
    CHNE CH2.......................... 145 L7
Fleming Industrial Estate
    WARR WA1 .... 5 J6
Flint Child Health Clinic
    FLINT CH6 .... 116 B6
Flint Football Club
    FLINT CH6 .... 116 B5
Flint Leisure Centre
    FLINT CH6 .... 116 A5
Flintshire County Council
    FLINT CH6 .... 116 A6
Flowcrete Business Park
    SBCH CW11 .... 203 J3
Flower Gallery
    WARRS WA4 .... 57 K1
Fordton Leisure Centre
    WARRN/WOL WA2 .... 37 G1
Forest School
    HALE/TIMP WA15 .... 42 F6
The Forge Shopping Centre
    WARRS WA4 .... 56 C3
Forum Leisure Centre
    WYTH/NTH M22 .... 63 J1
The Forum Shopping Centre
    CH/BCN CH1........................ 16 F5
The Framing Studio & Gallery
    EDGY/DAV SK3 .... 2 F6
Frodsham C of E
  Primary School
    FROD/HEL WA6 .... 99 J5
Frodsham County High School
    FROD/HEL WA6 .... 99 H4
Frodsham Golf Club
    FROD/HEL WA6 .... 99 H7
Frodsham Town Council
    FROD/HEL WA6 .... 99 G4
Frodsham Weaver Vale
  CP School
    FROD/HEL WA6 .... 99 J2
Fulshaw C of E CP School
    WILM/AE SK9 .... 83 M6
Furlong Medical Centre
    BURS/TUN ST6 .... 243 K8
Furness Vale Industrial Estate
    CHF/WBR SK23 .... 69 K8
Furness Vale Primary School
    CHF/WBR SK23 .... 89 K1
Gainsborough County
  Junior School
    CW/SHV CW2 .... 18 C7
Gainsborough Galleries
    MPL/ROM SK6 .... 48 C2
Gainsbourgh Galleries
    MPL/ROM SK6 .... 48 F6
The Gallery Furnishings
    OFTN SK2 .... 47 H7
The Gallery
    ALT WA14 .... 61 K1
The Gallery
    IRL M44.............................. 31 L7
Garden City Industrial Estate
    CQ CH5 .... 142 F4
Garden Lane Medical Centre
    CH/BCN CH1........................ 16 E3
Garrick Theatre
    EDGY/DAV SK3 .... 2 F6
Garven Place Clinic
    WARR WA1 .... 4 E7
Gas Works Industrial Estate
    ALS/KID ST7 .... 242 E2
Gateway Theatre
    CH/BCN CH1........................ 16 E5
Gateworth Industrial Estate
    WARRW/BUR WA5 .... 55 K1
Gatley Health Centre
    CHD/CHDH SK8 .... 45 G6
Gatley Primary School
    CHD/CHDH SK8 .... 45 G7
Gawsworth CP School
    MCFLDS SK11 .... 161 K2
Geldart Gallery
    MCFLDS SK11 .... 137 H4
Gemini Business Park
    WARRW/BUR WA5 .... 36 F1
Gilded Hollins School
    LEIGH WN7 .... 24 C3
Glazebury C of E
  Primary School
    GOL/RIS/CU WA3 .... 25 H5

Golborne All Saints RC School
    GOL/RIS/CU WA3 .... 23 H4
Golborne Clinic
    GOL/RIS/CU WA3 .... 23 H3
Golborne CP School
    GOL/RIS/CU WA3 .... 23 G4
Golborne High School
    GOL/RIS/CU WA3 .... 23 J3
Goldenhill Primary School
    BURS/TUN ST6.................... 243 J5
Golden Triangle
  Industrial Estate
    WDN WA8 .... 52 C6
Goostrey Business Park
    HOLMCH CW4 .... 156 F3
Goostrey County
  Primary School
    HOLMCH CW4 .... 157 M4
Gorse Covert Primary School
    GOL/RIS/CU WA3 .... 30 B6
Gorsewood CP School
    RUNC WA7 .... 74 E5
Gorsey Bank CP School
    WILM/AE SK9 .... 83 M5
Gorsthills CP School
    GTS/LS CH66 .... 120 C1
Goyt Valley Industrial Estate
    CHF/WBR SK23 .... 69 K8
Goyt Valley Medical Practice
    CHF/WBR SK23 .... 89 L4
Grandstands
    CH/BCN CH1........................ 16 D6
Grange CP School
    WSFD CW7 .... 177 H3
Grange Junior School
    NWCHW CW8 .... 129 G6
Grange Road C of E
  Primary School
    ALT WA14 .... 61 J3
Grange School
    NWCHW CW8 .... 129 H7
Grappenhall Clinic
    WARRS WA4 .... 57 H2
Grappenhall Cricket Club
    WARRS WA4 .... 57 G3
Grappenhall Hall School
    WARRS WA4 .... 57 H3
Grappenhall Sports Club
    WARRS WA4 .... 56 F3
Great Budworth C of E Primary
  School
    NWCHE CW9 .... 104 B4
Great Moor Clinic
    OFTN SK2 .... 47 J7
Great Moor Primary School
    OFTN SK2 .... 47 H8
Great Sankey Community
  High School
    WARRW/BUR WA5 .... 35 K4
Great Sankey Community
  Primary School
    WARRW/BUR WA5 .... 36 A7
Great Sutton Health Centre
    GTS/LS CH66 .... 94 D8
Greenbank Residential School
    NWCHW CW8 .... 12 D7
Greenbank School
    NSTN CH64 .... 92 F4
Greenbank Surgery
    NSTN CH64 .... 92 F4
Greencourts Business Park
    WYTH/NTH M22 .... 64 A5
Greenfields CP School
    WSFD CW7 .... 177 G3
Green Lane High School
    HALE/TIMP WA15 .... 62 A1
Green Lane School
    WARR WA1 .... 38 B4
Greenoaks Farm Industrial
  Estate
    WDN WA8 .... 7 M4
Gresty Brook Medical Centre
    CW/SHV CW2 .... 238 C4
Grosvenor Medical Centre
    CW/HAS CW1 .... 18 C2
Grosvenor Museum
    CH/BCN CH1........................ 16 F7
Grosvenor Nuffield Hospital
    CHSW/BR CH4 .... 169 J6
Grosvenor Shopping Centre
    CH/BCN CH1........................ 17 G6
Grove House Practice
    RUNC WA7 .... 9 H2
Guardian Medical Centre
    WARRW/BUR WA5 .... 4 C5
Guardian Street Industrial
  Estate
    WARRW/BUR WA5.................. 4 D5
Guilden Sutton C of E CP School
    CHSE CH3 .... 146 F7
Gwynedd CP Junior School
    FLINT CH6 .... 116 A6
Hague Bar Primary School
    NM/HAY SK22...................... 68 E4
Halebank C of E
  Controlled Primary School
    WDN WA8 .... 52 A8
Hale Barns Cricket Club
    HALE/TIMP WA15 .... 62 E4
Halebarns Cricket Club
    HALE/TIMP WA15 .... 62 D6
Hale C of E School
    SPK/HALE L24 .... 71 L3
Hale Preparatory School
    HALE/TIMP WA15 .... 61 L1
Hale Primary School
    SPK/HALE L24 .... 71 K3
Halewood C of E
  Primary School
    HLWD L26 .... 51 G3
Halewood Community
  Comprehensive School
    WLTN L25 .... 50 D5
Halewood Health Centre
    HLWD L26 .... 50 F5
Halewood Sports Centre
    HLWD L26 .... 51 G5

Hallwood Health Centre
    RUNC WA7 .... 73 M5
Hallwood Park CP School
    RUNC WA7 .... 73 L6
Halton Borough Council
    RUNC WA7 .... 73 M4
Halton Borough Council
    WDN WA8 .... 6 E7
Halton Borough Council
    WDN WA8 .... 7 J5
Halton Borough Council
    WDN WA8 .... 7 G7
Halton Borough Council
    WDN WA8 .... 52 B4
Halton College
    WDN WA8 .... 7 H6
Halton College of Further
  Education
    WDN WA8 .... 7 G5
Halton General Hospital
  NHS Trust
    RUNC WA7 .... 73 M6
Halton Health Authority
    WDN WA8 .... 53 K2
Halton Lodge County
  Junior & Infant School
    RUNC WA7 .... 9 M7
Halton Magistrates Court
    RUNC WA7 .... 73 M4
Halton St Marys C of E
  Primary School
    RUNC WA7 .... 74 A4
Hammond School
    CHNE CH2.......................... 146 C5
Handbridge Medical Centre
    CHSW/BR CH4 .... 17 G8
Handforth Health Centre
    WILM/AE SK9 .... 84 D1
Handley Hill CP School
    WSFD CW7 .... 177 J4
Happy Feet Health Centre
    FLINT CH6 .... 116 A5
The Harlequin Theatre
    NWCHE CW9........................ 13 G3
Harrytown RC High School
    MPL/ROM SK6 .... 48 A2
Hartford Business Centre
    NWCHW CW8 .... 128 F8
Hartford CP School
    NWCHW CW8 .... 129 H8
Hartford High School
    NWCHW CW8 .... 12 A7
Hartford Manor CP School
    NWCHW CW8 .... 12 B8
Harthill CP School
    CHSE CH3 .... 231 L1
Haslington CP School
    CW/HAS CW1 .... 222 D8
Haslington Cricket Club
    CW/HAS CW1 .... 222 D6
Haslington Surgery
    CW/HAS CW1 .... 222 D8
Havannah County
  Primary School
    CONG CW12 .... 184 F6
Haveley Hey Junior
  & Infant School
    WYTH/NTH M22 .... 44 C8
Hawarden Castle
    CQ CH5 .... 166 E5
Hawarden CP Infants School
    CQ CH5 .... 166 D4
Hawarden Health Centre
    CQ CH5 .... 166 D4
Hawarden High School
    CQ CH5 .... 166 B3
Hawarden Industrial Park
    CHSW/BR CH4 .... 167 H6
Hawthorne Business Park
    WARRW/BUR WA5 .... 4 E1
Hazel Grove Clinic
    BRAM/HZG SK7 .... 66 E1
Hazel Grove High School
    BRAM/HZG SK7 .... 66 C3
Hazel Grove Primary
  & Infant School
    BRAM/HZG SK7 .... 66 E1
Heald Green Medical Centre
    CHD/CHDH SK8 .... 64 B4
Health Authority
    SPK/HALE L24 .... 70 E1
The Health Centre Surgery
    HLWD L26 .... 50 F5
The Health Centre
    ALT WA14 .... 42 D7
The Health Centre
    CW/HAS CW1 .... 18 E4
The Health Centre
    NANT CW5 .... 20 F5
The Heath County
  Comprehensive School
    RUNC WA7 .... 9 K9
Heathfield County High School
    CONG CW12 .... 206 E1
Heath Lane Medical Centre
    CHSE CH3 .... 170 A3
Heath Road Medical Centre
    RUNC WA7 .... 9 J6
Heaton Moor Rugby
  Union Football Club
    HTNM SK4.......................... 46 B1
Heaton Norris Health Centre
    HTNM SK4............................ 2 D2
Hebden Green Special School
    WSFD CW7 .... 177 G5
Helsby County High School
    FROD/HEL WA6 .... 98 E7
Helsby Health Centre
    FROD/HEL WA6 .... 124 B1
Hempshaw Business Centre
    STKP SK1.............................. 3 M9
Henbury High School
    MCFLDN SK10 .... 137 L4
Heritage Centre
    CH/BCN CH1........................ 17 G6
The Heritage Gallery
    NANT CW5 .... 20 E6

Hermitage County
  Primary School
    HOLMCH CW4 .... 181 K1
Heyes Lane Junior
  & Infant School
    HALE/TIMP WA15 .... 43 H4
Higher Side Community
  Comprehensive School
    RAIN/WH L35 .... 33 G1
Highfield County Junior
  & Infant School
    CH/BCN CH1 .... 144 F8
Highfield County
  Primary School
    NANT CW5 .... 21 H3
Highfield School
    HLWD L26 .... 51 G5
High Lane Medical Centre
    MPL/ROM SK6 .... 67 L5
High Lane Primary School
    MPL/ROM SK6 .... 67 L4
High Legh CP School
    KNUT WA16 .... 59 J7
High Street CP School
    WSFD CW7 .... 177 K3
High Street Surgery
    ALS/KID ST7 .... 242 D6
Hillcrest Grammar School
    EDGY/DAV SK3 .... 46 F6
Hillgate Business Centre
    STKP SK1 .... 3 H8
Hillside CP School
    FROD/HEL WA6 .... 98 D8
Hill Top CP School
    ALS/KID ST7 .... 242 D5
Hill Valley Golf Club
    WHITCH SY13 .... 270 A2
Hill View CP School
    RUNC WA7 .... 73 L8
Hinderton School
    EP CH65 .... 121 G1
Historic House
    MCFLDS SK11 .... 161 L4
HM Remand Centre
    GOL/RIS/CU WA3 .... 29 L4
Holcroft Clinic
    GOL/RIS/CU WA3 .... 29 L1
Hollinhey CP School
    MCFLDS SK11 .... 162 F1
Holly House Estate
    MWCH CW10 .... 156 C5
Hollywall CP School
    BURS/TUN ST6 .... 243 J6
Holmes Chapel County
  Comprehensive School
    HOLMCH CW4 .... 181 G2
Holmes Chapel
  County Primary School
    HOLMCH CW4 .... 181 H1
Holmes Chapel Health Centre
    HOLMCH CW4 .... 181 J1
Holt CP School
    WRXS/E LL13 .... 228 D4
Holy Family Primary School
    WLTN L25 .... 50 D3
Holy Family RC
  Primary School
    WDN WA8 .... 33 K6
Holy Spirit School
    RUNC WA7 .... 73 K4
Hong Sing Chinese
  Medical Centre
    BRAM/HZG SK7 .... 66 D1
Hood Manor Community
  Primary School
    WARRW/BUR WA5 .... 36 C6
Hood Manor Medical Centre
    WARRW/BUR WA5 .... 36 C7
Hoole All Saints C of E
  County Infant School
    CHNE CH2 .... 170 A1
Horns Mill CP School
    FROD/HEL WA6 .... 124 A3
Hospital Contributory Scheme
    CW/SHV CW2 .... 18 F1
Howley Quay Industrial Estate
    WARR WA1 .... 5 L7
Hulme Hall School
    CHD/CHDH SK8 .... 65 G3
Hungerford County
  Primary School
    CW/HAS CW1 .... 19 L3
Hungerford Medical Centre
    CW/HAS CW1 .... 19 K3
Huntington CP School
    CHSE CH3 .... 170 A7
Hunts Cross CP School
    WLTN L25 .... 50 C6
Hunts Cross Group Practice
    WLTN L25 .... 50 B5
Hurdsfield CP School
    MCFLDS SK10 .... 15 M1
Hurdsfield Industrial Estate
    MCFLDS SK10 .... 138 F2
Hurdsfield Junior School
    MCFLDS SK10 .... 15 L1
Hursthead Infant
  & Primary School
    CHD/CHDH SK8 .... 65 J6
Huxley C of E CP School
    CHSE CH3 .... 196 A5
The Instructor College
    STKP SK1 .... 3 G6
Interchange Motorway
  Industrial Estate
    HUY L36 .... 32 A3
Irlam & Cadishead
  Community High School
    IRL M44 .... 31 L4
Irlam County Primary School
    IRL M44 .... 31 M3
Irlam Industrial Estate
    IRL M44 .... 31 L5
Ivy Bank CP School
    MCFLDS SK11 .... 138 A7
Ivy Bank Trading Estate
    KNUT WA16 .... 82 A8

Ivy Farm Court Doctors
  Surgery
    SPK/HALE L24 .... 71 K3
Jacksons Lane Recreation
  Centre
    BRAM/HZG SK7 .... 66 A3
James Brindley High School
    BURS/TUN ST6 .... 243 M6
Jeff Joseph Sale
  Moor Technology College
    SALE M33 .... 43 K2
J H Godwin CP School
    CH/BCN CH1 .... 144 D8
John Arnold Galleries
    BIDD ST8 .... 227 J4
John Street CP School
    EP CH65 .... 10 E5
John Street Medical Centre
    GOL/RIS/CU WA3 .... 23 C4
John Summers High School
    CQ CH5 .... 142 C1
Kelsall CP School
    TPLY/KEL CW6 .... 149 J8
Kelsall Medical Centre
    TPLY/KEL CW6 .... 149 K7
Kelsborrow Castle
    TPLY/KEL CW6 .... 149 L8
Kenmore Medical Centre
    WILM/AE SK9 .... 84 A6
Kerfoot Business Park
    WARRN/WOL WA2 .... 4 F1
Kidsgrove Medical Centre
    ALS/KID ST7 .... 243 J2
Kidsgrove Sports Centre
    ALS/KID ST7 .... 242 F3
Kiltearn Medical Centre
    NANT CW5 .... 20 E6
King School
    MCFLDN SK10........................ 15 K4
Kingsfield Co First
  & Secondary Schoo;
    BIDD ST8 .... 227 K4
Kings Grove County
  High School
    CW/SHV CW2 .... 18 B7
Kingsley CP School
    FROD/HEL WA6 .... 125 M2
Kings School
    CHSW/BR CH4 .... 169 H8
Kings School
    MCFLDN SK10........................ 14 F4
Kingsway County High School
    CHNE CH2 .... 145 M7
Kingsway School
    CHD/CHDH SK8 .... 45 J8
Kingsway Secondary School
    CHD/CHDH SK8 .... 45 J7
Kinsey Gallery
    NANT CW5 .... 253 G8
The Knoll Surgery Partnership
    FROD/HEL WA6 .... 99 H3
Knowles Industrial Estate
    CHF/WBR SK23 .... 89 J1
Knowsley Metropolitan
  Borough Council
    HLWD L26 .... 50 F5
Knutsford Civic Centre
    KNUT WA16 .... 107 G3
Knutsford County
  High School
    KNUT WA16 .... 106 F3
Knutsford Crown Courts
    KNUT WA16 .... 107 G3
Knutsford Cty High School
    KNUT WA16 .... 106 E3
Knutsford Football Club
    KNUT WA16 .... 106 F1
Knutsford Golf Club House
    KNUT WA16 .... 107 G1
Knutsford Leisure Centre
    KNUT WA16 .... 106 F3
Knutsford Sports Club
    KNUT WA16 .... 106 F1
Knutsford Squash
  Racquets Club
    KNUT WA16 .... 107 H3
Knypersley First School
    BIDD ST8 .... 227 H6
Knypersley Sports Club
    BIDD ST8 .... 227 J7
Kus Industrial Estate
    CQ CH5 .... 167 G6
Lacey Green CP School
    WILM/AE SK9 .... 84 A1
Lache County Junior
  & Infant School
    CHSW/BR CH4 .... 169 G7
Lache Health Centre
    CHSW/BR CH4 .... 169 G7
Lady Barn House School
    CHD/CHDH SK8 .... 64 D1
Ladybridge CP School
    CHD/CHDH SK8 .... 46 B7
Ladybrook Primary School
    BRAM/HZG SK7 .... 65 M5
Lakeside Surgery
    LYMM WA13 .... 58 D2
Lambs House School
    CONG CW12 .... 184 F8
Lane End Primary School
    CHD/CHDH SK8 .... 65 J2
Langley Road
  Industrial Estate
    WARRS WA4 .... 77 K2
Larkhill Junior & Infant School
    EDGY/DAV SK3 .... 2 B7
Latchford Medical Centre
    WARRS WA4 .... 56 E1
Laurel Bank Surgery
    MALPAS SY14 .... 258 B2
Lawnhurst Trading Estate
    CHD/CHDH SK8 .... 46 B7
Lawton House Surgery
    CONG CW12 .... 207 K2
Leaf Lane Infant School
    WSFD CW7 .... 178 N2
Leftwich County High School
    NWCHE CW9 .... 130 A8

Leftwich CP School
    NWCHE CW9 .... 130 A8
Leigh Cricket Club
    LEIGH WN7 .... 24 F2
Leigh Rugby Union
  Football Club
    LEIGH WN7 .... 24 E3
Leighton Hospital
    CW/HAS CW1 .... 220 E3
Leighton Park County
  Primary School
    CW/HAS CW1 .... 220 F4
Lime Tree Primary School
    SALE M33 .... 43 L1
Lindow CP School
    WILM/AE SK9 .... 109 K1
Linley Trading Estate
    ALS/KID ST7 .... 242 C3
Lisburne School
    OFTN SK2 .... 47 L6
Little Bollington C of E
  Primary School
    ALT WA14 .... 60 B2
Little Leigh CP School
    NWCHW CW8 .... 102 D7
Little Moreton Hall
    CONG CW12 .... 225 L2
Little Theatre
    KNUT WA16 .... 106 F2
The Little Theatre
    CH/BCN CH1 .... 17 G3
Liverpool Airport
    SPK/HALE L24 .... 70 C2
Liverpool University
    MCH SK11 .... 92 D5
L & M Business Park
    ALT WA14 .... 42 B6
Locking Stumps
  Community Primary School
    GOL/RIS/CU WA3 .... 29 J7
Lodgefields County
  Primary School
    CW/SHV CW2 .... 220 E8
The Lodge Victoria Infirmary
    NWCHW CW8 .... 12 F2
Longbarn Community
  Primary School
    WARRN/WOL WA2 .... 38 B3
Longford Street Surgery
    WARRN/WOL WA2 .... 5 G2
Long Lane Community
  Primary School
    WARRN/WOL WA2 .... 37 H3
Longton Medical Centre
    RAIN/WH L35 .... 33 H1
Loreto Convent
  Grammar School
    ALT WA14 .... 42 C7
Lostock Gralam C of E
  CP School
    NWCHE CW9 .... 131 G2
Lostock Gralam Football Club
    NWCHE CW9 .... 130 F2
Lostock Hall CP School
    POY/DIS SK12 .... 86 B1
Lostock Social & Sports Club
    NWCHE CW9 .... 130 E3
Loushers Lane Special School
    WARRS WA4 .... 56 D2
Lower Park CP School
    POY/DIS SK12 .... 66 C8
Lower Peover C of E
  Primary School
    KNUT WA16 .... 132 E3
Lowton High School
    GOL/RIS/CU WA3 .... 24 B4
Lowton Junior & Infant School
    GOL/RIS/CU WA3 .... 24 A5
Lowton St Marys C of E School
    GOL/RIS/CU WA3 .... 24 B4
Lowton West Primary School
    GOL/RIS/CU WA3 .... 23 J4
Ludworth Primary School
    MPL/ROM SK6 .... 49 C4
Lum Head Primary School
    CHD/CHDH SK8 .... 64 B1
Lunts Heath CP School
    WDN WA8 .... 34 B7
Lyme Park
    POY/DIS SK12 .... 88 B3
Lymm High School
    LYMM WA13 .... 59 H1
Lymm Rugby Football Club
    LYMM WA13 .... 58 E3
Lyon Industrial Estate
    ALT WA14 .... 42 B5
Mablins Lane CP School
    CW/HAS CW1 .... 221 H4
Macclesfield Borough Council
    POY/DIS SK12 .... 66 E8
Macclesfield College
    MCFLDS SK11 .... 14 D9
Macclesfield District
  General Hospital
    MCFLDN SK10........................ 14 C4
Macclesfield Golf Club
    MCFLDS SK11 .... 15 L9
Macclesfield Leisure Centre
    MCFLDN SK10....................... 137 L2
Macclesfield Silk Museum
    MCFLDS SK11 .... 15 G6
Macclesfield Town
  Football Club
    MCFLDS SK11 .... 138 D8
Macclesfield West
  Park Museum
    MCFLDN SK10........................ 14 E3
Macdonald Road
  Medical Centre
    IRL M44 .... 31 L4
Mackenzie Industrial Estate
    CHD/CHDH SK8 .... 46 B6
Mackets Primary School
    WLTN L25 .... 50 C3
Macon Business Park
    CW/HAS CW1 .... 19 J4
Madeley High School
    AUD/MAD/W CW3 .... 267 L6

Mads Little Theatre
    MCFLDS SK11 .... 15 H7
Magda House Medical Centre
    OFTN SK2 .... 47 K8
Malbank County High School
    NANT CW5 .... 20 B5
Manchester City Council
    NTHM/RTH M23....................... 44 B6
Manchester City Council
    NTHM/RTH M23....................... 44 B2
Manchester City Council
    SALE M33 .... 42 C2
Manchester City Council
    WYTH/NTH M22....................... 44 D7
Manchester Medical Centre
    KNUT WA16 .... 106 F2
Manchester Metropolitan
  University
    ALS/KID ST7 .... 224 B8
Manchester Metropolitan
  University
    CW/HAS CW1 .... 19 M6
Manchester Metropolitan
  University
    DID/WITH M20........................ 44 F1
Manchester Metropolitan
  University
    DID/WITH M20........................ 45 H2
Manchester Port Health
  Authority
    RUNC WA7 .... 9 G1
Mancot Clinic
    CQ CH5 .... 166 D2
Mancunian Community
  Health NHS Trust
    WYTH/NTH M22....................... 44 C4
Manley Village School
    FROD/HEL WA6 .... 125 C6
Manor House CP School
    FROD/HEL WA6 .... 99 J3
Manor Industrial Estate
    WARRS WA4 .... 37 L8
Manor Park County
  Primary School
    KNUT WA16 .... 107 J2
Mansfield CP School
    EP CH65 .... 120 F1
Manway Business Park
    ALT WA14 .... 42 E5
The Maples Medical Centre
    NTHM/RTH M23....................... 43 M8
Marcliffe Industrial Estate
    BRAM/HZG SK7 .... 66 F3
The Margaret Thompson
  Medical Centre
    SPK/HALE L24 .... 51 G8
Market Hall
    CH/BCN CH1 .... 16 F5
Market Hall
    EP CH65 .... 10 E9
Marlborough CP School
    MCFLDN SK10....................... 112 D8
Marlfield County
  Primary School
    CONG CW12 .... 207 J2
Marple Clinic
    MPL/ROM SK6 .... 48 F6
The Marple Cottage Surgery
    MPL/ROM SK6 .... 48 F7
Marple Gallery
    MPL/ROM SK6 .... 48 F6
Marple Hall School
    MPL/ROM SK6 .... 48 C5
Marsh Lane Trading Estate
    NM/HAY SK22......................... 69 K5
Marton & District
  C of E Primary School
    MCFLDS SK11 .... 160 C7
Marton Meadows Golf Club
    MCFLDS SK11 .... 160 C7
Maryhill CP School
    ALS/KID ST7 .... 243 H1
Massey Hall Special School
    WARRS WA4 .... 57 M2
Mcilvride Medical Practice
    POY/DIS SK12 .... 66 D8
Meadow County
  Junior School
    CTS/LS CH66 .... 120 E2
Meadows Special School
    BIDD ST8 .... 227 J5
Meadway Health Centre
    SALE M33 .... 42 E2
Megabowl
    CH/BCN CH1 .... 168 F1
Mellor CP School
    MPL/ROM SK6 .... 49 L6
Mellor Primary School
    MPL/ROM SK6 .... 49 L6
Mellor Sports Club
    MPL/ROM SK6 .... 49 K6
Melodys Antiques Galleries
    CH/BCN CH1 .... 17 J4
Menorah Synagogue
    WYTH/NTH M22....................... 44 E6
Mere Golf & Country Club
    KNUT WA16 .... 80 C4
Mersey Regional
  Health Authority
    RUNC WA7 .... 9 M1
Mersey Vale Primary School
    HTNM SK4 .... 46 A3
Merton House School
    CH/BCN CH1 .... 145 J8
Mickle Trafford
  County Primary School
    CHNE CH2 .... 146 E4
Mid Cheshire College
    NWCHE CW9 .... 13 H6
Mid Cheshire College
    NWCHW CW8 .... 12 F3
Mid Cheshire College
    WSFD CW7 .... 177 K3
Mid Cheshire Hospital
    CW/HAS CW1 .... 19 G4
Middlehurst Special School
    ALS/KID ST7 .... 243 M5

Middlewich Athletic
  & Supporters Club
    MWCH CW10 .... 179 H2
Middlewich County
  High School
    MWCH CW10 .... 179 J4
Middlewich County
  Junior & Infant School
    MWCH CW10 .... 179 H3
Middlewich Cricket Club
    MWCH CW10 .... 179 J2
Middlewich Leisure Centre
    MWCH CW10 .... 179 J4
Middlewich Medical Centre
    MWCH CW10 .... 179 J3
Middlewich Town Council
    MWCH CW10 .... 179 J3
Military Museum
    CH/BCN CH1 .... 16 F7
Millbank Business Centre
    NWCHE CW9 .... 13 L2
Millbrook Business Centre
    NTHM/RTH M23....................... 43 L6
Millbrook Industrial Estate
    NTHM/RTH M23....................... 43 L6
Millfields CP School
    NANT CW5 .... 20 B7
Mill Green Special School
    NEWLW WA12 .... 27 L1
Mill Hill CP School
    BURS/TUN ST6 .... 243 M8
Millingford Industrial Estate
    GOL/RIS/CU WA3 .... 23 H4
Mill Lane Industrial Estate
    EP CH65 .... 121 M1
Mill Street Medical Centre
    CW/SHV CW2 .... 19 G2
Millwood CP School
    SPK/HALE L24 .... 70 F2
Millwood Road
  Doctors Surgery
    SPK/HALE L24 .... 50 F8
Moat House School
    HTNM SK4 .... 2 E1
Mobberley C of E
  Primary School
    KNUT WA16 .... 82 C7
Mollington Church of England
  Controlled Primary School
    CH/BCN CH1 .... 144 E2
Monks Coppenhall
  County Primary School
    CW/HAS CW1 .... 221 L5
Moody Street Medical Centre
    CONG CW12 .... 207 K2
Moore CP School
    WARRS WA4 .... 55 G7
Moore Rugby Union
  Football Club
    WARRS WA4 .... 55 H6
Moorfield CP School
    WDN WA8 .... 53 K1
Moorfield Junior
  & Infant School
    BRAM/HZG SK7 .... 66 C3
Moor Lane Business Centre
    WDN WA8 .... 7 G7
Mosque
    BURS/TUN ST6 .... 243 K8
Mosscroft Primary School
    HUY L36 .... 32 A1
Moss Hey Primary School
    BRAM/HZG SK7 .... 65 J7
Moss Industrial Estate
    LEIGH WN7 .... 24 B3
Moss Lane Business Centre
    SBCH CW11 .... 203 K6
Moss Lane Surgery
    AUD/MAD/W CW3 .... 267 K3
Mossley C of E Primary School
    CONG CW12 .... 208 M3
Moss View Primary School
    PART M31 .... 41 G1
Mostyn House School
    NSTN CH64 .... 91 J4
Mottram St Andrew
  Grant Maintained
  Primary School
    MCFLDN SK10....................... 111 M1
Moulton CP School
    NWCHE CW9 .... 153 M4
Mow Cap Castle
    ALS/KID ST7 .... 226 D5
Murdishaw Health Centre
    RUNC WA7 .... 74 D5
Murdishaw West CP School
    RUNC WA7 .... 74 D6
Museum & Art Gallery
    WARR WA1 .... 4 F7
Nantwich & Border
  Counties Yacht Club
    NANT CW5 .... 236 B6
Nantwich Civic Hall
    NANT CW5 .... 20 F6
Nantwich Cricket
  & Rugby Union Football Club
    NANT CW5 .... 21 H2
Nantwich Museum
    NANT CW5 .... 20 E7
Nantwich Players Theatre
    NANT CW5 .... 20 E7
Nantwich Town Football Club
    NANT CW5 .... 21 H7
National Trading Estate
    BRAM/HZG SK7 .... 66 C1
Navigation Primary School
    ALT WA14 .... 42 D6
Neston County High School
    NSTN CH64 .... 91 M3
Neston CP School
    NSTN CH64 .... 91 L5
Neston Cricket Club
    NSTN CH64 .... 91 J4
Neston Medical Centre
    NSTN CH64 .... 91 L4
Neston Recreation Centre
    NSTN CH64 .... 91 M3

Neston St Marys
C of E Primary School
NSTN CH64 .... 91 M3
Neston Surgery
NSTN CH64 .... 91 M5
Nether Alderley CP School
MCFLDN SK10 .... 110 B8
Nether Alderley CP School
MCFLDN SK10 .... 110 A6
Netherpool County
Infant School
GTS/LS CH66 .... 94 E5
Network Clinic
MCFLDN SK10 .... 112 F5
Nevill Road Junior
and Infant School
BRAM/HZG SK7 .... 65 L2
Newall Green High School
NTHM/RTH M23 .... 43 M8
Newall Green Primary School
NTHM/RTH M23 .... 44 B8
Newby Road Industrial Estate
BRAM/HZG SK7 .... 66 D2
Newchurch Community
Primary School
GOL/RIS/CU WA3 .... 29 L2
Newfields Industrial Estate
BURS/TUN ST6 .... 243 K7
New Hutte Junior School
HLWD L26 .... 50 E6
Newman RC High School
WARRS WA4 .... 37 M7
New Mills CP School
NM/HAY SK22 .... 69 H4
New Mills Football Club
NM/HAY SK22 .... 69 K4
New Mills School
& Sixth Form Centre
NM/HAY SK22 .... 69 J5
New Mills Swimming Pool
NM/HAY SK22 .... 69 J4
New Mills Town Council
NM/HAY SK22 .... 69 H5
News Gallery
NSTN CH64 .... 91 L5
Newton Bank
Preparatory School
NEWLW WA12 .... 22 E8
Newton Community Hospital
NEWLW WA12 .... 27 H3
Newton CP School
CHNE CH2 .... 145 L8
Newton Health Clinic
NEWLW WA12 .... 22 B8
Newton Le Willows CP School
NEWLW WA12 .... 27 J1
Newton-le-willows Sports Club
NEWLW WA12 .... 22 C8
Newtown CP School
NM/HAY SK22 .... 69 H6
New Wellington School
HALE/TIMP WA15 .... 42 F6
Norbury Hall Primary School
BRAM/HZG SK7 .... 66 E3
Norfolk House
Preparatory School
SBCH CW11 .... 204 B5
Norley C of E CP School
FROD/HEL WA6 .... 127 G7
Norris Bank Medical Centre
HTNM SK4 .... 2 A5
Norris Bank Primary School
HTNM SK4 .... 46 B1
North Cheshire
Health Authority
RUNC WA7 .... 9 L1
North Cheshire Jewish
Primary School
CHD/CHDH SK8 .... 64 B2
Northenden Primary School
WYTH/NTH M22 .... 44 D3
Northern Moor Clinic
NTHM/RTH M23 .... 43 M3
Northgate Area
CHNE CH2 .... 17 G3
Northgate Medical Centre
CH/BCN CH1 .... 16 F3
Northgate Village Surgery
CHNE CH2 .... 16 F2
Northwich Rowing Club
NWCHE CW9 .... 13 G6
Northwich Sailing Club
WSFD CW7 .... 178 A6
Northwich Victoria
Football Club
NWCHE CW9 .... 13 J3
Norton Priory County
High School
RUNC WA7 .... 74 B3
Norton Priory
Recreation Centre
RUNC WA7 .... 74 B2
Oakdene Primary School
RAIN/WH L35 .... 33 J2
Oakenclough CP School
WILM/AE SK9 .... 84 D3
Oakfield County Junior
& Infant School
WDN WA8 .... 52 A4
Oaklands County Infant School
WILM/AE SK9 .... 84 E3
Oaklands Golf & Country Club
TPLY/KEL CW6 .... 174 D8
Oaklands Special Day School
WSFD CW7 .... 177 G5
Oakwood Avenue Community
Primary & Infant School
WARR WA1 .... 5 M2
Oakwood Medical Centre
NWCHW CW8 .... 129 G2
Oakwood Primary School
PART M31 .... 40 D1
Odeon Theatre
CH/BCN CH1 .... 16 F4
Offerton Green Clinic
OFTN SK2 .... 47 M7
Offerton Health Centre
STKP SK1 .... 3 M8

Offerton High School
OFTN SK2 .... 47 L5
Offley County Junior
& Infant School
SBCH CW11 .... 204 B5
The Old Bank Surgery
TPLY/KEL CW6 .... 149 K7
Oldfield CP School
CHSE CH3 .... 170 C1
Old Foundry Estate
WDN WA8 .... 7 K7
Old Hall Clinic
CHD/CHDH SK8 .... 45 H6
Old Hall Community
Primary School
WARRW/BUR WA5 .... 36 D4
Old Hall Surgery
EP CH65 .... 10 D9
The Old Surgery
CW/HAS CW1 .... 19 K4
Oldwood Primary School
WYTH/NTH M22 .... 63 H2
Old Wyche Studio Gallery
NANT CW5 .... 20 C6
Oriel Bank High School
EDGY/DAV SK3 .... 46 F7
Orrishmere Primary School
CHD/CHDH SK8 .... 65 G1
Ortenbrook School
PART M31 .... 40 E2
The Osteopathic Health Centre
CH/BCN CH1 .... 16 C1
Our Lady of Lourdes
RC Primary School
PART M31 .... 40 D1
Our Lady of Perpetual
Succour Junior School
WDN WA8 .... 51 M4
Our Lady of Perpetual
Succour RC Infant School
WDN WA8 .... 52 B3
Our Ladys Catholic
Primary School
WARRS WA4 .... 56 E1
Our Ladys RC Infant School
EP CH65 .... 121 G1
Our Ladys RC Junior School
EP CH65 .... 121 G1
Our Ladys RC Primary School
EDGY/DAV SK3 .... 2 D8
Our Ladys RC Primary School
RUNC WA7 .... 74 A6
Outlet Village
EP CH65 .... 121 L2
Outwood Primary School
CHD/CHDH SK8 .... 64 C5
Overdale Primary School
MPL/ROM SK6 .... 47 M3
Over Hall CP School
WSFD CW7 .... 177 H5
Overleigh St Marys C of E
County Primary School
CHSW/BR CH4 .... 169 K5
Over St Johns C of E County
Primary School
WSFD CW7 .... 177 H3
Owl Halt Industrial Estate
CQ CH5 .... 143 H6
Oxhey First School
BIDD ST8 .... 227 L3
Packmoor CP School
ALS/KID ST7 .... 243 M3
Padgate Business Centre
WARR WA1 .... 38 C3
Padgate Business Centre
WARR WA1 .... 38 A4
Padgate C of E Primary School
WARRN/WOL WA2 .... 38 A3
Padgate Community
High School
WARRN/WOL WA2 .... 37 M2
Padgate Medical Centre
WARRN/WOL WA2 .... 38 A3
Palacefields County
Infant School
RUNC WA7 .... 74 A6
Palace Theatre
WARR WA1 .... 5 G7
Palatine Industrial Estate
WARRS WA4 .... 56 C1
Paradise Silk Mill Museum
MCFLDS SK11 .... 15 H7
Park County Middle School
BIDD ST8 .... 227 J6
The Park CP School
RUNC WA7 .... 74 A3
Parkdale Industrial Estate
WARR WA1 .... 5 K8
Parkgate CP School
NSTN CH64 .... 91 J3
Park Green Surgery
MCFLDS SK11 .... 15 H6
Parklands CP Infant School
GTS/LS CH66 .... 94 C6
Parklands High School
WYTH/NTH M22 .... 63 J1
Park Lane Special School
MCFLDS SK11 .... 14 D9
Park Lane Surgery
MCFLDS SK11 .... 14 F8
Parkl Lane Gallery
POY/DIS SK12 .... 86 F1
Park Medical Centre
CHNE CH2 .... 145 M8
Park Medical Practice
HALE/TIMP WA15 .... 43 G4
Park Road Community Primary
School
WARRW/BUR WA5 .... 35 L6
Parkroyal CP School
MCFLDS SK11 .... 14 E6
Park School
NTHM/RTH M23 .... 43 M4
Parkside Hospital
MCFLDN SK10 .... 137 M3
Parkway Business Centre
CQ CH5 .... 142 E2

Parr Flat Community
Infant School
STHEL WA9 .... 26 A1
Parrs Wood High School
DID/WITH M20 .... 45 K3
Partington CP School
PART M31 .... 40 F1
Partington Health Centre
PART M31 .... 40 F1
Partington Shopping Centre
PART M31 .... 40 F1
Partington Sports Centre
PART M31 .... 40 F2
Patterdale Lodge
Group Practice
NEWLW WA12 .... 22 B8
Patterdale Lodge
Medical Centre
NEWLW WA12 .... 27 G1
Peacefield Primary School
MPL/ROM SK6 .... 48 E7
Pear Mill Industrial Estate
MPL/ROM SK6 .... 47 J2
Pebble Brook CP School
CW/SHV CW2 .... 238 C3
Peckforton Castle
TPLY/KEL CW6 .... 215 L3
The Peel Centre
STKP SK1 .... 3 H4
Peel Hall Primary School
WYTH/NTH M22 .... 63 M1
Peelhouse Lane Surgery
WDN WA8 .... 7 L2
Peerglow Industrial Estate
ALT WA14 .... 42 E4
Penarlag CP School
CQ CH5 .... 166 A2
Penketh Business Park
WARRW/BUR WA5 .... 36 B8
Penketh Community
High School
WARRW/BUR WA5 .... 36 A7
Penketh Community
Primary School
WARRW/BUR WA5 .... 35 K8
Penketh Health Clinic
WARRW/BUR WA5 .... 35 L8
Penketh South Community
Primary School
WARRW/BUR WA5 .... 54 F1
Penketh Swimming Baths
WARRW/BUR WA5 .... 35 L7
Penkford Technology School
NEWLW WA12 .... 26 E2
Pentre Industrial Estate
CQ CH5 .... 142 F8
Peover Superior
Endowed Primary School
KNUT WA16 .... 134 B4
Pewithall CP School
RUNC WA7 .... 9 J8
Phil Hughes Practice
CHD/CHDH SK8 .... 65 G1
Phoenix Medical Centre
STKP SK1 .... 3 H7
Pikemere County
Primary School
ALS/KID ST7 .... 224 B3
Pine Surgery
WARRS WA4 .... 76 D3
Pinnacle Business Centre
HTNM SK4 .... 2 F7
Piper Hill School
NTHM/RTH M23 .... 44 B2
Pius Xii RC School
GTS/LS CH66 .... 94 D6
Plantation Primary School
HLWD L26 .... 50 F4
Police Hq
CH/BCN CH1 .... 16 F7
Pooltown CP School
EP CH65 .... 94 F7
Portal Golf & Country Club
TPLY/KEL CW6 .... 197 K1
Portrait Gallery
WDN WA8 .... 7 H1
PO Sorting Office
CH/BCN CH1 .... 17 H2
Pott Shrigley C of E
Primary School
MCFLDN SK10 .... 113 K1
Poundswick Primary School
WYTH/NTH M22 .... 63 J2
Power Wash Trading Estate
BIDD ST8 .... 227 H8
Pownall Green Primary School
BRAM/HZG SK7 .... 65 L5
Pownall Hall School
WILM/AE SK9 .... 83 M4
Poynton Clinic
POY/DIS SK12 .... 66 E8
Poynton County High School
POY/DIS SK12 .... 86 F1
Poynton Leisure Centre
POY/DIS SK12 .... 86 F2
Poynton Parish Council
POY/DIS SK12 .... 66 E8
Poynton Sports Club
POY/DIS SK12 .... 66 E8
Prestbury C of E
Primary School
MCFLDN SK10 .... 111 M5
Prestbury Golf Club
MCFLDN SK10 .... 111 M8
Prestbury Village
Lawn Tennis Club
MCFLDN SK10 .... 111 M5
Priestley Business Centre
WARRW/BUR WA5 .... 4 C6
Priestley College
WARRS WA4 .... 56 C1
Priestnall School
HTNM SK4 .... 45 M1
Priorslegh Medical Centre
POY/DIS SK12 .... 66 E8
Prospect Vale Primary School
CHD/CHDH SK8 .... 64 B3

Pryors Hayes Golf Club
CHSE CH3 .... 173 G3
Public Baths
WHITCH SY13 .... 270 B4
Puss Bank County
Junior & Infant School
MCFLDN SK10 .... 15 L5
Quay Business Centre
WARRN/WOL WA2 .... 37 G1
Queensferry Industrial Estate
CQ CH5 .... 142 E8
Queensgate Primary School
BRAM/HZG SK7 .... 65 L8
Queens Park County
High School
CHSW/BR CH4 .... 17 H8
Queens Preparatory School
CH/BCN CH1 .... 145 J8
Queens Road Primary School
CHD/CHDH SK8 .... 65 G1
The Queen's School
CH/BCN CH1 .... 16 E5
Queensway Business Centre
WDN WA8 .... 52 F7
Quinta CP School
CONG CW12 .... 207 G2
Rackhouse Primary School
NTHM/RTH M23 .... 44 A3
Rainhill Clinic
RAIN/WH L35 .... 33 J1
Rainhill High School
RAIN/WH L35 .... 33 K2
Rainhill Village Surgery
RAIN/WH L35 .... 33 J1
Rainow CP School
MCFLDN SK10 .... 113 K8
Ramillies Hall School
CHD/CHDH SK8 .... 65 J2
Ravenbank Community
Primary School
LYMM WA13 .... 58 F1
Readesmoor Group Practice
CONG CW12 .... 207 K2
Reaseheath College
NANT CW5 .... 236 D3
Record Business Park
WARRN/WOL WA2 .... 4 F1
Recreation Centre
CHD/CHDH SK8 .... 65 H5
Red Bank School
NEWLW WA12 .... 27 L3
The Reginald Mitchell
County Primary School
ALS/KID ST7 .... 242 D3
Register Office
CH/BCN CH1 .... 16 F5
Richmond House Surgery
WHITCH SY13 .... 270 B5
The Ridge College
MPL/ROM SK6 .... 48 E7
Ridge Danyers College
CHD/CHDH SK8 .... 64 F1
Ridge Danyers College
MPL/ROM SK6 .... 48 F7
The Ridings County
Infant School
CH/BCN CH1 .... 144 B3
Ringstones Industrial Estate
CHF/WBR SK23 .... 89 K2
Rivacre Valley CP School
GTS/LS CH66 .... 94 E5
Riverside Trading Estate
NWCHW CW8 .... 13 G4
R L Hughes County
Junior & Infant School
AIMK WN4 .... 22 A1
The Roaches School
BIDD ST8 .... 227 H6
Robson Street Clinic
WARR WA1 .... 5 L5
Rock Surgery
FROD/HEL WA6 .... 99 H3
Rode Heath CP School
ALS/KID ST7 .... 224 F5
Romiley CP School
MPL/ROM SK6 .... 48 D2
Romiley Health Centre
MPL/ROM SK6 .... 48 C2
Rose Bank Special School
NWCHW CW8 .... 103 G8
Rose Cottage Surgery
WARRW/BUR WA5 .... 35 L8
Roseheath Primary School
HLWD L26 .... 50 F5
Rose Hill Primary School
MPL/ROM SK6 .... 48 E6
Rossett Clinic
WRX/GR/LL LL12 .... 210 C4
Rossmore CP School
GTS/LS CH66 .... 94 C5
Rother Drive Business Park
EP CH65 .... 10 B3
Roundwood Upper School
WYTH/NTH M22 .... 44 C5
Rowing Club
CH/BCN CH1 .... 17 J6
Royal Oak Industrial Estate
STKP SK1 .... 3 H8
Royal Oak Primary School
NTHM/RTH M23 .... 44 A5
Rudheath County High School
NWCHE CW9 .... 130 D5
Rudheath CP School
NWCHE CW9 .... 130 D6
Rudheath Dental
Health Centre
NWCHE CW9 .... 130 D5
Rudheath Leisure Centre
NWCHE CW9 .... 130 D5
Rugby Union Football Club
FLINT CH6 .... 116 B5
Runcorn All Saints
C of E Primary School
RUNC WA7 .... 9 G1
Runcorn County Court
RUNC WA7 .... 73 M4
Runcorn Football Club
RUNC WA7 .... 9 K1

Runcorn Rowing Club
RUNC WA7 .... 73 K8
Ruskin County High School
CW/SHV CW2 .... 18 E7
Rycroft Park Sports Club
CHD/CHDH SK8 .... 64 F3
Ryles Park County High School
MCFLDS SK11 .... 14 E9
Ryleys Preparatory School
WILM/AE SK9 .... 109 M3
Sacred Heart RC
Primary School
NTHM/RTH M23 .... 43 L6
Sacred Heart RC
Primary School
WARRW/BUR WA5 .... 4 A7
Saighton C of E Primary
School
CHSE CH3 .... 193 L3
St Aelreds RC High School
NEWLW WA12 .... 22 D8
St Aidan RC Primary School
NTHM/RTH M23 .... 44 B3
St Aidans C of E Community
Primary School
STHEL WA9 .... 34 E1
St Albans Catholic
Primary School
WARRW/BUR WA5 .... 4 D4
St Albans RC Primary School
MCFLDN SK10 .... 137 L3
St Ambrose College
HALE/TIMP WA15 .... 62 B3
St Ambrose Primary School
SPK/HALE L24 .... 71 G1
St Ambrose RC Primary School
EDGY/DAV SK3 .... 46 D7
St Andrews Ce Primary School
WARRN/WOL WA2 .... 37 J1
St Andrews School
CHSW/BR CH4 .... 17 G9
St Annes Ear Nose
& Throat Hospital
ALT WA14 .... 61 J4
St Annes RC Aided
Primary School
NANT CW5 .... 251 L1
St Anns C of E Primary School
RAIN/WH L35 .... 33 J1
St Anns C of E Primary School
WARRN/WOL WA2 .... 5 H1
St Anthonys RC Junior School
WYTH/NTH M22 .... 63 K3
St Anthonys RC School
CHSW/BR CH4 .... 168 E6
St Augustines Catholic
Primary School
WARRS WA4 .... 37 L8
St Augustines RC
Primary School
RUNC WA7 .... 74 A2
St Barnabas C E Aided
Primary School
WARRW/BUR WA5 .... 4 C6
St Barnabas C of E
Primary School
MCFLDS SK11 .... 15 H9
St Bartholomews RC
Primary School
RAIN/WH L35 .... 33 L3
St Basils RC Primary School
RAIN/WH L35 .... 52 A2
St Bedes RC Junior
& Infant School
WDN WA8 .... 7 H2
St Bedes RC Primary School
NWCHW CW8 .... 128 F5
St Benedicts Catholic
Primary School
WARRN/WOL WA2 .... 5 L2
St Benedicts RC Primary School
CHD/CHDH SK8 .... 64 E8
St Benedicts RC Primary School
WILM/AE SK9 .... 84 E1
St Bertelines Primary School
RUNC WA7 .... 74 C4
St Brides Preparatory School
MCFLDN SK10 .... 14 E4
St Bridgets Catholic
Primary School
WARRN/WOL WA2 .... 37 M1
St Catherines
Preparatory School
MPL/ROM SK6 .... 49 H5
St Catherines RC
Primary School
GOL/RIS/CU WA3 .... 23 L5
St Chads C of E
Primary School
WSFD CW7 .... 177 L4
St Chads RC School
RUNC WA7 .... 73 K5
St Christophers Infant School
SPK/HALE L24 .... 50 D8
St Christophers Junior School
SPK/HALE L24 .... 50 D8
St Christophers RC
Primary School
MPL/ROM SK6 .... 48 A2
St Clements RC Primary School
RUNC WA7 .... 9 G6
St Davids High School
CHSW/BR CH4 .... 168 C6
St Davids Trading Estate
CHSW/BR CH4 .... 168 D5
St Edmund Arrowsmith
RC High School
AIMK WN4 .... 22 B2
St Edwards RC Primary School
MCFLDS SK11 .... 138 C7
St Edwards RC Primary School
RUNC WA7 .... 9 K1
St Elizabeth RC Primary School
WYTH/NTH M22 .... 63 L2
St Ethelwolds School
CQ CH5 .... 142 B8

St Gabriels C of E
Primary School
HUY L36 .... 32 A2
St Gabriels RC CP School
ALS/KID ST7 .... 241 J1
St Georges C of E
Infant School
OFTN SK2 .... 46 F6
St Georges C of E
Junior School
OFTN SK2 .... 46 F6
St Georges C of E School
NM/HAY SK22 .... 69 J4
St Gregorys Catholic
High School
WARRW/BUR WA5 .... 36 D7
St Gregorys RC Primary School
MCFLDN SK10 .... 112 F4
St Helens C of E Primary
School
GOL/RIS/CU WA3 .... 40 B1
St Helens College
NEWLW WA12 .... 22 B8
St Helens Metropolitan
Borough Council
NEWLW WA12 .... 27 G1
St Hilarys School
WILM/AE SK9 .... 110 A3
St Hughs RC School
HALE/TIMP WA15 .... 42 F5
St James C of E Junior School
CHNE CH2 .... 170 A1
St James C of E Primary School
AUD/MAD/W CW3 .... 264 A7
St James C of E Primary School
WARRS WA4 .... 5 H9
St James RC High School
CHD/CHDH SK8 .... 64 F5
St John Fisher Junior
& Infant School
WDN WA8 .... 53 K3
St Johns C of E Primary School
FROD/HEL WA6 .... 126 C2
St Johns C of E Primary School
HTNM SK4 .... 45 L2
St Johns C of E Primary School
MCFLDN SK10 .... 113 G5
St Johns C of E Primary School
SBCH CW11 .... 204 E6
St Johns Medical Centre
ALT WA14 .... 61 J1
St Johns Primary School
MCFLDS SK11 .... 14 A1
St Johns RC CP School
ALS/KID ST7 .... 242 F3
St Johns RC Primary School
WYTH/NTH M22 .... 44 D8
St John's Wood School
KNUT WA16 .... 107 K2
St John Vianney School
HTNM SK4 .... 46 B2
St Josephs Catholic
Primary School
WARRW/BUR WA5 .... 35 L7
St Josephs College
MALPAS SY14 .... 246 A8
St Josephs RC CP School
BURS/TUN ST6 .... 243 K5
St Josephs RC Primary School
STKP SK1 .... 3 G5
St Josephs RC Primary School
WSFD CW7 .... 177 M1
St Julies High School
WLTN L25 .... 50 B3
St Leos Primary School
RAIN/WH L35 .... 32 E2
St Lewis's Catholic
Primary School
GOL/RIS/CU WA3 .... 29 H3
St Lukes C of E School
GOL/RIS/CU WA3 .... 23 L5
St Lukes RC Primary School
FROD/HEL WA6 .... 99 J4
St Margarets Ce Junior School
WARRN/WOL WA2 .... 37 J1
St Margarets C of E
Controlled Infant School
WARRN/WOL WA2 .... 37 J2
St Margarets Ward RC
Primary School
SALE M33 .... 42 C3
St Margaret Ward RC
High School
BURS/TUN ST6 .... 243 M7
St Marks R C Primary School
HLWD L26 .... 51 G4
St Martins Clinic
CH/BCN CH1 .... 16 F5
St Martins RC Primary School
RUNC WA7 .... 74 C5
St Mary's Centre
CH/BCN CH1 .... 17 G2
St Mary's C of E Primary School
IRL M44 .... 31 J6
St Marys C of E Primary School
MCFLDS SK11 .... 186 D4
St Marys RC Infant School
NEWLW WA12 .... 22 B8
St Marys RC Junior School
NEWLW WA12 .... 27 H1
St Marys RC Primary School
CONG CW12 .... 207 K1
St Marys RC Primary School
CW/SHV CW2 .... 18 A8
St Marys RC Primary School
MPL/ROM SK6 .... 49 H5
St Marys RC Primary School
MWCH CW10 .... 179 J4
St Marys RC Primary School
NM/HAY SK22 .... 69 H4
St Marys RC School
HTNM SK4 .... 2 F3
St Marys School
FLINT CH6 .... 116 B7
St Matthews C of E
Primary School
WARRS WA4 .... 76 E2

St Monicas Catholic
Primary School
WARRS WA4 .... 56 D5
St Nichols RC Aided High School
NWCHW CW8 .... 12 D7
St Oswalds Catholic
Primary School
WARR WA1 .... 37 M4
St Oswalds Primary School
AIMK WN4 .... 22 A1
St Paul of the Cross Catholic
Primary School
WARRW/BUR WA5 .... 26 E6
St Pauls RC High School
NTHM/RTH M23 .... 44 B8
St Pauls RC Primary School
POY/DIS SK12 .... 86 E2
St Peter & St. Paul High School
WDN WA8 .... 6 F1
St Peters Catholic Primary
School
WARR WA1 .... 38 C5
St Peters C of E Primary School
NEWLW WA12 .... 22 D8
St Peters Primary School
NTHM/RTH M23 .... 63 H1
St Peters RC Primary School
BRAM/HZG SK7 .... 66 D3
St Peters School
WRX/GR/LL LL12 .... 210 C1
St Philips Church & Community
Primary School
WARRW/BUR WA5 .... 36 B3
St Philips RC Primary School
OFTN SK2 .... 47 K6
St Richard Gwyn High School
FLINT CH6 .... 116 B7
St Saviours C of E
Primary School
ALS/KID ST7 .... 242 C3
St Saviours RC Aided School
GTS/LS CH66 .... 120 L1
St Simons RC Primary School
BRAM/HZG SK7 .... 66 E1
St Stephens C of E
Primary School
BRAM/HZG SK7 .... 47 M8
St Stephen's Primary School
WARRN/WOL WA2 .... 37 H1
St Teresas RC School
IRL M44 .... 31 L4
St Theresa Primary School
CH/BCN CH1 .... 144 F7
St Theresas RC Primary School
STHEL WA9 .... 34 C1
St Thomas Becket RC
High School
HUY L36 .... 32 A1
St Thomas Ce Primary School
WARRS WA4 .... 56 D3
St Thomas C of E Junior
& Infant School
GOL/RIS/CU WA3 .... 23 G3
St Thomas C of E
Primary School
STKP SK1 .... 3 H7
St Thomas C of E School
AIMK WN4 .... 22 C1
St Thomas Hospital
EDGY/DAV SK3 .... 2 F9
St Thomas More RC High School
CW/SHV CW2 .... 18 B8
St Thomas of Canterbury
C of E Junior School
CH/BCN CH1 .... 16 E2
St Thomas's C of E
Primary School
ALS/KID ST7 .... 243 G4
St Vincent RC Infant School
HALE/TIMP WA15 .... 42 F1
St Vincents Catholic
Primary School
WARRW/BUR WA5 .... 54 E1
St Vincents RC Primary School
KNUT WA16 .... 107 J2
St Weburgh C of E
Primary School
WARRS WA4 .... 56 B2
St Werburgh & St. Columba RC
Primary School
CHNE CH2 .... 17 M2
St Wilfreds C of E
Primary School
WARRS WA4 .... 57 H3
St Wilfreds RC Primary School
NWCHW CW8 .... 12 D8
St Wilfrids C of E
Primary School
WYTH/NTH M22 .... 44 E4
St Winefrides R C
Aided Primary School
NSTN CH64 .... 91 M5
St Winifreds RC Primary School
HTNM SK4 .... 46 A2
Sale Football Club
SALE M33 .... 43 H1
Sale Grammar School
SALE M33 .... 43 J1
Salford City Council
IRL M44 .... 31 K7
Salford City Council
IRL M44 .... 31 M4
Saltney Clinic
CHSW/BR CH4 .... 168 C6
Sandbach County High
School for Girls
SBCH CW11 .... 203 M5
Sandbach CP School
SBCH CW11 .... 204 A6
Sandbach Cricket Club
SBCH CW11 .... 204 B5
Sandbach R U F C
SBCH CW11 .... 204 B4
Sandbach School Foundation
SBCH CW11 .... 204 A6
Sandbach Town Hall
SBCH CW11 .... 204 B6

Sandilands Primary School
NTHM/RTH M23 .... 43 J4
Sandiway CP School
NWCHW CW8 .... 152 A1
Sandiway Golf Club
NWCHW CW8 .... 152 D2
Sandiway Surgery
NWCHW CW8 .... 152 A2
Sandycroft County
Primary School
CQ CH5 .... 166 E1
Sankey Bridge
Industrial Estate
WARRW/BUR WA5 .... 36 C8
Sankey Medical Centre
WARRW/BUR WA5 .... 35 L5
Sankey Valley Industrial Estate
NEWLW WA12 .... 27 H2
Saughall Village Surgery
CH/BCN CH1 .... 143 M3
Scholar Green CP School
ALS/KID ST7 .... 225 L6
The Schoolhouse Surgery
POY/DIS SK12 .... 68 C6
School Lane Farm
MPL/ROM SK6 .... 49 H1
Sealand Child Health Centre
CQ CH5 .... 142 F5
Sealand CP School
CQ CH5 .... 142 E6
Sett Valley Medical Centre
NM/HAY SK22 .... 69 J4
Shavington County
High School
CW/SHV CW2 .... 238 A7
Shavington CP School
CW/SHV CW2 .... 238 C7
Shavington Sports Centre
CW/SHV CW2 .... 238 A7
Shaw Heath Health Centre
EDGY/DAV SK3 .... 2 F9
Shay Lane Medical Centre
HALE/TIMP WA15 .... 62 C3
Shocklach Oviatt C of E
Primary School
MALPAS SY14 .... 244 D5
Shotton CP School
CQ CH5 .... 142 B6
Shotton Town Council Office
CQ CH5 .... 142 B6
Shrigley Hall Hotel Golf
& Country Club
MCFLDN SK10 .... 87 J8
Simms Cross County
Primary School
WDN WA8 .... 7 G5
Sir John Deanes College
NWCHE CW9 .... 13 H6
Sir John Offley C of E
Primary School
AUD/MAD/W CW3 .... 267 L7
Sir John Talbots School
WHITCH SY13 .... 270 B7
Sir Thomas Boteler
High School
WARRS WA4 .... 56 E1
Smallwood C of E
Primary School
SBCH CW11 .... 205 M7
Sound CP School
NANT CW5 .... 250 F7
South Cheshire College
CONG CW12 .... 207 K2
South Cheshire College
CW/SHV CW2 .... 18 C8
Southfields School
SALE M33 .... 42 F1
South Manchester High School
WYTH/NTH M22 .... 63 K1
South Manchester University
Hospitals NHS Trust
NTHM/RTH M23 .... 43 M8
Southmead Junior
& Infant School
RAIN/WH L35 .... 32 E2
Southmoor Business Park
NTHM/RTH M23 .... 43 L5
South Park Court
Business Centre
MCFLDS SK11 .... 15 G8
South Trafford College
ALT WA14 .... 42 D4
Speke Community
Comprehensive School
SPK/HALE L24 .... 70 D2
Speke Comprehensive School
SPK/HALE L24 .... 70 D1
Speke Family Health Clinic
SPK/HALE L24 .... 70 E1
Sports Centre
MPL/ROM SK6 .... 49 G5
Sports Stadium
BURS/TUN ST6 .... 243 L7
Springfield Special School
CW/HAS CW1 .... 239 G1
Springfield Surgery
BRAM/HZG SK7 .... 66 D1
Springhead CP School
ALS/KID ST7 .... 242 D6
Springwood Primary School
MPL/ROM SK6 .... 48 E1
Squirrel Hayes County
First School
BIDD ST8 .... 227 K5
Staffordshire County Council
AUD/MAD/W CW3 .... 267 L5
Staffordshire County Council
BURS/TUN ST6 .... 243 J5
Stag Industrial Estate
ALT WA14 .... 42 B6
Stamford Park Junior
& Infant School
HALE/TIMP WA15 .... 61 L1
Stanlaw Abbey CP School
EP CH65 .... 121 K2
Stanney Grange CP School
EP CH65 .... 121 J2

Stanney High School
EP CH65 .... 121 J2
Stanney Mill Industrial Estate
CHNE CH2 .... 121 M3
Stanney Mill Industrial Estate
EP CH65 .... 121 M1
Stapeley Broad Lane
C of E Primary School
NANT CW5 .... 252 A3
Statham Community
Primary School
LYMM WA13 .... 39 J8
Stella Maris School
HTNM SK4 .... 45 L2
Stepping Hill Hospital
OFTN SK2 .... 47 H8
Stepping Stones
Montessori School
MCFLDN SK10 .... 14 E4
Stewards Cottage Club House
MALPAS SY14 .... 247 M5
Stockport Acute Services
NHS Trust
OFTN SK2 .... 47 J8
Stockport College of Further
& Higher Education
EDGY/DAV SK3 .... 3 G8
Stockport County Court
STKP SK1 .... 2 F6
Stockport County Football Club
EDGY/DAV SK3 .... 46 D5
Stockport Cricket Club
EDGY/DAV SK3 .... 46 E6
Stockport Grammar School
OFTN SK2 .... 47 H7
Stockport Metropolitan
Borough Council
CHD/CHDH SK8 .... 65 G2
Stockport Metropolitan
Borough Council
EDGY/DAV SK3 .... 2 F7
Stockport Metropolitan
Borough Council
MPL/ROM SK6 .... 49 G6
Stockport Metropolitan
Borough Council
MPL/ROM SK6 .... 49 G2
Stockport Metropolitan
Borough Council
OFTN SK2 .... 47 K6
Stockport Road Medical
Practice
MPL/ROM SK6 .... 48 F6
Stockport Rugby Union
Football Club
BRAM/HZG SK7 .... 65 M3
Stockport School
OFTN SK2 .... 47 H7
Stockport Super Bowl
EDGY/DAV SK3 .... 2 F7
Stockport Trading Estate
HTNM SK4 .... 46 B4
Stockton Heath
Community Primary School
WARRS WA4 .... 56 C3
Stockton Heath Medical Centre
WARRS WA4 .... 56 C3
Stockton Wood JMI School
SPK/HALE L24 .... 70 C1
Styal Primary School
WILM/AE SK9 .... 63 L8
Summerbank Central
CP School
BURS/TUN ST6 .... 243 J8
Sutton County High School
GTS/LS CH66 .... 94 E7
Sutton Green CP School
GTS/LS CH66 .... 94 B7
Sutton Hall Golf Club
RUNC WA7 .... 100 A1
Sutton Manor Community
Primary School
STHEL WA9 .... 34 A2
Sutton Way County
Junior School
GTS/LS CH66 .... 94 E8
Swanlow Medical Centre
WSFD CW7 .... 177 J4
Sycamore Lane
Community Primary School
WARRW/BUR WA5 .... 36 B7
Syddal Park School
BRAM/HZG SK7 .... 65 K7
Tait Gallery
WHITCH SY13 .... 270 A4
Taliesin Junior School
CQ CH5 .... 142 A7
Talke Clinic
ALS/KID ST7 .... 242 D6
Tallarn Green School
MALPAS SY14 .... 256 E7
Tarporley Business Centre
TPLY/KEL CW6 .... 197 J3
Tarporley C of E
Primary School
TPLY/KEL CW6 .... 197 K3
Tarporley County High School
TPLY/KEL CW6 .... 197 K4
Tarporley War
Memorial Hospital
TPLY/KEL CW6 .... 197 J2
Tarvin CP School
CHSE CH3 .... 172 B3
Tarvin Road Medical Centre
CHSE CH3 .... 17 M5
Taxal Lodge School
CHF/WBR SK23 .... 89 K7
Tennis Club
WILM/AE SK9 .... 83 K8
Terra Nova Preparatory School
HOLMCH CW4 .... 158 D3
Thames Trading Centre
IRL M44 .... 31 M5
Thelwall Community
Infant School
WARRS WA4 .... 57 J1

Thelwall Community
Junior School
WARRS WA4 .... 57 K1
Thelwall New Road Surgery
WARRS WA4 .... 57 H1
Thomas Wedge School
CH/BCN CH1 .... 144 A3
Thornfield School
HTNM SK4 .... 45 H4
Thorn Grove Primary School
CHD/CHDH SK8 .... 65 G6
Thornsett CP School
NM/HAY SK22 .... 69 L1
Thursfield CP School
ALS/KID ST7 .... 243 K1
Tilston School
MALPAS SY14 .... 245 H1
Timperley Health Centre
HALE/TIMP WA15 .... 43 G5
Timperley Park Road
CP School
ALT WA14 .... 42 E4
Tone Up & Tan Health Centre
BRAM/HZG SK7 .... 66 D1
Torkington Primary School
BRAM/HZG SK7 .... 67 G2
Towers Business Park
DID/WITH M20 .... 45 H3
Town Hall & Mayors Parlour
FLINT CH6 .... 116 A5
Town House Practice
WDN WA8 .... 7 K3
Trafford Health Authority
HALE/TIMP WA15 .... 61 L2
Trafford Healthcare NHS Trust
SALE M33 .... 43 K1
Trafford Metropolitan Borough
Council
ALT WA14 .... 42 C8
Trafford Metropolitan Borough
Council
PART M31 .... 40 F1
Tregenna Health Centre
& Dental Surgery
WYTH/NTH M22 .... 63 J3
Tregenna Surgery
WYTH/NTH M22 .... 63 K3
Trevalyn Hospital
WRX/GR/LL LL12 .... 210 B6
Trident Industrial Estate
GOL/RIS/CU WA3 .... 29 K3
Tushingham Gallery
WHITCH SY13 .... 270 A5
Tushingham School
MALPAS SY14 .... 259 J3
Twiss Green Community
Primary School
GOL/RIS/CU WA3 .... 24 E8
Tyntesfield CP School
SALE M33 .... 42 E3
Tytherington County
High School
MCFLDN SK10 .... 138 D2
Tytherington Shopping Centre
MCFLDN SK10 .... 138 D2
Underwood Industrial Estate
CW/HAS CW1 .... 221 G6
The Unicorn Gallery
WILM/AE SK9 .... 84 B6
University College Chester
CH/BCN CH1 .... 16 E1
University of Liverpool
NSTN CH64 .... 92 B3
University of Liverpool
NSTN CH64 .... 92 D5
University of Manchester
MCFLDS SK11 .... 158 D2
Upton Acresfield CP School
CHNE CH2 .... 145 K4
Upton by Chester County
High School
CHNE CH2 .... 145 K4
Upton County Infants School
WDN WA8 .... 52 B1
Upton Medical Centre
WDN WA8 .... 52 B1
Upton Mill View CP School
CHNE CH2 .... 145 L6
Upton Priory County Junior
& Infant School
MCFLDN SK10 .... 137 M2
Upton St Marys C of E
Infant School
CHNE CH2 .... 145 L5
Upton Village Surgery
CHNE CH2 .... 145 K6
Upton Westlea CP School
CHNE CH2 .... 145 L6
Uri Jacobi Oriental
Carpet Gallery
CH/BCN CH1 .... 16 F5
Utkinton C of E Controlled
Primary School
TPLY/KEL CW6 .... 174 B4
Vale Football Club
CONG CW12 .... 207 K2
Vale Royal Abbey Golf Club
NWCHW CW8 .... 153 H4
Valley Brook Business Centre
CW/SHV CW2 .... 19 G6
Valley School
BRAM/HZG SK7 .... 65 H3
Verdin County High School
WSFD CW7 .... 177 J2
Vernon County Infant School
POY/DIS SK12 .... 86 E1
Vernon County Junior School
POY/DIS SK12 .... 86 E1
Vernon Industrial Estate
STKP SK1 .... 3 J4
Vernon Park Primary School
STKP SK1 .... 3 J3
Vicars Cross Golf Club
CHSE CH3 .... 171 G3
Victoria Community County
High School
CW/HAS CW1 .... 18 E1

Victoria Community
High School
CW/HAS CW1 .... 18 F3
Victoria County Infant School
CH/BCN CH1 .... 16 E2
Victoria Gallery & Gifts
CW/HAS CW1 .... 18 F3
Victoria Road CP School
NWCHE CW9 .... 13 L2
Victoria Road CP School
RUNC WA7 .... 9 G4
Victoria Trading Estate
RAIN/WH L35 .... 33 J1
The Village Gallery
SBCH CW11 .... 223 G1
Village Medical Centre
WLTN L25 .... 50 A2
The Village Surgery
BRAM/HZG SK7 .... 65 L6
Vine Tree County Primary
School
CW/SHV CW2 .... 18 B8
Virgin Cinemas
CH/BCN CH1 .... 168 F1
Virgin Cinemas
EDGY/DAV SK3 .... 2 F7
Wade Deacon High School
WDN WA8 .... 7 G1
Wallerscote County
Primary School
NWCHW CW8 .... 128 E4
Walray Pictures Gallery
NSTN CH64 .... 91 J5
Walton Hall
WARRS WA4 .... 56 A6
Walton Park Leisure Centre
SALE M33 .... 43 G2
Warford Hall Hospital
MCFLDN SK10 .... 109 J6
Warford Hall Hospital
WILM/AE SK9 .... 109 H6
Wargrave C of E Primary
School
NEWLW WA12 .... 27 J3
Wargrave House School
NEWLW WA12 .... 27 J3
War Memorial Hospital
CONG CW12 .... 207 M3
Warmingham C of E
Primary School
SBCH CW11 .... 202 E4
Warren Wood Primary School
OFTN SK2 .... 48 A6
Warrington Borough Council
COL/RIS/CU WA3 .... 29 M1
Warrington Borough Council
WARR WA1 .... 4 F7
Warrington Borough Council
WARR WA1 .... 5 L5
Warrington Borough Council
WARR WA1 .... 38 B5
Warrington Borough Council
WARR WA1 .... 38 F5
Warrington Borough Council
WARRN/WOL WA2 .... 37 H2
Warrington Borough Council
WARRN/WOL WA2 .... 37 M2
Warrington Borough Council
WARRS WA4 .... 37 M8
Warrington Borough Council
WARRS WA4 .... 56 E5
Warrington Borough Council
WARRW/BUR WA5 .... 36 F2
Warrington Business Park
WARRN/WOL WA2 .... 37 J3
Warrington Central
Trading Estate
WARRN/WOL WA2 .... 4 E4

Warrington Community
Health Care NHS Trust
WARRN/WOL WA2 .... 27 M6
Warrington Hospital NHS Trust
WARRW/BUR WA5 .... 4 B5
Warrington New Town
Cricket Club
WARRW/BUR WA5 .... 36 D7
Warrington Rugby
League Football Club
WARRS WA4 .... 56 B1
Warrington Sports Club
WARRS WA4 .... 56 A5
Warrington Town A F C
WARRS WA4 .... 56 E2
Warwick County
Primary School
MCFLDS SK11 .... 137 M6
Watergate School
WLTN L25 .... 50 B2
Waterloo Industrial Park
STKP SK1 .... 3 H1
Waters Green Clinic
MCFLDS SK11 .... 15 H1
Waterside Hotel
& Galleon Leisure Centre
DID/WITH M20 .... 45 J4
Water Street School
MCFLDN SK10 .... 113 H4
Waverton CP School
CHSE CH3 .... 171 G7
Weatherstone Business Centre
NSTN CH64 .... 92 C4
Weaver CP School
NANT CW5 .... 251 L2
The Weaver Gallery
NANT CW5 .... 20 F7
The Weaver Gallery
NWCHW CW8 .... 12 F3
Weaverham County
High School
NWCHW CW8 .... 128 C4
Weaverham Forest CP School
NWCHW CW8 .... 128 C3
Weaverham Special School
NWCHW CW8 .... 128 E4
Weaverham Surgery
NWCHW CW8 .... 128 D3
Weaver Park Industrial Estate
FROD/HEL WA6 .... 99 K2
Well Green Primary School
HALE/TIMP WA15 .... 62 B2
Werneth School
MPL/ROM SK6 .... 47 M2
West Bank County
rimary School
WDN WA8 .... 52 F8
West Bank Medical Centre
WDN WA8 .... 53 G7
Westbrook Medical Centre
WARRW/BUR WA5 .... 36 B3
West Cheshire College
CH/BCN CH1 .... 145 G7
West Cheshire College
EP CH65 .... 10 C8
Westcliffe Hospital
BURS/TUN ST6 .... 243 M5
Western Avenue
Medical Centre
CH/BCN CH1 .... 144 D8
Westfields County
Infant School
CW/SHV CW2 .... 237 K4
West Heath Shopping Centre
CONG CW12 .... 207 G1

Westlands County High School
CONG CW12 .... 207 G1
Westminster Industrial Park
EP CH65 .... 94 F6
Westminster Surgery
EP CH65 .... 10 E4
Weston County Primary School
CW/SHV CW2 .... 239 J7
Weston Point County
Primary School
RUNC WA7 .... 8 D8
Weston Primary School
RUNC WA7 .... 73 G6
Whaley Bridge Primary School
CHF/WBR SK23 .... 89 K5
Wharton C of E Controlled
Junior School
WSFD CW7 .... 177 M3
Wharton Health Centre
WSFD CW7 .... 177 M3
Wharton Retail Park
WSFD CW7 .... 177 M1
Whirley County Primary
School
MCFLDN SK10 .... 137 J3
Whiston Health Centre
RAIN/WH L35 .... 32 D1
Whitby County High School
GTS/LS CH66 .... 121 G3
Whitby Heath County
Primary School
EP CH65 .... 121 H1
Whitchurch C of E
Junior School
WHITCH SY13 .... 270 B4
Whitchurch C of E
Infant School
WHITCH SY13 .... 270 B5
Whitchurch Hospital
WHITCH SY13 .... 270 A4
Whitegate C of E
Primary School
NWCHW CW8 .... 152 F5
White House School
WHITCH SY13 .... 270 B7
Whitley County Primary School
WARRS WA4 .... 76 D8
Widnes Community
Midwifery & Ante Natal
WDN WA8 .... 7 G1
Widnes Cricket Club
WDN WA8 .... 34 B8
Widnes Public Baths
WDN WA8 .... 7 H5
Widnes Rugby Football Club
WDN WA8 .... 6 F5
Widnes Sixth Form College
WDN WA8 .... 33 L7
Wigan & Leigh College
LEIGH WN7 .... 24 D1
Wigan Metropolitan
Borough Council
COL/RIS/CU WA3 .... 23 H4
Wigan Metropolitan
Borough Council
COL/RIS/CU WA3 .... 24 A4
Willaston C of E Primary School
NSTN CH64 .... 92 C4
Willaston CP School
NANT CW5 .... 237 J6
William Beaumont
Community High School
WARRN/WOL WA2 .... 37 H3

William Stockton CP School
EP CH65 .... 10 C7
The Willows Primary School
HALE/TIMP WA15 .... 42 F6
Willow Wood County
Infant & Junior School
WSFD CW7 .... 178 A2
Wilmslow Albion
Football Club
WILM/AE SK9 .... 84 A1
Wilmslow Golf Club
KNUT WA16 .... 109 H3
Wilmslow Grange
County Primary School
WILM/AE SK9 .... 64 C8
Wilmslow Health Centre
WILM/AE SK9 .... 84 A6
Wilmslow High School
WILM/AE SK9 .... 84 B6
Wilmslow Leisure Centre
WILM/AE SK9 .... 84 B6
Wilmslow Preparatory School
WILM/AE SK9 .... 84 B5
Wilmslow Road Medical Centre
WILM/AE SK9 .... 64 D8
Wilmslow Rugby Club
WILM/AE SK9 .... 83 M3
Wimboldsley CP School
MWCH CW10 .... 178 F8
Wincham CP School
NWCHE CW9 .... 104 F7
Wincle C of E Primary School
MCFLDS SK11 .... 187 M3
Windmill Hill County
Primary School
RUNC WA7 .... 74 C2
Winnington Park CP School
NWCHW CW8 .... 12 C4
Winnington Park Rugby Club
NWCHW CW8 .... 12 A5
Winsford Darnall County
Primary School
WSFD CW7 .... 177 K6
Winsford Industrial Estate
WSFD CW7 .... 178 C2
Winsford Police Station
WSFD CW7 .... 177 L3
Winstanley Industrial Estate
WARRN/WOL WA2 .... 37 H3
Winwick C of E Primary School
WARRN/WOL WA2 .... 28 B6
Winwick Parish Leisure Centre
WARRN/WOL WA2 .... 28 B6
Wistaston Berkeley CP School
CW/SHV CW2 .... 238 B5
Wistaston County
Junior School
CW/SHV CW2 .... 237 L4
Witton Albion Football Club
NWCHE CW9 .... 130 D2
Witton Churchwalk C of E
Primary School
NWCHE CW9 .... 13 K3
Witton Street Surgery
NWCHE CW9 .... 13 K1
Woodcocks Weel C of E Primary
School
ALS/KID ST7 .... 226 C6
Woodend Industrial Estate
SPK/HALE L24 .... 50 D7
Woodfall County Junior
& Infant School
NSTN CH64 .... 92 A6

Woodfield County Junior
& Infant School
CHNE CH2 .... 146 A7
Woodford Aerodrome
MCFLDN SK10 .... 86 B2
Woodford Cricket Club
BRAM/HZG SK7 .... 85 L1
Woodford Lodge County
High School
WSFD CW7 .... 177 G5
Woodford Preparatory School
BRAM/HZG SK7 .... 85 K2
Woodheys Primary School
SALE M33 .... 42 E2
Woodhouse Park
Primary School
WYTH/NTH M22 .... 63 K4
Woodlands County
Infant School
GTS/LS CH66 .... 120 F2
Woodlands County
Junior School
GTS/LS CH66 .... 120 F3
Woodlands Industrial Estate
NEWLW WA12 .... 22 C6
Wood Memorial CP School
CHSW/BR CH4 .... 168 E6
Woodside County
Primary School
RUNC WA7 .... 73 L5
Woodside School
WYTH/NTH M22 .... 44 F8
Woolston C of E
Primary School
WARR WA1 .... 38 C4
Woolston Community
High School
WARR WA1 .... 38 B4
Woolston Community
Primary School
WARR WA1 .... 38 C5
Woolston Surgery
WARR WA1 .... 38 D5
Woolston County Infant School
WLTN L25 .... 50 B1
Woolton House Medical Centre
WLTN L25 .... 50 A2
Woolton Surgery
WLTN L25 .... 50 A2
Woolton Swimming Pool
WLTN L25 .... 50 A2
Worleston C of E
Primary School
NANT CW5 .... 219 L6
Worth County Primary School
POY/DIS SK12 .... 86 F1
Wrenbury County
Primary School
NANT CW5 .... 249 M8
Wybunbury Delves
C of E Primary School
NANT CW5 .... 253 H5
Wyche County Primary School
NANT CW5 .... 20 E5
Wythenshawe Hall
NTHM/RTH M23 .... 44 B4
York Road Group Practice
EP CH65 .... 10 E8
Yorston Lodge School
KNUT WA16 .... 106 F3

F6
1 Belgrave Av
2 Church St
3 Culchetch Av
4 Ellesmere Av
5 Gloucester Av
6 Highfield Rd
7 Queen St
8 Springfield Av
9 Union Rd

F7
1 Chadwick St
2 Cotefield Cl
3 Trinity St
4 Waterside Av
5 Willow Ct

F8
1 Goyt Rd
2 Outram Cl
3 Sherwood Cl
4 Sunwell Ter

Page 50

A1
1 Wootton Park Cl

A2
1 Berrington Av
2 The Old Quarry
3 St Mary's Pl

A3
1 Cam St

B1
1 Dove Ct
2 Meadow Hey Cl

B2
1 Bishops Ct
2 Deacon Ct

B4
1 Denstone Cl
2 Roedean Cl

B6
1 Enstone Rd
2 Faringdon Cl

B8
1 Bognor Cl
2 Lenham Wy
3 Sudbury Wy

C1
1 Davids Wk
2 Halewood Pl
3 Knotty Ms

C2
1 Budworth Dr
2 Felsted Av
3 Halewood Wy
4 Kingham Cl
5 Warton Cl
6 Whitney Pl

C4
1 Dunmow Wy

C6
1 Braydon Cl

C8
1 Ramsbrook Cl

D2
1 Blackberry Gv
2 Edenhall Dr
3 Hazelwood Gv
4 Honeysuckle Cl
5 Magnolia Cl
6 Riding Fold

D3
1 Lancing Rd

D4
1 Pembrey Wy

D8
1 Wellbrook Cl

E2
1 Comfrey Gv
2 Okell Dr
3 Openfields Cl
4 Pipit Cl
5 Rogerson's Gn
6 Ruscar Cl

E3
1 Bullfinch Ct
2 Chaffinch Cld
3 Chudleigh Cl
4 Goldcrest Ms
5 Greenfinch Cl
6 Lapwing Ct
7 Ransons Cl
8 Sandpiper Gv
9 Sparrowhawk Cl
10 Wren Gv

E4
1 Carlyon Wy
2 Cheriton Cl
3 Ravenfield Cl
4 Stainton Cl
5 Tarleton Cl

E5
1 Cotswolds Cresent
2 Mendip Cl

E6
1 Lonsdale Rd
2 Tiverton Rd

E8
1 Eastham Gn
2 Northern Rd
3 Penketh Gn

F3
1 Farnborough Gv
2 Yarcombe Cl

F4
1 Cambridge Dr
2 Catterick Cl
3 Fernwood Dr
4 Neasham Cl

F5
1 Penmann Cl
2 Stourvale Rd

F6
1 Blakeacre Cl
2 Georgian Cl
3 Romford Wy

F7
1 Garage Rd

Page 52

A1
1 Orchard Wy

A4
1 Beaufort Cl
2 Woodview Crs

B3
1 Acrefield Rd
2 Gainsborough Ct
3 Wilsden Rd

B4
1 Westminster Cl

B7
1 Church Meadow Wk
2 Cock Lane Ends

C1
1 Aubourn Cl
2 Broxton Cl
3 Burnham Cl
4 Caxton Cl
5 Chatsworth Dr
6 Fenton Cl
7 Hambleton Cl
8 Madeline Mckenna Ct
9 Newland Cl
10 Warkworth Cl

C2
1 Rufford Cl

C3
1 Gaisgill Ct
2 Graham Cl
3 Kendal Rd
4 Sherwood Cl

C4
1 Kenneth Rd
2 Winchester Pl

D1
1 Bloomsbury Wy
2 Shipton Cl
3 Turner Cl
4 Warnley Cl

D2
1 Brentfield
2 Lingwell Av
3 Moyles Cl
4 Revesby Cl
5 Tate Cl

D4
1 Alverton Cl
2 Poulton Dr

E3
1 Jubilee Wy
2 St Thomas Ct

E4
1 Rowthorn Cl
2 Thornton

F1
1 Battersea Ct
2 Burton Cl
3 Giltbrook Cl
4 Grundy Cl
5 Whickham Cl

F3
1 Clayton Crs
2 Holkham Cl
3 Marlowe Cl

F4
1 Millington Cl
2 Wordsworth Av

F5
1 Moorside Ct
2 Rhyl St

F6
1 Desoto Rd East
2 Desoto Rd West

Page 53

G1
1 Birchfield Rd
2 Devon Pl
3 Laurel Bank
4 Sefton Av
5 Victoria Gv

G2
1 Birchfield Av
2 Bradshaw St

G3
1 Shelley Rd
2 Timmis Crs
3 Towneley Ct

G4
1 Mond Rd
2 Wallace St

G5
1 Alexandra St
2 Alforde St
3 Bold St
4 Chapel St
5 Darlington Ct
6 Eleanor St
7 Ellis St
8 Emily St
9 Finlan Rd
10 Guest St
11 Lewis Crs
12 Luton St
13 Major Cross St
14 Market St
15 Millar Crs
16 Miners Wy
17 St Paul's Rd
18 Thomas St
19 Vicarage Rd
20 Victoria Rd
21 Violet St
22 Witt Rd

G6
1 Hutchinson St
2 Marsh St

G7
1 Chidlow Cl
2 Constance Wy
3 Dock Rd
4 Queensway
5 Short St
6 White St
7 Wilkinson Cl

G8
1 Beamont St
2 Bridge View Cl
3 Cholmondeley St
4 Hurst St
5 Parsonage Rd

H1
1 Boxgrove Cl
2 Durham Rd
3 Griffin Ms

H2
1 Hawthorn Av
2 Larch Av
3 Lime Av
4 Mount Pleasant
5 Pine Av

H3
1 Bradley Wy
2 Cross St
3 Lower Appleton Rd
4 Maple Av
5 Mount St
6 Robert St
7 Routledge St
8 Saxon Ter
9 Westmorland Av

H4
1 Alfred Cl
2 Elliot St
3 Gerrard St
4 Grenfell St
5 Hibbert St
6 Liebig St
7 Lugsdale Rd
8 Midwood St
9 Rylands St
10 Salisbury St
11 Timperley St
12 Travis St

H5
1 Batherton Cl
2 Caroline St
3 Elizabeth Ct
4 Lacey Ct
5 Margaret Ct
6 Pool St
7 Sutton's La
8 Trinity Pl

J2
1 Doward St
2 Stanley Cl
3 Susan St

J3
1 Bell House Rd
2 Black Denton's Pl
3 Cliffe St
4 Edwin St
5 Esther St
6 Harris St
7 Henry St
8 Parr St
9 Richmond St
10 Sadler St
11 Taylor St

K1
1 Crow Wood Pl
2 Selwyn Cl

K2
1 Barnes Cl
2 Drummond Ct
3 Moore Cl

K3
1 East St
2 Edward St
3 Hargreaves Ct
4 Norland St
5 Sussex St
6 Walter St

L1
1 Belgrave Cl
2 Chalgrave Cl
3 Fairburn Cl
4 Hampton Cl
5 Lamport Cl
6 Shetland Cl
7 Shevington Cl

L2
1 Egdon Cl
2 Ronaldshay
3 Shawell Ct
4 Swinford Av

M1
1 Shelton Cl

Page 56

C4
1 Bridgewater Ms
2 Carlisle St
3 Carlton St
4 Hawthorne Rd

F2
1 Stanley Pl

F6
1 Woodstock Gdns

F7
1 Chatwell Gdns
2 Eversley Cl

Page 63

G2
1 Beacon Dr
2 Compton Dr
3 Crowthorn Dr
4 Enford Av
5 Shepton Dr
6 Spalding Dr

H5
1 Chicago Av
2 Exit Rd West
3 Malaga Av
4 Terminal Rd East
5 Terminal Rd South

J1
1 Pembury Cl
2 Somerton Av

J2
1 Aldercroft Av
2 Brimscombe Av
3 Buttermere Av
4 Harry Rowley Cl
5 Hucclecote Av
6 Saintsbridge Rd
7 Twigworth Rd

J3
1 Cranesbill Cl
2 Daisyfield Cl
3 Goodridge Av
4 Herle Dr
5 Lullington Cl
6 Poynings Dr
7 Purbeck Cl
8 Ringmer Dr
9 Rottingdene Dr
10 Saltdene Rd
11 Somerby Dr

K1
1 Birch Tree Dr
2 Crawley Av
3 Longmere Av
4 Ryeburn Av

K3
1 Bardsea Av
2 Brayford Rd
3 Falmer Dr
4 Knowe Av
5 Mossack Av

M5
1 Emerald Rd

Page 64

B1
1 Crummock Rd
2 Ennerdale Rd
3 Loweswater Rd
4 Wasdale Dr

B3
1 Ainsdale Dr
2 Ashbrook Cl
3 Green Gables Cl
4 Hurstvale Av
5 Motcombe Farm Rd
6 Willow Tree Ms

D7
1 Beeston Rd
2 Durham Rd
3 Hurlbote Cl
4 Oakmere Rd
5 Ollerton Rd
6 Plumley Rd
7 Siddington Rd
8 Swettenham Rd

E2
1 Hampton Gv
2 Hurley Dr
3 Kingston Pl
4 Mostyn Av

F3
1 Bankfield Rd
2 Brantwood Rd
3 Cathill Cl
4 Courham Dr
5 Hadley Cl
6 West Oak Pl

F4
1 Moorland Dr
2 Waterfield Cl

F5
1 Sidmouth Gv

F6
1 Leafield Dr
2 St James' Wy

Page 65

G1
1 Kenilworth Av
2 Linden Rd
3 Northwood Av

G2
1 Woodthorpe Dr

G3
1 Almond Tree Rd
2 Hulme Hall Cl
3 Larch Av
4 Pinfold Dr

G4
1 Beechwood Gv
2 School La
3 Upton Av

G6
1 Fulbrook Dr
2 Newbury Cl
3 Rushton Rd

H1
1 Watersedge Cl
2 Windfields Cl

H2
1 Sedgemoor Cl
2 Station Rd
3 Warren Rd

H3
1 Bellfield Av
2 Butterfield Cl
3 Chase Briar Wd
4 Hill Top Ct
5 Ravenoak Rd

H4
1 Jesmond Gv
2 Ravenswood Dr
3 Summerlea

H6
1 Chapel Wks
2 Crowland Gdns
3 Lyncombe Cl
4 Melbury Rd

H7
1 Dickens Cl
2 Gorselands

J1
1 Ladybridge Ri

J2
1 Meadowside

J3
1 Park Gates Av
2 Ravenoak Rd

J5
1 Hollythorn Av
2 Orchard Cl

J6
1 Shrewsbury Gdns
2 Thorney Dr

J7
1 Derwent Dr

K3
1 Arden Ct
2 Cherry Orchard Cl
3 The Paddock
4 Roseneath

K5
1 Briarstead Cl
2 Convamore Rd
3 Glenholme Rd

K6
1 Briarlands Cl
2 Greenway
3 Victoria Cl

K7
1 Carlton Av
2 Kenwood Av
3 Norwood Av

L1
1 Chisworth Cl
2 Lausanne Rd
3 Midland Wk
4 North Park Rd
5 Parkside Wk
6 Zurich Gdns

L4
1 Lawton Av

L5
1 Barley Dr
2 Brixham Wk

L6
1 Bramley Cl
2 Bramley Dr
3 Manley Gv

M5
1 Helston Cl
2 Launceston Dr
3 Penhale Ms
4 Thorley Ms

M7
1 Bowen Cl

Page 66

A1
1 Duncombe Cl

A2
1 Hendham Cl
2 Reveton Gn
3 Southpool Cl
4 Winslade Cl

A3
1 Alston Cl
2 Harford Cl
3 Langston Gn
4 Modbury Cl

A5
1 Hillside Cl
2 Troon Cl

A8
1 Highfield Rd

B8
1 Widgeon Cl

C1
1 Norman Av
2 Walden Crs

C2
1 Shirley Cl

C3
1 Horsham Av
2 St Ann's Rd
3 St David's Rd

C8
1 Hazelbadge Cl

D1
1 Albert St
2 Albion Pl
3 Angel St
4 Ash St
5 Brewer's Gn
6 Buxton St
7 Charles St
8 Crown Ct
9 Gordon Av
10 Grosvenor St
11 John St
12 Lyme St
13 Newbourne Cl
14 Pownall St
15 Smithy St
16 Springfield Av
17 Stanley Av
18 Vernon St
19 Willard St
20 Yeoman Cl

D2
1 Marsland St
2 Norbury Gv
3 Wild St

D4
1 Charnwood Crs
2 Tamworth Cl

D7
1 Abbotsbury Cl
2 Covell Rd
3 Dundrennan Cl
4 Hartland Cl
5 Selby Cl

D8
1 Bylands Cl
2 Lambourn Cl
3 Tewkesbury Cl

E1
1 Back Chapel St
2 Bowden St
3 Grove St
4 Hazel St
5 Victoria Av
6 Vine St
7 Wesley St

E2
1 The Boulevard
2 Brook St
3 Daniel St
4 Grundey St
5 Spring V

E3
1 Barrule Av

E4
1 Lavenham Cl
2 Rowley Rd

E8
1 Mayfair Cl

F1
1 Cromdale Av
2 Wellington St

F2
1 Avondale Rd

F3
1 Carlton Pl
2 Kyle Rd
3 Lochmaddy Cl

F4
1 Capesthorne Cl

F8
1 Blenheim Cl
2 Brecon Cl
3 Ragley Cl
4 School La

Page 72

F1
1 Brackley St
2 Clarence St
3 Edith St
4 Egerton St
5 Greek St
6 Grove St
7 Handley St
8 Lord St
9 Speakman St

F3
1 Burland Cl
2 Curzon St
3 Drayton Cl
4 The Elms
5 Havergal St
6 Lightburn St
7 Queen's Cl
8 Southlands Ms
9 Stapley Cl
10 Westfield Ms

Page 73

G1
1 Alcock St
2 Bridgewater St
3 Canon St
4 Clarence Ter
5 Cooper St
6 Egerton St
7 Granville St
8 Loch St
9 Penketh's La
10 Princess St
11 Public Hall St
12 Wellington St

G2
1 Albert St
2 Arthur St
3 Back High St
4 Brook St
5 Devonshire Pl
6 Eaton St
7 Greenway Rd
8 High St
9 Nelson St
10 New St
11 Oakmere St
12 Queensway
13 Surrey St
14 Vine St
15 Walton St

G3
1 Cawley St
2 Chaucer St
3 Hawthorn Av
4 Salisbury St

H1
1 Ann St
2 Fredric Pl
3 Grosvenor St
4 Pinellas
5 St John's Brow
6 St John's St

H2
1 Malcolm St
2 Sewell St
3 Sutton St
4 Wilding Av
5 Windmill St

H3
1 Marina Gv

H4
1 Heath Road Crs

H6
1 Cheltenham Crs
2 Claverton Cl
3 Glenville Cl
4 Woodford Cl

J2
1 Cambridge St
2 Cartwright St
3 Grange Park Rd
4 Stenhills Crs
5 Vahler Ter

J3
1 Bickley Cl
2 Lavender Cl

J5
1 Laburnum Gv

J6
1 Kempton Cl
2 Thirsk Cl

K2
1 Henley Ct
2 Needham Cl
3 Tenby Dr

K3
1 The Winnows

K4
1 Davenport Rw

K5
1 Cranage Cl

K6
1 Cantley Cl
2 Danby Cl
3 Handforth La
4 Hyde Cl
5 Whitchurch Wy

K7
1 Braithwaite Cl
2 Kendal Ri

L2
1 Kingston Cl
2 Warrington Rd

L3
1 The Heys

L5
1 Earls Wy
2 Putney Ct
3 Spennymoor Ct

L6
1 Hobby Cl
2 Hunters Ct
3 Rothbury Cl
4 Seneschal Ct

L7
1 Bowland Cl
2 Brambling Cl
3 Mosedale Gv
4 Stonechat Cl
5 Whinfell Gv

L8
1 Bramble Wy
2 Dunmail Gv
3 Pippits Rw

M1
1 Marsh La

M3
1 Cheshyre Dr
2 The Green

M5
1 Thomas Ct

M6
1 Cote Lea Ct
2 Deer Park Ct

M7
1 Cherry Blossom Rd
2 Graylag Cl
3 Kingfisher Cl
4 Mallard Cl
5 Rosemary Av

M8
1 Ashbrook Av
2 Aster Crs
3 Audlem Cl
4 Azalea Gv
5 Bluebell Ct
6 Larkspur Cl
7 Lobelia Gv
8 Magnolia Dr
9 Millington Cl
10 Ovington Cl
11 Peckforton Dr
12 Stonecrop Cl
13 Verbena Cl
14 Weaverside Av

Page 74

A2
1 Castlefields Av North

A3
1 Constables Cl
2 Green Bridge Cl

A4
1 Brereton Cl
2 Castlefields Av South
3 Village Cl

A5
1 Iveagh Cl

A7
1 Hawkshead Cl
2 Oxmoor Cl
3 Peckfield Cl

A8
1 Skiddaw Cl

B5
1 Silkstone Crs

B6
1 Allendale
2 Bodmin Cl
3 Mullion Cl
4 Wharfedale

B7
1 Bartlegate
2 Broome Ct
3 Clover Ct
4 Coney Gv
5 Goulders Ct
6 Kilncroft

C2
1 Priory Rd
2 Southwood Av
3 Townfield Rd

C3
1 Sandalwood

C4
1 Kings Meadow
2 Saddlers Ri
3 Stoney Holt

C5
1 Cloverfield

C6
1 Camborne Cl
2 Launceston Cl
3 Newbridge Cl
4 Penare Gorran Hvn
5 Tintagel Cl
6 Truro Cl

C7
1 Backford Cl
2 Calverly Cl
3 Granby Cl
4 Halsall Cl
5 Linwood Cl
6 Wellbrook Cl

D2
1 Adlington Rd
2 Ashbury Cl
3 Harvard Cl
4 Haywood Crs
5 Swinden Cl

D3
1 Camden Ct
2 Chorlton Cl
3 Culford Cl
4 Gooseberry La
5 Winton Gv

D4
1 Dorrington Cl
2 Heron Cl
3 Mellor Cl
4 Ossett Cl

D5
1 Barton Cl
2 Baxter Cl
3 Chiswick Cl
4 Hitchen's Cl
5 Humphrey's Cl
6 Micklegate
7 Neptune Cl
8 Sabre Cl
9 Sovereign Cl

D6
1 Bournemouth Cl
2 Navigation Cl
3 Quadrant Cl
4 Schooner Cl

E1
1 Buckfast Ct

E5
1 Marina Village
2 Moresby Cl
3 Talisman Cl

E6
1 Aston Gn
2 Portsmouth Pl
3 Southampton Wy
4 Weymouth Cl

Page 84

A5
1 Hawthorn Pk
2 Hawthorn Vw
3 Hawthorn Wk
4 Kings Cl

A6
1 Kensington Ct
2 St James' Dr
3 Sandringham Wy

A7
1 Alderley Lodge

A8
1 Grosvenor Cl
2 Westminster Dr

B2
1 Styal Vw

B3
1 Carr Mill Ms
2 Marbury Rd

B5
1 Grove St
2 Warham St

B6
1 Covington Pl
2 Green Hall Ms

C2
1 Stanneylands Cl

C3
1 Chadwick Cl
2 Shargate Cl

C4
1 Calverley Cl
2 Connaught Cl
3 Fernwood Gv
4 Gladewood Cl

C6
1 Croftside Wy

D1
1 Anderton Wy
2 The Link
3 Thornton Dr
4 Wilmslow Rd

D2
1 Bankside Cl
2 Brandon Cl
3 Oakenclough Cl
4 Rodepool Cl
5 Rookerypool Cl
6 Viewlands Dr

D3
1 Fairywell Cl
2 Ringstead Cl
3 Rossenclough Rd
4 Sedgeford Cl

D4
1 Ashberry Cl
2 Carnoustie Cl
3 Cornwell Cl
4 Dorchester Cl
5 Gainsborough Cl
6 Gleneagles Cl
7 Muirfield Cl
8 Sandown Cl
9 Stanhope Cl

D5
1 Manor Gdns
2 Rodeheath Cl
3 Yew Tree Cl

D6
1 Avondale Ri

E1
1 Old Hall Crs
2 Wadsworth Cl

E2
1 Bidston Dr
2 Peckmill Cl

E3
1 Goosetrey Cl
2 Mosswood Rd

E4
1 Beechwood Dr
2 Brackenwood Ms
3 Broomfield Cl
4 Cherry Tree Cl
5 Chestnut Cl
6 Fieldhead Ms
7 Gorsefield Hey
8 Lymewood Dr
9 Reynolds Ms
10 Rowanside Dr
11 Thornfield Hey
12 Warren Hey
13 Welford Cl

E5
1 Overhill Dr

F3
1 Hunters Cl

Page 94

C7
1 Braeside Cl
2 Calder Wy
3 Chalfield Cl
4 Eden Cl
5 Innisfree Cl
6 Leas Cl

D8
1 Bidston Gn
2 Burton Gn
3 Heswall Rd
4 Oxton Gn

Page 120

E4
1 Canterbury Cl
2 The Furrows
3 Keats Cl
4 Wells Cl

F4
1 Badgers Cl
2 Bangor Cl
3 Bramley Cl
4 Gloucester Cl
5 Green Lawns Dr
6 Lambourne Cl
7 Larchdale Cl
8 Laxton Cl
9 St Georges Av
10 Salisbury Cl
11 Truro Cl
12 West Park Dr

F5
1 Backford Gdns
2 Kinnington Wy
3 Peterborough Cl
4 St Marks Crs

Page 121

K2
1 Buckingham Gdns
2 Caernarvon Ct
3 Criccieth Ct
4 Ewloe Ct
5 Flint Ct
6 Hawarden Gdns
7 Sandringham Gdns

Page 123

J1
1 Acacia Cl
2 Birchwood Cl
3 Manna Dr
4 Sorbus Cl

Page 129

H1
1 Goodwood Cl
2 Hill Top
3 Laburnum Crs
4 Townfield Ct

J5
1 Cloverdale
2 The Hawthorns
3 Kestrel Rd
4 Mulberry Ri
5 Sylvan Cl

J6
1 Milner Rd

J7
1 Kingsley Cl
2 Marshalls Ct
3 Thorn La
4 Woodlands Rd East

K6
1 Manor St

L5
1 Brocklebank Dr
2 Castle Bank
3 Castle Ct
4 Hooker St
5 Wallace St
6 Weaver Rd
7 Wellington St
8 Zion St

L8
1 Ashton Cl
2 Bishopgates Dr
3 Bladon Cl
4 Churton Cl
5 Littleton Cl
6 Mouldsworth Cl
7 Moulton Cl
8 Sandringham Cl
9 Sproston Wy

M4
1 Apple Market St
2 Market St
3 Naylor Ct
4 Theatre Ct
5 Timber La

M5
1 Athelbrae Cl
2 Chapel Ct
3 Dock Rd
4 Hayhurst Cl

M7
1 Headworth Cl
2 Lime Ct
3 Mereworth Dr

M8
1 Hatherton Cl
2 Lavister Cl
3 Picton Cl
4 Prestbury Cl
5 Stretton Wk
6 Tatton Cl

Page 130

A4
1 Crum Hl
2 Priory St
3 St Helens Rd

A8
1 Brooklands Dr
2 Christleton Av
3 Dunster Cl

C1
1 The Coppice
2 Hawthorn Wk
3 Hedgerow Dr

C6
1 Tennyson Cl

Page 137

L3
1 Birchgate Cl
2 Blyth Cl
3 Cornwall Cl
4 Cotswold Cl
5 Drummond Wy
6 Juniper Ri
7 Rayleigh Wy
8 Redruth Av
9 St Ives Cl
10 Tamar Cl
11 West House Ct

M3
1 Alveston Cl
2 Batemill Cl
3 Bracken Cl
4 Brookhouse Cl
5 Calveley Rd
6 Deerwood Cl
7 Home Farm Av
8 Leamington Rd
9 Merrydale Cl
10 Alveston Cl
11 Batemill Cl

M4
1 Abingdon Cl
2 Ashbourne Ms
3 Blandford Dr
4 Colville Rd
5 Dalesford Crs
6 Eldon Rd
7 Hedingham Cl
8 Kennet Wy
9 Livingstone Cl
10 Lutyens Cl
11 Maxfield Cl
12 Toll Bar Rd

Page 138

A2
1 Peterborough Cl
2 Woodstock Cl

A3
1 Argyll Cl
2 Atholl Cl
3 Blenheim Cl
4 Montrose Cl
5 Murray Cl
6 Roxburgh Cl

A4
1 Lea Bank Cl

A6
1 Park Mount Cl
2 Shadewood Rd

A7
1 Grisedale Wy
2 Manley Rd
3 Sussex Av

A8
1 Hillcrest Rd
2 Moss View Rd

B1
1 Hayfield Cl
2 Holcombe Dr
3 Portmarnock Cl
4 Weybridge Dr

B2
1 Folkestone Cl
2 Kirkstall Cl
3 Maidstone Cl
4 Merriden Rd
5 Sevenoaks Cl
6 Wetheral Rd

B4
1 Frances St
2 Hand St
3 West St

B5
1 Cherington Crs
2 Edward St
3 Horseshoe Dr
4 Stevenage Cl

B6
1 Cambridge Av
2 Cherington Crs
3 Rudyard Cl
4 Sycamore Ri

B7
1 Cloverdale Rd
2 Haddon Cl
3 Harewood Wy
4 Haworth Cl
5 The Roaches

C1
1 Barnside Wy
2 Haydock Cl
3 Moorlands Cl
4 Pasture Cl
5 Thetford Cl
6 Thirsk Wy

C2
1 Beechwood Ms
2 Cheveley Cl
3 Stoneleigh Cl
4 Woburn Cl

C4
1 Adlington St
2 Albert St
3 Anderson St
4 Boothby St
5 Charlton St
6 Cumberland St
7 George St West
8 Great Queen St
9 Grosvenor St
10 Hall St
11 Hope St West
12 King Edward St
13 Langford St
14 Pierce St
15 Pinfold St
16 Pownall Sq
17 Poynton St
18 Sharpley St
19 Tynedale Cl
20 Walker St
21 Waterloo St West
22 Westminster Rd
23 Whalley Hayes

C5
1 Back Paradise St
2 Blackshaw St
3 Crossall St
4 Crown St West
5 Hatton St
6 Henderson St
7 Holland St
8 Mansern Ter
9 Norbury St
10 Peter St West
11 St John's Rd
12 Water St
13 Whiston St

C6
1 Barton St
2 Grange Rd

C7
1 Marlowe Ct
2 Mayfield Ter
3 Stamford Rd
4 Stratford Wy

C8
1 Ash Ter
2 Cleaver Ms
3 Cornbrook Rd
4 Parkgate Rd
5 Torr Rd

D1
1 Bluebell Cl
2 Bluebell Ms
3 Cavendish Cl
4 Fitz Cl
5 Hall Gv
6 Orme Cl

D3
1 Brock St
2 Justice St
3 Old Hall St
4 Pearle St

D4
1 Back Wallgate
2 Brock St
3 Brunswick St
4 Buxton Rd
5 Churchside
6 Church St
7 Church St West
8 Cumberland St
9 Exchange Cl
10 Exchange St
11 Gas Rd
12 Queen St
13 Queen Victoria St
14 Unicorn Gateway
15 Waters Gn

D5
1 Bank St
2 Broken Banks
3 Crossall St
4 Hobson St
5 Lower Exchange St
6 Mill St
7 Nelson St
8 Newgate
9 Paradise St
10 Park Gn
11 Parsonage St
12 Roe St
13 Sunderland St
14 Townley Pl
15 Townley St
16 Wardle St
17 Wellington St

D6
1 Canton St
2 Cholmondeley St
3 Coronation St
4 Half St
5 Harpur Cl
6 Jackson St
7 Poplar Rd
8 St Barnabas Ct
9 St George's Pl
10 Smith St
11 Thistleton Cl

D7
1 Chantry Ct
2 Danes Sq
3 Goathland Wy
4 Lilford Sq
5 Lomas Sq
6 London Road Ter
7 Sanders Sq
8 Sherwood Rd

D8
1 Frith Ter
2 Moss Sq

E2
1 Elm Dr
2 Meadow Wy

E3
1 Adelaide St
2 The Crescent
3 Steeple St

E4
1 Cuckstoolpit Hl
2 Hope St

E5
1 Allen St
2 Bank St
3 Cawley St
4 Daintry St
5 Daintry Ter
6 Goodall St
7 Green St
8 Hallefield Crs
9 Hallefield Dr
10 Hallefield Rd
11 Jodrell Cl
12 Knight's Cl
13 Leigh St
14 Lower Bank St
15 Parker St
16 Pearson St
17 Quayside Wy
18 Stubbs Ter

E6
1 Bradley St
2 Byrons St
3 Coronation St
4 Cundiff Cl
5 Higginbotham Gn
6 Richmond Pl
7 River St
8 Square St
9 Tabor Street

E7
1 Mee St
2 Slack St

F2
1 Arundel Cl
2 Lathom Wy

F3
1 Delamere Dr
2 Howe St
3 Pleasant St
4 Timber St

F4
1 Wayside Rd
2 William St

F5
1 Capesthorne Wy
2 Eddisbury Ter
3 Hollands Pl
4 Roan Ms
5 Toll Bar Av
6 Watermill Dr

Page 142

B6
1 Ashfield Rd
2 Connaught Av
3 Gloucester Av
4 Health St
5 King Edward St
6 Lavender Ct
7 St David's Dr
8 Salisbury St
9 Windsor Av

B8
1 Castle Hill St
2 Elmwood Cl
3 St Ethelwold's St
4 South Bank

D8
1 Pembroke Cl
2 Radnor Cl

Page 145

C8
1 Hereford Pl

K5
1 Walnut Cl

M6
1 Ambleside
2 Dunham Wy
3 Shipbrook Rd
4 Shocklach Rd

Page 166

B1
1 Birchfield Crs
2 Moorfield Ct
3 Mountfield Rd
4 Wedgwood Rd

Page 168

E6
1 Beaumont Cl
2 Isabella Ct
3 Laburnum Gv
4 Mountain Vw

E7
1 Capeland Cl
2 Elm Gv
3 Halkett Cl
4 Kinnerton Cl
5 Shannon Cl
6 Sheringham Cl
7 Stanley Park Ct
8 Tatton Cl
9 Weybourne Cl

F6
1 Abingdon Crs
2 Bray Rd
3 Elm Sq
4 Fairford Rd
5 Guildford Cl
6 Lynton Cl
7 Newbury Rd
8 Redhill Rd
9 Shrewsbury Wy
10 Sunbury Crs
11 Telford Wy
12 Wenlock Wy
13 Westbury Wy
14 Wrekin Wy

Page 169

G5
1 Lansdowne Gv
2 Rothesay Rd

G6
1 Compton Pl
2 Waltham Pl

G7
1 Meadow Field Rd
2 Snowdon Crescent

H2
1 Cambrian Rd
2 Charlotte St
3 Goodwood Cl
4 Jesmond Rd
5 Kempton Cl

H7
1 Chiltern Cl
2 Johnsons Cl

J1
1 Abbot's Nook
2 Gaymoore Cl
3 Henshall St

J2
1 Brennus Pl
2 Cambrian Rd
3 Canal St
4 Canning St
5 Delamere St
6 Enderby Rd
7 Garden Ct
8 Hunter St
9 King St
10 Little Abbey Gateway
11 Mason St
12 Raymond St
13 The Yonne

J3
1 Bedward Rw
2 Crook St
3 Goss St
4 Grey Friars
5 Hamilton Pl
6 Hunters Wk
7 Linen Hall Pl
8 Nicholas Ct
9 Nicholas Street Ms
10 Old Hall Pl
11 Pierpoint Ct
12 Princess St
13 Sens Cl
14 Stanley Place Ms
15 Trinity St
16 Watergate St
17 White Friars

J4
1 Bunce St

J5
1 Powell's Orch
2 Selsdon Ct

K1
1 Church St
2 Eardswick Cl
3 Gloucester St
4 Gonsley Cl
5 Hankelow Cl
6 Trafford St
7 Wroxham Cl

K2
1 Back Queen St
2 Brook Pl
3 George St
4 Henry Pl
5 James St
6 Kaleyards
7 Oulton Pl
8 Queens Pl
9 St Anne St
10 Samuel St
11 Victoria Rd

K3
1 Bridge St
2 Leen La
3 Lumley Pl
4 Newgate St
5 Northgate St
6 Priory Pl
7 St Werburgh St
8 Souter's La

K4
1 Albion Pl
2 Lower Bridge St
3 St Mary's Hl
4 St Olave St
5 Steele St

K5
1 Belgrave Pl
2 Greenwood Av
3 Hugh St
4 Overleigh Ct
5 Pretoria St

L1
1 Gresford Av
2 Pickering St

L2
1 Albert St
2 Bold Sq
3 Francis Ct
4 Lee St
5 Seaville St
6 Seller St
7 Steam Mill St

L3
1 Bath St
2 Forest St

L4
1 Eastern Pathway
2 St John's Rear Rd
3 South Crescent Rd

L5
1 Allington La

M1
1 Bishop St
2 Burges St
3 Gosforth Pl
4 Kilmorey Park Rd
5 Law St
6 Longburgh Cl
7 Prescot St
8 Stone Pl
9 Sumpter Pathway
10 Tomkinson St

M2
1 Matthew Cl

M3
1 The Mount

Page 170

A2
1 Coppins Cl
2 Jamieson Cl
3 Stirling Cl
4 Woodlands La

A7
1 Blackthorn Cl

Page 177

G2
1 Birkdale Gdns
2 Wentworth Gv

G3
1 Badgers Cl
2 Beckenham Gv
3 Bridgewater Pl
4 Farriers Wy
5 Meadow Ri
6 Otters Bank
7 Pipers Ash
8 Redstone Dr
9 Thornycroft

G4
1 Brackenfield Wy
2 Hampstead Ct
3 Manor Sq
4 Newbury Av
5 St James Ter
6 Southwark Pl
7 Victoria Sq

G5
1 Quantock Cl

H2
1 Aston Av

H3
1 Delamere Ri

H4
1 Oak House La
2 Pentland Cl

H5
1 Caernarvon Av
2 Cheviot Ct
3 Launceston Cl
4 Llandovery Cl
5 Pembroke Wy
6 Snowdonia Wy

Notes

Notes

Notes

Notes

Notes